# NEW COMMENTARY
# ON THE WHOLE BIBLE:
# NEW TESTAMENT VOLUME

NEW TESTAMENT VOLUME

# New Commentary on the Whole Bible

Based on the classic commentary of
**Jamieson, Fausset, and Brown**

General Editor:
**J. D. Douglas**

New Testament Editor:
**Philip W. Comfort**

**Tyndale House Publishers, Inc.**
**Wheaton, Illinois**

# Contents

# Preface

Many years have passed since three scholars—two Scotts and an Irishman—collaborated in producing a commentary on the whole Bible. We are indebted to the original authors: Robert Jamieson (1802–80), Andrew R. Fausset (1821–1910), and David Brown (1803–97), the fruit of whose labours is still acknowledged in that any reference to "JFB" is readily identified with them.

"The Bible was never intended to be a book for scholars and specialists only," F. F. Bruce reminds us. "From the very beginning it was intended to be everybody's book, and that is what it continues to be." Yet we need those who will do for us what is conveyed by the Greek verb *hermēnuein:* "to make intelligible that which is obscure." Said Philip Melanchton, a commentator of Reformation times, "A good theologian and faithful interpreter of the heavenly teaching should be expert first in language, next in language, and then a witness."

Since not all of us are equipped for climbing the tree of knowledge, we enlist the help of specialists in biblical languages and background. We say to them, in effect, what James Stalker once said about the pastoral role at an induction service: "Look, brother, we are busy with our daily toils, and confused with cares, but we eagerly long for peace and light to illuminate our life, and we have heard there is a land where these are to be found, a land of repose and joy, full of thoughts that breathe and words that burn, but we cannot go thither ourselves. . . . Go thither for us, and . . . trade with that land and bring us its treasures and its spoils."

Biblical commentators tell us what words mean. They explain customs and life-styles, locate places, enlighten us on historical events. "He who would the poet know, must to the poet's country go." We owe a great deal to those who cast new light on old truths and never made the mistake of trying to interpret Scripture in terms of contemporary thinking. Too many have succumbed to the modern malaise of allowing biblical research to lapse into an arid academic exercise, and so inhibit the working of the Holy Spirit, the only source of true enlightenment.

Several editions and more than a century have passed since the work of Jamieson, Fausset, and Brown was first published, yet it still has wide appeal. It combines the best of evangelical scholarship with clarity of expression. With the appearance of new Bible versions and numerous books on biblical themes, we consider that readers will find helpful an updated and condensed version of JFB, both in content and style. Much of the original thought has been retained, and we still echo C. H. Spurgeon's verdict on it: "It contains so great a variety of information that if a man had no other exposition he would find himself at no great loss if he possessed this and used it diligently."

In embarking on this project, the editors were very conscious of being part of a great tradition and have sought to maintain the integrity and high academic standard set by what has been described as one of the best nineteenth-century commentaries. The revision of the material in this volume has been the work of Dr. Philip W. Comfort. Editorial and publishing colleagues have been impressed by the assiduous and enthusiastic manner in which he has approached and completed the task, and with the scholarly gifts which have enabled him to "trade with that land" for the glory of God and for the benefit of us all.

**J. D. Douglas**

## Introduction

The *New Commentary on the Whole Bible:* New Testament Volume, based on the work of Jamieson, Fausset, and Brown, presents a complete reworking of their classic commentary. While still retaining the choicest exegetical and devotional gems of the old classic, this new commentary should give the reader a clear, up-to-date exposition of the entire New Testament. The new commentary material illumines the Bible text (the Authorized Version, otherwise known as the King James Version) in that it provides new information gleaned from current commentaries, modern English translations (such as the RSV, NASB, and NIV), word studies, and New Testament textual criticism.

In the process of remaking the JFB commentary, my aim was to make a good commentary even better. Much of what Jamieson, Fausset, and Brown wrote over 130 years ago is still viable, understandable, and relevant to us today. Several of the commentators they relied upon and quoted from (such as Luther, Calvin, Bengel, and Alford) provided insights on Scripture that we—as much as they—treasure and consider helpful in understanding God's word. Thus, as I revised the commentary I was conscious that I was working with a tradition worthy of respect. Given this awareness, I attempted to revise the commentary stylistically and exegetically, as well as add to it new material that would reflect more contemporary scholarship, if such was needed to illumine the text.

I paid special attention to helping modern readers understand the Bible translation cited throughout this commentary, the King James Version, because the language of this version is often archaic and the textual authority behind it is frequently inadequate. I have often used renderings in various modern English translations to illumine the KJV text, and drawn upon the evidence of many early New Testament manuscripts to support a reading more likely original than that in the KJV. This perfectly follows the pattern set forth by Jamieson, Fausset, and Brown—who, while commenting on the Authorized Version, were always comparing it to the original biblical languages and earliest biblical manuscripts.

For every book of the New Testament there is an introduction, followed by a verse-by-verse commentary, with a bibliography at the end. The introduction provides information about the author, date, original readers, purpose of writing, and basic themes in each book. The commentary material follows the Bible text verse by verse, which is often quoted (in bold type) prior to the comments. Each book has been divided into logical segments clearly identified by descriptive subheads. The bibliography at the end of each book provides the source for each book whose author is cited in the commentary. Other reference works used in the commentary appear in abbreviated form and are listed on the following page.

I am indebted to the work of some scholars who began this project before I became involved; their names are listed on the contributor's page. I am also thankful for the participation of Wendell Hawley, editor-in-chief at Tyndale House Publishers, who greatly encouraged me in this work; Del Lankford, who typed the manuscript; Mark Norton, Richard Comfort, Daniel and Margaret Partner, who each assisted with reading the typed manuscript; and Dan Schmidt, who read over my edited manuscript on Matthew. Throughout this project I enjoyed the comradery of Dr. James K. Hoffmeier, editor of the Old Testament volume for the *New Commentary on the Whole Bible*. And finally, I want to express my deep appreciation for the work of Dr. J. D. Douglas in this project and for the opportunity I have been given to know him and labor with him. He was an inspiration to me as we worked together to make a commentary that would help readers understand the inspired New Testament text and the message of Christ it communicates.

**Philip W. Comfort**

## Abbreviations

| | |
|---|---|
| ASV | American Standard Version |
| BAG | Bauer, Ardnt, Gingrich (revised by Danker) *A Greek-English Lexicon of the New Testament and Other Early Christian Literature* |
| GAM | "Guide to the Ancient Manuscripts" in *Eight Translation New Testament*, Philip W. Comfort |
| KJV | Authorized King James Version |
| LXX | Septuagint |
| NA$^{26}$ | Nestle-Aland's 26th edition of *Novum Testamentum Graece* |
| NASB | *New American Standard Bible* |
| NBD | *New Bible Dictionary*, J. D. Douglas, editor |
| NEB | *New English Bible* |
| NIV | New International Version |
| NIVSB | *New International Version Study Bible*, Kenneth Barker, editor |
| NJB | *New Jerusalem Bible* |
| NT | New Testament |
| OT | Old Testament |
| RSV | Revised Standard Version |
| TDNT | *Theological Dictionary of the New Testament*, G. Kittel and G. Friedrich, editors, G. W. Bromiley, translator |
| TEV | Today's English Version |
| TLB | *The Living Bible* |
| TR | Textus Receptus |
| UBS$^3$ | *Greek New Testament*, United Bible Society, 3rd edition (corrected) |

## Contributors

Wallace Alcorn, A.B., A.M., M.Div., Th.M., Ph.D.
President, Alcorn Associates

Ralph H. Alexander, A.B., Th.M., Th.D.
Professor of Hebrew Scripture
Western Conservative Baptist Seminary

William G. Bellshaw, A.B., Th.M., D.D.
Professor of Theology
Northwest Baptist Theological Seminary

T. Miles Bennett, B.A., M.A., B.D., Th.D.
Professor of Old Testament
Southwestern Baptist Theological Seminary

W. Robert Cook, B.A., Th.M., Th.D.
Professor of Biblical Theology
Western Conservative Baptist Seminary

Virtus E. Gideon, B.A., B.D., M.Div., Th.D., D.D.
Professor of New Testament
Southwestern Baptist Theological Seminary

William F. Kerr, Th.D., S.T.D., D. D., LL.D.
Dean, International Graduate School of Theology

Richard D. Patterson, A.B., M.Div., Th.M., M.A., Ph.D.
Chairman of Department of Biblical Studies
Liberty University

# MATTHEW

## Introduction

The author of this Gospel was Matthew, one of the twelve apostles of the Lord Jesus. He was otherwise known as "Levi" (see Mark 2:14; Luke 5:27, 29). Before the Lord called him, he was a tax-collector (9:9ff.). It is interesting to note that Matthew called himself a tax-collector, while none of the other Gospel writers did. Perhaps he did this to show how great an ascendancy he had been granted when the Lord called him—for tax-collectors were despised and considered the lowest of people. The Gospel itself bears the impress of one knowledgeable of currency, for the Gospel writer speaks quite specifically about two-drachma tax (17:24), a four-drachma coin (17:27), and the various talents (18:24; 25:15ff.).

Scholars are divided about the date when Matthew was written primarily because there is still a debate about which Gospel was first written: Matthew or Mark? If Mark was written before Matthew, then Matthew was very indebted to Mark for a great deal of material; and vice versa. Those who argue for Matthew's priority do so on the basis that Matthew's Gospel was (1) recognized in the early church as the first Gospel, (2) written to those who first needed a written account—the Jews, and (3) was placed first in the NT canon. Whether it preceded or followed Mark, most scholars are certain that it was written before the destruction of Jerusalem (A.D. 70) because the temple is spoken of as still standing (24:15). Irenaeus indicated that Matthew wrote this Gospel while Peter and Paul were in Rome. This would make the time of writing in the sixties.

In the nineteenth century many Bible scholars suggested that Matthew originally wrote his Gospel in Hebrew (more specifically, Aramaic) for his Jewish audience. Later, it was translated into Greek. Most of the scholars founded this opinion on the basis of a statement made by Papias (c. 60–c. 130) concerning Matthew. According to Eusebius's *Ecclesiastical History,* Papias said, "Matthew compiled the sayings (*logia*) in the Hebrew language (or, Aramaic dialect); and everyone interpreted (or, translated) them as he was able." Although there is some ambiguity in this statement (see Carson's introduction), many scholars now think that Papias was referring to Matthew's composition of the "sayings of Jesus" only—which, quite naturally, he later worked into his Gospel narrative. Therefore, most scholars in this century espouse the view that Matthew did not originally write his Gospel in Hebrew, but in Greek. The Greek text bears no sign of having been a translation from Hebrew into Greek.

Traditionally, Matthew's Gospel has been described as the Gospel written for the Jews.

No one can deny its Jewish focus and flavor. More than any other Gospel, Matthew contains around fifty direct quotations from the OT and over seventy-five other allusions to the OT. Matthew commences his Gospel by tracing Jesus' descent from Abraham and David, and thus provides a bridge between the Old Testament and the New. Matthew, presuming a Jewish audience, did not explain Jewish customs (as opposed to Mark who wrote to a Gentile audience), and used Jewish terminology (e.g., replacing the expression "kingdom of God" with "kingdom of heaven"—in reverence for directly naming God). Jesus himself is constantly presented as the Son of David and the Messiah, who had come to fulfill all the prophetic proclamations (1:22, 23; 2:15, 17, 18, 23; 4:14-16; 8:17; 12:17-21; 13:35; 27:9, 10).

The gospel of the kingdom is first presented to the Jews (15:24); as they are the children of the patriarchs, the right to the kingdom inheritance was presented to them first. But the gospel of the kingdom would also go to the Gentiles; in fact, the Jews' place in the kingdom would be given over to the Gentiles because the Jews did not believe in the Messiah, while the Gentiles did. For example, after the Roman centurion exhibited faith that was greater than any Jesus had seen in Israel, he announced that people from all over the world (from "east and west") would enter into the kingdom (8:10-12). In fact, due to the Jews' rejection of the Messiah, the kingdom would be taken from the Jews and given over to "another nation" (21:33-43). Only a remnant of the Jews would enter the kingdom; the remainder would remain outside—which is a constant theme throughout this book (8:12; 25:10-12, 30).

Matthew wrote this Gospel to encourage more Jews to believe in Jesus as their Messiah and to enter into the kingdom of heaven. Of course, he also wrote it for the Gentiles—as they have a prominent place in God's economy. Jesus is presented as God's servant sent to the Gentiles (12:18-21), and the apostles are sent by Jesus to make disciples of all the nations (28:19). The Gentiles would become the major constituents of the kingdom God is establishing on earth.

According to Matthew's presentation, the kingdom of heaven (i.e., God's heavenly rule) came to earth and would yet come to earth in various phases. The advent of Jesus marked the first manifestation of the kingdom. God's heavenly rule came with his coming (3:2; 4:17). To believe in Jesus as the Messiah granted the believer entrance into the kingdom. It appears that the messianic kingdom could have come in all actuality if the Jews had not rejected Jesus (21:42). But this phase of the kingdom would be postponed until later. It can hardly be doubted that much of Jesus' language concerning the kingdom indicates a future reign. In the meantime, the kingdom would be coexistent with the church (16:18, 19) and would be an internal reign—in the hearts of men (13:3-23). Eventually, the kingdom (i.e., the messianic kingdom, the kingdom of David) would be displayed in full power and glory on the earth, after Christ's second advent.

*Chapter* **1**

## 1-17 GENEALOGY OF CHRIST
(SEE LUKE 3:23-38)

➤**1 The book of the generation**—an expression taken from Hebrew, meaning, "table of the genealogy." In Genesis 5:1 the same expression occurs in this sense. We have here, then, the title, not of the whole Gospel of Matthew, but only of the first seventeen verses. **of Jesus Christ**—For the meaning of these glorious words, see comments on 1:16, 21. "Jesus," the name given to our Lord at his circumcision (Luke 2:21), was that by which he was familiarly known while on earth. The word "Christ"—though applied to him as a proper name by the angel who announced his birth to the shepherds

(Luke 2:11), and once or twice used in this sense by our Lord himself (23:8, 10; Mark 9:41)—only began to be so used by others near the end of his earthly career (26:68; 27:17). The full form, "Jesus Christ," though once used by himself in his intercessory prayer (John 17:3), was never used by others until after his ascension and the formation of churches in his name. Its use, then, in the opening words of this Gospel (and in 1:17, 18) is in the style of the later period when Matthew wrote, rather than of the events he was going to record. **the son of David, the son of Abraham**—As Abraham was the first from whose family it was predicted that Messiah should spring (Gen. 22:18), so David was the last (2 Sam. 7:12-16; Isa. 9:6, 7; Jer. 23:5, 6). To a Jewish reader, accordingly, these were the two great starting points of any true genealogy of the promised Messiah; and thus this opening verse, as it stamps the first Gospel as one peculiarly Jewish, would at once tend to convince the writer's audience about Jesus' messianic identity. From the nearest of those two fathers came that familiar name of the promised Messiah, "the son of David" (Luke 20:41), which was applied to Jesus because, as David's son, he was the rightful king (see 9:27; 20:31).

➤**2 Abraham begat Isaac; and Isaac begat Jacob; and Jacob begat Judas and his brethren**—Only the fourth son of Jacob is here named, as it was from his loins that the Messiah was to come (Gen. 49:10).

➤**3-6 And Judas begat Phares** [Perez] **and Zara of Thamar** [Tamar]; **and Phares** [Perez] **begat Esrom; and Esrom begat Aram; and Aram begat Aminadab, and Aminadab begat Naasson; and Naasson begat Salmon; and Salmon begat Booz** [Boaz] **of Rachab** [Rahab]; **and Booz** [Boaz] **begat Obed of Ruth; and Obed begat Jesse; and Jesse begat David the king; and David the king begat Solomon of her that had been the wife of Urias** [Uriah]—Four women are introduced, two of them clearly Gentiles by birth—Rahab and Ruth, and three of them with a blot on their names in the OT—Tamar, Rahab, and Bathsheba (Gen. 38:24; Josh 2:1; 2 Sam. 11:2-5). According to popular Jewish legend (repeated in the Talmud), Tamar was considered a Gentile, and Bathsheba, through marriage

with Uriah, is linked with a Hittite. The Gentilic background for the Messiah is connected with God's promise to Abraham that his seed would bless many nations (Gen. 18:18). This feature in the present genealogy—herein differing from that given by Luke—comes well from him who styles himself in his list of the Twelve, as Matthew "the publican" [tax collector]. (In none of the other Gospels is he so named.) God's grace is able to reach those disreputable men and women who have faith in him and to use them in his divine plan. David is here twice emphatically identified as "David the king," and not only the first of that royal line from which Messiah was to descend, but the one king of all that line from which the throne that Messiah was to occupy took its name—"the throne of David" (see Isa. 9:7; Luke 1:32). Rahab seems to be here represented as the great-grandmother of David (see Ruth 4:20-22; and 1 Chron. 2:11-15), but genealogies must not necessarily include every generation. The fact is that Rahab was simply a distant ancestress of Jesus.

➤**7, 8 And Solomon begat Roboam** [Rehoboam]; **and Roboam begat Abia** [Abijah]; **and Abia begat Asa; and Asa** [Asaph in Gk., according to the best manuscripts] **begat Josaphat** [Jehoshaphat]; **and Josaphat begat Joram; and Joram begat Ozias** [Uzziah]—Three kings are here omitted—Ahaziah, Joash, and Amaziah (1 Chron. 3:11, 12). Some omissions were intentionally made to compress the whole into three fourteens (1:17). The reason why these, rather than other names, are omitted, must be sought in religious considerations—either in the connection of those kings with evil Ahab and Jezebel or because they themselves were so corrupt they were disqualified to be included in the royal line of the Messiah.

➤**11 And Josias begat Jechoniah and his brethren**—Jeconiah was Josiah's grandson, being the son of Jehoiakim, Josiah's second son (1 Chron. 3:15); but Jehoiakim might well be dropped in such a catalogue because he was a mere puppet in the hands of the king of Egypt (2 Chron. 36:4). The "brethren" of Jechoniah here evidently means his uncles—the chief of whom, Mattaniah or Zedekiah, who came to the throne (2 Kings 24:17), is, in 2 Chronicles 36:10, as well as here, called "his brother."

**about the time they were carried away to Babylon**—lit. "of their migration," for the Jews avoided the word "captivity" as too bitter a recollection, and Matthew studiously respects the national feelings.

**►12 And after they were brought to** [after the migration of] **Babylon, Jechoniah begat Salathiel** [Shealtiel]—See 1 Chronicles 3:17. The inclusion of Jechoniah in Christ's genealogy does not contradict Jeremiah 22:30, "Thus saith the Lord, Write ye this man [Coniah, or Jeconiah] childless"; for what follows explains in what sense this was meant—"for no man of his seed shall prosper, sitting upon the throne of David." He was to have seed, but no reigning child. And, in fact, none of Jechoniah's sons ruled upon the throne. **and Salathiel** [Shealtiel] **begat Zorobabel** [Zerubbabel]—See Ezra 3:2; Nehemiah 12:1; Haggai 1:1. But it would appear from 1 Chronicles 3:19 that Zerubbabel was Shealtiel's grandson, being the son of Pedaiah, whose name, for some reason unknown, is omitted. Zerubbabel took the lead among the returned captives from Babylon to rebuild the temple in Jerusalem (Ezra 3:2). After him, the OT gives no record of any other ruler in the messianic lineage.

**►13-15 And Zorobabel begat Abiud . . .** —After Zerubbabel, none of the names is found in the OT; but they were doubtless taken from the public or family registers, which the Jews carefully kept, and their accuracy was never challenged.

**►16 And Jacob begat Joseph, the husband of Mary, of whom** [referring to Mary] **was born Jesus**—From this it is clear that the genealogy here given is not that of Mary, but of Joseph; nor has this ever been questioned. And yet it is here studiously proclaimed that Joseph was not the natural, but only the legal father of our Lord. Jesus' birth by a virgin was known only to a few; but the acknowledged descent of his legal father from David secured that the descent of Jesus himself from David should never be questioned (see comments on 1:20). **who is called Christ**—signifying "anointed One." It is applied in the OT to the kings (1 Sam. 24:6, 10); to the priests (Lev. 4:5, 16); and to the prophets (1 Kings 19:16)—these all being anointed with oil, the symbol of the needful spiritual gifts to consecrate them to their respective offices; and it was applied, in its most sublime and comprehensive sense, to the promised Deliverer, inasmuch as he was to be consecrated to an office embracing all three by the immeasurable anointing of the Holy Spirit (Isa. 61:1; cf. John 3:34).

**►17 So all the generations from Abraham to David are fourteen generations; and from David until the carrying away** [or, migration] **into Babylon are fourteen generations; and from the carrying away into** [the migration of] **Babylon unto Christ are fourteen generations**—that is, the whole may be conveniently divided into three fourteens, each embracing one marked era, and each ending with a notable event, according to the Jewish annals. Such artificial aids to memory were familiar to the Jews, and much larger gaps than those here are found in some of the OT genealogies. In Ezra 7:1-5 no fewer than six generations of the priesthood are omitted, as will appear by comparing it with 1 Chronicles 6:3-15. It should also be noted that the number fourteen had symbolic meaning to the Jews, for the numerical value of each of the Hebrew letters in David's name equals fourteen. This shows the connection between David and Jesus. Finally, it will be observed that the last of the three divisions of fourteen appears to contain only thirteen distinct names, including Jesus as the last. Some commentators think that this was meant as a tacit hint that Mary was to be supplied, as the thirteenth link of the last chain, as it is impossible to conceive that Matthew could have made any mistake in the matter. But there is a simpler way of accounting for it. As Matthew reckons David twice—as the last of the first fourteen and the first of the second—so, if we reckon the second fourteen to end with Josiah, who was coeval with the "carrying away into captivity" (1:11), and the third to begin with Jeconiah, it will be found that the last division as well as the two others embrace fourteen names, including that of our Lord.

## 18-25 BIRTH OF CHRIST

**►18 Now the birth of Jesus Christ was on this wise** [or, thus]**: When as his mother Mary was espoused** [rather, betrothed, or engaged] **to Joseph, before they came together, she was found** [discovered to be] **with child of the Holy Ghost** [Spirit]—It was, of course, the fact only that was discovered; the explanation of the fact here given is the evangelist's own. That the Holy Spirit is a living, conscious "person" is plainly implied here, and is elsewhere clearly taught (Acts 5:3, 4, etc.). On the miraculous conception of our Lord, see comments on Luke 1:35.

➤**19 Then Joseph her husband**—cf. 1:20, "Mary, thy wife." Engagement was, in Jewish law, as binding as marriage. In giving Mary up, therefore, Joseph would have had to take legal steps to effect the separation. **being a just man**—or, righteous man. His righteousness was expressed in his unfailing obedience to God's directions (1:24; 2:13, 22). **and not willing to make her a public example**—to expose her (see Deut. 22:23, 24) **was minded to put her away privily**—i.e., privately by giving her the required writing of divorce (Deut. 24:1), in the presence of only two or three witnesses, and without cause assigned, instead of having her before a magistrate.

➤**20 But while he thought on these things**—As he brooded over the matter alone, his domestic prospects darkened and his happiness blasted for life, he began to plan the painful step of filing for divorce in the least offensive way. Then the Lord intervened. **behold, the angel of the Lord appeared to him in a dream, saying, Joseph, thou son of David**—This way of address would have reminded him of what all the families of David's line coveted, and thus, it would prepare him for the marvelous announcement which was to follow. **fear not to take unto thee Mary thy wife; for that which is conceived in her is of the Holy Ghost** [Spirit]—The conception of Jesus in Mary's womb originated from the Holy Spirit.

➤**21 And she shall bring forth a son**—i.e., she shall give birth to a son. **and thou** [as his legal father] **shalt call his name Jesus**—from the Hebrew meaning "Jehovah the Savior." **Jesus**—to the Christian, the sweetest and most fragrant of all names, expressing so melodiously and briefly his whole saving office and work! **for he shall save**—The "he" is here emphatic—*he* it is that shall save. His name, Jesus [Jehovah the Savior or Jehovah the Deliverer], expresses his work—salvation and deliverance. **his people**—the lost sheep of the house of Israel, in the first instance, for they

were the only people he then had. But, after the breaking down of the middle wall of partition (Eph. 2:14), the saved people embraced the "redeemed unto God by his blood out of every kindred and people and tongue and nation." **from their sins**—in the most comprehensive sense of salvation from sin (Rev. 1:5; Eph. 5:25-27).

➤**22, 23 Now all this was done, that it might be fulfilled which was spoken of the Lord by the prophet**—Isaiah 7:14. **saying, Behold, a virgin**—It should be *the* virgin, meaning that particular virgin destined to this unparalleled distinction. **shall be with child, and shall bring forth a son, and they shall call his name Emmanuel, which being interpreted is, God with us**— Not that he was to have this for a proper name (like "Jesus"), but that he should come to be known in this character, as God manifested in the flesh among men, and the living bond of holy and most intimate fellowship between God and men from henceforth and forever.

➤**24 Then Joseph, being raised from sleep** [and all his difficulties now removed], **did as the angel of the Lord had bidden him, and took unto him his wife**—With what deep and reverential joy would this now be done on his part; and what balm would this minister to his betrothed one, who had until now been suspected of unchastity.

➤**25 And knew her not**—i.e., they did not have sexual union—**till she had brought forth her firstborn son: and he called his name Jesus**—the expression "firstborn son" is found in later manuscripts (taken from Luke 2:7); the earliest manuscripts read simply "son."

*Chapter* 2

## 1-12 VISIT OF THE MAGI TO JERUSALEM AND BETHLEHEM

➤**1 Now when Jesus was born in Bethlehem of Judaea**—so called to distinguish it from another Bethlehem in the tribe of Zebulun, near the Sea of Galilee (Josh. 19:15); called also Bethlehem-judah, as being in that tribe (Judg. 17:7); and Ephrath (Gen. 35:16); and combining both, Bethlehem Ephratah (Mic. 5:2). It lay about six miles southwest of

Jerusalem. But how did Joseph and Mary move there from Nazareth, the place of their residence? Not of their own accord, and certainly not with the view of fulfilling the prophecy regarding Messiah's birthplace. In fact, they stayed at Nazareth until it was almost too late for Mary to travel with safety, and they would not have left at all, had not an order concerning a census forced them to the appointed place. God's sovereign hand was in all these movements. (See comments on Luke 2:1-6.) **in the days of Herod the king**—called the Great; son of Antipater, an Edomite, made king by the Romans. Thus, the scepter (i.e., kingship) had departed from Judah (Gen. 49:10), a sign that Messiah was now at hand. As Herod is known to have died in the year of Rome 750, in the fourth year before the beginning of our Christian era, the birth of Christ must be dated at least four years before the date usually assigned to it. Most scholars add two more years to the four because Herod was still alive when Jesus was two years old. **there came wise men**—lit. "magi," probably of the learned class who cultivated astrology and kindred sciences. Balaam's prophecy (Num. 24:17), and perhaps Daniel's (Dan. 9:24), might have come down to them by tradition; but nothing definite is known of the Magi. **from the east**—but whether from Arabia, Persia, or Mesopotamia is uncertain. **to Jerusalem**—as the Jewish metropolis.

**►2 Saying, Where is he that is born King of the Jews?**—From this it would seem they were not themselves Jews (cf. the language of the Roman governor, John 18:33, and of the Roman soldiers, 27:29, with the very different language of the Jews themselves, 27:42). The Roman historians, Suetonius and Tacitus, bear witness to an expectation, prevalent in the East, that out of Judea should arise a sovereign of the world. **for we have seen his star in the east**—Much has been written on the subject of this star; but from all that is here said it is perhaps safest to regard it as an astral phenomenon (the conjunction of several planets and stars) or simply a miraculous event, outside the normal realm of astronomy. **and are come to worship him**—or, to do him homage, as the Greek word can be translated— the nature of that homage depending on the circumstances of the case. That not civil but religious homage

is meant here is plain from the whole flavor of the narrative, and particularly 2:11. Doubtless these simple strangers expected all Jerusalem to be full of excitement about its newborn King, and the time, place, and circumstances of his birth to be familiar to everyone. Little would they think that the first announcement of his birth would come from themselves, and still less could they anticipate the startling, instead of transporting, effect which it would produce—else they would probably have sought their information regarding his birthplace in some other quarter. But God overruled it to draw forth a noble testimony to the predicted birthplace of Messiah from the highest ecclesiastical authority in the nation.

**►3 When Herod the king had heard these things, he was troubled**—viewing this as a danger to his own throne. Perhaps his guilty conscience also suggested other grounds of fear. **and all Jerusalem with him**—from a dread of revolutionary commotions, and perhaps also of Herod's rage.

**►4 And when he had gathered all the chief priests and scribes of the people together**—The class of the "chief priests" included the high priest of the present time, together with all who had previously filled this office; for although the then head of the Aaronic family was the only rightful high priest, the Romans removed them at will to make way for their own selections. In this class probably were included also the heads of the twenty-four courses of the priests. The "scribes" were at first merely transcribers of the law and synagogue-readers; afterwards interpreters of the law, both civil and religious, and so both lawyers and religious scholars. The first of these classes, a portion of the second, and "the elders," constituted the supreme council of the nation, called the Sanhedrin, the members of which, at their full complement, numbered seventy-two. That this was the council which Herod now convened is most probable, from the solemnity of the occasion; for though the elders are not mentioned, we find a similar omission where all three were certainly meant (cf. 26:59; 27:1). As Meyer says, it was all the theologians of the nation whom Herod convened because it was a theological response that he wanted. **he demanded of them**—as the authorized interpreters of Scripture. **where**

**Christ**—the Messiah. **should be born**—according to prophecy.

➤**5 And they said unto him, in Bethlehem of Judaea**—a prompt and involuntary testimony from the highest tribunal, which yet at length condemned him to die, **for thus it is written by the prophet**—Micah (5:2).

➤**6 And thou, Bethlehem, [in] the land of Juda**—the "in" being familiarly left out, as we say, Chicago, Illinois. **art not the least among the princes of Juda: for out of thee shall come a Governor ...**—This quotation, though differing verbally, agrees substantially with the Hebrew text and the Septuagint. Micah the prophet said, "But you, Bethlehem Ephrathah, though you are small among the clans of Judah, out of you will come for me one who will be ruler over Israel ... " (NIV). The honor of being the birthplace of Israel's ruler more than compensates for its smallness. Matthew, by a simple turn of phrase, has Micah say, "You are not the least." This distinction lifts it from the lowest to the highest rank. While Matthew says, "princes of Judah," the Septuagint reads, "thousands of Judah." Each tribe was divided into clans consisting of one thousand members, and each clan was ruled by a prince or governor. Bethlehem contained one clan of Judah, with one governor. One day, the ruler (or, governor) of all Israel would come from Bethlehem. **that shall rule**—lit., "that will shepherd." **my people Israel.**—In the OT, kings are, by a beautiful figure, called "shepherds" (Ezek. 31). The classical writers used the same figure. The pastoral rule of Jehovah and Messiah over his people is a representation pervading all Scripture (see Ps. 23; Isa. 40:11; Ezek. 37:24; John 10:11; Rev. 7:17). That this prophecy of Micah referred to the Messiah was admitted by the ancient rabbis.

➤**7 Then Herod, when he had privily called the wise men**—Herod had so far succeeded in his murderous design: he had tracked the spot where his victim was. But he had another point to fix—the date of his birth—without which he might still miss his mark. The one he had got from the Sanhedrin; the other he would obtain from the sages; but secretly, lest his object should be suspected and defeated. So he **inquired of them diligently**—rather, "precisely," **what time the star appeared**—presuming that this would be the best clue to the age of the child. The unsuspecting strangers told him all. Now he could locate the baby, for it was not likely that he would have been removed from his birthplace.

➤**8 And he sent them to Bethlehem, and said, Go and search diligently**—"Search out carefully." **for the young child; and when ye have found him, bring me word again, that I may come and worship him also**—The cunning hypocrite! Yet this royal mandate would in the meantime serve as a safe-conduct to the strangers.

➤**9 When they had heard the king, they departed**—But where were the Jewish ecclesiastics, the chief priests and scribes of the people? Why didn't they go to see the newborn king? They could tell Herod where Christ would be born and could hear of these strangers from the East that the Christ had actually come. But they did not go to see the One they had knowledge of—so their knowledge was theoretical and even superficial. Yet God allowed them to remain in this condition, for had they come, the news of the babe's birthplace would have quickly reached the tyrant's ears. **and lo, the star, which they saw in the east**—implying apparently that it had disappeared in the interval. **went before them, till it came and stood over where the young child was**—Surely this could hardly be but a luminous meteor, and not very high.

➤**10 When they saw the star, they rejoiced with exceeding great joy**—The language is very strong, expressing exuberant joy.

➤**11 And when they were come into the house**—not the stable; for as soon as Bethlehem was emptied of its strangers, they would have no difficulty in finding a dwelling house. **they saw**—The Textus Receptus has "found"; but here the KJV translators rightly depart from it, for it has no ancient authority. **the young child with Mary his mother**—The blessed babe is naturally mentioned first, then the mother. **and fell down and worshipped him**—Clearly this was no civil homage to a petty Jewish king. These star-guided strangers, who had come so far, and inquired so eagerly, and rejoiced with such exceeding joy at the sight of the star, now—when they see the object of their search, the babe in Bethlehem—fall down and worship him. **and when they had opened their treasures they presented**—rather, "offered." **unto him gifts**—This expression, used frequently in the OT of the oblations presented to God, is in the NT employed seven times, and always in a spiritual sense of offerings to God. Beyond doubt, therefore, we are to understand the presentation of these gifts by the magi as a spiritual offering. **gold, and frankincense, and myrrh**—Visits were seldom paid to sovereigns without a present (see 1 Kings 10:2; Ps. 72:10, 11, 15; Isa. 60:3, 6). "Frankincense" was an aromatic used in sacrificial offerings; "myrrh" was used in perfuming ointments. These, with the "gold" which they presented, seem to show that the offerers were persons in affluent circumstances. That the gold was presented to the infant King in token of his royalty; the frankincense in token of his divinity; and the myrrh, of his sufferings; or that they were designed to express his divine and human natures; or that the prophetical, priestly, and kingly offices of Christ are to be seen in these gifts; or that they were the offerings of three individuals respectively, each of them kings, the very names of whom tradition has handed down—all these are, at the best, interesting but unfounded suppositions. But that the feelings of these devout givers are to be seen in the richness of their gifts, and that the gold, at least, would be highly serviceable to the parents of Jesus in their unexpected journey to Egypt and subsequent stay there—that much at least is beyond dispute.

►**12 And being warned of God in a dream**—the Greek word for "being warned" means "receiving an answer from an oracle" (which implies that the magi may have asked God for direction) or "a divine warning or command." **that they should not return to Herod, they departed** [or, withdrew] **to their own country another way**—What a surprise this vision would be to the sages, just as they were preparing to carry the glad news of what they had seen to the pious king!

13-25 THE FLIGHT INTO EGYPT AND THE RETURN TO NAZARETH (See Luke 2:3.)

►**13 And when they were departed, behold, the angel of the Lord appeareth to Joseph in a dream, saying, Arise and take the young child and his mother**—Observe this form of expression, repeated in the next verse—another indirect hint that Joseph was

no more than Jesus' guardian. **and flee into Egypt**—which, being near, as Alford says, and a Roman province independent of Herod and much inhabited by Jews, was an easy and convenient refuge. Egypt had been a place of refuge for the patriarchs and the infant community of Israel; now it was a place of refuge for Jesus' parents and the infant Messiah (see comments on 2:15). **and be thou there until I bring thee word; for Herod will seek the young child to destroy him**—Herod's murderous purpose was formed before the magi had reached Bethlehem.

►**14 When he arose, he took the young child and his mother by night**—doubtless the same night.

►**15 And was there until the death of Herod**—which took place shortly thereafter (4 B.C.) by a terrible disease, the details of which will be found in Josephus's *Antiquities,* 17.6.1, 5, 7, 8. **that it might be fulfilled which was spoken of the Lord by the prophet, saying, Out of Egypt have I called my son**—Matthew here quotes Hosea 11:1 directly from the Hebrew, warily departing from the Septuagint, which renders the words, "From Egypt have I recalled his children," meaning Israel's children. The prophet was reminding God's people how dear Israel was to him (God) in the days of Israel's youth; how Moses said to Pharaoh, "Thus saith the Lord, Israel is my son, my firstborn; and I say unto thee, Let my son go, that he may serve me; and if thou refuse to let him go, behold I will slay thy son, even thy firstborn" (Exod. 4:22, 23); how, when Pharaoh refused, God killed all his firstborn and "called his own son out of Egypt" by a stroke of high-handed power and love. Viewing the words in this light, it is apparent that Matthew applied the verse in Hosea to Jesus because he saw the history of the infant community of Israel recapitulated in the life of the infant Jesus. Both were God's beloved sons, went to Egypt as infants, and were then called out (Carson).

►**16 Then Herod, when he saw that he was mocked of the wise men**—actually he was mocked (tricked) by God. **was exceeding wroth**—To be made a fool of is what none likes, and proud kings cannot stand. Herod burned with rage and was like a wild bull in a net. So he **sent forth** [a band of hired murderers], **and slew all the children** [young boys, according to the Gk.] **that were in Bethlehem, and in all the coasts** [districts] **thereof, from two years old and under, according to the time which he had diligently** [carefully] **inquired of the wise men**—In this ferocious step Herod was like himself—as crafty as cruel. He took a large sweep, not to miss his mark. He thought this mass murder would take care of his single victim. And it would, if he had been there. Why, ask skeptics and skeptical critics, is not this massacre, if it really occurred, recorded by Josephus, who was usually thorough in detailing the cruelties of Herod? To this the answer is not difficult. If we consider how small a town Bethlehem was, it is not likely there would be many male children in it of two years old and under; and when we think of the number of fouler atrocities that Josephus has recorded of Herod (e.g., he murdered some of his own children and some of his wives because he thought they were plotting against him), it is unreasonable to make anything of his silence on this.

►**17 Then was fulfilled that which was spoken by Jeremy** [Jeremiah] **the prophet, saying**—That which follows is Matthew's rendering of the Hebrew text of Jeremiah 31:15.

►**18 In Rama was there a voice heard, lamentation, and weeping, and great mourning, Rachel weeping for her children, and would not be comforted, because they are not**—These words, as they stand in Jeremiah, undoubtedly relate to the Babylonian captivity. Rachel, the mother of Joseph and Benjamin, was buried near Bethlehem (Gen. 35:19). Ramah, five miles north of Jerusalem, was one of the towns through which the Jews passed on their way to exile in Babylon (Isa. 10:29; Jer. 40:1). According to Jeremiah 31:15, Rachel (often thought of as the mother of the nation of Israel) is depicted as weeping for the children of Israel taken away into captivity. Matthew indicates that Rachel's lament was for yet another tragic event—the massacre of the male children in Bethlehem. Obviously, Matthew drew upon Rachel's association with Bethlehem and the connection of the women weeping for lost children. Perhaps this is all Matthew wanted to link together, but some commentators think Matthew selected the message from Jeremiah 31 because this chapter as a whole speaks of new hope (31:16,

17) and even a new covenant. (31:31-34) in contrast to a dreadful situation (i.e., the Babylonian captivity). In like manner, the dismal situation in Bethlehem would soon be turned around by the glorious appearing of Israel's deliverer and Messiah (Carson).

►**19 But when Herod was dead, behold, an angel of the Lord**—The same angel appears to have been employed on all these high occasions—and most likely he whom Luke names "Gabriel" (1:19, 26).

►**20 Saying, Arise, and take the young child and his mother, and go into the land of Israel**—not to the land of Judea, for he was afterward expressly warned not to settle there, nor to Galilee, for he only went there when he found it unsafe to settle in Judea, but to "the land of Israel," in its most general sense; meaning the Holy Land at large—the particular province being not as yet indicated. So Joseph and the Virgin had, like Abraham, to "go out, not knowing whither they went," until they should receive further direction. **for they are dead which sought the young child's life**—a common expression in most languages where only one is meant, who here is Herod. But the words are taken from the strikingly analogous case in Exodus 4:19, which probably suggested the plural here; and where the command is given to Moses to return to Egypt for the same reason that the greater than Moses was now ordered to be brought back from it—the death of him who sought his life. Herod died in the seventieth year of his age, and thirty-seventh of his reign.

►**21 And he arose, and took the young child and his mother, and came into the land of Israel**—intending, as is plain from what follows, to return to Bethlehem of Judea, there, no doubt, to rear the infant King, as at his own royal city.

►**22 But when he heard that Archelaus did reign in Judaea in the room of his father Herod**—Archelaus succeeded to Judea, Samaria, and Idumea; but Augustus refused him the title of king until it was observed how he conducted himself, giving him only the title of ethnarch (Josephus, *Antiquities,* 17.11.4). Above this, however, he never rose. The people, indeed, recognized him as his father's successor; and so it is here said that he **reigned** in his father

Herod's place. But, after ten years' defiance of the Jewish law and cruel tyranny, the people lodged heavy complaints against him, and the emperor banished him to Vienne in Gaul, reducing Judea again to a Roman province. **he was afraid to go thither**—and no wonder, for the reason just mentioned. **notwithstanding** [or more simply, "but"], **being warned of God** in a dream [see note on 2:12], **he turned aside** [withdrew] **into the parts of Galilee**—or, the Galilean parts. The whole country west of the Jordan was at this time divided into three provinces—Galilee being the northern, Judea the southern, and Samaria the central province. The province of Galilee was under the jurisdiction of Herod Antipas, the brother of Archelaus, his father having left him that and Perea, on the east side of the Jordan, as his share of the kingdom, with the title of tetrarch, which Augustus confirmed. Though crafty and licentious, according to Josephus—which is precisely what the Gospel history shows him to be (see Mark 6:14-30, and comments on Luke 13:31-35)—he was of a less cruel disposition than Archelaus. At any rate, it was safer for Joseph's family to settle in Nazareth because it was a good way off from the seat of government and considerably secluded.

►**23 And he came and dwelt in a city called Nazareth**—a small town in lower Galilee, lying in the territory of the tribe of Zebulun, and about equally distant from the Mediterranean Sea on the west and the Sea of Galilee on the east. According to Luke 1:26, 27; 2:39, Nazareth was the former home of Joseph and Mary. Thus, it was natural for them to go there when they were warned not to go into Judea. **that it might be fulfilled which was spoken by the prophets, He shall be called a Nazarene**—There are two ways to explain this statement about the prophets predicting that Messiah would be called a Nazarene. The first explanation of the origin of this name appears to be that which traces it to the word *netzer* in Isaiah 11:1—the small twig or sprout which the prophet there says "shall come forth from the stump of Jesse." Like a tree that had been stumped, the royal line was all but destroyed in the Babylonian captivity—yet not completely destroyed, for a twig (namely, Christ)

would come from that stump. This twig of royal stock would appear lowly and humble. The second explanation is based on the fact that the city of Nazareth was held in contempt by the Jews (see John 1:46)—even over and above the general contempt for Galilee, because the number of Gentiles that settled in the upper territories of it (in the estimation of the Jews) debased it. Thus, in the providential arrangement by which our Lord was brought up at the insignificant and opprobrious town called Nazareth, there was involved, first, a local humiliation (he was always known as a Nazarene, instead of as a Bethlehemite); next an allusion to Isaiah's prediction of his lowly, twig-like upspringing from the branchless, dried-up stump of Jesse; and yet further, a standing memorial of that humiliation that the prophets in a number of the most striking predictions had attached to the Messiah (Carson). It should be noted that Matthew did not directly quote one prophet (as had been his pattern up until now in this Gospel—1:22-23; 2:15, 17, 18—each time adding the word "saying" directly before the quote). Rather, Matthew says that the prophets (in general) spoke of him as being a Nazarene, which, in Matthew's time, was the same as saying he was the despised object of opprobrium. Many prophets predicted this (see Ps. 22:6-8; 69:8, 20, 21; Isa. 11:1; 49:7; 53:1-3; Dan. 9:26).

*Chapter* **3**

## 1-12 THE PREACHING AND MINISTRY OF JOHN (See Mark 1:1-8; Luke 3:1-18.)

For the proper introduction to this section, we must go to Luke 3:1, 2. Here, as Bengel well observes, the curtain of the NT is, as it were, drawn up, and the greatest of all epochs of the church begins. Even our Lord's own age is determined by it (Luke 3:23). No such elaborate chronological precision is to be found elsewhere in the NT, and it comes fitly from Luke, who claims it as the particular recommendation of his Gospel, that "he had traced down all things with precision from the very first" (1:3). Thus, the reader should see the comments on Luke 3:1, 2 because they introduce the reader to material that precedes this narrative.

➤1 **In those days**—of Christ's secluded life at Nazareth (2:23). **came John the Baptist, preaching**—about six months before his Master. **in the wilderness of Judaea**—the desert valley of the Jordan, thinly peopled and with hardly any vegetation, a little north of Jerusalem.

➤2 **And saying, Repent ye**—Though the word strictly denotes "a change of mind," it has respect here (and whenever it is used in connection with salvation) primarily to that sense of sin which leads the sinner to turn away from his sin to God for salvation. **for the kingdom of heaven is at hand** [or, near]—This sublime phrase, used in none of the other Gospels, occurs in this peculiarly Jewish Gospel nearly thirty times, alluding to Daniel's grand vision of the Son of man coming in the clouds of heaven to the Ancient of days, to receive his investiture in a worldwide kingdom (Dan. 7:13, 14). John declared that this kingdom was near. This heavenly kingdom may not have been the kind of kingdom the Jews were anticipating, for they were looking for an earthly kingdom in the political domain. Christ's coming would bring a heavenly kingdom with a spiritual domain—inside the hearts of men. Such a kingdom required repentance from its participants, so that they might receive deliverance from sin's rule in their lives. John's great work, accordingly, was to awaken this feeling and hold out the hope of a speedy and precious remedy.

➤3 **For this is he that was spoken of by the prophet Esaias** [Isaiah] **saying, The voice of one crying in the wilderness**—see comments on Luke 3:2. **Prepare ye the way of the Lord, make his paths straight**—This prediction is quoted in all the four Gospels, showing that it was regarded as an outstanding one and the predicted forerunner as the connecting link between the old and the new economies. Like the great ones of the earth, the Prince of Peace was to have his immediate approach heralded and his way prepared; and the call here—taking it generally—is a call to put out of the way whatever would obstruct his progress and hinder his complete triumph, whether those hindrances were public or personal, outward or inward. In Luke (3:5, 6) the quotation is thus continued: "Every valley shall be filled and every mountain and hill shall be brought low;

and the crooked shall be made straight, and the rough ways shall be made smooth; and all flesh shall see the salvation of God." Leveling and smoothing are here the obvious figures whose sense is conveyed in the first words of the proclamation—"Prepare ye the way of the Lord." The idea is that every obstruction shall be so removed as to reveal to the whole world the salvation of God in him whose name is the "Savior" (cf. Ps 98:3; Isa. 11:10; 49:6; 52:10; Luke 2:31, 32; Acts 13:47).

➤4 **And the same John had his raiment of camel's hair** [woven of it] **and a leathern girdle about his loins**—the prophetic dress of Elijah (2 Kings 1:8; and see Zech. 13:4). **and his meat was locusts**—the great well-known Eastern locust, a food of the poor (Lev. 11:22), **and wild honey**—made by wild bees (1 Sam. 14:25, 26). This dress and diet, with the shrill cry in the wilderness, would recall the stern days of Elijah.

➤5 **Then went out to him Jerusalem, and all Judaea, and all the region round about Jordan**—From the metropolitan center to the extremities of the Judean province the cry of this great preacher of repentance and herald of the approaching Messiah brought myriad penitents.

➤6 **And were baptized of him in Jordan, confessing** [aloud] **their sins**—This baptism was at once a public seal of their felt need of deliverance from sin, of their expectation of the coming deliverer, and of their readiness to welcome him when he appeared. The baptism itself startled them and was intended to do so. They were familiar enough with the baptism of proselytes from heathenism; but this baptism of Jews themselves was quite new and strange to them.

➤7 **But when he saw many of the Pharisees and Sadducees come to his baptism**—presumably, to be baptized by John, **he said unto them, O generation of vipers**—"Viper-brood," expressing the deadly influence of both sects alike upon the community. Mutually and entirely antagonistic as were their religious principles and spirit, the stern prophet charged both alike with being the poisoners of the nation's religious principles. In 12:34 and 23:33, the same strong language is applied by the faithful and true Witness to the Pharisees specifically—the only party that had enough zeal to diffuse this poison. **who hath warned you** [given you the hint] **to flee from the wrath to come?** One commentator said that they came to John's baptism "from a sense of fear like snakes fleeing from a forest fire" (Nixon). However, it seems that John more than suspected it was not so much their own spiritual anxieties as the popularity of his movement that had drawn them there. What an expression this is, "The wrath to come!" God's "wrath," in Scripture, is his righteous displeasure against sin and consequently against all in whose lives sin is found. This wrath arises out of the essential and eternal opposition of his nature to all moral evil. This is called "the coming wrath," not as being wholly future—for as a pronounced sentence it lies on the sinner already, and its effects, both inward and outward, are to some extent experienced even now—although the impenitent sinner will not have sentence publicly and irrevocably passed upon him and will not have it discharged upon him until "the judgment of the great day." Nevertheless, the unrepentant are storing up wrath for themselves on the day of wrath when God's righteous judgments will be revealed (see Rom. 2:5, RSV). But all true believers are saved from the wrath to come (1 Thess. 1:10). Doubtless, those coming to John's baptism did not have all this understanding concerning "the wrath to come," but those who came to be baptized with all sincerity sensed that they were fleeing from the coming wrath.

➤**8 Bring forth therefore fruits** [the true reading clearly is "fruit"] **meet for repentance**—that is, such fruit as befits true repentance. John, now being gifted with a knowledge of the human heart like a true minister of righteousness and lover of souls, here directs them how to evidence and carry out their repentance, supposing it genuine; and in the following verses he warns them of their danger in case it was not.

➤**9 And think not to say within yourselves, We have Abraham to our father**—The Jews believed quite confidently that they would be the heirs of the Messiah's kingdom because (and only because) they were the children of Abraham. But, as Paul so thoroughly argues in the Epistle to the Romans, the children of Abraham are the children of faith. **for I say unto you, that God is able of these stones to raise up children unto Abraham**—i.e., "Flatter not yourselves with the delusion that God stands in need of you to make good his promise of a seed to Abraham; for I tell you that, though you were all to perish, God is able to raise up children to Abraham out of stones." Though the stern speaker may have pointed as he spoke to the pebbles of the bare clay hills that lay around, John was clearly alluding to the remnant of Jewish believers and vast number of Gentile believers. The Gentiles, at that time stone-dead in their sins, would soon take the place of the Jews in becoming the true children of Abraham (see Rom. 4 and 11).

➤**10 And now also** [And even already] **the axe is laid unto the root of the trees**—as it were ready to strike: an expressive figure of impending judgment, only to be averted in the way next described. **therefore every tree which bringeth not forth good fruit is hewn down, and cast into the fire**—Language so personal and individual as this can scarcely be understood of any national judgment like the approaching destruction of Jerusalem, in which the chosen people were extruded from their holy land and holy privileges, but John's warning would serve as a dark shadow, cast before, of a more terrible retribution to come. The "fire," which in another verse is called "unquenchable," can be no other than that future "torment" and "everlasting punishment" (Matt. 25:46). The third Gospel here adds several important particulars (Luke 3:10-16).

➤**11 I indeed baptize you with water unto repentance** [see comments on 11:6]: **but he that cometh after me is mightier than I**—In Mark and Luke this is more emphatic—"But there cometh the mightier than I," **whose shoes** [sandals] **I am not worthy to bear**—The sandals were tied and untied, and borne about by the lowest servants. **he shall baptize you**—the emphatic "He": "He it is," to the exclusion of all others, "that shall baptize you." **with the Holy Ghost** [Spirit]—In saying this John demonstrated that, far from thinking that he had any equality with the Messiah, he considered himself to be Christ's lowest servant. He, the servant, would baptize with water (the outward symbol of purification); the Lord Messiah would baptize with the Holy Spirit himself, and so dispense the inward, spiritual reality. **and with fire**—To take this as a distinct baptism from that of the Spirit—a baptism of the impenitent with hell-fire—is exceedingly unnatural. Yet this was the view of Origen among the Fathers and among several modern commentators. Nor is it much better to refer it to the fire of the great day, by which the earth and the works that are therein shall be burned up. The Greek has but one preposition, "in" (*en*), before the two nouns: "Spirit" (*pneuma*) and "fire" (*puri*), which indicates two aspects of one event. Thus, the Spirit-baptism is also a fire-baptism. The expression "fire" indicates the fiery character of the Spirit's operations upon the soul—searching, consuming, refining, sublimating— as nearly all good interpreters understand the words. And thus, in two successive clauses, the two most familiar emblems—water and fire—are employed to set forth the same purifying operations of the Holy Spirit upon the soul. It was prophesied in the OT that the Messiah would come to purify Israel with the refiner's fire (see Mal. 3:2-5).

➤**12 Whose fan** [winnowing fork] **is in his hand**—ready for use. The winnower would throw the wheat stalks into the air with a winnowing fork. The chaff would be blown away, while the grain, being heavier, would fall to the ground. The grain would be collected for use, the chaff collected and burned; and thus the threshing floor would be totally cleansed. The image shows how Christ separates the genuine and useful believers from the false and worthless. **and he will thoroughly purge his floor**—that is, the visible church. **and gather his wheat**—his true-hearted saints; so called for their solid worth (cf. Amos 9:9; Luke 23:31). **into the garner** [barn]—"the kingdom of their Father," as this "garner" or "barn" is beautifully explained by our Lord in the parable of the wheat and the tares (13:30, 43). **but he will burn up the chaff**—empty, worthless professors of religion, void of all spiritual reality and character (see Ps. 1:4). **with unquenchable fire**—the strength of this apparent contradiction of figures: to be burnt up, but with a fire that is unquenchable; the one expressing the utter destruction of all that constitutes one's true life, the other the continued consciousness of existence in that awful condi-tion. Luke 3:18-20 provides further details of John's speech.

## 3:13-17 THE BAPTISM OF CHRIST AND DESCENT OF THE SPIRIT (See Mark 1:9-11; Luke 3:21, 22; John 1:31-34.)

➤**13 Then cometh Jesus from Galilee to Jordan unto John, to be baptized of him**— Moses rashly anticipated the divine call to deliver his people, and for this was forced to flee the house of bondage and wait in obscurity for forty years more (Exod. 2:11). Not so this greater-than-Moses. He had now spent thirty years in privacy at Nazareth, gradually ripening for his public work and calmly waiting for the time appointed of the Father. Now it had arrived. Luke (3:21) has this important addition—"Now when all the people were baptized, it came to pass that Jesus also being baptized . . ."—implying that Jesus waited until all other applicants for baptism that day had been taken care of before he stepped forward, that he might not seem to be merely one of the crowd. Thus, as he rode into Jerusalem upon a colt "which no one has ever ridden" (Luke 19:30, NIV) and lay in "a new tomb, in which no one had ever been laid" (John 19:41, NIV), so in his baptism, too.

➤**14 But John forbade him**—rather, "was [in the act of] hindering him," or "attempting to hinder him" (as is indicated by the Gk. imperfect tense). **saying I have need to be baptized of thee, and comest thou to me?**— The emphasis of his most remarkable speech lies all in the pronouns: I (the servant) need to be baptized by you (the Master), and you (the Master) come to me (the servant)? That this was the emphasis in the Baptist's words will be clearly seen if it be observed that he evidently regarded Jesus as himself needing no purification but rather qualified to impart it to those who did. And do not all his other testimonies to Christ fully bear out this sense of the words? But it were a pity if, in the glory of this testimony to Christ, we should miss the beautiful spirit in which it was borne—"Lord, must I baptize *you?* Can I bring myself to do such a thing?"

➤**15 And Jesus answering said unto him, Suffer it to be so now**—"Let it pass for the present." **for thus it becometh us to fulfil all righteousness**—i.e., it is fitting for both of us (John and Jesus) to go through with the baptism—John to perform it and Jesus to receive it—because it was God's will. Jesus was not fulfilling the righteous requirements of the law, for there was no law that required baptism. Jesus was complying with the Father's demands and thus doing what was right and proper in accordance with the divine will. He did not *need* to be baptized, but by doing so he identified with a humanity that needed repentance and baptism, and presented himself as a model of obedience to the divine will. **Then he suffered him**—i.e., John permitted him to be baptized.

**►16 And Jesus, when he was baptized, went up straightway out of** [from] **the water**—Mark has "out of the water." "and," adds Luke (3:21), "while he was praying"; a grand piece of information. **the heavens were opened**—Mark says, "He saw the heavens, being split open" (Gk.) The "open heaven" is referred to in prophetic visions (Ezek. 1:1; Rev. 4:1; 19:11) and times of heavenly unveilings (Acts 7:56). **and he saw the Spirit of God descending**—that is, he only saw it, with the exception of his honored servant, as he tells us himself (John 1:32-34); the bystanders apparently saw nothing. **like a dove, and lighting** [coming] **upon him**—The simile of "Spirit" and "dove" primarily indicates here that the Spirit of God's descent was like the descent of a dove; the other meaning (and this is the one made explicit in Luke 3:22) is that the Spirit had a form like a dove's. And the fourth Gospel gives us one more piece of information here, on the authority of one who saw and testified of it: "John bare record, saying, I saw the Spirit descending from heaven like a dove, and it abode upon him." And he adds that this last particular was expressly given him as part of the sign by which he was to recognize and identify him as the Son of God: "And I knew him not: but he that sent me to baptize with water, the same said unto me, Upon whom thou shalt see the Spirit descending, and remaining on him, the same is he which baptizeth with the Holy Ghost [Spirit]. And I saw, and bare record that this is the Son of God" (John 1:32-34). This perfectly compares with the predicted descent of the Spirit upon Messiah (Isa. 11:2): "And the Spirit of the Lord shall rest upon him." We cannot doubt that it

was this permanent and perfect resting of the Holy Spirit upon the Son of God that was here visibly manifested.

**►17 And lo a voice from heaven, saying This is**—Mark and Luke give it in the direct form, "Thou art." **my beloved Son, in whom I am well pleased**—The verb in Greek is a constative aorist; it expresses the Father's constant delight and pleasure in his Son. This declaration from the Father to the Son echoes the prophetic statement made by God through Isaiah: "Behold, My Servant, whom I uphold; My chosen one in whom my soul delights. I have put My Spirit upon Him; He will bring forth justice to the nations" (Isa. 42:1, NASB). Was this voice heard by the bystanders? From Matthew's form of it, one might suppose it so designed; but it would appear that it was not, and probably only John heard and saw anything peculiar about the great baptism.

*Chapter* 4

## 1-11 THE TEMPTATION OF CHRIST
(See Mark 1:12, 13; Luke 4:1-13.)

**►1 Then**—an indefinite note of sequence. But Mark's word (1:12) fixes what we should have presumed was meant, that it was "immediately" after his baptism; and with this agrees the statement of Luke (4:1). **was Jesus led up**—i.e., from the low Jordan valley to some more elevated spot. **of the spirit**—the Holy Spirit immediately before spoken of as descending upon him at his baptism and abiding upon him. Luke, connecting these two scenes, as if the one were but the sequel of the other, says, "Jesus, full of the Holy Spirit, returned from Jordan and was led by the Spirit . . ." (4:1, NIV). Mark's expression has a startling sharpness about it—"Immediately the Spirit driveth him" (lit. "thrust him out"). (See the same word in Matt. 9:25; 13:52; Mark 1:43; 5:40; John 10:4.) The thought thus strongly expressed is the mighty constraining impulse of the Spirit under which he went; while Matthew's more gentle expression, "was led up," intimates how purely voluntary on his on part this action was. **into the wilderness**—probably the wild Judean desert. The particular spot which tradition has fixed upon has hence got the name of *Quarantana* or *Quarantaria,* from the forty days. **to be tempted**—The Greek word *peirazein* means simply to try or make proof of; and when ascribed to God in his dealings with men, it means and can mean no more than this. Thus, Genesis 22:1, "It came to pass that God did tempt Abraham," or put his faith to a severe proof. (See Deut. 8:2.) But for the most part in Scripture the word is used in a bad sense and means to entice, solicit, or provoke to sin. Hence the name here given to the wicked one—"the tempter" (4:3). Accordingly, "to be tempted" here is to be understood both ways. The Spirit conducted him into the wilderness simply to have his faith tried; but as the agent in this trial was to be the wicked one, whose whole object would be to seduce him from his allegiance to God, it was a temptation in the bad sense of the term. Yet since he was God and could not sin in any way, whether by action, word, or inner desire (2 Cor. 5:21; Heb. 7:26), we must not think that the devil could have succeeded in the temptation. The temptation, nevertheless, was real, for Hebrews 4:15 says he was "tempted in every way, just as we are—yet was without sin" (NIV and NIV Study Bible). Jesus took the position of man, as a true human being, to defeat Satan (Heb. 2:14; 1 John 3:8). Satan tempted him to leave that position and reassume only his divine office. Jesus resisted and thereby defeated Satan for the sake of all humanity. Now, as a trustworthy high priest, he can help all who are tempted (Heb. 2:18). There is an obvious parallel to Jesus' success in overcoming the devil in contrast to Adam and Eve's failure in resisting the devil. But the connection between Jesus' wilderness temptation and Israel's wilderness trial is even more noticeable. Each of Jesus' retorts came from the Scripture, specifically from Deuteronomy 6–8. In that part of Deuteronomy, Moses recounted the wilderness trials and gracious provision of God. **of the devil**—The word signifies a slanderer, an accuser—one who accuses another. Hence that other name given him (Rev. 12:10): "The accuser of the brethren, who accuseth them before our God day and night." Mark (1:13) says, "He was forty days tempted of *Satan*," a word signifying an adversary, one who lies in wait for, or sets himself in opposition to another. These and other names of the same fallen spirit point to different features in his character or operations.

**➤2 And when he had fasted forty days and forty nights**—Luke says, "When they were quite ended." **he was afterward an hungered**—evidently implying that the sensation of hunger was unfelt during all the forty days; coming on only at their close. It was apparently so with Moses (Exod. 34:28) and Elijah (1 Kings 19:8) for the same period. A supernatural power of endurance was of course imparted to the body, but this probably operated through a natural law—the absorption of the Redeemer's Spirit in the dread conflict with the tempter. (See comments on Acts 9:9.) Had we only this Gospel, we should suppose the temptation did not begin until after this. But it is clear, from Mark's statement, that "he was in the wilderness forty days tempted of Satan," and Luke's, "being forty days tempted of the devil," that there was a forty days' temptation *before* the three specific temptations afterwards recorded. **➤3 And when the tempter came to him**—Evidently we do not have here a new scene. **he said, if thou be the Son of God**—In the first two tests, Satan said, "If you are the Son of God" not because he disbelieved Jesus' divine sonship but becasue he wanted Jesus to act in accordance with his divine prerogatives and thereby fail to pass the test as a man. But the whole point of the test was for Jesus to take a man's position in submission to God and to thwart Satan's attacks on his humanity. **command that these stones be made bread**—rather, "loaves," answering to "stones" in the plural; whereas Luke, having said, "Command this stone," in the singular, adds, "that it be made bread," in the singular. The sensation of hunger seems now to have come on in all its keenness—no doubt to open a door to the tempter, of which he is not slow to avail himself. **➤4 But he answered and said, It is written**—in Deuteronomy 8:3. **Man shall not live by bread alone**—more emphatically, as in the Greek, "Not by bread alone shall man live." **but by every word that proceedeth out of the mouth of God**—Of all passages in OT Scripture, none could have been more appropriate: "The Lord . . . led thee [said Moses to Israel, at the close of their journeyings] these forty years in the wilderness, to humble thee, and to prove thee, to know what was in thine heart, whether thou wouldest keep his commandments, or no. And he humbled thee, and suffered thee to hunger, and fed thee with manna, which thou knewest not, neither did thy fathers know; that he might make thee know that man doth not live by bread only, but by every word that proceedeth out of the mouth of the LORD" (Deut. 8:2, 3). Now, if Israel spent not forty days but forty years in a wilderness, where there were no means of human subsistence, not starving but divinely provided for, to prove to every age that human support depends not upon bread but upon God's unfailing word of promise and pledge of all needful providential care, could Jesus depend upon any other sustenance but that which the Father would provide? True, the Son of God was able enough to turn stones into bread; but what the Son of God is able to do is not the present question, rather, What is man's duty under want of the necessities of life? As man, therefore, Jesus would await the divine supply, not doubting that at the right time it would arrive. The second temptation in this Gospel is in Luke's the third. That Matthew's order is the right one will appear quite clearly in the sequel.

➤5 Then the devil taketh him up into the holy city—so called (as in Isa. 48:2; Neh. 11:1) from its being "the city of the Great King" (Ps. 48:2), the seat of the temple, the metropolis of all Jewish worship. and setteth him on a pinnacle [rather, the pinnacle] of the temple—a certain well-known projection. Whether this refers to the highest summit of the temple, which bristled with golden spikes (Josephus, *Antiquities,* 5.5, 6); or whether it refers to another peak, on Herod's royal portico, overhanging the ravine of Kidron, at the valley of Hinnom—an immense tower built on the very edge of this precipice, from the top of which dizzy height Josephus says one could not look to the bottom (*Antiquities,* 15.11, 5)—is not certain; but the latter is probably meant. Some commentators have thought that Satan was tempting Jesus to make a public display of his divinity—perhaps even prove by a sudden descent from the sky that he was the Messiah (a sign for which the Jews were looking—Mal. 3:1). But since Matthew says nothing about any people being present at this scene, the temptation must not have been related to a public manifestation.

➤6 And saith unto him, If thou be the Son of God—As this temptation starts with the same point as the first—Satan's determination to get Jesus to leave his standing as a man and seize upon his divine prerogatives—it seems clear to us that the one came directly after the other; and as the third temptation shows that the hope of carrying that point was abandoned, and all was staked upon a desperate venture, we think that the third temptation is thus shown to be the last, as will appear still more when we come to it. cast thyself down—"from hence" (Luke 4:9). for it is written—in Psalm 91:11, 12. Doubtless the tempter, having felt the power of God's Word in the former temptation, was eager to try the effect of it from his own mouth (see 2 Cor. 11:14). He shall give his angels charge concerning thee; and in [rather, on] their hands they shall bear thee up, lest at any time thou dash thy foot against a stone—The quotation is precisely as it stands in the Hebrew text and in the Septuagint except that after the first clause the words "to keep thee in all thy ways" are here omitted. Not a few good expositors have thought that this omission was intentional, to conceal the fact that this would not have been one of "his ways," i.e., of duty. But as our Lord's reply makes no allusion to this but seizes on the great principle involved in the promise quoted, so when we look at the promise itself, it is plain that the sense of it is precisely the same whether the clause in question is inserted or not.

➤7 Jesus said unto him, It is written again—in Deuteronomy 6:16. In essence, Jesus said, "True, it is so written, and on that promise I implicitly rely; but in using it there is another Scripture which must not be forgotten: Thou shalt not tempt the Lord thy God—Preservation in danger is divinely pledged; Jesus would not create danger, either to put the promised security to the test, or to demand a display of it. To do so would be "to tempt the Lord thy God," which, being expressly forbidden, would forfeit the right to expect preservation.

➤8 Again, the devil taketh him up [or unto] an exceeding high mountain, and showeth him all the kingdoms of the world, and the glory of them—Luke (4:5) adds the important clause, "in a moment of time"—a clause that seems to furnish a key to the true meaning. That a scene was presented to our

Lord's natural eye seems plainly expressed. But to limit this to that which the natural eye could take in, is to distort the expression "all the kingdoms of the world." It remains, then, to gather from the expression "in a moment of time"—which manifestly is intended to intimate some supernatural operation—that it was permitted to the tempter to extend preternaturally for a moment our Lord's range of vision and throw a "glory" or glitter over the scene of vision: a thing not inconsistent with the analogy of other scriptural statements regarding the permitted operations of the wicked one. In this case, the "exceeding height" of the "mountain" from which this sight was beheld would favor the effect to be produced.

➤**9 And saith unto him, All these things will I give thee**—"and the glory of them," adds Luke. But Matthew, having already said that this was "showed him," did not need to repeat it here. Luke (4:6) adds these other very important clauses, here omitted—"for it has been given to me, and I can give it to anyone I want to" (NIV). Was this wholly false? We answer, Is not Satan three times called by our Lord himself "the prince of this world" (John 12:31; 14:30; 16:11)? Does not the apostle call him "the god of this world" (2 Cor. 4:4)? And still further, is it not said that Christ came to destroy by his death "him that hath the power of death, that is, the devil" (Heb. 2:14)? No doubt these passages only express men's voluntary subjection to the rule of the wicked one while they live. In this sense he speaks what is not devoid of truth when he says, "It has been given to me." But how does he deliver this to whomsoever he wants? As employing whomsoever he pleases of his willing subjects in keeping men under his power. In this case his offer to our Lord was that of a deputed supremacy commensurate with his own, though as his gift and for his purposes. **if thou wilt fall down and worship me**—This was the sole but monstrous condition. No Scripture, it will be observed, is quoted now, because none could be found to support so blasphemous a claim. In fact, he has ceased now to present his temptations under the mask of piety, and he stands out unblushingly as the rival of God himself in his claims on the homage of men. Despairing of success as an angel of light, he throws off all disguise and with a splendid bribe solicits divine honor. This

again shows that we are now at the last of the temptations and that Matthew's order is the true one.

➤**10 Then saith Jesus unto him, Get thee hence, Satan**—Since the tempter has now thrown off the mask and stands forth in his true character, our Lord no longer deals with him as a pretended friend and pious counsellor but calls him by his right name—his knowledge of which from the outset he had carefully concealed till now—and orders him off. **for it is written**—in Deuteronomy 6:13. **Thou shalt worship**—In the Hebrew text and in the Septuagint it is, "You shall fear"; but as the sense is the same, so "worship" is here used to show emphatically that what the tempter claimed was precisely what God had forbidden. **the Lord thy God, and him only shalt thou serve**—The word "serve" in the second clause is one never used by the Septuagint of any but religious service; and in this sense exclusively is it used in the NT as we find it here. Once more the word "only," in the second clause—not expressed in the Hebrew text and the Septuagint—is here added to bring out emphatically the negative and prohibitory feature of the command. (See Gal. 3:10 for a similar supplement of the word "all" in a quotation from Deut. 27:26.)

➤**11 Then the devil leaveth him**—cf. Luke 4:2. **and, behold, angels came and ministered unto him**—or supplied him with food, as the same expression means in Mark 1:31 and Luke 8:3. Thus did angels to Elijah (1 Kings 19:5-8). Several good commentators think they ministered not only food, but supernatural support and cheer also. But this would be the natural effect rather than the direct object of the visit. And after having refused to claim the illegitimate ministry of angels in his behalf, oh, with what deep joy would he accept their services when sent, unasked, at the close of all this temptation, direct from him whom he had so gloriously honored!

12-25 CHRIST BEGINS HIS GALILEAN MINISTRY. THE CALLING OF PETER AND ANDREW, JAMES AND JOHN. JESUS' FIRST GALILEAN CIRCUIT (See Mark 1:14-20; 35-39; Luke 4:14, 15.)

There is here a notable gap in history, which but for the fourth Gospel we should never have discovered. If we took the history of the Synoptic Gospels only, we could draw three inferences, each of which would be erroneous according to the testimony of the fourth Gospel: first, that our Lord awaited the close of John's ministry, by his arrest and imprisonment, before beginning his own; next, that there was but a brief interval between the baptism of our Lord and the imprisonment of John; and further, that our Lord not only opened his work in Galilee, but never ministered outside of it, and never visited Jerusalem at all, nor kept a Passover until he went there to become "our Passover, sacrificed for us." The fourth Gospel alone gives the true succession of events; not only recording those important openings of our Lord's public work that preceded the Baptist's imprisonment—extending to the end of the third chapter—but so specifying the Passovers which occurred during our Lord's ministry as to enable us to line up, with a large measure of certainty, the events of the first three Gospels according to the successive Passovers which they embraced. Eusebius, the ecclesiastical historian, who, early in the fourth century, gave much attention to this subject, in noticing these features of the Evangelical Records, says (3:24) that John wrote his Gospel at the entreaty of those who knew the important materials he possessed, and he filled up what was lacking in the first three Gospels.

►**12 Now when Jesus had heard that John was cast into prison**—more simply, "was delivered up," as recorded in 14:3-5; Mark 6:17-20; Luke 3:19, 20. **he departed into Galilee**—as recorded, in its proper place, in John 4:1-3.

►**13 And leaving Nazareth**—The reason he left Nazareth is explained in Luke 4:16-30; in short, he was violently ousted by his own townspeople. **he came and dwelt in Capernaum, which is upon the sea coast**—maritime Capernaum, on the northwest shore of the Sea of Galilee; but the precise spot is unknown. (See comments on 11:23.) Our Lord seems to have chosen it for several reasons: four or five of the twelve disciples lived there; it had a considerable and mixed population, securing some freedom from that intense bigotry that characterized all places where Jews in large numbers dwelt nearly alone; it was central, so that not only on the approach of the annual

festivals did large numbers pass through it or near it, but on any occasion multitudes could easily be collected about it; and for crossing and recrossing the lake, which our Lord had so often occasion to do, no place could be more convenient. But one other reason for the choice of Capernaum remains to be mentioned—the only one specified by Matthew—i.e., Jesus went there to fulfill prophecy. **in the borders of Zabulon and Nephthalim**—the one lying to the west of the Sea of Galilee, the other to the north of it; but the precise boundaries cannot now be traced out. Matthew names these locations because of the messianic prophecy connected with them.

►**14, 15 That it might be fulfilled which was spoken by Esaias** [Isaiah] **the prophet**—see Isaiah 9:1, 2, or, as in the Hebrew text, 8:23 and 9:1. **saying, The land of Zabulon, and the land of Nephthalim, by the way of the sea**—the coast skirting the Sea of Galilee westward—**beyond Jordan**—a phrase commonly meaning eastward of Jordan, but here and in several places it means westward of the Jordan. The word seems to have the general meaning of "the other side"; the nature of the case determining which side that was. **Galilee of the Gentiles**—so called from its position, which made it the frontier between the Holy Land and the external world. While Ephraim and Judah were separated from the world by the Jordan Valley on one side and the hostile Philistines on another, the northern tribes were on the direct highway of all the invaders from the north, in unbroken communication with the promiscuous races who had always occupied the heights of Lebanon, and in close and peaceful alliance with the most commercial nation of the ancient world, the Phoenicians. Twenty of the cities of Galilee were actually annexed by Solomon to the adjacent kingdom of Tyre, and formed, with their territory, the "boundary" or "offscouring" (*Gebul* or *Cabul*) of the two dominions—at a later time still known by the general name of "the boundaries [coasts or borders] of Tyre and Sidon." In the first great deportation of the Jewish population, Naphtali and Galilee suffered the same fate as the transjordanic tribes before Ephraim or Judah had been molested (2 Kings 15:29). In the time of the Christian era this original disadvantage of their position was still felt; the speech of the

Galileans betrayed them by its uncouth pronunciation (Matt. 26:73); and their distance from the seats of government and civilization at Jerusalem and Caesarea gave them their character for turbulence or independence, depending on whether it was viewed by their friends or their enemies.

►16 The people which sat in darkness saw great light; and to them which sat in the region and shadow of death light is sprung up—The prophetic strain to which these words belong begins with Isaiah 7, to which chapter 6 is introductory, and goes down to the end of chapter 12. It belongs to the reign of Ahaz and turns upon the combined efforts of the two neighboring kingdoms of Syria and Israel to crush Judah. In these critical circumstances Judah and her king were, by their ungodliness, provoking the Lord to sell them into the hands of their enemies. What, then, is the relationship of this prophetic strain to the passage here quoted? First, Judah shall not perish because Immanuel, the virgin's son, is to come forth from his loins. Next, one of the invaders shall soon perish, and the kingdoms of neither be enlarged. Further, while the Lord will be the sanctuary of such as confide in these promises and await their fulfillment, he will drive to confusion, darkness, and despair the vast multitude of the nation who despised his oracles. This carries us down to the end of the eighth chapter of Isaiah. At the opening of the ninth chapter a sudden light is seen breaking in upon one particular part of the country, the part which was to suffer most in these wars and devastations—"the land of Zebulun, and the land of Naphtali, the way of the sea, beyond Jordan, Galilee and the Gentiles." The rest of the prophecy stretches over both the Assyrian and the Chaldean captivities and terminates in the glorious messianic prophecy of chapter 11 and the choral hymn of chapter 12. This is the point seized on by Matthew. By Messiah's taking up his abode in those very regions of Galilee and shedding his glorious light upon them, the prediction was now fulfilled. The Light of life had come to those who dwelt in the darkness and lived under the shadow of death; in fact, the Light "dawned" (or, "sprung up") upon them. This indicates that the dawning of Jesus' ministry began with the people most alienated from God, the people—both Jews and Gentiles—who desperately needed the Light of life. Jesus had come to give this living light to all men (see John 1:5, 9; 12:46; and especially 8:12, which is nearly a paraphrase of Isa. 9:2 and Matt. 4:16).

►17 From that time Jesus began to preach, and to say, Repent: for the kingdom of heaven is at hand—Jesus repeated the identical summons of his honored forerunner. Our Lord sometimes speaks of the new kingdom as already come—in his own person and ministry; and he sometimes speaks of a kingdom yet to come. In other words, Jesus' message concerning the kingdom carried with it a sense of "already here but not yet here." On one hand, the kingdom had already come because Jesus had come to be with his people and to call them to himself; on the other hand, the kingdom in its consummate manifestation was yet to come.

18-22 THE CALLING OF PETER AND ANDREW, JAMES AND JOHN

►18 And Jesus, walking—The word "Jesus" here does not appear in any Greek manuscripts; it was inserted by the KJV translators for the sake of continuity in the narrative. by the sea of Galilee, saw two brethren, Simon called Peter—for the reason mentioned in 16:18.

►19 And he saith unto them, Follow me—rather, as the same expression is rendered in Mark, "Come ye after me." and I will make you fishers of men—raising them from a lower to a higher fishing, as David was from a lower to a higher form of shepherding (Ps. 78:70-72).

►21 And going on from thence, he saw other two brethren, James the son of Zebedee, and John his brother, in a ship—rather, "in the ship," their fishing boat.

►22 And they immediately left the ship and their father—Mark adds an important clause: "They left the ship and their father Zebedee in the ship with the hired servants" ; showing that the family was well-off. and followed him—Two harmonistic questions here arise: First, was this the same calling as that recorded in John 1:35-42? Clearly not. For, (1) that call was given while Jesus was yet in Judea: this, after his return to Galilee. (2) Here, Christ calls Andrew; there, Andrew solicits an interview with Christ. (3) Here, Andrew and

Peter are called together: there, Andrew having been called, with an unnamed disciple, who was clearly the beloved disciple (see comments on John 1:40), went and brought Peter his brother to Christ, who then called him. (4)Here, John is called along with James his brother: there, John is called along with Andrew, after having had an interview with Jesus; no mention being made of James, whose call, if it then took place, would not likely have been passed over by his own brother. Thus far nearly all are agreed. But on the next question opinion is divided: Was this the same calling as that recorded in Luke 5:1-11? Many able critics think so. But the following considerations are against it. First, here in Matthew the four are called separately, in pairs: in Luke, all together. Next, in Luke, after a glorious miracle: here, the one pair are casting their net, the other are mending theirs. Further, here our Lord had made no public appearance in Galilee and so had gathered none around him; he is walking alone by the shores of the lake when he accosts the two pairs of fishermen: in Luke, the multitude are pressing upon him and hearing the word of God, as he stands by the Lake of Gennesaret—a state of things implying a somewhat advanced state of his early ministry and some popular enthusiasm. Regarding these successive callings, see comments on Luke 5:1.

23-25 FIRST GALILEAN CIRCUIT

►23 And Jesus went about all Galilee, teaching in the synagogues—These were houses of local worship. It cannot be proved that they existed before the Babylonian captivity; but as they began to be erected soon after it, probably the idea arose among the captives who did not have the Temple to go to. In our Lord's time, the rule was to have a synagogue wherever ten learned men or professed students of the law resided; and they extended to Syria, Asia Minor, Greece, and most places of the dispersion. The larger towns had several, and in Jerusalem the number approached 500. In terms of eldership and mode of worship, the early Christian churches were modeled after the synagogue. and preaching the gospel [proclaiming the glad tidings] of the kingdom, and healing all manner of sickness [every disease] and all manner of disease [every complaint]—The word means any incipient malady.

►24 And his fame went throughout all Syria—reaching first to the part of it adjacent to Galilee, called Syro-Phoenicia (Mark 7:26), and then extending far and wide. and they brought unto him all sick people—all that were ailing or unwell. [those] that were taken with divers diseases and torments—i.e., acute disorders. and those which were possessed with devils—that were demonized or possessed with demons. and those which were lunatick—lit. "moon-struck." and those that had the palsy—paralytics, a word not naturalized when the KJV was made. and he healed them—These healings became his credentials and illustrations of "the glad tidings" which he proclaimed. After reading this account of our Lord's first preaching tour, can we wonder at what follows?

►25 And there followed him great multitudes of people from Galilee, and from Decapolis [lit. "ten cities"]—a region lying to the east of Jordan, so called as containing ten cities, founded and chiefly inhabited by Greek settlers. and from Jerusalem and from Judaea, and from beyond Jordan—meaning from Perea. Thus not only was all Palestine moved by Jesus, but all the adjacent regions. But the more immediate object for which this is here mentioned is to give the reader some idea both of the vast concourse and of the varied complexion of eager attendants upon the great Preacher, to whom the astonishing discourse of the next three chapters was addressed. (Concerning the importance which our Lord himself attached to this first preaching circuit, and the preparation which he made for it, see comments on Mark 1:35-39.)

CHAPTERS 5–8

*Sermon on the Mount*

That this is the same discourse as that in Luke 6:17-49—only reported more fully by Matthew, and less fully, as well as with considerable variation, by Luke—is the opinion of many very able critics. The prevailing opinion of these critics is that Luke's is the original form of the discourse, to which Matthew has added a number of sayings, uttered on other occasions, in order to give in one sweep the great outlines of our Lord's ethical teaching. But that they are two distinct discourses—the one delivered about the close of his first missionary tour and the other after a second such tour and the solemn choice of the Twelve—is the judgment of others who have given much attention to such matters. The weight of argument appears to lie with those who think them two separate discourses. It seems hard to conceive that Matthew should have put this discourse before his own calling if it was not uttered until long after and was spoken in his own hearing as one of the newly chosen Twelve. And to this, that Matthew introduces his discourse between very definite markings of time, which fix it to our Lord's first preaching tour; while that of Luke, which is expressly said to have been delivered immediately after the choice of the Twelve, could not have been spoken until long after the time noted by Matthew. It is hard, too, to see how either discourse can well be regarded as the expansion or contraction of the other. And as it is beyond dispute that our Lord repeated some of his weightier sayings in different forms and with varied application, it ought not to surprise us that, after the lapse of perhaps a year—when, having spent a whole night on the hill in prayer to God, and having set the Twelve apart, he found himself surrounded by crowds of people, few of whom probably had heard the Sermon on the Mount, and fewer still remembered much of it—he should go over its principal points again, with just as much sameness as to show their enduring gravity, but at the same time with the difference that shows his inexhaustible fertility as the great Preacher.

*Chapter* **5**

## 1-16 THE BEATITUDES AND THEIR BEARING UPON THE WORLD

➤**1 And seeing the multitudes**—those mentioned in 4:25. **he went up into a mountain**—one of the dozen mountains in the vicinity of the Sea of Galilee, any one of them answering about equally well to the occasion. **and when he was set** [had sat or seated himself] **his disciples came unto him**—already a large

circle, more or less attracted and subdued by his preaching and miracles, in addition to the smaller band of devoted adherents. Though the latter only answered to the subjects of his kingdom, described in this discourse, there were drawn from time to time into this inner circle souls from the outer one, who, by the power of his matchless word, were constrained to forsake their all for the Lord Jesus.

➤**2 And he opened his mouth**—from a Hebrew idiom, indicating the beginning of instruction.

➤**3 Blessed . . .**—Of the two words which the KJV translators render "blessed," the one used here points more to what is inward and so might be rendered "happy," in a lofty sense; while the other denotes rather what comes to us *from without* (as 25:34). But the distinction is not always clearly made. One Hebrew word expresses both. On these precious Beatitudes, observe that though eight in number, there are here but seven distinct features of character. The eighth one—the "persecuted for righteousness' sake"—denotes merely the possessors of the seven preceding features, on account of which they are persecuted (2 Tim. 3:12). Accordingly, instead of any distinct promise to this class, we have merely a repetition of the first promise. This has been noticed by several critics, who by the sevenfold character thus set forth have rightly observed that a complete character is meant to be depicted, and by the sevenfold blessedness attached to it, a perfect blessedness is intended. Observe, again, that the language in which these Beatitudes are couched is purposely borrowed from the OT to show that the new kingdom is but the old in a new form; while the characters described are but the varied forms of the spirituality that was the essence of real piety all along, but which almost disappeared under corrupt teaching. Further, the things promised here, far from being mere arbitrary rewards, will be found in each case to grow out of the characters to which they are attached, and in their completed form are but the appropriate coronation of them. Once more, as "the kingdom of heaven," which is the first and the last thing promised here, has two stages—a present and a future, an initial and a consummate stage—so the fulfillment of each of these promises has two stages—a present and a future, a partial and a perfect stage.

►**3 Blessed are the poor in spirit**—All familiar with OT phraseology know how frequently God's true people are styled "the poor" (the "oppressed," "afflicted," "miserable") or "the needy"—or both together (as in Ps. 40:17; Isa. 41:17). The explanation of this lies in the fact that it is generally "the poor of this world" who are "rich in faith" (James. 2:5; cf. 2 Cor. 6:10 and Rev. 2:9); while it is often "the ungodly" who "prosper in the world" (Ps. 73:12). And so in Luke (6:20, 21), it seems to be this class of people—the literally "poor" and "hungry"—that is specially addressed. But since God's people are in so many places styled "the poor" and "the needy," with no evident reference to their temporal circumstances (as in Ps. 68:10; 69:29-33; 132:15; Isa. 61:1; 66:2), it is plainly an internal condition those terms are meant to express. Accordingly, the KJV translators sometimes render such words "the humble" (Ps. 10:12, 17), "the meek" (Ps. 22:26), "the lowly" (Prov. 3:34), as having no reference to outward circumstances. But here the explanatory words "in spirit" fix the sense to "those who in their deepest consciousness realize their entire need" (cf. the Gk. of Luke 10:21; John 11:33; 13:21; Acts 20:22; Rom. 12:11; 1 Cor. 5:3). This self-emptying conviction, that "before God we are void of everything," lies at the foundation of all spiritual excellence, according to the teaching of Scripture. Without it we are inaccessible to the riches of Christ; with it we are in the fitting state for receiving all spiritual supplies (Rev. 3:17, 18; Matt. 9:12, 13). **for theirs is the kingdom of heaven**—See comments on 3:2. The poor in spirit not only shall have—they already have—the kingdom. While others walk in vanity—in a shadow, an image—in an unreal world, taking a false view of themselves and the world around them, the poor in spirit are rich in the knowledge of their real case. Having courage to look this in the face and own it guilelessly, they feel strong in the assurance that "light arises in the darkness for the upright" (Ps. 112:4, NASB); and soon it breaks forth as the morning. We can do nothing to pay the price for God's riches; we have but to feel our total destitution and cast ourselves upon his compassion (Job. 33:27, 28; 1 John 1:9). So the poor in spirit are enriched with the fullness of Christ, which is the kingdom in substance; and

when he shall say to them from his great white throne, "Come, ye blessed of my Father, inherit the kingdom prepared for you" (25:34), he will invite them merely to the full enjoyment of an already possessed inheritance.

►**4 Blessed are they that mourn: for they shall be comforted**—This "mourning" must not be taken loosely for that feeling which is wrung from men under pressure of the ills of life, nor yet strictly for sorrow on account of committed sins. Evidently it is that entire feeling which the sense of our spiritual poverty begets, and so the second beatitude is but the complement of the first. The one is the intellectual, the other the emotional aspect of the same thing. It is poverty of spirit that says, "I am undone"; and it is the mourning this causes that makes it break forth in lamentation. The spiritual life, according to the Bible, is neither a set of intellectual convictions nor a bundle of emotional feelings, but a compound of both, the former giving birth to the latter. Thus closely do the first two beatitudes cohere. The mourners shall be "comforted." Even now they get beauty for ashes, the oil of joy for mourning, the garment of praise for the spirit of heaviness (see Isa. 61:3). Sowing in tears, they reap even here in joy. Still, all present comfort, even the best, is partial, interrupted, shortlived. But the days of their mourning shall soon be ended, and then God shall wipe away all tears from their eyes. Then, in the fullest sense, shall the mourners be "comforted."

►**5 Blessed are the meek: for they shall inherit the earth**—This promise to the meek is but a repetition of Psalm 37:11. Meekness denotes a gentle demeanor. Jesus himself said that he was meek: "Take my yoke upon you, and learn of me; for I am meek and lowly in heart: and ye shall find rest unto your souls" (11:29). The apostle Paul besought one of the churches by "the meekness and gentleness of Christ" (2 Cor. 10:1). In what esteem meekness is held by him who sees not as man sees, we may learn from 1 Peter 3:4, where the true adorning is said to be that of "a meek and quiet spirit, which in the sight of God is of great price." This disposition is the opposite of high-mindedness and a quarrelsome and revengeful attitude. "The earth," which the meek are to inherit, might be rendered "the land"—bringing out the more immediate reference to Canaan as the Promised Land, the secure possession of which was to the OT saints the evidence and manifestation of God's favor resting on them and the ideal of all true and abiding blessedness. Even in the Psalm (37) from which these words are taken, the promise to the meek is not held forth as an arbitrary reward but as having a kind of natural fulfillment. When they delight themselves in the Lord, he gives them the desires of their heart. When they commit their way to him, he brings it to pass, bringing forth their righteousness as the light and their judgment as the noonday. The little that they have, even when despoiled of their rights, is better than the riches of many wicked. All things, in short, are theirs—in the possession of that favor which is life, and of those rights that belong to them as the children of God—whether the world, or life, or death, or things present, or things to come; all are theirs (1 Cor. 3:21, 22); and eventually, overcoming, they "inherit all things" (Rev. 21:7).

►6 Blessed are they which do hunger and thirst after righteousness: for they shall be filled—or, shall be satisfied. What is the precise meaning of "righteousness" here? Some expositors espouse the more restricted sense of the term in which it is used with reference to the sinner's justification before God. (See Isa. 45:24; Jer. 23:6; Rom. 4:6; 2 Cor. 5:21.) But in so comprehensive a saying as this, it is clearly to be taken—as in 5:10 also—in a much wider sense, as denoting that spiritual and entire conformity to the law of God. The OT dwells much on this righteousness, as that which alone God regards with approbation (see Ps. 11:7; 23:3; 106:3; Prov. 12:28; 16:31; Isa. 64:5). As hunger and thirst are the keenest of our appetites, our Lord, by employing this figure here, plainly means "those whose deepest cravings are to live in a right relationship with God." And in the OT we find this craving variously expressed: "Listen to me, you who pursue righteousness, who seek the Lord" (Isa. 51:1, NASB); "I have waited for thy salvation, O Lord," exclaimed dying Jacob (Gen. 49:18); "My soul," says the psalmist, "is consumed with longing for your laws at all times" (Ps. 119:20, NIV)—and in similar breathings does he give vent to his deepest longings in that and other Psalms. Our Lord takes up here this

blessed frame of mind, representing it as the surest pledge of the coveted supplies, as it is the best preparative and indeed itself the beginning of them. "They shall be satisfied" (or, saturated), he says; they shall not only have what they so highly value and long to possess, but they shall have their fill of it. Not here, however. Even in the OT this was well understood: "in righteousness I will see your face; when I awake, I will be satisfied with seeing your likeness" (Ps. 17:15, NIV). The foregoing beatitudes—the first four—represent the saints rather as conscious of their need of salvation, and acting suitably to that character, than as possessed of it. The next three are of a different kind—representing the saints as having now found salvation and conducting themselves accordingly.

►7 Blessed are the merciful: for they shall obtain mercy—Beautiful is the connection between this and the preceding beatitude. The one has a natural tendency to beget the other. As for the words, they seem directly drawn from Psalm 18:25: "With the merciful thou wilt show thyself merciful." Not that our mercifulness comes absolutely first. On the contrary, our Lord himself expressly teaches us that God's method is to awaken in us compassion toward our fellowmen as he has exercised it (in so stupendous a way and measure) toward us. In the parable of the unmerciful debtor, the servant to whom his lord forgave ten thousand talents was naturally expected to exercise the small measure of the same compassion required for forgiving his fellow servant's debt of a hundred pence; and it is only when, instead of this, he relentlessly imprisoned him until he should pay it up that his lord's indignation was roused, and he who was designed to be a vessel of mercy is treated as a vessel of wrath (18:23-35; and see 5:23, 24; 6:15; James 2:13). "According to the view given in Scripture," says Trench most justly, "the Christian stands in a middle point, between a mercy received and a mercy yet needed." Sometimes the first is urged upon him as an argument for showing mercy—"forgiving one another, as Christ forgave you" (Eph. 4:32; Col. 3:13); sometimes the last—"Blessed are the merciful: for they shall obtain mercy"; "Forgive, and ye shall be forgiven" (Luke 6:37; James 5:9). And thus, while he is ever to look back on the mercy received as the source and motive of the mercy that he shows, he also looks forward to the mercy that he yet needs.

➤8 **Blessed are the pure in heart: for they shall see God**—Here, too, we are on OT ground. There the difference between outward and inward purity and the acceptableness of the latter only in the sight of God are everywhere taught. Nor is the "vision of God" strange to the OT; and though it was an understood thing that this was not possible in the present life (Exod. 33:20; cf. Job. 19:26, 27; Isa. 6:5), yet spiritually it was known and felt to be the privilege of the saints even here (Gen. 5:24; 6:9, 17:1; 48:15; Ps. 27:4; 36:9; 63:2; Isa. 38:3, 11). But oh, with what grand simplicity, brevity, and power is this great fundamental truth here expressed! And in what striking contrast would such teaching appear to what was then current, in which exclusive attention was paid to ceremonial purification and external morality! To "see" God is almost another way of saying to "know" God—quite intimately and personally. This experiential knowledge requires purity of heart, which begins with a "heart sprinkled from an evil conscience," or a "conscience purged from dead works" (Heb. 10:22; 9:14; see Acts 15:9); this also is taught in the OT (Ps. 32:1, 2; cf. Rom. 4:5-8 and Isa. 6:5-8). The conscience thus purged—the heart thus sprinkled—there is light within wherewith to see God (see 1 John 1:6, 7). The inward vision thus clarified, and the whole inner man in fellowship with God, each looks upon the other with satisfaction and joy, and those who behold God mirror God and are "changed into the same image from glory to glory" (2 Cor. 3:18). But the full and beatific vision of God is reserved for that time to which the psalmist stretches his views—"And I—in righteousness I will see your face; when I awake, I will be satisfied with seeing your likeness (Ps. 17:15, NIV). Then shall his servants serve him: and they shall see his face; and his name shall be in their foreheads (Rev. 22:3, 4). They shall see him as he is (1 John 3:2). But, says the writer of Hebrews, expressing the converse of this beatitude—"Follow holiness, without which no man shall see the Lord" (Heb. 12:14).

➤9 **Blessed are the peacemakers**—who not only seek peace, but diffuse it. **for they shall be called the children** [sons] **of God**—

The OT predicted that the Messiah would come as "the Prince of peace" (Isa. 9:6), proclaiming the gospel of peace (Isa. 52:7). When Christ came, he made peace by the blood of the cross and reconciled the enemies of God through his death (Eph. 2:14-18). When this reconciliation actually takes place, and one has "peace with God through our Lord Jesus Christ" (Rom. 5:1), then the peace-receivers become transformed into peace-diffusers. God is thus seen reflected in them; and by the family likeness these peacemakers are recognized as the children of God. In now coming to the eighth or supplementary beatitude, it will be seen that all that the saints are in themselves has already been described, in seven features of character; that number indicating completeness of delineation. The last feature, accordingly, is a passive one, representing the treatment that the kind of people already described may expect from the world.

➤10 **Blessed are they which are persecuted for righteousness' sake**—That this final beatitude has its ground in the OT is evident from the concluding words, where the encouragement given to endure such persecutions consists in its being but a continuation of what was experienced by the OT servants of God. But how, it may be asked, could such beautiful features of character provoke persecution? The Scripture abounds with statements declaring the hatred and animosity of the world against the people who live righteously because their righteous lives expose its unrighteous living (e.g., see John 3:20; 7:7; 15:19). More particularly, the seven characters here described are all contrary to the spirit of the world. Poverty of spirit runs counter to the pride of men's hearts; a pensive disposition, in the view of one's universal deficiencies before God, is ill relished by the callous, indifferent, laughing, self-satisfied world; a meek and quiet spirit is regarded as pusillanimous and rasps against the proud, resentful spirit of the world. Craving after spiritual righteousness exposes those who live to satisfy the lust of the flesh, the lust of the eye, and the pride of life; so does a merciful spirit the hardheartedness of the world; purity of heart contrasts painfully with painted hypocrisy; and the peacemaker cannot easily be endured by the contentious, quarrelsome world. Thus do the "righteous" come to be "persecuted." But blessed are they who, in spite of this, dare to be righteous. **for theirs is the kingdom of heaven**—As this was the reward promised to the poor in spirit—the leading one of these seven beatitudes—of course it is the proper portion of such as are persecuted for exemplifying them.

▶**11 Blessed are ye when men shall revile you**—or abuse you to your face (see Mark 15:32). **and persecute you, and shall say all manner of evil against you, falsely, for my sake**—Observe this: He had said, "for righteousness' sake." Here he identifies himself and his cause with that of righteousness, binding up the cause of righteousness in the world with the reception of himself, for he is righteousness incarnate (see Acts 3:14; 1 Cor. 1:30; 2 Cor. 5:21).

▶**12 Rejoice, and be exceeding glad**—exult. In the corresponding passage of Luke (6:22, 23), he says "leap for joy!" **for great is your reward in heaven: for so persecuted they the prophets which were before you**—i.e., "You will become heirs of their character and sufferings, and you will be rewarded with what the prophets were rewarded with."

## 13-16 THE APPLICATION OF THE FOREGOING PRINCIPLES TO THOSE DISCIPLES WHO SAT LISTENING TO THEM, AND TO THEIR SUCCESSORS IN ALL TIME

Our Lord, though he began by pronouncing certain kinds of people to be blessed—without express reference to any of his hearers—does not close the beatitudes without intimating that such people were in existence and that already they were before him. Accordingly, from kinds of people he comes to persons possessing them, saying, "Blessed are ye when men shall revile you . . ." And now, continuing this mode of direct personal address, he startles those humble, unknown men by pronouncing them the exalted benefactors.

▶**13 Ye are the salt of the earth**—to preserve it from corruption, to season its insipidity, to freshen and sweeten it. The value of salt for these purposes is abundantly referred to by classical writers as well as in Scripture. In Scripture, mankind, under the unrestrained workings of their own evil nature, are represented as entirely corrupt: before the flood (Gen. 6:11, 12); after

the flood (Gen. 8:21); in the days of David (Ps. 14:2, 3); in the days of Isaiah (Isa. 1:5, 6); and in the days of Paul (Eph. 2:1-3; see also Job 14:4; 15:15, 16; John 3:6; cf. Rom. 8:8; Titus 3:2, 3). The remedy for this, says our Lord here, is the active presence of his disciples among their fellows. The character and principles of Christians, brought into close contact with it, are designed to arrest the festering corruption of humanity and season its insipidity. But how, it may be asked, are Christians to do this for their fellowmen if their righteousness only exasperates them and causes them to recoil in every form of persecution? The answer is: that is but the first and partial effect of their Christianity upon the world; though the great population would dislike and reject the truth, some would receive and hold it fast. **but if the salt have lost his savour**—"become unsavory" or "insipid," losing its saline or salting property. The meaning is: if that Christianity on which the health of the world depends does in any age, region, or individual, exist only in name, **wherewith shall it be salted?**—that is, how shall the salting qualities be restored to it (cf. Mark 9:50)? Whether salt ever does lose its saline property—about which there is a difference of opinion—is not the question here. The point of the case lies in the supposition that if it should lose it, the consequence would be as here described. So with Christians, the question is not: can, or do, the saints ever totally lose that grace that makes them a blessing to their fellowmen? but, what is to be the issue of that Christianity that is found lacking in those elements which can alone restrain the corruption and season the tastelessness of an all-pervading carnality? Again, the question is not, if a man lose his grace, how shall that grace be restored to him? but, since living Christianity is the only "salt of the earth," if men lose that, what else can supply in its place? What follows is the appalling answer to this question. **it is thenceforth good for nothing, but to be cast out**—a figurative expression of indignant exclusion from the kingdom of God (cf. 8:12; 22:13; John 6:37; 9:34). **and to be trodden under foot of men**—expressive of contempt and scorn. It is not the mere lack of a certain property, but the lack of it in those whose profession and appearance were fitted to beget expectation of finding it.

➤**14 Ye are the light of the world**—This being the distinctive title which our Lord appropriates to himself (John 8:12; 9:5; and see John 1:4, 9; 3:19; 12:35, 36)—a title expressly said to be unsuitable even to the highest of all the prophets (John 1:8); it must be applied here by our Lord to his disciples only as they shine with his light upon the world, in virtue of his Spirit dwelling in them, and the same mind being in them which was also in Christ Jesus. Nor are Christians anywhere else so called. Rather, as if to avoid the august title that the Master has appropriated to himself, Christians are said to "shine"—not as "lights," as the KJV renders it, but—"as luminaries in the world" (Phil. 2:15); and the Baptist is said to have been "the burning and shining"—not "light," as in the KJV, but "lamp" of his day (John 5:35). **a city set on a hill** [lit. "mountain"] **cannot be hid**—nor can it be supposed to have been so built except to be seen by many eyes.

➤**15 Neither do men light a candle** [or, lamp], **and put it under a** [the] **bushel, but on a candlestick** [the lampstand]. The article is inserted in both cases to express the familiarity of everyone with those household utensils.

➤**16 Let your light so shine before men, that they may see your good works, and glorify your Father which is in heaven**—As nobody lights a lamp only to cover it up, but places it so conspicuously as to give light to all who need light, so Christians, being the light of the world, instead of hiding their light, are so to hold it forth before men that they may see what a life the disciples of Christ lead, and seeing this, may glorify their Father for so redeeming, transforming, and ennobling earth's sinful children, and opening to themselves the way to redemption and transformation.

17-48 THE IDENTITY OF THESE PRACTICES WITH THOSE OF THE OT ECONOMY, IN CONTRAST WITH THE PREVAILING TRADITIONAL TEACHING

➤**17 Think not that I am come** [that I came] **to destroy the law, or the prophets**—i.e., "the authority and principles of the OT." (On that phrase, see 7:12; 22:40; Luke 16:16; Acts 13:15.) This general way of taking the phrase is much better than understanding "the law" and "the prophets" separately, and inquir-

ing, as many good critics do, in what sense our Lord could be supposed to mediate the subversion of each. To the various classes of his hearers, who might view such supposed abrogation of the law and the prophets with very different feelings, our Lord's announcement would, in effect, be such as this—"Ye who tremble at the word of the Lord, fear not that I am going to sweep the foundation from under your feet: Ye restless and revolutionary spirits, do not think that I am going to head any revolutionary movement; and ye who hypocritically affect great reverence for the law and the prophets, pretend not to find anything in my teaching derogatory to God's living oracles." **I am not come to destroy, but to fulfil**—Not to subvert, abrogate, or annul, but to establish the law and the prophets—to unfold them, to embody them in living form, and to enshrine them in the reverence, affection, and character of men, am I come.

➤**18 For verily I say unto you**—Here, for the first time, does that august expression occur in our Lord's recorded teaching, with which we have grown so familiar as hardly to reflect on its full import. It is the expression manifestly of supreme legislative authority; and as the subject in connection with which it is uttered is the moral law, no higher claim to an authority strictly divine could be advanced. For when we observe how jealously Yahweh asserts it as his exclusive prerogative to give law to men (Lev. 18:1-5; 19:37; 26:1-4; 13-16, etc.), such language as this from our Lord expresses his divinity. When the Baptist's words—"I say unto you" (3:9)—are compared with those of his Master here, the difference of the two cases will be at once apparent. **Till heaven and earth pass**—Though even the OT announces the ultimate destruction of the heavens and the earth, in contrast with the immutability of Yahweh (Ps. 102:24-27), the prevalent representation of the heavens and the earth in Scripture, when employed as a popular figure, is that of their stability (Ps. 119:89-91; Eccles. 1:4; Jer. 33:25, 26). It is the enduring stability, then, of the great truths and principles, moral and spiritual, of the OT revelation that our Lord thus expresses. **one jot**—the smallest of the Hebrew letters (*yodh*). The Greek says, "one iota"—the smallest of the Greek letters. **one tittle**—one of those little strokes by which alone some of the Hebrew letters are distinguished from others like them. The Greek says, "one horn" (lit.)—i.e., one stroke of the pen. In both cases Matthew used a Greek translation of a Hebrew word, and the KJV translators gave an English translation of the Hebrew, not the Greek. One slight difference in a letter could change a word and thus alter the meaning of the law. Jews defended the authority of the OT right down to the least stroke of the pen (Carson). **shall in no wise pass from the law, till all be fulfilled**—The meaning is that "not so much as the smallest loss of authority or vitality shall ever come to the law." The expression "till all be fulfilled," is much the same in meaning as "until all be accomplished." Christ himself would accomplish, complete the moral law and prophetic law.

➤**19 Whosoever therefore shall break**— rather, dissolve, annul, or make invalid. **one of these least commandments**—an expression equivalent to "one of the least of these commandments." **and shall teach men so**—referring to the Pharisees and their teaching, as is plain from the next verse, but of course embracing all who would teach so. **he shall be called the least in the kingdom of heaven**—as the thing spoken of is not the practical breaking or disobeying of the law, but annulling or enervating its obligation by a vicious system of interpretation, and teaching others to do the same; so the thing threatened is not exclusion from heaven, and still less the lowest place in it, but a degraded and contemptuous position in the present stage of the kingdom of God. In other words, they shall be reduced by the retributive providence that overtakes them, to the same condition of dishonor to which, by their system and their teaching, they have brought down those eternal principles of God's law. **but whosoever shall do and teach them**—whose principles and teaching go to exalt the authority and honor of God's law, in its lowest as well as highest requirements. **the same shall be called great in the kingdom of heaven**—shall, by that providence which watches over the honor of God's moral administration, be raised to the same position of authority and honor to which they exalt the law.

➤**20 For I say unto you, That except your righteousness shall exceed the righteousness of the scribes and Pharisees**—The superiority

to the Pharisaic righteousness here required is plainly in kind, not degree; for all Scripture teaches that entrance into God's kingdom, whether in its present or future stage, depends, not on the degree of our excellence in anything, but solely on our having the character itself that God demands. Our righteousness, then—if it is to contrast with the outward and formal righteousness of the scribes and Pharisees—must be inward, vital, spiritual. Indeed, some of the scribes and Pharisees themselves might have the very righteousness here demanded; but our Lord is speaking, not of persons, but of the system they represented and taught. **ye shall in no case enter into the kingdom of heaven**—If this refers, as in the preceding verse, to the earthly stage of this kingdom, the meaning is that without a righteousness exceeding that of the Pharisees, we cannot be members of it at all, except in name. But our Lord's teaching here stretches beyond the present scene to that everlasting stage of the kingdom, where without purity of heart none "shall see God."

## 21-26 THE SPIRITUALITY OF THE TRUE RIGHTEOUSNESS, IN CONTRAST WITH THAT OF THE SCRIBES AND PHARISEES, ILLUSTRATED FROM THE SIXTH COMMANDMENT

➤**21 Ye have heard that it was said by them of old time**—or, "to them of old time" (i.e., to the ancients). Which of these translations is the right one has been much debated. Either of them is grammatically defensible, though the latter—"to the ancients"—is more consistent with NT usage (see the Gk. of Rom. 9:12, 26; Rev. 6:11; 9:4); and most critics decide in favor of it. But it is not a question of Greek only. Nearly all who would translate "to the ancients" take the speaker of the words quoted to be Moses who gave the law; "the ancients" to be the people to whom Moses gave the law; and the intention of our Lord here to be to contrast his own teaching, more or less, with that of Moses; either as opposed to it—as some go the length of affirming—or at least as modifying, enlarging, elevating it. But who can reasonably imagine such a thing, just after the most solemn and emphatic proclamation of the perpetuity of the law, and the honor and glory in which it was to be held under the new economy? It seems as plain as possible that our

Lord's one object is to contrast the traditional perversions of the law with the true sense of it as expounded by himself. Thus, "by the ancients" must have been what our Lord meant here, referring to the corrupt teachers. **Thou shalt not kill; and whosoever shall kill shall be in danger of** [liable to] **the judgment**—i.e., of the sentence of those inferior judiciary courts which were established in all the principal towns, in compliance with Deuteronomy 16:16. Thus was this commandment reduced from a holy law of the heart-searching God to a mere criminal statute, taking cognizance only of outward actions, such as that which we read in Exodus 21:12 and Leviticus 24:17.

➤**22 But I say unto you**—Note the authoritative tone in which—as himself the Lawgiver and Judge—Christ now gives the true sense, and explains the real meaning of the commandment. **That whosoever is angry with his brother without a cause** [the words "without a cause" are not present in the three earliest manuscripts] **shall be in danger of the judgment: and whosoever shall say to his brother, Raca, shall be in danger of the council: but whosoever shall say, Thou fool, shall be in danger of hell fire**—It is unreasonable to deny that three degrees of punishment are here meant to be expressed and to say that it is but a threefold expression of one and the same thing. But some expositors err greatly in taking the first two—"the judgment" and "the council"—to refer to degrees of temporal punishment with which lesser sins were to be visited under the gospel, and only the last—"hell fire"—to refer to the future life. All three clearly refer to divine retribution, and that alone, for breaches of this commandment; though this is expressed by an allusion to Jewish tribunals. The "judgment," as already explained, was the lowest of these; the "council" or "Sanhedrin"—which sat at Jerusalem—was the highest; while the word used for "hell fire" contains an allusion to the "valley of the son of Hinnom" (Josh. 18:16). In this valley the Jews, when steeped in idolatry, went to the length of burning their children to Molech "on the high places of Tophet"—in consequence of which Josiah defiled it, to prevent the repetition of such abominations (2 Kings 23:10); and from that time forward, if we may believe the Jewish writers, a fire was kept burning in it to consume

the carrion and all kinds of impurities that collected about Jerusalem. Certain it is that while the final punishment of the wicked is described in the OT by allusions to this valley of Tophet or Hinnom (Isa. 30:33; 66:24), our Lord himself describes the same by merely quoting these terrific descriptions of Isaiah (see Mark 9:43-48). What precise degrees of unholy feeling toward our brothers are indicated by the words "Raca" and "fool" are difficult to ascertain. Every age and every country has its modes of expressing such things; and no doubt our Lord seized on the then current phraseology of unholy disrespect and contempt merely to express and condemn the different degrees of such feeling when brought out in words, as he had immediately before condemned the feeling itself. In fact, we are not to make much of mere words, apart from the feeling which they express. Furthermore, anger is expressly said to have been felt by our Lord toward his enemies though mixed with "grief for the hardness of their hearts" (Mark 3:5), and Paul teaches us that there is anger that is not sinful (Eph. 4:26); so in the Epistle of James (2:20) we find the words, "O vain [or, empty] man"; and our Lord himself applies the very word "fools" twice in one breath to the blind guides of the people (23:17, 19). The spirit, then, of the whole statement may be thus given: "For ages you have been taught that the sixth commandment is broken only by the murderer, to pass sentence upon whom is the proper business of the recognized tribunals. But I say unto you that it is broken even by causeless anger, which is but hatred in the bud, as hatred is incipient murder (1 John 3:15); and if by the feelings, much more by those words in which all ill feeling from the slightest to the most envenomed are directed toward a brother: and just as there are gradations in judiciary courts and in the sentences they pronounce according to the degrees of criminality, so will the judicial treatment of all the breakers of this commandment at the divine tribunal be according to their real criminality before the heart-searching Judge." Oh, what holy teaching this is!

➤**23, 24 Therefore**—to apply the foregoing, and show its paramount importance. **if thou bring thy gift to the altar, and there rememberest that thy brother hath ought** [of just complaint] **against thee; leave there thy**

**gift before the altar, and go thy way; first be reconciled to thy brother**—The meaning evidently is not, "dismiss from your own heart all ill feeling," but "get your brother to dismiss from his mind all grudge against you." **and then come and offer thy gift**—"The picture," says Tholuck, "is drawn from life. It transports us to the moment when the Israelite, having brought his sacrifice to the court of the Israelites, awaited the instant when the priest would approach to receive it at his hands. He waits with his gift at the rails that separate the place where he stands from the court of the priests, into which his offering will presently be taken, there to be slain by the priest, and by him presented upon the altar of sacrifice." It is at this solemn moment, when about to cast himself upon divine mercy and seek in his offering a seal of divine forgiveness, that the offerer is supposed, all at once, to remember that some brother has a just cause of complaint against him through a breach of this commandment in one or other of the ways just indicated. What then? Is he to say, As soon as I have offered this gift I will go straight to my brother, and make it up with him? No, but before another step is taken—even before the offering is presented—this reconciliation is to be sought, though the gift has to be left unoffered before the altar. The converse of the truth taught here is very strikingly expressed in Mark 11:25, 26. "And when ye stand praying [in the very act], forgive, if ye have ought [of just complaint] against any: that your Father also which is in heaven may forgive you your trespasses. But if ye do not forgive, neither will your Father which is in heaven forgive you . . . " Hence the beautiful practice of the early church, to see that all differences among brothers and sisters in Christ were made up, in the spirit of love, before going to the Lord's Supper. Certainly, if this be the highest act of worship on earth, such reconciliation—though obligatory on all other occasions of worship—must be peculiarly so then.

➤**25 Agree with thine adversary**—your opponent in a legal dispute. **quickly, whiles thou art in the way with him**—"to the magistrate," as in Luke 12:58. **lest at any time**—here, rather, "lest at all," or simply "lest." **the adversary deliver thee to the judge, and the judge** [having pronounced you guilty] **deliver thee to the officer**—the official whose business it is to see the sentence carried into effect.

➤**26 Verily I say unto thee, Thou shalt by no means come out thence, till thou hast paid the uttermost farthing**—a fractional Roman coin, worth about half a cent. The language is designedly general; but it may safely be said that the unending duration of future punishment—elsewhere so clearly and awfully expressed by our Lord himself, as in 5:29 and 30, and Mark 9:43, 48—is the only doctrine with which his language here quite naturally and fully accords (cf. 18:30, 34).

## 27-32 THE SAME SUBJECT ILLUSTRATED FROM THE SEVENTH COMMANDMENT

➤**27 Ye have heard that it was said by them of old**—The words "by [or, to] them of old" are not in the earliest Greek manuscripts. **Thou shalt not commit adultery**—Interpreting this seventh, as they did the sixth commandment, perverters of the law restricted the breach of it to acts of unlawful intercourse between, or with, married persons exclusively.

➤**28 But I say unto you, That whosoever looketh on a woman to lust after her**—with the intent to do so, as the same expression is used in 6:1; or, with the full consent of his will, to feed thereby his unholy desires. **hath committed adultery with her already in his heart**—We are not to suppose, from the word here used ("adultery") that our Lord means to restrict the breach of this commandment to married persons, or to unlawful intercourse with such. The expressions "whosoever looketh" and "looketh upon a woman" seem clearly to extend the range of this commandment to all forms of impurity and the counsels which follow—as they most certainly were intended to confirm this. As in dealing with the sixth commandment, our Lord first expounds it and then in the four following verses applies his exposition, so here he first expounds the seventh commandment and then in the four following verses applies his exposition.

➤**29 And if thy right eye**—the readier and the dearer of the two. **offend thee**—be a "trap-spring" (the spring that triggers a trap), or as in the NT, be "an occasion of stumbling." **pluck it out and cast it from thee**—implying a certain indignant promptness, heedless of whatever cost to feeling the act may involve. Of course, it is not the physical eye of which our Lord speaks—as if execution were to be done upon the bodily organ—though there have been fanatical ascetics who have both advocated and practiced this, showing a very low apprehension of spiritual things—but the offending eye, or the eye considered as the occasion of sin; and consequently, only the sinful exercise of the organ is meant. Just as by cutting off a hand, or plucking out an eye, the power of acting and of seeing would be destroyed, our Lord certainly means that we are to strike at the root of such unholy dispositions, as well as cut off the occasions which tend to stimulate them. **for it is profitable for thee that one of thy members should perish, and not that thy whole body should be cast into hell**—He who despises the warning to cast from him, with indignant promptness, an offending member, will find his whole body "cast," with a retributive indignation, "into hell."

➤**30 And if thy right hand** [the organ of *action,* to which the eye excites] **offend thee, cut it off, and cast it from thee: for it is profitable**—See comments on 5:29. The repetition, in identical terms, of such stern truths and awful lessons seems characteristic of our Lord's manner of teaching (cf. Mark 9:43-48).

➤**31 It hath been said**—This shortened form was perhaps intentional, to make a transition from the commandments of the Ten Commandments to a civil enactment on the subject of divorce, quoted from Deuteronomy 24:1. The law of divorce—according to its strictness or laxity—has so intimate a bearing upon purity in the married life, that nothing could be more natural than to pass from the seventh commandment to the loose views on that subject then current. **Whosoever shall put away his wife, let him give her a writing of divorcement**—as a legal check upon reckless and tyrannical separation. The one legitimate ground of divorce allowed by the enactment just quoted was "some uncleanness"—in other words, conjugal infidelity. But while one school of Jewish interpreters (that of Shammai) explained this quite correctly, as prohibiting divorce in every case except that of adultery, another school (that of Hillel) stretched the expression so far as to include

everything in the wife offensive or disagreeable to the husband—a view of the law too well fitted to minister to caprice and depraved inclinations. It was to meet this that our Lord uttered what follows:

➤**32 But I say unto you, That whosoever shall put away his wife, saving for the cause of fornication, causeth her to commit adultery**—i.e., drives her into it in case she marries again. **and whosoever shall marry her that is divorced** [for anything short of conjugal infidelity] **committeth adultery**—for if the commandment is broken by the one party, it must be by the other also. But see comments on 19:4-9. Whether the innocent party, after a just divorce, may lawfully marry again is not treated here.

## 33-37 SAME SUBJECT ILLUSTRATED FROM THE THIRD COMMANDMENT

➤**33 Again, ye have heard that it hath been said by them of old time, Thou shalt not forswear thyself**—i.e., you shall not perjure. These are not the precise words of Exodus 20:7; but they express all that it was currently understood to condemn, viz., false swearing (Lev. 19:12). This is plain from what follows. **But I say unto you, Swear not at all**—That this was meant to condemn swearing of every kind and on every occasion is not the thought here. For even Yahweh is said again and again to have sworn by himself; and our Lord certainly answered upon oath to a question put to him by the high priest; and the apostle Paul several times, and in the most solemn language, made God his witness that he spoke and wrote the truth. Evidently, it is swearing in common conversation and on frivolous occasions that is here meant. Frivolous oaths were indeed severely condemned in the teaching of the times. But so narrow was the circle of them that a man might swear, says Lightfoot, a hundred thousand times and yet not be guilty of vain swearing. Hardly anything was regarded as an oath if only the name of God were not in it; just as among ourselves, as Trench well remarks, a certain lingering reverence for the name of God leads to cutting off portions of his name, or uttering sounds nearly resembling it, or substituting the name of some heathen deity, in profane exclamations or affirmations. Against all this our Lord now speaks decisively, teaching his audience that every oath carries an appeal to God whether named or not.

►**34, 35 neither by heaven; for it is God's throne: nor by the earth; for it is his footstool**—quoting Isaiah 66:1, **neither by Jerusalem, for it is the city of the great King**—quoting Psalm 48:2.

►**36 Neither shalt thou swear by thy head, because thou canst not make one hair white or black**—In the other oaths specified, God was profaned as if his name had been uttered, because his name was instantly suggested by the mention of his "throne," his "footstool," his "city." But in swearing by one's head and the like, the objection lies in their being beyond one's control, and therefore profanely assumed to have a stability which they have not.

►**37 But let your communication**—in ordinary interchange, **be Yea, yea; Nay, nay**—Let a simple yes and no suffice in affirming the truth or the untruth of anything. (See James. 5:12, and 2 Cor. 1:17, 18.) **for whatsoever is more than these cometh of evil**—not "of the evil one," though an equally correct rendering of the words, and one which some expositors prefer. It is true that all evil in our world is originally of the devil, that it forms a kingdom at the head of which he sits, and that, in every manifestation of it he has an active part. But any reference to this here seems unnatural, and the allusion to this passage in the Epistle of James (5:12) seems to show that this is not the sense of it: "Let your yea by yea; and your nay, nay; lest ye fall into condemnation." The untruthfulness of our corrupt nature shows itself not only in the tendency to deviate from the strict truth, but in the disposition to suspect others of doing the same; and as this is not diminished but rather aggravated by the habit of confirming what we say by an oath, we thus run the risk of having all reverence for God's holy name, and even for strict truth, destroyed in our hearts, and so "fall into condemnation." The practice of going beyond yes and no in affirmations and denials—as if our word for it were not enough, and we expected others to question it—springs from the vicious root of untruthfulness, which is only aggravated by the very effort to clear ourselves of the suspicion of it.

## 38-42 SAME SUBJECT—RETALIATION

We have here the converse of the preceding lessons. They were negative; these are positive.

►**38 Ye have heard that it hath been said**—See Exodus 21:23-25; Leviticus 24:19, 20; Deuteronomy 19:21. **An eye for an eye, and a tooth for a tooth**—i.e., whatever penalty was regarded as a proper equivalent for these. This law of retribution—designed to take vengeance out of the hands of private persons and commit it to the magistrate—was abused. This judicial regulation was held to be a warrant for taking redress into one's own hands, contrary to the injunctions of the OT itself (Prov. 20:22; 24:29).

►**39 But I say unto you, That ye resist not evil: but whosoever shall smite thee on thy right cheek, turn to him the other also**—Our Lord's own meek yet dignified bearing when smitten rudely on the cheek (John 18:22, 23) and not literally presenting the other, is the best comment on these words. It is the preparedness, after one indignity, not to invite but to submit meekly to another, without retaliation, which this strong language is meant to convey.

►**40 And if any man will sue thee at the law, and take away thy coat**—the inner garment in pledge for a debt (Exod. 22:2, 27). **let him have thy cloak also**—the outer and more costly garment. This overcoat was not allowed to be retained overnight as a pledge from the poor because they used it for a bedcovering.

►**41 And whosoever shall compel thee to go a mile, go with him twain** [two]—an allusion, probably, to the practice of the Romans and some Eastern nations, who, when government dispatches had to be forwarded, obliged the people not only to furnish horses and carriages, but to give personal attendance, often at great inconvenience, when required. But the thing here demanded is a readiness to submit to unreasonable demands of whatever kind, rather than raise quarrels, with all the evils resulting from them. What follows is a beautiful extension of this precept.

►**42 Give to him that asketh thee**—The sense of unreasonable asking is here implied (cf. Luke 6:30). **and from him that would borrow of thee turn not thou away**—Though the Greek word for "borrow" in classical usage signified "to have money lent to one on security," or "with interest," yet as this was not the original sense of the word, and as usury was forbidden among the Jews (Exod. 22:25, etc.), it is doubtless simple borrowing which our Lord here means, as indeed the whole strain of the exhortation implies. This shows that such counsels as "owe no man anything" (Rom. 13:8) are not to be taken absolutely for then the Scripture commendations of the righteous for "lending" to his needy brother (Ps. 37:36; 112:5; Luke 6:37) would have no application. **turn not thou away**—a graphic expression of refusal to relieve a brother in need.

43-48 SAME SUBJECT—LOVE TO ENEMIES

➤**43 Ye have heard that it hath been said**—in Leviticus 19:18. **Thou shalt love thy neighbour and hate thine enemy**—as if the one were a legitimate inference from the other.

➤**44 But I say unto you, Love your enemies**—The word here used (*agapaō*) denotes moral love, as distinguished from the other word (*phileō*), which expresses personal affection. The former denotes compassionate outgoing of desire for another's good. **bless them that curse you, do good to them that hate you**— These words are not found in the two oldest manuscripts (Codex Sinaiticus and Codex Vaticanus). **and pray for them which despitefully use you, and persecute you**—The words "which despitefully use you, and" are not found in the two oldest manuscripts (Codex Sinaiticus and Codex Vaticanus). Thus, the second part of the verse reads simply, "Pray for them who persecute you." The best commentary on this matchless counsel is the bright example of him who gave it. (See 1 Pet. 2:21-24; and cf. Rom. 12:20, 21; 1 Cor. 4:12; 1 Pet. 3:9.)

➤**45 That ye may be the children** [sons] **of your Father which** [who] **is in heaven**—The meaning is, "that ye may show yourselves to be such by resembling him" (cf. 5:9 and Eph. 5:1). This was spoken of elsewhere in Scripture (see Lev. 19:2; 20:26; and cf. 1 Pet. 1:15, 16). **for he maketh his sun to rise on the evil and on the good, and sendeth rain on the just and on the unjust**—rather (without the article) "on evil and good, and on just and unjust."

➤**46 For if ye love them which love you, what reward have ye? do not even the publicans** [tax collectors] **the same?**—The publicans, as collectors of taxes due to the Roman government, were obnoxious to the Jews, who sat uneasy under a foreign yoke and disliked whatever brought this unpleasantly before them. But the extortion practiced by this class made them hateful to the community, who in their current speech ranked them with "harlots." The meaning, then, is "In loving those who love you, there is no evidence of superior principle: the worst of men will do this: even a publican will go to that length."

➤**47 And if ye salute your brethren only**—of the same nation and religion as yourselves. **what do ye more [than others]?**—what do ye uncommon or extraordinary (i.e., wherein do ye excel?)? **do not even the publicans so?**—The meaning here appears to be "Do not even the heathens the same?" see 18:17, where the excommunicated person is said to be "as an heathen man and a publican."

➤**48 Be ye therefore**—or, "you will be"— the verb in Greek is future active, not present imperative. Therefore, this is not a demand but a promise. This is very significant because Christ is not demanding perfection from us—which would be impossible for us to fulfill; rather, Christ is promising us perfection—which is maturation, and completion. **perfect**—or complete. Manifestly, our Lord here speaks, not of degrees of excellence, but of the kind of excellence that was to distinguish his disciples and characterize his kingdom. When therefore he adds, **even as your Father which is in heaven is perfect,** he refers to that glorious completeness that is in the great divine model, "their Father which is in heaven."

*Chapter* **6**

1-18 SERMON ON THE MOUNT CONTINUED

1-4 ALMS GIVING

➤**1 Take heed that ye do not your alms**—But the true reading seems clearly to be "your righteousness," not "your alms." The external authority (of the manuscripts) and internal evidence is decidedly in favor of "righteousness." The subject of the second verse being "almsgiving," that word—so like the other in Greek (righteousness is *dikaiosunēn*; almsgiving is *eleēmosunēn*—the last six letters are identical)—might easily be substituted for it by the copyist, whereas the opposite would not be so likely. Even more in favor of "righteousness" is the idea that the first verse then becomes a general heading for this whole section of the discourse, inculcating unostentatiousness in all deeds of righteousness—almsgiving, prayer, and fasting being in that case but selected examples of this righteousness; whereas, if we read, "Do not your alms...," this first verse will have no reference but to that one point. By "righteousness," in this case, we are to understand that same righteousness of the kingdom of heaven. The main point of this discourse is to expound on that righteousness of which the Lord says, "Except your righteousness shall exceed the righteousness of the scribes and Pharisees, ye shall in no case enter into the kingdom of heaven" (5:20). To do this righteousness was an old and well-understood expression. Thus, "Blessed is he that doeth righteousness at all times" (Ps. 106:3). It refers to the actings of righteousness in the life—the outgoings of the gracious nature—of which our Lord afterwards said to his disciples, "Herein is my Father glorified, that ye bear much fruit; so shall ye be my disciples" (John 15:8). **before men, to be seen of them**—with the view of intention of being beheld of them. See the same expression in 5:28. True, he had required them to let their light so shine before men that they might see their good works and glorify their Father which is in heaven (5:16). But this is quite consistent with not making a display of our righteousness for self-glorification. In fact, the doing of the former necessarily implies our not doing the latter. **otherwise ye have no reward of your Father which** [who] **is in heaven**—When all duty is done to God, he will take care that it be duly recognized; but when done purely for ostentation, God cannot own it, nor is his judgment of it even thought of—God accepts only what is done to himself. So much for the general principle. Now follow three illustrations of it.

►**2 Therefore, when thou doest thine alms, do not sound a trumpet before thee**—The expression is to be taken figuratively for blazoning it. Hence our expression "to trumpet." **as the hypocrites do**—This word (of such frequent occurrence in Scripture, signifying primarily "one who acts a part") denotes one who either pretends to be what he is not (as here), or dissembles (disguises) what he really is (as in Luke 12:1, 2). **in the synagogues and in the streets**—the places of religious and of secular resort. **that they may have glory of men. Verily I say unto you**—In such august expressions, it is the Lawgiver and Judge himself that we hear speaking to us. **They have their reward**—All they wanted was human applause, and they have it—and with it, all they will ever get.

►**3 But when thou doest alms, let not thy left hand know what thy right hand doeth**—So far from making a display of it, dwell not on it even in thine own thoughts, lest it minister to spiritual pride.

►**4 That thine alms may be in secret, and thy Father which seeth in secret himself shall reward thee openly**—The words "himself" and "openly" do not appear in the earliest manuscripts.

5, 6 PRAYER

►**5 And when thou prayest, thou shalt** [or, preferably, when ye pray ye shall] **not be as the hypocrites are: for they love to pray standing in the synagogues and in the corners of the streets**— The standing posture in prayer was the ancient practice, alike in the Jewish and in the early Christian church, but of course this conspicuous posture opened the way for the ostentatious. (See comments on 6:2.)

►**6 But thou, when thou prayest, enter into thy closet** [a private room]**, and when thou hast shut thy door, pray to thy Father which is in secret; and thy Father which seeth in secret shall reward thee openly**—The word "openly" is not found in the best manuscripts. At any rate, it is not the simple publicity of prayer that is here condemned. It may be offered in any circumstances, however open, if not prompted by the spirit of ostentation but dictated by the great purposes of prayer itself. It is the private character of true prayer that is here taught.

## 7-15 SUPPLEMENTARY DIRECTIONS, AND MODEL PRAYER

➤**7 But when ye pray, use not vain repetitions**—"Babble not" would be a better rendering, both for the form of the word—which in both languages is intended to imitate the sound—and for the sense, which expresses not so much the repetition of the same words as a senseless multiplication of them as appears from what follows. **as the heathen** [lit., "Gentiles"] **do: for they think that they shall be heard for their much speaking**—This method of heathen devotion is still observed by Hindu and Muslim devotees. With the Jews, says Lightfoot, it was a maxim, that "every one who multiplies prayer is heard." In the Roman Catholic church, not only was it done far too much, but, as Tholuck justly observes, the very prayer that our Lord gave as an antidote to vain repetitions is the most abused to their superstitious end; the number of times it is repeated counting for so much more merit. Is not this just that characteristic feature of heathen devotion that our Lord here condemns? But praying much, and using at times the same words, is not here condemned and has the example of our Lord himself in its favor.

➤**8 Be not ye therefore like unto them: for your Father knoweth what things ye have need of, before ye ask him**—and so he does not need to be informed of our wants, any more than to be roused to attend to them by our incessant speaking. What a view of God is here given, in sharp contrast with the gods of the heathen! But let it be carefully noted that it is not as the general Father of mankind that our Lord says, "Your Father" knoweth what ye need before ye ask it; for it is not men, as such, that he is addressing in this discourse but his own disciples—the poor in spirit, the mourners, the meek, hungry and thirsty souls, the merciful, the pure in heart, the peacemakers, who allow themselves to have all manner of evil said against them for the Son of man's sake—in short, the newborn children of God, who, making their Father's interests their own, are here assured that their Father, in return, makes their interests his and needs neither to be told nor to be reminded of their wants. Yet he will have his children pray to him and

links all his promised supplies to their petitions for them, thus encouraging us to draw near and keep near to him.

➤**9 After this manner** [more simply "Thus"] **therefore pray ye**—The "ye" is emphatic here, in contrast with the heathen prayers. That this matchless prayer was given not only as a model but as a form might be concluded from its very nature. If it consisted only of hints or directions for prayer, it could only be used as a directory; but because it is an actual prayer—designed, indeed, to show how much real prayer could be compressed into the fewest words, but still, as a prayer, only the more incomparable for that—it is strange that there should be a doubt whether we ought to pray that very prayer. Surely the words with which it is introduced, in the second utterance and varied form of it that we have in Luke 11:2, ought to make this clear: "When ye pray, say, Our Father." Nevertheless, since the second form of it varies considerably from the first, and since no example of its actual use, or express quotation of its phraseology, occurs in the sequel of the NT, we are to guard against a superstitious use of it. How early this began to appear in the church services and to what extent it was afterwards carried is known to everyone versed in church history.

### 9-13 MODEL PRAYER

According to the Latin fathers and the Lutheran church, the petitions of the Lord's prayer are seven in number; according to the Greek fathers, the Reformed Church, and the Westminster scholars, they are only six—the last two being regarded as one. The first three petitions have to do exclusively with God: *"Thy* name be hallowed"—*"Thy* kingdom come"—*"Thy* will be done." And they occur in a descending scale—from himself down to the manifestation of himself in his kingdom; and from his kingdom to the entire subjection of its subjects, or the complete doing of his will. The remaining four petitions have to do with us: "Give us our daily bread"—"Forgive *us* our debts"—"Lead *us* not into temptation"—"Deliver *us* from evil." But these latter petitions occur in an ascending scale—from the bodily needs of every day up to our final deliverance from all evil.

*Invocation*

➤9 **Our Father which art** [who are] **in heaven**—In the first two words we express his nearness to us; in the last four words, his distance from us (see Eccles. 5:2; Isa. 66:1). Loving familiarity suggests the one; reverence the other. In calling him "Father" we express a relationship we have known and felt from our infancy; but in calling him our Father "who art in heaven," we contrast him with the fathers we have here below and so raise our souls to that "heaven" where he dwells in majesty and glory. These first words of the Lord's Prayer spark the whole prayer with brightness and warmth. These words usher the praying believer into a sphere of accessible love. It is true that the paternal relationship of God to his people is by no means strange to the OT (see Deut. 32:6; Ps. 103:13; Isa. 63:16; Jer. 3:4, 19; Mal. 1:6; 2:10).

*First petition*

**Hallowed be**—i.e., Be held in reverence; regarded and treated as holy. **thy name**—God's name means "himself as revealed and manifested." Everywhere in Scripture God defines the faith, love, reverence, and obedience he wants from men by the disclosures he makes to them of what he is—to both shut out false conceptions of him and to make all their devotion take the shape of his own teaching. Too much attention cannot be paid to this.

*Second petition*

➤10 **Thy kingdom come**—The kingdom of God is that moral and spiritual kingdom in which God rules. When Christ appeared, it was as a visible kingdom "at hand." His death laid the foundations of it. His ascension on high and the effusion of the Spirit into thousands upon thousands of believers was a glorious "coming" of this kingdom. But it is still to come, and this petition, "Thy kingdom come," must not cease to ascend so long as one subject of it remains to be brought in.

*Third petition*

**Thy will be done in earth, as it is in heaven**—or, as the same words are rendered in Luke, "as in heaven, so upon earth." But some will ask, will this ever be? The answer: if the "new heavens and new earth" are to be our present material universe purified by fire and transfigured, of course it will. But the aspira-

tion which we are taught in this beautiful petition to breathe forth may have no direct reference to any such physical fulfillment and is only the spontaneous and restless longing of the renewed soul—put into words—to see the whole inhabited earth in entire conformity to the will of God. It asks not if ever it shall be—or if ever it can be—in order to pray this prayer. Another way to look at this prayer is to see it as an encouragement to action—to the carrying out of God's will on earth. Believers are to carry out God's will in the same way as those in heaven carry it out: eagerly, willingly, and absolutely.

*Fourth petition*

➤11 **Give us this day our daily bread**—The compound word here rendered "daily" *(epiousion)* appears nowhere else in Greek literature prior to the time of the NT and so must be interpreted by the analysis of its component parts. The word can mean "that which gives substance or being" (from the Gk. word, ousia), or, "that which follows" (from the Gk. participle, *epiousa*), or, "for the coming day" (from the Gk. expression, *hēepiousa hemera*). According to the parallel verse in Luke (11:3), it undoubtedly suggests the sustenance that comes day by day. In any case, the petition indicates that we are to ask each day for the bread that will sustain our physical existence. We must remember that Jesus was speaking to a people who in fact lived a day-to-day and hand-to-mouth existence. This prayer was vital to their daily life. And though many of us in this modern age live according to longer increments of pay and provision, we still need to pray for our physical existence and realize that we are completely dependent on him. Some commentators have indicated that the daily bread is spiritual bread, but this kind of exposition goes beyond the context and nature of this prayer.

*Fifth petition*

➤12 **And forgive us our debts**—This conveys a vitally important view of sin; it is an offense against God demanding reparation to his dishonored claims upon our absolute subjection. As the debtor in the creditor's hand, so is the sinner in the hands of God. This idea of sin had indeed come up before in this discourse—in the warning to agree with our adversary quickly, in case of sentence being passed upon us, adjudging us to payment of the last farthing, and to imprisonment until then (5:25, 26). And it comes up over and over in our Lord's subsequent teaching—as in the parable of the creditor and his two debtors (Luke 7:41), and in the parable of the unmerciful debtor (18:23). But by embodying it in this brief model of acceptable prayer, and as the first of three petitions more or less bearing upon sin, our Lord teaches us, in the most emphatic manner conceivable, to regard this view of sin as the primary and fundamental one. Answering to this is the "forgiveness" which it directs us to seek—the removal of any debt in God's "book of remembrance" (see Mal. 3:16). **as we forgive our debtors**—The best manuscripts read, "as we have forgiven our debtors." The perfect tense indicates that the petitioner has already forgiven other people's debts when he asks God for forgiveness. This does not mean, however, that God will forgive us *only* when we have exercised forgiveness toward others—other Scriptures indicate that God's forgiveness is unconditional. But as no one can reasonably imagine himself to be the object of divine forgiveness who is deliberately and habitually unforgiving toward his fellowmen, so it is a beautiful provision to make our right to ask and expect daily forgiveness of our daily shortcomings and our final acquittal at the great day of admission into the kingdom dependent upon our consciousness of a forgiving disposition toward our fellows and our preparedness to protest before the Searcher of hearts that we do actually forgive them (see Mark 11:25, 26). God sees his own image reflected in his forgiving children; but to ask God for what we ourselves refuse to men is to insult him. So much stress does our Lord put upon this that immediately after the close of this prayer, it is the one point to which he comes back (6:14, 15), for the purpose of solemnly assuring us that the divine procedure in this matter of forgiveness will be exactly what our own is.

*Sixth petition*

➤ **13 And lead us not into temptation**—He who honestly seeks and has the assurance of forgiveness for past sin will strive to avoid committing it in the future. But conscious that "when we would do good evil is present with

us," we are taught to offer this sixth petition, which comes naturally close upon the preceding, and flows, indeed, instinctively from it in the hearts of all earnest Christians. There is some difficulty in the form of the petition, as it is certain that God does bring his people—as he did Abraham, and Christ himself—into circumstances both fitted and designed to try them or test the strength of their faith. Some deal with this by regarding the petition as simply a humble expression of self-distrust and instinctive shrinking from danger; but this seems too weak. Others take it as a prayer against yielding to temptation, and so equivalent to a prayer for support and deliverance when we are tempted; but this seems to go beyond the precise thing intended. Perhaps it is best to take it as a prayer against being drawn or sucked, of our own will, into temptation, to which the word used here seems to lend some validity—"Introduce us not." This view, while it does not put into our mouths a prayer against being tempted, does not, on the other hand, change the sense of the petition into one for support under temptation, which the words will hardly bear; but it gives us a subject for prayer, in regard to temptation, most definite, and of all others most needful. It was precisely this that Peter needed to ask, but did not ask, when—of his own accord and in spite of difficulties—he pressed for entrance into the palace-hall of the high priest, and where, once sucked into the scene and atmosphere of temptation, he fell so terribly. And if so, does it not seem very clear that this was exactly what our Lord meant his disciples to pray against when he said in the garden, "Watch and pray, that ye enter not into temptation" (26:41)?

*Seventh petition*

**But deliver us from evil**—As the expression "from evil" may be equally well rendered "from the evil one," a number of good commentators think the devil is intended, especially from its following close upon the subject of "temptation." But the comprehensive character of these brief petitions, and the place which this one occupies, as that on which all our desires die away, seems to be against so contracted a view. Nor can there be a reasonable doubt that Paul, in some of the last sentences that he penned before he was brought forth to suffer for his Lord, alludes to this very petition in the language of calm assurance—"And the Lord shall deliver me from every evil work [cf. the Gk. of the two passages], and will preserve me unto his heavenly kingdom" (2 Tim. 4:18). The final petition, then, is only rightly grasped when regarded as a prayer for deliverance from all evil of whatever kind—not only from sin, but from all its consequences—fully and finally. Fitly, then, are our prayers ended with this. **For thine is the kingdom, and the power, and the glory, for ever. Amen**—This doxology can hardly be considered part of the original text. It is missing in all the most ancient manuscripts (Codices Vaticanus, Sinaiticus, Bezea, and another fifth-century uncial—0170). It is not in the Old Latin version, the Vulgate, and some of the Coptic Boharic versions. As might be expected from this, it is passed by in silence by the earliest Latin fathers; but even the Greek commentators, when expounding this prayer, pass by the doxology. On the other hand, it is found in a majority of manuscripts, though not the oldest; it is found in all the Syriac versions, even the Peshitta. It is found in the Sahidic or Thebaic version made for the Christians of Upper Egypt, possibly as early as the Old Latin; and it is found in perhaps most of the later versions. But since the earliest manuscripts do not contain the doxology and no good reason can be given to explain why it would have been dropped if it were original, it seems very likely that later copyists added the doxology for liturgical purposes, modeling it after 1 Chronicles 29:11.

►**14, 15** See comments on 6:12.

## 16-18 FASTING

Having concluded his supplementary directions on the subject of prayer with the divine pattern, our Lord now returns to the subject of unostentatiousness in our deeds of righteousness, in order to give one more illustration of it in the matter of fasting.

►**16 Moreover, when ye fast**—referring, probably, to private and voluntary fasting, which was to be regulated by each individual for himself, though it would essentially apply to any fast. **be not, as the hypocrites, of a sad countenance: for they disfigure their faces**—lit., "make unseen"; very well rendered "disfigure." They went about with a slovenly appearance and ashes sprinkled on their head.

**that they may appear unto men to fast**—it was not the deed but reputation for the deed that they sought; and with this in view those hypocrites multiplied their fasts.

►**17 But thou, when thou fastest, anoint thine head, and wash thy face**—as the Jews did, except when mourning (Dan. 10:3); so that the meaning is, "Appear as usual"—appear so as to attract no notice.

►**18 That thou appear not unto men to fast, but unto thy Father which is in secret: and thy Father, which seeth in secret, shall reward thee openly**—The word "openly," a later addition to the text, is taken from 6:4, 7. It does not appear in all the earliest manuscripts.

## 19-34 CONCLUDING ILLUSTRATIONS OF THE RIGHTEOUSNESS OF THE KINGDOM—HEAVENLY-MINDEDNESS AND FILIAL CONFIDENCE

►**19 Lay not up for yourselves** [hoard not] **treasures upon earth, where moth**—a "clothes moth." Eastern treasures, consisting partly in costly dresses stored up (Job. 27:16), were liable to be consumed by moths (Job 13:28; Isa. 50:9; 51:8). In James 5:2 there is an evident reference to our Lord's words here. **and rust**—any "eating into" or "consuming"; here, probably, "wear-and-tear." **doth corrupt**—cause to disappear. By this reference to moth and rust our Lord would teach how perishable are such earthly treasures.

►**20 But lay up for yourselves treasures in heaven**—cf. Luke 12:33; Col. 3:2.

►**21 For where your treasure is** [that which you value most], **there will your heart be also**—"What a man loves," says Luther, "that is his God. For he carries it in his heart, he goes about with it night and day, he sleeps and wakes with it; be it what it may—wealth or pelf, pleasure or renown." But because "laying up" is not in itself sinful, and in fact in some cases is encouraged (2 Cor. 12:14), and honest industry and sagacious enterprise are usually rewarded with prosperity, many flatter themselves that all is right between them and God, while their closest attention, anxiety, zeal, and time are exhausted upon these earthly pursuits. To put this right, our Lord adds what follows, in which there is profound practical wisdom.

➤22 **The light** [the lamp] **of the body is the eye: if therefore thine eye be single**—simple, clear. As applied to the outward eye, this means general soundness; particularly, not looking two ways. Here, as also in classical Greek, it is used figuratively to denote the simplicity of the mind's eye, singleness of purpose, looking right at its object, as opposed to having two ends in view (see Prov. 4:25-27). **thy whole body shall be full of light**—illuminated. As with the bodily vision, the man who looks with a good, sound eye, walks in light, seeing every object clearly; so a simple and persistent purpose to serve and please God in everything will make the whole character consistent and bright.

➤23 **But if thine eye be evil**—distempered, or, as we say, if we have an evil eye—**thy whole body shall be full of darkness**—darkened. As a vitiated eye, or an eye that does not look straight and full at its object, sees nothing as it is, so a divided mind is dark. **If therefore the light that is in thee be darkness, how great is that darkness!**—As the conscience is the regulative faculty, and a man's inward purpose, scope, aim in life, determines his character—if these be not simple and directed to God, but distorted and double, what must all the other faculties and principles of his nature be which take their direction and character from these, and what must the whole man and the whole life be but a mass of darkness? In Luke (11:36) the converse of this statement very strikingly expresses what pure, beautiful, broad perceptions the clarity of the inward eye imparts: "If then your whole body is full of light, having no part dark, it will be wholly bright, as when a lamp with its rays gives you light" (RSV). But now for the application of this.

➤24 **No man can serve**—or, "be a slave to." The word means to "belong wholly and be entirely under command to." **two masters: for either he will hate the one, and love the other; or else he will hold to the one, and despise the other**—Even if the two masters be of one character and have but one object, the servant must take law (commandments) from one or the other: though he may do what is agreeable to both, he cannot, in the nature of the thing, be servant to more than one. Much less if, as in the present case, their interests are quite different, and even conflicting. In this case, if our affections be in the service of the one—if we "love the one"—we must of necessity "hate the other"; if we determine resolutely to "hold to the one," we must at the same time disregard and (if he insist on his claims upon us) even "despise the other." **Ye cannot serve God and mammon**—The word "mammon" in Greek is a transliteration of an Aramaic word *mamona,* which means "wealth," "money," or "property." It is impossible to serve this god and the true God at the same time. Here, there can be no doubt it is used for "riches," considered as an idol master, or god of the heart. But since the teaching of the preceding verses might seem to endanger our falling short of what is requisite for the present life, our Lord now comes to speak to that point.

➤25 **Therefore I say unto you, Take no thought**—"Be not anxious." The English word "thought," when the KJV was made, expressed this idea of "solicitude," "anxious concern"— as may be seen in any old English classic; and in the same sense it is used in 1 Samuel 9:5. But this sense of the word has now nearly gone out, and so the mere English reader is apt to be perplexed. Thought or forethought, for temporal things—in the sense of reflection, consideration—is required alike by Scripture and common sense. It is that anxious solicitude, that oppressive care, which springs from unbelieving doubts and misgivings, which alone is here condemned (see Phil. 4:6). **for your life, what ye shall eat, or what ye shall drink; nor yet for your body, what ye shall put on**—In Luke (12:29) our Lord adds, "Do not worry about it" (NIV). When we turn our souls to God in prayer, Paul assures us that "the peace of God, which passeth all understanding, shall keep our hearts and minds in Christ Jesus" (Phil. 4:6, 7); i.e., shall guard both our feelings and our thoughts from undue agitation and keep them in a holy calm. But when we commit our whole temporal condition to the intelligence of our own minds, we get into that unsettled state against which our Lord exhorts his disciples. **Is not the life more than meat** [food], **and the body than raiment?**—If God, then, gives and keeps up the greater—the life, the body—will he withhold the less, i.e., food to sustain life and raiment to clothe the body?

➤26 **Behold the fowls of the air**—in 6:28, "observe well," and in Luke 12:24, "consider"—so as to learn wisdom from them. **for they sow not,**

**neither do they reap, nor gather into barns; yet your heavenly Father feedeth them. Are ye not much better than they?**—The argument here is from the greater to the less; but how rich in detail! The birds—void of reason—are incapable of sowing, reaping, and storing; yet your heavenly Father does not allow them to perish helplessly but sustains them without any of those processes. Will he see, then, his own children using all the means that reason dictates for procuring the things needful for the body—depending on him for everything—and yet leave them to starve?

➤**27 Which of you, by taking thought** [anxious solicitude] **can add one cubit unto his stature?**—"Stature" can hardly be the thing intended here: first, because the subject is the prolongation of life by the supply of its necessities of food and clothing; next, because no one would dream of adding a cubit—or a foot and a half—to his stature; and finally, in the corresponding passage in Luke (12:25, 26) the thing intended is represented as "that thing which is least." But if we take the word in its primary sense of "age" (for "stature" is but a secondary sense) the idea will be this, "Which of you, however anxiously you vex yourselves about it, can add any time to your life (i.e., lengthen your life)?" To compare the length of life to measures of this nature is not foreign to the language of Scripture (cf. Ps. 39:5; 2 Tim. 4:7). So understood, the meaning is clear and the connection natural.

➤**28 And why take ye thought for raiment? Consider** [observe well] **the lilies of the field, how they grow; they toil not**—as men, planting and preparing the flax. **neither do they spin**—as women.

➤**29 And yet I say unto you, That even Solomon in all his glory was not arrayed like one of these**—What incomparable teaching!—best left in its own transparent clearness and rich simplicity.

➤**30 Wherefore, if God so clothe the grass of the field, which to day is, and to morrow is cast into the oven**—wild flowers cut with the grass, withering by the heat, and used for fuel (see James 1:11). **shall he not much more clothe you, O ye of little faith?**—The argument here is something fresh. Lovely as is the array of the flowers that deck the fields, surpassing all artificial human grandeur, it is for

but a brief moment; you enjoy it today and tomorrow it is gone; your own hands have seized and cast it into the oven. Shall, then, God's children, so dear to him, be left naked? He does not say, "Shall they not be more beauteously arrayed?" but, "Shall he not much more *clothe* them?" (cf. Heb. 13:5). The expression "little-faithed ones," which our Lord applies again and again to his disciples (8:26; 14:31; 16:8), can hardly be regarded as rebuking any actual manifestations of unbelief at that early period and before such an audience. It is his way of gently chiding the spirit of unbelief, so natural even to the best, who are surrounded by a physical world.

➤**31, 32 Therefore take no thought** [be not anxious], **saying, What shall we eat? or, What shall we drink? or, Wherewithal shall we be clothed? (For after all these things do the Gentiles seek:)**—Knowing nothing definitely beyond the present life to kindle their aspirations and engage their supreme attention, the heathen naturally pursue present objects as their chief and only good. **for your heavenly Father knoweth that ye have need of all these things**—How precious this word! Food and raiment are pronounced needful to God's children; and he who could say, "No man knoweth... the Father, save the Son, and he to whomsoever the Son will reveal him" (11:27), says with an authority which none but himself could claim, "Your heavenly Father knoweth that ye have need of all these things."

➤**33 But seek ye first the kingdom of God, and his righteousness; and all these things shall be added unto you**—This is the great summing up. Strictly speaking, it has to do only with the subject of the present section—the right state of the heart with reference to heavenly and earthly things; but being positioned in the form of a brief, general directive, it is so comprehensive as to embrace the whole subject of this discourse. And, as if to make this the more evident, the two keynotes of this great sermon resound in this verse: "the kingdom" and "the righteousness" of the kingdom. They are the grand objects of our supreme pursuit in this life. The precise sense of every word in this golden verse should be carefully weighed. **"The kingdom of God"** is the primary subject of the Sermon on the Mount. The kingdom of God is the sphere and realm of God's ruling in the lives of all those who have accepted Christ as Lord and King. "The righteousness thereof" is the character of all such, so amply described and variously illustrated in the foregoing portions of this discourse. The "seeking" of these is the making of them the object of supreme choice and pursuit; and the seeking of them "first" is the seeking of them before and above all else. The "all these things," which shall in that case be added to us, are just the "things" the last words of the preceding verse assured us "our heavenly Father knoweth that ye have need of"; i.e., all we require for the present life. And when our Lord says they shall be "added," it is implied, as a matter of course, that the seekers of the kingdom and its righteousness shall have these as their proper and primary portion: the rest being their gracious reward for not seeking them. (See an illustration of this principle in 2 Chron. 1:11, 12.) What follows is but a reduction of this great general direction into a practical and ready form for daily use.

➤34 **Take therefore no thought** [anxious care] **for the morrow: for the morrow shall take thought for the things of itself**—(or, according to other authorities, "for itself") shall have its own causes of anxiety. **Sufficient unto the day is the evil thereof**—An admirable practical maxim. Every day brings its own cares; and to anticipate is only to double them.

Chapter 7

## 1-29 SERMON ON THE MOUNT CONCLUDED

### 1-5 CENSORIOUS JUDGMENT

➤1 **Judge not, that ye be not judged**—To "judge" here does not exactly mean to pronounce condemnatory judgment, nor does it refer to simple judging at all, whether favorable or the reverse. The context makes it clear that the thing here condemned is that disposition to look unfavorably on the character and actions of others, which leads invariably to the pronouncing of rash, unjust, and unlovely judgments upon them. No doubt it is the judgments so pronounced that are here spoken of, but what the Lord aims at is the spirit out of which they spring. Provided we avoid this unlovely spirit, we are not only warranted to exercise judgment

upon a brother's character and actions but, in the exercise of a necessary discrimination, are often constrained to do so for our own guidance. It is the violation of the law of love involved in the exercise of a censorious disposition that alone is here condemned. And the argument against it—"that ye be not judged"— confirms this: "that your own character and actions be not pronounced upon with the like severity"; i.e., at the great day of judgment.

➤2 **For with what judgments ye judge, ye shall be judged: and with what measure ye mete** [whatever standard of judgment you apply to others], **it shall be measured to you again**—This proverbial maxim is used by our Lord in other connections (as in Mark 4:24, and with a slightly different application in Luke 6:38) as a great principle in the divine administration. Unkind judgment of others will be judicially returned upon ourselves, in the day when God shall judge the secrets of men by Jesus Christ. But, as in many other cases under the divine administration, such harsh judgment gets punishment even here. For people shrink from contact with those who systematically deal out harsh judgment upon others—naturally concluding that they themselves may be the next victims—and feel impelled in self-defense, when exposed to it, to return to the assailant his own censures.

➤3 **And why beholdest thou the mote**— "splinter," or, "speck," denoting any small fault. **that is in thy brother's eye, but considerest not the beam** [or, plank] **that is in thine own eye?**—denoting the much greater fault we overlook in ourselves.

➤5 **Thou hypocrite, first cast out the beam out of thine own eye; and then shalt thou see clearly to cast out the mote out of thy brother's eye**—The Lord uses a most hyperbolical, but not unfamiliar, figure to express the monstrous inconsistency of this conduct. They are hypocrites because they pretend to have a concern for their brother, while they have worse faults uncorrected in themselves. He only is fit to be a reprover of others who jealously and severely judges himself. Such persons will not only be slow to undertake the office of censor on their neighbors, but, when constrained in faithfulness to deal with them, will make it evident that they do it with reluctance and not satisfaction, with moderation and not exaggeration, with love and not harshness.

## 6 PROFANATION OF HOLY THINGS

The opposite extreme to that of censoriousness is condemned here, i.e., lack of discrimination of character.

►**6 Give not that which is holy unto the dogs**—savage or snarling haters of truth and righteousness. **neither cast ye your pearls before swine**—the impure or coarse, who are incapable of appreciating the priceless jewels of Christianity. In the East, dogs were wilder and more gregarious and, feeding on carrion and garbage, were coarser and fiercer than the same animals in the West. Dogs and swine, besides being ceremonially unclean, were peculiarly repulsive to the Jews, and indeed to the ancients generally. **lest they trample them under their feet**—as swine do—**and turn again and rend you**—as dogs do. Spiritual riches are brought into contempt and its possessors insulted when they are forced upon those who cannot value them and will not have them. But while the indiscriminately zealous have need of this caution, let us be on our guard against too readily putting our neighbors down as dogs and swine and excusing ourselves from endeavoring to do them good.

## 7-11 PRAYER

One might think enough had been said on this subject in 6:5-15. But the difficulty of carrying out the Lord's forementioned commands seems to have recalled the subject, and this gives it quite a new turn. "How shall we ever be able to carry out such precepts as these, of tender, holy, yet discriminating love?" might the disciple inquire. "Go to God with it," is our Lord's reply.

►**7 Ask, and it shall be given you; seek, and ye shall find; knock, and it shall be opened unto you**—There seems to be a climax here, expressive of more and more importunity; yet each of these terms used presents different aspects of what we desire of God. We ask for what we wish; we seek for what we miss; we knock for that from which we feel ourselves shut. Answering to this threefold representation is the triple assurance of success to our believing efforts.

►**8 For every one that asketh receiveth; and he that seeketh findeth; and to him that knocketh it shall be opened**—Of course, it is presumed that he asks aright—i.e., in faith—and with an honest purpose to make use of what he

receives. "If any of you lack wisdom, let him ask of God.... But let him ask in faith, nothing wavering [undecided whether to be altogether on the Lord's side]. For he that wavereth is like a wave of the sea driven with the wind and tossed. For let not that man think that he shall receive any thing of the Lord" (James 1:5-7). Hence, "When you ask, you do not receive, because you ask with the wrong motives, that you may spend what you get on your pleasures" (James 4:3, NIV).

►**9 Or what man is there of you, whom if his son ask bread** [a loaf] **will he give him a stone?**—round and smooth like such a loaf or cake as was much in use, but only to mock him.

►**10 Or if he ask a fish, will he give him a serpent?**—like it, indeed, but only to sting him.

►**11 If ye then, being evil, know how to give good gifts unto your children, how much more shall your Father which is in heaven give good things to them that ask him!**—Bad as our fallen nature is, the paternal nature in us is not extinguished. What a heart, then, must the Father of all fathers have toward his pleading children! In the corresponding passage in Luke (see comments on 11:13), instead of "good things," our Lord asks whether he will not much more give *the Holy Spirit* to them that ask him.

## 12 GOLDEN RULE

►**12 Therefore**—introduces a summary. **all things whatsoever ye would that men should do to you, do ye even so** [the same thing and in the same way] **to them: for this is the law and the prophets**—This is the substance of all moral duty and all Scripture in a nutshell. Incomparable summary! How well it is called "the royal law" (James 2:8; cf. Rom. 13:9). It is true that similar maxims are found in the writings of the cultivated Greeks and Romans, and naturally enough in the rabbinical writings. But so expressed as it is here—in immediate connection with, and as the sum of such duties as have just been enjoined, and such principles as had been taught before—it is to be found nowhere else. And the best commentary upon this fact is that this was not effectually and widely exemplified in men's lives before the time of Christ. The precise sense of the maxim is best referred to common sense. It is not, of course, what—in our wayward, capricious, grasping moods—we should wish men would do to us, that we are to hold ourselves bound to do to them; but only what—in the exercise of an impartial judgment, and putting ourselves in their place—we consider reasonable that they should do to us, that we are to do to them.

## 13-29 CONCLUSION AND EFFECT OF THE SERMON ON THE MOUNT

We have here the application of the whole preceding discourse. "The righteousness of the kingdom," so amply described both in principle and detail, would be seen to involve self-sacrifice at every step. Multitudes would never face this. But it must be faced, else the consequences will be fatal. This would divide all within the sound of these truths into two classes: the many, who will follow the path of ease and self-indulgence—end where it may; and the few, who, bent on eternal safety above everything else, take the way that leads to it—at whatever cost. This gives occasion to the two opening verses of this application.

►13 **Enter ye in at the strait** [narrow] **gate**—as if hardly wide enough to admit anyone at all. This expresses the difficulty of the first right step in the Christian life, involving, as it does, a triumph over all our natural inclinations. Hence the still stronger expression in Luke 13:24, "Struggle to enter through the strait door" (lit.).

►14 **Because strait is the gate, and narrow is the way, which leadeth unto life**—In other words, the whole course is as difficult as the first step; and (so it comes to pass that)—**few there be that find it**—i.e., life. The Greek word for "life" here is $z\bar{o}e$. In the NT it is almost always used to designate the divine life, the eternal life—in contrast to the personal life, the psychological life (Gk. $psuch\bar{e}$). To find life is to obtain God's life and gain access to life eternal. Those who go the broad way miss obtaining this life and hence find themselves on the way to destruction. Since destruction is the natural end of all fallen men, men do not need to try to get there. Life (God's life) is not man's by nature; he must seek to enter into it. Its very first step involves a revolution in all our purposes and plans for life and a surrender of all that is dear to natural inclination, while all that follows is but a repetition of the first great act of self-sacrifice. No wonder, then, that few find and few are

found in it. But since such teaching would be as unpopular as the way itself, the Lord next forewarns his hearers that deceptive preachers—the true heirs and representatives of the false prophets of old—would be active in the new kingdom.

►15 **Beware of false prophets**—i.e., of teachers coming as self-authorized expounders of the mind of God (see Acts 20:29, 30; 2 Pet. 2:1, 2). **which come to you in sheep's clothing**—with a gentle, plausible exterior, persuading you that the gate is not strait nor the way narrow and that to teach so is illiberal. These false prophets would be like those characterized in Ezekiel 13. **but inwardly they are ravening wolves**—bent on devouring the flock for their own gain (2 Cor. 11:2, 3, 13-15).

►16 **Ye shall know them by their fruits**—not their doctrines—as many of the ancient interpreters and some later ones explain it, for the doctrines correspond to the tree itself, but the practical effect of their teaching is the proper fruit of the tree. **Do men gather grapes of thorns, or figs of thistles?**—The general sense is obvious—every tree bears its own fruit.

►17, 18 **Even so every good tree bringeth forth good fruit; but a corrupt tree bringeth forth evil fruit. A good tree cannot bring forth evil fruit, neither can a corrupt tree bring forth good fruit**—This simple truth cannot be overlooked; the law of nature corresponds to the law of spiritual life. Each living entity can produce only that which is by nature, so he who has a new nature—indeed, is even a partaker of the divine nature (2 Pet. 1:4)—will produce fruit that expresses that nature. Whereas he who has only a fallen, corrupt nature—no matter how hard he would try to do otherwise—will produce corrupt fruit.

►19 **Every tree that bringeth not forth good fruit is hewn down, and cast into the fire**—See comments on 3:10.

►20 **Wherefore by their fruits ye shall know them**—We cannot know the nature of a man, but his fruits (his deeds) will express and expose that nature. Therefore, the way to detect false prophets is by their deeds. A person's speech will not always correspond to his true nature, as is implied in the next verse.

►21 **Not every one that saith unto me, Lord, Lord**—The duplication of the title

"Lord" denotes zeal. Yet our Lord claims and expects this of all his disciples, as when he washed their feet: "Ye call me Master and Lord: and ye say well, for so I am" (John 13:13). **shall enter into the kingdom of heaven; but he that doeth the will of my Father which is in heaven**—that will which it had been the great object of this discourse to set forth.

➤**22 Many will say to me in that day**— What day? It is emphatically unnamed. But it is in the day to which he had just referred when men shall "enter" or not enter "into the kingdom of heaven." (See a similar way of speaking of "that day" in 2 Tim. 1:12; 4:8.) **Lord, Lord**—The reiteration denotes surprise. "What, Lord? How is this? Are *we* to be disowned?" **have we not prophesied**—or, "publicly taught." As one of the special gifts of the Spirit in the early church, it has the sense of "inspired and authoritative teaching," and is ranked next to apostleship (see 1 Cor. 12:28; Eph. 4:11). In this sense it is used here, as appears from what follows. **in thy name**—or, "to thy name," and so in the two following clauses—"having reference to your name as the sole power in which we did it." **and in thy name have cast out devils? and in thy name done many wonderful works**— or, miracles. These are selected as three examples of the highest services rendered to the Christian cause and through the power of Christ's own name. And the threefold repetition of the question, each time in the same form, expresses the astonishment of the speakers at the view now taken of them.

➤**23 And then will I profess unto them**—or, openly proclaim. The verb means "to make confession"—in the legal sense, "to bear witness." Here, Jesus is functioning as a judge. **I never knew you**—The Greek word for "know" is used in the NT for personal knowledge, intimate knowledge. Christ here claims that he did not have any personal relationship with these who claimed to be his servants. In effect, Christ said, "Our acquaintance, our relationship was not broken off; there never was any." It should also be noted that the words "I never knew you" were used by rabbis to banish people. **depart from me**—cf. 25:41. The connection here gives these words an awful significance. They claimed intimacy with Christ and in the corresponding passage, Luke 13:26, are represented as having been on familiar terms with him. Jesus' words came

from Psalm 6:8. **ye that work iniquity**—lit., "lawlessness." Their works were not authorized by Christ. (See the almost identical, but even more vivid and awful, description of the scene in Luke 13:24-27.) Paul alluded to these words in 2 Timothy 2:19—"Nevertheless the foundation of God standeth sure, having this seal, The Lord knoweth them that are his. And, Let every one that nameth the name of Christ depart from iniquity."

➤**24 Therefore**—to bring this discourse to a close. **whosoever heareth these sayings of mine, and doeth them**—See James 1:22, which seems a plain allusion to these words; also Luke 11:28; Romans 2:13; 1 John 3:7. **I will liken him unto a wise man**—a prudent, sensible man. **which built his house upon a rock**—the rock of true discipleship or genuine subjection to Christ.

➤**25 And the rain descended, and the floods came, and the winds blew, and beat upon that house; and it fell not: for it was founded upon a rock**—See 1 John 2:17.

➤**26 And every one that heareth these sayings of mine**—in the attitude of discipleship—**and doeth them not, shall be likened unto a foolish man, which built his house upon the sand**—denoting a loose foundation—that of an empty profession and mere external services.

➤**27 And the rain descended, and the floods came, and the winds blew, and beat upon** [struck against] **that house; and it fell: and great was the fall of it**—terrible the ruin! How appropriate and lively this imagery must have been to an audience accustomed to the fierceness of an Eastern tempest and the suddenness and completeness with which it sweeps everything unsteady before it!

➤**28 And it came to pass, when Jesus had ended these sayings, the people were astonished at his doctrine**—rather, "his teaching," for the reference is to the manner of it quite as much as the matter, or rather more so.

➤**29 For he taught them as one having authority**—The word "one," which the KJV translators have here inserted, only weakens the statement. **and not as the scribes**—The consciousness of divine authority, as Lawgiver, Expounder and Judge, so beamed through his teaching that the scribes' teaching was eclipsed.

*Chapter* **8**

## 1-4 HEALING OF A LEPER (See Mark 1:40-45; Luke 5:12-16.)

➤**1, 2 When he was come down from the mountain, great multitudes followed him. And, behold, there came a leper**—"a man full of leprosy," says Luke 5:12. Much has been written on this disease of leprosy, but certain points remain still doubtful. All that needs be said here is that it was a cutaneous disease of a loathsome, diffusive, and usually incurable character; that though in its distinctive features it is still found in some countries, it prevailed in the form of what is called white leprosy to an unusual extent and from a very early period, among the Hebrews; and that it thus furnished to the whole nation a familiar and profound symbol of sin, considered as (1) loathsome, (2) spreading, (3) incurable. And while the ceremonial ordinances for detection and cleansing prescribed in this case by the law of Moses (Lev. 13, 14) provided a remedy "for sin and for uncleanness" (Ps. 51:7; 2 Kings 5:1, 7, 10, 13, 14), the numerous cases of leprosy with which our Lord came in contact and the glorious cures he wrought were a fitting manifestation of the work he came to accomplish. In this view, it deserves to be noticed that the first of the Lord's miracles of healing recorded by Matthew is this cure of a leper. **and worshipped him**—in what sense we shall presently see. Mark says (1:40), he came, "beseeching and kneeling to him," and Luke says (5:12), "he fell on his face." **saying, Lord, if thou wilt, thou canst make me clean**—This leper's faith in the power of Christ must have been formed in him by what he had heard of his other cures. And how remarkable a faith! He did not say that he believed He was able, but with simple confidence he said, "You are able." But he was not sure Christ was willing to do it; he needed more knowledge of Jesus before he could determine that. But one thing he was sure of, that Christ had but to "will" it into being. This manifests that the leper knew the divinity of the One he worshiped. Clear theological knowledge of the person of Christ was not then possessed even by those who were most with him and nearest to him. Much less could full insight into all that we know of the only-begotten of the Father be expected of this leper. But he who at that moment felt that to heal an incurable disease needed but the *fiat* of the person who stood before him had assuredly the same faith of all who have come to love him and would at any time die for his blessed name.

➤**3 Jesus**—or "he," according to some early manuscripts—"moved with compassion," says Mark (1:41), a precious addition. **put forth his hand, and touched him**—Such a touch occasioned ceremonial defilement (Lev. 5:3); even as the leper's coming near enough for contact was against the Levitical regulations (Lev. 13:46). But as the man's faith told him there would be no case for such regulations if the cure he hoped to experience should be accomplished, so he who had "healing in his wings" transcended all such statutes. **saying, I will; be thou clean**—How majestic those words! By assuring him of the one thing of which he had any doubt, and for which he waited—Jesus' will to do it—he made a claim as divine as the cure that immediately followed it. **And immediately his leprosy was cleansed**—Mark, more emphatic, says (1:42), "And as soon as he had spoken, immediately the leprosy departed from him, and he was cleansed"—as perfectly as instantaneously.

➤**4 And Jesus** ["straitly charged him, and forthwith sent him away"—Mark 1:43] **saith unto him, See thou tell no man**—This would be difficult for one who most naturally would like to proclaim, "Come, and hear, all ye that fear God, and I will declare what he hath done for my soul" (Ps. 66:16). **but go thy way, show thyself to the priest, and offer the gift that Moses commanded** [Lev. 14] **for a testimony unto them**—a palpable witness that the great Healer had indeed come and that "God had visited his people." What the sequel was, Matthew does not say; but Mark (1:45) gives it: "Instead he went out and began to talk freely, spreading the news. As a result, Jesus could no longer enter a town openly but stayed outside in lonely places. Yet the people still came to him from everywhere" (NIV). Thus—by an over-zealous, though most natural and not very culpable, infringement of the injunction to keep the matter quiet—was our Lord limited in his movements. As a result, we find him repeatedly taking steps to prevent matters prematurely coming to a crisis with him. (But see comments on Mark 5:19, 20.) "And he withdrew himself," adds Luke (5:16), "into the wilderness, and prayed"—retreating from the popular excitement into the secret place of the Most High. And this is the secret both of strength and of sweetness in the servants and followers of Christ in every age.

## 5-13 HEALING OF THE CENTURION'S SERVANT

This incident belongs to a later stage. For the exposition, see comments on Luke 7:1-10.

## 14-17 HEALING OF PETER'S MOTHER-IN-LAW, AND MANY OTHERS

See comments on Mark 1:29-34.

## 18-22 INCIDENTS ILLUSTRATIVE OF DISCIPLESHIP (See Luke 9:57-62)

The incidents here are two: in the corresponding passage of Luke they are three. Here they are introduced before the mission of the Twelve: in Luke, when our Lord was making preparation for his final journey to Jerusalem. But to conclude from this, as some good critics do, that one of these incidents at least occurred twice—which led to the mention of the others at the two different times—is too artificial. Taking them, then, as one set of occurrences, the question arises: are they recorded by Matthew or by Luke in their proper place? The critics are divided. Probably the first incident is here in its right place. But as the command, in the second incident, to preach the kingdom of God, would scarcely have been given at so early a period, it is likely that it and the third incident have their true place in Luke. "Apparently Matthew chose to insert these two vignettes here because they help show the nature of Jesus' ministry and the disciples he was seeking" (Carson).

## 19, 20 THE RASH OR PRECIPITATE DISCIPLE

►**19, 20 And a certain scribe came, and said unto him, Master [lit., "Teacher"], I will follow thee whithersoever thou goest. And Jesus saith unto him, The foxes have holes, and the birds of the air have nests; but the Son of man hath not where to lay his head**—Since there were so few scribes who attached themselves to Jesus, it would appear, from his calling him Teacher, that this one was a "disciple" in that looser sense of the word in which it was applied to the crowds who flocked after

him with more or less conviction that his claims were well founded. But from the answer he received we are led to infer that there was more of transient emotion—of temporary impulse—than of intelligent principle in the speech. The preaching of Christ had charmed him; his heart had swelled; his enthusiasm had been kindled; and in this state of mind he would go anywhere with him and felt impelled to tell him so. "Will you?" replied the Lord Jesus. "Do you know whom you are pledging yourself to follow, and where he might lead you?" No warm home, no pillow; he has them not for himself. The foxes are not without their holes, nor do the birds of the air lack their nests; but the Son of man has to depend on the hospitality of others and borrow the pillow whereon he lays his head. What an effective reply! And yet he did not reject this man's offer nor refuse him the liberty to follow him. But Jesus wanted him to know what he was doing and "count the cost." He would have him weigh the real nature and the strength of his attachment, whether it be such as would abide in the day of trial. If so, he would be most welcome, for Christ received all who came to him. But it seems plain that in this case this man did not follow Jesus. And so we have called this one the rash or precipitate disciple.

## 21, 22 THE PROCRASTINATING OR ENTANGLED DISCIPLE

As this is more fully given in Luke, we must take both together. "And he said unto another of his disciples, Follow me." But he said, **Lord, suffer me first to go and bury my father. But Jesus said unto him, Follow me; and let the dead bury their dead**—or, as more definitely in Luke, "Let the dead bury their dead: but go thou and preach the kingdom of God." This disciple did not, like the former, volunteer his services but is called by the Lord Jesus, not only to follow, but to preach him. And he is quite willing; only he is not ready just yet. "Lord, I will; but there is a difficulty in the way just now; but that once removed, I am yours." What now is this difficulty? Was his father actually dead—lying a corpse—having only to be buried? Unlikely. As it was the practice, as noticed in the comments on Luke 7:12, to bury on the day of death, it is not very likely that this disciple would have been here at all if his father had just breathed his last; nor would the Lord, if he was there, have hindered him discharging the last duties of a son to a father. No doubt it was the common case of a son having a frail or aged father who was not likely to live long. And so the son felt obligated to stay with him until he was put into the grave. This view of the case will explain Jesus' curt reply, "Let the dead bury their dead: but go thou and preach the kingdom of God." Like all the other paradoxical sayings of our Lord, the key to interpreting it comes from the different senses—a higher and a lower—in which the same word "dead" is used. There are two kingdoms of God in existence upon earth: the kingdom of nature and the kingdom of grace. To the one kingdom all the children of this world, even the most ungodly, are fully alive; to the other, only the children of light. The reigning impiety consists, not in indifference to the common humanities of social life, but to things spiritual and eternal. In essence, then, Jesus was saying to this disciple: "Fear not that your father will, in your absence, be neglected, and that when he breathes his last there will not be relatives and friends ready enough to give him kindness. Your wish to be there yourself is natural, and to be allowed to do it a privilege not easily neglected. But the kingdom of God lies now all neglected and needy. Its more exalted character few discern; to its paramount claims few are alive; and to 'preach' it fewer still are qualified and called. But you are. The Lord therefore needs you. Leave, then, those claims of nature, high though they be, to those who are dead to the still higher claims of the divine kingdom, which God is now erecting upon earth—Let the dead bury their dead; but go and preach the kingdom of God." And so we have here the genuine, but procrastinating or entangled disciple. The next case is recorded only by Luke; see comments on Luke 9:61, 62.

## 23-27 JESUS, CROSSING THE SEA OF GALILEE, MIRACULOUSLY STILLS A TEMPEST

See comments on Mark 4:35-41.

## 28-34 JESUS HEALS THE GERGESENE DEMONIACS

See comments on Mark 5:1-20.

Chapter **9**

## 1-8 HEALING OF A PARALYTIC

This incident appears to follow next in order of time to the cure of the leper (8:1-4). For the exposition, see comments on Mark 2:1-12.

## 9-13 MATTHEW'S CALL AND FEAST
(See Mark 2:14-17; Luke 5:27-32.)

## 9 THE CALL OF MATTHEW

**➤9 And as Jesus passed forth from thence**—i.e., from the scene of the paralytic's cure in Capernaum, toward the shore of the Sea of Galilee, on which that town lay. Mark, as usual, pictures the scene more in detail, thus (2:13): "And he went forth again by the sea side; and all the multitude resorted unto him, and he taught them"—or, "kept teaching them." "And as he passed by" **he saw a man, named Matthew**—the writer of this precious gospel, who here, with modesty and brevity, relates the story of his own calling. In Mark and Luke he is called Levi, which seems to have been his family name. In their lists of the twelve apostles, however, Mark and Luke give him the name of Matthew, which seems to have been the name by which he was known as a disciple. While he himself omits his family name, he is careful not to hide his occupation. As a tax collector (publican), he would be despised by all Jews. But Matthew exposed his despicable occupation in order to show how God's grace extended to him and transcended natural animosities. (See comments on 10:3.) Mark (2:14) alone tells us that he was "the son of Alphaeus"—probably the same father of James the Less. From this and other considerations it can be assumed that he must at least have heard of Christ before this meeting. **sitting at the receipt of custom**—as a tax collector (publican), which Luke (5:27) calls him. It means the place of receipt, the toll-house or booth in which the collector sat. Being in this case by the seaside, it might be the ferry tax for the transit of persons and goods across the lake that he collected. (See comments on 5:46.) **and he saith unto him, Follow me**—Jesus' call to each of his disciples was charged with a magnetism hard to resist. **And he** ["left all" (Luke 5:28)] **arose and followed him.**

## 10-13 THE FEAST

➤**10 And it came to pass, as Jesus sat at meat in the house**—Matthew's modesty especially appears here. Luke (5:29) says that "Levi made him a great feast," or "reception," while Matthew merely says, "He sat at meat"; and Mark and Luke say that it was in Levi's "own house," while Matthew merely says, "He sat at meat in the house." Whether this feast was made immediately after Matthew's call or not until afterwards is a point of some importance in the order of events and not agreed among harmonists. The probability is that it did not take place until a considerable time afterwards. For Matthew, who ought surely to know what took place while his Lord was speaking at his own table, tells us that the visit of Jairus, the ruler of the synagogue, occurred at that moment (9:18). But we know from Mark and Luke that this visit of Jairus did not take place until after our Lord's return, at a later period, from the country of the Gadarenes. (See Mark 5:21ff. and Luke 8:40cf.) As such, it appears that the feast was not made in the budding of his discipleship but after Matthew had had time to be somewhat established in the faith; when returning to Capernaum, his compassion for old friends of his own occupation and character led him to gather them together, that they might have an opportunity of hearing the gracious words that proceeded out of his Master's mouth, if perhaps they might experience a similar change of heart. **behold, many publicans and sinners**—Luke says, "a great company" (5:29)—**came and sat down with him and his disciples.** In all such cases the word rendered "sat" is "reclined," referring to the ancient practice of lying on couches at meals.

➤**11 And when the Pharisees**—"and scribes" add Mark and Luke. **saw it, they** "murmured" or "muttered," says Luke (5:30). **said unto his disciples**—not venturing to put their question to Jesus himself. **Why eateth your Master with publicans and sinners?**—See comments on Luke 15:2.

➤**12 But when Jesus heard that, he said unto them**—to the Pharisees and scribes—addressing himself to them, though they had shrunk from addressing him. **They that be whole need not a physician, but they that are sick**—i.e., "Ye deem yourselves whole; my mission, therefore, is not to you. The physician's business is

with the sick; therefore I eat with publicans and sinners." How many broken hearts or sin-sick souls have been healed by this matchless saying!

➤**13 But go ye and learn what that meaneth** [Hos. 6:6], **I will have mercy, and not sacrifice**—i.e., the one rather than the other. "Sacrifice," the chief part of the ceremonial law, is here put for a religion of literal adherence to mere rules; while "mercy" expresses such compassion for the fallen as seeks to lift them up. The duty of keeping aloof from the polluted, in the sense of "having no fellowship with the unfruitful works of darkness," is obvious enough; but to understand this as prohibiting such contact with them as is necessary to their recovery is to abuse it. This was what these religionists did, and this is what our Lord here exposes. **for I am not come to call the righteous, but sinners to repentance**—The last two words are of doubtful authority here and more than doubtful authority in Mark 2:17; but in Luke 5:32 they are undisputed. The "righteous" are the whole (healthy); "sinners," the sick. When Christ "called" the latter, as he did Matthew and probably some of those publicans and sinners whom he had invited to meet him, it was to heal them of their spiritual maladies and to save their souls: "The righteous," like those miserable self-satisfied Pharisees, "he sent empty away."

## 14-17 DISCOURSE ON FASTING

See comments on Luke 5:33-39.

## 18-26 THE WOMAN WITH THE ISSUE OF BLOOD HEALED. THE DAUGHTER OF JAIRUS RAISED TO LIFE

See comments on Mark 5:21-43.

## 27-34 TWO BLIND MEN AND A DUMB DEMONIAC HEALED

These two miracles are recorded by Matthew alone.

## 27-31 TWO BLIND MEN HEALED

➤**27 And when Jesus departed thence, two blind men followed him**— hearing, doubtless, as in a later case is expressed, "that Jesus passed by" (20:30). **crying, and saying, Thou son of David, have mercy on us**—It is remarkable that in the only other recorded case in which the blind applied to Jesus for their sight and obtained it, they addressed him over and over again by this one messianic title, so well known—"Son of David" (20:30). Can there be a doubt that their faith fastened on such great messianic promises as this, "Then the eyes of the blind shall be opened . . ." (Isa. 35:5)? And if so, this appeal to him, as the Messiah, to do his predicted office, would be very compelling to Jesus.

➤**28 And when he was come into the house**—To try their faith and patience, he seems to have made them no answer. But **the blind men came to him: and Jesus said unto them, Believe ye that I am able to do this? They said unto him, Yea, Lord**—Doubtless our Lord's design was not only to put their faith to the test by this question but to deepen it, to raise their expectation of a cure, and so prepare them to receive it.

➤**29 Then touched he their eyes, saying, According to your faith be it unto you**—not, "Receive a cure proportioned to your faith," but, "Receive this cure as granted because of your faith."

➤**30 And their eyes were opened; and Jesus straitly charged them**—The expression is very strong, denoting great earnestness.

➤**31 But they, when they were departed, spread abroad his fame in all that country**—See comments on 8:4.

## 32-34 A DUMB DEMONIAC HEALED

➤**32 As they went out, behold, they brought to him a dumb man possessed with a devil**—"demonized," or "demon-possessed." The dumbness was not natural but was the effect of the possession.

➤**33 And when the devil [demon] was cast out, the dumb spake**—The particulars in this case are not given—the purpose being simply to record the instantaneous restoration of the natural faculties when the malignant oppressor was removed. **and the multitudes marvelled, saying, It was never so seen in Israel**—referring, probably, not to this case only, but to all those miraculous displays of healing power that seemed to promise a new era in the history of Israel. Probably they meant by this language to indicate, as far as they thought it safe to do so, their inclination to regard him as the promised Messiah.

➤**34 But the Pharisees said, He casteth out devils through the prince of the devils**—"the demons through the prince of the demons." This seems to be the first muttering of a theory of such miracles that soon became a fixed mode of calumny—a theory both ridiculous and devilish. (See comments on 12:24.)

## 9:35–10:5 THIRD GALILEAN CIRCUIT. MISSION OF THE TWELVE APOSTLES

As the mission of the Twelve supposes the previous choice of them—of which Matthew gives no account, and which did not take place until a later stage of our Lord's public life—it is introduced here out of its proper place. It should follow Luke 6:12-19.

## 35 THIRD GALILEAN CIRCUIT

➤**35 And Jesus went about all the cities and villages, teaching in their synagogues, and preaching the gospel of the kingdom, and healing every sickness and every disease** [among the people]—The bracketed words are not found in any of the best manuscripts and were probably introduced here from 4:23. The language here is so identical with that used in describing the first circuit (4:23) that we may presume the work done on both occasions was much the same. It was just a further preparation of the soil and a fresh sowing for the precious seed. (See comments on 4:23.) Peter probably alluded to these journeys when, in his address to the household of Cornelius, he said that "Jesus of Nazareth was anointed by God with the Holy Spirit and with power, and he went around doing good and healing all who were possessed by demons, for God was with him" (Acts 10:38, TLB).

## 36-38 JESUS, HAVING COMPASSION ON THE MULTITUDES, ASKS FOR LABORERS

He had now returned from his preaching and healing circuit, and the result, as at the close of the first one, was the gathering of a vast and motley multitude around him. After a whole night spent in prayer, he had called his more immediate disciples and from them had solemnly chosen the Twelve: then he came down from the mountain, on which this was transacted, to the multitudes that waited for him below. He had addressed to them that discourse which bears so strong a resemblance to the Sermon on the Mount. (See comments on Luke 6:12-49 and introductory remarks on chapter five.) Soon after this, it would seem, the multitudes still hanging on him, Jesus was touched with their wretched and helpless condition.

➤**36 But when he saw the multitudes, he was moved with compassion**—i.e., he had deep sympathy. **on them, because they fainted**—This reading, however, has hardly any authority among the manuscripts. The true reading is "were harassed" or "were distressed." **and were scattered abroad**—rather, "lying about," "abandoned," or "neglected." **as sheep, having no shepherd**—Jesus was moved by their pitiful condition. Wearied under bodily fatigue, disorganized, souls uncared for by the religious leaders of their day, yet drawn after and hanging upon Jesus, this vast mass of humanity needed a Shepherd, a Savior.

➤**37 Then saith he unto his disciples, The harvest truly is plenteous**—speaking of Jewish believers and extending beyond to the vast field of "the world" (13:38). **but the labourers**—men divinely qualified and called to gather them in.

➤**38 Pray ye therefore the Lord of the harvest**—the great Lord and Proprietor of all. Cf. John 15:1, "I am the true vine, and my Father is the husbandman." **that he will send forth labourers into his harvest**—The words "send forth" properly mean "thrust forth"; but this emphatic sense disappears in some places, as in 9:25.

*Chapter* **10**

1-5 MISSION OF THE TWELVE
APOSTLES (See Mark 6:7-13; Luke 9:1-6.)

The last three verses of chapter 9 form the proper introduction to the mission of the Twelve, as is evident from the remarkable fact that the mission of the Seventy was prefaced by the very same words (see Luke 10:2).

➤**1 And when he had called unto him his twelve disciples, he gave them power**—The word signifies both "power" and "authority" or "right." Even if it were not evident that both ideas are included here, we find both words expressly used in the parallel passage of Luke (9:1)—"He gave them power and authority"—in other words, He both qualified and authorized them. **against**—or "over."

➤**2 Now the names of the twelve apostles are these**—The other Gospel writers enumerate the Twelve in immediate connection with their appointment (Mark 3:13-19; Luke 6:13-16). But Matthew, not intending to record the appointment but only the mission of the Twelve, gives their names here. And as in the Acts (1:13), we have a list of the Eleven who met daily in the upper room with the other disciples after their Master's ascension until the day of Pentecost. We have four catalogues in all for comparison. **The first, Simon, who is called Peter**—See comments on John 1:42. **and Andrew his brother; James [the son] of Zebedee, and John his brother**—named after James, as the younger of the two.

➤**3 Philip, and Bartholomew**—That the latter is the same as "Nathanael of Cana in Galilee" is justified by the three following reasons: first, because Bartholomew is not so properly an individual's name as a family surname (the name means "Son of Tolmai"); next, because not only in this list, but in Mark's and Luke's, he follows the name of "Philip," who was the instrument of bringing Nathanael first to Jesus (John 1:45); and again, when our Lord, after his resurrection, appeared at the Sea of Tiberias, "Nathanael of Cana in Galilee" is mentioned along with six others, all of them apostles, as being present (John 21:2). **Matthew the publican**—In none of the four lists of the Twelve is this apostle so branded but in his own, as if he would have all to know how deep a debtor he had been to his Lord. (See comments on 1:3, 5, 6; 9:9.) **James the son of Alphaeus**—Alphaeus was sometimes called Cleopas or Clopas (Luke 24:18; John 19:25). Alphaeus (or, Clopas) was Joseph's brother; therefore, his wife Mary was the Virgin's sister-in-law. So this James would have been "James the younger" (Mark 15:40), the cousin of Jesus. It is also possible that James the son of Alphaeus was Matthew's brother because Matthew's father was called Alphaeus (Mark 2:14). **and Lebbaeus, whose surname was Thaddaeus**—The best manuscripts read simply, "Thaddaeus" (meaning "beloved"). This apostle could be the same as "Judas, the brother of James," mentioned in both the lists of Luke (6:16; Acts 1:13), while no one of the name of Lebbaeus or Thaddaeus is so. It is he who in John (14:22) is called "Judas, not Iscariot."

➤**4 Simon the Canaanite**—rather "Kananite," but better still, "the Zealot," as he is called in Luke 6:15, where the original term should not have been retained as in the KJV ("Simon, called Zelotes"), but rendered "Simon, called the Zealot." The word "Kananite" is just the Aramaic, or Syro-Chaldaic, term for "Zealot." Probably before his acquaintance with Jesus, he belonged to the Zealots, a Jewish revolutionary group that sought to throw off Roman rule. **and Judas Iscariot**—i.e., Judas of Kerioth, a town of Judah (Josh. 15:25); so called to distinguish him from "Judas the brother of James" (Luke 6:16). Some commentators have pointed out that "Iscariot" could be a surrogate for "Sicari," the name of a political group known for carrying small daggers (*sicarii*) used in assassinations. **who also betrayed him**—a note of infamy attached to his name in all the catalogues of the Twelve.

5-42 THE TWELVE RECEIVE
THEIR INSTRUCTIONS

This section is divided into three distinct parts. The *first* part—extending from 10:5 to 10:15—contains directions for the brief and temporary mission on which they were now going, regarding the places they were to go to, the works they were to do, the message they were to bear, the manner in which they were to conduct themselves. The *second* part—extending from 10:16 to 10:23—contains directions for the ongoing exercise of the gospel ministry. The *third* part—extending from 10:24 to 10:42—is of wider application still, reaching not only to the ministry of the gospel in every age, but to the service of Christ in the widest sense. It is a strong confirmation of this threefold division, that each part closes with the words, **Verily I say unto you** (10:15, 23, 42).

5-15 DIRECTIONS FOR THE MISSION

➤**5 These twelve Jesus sent forth, and commanded them, saying, Go not into the way of the Gentiles, and into any city of the Samaritans enter ye not**—The Samaritans were Gentiles by blood; but being the descendants of those whom the king of Assyria had transported from the East to supply the place of the ten tribes carried captive, they had adopted the region of the Jews, though with admixtures of their own; and, as the nearest neighbors of the Jews, they occupied a place intermediate between them and the Gentiles. Eventually this prohibition was taken away. The apostles were later told that they should be Christ's witnesses first "in Jerusalem, and in all Judea," then "in Samaria," and lastly, "unto the uttermost part of the earth" (Acts 1:8).

➤**6 But go rather to the lost sheep of the house of Israel**—Until Christ's death, which broke down the middle wall of partition (Eph. 2:14), the gospel commission was to the Jews only, who, though the visible people of God, were "lost sheep," not merely in the sense that all sinners are (Isa. 53:6; 1 Pet. 2:25; cf. Luke 19:10), but as abandoned and left to wander from the right way by faithless shepherds (Jer. 50:6, 17; Ezek. 34:2-6).

➤**7 And as ye go, preach, saying, The kingdom of heaven is at hand**—See comments on 3:2.

➤**8 Heal the sick, cleanse the lepers, raise the dead, cast out devils**—The words "raise the dead" are not found in many late manuscripts; but their presence assures us of their genuineness. Here we have the first communication of supernatural power by Christ himself to his followers—thus anticipating the gifts of Pentecost. **freely ye have received, freely give**—Divine saying, divinely said! (cf. Deut. 15:10, 11; Acts 3:6). It reminds us of that other golden saying of our Lord, repeated by Paul. "It is more blessed to give than to receive" (Acts 20:35).

➤**9 Provide neither gold, nor silver, nor brass in** [for] **your purses**—lit. "your belts," in which they kept their money.

➤**10 Nor scrip for your journey**—the bag used by travelers for holding provisions. **neither two coats**—or tunics, worn next to the skin. The meaning is, Take no change of dress, no additional articles. **neither shoes**—i.e., change of them. **nor yet staves** [staffs]—The Textus Receptus here has a "a staff," but the KJV follows another reading, "staves," which is found in the Textus Receptus of Luke 9:3. The true reading, however, is "a staff," according to the best manuscripts. **for the workman is worthy of his meat**—his "food" or "maintenance"—a principle which, being universally recognized in secular affairs, is here authoritatively applied to the service of the Lord's workmen and repeatedly and touchingly employed by Paul in his appeals to the churches (Rom. 15:27; 1 Cor. 9:11; Gal. 6:6; 1 Tim. 5:18).

➤11 And into whatsoever city or town—town or village. ye shall enter, enquire who in it is worthy—to entertain such messengers; not in point of rank, of course, but of congenial disposition. and there abide till ye go thence—not shifting about, as if discontented, but returning the welcome given with a courteous, contented, accommodating disposition.

➤12 And when ye come into an house—or "the house," but it means not the worthy house, but the house they would first enter. salute it—show it the usual civilities.

➤13 And if the house be worthy—showing this by giving you a welcome. let your peace come upon it—This is best explained by the injunction to the Seventy, "And into whatsoever house ye enter, first say, Peace be to this house" (Luke 10:5). This was the ancient salutation of the Middle East, and it exists to this day. But from the lips of Christ and his messengers, it means something far higher, both in the gift and the giving of it, than in the current salutation. (See comments on John 14:27.) but if it be not worthy, let your peace return to you—If your peace finds a shut instead of an open door in the heart of any household, take it back to yourselves, who know how to value it; and it will taste the sweeter to you for having been offered, even though rejected.

➤14 And whosoever shall not receive you, nor hear your words, when ye depart out of that house or city—for possibly a whole town might not have one "worthy" household. shake off the dust of your feet—"for a testimony against them," as Mark and Luke add. By this symbolical action they vividly shook themselves from all connection with such and from all responsibility for the guilt of rejecting them and their message. Such symbolical actions were common in ancient times even among others than the Jews, as strikingly appears in Pilate (27:24).

➤15 Verily I say unto you, It shall be more tolerable [bearable] for the land of Sodom and Gomorrha in the day of judgment, than for that city—Those cities, which were given over to destruction for their loathsome impurities, shall be treated as less criminal, we are here taught, than those places

which, though morally respectable, reject the gospel message and affront those that bear it.

## 16-23 DIRECTIONS FOR THE FUTURE AND PERMANENT EXERCISE OF THE CHRISTIAN MINISTRY

➤16 Behold, I send you forth—The "I" here is emphatic, holding up himself as the originator of the gospel ministry. as sheep—defenseless. in the midst of wolves—ready to make a prey of you (John 10:12). To be left exposed as sheep to wolves would have been startling enough; but that the sheep should be sent among the wolves would sound strange indeed. No wonder this announcement begins with the exclamation, "Behold." be ye therefore wise as serpents, and harmless as doves—Wonderful combination! Alone, the wisdom of the serpent is mere cunning, and the harmlessness of the dove little better than weakness; but in combination, the wisdom of the serpent would save them from unnecessary exposure to danger; the harmlessness of the dove, from sinful expedients to escape it. In the apostolic age of Christianity, how harmoniously were these qualities displayed! Instead of the fanatical thirst for martyrdom, to which a later age gave birth, there was a manly combination of unflinching zeal and calm discretion, before which nothing was able to stand.

➤17 But beware of men: for they will deliver you up to the councils—the local courts, used here for civil authorities in general. and they will scourge you in their synagogues—By this is meant persecution at the hands of the Jews.

➤18 And ye shall be brought before governors—provincial rulers. and kings—the highest tribunals. for my sake, for a testimony against them—rather, "to them," in order to bear testimony to the truth and its glorious effects. and [to] the Gentiles—a hint that their message would not long be confined to the lost sheep of the house of Israel. The Acts of the Apostles is the best commentary on these warnings.

➤19 But when they deliver you up, take no thought—be not solicitous or anxious. (See comments on 6:25.) how or what ye shall speak—i.e., either in what manner ye shall make your defense, or of what matter it shall consist. for it shall be given you in that same hour what ye shall speak—See Exodus 4:12; Jeremiah 1:7.

►20 For it is not ye that speak, but the Spirit of your Father [a unique expression in the NT] which speaketh in you—How remarkably this has been verified by the whole history of persecution, from the Acts of the Apostles to the latest martyrology.

►21 And the brother shall deliver up the brother to death, and the father the child: and the children shall rise up against their parents, and cause them to be put to death—for example, by providing information against them to the authorities. The deep and virulent hostility of the old nature and the new was to cause tortuous separations of the dearest ties; and the disciples, in the prospect of their cause and themselves being launched upon society, were here prepared for the worst.

►22 And ye shall be hated of all men for my name's sake—The universality of this hatred would make it evident to them that since it would not be owing to any temporary excitement, local virulence, or personal prejudice, on the part of their enemies, so no amount of discretion on their part, consistent with entire fidelity to the truth, would avail to stifle that enmity—though it might soften its violence, and in some cases avert the outward manifestations of it. but he that endureth to the end shall be saved—a great saying, repeated, in connection with similar warnings, in the prophecy of the destruction of Jerusalem (24:13) and often reiterated by the writer of Hebrews as a warning against drawing back unto destruction (3:6, 13; 6:4-6; 10:23, 26-29, 38, 39). As "drawing back unto destruction" is merely the palpable evidence of the lack of "root" from the first in the Christian profession (Luke 8:13), so "enduring to the end" is just the proper evidence of its reality and solidity.

►23 But when they persecute you in this city, flee ye into another—"into the other." This, though applicable to all time, and exemplified by our Lord himself again and again, had special reference to the persecutions the disciples would experience. for verily I say unto you, Ye shall not have gone over—Ye shall in no wise have completed: the cities of Israel, till the Son of man be come—This does not refer to his second coming as such but to his coming in judgment upon Israel. The title "Son of man" is associated with Jesus' position as judge (see John 5:27).

"The coming of the Son of man" has a fixed doctrinal sense, here referring immediately to the crisis of Israel's history as the visible kingdom of God when Christ was to come and judge it, when "the wrath would come upon it to the uttermost," and when, on the ruins of Jerusalem and the old economy, he would establish his own kingdom. This, in the uniform language of Scripture, is more immediately "the coming of the Son of man," "the day of vengeance of our God" (16:28; 24:27, 34; cf. Heb. 10:25; James 5:7-9). This judgment was imminent (c. A.D. 70); and yet it also foreshadowed the judgment yet to come—at the time of Christ's second advent. So understood, it is parallel to 24:14.

## 24-42 DIRECTIONS FOR THE SERVICE TO THE WORLD

►24 The disciple is not above his master—teacher. nor the servant above his lord—another maxim which our Lord repeats in various connections (Luke 6:40; John 13:16; 15:20).

►25 It is enough for the disciple that he be as his master, and the servant as his lord. If they have called the master of the house Beelzebub—Most of the Greek manuscripts read "Beelzebul," which undoubtedly is the right form of this word. The other reading probably came from the OT "Baalzebub," an idol, the god of Ekron (2 Kings 1:2). As all idolatry was regarded as devil worship (Lev. 17:7; Deut. 32:17; Ps. 106:37; 1 Cor. 10:20), so there seems to have been something peculiarly satanic about the worship of this hateful god, which caused his name to be a synonym of Satan. Though we nowhere read that our Lord was actually called "Beelzebul," he was charged with being in league with Satan under that hateful name (12:24, 26), and more than once was charged with "having a devil" or "demon" (Mark 3:30; John 7:20; 8:48). Here it is used to denote the most opprobrious language could be applied by one to another. how much more shall they call them of his household—Three relations in which Christ stands to his people are here mentioned: he is their Teacher—they his disciples; he is their Lord—they his servants; he is the Master of the household—they its members. In all these relations, he says here, he and they are so bound up together that they cannot look to fare better than he and should think it enough if they fare no worse.

➤**26 Fear them not therefore: for there is nothing covered, that shall not be revealed; and hid, that shall not be known**—i.e., There is no use, and no need, of concealing anything; right and wrong, truth and error, are about to come into open and deadly collision; and the day is coming when all hidden things shall be disclosed, everything seen as it is, and everyone receive his or her recompense (1 Cor. 4:5).

➤**27 What I tell you in darkness, that speak ye in light: and what ye hear in the ear, that preach ye upon the housetops**—Give free and fearless utterance to all that I have taught you while yet with you. Objection: but this may cost us our life! Answer: it may, but their power ends there.

➤**28 And fear not them which kill the body, but are not able to kill the soul**—In Luke 12:4, "and after that have no more that they can do." **but rather fear him**—in Luke this is especially solemn: "I will forewarn you whom he shall fear," **which is able to destroy both soul and body in hell** [Gk. *gehenna*]—This is a decisive proof that there is a hell for the body as well as the soul in the eternal world; in other words, that the torment that awaits the lost will have elements of suffering adapted to the material as well as the spiritual part of our nature, both of which, we are assured, will exist forever. In the corresponding warning contained in Luke, Jesus calls his disciples "my friends," as if he had felt that such sufferings constituted a bond of peculiar tenderness between him and them.

➤**29 Are not two sparrows sold for a farthing?**—In Luke 12:6 (RSV), it is "five sparrows for two pennies"; so that, if the purchaser took two pennies' worth, he got one in addition—of such small value were they. **and one of them shall not fall on the ground without your Father**—i.e., without your Father knowing about it.

➤**30 But the very hairs of your head are all numbered**—See Luke 21:18 (and cf. for the language 1 Sam. 14:45; Acts 27:34).

➤**31 Fear ye not therefore, ye are of more value than many sparrows**—Was ever language of such simplicity felt to carry such weight as this does? Here lies much of the charm and power of our Lord's teaching.

➤**32 Whosoever therefore shall confess me before men, him will I confess also before my Father which is in heaven**—i.e., I will not be ashamed of him, but will own him before the Father.

➤**34 Think not that I am come to send peace on earth: I came not to send peace, but a sword**—strife, discord, conflict; deadly opposition between eternally hostile principles, penetrating into and rending asunder the dearest ties.

➤**35 For I am come to set a man at variance against his father, and the daughter against her mother, and the daughter in law against her mother in law**— See comments on Luke 12:51-53.

➤**36 And a man's foes shall be they of his own household**—This saying (and most of 10:35) is quoted from Micah 7:6. This is clearly illustrated in Judas' betrayal of Jesus.

➤**37 He that loveth father or mother more than me is not worthy of me: and he that loveth son or daughter more than me is not worthy of me**—This thought is similar to that found in Deuteronomy 33:9. As the preference of the one would, in the case supposed, necessitate the abandonment of the other, our Lord here asserts his own claims to supreme affection.

➤**38 And he that taketh not his cross, and followeth after me, is not worthy of me**—a saying that our Lord emphatically reiterates (16:24; Luke 9:23; 14:27). We have become so accustomed to this expression—"taking up one's cross"—in the sense of "being prepared for trials in general for Christ's sake," that we might lose sight of its primary and proper sense here—"a preparedness to go forth even to crucifixion," as when Jesus had to bear his own cross on his way to Calvary. Given the time this was spoken, this saying was quite remarkable because our Lord had not as yet given a hint that he would die this kind of death (nor was crucifixion a Jewish mode of capital punishment).

➤**39 He that findeth his life shall lose it: and he that loseth his life for my sake shall find it**—another of those pregnant sayings which our Lord so often reiterated (16:25; Luke 17:33; John 12:25). The pith of such paradoxical maxims depends on the double sense attached to the word "life"—a lower and a higher, the natural and the spiritual, the temporal and eternal. An entire sacrifice of the lower, with all its relationships and interest—or, a willingness to make it so, which is the same thing—is indispensable to the preservation of the higher life; and he who cannot bring himself to surrender the one for the sake of the other shall eventually lose both.

▶40 **He that receiveth you receiveth me, and he that receiveth me receiveth him that sent me**—As the treatment which an ambassador receives is understood and regarded as expressing the light in which he that sends him is viewed, so, says our Lord here, "Your authority is mine, as mine is my Father's."

▶41 **He that receiveth a prophet**—one divinely commissioned to deliver a message from God. Predicting future events was not necessarily part of a prophet's office, especially as the word is used in the NT. **in the name of a prophet**—for his office' sake and love for his master. (See 2 Kings 4:9, 10.) **shall receive a prophet's reward**—What an encouragement to those who are not prophets! **and he that receiveth a righteous man in the name of a righteous man**—from sympathy with his character and esteem for himself as such: **shall receive a righteous man's reward**—for he must himself have the seed of righteousness in him because of his real sympathy with it and service to him who is righteous.

▶42 **And whosoever shall give to drink unto one of these little ones**—Beautiful epithet, originally taken from Zechariah 13:7. The reference is to their lowliness in spirit, their littleness in the eyes of an undiscerning world, while high in heaven's esteem. **a cup of cold water only**—meaning, the smallest service. **in the name of a disciple**—or, as it is in Mark 9:41, because ye are Christ's. **verily I say unto you, he shall in no wise lose his reward**—There is here a descending climax—"a prophet," "a righteous man," "a little one," signifying that however low we come down in our services to those that are Christ's, all that is done for his sake, and that bears the stamp of love to his blessed name, shall be divinely appreciated, owned, and rewarded.

# Chapter 11

1-19 THE IMPRISONED BAPTIST'S MESSAGE TO HIS MASTER. THE REPLY, AND DISCOURSE, AFTER THE

DEPARTURE OF THE MESSENGERS, REGARDING JOHN AND HIS MISSION
(See Luke 7:18-35.)

▶1 **And it came to pass, when Jesus had made an end of commanding his twelve disciples, he departed thence to teach and to preach in their cities**—Jesus went out to certain places either not reached at all before, or too rapidly passed through, while he waited for the return of the Twelve. Matthew says nothing about their labors. But Luke (9:6) says, "They departed, and went through the towns," or "villages," "preaching the gospel, and healing every where." Mark (6:12, 13), as usual, is more explicit: "And they went out, and preached that men should repent. And they cast out many devils [demons], and anointed with oil many that were sick, and healed them." Though this "anointing with oil" was not mentioned in Jesus' instructions (at least in any of the records of them), we know it to have been practiced long after this in the early church (see James 5:14 and cf. Mark 6:12, 13)—not medicinally, but as a sign of the healing virtue that was communicated by their hands.

▶2-19 **Now when John had heard in the prison**—For the account of this imprisonment, see comments on Mark 6:17-20. On the whole passage, see comments on Luke 7:18-35.

20-30 JESUS' REACTION TO THE RESULT OF HIS LABORS IN GALILEE

The connection of this with what goes before it and the similarity of its tone make it evident that it was delivered on the same occasion, and that it is but a new and more comprehensive series of reflections in the same strain.

▶20, 21 **Then began he to upbraid the cities wherein most of his mighty works were done, because they repented not: Woe unto thee, Chorazin!**—not elsewhere mentioned, but it must have been near Capernaum. **woe unto thee, Bethsaida**—lit. "fishing-house," a fishing station on the western side of the Sea of Galilee and to the north of Capernaum: the birthplace of three of the apostles—the brothers Andrew and Peter, and Philip. These two cities appear to be singled out to denote the whole region in which they lay—a region favored by the Redeemer's presence, teaching, and mighty works. **for if the mighty works**—the miracles. **which were done in**

you had been done in Tyre and Sidon—
ancient and celebrated commercial cities, on
the northeastern shores of the Mediterranean
Sea, lying north of Palestine, and the latter the
northernmost. As their wealth and prosperity
engendered luxury and its concomitant
evils—impiety and moral degeneracy—their
overthrow was repeatedly foretold in ancient
prophecy and repeatedly fulfilled by victorious
enemies. Yet they were rebuilt, and at this time
were in a flourishing condition. **they would
have repented long ago in sackcloth and
ashes**—remarkable language, showing that
they were less guilty than the region here spoken of.

➤**23 And thou, Capernaum**—See comments on 4:13. **which art exalted unto
heaven**—Since Jesus lived at Capernaum during the whole period of his public life which he
spent in Galilee, it was the most favored spot
upon earth, the most exalted in privilege. **shalt
be brought down to hell: for if the mighty
works, which have been done in thee, had been
done in Sodom**—destroyed for its licentiousness. **it would have remained until this day**—
At the time of Jesus, it was a well-known fact
that Sodom had been completely obliterated.

➤**24 But I say unto you, That it shall be
more tolerable for the land of Sodom, in the
day of judgment, than for thee**—Capernaum,
as well as Chorazin and Bethsaida, today are in
ruins. And yet the inhabitants of these Galilean
cities who did not respond to Jesus' presence
among them await a greater and final judgment.

➤**25 At that time Jesus answered and
said**—We are not to understand by this that the
previous discourse had been concluded and that
this is a record only of something said about the
same period. For the connection is most close, and
the word "answered"—which, when there is no
one to answer, refers to something just before
said, or rising in the mind of the speaker in
consequence of something said—confirms this.
What Jesus here "answered" evidently was the
disappointing results of his ministry, lamented
over in the foregoing verses. It is as if he had said,
"Yes, but there is a brighter side to the picture;
even in those who have rejected the message of
eternal life, it is the pride of their own hearts only
which has blinded them, and the glory of the truth
does but the more appear in their inability to
receive it. But not all have rejected it; there were

some whose hearts were simple and pure, seeking after God. To these, the Father revealed the
splendor of his Son." **I thank thee**—rather, "I
assent to thee" or "I confess my agreement to
thee." The thing expressed is adoring acquiescence, holy satisfaction in that law of the divine
procedure about to be mentioned. And as, when
he afterwards uttered the same words, he "exulted
in spirit" (see comments on Luke 10:21), probably he did the same now, though not recorded. **O
Father, Lord of heaven and earth**—He so
addresses his Father here, to signify that he has
mastery over all the universe, as well as over
every man's heart. **because thou hast hid these
things**—the knowledge of these saving truths.
**from the wise and prudent**—The former of
these terms points to the men who pride themselves in their speculative or philosophical
attainments; the latter to the men with worldly
cleverness, the sharp-witted, the men "in the
know." The distinction is a natural one, and was
well understood (see 1 Cor. 1:19). But why had
the Father hid from such people the things that
would have given them eternal life and divine
light, and why did Jesus so emphatically set his
seal to this arrangement? Because human wisdom
and intelligence are not the prerequisites for
receiving divine revelation. God gives revelation
to those who are open to him and to those who,
by his mercy, have been selected to receive the
spiritual truths (see 1 Cor. 2:6-12). **hast revealed
them unto babes**—to babelike men: men of
unassuming docility, men who, conscious that
they know nothing, are eager to hear what God
will speak. Such are well called "babes."

➤**26 Even so, Father: for so it seemed
good**—or, "for so it was well-pleasing" (ASV).
**in thy sight**—or, "in your presence."

➤**27 All things are delivered unto me of my
Father**—He does not say, They are revealed—as
to one who did not know them, and was an entire
stranger to them but, They are "delivered over,"
or "committed," to me of my Father; meaning the
whole administration of the kingdom of grace. So
in John 3:35, "The Father loveth the Son, and hath
given all things into his hand" (see comments on
that verse). But though the "all things" in both
these passages refer properly to the kingdom of
grace, they of course include all things necessary
to the full execution of that trust—that is, unlimited power and authority. (See 28:18; John 17:2;
Eph. 1:22.) **and no man knoweth the Son, but**

the Father; neither knoweth any man the Father, save the Son, and he to whomsoever the Son will [decides to] reveal him—What a saying this is, that the Father and the Son are mutually and exclusively known to each other! A higher claim to equality with the Father cannot be conceived. Either we have here one of the most revolting assumptions ever uttered, or the truth concerning the divinity of Christ. As God, the Son fully and personally knows the Father; and the Father fully and personally knows the Son. (The Greek word for "knows" here is *epiginōsko*; it indicates a thorough and experiential knowledge between persons.) The Son decides on or chooses (Gk. *boulē*, denoting a counseled decision) those to whom he will reveal (or, unveil) the Father. No one can come to know God the Father without the Son revealing him (see John 1:14-18; 14:6-11).

➤28 Come unto me, all ye that labour and are heavy laden, and I will give you rest— Encouraging words to a weary, groaning world! What gentleness, what sweetness is there in the very style of the invitation—"Come to me": and in the words, "All ye that toil and are burdened," the universal struggle of man is depicted, on both its sides—the active and the passive forms of it.

➤29 Take my yoke upon you—the yoke of subjection to Jesus. and learn of me; for I am meek and lowly in heart: and ye shall find rest unto your souls—As Christ's willingness to empty himself to the utmost and heed his father's requirements was the spring of ineffable repose to his own Spirit, so in the same Spirit does he invite all to follow him, with the assurance of the same experience.

➤30 For my yoke is easy, and my burden is light—Matchless paradox! The rest which we experience when we are united to Christ makes all yokes easy, all burdens light.

## Chapter 12

1-8 PLUCKING GRAIN ON THE SABBATH DAY (See Mark 2:23-28; Luke 6:1-5.)

The season of the year when this occurred is determined by the event itself. Ripe heads of grain are found in the fields only just before harvest. The barley harvest seems clearly intended here, at the close of our March and beginning of April. It coincided with the Pass-

over season, as the wheat harvest with Pentecost. And if we are right in regarding the "feast" mentioned in John 5:1 as a Passover, and consequently the second during our Lord's public ministry (see comments on that passage), this plucking of the grain must have occurred immediately after the scene and the discourse recorded in John 5, which, doubtless, would induce our Lord to hasten his departure for the north, to avoid the wrath of the Pharisees, which he had kindled at Jerusalem. Here, accordingly, we find him in the fields—on his way probably to Galilee.

➤1 At that time Jesus went on the sabbath day through the corn—"the cornfields" (in British English), "the fields of grain" (in American English)—See Mark 2:23; Luke 6:1. and his disciples were an hungred—not as one may be before his regular meals, but evidently from shortness of provisions: for Jesus defends their plucking the heads of grain and eating them on the plea of necessity. and began to pluck the ears of corn [or, heads of grain], and to eat— "rubbing them in their hands" (Luke 6:1).

➤2 But when the Pharisees saw it, they said unto him, Behold, thy disciples do that which is not lawful to do upon the sabbath day—The act itself was expressly permitted (Deut. 23:25), but as being "servile work," which was prohibited on the Sabbath day, it was regarded as unlawful.

➤3, 4 But he said unto them, Have ye not read—or, as Mark has it, "Have ye never read." what David did [See 1 Sam. 21:1-6], when he was an hungred, and they that were with him; how he entered into the house of God, and did eat the showbread, which was not lawful for him to eat, neither for them which were with him, but only for the priests?—No example could be more appropriate than this. The man after God's own heart, of whom the Jews ever boasted, when suffering in God's cause and lacking provisions, asked and obtained from the high priest what, according to the law, it was illegal for anyone except the priests to touch. Mark (2:26) says this occurred "in the days of Abiathar the high priest." But this means not during his high priesthood—for it was under that of his father Ahimelech—but simply, in his time. Ahimelech was soon succeeded by Abiathar, whose connection with David, and prominence during his reign, may account for his name, rather than his father's, being here introduced.

►**5 Or have ye not read in the law, how that on the sabbath days the priests in the temple profane the sabbath**—by doing "servile work." **and are blameless?**—The double offerings required on the Sabbath Day (Num. 28:9) could not be presented every Sabbath morning without a good deal of servile work on the part of the priests; not to speak of circumcision, which, when the child's eighth day happened to fall on a Sabbath, had to be performed by the priests on that day. (See comments on John 7:22, 23.)

►**6 But I say unto you, That in this place is one greater than the temple**—The earliest manuscripts read, "something [neuter] greater"; some later manuscripts read, "someone [masculine] greater." The neuter reading is more comprehensive; it includes Jesus' personal presence and the event of his epiphany on earth. His presence took priority over the temple and all the regulations pertaining to it. Therefore, Jesus' argument was thus: "The ordinary rules for the observance of the Sabbath give way before the requirements of the temple; but even the temple itself must give way to One whose presence demands greater authority."

►**7 But if ye had known what this meaneth, I will have mercy, and not sacrifice**—See Hosea 6:6; Micah 6:6-8, and see comments on 9:13. **ye would not have condemned the guiltless**—i.e., Had you understood the great spiritual principle, which the Scripture everywhere recognizes—that ceremonial observances must give way before moral duties, and particularly the necessities of nature—ye would have refrained from these complaints against men who in this matter are blameless. But our Lord added a specific application of this great principle to the law of the Sabbath, preserved only in Mark: "And he said unto them, the sabbath was made for man, and not man for the sabbath" (Mark 2:27).

►**8 For the Son of man is Lord even of the Sabbath day**—In what sense now is the Son of man Lord of the sabbath day? Not surely to abolish it—that would be a strange lordship, especially just after saying that it was made or instituted for man—but to own it, to interpret it, to preside over it, and to ennoble it by breathing into it an air of liberty and love

unknown before, and thus making it the nearest resemblance to the eternal Sabbath rest. The title "Son of man" is the unique title chosen by Jesus for himself. In calling himself "the Son of man" he was identifying his messianic offices as (1) the Man of Sorrows who would suffer humiliation and crucifixion, and (2) the coming King (cf. Dan. 7:13, 14 and Matt. 26:63, 64).

## 9-21 THE HEALING OF A WITHERED HAND ON THE SABBATH DAY, AND RETREAT OF JESUS TO AVOID DANGER
(See Mark 3:1-12; Luke 6:6-11.)

## 9-14 HEALING OF A WITHERED HAND

►**9 And when he was departed thence**—"on another sabbath" (Luke 6:6). **he went into their synagogue**—"and taught" (Luke 6:6). He had now, no doubt, arrived in Galilee: but this, it would appear, did not occur at Capernaum, for after it was over, he "withdrew himself," it is said, "to the sea" (Mark 3:7), whereas Capernaum was *at* the sea.

►**10 And, behold, there was a man which had his hand withered**—disabled by paralysis (as in 1 Kings 13:4). It was his right hand, as Luke graphically notes. **And they asked him, saying, Is it lawful to heal on the sabbath days? that they might accuse him**—Matthew and Luke say they "watched him whether he would heal on the sabbath day." They were now dogging his steps, to collect materials for a charge of impiety against him. It is probably that it was to their thoughts rather than their words that Jesus addressed himself in what follows.

►**11, 12 And he said unto them, What man shall there be among you, that shall have one sheep, and if it fall into a pit on the sabbath day, will he not lay hold on it, and lift it out? How much then is a man better than a sheep?**— Resistless appeal! "A righteous man has regard for the life of his beast" (Prov. 12:10, NASB) and would instinctively rescue it from death or suffering on the Sabbath day; how much more his nobler fellowman! But the reasoning, as given in the other two Gospels, is singularly striking: "But he knew their thoughts, and said to the man which had the withered hand, Rise up, and stand forth in the midst. And he arose and stood forth. Then said Jesus unto them, I will ask you one thing; Is it lawful on the sabbath days to do good, or to do evil? to save life, or to destroy it?" (Luke 6:8, 9). Here we must turn for a moment to Mark, whose graphic details make the second Gospel so exceedingly precious. "When he had looked round about on them with anger, being grieved for the hardness of their hearts, he said unto the man" (Mark 3:5). This is one of the very few passages in the Gospel history which reveal our Lord's feelings. How holy this anger was appears from the "grief" which mingled with it at "the hardness of their hearts."

**➤13 Then saith he to the man, Stretch forth thine hand. And he stretched it forth**—the power to obey going forth with the word of command. **and it was restored whole, like as the other**—The poor man, having faith in this wonderful Healer, was healed; the Pharisees were put to shame.

**➤14 Then the Pharisees went out, and held a council against him, how they might destroy him**—This is the first explicit mention of their murderous designs against our Lord. Luke (6:11) says they were filled with madness and communed one with another what they might do to Jesus. But their discussion was not whether to get rid of him, but how to do it. Mark (3:6), as usual, is more definite: "The Pharisees went forth, and straightway took counsel with the Herodians against him, how they might destroy him." These Herodians were supporters of Herod's dynasty, created by Caesar—a political rather than religious party. The Pharisees regarded them as untrue to their religion and country. But here we see them combining together against Christ as a common enemy, as on a subsequent occasion (22:15, 16).

## 15-21 JESUS RETREATS TO AVOID DANGER

**➤15 But when Jesus knew it, he withdrew himself from thence**—where, Matthew does not say, but Mark (3:7) says "it was to the sea"—to some distance, no doubt, from the scene of the miracle, the madness, and the plotting just recorded. **and great multitudes followed him, and he healed them all**—Mark provides the details of this scene (see comments on Mark 3:7-12).

**➤16 And charged them** [i.e., those healed] **that they should not make him known**—See comments on 8:4.

**➤17-20 That it might be fulfilled which was spoken by Esaias the prophet, saying, Behold my servant, whom I have chosen: my beloved, in whom my soul is well pleased: I will put my spirit [Spirit] upon him, and he shall shew judgment to the Gentiles. He shall not strive nor cry; neither shall any man hear his voice in the streets. A bruised reed shall he not break, and smoking flax shall he not quench, till he send forth judgment unto victory**—Matthew's citation does not exactly follow the text of Isaiah 42:1-4. The OT reads "whom I uphold," Matthew says, "whom I have chosen"; the OT reads "establishes justice," Matthew says, "send forth judgment unto victory" (i.e., brought justice to a victorious conclusion). The Messiah-Servant would execute judgment in a gentle way, not with ruthlessness and ill regard for the people. But Matthew appropriated the spirit instead of the letter of the prediction in this point. Whereas one rough touch will break a bruised reed and quench the flickering, smoking flax, his would be with matchless tenderness, love, and skill, to lift up the meek, to strengthen the weak hands and feeble knees, to comfort all that mourn, to say to them that are of a fearful heart, be strong, fear not.

**➤21 And in his name shall the Gentiles trust**—Again, Matthew's citation of the OT text (Isa. 42:4b) is not exact; in fact, it is more like a paraphrase. The OT reads, "coastlands"; Matthew interpreted this as equalling "the Gentiles." The OT reads, "will wait expectantly"; this becomes "hope" in Matthew. Both paraphrases are legitimate. Finally, Matthew used the Septuagint, which reads, "in his name," rather than the Hebrew text, which reads, "in his law." At any rate, the OT Scripture was taken by Matthew to be a predictive prophecy concerning the Gentiles. Part of his present audience were Gentiles—from Tyre and Sidon—firstfruits of the great Gentile harvest contemplated in the prophecy.

## 22-37 A BLIND AND DUMB DEMONIAC HEALED, AND JESUS' REPLY TO THE MALIGNANT EXPLANATION PUT UPON IT  (See Mark 3:20-30; Luke 11:14-23.)

The precise time of this section is uncertain. Judging from the statements with which Mark introduces it, we should conclude that it was when our Lord's popularity was approaching its zenith, and so before the feeding of the five thousand. But, on the other hand, the advanced state of the charges brought against our Lord, and the plainness of his warnings and denunciations in reply, seem to favor the later period at which Luke introduces it. "And the multitude," says Mark (3:20, 21), "cometh together again," referring back to the immense gathering which Mark had before recorded (2:2)—"so that they could not so much as eat bread. And when his friends"—or, rather "relatives" (as appears from 3:31, and see comments on 12:46)—"heard of it, they went out to lay hold on him: for they said, He is beside himself." Cf. 2 Corinthians 5:13, "For whether we be beside ourselves, it is to God."

➤**22, 23 Then was brought unto him one possessed with a devil** [a demon-possessed person] **blind and dumb, and he healed him, insomuch that the blind and dumb** [i.e., the one both blind and dumb] **both spake and saw. And all the people were amazed, and said, Is not this the son of David?**—The form of the interrogative requires this to be rendered, "This man cannot be the Son of David, can he?" (NASB). And as questions put in this form (in Gk.) suppose doubt and expect a negative answer, the meaning is, "Can it possibly be?"— the people thus indicating their secret impression that this might be the One, yet saving themselves from the wrath of the Jewish leaders that a direct assertion of it would have brought upon them. (See a similar question in John 4:29; and on the phrase, "Son of David," in the comments on 9:27.)

➤**24 But when the Pharisees heard it**— Mark (3:22) says, "the scribes which came down from Jerusalem"; so this had been a hostile party of the Jewish leaders who had come all the way from Jerusalem to collect materials for a charge against him. (See comments on 12:14.) **they said, This fellow doth not cast out devils** [demons], **but by Beelzebub**—rather, Beelzebul, the prince of the devils (demons). Two things are here implied—first, that the bitterest enemies of our Lord were unable to deny the reality of his miracles; and next, that they believed in an organized internal kingdom of evil, under one chief. This belief would be of small consequence, had not our Lord set his seal to it; but this he immediately does. Stung by the testimony of "all the people," they had no way of holding out against his claims but to make the desperate shift of ascribing his miracles to Satan.

➤**25, 26 And Jesus knew their thoughts and said unto them, Every kingdom divided against itself is brought to desolation; and every city or house** [household] **divided against itself shall not stand: And if Satan cast out Satan, he is divided against himself; how shall then his kingdom stand?**—The argument here is irresistible. No organized society can stand (whether kingdom, city, or household) when turned against itself; such internal war is suicidal. But the works Jesus did are destructive of Satan's kingdom. That he should be in league with Satan, therefore, is incredible and absurd.

➤**27 And if I by Beelzebub cast out devils** [demons], **by whom do your children**—"your sons," meaning here the "disciples" or pupils of the Pharisees, who were so termed after the familiar language of the OT in speaking of the sons of the prophets (1 Kings 20:35; 2 Kings 2:3). Our Lord here seems to admit that such works were wrought by them, in which case the Pharisees stood self-condemned, as expressed in Luke (11:19), "Therefore shall they be your judges."

➤**28 But if I cast out devils** [demons] **by the Spirit of God**—In Luke (11:20) it is "with" (or "by") "the finger of God." This latter expression is just a figurative way of representing the power of God, while the former tells us the living Personal Agent was used by the Lord Jesus in every exercise of that power. **then**—"no doubt" (Luke 11:20). **the kingdom of God is come unto you**—rather "upon you," as the same expression is rendered in Luke. The meaning is as follows: "If this expulsion of Satan is, and can be, by no other than the Spirit of God, then is Satan's destroyer already in your midst, and that kingdom which is destined to supplant his has already come."

➤**29, 30 Or else how can one enter into a** [or rather, "the"] **strong man's house, and spoil his goods, except he first bind the strong man? and then he will spoil his house. He that is not with me is against me; and he that gathereth not with me scattereth abroad**— On this important parable, in connection with the corresponding one (12:43-45), see comments on Luke 11:21-26.

➤**31, 32 Wherefore I say unto you, All manner of sin and blasphemy shall be forgiven unto men**—The word "blasphemy" properly signifies "slander." In the NT it is applied, as it is here, to vituperation directed against God as well as against men; and in this sense it is to be understood as an excessive form of sin. All sin—whether in its ordinary or its more excessive forms—shall find forgiveness with God. There is no sin whatever, it seems, of which it may be said, "That is not a pardonable sin." This glorious assurance is not limited by what follows; but, on the contrary, what follows is to be explained by this. **but the blasphemy against the Holy Ghost** [Spirit] **shall not be forgiven unto men. And whosoever speaketh a word against the Son of man, it shall be forgiven him: but whosoever speaketh against the Holy Ghost** [Spirit], **it shall not be forgiven him, neither in this world, neither in the world to come**—In Mark (3:29) the language is awfully strong, "hath never forgiveness, but is in danger of eternal damnation"—or rather, according to what appears to be the preferable though very unusual reading, "in danger of eternal sin." Mark has the important addition (3:30), "Because they said, He hath an unclean spirit." What, then, is this unpardonable sin against the Holy Spirit? One thing is clear: its unpardonableness cannot arise from anything in the nature of sin itself; for that would be a contradiction to the emphatic declaration of 12:31, that all manner of sin is pardonable. And what is this but the fundamental truth of the gospel? (See Acts 13:38, 39; Rom. 3:22, 24; 1 John 1:7.) Then, again when it is said (12:32) that to speak against or blaspheme the Son of man is pardonable, but the blasphemy against the Holy Spirit is not pardonable, it is not to be conceived that this arises from any greater sanctity in the one blessed person than the other. These remarks so narrow the question that the true sense of our Lord's words is immediately clear. It is a contrast between slandering "the Son of man" in his veiled condition and unfinished work—which might be done "ignorantly, in unbelief" (1 Tim. 1:13) and slandering the same blessed person after actually seeing the glory the Holy Spirit expressed through Jesus' mighty deeds. This would be to slander him with eyes open, or to do it "presumptuously."

To blaspheme Christ in the former condition—when even the apostles stumbled at many things—left them still open to conviction on fuller light; but to blaspheme him in the latter condition would be to hate the light the clearer it became and resolutely to shut it out—which, of course, precludes salvation. (See comments on Heb. 10:26-29.) The Pharisees had not as yet done this; but in charging Jesus with being in league with Satan, they were displaying beforehand a malignant determination to shut their eyes to all evidence, and so were very close to committing the unpardonable sin.

➤**33, 34 Either make the tree good . . . O generation of vipers**—See comments on 3:7. **how can ye, being evil, speak good things? for out of the abundance of the heart the mouth speaketh**—a principle obvious enough, yet of deepest significance and vast application. In Luke 6:45 we find it uttered as part of the discourse delivered after the choice of the apostles.

➤**35 A good man, out of the good treasure of the heart, bringeth** [or, puts] **forth good things: and an evil man out of the evil treasure bringeth** [or, puts] **forth evil things**—The word "puts" (lit., "casts out") indicates the spontaneity of what comes from the heart; for it is out of the abundance of the heart that the mouth speaks. We have heard a new application of a former saying (see comments on 7:16-20). Here the thought is, "There are but two kingdoms, interests, parties—with the proper workings of each: If I promote the one, I cannot belong to the other; but they that set themselves in willful opposition to the kingdom of light openly proclaim to what other kingdom they belong. As for you (the Pharisees), in what you have now uttered, you have revealed the venomous malignity of your hearts."

➤**36 But I say unto you, That every idle word that men shall speak, they shall give account thereof in the day of judgment**—They might say, "It was nothing: we meant no evil; we merely threw out a supposition, as one way of accounting for the miracle we witnessed; if it will not stand, let it go; why make so much of it, and bear down with such severity for it?" Jesus might reply, "It was *not* nothing, and at the great day will not be treated as nothing. Words, as the index of the heart, however idle they may seem, will be taken account of, whether good or bad, in estimating character in the day of judgment."

## 38-45 A SIGN DEMANDED AND THE REPLY

The occasion of this section was the same with that of the preceding.

➤**38 Then certain of the scribes and of the Pharisees answered, saying, Master—** "Teacher," equivalent to "Rabbi." **we would see a sign from thee—**"a sign from heaven" (Luke 11:16); something of an immediate and decisive nature, to show, not that his miracles were real—that they seemed willing to concede—but that they were from above, not from beneath. These were not the same class with those who charged him with being in league with Satan (as we see from Luke 11:15, 16); but as the spirit of both was similar, the tone of severe rebuke is continued.

➤**39, 40 But he answered and said unto them, An evil and adulterous generation—** This latter expression is best explained by Jeremiah 3:20, "Surely as a woman treacherously departs from her lover, so treacherously you have dealt with me, O house of Israel, declares the Lord" (NASB). For this was the relationship in which he stood to the covenant people—he was married to them, but they departed from him and so committed spiritual adultery. **seeketh after a sign—**In the eye of Jesus this class were but the spokesmen of their generation, the exponents of the reigning spirit of unbelief. **and there shall no sign be given to it, but the sign of the prophet Jonas—**"a sign unto the Ninevites, so shall also the Son of man be to this generation" (Luke 11:30). **For as Jonas was three days and three nights in the whale's belly—**Jonah 1:17. **so shall the Son of man be three days and three nights in the heart of the earth—**This was the second public announcement of his resurrection to occur three days after his death. (For the first, see John 2:19.) Jonah's case was analogous to this, as being a signal judgment of God. After three days and nights, Jonah was resuscitated and then went on to a glorious mission to the Gentiles. The expression "in the heart of the earth," suggested by the expression of Jonah concerning the sea (see Jonah 2:3 LXX), means simply the grave. Jesus would be in the grave for three

days. This time period is here expressed in general terms, according to the Jewish way of speaking, which was to regard any part of a day, however small, included within a period of days, as a full day (see 1 Sam. 30:12, 13; Esther 4:16; 5:1; Matt. 27:63, 64).

➤**41 The men of Nineveh shall rise in judgment with this generation—**The Ninevites, though heathens, repented at a man's preaching; while they, God's covenant people, repented not at the preaching of the Son of God.

➤**42 The queen of the south shall rise up in the judgment with this generation—**The queen of Sheba (a part of Arabia, near the shores of the Red Sea) came from a remote country, "south" of Judea, to hear the wisdom of a mere man, though a gifted one, and was enthralled with what she saw and heard (1 Kings 10:1-9). They, when a Greater than Solomon had come to them, despised and rejected, slighted and slandered him.

➤**43-45 When the unclean spirit is gone out of a man—**On this important parable, in connection with the corresponding one (12:29) see comments on Luke 11:21-26.

## 46-50 HIS MOTHER AND BROTHERS SEEK TO SPEAK WITH HIM

➤**46 While he yet talked to the people, behold, his mother and his brethren—**See comments on 13:55, 56. **stood without, desiring to speak with him—**"and could not come at him for the press" (Luke 8:19). For what purpose these came, we learn from Mark 3:20, 21. In his zeal and ardor he seemed indifferent both to food and repose, and "they went to lay hold of him" as one "beside himself."

➤**47, 48 Then one said unto him, Behold, thy mother and thy brethren stand without, desiring to speak with thee—**Absorbed in the awful warnings he was pouring forth, he felt this to be an unseasonable interruption, fitted to dissipate the impression made upon the large audience. But instead of a direct rebuke, he seizes on the incident to convey the truth that those who do God's will are Jesus' mother and brothers.

➤**49, 50 And he stretched forth his hand toward his disciples—**How graphic this is! It is evidently the language of an eyewitness. **and said, Behold my mother and my brethren! For whosoever shall do the will of my Father** which is in heaven, the same is my brother, and sister, and mother—i.e., "There stand here the members of a family transcending that of earth. Filial subjection to the will of my Father in heaven is the indissoluble bond of union between me and all its members; and whosoever enters this hallowed circle becomes to me brother, and sister, and mother!"

# Chapter 13

1-52 JESUS' PARABLES (See Mark 4:1-34; Luke 8:4-18; 13:18-20.)

## 1-3 INTRODUCTION

►1, 2 The same day went Jesus out of the house, and sat by the sea side. And great multitudes were gathered together unto him, so that he went into a ship, and sat; and the whole multitude stood on the shore—How graphic this picture!—no doubt from the pen of an eyewitness, himself impressed with the scene. It was "the same day" on which the foregoing solemn discourse was delivered,— when his kindred thought him "beside himself" for his indifference to food and repose—that same day he retired to the seashore of Galilee; and there seating himself, perhaps for coolness and rest, the crowds again flocked around him and he may have desired to push off from them in the boat usually kept in readiness for him. Yet he began a new course of teaching, by parables, to the eager multitudes that lined the shore. There is nothing in all language that compares to Jesus' parables in simplicity, grace, fullness, and variety of spiritual teaching. They are adapted to all classes and stages of advancement, being understood by each according to the measure of his spiritual capacity.

►3 And he spake many things unto them in parables—There are seven parables; and it is not a little remarkable that while this is a typically sacred number, the first four of them were spoken to the mixed multitude, while the remaining three were spoken to the Twelve in private—these divisions, four and three, being themselves notable in the symbolical arithmetic of Scripture. Another thing remarkable in the structure of these parables is, that while the first of the seven—that of the sower—is

of the nature of an introduction to the whole, the remaining six consist of three pairs—the second and seventh, the third and fourth, and the fifth and sixth, corresponding to each other; each pair setting forth the same general truths, but with a certain diversity of aspect. All this can hardly be accidental.

## 3-9, 18-23 FIRST PARABLE: THE SOWER

For the exposition of this parable, see comments on Mark 4:1-9, 14-20.

## 10-17 REASON FOR TEACHING IN PARABLES

►10 And the disciples came, and said unto him—"they that were with him, when they were alone" (Mark 4:10). Why speakest thou unto them in parables?—Though before this he had phrased some statements in the parabolic form for more vivid illustration, it would appear that he now, for the first time, formally employed this method of teaching.

►11 He answered and said unto them, Because it is given unto you to know the mysteries of the kingdom of heaven—The word "mysteries" in Scripture does not signify things incomprehensible but things that were secrets until revealed by God. Many things in the OT economy were kept secret—until Christ came and revealed long-kept ancient mysteries known only to God (see 1 Cor. 2:6-10; Eph. 3:3-6, 8, 9). The OT believers knew that God wanted to establish his kingdom on earth, but they did not realize that Christ had come to do so in an unexpected way. He would establish the kingdom of God not among men but in men—by entering into their lives and ruling them from within. This was a mystery, a secret hidden in the councils of the Godhead (see Col. 1:27; 2:2; 4:3). but to them it is not given—(see comments on 11:25). Parables serve the double purpose of revealing and concealing; presenting "the mysteries of the kingdom" to those who know and relish them, though in never so small a degree, in a new and attractive light; but to those who are insensible to spiritual things, yielding only, as so many tales, some temporary entertainment.

►12 For whosoever hath—i.e., keeps, as a thing which he values. to him shall be given, and he shall have more abundance—He will be rewarded by an increase of what he so much prizes. but whosoever hath not—who lets this go or lie unused, as a thing on which he sets no value. **from him shall be taken away even that he hath**—or as it is in Luke (8:18), "what he seemeth to have," or, thinks he has. This is a principle of immense importance and, like other weighty sayings, appears to have been uttered by our Lord on more than one occasion and in different connections. (See comments on 25:9.)

➤**13 Therefore speak I to them in parables**—which our Lord, be it observed, did not begin to do until his miracles were malignantly ascribed to Satan. After the Jews rejected him so, he began to unveil the mysteries concerning God's plan for the coming ages—a plan that would extend beyond Israel and encompass all believers, whether Jewish or Gentile. **because they seeing see not**—They "saw," for the light shone on them as never light shone before; but they "saw not," for they closed their eyes. **and hearing they hear not, neither do they understand**—They "heard," for he taught them who "spake as never man spake"; but they "heard not," for they took nothing in, not apprehending the soul-penetrating, life-giving words addressed to them. In Mark and Luke, what is here expressed as a human fact is represented as the fulfillment of a divine purpose—"that seeing they may see, and not perceive." The explanation of this lies in the statement of the foregoing verse—that, by a fixed law of the divine administration, that which men voluntarily refuse to do, and in point of face do not do, at length becomes impossible to do.

➤**14 And in them is fulfilled**—rather, is fulfilling, or is receiving its fulfillment. **the prophecy of Esaias** [Isaiah], **which saith**—Isaiah 6:9, 10—here quoted according to the Septuagint. **By hearing ye shall hear, and shall not understand**—They were thus judicially sealed up under the darkness and obduracy which they deliberately preferred to the light and healing which Jesus brought to them. Jesus used the same OT passage in John 12:40 to summarize the universal rejection of his ministry. As John 12 marks a turning point in that Gospel (i.e., from that time, Jesus no longer ministered publicly, but only to his disciples in private), so Matthew 13 marks a critical junction in this Gospel.

➤**16 But blessed are your eyes, for they see: and your ears, for they hear**—i.e., "Happy you

whose eyes and ears, voluntarily and gladly opened, are absorbing the divine light."

➤**17 For verily I say unto you, That many prophets and righteous men have desired to see those things which ye see, and have not seen them; and to hear those things which ye hear, and have not heard them**—Not only were the disciples blessed above the blinded just spoken of, but they were favored above the most honored and the best that lived under the old economy, who had but glimpses of the things of the new kingdom just sufficient to kindle in them desires that would not be fulfilled in their day. In Luke 10:23, 24, where the same saying is repeated on the return of the Seventy—the words "many prophets and righteous men" should be "many prophets and kings," for several of the OT saints were kings.

## 24-30, 36-43, 47-50 SECOND AND SEVENTH PARABLES, OR FIRST PAIR: THE WHEAT AND THE TARES, AND THE GOOD AND BAD FISH

The subject of both these parables—which teach the same truth with a slight diversity of aspect—is: the mixed character of the kingdom in its present state, and the final, absolute separation of the two classes.

## 24-30, 36-43 THE PARABLE OF THE WHEAT AND THE TARES—AN INTERWEAVING OF THE STORY AND THE EXPLANATION

➤**24 Another parable put he forth unto them, saying, The kingdom of heaven is likened unto a man which sowed good seed in his field**—At this point, it should be noted that Matthew uses the phrase "kingdom of heaven," whereas the other gospel writers use the expression "kingdom of God." For the most part, the terms are synonymous, especially when we consider that Matthew may have used "heaven" as a surrogate for "God" in accordance with the Jewish practice of refraining from using God's name. However, Matthew also used the expression "kingdom of God" (12:28; 19:24; 21:31, 43). Thus, he could have intended a distinction: "the kingdom of God" is that realm which includes only genuine children of God; whereas "the kingdom of heaven" includes both real and false believers (Barbieri). If this is true, it helps us understand the mixture (of true and false believers) that is spoken of in several of the following parables—beginning with the parable of the good seed and the tares. Happily for us, this exquisite parable is with simplicity and clarity expounded to us by the great Preacher himself. Accordingly, we go on to the next section.

➤**36-38 Then Jesus sent the multitude away, and went into the house: and his disciples came unto him, saying, Declare unto us the parable of the tares of the field**—In the parable of the sower, "the seed is the word of God" (Luke 8:11). But here that word has been received into the heart and has made him that received it a new creation, a "child of the kingdom," according to that saying of James (1:18): "He chose to give us birth through the word of truth, that we might be a kind of firstfruits of all he created" (NIV). It is worthy of notice that this vast field of the world is here said to be Christ's own ("his field").

➤**26 But when the blade was sprung up, and brought forth fruit, then appeared the tares also**—the growth in both cases running parallel, as antagonistic principles are seen to do.

➤**27 So the servants of the householder came** [i.e., Christ's ministers] **and said unto him, Sir, didst not thou sow good seed in thy field? from whence then hath it tares?**—This well expresses the surprise, disappointment, and anxiety of Christ's faithful servants and people at the discovery of "false brethren" among the members of the church.

➤**28 He said unto them, An enemy hath done this**—These words clear his faithful servants of the wrong done to his field. **The servants said unto him, Wilt thou then that we go and gather them up?**—Compare with this the question of James and John in Luke 9:54.

➤**29 But he said, Nay; lest, while ye gather up the tares, ye root up also the wheat with them**—Nothing could more clearly or forcibly teach the difficulty of distinguishing the two classes, and the high probability that in the attempt to do so these will be confounded.

➤**38 The tares are the children of the wicked one**—As this sowing could only be "while men slept" (13:25), no blame seems intended, and certainly none is charged upon "the servants."

➤**39 The enemy that sowed them is the devil**—emphatically "*his*" enemy" (13:25). (See Gen. 3:15; 1 John 3:8.) Tares were noxious plants, probably darnels. "The tares are the children of the wicked one"; and by their being sown "among the wheat" is meant their being deposited within the territory of the visible church. As they resemble the children of the kingdom, so they are produced, it seems, by a similar process of "sowing"—the seeds of evil being scattered and lodging in the soil of those hearts upon which falls the seed of the word. The enemy, after sowing his "tares," "went his way"—his dark work soon done, but taking time to develop its true character.

➤**30, 39 Let both grow together**—i.e., in the visible church, or what we might call the visible manifestation of the kingdom of heaven (i.e., Christendom). **until the harvest**—until the one has ripened for full salvation, the other for destruction. **the harvest is the end of the world**—the period of Christ's second coming and of the judicial separation of the righteous and the wicked. Until then, no attempt is to be made to effect such separation. But to stretch this so far as to justify allowing openly scandalous persons to remain in the communion of the church, is to twist and misapply the teaching of this parable. **and in the time of harvest I will say to the reapers . . . and the reapers are the angels**—These angels are the Messiah's angels: "The Son of man shall send forth his angels" (13:41; see 1 Pet. 3:22). **Gather ye together first the tares, and bind them in bundles to burn them**—"in the fire" (13:40). **but gather the wheat into my barn**—Christ, as the Judge, will separate the two classes (as in 25:32). It will be observed that the tares are burned before the wheat is housed; in the exposition of the parable (13:41, 43) the same order is observed (see also 25:46).

➤**41 The Son of man shall send forth his angels, and they shall gather out of his kingdom**—to which they never really belonged. They usurped their place and name and outward privileges; but "the ungodly shall not stand in the judgment, nor sinners [abide] in the congregation of the righteous" (Ps. 1:5). **all things that offend**—all those who have proved a stumbling block to others. **and them which do iniquity**—The former class, as the worst, are mentioned first.

➤**42 And shall cast them into a** [rather, "the"] **furnace of fire: there shall be wailing and gnashing of teeth**—What terrific strength of language—the "casting" or "flinging" expressive of indignation, abhorrence, contempt (cf. Ps. 9:17; Dan. 12:2); "the furnace of fire" denoting the fierceness of the torment; the "wailing" signifying the anguish this causes; the "gnashing of teeth" graphically expressing the despair of regret and remorse (see comments on 8:12).

➤**43 Then shall the righteous shine forth as the sun in the kingdom of their Father**—as if they had been under a cloud during their association with ungodly pretenders to their character, false claimants of their privileges, and obstructors of their course. **Who hath ears to hear, let him hear**—See comments on Mark 4:9.

### 47-50 THE GOOD AND BAD FISH

The object of this brief parable is the same as that of the tares and wheat. But as its details are fewer, so its teaching is less rich and varied.

➤**47 Again, the kingdom of heaven is like unto a net, that was cast into the sea, and gathered of every kind**—The word here rendered "net" signifies a large dragnet, which draws everything after it, allowing nothing to escape, as distinguished from a casting-net (Mark 1:16, 18). The far-reaching efficacy of the gospel is thus denoted. This gospel net "gathered of every kind," meaning every variety of character.

➤**48 Which, when it was full, they drew to shore**—for the separation will not be made until the number of the elect is complete (or, full)—see Romans 11:25. **and sat down**—expressing the deliberateness with which the judicial separation will be made. **and gathered the good into vessels, but cast the bad away**—lit., "the rotten," but here meaning, "the foul" or "worthless" fish, corresponding to the "tares" of the other parable.

➤**49 So shall it be at the end of the world**—See comments on 13:42. We have said that each of these two parables holds forth the same truth under a slight diversity of aspect. What is that diversity? First, the bad, in the former parable, are represented as vile seed sown among the wheat by the enemy; in the latter, as foul fish drawn forth out of the great sea of human beings by the gospel net itself. Both are important truths—that the gospel draws into the visible church multitudes who are Christians only in name; and that the injury thus done to the church on earth is to be traced to the wicked one. But further, while the former parable gives chief prominence to the present mixture of good and bad, in the latter,

the prominence is given to the future separation of the two classes.

### 31-33 THIRD AND FOURTH PARABLES, OR SECOND PAIR: THE MUSTARD SEED AND THE LEAVEN

The subject of both these parables, as of the first pair, is the same, but under a slight diversity of aspect: namely the growth of the kingdom from the smallest beginnings to ultimate universality.

### 31, 32 THE MUSTARD SEED

➤**31, 32 Another parable put he forth unto them, saying, The kingdom of heaven is like to a grain of mustard seed, which a man took, and sowed in his field; which indeed is the least of all seeds**—not absolutely, but popularly and proverbially, as in Luke 17:6, "If ye had faith as a grain of mustard seed." **but when it is grown, it is the greatest among herbs**—not absolutely, but in relation to the small size of the seed, and in warm latitudes proverbially great (12-15 feet). **and becometh a tree, so that the birds of the air come and lodge in the branches thereof**—This is added, no doubt, to express the amplitude of the tree. Most commentators understand this image to convey how the kingdom, from a small beginning, grew into a great entity. This is usually viewed as positive, but OT portions portraying the same image (see Judg. 9:15; Ezek. 17:22-24; 31:3-14; Dan. 4:7-23) present the great tree as a great worldly kingdom. Perhaps Jesus intended to convey that the seed grew out of proportion, in the same way that Christendom would become a great, earthly kingdom—so big that birds (denoting evil characters?) would lodge in its branches. If this interpretation has any validity, the parable again shows mixture and imbalance in the visible church.

### 33 THE LEAVEN

➤**33 Another parable spake he unto them; the kingdom of heaven is like unto leaven, which a woman took, and hid in three measures of meal, till the whole was leavened**—This parable probably teaches the same general truth as the foregoing one—namely, both deal with the growth of the kingdom. Again, most commentators understand the picture of leaven expanding into the flour to convey how the gospel will penetrate into all the world. They prefer to think that Jesus was using the image of "leaven" positively. But since leaven is almost always used in the Bible negatively (i.e., to demonstrate the evil effect of sin or worldliness in God's people, etc.), other commentators hesitate to say that this parable presents a positive image. Could it be that Jesus was (again) relating that a little evil entering God's kingdom would spoil the entire community? This interpretation (and the one posited before) can only be valid if, in fact, Jesus was speaking about the appearance of the kingdom in these parables. If he was not, then the parable of the mustard seed and leaven must be seen as speaking of positive growth.

➤**34 All these things spake Jesus unto the multitude in parables; and without a parable spake he not unto them**—i.e., on this occasion, refraining not only from all plain discourse, but even from all interpretation of these parables to the multitude.

➤**35 That it might be fulfilled which was spoken by the prophet, saying** [Ps. 78:2, nearly as in LXX] **I will open my mouth in parables**—Though the psalm seems to contain only a summary of Israel's history, the psalmist himself calls it "a parable," and "dark sayings from old," for the psalmist brought out hidden truths by arranging Israel's history according to a certain perspective. (Stephen did the same in Acts 7.)

## 44-46 FIFTH AND SIXTH PARABLES, OR THIRD PAIR: THE HIDDEN TREASURE AND THE PEARL OF GREAT PRICE

The subject of this last pair, as of the two former, is the same, but also under a slight diversity of aspect: namely, the priceless value of the blessings of the kingdom. And while the one parable represents the kingdom as found without seeking, the other presents the kingdom as sought and found.

## 44 THE HIDDEN TREASURE

➤**44 Again, the kingdom of heaven is like unto treasure hid in a field**—no uncommon thing in unsettled and half-civilized countries, when there was no other way of securing it from the rapacity of neighbors or marauders (Jer. 41:8; Job 3:21; Prov. 2:4). **the which when a man hath found**—i.e., unexpectedly found. **he hideth, and for joy thereof**—on perceiving what a treasure he had found, surpassing the worth of all he possessed. **goeth and selleth all that he hath, and buyeth that**

**field**—in which case, by Jewish law, the treasure would become his own. Since Jesus did not interpret this parable, we are left to explicate it on our own. The explications are innumerable. The most plausible one is that Jesus relinquished everything (Phil. 2:6) to come and purchase his people, who were a great treasure to him (Exod. 9:5; Ps. 135:4).

## 45, 46 THE PEARL OF GREAT PRICE

➤**45, 46 Again, the kingdom of heaven is like unto a merchantman, seeking godly pearls: Who, when he had found one pearl of great price, went and sold all that he had, and bought it**—The one pearl of great price, instead of being found by accident, as in the former case, is found by one whose business it is to seek for such and who finds it just in the way of searching for such treasures. But in both cases the surpassing value of the treasure is alike recognized, and in both all is parted with for it. Again, we can only offer a plausible interpretation: Jesus is the merchant who sold everything to purchase the church at a great price (1 Cor. 6:20; 7:23).

➤**51 Jesus saith unto them**—i.e., to the Twelve. He had spoken the first four parables in the hearing of the multitude: the last three he reserved until, on the dismissal of the audience, he and the Twelve were alone (13:36).

➤**52 Then said he unto them, Therefore**—or as we should say, "Well, then." **every scribe**—or Christian teacher, here so called from that well-known class among the Jews (see 23:34). **which is instructed unto the kingdom of heaven**—lit., "made a disciple to the kingdom of the heavens." **is like unto a man that is a householder which bringeth forth out of his treasure**—his store of divine truth. **things new and old**—old truths in ever new forms, aspects, applications, and with ever new illustrations.

## 53-58 HOW JESUS WAS REGARDED BY HIS RELATIVES (See Mark 6:1-6; Luke 4:16-30.)

➤**53, 54 And it came to pass, that when Jesus had finished these parables, he departed thence. And when he was come into his own country**—i.e., Nazareth, as is plain from Mark 6:1. See John 4:43, where also the same phrase occurs. This visit to Nazareth must coincide with the one recorded in Luke 4:16-30. **Whence hath this man this wisdom, and these mighty** works?—"these miracles." These surely are not like the questions of people who had asked precisely the same questions before, who from astonishment had proceeded to rage, and in their rage had hurried him out of the synagogue and away to the brow of the hill whereon their city was built, to thrust him down headlong, and who had been foiled even in that object by his passing through the midst of them and going his way. Thus, it is very unlikely that Jesus' visit to Nazareth, as recorded in Luke 4:16-30, could have preceded this one.

➤**55, 56 Is not this the carpenter's son?**—In Mark (6:3) the question is, "Is not this the carpenter?" In all likelihood, Jesus, during his stay under the roof of his earthly parents, worked along with his legal father—probably building plows and yokes (according to Justin Martyr). **Is not his mother called Mary?**—"Do we not know all about his parentage? Has he not grown up in the midst of us? Are not all his relatives our own townsfolk? How, then, such wisdom and such miracles?" These particulars of our Lord's human history constitute a most valuable testimony: first, to his true and real humanity—for they prove that during all his first thirty years his townsmen had discovered nothing about him different from other men; second, to the divine character of his mission— for these Nazarenes proclaim both the unparalleled character of his teaching and the reality and glory of his miracles, as transcending human ability; and third, to his wonderful humility and self-denial—in that when he was such as they now saw him to be, he never gave any indication of it for thirty years. **And his brethren, James, Joses, and Simon, and Judas? And his sisters, are they not all with us? Whence then hath this man all these things?**—An exceedingly difficult question here arises—What were these "brethren" and "sisters" to Jesus? Were they his full brothers and sisters? Or were they his step-brothers and step-sisters, children of Joseph by a former marriage? Or were they his cousins, according to a common way of speaking among the Jews respecting persons of collateral descent? On this subject an immense amount has been written, nor are opinions yet by any means agreed. For the second opinion there is no ground but a vague tradition, arising probably from the wish for some such explanation. The third

opinion is unlikely. The first opinion undoubtedly suits the text best in all the places where the parties are certainly referred to (see 12:46; and its parallels, Mark 3:31, and Luke 8:19; our present passage and its parallels, Mark 6:3; John 2:12; 7:3, 5, 10; Acts 1:14). As to the names here mentioned, the first of them, James, is afterwards called "the Lord's brother" (see comments on Gal. 1:19). After Christ's resurrection, he became a believer (1 Cor. 15:7). Then he became a prominent elder in the church in Jerusalem (Acts 15:13ff.). The epistle bearing his name is usually attributed to him. The second of those here named, "Joses" (or Joseph), must not be confused with "Joseph called Barsabas, who was surnamed Justus" (Acts 1:23); and the third here named, "Simon," is not to be confounded with Simon the Kananite or Zealot (see 10:4). The fourth and last-named, "Judas," can hardly be identical with the apostle of that name, but it is quite possible that he wrote the epistle according to Jude (see the Introduction to Jude)

➤**58 And he did not many mighty works there, because of their unbelief**—See Luke 4:16-30.

Chapter **14**

**1-12 HEROD THINKS JESUS A RESURRECTION OF THE MURDERED BAPTIST, FOLLOWED BY AN ACCOUNT OF JOHN'S IMPRISONMENT AND DEATH** (See Mark 6:14-29; Luke 9:7-9.)

The time of Herod Antipas's fear that Jesus was John raised from the dead appears to have been during the mission of the Twelve, and shortly after the Baptist—who had been in prison for probably more than a year—had been cruelly put to death.

**1, 2 HEROD'S THEORY OF THE WORKS OF CHRIST**

➤**1 At that time Herod the tetrarch**—Herod Antipas, one of the three sons of Herod the Great, and brother of Archelaus (2:22), who ruled as ethnarch over Galilee and Perea. **heard of the fame of Jesus**—"for his name was spread abroad" (Mark 6:14).

➤**2 And said unto his servants**—his counsellors or court-ministers. **This is John the**

**Baptist; he is risen from the dead**—The murdered prophet haunted his guilty conscience like a specter and seemed to him alive again and clothed with unearthly powers in the person of Jesus.

### 3-12 ACCOUNT OF THE BAPTIST'S IMPRISONMENT AND DEATH

For the exposition of this portion, see comments on Mark 6:17-29.

### 13-21 HEARING OF THE BAPTIST'S DEATH, JESUS CROSSES THE LAKE WITH THE TWELVE AND MIRACULOUSLY FEEDS FIVE THOUSAND (See Mark 6:30-44; Luke 9:10-17; John 6:1-14.)

For the exposition of this section—one of the very few where all the four evangelists run parallel—see comments on Mark 6:30-44.

### 22-36 JESUS CROSSES TO THE WESTERN SIDE OF THE LAKE, WALKING ON THE SEA. INCIDENTS ON LANDING (See Mark 6:45; John 6:15-24.)

For the exposition, see comments on John 6:15-24.

Chapter **15**

### 1-20 DISCOURSE ON CEREMONIAL DEFILEMENT (See Mark 7:1, 23.)

The time of this section was after the Passover that followed the feeding of the five thousand (John 6:4)—i.e., the third Passover since his public ministry began, but which he did not keep at Jerusalem for the reason mentioned in John 7:1.

➤**1-3 Then came to Jesus scribes and Pharisees, which were of** [or, from] **Jerusalem**—Mark says they "came from" it: a deputation probably sent from the capital expressly to watch him. As he had not come to them at the last Passover, which they had reckoned on, they now come to him. "And," says Mark (7:2-5), "when they saw some of his disciples eat bread with defiled, that is to say, with unwashen hands"—hands not ceremonially cleansed by washing—"they found fault. For the Pharisees, and all of the Jews, except they wash their hands oft"—lit., "in" or "with the first"; i.e., probably washing the one hand by the use of the other—though some understand it, with the KJV, in the sense of "diligently," "sedulously"—"eat not, holding the tradition of the elders" (i.e., acting religiously

according to the custom handed down to them). "And when they come from the market"—After any common business, or after attending a court of justice, where the Jews came in contact with Gentiles, they would not eat unless they first washed. "And there are many other things which they have received in order to observe, such as the washing of cups and pitchers and copper pots" (NASB). "Then the Pharisees and scribes asked him," **saying, Why do thy disciples transgress the tradition of the elders? for they wash not their hands when they eat bread. But he answered and said unto them, Why do ye also transgress the commandment of God by your tradition?**—The charge is retorted with startling power. The tradition they transgressed was but *man's* and was itself the occasion of heavy transgression, undermining the authority of *God's law.*

➤**4-6 For God commanded, saying, Honour thy father and mother**—See Deuteronomy 5:16. **and, He that curseth father or mother, let him die the death**—See Exodus 21:17. **But ye say, Whosoever shall say to his father or his mother, It is a gift**—or simply "A gift!" In Mark it is *Corban!* i.e., "an oblation!" meaning, any bloodless offering or gift dedicated to sacred uses. **by whatsoever thou mightest be profited by me; and honour not his father or his mother** [he shall be free]—These verses are difficult to understand. A better rendering helps clarify them: "But you say that if a man says to his father or mother, 'whatever help you might otherwise have received from me is a gift devoted to God'" (NIV). One cannot offer something to God if that offering robs his care for his parents. To dedicate property to God is indeed lawful and laudable, but not at the expense of filial duty. **Thus have ye made the commandment of God of none effect**—cancelled or nullified it—**by your tradition.**

➤**7 Ye hypocrites, well did Esaias** [Isaiah] **prophesy of you, saying**—See Isaiah 29:13.

➤**8 This people draweth nigh unto me with their mouth**—By putting the commandments of men on a level with the divine requirements, their whole worship was rendered vain.

➤**10 And he called the multitude, and said unto them**—The foregoing dialogue, though within the people's hearing, was between Jesus and the Pharisees and scribes, whose object was to disparage him with the people. But Jesus, having exposed them, turned to the multitude, who at this time were prepared to drink in everything he said, and with admirable plainness, strength, and brevity, set forth the great principle of real defilement.

➤11 Not that which goeth into the mouth defileth a man; but that which cometh out of the mouth, this defileth a man—This is expressed even more emphatically in Mark (7:15, 16), and it is there added. "If any man have ears to hear, let him hear." As in 13:9, this so oft-repeated saying seems designed to call attention to the fundamental and universal character of the truth it refers to.

➤12 Then came his disciples, and said unto him, Knowest thou that the Pharisees were offended, after they heard this saying?—The Pharisees had given vent to their irritation, and perhaps threats, not to our Lord himself, but to some of the disciples, who report it to their Master.

➤13 But he answered and said, Every plant, which my heavenly Father hath not planted, shall be rooted up—Israel was depicted in the OT as God's plant (Ps. 1:3; Isa. 5:1-7; 60:21). But these Pharisees, although living among Israel, were not the Father's. (In the Gospel of John, Jesus says they were not his sheep—10:26.) They would be plucked up in judgment (see 3:9, 10; 8:11, 12).

➤14 Let them alone: they be blind leaders of the blind. And if the blind lead the blind, both shall fall into the ditch—A striking expression of the ruinous effects of erroneous teaching! (See John 9:40, 41.)

➤15, 16 Then answered Peter and said unto him—"when he was entered into the house from the people," says Mark. Declare [explain] unto us this parable. And Jesus said, Are ye also yet without understanding?—Slowness of spiritual apprehension in his genuine disciples grieved the Savior; from others he expected no better (13:11).

➤17, 18 Do not ye yet understand, that whatsoever entereth in at the mouth—Though these sayings have now become so familiar, what freedom from bondage to outward things do they proclaim, on the one hand; and on the other, how searching is the truth they express—that nothing that enters from without can really defile us; and only the evil that is in the heart, that is allowed to stir there, to rise up

in thought and affection, and to flow forth in voluntary action, really defiles a man!

➤19 For out of the heart proceed evil thoughts—referring here immediately to those corrupt reasonings that had stealthily introduced and gradually reared up the system of tradition that attempted to nullify the unchangeable principles of the moral law. But the statement is far broader than this. It declares that the first step evil in the heart takes, when it begins actively to stir, is that of "considerations" or "reasonings" on certain suggested actions. murders, adulteries, fornications, thefts, false witness, blasphemies—all of which transgress the sixth through ninth commandments. Mark adds "covetousness"—related to the tenth commandment.

➤20 These are the things which defile a man: but to eat with unwashen hands defileth not a man—Thus does our Lord sum up this whole searching discourse.

## 21-28 THE WOMAN OF CANAAN AND HER DAUGHTER
See comments on Mark 7:24-30.

## 29-39 MIRACLES OF HEALING—FOUR THOUSAND MIRACULOUSLY FED
See comments on Mark 7:31; 8:10.

*Chapter* # 16

## 1-12 A SIGN FROM HEAVEN SOUGHT AND REFUSED. CAUTION AGAINST THE LEAVEN OF THE PHARISEES AND SADDUCEES
See comments on Mark 8:11-21.

## 13-28 PETER'S NOBLE CONFESSION OF CHRIST, AND THE BENEDICTION PRONOUNCED UPON HIM. CHRIST'S FIRST EXPLICIT ANNOUNCEMENT OF APPROACHING SUFFERINGS, ANNOUNCEMENT OF HIS OF HIS DEATH AND RESURRECTION. HIS REBUKE OF PETER AND WARNING TO ALL THE TWELVE (See Mark 8:27; 9:1; Luke 9:18-27.)

## 13-20 PETER'S CONFESSION, AND THE BLESSING PRONOUNCED UPON HIM
➤13 When Jesus came into the coasts—lit., "the parts," i.e., the territory or region. In Mark (8:27) it is "the towns" or "villages."

of Caesarea Philippi—It lay at the foot of Mount Lebanon, near the sources of the Jordan, in the territory of Dan, and at the northeast extremity of Palestine. It was originally called Panium (from a cavern in its neighborhood dedicated to the god Pan). Philip, the tetrarch, the only good son of Herod the Great, in whose dominions Paneas lay, having beautified and enlarged it, changed its name to Caesarea, in honor of the Roman emperor, and added Philippi after his own name, to distinguish it from the other Caesarea (Acts 10:1) on the northeast coast of the Mediterranean Sea (Josephus, *Antiquities,* 15.10.3; 18:2, 1). Jesus probably chose this quiet and distant retreat so as to have time alone with his disciples, reviewing his past labors, and telling them for the first time the news of his approaching death. **he asked his disciples**—"by the way," says Mark (8:27), and "as he was alone praying," says Luke (9:18). **saying, Whom [Who] do men say that I the Son of man am?**—i.e., "What are the views generally entertained of me, the Son of man, after going up and down among them so long?" He had now closed the first great stage of his ministry and was just entering on the last dark one. His spirit, burdened, had sought relief in solitude, not only from the multitude, but even for a season from the Twelve. He retreated into "the secret place of the Most High," pouring out his soul in "prayers and supplications with strong crying and tears" (Heb. 5:7). On rejoining his disciples, as they were pursuing their quiet journey, he asked them this question.

**►14 And they said, Some say that thou art John the Baptist**—risen from the dead. So that Herod Antipas was not alone in his surmise (14:1, 2). **some, Elias [Elijah]**—cf. Mark 6:15. **and others, Jeremias**—Elijah and Jeremiah were expected by Jewish apocalyptists as heralds of the final day of judgment. Jesus, with his strong authority and incredible power, was probably viewed as one of those figures whose coming prepared the way for the Messiah. **or one of the prophets**—or, as Luke (9:8) expresses it, "That one of the old prophets was risen again." In another report of the popular opinions which Mark (6:15) gives us, it is thus expressed, "That it is a prophet [or], as one of the prophets": in other words, that he was a prophetical person, resembling those of old.

**►15 He saith unto them, But whom [rather, who] say ye that I am?**—He had never put this question before, but the crisis he was reaching made it fitting that he should now hear it from them. We may suppose this to be one of those moments of which the prophet says, in his name, "But, I said, 'I have toiled in vain, I have spent My strength for nothing and vanity' " (Isa. 49:4, NASB). "Lo, these three years he came seeking fruit on the fig tree; and where is it?" As the result of all, he was taken for John the Baptist, for Elijah, for Jeremiah, for one of the prophets. So he wanted to hear what his disciples would say.

**►16 And Simon Peter answered and said, Thou art the Christ, the Son of the living God**—He does not say, "Scribes and Pharisees, rulers and people, are all perplexed; and shall we, unlettered fishermen, presume to decide?" But feeling the light of his Master's glory shining in his soul, he breaks forth in the language of adoration—such as one uses in worship, "Thou art the Christ, the Son of the living God!" He first claims him as the promised Messiah (see comments on 1:16); then he rises higher, echoing the voice from heaven—"This is my beloved Son, in whom I am well pleased"; and in the important addition—"Son of the living God"—he recognizes the essential and eternal life of God—in this his Son.

**►17 And Jesus answered and said unto him, Blessed art thou**—Though it is possible that Peter, in this noble testimony to Christ, expressed the conviction of all the Twelve, yet since he alone seems to have had clear enough revelation to put that conviction in proper and suitable words, and courage enough to speak them out, and readiness enough to do this at the right time—so he only, of all the Twelve, seems to have met the present need. How refreshing Peter's confession must have been to Jesus! Jesus indicated the deep satisfaction that this speech gave him, for he quickly responded to it by a signal acknowledgment of Peter in return. **Simon Bar-jona**—or, "son of Jona" (John 1:42), or "Jonas" (John 21:15). This name, denoting his human origin, seems to have been purposely mentioned here, to contrast the more vividly with the spiritual elevation to which divine illumination had raised him. **for flesh and blood hath not revealed it unto thee**—This was not the result of human

teaching. **but my Father which is in heaven**—
The Father is the source of divine revelation.

➤**18 And I say also unto thee**—i.e., "As
you have given testimony to me, I will return
testimony to you." **That thou art Peter**—As
his first calling, this new name was given to
him (John 1:43). Now its significance is conveyed. **and upon this rock**—As "Peter" and
"Rock" are one word in the dialect familiarly
spoken by our Lord—the Aramaic or Syro-
Chaldaic, which was the mother tongue of the
country—this word-play can be fully seen only
in languages that have one word for both. In the
Greek, the word for "Peter" is *petros* (stone or
fragment of a rock); the word for "rock" is
*petra* (rock or rock-mass). Some commentators have indicated that, though the two
words are nearly synonymous, Jesus intended a distinction—Peter is but a fragment
of the whole, while Christ himself is the
entire Rock. Thus, it could be said that the
church would be built on Christ, the Rock.
But if this exposition stretches the point, at
least it can be said that the context allows that
the rock upon which the church is built is
Peter's revelation of Christ, the Son of God.
This revelation is the foundation of the
church. And had not the Roman Catholics
taken too much liberty with the notion of the
church's being founded on Peter, we could
plainly say that, in fact, the church is built,
at least in part, upon Peter—but not on Peter
alone; rather, on all the apostles (Eph. 2:20)
and with all the living stones (1 Pet. 2:5). **I
will build my church**—This statement is
emphatic, prophetic, and promisory. Jesus,
taking full responsibility, declares that he
himself will build his church. This is the
first mention of the church in the NT. What
a wonderful proclamation to inaugurate
its inception! **and the gates of hell**—"of
Hades," or, the unseen world; meaning, the
gates of Death; in other words, "It shall never
perish." Some explain it as "the assaults of
the powers of darkness"; but though that
expresses a glorious truth, probably the former is the sense here.

➤**19 And I will give unto thee the keys of
the kingdom of heaven**—the kingdom of God
about to be set up on earth. **and whatsoever
thou shalt bind on earth shall be bound in
heaven: and whatsoever thou shalt loose on
earth shall be loosed in heaven**—Whatever
this means, it was soon expressly extended to
all the apostles (18:18). As first in confessing
Christ, Peter received this commission before
the rest; and with these "keys," on the day of
Pentecost, he first "opened the door of faith" to
the Jews, and then, with Cornelius, he was
honored to do the same to the Gentiles. Hence,
in the lists of the apostles, Peter is always first
named. See comments on 18:18. One thing is
clear, that nowhere in the NT is there the ves-
tige of any authority either claimed or exercised by Peter, or conceded to him, above the
rest of the apostles.

➤**20 Then charged he his disciples that
they should tell no man that he was Jesus the
Christ**—The word "Jesus" is not present in
several good manuscripts. Now that he had
been so explicit, they might naturally think
the time had come for openly declaring his
identity; but here they were told not to.

21-28 ANNOUNCEMENT OF HIS
APPROACHING DEATH, AND REBUKE
OF PETER

➤**21 From that time forth began Jesus to
show unto his disciples**—i.e., with an explicitness and frequency he had never observed
before. **how that he must go unto Jerusalem
and suffer many things**—"and be rejected"
(Matthew and Mark). **of the elders and chief
priests and scribes**—not as before, merely by
not receiving him, but by actual aggressive
opposition. **and be killed, and be raised again
the third day**—Mark (8:32) adds, that "he
spake that saying openly"—"explicitly" or
"without disguise."

➤**22 Then Peter took him**—aside, apart from
the rest, presuming on the distinction just conferred on him. **and began to rebuke him**—affectionately, yet with a certain indignation, to
chide him. **saying, Be it far from thee, Lord:
this shall not be unto thee**—i.e., "If I can help
it"—which was the same spirit that prompted him
in the garden to draw the sword in Christ's behalf
(John 18:10).

➤**23 But he turned, and said**—in the hearing
of the rest; for Mark (8:33) expressly says, "When
he had turned about and looked on his disciples,
he rebuked Peter," perceiving that he had
uttered what others felt, and that the check
was needed by them also. **Get thee behind**

me, Satan—Although many commentators have interpreted this rebuke as indicating that Peter was somehow united to Satan when he attempted to hinder Jesus from going to the cross, it should be noted that, according to the Greek, Jesus could have simply been saying, "Get behind me, adversary." In the Greek, Satana (especially when used without the article) means adversary, opposer; it may not indicate the devil, the Satan—although, of course, no one can deny the association. Since Peter was opposing Jesus' cooperation with the divine plan, Jesus called him a "satan," an adversary. **thou art an offence**—a stumbling block, a snare. Jesus was destined to go to the cross; Peter could not alter this destiny. But he could impede Jesus' progress. **for thou savourest not** [you think not] **the things that be of God, but those that be of men**—Peter's thinking was preoccupied with the natural concepts concerning the establishment of Messiah's kingdom, quite contrary to those of God. Jesus spoke kindly, not to take off the sharp edge of the rebuke, but to explain and justify it, as it was evident Peter did not know the source of his rash speech.

➤**24-25 Then said Jesus unto his disciples**—Mark (8:34) says, "When he had called the people unto him, with his disciples also, he said unto them"—turning the rebuke of one into a warning to all. **If any man will come after me, let him deny himself, and take up his cross, and follow me. For whosoever will save**—is minded to save, or bent on saving—**his life** [or, soul] **shall lose it: and whosoever will lose his life** [or, soul] **for my sake shall find it**—See comments on 10:38, 39.

➤**26 For what is a man profited, if he shall gain the whole world, and lose** [or, forfeit] **his own soul? or what shall a man give in exchange for his soul?**—Instead of these weighty words, which we find in Mark also, it is thus expressed in Luke: "If he gain the whole world, and lose himself, or be cast away," or better, "If he gain the whole world, and destroy or forfeit himself." How awful is the stake as here set forth! If a man makes the present world—in its various forms of riches, honors, pleasures, and such—the object of supreme pursuit, then he forfeits his own soul. Not that any ever did, or ever will gain the whole world—a very small portion of it, indeed, falls to the lot of the most successful people. Yet

some seek to gain as much as they can—or, at least, some part of the world. But what can a man give in exchange for his soul? Nothing is comparable. A man's soul is his mind and his personal being—which needs salvation (cf. 1 Pet. 1:9). To give one's soul over to anything other than the Lord is to waste it and to lose it.

➤**27 For the Son of man shall come in the glory of his Father with his angels**—in the splendor of his Father's authority and with all his angelic ministers, ready to execute his will.

➤**28 Verily I say unto you, There be some standing here**—"some of those standing here." **which shall not taste of death, till they see the Son of man coming in his kingdom**—or, as in Mark (9:1), "Till they have seen the kingdom of God come with power"; or, as in Luke (9:27), more simply still, "Till they see the kingdom of God." The reference, beyond doubt, is to the firm establishment and victorious progress, in the lifetime of some then present, of that new kingdom of Christ, which was destined to work the greatest of all changes on this earth and be the grand pledge of his final coming in glory—which glory was soon to be

Chapter **17**

## 1-13 JESUS IS TRANSFIGURED. CONVERSATION ABOUT ELIJAH
See comments on Luke 9:28-36.

## 14-23 HEALING OF A DEMONIAC BOY. SECOND EXPLICIT ANNOUNCEMENT BY OUR LORD OF HIS APPROACHING DEATH AND RESURRECTION (See Mark 9:14-32; Luke 9:37-45.)

The time of this section is sufficiently marked by the events which all the narratives show to have immediately preceded it—the first explicit announcement of his death, and the transfiguration—both being between his third and his fourth and last Passover.

## 14-21 HEALING OF THE DEMONIAC AND LUNATIC BOY
See comments on Mark 9:14-32.

## 22, 23 SECOND ANNOUNCEMENT OF HIS DEATH
➤**22, 23 And while they abode in Galilee, Jesus said unto them**—Mark (9:30), as

usual, is very precise here: "And they departed thence"—i.e., from the scene of the last miracle—"and passed through Galilee; and he would not that any man should know it." So this was not a preaching, but a private, journey through Galilee. Indeed, his public ministry in Galilee was now all but concluded. Though he sent out the Seventy after this to preach and heal, he himself was hardly in public there, and he was soon to bid it a final farewell. Until this hour arrived, he was chiefly occupied with the Twelve, preparing them for the coming events. **The Son of man shall be betrayed into the hands of men . . . And they were exceeding sorry**—Though the shock would not be so great as at the first announcement (16:21, 22), their "sorrow" would be greater because the reality of this statement would begin to sink down into their hearts. Accordingly, Luke (9:43, 44), connecting it with the scene of the miracle just recorded and the teaching which arose out of it—or possibly with all his recent teaching—says our Lord forewarned the Twelve that they would soon stand in need of all that teaching. "But while they wondered every one at all things which Jesus did, he said unto his disciples, Let these sayings sink down into your ears: for the Son of man shall be delivered . . ." Remarkable is the antithesis in those words of our Lord preserved in all the three narratives—"The Son of *man* shall be betrayed into the hands of *men*." Luke (9:45) adds that "they understood not this saying, and it was hid from them, that they perceived it not."

## 24-27 THE TRIBUTE MONEY

The time of this section is evidently in immediate succession to that of the preceding one. The brief but most pregnant incident which it records is given only by Matthew—for whom, no doubt, it would have a peculiar interest, from its relation to his own town and his own familiar lake.

►**24 And when they were come to Capernaum, they that received tribute money**—Greek didrachma, the double drachma—a sum equal to two Attic drachmas, and corresponding to the Jewish "half-shekel," payable, toward the maintenance of the temple and its services, by every male Jew of twenty years old and upward. For the origin of this annual tax,

see Exodus 30:13, 14; 2 Chronicles 24:6, 9. Thus, it will be observed, it was not a civil, but an ecclesiastical tax. The tax mentioned in the next verse was a civil one. The whole teaching of this very remarkable scene depends upon this distinction. **came to Peter**—at whose house Jesus probably resided while at Capernaum. This explains several things in the narrative. **and said, Doth not your master pay tribute?** [Gk. didrachma]—The question seems to imply that the payment of this tax was voluntary, but expected; or what, in modern phrase, would be called a "voluntary assessment."

►**25 He saith, Yes**—i.e., "To be sure he does," as if eager to remove even the suspicion of the contrary. **And when he was come into the house** [Peter's], **Jesus prevented him**—anticipated him; according to the old sense of the word "prevent." **saying, What thinkest thou, Simon?**—using his family name for familiarity. **of whom do the kings of the earth take custom**—meaning custom on goods exported or imported. **or tribute** [Gk. *k*enson]—meaning the poll-tax, payable to the Romans by everyone whose name was in the census. This, therefore, it will be observed, was strictly a *civil* tax. **of their own children** [sons], **or of strangers?**—This cannot mean "foreigners," from whom sovereigns certainly do not raise taxes, but those who are not of their own family, i.e., their subjects.

►**26 Peter saith unto him, Of strangers**—"of those not their children." **Jesus saith unto him, Then are the children free**—The "children" (better translated as "sons") are the members of the ruling family; none of which is subject to pay taxes. Thus, Jesus as the Son of God was not subject to pay the tax. He was free from the tax, especially the temple tax, because it was paid for the temple, the house of Jesus' Father.

►**27 Notwithstanding, lest we should offend** [stumble] **them**—all ignorant as they are of my relation to the Lord of the temple, and should misconstrue a claim to exemption as indifference to God. **go thou to the sea**—Capernaum lay on the Sea of Galilee. **and cast an hook, and take up the fish that first cometh up; and when thou hast opened his mouth, thou shalt find a piece of money**—a stater. So it should have been rendered, and not indefinitely, as in the KJV, for the coin was an

Attic silver coin equal to two of the afore-mentioned "didrachmas" of half a shekel's value, and so, was the exact sum required for both Jesus and Peter. Accordingly, the Lord adds—**that take, and give unto them for me and thee**—lit., "instead of [indicating substitution] me and thee"; perhaps because the payment was a *redemption of the person* paid for (Exod. 30:12), in which view Jesus certainly was "free." If the house was Peter's, this will account for payment's being provided on this occasion, not for all the Twelve, but only for him and his Lord.

# Chapter 18

1-9 STRIFE AMONG THE TWELVE
ABOUT WHO SHOULD BE GREATEST
IN THE KINGDOM OF HEAVEN
See comments on Mark 9:33-50.

10-20 FURTHER TEACHING ON THE SAME
SUBJECT, INCLUDING THE PARABLE OF
THE UNMERCIFUL DEBTOR

➤**10 Take heed that ye despise not one of these little ones; for I say unto you, That in heaven their angels do always behold the face of my Father which is in heaven**—This refers to guardian angels (Ps. 34:7; 91:11; Heb. 2:14) who serve God's children.

➤**11 For the Son of man is come to save that which was lost**—This verse is not present in the earliest manuscripts. It was added, probably from Matt. 9:13 or Luke 19:10.

➤**12, 13 How think ye? if a man have an hundred sheep, and one of them be gone astray**—This is another of those pregnant sayings which Jesus uttered more than once. See comments on the parable of the lost sheep in Luke 15:4-7. The purpose of the parable in Luke is to show what the good Shepherd will do, when even one of his sheep is lost, to find it; here the purpose is to show, when found, how reluctant he is to lose it. Accordingly, we come to the next verse:

➤**14, 15 Even so it is not the will of your Father which is in heaven, that one of these little ones should perish. Moreover if thy brother shall trespass** [sin] **against thee**—"against thee [you]" is absent in some manuscripts. **go and tell him his fault between thee and him alone: if he shall hear thee, thou**

**hast gained thy brother**—The Lord puts forth the procedure we should follow in trying to reconcile problems among Christian brothers. First, the offended (or, sinned against) party should approach the offended alone. If the offender will not listen to him, the offender one should take witnesses and go a second time. If the offender will not still listen, the matter should be brought before the church (the local assembly in this case). If he will still not listen, then he is acting as an unbeliever and should be treated as such.

➤**17 tell it unto the church**—the local church. It is interesting to note that this is the second mention of the church in the NT. The first speaks of the universal church (16:18); the second of the local.

➤**18 Verily I say unto you, Whatsoever ye shall bind on earth shall be bound in heaven: and whatsoever ye shall loose on earth shall be loosed in heaven**—Here, what had been granted but a short time before to Peter only (see 16:19) is plainly extended to all the Twelve. The binding and loosing is exercised for the admission to and/or rejection from membership in the church. (See comments on John 20:23.)

➤**20 For where two or three are gathered together in my name**—lit., "into my name." The Greek expression *eis to onoma* in the papyri means "to the account of" or "into the possession of"—i.e., "they meet as the conscious possession of Jesus" (Ellison). **there am I in the midst of them**—The Lord's presence is manifest among those who meet with the conscious awareness that they belong to Jesus Christ. In connection with the previous verses, such assembling together can and should be exercised in the church (18:17, 18) or in any meeting together of the believers (18:15, 16). In any kind of Christian gathering it is essential that the believers be conscious of Christ's presence and pray together in one accord. Their prayers will be heard and answered.

21-35 PARABLE OF THE UNMERCIFUL
DEBTOR

➤**21 Then came Peter to him, and said, Lord, how oft shall my brother sin against me, and I forgive him?**—While 18:15ff. addressed the matter of how to deal with a brother who sins against another brother, this portion addresses the other side—i.e., how to forgive the brother who sins against us. Both aspects are needed for a balanced Christian life. **till seven times?**—This being the typical number for completeness, perhaps his meaning was, Is there to be a limit at which the needful forbearance will be full?

➤**22 Jesus saith unto him, I say not unto thee, Until seven times; but, Until seventy times seven**—i.e., so long as it shall be needed and sought: you are never to come to the point of refusing forgiveness sincerely asked. (See comments on Luke 17:3, 4.)

➤**23 Therefore** [with reference to this matter] **is the kingdom of heaven likened unto a certain king, which would take account of his servants** [lit., "slaves"]—would scrutinize the accounts of his revenue-collectors.

➤**24 And when he had begun to reckon, one was brought unto him, which owed him ten thousand talents**—If Attic talents are here meant, 10,000 of them would amount to more than $10,000,000; if Jewish talents, to a much larger sum.

➤**25 But forasmuch as he had not to pay, his lord commanded him to be sold, and his wife, and children, and all that he had, and payment to be made**—See 2 Kings 4:1; Nehemiah 5:8; Leviticus 25:39.

➤**26 The servant** [slave] **therefore fell down, and worshipped him**—or, did humble obeisance to him.

➤**27 Then the lord of that servant was moved with compassion, and loosed** [released] **him, and forgave him the debt**—Payment being hopeless, the master was first moved with compassion; next, liberated his debtor from prison; and then cancelled the debt freely.

➤**28 But the same servant** [slave] **went out, and found one of his fellowservants** [slaves]—Mark the difference here. The first case is that of master and servant (slave); in this case, both are on a footing of equality. **which owed him an hundred pence**—If Jewish money is intended, this debt was to the other less than one to a million. **and he laid hands on him, and took him by the throat, saying, Pay me that thou owest**—Mark the mercilessness even of the tone.

➤**29 And his fellowservant** [slave] **fell down at his feet, and besought him, saying, Have patience with me, and I will pay thee**

**all**—The same attitude, and the same words which drew compassion from his master, are here employed toward himself by his fellowservant (slave).

➤**30 And he would not: but went and cast him into prison, till he should pay the debt**—Jesus here vividly conveys the intolerable injustice of this act.

➤**32, 33 Then his lord, after that he had called him, said unto him, O thou wicked servant** [slave]—Before bringing down his vengeance upon him, he calmly pointed out to him how shamefully unreasonable and heartless his conduct was, which would give the punishment inflicted on him a double sting.

➤**34 And his lord was wroth, and delivered him to the tormentors**—more than *jailers,* denoting the severity of the treatment that he thought such a case demanded.

*Chapter* **19**

1-12 FINAL DEPARTURE FROM GALILEE. JESUS' WORDS ABOUT DIVORCE (See Mark 10:1-12; Luke 9:51.)

1, 2 FAREWELL TO GALILEE

➤**1 And it came to pass, that when Jesus had finished these sayings, he departed from Galilee**—This marks a very solemn period in our Lord's public ministry. So slightly is it touched here, and in the corresponding passage of Mark (10:1), that few readers probably realize it was Jesus' farewell to Galilee. **and came into the coasts** [or, boundaries] **of Judaea beyond Jordan**—i.e., to the farther, or east side of the Jordan, into Perea, the dominions of Herod Antipas. But though one might conclude from our Evangelist that our Lord went straight from the one region to the other, we know from the other Gospels that a considerable time elapsed between the departure from the one and the arrival at the other, during which many of the most important events in our Lord's public life occurred—probably a large part of which is recorded in Luke 9:51–18:15, and part of John 7:2-11, 54.

➤**2 And great multitudes followed him; and he healed them there**—Mark (10:1) says further that "as his custom was, he taught them" (RSV). What we now have on the subject of divorce is some of that teaching.

## 3-12 DIVORCE

**➤3 Is it lawful for a man to put away his wife for every cause?**—Two rival schools (as we saw on 5:31) were divided on this question. The schools of Hillel and Shammai differed on the interpretation of Deuteronomy 24:1-4. Shammai taught that divorce was permissible only if the wife was unfaithful; Hillel taught that divorce was lawful if the husband did not like the wife. Jesus sided with Shammai (*NIVSB*).

**➤4, 5 And he answered and said unto them, Have ye not read, that he which made** [created] **them at** [from] **the beginning made them male and female, and said, For this cause**—to carry out this divine arrangement—**shall a man leave father and mother, and shall cleave to his wife: and they twain shall be one flesh?**—Jesus here brings them back to the original constitution of their being man as one pair, a male and a female; to their marriage, as such, by divine appointment; and to the purpose of God throughout all time that one man and one woman should by marriage become one flesh—so to continue as long as both are in the flesh. This being God's constitution, let not man break it up by causeless divorces.

**➤7 They say unto him, Why did Moses then command to give a writing of divorcement, and to put h er away?**—See Deuteronomy 24:1-4.

**➤8 He saith unto them, Moses**—as a civil lawgiver. **because of**—or "having respect to." **the hardness of your hearts**—looking to your low moral state and your inability to endure the strictness of the original law. **suffered you to put away your wives**—tolerated a relaxation of the strictness of the marriage bond—not as approving of it, but to prevent still greater evils. **but from the beginning it was not so**—This is repeated in order to impress upon his audience the temporary and purely civil character of this Mosaic relaxation.

**➤9 And I say unto you, Whosoever shall put away his wife, except it be for fornication**—See comments on 5:31.

**➤10 His disciples say unto him, If the case of the man be so with his wife, it is not good to marry**—i.e., "In this view of marriage, surely it must prove a snare rather than

a blessing and had better be avoided altogether."

**➤11 But he said unto them, All men cannot receive this saying, save** [except] **they to whom it is given**—i.e., "That the unmarried state is better is a saying not for everyone and indeed only for such as it is divinely intended for." "But who are these?" they would naturally ask. Jesus identified them, in three categories.

**➤12 For there are some eunuchs which were so born from their mother's womb**—persons constitutionally either incapable of or indisposed to marriage. **and there are some eunuchs which were made eunuchs of men**—persons rendered incapable by others. **and there be eunuchs which have made themselves eunuchs for the kingdom of heaven's sake**—persons who, to do God's work better, deliberately choose this state. Such was Paul (1 Cor. 7:7). **He that is able to receive it, let him receive it**—"He who feels this to be his proper vocation, let him embrace it"; which, of course, is as much as to say—"he only." Thus, all are left free in this matter.

## 13-15 LITTLE CHILDREN BROUGHT TO CHRIST

See comments on Luke 18:15-17.

## 16-30 THE RICH YOUNG RULER

See comments on Luke 18:18-30.

*Chapter* **20**

## 1-16 PARABLE OF THE LABORERS IN THE VINEYARD

This parable, recorded only by Matthew, is closely connected with the end of chapter 19, being spoken with reference to Peter's question as to how it should fare with those who, like himself, had left all for Christ. It is designed to show that while *they* would be richly rewarded, a certain equity would still be observed toward *later* converts and workmen in his service.

**➤1 For the kingdom of heaven is like unto a man that is a householder, which went out early in the morning to hire labourers into his vineyard**—The figure of a vineyard to represent the spiritual growth of believers, the cultivation required and provided for that purpose, and the care and pains God takes in the whole matter, is familiar to every reader of the Bible (Ps. 80:8-16; Isa. 5:1-7; Jer. 2:21; Luke 20:9-16; John 15:1-8). At vintage time, labor was scarce, and masters had to go to the marketplace early in the morning to find workers. The "laborers," as in 9:38, are first, the *original* servants of the church, but after them and along with them *all* the servants of Christ, whom he has chosen to work in his service.

➤**2 And when he had agreed with the labourers for a penny** [denarius]—a day's normal salary.

➤**3 And he went out about the third hour**—about nine o'clock, or after a fourth of the working day had expired; the day of twelve hours was reckoned from six to six. **and saw others standing idle**—unemployed.

➤**4 And said unto them; Go ye also into the vineyard, and whatsoever is right**—just, equitable, in proportion to their time.

➤**5 Again he went out about the sixth and ninth hour**—about noon, and about three o'clock in the afternoon. **and did likewise**—hiring and sending into his vineyard fresh laborers each time.

➤**6 And about the eleventh hour**—but one hour before the close of the working day, a most unusual hour for hiring workers. **and found others standing idle, and saith unto them, Why stand ye here all the day idle?**—Of course they had not been there to offer themselves at the proper time; but as they were now willing, and the day was not over, they also were employed, and on similar terms with all the rest.

➤**8 So when even[ing] was come**—i.e., the reckoning time between masters and laborers (see Deut. 24:15); pointing to the day of final account; **the lord of the vineyard saith unto his steward**—representing Christ himself, "as a Son over his own house" (Heb. 3:6; see 11:27; John 3:35; 5:27).

➤**9 And when they came that were hired about the eleventh hour, they received every man a penny**—a denarius (a full day's wage).

➤**10 But when the first came, they supposed that they should have received more**—This is that calculating, mercenary spirit that had slipped out—though perhaps very slightly—in Peter's question (19:27), and which this parable was designed once for all to put down among the servants of Christ.

➤**11 And when they had received it, they murmured against the goodman of the house**—rather, "the householder," the word being the same as in 20:1.

➤**12 Saying, These last have wrought but one hour, and thou hast made them equal unto us, which have borne the burden and heat** [the burning] **of the day**—who have not only worked longer but during a more trying period of the day.

➤**13 But he answered one of them**—probably the spokesman of the complaining party. **and said, Friend, I do thee no wrong: didst not thou agree with me for a penny?**—a denarius (a full day's wage).

➤**15 Is it not lawful for me to do what I will with mine own? Is thine eye evil, because I am good?**—i.e., "You appeal to justice, but I was absolutely just in giving you the sum you agreed to work for. Now, you have nothing to do with the terms I make with other laborers; and to grudge the benevolence shown to others, when by your own admission you have been honorably dealt with, is both unworthy envy of your neighbor and discontent with the goodness that engaged and rewarded you in his service at all."

➤**16 So the last shall be first, and the first last**—The Lord was warning the first laborers not to become proud, for the last laborers, realizing their position, would naturally not have any pride. The Lord delights in exalting the humble (putting them first) and debasing the proud (putting them last). **many be called, but few are chosen**—This statement does not appear in the earliest manuscripts; it was probably taken from 22:14 (see comments there).

**17-28 THIRD EXPLICIT ANNOUNCEMENT OF HIS APPROACHING SUFFERINGS, DEATH, AND RESURRECTION. THE AMBITIOUS REQUEST OF JAMES AND JOHN AND THE REPLY**

See comments on Mark 10:32-45.

**29-34 TWO BLIND MEN HEALED**

See comments on Luke 18:35-43.

*Chapter* **21**

## 1-9 CHRIST'S TRIUMPHAL ENTRY INTO JERUSALEM ON THE FIRST DAY OF THE WEEK (See Mark 11:1-11; Luke 19:29-40; John 12:12-19.)

For the exposition of this majestic scene—recorded, as will be seen, by all the Evangelists—see comments on Luke 19:29-40.

## 10-22 DEBATE ABOUT HIM IN THE CITY. SECOND CLEANSING OF THE TEMPLE, AND MIRACLES THERE. GLORIOUS VINDICATION OF THE CHILDREN'S TESTIMONY. THE BARREN FIG TREE CURSED, WITH LESSONS FROM IT

See comments on Mark 11:12-26 and on Luke 19:45-48.

## 23-46 THE AUTHORITY OF JESUS QUESTIONED, AND THE REPLY—THE PARABLES OF THE TWO SONS, AND OF THE WICKED HUSBANDMAN (See Mark 11:27—12:12; Luke 20:1-19.)

Here begins, as Alford remarks, that series of parables and discourses of our Lord with his enemies, in which he develops, more completely than ever before, his hostility to their hypocrisy and iniquity: and so they are stirred up to hasten his death.

## 23-27 THE AUTHORITY OF JESUS QUESTIONED, AND THE REPLY

**➤23 By what authority doest thou these things?**—referring particularly to the expulsion of the buyers and sellers from the temple (21:12).

**➤25 The baptism of John**—meaning his whole mission and ministry, of which baptism was its chief characteristic. **whence was it? from heaven, or of men? And they reasoned with themselves saying, If we shall say, From heaven; he will say unto us, Why did ye not then believe him?**—In other words, Jesus was saying, "Why did you not believe the testimony he bore to me, as the promised and expected Messiah?" for that was the central theme of John's whole ministry.

**➤26 But if we shall say, Of men; we fear the people**—rather the multitude. In Luke (20:6) it is "all the people will stone us."

**➤27 And they answered Jesus, and said, We cannot tell**—Their difficulty was how to answer, so as neither to shake their determination to reject the claims of Christ nor damage their reputation with the people. They cared nothing for the truth. **Neither tell I you by what authority I do these things**—What composure and dignity of wisdom does our Lord here display, as he turns their question upon themselves, and, while revealing his knowledge of their hypocrisy, closes their mouths! Taking advantage of the surprise, silence, and awe produced by this reply, our Lord followed it up immediately by the two following parables.

## 28-32 PARABLE OF THE TWO SONS

**➤28 But what think ye? A certain man had two sons; and he came to the first, and said, Son, go work to day in my vineyard**—for true faith is a practical thing, a "bringing forth fruit unto God."

**➤29 He answered and said, I will not**—Trench notices the rudeness of this answer and the total absence of any attempt to excuse such disobedience as representing the careless, reckless attitude of sinners resisting God to his face. **but afterward he repented**—changed his mind, turned his course, **and went.**

**➤30 And he came to the second, and said likewise. And he answered and said, I go, sir**—lit., "I, sir." The emphatic "I" here denotes the self-righteous attitude which says, "God, I thank thee, that *I* am not as other men" (Luke 18:11). **and went not**—He did not "afterward repent" and refuse to go; for there was here no intention to go. He belonged to that group of people who "say and do not" (23:3)—a falseness more abominable to God than those who originally refuse.

**➤31 Whether of them twain did the will of his father? They say unto him, The first**—Now comes the application. **Jesus saith unto them, Verily I say unto you, That the publicans and the harlots go**—or, "are going" and are even now entering (while you hold back) **into the kingdom of God before you.** The publicans and the harlots were the first son, who, when told to work in the Lord's vineyard, said, "I will not," but afterwards repented and went. Their early life was a flat and flagrant refusal to do what they were commanded; it was one of continual rebellion against the authority of God. The chief priests and the elders of the people, with whom our Lord was now speaking, were the second son, who said, "I go, sir," but went not. They were called early, and all their life professed obedience to God but never rendered it; their life was one of continued disobedience.

**➤32 For John came unto you in the way of righteousness**—i.e., calling you to repentance and righteous living. He, like Noah, was "a preacher of righteousness" (2 Pet. 2:5). **ye believed him not**—They did not reject him; in fact, they "were willing for a season to rejoice in his light" (John 5:35). **but the publicans and harlots believed him**—of the publicans this is twice expressly recorded (Luke 3:12; 7:29); of the harlots, then, the same may be taken for granted, though the fact is not expressly recorded. These outcasts gladly believed the testimony of John to the coming Savior, and so believed in Jesus when he came. See Luke 7:37; 15:1. **and ye, when ye had seen it, repented not afterward, that ye might believe him**—Instead of being "provoked to jealousy" by their example, you have seen them flocking to the Savior and yet remain unmoved.

## 33-46 PARABLE OF THE WICKED HUSBANDMEN

**➤33 Hear another parable: There was a certain householder, which planted a vineyard**—See comments on Luke 13:6. **and hedged it round about, and digged a winepress in it, and built a tower**—These details are taken, as is the basis of the parable itself, from that beautiful parable of Isaiah 5:1-7, in order to sustain it by OT authority. **and let it out to husbandmen**—These were just the ordinary spiritual guides of the people, under whose care and cultivation the fruits of righteousness were expected to spring up. **and went into a far country**—"for a long time" (Luke 20:9), leaving the vineyard during the whole time of the Jewish economy. On this expression, see comments on Mark 4:26.

**➤34 And when the time of the fruit drew near, he sent his servants to the husbandmen**—By these "servants" are meant the prophets and other extraordinary messengers raised up from time to time (see 23:37). **that**

they might receive the fruits of it—See again Luke 13:6.

**➤35 And the husbandmen took his servants, and beat one**—see Jeremiah 37:15; 38:6. **and killed another**—see Jeremiah 26:20-23. **and stoned another**—see 2 Chronicles 24:21; cf. 23:37, where our Lord reiterates these charges.

**➤36 Again, he sent other servants more than the first: and they did unto them likewise**—see 2 Kings 17:13; 2 Chronicles 36:16, 18; Nehemiah 9:26.

**➤37 But last of all he sent unto them his son, saying, They will reverence my son**—In Mark (12:6) this is most touchingly expressed: "Having yet therefore one son, his well-beloved, he sent him also last unto them, saying, They will reverence my son." Luke's version of it too (20:13) is striking: "Then said the lord of the vineyard, What shall I do? I will send my beloved son: it may be they will reverence him when they see him." Who does not see that our Lord here severs himself, by the sharpest line of demarcation, from all merely human messengers and claims for himself Sonship in its loftiest sense? The expression "It may be they will reverence my son," is designed to teach the guilt of not reverentially welcoming God's Son.

**➤38 But when the husbandmen saw the son, they said among themselves**—cf. Genesis 37:18-20; John 11:47-53. **This is the heir**—This expresses a great truth: God's inheritance was designed for, and in due time is to come into, the possession of his own Son (Heb. 1:2). **come, let us kill him, and let us seize on his inheritance**—so that from mere *servants* we may become *lords*. This is the deep aim of the depraved heart; this is emphatically the source of all evil.

**➤39 And they caught him, and cast him out of the vineyard**—cf. Heb. 13:11-13 ("without the gate . . . without the camp").

**➤40 When the lord therefore of the vineyard cometh**—This represents "the time of settling accounts," which, in the case of the Jewish leaders, was that judicial trial of the nation and its leaders that issued in the destruction of their whole state.

**➤41 They say unto him, He will miserably destroy those wicked men**—an emphatic alliteration not easily conveyed in English: "He will badly destroy those bad men," or "miserably destroy those miserable men," is something like it. **and will let out his vineyard unto other husbandmen, which shall render him the fruits in their seasons**—If this answer was given by the Pharisees, to whom our Lord addressed the parable, they thus unwittingly pronounced their own condemnation: as David did to Nathan the prophet (2 Sam. 12:5-7), and Simon the Pharisee to our Lord (Luke 7:43). But if it was given, as Mark and Luke represent it, by our Lord himself (and the explicitness of the answer would seem to favor that supposition), then we can better explain the exclamation of the Pharisees that followed it, in Luke's report—"And when they heard it, they said, God forbid"—the whole meaning of the parable now dawning upon them.

►**42 Jesus saith unto them. Did ye never read in the scriptures**—Psalm 118:22, 23. **The stone which the builders rejected**—A bright messianic prophecy, which reappears in various forms (Isa. 28:16), and was used by Peter before the Sanhedrin (Acts 4:11) and in his first epistle (1 Pet. 2:4-6). **the same is become the head of the corner**—i.e., the cornerstone, which is the keystone of the entire building. The Jewish builders rejected Christ; but God made him the cornerstone and foundation of the church (Eph. 2:20-22).

►**43 Therefore say I unto you, The kingdom of God**—God's visible kingdom, or church, upon earth, which up to this time came from the seed of Abraham. **shall be taken from you, and given to a nation bringing forth the fruits thereof**—i.e., the great evangelical community of the faithful, which, after the extrusion of the Jewish nation, would consist chiefly of Gentiles, until the time that "all Israel should be saved" (Rom. 11:25, 26). This vastly important statement is given by Matthew only.

►**44 And whosoever shall fall on this stone shall be broken: but on whomsoever it shall fall, it will grind him to powder**—The kingdom of God was depicted as a temple, in the erection of which a certain stone, rejected as unsuitable by the spiritual builders, was by the great Lord of the house, made the keystone of the whole. Now in this verse it is indicated that the builders were "falling" on that stone and being "broken" (Isa. 8:15). They were sustaining great spiritual hurt; but soon that Stone

should "fall upon them" and "grind them to powder" (Dan. 2:34, 35; Zech. 12:2)—in their corporate capacity, in the tremendous destruction of Jerusalem, but personally, as unbelievers, in a more awful sense yet to come.

►**45 And when the chief priests and Pharisees had heard his parables**—referring to that of the two sons and this one of the wicked husbandmen: **they perceived that he spake of them**—this was one of the few times that the Jewish leaders clearly comprehended one of Jesus' parables.

►**46 But when they sought to lay hands on him**—which Luke (20:19) says they did "the same hour." They were hardly able to restrain their rage. **they feared the multitude, because they took him for a prophet**—just as they feared to say John's baptism was of men because the masses took him for a prophet (21:26).

# Chapter 22

## 1-14 PARABLE OF THE MARRIAGE OF THE KING'S SON

This is a different parable from that of the Great Supper, in Luke 14:15, and is recorded by Matthew alone.

►**2 The kingdom of heaven is like unto a certain king, which made a marriage for his son**—"In this parable," as Trench admirably remarks, "we see how the Lord is revealing himself in ever clearer light as the central Person of the kingdom, giving here a far plainer hint than in the last parable of the nobility of his descent. There he was indeed the Son, the only and beloved one (Mark 12:6), of the Householder; but here his race is royal, and he appears as himself at once the king and the king's son (Ps. 72:1). The last was a parable of the OT history; and Christ is rather the last and greatest of the line of its prophets and teachers than the founder of a new kingdom. In that, God appears demanding something from men; in this, a parable of grace, God appears more as giving something to them. Thus, as often, the two complete each other: this taking up the matter where the other left it." The "marriage" of Yahweh to his people Israel was familiar to Jewish ears; and in Psalm 45 this marriage is seen consummated in the person of the Messiah. But observe carefully that the bride does not come into view in this parable; its design being to teach certain truths under the figure of guests at a wedding feast and the need of a wedding garment.

➤3 And sent forth his servants—representing all preachers of the gospel. **to call them that were bidden** [invited]—here meaning the Jews, who were invited time and time again by the prophets to be prepared for the appearing of their King. **to the wedding**—rather, the wedding feast or marriage festivities. **and they would not come**—as was demonstrated throughout the whole ministry of the Baptist, our Lord himself, and his apostles thereafter.

➤4 **my oxen and my fatlings are killed, and all things are ready: come unto the marriage**—This points to the gospel call after Christ's death, resurrection, ascension, and effusion of the Spirit. Then all things were ready. Cf. 1 Corinthians 5:7,8 ("Christ our passover is sacrificed for us: therefore let us keep the feast"); also John 6:51 ("I am the living bread which came down from heaven: if any man eat of this bread, he shall live for ever: and the bread that I will give is my flesh, which I will give for the life of the world").

➤6 **And the remnant took his servants, and entreated them spitefully** [insulted them], **and slew** [killed] **them**—These are two different classes of unbelievers: the one, contemptuous scorners; and the other, bitter persecutors.

➤7 **But when the king**—the great God, who is the Father of our Lord Jesus Christ. **heard thereof, he was wroth** [angry]—at the affront to his Son and himself. **and he sent forth his armies**—the Roman army used by God to carry out his judicial vengeance (cf. Isa. 10:5). **and destroyed those murderers and burned up their city**—This probably looks ahead to the destruction of Jerusalem by the Roman armies in A.D. 70. (See 23:38 and Luke 19:43, 44.)

➤8 **The wedding** [feast] **is ready, but they which were bidden** [invited] **were not worthy**—for how should those be considered worthy to sit down at his table who had affronted him and rejected his gracious invitation?

➤9 **Go ye therefore into the highways**—the great outlets and thoroughfares, whether of town or country, where people are to be found.

**and as many as ye shall find, bid** [call] **to the marriage** [feast]—i.e., just as they are.

➤10 **So those servants went out into the highways, and gathered together all as many as they found, both bad and good**—i.e., without making any distinction between manifest sinners and the morally correct. The gospel call brought in Jews, Samaritans, and outlying heathen alike. So far, the parable corresponds to that of the Great Supper (Luke 14:16). But the distinguishing feature of Matthew's parable is what follows.

➤11 **And when the king came in to see the guests**—This suggests the Lord's inspection of every professed disciple. **he saw there a man** — This shows that it is the judgment of individuals that is intended in this latter part of the parable, while the first part represents national judgment. **which had not on a wedding garment**—The thought here may be drawn from Zephaniah 1:7, 8 ("Be silent before the Lord God! For the day of the Lord is near, for the Lord has prepared a sacrifice, He has consecrated His guests. Then it will come about on the day of the Lord's sacrifice, that I will punish the princes, the king's sons, and all who clothe themselves with foreign garments"—NASB). The custom in the Middle East of the host presenting festival garments to the guests (see Gen. 45:22; 2 Kings 5:22), even though not clearly proved, is certainly presupposed here. How could they have any such garment when they came in directly from the highways? Once they arrived, they must have been given an appropriate garment. Spiritually speaking, that garment must be the garment of righteousness (Isa. 61:10). And since Christ is our righteousness, we are to put on him and be clothed with him (1 Cor. 1:30 [in NASB]; 2 Cor. 5:21; Rom. 13:14; Gal. 3:27).

➤12 **Friend, how camest thou in hither not having a wedding garment?**—This individual did not take the righteousness offered to him. **And he was speechless**—being self-condemned.

➤13 **Then said the king to the servants**—the angelic ministers of divine vengeance (as in 13:41). **Bind him hand and foot**—putting it out of his power to resist. **and take him away, and cast him into outer darkness**—see 8:12; 25:30. The expression is emphatic—"the darkness which is outside." To be "outside" at all—or, in the language of Revelation 22:15, to be "without" the heavenly city, excluded from its festivities—is sad enough of itself, without anything else. But to find themselves not only excluded from the brightness, glory, joy, and felicity of the kingdom but thrust into a region of "darkness," with all its horrors, this is the dismal retribution that awaits the unworthy at the great day of judgment. **there**—in that region and condition. **shall be weeping and gnashing of teeth**—See comments on 13:42.

➤**14 For many are called, but few are chosen**—This is another of our Lord's terse and pregnant sayings (see 19:30). The "calling" of which the NT almost invariably speaks is what theologians have named "effectual calling," carrying with it a supernatural operation on the will to secure its consent. But that cannot be the meaning of it here because the "called" are emphatically distinguished from the "chosen." It can only mean here the "invited." And so the sense is, many are given the opportunity to receive the invitation of the gospel; those who do are manifestly the chosen ones of God.

15-40 ENTANGLING QUESTIONS ABOUT TRIBUTE, THE RESURRECTION, AND THE GREAT COMMANDMENT, WITH THE REPLIES

See comments on Mark 12:13-34.

41-45 CHRIST BAFFLES THE PHARISEES BY A QUESTION ABOUT DAVID AND MESSIAH

See comments on Mark 12:35-37.

*Chapter* **23**

1-39 DENUNCIATION OF THE SCRIBES AND PHARISEES, LAMENTATION OVER JERUSALEM, AND FAREWELL TO THE TEMPLE (See Mark 12:38-40; Luke 20:45-47.)

For this long and terrible discourse we are indebted, with the exception of a few verses in Mark and Luke, to Matthew alone. But as it is only an extended repetition of denunciations uttered not long before at the table of a Pharisee, and recorded by Luke (11:37-54), we may take both together in the exposition.

1-36 DENUNCIATION OF THE SCRIBES AND PHARISEES

The first twelve verses were addressed more immediately to the disciples, the rest to the scribes and Pharisees.

➤**2 Saying, The scribes and the Pharisees sit**—The Jewish teachers stood to read, but sat to expound the Scriptures, as will be seen by comparing Luke 4:16 with 23:20. **in Moses' seat**—i.e., as "the authorized successors of Moses as teachers of the law" (*NIVSB*).

➤**3 All therefore whatsoever they bid you observe, that observe and do**—It should be noted that the warning to beware of the scribes is given by Mark and Luke without any qualification; the charge to respect and obey them being reported by Matthew alone, indicating for whom this Gospel was especially written and the writer's desire to conciliate the Jews.

➤**4 For they bind heavy burdens and grievous to be borne, and lay them on men's shoulders; but they themselves will not move them with one of their fingers**—referring not so much to the irksomeness of the legal rites, though they were irksome enough (Acts 15:10), as to the heartless rigor with which they were enforced.

➤**5 But all their works they do for to be seen of men**—Whatever good they do or zeal they show has but one motive—human applause. **they make broad their phylacteries**—strips of parchment with Scripture texts on them, worn on the forehead, arm, and side, in time of prayer. **and enlarge the borders of their garments**—fringes of their upper garments (Num. 15:37-40).

➤**6 And love the uppermost rooms**—The word "room" is now obsolete in the sense here intended. It should be "the uppermost place," i.e., the place of highest honor. **at feasts, and the chief seats in the synagogues**—See Luke 14:7, 8.

➤**7 And greetings in the markets, and to be called of men, Rabbi, Rabbi**—The reiteration of the word "Rabbi" shows how it tickled the ear and fed the "spiritual pride."

➤**8 But be not ye called Rabbi: for one is your Master**—rather, your Teacher.

➤**9 And call no man your father upon the earth: for one is your Father, which is in heaven**—We should be careful not to take this command to an extreme. It was intended to guard against attributing too much honor to any man (and thus inducing pride).

►11 But he that is greatest among you shall be your servant—This plainly means, "shall show that he is so by becoming your servant," as in 20:27, compared with Mark 10:44.

►12 And whosoever shall exalt himself shall be abased—See Luke 18:14. What follows was addressed to the scribes and Pharisees.

►13 But woe unto you, scribes and Pharisees, hypocrites! for ye shut up the kingdom of heaven against men—Here they are charged with shutting heaven against men; in Luke 11:52 they are charged with what was worse, "taking away the key of knowledge," which means, not the key to open knowledge, but knowledge as the only key to open heaven. A right knowledge of God's revealed word is eternal life, as our Lord says (John 17:3 and 5:39); but this they took away from the people, substituting for it their man-made traditions.

►14 This verse is not present in the earliest manuscripts. It was taken probably from Luke 12:40 or Luke 20:47 and inserted in later manuscripts either before or after 23:13.

►15 Woe unto you, scribes and Pharisees, hypocrites! for ye compass sea and land to make one proselyte—i.e., to make a Gentile convert to Judaism. We have evidence of this in Josephus's writings. and when he is made, ye make him twofold more the child of hell [son of gehenna] than yourselves—condemned, for the hypocrisy he would learn to practice, both by the religion he left and that he embraced.

►16 Woe unto you, ye blind guides—A striking expression of the ruinous effects of erroneous teaching. Our Lord, here and in some following verses, condemns the subtle distinctions they made as to the sanctity of oaths—distinctions invented only to promote their own avaricious purposes. which say, Whosoever shall swear by the temple, it is nothing—He has incurred no debt. but whosoever shall swear by the gold of the temple—meaning not the gold that adorned the temple itself, but the *Corban,* set apart for sacred uses (see comments on 15:5). he is a debtor!—i.e., it is no longer his own, even though the necessities of the parent might require it.

►18 but whoever sweareth by the gift that is upon it, he is guilty—It should have been rendered, "he is a debtor," as in 23:16.

►19 Ye fools, and blind: for whether is greater, the gift, or the altar that sanctifieth the gift?—See Exodus 29:37.

►20-22 See comments on 5:33-37.

►23 Woe unto you, scribes and Pharisees, hypocrites! for ye pay tithe of mint and anise [rather, "dill"] and cummin—They founded this practice on Leviticus 27:30, which they interpreted rigidly. Our Lord purposely names the most trifling products of the earth as examples of what they punctiliously exacted the tenth of. and have omitted the weightier matters of the law, judgment, mercy, and faith—In Luke (11:42) it is "judgment and the love of God"—the expression being probably varied by Jesus himself on the two different occasions. In both, his reference is to Micah 6:6-8, where the prophet makes all acceptable religion to consist of three elements—"doing justly, loving mercy, and walking humbly with our God" (the third element presupposes and comprehends both the "faith" of Matthew and the "love" of Luke). See Mark 12:29, 32, 33. these ought ye to have done, and not to leave the other undone—There is no need for one set of duties to preempt another; but it is to be carefully noted that of the greater duties Jesus says, "Ye ought to have done" them, while of the lesser he merely says, "Ye ought not to leave them undone."

►24 Ye blind guides, which strain at a gnat—The proper rendering—as in the older English translations, and perhaps the KJV as it came from the translators' hands—evidently is, "strain out." It was the custom, says Trench, of the stricter Jews to strain their wine, vinegar, and other liquids through linen or gauze, so that they would not drink some little unclean insect and thus transgress the law (Lev. 11:20, 23, 41, 42)—just as the Buddhists do in some Asian countries. and swallow a camel—the largest animal the Jews knew, as the "gnat" was the smallest; both were by the law unclean.

►25 within they are full of extortion—In Luke (11:39) the same word is rendered "ravening," i.e., "rapacity."

►26 Thou blind Pharisee, cleanse first that which is within the cup and platter, that the outside of them may be clean also—In Luke 11:40) it is, "Ye fools, did not he that made that which is without make that which is within also?" This is a remarkable example of our Lord's power to draw the most striking illustrations of great truths from the most familiar objects and incidents in life.

➤27 Woe unto you, scribes and Pharisees, hypocrites! for ye are like unto whited [white-washed] sepulchres—cf. Acts 23:3. The process of white-washing the sepulchres, as Lightfoot says, was performed on a certain day every year, not for ceremonial cleansing, but, as the following words seem rather to imply, to beautify them. which indeed appear beautiful outward, but are within full of dead men's bones, and of all uncleanness—What a powerful way of conveying the charge that with all their fair show their hearts were full of corruption! (cf. Ps. 5:9; Rom. 3:13).

➤31 Wherefore ye be witnesses unto yourselves, that ye are the children of them which killed the prophets—i.e., "ye be witnesses that ye have inherited and voluntarily served yourselves heirs to the truth-hating, prophet-killing, spirit of your fathers." Out of pretended respect and honor, they repaired and beautified the sepulchres of the prophets, and with hypocrisy said, "If we had been in their days, how differently should we have treated these prophets?" While all the time they were witnesses to themselves that they were the children of them that killed the prophets, convicting themselves daily of as exact a resemblance in spirit and character to the very classes over whose deeds they pretended to mourn, as child to parent. In Luke 11:44 Jesus gives another turn to this figure of a grave: "Ye are as graves which appear not, and the men that walk over them are not aware of them." As one might unconsciously walk over a grave concealed from view and thus contract ceremonial defilement, so the plausible exterior of the Pharisees kept people from perceiving the pollution they contracted from coming in contact with such corrupt characters.

➤33 Ye serpents, ye generation of vipers, how can ye escape the damnation of hell?—lit., "the judgment of gehenna." At the end of his ministry, Jesus echoed the words of John the Baptist at the outset of his. There had been no change in the interim. They would receive their just retribution.

➤34 Wherefore, behold, I send unto you prophets, and wise men, and scribes—The *I* here is emphatic: "I am sending," i.e., "am about to send" (cf. Luke 11:49). He would be sending evangelical messengers, but called by the familiar Jewish names of "prophets, wise men, and scribes," whose counterparts were the inspired and gifted servants of the Lord Jesus, for in Luke (11:49) it is "prophets and apostles."

➤35 From the blood of righteous Abel unto the blood of Zacharias son of Barachias, whom ye slew between the temple and the altar—The murder of Abel is recorded in Genesis 4:8 and that of Zechariah (son—or perhaps—grandson of Jehoida and therefore son of Barachias—see Carson) in 2 Chronicles 24:20-22. Since the Hebrew OT began with Genesis and ended with 2 Chronicles, this was Jesus' way of saying "from the beginning to the end of Scripture." Jesus, therefore was summarizing the OT history of martyrdom.

➤36 Verily I say unto you, All these things shall come upon this generation—The iniquity of Israel was allowed to accumulate from age to age until in that generation it came to the full.

37-39 LAMENTATION OVER JERUSALEM, AND FAREWELL TO THE TEMPLE

➤37 O Jerusalem, Jerusalem, thou that killest the prophets, and stonest them which are sent unto thee, . . .—How much this sounds like Jeremiah the prophet who wept for Israel and lamented Jerusalem's downfall (see Lamentations). God's grief was expressed through that weeping prophet. Now God himself, God incarnate, utters this lament! It is the very heart of God pouring itself forth through human flesh and speech. It is this incarnation of the innermost life and love of Deity, pleading with men, bleeding for them, and opening his arms to them that will yet "draw all men unto him." "Jerusalem" here does not mean the mere city or its inhabitants; nor is it to be viewed merely as the metropolis of the nation, but as the center of their religious life. It is the whole family of God, then, which is here apostrophized by a name dear to every Jew, recalling to him all that was distinctive and precious in his religion. The intense feeling that sought expression in this utterance comes out first in the redoubling of the opening word—"Jerusalem, Jerusalem!" but, next, in the picture of it which he draws—"that killest the prophets, and stonest them which are sent unto thee!" He was speaking in God's stead, even as the God of the OT now manifest in the flesh. Throughout the OT there are references to God's exercising his care for his people in the same way a mother bird cares for her young (see Deut. 32:10-12; Ruth 2:12; Ps. 17:8; 36:7; 61:4; 63:7; 91:4; Isa. 31:5; Mal. 4:2). Many of these references speak of God's protective wings, under whose shelter the frightened could find refuge. The ancient rabbis had a beautiful expression for proselytes from the Gentiles—they had "come under the wings of the Shekinah" (see Ruth 2:12). But God's people, as characterized and epitomized as "Jerusalem," had rejected that care and tender affection again and again. They rejected Yahweh and his visitations to them through the prophets, and they rejected him manifest in the flesh.

►38 Behold, your house—the temple, beyond all doubt; but *their* house now, not the Lord's. Having disowned the temple, he calls it "your house." is left unto you desolate—The word "desolate" is present in some early manuscripts but absent in others. Either way, the statement bears the same meaning: God's house, now disowned by God, would be left to the Jews without God's presence.

►39 For I say unto you—and these were his last words to the impenitent nation (see opening remarks on Mark 13). Ye shall not see me henceforth—Does Jesus mean that he himself was the Lord of the temple, and that it became deserted when he finally left it? It is even so. That glory, once visible in the holy of holies over the mercy seat, called by the Jews the *Shekinah,* or the *Dwelling,* as being the visible pavilion of Jehovah—that glory, which Isaiah saw in vision, the beloved disciple says was the glory of Christ (John 12:41). That glory had left the first temple, due to Israel's and Jerusalem's apostasy (see Ezek. 10) and did not visibly return to the second temple, although Haggai said that "the glory of that latter house

should be greater than of the former" (2:9). Either this refers to the glory returning to the second temple (of which there is no record in Scripture) or to the glory returning when Christ would come to the temple. As Malachi (3:1) said, "The Lord whom they sought would suddenly come to his temple"—not in a bright cloud, but enshrined in living humanity. Yet this manifestation would be sudden and brief, for he was on the verge of departing from Israel until his second advent. till ye shall say, Blessed is he that cometh in the name of the Lord—i.e., until those "Hosannas to the Son of David" with which the multitude had welcomed him into the city should break forth from the whole nation, as their glad acclaim to their once pierced, but now acknowledged, Messiah. That such a time will come is clear from Zechariah 12:10; Romans 11:26; 2 Corinthains 3:15, 16. In what sense they shall then "see him" may be gathered from Zechariah 2:10-13; Ezekiel 37:23-28; 39:28, 29.

Chapter **24**

1-51 CHRIST'S PROPHECY OF THE DESTRUCTION OF JERUSALEM AND WARNINGS TO PREPARE FOR HIS SECOND COMING
See comments on Mark 13:1-37.

Chapter **25**

1-13 PARABLE OF THE TEN VIRGINS
This and the following parable are in Matthew alone.

►1 Then—at the time referred to at the close of the preceding chapter, the time of the Lord's second coming to reward his faithful servants and take vengeance on the faithless. shall the kingdom of heaven be likened unto ten virgins, which took their lamps, and went forth to meet the bridegroom—This supplies a key to the parable, whose object is, in the main, the same as that of the last parable—to illustrate the vigilant and expectant attitude of faith, in respect of which believers are described as "they that look for him" (Heb. 9:28), and "love his appearing" (2 Tim. 4:8). In the last parable it was that of servants waiting for their absent Lord; in this it is that of virgin attendants of a bride, whose duty it was to go forth at night with lamps and be ready on the appearance of the bridegroom to conduct the bride to his house and go in with him to the marriage feast. This entire and beautiful change of figure brings out the lesson of the former parable in quite a new light. But let it be observed that, just as in the parable of the Marriage Supper, so in this—the bride does not come into view at all in this parable; the virgins and the bridegroom present all the intended instruction.

➤2 And five of them were wise, and five were foolish—They are not distinguished as good and bad, but as "wise" and "foolish"— just as in 7:25-27 those who built their houses are distinguished as "wise" and "foolish" builders because in both cases a certain degree of spiritual understanding is assumed. To make anything of the equal number of both classes would be precarious, except to warn us how large a number there will be of those who seem to love the Lord's appearing but will not be ready when he comes.

➤3, 4 They that were foolish took their lamps, and took no oil with them: But the wise took oil in their vessels with their lamps—or, torches (which, according to the picture portrayed in this parable, would have been long poles with oil-drenched rags attached to the tops). But what do the lamps (torches) signify? Many answers have been given. But since the foolish as well as the wise took their lamps and went forth with them to meet the bridegroom, these lighted lamps probably denote that Christian testimony which is common to all who bear the Christian name. This testimony must be kept alive throughout the course of the Christian life. The testimony, like a lamp, should not die out (see 2 Tim. 1:6-8 in TLB, NIV). In order for the lamps to keep burning, there had to be a constant and sufficient supply of oil. Throughout the Bible, oil typifies the Spirit of God (Ps. 45:7; Zech. 4:2-6; Luke 4:18). Thus, the Christian testimony is sustained by the divine Spirit; any lack of the supply of the Spirit of Jesus Christ (Phil. 1:19) in a believer's life will cause the testimony to flicker and wane. In the ancient times, it was essential to keep one's lamp burning—even throughout the night; the virtuous woman did not let her lamp go out at night (Prov. 31:18—in NASB, NIV).

➤5 While the bridegroom tarried—The Jews had a custom for marriages in which the bridegroom would come to get his bride in the evening and then take her to his home for the marriage feast. The procession to and fro included attendants carrying lamps (which were torches). In this story, the bridegroom did not come at the expected time (see also 24:48). In the first century of the church, the believers expected the Lord to return at any moment. But even now, two thousand years later, he still tarries. Nevertheless, we must expect him to come at any time. they all slumbered and slept—the wise as well as the foolish. The word "slumbered" signifies "became drowsy"; while the word "slept" is the usual word for lying down to sleep. In the context of this parable, this is difficult to interpret. Does it mean that all the virgins became lethargic in their spiritual life? Does it mean that all of them died?—as "sleep" is a typical euphemism for death. Or does it mean that all of the virgins grew weary of waiting for the bridegroom? Whatever the meaning, it must be applied to all alike.

➤6 And at midnight—i.e., the time when the bridegroom will be least expected; for "the day of the Lord so cometh as a thief in the night" (1 Thess. 5:2).

➤7 Then all those virgins arose, and trimmed their lamps—To trim a lamp was to cut off the charred end of the rag and to add oil. Both the foolish and the wise did this.

➤8 And the foolish said unto the wise, Give us of your oil; for our lamps are gone out—rather, "are going out"—for oil will not light an extinguished lamp, though it will keep a burning one from going out. The torches they carried "required large amounts of oil in order to keep burning, and the oil had to be replenished about every 15 minutes" (NIVSB). The wise virgins had enough oil to replenish their lamps, but the foolish did not. And this was the factor that made all the difference. Now, various interpretations have been given to explain this critical factor; and it seems that each interpretation depends on the theology of the interpreter. Those who think the foolish virgins to be false believers say that their lack of oil proves their lack of genuineness. Those who think both kinds of virgins were genuine believers say the lack of oil demonstrates the failure to maintain a vibrant Christian testimony to the end.

►**9 But the wise answered, saying, Not so; lest there be not enough for us and you**—The words "Not so" are not in the original, where the reply is very elliptical—"In case there be not enough for us and you." **but go ye rather to them that sell, and buy for yourselves**—Again, interpretations are here applied on the basis of certain theological suppositions. But this much seems clear—if the foolish virgins were false believers, how could they be given the chance to appropriate a sufficient supply of oil? It could be, however, that the words here are to be understood as a general principle—i.e., as oil is only obtained with a price, so the Christian life demands a price—that must be paid in this lifetime, for it cannot be paid later (see 25:11).

►**10 And while they went to buy, the bridegroom came; and they that were ready went in with him to the marriage: and the door was shut**—Whatever the interpretation of the details of this verse (and again, they greatly vary), the main point is very clear: only those who are ready will enter the marriage feast. In fact, it should be said that readiness is the central theme of this parable.

►**11 Afterward came also the other virgins, saying, Lord, Lord, open to us**—In 7:22 this reiteration of the name was an exclamation rather of surprise; here it is a piteous cry of urgency, bordering on despair.

►**12 But he answered and said, Verily I say unto you, I know you not**—In 7:23 Jesus said, "I never knew you." The Greek word for "knew" (from the verb *ginosko*) indicates personal knowledge. Thus, Jesus told those "workers of lawlessness" that he did not personally know them—i.e., they were not personally his own. In this verse, a different word for "know" is used: *oida*—which indicates absolute knowledge, recognition, or perception. Some commentators think there is a difference (see, for example, Alford); others think the same meaning was intended. In either case, Jesus claimed not to know them.

►**13 Watch therefore, for ye know neither the day nor the hour wherein the Son of man cometh**—This is the practical lesson of the whole parable.

## 14-30 PARABLE OF THE TALENTS

This parable, while closely resembling it, is yet a different one from that in Luke 19:11-27. For the difference between the two parables, see the opening remarks on Luke 19:11-27. This parable closely follows the theme of the previous one—with this difference: the parable of the virgins speaks of inward preparedness; this parable of outward profitableness. Trench said, "While the virgins were represented as waiting for their Lord, we have the servants working for him; there the inward spiritual life of the faithful was described; here his external activity. It is not, therefore, without good reason that they appear in their actual order—that of the virgins first, and of the talents following—since it is the sole condition of a profitable outward activity for the kingdom of God, that the life of God be diligently maintained within the heart."

►**14 For [the kingdom of heaven is] as a man**—The ellipsis in the Greek must be supplied in English, with either what we have in the KJV (the kingdom of heaven), taken from 25:1, or perhaps it would be better to supply "the Son of man" (as in Mark 13:34). **travelling into a far country**—or more simply, "leaving home." **who called his own servants, and delivered unto them his goods**—Between master and slaves this was not uncommon in ancient times. Christ's "servants" here mean all who, by their Christian profession, stand in the relation to him of entire subjection. His "goods" mean all their gifts and endowments, whether original or acquired, natural or spiritual. As all that slaves have belongs to their master, so Christ has a claim to everything that belongs to his people, and he demands its appropriation to his service.

►**15 And unto one he gave five talents**—a talent was first used as a term to designate a unit of weight (about 70 pounds), then a monetary unit (about $1,000). Its modern day meaning (i.e., "natural endowment" or "special aptitude") was derived from the use of the word in this parable. **to another two, and to another one**—While the proportion of gifts is different in each, the same fidelity is required of all and equally rewarded. And thus there is perfect equity. **to every man according to his several ability**—his natural capacity and his providential opportunities for employing the gifts given to him. **and straightway took his journey**—Cf. 21:33, where the same departure is ascribed to God, after setting up the OT economy.

►**16, 17 Then he that had received the five talents went and traded with the same**—expressive of the activity that he put forth and the labor he expended. **and made them other five talents. And likewise he that had received two he also gained other two**—each doubling what he received, and therefore both equally faithful.

►**18 But he that had received one went and digged in the earth, and hid his lord's money**—not misspending, but simply making no use of it. In fact, his action seems that of one anxious that the gift should not be misused or lost, but ready to be returned, just as he got it.

►**19 After a long time**—suggests a long interval between the Lord's first and second coming. **the lord of those servants cometh and reckoneth with them**—lit., "takes up account with them."

►**20 Lord, thou deliveredst unto me five talents: behold, I have gained beside them five talents more**—How beautifully does this illustrate what John said of "boldness in the day of judgment," and his desire that "when he shall appear, we may have confidence, and not be ashamed before him at his coming" (1 John 4:17; 2:28).

►**21-23 His lord said unto him, Well done**—a single word, but of warm and delighted commendation. And from what lips! **thou hast been faithful over a few things, I will make thee ruler over many things . . . He also that had received two talents came . . . good and faithful servant; thou hast been faithful over a few things, I will make thee ruler over many things**—Both are commended in the same terms, and the reward of both is precisely the same. Observe also the contrasts: "Thou hast been faithful as a servant; now be a ruler—thou hast been entrusted with a few things; now have dominion over many things." **enter thou into the joy of thy lord**—your Lord's own joy (see John 15:11; Heb. 12:2).

►**24 Then he which had received the one talent came and said, Lord, I knew thee that thou art a hard man**—harsh. The word in Luke (19:21) is "austere." **reaping where thou hast not sown, and gathering where thou hast not strawed** [scattered seed]—The sense is obvious: "I knew you were the one whom it was impossible to serve, one whom nothing would please: exacting what was impracticable and dissatisfied with what was attainable." Thus do men secretly think of God as a hard master and virtually throw on him the blame of their fruitlessness.

►**25 And I was afraid**—of making matters worse by meddling with it at all. **and went and hid thy talent in the earth**—This depicts the conduct of all those who shut up their gifts from the active service of Christ.

►**26 Thou wicked and slothful servant**—The word "slothful" marks the precise nature of his wickedness; it consisted, it seems, not in his doing anything against, but in doing nothing for his master. **thou knewest that I reap where I sowed not, and gather where I have not strewed**—He takes the servant's own account of his demands, as expressing graphically enough, not the hardness he had basely imputed to him, but simply his demand of a profitable return for the gift entrusted.

►**27 Thou oughtest therefore to have put my money** [silver] **to the exchangers**—to the banker. **and then at my coming I should have received mine own with usury**—interest.

►**29 See 13:12.**

►**30 And cast**—cast out. **the unprofitable servant**—i.e., the useless servant. On this expression see comments on 22:13. **there shall be weeping and gnashing of teeth**—The same expression appears in 13:42, 50 and 24:51, but different punishments cause the same anguish. In 13:4 the tares—i.e., false believers—are burned with everlasting fire. In 13:50 the bad fish (i.e., the wicked) are cast into the furnace of fire. In this verse, however, it seems that a genuine—albeit, useless—servant is cast into outer darkness. In 25:41 the goats (i.e., the unrighteous) are sent into everlasting fire. Tares, bad fish, and goats get "everlasting fire"; unprofitable servants get "outer darkness." The distinction is important, for it shows that unbelievers will suffer eternal punishment, while an unprofitable servant (who is most likely a believer) will suffer punishment (or, loss of reward) but not eternal punishment. The kingdom involves reward and/or punishment for the believers depending on how they have served throughout their Christian life. The reward involves certain granted privileges (i.e., participation in the wedding feast [25:10], fellowship in the Lord's joy [25:21, 23], and ruling with Christ [25:21, 23]). The punishment is primarily a loss of such rewards—or not being permitted to participate in the millennial privileges (i.e., being in outer darkness). But such punishment does not entail loss of salvation or loss of eternal life. For further discussion on the Christian and the kingdom reward, see Robert Govett's *Entrance into the Kingdom*.

31-46 THE LAST JUDGMENT
➤31 **When the Son of man shall come in his glory**—his personal glory. **and all the holy angels with him**—See Deut. 33:2; Dan. 7:9, 10; Jude 14; with Heb. 1:6; 1 Pet. 3:22. **then shall he sit upon the throne of his glory**—the glory of his judicial authority.

➤ 32 **And before him shall be gathered all nations**—or, "all the nations." This is understood by many excellent commentators to mean the Gentiles, or all except believers in Christ. Their chief argument is the impossibility of any Christian wondering, at the time of judgment, that one should be thought to have done—or left undone—anything "unto Christ." These commentators say that this is a judgment on the Gentiles who have survived the tribulation, and that the judgment will be based on their treatment of the Jews, called Christ's "brothers" (25:40). But another view is that the scene describes a personal, public, final judgment on men, according to the treatment they have given to Christ—and consequently pertains to men within the Christian faith. If this is not the most obvious view, we shall have to consider again whether our Lord's teaching on the greatest themes of human interest does indeed possess that incomparable simplicity and transparency of meaning which, by universal consent, has been ascribed to it. **and he shall separate them**—now for the first time: the two classes having been mingled all along up to this awful moment. **as a shepherd divideth his sheep from the goats**—See Ezekiel 34:17.

➤33 **And he shall set the sheep on his right hand**—the side of honor (1 Kings 2:19; Ps. 45:9; 110:1). **but the goats on the left**—the side of dishonor.

➤34 **Then shall the King say unto them on his right hand, Come ye blessed of my Father, inherit the kingdom prepared for you from the foundation of the world**—Paul speaks of this blessed inheritance in the opening words of his epistle to the Ephesians (1:3-6). The believers were chosen from everlasting to possess and enjoy all spiritual blessings in Christ, and so chosen in order to be holy and blameless in love. This is the holy love whose practical manifestations the king is about to recount in detail; and thus we see that their whole life of love to Christ is the fruit of an eternal purpose of love to them in Christ. As to the view that this judgment is for Gentiles who survive the tribulation, how could it be said that the blessed Gentiles would inherit the kingdom prepared from the foundation of the world? Would God prepare a separate, special kingdom for them?

➤35-40 The dialogue between the king and the blessed ones indicates that both parties knew each other. These could hardly be the heathen talking to One they never knew. For, in fact, these are called "the righteous," those justified believers in Christ. Then why the surprise? Their surprise was not at their being told that they acted from love to Christ, but that Christ himself was the personal object of all their deeds; that they found him hungry and supplied him with food; that they brought water to him and satisfied his thirst; that seeing him naked and shivering, they put warm clothing upon him, paid him visits when lying in prison for the truth, and sat by his bedside when laid down with sickness. This is the astonishing interpretation that Jesus says "the King" will give to them of their own actions here on this earth.

➤41 **Then shall he say also unto them on the left hand, Depart from me, ye cursed, into everlasting fire, prepared for the devil and his angels**—This terrible curse pronounces eternal punishment. The everlasting fires of eternal judgment were originally (and probably exclusively) prepared for the devil and his angels, but the cursed will share their lot.

➤**46 And these shall go away into ever-lasting punishment**—cf. 13:42; 2 Thessalonians 1:9. **but the righteous into life eternal**—i.e., "life everlasting." This is the portion for all those who have been justified and made right with God (see Rom. 5:27-21).

Chapter **26**

1-16 CHRIST'S FINAL ANNOUNCEMENT OF HIS DEATH, NOW WITHIN TWO DAYS, AND THE SIMULTANEOUS CONSPIRACY OF THE JEWISH AUTHORITIES TO HAVE HIM KILLED. THE ANOINTING AT BETHANY. JUDAS AGREES WITH THE CHIEF PRIESTS TO BETRAY JESUS
See comments on Mark 14:1-11.

17-30 PREPARATION FOR AND LAST CELEBRATION OF THE PASSOVER, ANNOUNCEMENT OF THE TRAITOR, AND INSTITUTION OF THE SUPPER
See comments on Luke 22:7-23.

31-35 THE DESERTION OF JESUS BY HIS DISCIPLES AND THE DENIAL OF PETER FORETOLD
See comments on Luke 22:31-38.

36-46 JESUS' AGONY IN THE GARDEN
See comments on Luke 22:39-46.

47-56 BETRAYAL AND ARREST OF JESUS. FLIGHT OF HIS DISCIPLES
See comments on John 18:1-12.

57-75 JESUS ARRAIGNED BEFORE THE SANHEDRIN, CONDEMNED TO DIE, AND SHAMEFULLY ENTREATED. THE DENIAL OF PETER
See comments on Mark 14:53-72.

Chapter **27**

1-10 JESUS LED AWAY TO PILATE. REMORSE AND SUICIDE OF JUDAS (See Mark 15:1; Luke 23:1; John 18:28.)

1, 2 JESUS LED AWAY TO PILATE
See comments on John 18:28ff.

3-10 REMORSE AND SUICIDE OF JUDAS
This portion is peculiar to Matthew. On the progress of guilt in the traitor, see comments on Mark 14:1-11 and on John 13:21-30.

➤**3 Then Judas, which had betrayed him, when he saw that he was condemned**—The condemnation, even though not unexpected, might well fill him with horror. But perhaps this unhappy man expected that, while he got the bribe, the Lord would miraculously escape, as he often had done before, out of his enemies' power. **repented**—but, as the result too sadly showed, it was "the sorrow of the world, which worketh death" (2 Cor. 7:10). **and brought again the thirty pieces of silver to the chief priests and elders**—A remarkable illustration of the power of an awakened conscience. A short time before, the promise of this reward was temptation enough to his covetous heart to outweigh the most overwhelming obligations of duty and love; now the possession of it so troubled him that he could not use it, could not even keep it.

➤**4 Saying, I have sinned in that I have betrayed the innocent blood**—What a testimony this is to Jesus! Judas had been with him in all circumstances for three years; his post, as treasurer to him and the Twelve (John 12:6), gave him special opportunity to watch the spirit, disposition, and habits of his Master; while his covetous nature and thievish practices would incline him to dark and suspicious, rather than frank and generous, interpretations of all that Jesus said and did. If, then, he could have fastened on one questionable feature in all that he had so long witnessed, we may be sure that no such speech as this would have ever escaped his lips, nor would he have been so stung with remorse as not to be able to keep the money and survive his crime. **And they said, What is that to us? see thou to that**—"Guilty or innocent is nothing to us; we have destroyed him now." What hardened, hellish speech!

➤**5 And he cast down the pieces of silver**—The sarcastic, diabolical reply he received, in place of the sympathy that perhaps he expected, would deepen his remorse into a agony. Thus were fulfilled the words of the prophet—"So I took the thirty shekels of silver and threw them to the potter in the house of the Lord" (Zech. 11:13, NASB). **and departed, and went and hanged himself**—See comments on Acts 1:18 for the details.

➤**6 And the chief priests took the silver pieces, and said, It is not lawful for to put**

**them into the treasury**—"the *Corban*," or chest containing the money dedicated to sacred purposes (see comments on 15:5). **because it is the price of blood**—How scrupulous now! But those punctilious scruples made them unconciously fulfill the Scripture.

**►9 Then was fulfilled that which was spoken by Jeremy the prophet, saying**—The quotation that follows comes mainly from Zechariah 11:12, 13 but also from Jeremiah 19:1-11; 32:6-9. Zechariah's words do not mention the purchase of a field, but Jeremiah's words do. In fact, it is Jeremiah who speaks of innocent blood (Jer. 19:4) and of changing the name of a potter's field (Jer. 19:6). And it is Jeremiah who purchases a potter's field (Jer. 32:6-9). Thus, Jeremiah's prophecy contributed to Matthew's citation, and he received the credit because he was the more prominent prophet (see Archer, Carson).

**11-26 JESUS IS BROUGHT BEFORE PILATE AGAIN. PILATE SEEKS TO RELEASE HIM BUT FINALLY DELIVERS HIM TO BE CRUCIFIED**

See comments on Luke 23:1-25 and on John 18:28-40.

**27-33 JESUS, SCORNFULLY AND CRUELLY ENTREATED OF THE SOLDIERS, IS LED AWAY TO BE CRUCIFIED**

See comments on Mark 15:16-22.

**34-50 CRUCIFIXION AND DEATH OF THE LORD JESUS**

See comments on Mark 15:25-37; Luke 23:33-6; John 19:18-30.

**51-66 SIGNS AND CIRCUMSTANCES FOLLOWING THE DEATH OF THE LORD JESUS. HE IS TAKEN DOWN FROM THE CROSS AND BURIED. THE SEPULCHRE IS GUARDED (See Mark 15:38-47; Luke 23:47-56; John 19:31-42.)**

**51 THE VEIL RENT**

**►51 And, behold, the vail of the temple was rent in twain from the top to the bottom**—This was the thick and gorgeously fashioned veil which was hung between the "holy place" and the "holiest of all," shutting out all access to the presence of God as manifested "from above the mercy seat and from between

the cherubim"—"the Holy Ghost [Spirit] this signifying, that the way into the holiest of all was not yet made manifest" (Heb. 9:8). Into this holiest of all none might enter, not even the high priest, except once a year, on the great Day of Atonement, and then only with the blood of atonement in his hands, which he sprinkled "upon . . . and before the mercy seat . . . seven times" (Lev. 16:14)—to signify that access for sinners to a holy God is only through atoning blood. But as they had only the blood of bulls and of goats, which could not take away sins (Heb. 10:4), during all the long ages that preceded the death of Christ, the thick veil remained; the blood of bulls and of goats continued to be shed and sprinkled; and once a year access to God through an atoning sacrifice was permitted as a preview of the coming opened way. But *now,* the one atoning Sacrifice being provided in the precious blood of Christ, access to this holy God could no longer be denied; and so the moment Jesus expired on the cross (symbolizing the altar), the thick veil that for so many ages had been the symbol of separation between God and guilty men was, without a hand touching it, mysteriously "rent in twain from top to bottom." Now the way into the holiest of all is permanently and eternally opened. Now we can come boldly to the throne of grace to find mercy and grace (Heb. 4:16) because the blood of Jesus has opened to us a new and living way (Heb. 10:19-22).

**51-53 AN EARTHQUAKE OPENED THE GRAVES OF MANY SAINTS, WHO AROSE AFTER CHRIST'S RESURRECTION**

**►51 and the earth did quake**—From what follows it would seem that this earthquake was local, having for its object the rending of the rocks and the opening of the graves. **and the rocks rent**—were split.

**►52 And the graves were opened; and many bodies of the saints which slept arose**—This verse is clarified by the next one. The sequence is as follows: At the time of Jesus' death there was an earthquake that split the rocks, thus opening the graves of many deceased OT saints—who remained in their graves until the time of Jesus' resurrection, after which time they arose from their graves and then appeared to many people in the Holy

City, Jerusalem. The only ambiguous factor is the precise time of their quickening: at the moment of Jesus' death or at the time of Jesus' resurrection? The Scripture is not explicit here, but it would seem to be the latter. In the opening of the graves at the moment of the Redeemer's death, there was a glorious symbolical proclamation that the death that had just taken place had "swallowed up death in victory." And the saints that slept were awakened by their risen Lord, to accompany him out of the tomb, so it was fitting that the Prince of Life should be the first that should rise from the dead (Acts 26:23; 1 Cor. 15:20, 23; Col. 1:18; Rev. 1:5).

►**53 And came out of the graves after his resurrection, and went into the holy city**— Jerusalem. **and appeared unto many**—that there might be undeniable evidence of their own resurrection first, and through it of their Lord's. Thus, while it was not considered fitting that he himself should appear again in Jerusalem except to the disciples, provision was made that the fact of his resurrection should not be left in doubt. It must be observed, however, that the resurrection of these sleeping saints was probably not like those of the widow of Nain's son, of Jairus's daughter, of Lazarus, etc.—which were mere temporary recalling of the departed spirit to the mortal body, to be followed by a final departure. But this was probably a resurrection once for all, to life everlasting.

## 54 THE CENTURION'S TESTIMONY

►**54 Now when the centurion**—the military superintendent of the execution. **and they that were with him, watching Jesus, saw the earthquake**—or witnessed its effects. **and those things that were done**—reflecting upon the entire transaction. **they feared greatly**—convinced of the presence of a divine hand. **saying, Truly this was the Son of God**—or, God's Son. Although spoken by a Roman, this expression was uttered with its full biblical meaning in that it underscored and affirmed the claim that Jesus made to be the Son of God. In other words, the centurion was not just saying that he was a deity or divine or a son of God. His exclamation concurred with Jesus' self-declaration (26:63, 64).

## 55, 56 THE GALILEAN WOMEN

►**55 And many women were there beholding afar off, which followed Jesus**—The sense here would be better brought out by the use of the pluperfect, "which had followed Jesus." **from Galilee, ministering unto him**—As these dear women had ministered to him during his glorious preaching tours in Galilee (see Luke 8:1-3), so from this statement it should seem that they accompanied him and ministered to his needs from Galilee on his final journey to Jerusalem.

►**56 Among which was Mary Magdalene**—See Luke 8:2. **and Mary the mother of James and Joses**—the wife of Cleophas, or rather Clopas, and sister-in-law of Jesus' mother (John 19:25). See comments on 13:55, 56. **and the mother of Zebedee's children**—i.e., Salome (cf. Mark 1:40). All this about the women is mentioned for the sake of what is afterwards to be related concerning their purchasing spices to anoint their Lord's body.

## 57-60 THE TAKING DOWN FROM THE CROSS AND THE BURIAL

See comments on John 19:38-42.

## 61 THE WOMEN MARK THE PLACE OF BURIAL

►**61 And there was Mary Magdalene, and the other Mary**—"the mother of James and Joses," mentioned before (27:56) **sitting over against the sepulchre**—See comments on Mark 16:1.

## 62-66 THE SEPULCHRE GUARDED

►**62 Now the next day, that followed the day of the preparation**—i.e., after six o'clock of our Saturday evening. The Crucifixion took place on the Friday and all was not over until shortly before sunset, when the Jewish Sabbath began; and "that sabbath day was an high day" (John 19:31), being the first day of the feast of unleavened bread.

►**63 Saying, Sir, we remember that that deceiver**—The leaders of the Jews betrayed their uneasiness, which one almost imagines they only tried to stifle in their own minds, as well as in Pilate's, in case he should have any lurking suspicion that he had done wrong in yielding to them. **said, while he was yet alive**—In light of the heresies that denied Christ's actual death, this testimony from the mouths of Jesus' bitterest enemies concerning his death is very important. **After three days**—which, according to the customary Jewish way of reckoning, need signify no more than "after the beginning of the third day." **I will rise again**—"I rise," in the present tense, thus reporting not only the fact that this prediction of his had reached their ears, but that they understood him to look forward confidently to its occurring on the very day named.

➤**64 Command therefore that the sepulchre be made sure** [secure]—by a Roman guard. **until the third day**—after which, if he still lay in the grave, the imposture of his claims would be manifest to all. **and say unto the people, He is risen from the dead**—Did they really fear this? **so the last error** [deceit] **shall be worse than the first**—the imposture of his pretended resurrection worse than that of his pretended messiahship.

➤**65 Pilate said unto them, Ye have a watch**—The guards had already acted under orders of the Sanhedrin, with Pilate's consent, but probably they were not clear about employing them as a night-watch without Pilate's express authority. **go your way, make it as sure as ye can**—Though there may be no irony in this speech, it evidently insinuated that if the event should be contrary to their wish, it would not be for lack of sufficient human securities to prevent it.

➤**66 So they went, and made the sepulchre sure** [secure], **sealing the stone**—i.e., setting a clay seal on the great stone covering the entrance, which—if broken—would signal that someone had trespassed into the tomb. **and setting a watch**—to guard it.

*Chapter* **28**

1-15 A GLORIOUS ANGELIC ANNOUNCEMENT ON THE FIRST DAY OF THE WEEK THAT CHRIST IS RISEN. HIS APPEARANCE TO THE WOMEN. THE GUARDS BRIBED TO GIVE A FALSE ACCOUNT OF THE RESURRECTION (See Mark 16:1-8; Luke 24:1-8; John 20:1.)

1-8 THE RESURRECTION ANNOUNCED TO THE WOMEN

➤**1 In the end of the sabbath, as it began to dawn**—after the Sabbath, as it grew toward daylight. **toward the first day of the week**—Luke (24:1) has it, "very early in the morning"—properly, "at the first appearance of daybreak"; and corresponding with this, John (20:1) says, "when it was yet dark." (See comments on Mark 16:2.) Not an hour, it would seem, was lost by those dear lovers of the Lord Jesus. **came Mary Magdalene and the other Mary**—"the mother of James and Joses" (see 27:46, 61). **to see the sepulchre**—with a view of the anointing of the body, for which they had made all their preparations. (See comments on Mark 16:1, 2.)

➤**2 And, behold, there was**—i.e., there had been, before the arrival of the women. **a great earthquake; for the angel of the Lord descended from heaven ...**—And this was the state of things when the women drew near. The angel sat upon the huge stone, to overawe, with the brilliance that darted from him, the Roman guard, and to do honor to his risen Lord.

➤**3 His countenance** [appearance] **was like lightning, and his raiment white as snow**—the one expressing glory, the other purity.

➤**5 And the angel answered and said unto the women, Fear not ye**—The "ye" (you, plural) here is emphatic, to contrast their case with that of the guards. The guards needed to fear. **for I know that ye seek Jesus, which was crucified**—Jesus the crucified.

➤**6 He is not here: for he is risen, as he said**—See comments on Luke 24:5-7. **Come, see the place where the Lord lay**—Since these women had seen the place of his burial, his absence from that place would prove his resurrection. But see comments on John 20:12.

➤**7 And go quickly, and tell his disciples**—For a precious addition to this, see Mark 16:7. **that he is risen from the dead; and, behold, he goeth before you into Galilee**—their native land (27:55). **there shall ye see him**—This must refer to those more public manifestations of himself to large numbers of disciples at the same time—which happened only in Galilee; for individually he was seen by some of those very women almost immediately after this (28:9, 10). Prior to his death, Jesus had told his disciples that he would appear to them in Galilee after his resurrection (26:32; Mark 14:28), but due to their unbelief and fear they remained in Jerusalem. So Jesus appeared to them in Jerusalem and then, later, in Galilee. This explains why there are two categories of post-resurrection appearances: those in Jerusalem and those in Galilee.

►8 And they departed quickly—Mark (16:8) says "they fled," from the sepulchre with fear and great joy—How natural this combination of feelings! (See Mark 16:11.) and did run to bring his disciples word—"Neither said they anything to any man [by the way]; for they were afraid" (Mark 16:8).

## 9, 10 APPEARANCE TO THE WOMEN

This appearance is recorded only by Matthew.

►9 And as they went to tell his disciples, behold, Jesus met them, saying, All hail—the usual salute, but from the lips of Jesus bearing a higher signification.

►10 Be not afraid: go tell my brethren—Jesus' disciples are now called his "brothers" because of what the resurrection has accomplished. The resurrection issued forth the new creation and the fresh availability of the divine life. Prior to Christ's resurrection, the disciples could not be indwelt by the divine life and be partakers of the divine nature. But, as Peter later says, we were "born again to a living hope through the resurrection of Jesus Christ from the dead" (1 Pet. 1:3). Therefore, Jesus now calls his disciples his "brothers"; and he now announces, according to John's record (20:17), that his God is their God, and his Father, their Father. that they go into Galilee, and there shall they see me—According to what he had told them prior to his death and resurrection, they should have waited for him in Galilee. See comments on 28:7.

## 11-15 THE GUARDS BRIBED

This is recorded only by Matthew.

►11 Now when they were going—while the women were on their way to deliver to his brethren the message of their risen Lord.

►12 And when they were assembled with the elders—But Joseph at least was absent, Gamaliel probably also, and perhaps others. and had taken counsel, they gave large money unto the soldiers—It would need a good deal; but the whole case of the Jewish authorities was now at stake.

►13 Saying, Say ye, His disciples came by night, and stole him away while we slept—which, as we have observed, was a capital offense for soldiers on guard.

►14 And if this come to the governor's ears—rather, "If this come before the governor"; i.e., not in the way of mere report, but for judicial investigation. we will persuade him, and secure you—The "we" and the "you" are emphatic here—"we shall [take care to] persuade him and keep you from trouble," or "save you from harm." The grammatical form of this clause implies that the thing supposed was expected to happen. The meaning then is, "If this come before the governor—as it likely will—we shall see to it that you will not be blamed." The "persuasion" of Pilate meant, doubtless, quieting him by a bribe, which we know he was by no means above taking (like Felix afterwards, Acts 24:26).

►15 So they took the money, and did as they were taught—thus consenting to brand themselves with infamy. and this saying is commonly reported among the Jews until this day—to the date of the publication of this Gospel. The wonder is that so clumsy and incredible a story lasted so long. Justin Martyr (A.D. 170), says, in his *Dialogue with Trypho the Jew* that the Jews dispersed the story by means of special messengers sent to every country.

## 16-20 JESUS MEETS WITH THE DISCIPLES ON A MOUNTAIN IN GALILEE, AND GIVES FORTH THE GREAT COMMISSION

►16 Then the eleven disciples went away into Galilee—but certainly not before the second week after the resurrection, and probably somewhat later, into a mountain where Jesus had appointed them—It should have been rendered "the mountain," meaning some certain mountain, which he had specified the night before he suffered, when he said, "After I am risen, I will go before you into

Galilee" (26:32; Mark 14:28). It has been conjectured that it was the same mountain on which he delivered the Beatitudes, especially because of the nearness to the Sea of Galilee— another scene of one of his post-resurrection appearances (John 21:1ff.). Many Bible scholars believe that this meeting is the same one referred to in 1 Corinthians 15:6—"He was seen of above five hundred brethren at once; of whom the greater part remain unto this present, but some are fallen asleep." Nothing can account for such a number as five hundred assembling at one spot but the expectation of some promised manifestation of their risen Lord, and the promise before his resurrection, twice repeated after it, best explains this immense gathering.

➤17 And when they saw him, they worshipped him: but some doubted— certainly none of "the Eleven," after what took place at previous interviews in Jerusalem. But if the five hundred were now present, we may well believe this of some of them.

➤19 Go ye therefore, and teach all nations—rather, "make disciples of all nations"; for "teaching," in the more usual sense of that word, comes in afterwards, and is expressed by a different term. In this final commission, the disciples were charged to disciple all nations—not just the Jews. As is evident in the book of Acts, it took awhile before the disciples took the gospel beyond the Jews to the Gentiles. baptizing them in the name—It should be, "into the name"; as in 1 Corinthians 10:2 ("And were all baptized unto [or rather, into] Moses") and Galatians 3:27 ("For as many of you as have been baptized into Christ"). The result of being baptized into Christ is union with Christ. of the Father, and of the Son, and of the Holy Ghost [Spirit]—our one God has one triune name: Father, Son, and Holy Spirit. To be baptized into the name of the triune God is to be united with him.

➤20 Teaching them—This is teaching in the moral usual sense of the term; or instructing the converted and baptized disciples. to observe all things whatsoever I have commanded you: and, lo, I—The "I" here is emphatic. am with you alway—"all the days"; i.e., until making disciples, baptizing, and building them up by Christian instruction, shall be no more. Christ's continual, abiding presence is one of the greatest, most precious promises and the sweetest reality. Since the book of Matthew does not record Christ's ascension, this book leaves the reader with the lasting impression that Christ never left this earth. And this much is true: the church has always had his invisible, spiritual presence. even unto the end of the world—rather, the completion of the age, pointing to the completion of this present dispensation. Amen—This word is not present in the best manuscripts.

The great commission—the title given to Matthew 28:18-20—contains an evangelical commission and a pastoral commission. The evangelical (or, missionary) charge is contained in the words, "Go, make disciples of all the world." This was addressed to all the disciples then with Jesus (over five hundred then present) and those throughout this age. Then each new disciple was baptized into the reality of the triune God, thus setting a seal of visible discipleship upon each new convert. The pastoral charge is found in the words "teach them to observe whatsoever I have commanded you." In the teaching there is the feeding and shepherding. Every new believer needs this pastoral teaching. For these two aspects of the great commission, Jesus grants strong encouragement. First, we can go forth into all the world and make disciples of all nations knowing that all authority in heaven and on earth has been given to Christ. Second, we can always know that Christ is with us, even to the end of this age.

BIBLIOGRAPHY

Alford, Henry. *The Greek New Testament.* 1852. Reprint. Grand Rapids: Guardian Press, 1973.

Archer, Gleason. *Encyclopedia of Bible Difficulties.* Grand Rapids: Zondervan, 1982.

Barbieri, Louis. "Matthew" in *The Bible Knowledge Commentary.* Wheaton, Ill.: Victor Books, 1983.

Bengel, John A. *New Testament Word Studies.* 1742. Reprint. Grand Rapids: Eerdmans, 1971.

Carson, D. A. "Matthew" in *The Expositor's Bible Commentary.* Vol. 8. Grand Rapids: Zondervan, 1984.

Ellison, H. L. "Matthew" in *The New Layman's Bible Commentary.* Glasgow: Pickering & Inglis, 1979.

Govett, Robert. *Entrance into the Kingdom,* or *Reward According to Works.* London: Charles J. Thynne, 1922.

Lightfoot, Neil. *Parables of Jesus.* Grand Rapids: Baker Book House, 1963.

Nixon, R. E. "Matthew" in *New Bible Commentary: Revised.* London: InterVarsity Press, 1970.

Tholuck, August. *Commentary on the Sermon on the Mount.* Philadelphia: Smith, 1860.

Trench, R. C. *Studies in the Gospels.* London: Macmillan, 1878.

Walvoord, John. *Matthew: Thy Kingdom Come.* Chicago: Moody, 1974.

# MARK

## Introduction

It is universally agreed that this Gospel was written by Mark. But which Mark? The great majority of critics take the writer to be "John, whose surname was Mark," of whom we read in the Acts, and who was "sister's son to Barnabas" (Col. 4:10). John, surnamed Mark, was the son of Mary, in whose home some believers met to pray for Peter's release from prison (Acts 12:12). He accompanied Paul and Barnabas in their apostolic journeys when these two traveled together (Acts 12:25; 13:5). And when afterwards a dispute about Mark caused a separation between them, Mark accompanied his uncle Barnabas, and Silas went with Paul. When he was reconciled to Paul, which was probably soon after, we find Paul again employing Mark's assistance, recommending him and giving him a very honorable testimony (Col. 4:10; Philem. 1:24).

At the end of his life, Paul asked Timothy to bring Mark to Rome so that he could assist Paul there in prison (2 Tim. 4:11). Around the same time, Peter said that one called Mark was with him in Babylon (Rome). Peter called this Mark his son—i.e., his spiritual child through conversion (1 Pet. 5:13). Was this Mark the same Mark that helped Paul? Some scholars consider it unlikely, but most assume him to be the same Mark because there is no historical evidence that indicates there was any other Mark of note in the days of the early church.

The Mark that the Bible tells us about is one who mainly worked with Paul and *also* was with Peter—if, in fact, it is the same Mark. The Mark that many early church fathers tell us about is the Mark who accompanied Peter, heard his preaching in Rome, interpreted Peter's words, and wrote a gospel primarily based on Peter's testimony. Papias (c. 60–c. 130, a disciple of the apostle John) said that John (whom he calls "John the elder"—see 2 John 1; 3 John 1) made this comment about Peter's relationship to Mark's Gospel:

> The elder said this also: Mark, who became Peter's interpreter, wrote accurately, though not in order, all that he remembered of the things said or done by the Lord. For he had neither heard of the Lord nor been one of his followers, but afterwards, as I said, he had followed Peter, who used to compose his discourses with a view to the needs of his hearers, but not as though he were drawing up a connected account of the Lord's sayings. So Mark made no mistake in thus recording some things just as he remembered them. For he was careful of this one thing, to omit none of the things he had heard and to make no untrue statements therein. (Eusebius's *Ecclesiastical History*, 3.39.15)

Irenaeus said nearly the same: "Matthew published a Gospel while Peter and Paul were preaching and founding the church at Rome; and after their departure (or decease), Mark, the disciple and interpreter of Peter, also gave forth to us in writing the things which were preached by Peter" (*Against Heresies,* 3.1). And Clement of Alexandria is still more specific, in a passage preserved to us by Eusebius:

> Peter having publicly preached the word at Rome, and spoken forth the Gospel by the Spirit, many of those present exhorted Mark, as having long been a follower of his, and remembering what he had said, to write what had been spoken; and that having prepared the Gospel, he delivered it to those who had asked him for it; which when Peter came to the knowledge of, he neither decidedly forbade nor encouraged him. (*Ecclesiastical History,* 6.14)

Eusebius' own testimony, however, from other accounts, is rather different: that Peter's hearers were so penetrated by his preaching that they gave Mark, as being a *follower of Peter,* no rest until he consented to write his Gospel, as a memorial of Peter's oral teaching; and "that the apostle, when he knew by the revelation of the Spirit what had been done, was delighted with the zeal of these men, and sanctioned the reading of the writing (that is, of the Gospel of Mark) in the churches" (*Ecclesiastical History,* 2.15). Other church fathers, such as Origen and Jerome, also bear witness to the tradition that Mark was Peter's interpreter.

Whoever we understand Mark to be, it is the decided testimony of history that Mark wrote for Peter—hence, the Gospel of Mark is essentially the Gospel according to Peter. The Gospel definitely bears the impress of Peter's authorship. The vividness and striking detail in the narrative could have come only from one in Jesus' inner circle (see 1:16-20, 29-31, 35-38; 5:35-43; 9:14, 15; 10:32, 46-52; 14:32-42). Furthermore, the Gospel has a tendency to give special focus on Peter's words and deeds (8:29-33; 9:4-7; 10:28-31; 14:29-31, 66-72) and even on Peter himself (16:7).

What of Mark's intended audience? We are fairly certain that Mark wrote this Gospel in Rome for Gentile (specifically Roman) Christians. Because he wrote to a Gentile audience, he explained Jewish customs (7:3, 4; 14:12; 15:42), translated several Aramaic expressions into Greek (3:17; 5:41; 7:11, 34; 15:22, 34), used several Latin terms (5:9; 6:27; 12:15, 42; 15:16, 39), reckoned time according to the Roman way (6:48; 13:35), and, at the climax of the Gospel, recorded the faith of a Roman centurion (standing by the cross) in Jesus' death (15:39).

Since Mark's audience was composed of believers who already should have been familiar with the major events of Jesus' life, he did not write a biography as such. Rather, Mark (or should we say Peter via Mark) used the life and works of Jesus to present Christ as the dynamic model of Christian life and service—especially in the face of intense opposition. At the time this Gospel was written (late 50s), the Christians at Rome were living under the reign of Nero (54-68), the first and probably severest persecutor of the church. Many of these Christians would die for their faith. This Gospel would have greatly encouraged the Roman believers because they would have seen in Mark's narrative how their Lord labored in the face of constant opposition and resolutely determined to meet his destiny with death on the cross. Mark's Gospel does contain theology—especially in its presentation of Jesus as God's Son (1:1, 11; 3:11; 5:7; 12:35-57; 14:61; 15:39) and man's servant (1:31; 10:43-45). But the theology is practical in that it serves to reinforce the pastoral nature of the work.

*Chapter* 1

## 1-8 JOHN'S PREACHING AND BAPTISM

**➤1 The beginning of the gospel of Jesus Christ, the Son of God**—This verse (without a verb) is a comprehensive title for Mark's Gospel; it introduces this Gospel's theme: the good news about (or, preached by) Jesus Christ, God's Son. It is abrupt, but to the point, and characterizes the writer's energetic style. As is implicit in this title, Mark was more intent on presenting the gospel of Jesus Christ than the biography of Jesus Christ. Thus he quickly moves into the public part of Jesus' ministry. **The beginning**—The Bible records several significant beginnings. John speaks of the beginning before all beginnings, the timeless, eternal beginning, the beginning in which the Word was (John 1:1). The first verse of our Bible tells of the beginning of God's creation (Gen. 1:1). And the Gospel writers Matthew and Luke commence their accounts with Jesus' genealogy, birth, and the beginning of his life on earth. Mark, foregoing Christ's genealogy and early life, immediately focuses the reader's attention on the beginning of Christ's message and ministry. Some have thought that Mark did not include Christ's genealogy because he was interested in presenting Christ as a servant— and a servant does not need a genealogy. His worth is proven by his work, not his pedigree. Others have thought that Mark omitted the genealogy and instead used Christ's herald (John the Baptist) to introduce his narrative because a herald's announcement signaled the arrival of an eminent person more effectively and more immediately than a historical pedigree. Mark's Roman audience, familiar with the function of a herald, would have appreciated the way Mark chose to introduce Jesus Christ. **The gospel**—The Greek word means "good news." It was only as followers of Christ applied the term to him and his teachings that it took on any special meaning. After Justin Martyr (2nd century) the "good news" came to mean the actual written records of Jesus' life, including Mark's account. When Mark wrote, however, it was necessary to qualify whom the "good news" was about. This was the whole story of Jesus, the Messiah: how he lived and died, what he taught, and where he went. "It is

in Mark's Gospel that Jesus identifies 'gospel' so closely with his own person that the two are practically one entity"—see 8:35; 10:29 (Franzmann). **Jesus Christ**—His human name is Jesus, and that is the name he went by on earth. It was a common Jewish name that meant "the delivering one." The historian Josephus mentions about twenty men by the same name, and ten of them lived at the same time as this Jesus. That is why Mark makes sure his readers know which Jesus he is talking about. Messiah, or Christ, meant "the Anointed One" of God. There could be only one "Jesus, the Messiah." Throughout his short book Mark adequately portrays the human side of Jesus, alongside his uniquely divine character. **The Son of God**— or, God's Son. This title, while absent in a few early manuscripts, is present in many ancient witnesses and should be considered a genuine part of this Gospel. In fact, Mark makes Jesus' divine sonship a major theme (see 1:11; 3:11; 5:7; 9:7; 13:32; 14:36, 61-62; 15:39). Mark is completely convinced this Jesus is the Son of God and he emphatically identifies him as such in his opening statement. (See also note on 15:39.)

**➤2 As it is written in the prophets**— This is a reading found in some manuscripts, but the best authorities read "Isaiah the prophet" instead of "the prophets." While Matthew and Luke made their connection with the OT by tracing Christ's lineage through OT persons to Jesus Christ, Mark makes his connection by immediately citing OT passages that predicted the coming of Christ and his forerunner. In 1:2 he quotes from Malachi 3:1 (and perhaps also from Exod. 23:20, LXX) and in 1:3 he quotes Isaiah 40:1. But he mentions only Isaiah's name. It may be that he was more familiar with Isaiah, or simply felt that Isaiah's name was the one which his readers most often associated with prophecies about the Messiah. The Malachi quote speaks of a messenger who will prepare the way for Jesus. Both quotes refer specifically to verses 4-8, but in another sense, they introduce the theme of the entire book: Jesus the Messiah is the culmination of God's plan for Israel and for the whole world.

**➤3 The voice of one crying in the wilderness, Prepare ye the way of the Lord, make his paths straight**—The Isaiah quote (from

Isa. 40:3) referred specifically to a person who was to deliver Israel from the Babylonian captivity. But it had a more far-reaching implication as a messianic prophecy. The fact that everyone who recorded Christ's life in Scripture recognized this OT passage as prediction of the coming Messiah and quoted it in connection with Christ, indicates what an important prophecy they considered it to be. Matthew and Luke save the quote until they talk about John's imprisonment and death, using it as a sort of epitaph that summed up his whole life (Matt. 11:10; Luke 7:27). The Isaiah image is a picture of the man whose job it was to go ahead of the king in order to level and smooth out the roadway for the royal party. Spiritually speaking, that is exactly what John did for Jesus.

➤**4 John**—the Baptist; see Matthew 3:1-12 and Luke 3:1-18, for both have much fuller accounts of his ministry than Mark's very matter-of-fact sentence statement. Luke goes so far as to pinpoint the actual dates when he preached in relation to the Roman rulers and Jewish high priests of his day. (See Luke 1:5-25 and 57-80 for John's full story.) **wilderness**—John probably preached in the Jordan valley north of Jerusalem, although some people think he might have preached in Perea since he was later killed in Machaerus. **preach the baptism of repentance**—i.e., a baptism accompanied by repentance. Cole says that "John's baptism was not Christian baptism, nor was it associated with the gift of the Holy Spirit. John's baptism was therefore one of the initiatory and purification rites of later Judaism, and was an outward sign and symbol of the message John preached." That message was repentance, the turning of one's back on sin. Repentance involves a change in mind, a change in attitude, and an alteration of purpose. Repentance is more than mere regret. It is not just being sorry for sin, but actually being sorrowful about it. The result is a complete change of mind and purpose. **for the remission of sins**—i.e., for the forgiveness of sins. The baptism (accompanied by repentance) led to (Gk. *eis*) the forgiveness of sins—all of which prepared the baptized and forgiven to receive Jesus as the Christ and the salvation he would bring. Matthew (3:11) and Luke (3:7-14) give fuller descriptions of John's emphasis on repentance accompanying baptism.

➤**5 went out unto him**—lit. "kept going out to him." **all the land of Judaea, and they of Jerusalem**—John's popularity is confirmed by historians (see Josephus's *Antiquities*, 18.118). Even Jesus traveled to the Jordan to be baptized by him. **were all baptized of him . . . confessing their sins**—The confession of sin (and simultaneous repentance) accompanied their baptism.

➤**6 clothed with camel's hair**—Although Mark doesn't mention Elijah's name, this was the way Jews traditionally pictured the Old Testament prophet (see 2 Kings 1:8). **locusts and wild honey**—The Jewish law allowed eating locusts (Lev. 11:22). They were the poor man's meat then, just as they are today, but now the Bedouin eat them salted or roasted. John probably found the honey in rocks or else drew of a sweet sap from some trees. Notice that he never asked his disciples to follow his diet, just his message.

➤**7, 8** John's whole message is packed into this short sample. God never intended him to have the prominent place in his plan to save man. John's job was to introduce Jesus, and he knew it. He was only a signpost that pointed to the coming Messiah. It was up to the lowest slave in the house to undo a visitor's sandals at the door, and that's just how John saw himself in comparison to the One who was coming.

John's baptism was as inferior to Jesus' baptism as John himself was to the coming Messiah. Instead of just getting their bodies wet with river water, men's whole beings would now be saturated with God's Holy Spirit when Jesus baptized them.

**9-11 THE HOLY SPIRIT COMES DOWN FROM HEAVEN AT CHRIST'S BAPTISM**
See comments on Matthew 3:13-17.

**12, 13 CHRIST'S TEMPTATION**
See comments on Matthew 4:1-11.

**14-20 JESUS BEGINS HIS MINISTRY IN GALILEE BY CHOOSING FOUR DISCIPLES**
See comments on Matt. 4:12-22.

**21-34 A SERIES OF HEALINGS**
➤**21 they went into Capernaum**—See Matthew 4:13. **and straightway on the sabbath day he entered into the synagogue, and taught**—The Greek here indicates that Jesus

taught on successive sabbath days. Jesus' message was revolutionary but he didn't upset the system in order to preach it. He taught within the established religious order even though it was rotten through and through.

➤**22 they were astonished at his doctrine**—Jesus' first sermon is remembered not for what he said, but for how he said it. Mark notes the people's attentive response to his authoritative style. **he taught them as one that had authority**—see Matthew 7:28, 29. Rather than offer a personal opinion on a subject, the religious teachers of that day relied on a whole series of quotations from great men of the past to support what they said. Jesus was not the typical theologian they were used to hearing, and the people who had been accustomed to secondhand sermons for so long responded quickly to his fresh style.

➤**23 a man with an unclean spirit**—i.e., "a man possessed by a demon" (TLB). The man's conduct indicates that his personality was completely controlled by the evil power inside him. People have been too quick to explain away such incidents, either in the name of superstition or in the name of science. The Scriptures treat them as neither psychic belief nor psychotic behavior. Jesus recognized demons as very real spiritual beings, and they in turn recognized him as the Son of God, long before any of his disciples did.

➤**24 Let us alone; what have we to do with thee, thou Jesus of Nazareth?**—It is ironic that what the man needed most, he wanted least. His question implied that the demons and Jesus had nothing in common. "We don't want you; what do you want with us?" At first only people who wanted to make fun of Jesus called him "Jesus, you Nazarene," but soon even those who loved him were using the name with affection (see Luke 18:37; Acts 2:22). **art thou come to destroy us?**—Because they knew Jesus would someday destroy them, every time they met him they were afraid that the time had come. They knew that their control over this man could only last as long as he allowed it, so they gave up their grip on the victim without a fight. **I know thee who thou art, the Holy One of God**—The demons hoped they could make people think that Jesus was really one of them if they said they knew him. Jesus faced this accusation on other occa-

sions, and answered it well (Matt. 12:24-30; Mark 3:22-30), so that the demons' plan always backfired. What they thought would hurt his cause only helped to convince people of who he really was. They were actually quoting Scripture when they called Jesus the "Holy One of God." It was the same expression that David used in Psalm 16:10 when he predicted the death and resurrection of the "Holy One," the Messiah.

➤**26 the unclean spirit had torn him**—i.e., "the evil spirit convulsed the man violently" (TLB). Luke 4:35 recalled that he actually threw the man down before he left him. The demon is having his final fling with the man and goes as far as he can with him, just to show how much power he really had over the person. But he leaves with a scream of angry defeat, and Luke adds that he didn't hurt the man anymore.

➤**27 what new doctrine is this?**—The people who were there soon made the connection between what Jesus had been saying and what he had just done. They knew it had something to do with his teaching, but they had never seen anything like it before. The Greek word Mark used for "new" is *kainē*, or "new in kind," rather than *neos,* which means "new in time." This was not just something they had heard about before and now were seeing for the first time; it was something completely new.

➤**29 forthwith**—immediately. Mark's favorite expression tells us something about his Roman readers. They were impulsive men of action, and he uses the term frequently to keep the story moving by showing that Jesus himself was a man of action. The same Greek word (translated "anon") appears in 1:30. **house of Simon and Andrew**—During Jesus' Galilean ministry he stayed with Simon and Andrew (12:1; 3:19; 9:33; 10:10). Since John 1:44 says they were from Bethsaida, they had either moved to Capernaum, or else they lived in a fishing quarter of Capernaum known as Bethsaida. (See comments on Mark 6:46.)

➤**30 Simon's wife's mother lay sick of a fever**—Luke uses a more technical Greek term to describe her fever than Mark does (Luke 4:38). Luke's term indicated she had a high fever (see NIV). Since he was a doctor (Col. 4:14), he was careful to record exactly how sick she really was, while Mark is more concerned about listing everyone who saw her in that condition. This is probably the first of several evidences to support the claim that Mark worked with Peter in writing this document (see Introduction). His personal involvement in the episode is obvious. Paul confirms the fact that Peter was married (1 Cor. 9:5). Therefore the house was likely his. It was his mother-in-law who was sick, and it was also the first of many times that Peter joined James and John in sharing an exclusive experience in Jesus' life. Since Mark wrote from Peter's memory of his days with Jesus, it is easy to see why he is so precise about this particular event. Peter would have been anxious to authenticate everything that happened by naming all the reliable witnesses.

➤**31 took her by the hand, and lifted her up**—Jesus' bedside manner is deliberate, but marked by the warmth of a personal touch. **immediately the fever left her, and she ministered** [or, served] **unto them**—The fact that she goes straight into the kitchen not only shows her appreciation for what Christ has done, but also indicates how quickly and completely Jesus healed her. And she probably served them more than just a light lunch since they had come straight from the synagogue service (1:29). The Jews' sabbath meal was like our Sunday dinner. It was an elaborate affair, and in all likelihood this was a rather substantial meal.

➤**32** It was against the law to bring sick people for healing on the Jewish sabbath (Jesus got in trouble over it, according to Luke 13:14). That's why these people waited almost until sunset before they brought all their sick and demon-filled friends to Jesus. As soon as they could see three stars in the sky they knew it was safe to travel, for a new day had officially begun. Time and again Jesus showed them how silly it was to stretch the law to such superstitious extremes.

➤**33 all the city was gathered together**— Jesus' ministry attracts three kinds of people: those who need help, those who bring others for help, and those who just come "to watch." There were a lot of spectators here but Mark sees them as just so many more people to witness what Jesus was doing.

➤**34** Matthew confirms the success of Jesus' ministry that evening (Matt. 8:16). **and suffered not the devils to speak**—i.e., "refused to allow the demons to speak" (TLB). According to the parallel account in Matthew, Jesus cast out the demons "with a word" (see Matt. 8:16). The incident in the synagogue had been one too many for Jesus (1:23-37). He does not give these demons a chance to say a single word because he is afraid they will identify him. Later he tells the sick people he heals not to say anything about him either (1:44).

## 35-39 JESUS PRAYS IN THE WILDERNESS BEFORE REFUSING AN INVITATION TO RETURN TO CAPERNAUM

➤**35 in the morning**—Jesus began the next stage of his ministry on the first day of the week. **rising up a great while before day**— while it was yet night. **departed into a solitary place, and there prayed**—Jesus is ready to set out on his first assignment. But before doing so, he wanted to spend time with his Father in prayer. On this occasion, as in many others yet to come, Jesus spent time in prayer before taking an important step in his ministry (Luke 5:16; 6:12). It would have been good to hear him talking to God about beginning the work he had been sent to do. He was most likely excited and eager. It would not have sounded anything like the heavy-hearted prayer before he was arrested and killed.

➤**36, 37 And Simon and they that were with him followed after him**—His new companions must have been surprised when they got up to find his bed empty after such a busy evening. They had, in all probability, thought they would let him sleep in after all that excitement. Now they thought they had lost him, so Peter organizes a search party. The Greek word for "followed" (*katadiōkein*—"to track down" or "hunt") suggests that they were worried, and hurried to find him. Since Mark heard about it only from Peter, he tells only Peter's story. Actually everybody was looking for him (see Luke 4:42). Despite their numbers, Jesus probably prayed for quite a while before they found him. **All men seek for thee**—The first place people would have looked was Peter's house. News that a search party had been organized spread like wildfire and before you knew it everybody in town was on the lookout for Jesus.

➤**38 next towns**—The western shore of Galilee was dotted with towns and tiny fishing villages where Jesus felt he must take his message. **therefore came I forth**—i.e., "That is why I have come" (NIV). Compare John 16:28 where Jesus says, "I came forth from the Father." Jesus' sense of mission motivated everything he did (Luke 4:43). It must have been hard to say "no" to the invitation to return to a city where his ministry had been so successful and where he had been so well received. Yet Jesus knew why he had come to earth, and not even the prospect of a popular healing ministry could make him lose that sense of direction.

## 40-45 JESUS HEALS A LEPER
See comments on Matthew 8:1-4.

*Chapter* 2

## 1-12 HEALING A PARALYTIC (See Matt. 9:1-8; Luke 5:17-26.)

According to Matthew 9:1, this is the very next thing Jesus did after he healed the leper (Mark 1:40-45).

**➤1 Capernaum**—The city, located on the northwestern shore of Galilee, became Jesus' adopted home as long as he lived and taught around the sea. Matthew called it Jesus' home town (9:1).

**➤2 many were gathered together**—at Peter's house. He was probably watching from his doorstep or, more likely, trying to find room for everyone, so he was able to give Mark a firsthand account of everything that happened. **he preached the word unto them**—Though Jesus was in the house, there was quite a crowd outside, listening to what he had to say. It's a good thing he didn't go outside to preach to them because the lame man and his friends wouldn't have had the chance to show how much they believed Jesus could heal him. When the man came to Jesus the hard way, through the roof, and left through the door, everybody could see what happened, both inside and out. Luke added a very important detail to his description of the scene when he observed that Jewish religious leaders had come to hear Jesus from all over the country, and as far away as the capital (Luke 5:17). Nothing could speak better of Jesus' expanding influence in Palestine than the fact that these men had come all that way just to hear him.

They came at the right time. Few of Jesus' miracles equal the dramatic way in which the lame man demonstrated his faith, and the decisive manner in which Jesus healed him.

**➤3 four** [men]—Mark is the only writer who reports that it took four men to carry him.

**➤4 they uncovered the roof where he was**—or, "they dug through the clay roof above his head" (TLB). The typical flat terrace roof of that part of the world was made of branches plastered with mud that had to be repaired every fall before the rainy season started. Apparently Peter's roof had to be fixed early that year. Luke (5:19) adds that they took out some tiles. **let down the bed**—The house was probably one large room with a smaller attic accessible from an outside stairway; but unless we knew exactly what it was like and just where Jesus was standing, it would be impossible to say precisely how the men got him to Jesus. The important thing is that they did, and there were plenty of witnesses.

**➤5 When Jesus saw their faith**—Matthew, Mark and Luke all agree that Jesus spoke of *their* faith, not *his*. The four men were not just being nice in carrying their friend to Jesus. They were just as convinced that Jesus could take care of their own sickness and sin, as he could their friend's. We know the lame man had faith because Jesus forgave his sin, but we know his friends also had faith because Jesus tells us they did. He always recognized real faith and never passed it by without pointing it out. **Son, thy sins be forgiven thee**—lit. "your sins are forgiven you." Jesus does not command forgiveness; he announces it. Later the religious leaders present accuse him of giving out something that was not in the power of a man to give. Jesus agrees with them, but goes on to claim that because he is the Son of man he does have the right.

**➤6 certain of the scribes**—These were the men who had come all that distance just to observe Jesus. Even though they were not yet openly hostile they did not have the Spirit to receive what Jesus taught.

**➤7 who can forgive sins but God only?**—They wondered how a man, by all appearances as mortal as they, could presume the authority to forgive sins. God is the only one who can forgive sins. Jesus was either blaspheming or claiming an authority which was rightly his. Of course, Jesus did have the power to forgive sins because it was granted to him by the Father (see 1:10 and John 5:22, 27).

➤8 **immediately**—Mark's favorite means of maintaining the story's rapid action-packed pace is with this expression. Because Jesus knows what the religious men are thinking, he is able to respond without hesitation. **Jesus perceived** [Gk."fully recognized"] **in his spirit**—This spiritual perception was immediate, accurate, and complete. Jesus forgave the man's sin before he healed his body because he anticipated their reaction. Since he knew that they would challenge him for claiming to be able to forgive sins, Jesus was ready for them.

➤9 **Whether is it easier to say to the sick of the palsy, Thy sins be** [are] **forgiven thee; or to say, Arise and take up thy bed, and walk?**—Jesus performed the miracle to demonstrate that forgiveness is as real as healing.

➤10 **The Son of man hath power** [or, authority] **on earth to forgive sins**—God gave Jesus, the Son of man (the first appearance of this title in Mark) the authority on earth to forgive men's sins.

➤11 **take up thy bed** [mat] **and go**—Jesus knew that when the man picked up his mat everybody would see that he had been instantly and completely healed. Those outside who saw him go in through the roof lying on it would now see him coming out through the door with it tucked under his arm.

➤12 **And immediately he arose, took up the bed, and went forth before them all**—What had once been a symbol of his miserable confinement was now a trophy of his total freedom. While the people followed the man with their eyes, their ears must have been ringing with Jesus' words, "I, the Son of man, have authority on earth to forgive sins." Jesus had made his point. **We never saw it on this fashion**—i.e., "We have never seen anything like this!" (NIV). Forgiveness was nothing new to the Jews, but seeing a man like themselves actually forgive sins was a first. Jesus often referred to himself as the "Son of man" (2:28), a messianic title (see Dan. 7:13, 14). At the same time he claimed authority that belonged to God. Those who witnessed what he had just done must have sensed that he was more than

just a man, for they praised God because of what they had seen.

## 13-17 LEVI (MATTHEW) FOLLOWS JESUS AND INVITES HIM TO A BANQUET
See comments on Matthew 9:9-13.

## 18-22 DISCUSSION ON FASTING
See comments on Luke 5:33-39.

## 23-28 EATING GRAIN ON THE SABBATH
See comments on Matthew 12:1-8.

*Chapter* **3**

## 1-12 JESUS HEALS A DEFORMED HAND AND LEAVES TOWN TO AVOID TROUBLE
See comments on Matthew 12:9-21.

## 13-19 JESUS CHOOSES TWELVE COMPANIONS
See comments on Luke 6:12-19.

## 20-30 JESUS ACCUSED OF INSANITY AND DEMON POSSESSION
See comments on Matthew 12:22-37 and Luke 11:21-26.

## 31-35 JESUS' FAMILY LOOKS FOR HIM
See comments on Matthew 12:46-50.

*Chapter* **4**

## 1-9 THE PARABLE OF THE SOWER (See also Matt. 13:3-9; Luke 8:5-8.)
➤1 **he entered into a ship**—Jesus was prepared for the problem of being crowded off the beach. He had anticipated the situation earlier, and had asked for a boat (3:9). Now when he needed it, it was ready.

➤2 **He taught** [Gk. "began to teach"] **them many things by parables**—The use of parables to illustrate one basic idea or lesson was a popular teaching technique in Jesus' day. These parables were usually not like allegories that have many details calling for separate interpretation. Jesus used parables to describe the mysteries of God's kingdom to those who could understand the things of God; to those who could not understand or did not believe in Jesus, the parables were enigmas (see 4:11). But Mark is not the best place to study Jesus' parables since he was writing to men of action who were more interested in what Jesus did than what he said. A bare sample of the stories is recorded by Mark. (More information on the parables of Jesus can be found in C.E.B. Cranfield's *The Gospel According to St. Mark* in The Cambridge Greek Testament Commentary, pp. 148, 149.)

➤**3 Hearken**—Mark is the only one who uses this word at the beginning of Jesus' story about the sower. (It might have had something to do with getting the attention of an audience that was geared for action, by emphasizing the importance of what Jesus said as well as what he did.) **There went out a sower to sow**—The metaphor of a man sowing seed had been popular with teachers since the time of Plato. Jesus' Jewish audience pictured a Palestinian farmer with a bag of seed on his shoulder, scattering it across the freshly cultivated earth.

➤**4 some fell by the way side, and the fowls of the air came and devoured it up**—The path had not been prepared for seeding and so the seed was easy picking for the birds. Even though the Jewish farmer would cultivate his field again to cover the seed, he would not plough up his path.

➤**5 stony ground**—There is at least enough soil to cover the seed, but not much more.

➤**6 withered away**—Shallow seeds will germinate faster, but it takes deep seeds to grow strong plants.

➤**7 some fell among thorns**—This patch of ground had not been weeded well. Because it was not clean, the weeds soon shot past the grain, cut off the sun, and sapped the soil of all its moisture and nutrients. The grain grew, but it was stunted and did not amount to anything (Matt. 13:22). It had been starved out by the weeds.

➤**8 other fell on good ground**—Good soil is soft, deep, and clean. It provides a soft bed, plenty of room for root development and moisture storage, and a wholesome environment that is free from unwanted weeds that drain its richness. The yield of a crop depends on the extent to which its soil has these qualities.

➤**9 let him hear**—Jesus' sharp words reminded them that this was more than just a story. It's easy to get caught up in the excitement of how something is being taught without realizing that it actually applies to you.

**10-20 QUESTIONS AND ANSWERS ABOUT THE PARABLE OF THE SOWER**

➤**10 And when he was alone, they that were about him** [around him—i.e., in his circle] **with the twelve**—Besides the twelve there was another group of followers who stayed closer to Jesus than the rest of the crowd. He includes them in this particular lesson as well. **asked of him the parable**—The Greek is plural, "parables." This suggests that there were other parables that Jesus told at the same time, but that the parable of the sower was central to the rest and that is why Mark chose to record only it.

➤**11, 12 the mystery of the kingdom of God**—God's kingdom is a mystery. The Greek word for "mystery" indicates a secret revealed to the initiates (i.e., those in the inner circle) and, at the same time, an enigma to those outside the circle. Jesus was revealing the secrets of God's kingdom to his disciples and to the believers (see Matt. 13:10-17).

➤**13 Know ye not this parable?**—The Greek negative (*ouk*) implied very strongly that they did not understand the parable, and that Jesus knew it. Jesus explained this parable so that his disciples would be able to interpret the rest of his parables. Most commentators think he was not being critical of his disciples here, but merely wanted to be sure they listened to his explanation so that they would know how to understand his other parables. Jesus was not content just to have them understand this one parable of the sower. He wanted them to be capable of handling his teaching method competently.

➤**14 The sower soweth the word**—Luke says, "the seed is the word of God" (8:11). The real question is, "Who is the sower?" According to Matthew 13:37, the Son of man, Jesus, is the sower. It is obvious that right in this situation and as long as he was on earth, Jesus was a sower spreading God's message, but it is also clear that the whole point of his teaching was to train his disciples to be sowers as well, in spreading God's message to other men. In this parable it is the same sower and the same seed from start to finish. But it is what the sower does with the seed, and what happens to it as a result, that makes the story important. The whole point is to examine the various kinds of soil in which a person can plant.

These different soils represent, of course, different types of human beings. In one sense, it might be more appropriate to call this "the parable of the soils" rather than "the parable of the sower." Some people have called it "the Parable of Parables" because it describes how men will react to all of Jesus' teachings.

►**15 these are they by the way side**—See Matthew 13:19. The path through the field was beaten rock hard by the traffic of men and animals. It is a good picture of how calloused some men become by the traffic of life, so that they have become totally insensitive to what God wants to say to them. Nothing sinks in. They cannot understand God's word when it comes to them, and Satan whisks it away as fast as a bird who spots a seed lying on a beaten path. Unfortunately, a lot of people are in this category.

►**16, 17 stony ground**—This soil represents men who receive God's Word eagerly, but superficially. They get all excited about him until the first little test or bit of ridicule comes along. Then, when the heat is on, they cannot take it. They lose all their enthusiasm and are a total loss for God. These people are a big disappointment to those who have planted the seed and expected so much from them because of their fast start.

►**18, 19 among thorns**—Thorns, like weeds, rob the plant of its nourishment; they take its moisture and sunlight—not totally, but enough to choke its growth and make it unfruitful. The thorns in our lives (i.e., **the cares of this world, and the deceitfulness of riches, and the lusts of other things entering in**) can choke the growth of the word in us because they rob us of our spiritual nourishment. And although we may not die spiritually, we will never produce fruit for God.

►**20 good ground**—The soft, sensitive person who lets God's word work itself deep into every area of his life and gets rid of anything that might crowd God out of his life is the person who will enjoy a fruitful Christian experience, and his fruitfulness will be in direct proportion to his ability to keep the soil of his soul in this kind of shape.

## 21-25 WHY JESUS USED THE PARABLE METHOD (See Luke 8:16 and Matthew 5:15.)

►**22 For there is nothing hid, which shall not be manifested**—See comments on Matthew 10:26, 27. Jesus seems to suggest here that what he has told them in private they must soon preach in public.

►**23 If any man have ears to hear, let him hear**—This is the second time Jesus uses this attention-getter in the same chapter (see 4:9).

►**24 Take heed what ye hear**—He not only wants them to be careful *what* they listen to, but also *how* they listen (according to Luke 8:18). **with what measure ye mete, it shall be measured to you**—See comments on Matthew 7:2.

## 26-29 THE PARABLE OF HOW SEED GROWS BY ITSELF

Mark is the only NT writer who records this particular parable. Jesus was elaborating on the parable of the sower in order to illustrate the fact that God's law for spiritual growth functions like God's law for natural growth. He wanted to show the gradual growth of God's word in a human life until it finally yields the fruit God is looking for.

►**26, 27 So is the kingdom of God, as if a man should cast seed in the ground; and should sleep, and rise night and day**—The farmer went about his daily business and let nature take its course. Nothing he could do would help the seeds grow. He knew that it was only the soil that made the seeds grow (4:28).

►**28 For the earth bringeth forth fruit of herself**—lit. "the earth bears fruit automatically," **first the blade** [or, sprout], **then the ear** [better, the head—the image is wheat, not corn], **after that the full corn** [head]—What a wonderful picture of the automatic, spontaneous growth that occurs in the life of a healthy Christian.

►**29 the harvest is come**—Jesus' story moves to a beautiful climax as he points to God's final harvest when his church will be gathered up to heaven. This is the ultimate end of the successful planting of God's Word in many believers' hearts.

## 30-32 THE PARABLE OF THE MUSTARD SEED

See comments on Matthew 13:31.

## 33, 34 A STATEMENT ON JESUS' USE OF PARABLES

►**33 many such parables**—Mark makes clear that he has only given a sample of Jesus' parables here. Most, if not all, of the rest are recorded in Matthew 13.

➤**34 without a parable spake he not**—See Matthew 13:34. **he expounded**—lit. "he kept on explaining" or, he continued to unravel the meaning. See comment on 4:22. Jesus' explanations must have shattered many of the current concepts and popular theories on what the kingdom of God actually was.

## 35-41 JESUS CROSSES THE SEA OF GALILEE

Mark follows up this account of the parable Jesus told with a series of true stories of Jesus in action. Matthew (8:23-34) and Luke (8:22-39) both give parallel accounts of the storm at sea as well as the healing of the demon-possessed man on the other shore (ch. 5), but Mark is the only one of the three to pinpoint exactly when the incident occurred.

➤**35 When the even[ing] was come**—Mark reveals that the day Jesus told the parable of the sower was the day of the storm. It must have only been late afternoon when they left because when Jesus came back across the lake later the same day, there was still a crowd waiting for him (5:21). **Let us pass over unto the other side**—On the eastern shore Jesus confronts a desperate case of demon possession, but releases the man and leaves him there to share what God has done for him with his own people.

➤**36 they took him even [just] as he was in the ship**—By "even [just] as he was" we understand that he never left the boat he had been teaching in all day (4:1), but headed straight across the lake. **there were also with him other little ships**—They were undoubtedly packed with passengers who wanted to go along with Jesus.

➤**37 there arose a great storm of wind**— Such sudden squalls are common on the Sea of Galilee. The lake is like a deep basin formed by high eastern mountain ranges and the western hills with their narrow gorges through which the wind whistles down out across the lake, whipping the waves into a storm with little warning. **waves beat [were breaking] into the ship**—The Greek imperfect tense indicates that they "kept on breaking" over the ship; it was a repeated action. This was no small storm, and it showed no signs of letting up. **so that it was now full**—Matthew, who was in the boat, says that "the ship was covered with the waves" (8:24).

➤**38 he was . . . asleep on a pillow**—This is the only time in the entire Bible we ever read of Jesus sleeping. His pillow was either a special headrest that was a part of the boat itself, or else a cushion that had been provided. Mark is the only writer who mentions it, but the picture of Jesus sleeping on a pillow graphically depicts his total humanity. He was exhausted after teaching all day from the same cramped boat in which he now tries to make himself comfortable enough to catch a little sleep. He falls so sound asleep that even the storm cannot stir him. **Master, carest thou not that we perish?**—i.e., "don't you even care that we are all about to drown?" (TLB). When men who had spent their whole lives on the water talked about drowning, it must have been serious. They were so scared they forgot all about who was with them in the boat, and all the amazing things they had seen him do. They could think of only one thing—their own safety. When they wake Jesus up it is more to criticize him for sleeping than to call on him for help.

➤**39 Peace, be still**—lit. "be muzzled." This is the same verb Jesus used when he told the demon to be quiet (1:25). **the wind ceased, and there was a great calm**—The high waves dropped instantly and the sea was as smooth as glass. There was not a breath of wind. It wouldn't have been enough just to turn off the wind since a rough sea would take quite a while to settle down. That is why Jesus commanded both the wind and the sea to obey him. One minute Jesus was curled up on a cushion sleeping—the perfect picture of humanity. The next minute he was ordering the elements to obey him with all the divine authority of the One who made them.

➤**40** Jesus did not try to deal with the disciples' fear while the storm is still going on. He stopped the storm, which was the reason they were afraid, and then dealt with the real root of their fear, their faith.

➤**41 What manner [kind] of man is this, that even the wind and the sea obey him?**— They all knew the Psalms that spoke of Yahweh's majestic mastery of the elements (see Ps. 89:9; 93:4), but right there in the boat with them was a man, just like them, who had just demonstrated the same power, and with only a few words. They were amazed beyond words that someone who had been so sound asleep could so quickly and so quietly take charge and command calm. They asked the only possible question that could come to their minds, "What kind of man is this?" It is a question that men are still asking today.

Chapter **5**

## 1-20 JESUS CURES A DEMON POSSESSED MAN

**➤1 they came over unto the other side of the sea, into the country of the Gadarenes**—Some ancient manuscripts read "Gadarenes," others "Gergesenes," but the best authorities read "Gerasenes." Jesus' arrival on the other side marks a break in his story-style teaching, and the beginning of a series of healings. His first healing-miracle takes place somewhere in the neighborhood of Gerasa, although there is some confusion in the early manuscripts as to the exact location. Most scholars think that Mark identified "the other side" as the home country of the Gerasenes but that his early readers thought he meant Gerasa. Gerasa was a well-known town thirty miles from the lake, but Jesus couldn't possibly have done everything he did on this particular day if that was where he went. Most likely the name mentioned in Mark's Greek manuscript was actually a place near the lake now known as Khersa.

**➤2 there met him . . . a man with an unclean spirit**—i.e., "a demon-possessed man" (TLB). Matthew says there were two men who came out to meet Jesus (8:28). This must represent a variation between those who reported the incident since it is difficult to imagine two separate episodes so similar in every detail. Mark seems to take a special interest in the whole affair since he goes to great lengths in describing the man (1-10), the herd of hogs (11-13), the townspeople (14-17), and the released victim again (18-20).

**➤3** This man lived among **the tombs.** Luke says he was "homeless and naked" (8:27, TLB). The gravestones were actually rocky caves carved out of the countryside that were often used by men like himself for shelters or hideouts (Luke 8:26).

**➤4 he had been often bound with fetters and chains**—Matthew says that the men "were

so violent that no one could pass that way" (8:28, NIV), while Luke writes that the demon often "took control of the man so that even when shackled with chains he simply broke them and rushed into the desert" (8:29, TLB).

**➤5** The terror that the man created in public was nothing compared to the personal torture he suffered. The man lived in misery and tried to get rid of the demons by cutting himself.

**➤6 he ran and worshipped him**—or, paid homage to him. This man is attracted to Jesus, not out of eagerness, but out of compulsion. The demons know that they are subject to Jesus and come directly, but unwillingly, to be expelled from the man.

**➤7 What have I to do with thee**—lit., "what to me and to you." This is a common idiom in the NT that was carried over from the OT; it means "what do you and I have in common?" The demons live in constant dread of the day when Jesus will punish them. They sense his presence, and as soon as they see him they are afraid that the time of their judgment has come. **Jesus, thou Son of the most high God**—In addressing Jesus, the demon uses a title for God that was commonly used by Gentiles to express the superiority of the one true God over all gods. (The expression appears in Gen. 14:18; Isa. 14:14; Acts 16:17.)

**➤9 What is thy name?**—There are several possible reasons why Jesus asked the man for his name. Perhaps he wanted him to admit who it was that actually had control of him. It was a traditional belief that if you knew the name of the demon you could have power over it. It has also been suggested that he might have wanted the man to identify his own personality, something that had been obscured by the presence of the demon. **My name is Legion: for we are many**—Jesus' reason for asking the question is now made clear. There is more than one demon in the man and at his word they must identify themselves. The Jews believed that a man usually had only one demon at a time. Mary Magdalene was possessed by seven, but some people felt that since the number "seven" represented completion in Jewish numerology, this simply meant she was totally demon-possessed. The man standing before Jesus is possessed by a whole army of demons and is completely controlled by Satan. Their name comes from the Roman term for a company of soldiers numbering six thousand men. Whether or not this is to be taken literally, we do know that there were enough demons in the man to enter two thousand pigs and kill them all (5:13).

➤**10 he besought him**—lit., "he kept on begging him." There is one demon who speaks for the rest. They make the request because they have something in mind (see 1:12).

➤**11 nigh** [near] **unto the mountains a great herd of swine**—Some discussion has centered on the matter of whether these pigs were owned by Jews or Gentiles. On one hand, one would think the people here were Jews since Jesus came as their Messiah and only ministered to Gentiles as he encountered them incidentally. On the other hand, the pig was an unclean animal according to Jewish law. So it is much more likely that these people were Gentiles in the hog industry. The east side of Galilee, around Decapolis ("Ten Cities") was predominantly Gentile.

➤**12 Send us into the swine**—Since they knew they must be expelled, the demons probably thought they would at least turn the local people against Jesus by getting him blamed for destroying their property.

➤**13 Jesus gave them leave**—According to Matthew, all he said was "Go" (8:32). If Jews owned the pigs, they were involved in an illegal business. If Gentiles owned them, they were insulting the national Jewish religion by raising them. Either way, Jesus shows that his priority is people, not property. By actually seeing the demons going down the hill inside the hogs, the man's faith in what Jesus had done would be dramatically strengthened. If Jesus had to destroy animals in order to save a human life, there was really no question but that he would do it. **the herd . . . about two thousand**—of them. Mark is the only gospel writer to give an actual figure.

➤**14 they that fed the swine fled, and told it in the city,**—Matthew says they told the whole story of what had happened wherever they went (8:33). **And they went out to see**—If they didn't believe what the herdsmen said, they could soon see for themselves what Jesus had done. The pigs were gone and the man was standing quietly with Jesus.

➤**15 they come to Jesus**—Matthew says, "Behold, the whole city came out to meet Jesus" (8:34). The man was **sitting, and clothed, and in his right mind**—What a contrast to the naked terror they were used to seeing! Jesus made him a new man, physically, mentally and spiritually. Luke is the one who tells us that when they first saw the man who had been naked (8:27), **they were afraid**—This was not just surprise, or even shock, at what Jesus had done. It was a dark fear of the powerful forces they sensed had been unleashed.

➤**17 And they began to pray** [plead with] **him to depart out of their coasts**—It seems quite clear that it was not only the pig farmers who wanted him to leave. Luke says that "everyone begged Jesus to go away" because a "deep wave of fear had swept over them" (8:37, TLB). Although the people certainly must have been angry at the loss of the hogs, they were too scared to order him off their property so they begged him to leave.

➤**18 he that had been possessed with the devil** [demon] **prayed** [begged] **him that he might be with him**—It was only natural that the man would want to stay close to the one who had set him free from such a frightening experience. While everyone else wanted Jesus to get as far away as possible, the healed man wanted to be as close to Jesus as he could.

➤**19 Jesus suffered him not**—i.e., Jesus did not allow him. Jesus knew that the man had a job to do right in his own country that would have been impossible for Jesus himself to accomplish. Certainly the man would have been more comfortable with Jesus, but Jesus wanted him to stay at home because he would become an excellent witness among those who had known him as a demoniac.

➤**20 he . . . began to publish** [proclaim] **in Decapolis how** [what] **great things Jesus had done for him**—Jesus had only told him to go home to his friends and tell them what God had done for him, but he was not content to stop there. He set out for the ten Greek cities (all but one of them east of the lake) and told the good news there. **all men did marvel**—There is no way of knowing the tremendous impact his testimony must have made on the region, but we can be sure that there were some who did more than merely marvel, and who actually committed their lives to the One who had delivered this man from demons.

## 21-43 JAIRUS' DAUGHTER IS RAISED FROM THE DEAD AND A WOMAN WITH A HEMORRHAGE IS HEALED

Mark's next vivid account is actually a miracle within a miracle as Jesus demonstrates his power over death as well as disease.

➤**21 And when Jesus was passed over again by ship unto the other side**—Leaving the Gadarene country he returned to the western shore, landing near Capernaum. **much people gathered unto him**—Luke says they "gladly received him: for they were all waiting for him" (8:40). Even though it must have been late, what they had heard earlier in the day was so fresh and new that when Jesus left late in the afternoon to cross the lake, many of them had stayed around the beach with the hope that he would come back that way.

➤**22 one of the rulers of the synagogue**—A ruler of the synagogue was a lay official who supervised administrative duties in the synagogue and oversaw the worship. It would seem, from the gospel accounts, that most of the rulers did not receive Jesus (John 7:48); but, in fact, many did believe in him (John 12:42). However, they would not confess their belief. Jairus was among the minority who expressed their faith openly. It appears from what Mark says that Jairus was one of those who had been waiting on the shore for Jesus to come back. When he arrived the religious leader stepped out of the crowd to ask him for help. **Jairus by name**—This is the same as the OT name, "Jair" (Num. 32:41; Judg. 10:3). **he fell at his feet**—Matthew 9:18 simply says he "worshipped him," but Mark paints the picture more precisely, and for a religious ruler this was a humbling experience.

➤**23 besought him greatly**—Luke, with typical physician's precision, reports that this was the man's only daughter, and that she was twelve years old, almost a young woman by now (8:42). **at the point of death**—Matthew 9:18 abbreviates his story by saying that the man came to Jesus and told him his daughter was dead, when in fact Jairus did not find this out until after Jesus healed the woman in the crowd (5:28). **come and lay thy hands on her**—Here was a man who was in charge of the business end of the Jewish synagogue, asking Jesus to come and heal his daughter. Most of the members of his class expressed their disapproval of Jesus, but this man was desperate. By asking Jesus to place his hands on his daughter he was recognizing Jesus' ability to heal her, for that was a sign traditionally reserved for those who had blessings to bestow or commissions to grant to others.

➤**24 thronged him**—The crowd around Jesus was so thick that Luke says that the crowd lit., "stifled" or "choked" him. The NIV says, "almost crushed him."

➤**25 a certain woman, which had an issue [flow] of blood twelve years**—Her problem was likely associated with an irregular menstrual flow, which meant according to Jewish law that she would have been considered unclean (Lev. 15:25-30).

➤**26 And had suffered many things of many physicians**—This does not necessarily mean she was abused by the doctors, but simply that the endless number of assorted treatments over the years had been almost more than she could take. It was not the treatments themselves, but rather how many of them, and how costly they had been, that caused the suffering. **had spent all that she had and was nothing bettered, but rather grew worse**—Doctor Luke says that his colleagues "could find no cure" (8:43, TLB). She was in a very sad condition, a condition that epitomizes the fallen state of man and the hopelessness of all human remedies for spiritual maladies.

➤**27 she had heard of Jesus**—She had tried everywhere and everyone else and had all but given up hope when the reports of people who had been healed by Jesus gave her new confidence to try him. If this man had been so ready to help others, he could hardly refuse someone in her condition. **came in the press [crowd] behind**—Though she knew what she needed, she was still hesitant. Perhaps it was the nature of her problems or the presence of so many people that made her afraid to contact him. **and touched his garment**—The woman knew that the law said anyone she touched would be made unclean like herself (Lev. 15:27). That may be why she decided to sneak up behind Jesus. However, something told her that if she could be made clean by touching him, there was no way he would be made unclean by the same touch. He must be above such laws. Later the apostles follow a similar pattern in healing men whose faith is expressed through indirect contact with them (Acts 5:15; 19:12).

➤**28 If I may touch but his clothes, I shall be whole**—i.e., I shall be healed. Her faith in him is so strong that she believes she will be healed if she can contact Christ.

➤**29 And straightway** [immediately] **the fountain of her blood was dried up**—a good, literal rendering; it indicates that Jesus' healing took care of the very source of her disease. Not only did the bleeding stop instantly (Luke 8:44), but the healing was so thorough that **she felt in her body that she was healed.** (The Greek word for "felt" means "knew experientially.")

➤**30 Jesus, immediately knowing in himself that virtue** [power] **had gone out of him**—Unlike the prophets and apostles who used God's power to do supernatural things, Jesus' power came right from inside himself because he was God, and he knew the minute any of that power had been unleashed. **turned . . . and said**—Jesus turned around, not to criticize the person for what she had done, but to confront her with who he is.

➤**31 his disciples said unto him**—Luke says (8:45) that everyone denied touching him, and then Peter called Christ's attention to the crowd that was packed around him. **Who touched me?**—Jesus' question seems unreasonable with so many people around, but he has in mind a specific person who has deliberately touched him, not the many who have accidentally bumped into him in the normal pressure of the crowd. That person's touch had made contact with his body in a way that none of these others had, even though she actually only touched the edge of his robe (Luke 8:44). His awesome power passed through that point of contact like electricity through a live circuit, and he wanted to know whose faith was responsible for drawing it from him.

➤**32 he looked round about** [kept looking around] **to see her who had done this thing**—He is not looking for a confession from a culprit in order to punish her. He is looking for a confession from a person whose faith had released his power. Jesus has no personal need to hear the confession, but he wants the person to confirm in her own mind who it is that has healed her, and he wants the people to hear

again from someone who has felt the healing touch of his power. (Her testimony may have been just what Jairus needed to give him the faith to trust Jesus even after he discovered that his daughter was dead.)

➤**33 the woman fearing and trembling, knowing what was done in her, came and fell down before him**—She was just as embarrassed as anyone who is about to be publicly exposed, but she was ready to let her story speak for itself. **and told him all the truth**—Luke says she also told him "why she had touched him" (8:47, TLB). The details of her case were difficult to talk about in public, but Jesus wanted the crowd to realize that her case was incurable until faith in his power prompted a quick and complete cure.

➤**34** Her reluctance to reveal herself suggests a criminal complex. Jesus assured her that she did not steal the cure by sneaking up on him. When he exposed her, he placed his authoritative seal of approval on what had happened and sent her home with the peace and confidence that he had healed her and that she stood healed for all time. The Greek verb for **hath made thee whole**—better rendered as "has healed" or "has delivered"—is in the perfect tense, which indicates the present, durative effect of a completed action. The parting word, "go in peace," was an OT expression that meant more than peace of mind, but implied the kind of peace that comes from being right with God (Judg. 18:6; 1 Sam. 1:17; 2 Sam. 15:9). This was more than a casual good-bye. Jesus actually granted her God's peace, and declared her to be in right standing with God. (Calvin used this passage to show that belief in relics is little more than superstition. The woman was healed by placing her faith in Jesus, not by placing her hand on his clothes.)

➤**35 Thy daughter is dead; why troublest thou the Master** [Teacher] **any further?**—The messengers' advice is given on the assumption that death is too big for even Jesus.

➤**36 Be not afraid**—present imperative in Greek—"Stop fearing." **only believe**—present imperative in Greek—"keep believing." Jesus builds trust in himself by identifying with the sudden fear that struck the man at the news of his daughter's death. He first recognizes the man's feelings and then goes on to reassure him that he is able to handle this new problem equally well. How clearly we see Jesus' sensitivity to human feelings in this situation! Here is the One who understands our weaknesses (Heb. 4:15) because he went through every human experience we ever face.

➤**37 Peter, and James, and John**—These three men became known as the "inner circle." Although this is the first time Jesus specifically singles them out, they have been together before (see comment on 1:29). Later they will accompany him up the mount of his transfiguration (9:2) and into the Garden of Gethsemane (14:33). These are the men who would become prominent leaders in the early church.

➤**38 seeth the tumult, and them that wept and wailed greatly**—Matthew says that "noisy crowds and funeral music" (9:23, TLB) greeted Jesus as he stepped in the door. The Jews hired professional mourners and flutists before a person died, so that as soon as he did die they would be ready with wails and screams that helped to express the grief the family felt. Most of the professional mourners were women, and Matthew's description leads us to believe they were present here. Josephus notes that "even the poorest in Israel provide no fewer than two flutists and one female mourner."

➤**39 the damsel is not dead, but sleepeth**—There has been considerable discussion as to what Jesus really meant when he said the girl was only asleep. Some suggest she had been dead for such a short time that it almost seemed like she had only gone to sleep, and so Jesus chose a more soothing word to describe the cruel reality which confronted them. The Greeks, Romans, and even the Jews all substituted "sleep" for "death" whenever they wanted to soften its harshness and de-emphasize its finality. Jesus used the euphemism of sleep when speaking of Lazarus's death (John 11:11-14) and Paul used this expression in the Greek of 1 Thessalonians 4:13, 14. Others say that since Matthew and Luke wrote about this incident much later than Mark, their accounts of her death were probably inaccurate, and in fact the girl was only asleep, as Jesus says here. However, Mark's next statement disproves all these theories. The people's derision when Jesus suggested she was sleeping says only too well that they knew the girl was dead.

➤**40 they laughed him to scorn**—or, they ridiculed him. Luke says they scoffed because they all knew she was dead (8:53). This also meant there were a lot of people who could give evidence later that the girl was actually dead before Jesus got there. **When he had put them all out**—The Greek suggests that he did this very forcefully. He had the mourners and all those who were making the racket "put out." Jesus only wanted people who were directly involved, and the three witnesses he had brought, to be there in the room. That meant the parents, and Peter, James, and John. Six people, including Jesus, witnessed the event.

➤**41 took the damsel by the hand**—This is the same way Jesus raised Peter's sick mother-in-law (1:21). **and said unto her, Talitha cumi**—Mark quotes Jesus' exact Aramaic words, rather than their Greek translation, the language he was writing in. The Aramaic words mean, "Little girl, I say to you, Arise." Jesus spoke Aramaic (as his mother tongue), Greek (as that was the lingua franca, the common language of his times), and Hebrew (the language of the OT—used in the synagogues).

➤**42 the damsel arose, and walked**—Mark uses a different word for "girl" here than the one he has used in 39, 40; here and in 1:41 the word means "little girl." The observation that she walked around must have come from Peter's eyewitness report to Mark.

➤**43 he charged them straitly** [strictly] **that no man should know it**—The only imaginable reason why Jesus would have made such a request was to prevent a frenzied public reaction to his superhuman ability. He came with a powerful message that he did not want lost in the drama and spectacle of what he did to demonstrate it. **and commanded that something should be given her to eat**—Jesus' final touch proves beyond question that the girl is not only alive, but perfectly healthy. Mark has now presented Jesus as master over death as well as disease.

*Chapter* **6**

1-6 JESUS REJECTED AT NAZARETH
See comments on Luke 4:16-30.

## 7-13 THE DISCIPLES SENT ON A MISSION

See comments on Matt. 10:1; 5:15.

## 14-29 HEROD'S REACTION TO JOHN THE BAPTIST. THE ACCOUNT OF JOHN'S IMPRISONMENT AND DEATH

➤**14 king Herod**—This is Herod Antipas, one of the three sons of Herod the Great. It was Antipas's brother, Archelaus, who succeeded his father as King of Judea (Matt. 2:22), while Antipas became the Ethnarch (ruler of one fourth) of Galilee and Perea. Antipas ruled the region from 4 B.C. to A.D. 39. **for his name was spread abroad**—Jesus' fame had reached as far south as the court of Antipas, son of the unpopular king who had attempted to kill Jesus when he was a baby. **That John the Baptist was risen from the dead**—John's murder bothered Herod so much that he was convinced Jesus was actually John come back from the dead to haunt him. There were probably others who had the same guilty suspicions about Jesus.

➤**15 Others said, That it is Elias** [Elijah]—See comments on Matthew 16:14. Elijah was one of the Jews' most celebrated prophets.

➤**16 Herod . . . said, It is John**—Even though he was the one who had killed John, Herod was still convinced that this man was John, who had been brought back to life because of his innocence.

➤**17 John . . . in prison**—John was kept in the castle at Machaerus, a combination palace, fortress and prison near the southern tip of Herod's territory (Josephus's *Antiquities,* 18.5.2). **for Herodias' sake, his brother Philip's wife**—This is not the first time Herodias had ignored Jewish laws. Her original husband was also her uncle. Herodias was the granddaughter of King Herod, father of both Philip and Antipas, her father's brothers. Philip was not the brother of Herod the Great mentioned in Luke 3:1, but his disinherited son, Herod Philip. Antipas was apparently not content with seeing his half-brother lose his share of the inheritance. He decided to take Philip's wife as well. Though already married to the daughter of Aretas, King of Arabia, he agreed to get rid of her if Herodias would come and live with him (Josephus's *Antiquities,* 18.5.1).

Aretas eventually defeated Antipas in battle in A.D. 36, some time after John's death, but tradition has it that the Jews considered the defeat a divine punishment for his murder.

➤**18 For John had said unto Herod, It is not lawful for thee to have thy brother's wife**—John spoke out against a very tangled family situation. The marriage was wrong in the first place because Herod's wife and Herodias's husband were both alive. Besides that, Herodias was the niece of the man she was now living with, since she was the daughter of Aristobulus, Antipas's half-brother (Josephus's *Antiquities,* 18.5.4). Therefore, according to Jewish law, she was outside the legal limit of blood-relationship marriages (Lev. 20:21).

➤**19 Therefore Herodias had a quarrel against him** [or, "had a grudge against him," NASB] **and would have killed him**—Mark's account makes it unmistakably clear that this was her intention. Her pride would not even allow her to speak to him, much less to argue about the matter. She planned to take care of John in her own way and her own time.

➤**20 Herod feared John**—but John obviously wasn't afraid of Herod or he wouldn't have spoken out as he did. **knowing that he was a just man and an holy** [man]—Evil men often recognize the goodness of holy men, though they themselves will not repent of their evil. **observed him**—is better translated as "protected him" (NIV) or "kept him safe" (NASB). He was protecting John against Herodias, who was looking for an opportunity to do away with him. **and when he heard him, he did many things**—The statement "he did many things" is found in several good manuscripts, but the earliest manuscripts read, "he was very perplexed" (or, "he was very disturbed"). What John had to say disturbed Herod's conscience by exposing the conflict between his moral principles and his personal life. He was torn between John's message and a passion for Herodias (Swift). Mark is the only writer who notes that in spite of how much John's message bothered Herod, Herod still **heard him gladly.** There could hardly be a stronger statement of the powerful influence that Herodias must have held over this man. (Cf. Herodias's influence over Herod to Jezebel's control over Ahab.)

➤**21 on his** [Herod's] **birthday**—The graphic detail of this wild celebration only heightens the drama of the story's tragic climax.

➤**22 the daughter of the said Herodias**—i.e., the daughter of Herodias herself (a reading found in several ancient manuscripts). But other very ancient manuscripts read, "his daughter Herodias" (i.e., Herod's daughter). Josephus identifies her as "Salome" (*Antiquities,* 18.5.4). In all probability her dance was a degrading sexual display in front of all these men.

➤**23 he sware unto her**—People usually live to regret the rash promises they make when they let passion and pleasure rule their lives for even a moment.

➤**24** Women who have abandoned all moral principles can be even more bold and more brutal than men. John's faithful devotion to God may have reminded Herodias of her own unfaithfulness, and she could not enjoy her promiscuity until he was gone; so she jumped at the chance to get rid of him.

➤**25 I will**—i.e., I want. She does not say, "My mother wants . . ." What her mother wanted, she wanted as well.

➤**26 the king was exceeding sorry**—All he could think of was the trap he had finally fallen into after having fought so long to keep this man he liked and who spoke with such powerful truth out of the hands of his vicious wife. **yet for his oath's sake**—Because he had made a rash promise in front of his friends, Herod was willing to commit a worse crime in order to save face, rather than admit he was wrong. Often the fear of embarassment prevents us from making wrong things right as soon as they happen, and makes us do things that are even worse just to cover up.

➤**27 the king sent an executioner**—Mark uses a Roman military term for "executioner," which leads us to assume that the man was a member of the Imperial Guard. **he went and beheaded him in the prison**—John faced a cold-blooded death alone in the same dark room where he had lived for over twelve months. His consolation was the confidence that he had been faithful to his ministry to the end.

➤**28** Herodias did not raise a finger in the whole gruesome affair she had set in motion.

We are not told whether she even looked at the evidence of her cruel plot once it was carried out, and it is difficult to imagine the reaction of such a woman to the repulsive sight of something she herself had ordered.

➤**29 his disciples . . . came and took up his corpse, and laid it in a tomb**—Matthew adds that they "went and told Jesus" (14:12). If there was any rivalry between the disciples of Jesus and the disciples of John it was now over. Though they may have regretted that Jesus hadn't intervened on John's behalf, his disciples were like orphans who, from now on, would be joining Jesus. His response to the news is not recorded, but if he cried at Lazarus's graveside we can only imagine how John's death affected him.

30-44 FIVE THOUSAND MEN EAT A MIRACLE MEAL (See Matt. 14:13-21; Luke 9:10-17; John 6:1-15.)

The feeding of the five thousand is the first event recorded by all four gospel writers. Here, for the first time, all the four streams of the sacred text run parallel.

➤**30 the apostles gathered themselves together**—It is assumed that they met Jesus at Capernaum after their preaching tour (6:7-13). This is the only time Mark refers to Jesus' twelve companions as apostles. (The word "apostles" appears in 3:14 in some very ancient manuscripts.) An apostle is one who is sent out with a special commission—from the Greek word *apostellō* ("to send from").

➤**31 Come . . . into a desert place, and rest awhile**—There are several possible reasons why Jesus wanted to get away. Matthew says that as soon as he heard the news of John's death he went off by himself in a boat (14:13). The increased pressure of public life along with the mounting opposition to his ministry were no doubt secondary to his desire to be alone after the death of a friend. The successful report of his disciples was another good reason for retreating in order to allow them time to share their experiences and reevaluate their ministry. He must have been just as anxious to hear these reports as he was when he listened with such excitement to the stories of the seventy men he sent out later (Luke 10:17-22). After the emotional strain of a long tour, and now the sad news of John's death, he knew that they all needed a good rest.

➤**32 And they departed into a desert place by ship privately**—Luke and John identified where they went more precisely. John, who wrote about the incident much later, and to people who weren't as familiar with the details of Jesus' life as those who read the other accounts, added that they crossed the Sea of Galilee in order to get away (John 6:1). Luke notes that Jesus "withdrew privately to a city called Bethsaida" (9:10, NASB). There was a Bethsaida on the western shore (Matt. 11:21), but this Bethsaida lay on the northeastern side, close to the place where the Jordan River empties into the lake. It offered the added security of being in Gaulonitis, which was under the administration of Philip the Tetrarch (see Luke 3:1 and Josephus's *Antiquities,* 18.2.1), and therefore outside the control of Herod Antipas, the man who had just killed John.

➤**33 the people . . . ran afoot . . . and outwent them**—i.e., got there before them. The land route meant circling the lake and crossing the river at one of the many fords. Those who went on foot actually made it faster than the disciples did by water. Mark's account sounds as authentic as John's eyewitness report. John adds that Jesus actually took his disciples "up on a mountainside" (6:3, NIV) and sat them on the grassy slopes, but it was not long before he "saw a great crowd coming toward him" (6:5, NIV). His description helps to identify the place as the green tableland of hills on the eastern shore.

➤**34 Jesus . . . saw much people and was moved with compassion toward them, because they were as sheep not having a shepherd**—As soon as he saw them Jesus was ready to give up his privacy and needed rest in order to minister to their needs. John gives a clue as to why the crowds were unusually heavy at this time when he indicates that many of them were on their way to Jerusalem for the annual Passover feast (6:4). On their way to the festival they followed Jesus, but they must have left him soon after because, with the threat of death at the hands of the city's religious leaders, Jesus didn't go to Jerusalem that year (John 7:1). Yet while the people were with him, he cared for them as a shepherd does for his sheep. Specifically, he taught them—for in

teaching them he fed them and nourished them with the spiritual food they desperately needed.

➤**35 And when the day was now far spent**—i.e., late in the day. Matthew (14:15) and Luke (9:12) both agree about the time of day. This is the only one of Jesus' miracles that is recorded by all four of his reporters (Matt. 14:13-21; Luke 9:1-17; John 6:1-15).

➤**36 Send them away, that they may go . . . buy themselves bread**—According to John 6:5, 6, Jesus exposed the weakness of the disciples' suggestion by asking Philip where he could buy enough bread for the crowd. Philip's reply that it would take a great deal of money to feed so many pointed out a double problem. There was neither enough food available in the immediate area nor the funds to finance it, if it was. John adds that Jesus was just testing Philip and that he already knew what he was going to do.

➤**37 Give ye them to eat**—or, You (emphatic) feed them. The Greek could also be rendered, "You feed them yourselves." The order was designed to help them realize that what he was about to do was too big for them. **two hundred pennyworth**—Greek, two hundred denarii. John says Philip estimated it would take two hundred denarii, which amounted to a full year's salary since one denarius was an average day's pay.

➤**38 Five [loaves], and two fishes**—John adds that the loaves were "barley" (6:8, 9). What an embarassment to have to report back to Jesus that all they could get out of 5,000 men was one boy's lunch!

➤**39 make all sit down . . . upon the green grass**—As soon as he heard about the boy's lunch he called for the boy and had the people sit down on the grass. Mark is the only one to observe that the grass was "green" but it must have been a prominent feature of the landscape since John also observes the grassy slopes (6:10). John's observation can be translated literally from the Greek, "there was a lot of grass there."

➤**40 in ranks, by hundreds, and by fifties**—Jesus is the one who orders the seating arrangement. The Greek word for "ranks" is actually a garden term and was used in the same way that we speak of a row of vegetables or a patch of potatoes. This orderly seating plan not only facilitated feeding but made it easy for anyone who was there to estimate at a glance how many were being fed. Jesus' concern for order and accuracy is demonstrated in this detail.

➤**41 when he had taken the five loaves and the two fishes, he looked up to heaven**—so that even people who were at a great distance could see what he was doing. **and blessed**—John says that he gave thanks to God (6:11), but Mark implies this in the fact that Jesus directed his thanks heavenward. It was when Jesus gave thanks for what they had that the miracle happened. **and brake the loaves, and gave them to his disciples to set before them**—Jesus wanted the crowd to identify these men with him and with his message, because he knew that they would be his future representatives. The similarity between the way he served this meal and the manner in which he served the Last Supper was not necessarily peculiar to Jesus, but, according to Swift, his actions were probably "associated with any meal on the part of the host, and were later invested with new and richer meaning by the Lord in the fellowship of his disciples."

➤**42 And they did all eat, and were filled**—Each of the four men who report this event mentions this fact, as well as the fact that there were twelve baskets of leftovers. Despite the little he had to work with, and the large number he had to feed, Jesus was more than adequate for the emergency. In fact, everyone went home full and satisfied.

➤**43 they took up twelve baskets full of the fragments**—All four gospel writers used the same Greek word for "baskets": *kophinoi* (small wicker baskets). In the feeding of the 4,000, the baskets were *spurioi* (larger baskets). Mark uses the same Greek word to speak of the "fragments" as he does when he speaks of the broken pieces that Jesus distributed in the first place. The baskets used by the disciples were like suitcases, not serving bowls. They were an indispensable part of a Jew's luggage whenever he traveled, and were large enough to carry a day's food supply as well as his rolled-up bed, a bulky blanket the size of a sleeping bag (or enough hay to sleep on). A Jew never went far without such a well-stocked basket for fear of being forced to depend on a Gentile for these necessities, and in that way run the risk of being ceremonially defiled. (See

comment on 8:9 for the difference between the baskets used then and here.)

➤**44 about five thousand men**—Matthew adds that this does not include the women and children (14:21), but there may not have been many of them since only the men were required to go to the Passover festival in Jerusalem. Interpreters studying the accounts of this amazing event have usually attempted to explain what happened in five different ways. Some say it is an exaggeration, yet even if the number is exaggerated, Jesus still fed a lot of people with one small lunch. Others say the feeding of the five thousand is a legend, and that it was one of Jesus' stories that was repeated so often people eventually began to believe it. Yet what the four writers say about this miracle is no more unbelievable than anything else they say about Jesus. Then there are those who interpret the event as a sacrament at which everyone only got a little piece of food as a symbol of the great feast they would someday share in heaven. People who hold this view point to the fact that Jesus himself compared his coming kingdom to a feast. Still others believe that what Jesus really did was set an example for the crowd by sharing his lunch with others. When the disciples and the little boy followed Jesus' example, soon everyone who had a lunch in his basket reached in and shared it with his neighbor. However, the most acceptable explanation is to view the meal as a literal event. In reporting the life of Jesus, Mark, as well as the other writers, had no reason to fabricate a fictitious miracle when he had so many other amazing accounts of how Jesus met people's needs in a supernatural way.

## 45-56 JESUS TRAVELS TO THE WESTERN SHORE

John provides an important explanation of what Jesus did immediately after the miracle meal: "Jesus, knowing that they intended to come and make him king by force, withdrew again to a mounatin by himself" (John 6:15, NIV).

➤**45 And straightway** [immediately] **he constrained** [made] **his disciples to get into the ship, and to go to the other side before unto Bethsaida**—John says that they actually headed for Capernaum (6:17), which suggests that the storm they encountered made it impossible to head for Bethsaida (most likely a western suburb of Bethsaida-Julias). **while he sent away the people**—It seems that Jesus wanted to check the rising tide of popularity that he considered to be unhealthy in terms of his ultimate objective (cf. John 6:15). He had no designs for a kingdom on earth. It may be that his disciples had been drawn into similar speculations and so he *made* them go away. The Greek word for "constrained" or "made" indicates urgent force.

➤**46 he departed into a mountain to pray**—At last Jesus was able to get the rest and privacy he had been looking for and needed so badly. The isolated mountain spot provided a quiet place to talk with God about his ministry as well as an excellent lookout on the lake, from which he could keep his eye on the progress of his disciples as they worked their way across the rough water. He had told them to head for Bethsaida, but there is some confusion as to which Bethsaida Jesus had in mind. Most likely, he was speaking of the Bethsaida that was a western suburb (i.e., on the western bank of the Jordan) of Bethsaida-Julias, which was located on the eastern shores of the Jordan. The disciples, beginning from the northeastern shore of Galilee, started for this town, but were blown off course toward Gennesaret on the western shore.

➤**47 when even** [night] **was come**—It had been late afternoon when the disciples first mentioned the food shortage to Jesus, and both Matthew (14:23) and John (6:16) agree that it was dark by the time they were on their way. **the ship was in the midst of the sea, and he alone on the land**—The disciples did not appear to have been in any rush to get started and their reluctance to leave may explain why they are caught on the water at night, rowing against a strong wind (John 6:18).

➤**48 he saw them toiling in rowing; for the wind was contrary unto them** [against them]—From where he was Jesus could see that they were getting nowhere. Though he knew how they felt, he would not rescue them right away. **about the fourth watch of the night**—i.e., "about three o'clock in the morning" (TLB). The Jews normally divided the night into three four-hour watches, but by the time Mark wrote they had adopted the Roman system of four three-hour watches.

The first began at 6 p.m. Thus, when Mark says "about the fourth watch," we know that he was using the Roman system and that it was sometime around 3 a.m. when Jesus finally came to the disciples. John adds that they were three or four miles out by this time (6:19), which means it had taken them eight or nine hours to row only halfway across the lake. **he cometh unto them, walking upon the sea, and would have passed by them**—Barclay says Mark's curious observation that Jesus actually would have passed them by "is clothed in mystery which defies explanation." However, we can be sure of one thing: Jesus did not intend to walk right by without helping them. He may have wanted to go further only in the same sense as in Luke 24:28, perhaps planning to walk with them through the storm rather than climb into the boat. Or perhaps the expression "pass by" suggests a divine appearance, as in an OT theophany—Exodus 33:22; 1 Kings 19:11 (Grassmick). In any case, the lesson Jesus teaches here is graphically clear and should not be lost in attempting to unravel one detail. As Augustine puts it: "He came treading the waves, and so he puts the swelling tumults of life under his feet. Christians— why afraid?"

➤**49 but when they saw him walking upon the sea, they supposed it had been a spirit, and cried out**—The Greek word for "spirit" is *phantasma* (phantom). It is easy to imagine how a strange object coming across the water toward them on a dark stormy night, and looking more and more like a person all the time, would make them think of a phantom.

➤**50 For they all saw him**—This was not the figment of one man's imagination on a dark and windy night. Mark underlines the fact that they "all" saw him. **immediately he talked with them . . . Be of good cheer: It is I; be not afraid**—It's impossible to imagine the impact of Jesus' simple words on these terrified men. He realized that, with their boat bobbing like a cork in the rough sea, there was only one thing they needed to know: that he was there. The same words spoken by any other man in that situation would have sounded ridiculous; but coming from this man, standing there in the middle of the threatening waves, the words brought all the calm and confidence that were needed. They had the same authoritative ring as God's brief declaration to Moses: "I am" or "I, even I, am He" (Exod. 3:14; cf. John 18:5, 6; 8:58). And they seem to have been said with a similar purpose. It's hard to estimate how far such simple words, spoken in this desperate situation, may have gone in convincing the disciples that Jesus was actually God. Peter, for one, finds enough faith from those words to commit himself to Jesus in an unusual way. (See Matt. 14:28-32 for the story of his attempt to walk to Jesus on the water.)

➤**51 And he went up unto them into the ship**—John's words, "they were willing to take him in" (6:21, NIV), indicates that they had not been willing when they thought he was a phantom or ghost. **and the wind ceased**—John describes a second miracle when he says that "immediately the boat was where they were going" (6:21, TLB). The same power that silences the storm speeds the boat to land. Perhaps the disciples' dumbfounded response to what they have just witnessed makes them miss this extra expression of Jesus' power, for Mark does say that "they were greatly astonished" (NASB).

➤**52 For they considered not the miracle of the loaves; for their heart was hardened**—Mark's implication is that the disciples had not really thought about the miracle meal because, if they had, they wouldn't have been shocked at anything Jesus did. That he was capable of anything was clear, had they only stopped to consider it. Disbelief in this miracle persists. Some critics object to viewing the events of 6:48-51 as a miracle at all, claiming that the disciples weren't really in serious trouble, and that the mysterious way in which Christ came to them could evoke the image of a phantom-Christ in human disguise. (The Docetists of John's day erroneously believed that Jesus was a spirit-creature in human disguise.) However, no one is qualified to question Jesus' intentions in coming to the disciples the way he did. The whole phantom argument is unacceptable since Mark says plainly that he walked out to them on the water (6:48) and they all recognized him (6:50). Just because Peter did not have Mark record his attempt to walk on the water is no reason to discount the epi-

sode, either. He had a tendency to omit incidents that might sound like bragging (see Matt. 14:28-31).

### 53-56 THE LANDING

This brief section is typical of the rich detail of Mark's style.

➤**53 they came into the land of Gennesaret**—Gennesaret was the fertile and well-populated western shore region from which the lake itself sometimes took its name. Jesus and the disciples docked at or near Capernaum, a major center of the area (John 6:24, 25). **drew to the shore**—is better translated as "anchored" or "moored." Typical of Mark's penchant for technical terms is this use of a nautical expression that appears nowhere else in the NT.

➤**54 straightway they knew him**—i.e., they recognized him immediately. It was now impossible for Jesus to escape notice, for wherever he went there was someone who had seen or heard him before. They immediately associated him with supernatural healing and brought their sick friends and relatives as soon as they knew he was in the neighborhood.

➤**56 besought** [begged] **him that they might touch . . . the border** [fringes] **of his garment**—The news of what Jesus had done for the woman who touched his clothes (5:25-29), and perhaps for others we aren't told about, encouraged these sick people to expect the same thing in their own lives. The "fringe" of a Jewish robe was often decorated with tassels if a man wanted to show that he was religious (Num. 15:37; Deut. 22:12), so that the hem of a man's clothes soon became associated with piety. But it was only an external symbol that seldom reflected any inner spiritual depth. The fact that these people aspired to touch the hem of Jesus' robe implies indirectly that they were more concerned with the outward manifestation of his power than with the inner depth of his person and teaching. **as many as touched him were made whole**—i.e., were healed or were delivered (from their diseases). Despite their imperfect faith he responded to their touch and healed them all. The time of this event corresponds to that mentioned in John 7:1, when, instead of going to the Jerusalem Passover celebration (where religious leaders were plotting to kill him), he stayed in Galilee

# Chapter 7

## 1-23 A DISCUSSION OF RELIGIOUS RULES CONCERNING PURIFICATION

See comments on Matthew 15:1-20.

## 24-30 THE SYROPHOENICIAN WOMAN AND HER DAUGHTER (See Matt. 15:21-31.)

Jesus' encounter with the Gentile woman comes immediately after his discussion with the Jewish religious leaders. His next three miracles after that confrontation all take place in Gentile country. As a reaction to the Jews who cherished their ceremonial laws above true faith, Jesus went to the Gentiles, with whom Jews were not supposed to associate because they would become ceremonially unclean. Jesus would bring the gospel to the Gentiles. Mark's readers, Gentile believers, would have appreciated this.

➤**24 he . . . went into the borders** [district] **of Tyre and Sidon**—The words "and Sidon" are absent in several manuscripts. If they had originally been present in Mark's text, there is no good reason for scribes to omit them. Most likely, the words were added from Matthew 15:21. Either way, the region so indicated is the Phoenician district in which both Tyre and Sidon were major seaports. There has been some question as to whether Jesus actually went into this foreign country. But Mark says that he did, and goes on to give the reason why. This was a secret trip. Pressure from the Pharisees had been mounting, and Jesus' scathing exposure of their bogus religious rituals had only intensified the hostility (7:1-23). Jesus clearly wanted to get away from them for awhile. **entered into a house and would have no man know it**—he wanted to keep his presence in Phoenicia a secret. Jesus was the Jewish Messiah who was sent to the lost sheep of Israel (Matt. 15:24). He had not been sent to the Gentiles. However, that does not mean that he would turn away any of the lost sheep among the Gentiles, if they came to him. **but he could not be hid**—People here had heard about Jesus long before, so he could not avoid being recognized (Mark 3:8; Luke 6:17).

➤**25 a certain woman . . . heard of him**—People in trouble seem to have an ear for anyone who might possibly help.

➤**26 The woman was a Greek**—The word "Greek" here does not mean that she was from Greece, but that she was a Gentile (as distinct from a Jew). The word also indicates that she spoke Greek, and there is no reason to doubt that Jesus conversed with her in Greek. **a Syrophenician by nation**—She was "born in Syrian Phoenicia" (NIV). The term distinguishes the woman from the Phoenicians of Africa. At that time Phoenicia was a Syrian province. **and she besought him that he would cast forth the devil** [demon] **out of her daughter**—Mark summarizes the initial encounter, but Matthew tells us exactly what the woman said (Matt. 15:22, 23). Though not a Jew herself she had addressed Jesus as King David's son, in that way recognizing him as the Messiah who had been promised to Israel. Matthew also reports that Jesus never answered the woman. He had not been sent to the Gentiles, and he had instructed his disciples not to go to them either (Matt. 10:5). Now when he is in their country he wants to make sure his companions understand that he has not come there to preach, so he does not answer the woman. Matthew's account implies that they may have already been on their way home when the woman came after Jesus and then kept on bothering the disciples as they walked along (Matt. 15:23). Her shouting was just as bothersome to them as the children who constantly pestered Jesus, and the disciples complained, but Jesus could not keep quiet any longer. Matthew says that he finally told her why he had not been paying attention to her. "I am not sent but unto the lost sheep of the house of Israel" (15:24). Part of the reason for his silence was that he was testing her faith, but Jesus probably delayed his response more for his disciples' benefit than for hers. It was a reminder that he had not been sent specifically to do what he was going to do, nor had he gone out of his way to do it. Although he had been sent to the Jews, he did not say that he must minister strictly to them. But the woman was finished with talking. She bowed to worship him and said, "Lord, help me" (Matt. 15:25).

➤**27** Mark picks up the narrative at this point. **But Jesus said unto her, Let the children first be filled**—When she heard him say "first," her immediate reaction must have been, "And then it will be my turn." That Jesus used the word "first" indicates he had a time-frame in mind. He had come to give God's chosen people, Israel, the *first* privilege of accepting his ministry; then that privilege would be extended to the Gentiles. **for it is not meet [good] to take the children's bread, and to cast it unto the dogs**—Jesus gave the woman a crude yet profound proverb to explain why he had avoided her request. He had been sent to supply God's children, Israel, with the bread of life—indeed, he himself was (and is) that bread of life (John 6:48). So it was not good to take that bread from children and give it to the dogs (i.e., the Gentiles).

➤**28 she answered . . . Yes, Lord**—This is the only place in Mark's book where Jesus is called "Lord." **yet the dogs** [lit. "puppies"] **under the table eat of the children's crumbs**—Rather than take offense at being compared to a dog, the woman eagerly accepted the implication because she knew that the children's puppies get fed (and that was all she needed). She was so convinced of Jesus' resources she would be content with scraps. Just a little bit of his power would be more than enough to put the demon completely out of her daughter. It is difficult to say what Jesus meant by comparing Gentiles to dogs. The possibilities are numerous. Some feel he was using common slang in speaking to a woman, but if that is what he intended he would certainly have used the singular. Others think that he was just being a typical Jew. They were in the habit of calling all Gentiles "dogs." It has been pointed out that Jesus used the diminutive form here ("puppies"), possibly to soften the sharpness of the word and to prevent a misunderstanding. However the woman may have understood what Jesus said, the picture he painted was very clear. The Jews were God's chosen people and he was their Messiah. To take what had been promised to them and to give it to others would be just like taking food from children in order to feed dogs. The fact that the woman kept after Jesus shows that being compared to a dog did not bother her as much as it has others. And the fact that Jesus gave her what she asked for proves that he never intended anything harmful or disrespectful by what he said.

➤**29 For this saying**—Jesus was impressed with her wit and insight. She had perceived the meaning of his words and found a way to make them applicable to her positively, rather than negatively. According to Matthew, Jesus also marvelled at her faith (15:28). **Go thy way, the devil [demon] is gone out of thy daughter**—Jesus threw out the demon the minute he saw that her faith was real. She demonstrated her complete confidence in him by going straight home. This obedience was proof that her faith was genuine.

➤**30** Matthew says "her daughter was healed right then" (15:28, TLB). The event has stood for centuries as a monument of Jesus' ability to meet human needs whatever they may be.

## 31-37 THE HEALING OF A DEAF AND DUMB MAN

➤**31 And again, departing from the coasts of Tyre and Sidon**—According to the best manuscript evidence, this could read, "And again, departing from the district of Tyre, he came through Sidon"—and then on to **Galilee.** Rather than going straight south to Galilee after ministering as far north as Tyre (in present-day Syria), Jesus headed even farther north, up the coast to Sidon, before turning back. There is no record of any preaching or miracles in Sidon and none of the NT writers gives any indication of a reason for the detour. Just the same, there is no reason why Jesus should have taken this roundabout route with his disciples. **through the midst of the coasts of Decapolis**—Even then, Jesus did not go straight back to Galilee, but crossed the Jordan first, and came through the region of the Ten Towns east of his home country. He had almost completely circled Galilee. Although Matthew does not record Jesus' experience with the deaf and dumb man, he does mention that Jesus performed several healings on his way through the region (Matt. 15:29-31). Mark, on the other hand, prefers to illustrate what Jesus did by elaborating on one specific example, and chooses the story of the deaf and dumb man.

➤**32 And they bring unto him one that was deaf, and had an impediment in his speech**—The Greek word for "speech impediment," *mogilalon,* appears only twice in Scripture: here, and in the Greek Septuagint version of Isaiah 35:6, which appears in a passage that foretold the Messianic age and the display of God's power on earth. Jesus' healing of the deaf man signaled the advent of that age. **and**

**they beseech him to put his hand upon him**—Whether out of compassion or just plain curiosity, the people seemed a little over-anxious to see Jesus heal the man. He showed by his response to their request that he would not be pushed into doing anything.

➤**33 he took him aside from the multitude**—Perhaps to avoid a spectacle, perhaps to insure the man's undivided attention, Jesus dealt with the man privately just as he would do later with the blind man (8:23). **put his fingers into his ears**—Since the man's indistinct articulation was a result of his own deafness, Jesus dealt with that first. He communicated with him in the only vocabulary the man understood—sign language—and symbolically indicated what he was going to do by this particular gesture. **he spit, and touched his tongue**—with the spittle. When Jesus wet the man's parched tongue with his own saliva, he again symbolically signalled what he was about to do. He alone would be the source of healing that would loosen and liberate the man's tongue.

➤**34 looking up to heaven**—Even though it was Jesus who healed the man, he wanted him to acknowledge God's power and presence in the act. **he sighed**—There are two ways to understand Jesus' act of sighing, neither of which excludes the other: (1) the sigh was a sign of Jesus' grief over man's sinful condition, (2) the sigh was a sign of Jesus' unutterable prayer to the Father. Undoubtedly the first leads to the second—in that the sighs for a fallen creation become the groans of inexplicable petition. (See Rom. 8:22, 27 and note that the same Greek word for "sigh" or "groan" is used there, as in Mark 7:34.) Trench says Jesus was sighing "over the wreck which sin had brought about, and the malice of the devil in defoming the fair features of God's original creation." This sigh was only a hint of the deep despair he would sense at his death, when he would take on himself all of humanity's sickness and sin (Matt. 8:17). **and saith unto him, Ephphatha, that is, Be opened**—Again Mark invigorates his Greek text with Jesus' exact Aramaic expression, "Ephphatha" (see 5:41).

➤**35 And straightway** [immediately] **his ears were opened**—Jesus corrected the hearing deficiency that had been at the root of his speech impediment, first. **the string**

**of his tongue was loosed**—i.e., that which bound his tongue was loosed. **he spake plain**—At the same instant as he heard, his speech difficulty was remedied.

➤**36 he charged them that they should tell no man**—This was the very same area into which Jesus had sent the man delivered from the legion of demons, and with the specific task of telling what Jesus had done for him (5:19). Now Jesus turns around and tells the crowd not to talk about him. The difference is that now Jesus plans to stay in the area. Before, he had left immediately. Jesus was constantly concerned that his miracles would not detract from his message, and that people would not be distracted from what he said by what he did to demonstrate the power of his words. **but the more he charged them, so much the more a great deal they published it**—Some people feel that Jesus did this deliberately in order to speed up his message, because he knew that the more he asked them not to talk about him, the more determined they would be to tell everyone. However, such a position is inconsistent with everything else we know about Jesus.

➤**37 And were beyond measure astonished, saying, he hath done all things well**—Trench notes the similarity between the perfection of everything that Jesus did, and the flawless character of God's original creation that was excellent in every way (Gen. 1:31, LXX). This certainly makes sense since Jesus came to make men a "new creation." **he maketh both the deaf to hear and the dumb to speak**—Jesus did exactly what the OT predicted that the Messiah would do: "Then will the eyes of the blind be opened and the ears of the deaf unstopped" (Isa. 35:5, NIV).

*Chapter* **8**

## 1-10 FOUR THOUSAND PEOPLE ARE FED AT JESUS' SECOND MIRACLE MEAL

Various commentators have suggested that the events in Mark 8:1-30 parallel the sequence of events in 6:31–7:37 as follows: feeding the multitude (6:31-44 and 8:1-9), crossing the sea (6:45-56 and 8:10), conflict with the Pharisees (7:1-23 and 8:11-13), discourse about bread (7:24-30 and 8:13-21), healing (7:31-36 and

8:22-26), confession of faith (7:37 and 8:27-30)—see Wessel.

➤**1 In those days**—i.e., the time of Jesus' ministry in Decapolis (7:31).

➤**2 I have compassion on the multitude because they have now been with me three days, and have nothing to eat**—Whenever Jesus expressed concern for people, he did something about it (Matt. 14:14; 20:34; Mark 1:41). These people had remained with Jesus constantly, for three days and nights, and they had not had anything to eat. So Jesus was about to perform another miracle to meet their need. Some interpreters feel that the similarities between this episode and the feeding of the five thousand make it quite likely that the two stories are simply variations of the same event. However, there are too many differences to consider such a theory. Whereas Jesus had left Capernaum and the crowd had followed him to the scene of the first feeding, this time he has just returned to that city and the crowd is already waiting for him there. At the earlier feeding Jesus had been with the people for just that one day, while here he remarks that they have been following him for three days. Mark makes a special point of being sure his readers do not confuse the two events by recording Jesus' personal concern that the disciples differentiate between the two (8:12, 20). Perhaps the strongest evidence for the "same event" theory is the fact that the disciples ask a similar question prior to both feedings: "Are we supposed to find food for them here in the desert?" How could they possibly doubt Jesus' ability to supply food after witnessing the first miraculous feeding? But such forgetfulness was characteristic of their entire time with Jesus. This was another indication of their repeated refusal to believe that Jesus was adequate for every situation.

➤**3 And if I send them away fasting to their own houses, they will faint by the way**—In the excitement of following Jesus wherever he went, they had not brought enough food. This time Jesus anticipated the disciples' thinking. At the feeding of the five thousand they were the ones who suggested that the people be sent to get food. On this occasion Jesus realized that the people had been without food too long to go for it, so he rejected the idea of sending them away before his companions can even suggest it.

➤**4 From whence can a man satisfy these men with bread here in the wilderness?**—Jesus did not pursue their question the same way he did when they asked a similar question before the feeding of the five thousand (6:35, 36). Perhaps they were only informing Jesus that if he was not going to send the people home he had better be prepared to do something supernatural since there was no natural food supply available. Instead of his previous sharp reply, "You feed them," Jesus simply asked them how much food there was on hand and proceeded with instructions for feeding the people.

➤**5-9 How many loaves have ye? And they said, Seven**—Jesus wanted to know exactly how many loaves of bread were available. This kind of precise detail helps to maintain the distinctiveness of the two miracles. There is no way of reading any significance into the actual number other than that it provides another clear means of distinguishing between the two events. One time there were five loaves, another, seven. Although Jesus followed the same basic pattern of seating the people, breaking the bread, blessing it, and giving it to the disciples to distribute, there are other differences that clearly indicate this as a separate and unique event. This time Jesus did not divide the crowd into any specific seating arrangement, and this time, besides the fact that there are seven baskets of leftovers rather than twelve, the baskets themselves are of a different design. They were not the Jewish *kophinos* baskets used after the feeding of the five thousand, but woven twig *spuris* baskets carried by Gentiles. They were "very large" baskets (8:9), even bigger than the good-sized *kophinos* basket. In fact, they were big enough to support a man—since Paul was let down over the Damascus wall in a *spuris* basket (or, hamper)—(Acts 9:25). As a final evidence that the feeding of the four thousand was a distinct event, we observe that there was no popular movement to make Jesus king after this meal, as had happened after the feeding of the five thousand.

10-13 SOME RELIGIOUS LEADERS REQUESTED A SIGN

➤**10 he entered into a ship with his disciples, and came into the parts of Dalmanu-**

tha—Matthew says they went to "Magadan" (15:39). Both places were obviously on the western shore of the lake and no doubt quite close together. Mary Magdalene was probably from the Magadan area and took her surname from her home town as was customary.

**➤11 the Pharisees came forth and began to question** [debate] **with him**—Mark shows both sides of Jesus' ministry. As his popularity increased, opposition mounted toward antagonism and open hostility. **seeking of him a sign from heaven, tempting him**—Their whole purpose in coming to Jesus was not to be convinced of who he was, but to argue with him. The Jewish people had expected their Messiah to come with spectacular demonstrations of supernatural power that would prove he was God. These men were apparently looking for something completely out of the ordinary, like sending fire from out of the clouds, but Jesus was not concerned with magic in the sky. His miracles touched people with real problems. He had already said and done everything necessary to convince them he was their Messiah; he refused to do anything more. Matthew records the first part of his answer: "You are good at reading the weather signs of the skies but you cannot read the obvious signs of the times" (16:2, 3, TLB).

**➤12 he sighed deeply in his spirit**—This expresses Jesus' deep agitation and exasperation. After everything he had done to demonstrate his divinity, this critical taunt hurt deeply. Mark's Gospel is especially full of these insights into Jesus' emotions. **Why doth this generation seek after a sign?**—Henry E. Turlington defines what Jesus meant by "this generation" as "those whose spirit and attitude were like the Pharisees." And other commentators indicate that "this generation" encompasses the entire nation of Israel, as represented by the religious leaders. There was more than enough evidence in his teachings and miracles to show who he was if they had really wanted to know. One more miracle would not have proved anything. Matthew says that Jesus added, "and there shall no sign be given unto it, but the sign of the prophet Jonas [Jonah]" (16:4). Then he walked away in disgust. The miracle of the resurrection was not the kind of sign they were looking for either.

**➤13 And he left them, and entering into the ship again departed to the other side**—Jesus was visibly irritated by the reaction to him in this region. His displeasure and disappointment were obvious from his quick exit. He had no time for stubborn theologians with their appetite for argument. He had promised them a sign that was greater than anything they ever asked for; but when he could see that all they wanted was an argument, he simply walked away.

## 14-21 A WARNING ABOUT THE LEAVEN OF HEROD AND THE PHARISEES

**➤14 the disciples had forgotten to take bread, neither had they in the ship with them more than one loaf**—Probably they did not have time to stock up on any food because they departed so quickly. At any rate, there was one loaf present. This one loaf may have symbolized Christ's presence with the disciples. "The disciples failed to see that the one loaf they had with them was none other than Jesus himself, and that was sufficient" (Wessel).

**➤15 And he charged them, saying, Take heed, beware of the leaven of the Pharisees and of the leaven of Herod**—Matthew says Jesus included the Sadducees in this list (16:6). Leaven was a "common Jewish metaphor for an invisible, pervasive influence. It often, as here, connoted a corrupting influence" (Grassmick). It was an appropriate image to use in describing the subtle but pervasive influence these men had on society. Like leaven that works its way into fresh dough, spreading out through the bread until its effects are evident in the entire batch, so their ideas gradually infiltrated men's minds until they had penetrated and permeated every part of their thinking. In this context, the leaven of the Pharisees must be linked with their desire to see a sign, because they did not believe in Jesus' identity. Herod also wanted a sign (Luke 23:8). This unbelieving attitude, like leaven, had started to permeate all the Jews.

**➤16 And they reasoned among themselves, saying, It is because we have no bread**—Jesus had hardly recovered from his encounter with the thick-headed religious men when he was immediately faced with the dullness of his disciples. His rapid-fire response in the next four verses indicates how annoyed, and even offended, he must have been at their narrow conception of his teachings and their shallow estimate of his character. He fired nine questions their way, all implying how hard it was for him to imagine them thinking he could talk so seriously about something as insignificant as their stomachs. His surprised reaction shows that he expected them to understand what he was saying by this time. They had just witnessed their second miracle meal at which he fed thousands out of just a little, and yet they still could not comprehend his ability to take care of their physical needs.

➤17 Perceive ye not yet, neither understand?—He was amazed that they had not caught on to the simple illustration. Their perception was very dull, so dull they could only think in physical terms. have ye your heart yet hardened?—i.e., "Are your hearts too hard to take it in?" (TLB). Jesus' accusation that his faithful traveling companions were not even trying to understand him must have stunned these disciples.

➤18 Having eyes, see ye not? and having ears, hear ye not?—See Jeremiah 5:21; Ezekiel 12:2.

➤19-21 How is it that ye do not understand?—There had been a point to the miracles apart from the immediate needs that were met. Now Jesus uses the familiar details of these experiences to drive home his message. His precision in pursuing the particulars of each miracle feeding went right down to the kind of basket that was used to pick up the scraps. He carefully repeated the exact technical term for the two types of baskets the disciples used in order to emphasize the details. He wanted them to remember everything he ever did with them. The harsh tone of the lecture should have awakened their realization of who he is and how he thinks.

## 22-26 A BLIND MAN FROM BETHSAIDA IS GIVEN BACK HIS SIGHT

Mark reports only two miracles that are not recorded in any of the other accounts of Jesus' ministry. They are the healing of the deaf-mute (7:31-37) and the healing of the blind man from Bethsaida. These miracles have several things in common. Jesus isolated both men from public view while he performed the miracle. He used his own saliva both times, he touched the two men, and he avoided publicizing what he

did for them. The healing of the blind man, however, is unique among the miracles of Jesus because he healed him in stages.

➤22 he cometh to Bethsaida—This is Bethsaida-Julias on the northeastern shore of the lake. From here, Jesus and his men would travel straight north to Caesarea Philippi (8:27). and they bring a blind man unto him and besought him to touch him—People everywhere now associate Jesus' healing power with his personal touch. They know that the source of power comes from inside the man (7:32).

➤23 And he took the blind man by the hand, and led him out of the town—Though Jesus also led the deaf man with the speech impediment away from the crowd, here we are told that he personally took the blind man by the hand in order to take him out of town. Bengel and others point to this gesture as an indication of Jesus' humility (since he could easily have asked one of his disciples to bring the man along); however, Jesus clearly intended the personal touch to instill the man's confidence in him. when he had spit on his eyes—Just as with the deaf man (7:32), Jesus put saliva on the body organ he planned to heal. Blindness was common in Palestine. Its prevalence can probably be attributed to the dusty climate, the bright sun, and the fact that many people slept outside with little or no protection for the eyes, as well as the presence of a considerable amount of ophthalmia. Some commentators have suggested that this man was born blind. he asked him if he saw ought [anything]—Jesus' question indicates his awareness of a problem that was not going to be solved instantly. The healing would be gradual, as Jesus built the man's faith to the point where he could believe Jesus for complete restoration of his eyesight.

➤24 I see men as trees, walking—Or, "I see men, but they look like trees walking around." The only way the man could distinguish between the blurred objects he saw was that some of them were moving. Alford suggests that this gradual perception of the real world parallels his gradual loss of sight.

➤25 After that he put his hands again upon his eyes, and made him look up; and he was restored, and saw every man clearly—To our knowledge, this was the only time Jesus ever healed anyone in stages. Mark gives no reason why he did it. Although Jesus used an identical approach with the deaf-mute (7:33), that man was healed instantly. Since it is doubtful that Jesus prolonged the cure just so that he could enjoy seeing the man rediscover the physical world, it is much safer to assume that he healed the man gradually in order to build his faith to the point where he could believe Jesus for perfect vision. Jesus' question, "Can you see anything?" (8:23), indicates that he sensed something was wrong. He may have detected that the man's faith was weak and so asked the question in order to encourage him to believe. The fact that Jesus had to touch the man twice before he was able to see clearly only makes these historical accounts of his life more believable. Mark was not afraid to tell it the way it happened, and this honesty builds reliability into his report. It certainly does not detract from Jesus' record of perfect healings, but only shows, as Swift suggests, that Jesus never quit until the job was complete. In his ministry on earth Jesus healed four blind men that we know of. They all came to him (or were brought), with the exception of the man who was born blind. Jesus went to him instead. It did not seem to matter how a person met Jesus. Jesus was always ready and able to meet his need.

►26 he sent him away to his house, saying, Neither go into the town, nor tell it to any in the town—Jesus may have had more than one reason for sending him straight home. Besides his own distaste for publicity, Jesus knew that this man needed a good rest and time to think about what had happened.

27-38 PETER DECLARES JESUS TO BE THE CHRIST
See comments on Matthew 16:13-28.

Chapter 9

1-13 JESUS' TRANSFIGURATION
See comments on Luke 9:28-36.

14-32 JESUS HEALS A DEMON-
POSSESSED BOY AND MAKES A SECOND
CLEAR-CUT ANNOUNCEMENT OF HIS
APPROACHING DEATH AND RESURRECTION
(See Matt. 17:14-23; Luke 9:37-45.)
Several interpreters have observed the definite contrast between Jesus' exciting mountain-top experience and the grim reality of life in the valley. Some have even gone so far as to suggest that the contrast is deliberate, and that the encounter with the boy symbolizes the existing world of evil while the mountaintop experience represents everything that is divine.

►14 And when he came to his disciples, he saw a great multitude about them, and the scribes questioning [debating] with them—Luke says this happened the day after the mountain experience and just as Jesus was coming down the hill (9:37). He had apparently spent the night on the mountain with Peter, James and John, and returned in the morning just in time to rescue the rest of his disciples from an embarrassing argument. It all began when Jewish religious leaders had seized the opportunity to confront the disciples for failing to throw a demon out of a boy. In the process of insulting the disciples for their inability to perform the miracle, they probably insinuated that Jesus could not have done it either. An argument developed, as the disciples no doubt defended Jesus on the basis of his past miracles.

►15 And straightway [immediately] all the people, when they beheld him, were greatly amazed, and running to him saluted him—The only imaginable reason why the people could have been so awestruck at his appearance is that he still retained some of the glow of his transfiguration glory. Jesus may have looked like Moses, who did not realize as he came down the mountain "that his face glowed from being in the presence of God" (Exod. 34:29, TLB). The circumstances are certainly similar, and if this was the case it is no wonder the people ran to greet him. But Jesus apparently was oblivious to whatever it was that attracted them to him. He went straight to the men who had been intimidating his disciples.

►16 And he asked the scribes, What question ye with them—i.e., "what are you arguing with them about" (NIV). Jesus asked the obvious question but may not have expected to get an answer from where he did. Rather than hearing from a representative of one of the two groups who were arguing, the reply came from a man in the crowd who happened to be the boy's father. What appears to have happened is that, in the heat of the argument which began over his son, the father had been left completely out of the picture while the disciples and religious leaders went on squabbling over things that did not matter to him. He seized the opportunity to get the argument back on track by telling Jesus how it started in the first place. He described the whole sad story of his son to Jesus, along with the disciples' failure to help him. The symptoms he described have been identified by modern medical men as characteristic of an epileptic seizure. Such a diagnosis in no way contradicts the fact that the boy was demon-possessed, nor does it discredit the miracle that was needed to cure him.

➤**17 Master, I have brought unto thee my son**—It had been his intention to bring him directly to Jesus. Luke says it was his only son (9:38). **which hath a dumb spirit**—i.e., he was "possessed with a spirit which makes him mute" (NASB). Matthew says he was "an epileptic" (17:15, NIV). The Greek expression is "moonstruck"; it reflects an ancient belief that certain illnesses were in some way related to the moon. Although that is the way the boy is described by Matthew, his father has no illusions as to the true nature of his son's sickness. The boy may have been both a lunatic and an epileptic, but the real reason behind it was the demon that inhabited his body.

➤**18 And wheresoever he taketh him, he teareth him; and he foameth, and gnasheth with his teeth, and pineth away**—i.e., the spirit would cause him to foam at the mouth, grind his teeth, and become rigid. The rigidity can be translated most literally as "becomes withered" but has also been rendered "dried up," "stiffened," and "paralyzed." For a doctor's description see Luke's account (9:39). By the number of instances of demon-possession that Mark records and the thorough detail of his accounts, it would seem that he takes a special interest in the problem. **I spake to thy disciples that they should cast him out; and they could not**—The fact that these men were identified with Jesus meant that what they did was a direct reflection on Christ himself. Because they had misrepresented him in public, Jesus reprimanded them publicly. He did so as a means of drawing attention to what he was about to do.

➤**19 He answereth him**—actually, "them" (the disciples). **and saith, O faithless generation**—There is some question as to whom Jesus was speaking. Calvin believes Jesus was talk-ing to the religious leaders rather than the disciples, since they were the ones who had been causing the trouble. Several other interpreters suggest he was speaking to both disciples and religious leaders; however, it is probably safer to assume that the rebuke was aimed directly at the nine disciples who had failed to get rid of the demon. It is obvious that any criticism of their faith applied equally well to the men who laughed at it. Jesus points his finger at the nine because their faith should have been stronger by now. This incident is a good illustration of the intense training Jesus was putting his twelve men through. **how long shall I be with you?**—We detect a definite note of impatience in Jesus' tone of voice. **bring him unto me**—Jesus' blunt command prompts quick action. The boy is brought at once.

➤**20 And they brought him unto him: and when he saw him, straightway the spirit tare him** [violently threw him]—Demons always reacted the same way when they saw Jesus (cf. 5:6). They flew into a rage because they knew they were about to be thrown out, but they usually tried to do as much damage as possible before they left. **and he fell on the ground, and wallowed foaming** [at the mouth]—Instead of turning to help the tortured child immediately, Jesus kept on talking with the father. Several reasons have been offered for this strange delay in dealing with the demon. First of all, it was the father who could best describe the demon's destructive powers, and it was his faith that would have to be exercised if Jesus was to get rid of the demon. The delay would also allow the demon to demonstrate the full extent of its capabilities and to prepare even the most skeptical observers for the dramatic dismissal. Swift suggests that Jesus ignored the boy long enough to make sure the father's faith was completely restored in Jesus' ability following his disappointing experience with the disciples. He restored order and understanding to the confused scene before he acted, and left no question as to what he had done when he was finished.

➤**21 And he asked his father, How long is it ago since this came unto him? And he said, Of a child**—Though the father was earlier shattered by the disciples' defeat, while he related the familiar symptoms of his son's problem, his confidence in Christ was restored.

As he recalled the miserable conditions under which their family had lived, he again asked Jesus for help.

➤22 if thou canst do any thing, have compassion on us and help us—The father's cry for help is on behalf of his whole family. The boy's condition must have been a difficult burden for all of them.

➤23 Jesus said unto him, If thou canst—In Greek, Jesus' response to the man is, "as to the 'if you can' " (i.e., as to the statement "If you can"). Jesus turns the father's words back to him. (The word "believe" in KJV is not supported by the earliest Greek manuscripts.) all things are possible to him that believeth—The man had said, "If you can!" Jesus placed the responsibility right back on the man with his reply, "If *you* have faith." He was, in effect, saying, "What I do depends on how much you believe!" Jesus had been patiently building faith in the man to the point where he would believe him for the total deliverance of his son.

➤24 And straightway the father of the child cried out, and said with tears, Lord, I believe; help thou mine unbelief—The words "with tears, Lord" are not found in the best manuscripts. The man not only recognized his lack of faith but realized that Jesus was the only one who could supply the shortage. He recognized a power in Jesus far greater than simply the ability to cure his child.

➤25 Jesus showed that his principal concern was not performing before an audience but dealing with the personal need of this family. A crowd was gathering fast (in the Greek text Mark says that the people were actually "running together"), and now that the man's faith had been restored Jesus wasted no time in getting to the boy. Instead of waiting for those on their way to arrive, or even making sure everyone there had a good view, Jesus sent the demon out of the boy without further delay.

➤26 And the spirit cried, and rent him sore [convulsed him], and came out of him; and he was as one dead; insomuch that many said, He is dead—The evil spirit did everything in its power to kill the boy, but just as Jesus had proven in the past that he was adequate for all sorts of human sickness and sin, he now shows that he is more than capable of saving the boy from Satan's power.

After all, that is what he came to do (1 John 3:8). His intervention also proves that the man had finally found the faith that was necessary for Jesus to act.

➤28 And when he was come into the house his disciples asked him privately, Why could we not cast him out?—It was a natural enough question to ask after seeing him do what they had failed to do. The thing that must have bothered the disciples most was the fact that they had been given authority over unclean spirits (6:7) and had been able to cast them out before (6:13). Now for some reason, they do not experience that same miracle power, but at least they go to the right person to find out why.

➤29 And he said unto them, This kind can come forth by nothing but by prayer and fasting—The words "and fasting" do not appear in two of the earliest manuscripts (Codex Sinaiticus and Codex Vaticanus). Most likely, the words were added later (cf. 1 Cor. 7:5). The disciples were not expected to fast (2:19), nor was it expedient in this urgent situation for them to withdraw from the scene to fast. What was required was prayer—instantaneous and effectual prayer, which was the kind of prayer Jesus often would make right before he performed a miracle (see 7:34 and comments; see also John 11:41, 42).

## 30-32 JESUS' SECOND ANNOUNCEMENT OF HIS IMMINENT DEATH AND RESURRECTION

➤30 And they departed thence and passed through Galilee—From this point in Mark's narrative Jesus moves steadily toward Jerusalem and the death that awaits him there. This final trip with his disciples is documented in excruciating detail. and he would not that any man should know it—Both Matthew and Luke agree with Mark that Jesus wanted privacy so he could have time to talk to his twelve companions about the death and resurrection he was heading for (Matt. 17:22, 23; Luke 9:43, 44). He knew that it would take time to get the idea across. The first time he had mentioned it they had responded with shock and even resentment (8:31). This time they were silent (9:32). The next time he talked about his death they began speculating on the kind of kingdom he intended to set up and the place of honor they might have in it (10:32-40). Each repeated lesson brings them closer and closer to Jerusalem.

**➤31 For he taught his disciples**—in Greek, "for he was teaching his disciples." This clause connects 9:30 with 9:31. In some versions it is joined only with 9:30 (as in NIV, TLB), but in others it introduces 9:31 (as in RSV, NASB). Jesus wanted to be alone with his disciples because he was involved with instructing them about his destiny. **and said unto them**—Luke (9:44) recalls Jesus using rather strong language: "let these sayings sink down into your ears." The nearness of his death was very apparent to Jesus by the way he spoke, and this sense of urgency is expressed in the imperfect Greek tense, "he would say to them." It could be more literally translated, "he kept on saying to them." As he moved toward Jerusalem, he knew that religious men there had already taken steps to seal his death; so he tried to impress on his disciples the fact that he was coming quickly to the culmination of his ministry with them. **The Son of man is delivered into the hands of men**—The Greek word for "delivered" can mean "betrayed," "delivered up," or "handed over." Some commentators have thought the word here indicates that God handed over his Son to men for them to kill him—as is mentioned by all the synoptic writers, the Son of *man* is delivered into the hands of *men*. The futuristic present tense signals the imminence and eventuality of Jesus' betrayal. But Jesus could have also been alluding to Judas's betrayal. In either case, Jesus made sure his disciples had no false illusions of grandeur. They needed to know that he was headed for his death. **and after that he is killed, he shall rise the third day**—Jesus never predicted his death without reassuring the disciples that he would come back to life soon after.

**➤32 But they understood not that saying**—The Greek word for "saying" is *rhēma*; it was often used by the NT writers to indicate a special utterance or unique saying. Jesus' word about his death and resurrection was a special utterance the disciples did not understand. The Greek word for "understand" is in the imperfect tense; it indicates that they persisted in their inability to grasp the meaning of Jesus' saying. Luke (9:45) says that the word was veiled from them, so that they could not perceive what Jesus meant. **and were afraid to ask him**—Again, the predicate in the Greek is imperfect, so indicating that the disciples continued to be afraid to ask Jesus what he meant. Their reluctance may have resulted from the terrible tongue-lashing Peter had received for trying to talk Jesus out of such a plan not long before (8:32, 33). Even more so, they were afraid to think that Jesus would die. To do so would mean they would have to terminate all their ideas about the coming messianic kingdom and their place in it. Most of their trouble stemmed from a failure to comprehend who Jesus really was, so that when he talked about his kingdom they could only think in human terms of an actual political system.

## 33-37 JESUS SETTLES THE DISCIPLES' DISPUTE ABOUT WHICH OF THEM WOULD BE THE GREATEST IN HIS KINGDOM

**➤33** The disciples and Jesus are now back in Capernaum, the city where Jesus began his ministry with them and that served as their headquarters during his time in the country of Galilee. **What was it that ye disputed among yourselves by the way?**—After telling them he would soon be killed, Jesus had probably let his disciples walk on by themselves. He must have wanted them to think seriously about what he had said; at the same time, he wanted to be alone to contemplate the significance of what he was about to do.

**➤34 But they held their peace: for by the way they had disputed among themselves, who should be the greatest**—It is easy to see how the argument got started. With all the talk of a kingdom soon to be set up (Matt. 16:19-28), there was good reason for them to be wondering what place each of them would have in it. Three of the disciples had only recently been singled out for special attention when Jesus invited them up the mountain to share his transfiguration experience. This selection must have intensified the situation. An argument developed and Matthew (18:1) says that one of the disciples asked Jesus to settle it. Luke (9:47) reminds us that since "Jesus knew their thoughts" he was aware of what they were discussing without having to ask. Both accounts can be equally accurate. Perhaps Matthew knew of someone who had in fact asked Jesus to settle the matter right there on the road;

however, he had apparently ignored the request. Though he knew what they were arguing about, he also knew that this was no place to deal with the problem. One way or another, Jesus was aware of what was going on but waited until they were all together alone in the house before he brought up the subject. It is then that he confronted them with the question that brought their whole dispute out into the open. Mark starts his story from the time they arrived in Capernaum.

➤35 **If any man desire to be first, the same shall be last of all and servant of all**—In one short statement Jesus gets right to the root of the debate. If anyone of them had visions of being number one in his kingdom, he would have to be prepared to take the lowest position possible.

➤36 **And he took a child, and set him in the midst of them**—The child became a living object lesson of the quality of humility Jesus expected in his men. **taken him in his arms**—This beautiful picture is mentioned only by Mark.

➤37 **Whosoever shall receive one of such children in my name, receiveth me; and whosoever shall receive me, receiveth not me, but him that sent me**—Matthew's fuller account of Jesus' words helps us to understand Jesus' statement here. What Jesus really meant by receiving him was actually "entering" or "being received into" his kingdom (Matt. 18:3, 4). In order to get into this kingdom a person has to turn to God from his sin in the same spirit of simple humility that a child exhibits when he trusts himself into a person's arms. That is why no one can earn his way into the kingdom on the basis of any personal greatness or special favors he might do. Jesus only receives men who come to him with nothing to offer by way of personal recommendation or achievement, exactly as a child comes to an adult. And that is why the disciples were so far off base in their argument about who was the most qualified to be number one in the kingdom. Jesus said a person could not even get into the kingdom with that kind of attitude. The only entrance requirement was recognizing that Jesus himself had paid the entry fee, and that the path to genuine greatness lay in serving him and representing his majestic greatness.

➤38-41 In these verses John is reprimanded for thinking that the disciples were an exclusive group with unique privilege to Christ's power. From here to the end of the chapter, Mark records a series of instructions that seem to center on the subject of discipleship. The first lesson was prompted by a question from John. After hearing Jesus speak of the importance of his name (9:37), John remembered an incident in which the disciples had come across someone using Jesus' name to throw out demons. He recalled that they had told the man not to do it anymore because he was not one of them. Although John only related what happened, he appeared to be inviting Jesus' approval of their action. Jesus told him they were wrong and then went on to give the reason why.

➤39 **But Jesus said, Forbid him not: for there is no man which shall do a miracle in my name, that can lightly** [readily] **speak evil of me**—The man was obviously doing Jesus' work even though he was not one of them. In replying to John's innocent inquiry, Jesus actually condemned the intolerance of all the disciples. Rather than seeing him as an opponent, Jesus recognized the man's openness toward him, and warned his own men not to stop anyone who was working in his name.

➤40 **he that is not against us is on our part** [for us]—This was Jesus' standard for determining who was on his side.

➤41  See Matthew 10:42.

42-50 OTHER LESSONS PROMPTED BY THE DISCIPLES' DISPUTE

After answering John's question, Jesus returned to the matter at hand as if he had never been interrupted.

➤42 **And whosoever shall offend one of these little ones that believe in me**—The Greek word for "offend" means "cause to stumble" or "ensnare." Jesus was probably imagining the damaging effect the disciples' argument might have on someone who was just inquiring about him (see 9:39). **it is better for him that a millstone were hanged about his neck**—There were two common kinds of millstones in use at that time. One was a small slave-operated millstone; the other was a huge grindstone that required animal power. According to the Greek, Mark said that this millstone was a *mulos onikos* (lit. "mule [or, donkey] millstone"), a millstone empowered by a mule or donkey. **and he were**

**cast into the sea**—If this kind of treatment would prevent another person from stumbling and suffering the eternal consequences, then the punishment is fitting (Matt. 18:7).

►**43-47 if thy hand offend thee, cut it off: it is better for thee to enter life maimed than having two hands to go into hell**—The Greek word for "offend" is the same one used in 9:42. In this context, it appears that Jesus was adding more condemnation to the disciples' lust for ambition. This lust needed to be dealt with (cf. Matt. 5:29, 30). Their ambitious disposition could contribute to preventing another person from following Jesus, and so his sweeping statement was really intended to include anything that could cause another person to stumble. Jesus used three parallel examples to illustrate the same principle. Although these examples have at times been taken quite literally, Jesus was more concerned that his men learn the principle of getting at the root of whatever was causing the wrong. Just cutting off an offending limb or gouging out an eye that looked longingly at evil things would not necessarily uproot the deep inner core of sin that was responsible. However, Jesus did teach that drastic action was required to prevent people from stumbling.

►**48 Where their worm dieth not, and the fire is not quenched**—This verse is the same one as 9:44 and, again, 9:46. According to the earliest manuscripts, the verse should only appear once—here, at 9:48. Jesus used common images of decay and destruction to depict what hell (*gehenna*—9:43) would be like. The Greek word, *gehenna*, evoked some rather vivid sensations in the minds of these Jewish men, since the word was also used to refer to the smoldering garbage dump just outside of Jerusalem. The familiar stench of rotting, burning rubbish was easily recalled at the mention of the word. However, Jesus said that in the real *gehenna* the worm never dies and the fire never goes out. It is a place of perpetual decay and eternal fire (see Matt. 3:12; 5:30; Isa. 66:24).

►**49 For every one shall be salted with fire**—This verse has been explained in over a dozen ways. One of the most acceptable interpretations proceeds from the assumption that the "everyone" refers to everyone who follows Jesus. The "fire" can then be understood as a trial or test that a Christian must endure in order to be refined and perfected (see Isa.

33:14; Mal. 3:2; 1 Cor. 3:13, 15; 1 Pet. 1:7). But it is the expression, "salted with fire," that has created the most difficulty. The best explanation of the origin of this image lies in the Jewish practice of salting a sacrifice. The sacrifice was roasted first and then sprinkled with salt to symbolize the perfection of the offering. Since salt made the meat good to eat, this act indicated, in a figurative way, that the sacrifice was acceptable to God. Jesus may have had this OT ritual in mind when he said that everyone of his followers would have to be "salted with fire" in order to be made acceptable before God. Part of this prediction came true very literally during the fierce persecution of the Roman church shortly after his death. **and every sacrifice shall be salted with salt**—This clause, not found in the earliest manuscripts, was probably added by scribes who wanted to explain the difficult expression, "salted with fire."

►**50 Salt is good; but if the salt have lost his saltiness**—The real value of salt lies in its ability to make everything it touches taste like itself. **wherewith will ye season it**—The real difficulty comes in trying to put the saltiness back into the salt once it is gone. Obviously the job is impossible. That is why Jesus in this analogy encouraged his disciples never to lose their salty flavor (see Matt. 5:13). **Have salt in yourselves**—Always live the kind of life that will attract men to Jesus as they sense his goodness in the way you live. Build into your life those Christlike qualities that will make men taste Jesus whenever you are around. **and have peace with one another**—Jesus underscored the lesson that had been provoked by his disciples' argument with a final reminder. Like salt, they should exhibit a preservative influence on society, rather than contribute to its disintegration by personal quarrels. Paul echoed Jesus' instruction in 1 Thessalonians 5:13. Christians are to be the preserving element that prevents our world from total corruption.

*Chapter* **10**

**1 JESUS LEAVES GALILEE FOR THE LAST TIME**

**2-12 JESUS' INSTRUCTIONS ON MARRIAGE AND DIVORCE**
   See comments on Matthew 19:1-12.

## 13-17 JESUS' WARM RESPONSE TO CHILDREN

See comments on Luke 18:15-17.

## 17-31 A RICH RELIGIOUS RULER MEETS JESUS

See comments on Luke 18:18-30.

## 32-34 JESUS DESCRIBES IN DETAIL THE SUFFERING HE IS ABOUT TO GO THROUGH IN THIS THIRD ANNOUNCE-MENT OF HIS APPROACHING DEATH AND RETURN TO LIFE

The earlier announcements were in 8:31 and 9:31. (See Luke 18:31-34; Matt. 20:17-19.)

➤**32 And they were in the way going up to Jerusalem**—Jesus and his disciples were traveling in Perea, northeast of Jerusalem, and were somewhere on the road between Ephraim and Jericho. **and Jesus went before them**—Grotius points out that Jesus is the perfect picture of a courageous leader. **they were amazed**—lit. "kept on being astonished" at his courage in advancing to certain death. **and as they followed, they were afraid**—The disciples themselves began to sense what was waiting for Jesus in Jerusalem. Although they must have admired his determined stride, they were afraid that what Jesus was walking into would be their fate as well if they kept pace with him. Mark's contrast of Jesus' courageous pace alongside their cowardly attempt to keep up, yet keep their distance, is a graphic description of the disciples' dilemma. **And he took again the twelve**—Anticipating their apprehension, Jesus gathered them together again **and began to tell them what things should happen unto him**—when they arrived at Jerusalem. This prediction should have reassured his disciples that he was the Messiah.

➤**33 we go up to Jerusalem**—This was his last trip to Jerusalem. Luke (18:31) observed that everything the OT prophets had predicted about the Messiah would happen to Jesus there. **the Son of man shall be delivered unto the chief priests, and unto the scribes; and they shall condemn him to death, and shall deliver him to the Gentiles**—The "Gentiles" here refers to the Romans, since they had the power to exercise capital punishment. This was the first time Jesus linked the Romans with the Jews in sharing the responsibility for his death. The collaboration of the Gen-

tile world indicates that this would be more than the elimination of a local troublemaker, but the execution of an international criminal, for though the Jews would sentence him, it was the Romans who would execute him.

➤**34 And they shall mock him, and shall scourge him, and shall spit upon him, and shall kill him: and the third day he shall rise again**—Although Jesus spelled it out in black and white, Luke (18:34) tells us that the disciples still did not understand a word he said. They just could not see how what Jesus was saying had to do with their idea of a Messiah who would restore Israel to the ancient splendor and international prominence of David's reign. It is hard to imagine how they could hang onto this popular notion of a Messiah who would not have to suffer, especially after having heard the opposite from Jesus so many times. However, this strange insistence does make their complete reversal in thinking after Jesus had died and come back to life all that much more convincing, and gives added weight to their witness of a Savior who suffered and died for humanity.

## 35-45 JAMES AND JOHN ASK A SPECIAL FAVOR OF JESUS

➤**35 James and John, the sons of Zebedee, came to him, saying**—Matthew indicates that their mother, Salome, came with them. (This was probably Mary's sister—15:40; Matt. 27:56; John 19:25.) In fact, it may have been her idea to come to Jesus in the first place. However, since Jesus replied to her sons, the plan was likely theirs. They must have misconstrued Jesus' promise that his twelve companions would "sit on twelve thrones judging the twelve tribes of Israel" (Matt. 19:28), and it may be that they had asked their mother to do the talking because they were afraid of another reprimand like the one the disciples had just received for arguing about which of them was the greatest (9:33). **Master, we would that thou shouldest do for us whatsoever we shall desire**—i.e., "we want you to do for us whatever we ask" (NIV). By appealing to his charitable nature, the brothers hoped to avoid an unpleasant scene like the one that had resulted from their argument on the road to Capernaum (9:33, 34).

➤**36 What would ye that I should do for you?**—Jesus must have known what they were after but probably wanted the whole group to hear it.

➤**37 Grant unto us that we may sit one on thy right hand, and the other on thy left hand, in thy glory**—i.e., assign to us the two places of highest honor in thy kingdom. The brothers may have felt that they deserved the places of highest honor in the new kingdom because of the special treatment Jesus had been giving them during their travels together. Both of them were members of his select trio, and John always sat closest to Jesus at meals. According to Jewish etiquette the seat on the right of the host was always the most important seat in the house, and the place on his left, next in importance, with the other places of honor alternating down the table, first right, then left.

➤**38 But Jesus said unto them, ye know not what ye ask**—His answer was mild, to say the least. Jesus had just finished talking about his own torture and death, and all they could think of was their own ambitious plans. **can ye drink of the cup that I drink of? and be baptized with the baptism that I am baptized with?**—Jesus used two metaphors to describe the suffering he was about to go through. The object of his questioning was to see how willing these men were to share in that experience, since those who suffered the most for him would be the ones who received the highest place in his kingdom. In answering, Jesus adopted the same metaphor that the brothers had used. If they wanted to sit at the royal table beside him they would have to be willing to drink his cup. The expression, "to drink a cup," was the Hebrew way of saying, "to get your fill," or "to get everything that is coming to you," whether good or bad. The idiom is used in both senses throughout Scriptures (Ps. 16:5; Jer. 16:7; John 18:11; Rev. 14:10). It was customary at a royal banquet for the king to pass his cup around to his guests. By drinking from the king's cup they indicated that they were submitting to his authority and were willing to accept his way of life as theirs. This was what Jesus meant when he asked James and John if they were willing to drink his cup. Then Jesus turned to a second metaphor to explain more of what it would mean to drink his cup. Baptism meant to be "immersed" or "submerged." If

these men wanted to sit in the places of honor beside him, they would have to be willing to be submerged totally in his sufferings and to share in what he was about to go through.

➤**39 And they said unto him, We can**—It is at this point the brothers appear to admit that what their mother asked for was really their idea. But by the tone of their reply it seems obvious that they really meant what they said. They were completely willing to suffer anything Jesus did. Even though they had no idea what they were actually saying right then, the time would come when both of these men would fulfill their promise. James was the first disciple to be killed because of his faith in Christ (Acts 12:1, 2), while John went through years of persecution with the early Christians and spent the last years of his life in exile. It was probably because Jesus knew what suffering they would endure that he was so easy on them here, rather than making them sorry they had ever asked, as he could so easily have done. **And Jesus said unto them, Ye shall indeed drink of the cup that I drink of and with the baptism that I am baptized withal shall ye be baptized**—Jesus never promised they would sit at the place of honor beside him, but he did predict that they would share in his suffering and sorrow. When their sufferings actually came, this prediction must have cheered them with the assurance that their suffering could bring them into glory.

➤**40 But to sit on my right hand and on my left hand is not mine to give; but it shall be given to them for whom it is prepared** [has been prepared]—Jesus would not exercise any favoritism; besides, as Matthew (20:23) adds, the appointments had been made already by his Father (the Greek verb in the perfect tense—"has been prepared"—indicates that the appointment has already been made). It must have been a shock to the disciples to realize that there was actually something Jesus did not have the authority to do. He set the example for them again by recognizing his proper place of submission to God. Though he did not say "no" to James and John, he did not say "yes" either. The places of honor were simply not his to give. Alford points out that it was probably only when they saw the two thieves being crucified on Jesus' right and left hand that they finally realized what they had actually asked for. The sight must have been a bitter reminder of their ambitious request as they stared at the place where they should have been. (Only one of them [i.e., John] may have been present at the cross, but they would have both been sure to come to the same cruel realization as they were told the story of how he died.)

➤**41 And when the ten heard it, they began to be much displeased with James and John**—These ten were no better than the two who asked. Their reaction shows that they wanted the places of honor just as badly as James and John.

➤**42 Jesus called them to him, and saith unto them, Ye know that they which are accounted to rule over the Gentiles exercise lordship over them; and their great ones exercise authority upon them**—Society is based on a system of superiority in which the people who have made it to the top of the ladder got there by stepping on others on the way up.

➤**43 But so shall it not be among you: but whosoever will be great among you, shall be your minister** [servant]—The literal translation of "minister" is "servant" or "attendant." In Jesus' kingdom, it is the servants and attendants who are the greatest. Jesus is looking for that quality of character that makes a man willing to do the domestic duties and everyday chores for everyone else.

➤**44 And whosoever of you will be the chiefest** [first] **shall be servant** [slave] **of all**—If the great men in his kingdom will be servants, the greatest will be slaves. The one at the top of the ladder in Jesus' kingdom can expect to be stepped on by everyone else here on earth. The slave was on the lowest rung of the social ladder. Paul often described his own relationship to Jesus in just these terms, calling himself "a slave of Jesus," and living like someone who was chained to God's will (Rom. 1:1; Phil. 1:1).

➤**45 For even the Son of man came not to be ministered unto** [served], **but to minister** [serve], **and to give his life a ransom for many**—Many commentators think this is the key verse of Mark's Gospel. All of Jesus' ministry is summed up in the climactic contrast of one person giving himself for *many;* and the contrast is reinforced by the inclusion here of the two basic aims of his life: to serve and to give. The verse also marks the pivot point in Mark's story

of Jesus' life. Prior to this point in the account, Mark has shown how Jesus lived to serve man's need. From this point on he relates how Jesus died to give man salvation. The contrast between the "one" and the "many" is possibly an allusion to Isaiah 53:11, 12. By "many" Jesus meant not, "quite a good number," but "all." Romans 5:19 expresses an identical theme. The Greek word translated "for" (*anti*) has a distinct connotation of "substitution." Jesus gave his life "instead of," or "in the place of" others. It was this willingness to take the lowest place that gives him the right to the highest seat in God's kingdom. Because the word "ransom" means "the price of release," it graphically depicts what Jesus did for humanity. He "paid the demanded price" to release men from their sin. The word for "ransom" (*lutron*) appears only here and in Matthew 20:28. Two cognate words, *lutrōsis* and *apolutrōsis,* both usually translated "redemption," are used quite frequently in the NT. The first word indicates the act of freeing or releasing by paying a ransom price; the second, the act of buying back by paying a ransom price. Christ paid the ransom price with his own blood (1 Pet. 1:18) and thus freed us from the demands of the law and its curse (Gal. 3:13; 4:5).

## 46-52 THE BLIND BARTIMAEUS GETS BACK HIS EYESIGHT

See comments on Luke 18:35-42.

*Chapter* **11**

The rest of Mark's story about Jesus has to do with the last eight days of his life. This includes his ministry in Jerusalem, his death, and his return to life.

## 1-10 JESUS ENTERS JERUSALEM AS CHRIST, THE VICTORIOUS MESSIAH

See comments on Luke 19:29-40.

## 11-14 JESUS CURSES A FRUITLESS FIG TREE

This story is not completed until 11:20-26, where Mark gives the results of the curse and the reason behind it. In between the two parts of the story he relates the dramatic way in which Jesus cleansed the temple.

➤**11 And Jesus entered into Jerusalem, and into the temple: and when he had looked**

**round about upon all things**—Jesus made a thorough survey of the situation in the temple precinct (*hieron* in Gk.), not the sanctuary (which would be *naos* in Gk.). Despite how much the disgusting sight of his Father's house being defiled must have aroused Jesus' anger, he slept on the matter before he acted. The drastic measures he would take to cleanse the temple (11:15ff.) would not come from a reckless reaction but a controlled response. **and now the eventide was come, he went out unto Bethany with the twelve**—Luke and John's account of Jesus' first day in Jerusalem is similar to Mark's, but Matthew (21:10, 11, 14-16) supplies some extra details. Jesus and the disciples spent the night in Bethany outside the city because it was no longer safe for Jesus to sleep in Jerusalem. His only night in the city was the night of his arrest.

➤**12 on the morrow**—This was Monday, the day after his victorious entrance into the capital. **he was hungry**—There has been some speculation as to why Jesus was hungry so early in the morning. Perhaps he had spent the early hours in prayer as was his custom just before the important events in his life (1:35; Luke 6:12). One thing is certain: Jesus was actually looking for food, not just an excuse to teach another lesson.

➤**13 And seeing a fig tree afar off having leaves**—The village of Bethphage in the same neighborhood as Bethany actually got its name, "house of figs," from the fact that this was fig country. Around Jerusalem at this time of year (March/April) fig trees produced small, edible buds followed by large green leaves. The buds, which were eaten by peasants, would drop off when the figs would develop in June. **he came, if haply he might find anything thereon**—It was only natural to expect fruit on the tree. **he found nothing but leaves; for the time of figs was not yet**—This observation has caused considerable difficulty. If it was not fig season why were there leaves? One answer is that the leaves were premature and that is what led Jesus to think there would be fruit on the tree. However, critics are quick to accuse Jesus of being unreasonable in expecting anything on the tree at Passover time. This was definitely not fig season. He should have known better than to expect fruit even if there were leaves. Several attempts have been made

to account for what actually happened. The most worthy argument is that Jesus was looking for the small buds to eat (see comments above). Others have suggested that the fruit he was looking for was the leftover winter fruit that may have still been on the tree. Whatever Jesus was looking for, it is apparent he found no fruit of any kind.

➤**14 And Jesus . . . said unto it, No man eat fruit of thee hereafter for ever**—Jesus' curse did not make the tree barren; it simply sealed the way it had always been (see Matt. 13:13-15). Many commentators think this curse on the fig tree symbolizes Christ's judgment on Israel because Israel was often likened to a fig tree that failed to produce fruit (Jer. 8:13; Hosea 9:10, 16; Mic. 7:1). In Jesus' day, the Jewish religion was all show (leaves) with no reality (fruit). **And his disciples heard it**—Apparently they had not gone over to the tree with Jesus, but they heard what he said from where they were. This information helps link the first half of the event with what happened the next morning (11:20).

### 15-18 CLEANSING GOD'S TEMPLE A SECOND TIME

This part of Mark's story is covered in the comments on Luke 19:45-48.

### 20-26 LESSONS FROM A SHRIVELED FIG TREE

➤**20 And in the morning, as they passed by**—This was Tuesday, the third day of the final week before Jesus' death. He spent the nights in Bethany, the days in Jerusalem. **they saw the fig tree dried up from the roots**—A fruit tree without fruit is useless. The curse did more than condemn the tree to a barren life. It killed it completely. Matthew says that it withered as soon as it was cursed (21:19), but for some reason the disciples did not notice what had happened on their way back to Bethany that night. Whether because of the darkness, the dust, or simply because they were tired, it was not until morning that they saw the dying tree. It is quite possible, as Matthew says, that the tree did die right away, but it is also possible that Matthew simply compressed the specific facts of the incident in order to capsule the significance of the event. His book is more a summary of Jesus' teachings than a detailed diary of his life. Mark is always more concerned with the details of a matter than Matthew. At any rate, their contrasting styles only confirm and complement each other.

➤**21 And Peter calling to remembrance saith unto him**—Peter drew Jesus' attention to the result of his curse. His expression carried a note of surprise that the tree had actually shriveled as Jesus said it would. Perhaps Peter had thought yesterday's words were just a careless curse because Jesus had not found any fruit for his hunger. Now when he sees the withered tree he realizes Jesus meant what he said. A further reason for his surprise may have been the negative nature of the miracle. After all, the disciples were much more used to seeing Jesus use his power to produce blessing than to produce cursing. **Master, behold, the fig tree which thou cursedst is withered**—Peter seemed to think he had made quite a discovery by connecting Jesus' curse of the day before with the withered leaves he sees now. Matthew (21:20) is again content to simply summarize the disciples' surprise.

➤**22, 23 have faith in God. For verily I say unto you, That whosoever shall say to this mountain, Be thou removed . . . he shall have whatsoever he saith**—Jesus was quoting a familiar expression of the Jewish religious teachers when he talked about throwing mountains into the sea by faith. Since there was hardly any reason why the disciples would ever want to dump a mountain into the sea, it is safe to assume that Jesus was using a figure of speech to equate the spiritual obstacles they would face with the most formidable physical obstacle a man can face. What he was saying is that nothing is too big for God to handle if our faith is big enough to believe that he can.

➤**24 Therefore I say unto you, What things so ever ye desire, when ye pray, believe that ye receive them, and ye shall have them**—The verb for "receive" in the Greek is an aorist tense, which is always used to describe an accomplished past action. It should be translated "received." The Christian whose faith is of that quality that he believes he has "already received it" when he asks, will discover that he actually has. This verse simply expands on the preceding verse by setting out how far a person's faith can reach.

➤**25 And when ye stand praying, forgive, if ye have ought** [anything] **against any: that your Father also which is in heaven may forgive you your trespasses**—Jesus repeats a lesson he taught in his sermon on the mountain (Matt. 6:14, 15). Faith and forgiveness go hand in hand with successful prayer. If we cannot forgive others God cannot forgive us, and when we refuse his forgiveness in this way, he refuses our requests. A person just cannot receive forgiveness from God if he does not know how to forgive others.

## 27-33 JESUS' AUTHORITY IS QUESTIONED

See comments on Matthew 21:23-27.

## Chapter 12

### 1-12 THE PARABLE OF THE WICKED TENANT FARMERS

See comments on Matthew 21:33-46.

### 13-34 JESUS ANSWERS QUESTIONS ON TAXES, THE RESURRECTION, AND THE GREAT COMMANDMENT

Matthew 22:15-40 and Luke 20:2-47 give parallel reports of this "press conference." The incident probably occurred on the Tuesday of Jesus' last week in Jerusalem. Matthew plainly accuses the Pharisees of meeting together beforehand "to try to think of some way to trap Jesus into saying something for which they could arrest him" (22:15, TLB). Mark agrees with the accusation. Their questions were obviously "loaded," but Jesus handled them with articulate skill.

➤**13 And they send unto him certain of the Pharisees and of the Herodians**—Matthew observes that the Pharisees present were not the top leaders, but disciples of the Pharisees (Matt. 22:16). These representatives were undoubtedly some of their sharpest young scholars, who were no doubt bent on destroying Jesus by twisting his words until they could corner him. The Pharisees are first mentioned as a group during the reign of John Hyrcanus in the time between the writing of the Old and New Testaments. They were known for their strict adherence to the ceremonial law, with special emphasis on tithing and personal purity. While the Pharisees were religious separatists, the

Herodians were political nationalists. When the Roman tributary king, Herod the Great, died in 4 B.C., Palestine was divided among his sons. Herod Antipas became ruler of Galilee and Perea, Herod Philip became king of Trachonitis, Iturea and Abilene, and Archelaus became king of Judea and Samaria. As the Jews watched the decentralization of their country they realized that the only hope of ever being a free nation again would be to keep Herod's family together. That is why, more out of love for their country than devotion to the old king and his sons, they formed the Herodian party to preserve their Jewish national identity. It is curious how Jesus' presence brought these two groups with very different objectives together in one concerted effort to get rid of him. Apart from their mutual hatred of Jesus, they had nothing in common, but this new threat to their influence over the Jewish people had drawn them increasingly closer. In fact, it was soon after Jesus began his public ministry that they had begun their joint deliberations (3:6). The Herodians' obvious plan of attack was to trap him into saying something that could be taken as subversive to the administration of Rome. The Pharisees were on the lookout for something that might be construed as blasphemy against God and equally punishable by death. **to catch** [trap] **him in his words**—The word "trap" was most often used, as our English word, in a hunting context. Jesus' opponents were out to get him from both sides. If they could not catch him on a religious technicality, they would get him on a political misdemeanor.

►**14 we know that thou art true, and carest for no man; for thou regardest not the person of men, but teachest the way of God in truth**—The flattery was obviously intended to throw Jesus off guard. **Is it lawful to give tribute to Caesar, or not?**—A Gaulonite by the name of Judas had campaigned against taxes a few years before (A.D. 6) under the slogan "Taxation is no better than slavery." Rome silenced him shortly, but his words were still a popular rallying cry of the masses in Jesus' day. Taxes were oppressive by this time, and were designed to hit everybody at least once. There were three basic taxes: (1) a ground or produce tax

took one tenth of all the grain a man grew and one fifth of all his wine and fruits, (2) income tax took one percent of a man's earnings, and (3) everyone aged 14–65 paid a poll tax collected at the census enumeration. (Women began paying the poll tax, equivalent to one day's wages, at age 12.) It is not definite whether the question that was directed at Jesus referred to taxes in general, or just to the poll tax. At any rate, it was carefully worded. If Jesus supported taxation he would stand to lose his tremendous popularity with the people, but if he denounced taxation he could become another Judas.

►**15 he, knowing their hypocrisy, said unto them, Why tempt ye me? bring me a penny** [denarius]—Jesus, not fooled by their trick questions (Matt. 22:18), did not fall for their deception (Luke 20:23). He perceived their pretense, for although it was a very legitimate question to ask, Jesus knew they were not the least bit interested in his honest opinion on this controversial question. Jesus asked for a coin that was the exact amount of the poll tax. Just as today, the coin carried the stamp and authority of the government that circulated it. In that sense it belonged to the king whose picture appeared on its face.

►**16 Whose is this image and superscription? And they said unto him, Caesar's**—The familiar face of the emperor Caesar was clearly etched on one side and his royal title engraved on the outer edge of the other.

►**17 Render to Caesar the things that are Caesar's**—Jesus' reply packed a double punch. There was no way anyone could find a loophole in the answer, and it left no opportunity to pursue the matter further. Nobody could argue with the answer. **and to God the things that are God's**—Jesus' simple statement was loaded with meaning for these men. The person who uses the emperor's money pays the emperor's taxes because he has earned that right as ruler of the empire. However, Jesus says, there is another dominion that exceeds his authority at the same time it supports it. God's sphere of authority eclipses the emperor's but does not invalidate it. Cranfield states, "Here Jesus is not saying there are two separate independencies, that of Caesar and that of

God (for Caesar and all that is his belong to God); but he is indicating that there are obligations to Caesar which do not infringe the rights of God but are indeed ordained by God." Man has an obligation to both God and government (Rom. 13:1-7; 1 Tim. 2:1-6; 1 Pet. 2:13-17).

➤**18** Jesus' "press conference" had just begun. There were more questions to come. **Then cometh unto him the Sadducees, which say there is no resurrection**—With nothing to live for after death, these men made the most of their life on earth by surrounding themselves with material possessions. They were, for the most part, members of the rich ruling class of that day. Since they did not believe in a spirit world they were hardly friends of the Pharisees. Yet they felt they were on the right religious track anyway, because of their strict insistence on the written law. They condemned the Pharisees for putting equal weight on the written law and the traditional rules they had built up around them. At the same time, they rejected all of the OT except the Pentateuch. The Pharisees could not get along with the Sadducees any better than they could with the Herodians, but they all got together to "gang up" on Jesus.

➤**19-23** The Sadducees tried to make the resurrection look ridiculous by using a riddle of their own invention. Naturally, the riddle was based on the Levirate marriage laws they defended so religiously (Deut. 25:5-10). The law required that a man whose brother died before he had children was to take his brother's wife and have a son by her. This insured the dead brother of having an heir to carry on the family name even though he had no son of his own. It is interesting to see how Jesus handled the Sadducees' hypothetical question of a man who had seven brothers that all died childless. The moral and religious implications of their question, "Whose wife would the woman be in the resurrection," were not nearly as serious as those raised by the tax issue. The question was more like an insulting joke than something designed to start an argument.

➤**24 Do ye not therefore err, because ye know not the scriptures, neither the power of God**—Jesus responded to their clever little riddle by telling them they had made two mistakes. In effect, he answered their insult with one of his own, and shocked these men who were so proud of their stalwart defense of the Scripture by informing them that they did not even know what it says. If they had known the whole OT ("the scriptures") and not just Moses' writings, they would have been aware of all that it taught about life after death. The second deficiency in their question is that they had not taken into account the power of God. If they had known about God's power in an experiential way they would not have had any trouble believing in life after death.

➤**25 For when they shall rise from the dead, they neither marry nor are given in marriage but are as the angels which are in heaven**—Jesus' explanation clearly pinpoints the fallacy of this hypothetical case. Marriage is an institution that God designed specifically for the procreation of the human race. When death is no longer a possibility, procreation will no longer be a necessity. That is precisely God's plan (Luke 20:36). Man would not be governed by physical laws but will be "like angels" (there is no article in Gk.) instead. That is, he will share the immortal nature of angels. Since Jesus was speaking specifically about death, and life after death, it is safe to assume that immortality is the only angelic quality Jesus was talking about. In the same way, when Luke (20:36) says we will be the "sons of God" he qualifies it by adding that this is only in respect to the fact that we will be "sons of the resurrection" (Gk.). We can never be sons of God in the same sense that Jesus is, but we will be his sons in the sense that we will share his eternal nature.

➤**26 And as touching** [concerning] **the dead, that they rise: have ye not read in the book of Moses, how in the bush God spake unto him**—It was useless for the Sadducees to argue about the resurrection when they did not even believe in a spirit world. All of their problems related to their refusal to admit this fact. Because they had no concept of spiritual laws they tried to apply the physical laws of marriage in hypothesizing about a spiritual afterlife. This implied a denial of the divine power that would generate resurrection from the dead, and amounted to virtual atheism. Jesus pointed out this discrepancy in their reasoning by citing Moses' encounter with God at the burning bush. It was a skillful tactic in dealing with these rationalists since they had just finished quoting Moses' law to build their own hypothetical argument (12:19).

➤**27 He is not the God of the dead, but the God of the living**—lit. "he is not a God of dead persons but of living persons." The emphasis in the Greek is on the present tense predicate: *is*. Jesus demonstrated that God *is* the God of living men. Though Abraham, Isaac, and Jacob had long been dead by the time God spoke this to Moses, God still talked about them as if they were alive. The only possible explanation is that there is life after death, and that men retain a conscious relationship with God that never ends. It is generally admitted that Jesus chose a passage from Moses to prove his point about the resurrection because it was the only part of Scripture the Sadducees recognized. Some have further suggested that he chose it because every level of Hebrew society accepted the Pentateuch as the fundamental source of their religious and legal system.

➤**28 And one of the scribes came, . . . having heard them reasoning together**— This scribe performed the same duties as do our lawyers. He taught or interpreted the laws of the land. Though scribes were originally secretaries who duplicated copies of the law by hand, sometime during the intertestamental period they became professional people, trained to interpret and apply the law to living situations. The transition was natural for men who were so familiar with the books of the law. Their secretarial experience served them well, and they continued to record all the transactions and interpretations they had handled over the years until they had built up an enormous library of material similar to that in some of our law libraries. These records developed to the point where a person could find a precedent for almost any situation that might arise in the course of everyday affairs. By the time Jesus arrived, their stature as a national tradition was so prominent that they were the sole source of legal and religious advice in the country, and carried more weight than the Scriptures themselves. **perceiving**

**that he had answered them well, asked him**—The man appeared to approach Jesus with more honesty than anyone so far. Matthew (22:34) implies that the Pharisees got together (when they saw what Jesus had done to the Sadducees) in order to come up with another question. Whether the lawyer's question was his own idea or the product of their hasty conference is difficult to say, but it comes across as the first genuine question of the session. This is not to say that it was not aimed at testing and even trapping Jesus. However, Jesus' answers to the previous questions seem to have stimulated this man's thinking and challenged him to investigate the intriguing mentality of Jesus. He undoubtedly had a keen mind himself and wanted to test his own mental ability and grasp of the law against Jesus'. **Which is the first commandment of all?**—The lawyer tested Jesus on an issue that had been a standing debate between Jewish religious teachers for years. In fact it had been such a strong issue it had actually split the religious community into rival schools of thought. There seemed to be no end to the complex code of morality that had grown up around the original commandments. Every law had its own list of "dos and don'ts" and "ifs and buts," until the laws were virtually unintelligible to the average person. One man who wanted to become a follower of the Jewish religion challenged the famous Jewish teacher Hillel to give him the law in a nutshell, or at least in the same amount of time as he was able to stay standing on one leg. Hillel responded with the golden rule: Do not do anything to anyone else that you would not want done to you. "That is the whole law," he said. "The rest is commentary. Go and learn." Despite Hillel's simple reply to the inquirer, his colleagues continued to complicate matters by dividing the laws into "light" ones and "heavy" ones and then fighting among themselves over whether they had the right laws in the right category or not. However, Jesus recognized this man's honest interest in an important issue, and he replied in the same genuine manner in which the question was asked.

➤**29 And Jesus answered him, The first of all the commandments is**—the words "of all" do not appear in the best manuscripts. **Hear, O Israel; the Lord our God is one**

**Lord**—a direct quotation of Deuteronomy 6:4. Some critics of Christianity have maintained that there is no difference between God's universal laws and other rules of conduct which are subordinated to them and dependent on them. They insist that such a distinction between more important and less important laws is an artificial invention of later interpreters of the Bible. However, Jesus came out loud and clear in support of such a division (Matt. 23:23). He opens his reply by quoting the Shema, the national creed of Israel, and coupling it with the golden rule. The Shema was repeated twice a day by devout Jews, who wore miniature copies of it sewed in little boxes called phylacteries to their clothes or nailed a copy of it to their doorposts (Deut. 6:8, 9). It is still recited to this day as a national protest against every country and people who have more than one god, or who worship nature instead of its maker. In combining the Shema with the golden rule, Jesus joins the declaration of their relationship to God (Deut. 6:4, 5) with the law that is to be the guiding principle of their relationships with other men (Lev. 19:18).

➤**30 thou shalt love**—Love is the language of God's law. One word characterizes all God's law—and what a word! Had the essence of the divine law consisted in deeds, it could not possibly have been expressed in a single word; for no one deed is comprehensive of all others embraced in the law. But as it consists in an affection of the soul, one word suffices to express it—but only one. Though God wants us to fear him and deserves to be feared, he does not command it because he wants us to have a closer relationship to him than that. He does not even demand that we depend on him even though trust is an essential part of our relationship with him, because dependence implies that we only rely on God for what we can get out of him. Love builds a relationship that embraces both fear and dependence because love provides the spontaneous motivation to do what makes the other person happy. Love is the only thing that recognizes the total personality of the other person in a relationship. It is the warmest possible human response. While it is possible to fear some *thing* or to depend on some *thing,* you can only genuinely love some*one.* That is why love is the very nature of God himself, and the language of his laws (1 John 4:8). **the Lord thy God**—The object of our love is the one God who has always existed and who, though so far above the man he made, still wants to have an intimate relationship with him. He makes one demand: that we love him. But the love he demands has four aspects. The Scripture Jesus cited (Deut. 6:5) includes only three aspects—love with all one's heart, soul, and strength. Jesus added a fourth: love with all one's mind. **with all thy heart, and with all thy soul**—The heart has always been a symbol of man's inner self. Since Jesus made a distinction between man's heart and his soul, it may be proper to distinguish between these two dimensions, although the boundaries of each must overlap to some extent. Our soul is probably that part of us from which we derive our sense of who we are and where we are going. It is that combination of mental and emotional awareness which determines our desires and our intentions. In essence, our "soul" is our personal being. The heart may be more closely aligned with that warm and compassionate part of us which makes up our emotional nature. To love God with all our heart, then, must be to commit our undivided attention to the task of loving him. Everything we are must be focused on this love. To love God with all our heart is to involve our deepest emotions in this love. To love God with all our soul is to love him with all our being. **with all thy mind**—God made us with minds so that we could put all of our intellectual capacities to work in loving him. He could hardly be satisfied with a blind, uncomprehending love, for he knew that the more we understood him the more we would love him. **with all thy strength**—God demands an intense love that consumes all our energy. The kind of love he is looking for is genuine, warm, intelligent and energetic. In other words, he wants our total person to be involved in loving him.

➤**31 the second is like**—The word "like" does not appear in the best manuscripts; it was probably borrowed from Matthew. Matthew said Jesus described the second commandment as being like the first one (22:39). What he meant was that God required us to have the same quality of love for others as he expected us to have for him. **Thou shalt love thy neighbor as thyself**—Although God is to be the primary focus of our love, it is impossible to love him if we do not love the people he made. Jesus quoted the Greek version of the OT law that talked about man's relationship to man (Lev. 19:18). It is a principle he paraphrases in his golden rule (Matt. 7:12). Our actions and reactions toward other people should be nothing less than what we expect them to show toward us. **There is none other commandment greater than these**—Matthew reports Jesus as saying that all the rest of the law and the prophets hinges on these two laws. "This is the teaching of the laws of Moses in a nutshell" (Matt. 7:12, TLB). Hillel was right (12:28); the whole massive complex of Jewish rules and regulations could be boiled down to these two principles. They are simple enough for a child to understand, short enough for anyone to remember, sweeping enough to include every possibility, and strong enough to stand the test of time. God will never require anything less of his creation and he certainly has no reason to require anything more. It is all included in these two laws. **►32 And the scribe said unto him, Well, Master** [Teacher], **thou hast said the truth: for there is one God; and there is none other but he**—There is no manuscript evidence that supports the inclusion of the word "God." The scribe said, "there is one."

**►33 And to love him with all the heart . . . and to love his neighbor as himself, is more than all whole burnt offerings and sacrifices**—The man recognized the important difference between God's eternal principles and the earthly institutions he had established for man's use in serving him.

**►34 And when Jesus saw that he answered discreetly**—i.e., sensibly. Jesus not only observed the man's intelligent response and his positive inclination toward Jesus, but he also saw that the man had considerable insight into spiritual things. **he said unto him, Thou art not far from the kingdom of God**—It is one thing to be close,

but it is another thing to be right inside. We never have any indication that the lawyer, as close as he was, ever did what was necessary to get into God's kingdom (unless he did it secretly like Nicodemus and Joseph of Arimathea—John 19:38, 39). We do not know if he entered into God's sphere of ruling (i.e., God's kingdom) through faith in his Son, Jesus Christ. **And no man after that durst** [dared] **ask him any question**—Jesus was so unquestionably capable of handling himself against all types of arguments that after he defused the potential danger of these three questions, nobody dared to match wits with him anymore.

### 35-37 CHRIST BAFFLES THE PHARISEES REGARDING DAVID AND HIS SON

**►35 And Jesus answered and said, while he taught in the temple** [the temple courts], **How say the scribes that Christ is the Son of David?**—In Matthew, Jesus began his line of questioning by asking, "What think ye of Christ? whose son is he?" The Pharisees gathered there answered, "The son of David" (see Matt. 22:41-43).

**►36 For David himself said by the Holy Ghost** [Spirit], **the LORD** [Yahweh] **said to my Lord, Sit thou on my right hand, till I make thine enemies thy footstool**—See Psalm 110:1.

**►37 David therefore himself calleth him Lord; and whence is he then his son?**—There is only one answer to the question: the Messiah was as much God as he was man. According to his divinity, he was David's Lord; according to his humanity, he was David's son (see Rom. 1:3, 4). Even the sovereign David had admitted that the Messiah was Lord of a higher kingdom than his own, and had paid homage to him (see Ps. 110:1). Yet the Pharisees had continued to preach a Messiah who would come from David's lineage. They had not realized that the Messiah would have a divine origin. It was this puzzling paradox of the Messiah's human and divine natures and the difficulty of comprehending a spiritual kingdom that caused all the confusion among the Jews. Jesus was not asking a "trick" question or playing an academic game as his questioners had done. This was the most critical issue of his life and ministry. He even quoted a familiar OT passage (Ps. 110:1) that every religious Jew recognized as a prophecy of their coming Messiah, but they just could not make the connection between that and what he was saying. Comprehending Christ's human-divine origin is the key to unlocking all the enigmas about who the Messiah is.

## 38-40 JESUS DENOUNCES THE SCRIBES

➤**38 And he said unto them in his doc-trine**—Matthew (ch. 23) gives even a larger sample of Jesus' teaching on this theme. **Beware of the scribes**—See Matthew 23:5.

➤**39 the chief seats in the synagogues, and the uppermost rooms at feasts**—See Luke 14:7 and Matthew 6:5.

➤**40 Which devour widows' houses, and for a pretence make long prayers**—Matthew 23 records Jesus' lengthy warning that these men would be punished more severely, not just because of their conduct, but because of their attempt to hide behind a spiritual front.

## 41-44 THE WIDOW'S MITES

See comments on Luke 21:1-4.

*Chapter* **13**

## 1-37 JESUS PREDICTS THE DESTRUC-TION OF JERUSALEM AND WARNS MEN TO BE READY FOR HIS SECOND COMING (See Matt. 24:1-51; Luke 21:5-36.)

Jesus has just completed his most scathing attack on the leaders of the Jewish religious establishment. He has said that their hypocrit-ical lives will bring God's judgment on them-selves, as well as on their nation (Matt. 23). Now he concludes his last public message with an emotional expression of his own deep love for the city, a lament for its impending destruc-tion, and a final farewell to the temple before he leaves it for the last time (Matt. 24:1). Jesus' public ministry is now over, but he had more to reveal to his disciples. Their next lesson took place on the mountain overlooking Jerusalem and in response to questions prompted by his prediction of the destruction of the Temple. The disciples, reacting to this prediction, asked two questions: (1) "When shall these things be?"

and (2) "What shall be the sign when all these things shall be fulfilled?"—which is stated in Matthew 24:3 as, "What shall be the sign of thy coming and of the end of the world?" In the disciples' minds, the time of these events was probably the same. But Jesus distinguished the events; in response to their two questions, he predicted (1) the destruction of Jerusalem and the events involved with that catastrophe and (2) the signs of his second coming. "The former local event was a forerunner of the latter uni-versal event. In this way Jesus followed the precedent of OT prophets by predicting a far future event in terms of a near future event whose fulfillment at least some of his hearers would see" (Grassmick).

➤**1 as he went out of the temple, one of his disciples saith unto him**—Luke simply states that "some of his disciples were remarking about how the temple was adorned with beau-tiful stones" (21:5, NIV), while Matthew remembers that they "came along and wanted to take him on a tour of the various Temple buildings" (24:1 TLB). Obviously, someone was the spokesman, and though Mark does not say who it was, he tells us what he said. **Master** [Teacher], **see what manner of stones and what buildings are here**—Josephus gives a detailed description of the temple in *Jewish Wars,* 5.5.1. Some of the stones were over 60 feet long, and the marble porch pillars were 40 feet high and carved from a single solid stone. The walls withstood six days of battering with-out any visible effect, and the foundation was so solid that it is believed part of the original temple footings still remain. Jews were con-vinced of the permanent stability of the struc-ture, not only because of its sturdy construction but also because it represented God's residence with them. The disciple's exclamation at the amazing architecture seems to suggest the impossibility that the buildings could ever fall, as Jesus had implied in earlier statements about the temple (see Matt. 23:38).

➤**2 Seest thou these great buildings?**—Jesus' response intimates that although the dis-ciples had drawn his attention to the buildings, Jesus was quite aware of them already. How-ever, since the disciples seemed to be so impressed by the spectacular structure, perhaps they had better listen to what would soon become of them. **there shall not be left one** stone upon another, that shall not be thrown down—Herod's temple was one of the wonders of the ancient world, although it was still only under construction when Jesus walked with his disciples beneath its stately porches. Begun in 19 B.C., it was finally completed in A.D. 64, only six years before Titus' army moved in and demolished it along with the rest of the city (Josephus's *Jewish Wars*, 7.1.1). As he watched the foreign soldiers dig up the sacred temple and raze the city, Eleazar wrote that he wished they all would have been killed rather than have had to witness such a sight (*Jewish Wars,* 7.1.1). Since this magnificent structure had stood as a proud symbol of the Jewish people, the spirit of the Jews crumbled with it. Jesus warned his disciples about this ultimate humiliation of their nation long before it happened.

➤3 And as he sat upon the mount of Olives over against the temple—On their way back to Bethany that night they stopped off on the mountain to look back at the temple they had just been talking about. Jerusalem was spread out below them, with the temple projecting above the city's skyline. What a place to hear a warning about its destruction! Peter and James and John and Andrew asked him privately—It is typical of Mark not only to say there were four who asked him, but actually to name them. The other writers simply say "the disciples" here.

➤4 Tell us, when shall these things be? and what shall be the sign when all these things shall be fulfilled?—The disciples wanted to know when the catastrophe would happen and how they would know that it was about to happen. Matthew (23:24) reports them as also asking when the end of the world would be. This additional question has caused some speculation as to what exactly Jesus was talking about when he answered it. What did the disciples have in mind when they asked it? Schweizer thinks that "all these things" refers to the immediate destruction of the city, which Jesus then addresses in verses 5-23. However, Jesus also talked about the end of the world and his return to earth. Perhaps the disciples saw these future occurrences as one big event. At any rate, they, like us, wanted to know when it would be, but Jesus never gave a definite date.

## 5-13 PREDICTIONS ABOUT THE DESTRUCTION OF JERUSALEM

➤5, 6 And Jesus answering them began to say, Take heed lest any man deceive you: for many shall come in my name, saying, I am Christ—Jesus avoided specific dates but did identify the telltale signs that would indicate when destruction is near. The first indication would be an increase in the number of false messiahs, pretending to be Jesus himself. The expression "I am Christ" in Greek is actually "I am"—which could mean "I am he, the Christ": or "I am the One" or "I am that I am" (a declaration of deity). and shall deceive many—lit. "shall lead many astray." Throughout the first century, there were many such deceivers (see Acts 5:36, 37; 8:9-11; 2 Tim. 3; 2 Pet. 2; 1 John 2:18; 4:1-3).

➤7 wars and rumours of wars—Political turmoil would accompany the rise of religious frauds. but the end shall not be yet—Luke quotes Jesus as saying that "the end will not come right away" (21:9, NIV). Worse tribulation is yet to come.

➤8 For nation shall rise against nation, and kingdom against kingdom—Tacitus's journals document the fierce power struggles that crippled the Roman Empire shortly after Jesus spoke these words, and even before Jerusalem was destroyed. In A.D. 69 alone, civil strife was so intense that the throne changed hands four times. these are the beginnings of sorrows—lit. "These are [the] beginnings of birth-pangs," which is a typical biblical metaphor for the onset of travail and calamity (see Isa. 13:6-8; 26:16-18; Jer. 4:31; 22:20-23; Hos. 13:9-13). It was believed that these birth-pangs would precede the birth of the new, Messianic age.

➤9 they shall deliver you up to councils [Sanhedrins]; and in the synagogues ye shall be beaten—These refer to the persecutions the Christians would receive from the Jewish authorities. (See the book of Acts for the fulfillment of this word.) ye shall be brought before rulers and kings—This refers to the persecutions the Christians would receive from the Gentile civil authorities. The book of Acts is a running commentary on how the disciples put this advice into practice. They probably did more preaching in jails, and courtrooms, and government halls, than anywhere else.

►**10 And the gospel must first be published** [proclaimed] **among all nations**—God never sends judgment without warning. The Jews had Jesus himself living and preaching in their country just before it was destroyed. Every generation has a Christian witness, and man's responsibility is to respond to the provision that God has made in that particular generation. See Colossians 1:23.

►**11 But when they shall lead you and deliver you up, take no thought beforehand what ye shall speak, neither do ye premeditate**—the last clause, not found in the Greek, is a reiteration of the preceding one. This is not an excuse for the man who walks into the pulpit unprepared, but for the man who is brought into the courtroom unexpectedly. The man who is preaching Christ's message should know it inside out. The man who is persecuted for preaching it may not have time to even think about a personal defense. **but whatsoever shall be given you in that hour, that speak ye: for it is not ye that speak, but the Holy Ghost** [Spirit]—He should not worry about what to say because God promises to give him exactly what to say when the time comes. God's presence will bring peace and his Spirit will prepare the words of the defense.

►**13 And ye shall be hated of all men for my name's sake**—Matthew adds Jesus' further warning that "sin will be rampant everywhere and will cool the love of many" (24:12, TLB). This is one of the toughest tests the disciples will face in following Jesus: the loss of the love of their closest friends and family. John says Jesus commanded them to love each other because they would be hated by the world (15:18). William Temple notes in his commentary on that verse that "not all that the world hates is good Christianity, but it does hate good Christianity and always will." James witnessed just what Jesus predicted not many years later (c. A.D. 50) when he wrote about the way sin had cooled the love of many Christians. **but he that shall endure unto the end, the same shall be saved**—Jesus never promises immunity from persecution and death, but he does call for perseverance in the face of it. He has already mentioned the possibility of death to his disciples in 13:12, and his teaching on persisting in one's faith until the very end is supported by other Scripture. "Be faithful until

death, and I will give you the crown of life" (Rev. 2:10, NASB). It is one of the most important themes of Jesus' instructions to his followers. See comments on Matt. 10:21, 22.

►**14 But when ye shall see the abomination of desolation, spoken of by Daniel the prophet, standing where it ought not (let him that readeth understand)**—The exact expression that is here translated as the "abomination of desolation" appears in Daniel 9:27; 11:31; 12:11. It means "the abomination that causes desolation" (see NIV). Jesus referred to Daniel so that his hearers (and Mark's readers) would understand the OT context of this expression. The word abomination refers to pagan idolatry and sacrifice (Deut. 29:16-18; 2 Kings 16:3, 4; 23:12-14). The pagan idolatry that would occur in the temple would cause the temple to be abandoned and desolated. The first fulfillment of this prophecy came when Antiochus Epiphanes placed an altar to the Greek god Zeus in the temple (167 B.C.) and burnt a pig in sacrifice. This abominable act incited the Maccabean wars (1 Maccabees 1:41-64; 6:7; and Josephus's *Antiquities,* 12.5.4). The second fulfillment occurred when the Roman army destroyed Jerusalem, defiled the temple, and desecrated it in A.D. 70. Mark's readers, being Romans, could very well understand the expression "the abomination that causes desolation" as referring to the Roman army. It had a reputation for viciously disregarding the religious life and liberty of the people it overran. In fact, that expression was so commonly associated with that army that Luke records the same words of Jesus this way: "When ye shall see Jerusalem compassed with armies, then know that the desolation thereof is nigh" (21:20). The third fulfillment is yet to come. According to 2 Thessalonians 2:1-8, the antichrist will cause the ultimate desolation by proclaiming himself to be God and setting up an image of himself in the temple. In the Greek, the word for "standing" (*hestēkota*), which modifies "the abomination of desolation," is masculine and may possibly refer to a person—i.e., the antichrist. **then let them that be in Judaea flee to the mountains**—Eusebius, three centuries later, reported that the Jewish Christians had actually done this, crossing the Jordan River to Pella in the northern tip of Perea. There they escaped the atrocities of the Roman destruction of their country.

➤**15 And let him that is on the housetop not go down into the house**—This will be the time for a fast exodus, Jesus says. The extreme urgency of the hour is best described in his hypothetical illustration of a person who is in the second-floor room on the roof, not even bothering to go back through the house, but actually taking the outside steps down and heading straight out of the city. If anyone stopped to pick up a few of his things he would be sure to be caught in the attack, it was to come so suddenly.

➤**17 woe to them that are with child, and to them that give suck** (nurse) **in those days**—The warning is not a curse on those who are in such a condition at this time, but an expression of sorrow for those who are. The speed of the trip will be fast enough without these added burdens.

➤**18 And pray ye that your flight be not in the winter**—Winter will just make it that much more difficult to travel and that much easier to put off leaving. Matthew adds, "or on the Sabbath," to this phrase. The implication is that a Jew would be all the more hesitant to break the laws about traveling on the Sabbath and might postpone his departure one day too long.

➤**19 For in those days shall be affliction, such as was not from the beginning of the creation which God created unto this time, neither shall be**—It was not unusual to use such exclamatory language in Scripture, and this sort of hyperbole is often used in the OT to describe an impending disaster. Whether or not this statement is an intentional exaggeration is difficult to say, but from the reports of the Jewish historian, Josephus, it would seem that the intense suffering crammed into the brief period of the Jewish war can hardly be paralleled in history. He records 97,000 Jewish prisoners of war, and 1,100,000 deaths by starvation and slaughter.

➤**20 And except that the Lord had shortened those days, no flesh** [human] **should be saved** [i.e., delivered from death]: **but for the elect's sake, whom he hath chosen, he hath shortened the days**—There are usually two sides to God's predictions about the future; they point out his ultimate intentions as well as his immediate activity. Jesus' prediction here includes both sides, because he was talking about two judgments: the more immediate judgment on the Jews and God's ultimate judgment of the whole world. Much of what he says about the first applies just as easily to the second. Luke's account of what Jesus said helps us to realize the dual thrust of his predictions. He said that Jerusalem would be "trampled on by the Gentiles until the times of the Gentiles be fulfilled" (21:24, NIV). Some interpreters suggest that Jesus saw the fate of Jerusalem as a transparent object in the foreground of a much larger scheme, and through which he could see the ultimate end of the world in the distance. Just exactly what Jesus meant by the "time of the Gentiles" has been the subject of a good deal of speculation and controversy. Though it may refer to the general conversion of the world to Christ just before he returns, it is more likely Jesus was talking about the fact that the non-Jewish world would sustain the church, and actually be the church, until the time when Jerusalem and Israel were restored to their proper relationship with God (see Rom. 11).

➤**21 And then if any man shall say to you, Lo, here is Christ; or lo, he is there, believe him not**—See Luke 17:23. No one who has read Josephus's account of what happened just before Jerusalem was destroyed will ever argue that it did not happen exactly as Jesus said it would.

➤**22 to seduce** [lead astray], **if it were possible, even the elect**—It is encouraging to know that Jesus implied the impossibility of this ever happening (see 2 Thess. 2:9-12). The elect, God's chosen ones, as those who believe in Christ and follow him, will not be deceived by the false Christs.

➤**23 But take ye heed: behold I have foretold you all things**—Despite the encouragement of the previous verse, Jesus still cautioned them to be careful. He said that the Christians themselves would come close to being deceived, and the best way to guard against even coming close is to be always on the lookout for imposters. Matthew (24:26-28) records more of Jesus' warning to the disciples. His statements can

hardly be read as a detailed timetable of
what will happen, but they are a very adequate warning of what they could expect,
and even more important, when they would
know that the final events were near.

➤**24 But in those days, after that tribulation**—Now Jesus turns their attention to
the second crisis event of the future, his
return to earth. Since he talked about his
return coming right after "the tribulation"
(Gk.), many commentators think Jesus was
not talking just of the destruction of Jerusalem in the previous verses. The events so
described would announce his return: **the
sun shall be darkened, and the moon shall
not give her light.**

➤**25 And the stars of heaven shall
fall**—All of these expressions were employed in the OT to describe times of future
destruction. Trouble on earth was often predicted in conjunction with disturbances in
the sky (Isa. 13:10; 24:23).

➤**26 And then shall they see the Son of
man coming in the clouds with great
power and glory**—The prediction has an
obvious similarity to Dan. 7:13, and it is hard
to see how the disciples failed to link Jesus
with all the Messianic prophecies they knew
so well. It is almost certain that he was talking about his personal return to earth, but the
disciples never caught on. The words of his
prophecy sound just like Paul's teaching in
1 Thessalonians 4:13-18 and 2 Thessalonians 1:7 about the gathering of a church
on earth that will meet the Lord in the air
when he returns. The gathering together of
scattered people was characteristic of
many OT prophecies about the future, so
the language was very familiar to the disciples. However, there had been several gatherings of the Jewish people both predicted
and fulfilled in history, and for that reason it
must have been difficult for them to think in
terms of one ultimate ingathering (Isa. 11:12;
27:13). Many interpreters have been just as
confused—trying to figure out whether Jesus
was talking about something that would happen at the time of Jerusalem's destruction or
something that would occur much later in
time, or both. That is why it is so easy to see
how the disciples, with their particular perspective on history, would have had trouble

conceiving of anything beyond their immediate circumstances. One thing is certain,
however: Jesus' promise leaves no doubt
either for them or for us, that he is coming
back again.

➤**27 and shall gather together his
elect**—just as the tribes of Israel on many
occasions were gathered together by the
sound of the trumpet (Exod. 19:13, 16, 19;
Lev. 23:24; Ps. 81:3-5).

## 28-37 A PRACTICAL APPLICATION OF THE PREDICTIONS JESUS HAD JUST MADE

He punctuated the lesson with a reminder
that what he was saying applied to the disciples' generation as well as to everyone that
will come after them.

➤**28 Now learn a parable of the fig
tree; When her branch is yet tender, and
putteth forth leaves, ye know that summer is near**—The fig tree could be symbolic
of Israel (see comments on 11:13, 14) and
thus speaks of a time of revitalization among
the Jews prior to Christ's return, or the fig
tree is purely a "national" figure—i.e., its
life-pattern depicts the phenomenon that
will precede Christ's advent. In either case,
the figure is one of hope, newness, and
promise of life.

➤**29 when ye shall see these things come
to pass** [lit. "happening"], **know that it** [or, he]
**is nigh** [near], **even at the doors**—According
to the Greek, the subject of the main clause can
be "it" (the second advent) or "he" (Christ).
From our present vantage point in history we
know that Jesus was not only pointing to the
end of Jewish oppression, but to the final end
of all of man's trouble, when he comes back to
earth (1 Thess. 2:14-16; Luke 11:52).

➤**30 this generation shall not pass, till
all these things be done**—Both Matthew
and Luke record this discussion as well as
Mark, but their words do not make it any
easier to interpret. Again the argument is
over what Jesus meant by the expression,
"this generation." It probably has a dual significance. Most immediately, it refers to the
generation of Jews in Jesus' day, for they
were the ones who would see the destruction
of Jerusalem (A.D. 70). More distantly (and
secondarily), "this generation" could refer to

any Jews living until the end of the age, for "this generation" could mean "the Jewish race."

➤31 Heaven and earth shall pass away, but my words shall not pass away—Here is Jesus' strongest statement concerning the divine authority by which he spoke. Not even Paul or Moses could make such claims. It is more than any human would dare to say. This claim reinforces everything Jesus had been saying. These things will happen because he has said they will. Just as the buds on the fig tree tell you spring is coming, so the occurrence of the events he has predicted will tell us that Jesus himself is coming back soon.

## 32-37 A WARNING TO BE PREPARED FOR HIS RETURN

In these climactic verses Jesus looked beyond the impending crisis and the other disturbances that would mark the course of history to the time when he would come to bring all these troubles to an end. It is just this perspective that he wants us to have on life. There is only one way to face the unknown ahead, and that is to look beyond it to what we know for sure, and to live in the light of the knowledge of his return to earth.

➤32 But of that day and that hour knoweth no man, no, not the angels which are in heaven, neither the Son, but the Father—Mark is the only writer to record Jesus' admission that he himself did not even know when he was coming back to earth. The statement has been the subject of hot debate. How could he be God and not know everything? Luther was one of those who believed that this was something Jesus knew but did not have the authority to communicate. Calvin heads the list of those who insist on a literal interpretation of what Jesus said. If Jesus meant exactly what he said, this is the strongest possible warning we could have against speculating on the precise time when he will return. If he himself did not know, how are we to figure out the date from what he said? That date is locked in the mind of God. As in other areas of his life on earth, Jesus deliberately denied himself this knowledge (Phil. 2:5-8). "The Son of man" as *man* had emptied himself of certain divine preroga-

tives—one of which was prescience concerning the actual time of his return.

➤33 watch—Ignorance of the exact time of his return is no excuse for not being ready when he comes. The kind of trouble that will precede his return demands that we be watching and ready when he comes.

➤34 For the Son of man is as a man taking a far journey—The story starts out just like the story of the man who gave talents (money) to his servants for them to invest while he went on a trip (Matt. 25:14, 15) and commanded the porter to watch—Whether Jesus intended the "porter" to be equated with our church leaders and pastors in this analogy is difficult to say; however, his story does suggest that someone has responsibility for warning and reminding people of his return.

➤35 Watch ye therefore: for ye know not when the master of the house cometh, at even, or at midnight, or at the cock-crowing, or in the morning—Mark shows that he was writing for Gentile readers by his use of the four Roman watches rather than the three watches employed by the Jews.

➤36 See comments on Luke 12:35-40, 42-46.

➤37 I say unto all—Although the lesson was private, Jesus made it very clear that the information is public, and inferred that it was the disciples' responsibility to spread it to the world. Watch—Although the parable might suggest that the man plans to be away for some time, Jesus' advice was to expect him at any minute.

*Chapter* **14**

## 1-11 A WOMAN ANOINTS JESUS

The Jewish plot to execute Jesus is bolstered by Judas's offer to betray him. The final decision to do so appears to be inspired by an incident at supper in Bethany one evening at which Jesus is anointed with an expensive perfume. The events of these verses take place either Wednesday or Thursday of Jesus' last week in Jerusalem, but scholars have had trouble figuring out the exact order of everything Jesus did in those final two days. There is, however, an obvious connection between 14:1, 2 and 14:10, 11. It would seem that the religious leaders' plot to put Jesus away after the feast is only foiled by Judas's offer to turn him in earlier. Such an interruption in their plans merely indicates that it was God who was timing the events of his Son's death, not man. Swift explains in detail how Jesus was a servant in God's eternal plan, not a victim of some hasty human plot. His executioners were simply instruments in this sovereign plan, in the same way as Judas, who did everything God had planned for him to do, yet at the same time acted with absolute freedom in doing exactly what he wanted to do. (These events are paralleled in Matt. 26:1-16; Luke 22:1-6; John 12:1-11.)

**►1 After two days was the feast of the passover, and of unleavened bread**—Passover week fell in the month of Nisan on the Jewish calendar. The April 14 festival was a national holiday that began as a commemoration of the day God saved the oldest boy in each Jewish family from his death angel (Exod. 12). Later the celebration took on added significance when the Jews settled in Palestine, and it also became an agricultural feast marking the end of the barley harvest. The many details of the Passover tradition were perpetuated through regular religious instruction in the synagogue, and elaborate preparations were made well in advance of the week. The event began with the Passover feast and continued for seven days, during which time no bread made with leaven (yeast) could be eaten. An example of the massive participation of the Jewish people in the feast is the fact that during the reign of Nero approximately 265,000 lambs were killed for one Passover alone. Since one lamb was supposed to feed at least ten adults, nearly three million people must have taken part in that single feast. Some people believe that Jesus actually died at the precise moment when the Passover lamb was slaughtered; however, this has been a matter of argument for some time. The important thing is that he was crucified during this week, not after it, as the religious leaders had originally planned. In dying when he did, Jesus reinforced the fact that his death replaced the animal sacrifice which had made man acceptable before God. Now he had become the Passover Lamb (1 Cor. 5:6-8). **and the**

**chief priests and the scribes sought how they might take him by craft, and put him to death**—Matthew (26:3) says that they met in the palace of Caiaphas, the high priest, in order to decide what to do with Jesus. It was a meeting of the Sanhedrin, the Jewish Supreme Court. Matthew (26:2) also adds that Jesus was aware of their deliberations, or at least of the results of them, for he told his disciples: "Ye know that after two days is the feast of the Passover, and the Son of man is betrayed to be crucified." Matthew's account of these final two days is much more exhaustive than Mark's.

**►2 But they said, Not on the feast day**—It was agreed that any plans for his death would have to wait at least seven days. **lest there be an uproar** [riot] **of the people**—With somewhere between two and three million people crammed inside the walls of the capital for a week, anything might happen—especially when they were mostly men who had come in from all over the country. The feverish festival atmosphere was ripe for riot and violence. Even the Romans were particularly sensitive to the mood of the occasion and took heavy precautions against revolt at this time. That is why the Jewish authorities were so hesitant to arrest Jesus just then. Though they seem to have been talking about a plan, it does not appear to have been very well developed since they accepted Judas's proposal with scarcely any debate.

**►3 And being in Bethany, in the house of Simon the leper, as he sat at meat, there came a woman**—As Mark begins to tell how Judas sold out, he looks back at the episode which probably settled the idea of betrayal in Judas's mind. John (12:1) says that what happened at supper that night actually took place six days before the Passover. This would mean that Judas thought about it for four days before he went to the Jewish authorities. John (12:3) is also the one who tells us that the woman who came to Jesus was his friend, Mary. **having an alabaster box of ointment of spikenard very precious**—i.e., a "very expensive perfume, made of pure nard" (NIV). Mark notes that the flask was made of alabaster and that the perfume was pure nard. Nard came from a plant that grew in a cluster of spikes, each one about the size of a finger (thus its alternate name, spikenard). Oil from the nard was extremely expensive, and those Romans who could afford it used to pour a little on their head. John's Greek text (12:3) agrees with Mark that this was pure perfume, and John added that the flask held about a Roman pound (12 oz.) of genuine nard. **and she brake the box, and poured it on his head**— The "box" was actually a vial or jar—which she broke for this occasion. The act of pouring oil on a person's head was a custom that was used to express love and appreciation. Mary's gesture was an eloquent expression of her total love. She poured out the whole vial. John adds that she also spilled some on his feet and dried them with her hair. Though it was a deeply personal act that must have cost her everything she had, it gained greater significance than even Mary had intended and became symbolic of the devoted love that accompanies a believer's response to the gospel (see comments on 14:8, 9).

➤**4 And there were some that had indignation within themselves and said, Why was this waste of the ointment made?**— John (12:4) indicates that Judas Iscariot was their spokesman. But others felt the act was a "waste" too, and all it took was a little encouragement from him to get them going. (For an excellent devotional exposition of this act of "waste," see Watchman Nee's chapter "The Goal of the Gospel" in *The Normal Christian Life*.)

➤**5 For it might have been sold for more than three hundred pence** [denarii] **and have been given to the poor**—Both Mark and John report that Judas had already calculated the monetary value of the perfume before he spoke. He figured it to be worth about 300 denarii. A denarius was the average man's daily wage, so that the gift was worth almost a full year's salary. Today that would mean several thousand dollars. **And they murmured against her**—The Greek word for "murmured" conveys a much stronger reaction—one of anger, indignation, and displeasure. And John observes that while Judas spoke of making a charitable donation he was actually thinking of taking the money for himself. He would have much rather seen a cash contribution to the disciples' travel fund since he was their trea-

surer and since he "used to take what was put into it" (12:6, RSV). It is hard to imagine how such a man would be among Jesus' disciples— and even more so be the treasurer. His eleven companions seem to have been totally oblivious to what was going on, and even those closest to Jesus, like John, may not have suspected anything until he left them for the last time.

➤**6 And Jesus said, Let her alone; why trouble ye her? She hath wrought a good work on me**—The Greek word for "good" is *kalon* and can be translated "acceptable, appealing, beautiful." We know that it was acceptable because Jesus commended her for it. This expression of love must have appealed to Jesus because it came right at the close of his life on earth among people he had grown to love. It was a beautiful thing because it was such a genuine expression of her deepest love.

➤**7 For ye have the poor with you always**—Jesus quoted the Jewish law governing care of the poor (Deut. 15:11). **and whensoever ye will ye may do them good; but me ye have not always**—Jesus gave another reminder that he would not be with them very long. Quietly and unassumingly, he indicated how valuable his presence ought to be to them, but it was only after he was gone that the disciples realized it. It was Mary who had realized the preciousness of Jesus' presence while he was among them, and she demonstrated her appreciation with outpoured affection. It seems that she knew he might not be with them much longer, and so she took advantage of the occasion to express her love to him.

➤**8 She hath done what she could**—This is more than Jesus could say of any of the rest of them. His understatement must have been intentional, for Mary had given everything she could. **she is come aforehand to anoint my body to the burying**—i.e., she has anointed my body beforehand for burial. Mary probably never gave a thought to Jesus' burial when she poured out the perfume. If she had, she might have tried to save some for then. As it was, none of the women who followed Jesus got to anoint his body, even though embalming spices were purchased for that purpose (16:1). Jesus knew this ahead of time, so he accepted this anointing as having already been done.

➤**9 Wheresoever this gospel shall be preached throughout the whole world, this also that she hath done shall be spoken of for a memorial of her**—Olshausen observes that she erected a monument to herself that would survive as long as the Scriptures themselves. Because what she did involved forgetting about herself and what the gift might cost her for the rest of her life, Jesus promised that her act would be remembered for all time. John demonstrates what Jesus meant when he identifies Mary as the one "who poured the costly perfume on Jesus' feet and wiped them with her hair" (John 11:1, TLB). Wherever the Good News is preached and whenever it is published in a new language, the story of Mary's gift of love is repeated again and again, and she is remembered as the one who poured perfume on Jesus.

➤**10 And Judas Iscariot, one of the twelve, went unto the chief priests, to betray him unto them**—The details of Judas's bargaining with the authorities over how much they would pay him for the job are all recorded in Matthew 26. Judas finally settled on thirty silver coins, but it was not much for what he was about to do. This was the same amount that a man was required to pay in damages if another man's slave was accidentally killed by his animals or on his property (Exod. 21:32).

➤**11 And when they heard it, they were glad and promised to give him money**—Matthew gives us the exact amount they promised to pay him (thirty pieces of silver) because it was part of the fulfillment of an amazing prophecy (see Zech. 11:13). **And he sought how he might conveniently betray him**—Luke's additional information indicates that the Jewish authorities' concern to prevent a riot was probably one of the essential conditions of their agreement with Judas. Luke says he "watched for an opportunity to hand Jesus over to them when no crowd was present" (Luke 22:6, NIV). Earlier, Luke (22:3) stated that Satan actually entered Judas before he set out on this treacherous mission.

12-26 JESUS' LAST SUPPER WITH HIS DISCIPLES MARKS THE END OF THE PASSOVER FEAST AS AN INSTITUTION AND THE BEGINNING OF A NEW

SYMBOLIC INSTITUTION, THE CELEBRATION OF COMMUNION
See comments on Luke 22:14-20.

27-31 JESUS PREDICTS THAT HIS DISCIPLES WILL DESERT HIM AND PETER WILL DENY HIM
See comments on Luke 22:21-34.

32-42 JESUS SPENDS AN AGONIZING NIGHT IN THE GARDEN OF GETHSEMANE
See comments on Luke 22:39-46.

43-52 JESUS BETRAYED AND ARRESTED
See comments on John 18:1-12.

53-72 JESUS APPEARS BEFORE THE SANHEDRIN COURT, IS CONDEMNED TO DEATH, AND PHYSICALLY ABUSED. PETER DENIES HE EVER HAD ANYTHING TO DO WITH JESUS
If it were not for John's account of these events, we would have to assume that Jesus was taken directly to Caiaphas's house (the home of the high priest and assembly place for the Sanhedrin) following his arrest. But the Sanhedrin did not convene in the middle of the night. (In fact, it would have been very difficult to assemble the members at such short notice.) Luke (22:66) says they did make a special effort to assemble early the next morning at dawn, but it is John who tells us what they did with Jesus in the meantime. He says that after Jesus was arrested that night he was brought straight to Annas, the former high priest (John 18:13, 14). After his appointment as high priest by Quirinius in A.D. 12, Annas held office for several years before being deposed by Valerius Gratius, the man whom Pilate succeeded as procurator of Judea (Josephus's *Antiquities,* 18.2.1ff.). His tremendous influence in the country came from the fact that he managed to have his son Eleazar, his son-in-law Caiaphas, and four successive sons each hold the high priest's office after him (Josephus's *Antiquities,* 20.9.1). Though the Romans removed him, the Jews still revered him. Nothing he could have done short of gross misconduct or a serious breach of the law would have turned them against him. They still considered him their high priest and that is why they took Jesus there first.

➤**53 And they led Jesus away to the high priest: and with him were assembled all the chief priests and the elders and the scribes**—This was an official meeting of the Sanhedrin. They had probably been informed the night before to be ready to meet at any time, as soon as the man was arrested. It would seem from the accounts of these writers that Peter's denials of Jesus took place during the Sanhedrin trial while he stood outside by the fire. However, since the Sanhedrin never gathered until early morning it is much more likely that these denials took place before it had convened (with the exception of his final denial which took place just before the second cock crowing between 3 and 4 a.m.). The court was in session by this time. Annas and Caiaphas probably lived in the same building complex so that would only have been a matter of taking Jesus across a courtyard or into another chamber in order to have him before the court. This is likely why no mention is made of a trip from one place to the other.

➤**54 And Peter followed him afar off, even into the palace of the high priest**—Houses in those days were usually built around a square courtyard connected to the street by a passageway through the house. A heavy street gate kept intruders out of the passageway and a smaller gate guarded by porters insured that no one got into the courtyard. The courtyard, or Hall, was roofless but paved, and it was here that the servants had built a fire. When Jesus stood in front of the high priest he must have been in an open room just off the side of the courtyard, since he seemed to be aware of what was happening around the fire and even turned to look at Peter (Luke 22:61). Matthew (26:58) and John (18:18) add interesting details to the full account of this incident. While Peter sat by the fire, Jesus was answering to Annas. The actual interview with Annas, though unofficial, was still an important part of the complete record of Jesus' trial. There has been some question as to whether this private preliminary hearing actually took place. (See comments on John 18:19-24.) Mark's account begins with the official hearing itself and consists mainly of scraps of courtroom dialogue, mostly in the form of questions and answers.

➤**55 And the chief priests and all the council [Sanhedrin] sought for witness against Jesus to put him to death; and found none**—Matthew says, "the chief priests and the whole council kept trying to obtain false testimony against Jesus, in order that they might put him to death" (26:59, NASB). It was difficult building a case that would stand up before Pilate, but that was where they knew they had to go in order to get authorization for a death sentence.

➤**56 For many bare false witness against him**—The large number of witnesses, especially at this early hour, smacks strongly of bribery. Their only possible motive in testifying was mercenary. The same thing happened later to Stephen at his trial (Acts 6:11-14), and to David in earlier days. David said, "They accuse me of things I have never even heard about" (Ps. 35:11, TLB). **but their witness agreed not together**—Two corresponding testimonies were all that the Jewish court required in order to convict a man and condemn him to death (Deut. 17:6). However, the proceedings failed to produce even this slim evidence. It is hard to imagine that these men who were so anxious to convict Jesus, and who had paid a man to betray him, and bribed witnesses to testify against him, could not have made sure that the statements of their witnesses agreed. This is just another indication of God's controlling hand in the whole affair. Had the Jews managed to put together a legal case against Christ (no matter how corrupt), his cause might have suffered considerable damage for some time. However, just when Jesus' enemies were saying, "God hath forsaken him: persecute and take him; for there is none to deliver him" (Ps. 71:11), God was protecting him in order to prove his promise that man's futile wrath would only bring Him glory (Ps. 76:10).

➤**57 And there arose certain, and bare false witness against him**—Matthew records this trial incident more precisely. After initial attempts to produce similar stories failed, and since it was necessary to obtain corresponding testimony before conviction, two men finally got together on a statement (Matt. 26:60).

►58 **We heard him say, I will destroy this temple that is made with hands and within three days I will build another made without hands**—As eager as they were to lay a criminal charge against Jesus, his enemies had a hard time coming up with any concrete evidence. In fact, when they finally did concoct something, they had to twist a single speech he had made three years earlier during his first visit to the city. Though Jesus spoke very openly throughout his three-year ministry, there was nothing in what he said that they could charge him with. All that the prosecution had to work with was something they remembered him saying at the very start of his preaching. Even this they twisted, as can be seen by comparing John's record of the original speech with their version (John 2:18-22). John made it very clear that Jesus was talking about the destruction of the temple of his body, not of the Jerusalem temple. Even the religious leaders indicated that they were aware of what Jesus meant when they reminded Pilate (after Jesus' death) of his promise to come back to life in three days (Matt. 27:63). Therefore it would seem that everyone in the court was perfectly aware of what Jesus had been talking about when he spoke of destroying "this temple," but they chose to take his words out of context to suit their immediate purpose. Furthermore, Jesus never said, "*I* will destroy this temple"; he said, "*you* [understood] destroy this temple, and I will raise it up in three days." He had predicted what they were about to do—destroy his body.

►59 **But neither so did their witness agree together**—Few political or legal manipulations in the history of the world have been so badly bungled as the attempt to frame Jesus. Even with only a few words to say, the witnesses failed to perform it properly. It was essential that every word of the two stories harmonize if they were to have a conviction.

►60 **Answerest thou nothing? What is it which these witness against thee?**—The high priest's question was a wise move at this point in the trial. With the prosecution's case stalled on another contradicting testimony,

the only hope of a conviction seemed to lie in getting Jesus himself to say something that could be used against him. However, even this ploy failed.

►61 **But he held his peace, and answered nothing**—Though Jesus' refusal must have nonplussed the court, the high priest was not about to quit. **Again the high priest asked him, . . . Art thou the Christ, the Son of the Blessed?**—We would not understand why Jesus refused to answer the first question and then turned around and answered the second if it were not for Matthew's account of the trial. Matthew says that the high priest actually put Jesus under oath so that he was forced by law to answer (Lev. 5:1). The high priest demanded that Jesus answer in "the name of the living God" (Matt. 26:63, TLB).

►62 **Jesus said, I am, and ye shall see the Son of man sitting on the right hand of power, and coming in the clouds of heaven**—See Matthew 26:64; Luke 22:69. In predicting his return Jesus used the language of Psalm 110:1 and Daniel 7:13, verses that speak of the Son of man coming to earth as its judge and ruler. A few years later Stephen, just before he was stoned to death, said he saw Jesus standing at God's right hand (Acts 7:56). Jesus is there, just where he said he would be.

►63 **Then the high priest rent his clothes**—The act was a symbolic declaration that a blasphemy against God had been committed. The high priest was not allowed to do this on private occasions or when he had personal problems, but only in his official capacity as high priest. The traditional writings of the Talmud described exactly how he was to make the gesture.

►64 **Ye have heard the blasphemy: What think ye?**—There is really no need to even ask the question. Once the high priest had pronounced that this was blasphemy, the verdict was inevitable (John 10:33). **they all condemned him to be guilty of death**—Jewish law called for capital punishment in the case of those who blasphemed God (Lev. 24:16). But even in the face of this damning statement there were those of the court who did not agree with the decision. Joseph of Arimathea, for one, did not vote for the death penalty (Luke 23:50-52). It is quite possible that he and Nicodemus did not attend what they knew would be a kangaroo court.

➤**65 some began to spit on him, and to cover his face, and to buffet him**—i.e., hit him with their fists. Matthew adds that they spat in his face (26:67), while Luke tells how they began mocking him, and he also supports Mark's report that they hit him with their fists (22:63). Luke uses an even stronger word than Mark to describe the blindfolded beating. **and to say unto him, Prophesy**—They made a joke of Jesus' claim to be able to make predictions. Matthew's record (26:68) provides the information on exactly what they wanted Jesus to prophesy. **and the servants did strike him with the palms of their hands**—Jesus' response to the vicious treatment is a clear fulfillment of Isaiah 50:6: "I give my back to the whip, and my cheeks to those who pull out the beard. I do not hide from shame— they spit in my face" (TLB). Luke observes that "they said many other insulting things to him" (22:65, NIV). What we have here, then, is only a sample of the ugly abuse that Jesus received in the courtroom. It is incredible that the Supreme Court of a country could conduct itself in such a manner, but their behavior only demonstrates their deep hatred for Jesus.

➤**66 And as Peter was beneath in the palace** [courtyard]—It is important to remember that Peter himself was the one who told Mark what happened. What we are about to read is, for all intents and purposes, a firsthand account of the most dismal night in Peter's whole life. The one word "beneath" does a lot to set the scene for the next few verses. The trial we have just witnessed took place at the upper end of Caiaphas' courtyard, probably just up a short flight of stairs and in an open area overlooking the paved courtyard where Peter sat by the servants' fire. We know that the trial went on very close to this main courtyard because Jesus could see Peter from where he was standing (Luke 22:61). **one of the maids of the high priest**—The Greek text of John's account maintains that she was the one who "watched the gate" (John 18:17). It seems to have been customary to hire young girls as porters (Acts 12:13).

➤**67 when she saw Peter warming himself, she looked upon him**—How well Peter must have remembered the discomforting and wilting stare of this young servant girl, straining to recognize him in the dim light. Ironically, it was probably his reluctance to come out into the full light of the fire for fear of being recognized that created a suspicion and led to his recognition. **thou also wast with Jesus of Nazareth**—Again, John supplies the finer detail of this little drama when he reports that another disciple was actually in the courtyard before Peter—permission to be present probably being granted because he knew the high priest. It was this other disciple (quite likely John himself) who asked the servant girl in charge of the gate to let Peter in. In John's Greek version of the story the girl adds an "also" to her accusation that she had seen Peter with Jesus. Realizing that the other disciple was one of Jesus' men, she now was linking Peter with him (John 18:17). The fact that this other disciple asked her to let Peter in no doubt got her thinking that he knew Jesus too. Luke (22:56) suggests that she directed the accusation to another bystander, not to Peter himself. At any rate Peter heard what was said and denied any connection with Christ.

➤**68 But he denied, saying, I know not, neither understand I what thou sayest. And he went out into the porch**—Peter probably moved into the porch or vestibule connecting the courtyard with the street. Despite the cold night, things were getting too hot for Peter at the fire, so he moved away. In the dark there was less chance of being recognized and it allowed him an opportunity to try to untangle the inner conflicts that had been troubling him. As the Sanhedrin grappled with the issue of what they would do with Jesus in the upper courtroom, Peter battled with that same question in the dark courtyard below. **and the cock crew**—Since the some of the earliest manuscripts do not have this statement, it is questionable whether Mark originally wrote this, or whether it was added by scribes to account for the second rooster crowing in 14:72.

➤**69 And a maid saw him again**— Some of the accounts of what happened next appear to differ, but only because we do not have enough information from those who reported these events. Matthew (26:71) says that it was "another girl" who accused Peter this time, while from Peter's reply as recorded in Luke (22:58), it would seem that it was a man who confronted him with his involvement in the case. It is quite conceivable, however, that the accusation of one person was echoed by others and the incomplete reports of the event simply do not account for everything that was said.

➤**70 And he denied it again**—John indicates that the second denial was even more insistent than the first (18:25). **And a little after, they that stood by said again to Peter, Surely thou art one of them: for thou art a Galilean, and thy speech agreeth thereto**—Matthew (26:17) tells how they came to this conclusion. It was during the course of the fireside conversation that Peter's Galilaean accent gave him away. His dialect was closer to Syrian speech than to that of the Judean servants he was with. In trying to make himself one of them by joining in their conversation, Peter inadvertently revealed how obviously he was not. To add to his misfortune, a relative of Malchus, the man whose ear Peter had just cut off, happened to be there and confirmed the fact that Peter had been with Jesus earlier that night. Peter's own impetuous personality had gotten him into this predicament.

➤**71 he began to curse and to swear**—Peter's swearing was not profanity, but an oath that called God's curse on him if what he was about to say was not the truth. **saying, I know not this man of whom ye speak**—Peter's third denial shows how far he was willing to go in dissociating himself from Jesus.

➤**72 And the second time the cock crew**—Mark is the only writer to record both "crowings," and his report of the first crowing appears in only some manuscripts (see comments on 14:68). **And Peter called to mind the word that Jesus said unto him, Before the cock crow twice, thou shalt deny me thrice. And when he thought thereon he wept**—Both Matthew and Luke note how bitterly Peter wept, but it is Luke's short observation which tells us more than any adverbs possibly could, just how Peter must have felt. Luke tells us that Jesus turned and

looked at Peter right at that moment Peter denied him (22:61). This was no casual glance but a penetrating gaze. It told Peter that Jesus had been aware of what was going on around the fire all along, and it was this look which caused Peter to recall Jesus' words and to break into tears. The difference between Judas's betrayal and Peter's denial is dramatically reinforced by their personal reaction to what they did. One goes out in tears; the other goes out and hangs himself. Judas's betrayal must have been the culmination of years of resentment towards Jesus' miraculous ministry and resistance to his love, while Peter's denial was only a momentary lapse in an expanding love relationship that had developed over the years. We can only imagine what went through Peter's mind when Jesus looked at him. Maybe he remembered Jesus' prediction the night before, that Satan wanted to have him in order to sift him like wheat, or perhaps he remembered Jesus' promise that he had pled in prayer for Peter that his faith would not fail (Luke 22:32). Whatever he was thinking, we are made very aware of the fact that what happened in the courtyard is a direct fulfillment of Jesus' words. When Peter recalled Jesus' specific utterance (in Gk. to *rhēma*, indicating "the spoken word") concerning his denial, he was smitten with grief. While John is the only writer to omit the account of Peter's repentance, he is also the only writer to record the beautiful scene of Peter's complete restoration (John 21:15-17). Barclay is probably right when he says that Peter must have told this story over and over again, always remarking that in spite of all he had done to Jesus, Jesus never stopped loving him.

*Chapter* **15**

1-20 JESUS APPEARS BEFORE PILATE AND IS LED AWAY FOR EXECUTION
See comments on John 18:28—19:16.

21-37 HIS CRUCIFIXION AND DEATH
See comments on John 19:17-30.

38-47 THE EVENTS IMMEDIATELY FOLLOWING JESUS' DEATH, UP TO AND INCLUDING HIS BURIAL
See comments on Matt. 27:51-56 and John 19:31-42.

Chapter **16**

## 1-8 THE WOMEN VISIT THE TOMB (See
Matthew 28:1-10; Luke 24:1-11; John 20:1, 2.)

➤**1 when the sabbath was past**—This would mean sunset Saturday night. Luke (23:56) says that because it was the Sabbath the disciples rested the entire day. **Mary Magdalene**—See comments on Luke 8:2. **Salome**—This is the mother of Zebedee's sons, James and John (Mark 15:40 and Matt. 27:56). **Mary the mother of James**—This would be James the younger (15:40). **had bought sweet spices, that they might come and anoint him**—It is obvious that the women never expected to see Jesus alive again. They came to the tomb solely for the purpose of embalming the dead body. Luke (23:56) indicates that they actually bought and prepared the necessary spices the day he died, sometime during the few hours that remained between the time of his death Friday afternoon and sunset that evening, which marked the beginning of the Sabbath. According to Luke, by the time they had everything ready, it was already the Sabbath, so they had to wait until Sunday morning. It seems to have been their intention to anoint the body immediately, but there was not enough time. See comments on John 19:40.

➤**2 very early in the morning the first day of the week, they came unto the sepulchre at the rising of the sun**—Matthew (28:1) confirms the early hour, saying they went out at dawn. By this time Jesus had been in the grave three days, having been in the grave part of Friday, the whole of Saturday, and part of the following first day.

➤**3 they said among themselves, Who shall roll us away the stone from the door of the sepulchre?**—God took care of their problem before they even arrived. They were worrying about who would roll away the stone, but when they got there it was already moved. This is only the first of a whole series of overwhelming evidences that support the resurrection story. Jesus' friends could not have moved the stone and stolen his body because of the double Roman guard that was posted at the en-

trance. And his enemies certainly would not have removed the stone.

➤**5 entering into the sepulchre, they saw a young man sitting on the right side, clothed in a long white garment**—Matthew (28:2) calls him an "angel of the Lord," but Mark chose to describe him just as he appeared to the women. Matthew (28:6) also reports that the angel first met the women outside the tomb and then invited them to come in and see where Jesus' body had been lying. After moving the stone he had apparently been instructed to wait around and explain what had happened to Jesus. Alford suggests a likely synthesis of Matthew's account and Mark's when he says that the angel was probably sitting outside the tomb waiting, and then went in with the women. **they were affrighted** [astonished]—The angel's first task was to reassure the startled women. He not only told them the good news of Jesus' resurrection, but he pointed to further proof of that fact. Not only was there an *open* grave; he showed them that it was also *empty*.

➤**6 he saith unto them, Be not affrighted**—i.e., do not be so astonished. Matthew reports that the angel told them not to be "frightened" (28:5), but the word Mark uses might be translated just as easily, "Do not be shaken!" **Ye seek Jesus of Nazareth, which** [who] **was crucified: he is risen; he is not here**—The angel's encouragement began with a positive identification of the person they had come to embalm. There could be no confusion as to whose tomb this was or whom they were talking about. This was the name they were so familiar with, the person they loved. The declaration of his name spoke reassurance and comfort. But what greater encouragement than to hear that their Lord had risen from the dead. (See comments on Luke 24:5, 6.) **behold the place where they laid him**—The angel offered further visible evidence of the resurrection. (See comments on Matt. 28:6.)

➤**7 But go your way, tell his disciples and Peter**—Since it is commonly held that Peter was the source of Mark's information for this book, we can understand why Mark is the only one to report that the angel mentioned Peter's name separately. The other writers may not have felt it was necessary to distinguish Peter from the rest of the disciples since he had always been one of them. However, it must have been a constant cause of wonder to Peter, that after denying Jesus so vehemently, Jesus should make this special effort to include him in their fellowship again. **that he goeth before you into Galilee; there shall ye see him, as he said unto you**—See comments on Matthew 28:7.

➤**8 And they went out quickly, and fled from the sepulchre: for they trembled and were amazed**—The short encounter with the angel demonstrates Jesus' consideration for these women, and, brief as it was, this was all that was needed to send them away strengthened and encouraged, rather than disappointed and confused. They were probably trembling as much from excitement as from fear. In fact, they were so overwhelmed they did not tell anybody what happened: **neither said they anything to any man; for they were afraid**—Of course, they eventually did tell the disciples the good news—as we know from the other gospel accounts.

## 9-20 POST-RESURRECTION APPEARANCES

The ending of Mark according to all extant manuscripts has come to us in five basic forms:

(1) The Gospel ends with 16:8—supported by Codex Sinaiticus and Codex Vaticanus, some early translations (Syriac, Coptic, Armenian, Georgian), and attested to by Clement, Origen, Eusebius, Jerome and a few others.

(2) The Gospel ends with a short conclusion after 16:8—supported by one Old Latin, African manuscript, which reads:

But they reported briefly to Peter and those with him all that they had been told. And after this Jesus himself sent out by means of them, from east to west, the sacred and imperishable proclamation of eternal salvation. (See RSV mg and NEB mg.)

(3) The Gospel ends with the short conclusion above plus verses 9-20, supported by Codex Regius, Codex Athous Laurae and a few other manuscripts.

(4) The Gospel ends with 16:9-20—supported by Codices Alexandrinus, Ephraem Rescriptus, Bezae, several later manuscripts, several early translations (Old Latin, Syriac, Coptic) and attested to by the Diastessaron (fl. c. 185), Tertullian (born c. 165), and others.

(5) The Gospel ends with 16:9-20, incorporating a longer addition after 16:14—supported by Codex Washingtonianius and the testimony of Jerome about certain Greek manuscripts. The addition is as follows: And they excused themselves saying, This age of lawlessness and unbelief is under Satan, who does not allow the truth and power of God to prevail over the unclean things of the spirits. Therefore, reveal thy righteousness now—thus they spoke to Christ. And Christ replied to them, The term of years of Satan's power has been fulfilled, but other terrible things draw near. And for those who have sinned I was delivered over to death, that they may return to the truth and sin no more, in order that they may inherit the spiritual and incorruptible glory of righteousness which is in heaven. (Translation by Metzger.)

Most scholars would not consider the additions in #2 and #5 above to have any serious claim to originality. But debate still continues about verses 9 through 20 (see Farmer). Scholars have demonstrated that these verses are narratively and stylistically incongruous with 16:1-8. Indeed, any fair-minded reader can detect its non-Marcan flavor. The major consensus is that Mark did not write 16:9-20; it is the work of another writer (probably in the early second century) who provided an extended conclusion derived from various sources, including the other Gospels. Some have considered this appendage to be worthy of inclusion in the NT canon because they believe that (1) Mark himself, for whatever reason, was not able to complete his Gospel and thus had to stop at verse 8, or (2) the autographed ending was permanently lost and thus needed to be replaced. (The second conjecture is the more likely of the two because the early Christians used the codex [equivalent to our modern book with a spine] for making copies of the Gospels, and the last page of any of the Gospels could have easily been lost.) Almost all readers would have to admit that it is quite unlikely that Mark would stop his Gospel so abruptly. How could the Gospel close on such a negative note of fear and bewilderment? Undoubtedly, Mark wrote more or intended to write more, but of such we have no record. Since the two earliest and best manuscripts conclude with verse 8, we should accept this testimony—until more light can be shed on this textual problem (*GAM*).

➤**9 Now when Jesus was risen early the first day of the week, he appeared first to Mary Magdalene, out of whom he had cast seven devils** [demons]—The fact that Mary was alone here after accompanying the other women to the tomb has caused some difficulty. A possible explanation is that the women broke up after talking with the angel, and that Mary met Peter and John on their way to the grave, went along with them, and stayed with them until they returned to Jerusalem. It was shortly thereafter that she met Jesus, an encounter John describes in 20:11-18.

➤**11 they, when they had heard that he was alive, and had been seen of her, believed not**—All four writers report the same reaction to the news of the resurrection. This is especially significant when we consider that later on most of these men risked their lives to defend what they at first refused to believe.

➤**12 he appeared in another form**—The resurrection had transformed Jesus' body into a spiritual one. **unto two of them, as they walked**—Luke (24:13-31) gives a lengthier version of the meeting between Jesus and his two disciples on the road to Emmaus.

➤**15** See comments on John 20:19-23 and Luke 24:36-49.

➤**16 He that believeth and is baptized shall be saved**—Baptism, like a public testimony, is an external act that confirms the

faith a man has inside (Rom. 10:10). **but he that believeth not shall be damned**—actually, "condemned." The Scriptures make repeated references to the terrible consequences that will result for people who refuse to believe, but this is the only time those warnings are linked with Jesus' commission to preach the gospel. This fact ought to be a motivating force in our proclamation of the message of Jesus.

➤**17, 18** Similar promises are not recorded anywhere else in Scripture, and the source of these verses may be traced to apochryphal accounts of Jesus' life which existed at the time. There are, however, instances when Jesus' disciples did experience such unique power (see Acts 8:7; 28:3-5, 8).

➤**19 the Lord**—or, "the Lord Jesus," a reading found in some ancient manuscripts. Although the expression is much more common in Luke's writings, this is the only time Jesus is referred to as "Lord" in the entire book of Mark. Its presence here may indicate further the unlikelihood that Mark wrote these final verses. It is possible, however, that Mark could have used the expression for the first time here in order to dramatically punctuate his account of Jesus' life by acknowledging the risen Jesus as his Lord. **he was received up into heaven**—or, he was taken up into heaven. See comments on Luke 24:50, 51. **and sat on the right hand of God**—This is the first indication in the NT of Jesus' heavenly position following the completion of his earthly ministry. Shortly afterwards, Stephen saw him at God's right hand (Acts 7:55, 56). This is Jesus' exalted position in glory.

➤**20 And they went forth, and preached every where, the Lord working with them, and confirming the word with signs following**—This verse ties in well with the continuing account of Jesus' ministry through his disciples as it is recorded in Acts. The Jesus of Galilee now becomes the Lord of the church and his presence remains with them, as he promised when he said, "I am with you always" (Matt. 28:20, RSV).

BIBLIOGRAPHY

Calvin, John. *Commentary on the Harmony of the Evangelists*. 1564. Reprint. Grand Rapids: Baker Book House, 1979.

Cole, A. *The Gospel According to Mark*. Tyndale New Testament Commentary. Grand Rapids: Eerdmans, 1961.

Cranfield, C. E. B. *The Gospel According to Saint Mark*. Cambridge: Cambridge University Press, 1959.

Farmer, W. R. *The Last Twelve Verses of Mark.* Cambridge: Cambridge University Press, 1974.

Grassmick, John D. "Mark" in *The Bible Knowledge Commentary.* Wheaton: Victor Books, 1983.

Hunter, A. M. "The Gospel According to Saint Mark" in the *Torch Bible Commentary.* London: SCM, 1967.

Roehrs & Franzmann. *Concordia Self-Study Bible Commentary.* St. Louis: Concordia Publishing House, 1971.

Schweizer, Eduard. *The Good News According to Mark.* London: SPCK, 1971.

Taylor, Vincent. *The Gospel According to St. Mark.* London: Macmillan, 1952.

Trench, R. C. *Studies in the Gospels.* London: Macmillan, 1878.

Wessel, Walter. "Mark" in the *Expositor's Bible Commentary.* Grand Rapids: Zondervan, 1978.

# LUKE
## Introduction

The authorship of this Gospel, as well as the book of Acts, traditionally has been ascribed to Luke. Although he is not mentioned by name in either of these books, his authorship has rarely been challenged. The Muratorian Canon (c. A.D. 180) lists Luke as the author of the third Gospel, and so do Irenaeus (c. A.D. 175) and Marcion (c. A.D. 135). Luke is mentioned in Scripture always in connection with Paul. Paul speaks of him as "the beloved physician" in Colossians 4:14, as a fellow-laborer in Philemon 24, and as his sole remaining companion in 2 Timothy 4:11. Luke joined Paul in his missionary journeys just before Paul went to Macedonia. Thereafter Luke includes himself in the Acts narrative—as is noted by the second person, plural pronouns (see 16:10-17; 20:5-15; 21:1-18; 27:1–28:16).

The relationship with Paul had a profound impact on Luke's life and writing. Luke was most likely a Gentile, and a very well educated one. His style of writing demonstrates his grasp of classical Greek, but it also reveals his acquaintance with Semitic Greek (i.e., Greek mixed with expressions from Hebrew, Aramaic, and the Septuagint). Luke may unconsciously have picked up his Semitic Greek from Paul. The content of his writing also is similar to Paul's. Luke's account of the Last Supper is exactly the same as Paul's (cf. Luke 22:19, 20 with 1 Cor. 11:24, 25). The obvious conclusion is that Luke received his facts about this event from Paul. Further, when Paul mentions the post-resurrection appearances, he says that Jesus was seen by Cephas (Peter) and then by the Twelve (1 Cor. 15:4, 5). Luke alone among the Gospel writers affirms that Jesus appeared to Peter before he appeared to the Twelve (Luke 24:34ff.). Again, it seems that Luke received his facts from Paul.

Since Paul was the apostle to the Gentiles, it should not surprise us that his companion Luke would write a gospel for the Gentiles—specifically (with Acts), for a Gentile convert named Theophilus. Luke penned an account to verify the facts of Jesus' life and ministry and, in so doing, to establish and fortify Theophilus's faith. Of course, Luke's readership would extend beyond Theophilus to many readers with many needs, but this Gospel was initially aimed to help Gentile converts become grounded in their new-found faith.

Luke wrote his Gospel and the book of Acts as a two-part sequel sometime between A.D. 60 and A.D. 70. Acts was written shortly after Paul's two-year imprisonment mentioned in Acts 28:30. Most scholars think that those two years were around A.D. 60–62. It is quite possible that Luke wrote Acts around A.D. 63. This would mean that Luke was written just prior to A.D. 62–63.

Certain themes are impressively developed by Luke. The most important are: salvation, the work of the Holy Spirit, prayer, and praise. First and foremost, Luke presents Jesus as the One who offers salvation to all men. The word "save" appears sixteen times and "salvation" six times. As the Savior, Jesus brought both physical and spiritual deliverance.

Luke is the first book in the NT to present a picture of the Holy Spirit's work in the lives of certain godly people: John the Baptist (1:15, 80), Mary (1:35), Elizabeth (1:41) Zechariah (1:67), and Simeon (2:25-27)—and, more so, in the life and ministry of Jesus. Jesus was conceived of the Holy Spirit (1:35), anointed with the Holy Spirit for his ministry (4:18), was full of the Holy Spirit (4:1), and rejoiced in the Holy Spirit (10:21). He offered the gift of the Holy Spirit, promised by the Father (24:49; Acts 1:4), to those who ask for him (11:13). In the book of Acts, Luke continues to show how the Holy Spirit worked in the lives of the apostles and early believers.

Every reader of Luke will also notice how much attention is given to prayer and praise. Only Luke records that Jesus was praying at the time of his baptism (3:21) and at the time of his transfiguration (9:29). Luke also records Jesus' prayer before selecting the Twelve (6:12) and his agonizing petitions to his Father in the Garden of Gethsemane (22:40ff.). And it is quite fitting that as the Gospel of Luke begins with prayer (1:10, 13), it should end with praise (24:52, 53). Hardly any other book in the NT contains so many praises—and each is so joyful! Mary blessed and praised God (1:46-55); Zechariah eulogized the Lord God (1:68-79); the heavenly host praised God (2:13, 14); the shepherds praised and glorified God (2:20); Simeon extolled God for being able to see the Savior (2:28-32); the people of Nain (who witnessed a resurrection) praised God (7:16); Jesus rejoicingly magnified his Father (10:21); the people of Jericho (who witnessed the blind man's healing) gave glory and praise to God (18:43); the whole multitude of Jesus' disciples rejoiced and praised God as Jesus entered Jerusalem (19:37-38); and the apostles were praising and blessing God after seeing their risen Lord and witnessing his ascension (24:51-53).

*Chapter* **1**

## 1-4 THE PREFACE TO THE GOSPEL

It appears from the Acts of the Apostles and the apostolic epistles that the earliest preaching of the gospel consisted of a brief summary of the facts of our Lord's earthly history with a few words of pointed application to the parties addressed. Of these astonishing facts, notes would naturally be taken and digests put into circulation. It is to such records that Luke here refers; in terms of studied respect, he describes them as a testimony of "eyewitnesses and ministers of the word." But when he adds "it seemed good to me also, having had perfect understanding of all things from the very first, to write unto thee in order," this is a virtual claim for his own Gospel to supersede the many narrative accounts in existence at that time. Accordingly, while not one of them has

survived the ravages of time, this and the other canonical Gospels live and shall continue to live. The canonical Gospels are the only fitting vehicles of these life-bringing facts which have made all things new. Apocryphal or spurious Gospels, upheld by those unfriendly to the truths exhibited in the canonical Gospels, have not perished; but these well-meant and substantially correct narratives here referred to, used only while the four Gospels were not yet written, were by tacit consent allowed to merge in the four peerless documents accepted from age to age as the written charter of all Christianity. Verses 1-4, with their simplicity, modesty, and terseness, constitute a model preface for a historical work. Luke is the only gospel writer who speaks in the first person, and the only writer to make known his intentions and the purpose of his document. In the preface to his Gospel, Luke mentions at least four pertinent facts concerning gospel writing. First, it was popular. Luke obviously was not satisfied with the writings of others; therefore, he purposed to write a Gospel that Theophilus might know the truth of those things in which he had been instructed. Second, Luke tells us of the content of the writing. The events he records were delivered to him by "eyewitnesses and ministers of the word." He was a secondary witness, not a primary witness. Third, Luke's purpose in writing had a practical aim. He wrote so that Theophilus might have "full knowledge" concerning the events of Jesus' life. Fourth, Luke's method of research is defined as being comprehensive. He indicates that he investigated all things, examining the accounts carefully and accurately for the purpose of writing an orderly account.

➤1 Forasmuch as many have taken in hand to set forth in order a declaration of those things which are most surely believed among us—The word translated "Forasmuch" appears only here in the NT. This shows the extensiveness of Luke's vocabulary as well as introducing immediately the exalted form of his writing. "Many" (perhaps he even includes Mark at this point, although most interpreters would exclude Mark's Gospel and interpret Luke as referring to gospel accounts which have not been preserved) had attempted to compile an account. set forth in order a declaration—is better rendered, "to draw up an account" (NIV) or "to compile a narrative" (RSV). The idea of "setting forth in order," inherent in the Greek word and rendered in the KJV, indicates that Luke intended to provide a fresh arrangement of the events in Jesus' life. The word "believed" could also be rendered as "been accomplished" (RSV) or "been fulfilled" (NIV).

➤2 Even as they delivered them [lit., "handed them down"] unto us, which [who] from the beginning were eyewitnesses—from the beginning of Jesus' public ministry. The word "eyewitnesses" means "seeing with one's own eyes" (Robertson). The eyewitnesses were the apostles (see John 1:14; 2 Pet. 1:16; 1 John 1:1-3). and ministers—lit., "underrowers," or "attendants." These ministers were subservient to the Christ whose message they preached. of the word—capitalized "Word" in some translations (NASB, Marshall's Interlinear Greek-English New Testament), alluding to Christ's appellation as "the Word" (John 1:1), but probably meant to capture the idea of Christ's complete message.

➤3 It seemed good to me also, having had perfect understanding of all things from the very first—The Greek indicates that Luke accurately investigated (or, traced) all things from their source (or, from their beginning). It depicts the work of a historian. to write unto thee in order—i.e., to write an orderly account for you—not necessarily a chronological account, but rather a structured account, an account with organization. most excellent Theophilus—Theophilus is a Greek name, suggesting that the man was a Gentile. His identification is much debated. Some interpreters suggest that the word (which itself means "friend of God" or "lover of God") is a general name for Christians. Others believe Theophilus to have been a Gentile of importance, possibly a governmental official whom Luke addressed in the desire to secure Paul's release from prison. The titular address "most excellent" would in any case identify him as a significant individual. This title of rank is applied by Luke twice to Felix and once to Festus (Acts 23:26; 24:3; 26:25).

➤4 That thou mightest know the certainty—Perhaps the Greek tense of the verb (an inceptive aorist) suggests the initiation of an action; therefore, the translation might be "begin to know the certainty (or, reliability)." of those things wherein thou hast been instructed—The phrase could be translated "in which you have been instructed by word of mouth" (Gk. katēchēthēs, from where we get the word "catechism"). In this sense, the expression "catechetically taught" would be appropriate. With the conversion of many Gentiles to Christianity, early Christians needed some documents for use as sources of teaching material. This was not necessary so long as Christianity was predominantly a Jewish movement. The Jews were adept in memorizing extensive passages of Scripture, and they had a background in the Scripture that the Gentiles did not possess.

## 5-25 ANNOUNCEMENT OF THE FORERUNNER

➤5 Herod—See comments on Matthew 2:1. This Herod, of course, is Herod the Idumean, king of Judea, 37-4 B.C. He is known historically as Herod the Great. Although Herod was known to be extremely vile and wicked, the Roman emperor Augustus once insisted that Herod's domains were too small for the greatness of his soul. He is not mentioned again in Luke's Gospel. **of the course of Abia** [Abijah]—The eighth of the twenty-four orders or courses into which David had divided the tribes of Levi, the tribes of the priests (see 1 Chron. 24:1, 4, 10). Of these courses only four returned after the captivity (Ezra 2:24-29); however, these four were again subdivided into twenty-four—retaining the ancient name and order of each. Each group alternated in the temple responsibilities, except during the Feasts of Passover, Pentecost, and Tabernacles, when all served. During the remainder of the year each group served twice and that for a period of one week during responsibility of service. **his wife was of the daughters of Aaron**—The priests could marry into any tribe, but "it was most commendable of all to marry one of the priests' line" (Lightfoot).

➤**6 And they were both righteous before God**—Luke obviously places the emphasis upon the term "both." **walking in all the commandments and ordinances of the Lord blameless**—the one term expressing their moral, the other expressing their ceremonial obedience (Calvin and Bengel). Some scholars deny that any such distinction was known to either the Jews or NT writers, but Mark 12:33 and similar passages contradict such a viewpoint.

➤**7 And they had no child**—Children were considered a sign of God's blessing. Childlessness was a reproach to Jewish women (Gen. 30:23). **because that Elizabeth was barren, and they both were now well stricken** [advanced] **in years**—so with Abraham and Sarah, Isaac and Rebekah, Elkanah and Hannah, Manoah and his wife.

➤**8 while he performed the priest's office before God in the order of his course**—See 1:5.

➤**9 According to the custom of the priest's office, his lot was to burn incense**—The individual courses were determined by lot. The TLB marginal note suggests that throwing dice or drawing straws would be the contemporary equivalent. The duties of individual priests within the courses were likewise determined by lot. These duties were divided during six days, but all of the group served on the Sabbath. The burning of incense was a partic-

ularly significant responsibility, for it brought the priest near God. The people were praying outside while the incense was burned in the Holy Place, next to the Court of Israel. Three priests were employed at the offering of incense—one to remove the ashes of the former service; one to bring in and place on the golden altar the pan filled with hot burning coals taken from the altar of burnt offering; and one to sprinkle the incense on the hot coals, and while the smoke of it ascended, to make intercession for the people. This last function was the most distinguished part of the service (Rev. 8:3), and this was Zechariah's responsibility at the time. The priest who had the highest functions allotted to him was called "the chief of the course." One view suggests there must have been some twenty thousand priests in the days of Christ; therefore, the offering of incense could never be the responsibility of the same priest twice. This must have been a very memorable day in the life of Zechariah.

➤**10** Luke adds that the people were praying outside the court in front of the temple where the altar of burnt offering stood; the men and women were in separate courts, but the altar was visible to all of them. **the time of incense**—is an expression describing the offering of incense along with the morning and evening sacrifices. This was a beautiful symbol of the acceptability of the sacrifice offered on the altar of burnt offering. (Note: the coals from the altar of burnt offering were used to light the censer—see Lev. 16:12, 13.) This again was a symbol of the "living sacrifice" of themselves and their services offered daily to God by the worshipers.

➤**11 And there appeared unto him an angel of the Lord standing on the right side**—the south side, between the altar and the candlestick (lampstand). Zechariah was on the north side in front of the altar while offering incense. But why there? The right side was the favorable side.

➤**12 Fear** came on Zechariah when he saw the angel. The early Israelites spoke of God's presence as his "angel" (Gen. 22:11; Exod. 23:20), and "this manner of . . . speech later developed into a belief that God communicates with men through a host of messengers, among whom Gabriel was especially the angel of revelation" (Caird).

➤13 The angel sought to alleviate Zechariah's fear by stating, **Fear not, Zacharias, for thy prayer is heard**—doubtless a prayer for offspring. The angel predicted that Elizabeth would bear a son whose name would be **John**—the same as Johanan, frequent in the OT, meaning "Jehovah's gracious gift." Zechariah was instructed to call his son John and not name the boy after himself.

➤15 John would prove to be great in the sight of the Lord. He would be nearer to the Lord in official standing than all the prophets. (See comments on Matt. 11:10, 11.) He would drink no wine or strong drink. This suggests that he would be a Nazarite, or a "separated one" (see Num. 6:2). As the leper was the living symbol of *sin*, so was the Nazarite a living symbol of *holiness*. Nothing alcoholic was to come to his lips; no razor was to come on his head; no ceremonial defilement was to be contracted. This baby yet to be born was to be "holy to the Lord." It is fitting that the utmost severity of legal consecration should be seen in Christ's forerunner. He was to be **filled with the Holy Ghost** [Spirit] **... from his mother's womb**—Cf. 1:35.

➤16, 17 John was to be a religious and moral reformer like Elijah. He was to **go before him** as a herald to announce his approach and to serve as a pioneer to prepare his way. (See Mal. 3:1.) **in the spirit and power of Elias** [Elijah]—after the model of Elijah (see Mal. 4:5, 6). Jesus indicated that John would have been the fulfillment of Malachi 3:1, 4:5, 6 if the Jews had believed him (Matt. 11:10-14). Luke does not refer to John's miraculous power, because John did not perform miracles (John 10:41), but to his power in "turning the heart" to God. Elijah and John both came in degenerate times, both witnessed fearlessly for God, and neither appeared often except in the direct exercise of his ministry. Both men headed schools of disciples, and their successes were similar. **to turn the hearts of the fathers to the children**—i.e., to restore a pristine spirit, a spirit ready to receive the Messiah. This was predicted as Elijah's function (Mal. 4:5,6). **and the disobedient to the wisdom of the just**—If "the disobedient" are "the children," and "the fathers" have "the wisdom of the just" (Bengel), the meaning will be that John will bring back (or, revive) the ancient spirit of the nation.

**to make ready**—to make ready for the Lord a prepared people, **a people prepared** to welcome him. Such preparation requires an operation corresponding to John's ministry.

➤18 **And Zacharias said . . . Whereby shall I know this?**—Mary believed what was far more difficult, without a sign. Abraham, though older (and doubtless Sarah too), when given the same promise, did not disbelieve. Zechariah required a sign.

➤19 **Gabriel**—signifying "man of God," the same who appeared to Daniel at the time of incense (Dan. 9:21) and to Mary (1:26).

➤20 Zechariah requested a sign, and he was told that he would be silent and unable to speak until the day that these things came to pass (see 1:64).

➤21 **And the people waited**—to receive from Zechariah the usual priestly benediction following his offering of the prayers (cf. Num. 6:23-27). **marvelled that he tarried so long**—To do so was unusual, lest it should be thought divine vengeance had stricken the people's representative for something wrong.

➤22 **he could not speak**—See 1:62. Geldenhuys observes ". . . the officiating priest had then to pronounce over them the priestly blessings of Numbers 6:24-26, the other priests repeating it after him." But Zechariah was dumb.

➤24 After he returned home, **Elizabeth conceived,** and she **hid herself** for **five months.** Elizabeth hid herself until the event was beyond doubt and the angel's promise was apparent in its fulfillment.

26-38 ANNUNCIATION OF CHRIST (See Matthew 1:18-21.)

➤26 **In the sixth month**—of Elizabeth's pregnancy. **the angel Gabriel was sent from God unto a city of Galilee, named Nazareth**—This verse suggests the extensiveness and credibility of Luke's research. Note that he names the angel, as well as the city and province.

➤27 **to a virgin espoused** [engaged—pledged to be married] **to a man whose name was Joseph, of the house of David**—See Matt. 1:16.

➤28 **Hail, thou that art highly favoured, the Lord is with thee: blessed art thou among women**—This last clause does not appear in the earliest manuscripts. The expression "thou that art highly favored" or "O favored one" (RSV) is used only here in the NT. The mistaken Vulgate rendering "full of grace" has been used extensively by the Roman Catholic church. Verse 28 indicates that Mary had received favor but in no manner suggests that she confers favor.

➤**29 she was troubled at his saying, and cast** [considered] **in her mind**—Betrothal was sacred and any violation was judged as adultery. Betrothal lasted a year and could be dissolved only by divorce. Unfaithfulness on the part of the young girl was punishable by death.

➤**30 And the angel said unto her, Fear not, Mary**—lit., "stop fearing, Mary."

➤**31** Calvin notes that the angel purposely conformed his language to Isaiah's famous prophecy (7:14). Verses 32 and 33 are but an echo of the sublime prediction in Isaiah 9:6, 7.

➤**34 How shall this be . . . ?**—Mary does not express the unbelief of Zechariah exhibited in his question, "Whereby shall I know this?" On the other hand, she takes the fact for granted and inquires only concerning the manner of fulfillment. Instead of reproof, therefore, her question is answered in mysterious detail.

➤**35 The Holy Ghost** [Spirit]—See Matthew 1:18. **power of the Highest**—The immediate energy of the Godhead conveyed by the Holy Spirit. This power would **overshadow** Mary—an expression suggesting the gentle yet efficacious working of God's Spirit. **That holy thing** [a literal rendering] **which shall be born of thee**—This language is puzzling, for we would prefer that it read "that holy child." But Luke used a neuter expression: *to gennōmenon hagion* ("the holy thing being born"). Perhaps Luke phrased it this way because a new thing had happened—God had entered into humanity. A new entity, a God-man, was about to be born. He would be holy and would **be called the Son of God.** That Christ is the Son of God in his divine and eternal nature is evident from all the NT; yet, here we see that sonship entering into human manifestation by his being born through the working of the Holy Spirit. We must not think of a divided sonship (one human and another divine), or deny what is here plainly expressed—the union between his human birth and his personal divine sonship. The NT makes no attempt to prove the virgin birth; it simply asserts the virgin birth. It is not

the virgin birth that guarantees the stature of Jesus, but the stature of Jesus that makes the virgin birth credible. To speak of being born of a virgin would be incongruous in relationship to the life of any other historical character, but the virgin birth is in harmony with all that we know of Jesus' sinless life.

➤**36** The angel suggests that Mary's **cousin** [or, relative] **Elisabeth** had already conceived. This conception was an unsought sign to Mary, but nonetheless this came in reward of her faith.

➤**37 with God nothing shall be impossible**—In other early manuscripts, the reading is, "no word from God will be void of power" (see ASV). In other words, God's word has the dynamo to accomplish what had been uttered. What God had just promised to Mary he was well able to perform (see 1:45). Verse 38 records the marvelous faith of Mary under such circumstances.

### 39-56 VISIT OF MARY TO ELIZABETH

➤**39** Mary went into the **hill country,** the mountainous tract running along the middle of Judea from north to south. **with haste**—She rushed to Elizabeth's home, not only because of what Gabriel had announced concerning the coming of her own son, but also because of his announcement concerning Elizabeth's conception. The **city of Juda** is likely to be identified as Hebron (see Josh. 20:7; 21:11).

➤**40** Mary greeted Elizabeth, who had now returned from her seclusion (see 1:24). Elizabeth had either hidden herself to keep society from knowing of her pregnancy or, more likely, to glorify God in the quietness of her home.

➤**41** Elizabeth's **babe leaped** upon hearing the greeting of Mary. Verse 44 indicates that this maternal sensation was something extraordinary—a sympathetic emotion of the unconscious babe, at the presence of the mother of his Lord.

➤**42-44** What beautiful superiority to envy have we here! High as was the distinction conferred upon herself, Elizabeth loses sight of that distinction altogether in the presence of one more honored still. The only explanation for Elizabeth's calling Mary the mother of her Lord (1:43) is that, as the prophets of old, she was enlightened to perceive the Messiah's divine nature (Olshausen).

## 46-55 MARY'S HYMN OF PRAISE

This lyrical poem is Hebraic in thought and manner. It is composed almost entirely of OT quotations, closely following the song of Hannah (1 Sam. 2:1-10). This hymn of praise has been traditionally known as the "Magnificat," derived from the first word in the hymn of praise in the Vulgate translation. In Mary's song, as in Hannah's song, these holy women were filled with wonder to see that "the proud, the mighty, the rich" were not chosen to usher in the greatest events, but the lowly. They sang of this as no capricious movement, but as a great principle of God by which he delights to put down the mighty from their seats and to exalt them of low degree. In both songs the ultimate focus is on Christ. In Hannah's song, he is "Jehovah's King"; in Mary's song, he is **my Saviour.** Mary recognized her son to be her Savior. And, as such, she is not any different than the rest of fallen humanity—all of whom need Jesus the Savior.

➤**56** Mary remained with Elizabeth about three months; she left just before Elizabeth gave birth to John. **returned to her own house**—at Nazareth—after which took place what is recorded in Matthew 1:18-25.

## 57-66 THE BIRTH AND CIRCUMCISION OF JOHN

➤**57 Now Elizabeth's full time came that she should be delivered**—i.e., her time of delivery had come. This is additional evidence of the care with which Luke wrote his Gospel.

➤**58** Elizabeth's **neighbours and her cousins** [relatives]—rejoiced upon hearing of the baby's birth.

➤**59 eighth day**—The law (Gen. 17:12) was observed, even if the eighth day after a birth would be a Sabbath day (John 7:23; see also Phil. 3:5). **they called him Zacharias**—The Greek indicates that "they were calling him Zechariah" (or, "had been calling him Zechariah"). The naming of children at baptism had its origin in the Jewish circumcision (Gen. 21:3, 4), for the names of Abram and Sarai were changed at its first performance (Gen. 17:5, 15). Boys were named on the day of circumcision while girls were named anytime within thirty days of their birth.

➤**60 he shall be called John**—Jews chose meaningful names, but God had already named this son. Rather than having his aged father's

name, the baby was to be called John, "Jehovah was graciously given."

➤**61** The people sought to understand Elizabeth's choice of name, for none of the relatives bore the name John.

➤**62 made signs**—showing he was deaf, as well as unable to speak.

➤**63 And he asked for a writing table,** [tablet] **and wrote, His name is John**—This naming was not debatable. The issue had already been settled in the temple courts. **And they marvelled all**—at his giving the same name, not knowing of any communication between them on the subject.

➤**64 And his mouth was opened immediately and his tongue loosed**—thus palpably showing his full faith in the vision because he had been struck dumb as a result of his disbelief (1:13, 20). Zechariah spoke in the manner of praising God and not simply in expressing mere joy over the birth of a child.

➤**65 And fear came on all**—religious awe. The neighbors were under the impression that God's hand was particularly evident in these events (cf. 5:26; 7:16; 8:37).

➤**66 and all they that heard . . . , What manner of child shall this be!**—The evidence of God's hand at work in the birth of the child conveyed to the simple people a divine purpose beyond comprehension. **And the hand of the Lord was with him**—by special tokens marking him out as one destined to some great work.

## 67-74 THE SONG OF ZECHARIAH

This song is often called the Benedictus, so named for its first word in the Vulgate. This noble burst of divine song says little about his own child. Zechariah lost sight entirely of himself in the glory of One greater than both his child and himself.

➤**68 Blessed be the Lord God of Israel**—the God of the ancient covenant between him and his special people. **visited and redeemed**—lit., "visited and accomplished redemption" (the past tense for "redeemed" is used in anticipation of the action. God had returned after a long absence and had broken his prophetic silence. In the OT God is said to "visit" chiefly for judgment, but in the NT his visitation is for mercy. Zechariah had imperfect views of this "visiting and redeeming" and "saving and delivering out of the hands of enemies" (1:71, 74), for his concept of deliverance entailed military overthrow (1:74), not expiatory sacrifice. But this OT phraseology can be adapted to express the most spiritual conceptions of the redemption that is in Christ Jesus.

➤**69 horn of salvation**—"strength of salvation" or "mighty salvation." Surely this refers to the Savior himself (cf. 2:30). The metaphor is derived from a description of animals whose strength is in their horns (Ps. 18:2; 75:10; 132:17). **house of his servant David**—This phrase shows that Mary must have been known to be of the royal line, independent of Joseph.

➤**73 The oath which he sware to our father Abraham**—The whole work and kingdom of the Messiah is represented as a mercy pledged by oath to Abraham and his seed, to be realized at an appointed time. And at length, "in the fullness of time," this pledge was to be gloriously kept.

➤**74, 75** These two verses give us a comprehensive view of what would come as a result of God's deliverance. First is service to God: that we "might serve him without fear." The word for service signifies religious service distinctively—the priesthood of the NT. Then follows a description of the nature of this service: "in holiness and righteousness before him." This service is a result of our freedom from our enemies and is without fear and without end ("all the days of our life"). In this first part of the song, Zechariah defines redemption as a visitation from God and also describes the nature of salvation. The second portion of the song begins with verse 76 and relates to the child himself. But the song here passes not from Christ to John, but only from Christ direct to Christ as heralded by his forerunner.

➤**76 thou, child, shalt be called the prophet of the Highest** [or, the Most High]—As "the Most High" is an epithet in Scripture only of the supreme God, it is inconceivable that Luke would apply this term to Christ if he were not "God over all, blessed for ever" (Rom. 9:5).

➤**77 To give knowledge of salvation**—To sound the note of a needed and provided salvation was the noble office of John above all that preceded him, even as it is that of all subsequent ministers of Christ. **by the remission** [forgiveness] **of their sins**—This characterizes the spiritual nature of the salvation here intended and explains 1:71, 74.

➤**78 Through the tender mercy of our God**—which is the sole source of all salvation for sinners. **whereby the dayspring** [lit., "sunrising"] **from on high hath visited us**—or, "will visit us," according to other manuscript authority (including the three earliest manuscripts). Either way, it speaks of Christ's first advent, his dawning epiphany.

➤**79** This verse is taken from the prophetic word in Isaiah 9:2 (used also in Matt. 4:13-17). This verse, as well as the verses preceding, stands as still another evidence of the careful research and writing of Luke.

➤**80 The progress of John as a child.**

This is the only reference to the childhood of John. John lived in the desert area (at least from his twentieth year) while the Messiah lived in Nazareth, each awaiting the proper time to begin his public ministry. The paragraph indicates the bodily and mental development of John and quickly summarizes his life up to the period of his public appearance. The deserts were probably the wilderness places of Judea where John retired early in life in the Nazarite spirit and where, free from rabbinical influences and alone with God, his spirit would be educated for his future vocation. The term is plural, suggesting that he did not always remain in the same area. Some scholars have speculated that John spent some time in one of the Qumran communities, but no such contact or relationship with the Essenic communities can be proved. John preached to people and mingled with men, while the Essenes avoided society; he preached social righteousness, while they were ascetic; he preached Jesus as the Christ, while the Essenes wanted nothing to do with him. **his showing unto Israel**—i.e., his manifestation to Israel and the presentation of himself before his people as the Messiah's forerunner.

Chapter 2

## 1-7 BIRTH OF CHRIST

➤**1 Caesar Augustus**—Caesar was the first of the Roman emperors. He ruled from 31 B.C. to August 19, A.D. 14, and was absolute monarch over the Roman Empire. Augustus was also called "Savior." **all the world**—i.e., the vast Roman Empire; in those days called "the world." **should be taxed**—lit., "should be enrolled." The term used for "enrolled" is a term describing a provincial census. Taxation, of course, normally followed this registration. This enrollment occurred in 6 B.C.; a second enrollment, referred to in Acts 5:37, happened in A.D. 6.

►**2 first . . . when Cyrenius**—a very difficult verse, inasmuch as Cyrenius, or Quirinius, appears not to have been governor of Syria until approximately ten years after the birth of Christ, and the taxing under his administration was what led to the insurrection mentioned in Acts 5:37. Therefore, some scholars have thought that Luke mistook the second enrollment for the first. But there is some evidence that Cyrenius was serving a second term when the Acts 5:37 enrollment occurred. Also it is quite acceptable to translate the Greek word for "first" (*prōte*) as "before"; hence, the verse could be rendered "And this enrollment happened before Cyrenius governed Syria" (see Liefeld's comments and quotes from Bruce and Turner).

►**3 And all went to be taxed** [enrolled], **everyone into his own city**—the city of the man's lineage, not the city of his abode. The Jews had to return to the city where the records of their families were kept.

►**4, 5** David had been born in Bethlehem about one thousand years earlier. Therefore, Joseph returned to that city. It was unnecessary for Mary to journey with her husband, but she probably accompanied him because her pregnancy was full term. **his espoused** [betrothed—pledged to be married]. By this time, Joseph had taken Mary to his home, as related in Matthew 1:18.

►**6 while they were there**—Mary had been living at the wrong place for the Messiah's birth. A little longer stay at Nazareth, and the prophecy would have failed. But, with no intention certainly on her part to fulfill the prophecy, much less on the part of Caesar Augustus, she was brought from Nazareth to Bethlehem, and at that time her son was born.

►**7** How humble a birth! Jesus was born in a stable where animals were kept. Justin Martyr (died c. A.D. 165) described this as a cave. **firstborn son**—See note on Matthew 1:25. **swaddling clothes**—were the usual dress for a newborn baby. **a manger**—an eating trough

for farm animals. **no room for them in the inn**—a room where travelers stayed, often a square edifice with a stable built on to the back wall. Jesus could have been born in one of these stables or in a cave, as is stated in ancient tradition. This is quite feasible because of the rocky conditions of the country and the numerous caves. In Mary's condition the journey would be a slow one, and by the time they made the trek from Nazareth to Bethlehem (a distance of some eighty miles), any accommodations would be taken. Luke says that a stable was all that was available for Joseph and Mary.

## 8-20 THE ANGELIC ANNOUNCEMENT TO THE SHEPHERDS AND THEIR VISIT TO BETHLEHEM

►**8 shepherds abiding in the field**—probably living in huts or tents. **keeping watch over their flocks by night**—or, "night-watches," taking their turn of watching. From about Passover in April until autumn, the flocks pastured constantly in the open fields. The shepherds lodged with the flocks during that time. From this custom it seems evident that the period of the year usually assigned to Jesus' birth is too late. Were these shepherds chosen to have the first sight of the blessed babe without any respect to their own state of mind? At least, that is not God's usual way of working. It is possible that these were flocks owned by the temple, and the shepherds were caring for sheep that would later become sacrificial animals.

►**9 the angel of the Lord came upon them**—i.e., the angel appeared to them. **they were sore afraid**—lit., "feared a great fear." Men have never felt easy with the invisible world laid suddenly open to their gaze.

►**10 the angel said . . . , Fear not**—lit., "Stop being afraid." The Greek construction means to stop an action now in progress. This expression is characteristic of this section of Luke's Gospel. **I bring you good tidings of great joy**—The verbal expression in Greek is a word that can be translated "I preach the gospel." The term carries with it the idea of good news, a good message. Whereas the shepherds had "feared a great fear," the angel brings a "great joy," which is to be to **all people.** This last expression suggests the universality of the good news.

►**11 For unto you is born**—to you shepherds, to Israel, to mankind (cf. Isa. 9:6). **in the city of David**—Bethlehem, the city of David's and the promised Messiah's birth (Mic. 5:2). How dear to us should be these historic affirmations of our faith! With the loss of them, all substantial, Christianity is lost. **a Saviour**—not one who shall be a Savior, but one "born a Savior." Of the Synoptic writers, only Luke uses this term. **Christ the Lord**—lit., "Christ Lord," a magnificent appellation. This is the only place where these words come together. This "Lord" probably corresponds to the Hebrew "Jehovah" or "Yahweh" (see Alford). Thus, Messiah is Yahweh.

►**12 a sign**—lit., "the sign." **a babe . . . lying in a manger**—The sign was to consist solely in the overpowering contrast between the things just said of him and the lowly condition in which they would find him. Although born a Savior, he would be found "wrapped in swaddling clothes" and "lying in a manger."

►**13 suddenly**—as if only waiting until the first angel had finished his declaration. **with the angel**—The angel did not depart but was joined by others who came to seal and celebrate the tidings he had brought. **heavenly host**—or, army. An army celebrating peace!

►**14 Glory to God in the highest, and on earth peace, good will toward men**—According to better and earlier manuscript authority, the last phrase should read "among men of good will." Therefore, the verse should read, "Glory to God in the highest, and peace on earth among men of *his* good pleasure." (This good pleasure does not come from man but from God.) The angelic message meant that peace in the highest sense becomes a reality among men who are blessed by God's good favor. "Peace" with God is the grand necessity of a fallen world. To bring this condition was the prime errand of the Savior come to earth, and along with it heaven's whole "good will to men."

►**15 as the angels were gone** [went away] . . . **Let us now go**—The response of the shepherds was simultaneous. Although it is probable that these shepherds were keeping flocks for the temple sacrifices, the orthodox Jews despised the shepherds because of their lack of ceremonial purity. Yet it was to these simple shepherds that God chose to reveal first the communication of the Savior's birth. The

shepherds were not "taken up" with the angels, the glory that surrounded them, or the lofty strains with which they filled the air. Neither did they say, "Let us go and see if this be true." They had no such misgivings. Rather they suggested, "Let us go over to Bethlehem and see this thing that has happened, which the Lord has made known to us."

►**16 they came with haste**—Cf. 1:39; Matthew 28:8. The term "haste" means "to accelerate, to cut across." They likely "cut across the fields" in their haste to reach Bethlehem. **found Mary, and Joseph**—mysteriously guided by the Spirit through the darkness of the night to the right place.

►**17 they made known . . . the saying**—they reported the angelic message.

►**19 Mary . . . and pondered them**—She was placing all of these things together in order, for the purpose of comparing them much as one puts together the pieces of a jigsaw puzzle.

►**20 glorifying and praising God**—Both these terms are present tenses and describe continuous action. The latter word is used in 2:13 to describe the words of the angels. Luke here employs the term to describe the swelling emotions of simple hearts stirred by what "they have heard and seen."

21 CIRCUMCISION OF CHRIST

This is the only reference to the circumcision of Christ, and this reference is seemingly for the purpose of introducing his name. The male Jew was circumcised on the eighth day after birth even if the eighth day was a Sabbath. The rite of circumcision not only fulfilled the law but indicated that the Jew adhered to his covenant relationship with God. **his name was called Jesus**—equivalent to the OT name "Joshua," the "delivering One." Luke further adds that this was the name given by the angel even before Jesus was conceived. The circumcision of Christ had a profound bearing upon his work. Paul indicated that the circumcised one "is bound to keep the whole law" (Gal. 5:3, RSV). Therefore, Jesus bore in his very flesh the seal of a voluntary obligation to do the entire law—which only he, of all men, could actually do. And inasmuch as he was "born under the law and to redeem those who were under the law" (Gal. 4:4, 5, RSV), the obedience to which his

circumcision pledged him was a redeeming
obedience—that of a "Savior." And finally, as
Christ "redeemed us from the curse of the law"
(Gal. 3:13), we must regard him in his circumcision as brought under a pledge to be "obedient unto death, even the death on the cross"
(Phil. 2:8).

## 22-24 THE PURIFICATION OF MARY AND THE PRESENTATION OF JESUS IN THE TEMPLE

➤**22 And when the days of her purification**—according to the best manuscripts, "their
purification," i.e., the purification of the child
and mother. Leviticus 12:2, 4 indicate that "the
days" of this purification for a male were forty;
and on the expiration of the time, the mother
was required to offer a lamb for a burnt offering
and a turtle-dove or young pigeon for a sin
offering. If she could not afford a lamb, the
mother was to bring another turtle-dove or
young pigeon. And if even this was beyond her
means, then a portion of fine flour, but without
the usual fragrant accompaniments of oil and
frankincense, since this represented a sin offering (Lev. 12:6-8; 5:7-11). Luke indicates the
poverty of Joseph and Mary in a very subtle
way by saying (2:24) that they offered the birds
rather than a lamb and a pigeon.

➤**23 Every male that openeth the
womb**—The redemption of the firstborn as
specified in Exodus 13:2 required a redemption
payment to the temple treasury. All firstborn
males had been declared holy to God and set
apart for sacred uses in memory of how the
firstborn of Israel were saved from destruction
through the sprinkling of blood (Exod. 13:2).
In lieu of these, however, one whole tribe, that
of Levi, was accepted and set apart to occupations exclusively sacred (Num. 3:11-38).
Because there were 273 fewer Levites than the
firstborn of all Israel on the first counting, each
of these firstborn was to be redeemed by the
payment of five shekels, yet not without being
presented unto the Lord in token of his rightful
claim to them and their service (Num. 3:44-47;
18:15, 16). It was in obedience to this "law of
Moses" that Mary presented her baby unto the
Lord. By that baby, in due time, we would be
redeemed—"not with perishable things such as
silver or gold, but with the precious blood of
Christ . . ." (1 Pet. 1:18, 19, RSV). Luke, in

writing to present Jesus as the universal Savior,
significantly explains the rite of purification
(2:22) in 2:23, 24.

## 25-40 THE TEMPLE SCENE WITH SIMEON AND ANNA

This experience in the life of Jesus was
characterized by quietness; no banners were
flying, no armies advancing. The scene was
one of humility and devotion.

➤**25 there was a man in Jerusalem**—This
statement again characterizes Luke's deliberate
historical methodology. **whose name was
Simeon**—Again Luke deals in specific personalities and illustrates his interest in accurate
historical facts. **and the same man was just
and devout**—upright in his moral character
and of a religious frame of spirit. **waiting for
the consolation of Israel**—a beautiful title of
the coming Messiah. The Greek word (para-
klēsis) shares the same root as "comforter"
(paraklētos), which includes the functions of
consoler, encourager, and exhorter. Caird indicates that the term "'consolation' was a standard rabbinical term used by the Jews for the
messianic age" (cf. Isa. 40:1; 61:2 for OT
usage of the term "consolation") **and the Holy
Ghost [Spirit] was upon him**—The Greek language indicates that the Holy Spirit had been
upon him for an indefinite amount of time in
the past—probably during all the time he was
seeking the Messiah; it does not indicate that
the Holy Spirit came upon him at that instant.

➤**26** The Holy Spirit had **revealed** to him
that he would not see death prior to seeing the
Messiah. The Greek word for "revealed" is the
same used in Matthew 2:12, 22 to designate a
divine communication. The Holy Spirit had
already conveyed the divine message to
Simeon that before his own death he would see
the Messiah. **the Lord's Christ**—a unique
application, which equals "Yahweh's Messiah"
(cf. 2:11).

➤**27, 28** The Spirit guided him to the temple at the very moment when Mary was about
to present Jesus to the Lord. Here was a man
effused with the Holy Spirit (2:25), enlightened
by the Holy Spirit (2:26), and led by the Spirit
(2:27). Simeon took Jesus in his arms, recognizing the child with unhesitating certainty and
without needing Mary to inform him of what
had occurred in her life. The remarkable act of

taking the baby into his arms must not be overlooked. It was as if he had said, "This is all my salvation and my heart's desire."

➤**29 Lord**—"Master," *despota,* not *kurios,* a word rarely used in the NT and selected here with peculiar propriety when the aged saint, feeling that his last object in wishing to live had now been attained, awaited his Master's word of command to "depart." **now lettest**—more clearly, "now you are releasing your servant," a patient, yet reverential mode of expressing a desire to depart.

➤**30 seen thy salvation**—embodied in the Savior. Many saw this child, even the full-grown Jesus, who never saw in him "God's salvation." Simeon's estimate came from pure faith. From another perspective, Simeon's action was prior faith rewarded by present sight.

➤**31, 32 all people**—refers to mankind at large. **a light to lighten the Gentiles**—from Isaiah 49:6 better rendered, "a light for revelation to the Gentiles" (NIV). It had long been known to the Jews, through reading the prophets, that the Messiah would bring salvation to the Gentiles, but it is very significant that Simeon mentions the Gentiles before the Jews. **the glory of thy people Israel**—To the believing portion of Israel, Jesus was their boast, their pride and honor. It will be observed that this final song takes a more comprehensive view of the kingdom of Christ than that of Zechariah, though the kingdom they sing of is one. Some scholars have argued that Mary's and Joseph's surprise at Simeon's words is inexplicable because of the previous visits of Gabriel, but to argue in this manner is to ignore the human element of awe at God's working.

➤**34, 35 set [appointed] for the fall and rising again of many in Israel; and for a sign which shall be spoken against**—Perhaps the first phrase expresses the two stages of (1) a temporary "fall of many in Israel" through unbelief (during our Lord's earthly career), and (2) the subsequent "rising again" of the same persons after the effusion of the Spirit at Pentecost. The second phrase describes the determined enemies of the Lord Jesus.

➤**35 a sword shall pierce through thy own soul also**—Not only would Jesus suffer, Mary also would suffer from his enemies' attack. Those agonies of his that she was to witness at the cross and her desolate condition

thereafter would be as a sword piercing her soul. **that the thoughts of many hearts may be revealed**—This expression continues from the end of 2:34 (see punctuation in KJV). The unbelief and belief in Israel would expose the inmost thoughts of all who beheld the Messiah.

➤**36, 37 Anna, a prophetess**—"Luke's attention to the renewal of prophecy at the coming of the messianic age continues with the introduction of Anna as a 'prophetess'" (Liefeld). **of the tribe of As[h]er**—one of the ten tribes, of whom many were not carried captive and not a few reunited themselves to Judah after the return from Babylon. The distinction of tribes, though practically destroyed by the captivity, was well enough known up to their final dispersion (Rom. 11:1; Heb. 7:14), nor is it now entirely lost. **fourscore and four years**—84 years. The Greek could indicate that she had been a widow 84 years, or that she was a widow until the age of 84 (see RSV, NIV). If the former were true, she would have been over 105 years old—which seems unlikely. **departed not from the temple**—She likely lived in one of the temple buildings.

➤**38 And she coming in that instant gave thanks likewise unto the Lord**—There is no manuscript authority for the rendering "Lord"; all manuscripts read "God." Anna had been there already but is now found "standing by" as Simeon's testimony to the blessed child ends. **and spoke of him to all them that looked for redemption in Jerusalem**—saying in effect, "Your expectations are all fulfilled in this child." If this was at the hour of prayer when numbers flocked to the temple, it would account for her having such an audience as the words imply. Jerusalem is here used as a synonym for Israel.

➤**39** Nothing is more difficult than to fix the precise order in which the visit of the Magi, with the flight into Egypt, and return from Egypt (Matthew 2) occurred in relation to the circumcision and presentation of Jesus in the temple. It is perhaps best to leave this in the obscurity in which we find it, as the result of two independent narratives, although it is likely that the visit to Egypt must be fitted in here.

➤**40** This verse records 12 years of Jesus' life. His mental and spiritual growth were as genuine as his physical growth. The verbs "grew" and "became [**waxed**] strong" are both used in 1:80 to describe John. They are both in the imperfect tense (defining continuous action in past time), indicating that the child "was growing" and "was waxing strong." Luke adds "was being filled with wisdom" to Jesus' description—and this wisdom would be displayed in his discussions with the religious scholars (2:46ff.). **and the grace of God was upon him**—rested manifestly and increasingly upon him (see 2:52).

## 41-52 JESUS' VISIT TO JERUSALEM WHEN HE WAS TWELVE YEARS OF AGE

These verses alone record the only glimpse into the youth of Jesus.

➤**41 Now his parents went to Jerusalem every year at the feast of the passover**—Male Jews were expected to participate in the three principal feasts—Passover, Pentecost, and Tabernacles. However, it seems that many Jews living outside of Jerusalem attended only the Passover. Devout women went, as did Hannah (1 Sam. 1:7), and Mary in this instance. Josephus suggests that as many as 256,000 lambs were offered during this time. Since ten adults were required before one lamb could be offered, some 2.5 million people probably attended the average Passover.

➤**42 And when he was twelve years old, they went up to Jerusalem after** [according to] **the custom of the feast**—At this age every Jewish boy was styled "a son of the law," being put under a course of instruction and trained in fasting and attendance in public worship, in addition to learning a trade. At this age Jesus went for the first time to Jerusalem at the Passover season, the chief of the three annual festivals. But oh, with what thoughts and feelings must this youth have gone up! Long before he beheld the temple, he had doubtless "loved the habitation of God's house" (Ps. 26:8). This love was nourished by the word hidden within his heart. At the time of his first visit, he must have been unusually excited. (See Ps. 42:1; 87:2; 112:1, 2 for appropriate suggestions of his feelings.) As a devout child in company with his parents, he would go through the services so as to be prepared for participation the next year when he became a member of the community.

➤**43 And when they had fulfilled the days**—If the duties of life must give place to worship, worship in its turn must give place to the responsibilities of life. Jerusalem is good, but Nazareth is also good. Let him who neglects the one on pretext of attending the other consider this scene.

➤**44 they sought him among their kinsfolk and acquaintance**—On these sacred journeys, entire villages and districts traveled in groups, partly for protection and partly for company. This readily explains why Joseph and Mary were unaware of Jesus' absence. They surely believed him to be with other relatives or friends.

➤**45 And when they found him not**—After three stressful days, they found him still in Jerusalem, not gazing on its architecture or surveying its forms of busy life, but in the temple with the rabbis and scholars.

➤**46 hearing . . . and asking**—The method of question and answer was the customary form of rabbinical teaching. The teacher and learner took turns as a questioner and answerer. This would give meaning to for Luke's observation that the scholars were amazed "at his understanding and answers." Not that he assumed the office of teaching— "His hour" for that "was not yet come," and his preparation for that was not complete; for he had yet to "increase in wisdom" as well as "stature" (2:52). In fact, the beauty of Christ's example lies very much in his never at one stage of his life anticipating the duties of another. All would be in the style and manner of a learner—and now more than ever before, when finding himself for the first time in his Father's house.

➤**48 thy father and I**—the natural way to refer to herself and Joseph. This expression by no means invalidates the virgin birth.

➤**49 How is it that ye sought me? . . . I must be about my Father's business**—This is the first recorded word of Jesus, and this word is one of dedication. Jesus insists that he must be where God is found. Here he felt himself at home, breathing his own proper air. His words convey a gentle rebuke of their obtuseness for requiring him to explain this. Mary tells Jesus of the sorrow that he has caused herself and his father, Joseph. But Jesus speaks of God as being "my Father" and thus unveils, for the first time, his divine identity.

➤**50, 51 And he went down with them, and came to Nazareth, and was subject unto**

**them**—Just as Jesus' words surpassed Joseph's and Mary's understanding, his obedience is also incredible. He returned to Nazareth and was obedient to them in all things. **his mother kept all these sayings in her heart**—From this time, there is no additional mention of Joseph. The next that we read of Jesus' family is of his "mother and brothers" (John 2:12). It has been generally inferred, therefore, that between this time and the beginning of our Lord's public ministry, Joseph died, leaving Jesus as the oldest son, responsible for the family.

➤**52** See comments on 2:40. **increased**—"was increasing," or, "was progressing," or, "was pioneering ahead"—the Greek term means to "forge ahead as a pioneer cuts the way through the forest" (cf. Gal. 1:14; Phil. 1:12 in Gk.). Jesus was increasing in wisdom, age, and grace with God and men alike. Mark 6:3 indicates that Joseph and Mary had other sons and daughters. Jesus became a carpenter, probably the town carpenter of Nazareth.

*Chapter* **3**

## 1, 2 BACKGROUND OF JOHN'S MINISTRY

These verses follow Luke's careful methodology in specifying historical events and personalities. He states that his ministry was not performed somewhere in an isolated corner but that it occurred on the actual stage of history under these specific conditions. Here the curtain of the NT is raised, and the greatest of all epochs begins. Jesus' age (3:23) is determined by it (Bengel). No such elaborate chronological precision is to be found elsewhere in the NT, and it comes fitly from him who claims it as the peculiar recommendation of his Gospel (cf. 1:3). Here Luke begins his proper narrative. He does so by fitting this ministry into the political background. See Matthew 3:1-12; Mark 1:1-8; and John 1:19-28 for Gospel parallels.

➤**1 Now in the fifteenth year of the reign of Tiberius Caesar**—There are several approaches to the interpretation of this temporal element. (1) Tiberius became ruler when Augustus died in A.D. 14. (2) Tiberius had been made a colleague and co-ruler with his father as early as A.D. 11/12. (3) The "fifteenth year"

is a reference to the ecclesiastical year used for the reign of Jewish kings. This year began 1 Nisan (March-April), and the civil years used for foreign kings began six months later at 1 Tishri. The reigns were then reckoned from the new year preceding the ascension to the throne, so in this case Luke would be referring to 1 Tishri, c. A.D. 27/28. This practice was retained from the days of the Seleucidae. **Pontius Pilate being governor of Judaea**—The proper title was "procurator," but he had more than the usual powers of that office. After occupying this office for some ten years, he was ordered to Rome to answer charges brought against him; but before he arrived, Tiberius died, and soon thereafter Pilate committed suicide. He reigned as governor of Judea during A.D. 26-36. **Herod being tetrarch of Galilee**—Herod Antipas, son of Herod the Great, ruled Galilee from the time of his father's death in 4 B.C. until A.D. 39. **and his brother Philip tetrarch of Ituraea and of the region of Trachonitis**—a different Philip from the one whose wife Herodias went to live with Herod Antipas (see Mark 6:17). Philip reigned 4 B.C.-A.D. 34 over Ituraea (northeast Palestine) and Trachonitis (farther to the northeast, between Ituraea and Damascus). **Lysanias the tetrarch of Abilene**—Little is known concerning Lysanias, but Abilene is more particularly the Lebanon area and is some 18 miles from Damascus.

➤**2 Annas and Caiaphas, being the high priests**—or, "the high priesthood of Annas and Caiaphas" (RSV). Annas, who was high priest A.D. 6-15, was deposed by the Romans but nonetheless retained his place of importance among the Jews. Caiaphas was high priest during A.D. 18-36 and was a son-in-law of Annas. Luke employs the singular "priesthood," indicating that he looks upon this era as one period and not as two different priesthoods.

## 3-17 THE PREACHING AND MINISTRY OF JOHN THE BAPTIST

Judging from the general data concerning the time elements defined in the preceding verses, John must have begun his ministry between the years A.D. 26-29. Some scholars have conjectured that the year was likely A.D. 27. John's preaching is expanded in three brief sections. Verses 7-9 contain the warning that baptism apart from true repentance is worthless. Verses 10-14 state specific instructions for the people. Verses 15-17 underscore John's position in relationship to Jesus. He saw himself as merely the forerunner, not as the promised One of God.

➤**3 And he came into all the country about Jordan**—perhaps in the general area of Jericho. **preaching the baptism of repentance**—baptism characterized by repentance. Repentance is more than mere sorrow; it is "an about-face, a change in conduct." This "baptism" is described further as a baptism of repentance **for the remission of sins.** People were baptized by John because they had repented of their sins and their lives had been changed. Verses 10-14 reveal certain conversations with John concerning evidences of a changed life. Although the Jews had many ablutions, a baptism characterized by repentance was unique in Jewish thought.

➤**4** John viewed himself as the fulfillment of Isaiah 40:3. The "wilderness one" was preparing the way for the Messiah (see Mark 1:3).

➤**5** The figures in this verse speak of leveling and smoothing, the sense of which connects to the first words of the proclamation, "Prepare ye the way of the Lord." Where a man has deviated from God's ways, he must return to his pathway. The pathways must be made straight and all the rough places smoothed; only in this manner will all be in readiness for the coming of the Messiah.

➤**6 all flesh**—i.e., all humanity. This notes the universality of his mission. The idea is that every obstruction shall be removed so as to reveal to the whole world the salvation of God in him whose name is Savior. Men would be able to see salvation as revealed through the Messiah and his work, as well as how and in what ways it brought deliverance to them.

➤**7 generation** [offspring] **of vipers!**— Matthew (3:7) addresses this statement to the Pharisees and Sadducees.

➤**8** The application of this verse is seen in verses 10-14. The Jews trusted in their Abrahamic sonship and felt justified by it. But John affirmed that God was able of the wilderness stones to raise up children unto Abraham. He did not desire children of Abraham but children of faith. In Aramaic the words *stones* and *children* produce a pun.

➤**9** The **axe** depicts judgment. The coming of the kingdom brings judgment to all men; the tree bearing bad fruit is cut down.

➤**10-14 What shall we do then?**—to show the sincerity of our repentance. **two coats**— directed against the prevalent avarice. **Exact no more than that which is appointed you**— directed against that extortion which made the tax collectors a by-word. Soldiers supplemented their salaries by extortion and threat of fraud. They were commanded by John not to intimidate in order to extort money or other property. **neither accuse any falsely**—False accusation was also a favorite approach by many soldiers who acted as vexatious informers on frivolous or false grounds. **be content with your wages**—We may take this as a warning against mutiny, which the officers attempted to suppress by largesses and donations (Webster and Wilkinson). And thus the "fruits" that would evidence their repentance were just resistance to the reigning sins, particularly of the class to which the penitent belonged, and the manifestation of an opposite spirit. John the Baptist insisted that a man's entering the kingdom expressed itself in ethical and moral relationships.

➤**15 as the people were in expectation, and all men mused in their hearts of** [concerning] **John, whether he were the Christ, or not**—showing both how successful he had been in awakening the expectation of the Messiah's immediate appearing and also the high estimation and reverence that his own character commanded.

➤**16, 17 John answered**—either to the deputation from Jerusalem (see John 1:19) or on some other occasion, simply to remove the false impressions that he knew were to be taking hold of the popular mind. The worst thing John could do was give any kind of impression that he was the Christ. So he pointed to the mightier One. What a beautiful spirit distinguishes this servant of Christ! (See also comments on Matt. 3:11; 11:1ff.)

18-20 THE IMPRISONMENT OF JOHN
➤**18 many other things in his exhortation**—such as are recorded in John 1:29, 33, 34; 3:27-36.

➤**19, 20** See comments on Mark 6:14ff. **reproved by him . . . for all the evils which**

**Herod had done**—an important fact mentioned only by Luke, showing how thoroughgoing was the fidelity of John to his royal hearer and how strong must have been the workings of conscience in that slave of passion when, notwithstanding such plainness, he heard John gladly (Mark 6:20, 26).

►**21-22 The baptism of Jesus and the descent of the Holy Spirit upon him.** (See comments on Matt. 3:13-17.)

►**21 Now when all the people were baptized**—that he might not seem to be merely one of the crowd. **Jesus also being baptized, and praying**—Luke is the only Gospel writer who indicates that Jesus was praying. This clause suggests something of the worshipful atmosphere characterizing his Gospel. **the heaven was opened**—Mark says, literally, "split assunder," characteristic of the Marcan style.

►**22 and the Holy Ghost** [Spirit] **descended in a bodily shape like a dove upon him**—The words "bodily form" express the reality of the Spirit's equipping Jesus for his ministry. John indicates that the Spirit's coming upon Jesus proved to him that Jesus was the Messiah (1:33).

23-38 THE GENEALOGY OF JESUS

►**23 Jesus himself began to be about thirty years of age**—This is better translated as, "Now Jesus himself was about thirty years old when he began his ministry" (NIV). Luke now establishes Jesus as the central person before introducing his public ministry. As the OT priests began their service at the age of 30, so Jesus began his ministry when he was about 30 (c. A.D. 27). The genealogy is given to establish the fact that Jesus was legally a descendant of David. The existence of such a genealogical table extending to Joseph does not disprove the virgin birth. The author, in all probability, received much of his information from Mary. **being (as was supposed) the son of Joseph**—The expression "as was supposed" means "as was thought"—i.e., it was **thought** by Jesus' contemporaries that he was Joseph's son, when actually he was God's Son born through Mary. Have we in this genealogy, as well as in Matthew's, the line of Joseph? Or is this the lineage of Mary?—a point on which there has been great difference of opinion and much discussion. Those who are of the former

opinion contend that it is the natural sense of this verse and that no other would have been thought of had not there been problems with some of the details in this genealogy, especially as compared to Matthew's. But it is liable to another difficulty; that is, in his Gospel, Luke makes "Heli" to be Joseph's father, while Matthew makes "Jacob." Those who take the latter opinion, that we have herein the lineage of Mary, his real genealogy, explain the statement about Joseph (that he was "the son of Heli") to mean that he was his son-in-law, as the husband of his daughter Mary (as in Ruth 1:11, 12), and believe that Joseph's name is only introduced instead of Mary's in conformity with the Jewish custom in such tables. Perhaps this view is attended with fewest difficulties, as it certainly is the best supported. Thus, Matthew gives his royal lineage, while Luke gives his complete, human lineage, "probably with the intention of stressing the identification of Jesus with the entire human race" (Leister). In other words, Matthew, writing more immediately for Jews, deemed it enough to show that the King sprang from Abraham and David; whereas Luke, writing more immediately for Gentiles, traced the Savior's descent back to Adam, the parent stock of the whole human family, thus showing him to be the promised "seed of the woman."

*Chapter* 4

1-13 THE TEMPTATION OF CHRIST
See comments on Matthew 4:1-11.

14-32 JESUS BEGINS HIS PUBLIC MINISTRY BY MAKING A TRIP THROUGH GALILEE

There is a large gap of information missing at this point, covering the important events in Galilee and Jerusalem recorded in John 1:29–4:54, and which occurred before John's imprisonment (John 3:24). Jesus' visit to Nazareth recorded in Matthew 13:54-58 (and Mark 6:1-6) seems not to be a later visit but the same as this one. It is impossible to believe that the Nazarenes, after being so enraged at his first display of wisdom so as to attempt his destruction, should, on a second display of the same, wonder at it and ask how he came by it, as if they had never witnessed it before. Luke basically leaves out the materials contained in Mark 6:45–8:26, called the "great omission of Luke." Here he is very selective in what he records. Verses 14 and 15 serve as a brief summary stressing Jesus' teaching ministry and the excitement which it created.

➤**16 And he came to Nazareth, where he had been brought up**—Jesus had worked in the carpenter shop in Nazareth, a city of Galilee. It likely had a population of 20,000 people. **and as his custom was, he went into the synagogue on the sabbath day**—Jesus habitually worshiped in the synagogue, the most influential institution in Nazareth. The synagogue had a religious, educational, and a judicial function. In the meetings, there was a fixed reading from the law (called *Shema*—Deut. 6:4-9), followed by a free reading from the prophets (called *Haphtorah*), a translation of this into the vernacular and a running commentary, a sermon, the offering of prayers, and blessing. **stood up . . . to read**—A visiting rabbi might be expected to conduct a part of the synagogue services. Someone else had read from the law; now Jesus reads from the prophet Isaiah. He likely read the Hebrew and translated it into Aramaic (see Acts 13:15). The reader stood; the teacher sat during the synagogue services.

➤**18, 19** To have fixed on any passage announcing his sufferings (as Isa. 53) would have been unsuitable at this early stage of his ministry. So he selected a passage announcing the sublime object of his whole mission, its divine character, and his special endowments for it. Notice that the Scripture expresses itself in the first person and so was especially adaptable to the first opening of his mouth in his prophetic capacity. It is from the well-known section of Isaiah's prophecies where the central figure is that mysterious "Servant of the Lord," despised of man, abhorred of the nation, but before whom kings are to arise on seeing him and princes are to worship. The quotation is chiefly from the Septuagint, or it is a free rendering of the Hebrew (with one part taken from Isa. 58:6 and the rest from Isa. 61:1, 2). Isaiah 61:1, 2 pictures the deliverance of Israel from Babylon in the "Year of Jubilee" terminology. In this year all debts were to be cancelled, slaves were to be freed, and property was to be returned to its original owner. Jesus boldly links this coming age with himself—an age which the prophet must have had in mind since the people were still oppressed. **acceptable year**—an allu-

sion to the Jubilee year (Lev. 25:10). See also Isaiah 49:8 and 2 Corinthians 6:2. Here the expression obviously refers to the era of God's favor upon man in which he would accept all who come to him. As the maladies under which humanity groans are here set forth under the names of poverty, brokenheartedness, bondage, blindness, and bruisedness, so the glorious healer of all these maladies, Jesus Christ, announces himself in the act of reading this Scripture. He declares himself to be the Messiah, the Anointed One—anointed with the Spirit of the Lord. This anointing occurred at the time of his baptism, the time when the Holy Spirit descended on him (3:22).

➤**20 And he closed the book, and he gave it again to the minister** [attendant]—Having "rolled up" the scroll, he gave it to the synagogue official. **and sat down. And the eyes of all them that were in the synagogue were fastened on him**—astounded by his making such claims.

➤**21 And he began to say unto them, This day is this scripture fulfilled in your ears** [hearing]—His whole address was just a detailed application to himself of these verses and perhaps similar prophecies. Verse 21 summarizes the following truths: (1) Jesus himself is the Messiah; (2) in his word he conveys aid and comfort to this people; (3) the prophet Isaiah speaks of spiritual blessings, not material.

➤**22 And all bare him witness and wondered at the gracious words which proceeded out of his mouth**—referring both to the richness of his matter and the sweetness of his manner. This first reaction of the people was favorable; then they remembered that he was **Joseph's son.** They knew he had received no rabbinical education, and they seemed incapable of conceiving anything supernatural. The rapid transition from belief to disbelief has caused some scholars to insist that Luke combined three separate incidents (i.e., 4:16-22; 4:23, 24; 4:25ff.).

➤**23 Physician, heal thyself: whatsoever we have heard done in Capernaum, do also here in thy country**—Rumors had reached their ears concerning his works in Capernaum. If such power actually resided in Christ, then is it asking too much for him to perform similar works in his hometown, Nazareth? His choice of Capernaum as a place of residence since entering public life was already well known in Nazareth, it seems. Their pride was wounded because of his refusal to perform the same kinds of miracles here as he had done in Capernaum. Mark (6:5) records that Jesus had healed a few sick people, but this seems to have been done privately, the general unbelief precluding anything more open.

➤**24 No prophet is accepted in his own country**—He replied to the one proverb by employing another, equally familiar. His reply could well be expressed in this form: "Too much familiarity breeds contempt." Our Lord's long residence in Nazareth merely as a townsman had made him too common, insulating them from receiving him as others did who were less familiar with his everyday demeanor in private life. This is a most important principle to which the wise will pay due regard.

➤**25-27** Jesus drew upon the experiences of Elijah and Elisha to substantiate his position. Both these prophets, rejected by their own nation, ministered to Gentiles. So Jesus, rejected by his own townspeople, would minister to others of another city. (The choice of Gentiles in his illustration intimates that Jesus' ministry would extend, not just beyond Nazareth, but beyond all of Israel.)

➤**29 thrust him out of the city**—with violence, as though dealing with a prisoner. **brow of the hill**—Nazareth was located in the southern slopes of the Galilean hills. This was the first insult which the Son of God received, and it came from his own people.

➤**30 passing through the midst**—evidently in a miraculous way, though perhaps quite noiselessly, leading them to wonder afterwards what spell could have come over them that they allowed him to escape.

➤**31 And came down to Capernaum**—the headquarters of his Galilean ministry. The city was a Roman military post (7:1-10) and is called his own city (Matt. 9:1; Mark 2:1).

➤**32** The **power**—or, authority characterized Jesus' teaching, in contrast to the hollowness of the teaching of the scribes and Pharisees.

## 33-37 THE HEALING OF A DEMONIAC

Here Jesus shows his power over demons. The Jews accounted for the existence of demons by explaining that two angels came to earth, one returning to God while the other gratified his lust with mortal women. His children and his children's offspring became

demons. In the NT demons are mentioned essentially in relationship to exorcism. In Matthew 10:25 they are referred to as ministers of Satan.

➤**33 unclean**—The frequency with which this character of impurity is applied to evil spirits is worthy of notice. **cried out**—See comments on Matthew 8:29; Mark 3:11.

➤**35** Jesus silenced the demon because his words about Jesus' divine identity were untimely, inappropriate, and inflammatory. The people had never before witnessed such a manifestation of power.

➤**37 And the fame of him went out**—echoes of his power and word continued to be heard.

## 38-41 THE HEALING OF PETER'S MOTHER-IN-LAW

See comments on Matthew 8:14-17. Simon's mother-in-law is described as having a great fever. Greek medical writers describe fevers as minor or major. Luke, the physician, calls this a major illness.

➤**39** This verse indicates the thoroughness of the healing; the woman immediately ministered to the needs of those in the house.

➤**40 Now when the sun was setting**—the people brought many who were diseased. "The setting of the sun" characterized the conclusion of the day. A new day began when the Jews could observe three stars in the darkening sky. The people had refrained from bringing diseased friends because they would have broken the law of the Sabbath by carrying a burden on the Sabbath.

➤**41 he rebuking them suffered them not to speak** [did not allow them to speak]—Our Lord always silenced testimony from demons for the very reason they were eager to give it—because he and they would thus seem to have one interest, as his enemies actually alleged (see comments on Matt. 12:24).

## 42-44 JESUS' PRAYER IN THE EARLY MORNING HOUR

See comments on Mark 1:35-39, where we learn that he retired early, found solitude, and was engaged in prayer and contemplation when the people came seeking him. What a sharp contrast between the attitude of these people and that of the Gadarenes! The nature of his mission required him to keep moving that all might hear the glad tidings (Matt. 8:34).

## Chapter 5

### 1-11 THE MIRACULOUS CATCH OF FISHES AND THE CALL OF THE FIRST DISCIPLES

Not their first call, however, which is recorded in John 1:35-42, nor their second, recorded in Matthew 4:18-22. This is their third and last before their appointment to the apostleship. That these calls were all distinct and progressive seems quite plain.

➤**1 as the people pressed upon him to hear the word of God**—They were nearly pushing him into the water. **he stood by the lake of Gennesaret**—so called because the Plain of Gennesaret is on the west side of the lake. The sea may be referred to as the Sea of Galilee, the Sea of Tiberius, or the Lake of Gennesaret.

➤**2 And saw two ships standing by the lake: but the fishermen were gone out of them and were washing their nets**—Dip-type nets were used as well as the larger drag-nets. In either case, the nets had to be washed after a night of fishing.

➤**3 And he entered into one of the ships, which was Simon's, and . . . thrust out a little from the land**—Jesus planned to use the boat as a rostrum from which to speak, thereby no longer endangering the crowds or himself because of their desire to be near him. The content of Jesus' teaching is left unrecorded, and the emphasis of the story is on what follows. (See Matt. 13:2ff.)

➤**4** The command **let down your nets for a draught** is not simply to recompense Peter for the use of his boat. By this miracle, Jesus was attempting to teach Peter something concerning his own power.

➤**5 Master**—In Greek the word is *epistata*. It was used only by Luke in the NT, and only from the mouths of the disciples. The term means "officer" and is a surrogate for "teacher." Peter's use of this word indicates that a personal relationship between him and Jesus had already been formed. **all the night**—a normal time for fishing (John 21:3), and even now the expert fisherman knew how hopeless it was to let down the net again. Only at the Master's word

was he willing to cast the net into the sea. This willingness itself was an act of faith on the part of Peter.

➤**6 brake**—imperfect tense in Greek, "were breaking." Their nets were breaking, so great was the number of fish enclosed. The expert fishermen who had toiled all night and taken nothing had confidence in Jesus' word; this confidence was rewarded by an excessive catch of fish. This verse abounds in vivid detail and description.

➤**8 Depart**—in Greek, an aorist imperative, suggesting promptness and decisiveness of action. Peter asked for this separation because he realized how separate he, a sinful man, was from one so divine. Peter said in essence, "A sinner such as I am is not fit company for you."

➤**10 Fear not**—lit., "stop fearing," as spoken to Mary and Zechariah. **from henceforth**—marking a new stage of the disciples' relationship with Christ. **Thou shalt catch men**—It was not that Peter (and the other disciples) would simply be "fishing for fish"; they would be catching and bringing men into the kingdom.

➤**11 they forsook all**—They did this before (Matt. 4:20); now they do it again. Yet, after the Crucifixion, they are at their boats once more (John 21:3). After Pentecost, however, they appear to have finally abandoned their secular vocation.

### 12-16 A LEPER HEALED

See comments on Matthew 8:2-4.

### 17-26 A PARALYTIC HEALED

See comments on Matthew 9:1-8.

➤**17 Pharisees and doctors of the law** [lit., "law-teachers"] **sitting by**—The "Pharisees," a religious party, placed great stress on the law and ceremonial purity. The "law-teachers" were scribes who were initially copyists and secretaries but had become professional interpreters of the law. Because of Jesus' growing influence, many Jews felt compelled to see him for themselves and make some definite judgment regarding him. **the power of the Lord was present to heal them**—i.e., to heal the sick in the presence of the Pharisees and teachers of the law.

➤**19 the housetop**—or, roof. The houses had flat roofs generally made of beams, the spaces between them being filled with brush and mud.

➤**24 take up thy couch** [bed]—The bed had borne the man; now the man shall bear the bed (Bengel).

## 27-32 LEVI'S CALL AND FEAST

See comments on Matthew 9:9-13 and Mark 2:14.

## 33-39 THE TEACHING CONCERNING FASTING

See comments on Matthew 9:14-17.

The incongruities mentioned in verses 36-38 were intended to illustrate the difference between the genius of the old and new economies and the danger of attempting to mix one with the other. A mixture of the ascetic ritualism of the old with the spiritual freedom of the new economy disfigures and destroys both the old and the new. The additional parable in 5:39, which is peculiar to Luke, has been variously interpreted. But the "new wine" seems plainly to be the evangelical freedom that Christ was introducing, and the old, the opposing spirit of Judaism. Men long accustomed to the latter could not be expected straightway to take a liking to the former. These inquiries about the difference between Jesus' disciples and the Pharisees, and even John's, are not surprising. They were the effect of a natural revulsion against sudden change. The new wine will itself in time become old and so acquire all the added elements of antiquity. What lessons does this teach to those who unreasonably cling to what is getting antiquated, and, on the other hand, what lessons does this teach to hasty reformers who have no patience with the timidity of their weaker brothers?

Chapter **6**

## 1-5 PLUCKING EARS OF CORN (GRAIN) ON THE SABBATH (See Matt. 12:1-8 and Mark 2:23-28.)

➤**1 On the second sabbath after the first**—an obscure expression occurring here, generally understood to mean the first Sabbath after the second day of unleavened bread. But the most reliable and earliest manuscripts read simply, "on the sabbath."

➤**2 And certain of the Pharisees**—the legalistic religious sect. **said unto them, Why do ye that which is not lawful to do on the sabbath**

**days?**—The preceding passage, Luke 5:33-39, indicates Jesus' departure from traditional Judaism. The forms of Judaism were inadequate to express the spiritual experience that he brought to man. Luke 6:1-11 applies the principles of 5:33-39 to the Sabbath. Rigid observance of the law was one of the main constituents of Sabbath law. Sabbath keeping in Jesus' day may be described as an extreme formalism. However, it remained the most important institution for the survival of Judaism in a Gentile world. The Sabbath reminded the Jews weekly that God had created the world and had redeemed them from bondage. God had taught that the Sabbath is a holy day (Exod. 20:8-10). Therefore, one must not labor on the Sabbath. Rabbis had attempted to apply the law in its minutia and had divided work into thirty-nine categories. One specific labor forbidden was that of harvesting on the Sabbath.

➤**3 Have ye not read . . . what David did**—Employing David's action in the eating of the showbread as an example, Jesus defends the actions of his own disciples. What was right for David must surely be right for David's son, the Messiah. Showbread was placed in the Holy Place of the tabernacle every Sabbath morning. There were twelve loaves in two rows of six loaves each. The flour was sifted no fewer than eleven times. This bread reminded the people of God's presence and provision for them, and only the priests could eat it. Yet, when David was fleeing for his life, he came to the tabernacle in Nob and there he and his men ate the bread that was lawful only for the priests to eat.

➤**5 the Son of man is Lord also of the sabbath**—As Lord, he created the Sabbath and ordained its sanctity; therefore, he controlled the regulations pertaining to it. (See comments on Mark 2:28.) Joy in Sabbath observance is brought by a simple acquiescence in the lordship of Christ, not by a pharisaical ritual. Jesus had showed the people that the OT does not uphold the extreme legalistic ritual of Judaism as interpreted and practiced by the Pharisees.

## 6-11 A WITHERED HAND HEALED (See Matt. 12:9-15 and Mark 3:1-7.)

➤**6 On another sabbath**—Luke obviously selected a series of Sabbath controversies in order to teach the lordship of Christ and his superiority to the Sabbath law. This experience further illustrates the principles enunciated in 5:33-39.

**➤7 And the scribes and Pharisees watched him**—Luke indicates that they watched him for no good purpose, but Jesus was not deterred by them. He rather affirmed what must be done positively on the Sabbath.

**➤8 he knew their thoughts**—Jesus knew the state of their hearts and addressed himself to it even as if these thoughts had been overtly expressed.

**➤9 to do good, or to do evil? to save life, or to destroy it?**—By his novel way of stating his case, our Lord teaches the great ethical principle that for one to neglect any opportunity of doing good is to incur the guilt of doing evil, and by this law he bound his own spirit (see Mark 3:4). **Stretch forth thy hand**—Just as Jesus took the initiative in the conversation with the scribes and the Pharisees, he also took the initiative in coping with the problem of this man. When he commanded the man to stretch forth his hand, the hand was restored immediately.

**➤11 And they were filled with madness**—The Greek word for "madness," *anoias*, (lit., "without thinking") denotes senseless rage. **what they might do to Jesus**—not so much whether to get rid of him, but how to get rid of him.

## 12-16 THE CHOOSING OF THE TWELVE APOSTLES

**➤12 in those days**—The phrase again indicates the historical reliability of Luke's record. **he went out**—likely from Capernaum. **and continued all night in prayer. . . And when it was day**—The work with which the next day began shows what had been the burden of the night's devotions. As he directed his disciples to pray for "laborers" just before sending themselves forth (see Matt. 9:37; 10:1), so here we find the Lord himself in prolonged communion with his Father in preparation for the solemn appointment of the apostles. His choice would determine the future of the church.

**➤13-16** See comments on Matthew 10:2-4. These disciples were ordinary men, most of whom are not heard of by name after this record. Generally speaking the future of his church depended on these choices. From the disciples (a "learner" or "follower") he chose twelve apostles ("one sent with a message").

Men of all types were named: a tax collector, a fisherman, Galileans, a Judean. (Cf. Acts 1:13; Matt. 10:2-4; Mark 3:16-19 for a listing of the apostles. Peter is named first in each list.)

## 17-49 A SERIES OF HEALINGS AND TEACHINGS

**➤17 stood in the plain**—lit., "a level place," a piece of high tableland, a level place in the mountainous area. Many scholars take this following discourse to be but an abridged form of the Sermon on the Mount, and their arguments are indeed forceful. (Note: This discourse contains little more than one fourth of the other; it contains woes of its own, as well as beatitudes common to both.) But other scholars find difficulty with synchronizing the temporal element involved in the two sermons because Matthew's sermon was delivered some time prior to the choice of the Twelve while this one was spoken after the choice of the Twelve. Furthermore, these scholars add that there is little difficulty in making the discourses to be on different occasions inasmuch as Jesus often repeated his more important sayings.

**➤19 healed**—"kept healing" (according to the Gk.), denoting successive acts of mercy—until it went to "all" who needed healing. There is something unusually grand and pictorial in this description.

**➤20, 21** Verses 20-26 contrast two types of men. The first group would be pitied by outward appearance, but Jesus knows them to be "blessed" because of what is promised to them. The second group possess what the present world can offer, but they have no desire for the spiritual things that are desired by the former group. In the Sermon on the Mount the benediction is pronounced upon the "poor in spirit" and those who "hunger and thirst after righteousness." Here it is simply on the "poor" and the "hungry now." In this form of the discourse, our Lord seems to have had in view "the poor of this world, rich in faith and heirs of the kingdom which God hath promised to them that love him," as these very beatitudes are paraphrased by James (2:5, RSV). **laugh**—How charming is the liveliness of this word, to express what in Matthew is called being "comforted"!

**➤22 cast out your name**—lit., "exclude your person," or "exclude you personally," whether from their group by excommunication or from their society. **for the Son of man's sake**—Cf. Matt. 5:11.

➤**23 leap for joy**—a livelier expression than "rejoice and be glad" of Matthew 5:12.

➤**24, 25 rich . . . full . . . laugh**—who have all their good things and joyous feelings here and now in perishable objects. **received your consolation**—See 16:25. **shall hunger**—their inward craving strong as ever, but the materials of satisfaction forever gone.

➤**26 all men speak well of you**—alluding to the honor given to the false prophets of old (Mic. 2:11). For the principle of this woe and its proper limits see John 15:19.

➤**27-36** The first section of the sermon deals with man's relationship to God; this section with man's relationship to man.(See comments on Matt. 5:44-48; 7:12; Luke 14:12-14.)

➤**37, 38** See comments on Matthew 7:1, 2; but Luke's is much fuller and more graphic.

➤**39 Can the blind lead the blind?**—not in the Sermon on the Mount but recorded by Matthew in another and very striking connection (15:14).

➤**40 The disciple**—aspires to measure up to his master, and he thinks himself complete when he does so; if you then be blind leaders of the blind, the perfection of one's training under you will only make him the more certainly blind. And both teacher and disciple will end in ruin.

➤**41-49** See comments on Matthew 7:16-27.

*Chapter* **7**

1-10 THE HEALING OF THE CENTURION'S SERVANT (See Matt. 8:5-13.)

➤**1 Capernaum**—a border town between Galilee and the area ruled by Philip.

➤**2, 3 a certain centurion's servant**—probably a servant of Herod Antipas. The centurion was the backbone of the Roman army. He was roughly the equivalent of a captain in our armed forces. The **elders** sent to Jesus by the centurion were the leading men of the Jewish community. **was sick, and ready to die**—Again Luke clearly identifies the seriousness of the moment.

➤**4 And when they came to Jesus, they besought him**—Their testimony is a valuable word concerning the character of the centurion.

➤**5** Luke indicates that the centurion, according to the testimony of the Jewish elders, "loves our nation and he has built us our synagogue" (RSV). His love took a practical and appropriate form.

➤**7, 8 Say in a word, and my servant shall be healed. For I also am a man set under authority**—The centurion understood the principle of authority and knew that it was unnecessary for Jesus to come to his house in order to heal the servant. Verse 8 affirms the centurion's acquaintance with the authoritarian principle of command and obedience.

➤**9 I have not found so great faith, no, not in Israel**—Jesus employed this man's faith to challenge the Jews. This was the highest praise uttered by Jesus, and it was spoken of a Gentile—showing the universal Saviorhood of our Lord.

11-17 THE RAISING OF THE SON OF THE WIDOW OF NAIN

This account is recorded only in Luke. The miracle shows Jesus' authority to heal not only a diseased body but also to raise a lifeless body. Luke interestingly records this account of the raising of a dead man immediately after the record of healing one at the point of death. Jesus' sympathy was aroused for this widow when he met the funeral procession.

➤**11 Nain**—a small village not elsewhere mentioned in Scripture and probably visited only this one time by our Lord. It was south of Nazareth and may not have had a gate. If this be true, then Luke describes the city in terms that his readers would understand.

➤**12 there was a dead man carried out**—Dead bodies, being ceremonially unclean, were not allowed to be buried within the cities (except the kings of David's house who were buried in the city of David), and the funeral was usually on the same day as the death. This verse shows death at its worst. The mother was probably in front of the funeral bier, accompanied by friends, relatives, and curiosity seekers. There were also present professional mourners with flutes and cymbals. These mourners were usually women because of their high-pitched voices.

➤**13, 14 the Lord**—This appellation is more usual with Luke and John than Matthew. **saw her, he had compassion on her**—Jesus told the woman to "weep not," that is, "stop weeping" (a present imperative in Gk., preceded by *mē*, meaning to stop an act underway). What consolation to thousands of the bereaved has this single verse carried from age to age!

➤**14, 15** What majesty mingled with mercy shines in this scene! The Resurrection and the Life embodied in human flesh brings back life to a dead body with a word of command; Incarnate compassion summoning its absolute power to dry a widow's tears!

➤**16 a great prophet is risen up among us; and . . . God hath visited his people**—But this visitation was more than bringing back the days of the prophets Elijah and Elisha (cf. 1 Kings 17:17-24; 2 Kings 4:32-37; see comments on Matt. 15:31), although that may have been what was in the people's minds. This visitation was the divine epiphany, the manifestation of God in the flesh. It was "the Lord," not a prophet, who had performed this miracle. This is the first time Luke uses the term "Lord." This term was to become a favorite of Jesus' followers. The early Christians adopted the word from the master-slave relationship. Thus Paul thought of himself as a "bondsman, a slave" of Jesus Christ.

## 18-25 A WORD CONCERNING JOHN THE BAPTIST

See comments on Matthew 11:2-14.

John had been imprisoned because of his stern denunciation of Herod Antipas's relationship with Herodias, his half-brother's wife. The prophet's inquiry is logical. Various suggestions have been offered concerning the reason for the inquiry. Some have suggested that he made this inquiry for the sake of his disciples. Others have suggested that he sent the message to Jesus in an attempt to hasten the accomplishment of Jesus' purpose. John may have misunderstood the ministry of the Messiah. Acquainted with the Jewish ideas of a political Messiah, he may have expected an entirely different answer from his disciples, possibly even expecting to hear that the armies of Jesus were already massing, that Caesarea was on the verge of falling, etc. However, Jesus' answer is in terms of Isaiah (29:18, 19; 35:5, 6; 61:1). Verse 22 seems to suggest a lack of understanding on the part of John. The departure of John's messengers gives Jesus the opportunity to speak a word of genuine appreciation of John. Crowds went into the wilderness to see him, not just a blade of grass blown by the wind (7:24-28). He is described as the greatest of all prophets. His place was a place of preparation, and his work belongs to the preparatory stage; therefore, the most insignificant citizen of the kingdom is greater than John. Geldenhuys writes: "He belonged to the period of preparation and had not yet learned to know Jesus as the Crucified One . . . He will indeed . . . share fully his place in the redemption and blessings achieved by him, but as regards his place in the unfolding of the divine revelation which culminated in Christ, he still belongs to the preparatory stage and is therefore in this respect less than the most insignificant believer of the New Dispensation."

➤**29, 30 all the people**—These are the observations of Luke, not of our Lord. **and the publicans** [tax collectors], **justified God**—a striking clause. The meaning is that they acknowledged the divine wisdom in having John prepare them for the Messiah. But the Pharisees and the lawyers, true to themselves in refusing the baptism of John, rejected the design of God by rejecting the Savior himself.

➤**31-35** These verses describe the generation of John's day. They were like unresponsive, self-absorbed children. They would not dance to the pipe (characteristic of weddings), and they would not weep with the mourners (characteristic of funerals). So their generation rejected both John and his Master: the one because he was too unsocial—more like a demoniac than a rational man; the other because he was too much the reverse—given to indulgences and consorting with the lowest classes of society. But the children of wisdom recognize and honor her, whether in the austere garb of the Baptist, or in the more attractive style of his Master, whether in the law or the gospel, whether in rags or in royalty; for "he who is full loathes honey, but to the hungry even what is bitter tastes sweet" (Prov. 27:7, NIV). Regardless of the Jews' attitude toward Jesus, wisdom is recognized by all related to her and is honored in whatever form it appears, whether in John or in Jesus.

## 36-50 CHRIST'S FEET ARE WASHED WITH TEARS

➤**36 one of the Pharisees desired him that he would eat with him**—Verse 40 identifies the Pharisee as Simon, another evidence of Luke's careful historical accuracy.

➤37 And, behold, a woman in the city, which [who] was a sinner—one who had led a profligate life. Some interpreters have identified this woman as Mary Magdalene, but there is no ground for this identification. brought an alabaster box of ointment—a perfume vessel, in some cases very costly (John 12:5). This sinful woman had brought a precious possession to share with Jesus. "The ointment has here a peculiar interest, as the offering by a penitent of what had been an accessory in her unhallowed work of sin" (Alford).

➤38 And stood at his feet behind him weeping, and began to wash [wet] his feet with tears, and did wipe them with the hairs of her head, and kissed his feet, and anointed them with the ointment—the posture at meals being a reclining one, with the feet extending behind. The woman's tears, which were quite involuntary, poured down in a flood upon his naked feet as she bent down to kiss them and then use the long tresses of her own hair for a towel. The term translated "kissed" actually signifies "to kiss fondly, to caress," or "to kiss again and again." Verse 45 indicates that the latter is the intended meaning in this instance. What prompted this? Much love, springing from a sense of much forgiveness. So says he who knew her heart (7:47). Where she had met with Christ before or what words of his had brought life to her dead heart and a sense of divine pardon to her guilty soul, we do not know, but probably she was one of the crowd of "publicans and sinners" who heard Jesus' words of life, light, and love.

➤39 The Pharisee—had formed no definite opinion of our Lord and invited him apparently to make a judgment. This verse indicates Simon's true evaluation of Jesus' character.

➤40-43 As Nathan with David, our Lord conceals his telling point under the veil of a parable and makes his host himself pronounce a verdict on the case. Obviously, the two debtors represent the woman and Simon. The criminality of the one was ten times that of the other, but both are forgiven with equal frankness. Simon is made to recognize that the greatest debtor will cling to his or her divine forgiver with the deepest gratitude. Verse 43 suggests the proportionate relationship between the favor conferred and the response elicited.

➤45-47 Thou gavest me no kiss . . . [she] hath not ceased to kiss my feet . . . My head with oil thou didst not anoint . . . this woman hath anointed my feet with ointment—The customary marks of hospitality were missing. Where was the sign of Simon's love? What evidence was thus afforded of any feeling which forgiveness prompts? Our Lord speaks this with delicate politeness as if hurt by these inattentions of his host, which, though not invariably shown to guests, were the customary marks of respect and regard. The reference is plain—only one of the debtors was really forgiven. Her sins, which are many, are forgiven— This statement represents the stark reality of her relationship to Jesus. The second part of verse 47 contains the basic teaching of the parable: the greater the forgiveness, the greater the love. If one knows the depth of his sin and the depth of God's love, he cannot but love God as did this woman.

➤48 Thy sins are forgiven—The word translated "forgiven" is a perfect tense in Greek and indicates that the action was completed in the past, the results continuing to the present. She was forgiven and remains forgiven.

➤49, 50 And they that sat at meat with him began to say within [or, among] themselves, "Who is this that forgiveth sins also?"—No wonder they were startled by the one reclining at the same couch and partaking of the same hospitalities as themselves. But so far from receding from this claim or softening it, our Lord only repeats it with two precious additions: (1) Thy faith hath saved thee; (2) go in peace. The first announcement unveils the secret of the "forgiveness" she had experienced, and which carried "salvation" in its bosom; the second, a glorious dismissal of her sins in the "peace" that she had already felt, but is now assured that she has his full warrant to enjoy! This wonderful scene teaches two very weighty truths: (1) Though there be degrees of guilt, the inability to wipe out the dishonor done to God is common to all sinners. (2) As Christ is the great Creditor to whom all are indebted, so to him belongs the prerogative of forgiving the indebtedness. This latter truth is brought out in the structure and application of the present parable as it is nowhere else. Therefore, Jesus was either a blaspheming deceiver, or he was and is God manifest in the flesh.

# 8

*Chapter*

## 1-3 A CIRCUIT THROUGH GALILEE

This record is found only in Luke's account. It reveals that Jesus began to travel throughout the countryside after a somewhat settled period of ministry.

➤**1 went throughout**—traveled, made a progressive journey. **every city and village**—or, "city by city and village by village." **preaching . . . the glad tidings**—the prince of itinerant preachers scattering far and wide the seed of the kingdom.

➤**2 certain women, which had been healed of evil spirits and infirmities**—on whom Jesus had the double claim of having brought healing to their bodies and new life to their souls. They were drawn to him by an attraction more than magnetism, and they accompanied him on this tour as his financial supporters—ministering to him from their possessions. **Mary, called Magdalene**—probably of Magdala, on which see Matthew 15:39. **out of whom went seven devils** [demons]—It is incorrect to view this honored woman as the once profligate woman of 7:37 and to call all such penitents "Magdalenes." The mistake has arisen from confusing unhappy demoniacal possession with the conscious entertainment of diabolic impurity, or supposing the one to have been afflicted as a punishment for the other—for which there is not the least scriptural ground. The number "seven" suggests the worst conceivable state of demon possession.

➤**3 Joanna the wife of Chuza Herod's steward**—If the steward of such a godless, cruel, and licentious ruler as Herod Antipas differed greatly from his master, his post would be no easy or enviable one. That he was a disciple of Christ is very improbable, though he might be favorably disposed toward him. But what we do not know of him, we are sure his wife possessed. Healed either of "evil spirits" or of some one of the "infirmities" here referred to (i.e., the ordinary diseases of humanity), she joins in the Savior's train of grateful clinging followers. **and Susanna**—We know nothing of her but the name. She is mentioned only in this verse. Her services on this memorable occasion must have immortalized her name. **many others**—many other women (the Gk. is feminine). The reference is likely to healed women. All of these were ministering to him from their possessions (or, wealth), and he allowed them to do it and subsisted upon it. He who was the support of the spiritual life of his people disdained not to be supported by them physically. He gave all things to men, his brothers, and received all things from them, enjoying thereby the pure blessings of love.

## 4-18 THE PARABLE OF THE SOWER

See comments on Mark 4:3-9, 14-20.

## 19-21 JESUS' MOTHER AND BROTHERS DESIRE TO SPEAK WITH HIM

See comments on Matthew 12:46-50.

## 22-25 JESUS STILLS THE STORM

See comments on Matthew 8:23-27 and Mark 4:35-41.

## 26-39 THE HEALING OF THE DEMONIAC OF GADARA

See comments on Matthew 8:28-34 and Mark 5:1-20.

## 40-56 THE RAISING OF JAIRUS'S DAUGHTER AND THE HEALING OF THE WOMAN WITH THE ISSUE OF BLOOD

See comments on Mark 5:21-43.

➤**40** The people **gladly received him, for they were all waiting for him**—The abundant teaching of that day (cf. Matt. 13 and Luke 4:36) had only whetted the people's appetites. They seemed disappointed that he had left them in the evening to cross the lake and therefore remained around the beach, having a hint that he would return the same evening. This, of course, was on the Jewish side of the lake. Perhaps they witnessed at a distance the sudden calming of the tempest. Here at least they stood, watching for his return and welcoming him to the shore. The tide of his popularity was rising rapidly.

➤**45 Who touched me?**—Peter seemed surprised that Jesus would question the identity of the one who touched him in such a multitude and throng as this.

➤**46 Somebody hath touched me**—Jesus saw an individual, not simply a great host of people. In the group "being carried along" by the movement of the crowd, Jesus realized that someone had touched him. It was this touch and this only that Jesus acknowledged. Even so, as Augustine said so long ago, "Multitudes still come similarly close to Christ in the means of grace, but all to no purpose, being only sucked into the crowd." The voluntary, living contact of faith is that electric conductor that alone draws virtue out of him.

➤**47 declared unto him before all the people**—This, though a great trial to the shrinking modesty of the believing woman, was just what Jesus wanted in drawing her forth. Her public testimony to the facts of her case, both her disease and her abortive efforts at a cure, as well as the instantaneous and perfect relief her touch of the great Healer had brought, focused additional attention upon Jesus.

*Chapter* **9**

## 1-6 THE MISSION OF THE TWELVE APOSTLES

See comments on Matthew 10:1-15.

Luke (8:1) records the expansion of Jesus' work, and this expansion provided ample opportunity for Jesus to instruct his disciples. They were to live frugally, reside in one location, and avoid being identified with certain less reputable wandering preachers.

## 7-9 HEROD'S DISTURBED MIND BECAUSE OF REPORTS CONCERNING JESUS

See comments on Mark 6:14-30.

➤**7 perplexed**—an imperfect tense, suggesting continuous action in past time; it means "at a loss, embarrassed." A. T. Robertson suggests the meaning "unable to find a way out, thoroughly at a loss." **said of** [by] **some that John was risen from the dead**—Among many opinions this was the one which Herod himself adopted. The explanation is probably seen in Mark 6:14.

➤**9 desired to see him**—but did not, until as a prisoner he was sent to him by Pilate just prior to his death, as Luke indicates in 23:8.

## 10-17 THE FEEDING OF THE FIVE THOUSAND

See comments on Mark 6:31-44.

## 18-27 PETER'S CONFESSION OF CHRIST AND JESUS' FIRST EXPLICIT

## ANNOUNCEMENT OF HIS APPROACHING DEATH

See comments on Matthew 16:13-28 and Mark 8:34.

Luke omits the stories contained in Matthew and Mark between the feeding of the five thousand and the confession of Peter.

➤**22, 23** These verses contain Jesus' clear declaration of his future rejection, suffering, and death. Jesus knew that he was going to a cross to die. Note Jesus' usage of **Son of man,** his favorite term for himself. The expression is likely derived from Daniel 7:9-22 and stresses his sovereignty, deity, and humanity. His messianic role differed radically from what the contemporary Jew had expected. The Jews were looking for a political deliverer, and Jesus didn't fit this image. But the disciples (especially Peter) had come to realize that Jesus was, in fact, the Messiah of God. Peter's declaration (9:20) suggests that Jesus' teaching had borne fruit, and at the same time it also affirmed his messiahship. Closely allied with this is Jesus' challenge in verse 23. Jesus indicated that a man must **deny himself** (say no to himself) if he wills to follow the master. In addition to this, Jesus required **daily** cross-bearing.

➤**24 whosoever will save his life**—desires to save, is minded to save, is intent on saving his life. This pithy maxim depends upon the double sense attached to the term "life," a lower and higher, the natural and the spiritual, the temporal and the eternal. An entire sacrifice of the lower life, or a willingness to make such a sacrifice, is indispensable to the preservation of the higher life. The man who cannot bring himself to surrender the one for the sake of the other will eventually lose both.

➤**26 whosoever shall be ashamed of me and of my words**—The sense of "shame" is one of the strongest in our nature; it is one of those social reactions founded on our love of "reputation," which causes instinctive aversion to what is fitted to lower it, and it was given to us as a preservative from all that is properly "shameful." When one is "lost to shame" he is nearly past hope. But when Jesus and "his words" (particularly in their more spiritual uncompromising features) are unpopular, the same instinctive desire to stand well with others begets the temptation to be ashamed of him. **of him shall the Son of man be ashamed**—

Jesus will render to that man his own treatment; he will disown him before the most august of all assemblies and put him "to shame and everlasting contempt" (Dan. 12:2).

➤27 **some standing here, which shall not taste of death, till they see the kingdom of God**—Mark adds (9:1) "come with power." The reference is to the firm establishment and victorious progress of the kingdom of Christ in the lifetime of some then present. Suggestions as to a specific time and/or event are legion. Scholars have suggested the transfiguration, the resurrection of Jesus, the coming of the Holy Spirit, the destruction of Jerusalem, or the parousia. Since no such time or event is specified in the Scriptures, it is properly best to view this statement as referring to a gradual manifestation of God's kingdom through Jesus—beginning from the transfiguration and climaxing with his exaltation in resurrection and ascension—followed by the effusion of the Holy Spirit on the disciples. All this brought about a new age and a new dispensation, of which the disciples were the major witnesses and participants.

## 28-36 THE TRANSFIGURATION

➤28 **eight days after these sayings**—including the day on which this was spoken and the day of the transfiguration. Matthew and Mark say "after six days," excluding these two days. As the "sayings" so definitely connected with the transfiguration scene are those announcing his death, resurrection, and the visible manifestation of his kingdom, so Jesus' transfiguration was designed to give them a preview of that coming glory that would come as a result of his death and resurrection. **Peter and John and James**—constitute the inner circle of the disciples. They were partners in secular business. They were sole witnesses of the resurrection of Jairus's daughter (Mark 5:37), the transfiguration, and the agony in the garden (Mark 14:33). They accompanied Jesus **up into a mountain to pray.** The mountain was apparently near the lake and was not Mount Tabor as has been long supposed. Luke notes the purpose of the visit to the mountain inasmuch as this period of Jesus' ministry was extremely critical and anxiety-filled.

➤29 **And as he prayed, the fashion of his countenance was altered**—Luke is the only synoptic writer to state that Jesus was praying.

(Cf. 3:21, where again Luke is the only writer to indicate that Jesus was praying at his baptism.) As he prayed, his countenance was altered (lit., "the appearance of his face became different"), and his divine majesty shone gloriously through his human nature. Even his raiment glistened. Matthew (17:2) says that his face was as the sun, and Mark (9:3) says that his raiment became white as no fuller could make them white. Therefore, the light was not something that shone upon him from without, but shone out of him from within. He was all irradiated and was in one blaze of celestial glory. What a contrast to that "appearance . . . so marred, beyond human semblance, and his form beyond that of the sons of men" (Isa. 52:14, RSV).

➤30, 31 **Moses and Elias** [Elijah]—Moses stands as the representative of the law while Elijah represents the prophets. Luke does not indicate how these were identified, but in all probability they were identified either by their conversations or through divine revelation. Luke, however, is careful to indicate that these men discussed with Jesus his departure, or rather his "exodus" (as it is in Gk.). This is the very subject for which Peter had rebuked Jesus (Matt. 16). The exodus is a beautiful euphemism for death. Peter used this term in speaking of his own departure (2 Pet. 1:15), and the very mention of "exodus" seems to have brought to Peter's mind a sudden rush of remembrances and occasioned that marvelous recounting of the transfiguration scene (see 2 Pet. 1:15-18). **which he should accomplish at Jerusalem**—Jesus had an exodus to accomplish. He was about to make a great transition—from having an existence on earth in the flesh to having an existence in heaven, in spirit (see 1 Pet. 3:18). Jerusalem was the starting point of that exodus because Jerusalem would be the place of his death and resurrection. Nothing or no one could stop Jesus from going to Jerusalem (9:53) because that city marked his "rendezvous with destiny."

➤32 **when they were awake**—Perhaps the suggestion is that they "roused themselves up." The idea is that they "shook off their drowsiness." It was night, and the Lord seems to have spent the entire evening on the mountain (9:37). Luke alone mentions their "sleep." The same term is used by Matthew (26:43) to describe the disciples in the Garden of Geth-semane. **they saw his glory**—The emphasis lies on "saw," qualifying them to become "eyewitnesses of his majesty" (2 Pet. 1:16).

➤**33 And . . . as they departed from him**—Peter made the suggestion that the group remain on the mountain, making three booths, one for each of the primary characters. But Peter didn't realize that even Moses and Elijah should never be put on an equal standing with Jesus, God's Son. The heavenly voice asserted Jesus' preeminence above all others.

➤**34, 35 a cloud**—the Shekinah-cloud, the pavilion of the manifested presence of God with his people, called "the excellent" or "manifest glory" by Peter (2 Pet. 1:17). **a voice**—Peter says, "We heard this voice borne from heaven, when we were with him on the holy mountain" (2 Pet. 1:18). **This is my beloved Son**—According to the best manuscripts, this should read, "This is my Son, the chosen One." The reading in the KJV, appearing in later manuscripts, was probably taken from Mark 9:7.

➤**36 Jesus was found alone**—Moses and Elijah are now gone. The cloud too is gone, and the majestic Christ, braced in spirit and enshrined in the reverent affection of his disciples, is left—to suffer! **kept it close**—i.e., kept silent, accord-ing to the Lord's command (Mark 9:9). **those things which they had seen**—These three disci-ples were eyewitnesses of Jesus' transfiguration (2 Pet. 1:15-18; 1 John 1:1, 2). This experience was designed to reveal to these disciples the resplendent preeminence of the Son. Moses and Elijah, those great men who symbolized the two great facets of the OT economy—the law and the prophets—could not compare with the majestic Son, the uniquely chosen One of God. The divine voice heard by the disciples did not direct them to the law or the prophets, but to Jesus only. Thus, the transfiguration was not merely a stage in the education of the disciples, but it became also a crisis experience in Jesus' ministry. The transfiguration meant that Jesus was on his way to death, for the subject which he discussed with Moses and Elijah was his exodus to be accomplished in Jerusalem. The disciples had never seen the glory of God man-ifest in this fashion. His entire countenance was altered; the essence of deity shone through his humanity. But that divine glory expressed in humanity on the mount of transfiguration was

but a momentary preview of the permanent glory he was about to enter into (24:26) when his body would be completely transfigured via death and resurrection (1 Cor. 15:42-45; Phil. 3:21).

## 37-43A THE HEALING OF THE DEMONIAC BOY

See comments on Mark 9:14-32.

Luke 9:37-50 provides a record of the last experiences of Jesus' ministry in Galilee. Each demonstrates the disciples' need of additional instruction and teaching.

## 43B-45 CHRIST'S SECOND EXPLICIT ANNOUNCEMENT OF HIS DEATH AND RESURRECTION

➤**43b But while they** [i.e., the disciples] **wondered every one at all things which Jesus did**—lit., "was doing." The divine grandeur of Christ increasingly impressed the disciples. By comparing Matthew 17:22 and Mark 9:30, we assume that this had been the subject of con-versation between the Twelve and their Master as they journeyed along.

➤**44, 45 these sayings**—not what was pass-ing between them about his grandeur, but what he was now to repeat for the second time con-cerning his sufferings. The disciples were to permit these words to sink down into their ears. In essence, he was telling them: "Do not be carried off your feet by all this grandeur, but bear in mind what I have already told you and now distinctly repeat that the Son of man will be delivered into the hands of hostile people." Luke, as does Mark (9:32), stresses the obtuse-ness of the disciples. Luke attributes their dull-ness to the purpose of God. **They feared** to ask him concerning this saying. Their most cher-ished ideas were so completely dashed by such announcements that they were afraid of open-ing themselves to rebuke by asking him any questions. The disciples were so obtuse that Jesus' words seemed to mean less to them. They already had their preconceived ideas con-cerning the nature of the Messiah, and these ideas did not permit room for considering such suffering as this.

## 46-50 A DISCUSSION OF GREATNESS AND JESUS' REBUKE OF JOHN

The disciples' lack of understanding is fur-ther stressed by the two incidents recorded here.

➤**46-48** See comments on Matthew 18:1-5.

➤**49, 50 John answered**—The link here with the foregoing verses (46-48) lies in the words "in my name" (9:48). There are two principles of immense importance in Jesus' answer. He did not say that this man should *not* have followed him and the disciples, but simply taught how the man was to be regarded though he did not follow. He was to be regarded as a reverer of his name and a promoter of his cause. Surely this condemns not only those horrible attempts to shut up all within one visible pale of discipleship, but also the same spirit in its milder form of proud ecclesiastic sectarianism. Visible unity in Christ's kingdom is to be sought devoutly, but this is not the way to do it. Luke does not record the events contained in Mark 9:42–10:12. He returns to the Marcan framework at 18:15. Until then, he records voluminous material not contained in Mark. In many respects this is the most important section of the Gospel because of its unique contribution of new material. Leaney, agreeing with Conzelmann, indicates that Luke did not know Palestine, and therefore the journey was "less a departure to new places than a new stage in our Lord's mission." Marshall does not believe this is an account of one journey but represents a mass of material that Luke collected and used in this "travel account." Others (Robertson, Arndt, etc.) view this as the journey to the Feast of Tabernacles recorded in John 7.

➤**51 when the time was come that he should be received up**—This has been variously rendered, but the common meaning of all the translations indicates that Luke was speaking of Jesus' ascension into heaven. The action of Jesus being received up (or, taken up) into heaven by the Father has been made a substantive: "the receiving up" or "the taking up"—sometimes called "the assumption." The time had come for Jesus to fulfill the ultimate destiny of his ministry on earth. Therefore, the work of Christ is here divided into two great stages: all that preceded this belonging to the one, and all that follows it to the other. **he stedfastly set his face**—The "he" here is emphatic: "he himself set his face." (Cf. Isa. 50:7.) **to go to Jerusalem**—the city of his coming crucifixion and resurrection.

➤**52 And sent messengers before his face** [i.e., ahead of him]—He had not done this before. But now instead of avoiding publicity, he seems to have desired it.

➤**53 And they did not receive him**—In going to the festivals at Jerusalem, the Galileans usually had to take the Samaritan route (Josephus's *Antiquities,* 20.5.1), and yet they were not met with such inhospitality. But the citizens of Jerusalem would not receive this Galilean because he laid claim to the messiahship. As is evident from John 7:52, the Jews would never believe that the Messiah would come from Galilee.

➤**54 James and John**—not Peter, as would have been expected, but those "sons of thunder" (Mark 3:17), the younger of whom had been rebuked already for his exclusiveness (9:49, 50). The same fiery zeal is found in 2 John 10 and 3 John 10. **command fire to come down from heaven**—an allusion to what Elijah did in Samaria (2 Kings 1:10-12). (This accounts for the fact that later copyists added the words "as Elijah did" into the text. These words are not present in the earliest manuscripts.)

➤**55, 56** According to an impressive list of ancient manuscripts, these verses contain only these words: "But he turned, and rebuked them. And they went to another village." The added words, doubtless a gloss, serve as a commentary on Jesus' report. Having been rejected by Jerusalem, Jesus went to another village.

## 57-62 INCIDENTS ILLUSTRATIVE OF DISCIPLESHIP

Many men wished to follow Jesus, then as now, until they realized what was involved in "going to Jerusalem." The case of each of these three men stresses the idea of total and absolute commitment to Jesus.

➤**58** See comments on Matthew 8:19, 20.

➤**59, 60** See comments on Matthew 8:21, 22.

➤**61, 62 I will follow thee; but**—The second disciple also used "but," yet the different treatment of the two cases shows how different was the spirit of the two men, and to that difference our Lord addresses himself. The case of Elisha (1 Kings 19:19-21), though apparently similar to this, will be found quite different from the "looking back" of this case (as is explained by Jesus' illustration). As ploughing requires an eye intent on the furrow to be made and is marred the instant one turns about, so will a person not be qualified for God's kingdom who does the work of God with a distracted attention, a divided heart. Though the reference seems chiefly to ministers, the application is general. The expression "looking back" has a pointed reference to "Lot's wife" (see Gen. 19:26). It is not actual return to the world, but a reluctance to break with it.

## Chapter 10

### 1-24 THE MISSION OF THE SEVENTY DISCIPLES AND THEIR REPORT TO JESUS

➤1 the Lord appointed other seventy also—As the conclusion of Jesus' earthly ministry approached, the preparations for it were quickened. Luke alone records the fact that Jesus sent **seventy** disciples on this mission in addition to the Twelve. (Cf. 9:1-6 for the record of his commissioning of the Twelve.) Instead of **seventy,** some manuscripts read "seventy-two" (see also in 10:17). Since the manuscript support for both readings is equally good and good reasons can be given for the authenticity of either number, it can not be said for certain which one Luke wrote. Nevertheless, most versions adopt the reading **seventy.** Why did Jesus choose seventy? Probably he did so with allusion to the seventy elders of Israel on whom the Spirit descended in the wilderness (Num. 11:24, 25). Moses had seventy elders to assist him; Jesus had seventy assistants. The number seventy was symbolic to the Jews, for it suggested fullness and completion (it is the sacred number "seven" multiplied in the round number "ten"). Their mission, unlike that of the Twelve, was evidently temporary in nature. Their instructions were in keeping with a brief and pioneering mission, intended to supply general preparation for the Lord's own visit afterward to the same "cities and places." We never read again of the seventy after their return from this single missionary tour.

➤2 The harvest—See comments on Matthew 9:37, 38.

➤3-11 See comments on Matthew 10:7-16. **son of peace**—inwardly prepared to embrace the disciples' message of peace. This refers to one who is worthy of the messianic gift of peace. (See note on "worthy," Matt. 10:13.) Verse 7 is similar to Paul's teachings recorded in 1 Cor. 9:13, where the apostle teaches that he who receives the gospel should care for the proclaimer of the gospel.

➤12-15 See comments on Matthew 11:20-24. **Tyre and Sidon**—were ruined by commercial prosperity. Sodom sank through its vile pollutions, but the judgment on those cities who rejected the Savior, when he personally visited them, shall be greater than that received by Tyre and Sidon.

➤16 See comments on Matthew 10:40. (Cf. Luke 9:48 and John 15:23.)

➤17 returned again with joy—Evidently they were not too far removed from the Savior nor had the time element been extensive. **Lord, even the devils [demons] are subject unto us**—The possession of such power so as to perform these miracles filled them with more astonishment and joy than all else. **through thy name**—taking no credit to themselves but feeling lifted into a region of unimagined superiority over the powers of evil simply through their connection with Christ. Their power had extended even to exorcism of demons.

➤18 I beheld Satan . . . fall—Much of the force of this statement depends on the shade of meaning indicated by the imperfect tense in Greek and should therefore be translated, "I was beholding Satan as lightning falling. . . ." Jesus was therefore telling the seventy that he had followed their mission and had observed their triumphs. As they were casting out demons, he was watching the progressive decline of Satan's power. This "satanic fall" is not the same as Lucifer's original fall (Isa. 14:4-11). This fall is like that in Revelation 12:10, which depicts the downfall and demise of Satan as his kingdom is overpowered by the kingdom of God.

➤19 Behold, I give unto you power—is better translated, "I have given you authority" (RSV). **serpents and scorpions**—Scorpions are more venomous than serpents. (Cf. Deut. 8:15; Ps. 91:13.)

➤20 rather rejoice, because your names are written in heaven—So far from forbidding rejoicing, he takes occasion from it to tell them what had been passing in his own mind. If having power over demons brought exhilaration, he gave them a higher joy to balance it—the joy of having their names in heaven's register (cf. Phil. 4:3).

➤21, 22 **Jesus rejoiced in spirit**—This is the reading in some ancient manuscripts; but others read, "Jesus rejoiced in the Holy Spirit." The first reading could also be translated, "Jesus rejoiced in the Spirit." **and said . . .** —The very same words were uttered formally by our Lord on a similar occasion (Matt. 11:25-27). However, on that occasion Matthew simply indicates that he "answered and said"; here, he "rejoiced in [the] spirit and said . . ." On the former occasion, it was merely "at that season" he spoke, meaning with a general reference to the rejection of his gospel by the self-sufficient; here in Luke's record it is said that "in that hour . . ." The term "rejoiced" is too weak to express the full meaning of the verb used. It is "exulted"—evidently giving visible expression to his unusual emotions, while at the same time the words "in [the] spirit" are meant to convey to the reader the depth of them. This is one of those rare cases in which the veil is lifted from the Savior's inner man so that the reader may "look into it" for a moment (1 Pet. 1:12). Let us gaze on it with reverential wonder; and as we perceive what it was that produced that mysterious ecstasy, we shall find rising in our hearts an appreciation of our Lord's inner depths. Although the authenticity of 10:22 has been questioned by some interpreters, it is now generally recognized as thoroughly Jewish language.

➤23, 24 See comments on Matthew 13:16, 17.

## 25-27 THE PARABLE OF THE GOOD SAMARITAN

This parable and the question of the lawyer which occasioned it are related closely to the preceding section. This story is not to be confused with the one related in Mark 12:28-31. The reader quick to call Jesus' interpretation legalistic should note the general content of his teaching.

➤25 **And, behold, a certain lawyer stood up, and tempted him**—i.e., put him to the test. The lawyer was a man who was skilled in the interpretation of the law, rabbinical and Mosaic. He did not test Jesus with a hostile spirit; he was curious to see what insight this great Galilean teacher should share with him.

Notice that the conversation begins with the question of questions: **Master** [Teacher], **what shall I do to inherit eternal life?**

➤26 Jesus answered the lawyer's question with a question and in turn put the lawyer to the test. He referred the questioner to the law.

➤27 The lawyer's answer is the same answer which Christ himself gave to another inquirer (Mark 12:29-33).

➤29 **willing** [wishing] **to justify himself**—He wished to escape the difficulty which the correctness of his answer had made for himself by requiring Jesus to define the term "neighbor." The Jews interpreted this word in a very narrow manner and in a technical spirit, thus excluding Samaritans and Gentiles. Jesus' response in the following parable of the good Samaritan would break the narrowness of their interpretation.

➤30 **A certain man**—a Jew. **went down from Jerusalem to Jericho**—a distance of approximately seventeen miles northeast but with an extreme drop in altitude (3,300 feet from Jerusalem to Jericho). Thus, a traveler is described as one "going down" from Jerusalem to Jericho, a country dwelling of priests. **thieves**—The road, rocky and desolate, was a notorious haunt of robbers then and for ages after and even to the present time.

➤31, 32 **came down a certain priest that way . . . likewise a Levite**—Jericho, the second largest city of Judea, was a city of the priests and Levites; thousands of them lived there. The two here mentioned are believed to have been returning from their temple duties, but apparently they had not learned the true meaning of law and sacrifice. **when he saw him, he passed by**—although the law expressly required the opposite treatment—even of an animal (Deut. 22:4; Exod. 23:4, 5).

➤33 **a certain Samaritan**—one excommunicated by the Jews, a byword among them, synonymous with heretic and devil (John 8:48). No Samaritan, because of his ancestral difficulties, could be accepted by a Jew. Perhaps Jesus' hearers would naturally expect the third character to be a Jewish layman. **he had compassion**—His best is mentioned first. No doubt the priest and Levite had their excuses: it was not safe to linger there; they had been gone for some time from their homes; the man was past restoration to health; perhaps they would have been suspected by their countrymen if they assisted the man. The Samaritan could have reasoned in this way but did not. Nor did he say, "He is a Jew who would have had no dealings with me; why should I assist him?"

➤34 oil and wine—to cleanse the wounds and the oil to assuage their smartings. on his own beast—the Samaritan thus walking.

➤35 The two pence (denarii) are the equivalent of two days' wages of a laborer.

➤36, 37 Which now of these three . . . was neighbour unto him that fell among the thieves?—a most dexterous way of putting the question: thus (1) turning the question from, "Whom am I to love as my neighbor?" to "Who is the man that shows that love?"; (2) compelling the lawyer to give a reply very different from what he would like, not only condemning his nation but also his own people, who should be the most exemplary; and (3) making him commend one of a deeply-hated race. And he does it, but it is almost extorted. For he does not answer, "The Samaritan"—that would have sounded heterodox, heretical—but he that shewed [showed] mercy on him. It comes to the same thing, no doubt, but the circumlocution is significant. Jesus commanded the lawyer, Go and do thou likewise. Details of the discussion had been simple enough. The lawyer was dissatisfied with Jesus' answer and sought to be more specific. His ulterior motives prompted him to evade Jesus' initial answer. Although some interpreters insist that Jesus did not answer the lawyer's question, it seems quite evident that he answered the question by forcefully driving home his point. It is not simply, "Who was the neighbor?" but "Who acted as a neighbor?" True love does not ask for limitations but for opportunity. In summary, Jesus insists that life is not to be guided simply by the question "Who needs my help?" but "Who is able to help?" Jesus insists that the showing of mercy and acting neighborly is to be a constant in life. The two verbs "go" and "do" are present imperatives and carry with them the idea of continuous action—an action characteristic of any true neighbor.

38-42 THE STORY OF MARTHA AND MARY
Luke alone preserves this account for us.

➤38 he entered into a certain village— According to John (11:1), the village was Bethany. received him into her house—Martha is mentioned first likely because the house belonged to her, and she appears throughout the account to be the older sister.

➤39 Mary . . . sat at Jesus' feet—in contrast with Martha who was on her feet serving. Mary seated herself at Jesus' feet and gave rapt attention to all that he spoke. She "kept listening" to his words.

➤40 Martha was cumbered [distracted] about much serving—Her supreme interest seemed to be that of being an ideal hostess. But this distracted her from Christ. She rebuked her sister's action and inquired of Jesus concerning his own view of their activities. bid her therefore that she help me—She did not even think that by calling her sister away she would be causing Jesus to stop his teaching.

➤41 Martha, Martha—emphatically redoubling her name—thou art careful [anxious] and troubled about many things—the first word expressing the inward anxiety that her preparations should be worthy of her Lord; the other, the outward hassle of making these preparations. The "many things" would probably include her attitude toward service, which so engrossed her attention that she missed her Lord's teaching.

➤42 one thing is needful—There is one thing, above all else, that is necessary: to spend time exclusively with Jesus and to listen to his words with undistracted attention. Mary hath chosen that good part—Mary chose to be with the Lord himself rather than to do something for him. shall not be taken away from her—Martha's choice would be taken from her, for her services would die with her. Mary's would never be taken inasmuch as hers were spiritual and eternal. Both were true-hearted disciples, but the one was absorbed in the higher, the other in the lower of two ways of honoring their Lord. Yet neither despised the other's occupation. Some view Mary as representing the contemplative, and Martha the active style of the Christian character. A church filled with people of Mary's qualities would perhaps be as great an evil as a church filled with those of Martha's qualities. Both are needed since each complements the other. During the Middle Ages, Christian interpreters used this passage as a basis for declaring the superiority of the contemplative life. Contemporary interpreters note that the service of Jesus must not be so misdirected that the servant has no time to learn from him, nor should we permit ourselves to become agitated by the manner in which some serve, thus distracting from our own service.

*Chapter* **11**

## 1-13 TEACHING THE DISCIPLES TO PRAY

➤**1 one of his disciples**—who was probably impressed with either the matter or the manner of our Lord's prayers. **as John**—From this reference to John it is possible that disciple had not heard the Sermon on the Mount. Nothing of John's teaching to his own disciples has been preserved for us, but he probably did not teach his disciples to say, "our Father."

➤**2 Father**—*Pater,* the Greek translation of the Aramaic "Abba" used by Jesus. (Cf. 10:21; Mark 14:36.) Jesus now introduces his disciples to the same intimate, personal relationship that he enjoyed with the Father. **hallowed be thy name**—This indicates that his name be honored and revered above all other names, and it forms the basis for the petition, **thy kingdom come.** This prayer asks God to act speedily in bringing his kingdom and in hastening the great day of the Lord. Two forms of the prayer have come to us: this one and the account in Matthew. E. J. Tinsley states, "In Matthew it is a context dealing with prayer in general. Here in Luke . . . it comes after one of Jesus' periods of prayer and in a context dealing with discipleship." The two petitions are very similar but not identical. Certain scribes in the later history of the transmission of the Greek text added words to conform Luke's record to Matthew's. Thus, later manuscripts have the statement "Thy will be done, as in heaven, so on earth" (taken from Matt. 6:10). But this statement does not appear in the earliest witnesses.

➤**3, 4** See comments on Matthew 6:9-13. **day by day our daily bread**—The Greek term translated "daily" (*epiousios*) is found only here and in Matthew 6:11 (see comments there) in all of Greek literature; it probably designates that which comes "day by day." Some interpreters see this principle as applying also to forgiveness. A closing doxology, lacking here, is also lacking in all the best and most ancient manuscripts of Matthew's Gospel (see comments on Matt. 6:13).

## 5-13 PARABLES ENCOURAGING PRAYER FOLLOWING LUKE'S RECORD OF JESUS' PRAYER

➤**5-8 shall go unto him at midnight**—The heat in warm countries makes evening better for traveling than daytime. But midnight is everywhere a most unreasonable hour to call, and the hour is selected here for that very reason. **Trouble me not**—the trouble making him insensible both to the urgency of the case and the claims of friendship. **I cannot**—without exertion, which he would not make. **importunity**—The word is a very strong one; it means "shamelessness." In this context, it has the idea of persisting in the face of all that seems reasonable and refusing to accept a denial. **as many as he needeth**—His reluctance once overcome, all the claims of friendship and necessity are felt to the full. The sense is obvious. If the self-indulgent—deaf both to friendship and necessity—can, after a positive refusal, be won over by sheer persistence to do all that is needed, how much more may the same determined perseverance in prayer be expected to prevail with him whose very nature is ready to bestow "his riches upon all who call upon him" (Rom. 10:12, RSV). The contrast of the parable is obvious. If a man will not hear the plea of his brother, he will hear because of "importunity." If a man hears because of "importunity," how much sooner does God respond without "importunity"!

➤**9-13** See comments on Matthew 7:7-11. **give the Holy Spirit**—the gift of gifts descending on God's people through Christ.

## 14-36 THE HEALING OF THE BLIND AND DUMB DEMONIAC AND THE CHARGE AGAINST JESUS OF BEING IN LEAGUE WITH BEELZEBUB

See comments on Matthew 12:22-45.

➤**14 dumb**—blind also (Matt. 12:22).

➤**15-19** The Jews did not question Jesus' ability to exorcise demons; they simply said that he did this by the power of the prince of the demons. However, Jesus exposed the ridiculous nature of this accusation by referring to the divided kingdom and house. Satan would defeat himself if he cast out his own demons. Verse 19 is an assumption for the sake of argument. If Jesus did cast out demons by Beelzebub, then how did his accusers' sons exorcise them? Apparently the Jews found difficulty in believing that one stronger than Satan was stripping him of his power.

➤20 **finger of God**—"Spirit of God" in Matthew 12:28. The former figuratively denoting the power of God, the latter the living personal agent in every exercise of this power.

➤21, 22 The expression **strong man** means Satan. **armed**—pointing to all the subtle and varied methods by which he wields his dark power over men. **palace**—This is not to be construed as referring to an individual, but the illustration is of a man guarding his household. **in peace**—undisturbed, secure in his possession. **a stronger than he**—stronger than the previously described "strong man." Not a reference to Christ, although in actual fact, of course, Christ is stronger than Satan and overcomes him. **overcome[s] him ... taketh from him all his armour**—overpowers him and takes away his panoply, his complete armor.

➤23 There is no neutrality in religion. The absence of positive attachment to Christ involves hostility toward him. **gathereth ... scattereth**—referring probably to gleaners. The meaning seems to be, whatever is disconnected from Christ comes to nothing.

➤24-26 **dry** [or, waterless] **places**—were regarded by the Jews as places of natural habitation of demons, which preferred the bodies of men. Man's heart is no vacuum; it must be filled. When one refuses God's Spirit, he is practically inviting evil spirits to return to his heart. Either he fills the heart or Satan fills it.

➤27, 28 **as he spake these things, a certain woman of the company lifted up her voice, and said unto him . . .**—a charming little incident and profoundly instructive. With true feminine feeling, she envied the mother of such a wonderful Teacher. Our Lord did not condemn her. Rather, he pointed out that the hearers and keepers of God's word are the blessed ones; in other words, the humblest believer who keeps his word is more blessed than the one who bore him. (See comments on Matt. 12:49, 50.) How alien is this sentiment from the

teaching of those who magnify the Virgin Mary!

➤29-32 See comments on Matthew 12:39-42.

➤33-36 See comments on Matthew 5:14-16; 6:22, 23.

## 38-54 THE DENUNCIATION OF THE PHARISEES

In this passage Jesus indicates again that the kingdom is not composed of externals or of external relationships.

➤38 **marvelled**—See comments on Mark 7:2-4.

➤39-41 **the cup and the platter**—a remarkable example of our Lord's way of drawing the most striking illustrations of great truths from the most familiar objects and incidents of life. **did not he that made that which is without make that which is within also?**—"Did not the one who made the outside make the inside also?" (NIV). God is Lord of the outer man and the inner man. **alms ...** — Our Lord encouraged them to exemplify the opposite character and then their outside would be beautiful in the eyes of God and their meals would be eaten with clean hands.

➤42 **mint and rue**—founding the statement on Leviticus 27:30, which they interpreted rigidly. Our Lord purposely names the most minute products of the earth as examples of that from which they punctiliously exacted the tithe. **judgment and the love of God**—The reference is to Micah 6:6-8. (See comments on Mark 12:29, 32, 33.) The same tendency to merge greater duties in lesser besets us still; it is the characteristic of hypocrites. There is no need for one set of duties to jostle out another, but of the greater our Lord says, **These ought ye to have done.**

➤43 **uppermost seats in the synagogues**—See 14:7-11. **greetings**—See Matthew 23:7-10.

➤44 **the men that walk over them are not aware of them**—As one might unconsciously walk over a grave concealed from view and thus contract ceremonial defilement, so the plausible exterior of the Pharisees kept people from perceiving the pollution they contracted from coming in contact with such corrupted individuals. (See Ps. 5:9; Rom. 3:13.)

➤46 **burdens grievous to be borne**—hard to bear, referring not so much to the irksomeness of the legal rites as to the heartless rigor with which they were enforced and by men of shameless inconsistency.

➤47, 48 Out of pretended respect and honor, they repaired and beautified **the sepulchres of the prophets** and with whining hypocrisy said, "If we had been in the days of our father, we should not have been partakers with them in the blood of the prophets," while all the time they "were witnessing against themselves that they were the children of them that killed the prophets" (Matt. 23:29, 30).

➤**49-51 the wisdom of God**—In the parallel passage (Matt. 23:34), the speaker is not identified. Luke names him "the wisdom of God"—referring to God, or to God as identified with the oracle of God, or to Christ. Since the declaration ("I will send them prophets," etc.) is not taken directly from any OT passage, it must refer to Christ's present speaking, in which he steps in, so to speak, to continue an ancient divine oracle. In short, Christ speaks as God. **the blood of all the prophets . . . may be required of this generation**—The iniquity of Israel was allowed to accumulate from age to age until in that generation it came to the full, and the whole collected vengeance of heaven broke at once over its head. **From the blood of Abel unto the blood of Zacharias**—See comments on Matthew 23:35.

➤**52 Woe unto you, lawyers! for ye have taken away the key of knowledge**—In Matthew 23:13 they are accused of shutting heaven; here of taking away the key of knowledge. A right knowledge of God's word is eternal life (John 17:3), but this they took away from the people, substituting for it their traditions.

Chapter **12**

## 1-12 WARNING AGAINST HYPOCRISY

➤**1, 2 In the mean time**—in close connection with the foregoing scene, another note of Luke's careful historical accuracy. The first verse connects the passage with the previous verses on the Pharisees, whose teaching acted as leaven or yeast in its effect on society. Our Lord had been speaking more plainly than ever before, as matters were coming to a climax between himself and his enemies, and this seems to have suggested to his own mind the

warning here recorded. **his disciples first**—afterward he would speak to the multitudes (12:54). **covered**—hidden from view. **hid**—concealed from knowledge. Some day the most secret thoughts of men's hearts will be revealed (cf. 1 Cor. 4:3, 5).

➤**4, 5** The proclamation of the Lord's word may cost the disciples their lives. He calls them "friends" here, not in any loose or impersonal sense, but from the feeling he then had that in this "killing of the body" he and they were going to be one with another. **Fear him . . . Fear him**—fear God who has control over a man's final destiny. **hell**—lit., "gehenna," a Greek translation of the Hebrew words for "Valley of Hinnom" (*gehinnōm*), which is a ravine outside of Jerusalem in which there were infant sacrifices (2 Chron. 28:3; 33:6). The place was repulsive to the Jews; it came to be associated with future judgment in OT times (Jer. 7:32; 19:6). During the intertestamental period, *genimmōm* was described as a place of punishment after death (see Liefeld).

➤**6, 7 five sparrows sold for two farthings**—In Matthew 10:29 it is two for one farthing. So if one took two pennies' worth, he got one "in addition"—of such small value were they. **ye are of more value than many sparrows**—not "than millions of sparrows." The charm and power of our Lord's teaching is very evident in this simplicity.

➤**8, 9 confess . . . denieth**—The point lies in doing it "before men" because one has to do it "despising the shame." But when done, the Lord holds himself bound to repay it in kind by confessing such "before the angels of God." For the remainder, see comments on 9:26.

➤**10 Son of man . . . Holy Ghost** [Spirit]—See comments on Matthew 12:31, 32. The term "Son of man" was the favorite term Jesus used for himself. The term emphasizes his humanity as well as his deity and is likely derived from Daniel 7:13 where one like a "son of man" receives an everlasting kingdom."

## 13-53 TEACHINGS ON COVETOUSNESS, WATCHFULNESS, AND SUPERIORITY OF CHRIST TO EARTHLY TIES

Jesus was commonly regarded as a rabbi, and it is therefore understandable why his opinion was requested in this legal matter. It is likely that the younger man was being defrauded of his inheritance. Although Jesus refused to make any decision in the matter, he did speak a word of warning concerning covetousness, which was at the very foundation of the matter. The synagogue served as a place of worship, instruction, and judgment of civil matters. The rabbi was responsible in each of these areas.

➤**13** In this most inopportune intrusion upon the solemnities of our Lord's teaching, there is a mixture of the absurd and the irreverent, the one, however, occasioning the other. The man had not the least idea that his case was not urgent and was hardly worthy of our Lord's attention.

➤**14 Man**—Contrast this style of address with "my friends" (12:4). **who made me a judge?**—a question literally repudiating the office that Moses assumed (Exod. 2:14). The influence of religious teachers in the external relations of life has always been immense; but whenever they meddle directly with secular and political matters, the spell of that influence is broken.

➤**15 unto them**—i.e., the multitude assembled around him (12:1). **beware of covetousness**—lit., "beware of all covetousness." The man's desire for an equal share of the inheritance was actually covetousness. **a man's life**—a singularly weighty maxim, and not less so because its meaning and its truth are equally evident.

➤**16-19 a certain rich man**—Why is this man called a "fool"? (1) Because he treasured a life of secure and abundant earthly enjoyment as the essence of human happiness. (2) Because, possessing the means to obtain this happiness, he flattered himself that he had a long lease of such enjoyment and nothing to do but give himself to it. Nothing else is laid to his charge.

➤**20, 21 this night**—This sudden cutting short of his career is designed to express not only the folly of building securely upon the future but also of throwing one's whole soul into what may at any moment be gone. **So is he that layeth up treasure for himself**—Such is a picture of his folly here and its terrible result (see Ps. 39:6). **is not rich toward God**—He lives to amass and enjoy riches which terminate in self, but as to the riches of God's favor (such as eternal life, precious faith, good works, and

wisdom) he has none and thus dies a beggar (Cf. Ps. 30:5; Prov. 8:11; 1 Tim. 6:18; James 2:5; 2 Pet. 1:1).

➤**22-31** See Matthew 6:25-33 for comments on this material in Luke, which is parallel to the Matthean section of the Sermon on the Mount.

➤**25, 26 which of you . . . can add to his stature** [or, age] **one cubit?**—The term that is translated "cubit" may refer either to physical height or to one's life span. However, people would be more prone to worry concerning the extension of life than concerning the increasing of their physical height.

➤**32 little flock**—How sublime and touching a contrast between this tender appellation **little flock** and the **Father's good pleasure to give you the kingdom.** The former terms recall the insignificance and helplessness of the handful of disciples while the latter terms hold up to their view the eternal love that encircled them, the everlasting arms that were underneath them, and the great inheritance awaiting them!

➤**33, 34** This is but a more vivid expression of Matthew 6:9-21 (see comments there).

➤**35-40** Jesus now considers the disciples' attitude toward the future. Tinsley writes: "For Luke, as we shall see, the first signs of the *parousia* (the coming of the Son of man) have come with the resurrection. His disciples . . . live in the interval before the whole process is finished, and they must be ready for this at any moment." **loins be girded**—to fasten up the long outer garment, always done before travel and work (2 Kings 4:29; Acts 12:8). The meaning is "Be in readiness." **lights** [lamps] **burning**—See comments on Matthew 25:1. **return from the wedding** [feast]—not come to it, as in the parable of the virgins. Both have their spiritual significance, but preparedness for Christ's coming is the prominent idea. **gird himself**—i.e., prepare himself to serve. "Thus will the Bridegroom entertain his friends on the solemn Nuptial Day" (Bengel). **second watch . . . third**—To find the servants ready to receive their lord at any hour of day or night when they might least of all expect him. An unprepared servant does not have everything in such order and readiness for his master's return—as he both could and would have had if he had had notice of the time of his coming. Thus, he may not be willing to open to him "immediately," but hasten to prepare and let his master knock again before he admits him, and even then not with full joy. This is a too common case with Christians. But if the servant so disciplines himself and all under his charge in such a state that at any hour when his master knocks, he can open to him "immediately" and hail his "return"—that is the most enviable and blessed servant of all.

➤**41-48 this parable unto** [for] **us, or even to** [for] **all?**—for us, the Twelve, or all this vast audience? **who then**—answering the question indirectly by another question from which they were left to summarize that the answer would be: The disciples are represented by the "stewards" of the "household"; the rest of the people, generally speaking, by the "servants." **faithful and wise**—Fidelity is the first requisite in a servant; wisdom (discretion and judgment in the exercise of his function) is the next important requisite. **servant**—a house-steward, whose responsibility it was to distribute to the servants their allotted portion of food. **whom his lord shall make ruler over his household**—His lord will deem him fit to be advanced to the highest post. **beat the menservants and maidens**—In the confidence that his lord's return will not be speedy, he discards the servant's role and plays the role of the master, maltreating those faithful servants who refuse to join him, and seizes the opportunity to rebel in the fullness of his master's house. This servant intends to resume the mask of fidelity before the master appears. **will appoint him his portion with the unbelievers**—Those unworthy of trust. (Cf. Matt. 24:51.) Such are those who falsely call themselves "servants," or are those who, espousing true faith, mistreat God's people (see Acts 20:29, 30). **he that knew not**—i.e., did not have the same full knowledge as the steward concerning the seriousness of the entrusted responsibilities. **many stripes ... few stripes**—degrees of future punishment proportioned to the knowledge against which the servant sinned. Even heathen have some knowledge of God and of future judgment, but the reference here is not to such people. It is a solemn truth and discloses a tangible and momentous principle in its application. Christ's servants will be held accountable for their deeds (see Rom. 14:10; 2 Cor. 5:10).

➤**49-53** This passage notes the crisis upon men as a result of Christ's ministry, which itself will set the world on fire. Being involved in this ministry means suffering for Jesus personally because many of one's relatives will not become involved—and will even oppose. **fire on earth**—the higher spiritual element of life that Jesus came to introduce on the earth, with reference to its mighty effects in quickening all that is akin to it and destroying all that is opposed. To cause this element of life to take up its abode on earth and wholly to pervade human hearts with its warmth was the lofty destiny of the Redeemer. Jesus' ministry is one of spiritual fire and is divisive in its nature. Fire has a twofold effect: (1) It destroys what is combustible, and (2) it purifies noncombustible objects. **I have a baptism**—his own agony and suffering to occur on the cross. (Cf. Ps. 69:1-3, where being plunged into water carries with it the concept of agony and distress.) Mark 10:38ff. uses "baptism" as an expression of Jesus' passion. **how am I straitened** [constrained, pressed]—not the idea of longing for its accomplishment, but rather the pressure of the experience which rests upon him prior to its accomplishment. **peace ... ? Nay**—the reverse of peace, in the first instance. (See comments on Matt. 10:34-36.) The truth proclaimed by Jesus creates division within the household and within one's family.

## 54-59 NOT DISCERNING THE SIGNS OF THE TIME

➤**54 He said also to the people**—a word of special warning to the thoughtless crowd before dismissing them. (See comments on Matt. 16:2, 3.)

➤**56 ye do not discern this time**—unable to perceive what a critical period this was for the Jewish nation. The lack of personal integrity is illustrated by the Jews' inability to discern the signs of the time. They were not intelligent enough to discern that Jesus was the Messiah, although they were quite apt in interpreting the physical conditions relating to the weather.

➤**57 Why even of yourselves judge ye not what is right?**—i.e., "Why do you not judge for yourselves?" (RSV). They might reply, "To do this requires more knowledge of Scripture and providence than we possess." However,

Jesus spoke to their conscience enough to show them who he was and to win some of them to immediate discipleship.

➤**58 When thou goest**—See comments on Matthew 5:25, 26. The urgency of the case with them and the necessity, for their own safety, of immediate decision was the object of these striking words. The story employed by Jesus is couched in physical terminology but nonetheless relates spiritual truth. The man who fails to be reconciled with God through Christ indeed faces a bleak future. Marshall observes that "a doctrine of purgatory can be read out of this verse only if it is first read into it."

*Chapter* **13**

## 1-9 A COMMAND TO REPENT OR PERISH AND AN ILLUSTRATION OF THE COMMAND

These words are apparently directed to the Pharisees. Jesus had already noted that his coming created a crisis. The reference to the Galileans slain by Pilate and to the fruitless fig tree further emphasize the need of repentance.

➤**1-3** In these verses, Jesus indicates that repentance is essential for all who purpose to enter the kingdom. The Jews generally believed that calamities came because of man's sins. Jesus here points out that even the most religious must repent in order to enter the kingdom. **Galileans**—possibly the followers of Judas of Galilee, who some twenty years earlier had taught that Jews should not pay tribute to the Romans. From Acts 5:37 we learn that he drew a circle of followers about himself, but they were quickly dispersed after Judas's death. Although we know nothing of these "Galileans" except the above conjecture, there is nothing in the account that deviates from what is known of Pilate's character. Josephus (in *Antiquities,* 18.3.2) relates the account of Pilate's soldiers slipping among the crowds at the time of the Jewish opposition to the building of the aqueduct into Jerusalem and Pilate's subsequent murder of his opponents. Apparently the informer brought the report of "Galileans' murder" to Jesus so that he might learn Jesus' views of the event and whether it was a judgment of heaven. In response he simply pointed them to the practical view of the mat-

ter: "These men are not signal examples of divine vengeance, as you suppose; but every impenitent sinner—including you yourselves, except you repent—shall be like monuments of the judgment of heaven and in a more terrible sense."

➤**4, 5** The necessity of repentance on the part of all further is illustrated by the eighteen men killed by the fall of Siloam's tower. The **tower** is not mentioned elsewhere, although it is generally believed that it was one of the towers of the city wall, near the pool of Siloam (situated at an angle where the south and east walls of the city joined). Nothing is known of its fall. Its absence from the historical accounts surely does not disprove the integrity of Luke's report any more than the absence of household accidents from contemporary historical writing disproves their reality. Verse 5 emphatically insists upon the repentance of all.

➤**6-9** The parable of the barren fig tree concludes the section. Obviously, the fig tree refers to barren Israel, thus revealing that even Israel must repent. (Cf. Isa. 5:1-7; John 15:1-8.) The **vineyard** was a spot selected for its fertility, separated from the surrounding fields and cultivated with special care with a view solely to the bearing of fruit. **I came seeking fruit**— In the terms of the parable, Jesus is depicted by the man who came to a given tree and sought fruit. The spiritual application, of course, refers to a heart turned to God producing the fruits of righteousness. (Cf. Matt. 21:33, 34 and Isa. 5:2.) God has a right to it and will require it. **three years**—a period long enough to determine the productivity of a fig tree. But some insist that the tree matured in three years, and this is now "three years" later. The point, however, is not the specific number of years, but that the tree, now mature enough to bear fruit, bore no fruit. Although some suppose that this is an allusion to the duration of our Lord's ministry, such an interpretation is indeed precarious. **let it alone this year**—The husbandman is the intercessor and loathes to see the tree cut down so long as there is any hope of productivity. He insists that he be permitted to loosen the soil about the tree and fertilize it. Then if it bears no fruit, it is to be cut down. The parable evidently refers to Israel, who had been given full opportunity by God to bear fruit in his kingdom. It appears that Israel would remain fruitless; nonetheless, God would give them one last chance to bear fruit. If they bore fruit, this would be an indication of genuine repentance. However, if they did not bear fruit, he would **cut it down.** The final perdition of those that are found fruitless will be just.

## 10-17 THE HEALING OF THE WOMAN WITH AN INFIRMITY OF EIGHTEEN YEARS' DURATION

Jesus again comes under the criticism of the religious leaders because he healed on the Sabbath when there was no danger of immediate death. Yet, Jesus taught that the work of liberation must continue throughout the week. This event further illustrates the need of repentance on the part of the religious leaders.

➤**10 he was teaching in one of the synagogues on the sabbath**—Luke continues carefully his structured approach to the gospel and establishes the background for the difficulty soon to be described.

➤**11 spirit of infirmity eighteen years**—Cf. 13:16 (Satan bound her for eighteen years). One is likely to derive from this that her protracted infirmity was the effect of some milder form of possession.

➤**12, 13 Woman, thou art loosed**—freed, from both afflictions at once.

➤**14 ruler of the synagogue answered with indignation**—He was indignant because Jesus violated the Sabbath law in healing this woman (cf. Matt. 21:15). The ruler then addressed himself to the people, not daring directly to find fault with Christ, but seeking circuitously to condemn him through the people over whom he had tremendous influence by virtue of his synagogue position.

➤**15 The Lord**—See comments on 10:1. **hypocrite**—plural in Greek, "hypocrites." How "the faithful and true witness" rips the masks from men's faces! **his ox**—See comments on Matthew 12:9-13 and 6:9.

➤**16 ought not this woman . . . be loosed**—How gloriously the Lord vindicates the superior claims of this woman, for she, as a daughter of Abraham, was an heir of the promise. Jesus, by his miracle, insists that the woman is of far greater value than the animal who would be routinely watered and cared for on the Sabbath.

➤**17** The opponents of Jesus, to whom he earlier referred as "hypocrites," "were put to shame" (RSV). The verb translated "were put to shame" is an imperfect tense and would suggest that their shame was continuous as the Lord exposed them. However, the reaction of the multitude was just the opposite; they were "continuously rejoicing" (also an imperfect tense) because of Jesus' deeds. Therefore, Jesus concludes that the kingdom is not to be ruled by scribal legalism but by the law of love and mercy.

## 18-30 SOME MISCELLANEOUS TEACHINGS

➤**18-21 mustard seed . . . leaven**—The parable of the leaven speaks of the inward growth of the kingdom, while the parable of the mustard seed seems to point to the external growth of the kingdom. (But see comments on Matt. 13:31-33; Mark 4:30-32.)

➤**24 Strive**—The word signifies to "contend" as for the mastery, to "struggle," expressive of the difficulty of being saved as if one would have to force his way into the kingdom. **strait gate**—another figure of the same. (See note on Matt. 7:13, 14.) This figure expresses the idea of limited, difficult admission. **many . . . will seek to enter in, and shall not be able**—because it must be a life-and-death struggle. The word translated "strive" is employed in 22:44 to describe Jesus' struggle in Gethsemane. The word suggests a struggle as would be essential to the winning of an athletic contest.

➤**25 the master of the house is risen up, and hath shut . . . the door**—A sublime and vivid picture! At the present he is represented as being in a sitting posture, as if calmly looking on to see who will strive while entrance is available. But when this period has passed, the Master of the house himself rises and shuts the door, after which there will be no admittance. **Lord, Lord**—expressive of the earnestness now felt, but too late. (See comments on Matt. 7:21, 22.)

➤**26 We have eaten and drunk in thy presence**—We have sat with you at the same table. **thou hast taught in our streets**—Do we not remember listening in our own streets to your teaching? Surely we are not to be denied admittance?

➤**27 But he shall say . . . I know you not . . . ye workers of iniquity** [unrighteousness]—No nearness of external communion with Christ will avail at the great day in place of that holiness without which no man shall see the Lord. Observe the style that Jesus intimates he will then assume—that of absolute ruler of men's eternal destinies—and contrast it with his despised and rejected condition at that time.

➤**28, 29** See comments on Matthew 8:11, 12.

## 31-35 A MESSAGE TO HEROD

The Pharisees mentioned in this passage are probably friends of Herod, although it has been conjectured that they were friends of Jesus.

➤**31** Jesus was on his way out of Perea, east of Jordan, and was in Herod's dominion (Galilee and Perea) journeying toward Jerusalem. Haunted by guilty fears, Herod wanted to get rid of him (see comments on Mark 6:14). He seems to have sent these Pharisees under the pretense of a friendly hint to persuade him that the sooner he got beyond Herod's jurisdiction the better it would be for his own safety.

➤**32** Our Lord saw through this guise and sent the cunning ruler a message couched in dignified and befitting irony. **that fox**—that crafty, cruel enemy of God's innocent servants. **Behold, I cast out devils** [demons] **and I do cures to day and to morrow**—Jesus responded by asserting that he had *his* work to accomplish—no matter what Herod would do to stop him. Jesus' works of mercy were near completion, but some remained to be done. He had work for **today and tomorrow** too, and even for **the third day.** By that time he would be where Herod's jurisdiction could not reach. **the third day I shall be perfected**—This has two meanings: First, "the third day," figuratively speaking, means "the day something is finished." In connection with the next verse, this finishing points to the completion of Christ's suffering. Through suffering, he was perfected (Heb. 2:9). Second, "the third" clearly points to Christ's resurrection. In resurrection, Christ was perfected in glory.

➤**33 it cannot be that a prophet perish out of** [outside] **Jerusalem**—Note the awful severity of the satire! It is as if Jesus were saying, "Herod seeks to kill me, does he? Ah! I must be out of Herod's jurisdiction for my death to occur. Go tell him I neither flee from him nor fear him, but Jerusalem is the prophet's slaughter-house."

*Chapter* **14**

## 1-24 THE HEALING OF THE DROPSIED MAN AND VARIOUS TEACHINGS AT A SABBATH FEAST

Chapter 14 continues Luke's record of Jesus' debate with the Pharisees. This chapter begins another section dealing with the journeys of Jesus to Jerusalem; these journeys were first mentioned in 9:51. The chapter also begins a section of material unique to Luke's Gospel (14:1-17) as most of the "travel narrative" is peculiar to the Lucan account.

➤**2 a certain man before him which had the dropsy**—He was not one of the company, since this was apparently before the guests were seated, and probably the man came in hope of being cured, though not expressly soliciting the miracle. A dropsied condition exists when fluids are retained in the body tissues.

➤**3-6** See comments on Matthew 12:11, 12. Jesus used the dropsied man's condition as an opportunity to question the Pharisees, who wisely refused to comment about healing on the Sabbath. Verse 5 drives home the point of the Pharisees' inconsistency in their Sabbath law. The best manuscripts read "son" instead of "ass" (or, donkey). Copyists of other manuscripts felt that the combination of two animals (ass and ox) was more natural than "son and ox." In either case, the point is the same: when there is an emergency, the Sabbath restrictions should be put aside. If the Jews agreed to this, why should they oppose Jesus' healing on the Sabbath?

➤**7-11 a parable**—showing that his design was not so much to inculcate mere politeness or good manners, but to teach something deeper with a spiritual application (cf. 14:11). **highest room**—i.e., "place of honor" (RSV)—in the middle of the couch on which they reclined at meals. These places were esteemed the most honorable. **with shame**—to be lowest is only ignominious to him who desires the highest position. **the lowest**—not merely a lower. The term **friend** is spoken to the modest guest only, not the proud one. **shalt thou have worship in the presence of them**—better translated, "you will be honored in the presence of all" (NIV). The whole of this is but a reproduction of Prov. 25:6, 7. But it was reserved for the matchless Teacher to utter articulately and apply it to behavior in the kingdom of God (14:11). A man is given the place of importance because of the host's evaluation; the same is true of the man who is honored by God. Verse 11 summarizes the parable and suggests that the values of the present world-order will be turned about by the priorities in the kingdom of God.

➤12-14 call not thy friends—Jesus certainly did not mean for us to dispense with the duties of ordinary friendship and fellowship, but leaving these to their proper place, he inculcates what is better. lest . . . a recompence be made thee—The meaning is that one should not exercise hospitality with selfish motives (Matt. 5:46, 47).

➤15 When one . . . heard . . . he said unto him, "Blessed is he"—Our Lord's words seemed to hold forth the future "recompense" under the idea of a great feast. The thought passes through this man's mind that those invited to the feast would be honored and blessed. Jesus' reply in substance is: "The great feast is prepared already; the invitations are issued, but declined; the feast, not withstanding, shall not lack abundance of guests, but not one of its present scorners—who shall yet come to ask for admission—shall be allowed to taste of it."

➤16 A certain man made a great supper and bade [invited] many—Drawing from the custom and terminology of his day, Jesus spoke of the Jews who were invited to the messianic feast. The "messianic" banquet was just one of the numerous word pictures by which the Jews described the activities of this coming age. In their thinking, Gentiles and sinners would never find a place at this banquet table. When the meal was prepared, the host sent his servant to those who had been invited. In Palestine guests were invited to a feast on a specific day, but the hour was announced when all was in readiness. Contrary to current social customs, the Jews extended two invitations.

➤18-20 all with one consent began to make excuse—Cf. Matthew 22:5. Three excuses are given as specimens of the entire group. Mentioned are the claim of business (14:18), the claim of novelty (14:19), and the claim of one's family (14:20). Each excuse differs from the other and has its own plausibility, but all arrive at the same result. Those

invited had other things occupying them that seemed more pressing at the moment. Nobody is represented as saying, "I will not come." All of the excuses imply that but for certain events they would attend, and when these things had been cared for, they would come. So it is certainly in the case intended, for the last words clearly imply that the refusers will one day become petitioners.

➤21 The servant returned and reported this to his master. The householder became angry and commanded the servant to invite people from the streets and the lanes of the city to the banquet. Historically, these would likely be interpreted as being the publicans and sinners. They would normally have been overlooked in the first invitation list, but in anger the host instructed the servant to invite them to his meal.

➤22 yet there is room—implying that these people had embraced the invitation (Matt. 21:32; Mark 12:39; John 7:48, 49).

➤23 highways and hedges—outside the city altogether. compel them to come in—not as if they would make the excuses of the first group, but because it would be difficult for them to overcome two difficulties: (1) they were not fit company for such a feast; (2) they did not have the proper clothing or attire. How fitly does this represent the difficulties and fears of the sincere! How is this met? "Take no excuse—make them come as they are—bring them along with you." What a directory for ministers of Christ!

➤24 I say unto you, That none of those men bidden . . . shall taste of my supper—Our Lord here throws off the veil of the parable and proclaims the supper his own, intimating that when transferred and transformed into its final glorious form, and when the refusers themselves would give all for another opportunity, he will not allow one of them to taste it. The parable obviously indicates that many invited into the kingdom will refuse to enter; others will accept. An invitation alone is not adequate; one must accept the invitation extended.

25-35 AN ADDRESS TO HIS TRAVELING COMPANIONS CONCERNING THE COST OF DISCIPLESHIP

➤25 there went great multitudes with him—on his final journey to Jerusalem. The "great multitudes" were doubtless people journeying to Jerusalem for the Passover. These people moved along in clusters, family groups and fellow villagers traveling together (2:44). On this occasion, they had joined Jesus and had formed themselves into one mass of humanity.

➤**26, 27** See comments on Matthew 10:34-36 and Mark 8:34, 35.

➤**28-33** Although human leaders take tremendous pride in the masses following them, Jesus insisted that the multitudes must count the cost of discipleship. Common sense teaches men not to begin any costly work without first seeing that they have the supplies and material required to finish the project. And the man who otherwise exposes himself is open to general ridicule. Nor will any wise potentate enter a war with any hostile power without first seeing that, despite formidable odds (two to one), he will be able to stand his ground. If he has no hope of doing so, he will feel that nothing remains for him but to make the best terms he can. Jesus seems to be saying: "In the warfare you will each have to wage as my disciples, despise not your enemy's strength, for the odds are all against you; and you must see that despite every disadvantage you still have the means whereby to hold out and win the victory, or else do not begin at all, and make the best you can in such awful circumstances." If the disciple is to bring flavor to society, then he must possess the special qualities and characteristics of discipleship. If the disciple is tasteless, he is of no more value than salt that has lost its qualities of being "salty." Salt is valuable only when it flavors food as it is expected to do. Without the absolute surrender of self, the contest is hopeless (14:33). (For a further discussion of 14:34, 35, see comments on Matt. 5:13-16 and Mark 9:50.)

*Chapter* **15**

## 1-32 THREE PARABLES THAT EXPLAIN JESUS' WELCOMING OF PUBLICANS AND SINNERS

The theme of 14:1-24 (the heavenly banquet) is more fully discussed in the three parables contained in chapter 15. The Pharisees had constantly criticized Jesus for his ministry to the publicans and sinners. The rabbis had a saying,

"Let not a man associate with the wicked, not even to bring him to the Law," which summarized their feelings toward the outcast. Having earlier indicated his love of these people (5:29ff.) and suggested that he would extend God's love to them, he now declares in these parables God's love for the lost.

➤**1 The publicans** (tax collectors) **and sinners**—were considered outcasts of Jewish society. The Pharisees thought of them as non-lawkeepers, and as such were described as the "People of the Land."

➤**2** This explains the murmuring of **the Pharisees and scribes**—upon observing that Jesus formed relationships with people they considered to be social outcasts. The scribes and Pharisees were scandalized by him and insinuated that he must have some secret sympathy with their character. Jesus justified his attitude by revealing that it was also God's attitude. Three parables illustrate this love and concern.

### 3-7 THE LOST SHEEP

(Cf. Matthew 18:12-14.) In the Matthean account Jesus shows how precious one of his sheep is to the Good Shepherd; here, he shows that the shepherd will seek out the lost sheep, and having found it will rejoice in its recovery.

➤**4 doth not leave the ninety and nine in the wilderness**—All his attention and care, as it were, is given to the one goal of recovering the lost sheep. **go after . . . until he find it**—pointing to all the efforts of the shepherd's attempts to find the sheep. In Jesus' day the shepherd was responsible for the sheep. If one died, he must bring home the fleece to prove that it had died. The shepherd, therefore, could see no sacrifice too great to forbid an attempt to recover the lost sheep.

➤**6 Rejoice with me**—The thought here is that one feels exuberant joy to be almost too much for himself to bear alone and therefore wants to share it with others. **I have found my sheep which was lost**—To call a man "lost" is to pay him a high compliment, in that this shows God's love for the man. God is concerned with one person who is lost, not with one who is legalistically and rabbinically correct.

➤**7 ninety and nine just** [righteous] **persons, which need no repentance**—The reference is not to angels, whose place in these parables is very different from this. The reference is to those represented by the prodigal's well-behaved brother, who have served their father many years and not at any time transgressed his commandment (in the same outrageous sense as did the prodigal). (See comments on 15:29, 31.) In other words, these are such as have grown up from childhood in the fear of God and as the sheep of his pasture.

## 8-10 THE LOST COIN

➤8 Either—lit., "Or." This conjunction indicates that this parable continues the first one. Jesus often told parables in pairs or groups. The floor of the average Jewish home was hard earth that was covered with weeds, etc. Therefore, it would be easy to lose a coin. The parable stresses the fact that the woman searched thoroughly for the coin that had been lost. It has been suggested by some commentators that the headdress of a married woman was ten silver coins linked by a silver chain. If this be the case of the woman who is the subject of this story, then it would be quite easy to understand why she would miss the coin. On the other hand, we are not to understand that the woman was wealthy.

➤10 Likewise—On the same principle. joy—Note carefully the language here—not "joy on the part of the woman" but "joy before the angels of God over one sinner who repents" (RSV). This is basic to all the three parables. The great shepherd, the great owner himself, is he who has the joy over his own recovered property—or, as in the case of the father, over his own recovered son. As this is applied to the reception of those publicans and sinners who stood around our Lord, perhaps the meaning is this: "You turn from these lost ones with disdain, and because I do not the same, you murmur; but a very different feeling is cherished in heaven. There the recovery of even one outcast is watched with interest and hailed with joy; nor are they left to come home of themselves or perish; for lo! even now the great Shepherd is going after his lost sheep, and the owner is making diligent search for the lost property. He is finding it and bringing it back with joy, and all heaven is filled with that joy."

## 11-32 THE PRODIGAL SON

The account of the prodigal son is actually an account of the father who lost two sons—"one who strayed from home" and "one who stayed at home." Perhaps this parable of the Lost Son is the best loved of all Jesus' parables. It is described by many interpreters as the "gospel within the gospel." Marshall states that the father is the primary character of the parable.

➤12 the younger—the more thoughtless, weary of restraint, longing for independence, unable longer to abide the check of a father's eye. This is the man impatient of divine control who desires to be independent of God. He seeks to be his own master. The father is represented as dividing his living between the two sons. Property could be given to one's posterity either by making a will or simply as a gift. The older brother did not request anything, he apparently did not desire anything, and furthermore he did not enjoy anything even though he remained in the father's presence.

➤13 not many days after—intoxicated with his new-found resources and eager for the luxury of using them at will. a far country—beyond all danger of interference from home. The young man squandered his wealth in loose living.

➤14 And when he had spent all . . . there arose a mighty famine—The famine did not occur until the young man was in circumstances that would cause him to feel the famine in all its rigor and seriousness. Thus, like Jonah, whom the storm did not overtake until he was on the mighty deep at the mercy of the waves, this young man felt as if he were fighting against life itself. He is described as being in want—the first stage of his bitter experience.

➤15 The young man joined himself to a citizen of that country and became a caretaker of swine. This indicates the seriousness and extensiveness of his agony. He was simply glad to maintain his life at any cost. He who begins by using the world as a servant to minister to his own pleasure, ends by reversing the relationship (Trench).

➤16 He ate the husks, or the hulls of the leguminous plant, which in the East is the food of cattle and swine. It is known that the poor in time of distress also relied upon these pods for nourishment. No one cared enough for the young man to give him anything better.

➤17 when he came to himself—"When he finally came to his senses" (TLB), he realized that even the hired servants at home fared better than he. What a testimony to the nature of the home he had left! But did he not know all this before he departed? He did, and he did not. His heart was wholly estranged from home and steeped in selfish gratification; his father's house never came within the range of his vision except as another name for bondage, gloom, and subservience. Now he is empty, desolate, withered, perishing, and home with all its peace and plenty comes into full view for what it actually is.

➤18 I will arise and go to my father—The change in attitude has now been effected. The man expresses himself in simple terminology; the expression "father" speaks volumes of truth. Now the young man admits his sinfulness and that he is not worthy to be called his father's son. "I have sinned" are hard words to say, yet he utters them (Robertson). All he requests is to be made a hired servant. Perhaps **heaven** is used as a surrogate for "God."

➤20 His decision was not merely theoretical or academic; he acted immediately upon the basis of his thoughts. When he was still far removed from home, **his father saw him** and rushed to meet him. The father did not stand there in utter disgust and dismay! Rather, he threw his arms about the son's neck and kissed him. Was this his son? Yes. In all his rags? Yes. In all his haggard, shattered wretchedness? Yes.

➤21 His son's confession is open and truthful.

➤22 The father's response is precisely what all parents would expect. The son has not said all that he purposed because the father's demonstrations have rekindled the father-son relationship and swallowed up all servile feeling on the part of the young man. **Bring forth the best robe**—Cf. Zechariah 3:4, 5. **a ring on his hand**—a ring which would identify him as his father's son (cf. Gen. 41:42). **shoes on his feet**—slaves went barefoot.

➤23 kill **the fatted calf**—a calf fed for such festive occasions.

➤24 **my son**—now twice his son. The lad had been born his son, and now he had returned to his father's house after having been assumed **dead. lost**—to me, to himself, to my service, to my satisfaction, to his own dignity, to his own peace and profit. **alive again . . . found**—to all these things just mentioned. **merry**—See comments on 15:10.

➤25 The **elder son** was busily engaged in his father's business and was in the fields plying his agricultural trade.

➤28 **came his father out, and intreated him**—The elder brother in all his anger was wrong, but the same paternal compassion previously expressed toward the younger brother is now expressed toward the elder brother.

➤29 **Lo, these many years do I serve thee**—The elder son's definition of sonship was as perverted as the younger son's. He also had failed to understand the true spirit that must exist between father and son. Every word of the account displays some undesirable aspect of his personality. He insists upon contrasting his constancy (shown by the present tense in Gk.: "I am serving") of love and service with the conduct of his brother. **never gavest me a kid**—not to say a calf, not even a kid (a goat). **that I might make merry with my friends**—Here lay his misunderstanding. It was no entertainment for the gratification of the prodigal; it was a father's expression of the joy he felt at his recovery.

➤30 Note carefully the following response of the elder son. He refuses to call the younger brother "brother"; instead, he calls him **thy son.** How unworthy a reflection on the father of both, for the one not only to disown the other but to fling him over upon his father as if he should say, "Take him and have joy of him!"

➤31 This verse contains a sobering truth. The father, resenting the insult hurled at him by the elder son, attempts to explain his genuine feeling toward both sons: "Son, listen to reason. What need for special, exuberant joy over you? Did you not say, 'Lo, these many years I have served you?' You have spoken the truth, but just for that reason do I not set the whole household rejoicing over you. For you is reserved what is higher still—a tranquil lifelong satisfaction in you as a true-hearted and faithful son in your father's house."

➤32 **It was meet**—"It is proper to rejoice in the return of your brother simply because he has returned. You have always been with me." But this festivity is only a temporary experience. In time, the dutifulness of even the younger son would become the rule and not the exception. He too at length might venture to say, "Lo, these many years I have served you." And of him the father would say, "Son, you are always with me. In that case, therefore, it would not be fitting to make merry and be glad." The lessons are obvious and extremely beautiful: (1) The more profligate and the longer estranged any sinner is, the more exuberant is the joy when his recovery occurs. (2) Such joy is not the portion of those whose whole lives have been spent in the service of their Father in heaven. (3) Instead of grudging the lack of this, they should deem it the highest testimony to their lifelong fidelity that something better is reserved for them—the deep and abiding joy of their Father in heaven. T. W. Manson reminds us that this is not a complete compendium of theology. The parable illustrates God's concern for the lost. Jesus welcomed publicans and sinners into his kingdom, although the Pharisees questioned Jesus' contact with the publicans and sinners. If the Pharisees had not enjoyed God's blessings, this was not God's fault. Doubtless the attitude of the elder son depicts the conduct and selfishness of the Pharisees and the scribes. The three parables are closely knit together to illustrate God's concern and love for the lost in opposition to the attitude of the scribes and Pharisees toward those they considered social outcasts.

*Chapter* **16**

## 1-8 THE PARABLE OF THE UNJUST STEWARD, A PARABLE CONCERNING THE USE OF POSSESSIONS

Some of the instructions contained in this chapter are given to Jesus' disciples, some to Pharisees, but the truths are applicable to both. Jesus, in the parables of the last chapter, explained why he preached to sinners and social outcasts. This parable seems to suggest how possessions are to be used, although Jesus does not commend the lack of integrity on the part of the steward. The next parable teaches how possessions are *not* to be used.

➤**1 steward**—manager of the rich man's estate and business affairs. Charges were brought against the steward that he was wasting the master's goods.

➤**3 I cannot dig; to beg I am ashamed** therefore, the steward would be in utter need when he was dismissed.

➤**4 may receive me . . .**—Observe the steward's one object. When cast out of one home,

he wished to secure another. This is the key to the interpretation of the parable. Three basic approaches to interpreting the parable have been suggested, the third of which is the most plausible: (1) Perhaps it urges men to prepare for the crisis brought by Jesus' ministry. (2) The steward was merely releasing the debtors from exorbitant interests that had been imposed illegally. Thus, he was simply keeping the Jewish law. (3) Jesus was teaching that the men of the world are more astute than his followers. Therefore, they should learn from worldly men to use their money correctly, thereby making God their friend (see 16:7-9).

➤**6, 7 fifty . . . fourscore** [eighty]—deducting a half from the debt of one and a fifth from the indebtedness of the other man.

➤**8 the lord commended the unjust steward**—note that he did not commend him for his "injustice," but because of his prudence. He had acted with commendable foresight and skillful entrepreneurship. **children** [sons] **of this world** [age]—See 20:34; Psalm 17:14; Philippians 3:19. **are in their generation wiser than the children** [sons] **of light**—that is, for the purposes of the "age" or "generation" to which they belong. The people of any given age may exercise more wisdom in entrepreneurship than the children of light. Yet, this is only as night birds see better in the dark than do those of the day. But we may learn lessons from them, as our Lord now shows.

➤**9 make . . . friends**—Turn things to your advantage as the steward did. **mammon of unrighteousness**—treacherous, precarious. (See comments on Matt. 6:24.) **ye fail**—should be translated, "it [mammon] fails." **they may receive you**—not generally, but those you have relieved may rise up as witnesses for you at the great day. Then, as the steward when turned out of one home, you will be able to secure another.

➤**10 He that is faithful**—Fidelity depends not on the amount entrusted but on the sense of responsibility toward the trust.

➤**11, 12 unrighteous mammon**—He contrasts this disparaging term to the "true riches," (i.e., those with eternal value). **that which is another man's . . . that which is your own**—an important turn to the subject. In this life, what we have is what has been entrusted to us as stewards. Hereafter, what the faithful will possess will be their own property, being no longer on probation but in secure, undisputed, rightful, everlasting possession and enjoyment of all that is graciously bestowed on them. Thus, money is neither to be idolized nor despised; rather, it should be used for God's glory.

➤**13 can serve**—be entirely at the command of; and this is true even where the services are not opposed. **hate . . . love**—showing that the two here intended are in uncompromising hostility to each other: a penetrating and searching principle! The previous parable (that of the prodigal son) describes the son's waywardness and selfishness. The boy demanded his inheritance and then squandered it. This present parable describes selfishness in dealing with possessions that belong to another. Jesus shows that this man acted adroitly and wisely. The central teaching seems to be: use your earthly means wisely to provide benefits for yourself in the life to come. Nowhere does Jesus commend the man for his dishonesty and lack of integrity.

➤**14-18 covetous**—lit., "moneylovers." **derided him**—"scoffed at him" (RSV). To cover up their exposure, they sneered at him. **justify yourselves**—make a show of righteousness. **highly esteemed among men**—generally carried away by plausible appearances (see 14:11). **The law and the prophets**—See comments on Matthew 11:13. The law and prophets pointed to the ministry of the Savior (16:16). Jesus recognized the eternal quality of the law (cf. Matt. 5:17). For example, in 16:18 Jesus shows that adultery remains adultery even though the messianic age has come. The character of the law, therefore, is unalterable. **presseth into it**—Publicans and sinners were eagerly pressing into the kingdom. Yet the Pharisees, who were interested adherents of the mere forms of an economy that was passing away, would allow the flow to go past them and thus be found the stranded monument of blindness and obstinacy. **it is easier**—See comments on Matthew 5:17, 18.

## 19-31 THE PARABLE OF THE RICH MAN AND LAZARUS

Jesus told this story to reinforce the fact that the riches of the Pharisees were not necessarily a sign of God's approval. Some interpreters suggest that the kernel of the story was a popular story of those times and possibly derived from an Egyptian source (Caird). The main characters of the story are the rich man (some-times called Dives, a term meaning "wealth") and **Lazarus** (a term meaning "God is help"). A recently discovered manuscript (Bodmer Papyrus XIV, designated P75) cites the rich man's name as *Neuēs*. But it is almost certain that Luke never gave him a name. **purple and fine linen**—Cf. Revelation 18:12. The man lacked nothing which taste and appetite craved and money could secure.

➤**20, 21 a certain beggar named Lazarus . . . laid at his gate**—having to be carried and put down. **full of sores**—open, running (cf. Isa. 1:6). **desiring to be fed**—but was not. The words indeed may mean "gladly fed on," but the context rather favors the former. **dogs . . . licked his sores**—a touching act of brute pity, in the absence of human relief. It is a case of heartless indifference, amidst luxuries of every kind, to one of God's poorest and most afflicted ones presented daily before the eye.

➤**22 died**—His burial was so unimportant as to require no mention. While **the rich man . . . died, and was buried**— his body was carried in pomp to its earthly resting place.

➤**23 in hell**—hades, not the final place of the lost (for another word is used, but as we say, "the unseen world"). But as the object here is certainly to depict the whole torment of the one and the perfect bliss of the other, it comes in this case to have nearly the same meaning. The contrast is between the two men and their eternal destinies. In the thinking of the Jew, "plenty" was a sign of God's favor and "poverty" was a sign of God's judgment. **seeth Abraham**—His cry, "Father Abraham" is a claim of natural descent (3:8; John 8:37). **in his [Abraham's] bosom**—as if seen reclining next to him at the heavenly feast (Matt. 8:11).

➤**24 have mercy on me**—who never showed any (cf. James 2:3). **send Lazarus**—the victim of his merciless neglect. **dip the tip of his finger in water, and cool my tongue**—the least conceivable and most momentary abatement of his torment; that is all. But he was told that even this was not possible.

➤**25, 26 Son**—a stinging acknowledgment of the claimed relationship. **thou . . . Lazarus**—As it is a great law of God's kingdom that the nature of our present condition shall rule that of our future existence, so by that law he whose "good things" were all limited and circumscribed by "time" could look for none after his connection

with "time" had come to an end. But by this
law, he whose "evil things" drove him to seek
consolation in a life beyond the grave is by
death released from all evil and ushered into
unmixed and uninterrupted good. **And beside
all this**—independently of this consideration. **a
great gulf** [chasm]—By an irrevocable decree
there has been placed a vast impassable abyss
between the two states and the occupants of each.

➤**27-31 Then he said**—now abandoning all
hope for himself. **send him to my father's
house: For I have five brethren**—The answer
is that his brothers too have been sufficiently
warned. **Nay, father Abraham**—The rich man
argued against the adequacy of the warning. **if
one went unto them from the dead**—a principle of great magnitude and importance. But
the greatest miracle will have no effect on those
who are determined not to believe. Even a real
Lazarus was soon to rise from the dead, but the
sight of him only crowned the unbelief and
hastened the murderous plots of the Pharisees
against the Lord of glory. The selfish earthly
life of the rich man well illustrates the attitude
and characteristics of the Pharisees. The man
had not gone to Hades because he was rich, but
rather because of his unwillingness to recognize the lordship of Jesus. The parable points
out that poverty does not automatically bring
joy, nor does wealth automatically bring condemnation. The Pharisees continued in their
greed, and this led to their separation from God,
although they believed materialism to be a sign
of God's favor. The rich man was lost because
he did not listen and heed the warnings contained in the law and the prophets, although he
also had been blessed materialistically. This
account was given not to disclose the experiences of life after death but rather the seriousness of the responsibilities of this present life.

# Chapter 17

## 1-10 SOME MISCELLANEOUS TEACHINGS

### 1-4 CONCERNING OFFENSES
➤**1, 2** See comments on Matthew 18:6, 7.
Most commentators regard this section of
Luke's Gospel as a group of loose sayings that
have been connected by the author. The first
paragraph (17:1-4) repeats the emphasis of

life's stewardship. The expression **offences** is
a translation of a Greek term which means
"stumbling blocks." The term originally
referred to the trigger that springs a trap; then
the word came to refer to anything that causes
one to sin. Jesus emphatically warns that these
stumbling blocks are sure to occur. Nonetheless, he pronounced a woe upon those by whom
the occasions to sin came. He suggests that
death by drowning would be preferable rather
than **to offend one of these little ones.** There
is some question as to the identity of the "little
ones." Some have interpreted this as a reference merely to children, but most seem to agree
that this expression refers to disciples.

➤**3, 4** See comments on Matthew 18:15-17,
21, 22. The principle of care in dealing with
others is further illustrated by the suggestion
that the Christian is to forgive his brother. Just
as it is necessary to avoid putting obstructions
in the way of others, even so it is necessary for
Christians to be forgiving toward other people.
The Jews believed seven acts of forgiveness to
be adequate, but Jesus said that the Christian is
to practice unlimited forgiveness.

## 5, 6 CONCERNING FAITH
➤**5 Lord, Increase our faith**—a request
motivated by the difficulty of avoiding and
forgiving "offenses." This is the only instance
in which a spiritual operation upon their souls
was solicited of Christ by the Twelve.

➤**6 sycamine**—mulberry. (See comments on
Mark 11:22-24.) Although the transition between
this section and 17:1-4 lacks smoothness, there
can be no question of the relationship between
forgiveness and faith in the Christian life. The
sycamine tree was known for its strong roots.
Therefore, Jesus says that it is not a greater faith,
in the sense of more expansive faith that is
needed, but a deeper faith.

## 7-10 CONCERNING HUMILITY
The connection here is: "But when your
faith has been so increased as both to avoid and
forgive offenses and do things impossible to all
but faith, be not puffed up as though you had
laid the Lord under any obligations to you."
The principle is that the Christian is not to
permit his faith to exalt him, but he is to remember its source and his own servitude to God.
The master is not subservient to the servant's
obedience, nor does he feel any sense of

obligation because the servant has performed some menial task. Whatever the slave does, he is still a slave; he can never put his master in his debt. Nor can the Christian place God in his debt. This teaching is a warning against any proclivity toward a "bookkeeping and legalistic morality."

## 11-19 THE CLEANSING OF TEN LEPERS

➤**11-13** As Jesus traveled toward Jerusalem, he traveled along the boundary between Samaria and Galilee. Entering a certain village, **there met him ten men that were lepers, which stood afar off**—Cf. Leviticus 13:45, 46. These lepers were careful to observe the ceremonial rules applicable to them. They kept their distance and probably cried the usual cry of the leper, "Unclean, unclean!" Lepers were not permitted to travel on the roadway, nor could they have any social contact with "clean" people. **lifted up their voices**— Their common misery drew these poor outcasts together (2 Kings 7:3), causing them to forget the fierce national antipathy of Jew and Samaritan. **Jesus**—Cf. Matthew 20:30-33.

➤**14 Go show yourselves**—as cleaned persons (see Matt. 8:4). **And . . . as they went, they were cleansed**—in how many different ways were our Lord's cures wrought, and this different from all the rest.

➤**17, 18 Were there not ten cleansed?**— that is, the whole of them—an example of Christ's omniscience. The only one who returned to express gratitude to Jesus was the Samaritan. The language is that of wonder and admiration, as it is expressly said of another exhibition of Gentile faith (Matt. 8:10).

➤**19 Arise**—Cf. 17:16. **thy faith hath made thee whole**—healed you, not as the others, merely in body, but in that higher spiritual sense with which his constant language has so familiarized us. Nothing does more to frustrate one's own stewardship of life than the sin of ingratitude. Jesus indicated that the man's faith had made him whole—a perfect tense that signifies completed action in the past and results which continue into the present.

## 20-37 THE COMING OF THE KINGDOM OF GOD AND OF THE SON OF MAN

The discussion relating to the parousia (coming) was occasioned by the Pharisees. No question occupied more of their time or interest than the question of the kingdom's coming and

completion. To outline the paragraph is exceedingly difficult, but perhaps verses 20, 21 are to be related to the Jewish question of the initiation of the kingdom, and verses 22-37 could be related to the completion of the kingdom when Christ returns. In earlier situations Jesus spoke of the coming of the kingdom and the Son of man. The obvious question that his hearers asked was, "When will these events occur?"

➤**20-25 when the kingdom of God should come**—To meet the erroneous views not only of the Pharisees but of the disciples themselves, our Lord addressed both and announced the coming of the kingdom under different aspects. He insisted that it would not come with signs to be observed; that is, the domain of God's rule does not come in a way in which it can be watched. The alleged conflict between this idea and 21:5-36 has caused certain scholars to question the authenticity of one or the other. But Marshall notes that premonitory signs were a part of apocalyptic teaching; therefore, Jesus was warning against trusting them for security. **Lo, here! or, lo there!**—confined to this or that sharply defined and visible geographical or ecclesiastical limit. **the kingdom of God is within you**—is of an internal and spiritual character (as contrasted with their views of its being external in nature). Some commentators and translators favor the translation "the kingdom of God is among you" (Alford)—or, "in your midst" (NASB). This rendering gives ground to the interpretation that the kingdom as embodied in Jesus was present among them. But the Greek preposition (*entos*) is seldom used in this sense (Robertson); it is almost always used to mean "within." And the context here bears this out. But the kingdom of God also has its external side too. For example, his very presence reveals its external side. **The days will come**—when you will anxiously look for a deliverer, and deceivers will put themselves forth in this character (cf. 19:43). Perhaps the "days" immediately precede the coming of the Son of man. **one of the days of the Son of man**—himself again among them but for one day, as we say when all seems to be going wrong and the one person who could keep them right is removed. **they shall say to you, See here; or, see there**—a warning to all so-called expositors of prophecy and their followers who cry that the kingdom of God has come. **as the lightning, that lighteneth [flashes] . . . so shall also the Son of man be in his day**—i.e., his parousia will be clearly manifest. The Lord speaks here of his coming and manifestation in a prophetically indefinite manner, and in these preparatory words the distinctive epochs of apocalyptic prophecy blend into one. When the whole polity of the Jews, both civil and ecclesiastical, was broken and its continuance rendered impossible by the destruction of Jerusalem, it became manifest to all (as the lightning flashing from heaven) that the kingdom of God had ceased to exist in its old form and had entered into a perfectly different form. So it may be again before its final and greatest change at the personal coming of Christ—to which these words in their highest sense are addressed. **But first must he suffer**—This shows that the more immediate reference of the previous verse is to an event soon to follow the death of Christ. It was designed to withdraw the attention of his disciples from the glory his foregoing words had given to the approaching establishment of his kingdom.

➤**26-29 eat . . . drank . . . married**—all the ordinary occupations and enjoyments of life. Though the antediluvian world and the cities of the plain were unusually wicked, it was not their wickedness but their worldliness, their unbelief and indifference toward the future, and their unpreparedness, that was held up as a warning. Jesus referred to these recorded events of OT history as factual.

➤**31-33 let him not come down to take it away**—a warning against that lingering reluctance to part with present treasures, which induces some to remain in a burning house in hopes of saving this and that precious article until they themselves are consumed and buried in its ruins. The cases here supposed are similar. **Remember Lot's wife**—her "looking backward" and her doom are significant to Jesus' argument. Her heart was still in Sodom. She was so attached to earthly things that she turned to see what was happening and in so doing lost all (Gen. 19:26).

➤**34 two men in one bed**—The prepared and unprepared are in closest relationship together in the ordinary walks and fellowships of life until the moment of severance arrives. This warning was realized before the destruction of Jerusalem when the Christians found

themselves forced at once and forever away from their old associates (see 21:21). But most of all this will become a reality when the second coming of Christ shall burst upon a heedless world. The decisiveness of eternal separation is pointed out in 17:34, 35.

➤**37 Wheresoever the body is, thither will the eagles be gathered together**—a popular proverb of the day summarizing Jesus' thoughts concerning God's judgment. Where the conditions of decay exist, judgment follows. Where bodies are decayed physically, vultures gather; where men decay spiritually, judgments follow. As surely as the vulture finds a carcass, so surely will divine judgment come upon an immoral world. This proverbial saying was vividly verified in the destruction of Jerusalem, as illustrated by all her agony, suffering and death.

## *Chapter* 18

### 1-8 THE PARABLE OF THE WIDOW AND THE JUDGE

Luke obviously intends this parable to be linked with the preceding section. It is similar to the parable in 11:5-8 and makes its point by way of contrast. The ultimate question conceived is not whether Jesus will come but whether men will be found faithful at the time of his coming.

➤**1-5** Although the city and judge are left unidentified, Jesus carefully pointed out that the judge had no reverence for God or for his commands. **ought always**—"day and night" (cf. 18:7). **not to faint**—slacken, lose heart, or become discouraged. **widow**—weak, desolate, defenseless. **came unto him**—imperfect in Greek, "kept coming to him." The widow kept coming to him requesting that the judge vindicate her. She desired to be rid of her oppression. Perhaps the underlying dishonesty of the judge in waiting for a bribe is to be understood, but this woman could not bring a bribe. She was able only to be persistent. **I fear not God, nor regard man**—defying the vengeance of God and despising the opinion of men.

➤**6-8 the Lord**—a name expressive of the authoritative style in which he interprets his own parable. **shall not God avenge** [vindicate]—not as an unjust judge, but as the infinitely righteous Judge. He will redeem from oppression his own people (Zech. 2:8). **cry day and night unto him**—Their incessant cries enter his ears. **though he bear long with them?**—i.e., "will he keep putting them off?" (NIV). God will vindicate them **speedily,** as if pained by the long delay and impatient for the destined moment to interpose (cf. Prov. 29:1). **Nevertheless when the Son of man cometh, shall he find faith on the earth?**—The question relating to Christ's return has been answered. There is now no question at this point, but the question is whether Christ will find faith on the earth when he returns. Will the faithful persevere? The question posed here is a challenge to the Christian, that his faith will not waver even though the return of Christ seems to be delayed.

9-14 THE PARABLE OF THE PHARISEE AND THE PUBLICAN

In 18:1-8 Jesus showed the necessity of constant prayer. There he indicated that the character of the judge is unlike God's, but both God and the judge hear because of man's persistence. Here in 18:9-14 Jesus reveals that not all prayer is genuine. This parable is an example parable, or conduct parable, as in the account of the Good Samaritan. By the characters of the parable, Jesus shows us what we are and what we are not to do.

➤**9 unto certain** [ones] **which trusted in themselves that they were righteous, and despised others**—This is likely a reference to the Pharisees. The qualifications certainly describe the pharisaical attitude.

➤**10 Two men went up into the temple to pray**—to the temple mountain. The hours of prayer according to our temporal designations would have been 9:00 a.m., noon, and 3:00 p.m. The characters of the account are described as a **Pharisee** and a **publican** [tax collector].

➤**11, 12 stood**—as the Jews did during prayer (cf. Mark 11:25). **God, I thank thee**—This Pharisee seems quite representative of those generally met on the pages of the NT. To have been kept from gross iniquities was undoubtedly a just cause of thankfulness to God. Instead of the devoutly humble attitude this should inspire, he arrogantly severs himself from the rest of mankind and, with a contemptuous look at the poor publican, thanks

God that he must not stand afar off like the publican. However, these were the only moral excellencies he could mention. His religious merits complete his grounds for congratulation. Not confining himself to the one divinely prescribed fast (Lev. 16:29), that of the Day of Atonement, he was equal to the most rigid, who fasted on the second and fifth days of every week and who gave the tenth of all his gains (not simply what the law defined as commodities and possessions to be tithed). The strictest Jew fasted on Thursday and Monday, for Moses traditionally had gone to Sinai on Thursday and returned from the mount on Monday. To be legalistically correct about tithing, the most strict Jew tithed even what he bought lest the products had not been tithed by the initial owner. Therefore, in addition to doing all his duty, he did works of supererogation. He felt that he had no sins to confess and no spiritual needs to be supplied. What a tragic picture of the pharisaical character and religion!

➤**13 And the publican, standing afar off**—feeling unworthy to draw near (Ps. 34:18; Isa. 57:15). **would not lift up so much as his eyes unto heaven**—blushing and ashamed to do so (Ezra 9:6). He was beating his **breast** because of anguish and self-reproach, and his prayer was a simple prayer for mercy. The word translated **be merciful** is better translated, "be propitious." The term is used only one other time as a verb in the NT, and there it describes how Christ made reconciliation between God and man by his sacrifice on the cross (Heb. 2:17). The noun form appears in 1 John 2:2; 4:10; in both places Jesus is called "the propitiation for our sins." He himself, as our sacrifice, propitiated God concerning our sins. This publican, well aware of his sinful condition, was asking God for propitiation; that is, he was asking God for conciliation. **a sinner**—lit., "the sinner." This is as if the publican said, "If ever there was a sinner, I am he."

➤**14 justified rather than the other**—The meaning is "and not the other." The Pharisee was not seeking justification and felt no need of it. This great law of the kingdom of God is inscribed over its entrance gate and is repeated in many different forms (Ps. 138:6; 147:6; Luke 1:53). To be self-emptied is the fundamental and indispensable preparation for the reception of the grace of God that brings salvation. Self-exaltation brings humiliation, but humility, in turn, results in exaltation. Jesus was teaching that righteousness is internal, not external. The eye of God looks upon the heart; the eye of community sees the external conduct and action of mankind.

## 15-17 LITTLE CHILDREN ARE BROUGHT TO CHRIST

There are no Marcan parallels in Luke 9:51–18:14. Now, however, Luke comes to a series of incidents that do have Marcan parallels. The first record tells of Jesus receiving the children.

➤**15** The tense of the verbs **brought** and **rebuked** in Greek is imperfect. The people were in the process of bringing their children to Jesus, and just as they brought them the disciples were rebuking them. **touch them**—or, as more fully in Matthew, "that he might lay his hands on them and pray" (19:13). The suggestion is that the touch and prayer of Jesus invoked a blessing on them according to the venerable custom (Gen. 48:14, 15). **rebuked them**—lit., "were rebuking them." Repeatedly the disciples thus interposed to save annoyance and interruption to their Master; but, as the result showed, this was always against the intention of Jesus (Matt. 15:23; 18:39, 40). Here, it is plainly deduced from our Lord's reply that they thought the intrusion a useless one, inasmuch as infants were not capable of receiving anything from him. His ministry was intended for grown people!

➤**16, 17 for of such is the kingdom of God**—It is surely not to be conceived that all our Lord meant was to inform us that mature people must become childlike in order to be capable of the kingdom of God. According to Mark 10:16, he took the children in his arms and blessed them. Was it not just a grave mistake of the disciples that infants should not be brought to Christ because only mature people could profit by him? And though he took the irresistible opportunity of lowering their pride by informing them that in order to enter the kingdom they must become as little children, this was but an aside; and, returning to the children themselves, he took them up in his gracious arms, put his hands upon them and blessed them, for no reasonable reason but to show that they were thereby made capable of receiving his blessings. An acceptance and

wholehearted commitment similar to that of a little child are essential for entry into the kingdom of God. **shall in no wise enter**—This is the strongest construction by which a negative statement can be expressed in the Greek language. Under no conceivable circumstance will a person unlike a child in faith and humility enter into the kingdom.

## 18-30 THE ACCOUNT OF THE RICH YOUNG RULER

This case presents some remarkable points: (1) The man was of irreproachable moral character, and this amidst all the temptations of youth, for he was young (Matt. 19:22) and very rich (18:23). (2) But he was restless; his heart craved eternal life. (3) Unlike the rulers to whose class he belonged, he so far believed in Jesus as to be persuaded he could authoritatively direct him on this vital point. (4) He showed his earnestness by kneeling before Jesus when the Master was surrounded by travelers to the Passover Feast.

➤**19 none is good, save** [except] **one, that is, God**—Did our Lord mean to teach that God only ought to be called "good"? This is an impossible interpretation, for this would contradict all scriptural teaching and even his own (Ps. 112:5; Matt. 25:21; Titus 1:8). Our Lord could have had but one object—to raise the youth's ideas of himself, as not to be classed merely with other "good masters"; rather, the young man needed to realize that to call Jesus "good" was actually to call him "God." This is not overtly declared but discreetly implied.

➤**20** Matthew is a bit more complete here (cf. Matt. 19:17, 18). Our Lord purposely confined himself to the second table of the law, which he would consider easy to keep. He enumerated all the laws in that table, as seems obvious from Mark 10:19 where "defraud not" stands for the tenth commandment. In Matthew the summary of this second table of the law is added: "You shall love your neighbor as yourself" (19:19). It seems as if Jesus wondered whether the young man would venture to say that he had kept this summation.

➤**21** Matthew adds, "What lack I yet?" This gives a glimpse of the youth's heart. Doubtless he was perfectly sincere, but something within told him that the keeping of the commandments was not enough to obtain eternal life. He felt something beyond this was necessary. After keeping all the commandments, he was at a loss to know what that could be. He came to Jesus at this point. His sincerity, frankness, and nearness to the kingdom of God, in themselves most winning qualities, won our Lord's regard.

➤ **22 lackest thou one thing**—a fundamental and crucial lack. Our Lord, who understood that riches were the young man's idol, told him, **sell all that thou hast, and distribute unto the poor**—Jesus did not give a general mandate about the disposal of riches but simply insisted that a man is to place God before riches, thereby laying the riches at the feet of the One who gave them. He who does this with all he has, whether rich or poor, is a true heir of the kingdom of heaven.

➤ **23-25 he was very sorrowful**—He was very sorry to part with Christ, but to have parted with his riches would have caused him more pain and anguish. When riches or heaven were the alternative, the result showed to which side the balance was inclined. Therefore, the young man was seen to lack the one all-comprehensive requirement of the law: to love God with all one's heart, and this lack vitiated all his other obediences. **when Jesus saw**—Mark indicates that Jesus "looked around" as if first following the departing youth with his eye. **that he was very sorrowful**—is found in some ancient manuscripts but not in the two earliest (Sinaiticus and Vaticanus). **How hardly**—with what difficulty. **easier for a camel to go through a needle's eye**—a proverbial expression used to describe that which is nearly impossible to accomplish. Some interpreters think that Jesus was speaking of the needle-like gate in the city wall through which the loaded camel must stoop to enter after the main gate had been closed for the night. Others think that there has been a scribal error in transmitting the term "rope," very similar to the term "camel," in the Greek text. It seems best to take the statement as it stands, with the realization that Jesus purposely used this hyperbole. A Jewish proverb uses the figure of an elephant in a similar teaching.

➤ **26, 27 Who then can be saved?**—at that rate none can be saved. The response: "It surpasses human power, but not divine power."

The salvation of the rich is possible with God, although man cannot understand it.

➤ **28-30** Peter had surrendered all; he, and all others like him, would be rewarded with an abundant life now and eternal life thereafter. **for the kingdom of God's sake**—Mark says, "for my sake and the gospel's." **manifold more in this present time**—Matthew says "an hundred-fold" (19:29), while Mark (10:30) is all-inclusive and stipulates houses, brothers, sisters, mothers, children, and lands. We have here the blessed promise of a reconstruction of all human relationships and affections on a Christian basis. This he calls "manifold more" than they had sacrificed.

Our Lord was himself the first to exemplify this new adjustment of his own relationships. (See Matt. 12:49, 50.) But this "with persecutions" (Mark 10:30), for how could such a transfer take place without the most cruel agonies to flesh and blood? These promises are for everyone who forsakes his all for Christ. But in Matthew (19:28) this is prefaced by a special promise to the Twelve: "Truly, I say to you, in the new world, when the Son of man shall sit on his glorious throne, you who have followed me will also sit on twelve thrones, judging the twelve tribes of Israel" (RSV). In the new kingdom, those who followed Christ shall rule the great Christian world, here set forth as the twelve tribes, presided over by the twelve apostles on their judicial thrones. But if the promise refers to the coming glory, as many interpreters derive from Luke 22:28-30, it points to the highest personal distinction of the first founders of the church. At any rate, it is best to understand verses 29, 30 as comprising a precious promise to all who wholeheartedly and absolutely follow Jesus. No man gives to the kingdom without reward. He will receive what gladdens his heart in return, not necessarily many houses for one house, or many children for one child. His reward will rather correspond to the spiritual service he has rendered.

### 31-34 ANOTHER ANNOUNCEMENT OF HIS APPROACHING DEATH AND RESURRECTION

See comments on Mark 10:32-34.

➤ **31-34** Luke, in following his careful historical methodology, indicates that Jesus was addressing himself to the Twelve. This, of course, was not the first time that he had spoken to his apostles concerning his death and resurrection (see 9:22, 44 and 13:33). This, however, was the last, and the language went beyond the earlier announcements. He names **Jerusalem** as the place of death and indicates that everything written by the **prophets** concerning the Messiah would be fulfilled in his experience. Although verses 32, 33 reveal the details of his sufferings, it would not be until after his resurrection that the disciples would understand. Their total lack of understanding is reiterated three times in 18:34: (1) **they understood none of these things;** (2) **this saying** [Gk. *rhēma*— indicating what was just spoken] **was hid from them;** and (3) **neither knew they the things which were spoken.** They were void of understanding, revelation, and knowledge concerning the prophecies and eventualities of Christ's passion, crucifixion, and resurrection.

### 35-43 THE HEALING OF A BLIND MAN

In Matthew 20:29, *two* blind men are mentioned, as is true in the case of the demoniac of Gadara. In Matthew and Mark (10:46) the occurrence is connected with Christ's departure from Jericho; in Luke the event is mentioned in relationship to his approach to Jericho. Numerous explanations are offered to account for these slight divergences of detail. One suggestion is that the two towns of Jericho, the old and the new, lay close together, and the incident perhaps occurred between the two towns. Perhaps if we knew all the facts, we should see no difficulty. One thing is plain—there could have been no collusion among the authors of these Gospels, else they would have taken care to remove these "spots on the sun." At this time, Jesus was accompanied by a large group of pilgrims who were also traveling to Jerusalem for the Passover. One of the blights of Palestinian society was blindness created by heat, dust, sunlight, and ophthalmia.

➤**38 son of David**—See comments on Matthew 12:23. See also Isaiah 11:1-10; Jeremiah 23:5ff.; Ezekiel 34:23ff.; Luke 20:41-44.

➤**39** The crowds accompanying Jesus **rebuked** the man (called Bartimaeus by Mark) and ordered him to be quiet. However, Jesus' approaching nearness had just the opposite effect.

➤**40-43 Jesus stood**—i.e., stopped. The blind man had employed the expression "Son of David," a messianic title to describe Jesus. Now the Messiah stops and commands the blind person to be brought. The blind man's interview had been granted. What did he wish? **Lord, that I may receive my sight**—The willingness of the Lord is disclosed not only by the words that brought healing to the man's body (**Receive thy sight**), but also by the fact that Jesus permitted this man to address him as the Son of David, a surrogate for "Messiah" (see 4:35, 41; 9:21, 36). However, this is the beginning of Jesus' open claim to messiahship. The Lord ("Rabboni" in Mark 10:51) immediately healed the man and he **followed** Jesus, **glorifying God.**

*Chapter* **19**

### 1-10 ZACCHAEUS THE PUBLICAN

➤**1, 2** Zacchaeus is a Jewish name; he lived in **Jericho,** a very wealthy city lying in the Jordan Valley. The city, located on the main road from Trans-Jordan to Jerusalem, commanded the approach and crossings which gave access to the land in the east. Consequently, many tax collectors worked along this roadway. Zacchaeus was a chief tax collector and had chosen Jericho as his home, the logical place to collect taxes on the goods being transported from Egypt to Jordan. He obviously headed the publicans (tax collectors) in that area. Luke describes him as **rich.** His riches were ill-gotten through the misapplication of his power and authority. The tax collectors were hated by the Jews because of their tendencies to collect exorbitant taxes on every item possessed by the merchant, ranging from the goods being transported to the wheels of the cart or even to the animal which pulled the cart. Since Zacchaeus was a "chief tax collector" and was "rich," he was excluded from membership among the people of God.

➤**3** Nevertheless, he desired **to see** Jesus, his curiosity requiring a diligent effort on his part.

➤**4** Curiosity was apparently his only motive in climbing the **sycamore tree.** The sycamore tree is the Egyptian fig tree with leaves like the mulberry.

➤**5 looked up**—with the full knowledge of who was in the tree and preparatory to addressing him. **Zacchaeus**—whom he had never seen and likely of whom he had never heard (but see John 10:3). Jesus commanded Zacchaeus to **make haste and come down** from the tree. **I must abide at thy house**—Our Lord invited himself and announced the purpose of his invitation. Jesus speaks as knowing how the privilege would be appreciated.

➤**6 joyfully**—What is the source of this sudden "joy" in the cold bosom of an avaricious publican? The internal revolution was as perfect as instantaneous. Jesus spoke the command to Zacchaeus, and immediately Zacchaeus obeyed. Verse 5 indicates that Jesus revealed to Zacchaeus his purpose of staying at his house (likely overnight).

➤**7 they all murmured**—Jesus had done an unheard of thing for religious leaders. No man occupying the place of religious leadership would dare visit the home of a publican. **to be guest**—something more than "eating with" Zacchaeus (15:2). **a sinner**—a sinner a moment ago, but not now. This mighty change in his life was all unknown to those who murmured against Jesus' action. But they would know it presently. "Sinner" would refer both to his office, vile in the sight of the Jew, and to his character, which evidently was not good. His fellowmen failed to recognize that Zacchaeus, also a son of Abraham (19:9), had as much right to hear the gospel as they.

➤**8 Zacchaeus stood, and said unto the Lord, Behold, Lord**—Mark how frequently Luke uses this title and always where lordly authority, dignity, or power is intended. **if I have**—that is, "So far as I have," for evidently the "if" is so used (Phil. 4:8). **taken any thing from any man by false accusation**—i.e., defrauded anyone. **fourfold**—The Roman law required this; the Jewish required the principal and a fifth more to be returned (Num. 5:7). There was no demand made for either; but, as if to clear himself from this previous reigning sin and to testify to the change that he had experienced, Zacchaeus voluntarily determined to give up all of his ill-gotten materialism, quadrupled. He gratefully addressed this to the "Lord" to whom he owed the wonderful change. The **I give** and **I restore** are present tenses but used with the significance of the future.

➤**9 Jesus said unto him**—but also before all the Jews so that they too could hear. **This day is salvation come**—memorable saying! Salvation had already come, but it was not a day old in the experience of Zacchaeus. **to this house**—so expressed probably to meet the taunt, "He is gone in to be the guest of a man who is a sinner." The house is no longer polluted; it is now fit to receive Jesus. **son of Abraham**—He was that by birth, but here it means a partaker of Abraham's faith, being mentioned as the sufficient means to salvation, having come to him.

➤**10 lost**—and such "lost" ones as this Zacchaeus. (See comments on 15:32.) The publican, a descendant of Abraham, was now made a spiritual son of Abraham.

## 11-27 THE PARABLE OF THE POUNDS

This parable is the only parable in Luke's Gospel which has a historical basis. Most interpreters agree that the parable was spoken just a few days prior to the crucifixion. It was addressed primarily to the disciples and teaches that all who believe in him have the opportunity of working in the kingdom and storing up treasures in heaven. The historical basis seems to have been in the activities of the descendants of Herod. Herod the Great, upon his death, had left the kingdom to Herod Antipas, Herod Philip, and Archelaeus. The Jews sent approximately fifty men to Rome to express the fact that they did not wish to retain Archelaeus as their leader. Herod Antipas was also a contender for the throne of Judea and Samaria. This portion of Jewish history seems to serve as a historical basis for the parable. Some interpreters have believed this parable to be the same as the parable of the talents (Matt. 25:14-30). However, it must be noted that Luke places the account in Jericho; Matthew in Jerusalem. Matthew inculcates usage of one's gifts; Luke adds that the revelation of the messianic glory was not to be expected all at once. Matthew speaks of a businessman; Luke speaks of a king. Matthew speaks of all possessions being distributed; Luke speaks of the distribution of only ten pounds. Matthew shows different amounts distributed to given individuals; Luke indicates that each recipient received a pound. Matthew speaks of three slaves; Luke speaks of ten slaves. Matthew speaks of no distinctions and awards; Luke does make distinctions in the awards received. Luke speaks of enmity toward the king; Matthew does not. Matthew speaks of severe punishment of the unfaithful servant; Luke simply indicates that his pound is taken from him. Matthew spoke his parable only to the Twelve; Luke indicates that the parable was given to the crowd. In Matthew there is a reference only to the servants; in Luke there is a reference to both "servants" and "citizens." Therefore, it seems that the intended lesson is different. The one illustrating equal fidelity with different degrees of advantage; the other, different degrees of improvement of the same opportunities. Yet with all these differences, the parables are similar.

➤12 a far country—The man was on his way to set up his kingdom and to inaugurate it by his personal presence. to receive . . . a kingdom—to be invested with royalty, as when Herod went to Rome and was there made king. This striking expression reminds us of Christ's heavenly enthronement. and to return—from the far country. Some interpreters see this as a reference to Christ's return.

➤13 Occupy—is better translated, "trade." The term "trade" means to negotiate, do business with the money entrusted to them.

➤14 his citizens—were his proper subjects. This expression refers to the Jews, who expressly repudiated Jesus' claims.

➤15-26 See comments on Matthew 25:19-29.

➤27 bring hither [here], and slay them—referring to the awful destruction of Jerusalem, but pointing to the final destruction of all that are found in open rebellion against Christ. The parable contains in embryonic form the law of spiritual life. The man who does not employ his spiritual gifts loses them; the man who uses them increases them. The last verse of the parable predicts a curse that is to come upon the enemies of Christ.

## 28-44 CHRIST'S TRIUMPHANT ENTRY INTO JERUSALEM AND HIS TEARS OVER THE CITY

(Cf. Matt. 21:1-9; Mark 11:1-10; John 12:12-19.) See comments on Matthew 21:1-11. Jesus had warned his disciples of what would occur when they entered Jerusalem. It would not be according to their grand expectations. His humble entry contradicted the typical Jewish expectation of the Messiah and his era.

➤29-38 Bethphage—"house of figs," a village next to Bethany, situated along the farther side of Mount Olivet, east of Jerusalem. Jesus now provides instructions for his disciples, who leave Bethany, a village two miles from Jerusalem, and travel into the city to secure a donkey on which Jesus is to enter the city. The entry itself is a messianic act and fulfills the prophecy of Zechariah (9:9): "Rejoice greatly, O daughter of Zion! Shout in triumph, O daughter of Jerusalem! Behold, your king is coming to you; He is just and endowed with salvation, humble, and mounted on a donkey, even on a colt, the foal of a donkey" (NASB). In his entry, Jesus dramatizes this ancient prophecy. whereon yet never man sat—See comments on John 19:41. The Lord hath need—He both knew all and had the key of the human heart. (See 19:5.) they sat Jesus thereon—He allowed this as befitting the kingly position he was for the first time assuming. the whole multitude of the disciples began to rejoice and praise God . . . for all the mighty works that they had seen—The language here is very grand, intended to express a burst of admiration far wider and deeper than ever had been witnessed before.

➤38 Blessed be the King—Mark adds: "Hosanna" (that is, "Save now"), the words of Psalm 118:25, which were understood to refer to the Messiah. This was the loftiest style in which he could be saluted as the promised Deliverer.

➤40 the stones would immediately cry out—The secret of his messiahship is now revealed (cf. 4:35, 41; 9:21, 36). Hitherto the Lord had discouraged all demonstrations in his favor; now he begins an opposite course. On this one occasion he seems to yield his whole soul to the wide and deep acclaim with a mysterious satisfaction, regarding it as a necessary part of the regal dignity belonging to the Messiah. If this praise had not been offered by the multitude of his disciples, it would have been sounded out from the stones.

➤41-44 And when he was come near, he . . . wept—Cf. Lamentations 3:51. The heart again affects the eyes. Subject to the sympathetic law of the relationship of soul and body, Jesus was constituted even as we. What a contrast to the immediately preceding profound joy! He yielded himself alike freely to both. (See Matt. 23:37.) If thou hadst known . . . in this thy day, the things which

**belong unto thy peace**—This was to be Jerusalem's crowning day, the day of all days, because the King of all kings had entered her. Yet she would reject him and forfeit the peace he would have brought to her. Jerusalem, "the city of peace," would become the object of war and destruction. **they are hid from thine eyes**—It was among his last open efforts to "gather them," but their eyes were judicially closed. **a trench**—actually, a rampart, built in three days by the determined Roman army. This strategy cut off all hopes of escape and consigned the city to unparalleled horrors (see Josephus' *Jewish Wars,* 5.6.2; 12.3, 4). All events here predicted by Jesus were fulfilled with dreadful literalness.

### 45-48 THE SECOND CLEANSING OF THE TEMPLE

➤**45, 46** Some interpreters see the first cleansing as occurring on his first visit to Jerusalem (John 2:13-22) and this second cleansing on his last. Others believe them to be accounts of the same act. This purging was more than the work of a Jewish reformer; it was the sign of the advent of the Jewish Messiah. Mark 11:11ff. seems to indicate that Jesus entered the temple on Sunday afternoon, observed the activities and then retired to Bethany for the night. This temple area had become an area of merchandising. The activities were relegated to the Court of the Gentiles. Every male Jew was required to pay one half shekel temple tax. He was charged three or four cents to change the money if he possessed the coin of equivalent amount, and if not, he was charged an additional three or four cents for the giving of change. Animal sacrifices were as much as fifteen times more expensive inside the temple than outside. However, these sacrificial animals were "guaranteed acceptable" because they had been provided by the priests. These booths of this merchandizing area were called "Booths of Annas" and belonged to the high priest's family. Therefore, in cleansing the temple Jesus attacked not only the institution but likewise the personalities who had become very wealthy at the expense of the worshipers. **den of thieves**—banded together for plunder, void of moral principle. The milder term "house of merchandise" used on the former occasion was just as suitable.

➤**47, 48 sought to destroy him**—"kept on seeking to destroy him," that is, daily they sought

him even as he taught. However, they were unable to fulfill their purpose inasmuch as **all the people were very attentive to hear him**—lit., "all the people hung upon as they heard him"—or, "hung upon his words" (RSV). Yet this hurried his death. Either he was the Messiah and therefore belonged in the temple, or else he must be destroyed. The leaders were convinced that he was an impostor, and as such they were determined to do away with him. But Luke indicates that the people's attraction to Jesus prohibited the leaders from immediately destroying him.

*Chapter* **20**

### 1-8 THE QUESTIONING OF JESUS' AUTHORITY

(Cf. Matt. 21:23-27 and Mark 11:27-33.) This event occurred on Tuesday of Passion Week; the day itself may be construed as a day of questioning. It was an extremely active day in Jesus' ministry, and many of his opponents interrogated him. Luke already indicated to us that the rulers of the Jews desired to take Jesus and destroy him. However, they had to either discredit him before the people or disprove his claim to messiahship before this could be done. These questions, and particularly the one under consideration, represent an attempt to discredit Jesus with the people.

➤**1** Luke carefully indicates that Jesus **taught the people in the temple, and preached the gospel**—Luke's reference again fits into the structured account that characterized Luke's purpose in writing this Gospel. **chief priests and the scribes . . . with the elders**—came to Jesus with this question concerning authority. It is obvious that these men represented the Sanhedrin inasmuch as these groups represented the Sanhedrin's constituency. "Chief priests" were members of the high priests' families or occupied important priestly offices. "Elders" were the lay leaders of the people.

➤**2 by what authority doest thou these things?**—particularly the clearing of the temple area. Jesus' purification of the temple was a dramatic act and a severe interference in Jewish religious life. Jesus himself did not come from a priestly lineage or background, but he proposed to exercise authority over the ecclesiastical groups of his day. The question concerning authority is a very pointed one.

What is the source of his authority? Who gave him this authority? Obviously only an individual who claimed to be divine could take precedence over the authority that lay in the Sanhedrin, the high Jewish religious court. Jesus' approach in answering the question is an interesting study in debate tactics.

➤**3 I will also ask you one thing**—Here Jesus takes the offensive.

➤**4-7 The baptism of John**—his whole ministry and mission of which baptism was merely the seal. His interrogators immediately realized their dilemma. If they recognized that John's baptism was **from heaven,** then Jesus would ask why they did not **believe him.** On the other hand, if they described John's baptism as being **of men, all the people** would stone them since they believed **that John was a prophet.** The question of their disregard of John's testimony to Jesus, the sum of his whole witness, could not be lightly ignored. **they answered, that they could not tell**—crooked, cringing hypocrites! No wonder Jesus gave them no answer (Matt. 7:6). But what dignity and composure did our Lord display as he turned their question upon them! In analyzing the answer of Jesus, it becomes obvious that authority, in his thinking, was not merely settled by authoritarian answers. He could have answered very dogmatically, but the proof and substance of his person were more important than the dogmatism of his answer. In referring to John's baptism, he was referring to a baptism that required repentance, a change of mind, heart, and life. This was totally foreign to the thinking of the Sanhedrin's representatives. Jesus, by referring to the ministry of John, did give an indirect answer to their question. He spoke in terms of a prophet who had prepared the way for his coming, but the Sanhedrin had not heard his message.

➤**8 Neither tell I you**—They could not answer his question, and therefore their inadequacy forfeited their right to ask questions of Jesus.

## 9-10 THE PARABLE OF THE WICKED HUSBANDMEN

The above encounter provides the background for the parable of the wicked husbandmen. The parable elicited sorrow and sympathy from Jesus' hearers. While his questioners were still there, Jesus related this parable. The meaning of this parable is clear. Any Jew who knew the Scriptures would surely be reminded of Isaiah 1-7. His messiahship had been pronounced and verified by his triumphal entry into Jerusalem and his purging of the temple.

➤**9, 10 vineyard**—See 13:6. The "vineyard" obviously reminded the Jews of Israel. In Matthew 21:33 additional points are given, taken literally from Isaiah 5:2, to establish the application and to sustain it by OT authority. **husbandmen**—or, tenants—individuals responsible for the owner's vineyard. However, Jesus obviously is thinking in terms of the ordinary spiritual guides of the people under whose care and nurture the fruits of righteousness should come to fruition.

➤**11 another servant**—i.e., the prophets, extraordinary messengers raised up from time to time (cf. Matt. 21:35). Although the parable is couched in the terminology of everyday Jewish life, Jesus obviously was speaking in terms of Israel's relationship to God and was demonstrating the methodology by which God sought to bring Israel back to himself.

➤**13 send my beloved son**—This is precisely what God did in sending his Son to the Jews (cf. Mark 12:6). **it may be**—implying the almost unimaginable guilt of not doing so.

➤**14, 15 they reasoned among themselves**—Cf. Genesis 37:18-20; John 11:47-53. **the heir**—sublime expression of the great truth that God's inheritance was destined for and in due time would come into the possession of his Son. **inheritance may be ours**—and so from mere servants they sought to become lords of the property. This is the deep aim of the depraved heart and is literally "the root of all evil." **So they cast him out of the vineyard and killed him**—Cf. Heb. 13:11-13.

➤**16 He shall come and destroy**—This answer was given by the Pharisees themselves (Matt. 21:41), thus pronouncing their own righteous doom. Matthew (21:43) alone gives the unambiguous application that "the kingdom of God will be taken away from you and given to a nation producing the fruits of it" (RSV). In other words, the gospel was to be given to the community of the faithful, chiefly Gentiles. **God forbid**—Jesus' teaching now bursts upon them.

➤**17-19 written**—in Psalm 118:22, 23. (See 19:38.) This song was sung upon the completion of the walls of the city in 443 B.C. It was interpreted as a messianic song by the Jews of Jesus' day and is quoted by Peter (1 Pet. 2:7). In the psalmist's terminology, the kingdom of God is depicted as a temple. During the erection of this temple, a certain Stone was rejected as unsuitable by the spiritual builders, but the great Lord of the temple made this Stone to be the chief of the building (cf. Isa. 8:15). The people to whom Jesus had been sent were then stumbling over this Chief Stone. And, in the future, this Stone would fall in judgment on those who rejected him.

## 20-40 QUESTIONS CONCERNING PAYMENT OF TAXES AND LUKE'S ACCOUNT OF THE RESURRECTION

### 20-26 THE QUESTION OF TRIBUTE MONEY

The authority of Jesus is further illustrated in his answer concerning the payment of taxes. The previous parable so pertinently applied to the Jewish leaders that they would then have arrested him, but the time was not propitious. Therefore, they continued to collect evidence against him.

➤**20** Matthew 22:15, 16 indicates that the Sanhedrin discussed the best plan whereby Jesus might be trapped. Matthew also indicates that they sent a number of their young disciples in an attempt to ensnare him in his speech. But the Sanhedrin was never able to disguise their hatred for Jesus, although their representatives began their questioning with flattery (20:21). **spies**—of the Pharisees and Herodians (Mark 12:13). (See comments on Mark 3:6.)

➤**21 we know**—hoping by flattery to catch Jesus off guard. However, they moved quickly from their extreme flattery to a discussion of Roman taxation.

➤**22 tribute**—The question was designed to put Jesus in a dilemma. If Jesus answered the question affirmatively, then he would have incurred the disfavor of the Jews. On the other hand, if he answered negatively, he would deny the Roman power and in essence deny Roman authority. He could then be accused of treason before the Roman rulers. The question of taxation had long been divisive in nature. Judas of Gamala had declared that death was better than taxation. Roman taxation was extensive but

perhaps was not unduly heavy when compared to current tax programs. The publicans and tax collectors (cf. 19:1-10) had further aggravated the entire question.

➤**23** Jesus, however, **perceived their craftiness** and answered them in a very pragmatic way. Calling for a coin, he simply asked whose inscription was on it. Of course, Caesar's image was on the coin; therefore, in a sense the coin belonged to Caesar. A ruler's domain extended so far as his coins were valid.

➤**25, 26 Render therefore unto Caesar**—those things which belong to him, and give to God his own possessions. Jesus' answer was so straightforward and logical that no one dared continue the questioning. So long as Caesar provided a framework for man's life, he had a right to claim his taxes. Jesus recognized governmental authority and advocated it, but he also saw man's relationship to God as being of supreme importance. Later, the Jewish leaders were to accuse Jesus falsely of "perverting the nation," and "forbidding to give tribute to Caesar" (cf. 23:2). Luke concludes by stating that **they could not take hold of his words before the people**—i.e., "they could not catch him in his speech in the presence of the people." But they remained silent and marveled **at his answer.**

### 27-40 THE QUESTION OF RESURRECTION

(Cf. Matt. 22:23-33 and Mark 12:18-27.) In the last questioning experience, Jesus' opponents sought to lead him to teach treason against Rome. In this question his opponents sought to ridicule him.

➤**27** The irony of the question was heightened by the fact that **the Sadducees,** who said there was no resurrection, interrogated Jesus concerning it. The Sadducees had their stronghold in the temple and largely controlled the political life of the people from the time of Alexander the Great. They represented the aristocracy and "status quo." Their religion was based upon the books of Moses. They were materialists and denied the existence of the spirit world (cf. Acts 23:8).

➤**28-33** Their question to Jesus was based on the levirate (brother-in-law) law of marriage. This law was given in order to protect the childless wife. If a brother died leaving no child, the elder brother was to take the widow to wife and rear children to his brother. Apparently, the law was not practiced at the time of Jesus, so the question seems to be purely academic. The drama of the situation was further heightened because of the number of marriages involved. How would it be possible for a wife to have seven husbands at the time of resurrection?

➤**34-36** But Jesus cut through the hypocrisy of their theoretical construct and said, **The children of this world marry, and are given in marriage: But they which shall be accounted worthy to obtain that world, and the resurrection from the dead, neither marry, nor are given in marriage: Neither can they die anymore . . . being the children of the resurrection**—This first aspect of Jesus' comment on marriage reveals that the conditions of the resurrection will not be the same as in this current life. There will then be no death or need to replenish the earth. The immortality of the future life explains why marital relationships are not continued.

➤**37, 38** In supporting his answer, Jesus turned to the Pentateuch (the only portion of the OT accepted as authoritative by the Sadducees) to show that it teaches immortality. He does this by referring to **the God of Abraham . . . Isaac . . . and Jacob.** Only living people have a living God. This second aspect of his answer is based on the law of Moses. In Exodus 3:6, God said to Moses, "I . . . the God . . ."; no verb was used. Jesus understood the verbal to be present, not past. The God of Abraham did not permit death to disrupt this personal relationship. If the patriarchs were not immortal, then God could never be called the God of Abraham, Isaac, and Jacob. The Sadducees, then, made two mistakes: (1) they had misunderstood the OT and believed that it did not teach immortality; (2) they had made the mistake of attempting to recreate heaven in the image of the earth. Marriage is ordained to perpetuate the human family, but since there will be no breaches by death in the future state, this ordinance will cease. The saints of God sustain an abiding, conscious relationship with him. These sustained a gracious covenant relation to God that cannot be dissolved. In this sense, our Lord affirms that for Moses to call the Lord the "God" of his patriarchal

servants—if at that moment they had no existence—would surely be unworthy of him.

➤**39, 40 scribes**—possibly the scribes of the Pharisees, the antitheses of the Sadducees. The Pharisees believed in angels, resurrection, and the spirit world. The "scribes" enjoyed Jesus' victory over the Sadducees. No one dared question him further. For the time being, his opponents were utterly foiled.

## 41-47 CHRIST QUESTIONS THE PHARISEES CONCERNING DAVID AND THE MESSIAH

(See Matt. 22:41-44b; 23:6; Mark 12:35-40.) Jesus continued working with the Jews to the very end of his ministry in an attempt to bring them to their senses.

➤**41** The penetrating question, **How say they that Christ is David's son?** is a monumental attempt to force the leaders to recognize his true identity.

➤**42** David had called the Messiah **my Lord** in Psalm 110:1.

➤**44** It was clearly known that the Messiah would be David's descendant ("David's son"), but it was never imagined that David's **son** would be David's **Lord.** If David **calleth him Lord, how is he then his son?** Therefore, Jesus was a ruler from the Davidic line and ruler of the Davidic line. According to his humanity, he was a son of David (Rom. 1:3); according to his divinity, he was David's Lord—even the Son of God (Rom. 1:4). Choosing not to press home the implications of his arguments, Jesus turned to the matter of warning his disciples about the scribes.

➤**46, 47 Beware of the scribes**—See comments on Matthew 23:5 and on Luke 14:7. The formalism the scribes enjoyed is defined in Jesus' words concerning **long robes, . . . greetings in the markets,** their desire for the **highest seats in the synagogues,** and their interest in the **chief rooms** [lit., "chief couches"] **at feasts.** However, this external legalism and formalism in no fashion covered or disguised the true condition of their hearts. They **devour widows' houses** and **make long prayers.** But these long prayers of simulated earnestness had nothing to do with purity and cleanliness of heart. Although their offices were marked by the clothing they wore and the salutations they received in the market places, their inner character had not been altered.

# Chapter 21

## 1-4 THE WIDOW'S TWO MITES (See Mark 12:41-44.)

➤**1 looked up**—He had "sat down opposite the treasury" (Mark 12:41, RSV), probably to rest, for he had taught for a long time in the temple court (Mark 11:27), and he observed the widow, even as he had "looked up" and observed Zacchaeus in the fig-mulberry tree. **rich men**—Mark (12:41) indicates that the wealthy people made huge offerings. There were 13 trumpet-shaped receptacles in the Court of the Women into which the worshipers put their gifts.

➤**2** Perhaps Jesus was downcast from the lack of offering on the part of the Jewish leaders, but the offering of the widow encouraged him greatly. **two mites**—small copper coins worth very little.

➤**3 And he said**—obviously he addressed his disciples. **more than they all**—in proportion to her means, which is God's standard (cf. 2 Cor. 8:12).

➤**4 of their abundance**—What they had to spare, or beyond what they needed for living expenses. **of her penury**—lit., "of her lack" (cf. Mark 12:44). She gave of her deficiency, of what was less than her own needs required. Mark is even more emphatic and indicates that she gave everything she had.

## 5-38 THE ESCHATOLOGICAL DISCOURSE (See Mark 13 and Matt. 24, 25.)

➤**5-7** See comments on Matthew 24:1-3. Mark and Matthew indicate that the disciples had pointed to the grandeur of the temple. Solomon had built the temple one thousand years before Jesus' time, and it had existed since that time (except during the Babylonian exile and for some three years during the time of Antiochus Epiphanes, 168-165 B.C.). The current structure had been rebuilt by Herod the Great; in fact, it was not actually completed until A.D. 64. Jesus' disciples were attracted by its beauty and greatness just as the average Jew of their day. But Jesus, on this occasion, predicted its destruction.

➤**8** (Cf. Matt. 24:4-7 and Mark 13:5-8.) **the time**—of the kingdom's coming in its full glory. **go ye not . . . after them**—cf. 2 Thessalonians 2:1, 2.

➤**9-11 be not terrified**—See 21:19 and Isaiah 8:11-14. Jesus states that **the end is not by and by** [immediately]—cf. Matt. 24:6 and Mark 13:7. **Nation**—Matthew and Mark add that all of these things were merely the beginning of sorrows.

➤**12** His followers were to be **brought before kings and rulers;** the book of Acts verifies this. This would be a time for his followers to bear testimony.

➤**18 not an hair . . . perish**—Jesus had just said (21:16) they would be "put to death"; therefore, this precious promise does not provide immunity from physical death. Rather, it provides protection against eternal harm (see 12:4, 5). Matthew adds the following: "And because iniquity shall abound, the love of many shall wax cold" (24:12). However, the man who endures to the end shall be saved. Sad illustrations of the effect of the abounding iniquity in cooling the love of faithful disciples are seen in the Epistle of 2 Timothy and also in Hebrews. God never sends judgment without previous warning, and there can be no doubt that the Jews, already dispersed over most known countries, had nearly all heard the gospel "as a witness" before the end of the Jewish state. The same principle was repeated and will repeat itself to the end.

➤**20, 21** (Cf. Matt. 24:15-22 and Mark 13:14-20.) **compassed with armies**—surrounded by encamped armies, indicating that the city would be besieged. Note Mark 13:14: "But when you see the desolating sacrilege set up where it ought not to be (let the reader understand), then let those who are in Judea flee to the mountains . . . " (RSV). Eusebius says that the Christians fled to Pella at the north extremity of Perea.

➤**23 woe**—to the women with children. This would naturally involve greater suffering as would also a flight in the winter or on the Sabbath, against which they were to pray (Matt. 24:20). The flight in the winter would be more trying to the body, but the flight on the Sabbath would be more to the soul because of the Jewish legalistic interpretation of the Sabbath. **great distress**—will be upon the earth. Matthew (24:21, 22) indicates that no flesh would be saved apart from the shortening of **those days** of suffering. Except for this merciful "shortening" brought about by a remarkable concurrence of causes, the whole nation would have perished. In Matthew and Mark there are references to "false Christs" who would deceive the elect if possible. (Cf. 2 Thess. 2:9-11 and Rev. 13:13.)

➤**24 Jerusalem shall be trodden down of the Gentiles, until the times of the Gentiles be fulfilled**—implying (1) that one day Jerusalem shall cease to be trodden down by the Gentiles; (2) that this shall be at the completion of the "times of the Gentiles," which from Romans 11:25 means, until the Gentiles have had their full time of being in God's NT economy. After this, the Jews will be "grafted into their own olive tree" (see Rom. 11:17-24) and again take up their promised place in God's overall plan.

➤**25-28** (Cf. Matt. 24:29-31 and Mark 13:24-27.) **signs**—Though the grandeur of this language catapults over all ages to that of Christ's second coming, nearly every expression could be applied at one time or another to any number of intervening national judgments. From 21:28, 32, it seems undeniable that its immediate reference was to the destruction of Jerusalem, though its ultimate reference is to Christ's second coming. **redemption**—immediately, from the oppression of ecclesiastical despotism and legal bondage; ultimately, from the old creation and its bondage (Rom. 8:18-23). But the words are of far wider and more precious import. Matthew (24:30) says, "Then will appear the sign of the Son of man in heaven, and then all the tribes of the earth will mourn, and they will see the Son of man coming on the clouds of heaven with power and great glory . . . " (RSV). Interpreters do not agree concerning the meaning of this verse. But even as before Christ came to destroy Jerusalem, some appalling portents were seen in the air, so before his personal appearing it is likely that something analogous will be witnessed, although of what nature it is only vain to conjecture. Marshall reminds us that this final return of the Son of man is based on Daniel 7:13ff.

➤**32 This generation**—"this nation" as some interpret it, which, though admissible in itself, seems very unnatural here. It is rather as in 9:27.

➤**34-36 surfeiting, and drunkenness**—all "animal" excesses, quenching spirituality. **cares of this life**—See Mark 4:7, 19. **all these things**—must include the warnings Jesus gave, which occurred as he prophesied. These, however, will serve only as a precursor to his return. **watch . . . and pray**—The two great duties which in prospect of trial are constantly enjoined. These warnings, suggested by the need of preparedness for the tremendous calamities approaching and the total wreck of the existing state of things, carry the mind forward to judgment and vengeance of another kind and on a grander and more awful scale: not ecclesiastical or political, but personal; not temporal, but eternal—when all safety and blessedness will be found to lie in being able to "stand before the Son of man" in the glory of his personal appearing. These verses serve as a solemn warning against spiritual lethargy. One is to be alert lest his life be replete with the sins so mentioned.

➤**37, 38 in the day time**—every day of his last week. **abode in the mount**—that is, at Bethany (Matt. 21:17). A final note: This chapter is extremely difficult to structure inasmuch as Jesus discussed both the destruction of Jerusalem and his second coming. It seems that details related to one event may also refer to the other. Perhaps the chapter could be arbitrarily structured by construing 21:5-24 to refer to the destruction of Jerusalem and 21:25-38 to refer to the coming of the Son of man, but such a structure is, admittedly, artificial.

*Chapter* **22**

## 1-6 THE CONSPIRACY OF THE JEWISH AUTHORITIES TO PUT JESUS TO DEATH

➤**1, 2** See comments on Matthew 26:1-5. The Feast of Passover was instituted at the time of the death angel's passing (Exod. 12). Luke refers to it and to the Feast of Unleavened Bread, which began the night of Passover and continued for one week. Matthew (26:17) notes that the two feasts were popularly named as one. The Passover was celebrated on Nisan 14, 15. The Passover lambs were slain in the temple on the afternoon of Nisan 14. The feast was actually that evening, the beginning of Nisan 15. The days of unleavened bread extended from Nisan 15 to 21.

➤**3 Then entered Satan into Judas**—The stages of Satan's entrance into Judas may be seen progressively in the following: (1) He was enslaved to covetousness. The Lord let it reveal itself and gather strength by entrusting him with "the bag" (John 12:6), as treasurer for himself and the Twelve. (2) In the discharge of that most sacred trust he became "a thief," appropriating its contents from time to time for his own use. Satan, seeing this door into his heart standing open, determined to enter by it. First, Satan merely put the thought into Judas's mind to betray Jesus (John 13:2), perhaps suggesting to him that by this means he might enrich himself. (3) This thought was probably converted into a settled purpose, as is evident by what took place in Simon's house at Bethany. (See Matt. 26:6-11 and John 12:4-8.) (4) The determination to betray Jesus was not consummated until "Satan entered into him" (see John 13:27), and conscience, effectually stifled, only rose again to be his tormentor. What lessons in all this for everyone (Eph. 4:27; James 4:7; 1 Pet. 5:8, 9)!

➤**4 captains**—probably represented the priestly aristocracy in charge of the temple guard and were responsible for policing the temple area.

➤**5 money**—Matthew (26:15) indicates that the price agreed upon was thirty pieces of silver. (See comments on John 19:16.)

➤**6** Judas agreed and began the search for an **opportunity to betray him unto them in the absence of the multitude**—This resolved the problems of the Jews; they could perhaps arrest him without creating an uprising among his followers. (See Matt. 26:5.)

7-13 PREPARATION FOR THE PASSOVER
(Cf. Matt. 26:17-19 and Mark 14:12-16.) Wednesday's activities are left unrecorded. Jesus' activities on Thursday were confined essentially to ministering to the apostles. That evening he was arrested. The preparation for the Passover might be divided into two segments: (1) Earlier preparation: During this time, the roads were prepared for the great throngs that would be assembling in Jerusalem for the observance of the Passover. The bridges were made safe, tombs by the wayside were whitewashed (that no pilgrim would be contaminated by touching a tomb), and everything

was generally prepared for the great migration to Jerusalem. Josephus says that as many as 256,500 lambs were slain at a single Passover. Since ten adults were required before a lamb was eaten ceremonially as a Paschal lamb, this means that approximately 2,500,000 people assembled in Jerusalem to observe the Passover. The principles and the occasion of the feast were taught in the synagogues for at least two months prior to the date of the feast. (2) Later preparation: This began on the night before, that is, the 13th of Nisan. Houses were searched very carefully for leaven, and if any was found, it was burned the following day. The Paschal lambs were slain between 2:30 and 6:00 p.m. on the 14th of Nisan. The lamb had to be a perfect lamb, and it was slain by its owner. The blood of the lamb was caught in a utensil and passed along a long line of priests and finally dashed upon the altar.

➤**7 the day of unleavened bread**—strictly the 15th of Nisan (part of our March and April) after the Paschal lamb was killed.

➤**10-13 when ye are entered into the city**—He himself probably stayed at Bethany during the day. **a man meet you, bearing a pitcher of water**—See comments on 19:29-32. In Palestine only women normally carried water in pitchers. Some interpreters suggest that Jesus had arranged earlier for a place in which to eat the Passover, postulating that the house probably belonged to a disciple. In addition to the numerous preparations previously mentioned, those involved in the observance had to also select a lamb, herbs, spices, wine, etc.—all of the essential ingredients to the Passover meal. The large upper room was usually used by a rabbi for teaching his disciples.

14-34 THE LAST PASSOVER AND
INSTITUTION OF THE LORD'S SUPPER
See Matt. 26:20, 26-29 and Mark 14:17, 20-25; cf. also John 13:21-30.
The following represents the normal order of the Passover meal: (1) An initial blessing and prayer followed by the first of four cups of wine and a dish of herbs and sauce. (2) The story of the Passover's institution, singing of Psalm 113, and the second cup of wine. (3) Prayer of thanksgiving, followed by meal of roast lamb, unleavened bread, bitter herbs, another prayer after which the third cup of wine was

drunk. (4) singing of Psalms 114-118, and a fourth cup of wine.

➤**14-18 the hour**—about 6:00 p.m. Between three and six the lamb was killed (Exod. 12:6). **with desire I have desired**—The repetition expresses his earnestness. But why was he so desirous to share the Passover with his disciples? Because it was to be his last before he suffered and so became "Christ our passover . . . sacrificed for us" (1 Cor. 5:7); and because he would not dine again with the disciples until the kingdom of God had come (22:16, 18).

➤**17 he took the cup**—the first of several of which the participants partook during the meal. This cup (as distinguished from the cup in 22:20) was probably a cup drunk during a normal Passover celebration. The cup in 22:20 is the cup of the new covenant. **divide it among yourselves**—"It is to be your last as well as mine until the kingdom of God is fulfilled," or as it is beautifully stated in Matthew 26:29, "until that day when I drink it new with you in my Father's kingdom." It was the great point of transition between two economies and their two great festivals, the one about to close forever, the other immediately to open and run its majestic career until from earth it be transferred to heaven. Some interpreters view this as a reference to the messianic banquet.

➤**21, 22** See comments on John 13:21.

➤**24-30 strife among them**—referring probably to the symptoms of the former strife that had reappeared perhaps on account of the whole Paschal arrangements being committed to only two of the twelve disciples. (See comments on Mark 10:42-45.) **benefactors**—a title the vain princes eagerly coveted. **But ye shall not be so**—Of how little avail has this condemnation of "lordship" and vain titles been against the vanity of Christian ecclesiastics! Jesus tells his closest followers that status does not arise in the kingdom of God. However, the saying of 22:28-33 does allow the disciples some honor. They shared his trials and would eventually share his triumph. **Ye are they which have continued with me**—Personal and intimate evidence of Christ's tender susceptibility to human sympathy and support! **I appoint unto you a kingdom**—Who is this that dispenses the kingdom of kingdoms within an hour or two of his appre-

hension and less than a day away from his shameful death? These sublime contrasts augment the splendor of this history. **may eat and drink . . . in my kingdom**—See comments on 22:16 and on 18:28.

➤**31 Satan hath desired to have you**—plural in Greek, referring to all the disciples. Here Jesus, speaking to Peter, tells his disciples that Satan wanted to **sift** them **as wheat.** This imagery comes from Job 1:6-12; 2:1-6. Satan obtained permission from God to sift Job as wheat that he might find "the chaff" in his spiritual life.

➤**32 But I have prayed for thee** [you]—singular in Greek, referring specifically to Peter (see 22:61, 62). **that thy faith fail not**—that is, entirely, for partially it did fail. **when thou art converted**—i.e., "when you have turned." **strengthen**—make use of your bitter experience for fortifying and supplying your weak brothers.

➤**33, 34 I am ready**—an honest-hearted, warmly attached disciple, thinking he was as immovable as a rock. But in the hour of temptation he would be unstable as water. **The cock shall not crow**—twice, according to Mark 14:30.

➤**35-38** These verses constitute the fourth and final sayings of Jesus and conclude this section. In essence he said, "But now your methods must be different, for you are going forth, not as before on a temporary mission, provided with no purse or scrip, but into scenes of continued and severe trial. The purse and scrip will now be needed for support, and the usual means of defense will be required" (22:35, 36).

➤**37 this that is written must yet be accomplished in me**—alluding to the things divinely decreed and written in Scripture (Isa. 53:12). What had been written concerning Jesus had its **end** [fulfillment].

➤**38 two swords . . . enough**—They thought he referred to the present defense, while his answer showed he meant something else entirely.

39-46 THE AGONY IN THE GARDEN (See Matt. 26:36ff.; Mark 14:32-50; John 18:1-11.)

➤**39** After the meal, Jesus left the city of Jerusalem **and went, as he was wont** [according to his habit], **to the mount of Olives**—See John 18:2.

➤**40-46** He came to **the place** and there he prayed. The place is the Garden of Gethsemane, on the west or "city" side of the mountain. Comparing all the accounts of this mysterious scene, the facts appear to be these: (1) He requested eight of the Twelve to remain "here" while he went and prayed "yonder." (2) He took the three other disciples (Peter, James, and John) and was amazed by their inability to remain alert and awake during this time of his soul searching. It apparently strengthened Jesus just to have them near him. (3) But soon even they were too much for him; he must be alone. He withdrew himself from them about a stone's throw away, though near enough for them to be competent witnesses. There he knelt and prayed, uttering the prayer recorded in Mark 14:36: "Abba, Father, all things are possible to thee; remove this cup from me; yet not what I will, but what thou wilt" (RSV). This prayer implies that in itself the cup was so entirely revolting that only its being his Father's will would induce him to taste it; but further, in that view of it, he was perfectly prepared to drink it. It was no struggle between a reluctant and a compliant will, but between views of one event— an abstract and a relative view of it, the one of which is revolting and the other acceptable. By signifying how it felt in the one view, he demonstrated his oneness with our human nature and feeling. His true humanity hereby was expressed. By expressing how he regarded the Father's will, he revealed his absolute and obedient subjection to his Father. (4) Having a momentary relief, he returned to the three and found them sleeping. He addressed them personally, especially Peter (Mark 14:37, 38). (5) He then went back, not now to kneel, but to fall on his face, saying the same words but with this alteration: "My Father, if this cannot pass unless I drink it, thy will be done" (Matt. 26:42, RSV). (6) Again, seeking a moment of relief, he returned and found them "sleeping for sorrow" and warned them as before, indicating that "the spirit is willing but the flesh is weak." (7) Once more Jesus returned to his solitary spot; this time the surge of his inner feelings beat more tempestuously and seemed ready to overwhelm him. (The details of his praying so hard that he sweated great drops of blood, etc., as recorded in 22:43, 44 [KJV], are not found in several of the earliest manuscripts.) It was just shuddering

nature and indomitable will struggling together. But again the cry, "If it must be, thy will be done." He had anticipated and rehearsed his final conflict and won the victory—now in the theater of an invincible will, and then in the arena of the cross. The conclusion, "I will suffer," is the grand result of Gethsemane. The pronouncement "It is finished" is the shout that burst from the cross. (8) At the close of the whole scene, he found the disciples; the hour for the Son of man to be betrayed into the hands of sinners had come. Even while he spoke, Judas approached with his group of armed men. Therefore, they proved "miserable comforters." Thus, in his whole work he was alone; not one of his was with him.

## 47-54 BETRAYAL AND APPREHENSION OF JESUS

See comments on Matthew 26:47-56; Mark 14:43-50; John 18:3-11.

## 55-62 JESUS BEFORE CAIAPHAS AND THE DENIAL BY PETER

The particulars of these two sections require a combination of all the narratives, for which see comments on John 18:1ff.

## 63-71 JESUS IS CONDEMNED TO DIE. HIS SUFFERING PRIOR TO THE CROSS

See comments on Mark 14:53-63; John 18:19ff.

*Chapter* **23**

## 1-6 JESUS BEFORE PILATE

See comments on Mark 15:1-5 and John 18:23ff.

Luke indicates that the entire company— Sadducees, Pharisees, and scribes—put Jesus before Pilate. The Jewish right to try capital cases was taken from them some forty years prior to the destruction of the city, which would mean it was approximately at the time of Jesus' trial that the enactment of the Roman order prohibiting the Jewish court from trying such cases was effected. (See John 18:31.) A Roman ruler would refuse to be concerned with names and persons (cf. Acts 18:14), but the question couched in terms of sedition or a threat to Roman rule would receive a ready hearing. Therefore, the charge brought against Jesus was that he was socially and politically subversive.

## 7-12 JESUS BEFORE HEROD
See comments on Mark 15:6.

➤7 When Pilate learned Jesus was a Galilean, **he sent him to Herod**—Herod was in **Jerusalem** at that time for the observance of the Passover Feast. Pilate obviously hoped to escape the dilemma of an unjust condemnation or an unpopular release of Jesus. This episode is recorded only in Luke's account, thereby causing some critics to question whether the event actually occurred. Tinsley notes that this incident is mentioned in Acts 4:25-28, where it is in the context of Psalm 2:1, 2. Luke obviously wanted to show that the Jews were responsible for Jesus' death, not the Romans.

➤8 **hoped to have seen some miracle**—A miracle would have been great entertainment so far as Herod was concerned. This reminds one of the Philistines' experiences with Samson (Judg. 16:25). The coarse, crafty, cruel Herod is seen for what he actually was (see also 13:31-33). Jesus, however, gave no answer to Herod's questioning (see Matt. 7:6).

➤10 **stood and vehemently accused him**—No doubt both of treason before the king and also blasphemy, for the king was a Jew. Herod's soldiers (his bodyguards) joined in the taunting. This was their reaction to their stinging disappointment brought by Jesus' refusal to amuse them with miracles and answer any of Herod's questions.

➤11 **gorgeous robe**—lit., "a bright robe." If this means (as sometimes it does) a "shining white" robe, this being the royal color among the Jews, it may have been in derision of his claim to be "King of the Jews." But if so, "He in reality honored him, as did Pilate with his true title blazoned on the cross" (Bengel). Herod was entirely too wise to be trapped by Pilate and soon returned Jesus to the governor. Neither Pilate nor Herod was able to establish anything against Jesus. The confidence Pilate had exhibited in Herod and had demonstrated by sending Jesus to him created a certain friendship between them.

➤12 Luke carefully notes that they had been **at enmity** with each other prior to that time. Luke's careful research is again underscored by the including of this event, which is not mentioned in the other Gospels. Although Herod had beheaded John, he refused to sentence Jesus. The gorgeous robe of royalty, possibly a white mantle as worn by Jewish kings, suggests how lightly Herod treated Jesus. The king obviously considered Jesus of no importance.

## 13-32 JESUS AGAIN BEFORE PILATE AND THE TRIP TO GOLGOTHA. (See Mark 15:6-15 and John 19:2.)

The governor customarily released one criminal during the Passover season. Pilate attempted a second time to release Jesus, but realizing the unpopularity of this decision and desiring to maintain a friendship with the Jews, he wished simply to chastise him and release him as a scourged king. This would show the Jews that he was not indifferent to their desires. However, this did not please the Jews, and Pilate attempted a third time (23:21) to release Jesus. The threefold plea is recorded in 23:14-16, 20, and 22. (Cf. Matt. 27:19 for the pleas of Pilate's wife.)

➤26 **Simon, a Cyrenian**—Cyrene was in Libya, on the north coast of Africa, where many Jews lived (cf. Acts 6:9). Simon is identified by Mark (15:21) as the father of Alexander and Rufus, probably better known by later Christians than the father himself. Luke omits the events immediately following the sentencing; he alone seems to go out of his way in presenting Simon as the cross-bearer. **coming out of the country**—and casually drawn into that part of the crowd. **on him they laid the cross**—Caird says that Simon likely carried only the cross bar, that the remainder of the cross would have been too heavy for one man to carry. It appears that Jesus had first borne his own cross (John 19:17), but being exhausted and unable to proceed, the cross was laid on Simon, who followed him.

➤27 **women**—not the precious Galilean women (23:49) but part of the crowd.

➤28 **weep not for me**—What a noble spirit of compassion, rising above his own dreaded endurances in tender commiseration of sufferings yet in the distance and far lighter, but without his supports and consolations.

➤30 **mountains . . . hills**—The Jews did rush there in an attempt to find shelter during the time of the city's siege. **green**—that naturally resists the fire. **dry**—that attracts the fire, being its proper fuel. The proverb here means: "If such sufferings alight upon the innocent One, the very Lamb of God, what must be in store for those who are provoking the flames? If they do these terrible things to the green tree (Jesus), what will they do to the dry (people meriting suffering after Jesus is gone)?"

## 32-38, 44-46 THE CRUCIFIXION AND DEATH OF JESUS

See comments on John 19:17-30.

## 39-43 THE TWO THIEVES

➤**39** Two criminals were crucified with Jesus. One of them railed at him. He was caught up in the universal derision but with a characteristic tone and accusation all his own. Jesus, although reviled, did not revile in turn. Another voice from the cross shall nobly wipe out of his dishonor and turn it to the unspeakable glory of the dying Redeemer. Some interpreters believe this to have been irony on the part of the thief.

➤**40** The other criminal rebuked the first, saying, **Dost not thou fear God?**—so as to say, "Let others jeer, but do you? Have you no fear of meeting him so soon as thy righteous Judge? You are in an hour or two of eternity, and do you spend it in reckless disregard of coming judgment? You are under the **same** sentence of **condemnation.**"

➤**41 nothing amiss**—lit., "nothing out of place." Our Lord was not charged with ordinary crime, but only with laying claim to office and honors, which amounted to blasphemy. The charge of treason had not even a show of truth, as Pilate told his enemies. In this defense, then, there seems more than meets the eye. He made himself the promised Messiah, the Son of God; but in this he did nothing wrong. Jesus ate with publicans and sinners and invited all the weary and heavy laden to come and rest under his wing; but in this he did nothing wrong. He claimed to be Lord of the kingdom of God, to shut it at will, and also to open it according to his own pleasure; but in this he did nothing wrong. Does the thief's next speech imply less than this? Observe: (1) his frank confession and genuine self-condemnation; (2) his astonishment and horror at the very different state of his mind; (3) his anxiety to bring him to a

better mind while yet there was hope; (4) his noble testimony, not only to the innocence of Jesus, but to all that this implied concerning the righteousness of his claim.

➤**42 And he said unto Jesus, Lord, remember me when thou comest into thy kingdom**—Observe: (1) The kingdom referred to was one beyond the grave; for it is inconceivable that he should have expected Jesus to come down from the cross to erect any temporal kingdom. (2) This he calls Christ's own kingdom. (3) As such, he sees in Christ the absolute right to dispose of that kingdom to whom he pleased. (4) He does not presume to ask for a place in the kingdom, although that is what he means, but in humility just says, "Lord, *remember* me when thou comest into thy kingdom." Yet there was mighty faith in that saying. Contrast this bright act of faith with the darkness of the apostles' minds. They could hardly believe their Master would die, and now were almost despairing of him, burying all their hopes in his grave. Consider also this man's previous disadvantages and bad life. And then mark how his faith comes out, as having no shadow of doubt—he just says, "Lord, remember me when you come . . . " Was ever faith like this exhibited upon the earth? It looks as if the brightest crown had been reserved for the Savior's head at his darkest moment!

➤**43 And Jesus said**—The dying Redeemer spoke as if he himself viewed it in this light. It was a "song in the night." It ministered cheer to his spirit in the midnight gloom that now engulfed it. **Verily, I say unto thee**—Since you speak as to the king, with kingly authority I speak to you. **to day**—The thief was prepared for a long delay before Jesus came into his kingdom, but there would not be a day's delay for him. He would not be parted from Jesus even for a moment, but together they would go and even before the day expired be together **in paradise** (2 Cor. 12:4; Rev. 2:7). The term "paradise" was initially a Persian word and meant a garden place, a place of repose. It is extremely significant that Jesus chose this term to describe the place of relationship with a penitent thief. Perhaps the word here refers to the abode of the righteous dead prior to judgment.

## 47-56 SIGNS AND CIRCUMSTANCES FOLLOWING HIS DEATH AND HIS BURIAL

See comments on Matthew 27:51-56, 62-66; John 19:31-42.

*Chapter* **24**

## 1-12 THE ANGELIC ANNOUNCEMENT TO THE WOMEN THAT CHRIST IS RISEN, AND PETER'S VISIT TO THE EMPTY TOMB

See comments on Matthew 28:1-10; Mark 16:1-8; and John 20:1-10. An unidentified number of women of Galilee visited the tomb of Jesus on Sunday, found it open, but no body was inside. Two angels appeared to them, after which the women returned to the other disciples and related their story to them. There is no question about the basic facts, but it is difficult to harmonize the various gospel narratives at this point. The same difficulty would occur if several eyewitnesses of a plane crash should attempt to harmonize the accounts of what they observed.

➤**5 Why seek ye the living** [One] **among the dead?**—an astonishing question! Not "the risen One," but "the living One" (cf. Rev. 1:18). The surprise expressed in this statement implies an incongruity in his being there at all, though he might for a while submit to death. However, it was impossible that he should be "held by it" (Acts 2:24, RSV).

➤**6, 7 in Galilee**—To which these women themselves belonged (cf. 23:55). How remarkable it is to hear angels quoting a whole sentence of Christ's to the disciples, mentioning where it was uttered and wondering if it was not fresh in their memory, as doubtless it was in theirs! (See 1 Tim. 3:16, "seen of angels," and 1 Pet. 1:12.)

➤**10 Joanna**—See comments on 8:1-3.

➤**12 Peter**—See comments on John 20:1ff.

## 13-35 CHRIST APPEARS TO THE TWO DISCIPLES ON THE ROAD TO EMMAUS

(Cf. Mark 16:12ff.) This event occurred on the same afternoon Jesus arose. When Jesus joined the men, they were downcast and frustrated.

➤**13 two of them**—One was Cleopas (24:18), and the identity of the other remains mere conjecture. Marshall suggests that the second disciple was Cleopas's wife. **Emmaus**—approximately seven miles northwest of Jerusalem. This is not a great distance, but it is a long way when one's heart is broken. These disciples probably lived there and were returning to Emmaus following the Passover.

➤**14-16 talked together**—exchanged views and feelings, weighing afresh all the facts as detailed in 24:18-24. **Jesus himself drew near**—coming up behind them as from Jerusalem. **their eyes were holden** [held]—"their eyes were kept from recognizing him" (RSV). This must be explained partially upon the basis that he was "in another form" (Mark 16:12) and partially that there seems to have been an operation on their own vision. Inasmuch as they did not believe that he was alive, his company as a fellow traveler was the last thing they would expect. All of their hopes for the future had been destroyed by his crucifixion.

➤**17-24 what manner of communications**—The words imply the earnest discussion that appeared in their manner. **A stranger . . . hast not known**—If he did not know the events of the last few days in Jerusalem, he must be a mere sojourner; if he was aware of these events, how could he suppose they would be talking of anything else? As if feeling it a relief to have someone to unburden his thoughts and feelings to, one of the disciples repeated the main facts in his own despondent style, and apparently this was just what the Lord wished him to do. **We trusted**—is better translated, "we hoped." They expected the promised deliverance by his hand, but in the popular sense of deliverance, not by his death. **beside all this**—Not only did his death seem to give the fatal blow to their hopes, but he had been two days dead already, and this was the third. It was true, they added, some of their women gave them a surprise by telling about a vision of angels they had at the empty grave this morning. These angels reported that Jesus was alive, and some went there to confirm their statement, but no one saw Jesus.

➤**25-27 O fools, and slow of heart**—Senseless, without understanding. **Ought not**

**Christ**—lit., "the Christ," or, "the Messiah." **to have suffered . . . and enter into his glory**—that is, through the gate of suffering to enter into the glory of his resurrection. **Moses and all the prophets**—Here our Lord both teaches us the reverence due the OT Scriptures and their great testimony to himself. The OT Scriptures consisted of the Law, Prophets, and Writings (or Psalms). **in all the scriptures the things concerning himself**—What a wonderful message that must have been! Christ expounding on "Christ" in all the OT Scriptures!

➤**28-31 made as though** [pretended] **he would have gone further**—Cf. Mark 6:48. **constrained him**—for he had kindled a longing in the hearts of his traveling companions that was not to be so easily discarded. **He took bread, and blessed . . . And their eyes were opened**—The stranger must have startled the disciples by taking the place of the master at their own table, and on proceeding to that act which reproduced the whole scene of the Last Supper, he stood before their astonished gaze as their risen Lord! They wished to gaze on him, perhaps embrace him, but at that moment he was gone! This was testimony enough to the resurrection.

➤**32-34** They now relate to each other how their hearts were fired within them by his exposition of the Scriptures. They could not rest. They had to return and share this event with those in Jerusalem. They found the Eleven, but before they even had time to relate their experience, their ears were priced by the thrilling news, **The Lord is risen indeed, and hath appeared to Simon**—This appearance to Peter is affirmed by Paul in 1 Corinthians 15:5. The only one of the Eleven to whom he appeared alone was he who had so shamefully denied Christ. What occurred during this interview we shall never know here in this life. Probably it was too sacred for disclosure. (See Mark 16:7.)

➤**35** The two from Emmaus now relate what had happened to them, and while thus sharing news of their Lord's appearances, he himself stood in their midst. What encouragement to doubting and true-hearted disciples!

## 36-50 JESUS APPEARS TO THE ASSEMBLED DISCIPLES

Compare Matthew 28:16-20; Mark 16:14-20; John 20:19–23; Acts 1:6-11. Luke reveals only those appearances of Jesus in or near Jerusalem, while Matthew depicts those in Galilee. John records both. Luke's approach may have been partially influenced by the purpose of the Acts volume. If his Gospel deals with the mission of Jesus from Galilee to Jerusalem, then the theme of Acts must be Christ's work from Jerusalem to Rome (Tinsley).

➤**36 Jesus himself stood**—See comments on John 20:19. The travelers' excited story was interrupted by the appearance of Jesus with the greeting **Peace be unto you.**

➤**37, 38 a spirit**—They imagined they saw the ghost of their dead Lord, but not himself in the body (Acts 12:15; Matt. 14:26). **why do thoughts arise in your hearts?**—They were trying to determine whether he were risen or not and whether this was Jesus himself.

➤**39-43 handle me, and see**—lovingly offering them both visual and tangible demonstration of the reality of his resurrection. **a spirit hath not flesh and bones**—He says not "flesh and blood," for the blood is the life of the corruptible body that cannot inherit the kingdom of God (1 Cor. 15:50). He rather says "flesh and bones," implying the identity (but with diversity of laws) of the resurrection body. In resurrection, Christ was the glorified Godman, still retaining his humanity, but a humanity transfigured and transformed. **yet believed not for joy**—They did believe, else they had not rejoiced. But it seemed too good to be true. **did eat before them**—Let them see him doing it, not for his own necessity, but for their own conviction.

➤**44 These are the words**—See 18:31-34. **while I was yet with you**—A striking expression, implying that he was now, as the dead and risen Savior, virtually separated from this scene of mortality, and from all ordinary contact with his mortal disciples. **law . . . prophets . . . psalms**—The three Jewish divisions of the OT Scriptures.

➤**45 Then he opened**—A statement of unspeakable value, expressing, on the one hand, Christ's immediate access to the human spirit and absolute power to give it spiritual discernment, and on the other hand, making it certain that the manner of interpreting the OT the apostles would afterwards employ had the direct sanction of Christ himself.

➤**46 it behoved Christ**—See comments on 24:26.

➤**47 beginning at Jerusalem**—(1) as the metropolis and heart of the then existing kingdom of God. The gospel was to go to the Jew first (Rom. 1:16; Acts 13:46); (2) as the great repository of all the sin and crime of the nation, thus proclaiming for all time that there is mercy in Christ for the chief of sinners. (See Matt. 23:37.)

➤**48 witnesses**—See Acts 1:8, 22.

➤**49 I send**—the present tense. This intimates the nearness of the event. **the promise of my Father**—i.e., what the Father has promised, the Holy Spirit (cf. John 14:16). **endued with**—"invested," indicating that they would be immersed in a conscious supernatural power that would stamp divine authority on the whole exercise of their apostolic office, including, of course, their pen as well as their mouth. (See Rom. 13:14; 1 Cor. 15:53; Gal. 3:27.)

➤**50, 51 as far as to Bethany**—not to the village itself, but on the descent to it from the Mount of Olives (cf. Acts 1:12). **while he blessed them, he was parted from them**—The last picture of Jesus in this Gospel is that of the Savior **lifting up his hands** in a priestly gesture of blessing.

➤**52 worshipped him**—certainly in the strictest sense of adoration. **returned to Jerusalem**—as instructed to do—but not until after gazing, as if entranced, up into the blue vault into which he had disappeared. They were gently checked by two shining angels, who assured them he would come again in a similar manner in which he had gone into heaven. (See comments on Acts 1:10, 11.) This made them return, not with disappointment at his removal, but "with great joy." Note: Luke 24:52 along with several other verses in this chapter—24:3, 6, 12, 36, 40, and 51—are not found in Codex Bezae and several old Latin manuscripts. Certain scholars, chiefly Westcott and Hort, believed that these verses must have been interpolations. As a result, these verses (or parts of them) were not included in the Greek texts of Westcott and Hort, and Nestle, and certain English translations (NEB and RSV in part) followed suit. But most scholars today uphold the authenticity of these verses. All the earliest Greek manuscripts (including two of which were discovered in this century: the Freer Gospels and Papyrus Bodmer XIV) contain these verses. Thus, the most recent Nestle text (26th edition, 1979) has these verses in the text and so do most of the modern English versions (TEV, JB, NASB, TLB, NIV).

➤**53 were continually in the temple**—every day at the regular hours of prayer until the day of Pentecost. Luke begins his Gospel with a scene in the temple and concludes his record of Jesus' life by describing his disciples in the same manner. The break with the synagogue is recorded in Acts.

BIBLIOGRAPHY

Alford, Henry. *The Greek New Testament*. 1852. Reprint. Grand Rapids: Guardian Press, 1973.

Bengel, John A. *New Testament Word Studies*. 1792. Reprint. Grand Rapids: Eerdmans, 1971.

Caird, George B. *The Gospel of St. Luke*. Westminster Pelican Series. Philadelphia: The Westminster Press, 1964.

Calvin, John. *Commentary on the Harmony of the Evangelists*. 1564. Reprint. Grand Rapids: Baker Book House, 1979.

Conzelmann, Hans. *The Theology of St. Luke*. New York: Harper & Row, 1960.

Geldenhuys, Johannes. *Commentary on the Gospel of Luke*. New International Commentary. Grand Rapids: Eerdmans, 1951.

Keble, John. *The Christian Year: Thoughts in Verse for Sundays and Holidays throughout the Year*. Oxford: J. Parker, 1827.

Leaney, A. R. C. *A Commentary on the Gospel according to St. Luke*. Harper's New Testament Commentaries. New York: Harper & Brothers, 1958.

Liefeld, Walter. "Luke" in *The Expositor's Bible Commentary*. Grand Rapids: Zondervan, 1984.

Lightfoot, Neil. *Parables of Jesus*. Grand Rapids: Baker Book House, 1963.

Manson, T. W. *The Sayings of Jesus*. London: SCM, 1949.

Marshall, I. Howard. *Luke: Historian and Theologian*. Grand Rapids: Zondervan, 1971.

Nineham, D. E. *Studies in the Gospels*. Naperville, Ill.: Allenson, 1955.

Olshausen, Hermann. *Biblical Commentary on the New Testament*. New York: Sheldon, 1858.

Robertson, A. T. *Word Pictures in the Greek New Testament*. Nashville: Broadman Press, 1932.

Tinsley, E. J. *Gospel according to Luke*. Cambridge Bible Commentary on the New English Bible. Cambridge: Cambridge University Press, 1965.

Trench, R. C. *Studies in the Gospels*. London: Macmillan, 1878.

# JOHN

## Introduction

The author of the fourth Gospel was the younger of the two sons of Zebedee, a fisherman on the Sea of Galilee, who resided at Bethsaida (the town of Peter, Andrew, and Philip). John was a disciple of John the Baptist (1:35) before he followed Jesus. He and his brother James were called "the sons of thunder" (Mark 3:17), probably because of their natural vehemence and fiery zeal. They and Peter constituted the select inner circle among the Twelve. But the highest honor given to this disciple was that he was so dearly loved by Jesus that he was allowed to recline on Jesus' bosom during the Last Supper—and thus styled himself throughout this Gospel as "the disciple whom Jesus loved" (13:23; 19:26; 20:2; 21:7, 20, 24).

The Gospel itself points to John's authorship. The writer of this Gospel was a Palestinian Jew who was very familiar with Jewish customs, topography, and language. The writer was an eyewitness, as is shown by the many fine details presented throughout. Note how the writer points out the details of the marriage celebration in Cana, Jesus' encounter with the Samaritan woman at the well, Jesus' reactions outside the tomb of Lazarus, Jesus' feelings and thoughts at the Last Supper, John and Peter's interaction at the Last Supper, Jesus' trial, Jesus' crucifixion, and Jesus' post-resurrection appearances. None but an eyewitness could have penned these accounts with such exquisite detail. As "the disciple whom Jesus loved," John had a very intimate relationship with Jesus and thus could provide his readers with insights into Jesus' person that we do not find in the other Gospels. John alone of all the disciples followed Jesus to his trial (John evidently was known by the high priest's family and thereby gained access to the trial—18:15, 16) and then to the cross. As John beheld his Savior dying, Jesus entrusted the care of his mother to him (19:26, 27). John himself testified that he was an eyewitness of Jesus' crucifixion (John 19:35).

John's authorship of the fourth Gospel was attested by many of the early church fathers: Clement of Alexandria (c. 155–c. 220), Origen (c. 185–c. 254), Hippolytus (d. c. 236), Justin Martyr (c. 100–165), indirectly, and Tertullian (c. 165–cc. 217). Evidence for John's authorship has also been gathered from the Muratorian fragment (later 2nd century) and Tatian's *Diatessaron* (c. 150). John's authorship was not questioned until the eighteenth and nineteenth centuries. Various theories were advanced, the most popular of which propounded that John the presbyter (spoken of by Papias according to Eusebius) authored the last Gospel. But this opinion has no substance. Other critics (chiefly of the Tubingen school) advanced the theory that John's Gospel was written in the middle of the second century. But this theory was disproved by the discovery of a papyrus fragment dated A.D. 115–125 containing a portion of John's Gospel (18:31-33, 37-38). (The papyrus is known as the Ryland Papyrus, designated P52.)

Most conservative scholars date the writing of the fourth Gospel somewhere in the last decade of the first century (90–100). Apparently John was banished to the island of Patmos (see Rev. 1:9) sometime during the reign of Domitian (81–96). His return from exile took place during the brief but tolerant reign of Nerva, and then he died at Ephesus during the reign of Trajan sometime around A.D. 100. Most likely, John wrote his Gospel prior to his banishment, in the early 90s. According to tradition, he wrote the Gospel in Asia Minor (probably Ephesus) to confirm and strengthen the faith of the believers in that region, and his writing was certified by the elders at Ephesus (see comments on 21:24, 25).

Readers of this Gospel cannot help but notice how different it is from the Synoptic Gospels. Since John was familiar with the other Gospels—as were many other Christians of his day—he supplied material not found in the others. (For example, of the seven miracles recorded by John, only two—the feeding of the multitude and the walking on the water—repeat the Synoptic Gospels.) And unlike the Synoptic Gospels, John chose to present a portrait of the God-man, Jesus, rather than a narrative of Jesus' life and ministry.

Therefore, the Gospel of John is not event-oriented; it is person-oriented. There are events, but the events function as a platform for exhibiting Jesus. While writers like Mark narrate action upon action, John mainly selects those stories that will manifest some specific aspect of Christ's person. The well in Samaria serves as a good backdrop for portraying Jesus as the fountain of living waters, the multiplication of the loaves gives a good setting for showing Jesus as the bread of life, and the raising of Lazarus from the dead is a marvelous stage for presenting Jesus as the resurrection and the life.

No other book of the NT reveals as much about Christ's person as does the Gospel of John. The prologue (1:1-18) alone contains more items about Jesus than any other single pericope in the Bible. Jesus is presented as the Word, the One face to face with God, God, the One in the beginning, the agent of creation, the life, the light of men, the rejected One, the received One, the incarnate Word, the tabernacle of God, the glorified Son, the one-and-only Son, the preeminent One, the fullness, the full embodiment of grace and reality, the giver of constant grace, the Christ, the unique One in the Father's bosom, and God's interpreter. What a Christ!

John does not present Jesus' fullness in an objective way—as if he were providing a list or positing a creed. John's record is warm and personal, as one would find in a memoir. With fond recollection, John recounts the awe with which he (and the other disciples) gazed upon Jesus' special glory (1:14). As was noted earlier, the entire Gospel is delightfully enhanced by John's first-hand knowledge and personal interaction with Jesus.

At the end of this Gospel, John straightforwardly declares *why* he wrote this book: "These [things] are written that you might believe that Jesus is the Christ, the Son of God, and that believing ye might have life through his name" (20:31). This Gospel, focusing on the person Jesus, constantly affirms that he is the Christ (the Messiah, the anointed One of God) and he is the Son of God (the divine One, even God himself). In passage after passage, John asserts Jesus' claim to the Messiahship and deity. The tension of the Gospel gathers around Jesus' identity. Some believe in who he is; most do not. The believers become the receivers; they receive eternal life.

# Chapter 1

## 1-18 THE PROLOGUE

**➤1 In the beginning**—the beginning before all beginnings, prior to the beginning of Genesis 1:1. The phrase could be rendered "from all eternity." The expression in Greek "characterizes Christ as preexistent, thus defining the nature of his person" (Dana and Mantey). **was the Word**—Greek, *ho logos*, signifying primarily "the Expression"—God expressed, God explained, God defined (see 1:18). The Greek term *logos* in philosophical terminology also denoted the principle of the universe, even the creative energy that generated the universe (Morris). Thus, Christ as the *Logos* is the agent of and the personal expression of the Creator God. **the Word was with God**—The preposition translated "with" is *pros*. In Koine Greek *pros* (short for *prosopon pros prosopon*, "face to face") was used to show intimacy in personal relationships (see Matt. 13:56; 26:18; Mark 6:3; 14:49; 1 Cor. 13:12; 6:10; 2 Cor. 5:8; Gal. 1:18). Thus, for John to say "the Word was with God" was for him to mean "the Word was face to face with God" (see Williams's translation) or "the Word was having intimate fellowship with God." This speaks of the preincarnate Son's relationship with the Father prior to creation—in fact, prior to everything (see 1:18; 17:5, 24). **the Word was God**—The Greek clause underlying this clause stipulates, according to a rule of grammar, that "the Word" is the subject and "God" is the predicate nominative. Another particularity of the Greek is that the article is often used for defining individual identity and often absent in ascribing quality or character. In the previous clause ("the Word was with God"), there is an article before "God" (*ton theon*), thus pointing to God the Father; in this clause, there is no article before "God." The distinction, though a fine one, seems to be intended. In the previous clause, John indicates that the Son was with God, the Father; in this clause, John indicates that the Son was himself God (or should we say, deity) but not *the* God (i.e., God the Father). Therefore, some translators have attempted to bring out these distinctions by rendering the last clause as follows: "and what God was the Word was" (NEB) or "and he was the same as God" (TEV).

Thus, we see that John presents the Word as being eternal, as being with God (the Father), and as being himself God (or, deity). This is the One who became flesh and dwelt among men on earth.

**➤2 The same**—lit., "This one," the one just described in 1:1.

**➤3 All things were made by him**—is better rendered, "All things came into being through him" (NASB). The verse speaks of Christ's *instrumentality* in creation, not his authorship of it. God created *through* (Gk. *dia*) Christ, as is elsewhere affirmed in Scripture (1 Cor. 8:6; Col. 1:16; Heb. 1:2).

**➤4 In him was life**—Greek *zoe* in classical usage meant life in general, as that common element possessed by all living creatures. But John and the other NT writers took the word and uplifted its meaning to designate the eternal, divine life given to the believers. The NT writers were careful to distinguish this word from other words that mean life, such as *psuche*, the psychological life (see comments on 10:10, 11). **life was the light of men**—The divine life embodied in Christ illuminated the inner lives of men (cf. 8:12).

**➤5 shineth in darkness**—used metaphorically to describe unregenerated, fallen humanity (cf. Eph. 5:8). The divine light shined on darkened humanity (see Matt. 4:15, 16). **the darkness comprehended it not**—The Greek word (*katelaben*) in this context: (1) lay hold of, grasp, apprehend, comprehend; or (2) overcome, overpower. The darkness could not take the light in—i.e., men did not receive the light (1:9-11). Nevertheless, the light was not overpowered or conquered by the darkness.

**➤7 through him**—through John the Baptist. Jesus is the object of faith, John a vehicle through which people could believe in Christ.

**➤8 not that Light**—John was a lamp for the light (5:35), but not the light itself.

**➤9 lighteth every man that cometh into the world**—Most translators prefer to join the phrase "coming into the world" with "the true Light" and not with "every man" because John's prologue stresses the fact that the light came into the world.

**➤10 He was in the world**—i.e., in the habitat of mankind. **and the world was made by**

him—i.e., he was instrumental in creation of the universe and the men in it. **the world knew him not**—i.e., mankind did not recognize him. What tragic irony! (Note the three uses of "world": man's habitat, universe, mankind.)

►**11 his own**—neuter in Greek, "his own things" (property, possessions; hence, homeland). **and his own**—masculine in Greek, "his own people" (the Jews). **received him not**—speaking categorically of a national rejection.

►**12 But as many**—speaking of individuals. **as received him**—accepted him into their lives. **power**—authority and ability. **to become**—speaking of regeneration. **sons of God**—rather, children of God, speaking of a new, divine birth. **that believe**—indicates that belief is the means to regeneration. **on [in] his name**—i.e., in his person (in who and what he is, in all that is embodied in his person and work).

►**13 Which were born**—a sonship therefore not of mere title and privilege (as is conveyed in the word "adoption") but of nature; in short, an actual regeneration. **not of blood**—not of human descent. **nor of the will of the flesh**—not of human volition. **nor of the will of man**—not of a man's desire (or, a husband's desire). **but of God**—God himself is the unique source of each believer's regeneration.

►**14 And the Word**—continues the theme of the prologue and should therefore be connected with 1:1ff. and not directly with 1:13. **was made flesh**—is better translated "became flesh." The word "became" indicates a transformation process occurred. The Word, who is God, *became* what he never before was: man. **and dwelt**—lit., "tabernacled" or "pitched his tent." To the readers of this Gospel, the Greek word for "tabernacled" would have evoked the image of the OT tabernacle's being inhabited by God's shekinah glory. God in his glory tabernacled in the midst of his OT people. A new tabernacle was pitched among God's NT people: Jesus, God incarnate. The first believers **beheld** [gazed upon] **his glory.** His glory was special; he was the one and only Son come from the Father. And he was **full of grace and truth.** "Grace," a carryover from a Hebrew word for "loving-kindness," means "favor, kindness" and "gift that brings joy." Christ was full of grace—and truth, which means reality.

►**15** This verse, a parenthesis in the prologue, encapsulates John the Baptist's testimony concerning Jesus. In this testimony, John declares Christ's eternal existence (Mic. 5:2) and his preeminence. **is preferred before me: for he was before me**—i.e., Jesus has priority over me because he existed before me (see 8:58).

►**16** This verse, containing the words of John the apostle, continues the thought of the prologue, specifically 1:14. In 1:14 Jesus is said to be "full of grace and truth"; now John speaks of this fullness by way of personal testimony. He, speaking for all the apostles, received out of his fullness (cf. Col. 2:9). **grace for grace**—lit., "grace instead of grace," conveying the idea of continuous replacement, perpetual replenishment—one measure of grace replenishing the other in ever greater quantities.

►**17 grace and truth**—The two main elements of the NT economy are contrasted to the **law,** the main element of the OT economy. And note: the law **was given by Moses, but grace and truth came** [lit., "became"] **by Jesus Christ.** Moses gave something—the law. Christ himself brought something (grace and truth) in his very own person, for grace and truth were embodied in him.

►**18 No man hath seen God at any time**—i.e., no man has ever seen God *as God,* or known God *as God.* **the only begotten Son**—According to the earliest and best manuscripts (Papyrus Bodmer II [P66], Papyrus Bodmer XV [P75], Codex Sinaiticus, Codex Vaticanus), this should read "an only begotten, God." In 1:1, the word was called "God"; in 1:14 "an only begotten." Here, in 1:18 (the climax of the prologue), John combines the two appellations: "an only begotten, God." **in the bosom of the Father**—depicting the closeness of the Son to the Father. Their fellowship was eternally intimate (see comments on 1:1). **declared him**—lit., "explicated [him]." The Greek indicates Jesus was God's explainer, God's explicator, even God's exegete. The Greek word (*exēgeomai*) means "to narrate, to draw out, to lead through." Christ came to narrate God, to draw out the meaning of God, and to lead men, so to speak, on a tour through God. In short, he came to make God known to men. He was uniquely qualified to do this because (1) he himself was God; (2) he was God's one and only Son; and (3) he was in the bosom of the Father (i.e., he had the most intimate relationship with him). This verse 1:18 mirrors 1:1 and provides a grand climax to John's prologue.

## 19-34 THE TESTIMONY OF
## JOHN THE BAPTIST

➤**19 this is the record of John**—As the man whom God prepared to be the forerunner of Christ, John the Baptist was a truly effective witness to the Lamb of God. In statement after statement John disavowed any personal status and glorified Christ instead (1:15-18, 20, 21, 23, 26, 27, 29-34). John pointed out Christ's timelessness and preeminence (1:15).

➤**20, 21 he . . . confessed, I am not the Christ**—John rejected any suggestion that he himself was Israel's long-awaited Messiah, or the "Elijah" prophesied in Malachi 4:5, 6 (cf. 2 Kings 2:11), or the "Prophet" promised in Deuteronomy 18:15-19 (cf. John 6:14; 7:40). He had come in the spirit of Elijah (Luke 1:17) to prepare the way for the Messiah.

➤**23** In response to the priests' insistent questioning, John identified himself simply as the long-awaited **voice . . . in the wilderness** mentioned in Isaiah 40:3-5 (cf. Mal. 3:1a). With this identification, John presented himself as the Messiah's forerunner and herald.

➤**25 Why baptizest thou then . . . ?**—Since the Jewish priests and Pharisees were very credential conscious, they wanted to know what right John had to proselytize people through baptism (long recognized as an important symbol of change in religious convictions).

➤**26, 27 I baptise with water: but there standeth one among you . . . who coming after me is preferred before me**—John replied by de-emphasizing his own baptizing ministry (though it was an important symbol of repentance in God's sight—see Matt. 3:1-12; 21:32; Acts 19:4) and exalting the Spirit-baptizing ministry of Jesus, the true Messiah (1:26-33).

➤**28 Bethabara**—in some ancient manuscripts, but all the earliest manuscripts read, "Bethany." This Bethany is distinguished from the one near Jerusalem as being "beyond the Jordan."

➤**29 Behold the Lamb of God**—To help validate Christ's Messiahship in the eyes of the skeptical religious leaders, John pointed out Christ as the Lamb of God. To the Jews this was a very significant title, pregnant with OT imagery—of the passover lamb (Exod. 12), the lambs for the burnt offering (Exod. 29:38-46), and the sacrificial lamb (Isa. 53). **taketh away the sin**—or, "takes up [bears] the sin." The image could be that of disposal of sin or of bearing sin (as in Isa. 53). **of the world**—not just of Israel. The Lamb took upon him all the sin of the world.

➤**30** See comments on 1:15.

➤**31 knew him not**—John and Jesus, though relatives, lived at a distance from one another: John in the desert and Jesus in Nazareth. John knew that he was the herald of the Messiah, but he did not know Jesus was that Messiah until God gave him a sign—the descent of the Spirit upon Jesus.

➤**32, 33 the Spirit descending**—anointing Jesus for his ministry (Isa. 61:1; Luke 4:18). This One would baptize in the Holy Spirit.

➤**34 the Son of God**—A few early manuscripts read, "the chosen One of God."

## 35-51 THE FIRST GATHERING
## OF DISCIPLES

➤**36 Behold the Lamb of God!**—Though the religious leaders rejected John's testimony about Christ, many of the common people were not so skeptical. Within two days, four people had acknowledged Jesus' Messiahship through his own manifestation and the witness of John (1:35-51). Each of the four men responded to Christ in a slightly different way, showing that the one Lord Jesus Christ is accessible to every human need and every kind of personality.

➤**37 the two disciples**—of John the Baptist, who then became disciples of Jesus Christ. One of the disciples is named—Andrew, Simon Peter's brother (1:40); and the other is left unnamed, though undoubtedly it is the author of this Gospel—John.

➤**38-41 Andrew**—inquired about the personal life of Christ (1:38) and was so impressed by what he saw that he not only acknowledged Jesus as his own Messiah but persuaded his brother **Simon** [Peter] to also evaluate this unique person. Peter apparently received Jesus also, but in his case the call of Christ is given the greater emphasis.

➤**42 Simon . . . thou shalt be called Cephas, . . . A stone**—Jesus changed Simon's name to "Cephas" (Aramaic for "stone"). The

Greek translation is *petros* (stone). See comments on Matthew 16:18.

➤**43, 44 Philip**—was found by Christ and called by Christ to follow him.

➤**45-48 of whom Moses in the law, and the prophets, did write**—Moses had written about him in the law (see Deut. 18:15-18), and the prophets had foretold his coming. **Jesus of Nazareth, the son of Joseph**—the current way of speaking. Nathaniel's skepticism was overcome by a simple demonstration of omniscience on the part of Christ. Jesus told Nathaniel that he saw him **under the fig tree**— a euphemism for studying God's Scriptures. Nathaniel, no doubt, had been studying the Scriptures concerning the Messiah. Jesus said there was **no guile** in Nathaniel—that is, there was no deceit, cunning, or falsehood in him.

➤**49** Seeing a demonstration of Jesus' prescience and omniscience, Nathaniel called him **Son of God** (a description of the Messiah in Ps. 2:7) and **King of Israel** (also a description of the Messiah in Ps. 2:6; cf. Zeph. 3:15).

➤**51 ye shall see heaven open, and the angels of God ascending and descending upon the Son of man**—To a reader of the OT, the allusion would be plain. Jesus used Jacob's vision of the ladder connecting heaven to earth (Gen. 25:12-22) to point to himself as the real vehicle of communication between heaven and earth, divinity and humanity.

*Chapter* **2**

**1-12 CHRIST'S FIRST PUBLIC MIRACLE**

➤**1, 2 there was a marriage . . . the mother of Jesus was there . . . Jesus . . . and his disciples**—Unlike John the Baptist, who was called to a lonely and austere life (Mark 1:3-6), Christ identified himself with human society in every legitimate activity (cf. Luke 7:31-36). Jesus' presence at a wedding implied his unspoken approval of this God-ordained relationship. (Compare Christ's comments about marriage in Matthew 5:31, 32; 19:3-9.)

➤**3** When the supply of **wine** ran out, Mary the mother of Jesus apparently remembered the announced destiny of her son (Luke 1:26-56; 2:8-19) as well as his uniquely sinless human history and sensed that Jesus could alleviate the wine shortage miraculously if he chose to.

➤**4 Woman**—not a term of disrespect in those days (see 19:26). **mine hour is not yet come**—This phrase is used frequently in John (7:30, 39; 12:23, 24; 17:1) to designate the hour of Christ's glorification through death and resurrection. The occasion was premature for the commencement of Christ's ministry of miracles, but in response to his mother's faith (2:5) Jesus performed the desired miracles anyway as a preview of his coming glory. As with most of the miracles described throughout Scripture, Christ performed the necessary supernatural act with a minimum of fanfare or extravagance. God receives greater glory through quiet displays of divine power than through superficial showmanship.

➤**8-11** That Christ's miracle was genuine is attested by the **governor of the feast** (the master of ceremonies) and the fortified faith of Christ's recently-called **disciples** (cf.1:41-49). These men **believed** that this unique Person who could call them almost irresistibly (1:42, 43) and turn water into wine by a simple act of will must truly be God's heaven-sent Messiah. **manifested forth his glory**—Jesus' act of changing water into wine was a display of glory, and yet this display was but a preview of the glory he would manifest in resurrection. Then "his hour" would finally come, and then he could change every dying situation into a living one. The miracle of changing water into wine was a foretaste of what was to come when his hour of glorification would come.

**13-25 CHRIST CLEANSES THE TEMPLE**

➤**13 And the Jews' passover was at hand, and Jesus went up to Jerusalem**—The four Gospel accounts indicate that Christ attended every one of the official Jewish festivals in spite of the widespread hypocrisy and commercialism that accompanied them.

➤**14-16 he drove them all out of the temple**—Because Christ still regarded the Jewish temple in Jerusalem as **"my Father's house"** (cf. Luke 2:49), he exercised his prerogative as the "Son over his own house" (Heb. 3:6) to rid the outer courtyard **of the temple** (called *hieron* in Gk.) of greedy merchants and money-changers. His effectiveness in cleansing the sacred area of commercialism lay not so much in his small rope whip as in the intrinsic power of his spoken command. Jesus' cleansing of the temple was a partial fulfillment of Malachi 3:1-4.

►**17, 18** Both Christ's disciples and his critics sensed his supernatural authority, for the disciples recalled the messianic tone of Psalm 69:9, "zeal for your house consumes me" (NIV), while the critics demanded some further supernatural **sign.**

►**19 Destroy this temple**—Greek, *naos* (the inner sanctuary), as compared to *hieron* (the outer courtyard, the temple proper), used in 2:15. This saying was used against Jesus at his trial, but his accusers twisted his words (see Mark 14:58, 59). He did not say that he would destroy the temple, but that they would destroy him. **and in three days I will raise it up**— referring to his own authority over his resurrection (see 10:18). Thus, Christ employed veiled symbolism to offer the greatest sign of all—his eventual resurrection after three days in the grave.

►**20 Forty and six years**—From the eighteenth year of Herod until then was just forty-six years (see Josephus's *Antiquities,* 15.11.1).

►**21 temple of his body**—in which was enshrined the glory of the eternal Word. Jesus, indwelt by God, house on earth (see comments on 1:14). Through resurrection, the true temple of God would be set up on earth. So the allusion is not quite exclusively to himself, but may take in that temple of which he is the foundation, and all the believers are living stones (1 Pet. 2:4, 5).

►**22 they believed the scripture**—not an isolated passage, but the OT at large as it testifies to Christ's resurrection (e.g., Ps. 2:7; 16:9, 10; Isa. 25:8). **and the word**—the specific word concerning his death and resurrection in three days. Jesus' disciples eventually understood the meaning of Christ's strange prediction, but the obdurate Jewish leaders misinterpreted Christ's words as he spoke them (2:20) and disbelieved them even after they had been fulfilled (Matt. 28:11-15). The incident shows that faith in Christ depends more on inner attitudes than on intellectual conclusions, important as these can be.

►**23-25 many believed in his name . . . but Jesus did not commit himself unto them**—These verses show that the intellectually persuaded supporters of Christ were not truly his followers at all. The word-play John uses here brings this out; they are said to believe in him (or, trust in him), but Jesus would not commit himself (or, entrust himself) to them. In both instances, John plays upon the one Greek word, *pisteuō.* In any case, Jesus would not entrust himself to these men because he knew that what is in man can not always be trusted (see Jer. 17:9, 10).

*Chapter* **3**

## JESUS WITH NICODEMUS

►**1 Nicodemus**—Though most of the Jewish leaders scoffed at the words and works of Christ throughout his entire earthly ministry, a few religionists exercised the spiritual and intellectual honesty to approach Christ with a sincerely inquisitive attitude. Nicodemus was one of these. He has often been criticized for his secretive, nighttime rendezvous with Christ, but the fact remains that Nicodemus did come to hear and receive, as his later actions affirm (John 7:50, 51; 19:39).

►**2 a teacher come from God**—Nicodemus opened his interview with words of praise, but Jesus replied with a startling and humbling edict of new birth.

►**3 Except a man be born again**—born anew, born from above. The language describes an infusion of new, divine life which then causes a revolution in the person's entire life. Without this birth, a person cannot perceive the things in the spiritual realm, called **the kingdom of God.**

►**5 born of water and of the Spirit**—The "water" of this verse could refer to the OT symbol for inner spiritual cleansing (Ezek. 36:25-27), or to Holy Scripture as "the water of the Word" (Eph. 5:25, 26), or to John the Baptist's water of repentance (Matt. 3:11, 12; Mark 1:4, 5; Acts 13:24; 19:1-5). Most early Christian expositors held this last interpretation. But, according to the Greek, the new birth is said to be "of water and Spirit" (one experience with two aspects, as is designated by one preposition governing two nouns). Therefore, the "water" could very well signify the cleansing and life-imparting action of the Spirit (cf. 7:37-39). Thus, the Spirit brings about regeneration and inward cleansing simultaneously—the idea of a "washing of regeneration" (Titus 3:5).

➤**6 That which is born of the flesh is flesh**—flesh begets its own kind: flesh. **born of the Spirit is spirit**—the Spirit begets its own kind: spirit. The divine Spirit generates a new spirit in the believer (see Ezek. 36:26, 27).

➤**7 ye**—plural (not just Nicodemus, but all those Jews, of whom Nicodemus was here the representative). **must be born again**—or anew, from above.

➤**8 wind . . . Spirit**—are the same word in Greek: *pneuma*. We could also add "breath" as a word which translates *pneuma*. All three words are used to describe the revitalization of the dead bones in Ezekiel 37, a passage which Jesus alluded to here and apparently expected Nicodemus to understand (3:10). God's Spirit is like wind and like breath; it has free movement and vivification power. **so is everyone that is born of the Spirit**—"The believer shows by deed and word that an invisible influence has moved and inspired him. He is himself a continual sign of the action of the Spirit, which is freely determined, and incomprehensible by man as to source and end, though seen in its present result" (Westcott).

➤**10 a master**—lit., "the teacher." **knowest not these things?**—How could the teacher of Israel be ignorant of what the OT said about regeneration? It is spoken of in Ezekiel 36:26, 27; 37:1-14. But since Nicodemus did not grasp this allusion, Jesus turned to another OT passage—a quite familiar one: the pericope concerning the brass serpent (see comments on 3:14).

➤**11 we speak that we do know, and testify that we have seen**—Jesus was probably referring to himself and the Father, who acted in one accord. **ye receive not**—speaking of the Jews' obdurateness.

➤**12 how shall ye believe?**—The plural pronoun indicates that Jesus was speaking to Nicodemus as if Nicodemus represented the Jews (see comments on 3:7).

➤**13 no man hath ascended up to heaven, but he that came down from heaven, even the Son of man which is in heaven**—In many early manuscripts the last clause is omitted. However, it is generally thought that this statement was deleted very early in the transmission of the text because of the difficulty it presents—namely, how could Christ be located in heaven and earth simultaneously? Taking the last clause as genu-

inely Johannine, we can understand it to mean that Christ, while on earth, still had his being, his nature, even his habitation with the Father in heaven.

➤**14, 15** Jesus provided Nicodemus with another illustration from the OT (Num. 21:6-9), this time a very clear one (see comments on 3:13). Jesus compares his being **lifted up** on the cross to **Moses'** lifting up of **the serpent** on the pole. As the lifted-up serpent became the remedy for those rebellious, serpent-bitten Israelites who looked upon the brass serpent for deliverance, so Christ, lifted up on the cross, becomes the cure for sin and death to those who believe in him. Numbers 21:6-9 declares "look and live"; John 3:14-16 declares "believe and live." As the brass serpent was in the likeness of the fiery serpents (it did not contain the poison they possessed), so Christ came in the likeness of sinful flesh (he did not have any sin in him)—see Romans 8:3; 2 Corinthians 5:21. A look at the brass serpent brought life to those who were perishing; faith in Jesus brings eternal life to those who would otherwise perish forever.

➤**16 For God so loved the world, that he gave his only begotten Son**—This verse continues the thought of 3:14, 15 and summarizes it. How often has this verse been proclaimed! It is the gospel in a nutshell! It speaks of God's great love (*so* loved) for mankind (**the world**); so much so, that he **gave** "his one and only Son" (see NIV)—i.e., he gave him over to be crucified (see Rom. 8:32), so that everyone who **believeth in him** (the crucified Savior) would **not perish** (suffer eternal destruction) but **have** (here and now, as well as in the future) **everlasting** (eternal) **life.**

➤**18-21** Christ then closed his conversation with some very sobering words, which declare that all unbelievers are condemned in the sight of God until they believe in Christ and receive the light. (Note: some commentators think 3:16-21 are John's words, not Jesus'; but this is difficult to defend. Besides, some of the earliest manuscripts that contain paragraph breaks show a new paragraph beginning at 3:22, not 3:16.)

➤**22-24** Both John and Jesus (rather, Jesus' disciples) were baptizing as a symbol of repentance in two separate locations at the same time, showing the unity of Master and servant in the proclamation of the gospel message. **Aenon near to Salim**—on the west side of the Jordan.

➤**25, 26 Jews**—should read "Jew," according to the best manuscripts. The argument was **about purifying**—concerning baptism, the symbolic means of purification. When **John's disciples** told John that Christ's baptism was becoming more popular than his own, the godly prophet of repentance responded with a torrent of praise for the man who was eclipsing him (3:27-36). He did not share their competitive spirit.

➤**27, 28** John realized that a man can do nothing if it has not been **given** [to] **him from heaven.** In the divine plan, John was but the Messiah's forerunner and herald. Once the One heralded arrives, all eyes naturally (and rightly) go to him. The heralder must of necessity fade into the background.

➤**29** John compared Christ to a **bridegroom** at a gala oriental wedding and himself as a **friend** merely standing in the shadow of the honored guest. Christ's **bride** is the church, the holy people of God (see 2 Cor. 11:2; Eph. 5:25-32; Rev. 19:7; 21:2); she belongs only to him.

➤**30 He must increase, but I must decrease.**—John the Baptist realized that Jesus' following would increase, while his own would decrease. That was as it should be. At any rate, these words form a truly fitting motto for every aspiring servant of Christ.

➤**31-36** Then John burst forth into a glowing eulogy concerning the Savior from heaven, pointing out that the One who is filled with heavenly truth, endued with the limitless power of the Spirit, and endowed with all the Father's love and honors is certainly worthy of our faith. To receive him is to enjoy eternal life now and forever, and to reject him is to endure the just anger of God for eternity.

*Chapter* 4

## 1-42 JESUS AND THE WOMAN OF SAMARIA

➤**1 the Lord**—in most of the early manuscripts, but a few ancient manuscripts read, "Jesus."

➤**2 (Though Jesus himself baptized not, but his disciples.)**—This parenthetical remark emphasizes that it was Jesus' function to bap-

tize with the Holy Spirit (1:33), not water. The apostles, here as later (after Pentecost), performed water baptisms.

➤**3, 4 He left Judaea and departed again into Galilee**—See comments on 4:43, 44. Christ could easily have persevered in baptizing despite the rising tide of Pharisaic hostility (4:1), but he chose to defer an all-out confrontation with the Jewish leaders until the divinely appointed moment (18:1-12). Instead, our Lord embarked on one of the most touching missionary journeys of his entire earthly career. Shunning the usual easterly route which skirted despised Samaria, Jesus traveled directly into the heartland of the racially mongrel territory (4:3, 4). (The Samaritans were part-Jews who had returned from the Northern captivity with Assyrian and perhaps other Gentile intermarriages. They worshiped at Mount Gerizim [see Deut. 11:26-29; 27:1-8] instead of Jerusalem, rejected all the Hebrew Scriptures except the Pentateuch, and incorporated certain forms of idolatry into their worship of Jehovah. For these reasons strict Jews ostracized the Samaritans completely.)

➤**5 the parcel of ground that Jacob gave to his son Joseph**—The well was on a piece of land that was Joseph's gift from Jacob (see Gen. 33:19; 48:22; Josh. 24:32). Perhaps John mentioned that the land was a gift as a foreshadowing to Jesus' following statement concerning "the gift of God" in 4:10.

➤**6** Then our weary and human Lord sat on historic Jacob's well in the hot noonday sun (**the sixth hour**) before meeting the Samaritan woman.

➤**7-9** To break the communication barrier based on racial-religious bias between **Jews and Samaritans,** Jesus asked the **woman** for a simple favor: **give me to drink. the Jews have no dealings with the Samaritans**—lit., "the Jews do not share [things] in common with the Samaritans." In context, this statement could indicate that it was against Jewish custom to use a Samaritan's utensil—such as a bucket (see TEV, NIV mg.). For Jesus to drink from a Samaritan's bucket would violate Jewish custom. Thus, the Samaritan woman was startled by Jesus' request.

➤**10 the gift of God**—is Christ himself as living water. Christ followed his perfect approach with a startling offer to the now attentive woman: **living water** for the asking.

►**11, 12** The woman first misunderstood Christ's gracious offer; but after a few words of explanation from the master Teacher (4:13, 14), the spiritually thirsty woman recognized that Christ was offering exactly what she needed.

►**14 shall never thirst**—i.e., shall never need to go thirsty because **the water that I shall give him shall be** [become] **in him a well** [fountain] **of water springing up into everlasting** [eternal] **life**—the springing up of the water provides the drink of life. This inner well is none other than the indwelling Spirit of Christ (see 7:37-39).

►**16 Go, call thy husband**—One crucial hindrance stood in the way of the Samaritan woman's reception of Christ's living water: she was harboring unconfessed sin and an unrepentant heart (cf. Matt. 3:1-6, 11, 12).

►**17, 18 thou hast had five husbands; and he whom thou now hast is not thy husband**— So Christ exposed her sin with gentle candor.

►**19, 20** The woman parried by diverting the discussion from a personal exposé to a current religious controversy, but Jesus seized the opportunity to define the true worship of God and to expose the futility of ignorant Samaritan worship. **Our fathers worshipped in this mountain**—The Samaritans worshiped on Mount Gerizim (see comments on 4:3, 4). **ye say**—the Jews say. **in Jerusalem**—which, in fact, was the one appointed place of worship.

►**22 salvation is of the Jews**—salvation comes from the Jews; i.e., the Savior providing salvation would be a Jew, from Jewish heritage and lineage.

►**23 worship the Father in spirit**—This corresponds to the place of worship, which would not be in Gerizim or Jerusalem, but in man's spirit. **and in truth**—This contrasts with the falsehood of the Samaritans' worship and their ignorance of the scriptural truths (4:22).

►**24 God is a Spirit**—is better translated "God is Spirit." Since God is himself Spirit and Spirit is his nature, he must be worshiped in (and by) the realm (or medium) that is akin to his nature—namely, man's spirit. There is one part of man's being—his human spirit—that corresponds to God's nature and can even be united to God (see 1 Cor. 6:17; Rom. 8:16). **in**

**truth**—in reality, and with proper knowledge concerning the truth in God's Word.

►**25 I know that Messias cometh**—Though ignorant of many scriptural truths, this Samaritan woman did know that the Messiah was coming; and it appears that she was expecting his coming.

►**26 I . . . am he**—Jesus rarely told his own people this. To the Jews, he proved his Messiahship by his deeds; to this simple Samaritan he plainly stated that he was the Christ. His frank words of truth apparently produced the necessary repentance in the heart of his hearer, for she thereupon acknowledged her need for a coming Messiah (4:25) and subsequently acknowledged Christ's forthright self-identification as that very person (4:28, 29). The episode of the Samaritan woman shows that all of us need and can have the living water of eternal life if we turn to Christ in repentance and faith. No human being, no matter how sinful or despised, is ineligible for the redeeming grace of God poured out through the Lord Jesus Christ (cf. Mark 2:17; Rom. 5:6-10; Eph. 2:1-19).

►**27 And upon this came his disciples**— The disciples had gone into town to buy food while Jesus sat alone at Jacob's well (4:8), and they were surprised to find him talking with a woman, especially a Samaritan, when they returned.

►**28 The woman then left her waterpot, and went her way into the city**—The presence of strangers made her feel that it was time for her to withdraw, and he who knew her heart, and what she was going to the city to do, let her go without exchanging a word with her in the hearing of others.

►**29 is not this the Christ?**—The form of the question in the Greek (which expects a negative answer) is a modest way of only half-insinuating what it seemed hardly fitting for her to affirm.

►**34 My meat** [food] **is to do the will of him that sent me**—The conversion of a needy sinner had been food for Christ's soul, and he used the occasion to impart some of his own missionary urgency into the hearts of his disciples.

►**35, 36 they are white already to harvest**—Jesus realized that the Samaritans were ripe for the harvest; they were ready, like sheaves of wheat, to be brought into the experience of obtaining eternal life—just like grain is brought into the granary (which explains the statement, **gathereth fruit unto** [into] **life eternal.** (Cf. Matt. 13:30; Luke 3:17.)

➤**37 And herein is that saying true, One soweth, and another reapeth.**—This is a paraphrase taken from verses like Deuteronomy 6:11; Job. 31:8; Micah 6:15.

➤**38 I sent you to reap**—The Samaritans were ready to be harvested. So the Lord of the harvest sent his disciples to reap them in. **other men laboured**—referring to the OT prophets (specifically the writings of Moses) and John the Baptist. **ye are entered into their labours**—After the church began, the gospel went to the Samaritans—and there was a great harvest (see Acts 1:8; 8:1; 9:3). Even then, many in that Samaritan village believed that Jesus was the Messiah. Verses 37 and 38 stress the important principle that many witnesses are often involved in the conversion of a single soul, with the final witness often doing the least work. All credit for conversions should therefore await God's perfect evaluation.

➤**39-42** While Christ was talking to his disciples, the Samaritan woman forgot her water-drawing chore and rushed into the nearby village with the good news of the long-promised Messiah (4:28, 29). The village people responded to the enthusiastic words of Christ's first woman missionary by streaming out of the village to see this unique Man for themselves (4:30; cf. 4:39). After seeing Christ and hearing his words of grace and truth, large numbers of the despised Samaritans believed in Jesus as the Messiah and received eternal life. The missionary zeal of the Samaritan woman and the willing response of her compatriots is sadly ironic in its condemnation of the many privileged Jews who heard Christ for nearly three years but rejected him to the very moment of his crucifixion (Matt. 27:20-25, 39-43). The faith of the Samaritans is doubly ironic because millions of sophisticated people today persist in refusing the one Person who can rescue them from the eternal wrath of God (cf. John 3:18-20, 36).

43-54 JESUS AND THE RULER
OF CAPERNAUM
➤**43, 44 went into Galilee . . . For Jesus himself testified, that a prophet hath no honour in his own country**—This can be understood in two ways: (1) Jesus returned to the general region of Galilee, though not to his home town of Nazareth, since a prophet is honored everywhere except in his own country (cf. Mark 6:4; Luke 4:22-27), or (2) Jesus purposely returned to a region in which he knew he would be rejected. His popularity had been growing, so he needed to take an action which would restrain this. (John 4:1-3 tells us that Jesus left Judea to go to Galilee because he knew that the Pharisees were aware that he was gaining more disciples than John had.)

➤**45** The Galileans at large **received** [welcomed] Christ warmly on the basis of his earlier miracles **at Jerusalem** during **the feast** (cf. John 2:23). (Note, however, that their warm welcome was not necessarily synonymous with genuine faith—John 2:24, 25.)

➤**46, 47 a certain nobleman**—"a certain royal official" (NIV), a courtier, king's servant, or one connected with the royal household. After Christ arrived in Cana, a government official from Capernaum met him with a desperate plea for help: would the Master come and heal his dying son?

➤**48** Jesus replied with a strange answer: "Unless you people [i.e., the Je7ws] see signs and wonders, . . . you will never believe" (NIV). The Jews' insistence on seeing a sign blinded them to the fact that the greatest of all signs—God incarnate in Jesus Christ—was present among them.

➤**49-54** The penetrating test of the ruler's sincerity was met with a renewed plea: "Sir, come down before my child dies" (NIV). Sensing the ruler's genuine faith, Christ met his essential need in an even more immediate way than the ruler had requested (4:50). Christ's analysis of the man's faith proved correct, for the ruler started home with an inner assurance based solely on the words of Christ (4:50). This is the kind of faith God appreciates the most highly and rewards the most richly (John 20:29; Heb. 11:1-3). The ruler's faith was soon rewarded bountifully with the good news of his son's recovery (4:51, 52), and this dramatic confirmation of faith resulted in wholehearted reception of Christ by both the ruler and his entire household (4:53). "What is faith? It is the confident assurance that something we want is going to happen. It is the certainty that what we hope for is waiting for us even though we cannot see it up ahead" (Heb. 11:1, TLB).

# Chapter 5

## 1-14 CHRIST'S HEALING OF THE LAME MAN AT BETHESDA POOL

➤**1 a feast of the Jews**—perhaps the Passover.

➤**2 a pool . . . called in the Hebrew tongue Bethesda**—"house of mercy," named for the cures performed there. The "Bethesda Pool" is probably the pool rediscovered in 1888 near Saint Anne's Church in Jerusalem.

➤**3b, 4** The last half of verse 3 and all of verse 4 are absent from all the earliest Greek manuscripts, suggesting that these words were probably a well-intended gloss added by some early copyist (cf. 5:7).

➤**5-9 And a certain man was there, which had an infirmity thirty and eight years.**—Christ deliberately chose one of the most dramatically helpless sufferers in the waiting throng in order to display the limitless power and grace of God. And he deliberately healed him on the Sabbath (5:9) in order to expose the heartless hypocrisy of the Jewish leaders (5:10-12, 16, 18). The miraculously cured invalid played an almost passive role in the entire episode, serving mostly as a catalyst for the Jewish leaders' violent reaction to the love of Christ.

➤**14** Yet Jesus was personally interested in the invalid too, for he not only healed him (5:8) but searched him out in the crowded temple courtyard to warn him against the recurring judgment of God. The miracle and its aftermath show that all circumstances of life, including calamities, can eventuate in the glory of God.

## 15-47 CHRIST'S ANSWER TO HIS JEWISH CRITICS

➤**16 the Jews persecute[d] Jesus . . . because he had done these things on the Sabbath day**—The Sabbath had of course been ordained by God as a very holy day for all Jewish people (Exod. 20:8-11; 31:12-17; Deut. 5:12-14). But the Jewish leaders had long since lost any spiritual understanding of God's law and were simply interested in over-enforcing its mechanical requirements. Nor were they content to misinterpret the law themselves; they bitterly attacked anyone who presumed to violate their harsh traditions by glorifying God with works of mercy on the Sabbath (5:10, 12, 16, 18; cf. Matt. 12:1-14; Luke 13:10-17; 14:1-6;

John 9:1-16). The reason Christ condemned this cruelty so strongly is that these Jewish leaders were misrepresenting the nature of God to the common people. The Pharisees were depicting God as a cruel, austere tyrant who became enraged at trifles, while Jesus revealed God to all the world as an infinitely compassionate Father who poured out his wrath for mankind's sins on the suffering Savior at Calvary.

➤**17 My Father worketh hitherto, and I work**—In verse 17 Christ defended his ministry on the basis of his personal relationship to the Father in heaven, and the Jewish leaders immediately condemned this obvious claim to deity and Messiahship.

➤**18 he . . . said also that God was his Father, making himself equal with God**—The Jews realized that in his calling God "my Father" (5:17) Jesus was saying: "I am God's Son, equal to God." In other words, for Jesus to say that God himself was his very own Father was to make himself equal to the very God. (The Greek verifies this interpretation because both times the word for "God" is preceded by an article—so rendered literally "the God," i.e., the very God or God himself.) This was unthinkable to the Jews; in fact, it was outright blasphemy. From that day onward, they sought to kill him.

➤**19 these also doeth the Son likewise**—Instead of rescinding his strong claim in the face of the leaders' hostility, Christ bolstered his assertion of deity with claims of absolute harmony between him and the Father, thus asserting absolute equality (see Phil. 2:6).

➤**20 Father loveth . . . and showeth him all**—As love has no concealments, so it results from the perfect fellowship and mutual endearment of the Father and the Son (see comments on 1:1, 18), whose interests are one, even as is their nature. The Father communicates to the Son all his counsels, and what has been thus shown to the Son is executed by him in his mediatorial character. "With the Father, **doing** is *willing;* it is only the Son who *acts in time*" (Alford). Three things here are clear: (1) the personal distinctions in the Godhead; (2) unity of action among the Persons resulting from unity of nature; and (3) that their oneness of interest is no unconscious or involuntary thing, but a thing of glorious consciousness, will, and love.

**▶21** In the following verses (21-30) Jesus describes how he and the Father work together in raising the dead, imparting life, and executing judgment. Jesus, as the Son of man (his Messianic title carrying strong associations with judgment—Dan. 7:13, 14), exercised his divine prerogative to give life and to execute judgment. **raiseth up the dead, and quickeneth them**—one act in two stages. This is his absolute right as God. **so the Son quickeneth**—i.e., raiseth up and quickeneth. **whom he will**—not only doing the same divine act, but doing it as the result of his own will, even as the Father does it. This statement is of immense importance in relation to the miracles of Christ, distinguishing them from similar miracles of prophets and apostles, who as human instruments were employed to perform supernatural actions, while Christ did all as the Father's commissioned Servant indeed, but in the exercise of his own absolute right of action.

**▶22 For the Father judgeth no man**—rather, "For neither doth the Father judge any man," implying that the same thing was meant in the former verse of the quickening of the dead—both acts being done, not by the Father and the Son, as though twice done, but by the Father through the Son as his voluntary Agent. **all judgment**—judgment in its most comprehensive sense, or as we should say, all administration.

**▶23 honour the Son . . . as they honour the Father**—As he who believes that Christ in the foregoing verses has given a true account of his relation to the Father must of necessity hold him entitled to the same honor as the Father, so he here adds that it was the Father's express intention in giving all judgment to the Son that men should thus honor him.

**▶24 believeth on him that sent me**—i.e., believe in him as having sent me. **hath everlasting** [eternal] **life**—immediately on his believing (cf. 3:18; 1 John 5:12, 13). **is passed**—"has passed over" from death unto life. What a transition! (Cf. 1 John 3:14.)

**▶25 the dead**—the spiritually dead, as is clear from 5:28. Here Jesus rises from the calmer phrase "hearing his word" (5:24) to the grander expression "hearing the voice of the Son of God" to signify that as it finds men in a dead condition, so it carries with it a resurrection-power. **shall live**—in the sense of 5:24.

**▶26 the Son to have life in himself**—Does this refer to the essential life of the Son before all time (1:4) or to the purpose of God that this essential life should reside in the person of the incarnate Son and be manifested thus to the world? The question is as difficult as the subject is high. In his essential relationship with the Father, the Son possessed the same essential divine life; in his economical relationship, he has the authority to impart this life to men.

**▶27 because he is the Son of man**—This seems to confirm the last remark, that the life Jesus was referring to was the indwelling of the Son's essential life in humanity as the medium of divine dispensation to humanity, in both the great departments of his work—lifegiving and judgment. The appointment of a judge in our own nature is one of the most beautiful arrangements of divine wisdom in redemption.

**▶28 Marvel not at this**—this committal of all judgment to the Son of man. **for the hour is coming**—He adds not in this case (as in 5:25) "and now is" because this was not to be until the close of the whole dispensation of grace.

**▶29 resurrection of life**—i.e., to life everlasting (Matt. 25:46). **of damnation**—lit. "of judgment." The resurrection of both classes is an exercise of sovereign authority; but in the one case it is an act of grace, in the other of judgment. (Cf. Dan. 12:2, from which the language is taken.) How awfully grand are these unfoldings of his dignity and authority from the mouth of Christ himself! And they are all in the third person; in what follows he resumes the first person.

**▶30 of mine own self do nothing**—i.e., apart from the Father, or in any interest of my own. (See comments on 5:19.)

**▶31 witness**—The Lord now concludes his defense by providing the Jews with a five-fold witness. They had questioned his authority and assaulted his identity. In response, Jesus indicated that he had five very reliable witnesses: (1) John the Baptist (5:33-35), (2) his own works (5:36), (3) the Father himself (5:37), (4) the Scriptures (5:39, 40), and (5) Moses (5:45-47). All these witnesses were accessible to the Jews.

**▶33-35 He was a burning and a shining light**—lit., "lamp" (through which the light—Christ—shined). John the Baptist, that burning and shining lamp, pointed the Jews to Jesus the Christ.

**➤36 I have greater witness . . . the works**—Cf. 15:24.

**➤37 the Father himself . . . hath borne witness of me**—probably not the voice at Christ's baptism, but (as seems from what follows) to the testimony of the OT Scriptures (see 8:47). **Ye have neither heard his voice at any time, nor seen his shape**—God, as Spirit, is invisible; the Son, Jesus Christ, is his visible expression (see comments on 1:18).

**➤38 ye have not his word abiding in you**—They had the Scriptures—but only outwardly, for they did not indwell them (see 8:37).

**➤39 Search the scriptures**—or, you research the Scriptures. They researched the Scriptures daily, looking for statements about the coming Messiah. And yet they rejected him when he came. They thought their study of the Word would give them life, when actually their study should have pointed them to the living One who alone can give life (5:40).

**➤40-43 ye will not come to me, that ye might have life**—The tragic irony of the Jewish leaders' rejection of Christ lay in their willful inability to identify Jesus as the Messiah despite their professed expertise in the OT Scriptures (5:39, 40, 45-47).

**➤44 How can ye believe, which receive honour [glory] one of another**—Instead of welcoming Christ with open arms, the Jewish leaders banded together to flatter each other with pompous religious honors while at the same time rejecting the true Messiah from heaven. **honour [glory] that cometh from God only**—The three earliest manuscripts (Bodmer Papyri II and XV [P66 and P75] and Codex Vaticanus) read, "glory from the only One" or "glory from the unique One."

**➤45 there is one that accuseth you, even Moses**—For these Jews to be accused by Moses, the object of all their religious boastings, would be a hard blow. **in whom ye trust**—lit., "in whom you have hoped." To hope in Moses was to hope in what Moses gave—namely, the law (see Rom. 2:17). But the law cannot give life; rather, it condemns.

**➤46 he wrote of me**—Moses wrote about the Messiah specifically in Deuteronomy 18:15-18, and typologically in connection with Christ being the antitype of the brass serpent,

manna, and smitten rock (see comments on 3:14, 15; 6:32ff.; 7:37-39—all of which have connections with the Pentateuch written by Moses).

**➤47 his writings . . . my words**—The two are compatible, not contradictory, as the Jews mistakenly thought. By rejecting Jesus' words they would be rejecting Moses' writings and witness to him (Bruce).

*Chapter* **6**

## 1-15 CHRIST FEEDS THE FIVE THOUSAND

See comments on Mark 6:31-44. The feeding of the five thousand is one incident recorded by all four Gospel writers: Matthew 14:13-21; Mark 6:31-44; Luke 9:10-17; John 6:1-15.

**➤1 After these things Jesus went over the sea of Galilee**—See comments on Mark 6:31-44. Christ's many miracles (John 2:1-11, 23; 4:45-54; 5:1-9) produced the inevitable bevy of curiosity-seekers (6:1-5; cf. John 2:23; Matt. 19:2; Mark 5:20-24), so Jesus withdrew by boat to the hill country on the eastern side of the sea of Galilee (cf. Matt. 14:13).

**➤5 a great company**—But the curious throng was not that easily dissuaded, for they followed him even to his secluded hideaway. Instead of repelling the people angrily for their invasion of his privacy, Christ first healed the sick among them (Matt. 14:13, 14) and then turned to Philip with the compassionate words, "Where can we buy bread to feed all these people?" (TLB).

**➤7-9** But first **Philip** and then **Andrew** failed this gentle test of their faith in the time of need, for both of them overlooked the power of the Master and instead answered with the pessimism of despair.

**➤10-13 Make the men sit down**—Without a word of rebuke to his doubting disciples, Christ ordered the waiting throng to sit on the grass in orderly groups (cf. Mark 6:39, 40; Luke 9:14), and then the inexhaustible supply of **loaves** and **fishes** was distributed to the hungry people. When everyone had eaten abundantly, Christ ordered the leftovers (**fragments**) collected, for even our infinite God never wastes any of his resources. As in most biblical miracles, the basic human need at hand was abundantly met without waste or gaudy showmanship. Our God is too majestic to stoop to sideshow magic. For other details of this miracle, see Matthew 14:14-22; Mark 6:35-44; Luke 9:12-17.

➤**14 This is . . . that prophet that should come into the world**—The well-fed throng recognized the authenticity of Christ's miracle, so they correctly identified Jesus as the predicted "Prophet" of Deuteronomy 18:15-18 and rushed to acclaim Jesus as their miracle-working King.

➤**15 he departed again into a mountain himself alone**—Tragically, they missed completely the true redemptive purpose of the Prophet in their presence, and Christ was forced to withdraw into seclusion and prayer. What a calamity to acknowledge Christ as a "great Prophet" but reject him as the Savior of our souls!

16-21 JESUS STILLS THE STORM
    See comments on Mark 6:45-56.
➤**16-21** Christ told his disciples to cross the sea of Galilee without him (Matt. 14:22; Mark 6:45), but while they lingered it grew dark, and they were forced to set sail at night. But before the disciples could reach the western shore they were struck by a sudden squall (**a great wind**), and only the miraculous appearance of Jesus saved them from a watery grave (see Matt. 14:23-32; Mark 6:47-51). The disciples were learning that Christ is truly the Master of every situation!

22-71 CHRIST OFFERS THE
BREAD OF LIFE
➤**22, 23 The day following . . . the people . . . saw**—Many people in the miraculously-fed throng apparently stayed overnight near the western shore of the sea of Galilee, for they had witnessed the disciples' nighttime departure in that one boat (5:17).

➤**24 When the people therefore saw that Jesus was not there**—Mystified at Jesus' inexplicable absence in the morning, the crowd boarded several other small boats nearby and crossed the lake in search of Jesus.

➤**25 The searchers were delighted to have found him,** but Christ did not bother to explain his miraculous crossing of the lake to them because he knew they were already unduly enamored with the novelty of his miracles.

➤**26 Ye seek me, not because ye saw the miracles, but because ye did eat of the loaves, and were filled**—Jesus confronted the sensation-seekers with a blunt appraisal of their superficiality. Their motive for seeking him was entirely carnal—they wanted more food.

➤**27 the meat [food] which perisheth . . . that meat [food] which endureth [remains] unto everlasting life**—Two kinds of bread, the perishing and the living, become the subject of the long discourse that follows. **the Son of man**—taking that title of himself which denoted his incarnate life. **him hath God the Father sealed**—marked out and authenticated for that transcendent office, to provide the world with the bread of everlasting life.

➤**28, 29 work the works of God . . . This is the work of God, that ye believe on him**—The only action that God approves is belief in his Son.

➤**30, 31 What sign showest thou then?**—The people responded by asking for another sign. They had seen the miracle of the loaves, but they thought this was nothing greater than what their forefathers saw—through the agency of Moses, manna came down from heaven for forty years! They quoted the Scripture to Jesus, "He gave them bread from heaven to eat" (Ps. 78:24; 105:40).

➤**32 Moses gave you not . . . but my Father giveth**—It was not Moses who gave their forefathers the manna; it was God. And now that very same God gives the true bread from heaven—his Son, Jesus Christ. The manna that had been given to their forefathers in the wilderness had no present effect on the Jews of Jesus' day. Their boast in the ancient miracle could not give them life.

➤**33 For the bread of God is he which cometh down from heaven, and giveth life unto the world**—In the Greek, the verbs are in the present tense, emphasizing that Christ, as the true manna, is continually given as the ever-present bread. Just as the manna came down every day to supply the sojourning Israelites, the Lord, as the real manna, comes down from heaven and keeps on giving life to the world.

➤**34, 35** The people still did not understand that Jesus was talking about himself, so he emphatically told them, **I am the bread of life.**

➤**37 All that the Father giveth me**—In the Greek, the pronoun for "that" is in the neuter case and singular. It encompasses the one corporate entity of all believers. This unified entity was given as a gift from the Father to the Son (see comments on 6:39; 17:2, 24). **and him**— Here the Lord shifts from the impersonal neuter pronoun to the personal masculine pronoun. Each believer within that corporate whole receives Jesus' personal attention. He (or, she) can be assured that he will never be **cast out.**

➤**39 all which he hath given me**—Again, Jesus is speaking of that one corporate entity composed of all the believers, given to him as a gift from the Father (see comments on 6:37). **raise it up**—The neuter is used to keep the consistency with the previous remarks concerning the one corporate entity. Christ is saying that he will raise up the entire whole, each and every one included.

➤**40 every one which . . . believeth on him, may have everlasting life: and I will raise him up at the last day**—Jesus now shifts from the corporate to the individual—from the corporate resurrection to the individual's resurrection. An individual can know if he will be raised on the last day if he knows that he has eternal life here and now. The possession of eternal life now is a guarantee of participation in the future resurrection.

➤**41-43 The Jews then murmured at him**—The people were offended. How could he, a mere man, be **the bread which came down from heaven?** How could Jesus, **the son of Joseph** and Mary (people these Jews knew), come from heaven?

➤**44 No man can come to me, except the Father which has sent me draw him**—Without divine revelation and divine drawing, a man cannot realize Jesus' heavenly origin, his divine being—and then come to believe in Jesus.

➤**45 written in the prophets**—Isaiah 54:13; Jeremiah 31:33, 34. **all taught of God**—This teaching is not by external instruction but by inward revelation, corresponding to the "drawing" in the previous verse.

➤**46 Not that any man hath seen the Father, save** [except] **he which is of God**— i.e., Only the Son has seen the Father; therefore, the people should not think mistakenly that they could see and hear God himself directly. Only the Son had this privilege.

➤**47-50** Jesus then pointed out the infinite superiority of the **bread** from heaven to the **manna** in the wilderness. The ancient manna kept people alive for a few years, but Christ, **the bread of life,** gives his recipients spiritual life that begins right now and continues on into eternity.

➤**51 the bread that I will give is my flesh . . . for the life of the world**—The Greek word behind "for" (*huper*) denotes benefaction and even substitution. Christ had come to sacrifice his life so that the world might have eternal life.

➤**53** Jesus demanded that they **eat** his **flesh** and **drink** his **blood** in order to appropriate eternal life. Since he spoke of the blood as being separated from the flesh, he was speaking of death. Christ himself, by virtue of his sacrificial death, is the spiritual and eternal life of men; and unless men appropriate this death in its sacrificial virtue, so as to become the very life and nourishment of their inner man, they have no spiritual and eternal life at all.

➤**54 hath eternal life; and I will raise him up at the last day**—The believer is the recipient of eternal life here and now, and this life guarantees participation in the future resurrection.

➤**56 He that eateth my flesh, and drinketh my blood, dwelleth in me, and I in him.**—Whoever appropriates, by faith, Jesus' death and thereby receives his life has eternal life (6:54), dwells in God and is indwelt by him (6:56), lives by Jesus (6:57), and will live forever (6:58).

➤**57 I live by the Father**—lit., "I live because of the Father." Jesus, as the sent One, the Son of man, lived in dependence on the Father's life (see 5:26). **so he that eateth me**— Note the change from "eat my flesh and drink my blood" (in previous verses) to simply "eat me." This helps us understand that the expression "eat my flesh and drink my blood" is a metaphor for appropriating the person Jesus Christ. **even he shall live by me**—lit., "even that one will live because of me." As Jesus lived in union with the Father and depended on his life, so the eater of Jesus will live in union with Jesus and depend on his life. This union and life-dependency is elaborated later in Jesus' illustration of the vine and the branches (see 15:1-17).

➤**58** This verse summarizes Jesus' discourse on the bread of life.

➤**60, 61 Doth this offend you?**—Many of Jesus' disciples were offended by his statements. Yet at the very beginning of his message Christ had explained that eating the bread of life meant receiving him as the Son of God and appropriating eternal life (6:35-40). Had Christ's hearers been properly attentive to his words, they would never have suggested the grotesque thought of eating Christ's literal flesh (6:52).

➤**62 What and if ye shall see the Son of man ascend up where he was before?**—"What if you saw my ascension, my return to my heavenly abode—would you then be offended?" If they could believe his heavenly origin, they should be able to believe his words—no matter how difficult.

➤**63 words. . . are spirit . . . are life**—The whole essence of his message was "spirit," not flesh—spiritual, not material. And his words themselves should be taken spiritually, not literally. They were words of life, words that imparted life.

➤**64 some of you that believe not**—referring to some of the disciples in the outer circle (i.e., not among the Twelve) and to even one among the Twelve—Judas (6:70, 71).

➤**65** A repetition of 6:45, emphasizing the need for divine revelation. A man can't come to Christ without a divine revelation.

➤**66 many went back**—to their former way of life.

➤**67 Will ye also go away?**—In Greek, this question expects a negative response: "You will not also go away, will you?"

➤**68, 69** Peter's confession clears the air. **thou hast the words of eternal life**—i.e., your words contain and convey the divine, eternal life. **Christ, the Son of the living God**—According to the earliest manuscripts, this reads, "the holy One of God." The reading in the KJV was adapted from a reading borrowed from Matt. 16:16.

➤**70, 71** Judas, chosen by Jesus, is called **a devil**—Greek, *diabolos* (slanderer). He would betray Jesus, and Jesus knew it all along (see comments on 13:18).

# Chapter 7

## 1-53 CHRIST AT THE FEAST OF TABERNACLES

➤**1 After these things Jesus walked in Galilee: for he would not walk in Jewry, because the Jews sought to kill him**—Why

didn't Jesus go directly to Judea and face the hatred of the Jewish leaders head-on? Because it was not yet time to either resist their death-plot or submit to it. In Christ's life and in ours, timing can be extremely important. And he stayed away from the important feast of tabernacles until the divinely-appointed moment to appear.

➤**2 feast of tabernacles**—This was the last of the three annual feasts, celebrated on the fifteenth of the seventh month (September).

➤**3-5 neither did his brethren believe in him**—His brothers could not believe that their brother, Jesus, was the Messiah. Later, after his resurrection, they became believers (see Acts 1:14; 1 Cor. 15:7).

➤**6-10** The coarse taunts of his brothers (7:3-5) failed to rush Christ into premature action, for he replied in 7:6-9 with all the patience of deity. Yet Jesus did fulfill his self-imposed obligation to Jewish law by appearing inconspicuously at **the feast** (7:10; cf. Matt. 5:17). **I go not up yet unto this feast**—This is the reading in some early manuscripts; however, other manuscripts do not include the word "yet." This creates a difficult reading in light of the fact that after saying he would not go up to Jerusalem he then goes up. However, it could very well be that Jesus' response simply negates the urgings of his brothers; it does not mean that he was refusing to go up to the feast. (See Morris, who said that "the use of the present tense does not exclude subsequent action of a different kind" because the present tense could mean "I am not now going to this feast.")

➤**11-13 Where is he?**—The rumor apparently spread that Jesus was somewhere in the festal throng, for the Jewish leaders were on the lookout to capture him, and the common people found Jesus a wonderful conversation piece. But no one was willing to speak **openly** because they feared **the Jews.**

➤**14 Now about the midst of the feast Jesus went up into the temple, and taught**—About midway through the eight-day feast of tabernacles (see Lev. 23:33-43), the right time had come for Christ to reveal himself openly.

➤**15 How knoweth this man letters**—How has he been educated in the religious writings? **having never learned**—having not had any formal rabbinical training. Jesus replied that all his teaching came directly from God, and that any of his hearers who were sincere seekers of truth should be able to verify Christ's claim of divine wisdom. The very fact that Jesus continually honored the Father rather than himself was strong evidence of his deity.

►**19, 20** Then Christ turned to his critics with a challenge: "Since you blithely break Moses' laws yourselves, why do you try to kill me for my alleged violations (healing on the sabbath)?" (7:19, paraphrased). To this the crowd jeered, "You are demon-possessed . . . Who is trying to kill you?" (7:20, NIV).

►**21-24 Moses therefore gave unto you circumcision . . . and ye on the sabbath day circumcise a man**—Though servile work was forbidden on the sabbath, the circumcision of the males on that day (which certainly was servile work) was not considered an infringement of the law. Thus, if it is permitted to perform circumcision on the sabbath, how could it be wrong to perform a miracle (as an act of mercy) on this very same day?

►**25-27** To this argument Jesus' critics apparently had no rejoinder, for it was Christ's sympathetic listeners who spoke next. They were impressed with Christ's words and his apparent victory over his critics (7:26), but no one in the crowd seems to have bothered investigating the circumstances of Jesus' birth or even the OT Scripture which pinpointed Bethlehem (Mic. 5:2), for some of them said, **but when Christ cometh, no man knows whence he is.** There seems to have been a popular notion that Messiah's origin would be mysterious, which was not altogether wrong—for even Micah 5:2 indicates that his origins would be from eternity. They rejected Jesus' claims because they knew he was from Nazareth (see comments on 7:41, 42, 51).

►**28, 29 Ye both know me, and ye know whence I am**—It is better to take this as a question: "You know me, and you know where I come from?" (RSV). Jesus then rebuked these people for not recognizing his divine identity: **I am not come of myself. . . . I am from him.**

►**30 Then they sought to take him: but no one laid hands on him, because his hour was not yet come.**—The rebuke cut the Jewish leaders deeply (since they were well aware of Christ's claim to deity), but God's moment for

the capture of Christ had not yet arrived, so not a hand was laid on him.

►**31 And many of the people believed on him**—Christ's miracles and words of grace convinced many people that he must be the long-awaited Messiah, so they "believed on him" either intellectually or totally.

►**32** The jealous Pharisees were unable to contain their rage at Jesus' newly-won popularity, so they sent officers to arrest him.

►**33, 34 Yet a little while am I with you, and then I go unto him that sent me.**—But God's divinely permitted moment for Christ's arrest had still not come, so Jesus simply responded to their evil intent with a cryptic but concisely accurate prediction of his approaching death, resurrection, and ascension.

►**35, 36 Whither will he go, that we shall not find him?**—The spiritually blind leaders were totally baffled by Christ's carefully chosen words, and Jesus let them ponder this enigma without further comment.

►**37, 38 In the last day, that great day of the feast**—The feast of tabernacles, which lasted for eight days, was held in commemoration of the Israelites' journey in the wilderness, from Egypt to Canaan. They celebrated the memory of how God tabernacled with them in their sojourning, guiding their way and providing them with their daily supply through the manna, smitten rock, etc. Every day during this feast (except the last) a priest standing in front of the temple would take a golden pitcher of water and pour it out, in commemoration of the water flowing out of the smitten rock (see Exod. 17:6). While the water flowed out, the people standing by would chant, "Therefore with joy shall you draw water out of the wells of salvation" (Isa. 12:3). John A. Bengel remarked that a priest would also read Zechariah 14:8 on the first day of this feast: "And it shall come to pass in that day, that living waters shall go out from Jerusalem . . . " All these promises of living water were wonderful, yet they were merely promises. No one could take a drink, for all was symbolic and prophetic. Consequently, the people were still thirsty. Thus, on the last day of this feast, Jesus stood and cried, "If any man thirst, let him come to me and drink." By this action, Jesus designated himself as the true antitype of the smitten rock. **If any man thirst, let him come unto me, and**

**drink. He that believeth on me, as the scripture hath said, out of his belly** [innermost being] **shall flow rivers of living water**—This statement, as it reads in the KJV and several other translations, relates that the believer who drinks of Christ as the Rock will become one out from whom rivers of living water flow. Westcott said, "He who drinks of the Spiritual Rock becomes in turn himself a rock from within which the waters flow to slake the thirst of others." However, other commentators and translators prefer a different form of punctuation: "If anyone is thirsty let him come to me; whoever believes in me, let him drink. As Scripture says, 'Streams of living water shall flow out from within him' " (NEB). This rendering enables the interpeter to align the last statement with Jesus—not the believer—as being the source from which the living waters flow. This seems to be a more natural association, for Jesus is the smitten Rock from whom the living waters flow. The **scripture** the Lord referred to was not a particular OT verse, but the general tenor of Scripture that spoke of the living waters flowing forth (see Isa. 12:3; 44:3; 58:11; Ezek. 47:1-12; Joel 3:18).

➤**39 But this spake he of the Spirit, which they that believe on him should receive: for the Holy Ghost** [Spirit] **was not yet given; because that Jesus was not yet glorified**—After Jesus' declaration, John added an explanatory note, which according to the best manuscript evidence should read something like this: "And this he said concerning the Spirit whom those who believed in him were about to receive; for the Spirit was not yet because Jesus was not yet glorified." This explanatory note, in context, has nothing to do with whether or not the Spirit yet existed. Of course, the Spirit existed; but the Spirit about to be made available through the glorification of Jesus was not yet. In short, the Spirit of the glorified Jesus was not yet available for the believers to partake of. Once his glorification (through death and resurrection) happened, the believers could drink of the Spirit of the glorified Christ (Murray).

➤**40-52** After Jesus' profound exclamation on the last day of the feast of tabernacles, some believed that Jesus was **the Prophet,** and others even believed that he was **the Christ.** But still others demurred: **Shall Christ come out**

**of Galilee?** According to the traditional interpretation of the OT, the Jews were convinced that the Messiah must come from the seed of David and be born in Bethlehem. This was based accurately on many verses: 2 Samuel 7:12-16; Psalms 89:3, 4; 132:11; Isaiah 9:6, 7; 11:1; Micah 5:2. Jesus was indeed the son of David, born in Bethlehem, but due to his early flight to Egypt and return to settle in Galilee, he was known throughout his lifetime as a Galilean. The Pharisees held the same view as the crowd did about the origin of the Messiah. When Nicodemus tried to defend Jesus, they retorted, "Are you from Galilee too? Search and you will see that no prophet is from Galilee" (7:52, RSV). Jesus refuted their position, not by trying to prove that he had really been born in Bethlehem, but by declaring, "I am the light of the world: he that followeth me shall not walk in darkness, but shall have the light of life" (8:12). (In the original text of John, 8:12 immediately follows 7:52.) The story about the adultress was a later addition, interrupting the true narrative—see comments on 7:53-8:11. By making this declaration, Jesus was clearly alluding to Isaiah 9:1, 2, which states, " . . . beyond the Jordan, Galilee of the Gentiles. The people that walked in darkness have seen a great light; they that dwelt in the land of the shadow of death, upon them hath the light shined" (ASV). The reader cannot but notice how similar are Isaiah 9:2 and John 8:12. Both speak of the light shining on the people, both indicate that these people walked in darkness, and both relate light to life. The Pharisees were so confident in their knowledge of the Scriptures. They knew that the Scriptures did speak of a great light appearing to the Galileans, a great light intimately related to those people who lived in the land of the shadow of death. Jesus was that great light. (For more on this, see "The Pericope Adulteress" by P. Comfort in *The Bible Translator,* Jan. 1989.)

## 7:53–8:11 THE STORY OF THE ADULTEROUS WOMAN

This story is one of the best examples of an addition coming into the text from an oral tradition. This story is not included in the best and earliest manuscripts (Papyrus Bodmer II [P66], Papyrus Bodmer XV [P75], Codeces Sinaiticus, Vaticanus, Alexandrinus, Ephraemi

Rescriptus, Regius, the Freer Gospels, and others). In fact, it is absent from all witnesses earlier than the ninth century, with the exception of a fifth-century Greek-Latin manuscript. No Greek church father comments on the passage prior to the twelfth century—until Euthymius Zigabenus, who himself declares that the accurate copies do not contain it. When this story is inserted in later manuscripts, it appears in different places: after John 7:52, after Luke 21:38, at the end of John, etc., and when it does appear, it is often marked with obeli. The story is known to have been a piece of oral tradition first recorded in a Syriac version circulated in the Western church, eventually finding its way into the Latin Vulgate and from there into later Greek texts, from which the Textus Receptus was derived (Metzger).

# Chapter 8

## 1-11 CHRIST'S COMPASSION ON THE ADULTEROUS WOMAN

See comments on 7:53–8:11 concerning the absence of this passage in the earliest manuscripts.

➤**1** Verse 1 tells us that Jesus went to the Mount of Olives after his long and wearying confrontation with the mostly hostile throng at the tabernacle celebration (see John 7). In all probability the Son of God refreshed his soul with the communion of prayer during the long hours of the night (cf. Matt. 14:23; 26:36-44; Luke 5:16; 6:12; 9: 18, 28; 11:1), for he chose to receive his power for service the same way each of us must do today. It is not possible to serve God acceptably with a prayerless life.

➤**2** Undeterred by the continuing hostility of his enemies, Christ came again to **the temple** early in the morning for another full day of difficult service for the Father (cf. 8:28, 29, 49).

➤**3** Christ's words of instruction to his early-morning hearers were soon interrupted by the pompous approach of several **scribes and Pharisees** who had just caught a **woman . . . in adultery.** Perhaps they thought they could use her to discredit the teachings of Christ (8:5, 6).

➤**5, 6** The Pharisees were correct when they said that adulterers and adulteresses were to be killed (Lev. 20:10; Deut. 22:22) but tragically

mistaken when they assumed that they, as secret sinners, were qualified to render the capital punishment. The Son of God knew both their motives and their hypocritically sinful lives, so with ominous silence he began writing on the ground. He may have done this to show his aversion to enter on the subject.

➤**8, 9** As Jesus kept writing the Pharisees got the point, and all of them eventually conceded their own sinfulness by their quiet departure. Now Christ was left standing with the woman and his original audience.

➤**10** Since the woman had already been unofficially condemned and totally humiliated by her captors, Jesus now asked her whether anyone was left to officially condemn her.

➤**11 go, and sin no more**—Since Christ's earthly ministry was not a judgmental one (8:15, 16; 12:47, 48), our Lord released the contrite woman with a warning to **sin no more.** Since the woman's critics were guilty of even more numerous sins than she was, the most remarkable feature of this episode is not Christ's release of the woman with just a word of warning, but his release of her accusers with just a quiet hint of their guilt (8:6-8). Yet all the judgment that Christ has been withholding from that day to the present will be amply recompensed at the final day of judgment (12:47, 48; Rev. 20:11-15). It is only God's mercy that delays his judgment so that all have a chance to be saved (2 Pet. 3:8, 9, 15).

## 12-59 CHRIST'S CONFRONTATION WITH HIS HOSTILE CRITICS

➤**12 I am the light of the world**—As Christ stood in the treasury of the temple (8:20), he employed its two huge lampstands as an object lesson for the important truth of his own spiritual illumination. During the feast of tabernacles, it was customary to keep the lamps burning every evening. But it should be noted that 8:12 in the best manuscripts follows 7:52 (see comments on 7:53). Therefore, 8:12 is most likely Jesus' retort to the Jews who denied his Messiahship on the basis of Jesus coming from Galilee. They had failed to realize that Isaiah 9:1, 2 predicted that a great light would shine in Galilee, bringing illumination to those who lived and walked in darkness and death. As the language Jesus used in 8:12 nearly repeats Isaiah 9:2, he was pointing to himself as the fulfillment of that prophecy. He was the light that brought life so that the people might no longer have to walk in darkness.

►**13 Thou bearest record of thyself**—As usual (cf. John 2:18, 20; 5:10, 12, 16, 18), the hostile Pharisees challenged him immediately, this time with the accusation of false self-witness.

►**14 I know whence I came**—Christ answered that his self-witness was flawless because of his heavenly origin and destiny.

►**15** It was the Pharisees' testimony that was false. They judged according to **the flesh**—i.e., according to the outward appearance.

►**17, 18 It is also written in your law**—If the Pharisees still demanded a plurality of witnesses (based on a misapplication of Deuteronomy 17:6 and 19:15), then Christ would invite them to accept the Father's **witness** about his beloved Son (5:37, 38).

►**19** The Pharisees knew exactly what Christ was driving at (cf. 5:15-18), but they retorted with a sarcastic rebuttal: **Where is thy Father?** So Jesus silenced them with a blunt statement about their spiritual blindness and unbelief. They did not know the Father, so they did not recognize his Son (cf. 14:8-11).

►**20** The furious Pharisees would have loved to arrest Jesus, but his divine moment for capture had not yet arrived, so they once again found themselves unable to touch him (cf. 7:30, 44).

►**21 I go my way**—lit., "I am going away." On certain occasions Jesus spoke to his hearers in rather enigmatic statements in order to force them to ponder his words. And that was exactly the effect of the statement in this verse, for Christ's hearers felt compelled to discuss the meaning of his words among themselves (8:22). Having now gained the complete attention of his hearers, Christ expanded his condemnation of verse 21 with a warning to repent and an invitation to believe on him.

►**24 I am he**—or, I am the One or, I am the Christ. The predicate nominative has to be supplied. But his hearers knew what he meant. He was declaring his divine identity. (Cf. God's self-declarations of "I Am He" in Deut. 32:39; Isa. 43:10, 13; 46:4; 48:12.)

►**25 Even the same that I said unto you from the beginning**—This could be rendered, "I am principally (or, essentially) that which I also speak" (see Darby's *New Translation*), which is to say, "I am what I say I am—my

words present who I am." The Lord did not need to give them any further explanations; he had already repeatedly unveiled his identity to them through his previous speeches. In short, the Word revealed himself through his words.

►**26, 27 I have many things to say and to judge of you**—Cf. 16:12 ff.

►**28 When ye have lifted up** [on the cross] **the Son of man, then shall ye know that I am he**—This is the plainest intimation he had yet given in public of the *way* in which he would be killed, for "lifted up" was an unmistakable euphemism for "crucifixion." Once he was crucified, his true identity would be even more manifest. As he predicted, thousands of Jews in Jerusalem did indeed receive Christ as their Messiah within a few weeks of his death and resurrection (Acts 2:37-47; 4:4; 5:14; 6:7).

►**29 the Father hath not left me alone; for I do always those things that please him**—Due to their blindness, the Jews did not realize that Jesus had come from God the Father and was still accompanied by God the Father. Jesus was not alone; the Father who sent him came with him. He asserted this twice in this chapter (8:16, 29) and in 12:45. Jesus had not come on his own and did not do anything on his own initiative (8:28, 42). He was completely dependent on the Father. He spoke only what he heard from his Father, and he taught that which he had seen together with the Father (8:28, 38). In short, he lived to please the Father (8:28, 29).

►**31, 32 If ye continue in my word . . . ye shall know the truth, and the truth shall make you free**—The impression produced by our Lord by his last words may have been noticeable to him; so here he takes the chance to encourage them to continue in his words. Then they would "come to know by their own experience" (the meaning of the Gk. word used here, *ginōko*) the truth, and thus experience spiritual freedom.

►**33 They answered**—Although several commentators think these are the new believers who now respond to the Lord, that which follows seems to imply that these were other Jews among the crowd—probably the Pharisees (see 8:13). **were never in bondage to any man**—Christ did not bother pointing out the ludicrousness of the Jews' claim to eternal freedom (they had been slaves to the Egyptians,

Assyrians, Babylonians, Persians, Greeks, and now the Romans). But he did point out their obvious slavery to sin and Satan (8:34-45).

➤**35 And the servant abideth not in the house** [or, household] **forever; but the Son abideth ever**—This verse yields better sense if "Son" is not capitalized. In speaking of slavery and freedom, he made a distinction between the bond-slave who has no permanent place in the household and the son who remains in the household forever, a clear allusion to Ishmael and Isaac—see Galatians 4:22-30 (Alford).

➤**36 If the Son therefore shall make you free**—The Son has the power to liberate in reality.

➤**37 my word hath no place in you**—lit., "my word finds no room in you."

➤**38 your father**—the devil, according to 8:44.

➤**39-41** Christ's hearers argued vehemently that Abraham and God himself were their physical and spiritual fathers, but in tragic fact their real father was the devil, as confirmed by their persistent rejection of Christ as God's flawless personification of truth (8:37-47). They claimed they were not **born of fornication;** i.e., they were the genuine descendants of Abraham and children of the one true God. Their religious heritage was genuine.

➤**42 If God were your Father, ye would love me: for I proceeded forth and came from God**—Jesus designated his source: God the Father, the very One they claimed to own as Father. But they did not really know this Father, for they did not love his Son.

➤**44 ye are of your father the devil**—In bold language, Jesus identified their source: the devil. **He was a murderer from the beginning**—the beginning of the human race. The devil murdered Adam spiritually (see Rom. 5:12ff.) and thus the devil's murderous act brought death to all mankind. **abode not in the truth**—rather, "stood not in truth" according to some manuscripts, whereas other manuscripts (yielding a better testimony) read, "has not been standing in truth." Since the beginning the devil has lived in falsehood. In fact, he is the father of falsehood.

➤**45-48** Christ's hearers became so enraged by his stinging truthfulness and by their own inability to convict him of sin that they lashed out in a flood of passionate hatred.

➤**49, 50** Christ did not reply in kind, but instead responded with a restatement of the Son's and Father's goal of mutual honor.

➤**51 If a man keep my saying** [word] **he shall never see death**—Because Christ's words are spirit and life (6:63), a man could receive eternal life by keeping them (see 5:24; 6:68).

➤**52, 53** Christ's words fell on deaf ears, for the Jewish leaders sought to refute the Savior's invitation to eternal life by pointing to the death of **Abraham** and the OT **prophets.**

➤**54-56** But once again Jesus replied with words of truth and conviction, including the dynamic disclosure that **Abraham rejoiced** in the anticipation of Christ's coming (cf. Gen. 22:1-14).

➤**57 Thou art not yet fifty years old**— This claim was too much for the hostile Pharisees to take, so they jeered Christ with scornful sarcasm about his age. ("Fifty years old" was simply the Jewish equivalent for "full manhood.")

➤**58, 59 Before Abraham was, I am**—lit. "Before Abraham was brought into being, I exist." The statement, therefore, is not that Christ came into existence before Abraham did, but that he already existed before Abraham was brought into being; in other words, Christ existed before creation, or eternally (as 1:1). In that sense, the Jews plainly understood him, for they wanted to stone him for blasphemy. Jesus, in claiming to be I Am, was asserting equality with God himself (as in 5:18), who was revealed as the I Am That I Am—the self-existent, eternal God (Exod. 3:14).

# Chapter 9

## 1-41 THE EPISODE OF THE BLIND MAN HEALED

➤**1-3 he saw a man which was blind from birth**—Neither Christ's notice of the **blind** man nor his **disciples'** curiosity about him was accidental, as shown by Jesus' words in 9:3. Because the disciples held a popular but erroneous opinion about human suffering, Christ taught them the ultimate meaning of all forms of disorder in the universe. Christ's words do not imply that God heartlessly inflicted blindness on a newborn baby but simply that he allowed nature to run its course in this case so that the victim would ultimately bring glory to God through the reception of both physical and spiritual sight (see 9:30-38).

►**4, 5 I** [we, according to better manuscripts—referring to Jesus and the disciples] **must work the works of him that sent me . . . I am the light of the world**—In these verses Christ used the beggar's blindness as an illustration of the spiritual darkness which gripped the world and could only be alleviated by his work. He included the disciples in this work (although they did nothing for this blind man) because they would continue to shine forth his light after Jesus' departure (see Phil. 2:15).

►**6 he spat on the ground, and made clay of the spittle**—Why did Christ send the blind man away with clay (or, mud) on his face before he could be healed? As in the somewhat similar episode of Naaman and Elisha (2 Kings 5:9-14), it was to test the man's faith in Christ even in the face of puzzling humiliation.

►**7 Go, wash in the pool of Siloam, (which is by interpretation, Sent.)**—Siloam is a Greek translation of the Hebrew name, **Shiloah,** which means "sent." The water in Siloam came by being sent into the pool through a channel. It was said in Isaiah 8:6 that the Jews refused the waters of Siloam, just as in this chapter the Jews refused Jesus (Barrett). But the blind man obeyed the word of the sent One. He washed in the water of Siloam and received his sight. These waters symbolized the work that Jesus, the sent One, had come to do.

►**8, 9** So amazed were the beggar's friends at his newly gained sight that they temporarily questioned his identity, even as sometimes still happens when a darkened sinner gets saved (cf. Acts. 9:1-21).

►**10-11** The newly sighted man lost no time in testifying to the healing power of Jesus.

►**13 They brought** [him] **to the Pharisees**—The curious onlookers did not know how to respond to the joyous miracle they had just witnessed, so they took the healed man to the Pharisees for their official evaluation. What a grueling cross-examination followed!

►**15-23** First the Pharisees asked all about the healing (9:15), and then they condemned the healer for doing good on the sabbath (9:14, 16). Reacting to the questions of some of their colleagues (19:16), the staunchest Pharisees attacked the healed man with a renewed attempt to break down his testimony (9:17, 18). The newly sighted beggar responded with even warmer praise for his benefactor than he had offered previously—he called him **a prophet** (9:17). So the Pharisees called in the man's parents in the vain hope that they would refute their own son's testimony (9:18, 19). The parents refused to disavow their son's story but fell short of glorifying Christ for fear of the vindictive Jewish leaders (9:20, 23). What a sad example of the kind of religious persecution that has faced Christ's witnesses down through the centuries!

►**24 again called they the man that was blind**—Not content with their searching cross-examination of the healed man, the Pharisees called him in a second time with a command to stop glorifying Jesus. But the healed man fulfilled God's ultimate purpose in restoring his sight (9:3) by honoring both God the Father and the Son (9:25-33; cf. 5:22, 23). Christ's words of verse 3 may have seemed harsh to his disciples when they were first spoken, but the culmination of the story shows that the blind beggar's dramatic healing impelled him to glorify God in a way that few physically fit people were willing to duplicate (cf. 2:23, 24; 6:14, 15, 41, 42, 52, 66; 7:13; 18:15-17, 25-27).

►**26-33** The relentless questions (9:26) and even curses (9:28, 29, 34) of the ruthless Pharisees were unable to throttle the healed beggar's willingness to testify for Christ (9:25, 27, 30-33). In fact, the more the Pharisees questioned the man who received his sight, the clearer he became about Jesus. Their blind obstinacy augmented his clarity.

►**34** The healed man's condemnation of the Pharisees' irrational rejection of Jesus (9:30-33) proved too much for them to take, so they excommunicated (lit., "de-synagogued") him from the synagogue with a curse about his presumed guilt from birth.

►**35** Christ knew that this cruel act would be a severe test of the healed man's faith, so he soon approached the man with a crucial leading question: **Dost thou believe on the Son of God?**—which is the reading in some ancient manuscripts. But the most ancient read, "Do you believe in the Son of man?" If the reading in the KJV were original, there is no reason why "God" would have been changed to "man." But one can easily see how zealous scribes would have changed "Son of man" to "Son of God." Since "Son of man" is a title of the Christ, Jesus was asking the man if he believed him to be the Christ. He did believe, and he showed it by worshiping Christ, as one would worship God.

➤**39 And Jesus said, For judgment I am come into this world, that they which see not might see; and that they which see might be made blind**—Christ spoke these double-edged words to the healed man while he was still in the presence of the Pharisees. The Pharisees quickly understood that Jesus was attacking their unbelief, but they weren't fully sure of the meaning of his words (9:40), so Jesus expanded his statement with the rather cryptic condemnation found in verse 41. In contrast to the man who had received his double sight, the Pharisees had sight but no light. They were spiritually blind, though they thought they were enlightened. This was presumptuous. They presumed they knew all about the Messiah, but their knowledge blinded them from seeing the very Christ who stood in their midst. Because they thought they saw, they were blind. Those who admitted blindness could receive the light and see, but those who thought they saw would remain in their darkness (9:39-41).

# Chapter 10

## 1-21 AN ALLEGORY ABOUT THE GOOD SHEPHERD

The first 21 verses of this chapter are probably a continuation of Christ's remarks to the intransigent Pharisees (see 9:39-41 and compare with 10:19-21).

➤**1 He that entereth not by the door into the sheepfold, but climbeth up some other way, the same is a thief and a robber**—This chapter begins with an allegory. An allegory is different from a parable. In an allegory each item has a corresonding significance; in a parable all the items produce one total meaning— hence, each item in a parable may not have an equivalent signification. Most of the elements in this allegory can be readily assigned a corresponding antitype. The good Shepherd is Christ, the sheep are the believers, the sheepfold is Judaism, the doorkeeper is God, and the

stranger is a false Christ. But what is **the door into the sheepfold?** It would seem that the door is the "Messiahship"—i.e., the office of the Messiah. Only one person could qualify for entering into that position. Jesus was the one. Since he was the true Messiah, God the Father opened the door to him. He had the legitimate access into the sheepfold of Judaism. Anyone else who tried to enter that fold had to do so by some other means, for no one else was qualified to be the Christ.

➤**2-5** Only Jesus was the legitimate Christ, as this Gospel time and again declares. By this allegory Jesus was claiming his right to be the Christ, because the Father opened the door only to him, and the sheep knew only his voice. Within the fold of Judaism were some of God's people who had awaited the coming of their Shepherd-Messiah (see Isa. 40:1-11). When the Shepherd came, he would lead his people out to good pasture (see Ezek. 34). He would call his own sheep by name and lead them out of the fold. This was exactly what happened to the blind man in the previous chapter.

➤**7** After presenting the allegory, Jesus first expanded on the meaning of **the door of the sheep** (10:7-10) and then on "the shepherd of the sheep" (10:11-18). As **the door of the sheep,** he was the One uniquely qualified to fulfill the role of Messiah.

➤**8** All who ever **came before** him (meaning "all who ever came pretending to be the Christ") were actually thieves and robbers. **But the sheep did not hear them**—for none of them possessed the authentic voice of the Shepherd.

➤**9** Since Jesus was the genuine Messiah, the sheep could enter through him to find salvation, liberty, and provision. The expression **shall be saved** indicates spiritual salvation and spiritual security ("will be kept safe," see NIV). The statement **shall go in and out** comes from an OT expression describing "the free activity of daily life" (Dods)—i.e., the freedom to come and go as one pleases (see Deut. 28:6; Ps. 121:8; Jer. 37:4). In short, the Shepherd would provide his sheep with freedom. The language of Numbers 27:16, 17 is similar: "Let Jehovah . . . appoint a man over the congregation, who may go out before them, and who may lead them out and bring them in; that the congregation of Jehovah be not as sheep which have no Shepherd" (ASV).

►**10-15** As opposed to the **thief** (who may represent the false Christ, the Antichrist, the one in league with the devil, or just someone whose intention is to harm the sheep) and the **hireling** (who denotes the religious leader who shepherds God's people for self-gain), Christ is the devoted and dedicated Shepherd. He gives abundant, eternal life to his sheep. And he demonstrated his love in that he laid down his soul for the sheep. Four times in this passage Jesus indicated that he would lay down his life for the sheep (10:11, 15, 17, and 18). Jesus was, of course, alluding to his substitutionary death, in which he would sacrifice his soul, his life (*psuchē* in Gk.) so that the sheep might enjoy the abundant, divine life (*zoē* in Gk.). Isaiah 53:10 says the Messiah would offer "his soul a sacrifice for sins." What a difference between the good Shepherd and the thief and the hireling! The thief steals, slaughters, and destroys, and the hireling depicts those Jewish leaders who took their office for self-gain. In the OT these hirelings were severely reproved by God (e.g., see Ezek. 34, where "the shepherds of Israel" are rebuked for abusing their office). The leaders of Israel had not shepherded Israel properly prior to the captivity; thus, many of the Jews became like scattered sheep having no shepherd (again see Ezek. 34).

►**16 one fold**—should be translated, "one flock." The good Shepherd would come, however, to gather God's people together again and bring them into one flock (see Ezek. 34:11-14, 23). This flock would consist of Jewish and Gentile believers (called **other sheep . . . not of this fold**). All would be brought into one flock, with one shepherd (cf. Eph. 2:14; 3:6).

►**17, 18 I lay down my life, that I might take it again**—These verses show that Christ's death as the good Shepherd was not the demise of a captured martyr but the voluntary sacrifice of the omnipotent Son of God. Jesus himself had the authority to lay down his life (in death) and to take it up again in resurrection.

►**19-21** The gracious grandeur of Christ's words struck deep into the hearts of his hearers, and they responded with either scornful rejection (10:20) or timid acceptance (10:21). Yet none of these leaders seemed willing to acknowledge the presence of God the Son in their midst.

## 22-42 THE FEAST OF DEDICATION DISCOURSE

►**22 the feast of dedication**—The dedication celebration was not one of the official festivals prescribed by Pentateuchal Law (it was instituted by Judas Maccabeus to commemorate the purification of the temple from Antiochus Epiphanes' profanations in 170 B.C.), but Christ attended it anyway because he wanted to identify himself as fully as possible with every legitimate activity of his people. (Compare the commentary on 2:1, 2.) Despite all the evidentiary words and miracles which Jesus had produced in the previous weeks and months (2:1–10:18), the Jewish leaders refused to acknowledge his Messiahship.

►**24 If thou be the Christ, tell us plainly**—Their request was not a search for truth but a thinly-veiled accusation of blasphemy, as shown by the Pharisees' actions a few moments later (10:31, 33, 39).

►**25** In verses 25-30 Christ summarized all the works and teachings he had presented to his observers since the beginning of his ministry (see 2:1-10:18), with special emphasis on his important pastoral lesson of 10:1-16.

►**26, 27** Since the Jewish leaders had consistently ignored Christ's claims of Messiahship and his validating miracles (10:25, 26), Jesus turned to his true flock with words of unparalleled assurance and comfort (27-29). Only such landmark passages as Romans 8:31-39, Ephesians 1:1–2:22, and 1 John 5:1-15 rival these transcendently reassuring words of the good Shepherd.

►**28 I give unto them eternal life**—not "I will give," for it is a present gift. (See comments on 5:24.)

►**29 My Father, which gave them me**—See comments on 6:37-39. **is greater than all**—with whom no adverse power can contend. It is a general expression of an admitted truth, and what follows shows for what purpose it was uttered: "and none is able to pluck them out of my Father's hand." The impossibility of true believers being lost, in the midst of all the temptations which they may encounter, does not consist in their fidelity and decision, but is founded upon the power of God. Here the doctrine of predestination is presented in its sublime and sacred aspect; there is a predestination of the holy, which is taught from one end of the Scriptures to the other; not, indeed, of such a nature that an "irresistible grace" compels the opposing will of man (of course not), but so that the will of man that receives and loves the commands of God is produced only by God's grace (Olshausen). It should be noted that this verse appears in the ancient manuscripts in three ways. The first, as cited above; the second, "My Father, as to that which he has given me, is greater than all"; the third, "That which the Father has given me is greater than all." The last reading is the most difficult and perhaps original—it speaks of the Father's gift to the Son (i.e., the church—see comments on 6:37, 39; 17:2) as being able to overcome all outside forces.

➤ **30 I and my Father are one**—Since the word for "one" in Greek is neuter, it could be rendered "are one in purpose" (i.e., that of securing the sheep). But the oneness of purpose comes from their oneness of essence. This is also intimated by the use of the neuter case. This verse is widely regarded by conservative scholars as a succinct intimation of the essential unity and personal distinctiveness of the three members of the Godhead, even though only two members are specified in the verse. Augustine was right in saying that "we are" condemns the Sabellians (who denied the distinction of persons in the Godhead), while the "one" (as explained) condemns the Arians (who denied the unity of their essence). But no matter how we understand this bold statement, it is obvious that the Jews who heard it recognized it as a claim to deity, which to them was blasphemy.

➤ **31 They took up stones** to execute this blasphemer (Lev. 24:11-16).

➤ **33 thou, being a man, makest thyself God**—or, you, being human, make yourself deity. Twice before they understood him to advance the same claim, and both times they prepared themselves to avenge what they took to be the insulted honor of God, as here, in the way directed by their law (5:18; 8:59).

➤ **34-36 Is it not written in your law**—in Psalm 82:6 (the term "law" could encompass the entire OT), respecting judges or magistrates. **Ye are gods**—being the official representatives and commissioned agents of God. **If he called them**

**gods, unto whom the word of God came . . . Say ye of him whom the Father hath sanctified, and sent into the world, Thou blasphemest**—The whole force of this reasoning lies in what is said of the two parties compared. The comparison of himself with mere men, divinely commissioned, is intended to show that the idea of a communication of the divine Majesty to human nature was by no means foreign to the revelations of the OT. But there is also a contrast between himself and all merely human representatives of God—the One "sanctified by the Father and sent into the world"; the other, "to whom the word of God [merely] came." It is never said of Christ that "the word of the Lord came to him"; whereas this is the well-known formula by which the divine commission, even to the highest of mere men, is expressed, as with John the Baptist (Luke 3:2). The reason is that given by John the Baptist himself (see 3:31). The contrast is between those "to whom the word of God came"—men of the earth, earthy, who were merely privileged to get a divine message to utter (if prophets) or a divine office to discharge (if judges)—and "him whom (not being of the earth at all) the Father hath sanctified (or, set apart), and sent into the world," an expression never used of any merely human messenger of God, and used only of himself. **because, I said, I am the Son of God**—It is worthy of special notice that our Lord had not said, in so many words, that he was the Son of God, on this occasion. But he had said what beyond doubt amounted to it—namely, that he gave his sheep eternal life, and none could pluck them out of his hand; that he had got them from his Father, in whose hands, though given to him, they still remained, and out of whose hand none could pluck them; and that they were the property of both, inasmuch as "he and his Father were one." Our Lord considers all this as just saying of himself, "I am the Son of God: one nature with him, yet mysteriously of him." The parenthesis (10:35), "and the Scripture cannot be broken," referring to the terms used of the judges in Psalm 82, has an important bearing on the authority of the living oracles. "The Scripture, as the expressed will of the unchangeable God, is itself unchangeable and indissoluble" (Olshausen).

➤ **37-38 though ye believe not me, believe the works**—There was in Christ's words, independent of any miracles, a self-evidencing truth, majesty and grace, which those who had any spiritual susceptibility were unable to resist (7:46; 8:30). But, for those who lacked this, "the works" were a mighty help. **that ye may know, and believe, that the Father is in me, and I in him**—thus reiterating his claim to essential oneness with the Father. The Son and Father's oneness is described by John in terms of mutual indwelling. The two were one with one another because they dwelt in each other (see 14:10, 11; 17:21).

➤**39 Therefore they sought again to take him**—true to their original understanding of his words, for they saw perfectly well that he meant to "make himself God" throughout all this dialogue.

➤**40-42 went away again beyond Jordan . . . the place where John at first baptized**—See 1:28.

➤**41 many resorted unto him**—i.e., many on whom the ministry of John the Baptist had left permanent impressions. **John did no miracle: but all things that John spake of this man were true**—what they now heard and saw in Jesus only confirming in their minds the genuineness of his forerunner's mission, though unaccompanied by any of his Master's miracles.

➤**42** And thus, **many believed on him there.**

*Chapter* **11**

## 1-46 THE DEATH AND RESURRECTION OF LAZARUS

➤**1, 2 Lazarus, of Bethany, the town of Mary and her sister Martha . . . It was that Mary which anointed the Lord**—In keeping with the Lord's prediction (Matt. 26:13), this Mary was well known in the Christian community because of her display of love and devotion to Christ (Matt. 26:6-13; Mark 14:3-9). So John felt free to identify her with this event even before he described it (12:1-7).

➤**3 he whom thou lovest is sick**—Though Lazarus the brother of Mary and Martha is mentioned only in John 11 and 12, verses 3 and 5 of this chapter show that Jesus must have been his friend for quite some time.

➤**4 When Jesus heard that, he said, This sickness is not unto death, but for the glory of God**—This made Christ's answer to the two sisters' call for help seem all the more strange. How could the compassionate Messiah ignore the legitimate needs of one of his favorite families? As in many of our own trying experiences of life, the answer lay in a simple but sweeping principle: **that the Son of God might be glorified thereby**—Cf. 11:45; 12:1-19. As in the case of the blind beggar who was healed (9:1-5, 24-38), alleviated human suffering often gives God greater glory than the everyday blessings we enjoy (Matt. 5:45). Yet our goal should be to glorify God in everything—not just in sickness or adversity (Rom. 15:5, 6; 1 Cor. 10:30, 31).

➤**5, 6 Jesus . . . abode** [remained] **two days still in the same place where he was**—The lingerings of God seem unbearably trying at times, but their culminations are always glorious. The hesitation of God is never based on calloused indifference (11:5), but always on divinely perfect timing.

➤**7, 8** Christ's disciples, on the other hand, did not seem concerned at all about Lazarus, Martha, or Mary—just about the safety of the Master and perhaps themselves as well (but cf. 11:16).

➤**9, 10 Are there not twelve hours in the day?**—Our Lord's "day" had now reached the eleventh hour; and having until now walked in the day, he would not mis-time the remaining and more critical part of his work. **If any walk in the day, he stumbleth not, because he seeth the light of this world**—On one level, this refers to the actual sunlight and daylight of the physical world. Jesus' time to walk in the sunlight was now limited. He had work to do before his death. On another level, "the light of the world" refers to Christ's presence among mankind. While he was among men, he was their light (see 1:4; 8:12; 9:5). "Men should make the most of the presence of Christ, the Light of the world. For when he is withdrawn from them there is no possiblity of their 'walking' without stumbling" (Morris).

➤**11 Our friend Lazarus sleepeth**—The disciples missed the meaning of this euphemism for death (11:12, 13; cf. Dan. 12:2; 1 Cor. 11:30; 15:20, 51; 1 Thess. 4:14).

➤**14** So Jesus told them plainly, **Lazarus is dead.**

➤**15** His next words, **I am glad for your sakes that I was not there**—suggest that

Christ would not have allowed Lazarus to die in his very presence.

►16 Thomas apparently missed the whole tenor of Christ's words and volunteered all the disciples for what he saw as sure "suicide." Thomas realized that death awaited Jesus in Jerusalem (10:31, 39; 11:8)—and Bethany was Jerusalem's neighbor (11:18).

►20 Martha . . . went and met him: but Mary sat still in the house—This was true to character: Martha, energetic; Mary, placid.

►21 My brother had not died—Martha was confident that Jesus' presence would have prevented Lazarus' death. Mary makes the same comment later (11:32).

►22 whatsoever thou wilt ask of God, God will give it thee—even to the restoration of my dead brother.

►23, 24 But Martha did not take her own suggestion very seriously, for when Jesus replied with a simple affirmative answer (Thy brother shall rise again), she attributed it to the most distant event which Christ's words allowed (i.e., the future resurrection of the believers).

►25 I am the resurrection, and the life—Martha thought of an *event;* Jesus revealed that he, a *person,* is the resurrection and the life. Life (Gk., z̄oe) that is really life (1 Tim. 6:19) is by its very nature resurrection life because it can stand the trial of death. Only one kind of life—the life of God (Eph. 4:18), the indissoluble life (Heb. 7:16), designated z̄oe in the NT—is truly life. All else that is called "life" eventually dies. Jesus was (and is) this life; therefore, he was (and is) resurrection (cf. Rev. 1:18).

►26 And whosoever liveth and believeth in me shall never die—is better translated, ". . . shall not die forever." Lazarus had been a believer in Jesus; therefore, even though he died, he would live. Every believer who has died would yet live, and everyone who was (and is) still living and believing would certainly not die forever. Christ did not promise the prevention of death; He promised the life that guarantees resurrection and eternal life. Christ did not prevent Lazarus's death, but he would guarantee his eternal life.

►27 I believe—lit., "I have believed." The perfect tense indicates that her past belief was still very much present. But her statement (you

are **the Christ, the Son of God**)—be it ever so good—failed to capture the present Christ and the significance of the new title ("I am the resurrection and the life") he had pronounced for himself.

►28, 29 she went her way, and called Mary her sister—After this exchange, Martha quickly persuaded Mary to come and talk with the Master.

►30, 31 Mary was followed closely by an entourage of mourners, since in her society prolonged mourning for the dead was considered an essential part of every funeral. (Professional mourners were sometimes even hired for a fee.) It was this kind of excessive sorrow over physical death—and especially in the case of a believer like Lazarus—that grieved our Lord so very deeply (see comments on 11:33).

►32 if thou hadst been here, my brother had not died—Mary repeated Martha's statement (11:21).

►33 he groaned—or, "he was agitated," or, "he was indignantly angered." The underlying Greek verb is consistently used in the Septuagint (LXX) and NT to express anger or agitation (see Lam. 2:6; Dan. 11:30, LXX; Matt. 9:30; Mark 1:43; 14:5). The atmosphere all around Jesus must have angered and agitated him: the mourners with their excessive sorrow, Martha's lack of understanding, Mary's faithless rebuke, and the general unbelief.

►35 Jesus wept—lit., "Jesus shed tears." Jesus was so saddened by the faithless grief that surrounded him that tears filled his eyes before he reached the site of the tomb.

►36, 37 The misinterpretation of his tears, coupled with the mistrust of his motives and abilities, grieved Christ still further.

►38, 39 The Scripture says that Jesus was again groaning [the same word used in 11:3] in himself. The weight of the stone and the smell of the corpse would prove irrefutably that the raising of Lazarus was no clever illusion of a crafty magician.

►40 if thou wouldest believe, thou shouldest see the glory of God—The whole event was for Christ to display God's glory; Christ knew this all along (11:4).

►41, 42 Father, I thank thee that thou hast heard me.—While the crowd waited beside the open tomb Christ glorified his Father in testimony and prayer.

**➤43** He shouted the triumphant cry of resurrection: **Lazarus, come forth.**

**➤44** Lazarus walked out of the tomb in his **graveclothes.** Since God never wastes his power by using supernatural energy for ordinary tasks (cf. 2:7, 8; Luke 9:12-17), Jesus instructed the speechless onlookers to unwrap Lazarus themselves.

**➤45** The stunning display of power which they had just seen finally forced many of the Jews to acknowledge Jesus as the Messiah.

**➤46** Yet other Jewish onlookers felt that even the power of resurrection was inadequate evidence of Messiahship, so they reported Jesus to the Pharisees.

## 47-57 THE ARREST PLANS OF THE PRIESTS AND PHARISEES

**➤47, 48 Then gathered the chief priests and the Pharisees a council**—In one sense the Jewish leaders' fears were justified, since the Romans were known for their fear of rivalry (Matt. 2:16-18); yet in the larger outlook, the Pharisees' plottings were based on purely selfish motives, since Christ was challenging the Jewish leadership rather than the Roman government (cf. Matt. 23:1-36). Not one of Christ's followers was a political office-seeker.

**➤49, 50 Caiaphas,** the current **high priest,** then responded to his underlings' fears with a truly remarkable statement: **one man should die for the people.**

**➤51, 52 it is expedient for us, that one man should die for the people, and that the whole nation perish not**—Caiphas's immediate intent was certainly murderous, but verses 51 and 52 show that God used Caiaphas in his position as high priest to utter a striking prediction about the worldwide efficacy of Christ's death. **And not for that nation only, but that also he should gather together in one the children of God that were scattered abroad**—Jesus would die, not to save the nation from the Romans, but to gather together into one all the scattered children of God (see 10:16; 17:20-26).

**➤53** The vengeful Jewish leaders of course missed the higher theological implications of Caiaphas's statement and immediately began plotting Jesus' death.

**➤54** Because God's divinely appointed moment for Christ's capture had not yet arrived (cf. 7:30, 44; 8:59; 10:39), our Lord discontinued his public appearances in Jerusalem. It is not always God's will for his people to risk death in a storm of persecution (cf. Acts 8:1-4; 9:23-25).

**➤55** The **Jews' Passover was nigh at hand** [near]: **and many went . . . to purify themselves**—The Jewish people were right in preparing themselves for the Passover (cf. Exod. 12:14-20; 13:1-9) but tragically wrong in ignoring or rejecting the very sacrifice it pictured (1 Cor. 5:7, 8; 1 Pet. 1:19; Rev. 5:6-14).

*Chapter* **12**

## 1-8 THE ANOINTING AT BETHANY

**➤1 Jesus . . . came to Bethany**—Among those who loved him were his friends at Bethany. In a world that would not receive him, among his own people who would not own him (moreover, who were intending to kill him), how comforting it must have been for him to have a place of rest and love, a home to which he could resort. **Bethany**—was a place of sweetness and supply (Bethany means "a house of figs"). His friends were there to receive him and serve him (Luke 10:38). Whenever Jesus came to Jerusalem he did not lodge there, but he would go to Bethany to lodge with his friends Mary, Martha, and Lazarus (see Matt. 21:17). **six days before the passover**—Jesus came to Bethany. This would be his last visit, for Jesus was on his way to be sacrificed as the Passover Lamb at Calvary. We do not know if anyone was truly aware of this. According to the other Gospels as well as John's, Jesus had given his disciples plenty of warning. But his word about his death did not penetrate. Who, among his loved ones, realized that Jesus was about to die? Did his disciples, absorbed as they were with the coming glory? Did Lazarus, recently raised from the dead? Did Martha, obsessed with her serving? It seems that only Mary perceived that Jesus' death was imminent. Perhaps she realized that evening would be her last with him. This would be her last chance to demonstrate her love to him.

**➤3** She had been keeping a very costly precious ointment for just such an occasion. When supper was ended, she took the **spikenard . . . and anointed the feet of Jesus, and wiped his feet with her hair: and the house was filled**—with the fragrance!

►**4-6** The disciples were offended that Mary would waste this ointment (Mark 14:4), and **Judas Iscariot . . . a thief**—would have liked to pocket the money for which it could have been sold.

►**7, 8 Let her alone: against the day of my burying hath she kept this. For the poor always ye have with you; but me ye have not always.**—Jesus pointed out that this ointment was not wasted on him. Certainly, the money could have been given to the poor, but there would always be the poor. Yet they would not always have Jesus. Mary had perceived the preciousness of having him with them. And besides, her anointing would serve as a burial ointment. The ointment that Mary had kept for this occasion would keep until the day of his burial and, in effect, serve as the burial unguent.

## 9-19 CHRIST'S TRIUMPHANT ENTRY INTO JERUSALEM

►**9-11 they came not for Jesus' sake only, but that they might see Lazarus also**—The chief priests and Pharisees were too cowardly to arrest Christ in the presence of the welcoming throng (cf. Mark 11:26-33; Luke 20:19; 22:1, 2), so the common people were free to welcome both Jesus and Lazarus. Yet far from abandoning their plan to kill Jesus (11:53, 57), the Jewish leaders included innocent Lazarus in their postponed scheme of murder. The venom of unbelief is truly astonishing (cf. Acts 7:54-58). Lazarus's resurrection (11:37-44) had so enthralled the fickle crowd that they were now ready to acclaim Jesus as their Savior and king.

►**12-15** The next day Jesus made his triumphal entry into Jerusalem. The people were hailing him, crying out, **Hosanna, Blessed is the King of Israel that cometh in the name of the Lord**—As they shouted "Hosanna" (from Hebrew, meaning "save now"), they were expecting that the conquering Messiah had come to save them from Roman captivity. To their way of thinking, the one "who comes in the name of the Lord" would be "the *King* of Israel" (see Ps. 118:25, 26; Zeph. 3:15). The people were hailing the arrival of their King! Indeed, their King was coming to them—but not the kind of king they expected. Rather, Jesus came to them in the way prophesied by Zechariah: "Behold your king is coming to you; He is just and endowed with salvation,

Humble and mounted on a donkey, Even on a colt, the foal of a donkey" (9:9, NASB). The King, in this coming, would not be a conqueror, but a humble servant. And he would not be exalted to the Davidic throne, but lifted up on Calvary's cross. The Passover Lamb had come to be slaughtered (1 Cor. 5:7); the grain of wheat had come to be buried (12:24). Of course, the people at that time could never have imagined that his entrance into Jerusalem was an entrance into the throes of death. They never would have thought that Jesus was about to enter into glory through death and resurrection. As they shouted scriptures from Psalm 118:25, 26, they probably never thought that the very same Psalm (vs. 22) ironically foretold that the cornerstone would be rejected by the builders.

►**16 These things understood not his disciples at the first**—Not even Christ's closest followers understood the tremendous prophetic significance of his triumphant entry until after the resurrection. The Spirit of the glorified Jesus would open their eyes to the true sense of the OT and bring to their recollection this and other Messianic predictions.

►**18 For this cause the people also met him, for that they had heard that he had done this miracle.**—This reiterates the rather superficial enthrallment with Christ's miracles which characterized most of the cheering well-wishers (12:13). It is still possible to speak of Christ in glowing terms but reject him as our personal Savior. This is surely the ultimate human tragedy.

►**19** The Pharisees, however, were not concerned about the well-wishers' inner motivations, but only about their enthusiastic gossip. So their temporary despair only intensified their burning desire to eliminate Christ at any cost and at the very first opportunity. This helps to explain the almost instant hatred which the Jewish leaders later displayed at Christ's several fraudulent trials (Matt. 26:66-68; 27:22-25; John 18:29-31; 19:6, 7, 14, 15).

►**20, 21 there were certain Greeks among them that came up to worship at the feast . . . saying, Sir, we would see Jesus**—These visitors from Greece were apparently converts to Judaism and had very likely been among the Passover pilgrims who greeted Christ as he rode into Jerusalem on a donkey (12:12-15). And they almost surely heard about

Jesus' resurrection powers sometime during their Passover pilgrimage (cf. 12:17, 18). The Greek worshipers selected Philip (himself a visitor to Jerusalem from northern Galilee— 12:21) as their intermediary to Christ because of his Greek name and perhaps also because of his winsome personality (cf. John 1:43-46).

➤22 For a moment Philip hesitated to approach Jesus with the Greeks' request; but after discussing it with **Andrew,** both of them approached Jesus together. (Compare the intermediary role of these two men in 1:41-46. See also 6:59.)

➤23, 24 The whole world had gone after him (12:19)! Even the Greeks wanted to see him (12:20). That should have been the time for Jesus to seize the hour! But the hour had **come** for **the Son of man** to *be glorified* through death and resurrection. The hour had come for him, like a **corn** [grain] **of wheat,** to be buried in the earth. He would forego the momentary glory for the eternal. The buried grain would eventually bring forth much fruit, more fruit than could have been gained had he then and there taken the kingship on earth. Indeed, Jesus, through being lifted up on the cross, would draw all men to himself. His cross, like a charged magnet, would draw millions and millions to him (12:32). This has been evidenced by the history of the last two millennia. How many have been drawn to Christ! And how many grains have come from that one seed! Thank Jesus that he chose the way of death. If he had not gone to Calvary, he would have remained single and alone, like an unplanted grain. But his burial, like a planting, brought germination and multiplication.

➤25 See comments on Luke 9:24.

➤26 **If any man serve me, let him follow me**—i.e., let him follow my pattern of self-denial.

## 27-50 THE VOICE FROM HEAVEN AND THE PROCLAMATION OF CHRIST

➤27 **Now is my soul troubled**—The time of Christ's crucifixion was approaching so rapidly that Jesus concluded his remarks to Philip and Andrew (12:20-26) with a glimpse into his inner agony of expectation.

➤28 **Father, glorify thy name.**—Christ's burning desire to glorify the Father transcended his revulsion of sin's judgment, and God the Father responded to this noble motivation with his audible approval from heaven. All of Christ's words and works had truly **glorified** the Father (cf. 5:19-21, 30; 8:28, 29).

➤29 **The people . . . heard it**—The listening throng, however, totally missed the significance of Christ's words and the Father's response, and they attributed the voice from heaven to either **thunder** or an **angel.**

➤30-33 So Jesus explained to the audience that the voice was intended to show the imminence of his greatest God-glorifying act— death on the cross (which is described as being **lifted up from the earth**). At this great moment in history the sins of the world would be judged and the **prince** of the world's authority would be **cast out** (i.e., ejected from his rule). But Christ's majestic disclosure, coupled with a hint of his circumstances of death, only confused his listeners still further. They had believed in a figure called the Messiah—and when Jesus seemed to fit that image, they began to believe in him; but it was difficult to believe him when he continually spoke of his imminent death, and that on a cross. The signs he performed encouraged their faith, but his words about his death shattered the Messianic image.

➤34 The people had been taught from **the law** (i.e., the Scriptures) that the Messiah would never die, for he would have an eternal kingdom (see Ps. 89:4, 28, 29; 110:4; Isa. 9:6, 7; Dan. 2:44; 7:14).

➤35, 36 **Yet a little while is the light with you. Walk while ye have the light**—Rather than engage in a futile attempt to correct the people's misconceptions against their will, Jesus replied with an easily understood warning to take advantage of the light of the world while he was still with them (cf. 1:5-9; 3:18-21; 8:12; 9:4, 5). After delivering this ample warning, Christ withdrew from the crowds to prepare for his final pre-crucifixion activities.

➤37-41 These verses show that Christ's continued preaching or miracle-working would have rendered no additional useful purpose, since by now each observer had received ample evidence to make an intelligent choice. Only a small minority of Christ's audiences ever decided to believe in him. Yet even those few who accepted Christ chose to remain secret disciples for fear of the hostile Pharisees (12:42, 43).

In short, the Jews were blind and hardened. They did not see that Jesus was the Christ. This unbelief was predicted by Isaiah. In the opening of the great chapter on the suffering Savior and sacrificial Lamb, Isaiah declared, "To whom was the arm of the Lord revealed?" (Isa. 53:1). It took revelation from God to see that the suffering, death-bound Jesus was the glorious Lord. But God blinded the Jews and hardened their hearts (see Rom. 11:25) so that they did not see or understand. They did not turn to the Lord and receive his healing. But Isaiah had seen his glory, and because of his vision he predicted the blindness to come (see Isa. 6:1-10). Isaiah had foreseen so much concerning Christ; he was foremost among the prophets to speak of the sufferings of Christ (see Isa. 50, 52, 53) and the glories that followed (see Isa. 6, 9, 11 40, 60, 61). But he prophesied to a dull people.

➤**42 among the chief rulers also many believed on him**—such as Nicodemus and Joseph of Arimathea (19:38, 39).

➤**44-50** Jesus had left the skeptical crowds temporarily (12:36, 37), but here in one final public appearance he appealed to his hearers to believe in him as God (cf. 5:17-44; 6:27-65; 7:16-18; 8:14-58; 10:14-18) and thereby walk in his light. Verse 47 reiterates the important truth that Christ came not to judge the world but to save it (cf. 3:17; 8:15, 16), even though his rejected words would condemn all unbelievers in the final day of judgment (cf. 3:31-36). At that time Christ will indeed judge all mankind as the magistrate of the Father (5:22, 23, 26-30). Then Christ closed his message with one final appeal to accept the Father-guided words he had spoken and thereby receive eternal life (3:16, 17, 35, 36; 5:24-29, 39, 40). These verses (12:44-50) provide a summary of Jesus' entire testimony.

Chapter **13**

## 1-38 THE LAST SUPPER

➤**1 having loved his own which were in the world, he loved them unto the end**—or, to the utmost. But the meaning seems to be that Jesus continued his devotion to the disciples until the very end of his life—and this is all the more remarkable when we consider how Jesus could have been absorbed with his own conflicts.

➤**2 supper**—This was the yearly Passover supper (13:1), which Jesus and his disciples partook of before the "Lord's Supper" (cf. Matt. 26:17-30; Mark 14:12-26; Luke 22:7-39). **being ended**—"being served" or "going on," according to other ancient manuscripts. **the devil having now put into the heart of Judas Iscariot . . . to betray him**—This scene of Christ's humble servitude in the face of Judas's imminent betrayal forms one of the most touching episodes in all of Scripture.

➤**3-5 Jesus knowing . . . that he was come from God, and went to God**—Jesus had an absolute knowledge of his origin and destiny. He knew that he had come as God's servant to accomplish redemption, and he knew that he would rise again and return to the Father. His actions that evening illustrated what it means to him to have come from God and to return to God. The action of rising from supper and setting aside his garment depicted how he, who existed in God's form, equal with God (Phil. 2:6), was willing to divest himself of that reputation. And the action of taking the towel and girding himself with it illustrated how he humbled himself to take the form of a servant. After washing the disciples' feet (a sign of his cleansing ministry), he put his garments on again and returned to his former position (13:12). This exhibited his return to glory and to God. The entire scene is very close to what Paul verbalized in Philippians 2:5-11. John 13:3-12 provides the portrait, Philippians 2:5-11 the caption.

➤**6-11** In between the act of rising and returning, Jesus washed the disciples' feet. All the disciples accepted the washing—until Jesus came to Peter, who refused to let Jesus wash his feet: **Thou shalt never wash my feet.** But Jesus told him, **If I wash thee not, thou hast no part with me.** Then Peter wanted a bath! But a bath is not necessary for one who had been bathed, for such a one is completely clean except for his feet. What a bathed person needs is foot-washing. In speaking to Peter, Jesus used two different Greek words (*niptō* and *louō*) to convey two different kinds of washing. The two washings, one initial and the other continual, are very important to the Christian life. The Greek word *niptō* appearing in 13:5, 6, 8, and in the last part of 13:10, is used throughout the Septuagint and NT to indicate the washing of the extremities (i.e., the hands and the feet). *Louō* (from which is formed the perfect participle *lelouomenos* in 13:10) specifically means bathing. According to the customs of those times, once a person had bathed his body, he needed only to wash his feet before partaking of a meal. Jesus was going around to all the disciples washing their feet until Peter protested. In his response to Peter, the Lord appropriately used both words in order to advance a precious truth: as he who has been bathed needs only to wash his feet daily, so he who has been bathed by the Lord (through his word, the Spirit, and/or baptism—see John 15:3; Tit. 3:5; Eph. 5:26) needs only to wash himself day by day from the filth and defilement which he accumulates by his contact with the world.

➤**12-17** Besides the spiritual significance contained in the Lord's word about the two kinds of washing, the act of washing the feet demonstrated the service of love. Jesus, the Teacher and Master, had stooped to a position of humility and service because he loved those he served. Jesus commanded his disciples to love one another according to the model he provided. They were to serve one another in love and with humility. Again, this thought is paralleled in Philippians 2:3-5.

➤**18, 19  I speak not of you all: I know whom I have chosen**—See 6:70. **but that the scripture may be fulfilled**—See Psalm 41:9. Christ had, of course, known all along that Judas would betray him (see 6:64, 70, 71; Matt. 17:22, 23; 20:17-19), but he predicted the betrayal in the presence of his disciples so that they could regard the fulfilled prediction as an additional validation of Jesus' Messiahship at the time they most needed encouragement.

➤**20** Then Jesus reinforced his claim to deity still another time with his words in this verse (cf. 5:17-44; 6:27-65; 7:16-18; 8:14-58; 10:14-18; etc.) so that the disciples would continue to believe in their Master even as he hung dying on the cross.

➤**21** Since none of the disciples had responded to Christ's previous hints about Judas's betrayal (13:10, 18, 19), Jesus reiterated the awful prophecy even more explicitly.

➤**22-24** This time the disciples understood what Jesus meant, for Peter beckoned to John, the one **whom Jesus loved,** to find out from

Jesus exactly who the traitor would be (cf. Matt. 26:22-25; Mark 14:19, 20; Luke 22:23).

➤**26** Christ's disclosure to John involved a courtesy to the Satanically goaded traitor—the honor of receiving the traditional sauce-soaked bread (called **sop** in KJV—cf. the foot-washing honor—13:4, 5).

➤**27-30** So tactful was Christ's identification of Judas that all the disciples except John missed the significance of the act. Yet Judas, now indwelt by Satan, took Christ's courtesy as an immediate cue to betray the Son of God to the murderous Pharisees. What a chilling interplay of human avarice, Satanic hatred, and divine permission! Only God knows the eternal agonies that await these human and Satanic co-conspirators of betrayal (Matt. 26:20-24; Rev. 20:10).

➤**31 when he** [Judas Iscariot] **was gone out, Jesus said, Now is the Son of man glorified, and God is glorified in him**—As long as Judas Iscariot was in the room, Jesus had been unable to speak freely of his coming glory or of his intimate tie with his true disciples. But with the traitor gone Christ looked past the cross to his glorification in resurrection. The Lord's final discourse begins here (not in 14:1 as is usually stated), and this discourse begins on the theme of glorification. Once Judas went out to betray him, the Lord knew that his crucifixion and resurrection were imminent; he knew he was about to be glorified. Anticipating his glorification, he utters the proleptic proclamation in 13:31, **Now is** [lit., "was"] the Son of man glorified and God is [lit., "was"] glorified in him. This glorification is the keystone of the following discourse. All that follows is built upon the fact that Jesus viewed his glorification, through death and resurrection, as accomplished. As a result of this glorification, Jesus in resurrection would acquire a spiritual form which would enable him to indwell his disciples and they him. In other words, the essential thing to keep in mind when reading John 14 (and the following chapters) is that most of the discourse is framed in terms of Christ's anticipation of his resurrection and what that resurrection would generate in respect to his spiritual union with the disciples. Indeed, in John 15 the Lord envisions himself and the disciples already organically united as vine and branches, for he says, in the proleptic present tense, "I *am* the vine, you *are* the branches." This, of course, could not be realized until the Lord in resurrection, imparted his life to his believers (see 14:19). On the evening of the resurrection the Lord would come to his disciples and breathe the Spirit into them (20:22), and from then on he would live in them and they in him. All the references to his coming in chapters 14-16 are not to the second advent as such, but to his coming to them in resurrection. His absence from the disciples would be only for "a little while" (16:16). Then (after three days) they would see him again and rejoice, for on that day, the day of his resurrection, they would know that they were in him and he in them.

➤**32 If God be glorified in him**—This clause is not present in several ancient manuscripts. But the rest of the verse is unquestionably genuine. It indicates that the Father would be glorified in his Son's glorification.

➤**33 I go**—to the Father (14:6, 28).

➤**34 A new commandment . . . love one another**—Christ's **new commandment,** that of brotherly love, was not some radical new concept but simply an intensified emphasis on God's old commandments of love (Exod. 20:12-17; Lev. 19:18, 33, 34; Deut. 5:16-21; 22:1-4; Matt. 5:38-48; 7:12; 23:36-40; Luke 10:25-37).

➤**37** Christ's love to his disciples was the model and standard of the kind of love they should have for one another. Simon Peter thought he had already attained to this kind of love and would be willing to die for his Master, but how mistaken he turned out to be (cf. Matt. 26:69-75; Mark 14:66-72).

➤**38** See comments on Luke 22:31-34.

*Chapter* **14**

## 1-31 JESUS' LAST DISCOURSE: JESUS, THE ABODE OF GOD AND MAN

➤**1 Let not your heart be troubled**—speaking to Peter and all the other disciples.

➤**2 In my Father's house are many mansions**—lit., "abodes." The first portion of John 14 traditionally has been interpreted with the understanding that verse 2 refers to God's house in heaven. Accordingly, many commentators think that Jesus was speaking about his Father's house in heaven, to which he had to

go in order to prepare some rooms and from which he would return one day to take back his believers to be with him in heaven. The day of that return usually has been designated as the second advent (or perhaps the Lord's personal visitation to each believer when they depart this world—a favorite homily at funerals).

The traditional exegesis has serious problems. First of all, heaven is not mentioned in John 14. Second, the going away and coming again according to the context of John 14-16 would be but for "a little while" (see 14:19, 20; 16:16-23), not two or more millennia! Indeed, 14:20 and 16:20-22 make it more than evident that "that day" would be the day of Christ's resurrection, the day in which the disciples would realize that they had become united to the resurrected Christ. Third, John 14:4 and 6 indicate that Jesus was talking about the believers coming to the Father through him, the unique way. Surely this access to the Father is not reserved for the second advent or for the time of each saint's departure from this world. Jesus came to provide believers with a way to approach and indwell the Father here and now (see Eph. 2:18). Fourth, John 14:2, 3 reveal that Jesus' intention was to bring the disciples to be with him "where I am," not "where I will be." Where was the Lord then and there? Jesus repeatedly indicated that he was in the Father (10:38; 14:10, 11), and he prayed in John 17 that the disciples would also be with him in the Father (17:21-24). Of course, the Lord also indicated that he was going to the Father (14:12; 16:28) and that that ascent would take him to heaven. As such, it could be inferred that he was going to heaven, and that was where he wanted to take his disciples. But this seems to miss the mark. The goal of Jesus' mission, according to the Gospel of John, was to express the Father to mankind and to bring the believers to the Father. John 14:6 says it so clearly: "I am the way and the truth and the life; no one comes to the Father except through me."

Since the traditional exegesis of John 14:2, 3 has serious defects, some modern commentators have attempted to resolve the problems by suggesting that this passage could indicate: (1) the Lord's second advent and the believers' ascent to heaven; (2) the believers' ascent to heaven at the time of death; or (3) the believers' immediate access to God the Father through the

Son. Of the three possible meanings, the first is not very Johannine, although possible, but the second is highly unlikely (the Scriptures nowhere speak of the Lord's coming again and again for each deceased believer). Only the third seems valid. Nevertheless, most commentators think Jesus was talking about going to a place (heaven) and not to a person (the Father). **I go to prepare a place for you**—When Jesus said that he was going to prepare a place for the disciples in the Father's house, could he not have been suggesting that he himself was that house? Did not the Father dwell in him, and he in the Father? Then, the way for the disciples to dwell in the Father would be for them to come and abide in the Son. In other words, by coming into the One who was indwelt by the Father, the believers would come simultaneously into the Indweller, the Father. Clearly, this was the Lord's desire and design (see 14:20; 17:21-24). Therefore, when he said he was going to prepare a place for them, does it not mean that he, through the process of death and resurrection, was going to make himself ready to be inhabited by his disciples? In short, Jesus was (and is) the Father's house that needed to be prepared to receive the believers. The same expression, "Father's house," appears in John 2:16, in which it is clear that the temple in Jerusalem was the Father's house; yet in the next few verses (2:17-21) Jesus likens himself to the temple, a temple that would be destroyed and raised again in three days. Thus, the Son, through the process of crucifixion and resurrection, would become the temple, the Father's house, prepared to receive the believers. He, as the temple, the Father's house, would be the means through which the believers could come to dwell in the Father and the Father in them (see MacGregor). In other words, the Son would become the common abode of the believers and God.

Other commentators prefer to see "the Father's house" as being the church, the dwelling place of God (see 1 Cor. 3:16, 17; Eph. 2:20-22; Heb. 3:2). As such, the promise in 14:2, 3 is then thought to relate to the corporate fellowship that would be possible through Christ's departure and return in the Spirit (Gundry). In this view, the "many abodes" would be the many members of God's household. Christ went to prepare a place for each member in God's household

(cf. 1 Chron. 17:9)—the preparation was accomplished by his death and resurrection. If, however, the "many abodes" must be connected with Christ or God's house, the explanation is more difficult.

For how could the Lord contain many abodes? Answer: the same way in which the vine incorporates many branches. Note, the Lord does not say, "In my Father's house, there will be [future tense] many abodes." This was spoken proleptically, as also was John 15:2. The believers are viewed as having already inhabited the Son, or as having already been joined to him. Yet this could not be actualized until after the Lord's death and resurrection. It required preparation. Therefore, though the believers are viewed as already being abodes in the Father's house, a place needed to be prepared for them. Once the Lord was resurrected, God's house would be enlarged from one individual abode (i.e., the Father and the Son indwelling each other) to many abodes (i.e., the Father and the Son indwelling many believers and vice versa). The word "abodes" is used only twice in the entire NT, both places in John 14 (verses 2 and 23). Could the "abodes" be different abodes? According to John 14:23 each believer becomes an abode of the Father and the Son, and since there are many believers, these must be the many abodes in the Father's house. In verse 2, the abodes are spoken of as already existing; but in verse 23, we see how these abodes actually come into existence.

➤**3 I will come again** [lit., "I am coming again"], **and receive you unto myself**—Notice, the Lord does not say, "I am coming again and will receive you to *heaven*," but, "I am coming again and will receive you to *myself*." A person, not a place, is the destination. The present tense Greek verb (I am coming") shows the immediacy of the Lord's coming back. His coming to them again would be realized in a short while. (This is confirmed by 16:16—note the similar use of "again.") When the Lord said, "I am coming again," that "coming again" came on the day of his resurrection. However, many commentators say this is the parousia.

➤**4 And whither I go ye know, and the way ye know**—It should be pointed out that several modern translators of 14:4 offer expansions based upon the traditional exegesis explained previously (14:2). The translators of NIV, TEV, and NEB added words which indicate that the Lord was going *to a place*: NIV ("the way to the place"), TEV ("the way that leads to the place"), and NEB ("my way there"—a little less conspicuous). But, in context and in accordance with Johannine thought, the Lord was preparing the way through himself to the Father. The destination is not a place but a person. Thomas Merton said, "Where is this place? It is not a place, it is God."

➤6 God is the destination, and the Son is the way to him. **I am the way, the truth and the life: no man cometh unto the Father but by** [except through] **me.** Christ is the way to the Father; Christ is the truth (or reality) of all we find in the Father when we get to him; and Christ is all the life that shall ever flow to us and bless us from the Godhead.

➤7 **If ye had known me, ye should have known my Father also**—In the first six verses of John 14, Jesus has revealed the great truth that he is the unique way to the Father. In 14:7 and following, he will begin to unveil that he is the visible manifestation of the Father. If the disciples were to realize that coming to dwell in the Son was equivalent to coming to dwell in the Father, they would have had to realize that the Son was the Father revealed, the manifestation of the Father (see John 1:18; Col. 1:15; Heb. 1:3). If they had come to know the Son, they should have perceived the Father also. Another manuscript reading yields a translation like the one in TEV: "Now that you have known me, . . . you will know my father also." But the entire context of this portion seems to assert the opposite. It is not that the disciples *will* come to know the Father as they have known the Son, but that they should have already known the Father as manifest in the Son. The Lord was reproving them, not promising them some future knowledge of the Father. If he was making a promise, how could the Lord say in the very next sentence: **And from henceforth ye know him, and have seen him.**

➤8, 9 The Lord was not promising but reproving them, due to their lack of discernment—as again 14:9 asserts: "Jesus said to him, have I been with you so long and yet you do not know me, Philip? He who has seen me has seen the Father" (RSV). According to

Philip's concept, the Father was another "person" besides Jesus, a person who could perhaps show up in the room if Jesus called upon him to do so. And though it is true that the Father and Son each have their own distinct "person" (or *persona*), the Son and Father are essentially inseparable; thus, it is impossible to show the Father outside of the Son—for the Son has always been his unique expression. Philip (and the disciples) should have come to know and recognize that the One in their midst was the very expression of God the Father.

➤10, 11 **I am in the Father, and the Father in me**—To know the Son is to know the Father and vice versa because the two exist in one another. This coinherence (mutual indwelling) is the basis of the oneness between the Father and the Son (see 10:30, 38; 17:21-24). The reason the Son could boldly assert that seeing him was equivalent to seeing the Father is that he and the Father are one by virtue of their coinherence. This vital state makes it possible for the believers, because once the believers enter the Son, they come into the Father and the Father comes into them.

➤12 **greater works than these shall he do**—Even though Christ had performed some truly impressive miracles during his earthly ministry, his disciples would perform even greater ones in the post-resurrection era. Christ had fed thousands at a single sitting (6:1-14) but had never seen multitudes converted within a few minutes, so far as we know from the Gospel records. Yet Peter and his fellow preachers initiated unprecedented mass evangelism (Acts 2:37-43, 47; 4:1-4; 6:7) in addition to performing spectacular miracles of healing (Acts 3:1-11; 5:12-16; 6:8). Christ could obviously have converted thousands if he had chosen to, but he instead elected to glorify the Father through the gospel preaching of his Spirit-filled followers (14:13).

➤13, 14 **whatsoever ye shall ask in my name, that will I do**—The sweeping promise of answered prayer described in these verses is absolutely true within the context of Christ's words. When we approach the Father through Christ with a Spirit-inspired request, it will invariably be answered in God's proper time (cf. Matt. 7:7-11; John 15:7, 16; 16:23, 24; Jas. 1:5, 6; 4:1, 2; 1 John 5:14, 15).

➤15 If ye love me, keep my command-ments—True love is obedient love (cf. 14:21), and this kind of love is rewarded with intimate spiritual blessings which the world at large can never know (14:15-17, 21).

➤16 And I will pray the Father, and he shall give you another Comforter, that he may abide with you for ever—The first part of John 14 focuses on God as man's habitation; the second part (beginning with verse 16) cen-ters on man's becoming God's habitation. In the first part of the chapter, Jesus revealed his relationship with the Father because the disci-ples needed to see that their union with the Son meant union with the Father—for the two are one. In the second part Jesus revealed his rela-tionship with the Spirit because his union with the Spirit is the Son's way of indwelling the believers. Jesus himself provides man with the way to access to God, and the Spirit gives God a way of access to man. Therefore, indwelling the Son equals indwelling the Father, and being indwelt by the Spirit equals being indwelt by the Son. In 14:16 Jesus said that the Father would give the disciples **another Comforter.** The expression another Comforter (Gk., *allon paraklēton*) means "another comforter of the same kind as the first." This, of course, implies that Jesus was the first Comforter (see 1 John 2:1), and the Spirit would be the same kind of Comforter. Although it is difficult to reproduce in English the Greek word *paraklētos,* it fun-damentally denotes the office of one who comes to the aid of a person in need (lit., "one who comes to [our] side when called upon"— from *para* [by the side] and *klētos* [called]). Properly speaking, this is the office of an Advo-cate; but this title hardly suits the context of John 14 (cf. 1 John 2:1, where the title Advo-cate is very fitting). Titles like Comforter, Helper, Counselor, or Consoler fit the context of John 14; but neither one by itself seems to be adequate because a Paraclete does more than comfort, help, counsel, and console—he also advocates, exhorts, and teaches.

➤17 Even the Spirit of truth; whom . . . ye know . . . for he dwelleth with you and shall be in you—In this verse Jesus identifies the Comforter. He is **the Spirit of truth,**—or better, the Spirit of reality—inasmuch as he is the Spirit who reveals the reality about God (cf. TEV). The world cannot receive (or accept)

this Spirit of reality because the world does not see him or know him. And then Jesus declares, "you know him [lit., 'it'], because he abides with you and shall be in you." This statement indicates that (1) the Spirit embodied in Jesus was then and there abiding **with** the disciples, and (2) the same Spirit of Jesus would, in the future, be **in** the disciples. In other words, the one who was **with** them would be *in* them. Notice the shift of pronouns from verse 17 to verse 18: "He shall be in you . . . I am coming to you." Who is the "he"? The Comforter, the Spirit of reality. Who is the "I"? Jesus, the Son. Thus, Jesus through the Spirit would be coming to the disciples and indwelling them. (Notice that in verse 20, the Lord says, "I in you." Compare this with verse 17 where Jesus said that the Spirit "shall be in you.") When we put all these statements together, it should be clear that the coming of the Comforter is none other than the coming of the Lord in the Spirit. Sev-eral commentators have remarked on this won-derful truth. Leon Morris said, "He [Jesus] comes in the coming of the Spirit." A.B. Simp-son said, "The coming of the Comforter is just the coming of Jesus himself to the heart." And Watchman Nee affirmed the same: "This Com-forter, Who is the Holy Spirit, is just the Christ that will dwell in you." The Spirit did not come as the Son's replacement or representative, but as the Son himself in his spiritual form. And R.C. Moberly remarked, "It is not for an instant that the disciples are to have the presence of the Spirit instead of having the presence of the Son. But to have the Spirit is to have the Son."

Not all exegetes will agree with the interpre-tation presented above, especially those who do their utmost to distinguish the persons of the Trinity. Yet it must be admitted that according to Christian experience, there is no distinguish-able difference between the experience of Christ and the experience of the Spirit. The two are one and the same. Paul's practical theology affirms this (see Rom. 8:9-11; 1 Cor. 15:45; 2 Cor. 3:17-18), and so does John's (see 7:37-39; 16:11-13; 20:22). The unity between Jesus and the Spirit is essential to the proper interpreta-tion of the Lord's last discourse, and specific-ally to the verses (16-18) we have been discussing. One final citation, from Eric L. Titus, certifies this view:

A tendency to make a distinction between Jesus and the Spirit has been responsible, in part, for failure to recognize the unitive function which this doctrine of the Spirit provides. The references to the Spirit and to the Paraclete in the discourses become meaningful only when they, together with Jesus, become identified as the same thing. This is done in one passage: "I will ask the Father, and He will give you another Helper [Paraclete], that He may be with you always, the Spirit of Truth, whom the world cannot receive, because it neither sees him nor knows him; but you know him, for he abides with you, and he is in you" (14:16-17). This is like saying, "I, Jesus, will ask God for another Paraclete to be with you after I am gone. The world cannot recognize this Paraclete, but you are able to recognize him for I am talking about myself dwelling in your midst, and I will be with you as the indwelling Spirit of Truth." To say that the Father "will send another Paraclete" is the same as saying, "I will come to you," a statement which Jesus makes in the verse immediately following the above quoted passage (14:18).

➤**18 I will not leave you comfortless**—lit., "I will not leave you orphans." **I will come to you**—lit., "I am coming to you." After Jesus told the disciples that the Spirit's coming would be his coming to them, he told them that he would not leave them as orphans; he would father them.

➤**19** This coming would be but in **a little while,** during which time he would be crucified, buried, and resurrected. The world would never see him again, but they would see him in his resurrection appearances (see 20:20, 26; 21:1, 14). John 16:16-23 makes it more than clear that **the little while** indicates the span of time between Christ's death and resurrection. In resurrection, the living One would become the disciples' life because they would become united to him like branches in the vine. **because I live** [timeless and absolute], **ye shall live also**—Each believer's life is intrinsically dependent on Christ's life.

➤**20** In **that day,** the day of resurrection, the disciples would come to **know** (or, realize) that the Son is in the Father, and they are in the Son, and the Son is in them: **I am in my Father, and ye in me, and I in you**—This is the climax of John 14 because the mutual indwelling is made complete.

➤**21-23** This mutual indwelling is made personal in verses 21 through 23. To anyone who loves the Lord, he would **love him** and **manifest** himself to him (14:21). The Greek word underlying "manifest" means "to be brought into light—hence, to appear, to be made visible." The word is used in John 21:1 in connection with the Lord's final resurrection appearance. To the disciples the Lord manifested himself visibly and physically; thereafter, to all his other lovers in his invisible, spiritual presence (see 20:29; 2 Cor. 4:6). In verse 22, **Judas** asked Jesus how he was going to manifest himself to the disciples and not to the world. The Greek word behind "to reveal," as a present active infinitive, denotes a continual act of manifestation, revelation, and disclosure—not just a single event. Indeed, when the Lord related how he would perform the manifestation, it was evident that the manifestation is not once and for all. To the lover of Jesus, the Son and the Father would come and make a permanent abode with him (14:23). Note: it does not say, as might be expected by the context of John 14, that the Father and Son make an abode in the one who loves God—for that would implicate that the lover is but an instrument, a vessel for God. Though it is true that the believers are God's vessels (see Rom. 9:21), the preposition *para* is used here to indicate a side-by-side, mutual activity, as between two lovers who make a home with each other. The RSV and NIV capture this thought with their rendering, "we will come to him and make our home with him." Earlier in John 14 Jesus revealed how he and the Father were a habitation for the believers; now each believer becomes a dwelling place for the Father and the Son—and the Spirit (see 14:17, 18). The Triune God and the believers secure an abode in and with each other.

➤**26** See comments on 15:26; 16:13-15.

➤**27 Peace I leave with you, my peace I give unto you**—Christ bestowed this precious gift of peace on his disciples *before* his death and resurrection rather than after it so that they would have no cause to become unduly discouraged during the difficult hours that lay ahead. Though the faith of the disciples faltered during Christ's ordeal of suffering and death (Matt. 26:56, 69-75; Luke 24:11; John 20:24, 25), his divine gift of peace sustained them in a truly supernatural way during the ensuing years of post-resurrection persecution (Acts 4:5-35; 5:26-42; 1 Pet. 1:2-8).

➤**29 now I have told you before it come to pass**—True to Christ's prediction, his disciples did indeed remember Jesus' prophecies of death, resurrection, and ascension (cf. 14:19, 20) shortly after his resurrection (Luke 24:5-8; 44-48; cf. John 2:22). The total testimony of Christ—his predictions, his miracles, his words of grace, and most of all his resurrection—turned his disciples into burning witnesses for the remaining decades of their earthly lives.

➤**30, 31 Hereafter I will not talk much with you**—In these verses Christ shows that Satan's role in the crucifixion was strictly subordinate to the will of the Father and the voluntary submission of Christ himself. No omnipotent devil terminated the life of the Son of God! Of his own volition, operating in submission to the Father's will, the Son laid down his life.

*Chapter* **15**

## 1-27 JESUS' LAST DISCOURSE: THE VINE AND THE BRANCHES

John 15 follows John 14 thematically in that it dwells on the theme of God and man obtaining an abode in each other. Chapter 15 advances the image from an inorganic dwelling to an organic one: "house" and "abodes" become "vine" and "branches." The mutual indwelling expands from a cohabitation to an organic union.

➤**1 I am the true vine**—This may mean that he, in contrast to the physical vine tree, is the real one. But it probably means that he, in contrast to Israel, who should have been God's vine but failed (Isa. 5:1-7; Jer. 2:19-21), is the

**true vine**—the true fulfillment and actualization of the vine. In fulfillment of Psalm 80, the Son of man and of God's right hand is the vine planted by the Father. The whole race of Israel sprang from the patriarch Israel; the new race of God's people is here viewed as originating from Christ, organically united to him, as branches emanating from the vine—the entire economy being under the care of the Father, the Vinedresser. The union between the vine and the branches is characterized by the expressions "in me" and "in you."

➤**2, 3** In these verses, there are three Greek words whose meanings have troubled translator and exegete alike: *airei* ("lift up" or "take away"); *kathairei* ("cleanse," "purge," or "prune"); and *katharoi* ("cleansed," "purged," or "pruned"). The combination of words *airei* and *kathairei*—a definite wordplay which cannot be matched in English—is fascinating. Most take the first word to designate the action of taking away, though a few would say it means "lift up" (e.g., Pink). Both meanings are there in the NT, but can both be true in this verse? Vinedressers are known to lift up branches from the ground to enhance fruit bearing, and to clean a dirty vine for the same reason. Perhaps the combination of *airei* and *kathairei* describes this process. However, most commentators understand *airei* to describe cutting off (see 15:6) and *kathairei* to describe pruning (Morris). It seems Jesus has moved to a different level of abstraction. Purging, like pruning, is a spiritual cleansing, a taking away of the filth. Verse 3 indicates that the disciples were already clean (*katharoi*) on account of the Lord's word; this purging serves as a pruning, and pruning will cause fruit-bearing.

➤**4** This verse contains the theme of this passage: **Abide** [or, remain] **in me, and I in you**—Since each branch (each believer) has been positioned in the vine, he is charged to *remain* in union with Christ, not to *attain* this union. The Greek for "abide" is an imperative (*meinate*). Here it is constative; it encompasses the entire act of abiding and views it as a single event (Robertson). Then, in the following sentences, the Lord constantly uses present tense verbs to describe the continual activity involved in maintaining an organic union with Christ.

**➤5 the same bringeth forth much fruit**—Each branch that continues to remain in the vine will keep on bearing fruit. Some commentators say the fruit is new converts (cf. 15:6), and others, "the fruit of the Spirit" (Gal. 5:22). Andrew Murray said, "The essential idea of fruit is that it is the silent, natural, restful produce of our inner life." The fruit is the practical expression of the indwelling divine life. This expression in our lives should attract people to Christ and thus make them new members of God's vine.

**➤6 If a man abide not in me, he is cast forth as a branch . . . cast . . . into the fire . . . burned**—Each branch that does not continue to abide in the vine is expelled from the vine. This is a harsh reality, which may or may not implicate eternal destruction. Seen within its context, the verse is probably more experiential than doctrinal. The verse deals with the vital necessity of abiding in the vine and the consequences of not doing so (see Isa. 5:5-7; Ezek. 15:2-7; 19:10-14; Ps. 80:8-16).

**➤7, 8** On the positive side, Jesus assured fruitfulness to each branch abiding in the vine. However, abiding in the vine could be so subjective and mystical that each believer could determine for himself what it entails. So Jesus equated abiding in the vine with abiding in his **word** and with keeping his **commandments.** Every believer who abides in the Lord's word and keeps his commandments will be fruitful (15:7-10).

**➤9-11 As the Father hath loved me, so have I loved you**—The intimate fruitbearing relationship between the Father, the Son, and the believer (15:1-8) is based on a continuum of loving trust (15:9-15). If we as Christians love Christ the way the Father and the Son love each other, we will experience the daily joy of obedience to our Lord (15:9-11).

**➤12-13 love one another**—If we love Christ we should also love our brothers and sisters in Christ, for he has shown us the greatest degree of love that is possible—love unto death.

**➤14 Ye are my friends**—Though every true Christian is in one sense a slave of Christ (Matt. 25:14-23; Luke 17:6-10; John 12:26; 13:12-17; 15:20; Rom. 1:1; 6:1-23), in a still higher sense we are much more than slaves, since Christ has truly revealed the most intimate spiritual truths imaginable to us (John 13-17; Rom. 1-8; Gal. 1-5; Eph. 1-4; Col. 1, 2; Heb. 1-13; etc.).

**➤16 Ye have not chosen me, but I have chosen you**—Though in a subordinate sense human choice is involved in conversion (John 1:12, 13, 47-49; 2:11, 23; 3:15-18, 33-36; 4:42, 50; 5:24, 40; Rev. 22:17; etc.), in the final analysis it is Christ (as well as the Father and the Holy Spirit) who chose us (cf. John 1:43; 6:37, 40, 44-46, 65, 70; 2 Thess. 2:13; etc.). We were chosen not merely to escape hell, but to bear the beautiful fruit of Christian character and witness (cf. 15:8; Mark 4:20; Gal. 5:22, 23). If we fulfill this Christ-abiding and fruitbearing destiny to which we were called, we will enjoy the special blessing of regularly answered prayer (cf. 15:7; John 14:13, 14; 16:23, 24; 1 John 5:14, 15).

**➤18 If the world hate you**—Because the world at large hates the righteous Savior and all who share his holiness (cf. 1 John 3:12, 13), it is essential for all true believers to sustain each other with their daily, Christ-centered love (15:17-21). Any professing Christian who is warmly embraced by the world at large should re-examine the reality of his claim to discipleship (2 Tim. 3:10-12; Jas. 4:4; 1 John 2:15-17; 3:1; 4:5, 6).

**➤22 If I had not come and spoken unto them, they had not had sin**—This verse does not teach that the unevangelized heathen are totally guiltless in the sight of God (cf. Rom. 1:18-2:16) but simply that they are *relatively* guiltless—that is, **less** guilty than the full-enlightened rejectors of Christ (Rom. 2:25-27).

**➤25 They hated me without a cause**—quoted from Psalm 69:4.

**➤26 But when the Comforter is come, whom I will send unto you from the Father**—In 14:26 it was asserted that the Father would send the Comforter, the Spirit of truth, in the name of his Son, the Lord Jesus Christ. Just as the Son had come in the Father's name (i.e., the Son, as the very embodiment of the Father, came to express the Father), so the Spirit would come in the Son's name, as the embodiment of the Son, to make the Son real in the believers' experience. Perhaps this is why the Spirit in NT writings has taken on the name "Lord" ("the Spirit of the Lord," 2 Cor. 3:17, 18), "Jesus" ("the Spirit of Jesus," Acts

16:7), "Christ" ("the Spirit of Christ," Rom. 8:9; 1 Pet. 1:11), and "Jesus Christ" ("the Spirit of Jesus Christ," Phil. 1:19). In 14:26 it is said that the Father would send the Holy Spirit in Jesus' name; in this verse it is stated that the Son would send the Comforter, the Spirit of truth, from the Father. Who sent the Spirit? The Father (14:26) or the Son (15:26)? There is actually no contradiction, for the Lord says that he would send the Spirit **from the Father.** In fact, the Lord emphasizes that the Spirit proceeds out from the Father. Both 14:26 and 15:26 designated the Father as the source whence the Spirit would be sent. Chapter 15 adds an extra detail: the Son would also send the Spirit. Thus, the Father and Son together would send the Spirit.

➤**27 ye also shall bear witness, because ye have been with me from the beginning**—This statement refers especially to Christ's original disciples, since only they had been "with him from the beginning," but by application the verse could extend to all Christians as well (cf. Matt. 28:18-20; Acts 1:8; Rom. 10:14, 15).

*Chapter* **16**

## 1-33 JESUS' LAST DISCOURSE: THE COMING COMFORTER

➤**1 that ye should not be offended**—lit.,"stumbled," perhaps conveying the idea of "falling away" (see TEV). Christ's words of John 14 and 15 had been truly reassuring, and his post-resurrection followers found themselves recalling these promises often (cf. Acts 1:4-8). Throughout the many centuries of Christian persecution, thousands of believers have lived and died with the promises of Jesus at their lips.

➤**2, 3 the time cometh, that whosoever killeth you will think that he doeth God service**—Tragically, the post-resurrection enemies of Christ have misunderstood his words as grossly as his pre-crucifixion antagonists (cf. 2:19-22; 5:16-18; 6:28-66; 7:16-52; 8:12-59; 10:1-42), and many anti-Christian zealots have deluded themselves into thinking they were pleasing God by killing Christians, exactly as here predicted by Christ (cf. Acts 5:33-40; 7:54–8:3).

➤**4** Though Christ had intimated this kind of persecution early in his ministry (Matt. 5:10-12; 10:16-40), he had never before described the self-deluded zeal that would accompany the harassment (cf. 15:17-21).

➤**5 now I go my way to him that sent me**—The disciples had wondered previously about Christ's imminent fate (13:36; 14:4, 5), but had apparently never inquired about his subsequent resurrection and ascension to the Father.

➤**6, 7 It is expedient for you that I go away: for if I do not go away, the Comforter will not come unto you**—This exalted truth and its blessed consequence was far too lofty a concept for the disciples to comprehend in their immediate **sorrow.** Yet Jesus once again stressed the important ministries of the coming Holy Spirit (16:8-15; cf. 14:15-17, 26; 15:26) so that the disciples would remember these vital facts in their post-resurrection witness (cf. John 2:22; 12:16; 14:26).

➤**8-11 And when he is come, he will reprove** [convict] **the world of sin, and of righteousness and of judgment**—Jesus here declares that the Spirit will convict the world (prove mankind guilty) concerning sin, righteousness, and judgment. He will convict the world (1) of its sin **because they believe not on me**—(i.e., the world's unbelief is their sin); (2) concerning **righteousness, because I go to my Father, and ye see me no more**—(i.e., it will now be the Spirit's function to show men that righteousness is in Christ); (3) concerning judgment **because the prince of this world is judged**—(i.e., the Spirit will show to mankind that Christ judged Satan). Operating according to what Christ has accomplished, the Spirit convicts men concerning their sin of unbelief in Christ, concerning the righteousness that is found in Christ alone, and concerning the judgment over Satan accomplished by Christ on the cross (Morris).

➤**13-15** Having indicated what the Spirit would be doing **in the world** (16:7-11), Jesus then relates (in 16:13-15) to the disciples what the Spirit would be doing in the believers (Morris). Verses 13-15 display a sublime picture of the inner workings of the three members of the Godhead, and special detail is given to describe the Spirit's function of conveying the Father and the Son to the believers, and of leading the believers into the Son and the Father. Here the Spirit is seen in full submission to and in harmony with the Son and the Father. He does not act or speak from himself; nothing originates from him, for all comes from the Son and all is done to glorify the Son. Just as the Son did not do anything from himself, but only that which he heard and received from the Father (see 5:19, 30; 8:28, 38; 14:10, 24), so the Spirit never acts independently from the Son. The Spirit appropriates the aggregate totality of Christ's person and reveals it, item by item, to the believers. Yet in revealing Christ (and all that he is) the Spirit is actually revealing the Father, because all that Christ has is the Father's. Thus, the Spirit reveals the Son, who, in turn, expresses the Father. **he will guide you into all truth**—The prominent role of the Spirit of reality is to lead or guide the believers **into** (Greek *eis*) all the reality of Christ (16:13). According to Johannine usage, which seems to follow the classical distinction between *eis* and *en*, *eis* is used dynamically—indicating penetration into an object, person, or sphere. When the Spirit leads the believers **into** all the truth, he penetrates that sphere for them and guides them into a definite destiny, Christ (who is reality). **whatsoever he shall hear, that shall he speak**—In addition to revealing Christ and guiding the believers into the experience of Christ, the Spirit's function is to continue the spoken ministry of Jesus. According to 14:26, the Spirit would come to carry on Jesus' speaking both by way of teaching and by way of reminding the disciples of what Jesus had said during his ministry. (This reminding enabled the Gospel writers to recall and record the very words of Jesus.) The Spirit would also affirm Jesus' ministry by bearing witness to him (15:26). The Lord had many things he wanted to tell the disciples before he departed from them, but they were not able to bear them. When the Spirit would come, he would speak to the disciples whatever he heard from Jesus (16:12, 13). The Spirit's function throughout the church age has been to continue Jesus' spoken ministry. The Lord through the Spirit still speaks to the churches. In Revelation chapters 2 and 3 *the Lord Jesus* addressed each of the seven local churches, and yet it is said that the churches should hear what *the Spirit* says to the churches

(see Rev. 2:1 and 7, 8 and 11, 12 and 17, 18 and 29; 3:1 and 6; 7 and 13; 14 and 22).

➤**16-19 A little while, and ye shall not see me: and again, a little while, and ye shall see me, because I go to the Father**—Since his departure was imminent, Jesus had much he wanted to convey to his beloved disciples, who (by now) must have realized he was earnest about leaving. He knew something they didn't: he would be returning to them very soon. But they were so overwhelmed by their grief over his imminent departure (16:20) that Jesus had to assure them that the interim between his going and returning would be only for **a little while.** The saying "A little while and you will see me no more; again a little while and you will see me" (RSV) was troublesome to the disciples. They should, however, have realized from the Lord's discourse in chapter 14 that he was speaking of his going to the Father and his imminent return to them. The interim between his going and coming would be but for "a little while." Indeed, this "little while" would last only three days—during which time he would go to the cross, arise, ascend to the Father (20:17), and return to the disciples on the evening of the resurrection (20:19-23). The Lord had already spoken to the disciples about this "little while" in 14:19, 20. There he indicated that the disciples would not see him for a little while but then they would see him—and on that day (i.e., the day of resurrection) they would come to realize that he was in the Father, and they in him, and he in them.

➤**20-21** Following his explanation of the interim between his going and coming, Jesus used an allegory (see 16:25, 29) to depict how quickly the disciples' grief would turn to joy, and to convey a spiritual truth about his death and resurrection: **ye shall be sorrowful, but your sorrow shall be turned into joy. A woman when she is in travail hath sorrow, because her hour is come: but as soon as she is delivered of the child, she remembereth no more the anguish, for joy that a man is born into the world**—There is more to this allegory than depicting grief turned to joy: (1) The woman's hour of travail corresponds to the "hour" the Lord constantly referred to throughout his ministry, which would be the hour of his glorification via crucifixion and resurrection (see 2:4; 7:30; 8:20; 12:23, 24, 27; 13:1);

(2) The "man born into the world" represents Christ who was begotten from the dead (see Acts 13:33, 34; Col. 1:18). (3) The travailing woman, according to the context, depicts the grieving disciples who, in a greater sense, represent God's people that had the expectation of being delivered from their sorrows and travails by virtue of Christ's victory over death (see Isa. 26:16-19 and cf. Rev. 12:1-5). He is the **man** born into the world, the hope of all mankind: "Hence the proper import of the figure seems to be that the Death of Jesus Christ was as it were an anguish of birth belonging to all Humanity . . . in which the perfect Man was born into the world; and in this very birth of the new man lies the spring of eternal joy, never to be lost for all, inasmuch as through Him and His power the renovation of the whole is rendered possible" (Olshausen).

➤**23, 24 Whatsoever ye shall ask the Father in my name, he will give it you**—Christ's instruction to begin praying directly to the Father in Jesus' name after the resurrection was another reminder that he would not remain on earth indefinitely after he rose from the dead. Other verses in John (14:12-14; 15:7) and in the NT epistles (Eph. 5:20; 1 John 5:13-15) show that Christ's prayer instructions of verses 23 and 24 are valid directives for all of us today.

➤**25 These things have I spoken unto you in proverbs**—or, allegories (see comments on 16:21). Totally explicit predictions about future events would have overtaxed the disciples' weak faith at this point (cf. 16:12, 13), so Jesus spoke to his disciples in allegories. After the resurrection the disciples would remember Christ's words and understand their meaning (2:22; 12:16; 14:26; 20:8, 9), especially when Christ himself explained all these truths to them (Luke 24:13-32, 44-48; Acts 1:3-8).

➤**26-28** At that time it would be essential for the disciples to begin praying directly to the Father in Jesus' **name,** for in a few more weeks the resurrected Son of God would return to the Father in heaven (Luke 24:50-52; Acts 1:9-11).

➤**29-30 now speakest thou plainly**—Christ's final few words were no more explicit than any others he had spoken up to this point (remember that the "plain speaking" of verse 25 refers to Christ's resurrection ministry), but Jesus' repeated predictions of his imminent death, resurrection, and ascension (Matt.

17:22, 23; 20:17-19; John 7:33; 10:11-18; 12:23, 24, 30-36; 13:18-38; 14:1-5, 15-31; 16:5-7) finally left their mark on the disciples. Now they were convinced that Christ's impressive knowledge about future events marked him unquestionably as the Son of God come from God.

➤**31, 32** Though Christ must have appreciated this acknowledgment, he felt constrained to point out the disciples' coming faithlessness in the face of adversity. **ye shall be scattered**—an allusion to Zechariah 13:7, fully quoted in Matthew 26:31 and Mark 14:27. **yet I am not alone, because the Father is with me**—See comments on 8:29.

➤**33 I have overcome the world**—Cf. 1 John 5:4.

*Chapter* **17**

## 1-26 JESUS' INTERCESSORY PRAYER

John 17 contains Jesus' sublime, high-priestly prayer. This petition, which consummates his discourse begun in John 13:31, expresses the deepest desires of God's heart for his chosen ones. The Lord did not pray for the world, but for his own. He prayed for that group of men given to him as a gift from the Father, and he prayed for all who would believe on him through **their** word. He requested that all the believers would share with him in his glory and in his relationship with the Father. From eternity, the Father loved the Son, and the Son enjoyed co-equal glory with the Father. The two were (and are) essentially and coinherently one. The believers, he asked, should be brought into oneness by virtue of being in the triune God and the triune God being in them. Oneness among the believers was to issue from each believer's oneness with God. What a lofty petition!

➤**1 glorify thy Son**—Jesus began his petition by asking the Father to glorify him so that he might glorify the Father. As was stated earlier (see 13:31), Jesus' glorification is the central theme of Jesus' discourse in John 13:31 to 16:33. If the Father would glorify the Son in resurrection, the Son could in turn impart life to the believers (17:2) and so glorify the Father. Of course, Jesus viewed his glorification as being as certain as history (see 13:31, 32);

nevertheless, he prayed for that which he believed would most certainly take place.

➤**2** Jesus made his requests to the Father, knowing that the Father had **given him power** [authority] **over all flesh** [men] and that he could **give eternal life to as many as** [lit., "all which"] . . . [the Father] **hast given him**—As was discussed earlier in connection with John 6:37-39, Jesus used the neuter singular "all which" (Gk. *pan ho*) when referring to the one corporate gift of all believers given to him by the Father. But in the same breath he acknowledged the plurality and individuality of the members of that group by using a personal pronoun (*autois* in Gk.—"them"). (See 17:24 for the same pattern, and see 6:37-40; 10:29, 30 for a shift from the one corporate entity to each individual member.) Each and every member of that corporate "gift" would be given the gift of eternal life.

➤**3 this is life eternal**—Jesus defined eternal life. To experientially, progressively **know . . . God, and** his Son, **Jesus Christ,** is eternal life. In other words, eternal life is the ongoing knowledge of the Father and the Son. The Greek verb *ginōskōsin* signifies the continual action of "getting to know." In colloquial English, we could render this verse: "And this is eternal life: that they may get to know you, the only true God, and Jesus Christ, whom you have sent."

➤**4, 5 I have glorified thee on the earth**—In this statement, Jesus affirms that he had glorified the Father on earth by accomplishing the works he was given to do. Then in 17:5, he asks that the Father would glorify him with the glory he had with the Father before the world was. In saying this, Jesus lifted the veil to give us a glimpse of his eternal, premundane relationship with the Father. According to a literal interpretation of the Greek, Jesus was asking to be glorified alongside the Father (i.e., in the Father's presence) by means of (or, with) the glory he had with the Father before the world was. In other words, Jesus was praying to enter into that pristine state of coequal glory with the Father, a position he possessed from the beginning as the unique Son of God (see 1:1, 18). He prayed that that same glory would be the means by which he (now as a man) would be brought into that coequal glory with the Father.

➤**6-10 the men which thou gavest me . . . I pray for them**—After praying for his own glorification, Jesus turned the direction of his petition to the disciples. Jesus did not here pray for the world, but for the ones the Father had given him. **I am glorified in them**—Speaking proleptically (i.e., with a view to the certainty of a future event), Jesus proclaimed that he would be glorified in his disciples (cf. 15:8).

➤**11-17** Since he would be leaving the world to rejoin the Father, and since the disciples would be staying in the world, they needed to be preserved from the evils in the world. Jesus asked that the Father would keep them in the name that the Father had given him so that they would be one, even as the Son and Father were one (17:11, 12). In short, Jesus requested that the disciples would be sanctified from the world and from the evil one by means of his name (i.e., his person—17:11, 12), the word (17:14-17), and the truth (17:11, 12). These are the sanctifying elements, the elements that preserve Christians, who must live in the midst of an evil world.

➤**18 As thou hast sent me into the world, even so have I also sent them**—The Father's commission is passed on from the Son to his apostles (see 20:21).

➤**19 And for their sakes I sanctify myself**—i.e., I consecrate myself. Jesus consecrated himself to do the Father's will, to become an offering on the cross.

➤**20** After praying for his disciples, Jesus prayed for all those who would believe in him **through their word.** Since the apostles' word became the NT Scriptures (for the most part) and the very foundation of the faith (see Eph. 2:19), everyone who has become a believer has done so through the apostles' words. Therefore, Jesus was praying for all the believers that would ever be.

➤**21** First, Jesus prayed for the apostles to be one (17:11), and then he prayed for all the believers, including the apostles, to be one: **That they all may be one**. What a universal prayer! Look closely at the three things Jesus requested here. Each request begins with the word "that" (Gk. *hina*): (1) **That they all may be one; as thou, Father, art in me, and I in thee,** (2) **that they also may be** [one] **in us** (the word "one" does not appear in the earliest manuscripts), (3) **that the world may believe** that thou hast sent me—All the requests are subsequential: #2 depends upon #1, and #3 depends on both. In the first request, the Lord asked that all the believers may be one. This universal and all-encompassing petition includes all the believers throughout time. Then the first request is qualified by an astounding fact: the oneness among the believers is to be as the mutual indwelling of the Father and the Son. In other words, as the Father and Son's oneness is that of mutual indwelling (10:30, 38; 14:9-11), so the believers are to have a oneness as theirs (see 17:11, 22). Since the believers cannot indwell each other, their oneness is not exactly the same as the Father and Son's—but in the *same principle* as their oneness, i.e., the principle of mutual indwelling. The oneness of the believers would be realized by virtue of the mutual indwelling between each believer and the Triune God—much like each and every branch in the vine is one with all the other branches by virtue of their common participation of abiding in the vine.

➤22-23 The Lord, expanding upon the oneness, defined it in terms of mutual indwelling: **that they may be one, even as we are one: I in them, and thou in me, that they may be made perfect in one** [completed in their oneness]—In 17:21 Jesus asked that the believers be in the Father and Son; in 17:22, 23 he asked that the Father in the Son be in the believers. Now the mutual indwelling is complete and perfect. The reality and demonstration of this oneness will convince the world that the Father did indeed send the Son.

➤24 **they also, whom thou hast given me**—lit., "that which you have given me." Jesus again spoke of "that which" the Father had given him. The term "that which" designates all the believers as the one collective entity given as a gift to him from the Father (see comments on John 6:37, 39; 10:29; 17:2). This is the same corporate group referred to in 17:2; it includes all the ones who have received and will receive the gift of eternal life. This corporate whole, then, is the universal church, the one Body of Christ. The Lord requests that each one of the corporate whole may be with him where he is—i.e., in glory with the Father. There, in the Father, with the Son, they could view the glory which the Son received from the Father, because he loved him **before the foun-**

**dation of the world.** What a revealing statement: the Father loved the Son before the foundation of the world! Again, Jesus lifted the veil to give us a glimpse of his eternal, pre-incarnate relationship with the Father (see 1:1, 18).

➤26 And what is more astounding is that Jesus asked the Father to love the believers with the same love he had for his Son. Jesus asked that the Father's love would be in us and that he himself (Jesus) would be in us. Because of the Father's love, we are indwelt by the Son. **I in them**—what a conclusion to this sublime prayer! It expresses the kernel of God's desire, which is to have his Son (the "I") in a corporate people (the "them"): "I in them."

*Chapter* **18**

## 1-11 THE ARREST OF JESUS

➤1 **When Jesus had spoken these words, he went forth with his disciples over the brook Cedron** [Kidron]—All of John 15-17 was apparently spoken as Jesus and his disciples walked from an upper room somewhere in the heart of Jerusalem to the Garden of Gethsemane, located outside the eastern wall of the city, at the foot of the Mount of Olives (Matt. 26:30, 36; Luke 22:7-13; John 14:31; 18:1).

➤2 Though **Judas** had left the group while they were still in the upper room (13:26-31), he evidently guessed that Jesus would withdraw to Gethsemane for prayer, since he had often done so before.

➤3 So the heartless betrayer of Christ took advantage of his intimate knowledge of the Savior's devotional life to lead the Pharisees' hatchet men to the hallowed garden of prayer. But if the armed and lighted troops were savoring a bloody battle and conquest, they would be severely disappointed, for the omnipotent Son of God would voluntarily give himself up.

➤4 **Jesus therefore, knowing all things that should come upon him, went forth, and said unto them, Whom seek ye?**—Having a complete foreknowledge of what was to come and being fully cognizant that all things would happen as they had been predetermined, Jesus unswervingly walked into his own death. Unlike the other Gospels, there is no question in John about whether or not he would drink the cup the Father had given him (18:11). He would do as the Father had commanded. He would lay down his life voluntarily, and he would also take up his life again because he had received the authority to do so from the Father (see 10:18). All the things that happened in connection with Jesus' betrayal and crucifixion transpired according to the prearranged, divine plan. The hour was predetermined; it could not happen before or after the Passover. The betrayer, Judas Iscariot, was picked by Jesus. He knew from the beginning that Judas was a devil and would be his betrayer (see 6:64, 70). The method of death—crucifixion—was prearranged, so Jesus knew that he would be lifted up on the cross (see 12:32, 33). Thus, it was clear that his executors would be the Romans (for they were the unique administrators of this kind of capital punishment) and not the Jews, who executed by stoning (18:32). The Jews attempted to stone Jesus many times, but they never succeeded because it was not in accord with the divine plan. Now the time had come for Jesus to hand himself over to his executioners.

➤5 Jesus of Nazareth . . . I am he—lit., "I am," which some commentators assert is a declaration of deity (as in 8:58); but it is more natural to understand it as a normal response (as in 6:20). The power emanated from the One who said it, not the words themselves.

➤6 they . . . fell to the ground—It was the glorious effulgence of Christ's majesty which overpowered them. This would demonstrate that Jesus could have exercised his power to thwart his arrest, but he chose not to.

➤8 let these go their way—Jesus ordered the soldiers to release the eleven disciples.

➤9 That the saying might be fulfilled, which he spake—in 6:39; 17:12.

➤10 Then Simon Peter having a sword drew it, and smote the high priest's servant—Any mere man would have welcomed Peter's well-intentioned zeal, but the Son of God knew that his God-appointed time of suffering had come (cf. 17:1).

➤11 He chided Peter for his misguided act and reiterated his determination to drink the entire cup which God the Father had appointed him. (See comments on 18:4.) According to Luke (22:49-51), he healed the mutilated servant.

## 12-27 CHRIST'S FIRST TRIALS AND PETER'S DENIALS

➤12 the Jews took Jesus, and bound him—Christ himself or his thousands of angels (Matt. 26:52, 53) could easily have broken the soldiers' ropes, but then the whole foreordained plan of human redemption would have been in jeopardy (Matt. 26:54; John 12:27; Eph. 1:4, 5), so Jesus quietly accompanied the soldiers to his fraudulent civil and religious trials (18:33 ff.).

➤13 led him away to Annas first—The elderly Annas had been deposed as the Jewish high priest by the Romans in A.D. 15, but he still wielded great influence over the ruling high priest, his son-in-law Caiaphas. For this reason Annas was the first dignitary to interview Jesus (see 18:19-23). Because Annas was usurping the high priestly privileges through his own pride, Jesus answered his questions somewhat tersely (18:19-21) and was promptly punished for his integrity (18:22). Christ's response in 18:23 shows that a Christian defendant in a courtroom setting may rightfully elect to protect his legal rights rather than turn the other cheek. (Notice, however, that Christ did not always exercise this legitimate prerogative—Matt. 26:59-63; Mark 14:55-61.)

➤14 See 11:49, 50.

➤15-18 Peter, meanwhile, was defending himself with illegitimate and untrue denials (15-18, 25-27), just as Christ had predicted (13:37, 38; cf. Matt. 26:33-35; Mark 14:29-31). Peter's three denials were not merely instant impulses on an immediate threat, but were deliberate lies spaced over a period of several hours and uttered in at least two separate locations (18:15-18, 25-27; cf. Matt. 26:58, 69-74; Mark 14:66-72; Luke 22:54-62). That is why his repentance was so bitter (Matt. 26:75; Mark 14:72; Luke 22:62).

➤19-24 See comments on 18:13.

➤25-27 See comments on 18:15-18.

## 28-40 CHRIST'S TRIALS BEFORE PILATE

➤28 Then led they Jesus from Caiaphas unto the hall of judgment—lit., "the praetorium," which was the palace of the provincial Roman governor—in this case, Pilate's palace. Christ's illegal nighttime trial before Caiaphas and other Jewish leaders (cf. Matt. 26:59-68) was apparently followed by an equally secret and illegal trial by the entire Jewish Supreme Court (Luke 22:66-23:1) and then by Pilate's fraudulent civil trial (John 18:28–19:16; cf. Matt. 27:2, 11-26; Mark 15:1-15; Luke 23:1-25). (Christ's trial before Pilate was interrupted by a brief appearance before Herod, the representative of Caesar—Luke 23:6-11.) The multiplicity of false trials to which Jesus was subjected dramatizes the insane wickedness which sometimes impels men to reject the Son of God. **they themselves went not into the judgment hall, lest they should be defiled; but that they might eat the passover**— Christ's legalistically meticulous accusers worried about defiling themselves in the house of a Gentile at the very moment they were rejecting God's true Passover Lamb (Isa. 53:4-7; Acts 8:32-35; 1 Pet. 1:18-20)!

➤**29 What accusation bring ye against this man**—Pilate, the Roman governor, sensed the religious jealousy of Christ's accusers and pressed them for a bona fide charge of criminality against their captive.

➤**30-31 If he were not a malefactor**— Knowing they had no case which Pilate would recognize, they insinuated that they had already found him worthy of death by their own law; but not having the authority, under the Roman government, to carry their sentence into execution, had come for this sanction.

➤**32 signifying what death he should die**—The Jews executed capital punishment by stoning, the Romans by crucifixion. Jesus had always foretold his death in terms of crucifixion, not stoning.

➤**33-36 Art thou the King of the Jews?**— Since Christ's enemies had accused him of sedition against the Roman empire (Luke 23:1, 2), Pilate first asked Jesus if he really claimed to be a king. When Jesus explained that he was seeking no immediate earthly kingdom but was instead the king of all truth, Pilate mused on the desirability of attaining truth and then declared Christ "not guilty."

➤**38 I find in him no fault**—i.e., "I find no basis for a charge against him" (NIV).

➤**39** Since Pilate knew that Christ's Jewish accusers would reject this verdict, he attempted to resolve his thorny dilemma by declaring Jesus unofficially guilty and then pardoning him (see Mark 15:7-11).

➤**40** But Pilate's unethical ploy failed to placate the screaming Jewish officials, and they demanded that a convicted **robber, Barabbas,** be pardoned instead. The Greek word for "robber" was "used by Josephus the historian to describe rebels against Roman authority" (Lindsell). Therefore, the rendering in the NIV is quite suitable: "Now Barabbas had taken part in a rebellion."

*Chapter* **19**

## 1-15 LEGAL ACQUITTAL OF CHRIST

➤**1 Then Pilate therefore took Jesus, and scourged him**—in hope of appeasing the Jews. At this point in Jesus' trial, not a single human being was willing to testify in his defense. The disciples had long since fled (Matt. 26:56; Mark 14:50), the Jewish leaders were screaming for Christ's crucifixion (18:31, 40; cf. Matt. 27:21-25), and Pilate had now consented to a brazen miscarriage of justice (cf. 18:29-39).

➤**2 platted a crown of thorns**—i.e., plaited a crown using thorns. **put on him a purple robe**—in mockery of the imperial purple. According to Matthew 27:28, they first stripped him of his own outer garment. For other forms of mockery inflicted on Jesus, see Matthew 27:29.

➤**3 Hail, King of the Jews!**—giving him derisive homage in the form used when people approached the emperor. **they smote him with their hands**—The Roman soldiers were all too willing to mock and pummel their innocent prisoner (cf. Matt. 27:26-30).

➤**4 I find no fault in him**—Pilate could not help being moved by this gross travesty of justice, so for the second time he attempted to unburden his feeling of guilt by pronouncing Jesus not guilty (see 18:38).

➤**5** The sight of the robed and thorn-crowned Savior so moved the cowardly governor that he uttered the now-famous words, **Behold the man!**

➤**6** But the bloodthirsty chief priests and officials responded differently: **Crucify him, crucify him** poured forth from their hateful lips. **Take ye him, and crucify him: for I find no fault in him**—Pilate was so moved by the lynching scene before him that he dared the

Jewish leaders to usurp the exclusive Roman authority of capital punishment by crucifying their innocent captive themselves. The Jewish leaders were too shrewd to fall into this trap of forensic usurpation, however.

➤**7 We have a law, and by our law he ought to die, because he made himself the Son of God**—As a last resort, the Jews appealed to Pilate to punish Jesus with Roman crucifixion for violating a strictly Jewish tradition!

➤**8 When Pilate . . . heard that saying, he was the more afraid**—The Jews' charge of blasphemy backfired, for Pilate was now frightened rather than angered. What the Jewish officials were too blind to see, the Roman governor sensed intuitively—that the quiet captive in his presence was a truly unique Personality among men.

➤**9-11 Whence art thou?**—He therefore asked Jesus about his origin, but Jesus stood silently in the face of his previous declarations (18:36, 37). Pilate's officious threat of crucifixion did not frighten Christ but merely elicited an authoritative statement about the respective roles of Pilate and the Jewish leaders within the permissive will of God. **Thou couldest have no power at all against me, except it were given thee from above**—Pilate thought too highly of his own power. In fact, he had no power against Jesus, for Jesus lived and died according to the divine authority. **he that delivered me unto thee hath the greater sin**—This shows clearly that there are varying degrees of human guilt in the sight of God (cf. Matt. 12:39-42).

➤**12 Pilate sought to release him**—By this time Pilate was apparently sincerely convinced that Jesus was some kind of special prophet from God, so he tried still another time to release him. But the Jews were not about to let their prey escape from their hands at this point in the trial, so in a final desperate ploy they appealed to Pilate's friendship with Caesar: **If thou let this man go, thou art not Caesar's friend**—The Jews must have gagged as they spoke these words (since most Jews despised the Roman despot), but their hatred for Christ outweighed their hatred for the foreign king. Compare the desperation of the mutually antagonistic Pharisees and Sadducees as they temporarily joined forces in attacking the Son of God (Matt. 16:1ff.).

➤**13-15 Behold your King! . . . Shall I crucify your King?**—Pilate was too cowardly to acquit his innocent defendant but too guilt-ridden to summarily condemn him, so in one last desperate effort he challenged Christ's Jewish accusers to accept their king. But the Jews continued with their plea: **Away with him, away with him, crucify him. . . . We have no king but Caesar**—"Some of those who thus cried died miserably in rebellion against Caesar forty years afterwards. But it [their false exclamation] suited their present purpose." (Alford).

## 16-30 THE CRUCIFIXION OF CHRIST

➤**16 Then delivered he him therefore unto them to be crucified**—When Pilate saw that no kind of reasoning would appease Christ's bloodthirsty enemies, he reluctantly and guiltily released his innocent prisoner to them. The cowardly governor had earlier washed his hands in a public display of non-involvement (Matt. 27:19, 24), but Pilate's capitulation to a mob of murderers stands as an eternal witness to his guilt.

➤**17, 18 bearing his cross**—According to John's account, Jesus carried his own cross. The synoptic Gospels indicate that Simon, a Cyrenian, was forced to carry the cross for him (see Matt. 27:32; Mark 15:21; Luke 23:36). Most likely, Jesus carried the cross (usually the horizontal cross beam) at first; but then, having become weak because of the flogging, Simon took over (Morris). **Golgotha**—meaning "Hill of the Skull," where Jesus was crucified in between two robbers (19:17, 18; cf. Matt. 27:31-34; Mark 15:20-22; Luke 23:26-33).

➤**19-22** The three other Gospels point out additional gruesome and prophetic details of Christ's crucifixion (Matt. 27:33-44; Mark 15:22-32; Luke 23:32-43), but John's Gospel emphasizes Pilate's continuing attempt to assuage his guilty conscience. The chief priests wanted Christ's crime posted as a false claim to kingship, but in a final slap at the Jews, Pilate vented his inner torment with a bona fide tribute to Christ's kingship in a trilingual placard that all the world could read. He wrote, **JESUS OF NAZARETH THE KING OF THE JEWS . . . in Hebrew** [or perhaps, Aramaic—the language of the Jews], **and Greek** [the lingua franca, the common tongue], **and Latin** [the Roman language, the official language]. (In the Greek text, the order is Hebrew, Latin, Greek.) And this time no persuasion of the chief priests could induce him to change his mind (19:22). Pilate's guilt-ridden tribute to the Son of God presages that exultant moment when every creature in God's universe will bow the knee to Christ in willing or unwilling worship (Phil. 2:9-11; Rev. 5:13).

➤**23 Then the soldiers, when they had crucified Jesus, took his garments and made four parts**—Christ's hour of apparent defeat was in reality his moment of greatest triumph, for in addition to paying for the sins of the world, Jesus fulfilled many OT prophecies about his sufferings and death (compare the four Gospel accounts).

➤**24 that the scripture might be fulfilled, which saith, They parted my raiment** [garments] **among them and for my vesture** [outer garment] **they did cast lots**—The Roman soldiers' participation in the fulfillment of prophecy (Ps. 22:18) refutes any notion that Christ and his disciples plotted Jesus' death as a kind of martyr's death. Instead, God permitted Christ's enemies to vent their hatred only in ways that validated Scripture (cf. Ps. 76:10).

➤**25-27 Woman, behold thy son!**—speaking to Mary with respect to John the apostle. **Behold thy mother**—speaking to John with respect to Jesus' mother. As Jesus' mother and her friends grieved over the dying form which hung before them, Christ ignored his own agonies long enough to commit Mary to the keeping of John the Apostle. (Mary had apparently been previously widowed through the death of Joseph and was being cared for by Jesus himself.) Shortly after this act of compassion, the sky grew dark for three long hours as Christ agonized under the accumulated sins of a corrupt human race (Matt. 27:45, 46; Mark 15:33, 34).

➤**28** His vicarious sufferings nearly over, Jesus proclaimed, **I thirst,** another biblical prediction (Ps. 69:21).

➤**30 It is finished**—This final, glorious proclamation is pregnant with meaning. According to the Greek, the expression can also mean, "It is accomplished," "It is fulfilled," or even, "It is paid in full." His death accomplished redemption—paid in full; and his death fulfilled all the OT prophecies. **gave**

**up the ghost**—i.e., gave up his spirit. Jesus' life was not taken from him; he gave his life of his own free will (Matt. 20:28; John 10:11, 15, 17, 18; 15:13).

31-42 JESUS' BURIAL

➤**31, 32 that the bodies should not remain upon the cross on the sabbath day**—overnight, which was against the law (Deut. 21:22, 23). The two robbers crucified with Christ (cf. Matt. 27:38) were apparently also Jews, for the religious leaders were concerned that none of the three bodies remain hanging overnight. **besought Pilate that their legs might be broken**—Pilate agreed to this minor favor, and his soldiers smashed the legs of the still-living robbers with clubs in order to hasten their death. A person being crucified could use his legs to lift up his body in an attempt to take in more oxygen into his collapsing lungs. To break the legs of one being crucified would, therefore, hasten his death.

➤**33, 34** Seeing that Jesus **was dead already,** the soldiers omitted smashing his legs and instead pierced his side with a spear in order to prevent any possible resuscitation.

➤**35 he that saw it bare record**—John witnessed the entire crucifixion (19:26). **and his record is true**—See 20:30, 31.

➤**36, 37** Through their brutality the Roman soldiers unwittingly fulfilled two biblical prophecies: **A bone of him shall not be broken** (from Ps. 34:20; see also Exod. 12:46; Num. 9:12) and **They shall look on him whom they pierced** (from Zech. 12:10). By piercing Jesus' side, they provided the identifying scar by which the risen Christ would reveal himself to his hesitant disciples (20:19, 20, 24, 25, 27, 28) and later to the repentant Jewish nation as a whole (Rev. 1:7).

➤**38 Joseph of Arimathaea**—He had been a secret disciple while Jesus was alive (7:13; 12:42, 43), but now that his Lord's body hung dead on the cross, he found the courage to approach Pilate about a decent burial for the Master.

➤**39 Nicodemus**—another disciple of Jesus (3:1; 7:13, 50-52; 12:42, 43), joined wealthy Joseph of Arimathaea (cf. Matt. 27:57) in embalming and wrapping Jesus' body in regal style.

➤**40-42** The striking combination of Christ's degrading crucifixion and sumptuous burial fulfilled the predictions of Isaiah 52:13–53:12 and displayed to all the world that God would tolerate no further humiliation of his Son once the awesome work of redemption was accomplished. Little did Christ's disciples realize what further triumphs lay in store for the immortal Son of God!

Chapter **20**

## 1-18 CHRIST'S FIRST RESURRECTION APPEARANCE

➤**1 Mary Magdalene**—she had followed Jesus to the cross, watched his crucifixion, and then remained to see where he was buried (Matt. 27:61). Christ's tomb was apparently a rock-hewn, hillside burial vault which was sealed by a massive circular stone rolled into place across the entrance to the vault (Matt. 27:59, 60, 66; 28:2; Mark 15:46; 16:3, 4; Luke 23:53; 24:1, 2; John 19:41, 42; 20:1).

➤**2** When Mary Magdalene (with her companions—Matt. 28:1; Mark 16:1) saw that the huge stone had been rolled aside, she was sure that someone had stolen the body of her Lord.

➤**3, 4 they ran both together**—So Peter and John responded to Mary's alarm by rushing to the burial vault to see for themselves.

➤**5-7** John and Peter saw the neatly-arranged wrappings of Jesus' body lying in the tomb. The order showed that there was not a hasty removal of Jesus' body. Rather, it shows that Jesus must have arisen with all tranquility and dignity.

➤**8 he** [John] **saw, and believed**—Since there is no direct object after "believed," the reader has to imagine what John believed. The simplest explanation is that John believed Mary's story about the empty tomb; however, it could very well be that John believed in Jesus' resurrection. If the latter meaning was intended, we must understand the next verse (20:9) to indicate that, though John had come to believe in Jesus' resurrection, he had not yet known the Scripture about the resurrection (2:22). He had faith

but no knowledge; the knowledge would come later and affirm the faith.

➤**9 as yet they knew not the scripture, that he must rise again**—This does not refer to a specific OT passage, but to the whole OT testimony concerning Christ's resurrection (see comments on 2:22).

➤**11-15** After John and Peter left, Mary remained by the empty tomb in solitary grief, hoping against hope that she would somehow discover where the body had been hidden (see 20:13, 15). So grief-stricken was this devotee of Jesus that even the sight of two angels failed to assuage her sorrow or lessen her search for the body! Then something caused Mary to look behind her, and there in the morning dew of the garden stood another quiet figure (20:14). Through Mary's tear-stained eyes the form before her looked like that of a gardener, and his friendly question induced Mary to plead for information about the theft of Jesus' body.

➤**16 Mary . . . Rabboni; which is to say, Master**—Mary must have turned away in grief as she talked, for at the sound of her name (**Mary**) she turned back toward her living Lord with the one word "Rabboni"!

➤**17a Touch me not**—is better translated, "Stop clinging to me." The Greek verb underlying "clinging" is a present imperative. The action had already begun when Jesus told Mary, "Stop clinging to me." He was not preventing Mary from touching him (which would be the meaning if an aorist imperative had been used). Mary wanted to hold onto Jesus and so reinstate the former relationship with him, but Jesus, through resurrection, had entered into a new state of being and a new sphere of living. Mary could no longer know him according to the old way (see 2 Cor. 5:17, 18). Jesus affirmed this new change when he told Mary, **go to my brethren, and say unto them, I ascend** [I am ascending] **unto my Father, and your Father; and to my God, and your God**—Because of Christ's resurrection, his disciples had now become Jesus' brothers (see also Matt. 28:10). Resurrection creates this new relationship because it

providesfortheregenerationofevery believer.
First Peter 1:3 says that we have been born
again to a new hope through the resurrection of Jesus from the dead. As possessors
of the divine life (see Eph. 4:18) and partakers of the divine nature (2 Pet. 1:4), all the
believers have become Jesus' brothers, having the same God and same Father.

Jesus told Mary, "I am ascending to my
Father." The language gives no indication
that this ascension would be in the future. We
must be careful not to superimpose a timetable upon John's Gospel that is not indigenous
to John's narrative. According to John's
chronology, the Lord would arise from the
dead, ascend to the Father, and then come to
the disciples—all within "a little while" (see
14:2, 3, 18-20, 23; 16:16-22 and the comments on these verses).

## 19-31 CHRIST'S SUBSEQUENT RESURRECTION APPEARANCES

➤**19 Then the same day at evening,
being the first day of the week, when the
doors were shut . . . came Jesus and stood
in the midst**—Jesus met Mary on the morning of the resurrection. On the very same
evening Jesus made his first appearance to
his disciples. This appearance is astounding because Jesus probably penetrated the closed room and manifested
himself in their midst. He could do this
because resurrection and the subsequent
glorification had altered his form. In resurrection, he had become life-giving spirit (1
Cor. 15:42-45). At the same time, he still
retained his humanity—but a glorified
one. In resurrection, he was the same person in a different form (see Mark 16:12).
In this new spiritual form, he was able to
transcend all physical barriers. He was
able to penetrate matter and even penetrate
men.

➤**20** On the evening of his resurrection,
Jesus appeared to his disciples and showed
**them his hands and his side.** They
thought they were being visited by a ghost
or phantom (see Luke 24:37-39). His physical appearance reassured them that it was
Jesus himself in their midst.

➤**21** Jesus graced them with his peace
and then commissioned them just as he had

been commissioned by the Father. The disciples were to be his ongoing testimony, even
as he had been the Father's. As the Father
sent the Son, so the Son now sends the apostles. But before doing so, he imparted the
Holy Spirit into them.

➤**22** The impartation of the Holy Spirit
was accomplished by Jesus breathing the
Holy Spirit into his disciples: "He breathed
into them and said, Receive the Holy
Spirit" (a literal translation). In a sense this
verse consummates the Gospel of John
because the Spirit who had been promised
in John 7:37-39; 14:16-20, 26; 15:26; and
16:7-15 is now at last given to the disciples
(see note, *Recovery Version*). After the
Lord commissioned the disciples, he
breathed (*enephusēsen*) to them and said,
lit., "Receive Holy Spirit". Jesus' breathing into them recapitulates God's breathing into Adam (see Gen. 2:7, LXX, where
*enephusēsen* is used) and thus denotes
that Jesus' infusion inspired a new genesis, in which he regenerated the disciples
(see 1 Peter 1:3). With this "in-breathing"
came the actual impartation of the promised Holy Spirit. This impartation was not
a symbolic act or a mere prefiguration of
the Pentecostal outpouring. Some commentators and translators, however, have
asserted that since the Greek reads *pneuma
hagion* (without definite articles), it does
not designate the personal Holy Spirit but
rather an earnest of that gift or an effusion
of the Spirit (for example, see Bengel and
Vincent). But the expression *pneuma
hagion,* appearing eighty-six times in the
NT, is used thirty-seven times with an article and *forty-nine* times *without* an article.
Whether arthrous or anarthrous, *pneuma
hagion* designates the unique Holy Spirit.
The real reason some insist on saying that
the John 20:22 infusion was either a symbolic act or a foretaste is that they believe
that the Holy Spirit was given only at Pentecost and not until then. For example, J.B.
Phillips translated the last part of the verse
as "Receive the Holy Spirit"—to which he
appended a note, "Lit., 'receive holy
spirit.'" Historically the Holy Spirit was
not given until Pentecost." But the Gospel
doesn't fit this systematic theology, for it

has its own chronology. According to the entire context of John's Gospel, the Lord Jesus would first ascend to the Father and then come to the disciples to give them the promised Spirit. John, as a self-contained unit, has its own time frame. That the timing does not coincide with the Luke-Acts sequence does not mean it is invalid; nor do the two accounts contradict each other. The apostles received the Spirit into them on the evening of the resurrection and the Spirit came upon them on the day of Pentecost. They were infilled and endued with the same Spirit.

➤**23** sins . . . remitted . . . sins . . . retained—In any literal and authoritative sense, this power was never exercised by one of the apostles, and plainly was never understood by them as possessed by them or conveyed to them. (See comments on Matt. 16:19.) The power to intrude upon the relation between men and God cannot have been given by Christ to his ministers in any but a ministerial or declarative sense—as the authorized interpreters of his word, while in the actings of his ministers, the real nature of the power committed to them is seen in the exercise of church discipline.

➤**24, 25** Thomas missed the meeting. When the disciples told him that Jesus appeared to them, he did not believe. He insisted that he see Jesus with his eyes and touch his wounds with his hands.

➤**26-28** At their next meeting, eight days later, Thomas was present when Jesus appeared again. When he saw Jesus, doubting Thomas became believing Thomas; he exclaimed to Jesus, **My Lord and my God.** This is one of the clearest affirmations of Jesus' deity in the NT. (See also John 1:1, 18; 8:58; 10:30; Rom. 9:5; Phil. 2:6; Col. 2:9; Tit. 2:13; 2 Pet. 1:1; 1 John 5:20 in NASB or NIV.)

➤**29** Though Thomas hailed Jesus as his Lord and God, Jesus reproved Thomas's way of faith—for he first saw and then believed. The blessed ones are **they that have not seen, and yet have believed.** This blessing would be effective for the millions of Christians who have never seen Jesus yet believe in him (see 2 Cor. 5:7; 1 Pet. 1:8).

➤**30, 31** After recording this appearance, John explains why he wrote this Gospel: **And many other signs truly did Jesus in the presence of his disciples, which are not written in this book: But these are written, that ye might believe** [or, continue to believe] **that Jesus is the Christ, the Son of God; and that believing ye might have life through his name.** This Gospel's *raison d'étre* is very clear. To have read this Gospel and not believed that Jesus is the Christ, the Son of God, is to have missed John's purpose for writing it. This Gospel is focused on the person, Jesus. He is the Christ, the Son of God, who came to give life to those who believe in his name (i.e., his identity). This Gospel constantly dwells on this theme. Significantly, John wrote this Gospel primarily to encourage those who already believed to continue in their faith. This can be inferred because John used the present tense for the subjunctive verb *pisteuō*, rather than the aorist (according to the best manuscript evidence). The aorist would have indicated initial belief, but the present indicates continual belief. If indeed John intended this Gospel to go to those who already believed, we can understand why this Gospel has so much more theological, spiritual, and experiential depth than the Synoptic Gospels. Without detracting from the other Gospels, it is generally admitted that John's is the most profound. At the same time, it is the most simple. New believers benefit from it, and so do the most mature.

Chapter **21**

## 1-23 CHRIST'S APPEARANCE TO HIS DISCIPLES BY THE SEA OF TIBERIAS (GALILEE)

➤**1** Jesus showed himself again to the disciples at the sea of Tiberias—John 21, an epilogue, records Jesus' appearance to the disciples beside the sea of Tiberias (Galilee). Jesus had made at least six appearances in (or around) Jerusalem: to Mary Magdalene (Mark 16:9-11; John 20:11-18), to the other women (Matt. 28:8-10; Mark 16:8; Luke 24:9-11), to Peter (Luke 24:34; 1 Cor. 15:5), to two disciples (Luke 24:36-49; John 20:19-23), and to the disciples with Thomas (John 20:24-29). After the Jerusalem appearances, the disciples evidently returned to Galilee. Jesus made more appearances there: to the disciples on a mountain in Galilee (Matt. 28:16-20; Mark 16:15-18); to five hundred believers (1 Cor. 15:6); to James, his brother (1 Cor. 15:7); and to the seven disciples who went fishing on the sea of Tiberias. Prior to his resurrection, the Lord had told his disciples that he would meet them at an appointed place in Galilee after he arose (see Mark 14:28). But due to their unbelief and fear, they remained in Jerusalem. So Jesus first appeared to them in Jerusalem and then in Galilee. After the Galilean appearances, they were to return to Jerusalem, where he would again appear to them and tell them about the promised outpouring of the Holy Spirit.

➤3 I go . . . fishing—Having returned to Galilee, it was natural for some of the disciples to return to their old occupation, fishing. Peter took the lead, and six other disciples went with him. That night, however, they caught nothing. Perhaps this was a *déjà vu* for Peter. Just before the Lord appeared to Peter the first time, Peter had been out fishing, catching nothing. Peter might have been reminiscing about that first miraculous draught. That miracle caused Peter to fall on his knees and ask Jesus to depart from him, a sinful man (see Luke 5:1-11). Here he was again, fishing, catching nothing, lacking the presence of the Lord.

➤4-9 Little did Peter know that **Jesus** was standing **on the shore,** waiting for the coming of dawn, waiting for the chance to make another appearance to the disciples, especially Peter. The repeated miraculous draught of fish was particularly intended to affect Peter. It did. Peter did not say a word as he dragged the net full of fish to shore and then (with the other disciples) ate the breakfast the Lord had prepared even before they caught the fish.

➤11 Peter went up—into the boat. **and drew the net to land full of great fishes, an hundred and fifty and three: and for all there were so many, yet was not the net broken**—The manifest reference here to the former miraculous draught (Luke 5:1-11) furnishes the key to this scene. There the draught was *symbolical* of the success of their future ministry. Here, then, if but the same symbolic reference be kept in view, the design of the whole scene will, we think, be clear. The *multitude* and *size* of the fishes *they* caught symbolically foreshadowed the vast success of their now fast-approaching ministry.

➤14 This **third** manifestation of the Lord had a profound effect on the disciples. His presence silenced them, humbled them, and reinstated them. It seems that their going fishing was a kind of diversion from their commission or, at worst, a kind of backsliding to the former things. In this appearance, Jesus brought them into line with his purposes, for he specifically exhorted Peter to take care of shepherding the flock.

➤15 After breakfast Jesus asked Peter, **lovest thou me more than these?**—According to the Greek, this could also be rendered, "Do you love me more than these men love me?" or "Do you love me more than these men?" or "Do you love me more than these things?" (i.e., the fish, the boat, and all things related to the fishing occupation). All three renderings are compatible with the context (especially the first and third), but in the light of the fact that Peter had claimed, in the presence of all the disciples, that he would never forsake the Lord, even if all the others did (see Matt. 26:33; Mark 14:29; John 13:37), it seems that Jesus was exposing Peter for having thought he loved Him more than the other disciples did.

➤16, 17 lovest thou me?—Three times Jesus asked Peter if he loved him (21:15-17). The first two times Jesus used the Greek word *agapaō* and the last time *phileō* to express two different kinds of love. In all three of his responses, Peter used the word *phileō*. The Greek word *agapaō* designates the most noble action of love, for this word indicates volitional, responsible love, love that emanates, not so much from the emotion, as from the rational soul. This is the sort of love one uses in choosing to love the unlovely, the unattractive, and unbecoming. This is the kind of love God has for the world; it is a divine love, a love not easily appropriated by us self-centered mortals. The Greek word *phileo* designates the action of love that emanates from liking someone or something. It conveys the idea of fondness. Peter, quite honestly, told Jesus that he was fond of him. Peter could not say that he had demonstrated *agape* love. In fact, he had failed to exercise self-sacrificial love at the time of Jesus' trial. Three times Peter denied him; three times Jesus asked Peter if he loved him. The third time, stooping to Peter's level, Jesus asked Peter if he was fond of him. Peter told him what he already knew: "I am fond of you."

Each time Peter told Jesus, "I am fond of you," Jesus exhorted Peter to care for his **lambs** and **sheep** ("young lambs" and "little sheep"—terms of endearment). Peter was charged to care for them by feeding them and shepherding them. Peter never forgot this charge; he became a devoted shepherd of the flock (see 1 Pet. 5:1-4).

►**18, 19 When thou shalt be old, thou shalt stretch forth thy hands, and another shall gird thee, and carry thee whither thou wouldest not. This spake he, signifying by what death he should glorify God**—The image most likely depicts crucifixion, and tradition says that Peter was crucified. He, like the good Shepherd, would be led to the cross. Once Jesus told him this, Peter knew what death lay before him. This prophecy remained with Peter all his days (see 2 Pet. 1:14).

►**20-23** Having been told of his destiny, Peter wanted to know what would

happen to John (called "the disciple whom Jesus loved"). In essence, the Lord said that John *could* stay alive until his coming (if the Lord so willed), not that John *would* stay alive until his coming. The Lord's sovereignty over each man's life was the issue, not the duration of John's life. Each man is responsible to follow the Lord according to what the Lord has revealed to him. The command is clear: **follow thou me.**

## 24, 25 THE CONCLUSION

►**24, 25** The last two verses of the Gospel contain the colophon that attests to the veracity of John's written testimony. John's testimony is trustworthy because he was that disciple whom Jesus loved and that disciple who was an eyewitness of Jesus' life and ministry. The statement **we know that his testimony is true** is the attestation of some of John's contemporaries who knew that what John wrote was true. Some scholars think these contemporaries were the Ephesian elders. (John resided in Ephesus in his later years.) Westcott wrote, "The words were probably added by the Ephesian elders, to whom the preceding narrative had been given both orally and in writing." John's final statement (**I suppose that even the world itself could not contain the books that should be written**) is not a mere hyperbolic expression but an affirmation of the fact that his materials were far from being exhaustive.

BIBLIOGRAPHY

Alford, Henry. *The Greek New Testament.* 1952. Reprint. Grand Rapids: Guardian Press, 1973.

Barrett, C. K. *The Gospel According to St. John.* Philadelphia: The Westminster Press, 1978.

Bengel, John. *New Testament Word Studies.* 1742. Reprint. Grand Rapids: Eerdmans, 1971.

Bruce, F. F. *The Gospel of John.* Grand Rapids: Eerdmans, 1982.

Dana and Mantey. *A Manual Grammar of the Greek New Testament.* New York: MacMillan, 1957.

Dods, Marcus. "The Gospel of St. John" in *The Expositor's Greek Testament.* London: Hodder and Stoughton, 1899.

Gundry, Robert H. "In My Father's House are Many Monai" in *Zeitschrift für die Neutedstamenliche Wissenschaft.*

Lindsell, Harold. *The People's Study Bible.* Wheaton: Tyndale House Publishers, 1986.

MacGregor, G.H.C. "The Gospel of John" in *The Moffat New Testament Commentary.* London: Hodder and Stoughton, Ltd., 1928.

Moberly, R. C. *Atonement and Personality.* London: John Murray, 1909.

Morris, Leon. *The Gospel According to John.* Grand Rapids: Eerdmans, 1971.

Olshausen, Hermann. *Biblical Commentary on the New Testament.* New York: Sheldon, 1858.

Pink, A. W. *Exposition of the Gospel of John.* Grand Rapids: Zondervan, 1973.

*Recovery Version: Gospel of John* (Lee, Ingalls). Anaheim, Calif.: Living Stream Ministry, 1975.

Robertson, A. T. *Word Pictures in the Greek New Testament.* Nashville: Broadman Press, 1932.

Titus, Eric L. *The Message of the Fourth Gospel.* Nashville: Abingdon Press, 1967.

Trench, R. C. *Synonyms of the New Testament*. 1880. Reprint. Grand Rapids: Eerdmans, 1978.

Vincent, M. R. *Word Studies in the New Testament*. 1880; Reprint. Grand Rapids: Eerdmans, 1978.

Westcott, B. F. *The Gospel According to St. John*. 1881. Reprint. Grand Rapids: Zondervan, 1973.

Note: Some portions of the commentary on John were excerpted from two volumes written by the New Testament editor, Philip W. Comfort:

Comfort, Philip. *A Study Guide to Translating the Gospel of John*. Vol. 1, Studies in the Greek New Testament for English Readers, Wheaton, Ill., 1985.

Comfort, Philip. *Portraits of Jesus in the Gospel of John*. Vol.

2. Studies in the Greek New Testament for English Readers, Wheaton, Ill., 1986.

Devotional works cited:

Merton, Thomas. *The New Man*. New York: Farrar, Straus, and Giroux, 1961.

Murray, Andrew. *The True Vine*. Chicago: Moody Press, 1982.

Murray, Andrew. *The Spirit of Christ*. New York: Anson D. F. Randolf Co., 1888.

Nee, Watchman. *The Normal Christian Faith*. Hong Kong: Hong Kong Church Book Room, 1977.

Simpson, A. B. *When the Comforter Came*. Harrisburg, Pa.: Christian Publications, n.d.

# ACTS

## Introduction

The book of Acts, in addition to the third Gospel, most likely was written by Luke. Originally Luke and Acts were two parts of one volume written to the same man, Theophilus (cf. Luke 1:1-4 with Acts 1:1-3). During the last part of the first century and/or the first part of the second century, the Gospel of Luke was detached from Acts when it was added to the three other Gospels to form one collection. From that time forward, Acts went on its own separate journey. But every reader of Acts must realize that it is a continuation of the Gospel of Luke. The same author, "the beloved physician" (Col. 4:14) and faithful co-worker with Paul (2 Tim. 4:11; Philem. 24), wrote both works. The language is the same: the two books are written in a style approximating classical Greek, mingled with Semitic Greek (i.e., Greek infiltrated with expressions borrowed from Hebrew, Aramaic, and the Septuagint). And Paul's influence on Luke is evident in both Luke (see Introduction to Luke) and Acts. Luke was with Paul during a great portion of Paul's missionary journeys. He joined Paul just before Paul went to Macedonia, at which point Luke includes himself in the narrative—as is noted by the first person, plural pronoun: "we," used in 16:10-17; 20:5-15; 21:1-18; 27:1–28:16.

The book of Acts (sometimes called "the Acts of the Apostles") begins with the effusion of the promised Holy Spirit and the commencement of the proclamation (*kerygma*) of the gospel of Jesus Christ. A new age in God's plan and economy here begins. Jesus, as the grain of wheat who fell into the ground to die (John 12:24), is now bringing forth much fruit. And he does this through the Holy Spirit and by the preaching of the apostles. No longer is Jesus among the disciples (as in the Gospels); he now indwells them through the Holy Spirit and ministers through their deeds. Thus, the acts of the apostles are actually the activities of the Holy Spirit through the apostles.

This Spirit-inspired activity began in Jerusalem and spread to Rome, eventually covering most of the Roman Empire. The gospel first went to the Jews, but they, as a nation, continually rejected it. A remnant of Jews, of course, gladly received the word. But the continual rejection of the gospel by the vast majority of the Jews, both in Judea and abroad, led to ever-increasing promulgation of the gospel to the Gentiles. But this was according to Jesus' plan; the gospel was to go from Jerusalem, to Judea, to Samaria, and to the uttermost parts of the earth (1:8). This, in fact, is the pattern that the Acts narrative follows. The glorious proclamation began in Jerusalem (chapters 1–7), went to Judea and Samaria (8:1ff.), and then to countries beyond Judea (11:19; 13:4ff.).

The church began with only Jewish believers. As the gospel spread, the circle widened to include Gentile proselytes (as the Ethiopian eunuch); Samaritans (8:5ff.); "God-fearers" and "God-worshipers" (Gentiles attracted to the Jewish faith—see comments on 10:2), among whom were Cornelius, Lydia, and Justus; and non-religious Gentiles. The gift of grace and of the Holy Spirit was given to them as it had been to the Jews. But there were certain Jewish Christians (especially from Jerusalem) who wanted to make all the non-Jewish Christians adhere to the Mosaic law and receive circumcision. This became a critical point of contention between the Jewish and Gentile believers in the early church. The problem was partially solved by the council held in Jerusalem (Acts 15), but Paul's ministry to the Gentiles was continually plagued by the Judaizers. Paul was left to struggle with this problem throughout his lifetime. Peter, who had opened the door of the gospel to the Gentiles (Acts 10) and affirmed Paul's position at the Jerusalem council (15:7-11), had not been committed with the gospel to the circumcised. So the second half of Acts (i.e., from the Jerusalem council on) is entirely focused on Paul's ministry to the Gentiles and his ongoing struggle with the Jews.

Thus, the book of Acts is primarily focused on the activities of two apostles: Peter (in the first half) and Paul (in the second half). Both apostleships are equally confirmed by the signs that accompanied their ministries (Bruce). Both Peter and Paul heal a lame man (3:2; 14:8), have extraordinary healing powers (5:15; 19:12), exorcise evil spirits (9:36; 20:9), receive visions to evangelize the Gentiles (10:9; 22:17-21), and are miraculously released from prison (12:7; 16:26). But Paul, in the end, looms larger than Peter because Luke's narrative follows him on his apostolic journeys to the Roman world, in which Paul plants churches that eventually become the recipients of many Pauline epistles, whose contents have provided a large portion of NT doctrine.

In his book The New Testament: Its Background, Growth, and Content, Bruce Metzger provides an excellent outline for the book of Acts, in which he divides it into six periods: 1:1–6:7 (early episodes in the Jerusalem church); 6:8–9:31 (extension of the church through Palestine); 9:32–12:24 (extension of the church to Antioch); 12:25–16:5 (extension of the church to southern and central Asia Minor); 16:6–19:20 (extension of the church to Europe); 19:21–28:31 (extension of the church to Rome). The last verse in each of these six sections summarizes the section by providing a positive statement concerning either the increase of God's word being proclaimed or the growth of the church.

Chapter **1**

## 1-11 INTRODUCTION.
### JESUS' LAST DAYS ON EARTH

➤**1 The former treatise**—This refers to the book of Luke. **Theophilus**—The Gospel of Luke was addressed to the same. **of all that Jesus began both to do and teach**—Jesus' work, begun in person while he was present in this world, would continue from heaven through the Spirit. Jesus' teachings were carried on by the apostles under Jesus' authority and by the power of his Spirit.

➤**2 Until the day . . . he was taken up**—his ascension. **after that he through the Holy Ghost [Spirit] had given commandments**—referring to the charge given in Matthew 28:18-20; Mark 16:15-18; Luke 24:44-49; John 20:19-23. In resurrection, Christ's relationship with the believers (the church) took a new turn. All communications would come from Christ through the Spirit to the believers. Prior to the Pentecostal outpouring of the Spirit, Jesus had already breathed the Spirit into the disciples (John 20:22)—thus creating this new relationship. The Spirit that had remained within Christ was now the Spirit that flowed from Christ to his disciples.

►3 To whom also he showed himself alive—Acts repeatedly asserts the resurrection of Christ as the central message of the apostles. As an introduction, Luke (the author of this book) refers to the most important evidence of Christ's resurrection. It is important to remember that the apostles were skeptical and had to see Christ repeatedly after his resurrection. after his passion—i.e., his suffering on the cross. many infallible proofs—See the last chapter of all four Gospels. being seen—middle voice in Greek, "allowed himself to be seen." During the forty days after his resurrection, Jesus was constantly with his disciples in his invisible, spiritual presence. For their sake, he would allow himself to be seen by them on various occasions. He was always there, but to encourage their faith, he would let them see him. Each time he did this as "an appearance." the kingdom of God—the central theme of Jesus' teaching. The visible expression of that kingdom was just beginning to form.

►4 they should not depart from Jerusalem—The Spirit was going to work through the existing economy and structure of that great city to bring the good news of Christ via the apostolic testimony to the whole world (Isa. 2:3). wait for the promise of the Father—the promised effusion of the Spirit (Luke 24:49).

►5 ye shall be baptized with the Holy Ghost [Spirit] not many days hence—It was actually ten days (see comments on 2:1), but was expressed indefinitely to test their faith.

►6 wilt thou at this time restore again the kingdom to Israel?—The apostles were just beginning to understand the nature of God's new kingdom. They had always expected that Christ would one day restore the messianic kingdom in Israel; they wondered if the promised Spirit signaled that event.

►7 It is not for you to know—This was not the time for Israel to be given her freedom, nor was that fact important to the present or future work of the apostles.

►8 receive power—See Luke 24:49. ye shall be witnesses unto me both in Jerusalem, and in all Judaea, and in Samaria, and

unto the uttermost part of the earth—This progression outlines the spread of the gospel in the book of Acts.

►9 while they beheld, he was taken up—a repetition of Luke 24:50-53. Christ ascended while the disciples watched; he didn't leave them to guess what had happened to him (see also 2 Kings 2:10, 12; Luke 9:32).

►10 while they looked stedfastly toward heaven—They were amazed at what they had seen. This further supports the fact of Christ's resurrection, which was essential to the ministry of the apostles. two men stood by them in white apparel—These were angels in human form (Luke 24:4).

►11 men of Galilee, why stand ye gazing up into heaven?—They felt as if their Master had gone forever. this same Jesus . . . shall so come in like manner—i.e., "Jesus will return with the same glory and just as visibly as he left. Do not be sad about his leaving; rather, look forward to his return."

12-26 THE ELEVEN DISCIPLES RETURN TO JERUSALEM; EVENTS IN THE UPPER ROOM FROM THEN UNTIL THE SPIRIT COMES

►12 the mount called Olivet, which is from Jerusalem a sabbath's day journey—According to the Mishna, travel on the Sabbath day was limited to 2,000 cubits, which is about one kilometer or two-thirds of a mile.

►13 an upper room—This may have been the same room where they had celebrated the last Passover supper with Jesus (Luke 22:12). abode—The Greek word indicates that the disciples did not live there but frequently stayed there for meetings. Peter—the eleven apostles (Matt. 10:2-4).

►14 These all continued with one accord in prayer and supplication—Most likely they were praying for the promised effusion of the Spirit. the mother of Jesus—This is the last mention of Mary in the NT. his brethren—who must have become believers during Jesus' post-resurrection appearances (see 1 Cor. 15:6, 7).

►15 in those days—The nature of the disciples' work was becoming clearer to them. The Holy Spirit, who had already "breathed" on them (John 20:22), was beginning to move Peter to become the leader of the new community (Matt. 16:19). about an hundred and

**twenty**—Most of the 500 (1 Cor. 15:6) who had seen Jesus ascend to heaven remained in Galilee.

➤**18 falling headlong**—This supplements what is said in Matthew 27:5.

➤**20 Let his habitation** [estate] **be desolate, and let no man dwell therein**—from Psalm 69:25. **and his bishoprick** [office of overseeing] **let another take**—from Psalm 109:8. Luke combines these two verses from Psalms as applying not just to David's counselor Ahithophel (who betrayed David) but to Jesus' "false" apostle, Judas Iscariot (who betrayed Jesus). His vacant office needed to be filled.

➤**21, 22** These verses establish the criteria for apostleship. An apostle had to be a **witness** of Christ's **resurrection.** The work of the apostles was (1) to tell others that they had seen the resurrected Christ, and (2) to show how Jesus' ascension established his claim to be the Son of God. **from the baptism of John, unto that same day that he was taken up**—i.e., from the beginning to the end of his earthly ministry, a period of three and a half years.

➤**23 they**—This was a group of 120, for which Peter served as spokesman.

➤**24 Thou, Lord**—referring to the Son of God. **knowest the hearts of all men**—See John 2:24, 25; 21:15-17; Revelation 2:23.

➤**25 That he might go to his own place**—This was a polite way of describing the terrible state in which Judas would permanently reside.

➤**26 they gave forth their lots**—See Proverbs 16:33. This is the last time the Bible mentions the casting of lots. **he was numbered with the eleven apostles**—This completed the twelve once more.

## Chapter 2

### 1-13 THE HOLY SPIRIT COMES ON THE DISCIPLES

➤**1 the day of Pentecost**—This was fifty days after the first Passover Sabbath (Lev. 23:15, 16).

➤**2 suddenly there came a sound from heaven as of a rushing mighty wind**—This passage is so descriptive as to suggest that it was written by someone who witnessed the event. Wind was a common sign for the Spirit (Ezek. 37:9; John 3:8; 20:22).

➤**3 cloven tongues like as of fire**—These flames rose from a common source and descended on the heads of those present; this was a striking image appropriate to the context. Fire is a symbol of God's holiness and purity (Exod. 3:2; Heb. 12:29).

➤**4 filled with the Holy Ghost**—in fulfillment of Luke 24:49; Acts 1:5, 8. The expression "filled with the Holy Ghost" appears eight times in Luke's writings (Luke 1:15, 41, 67; Acts 2:4; 4:8, 31; 9:17; 13:9). In every case, the filling or effusion of the Holy Spirit enables the person so endowed to speak or preach for God. Thus, the filling of the Spirit is directly related to the prophetic ministry. **began to speak with other tongues**—or, languages. They spoke in authentic languages and probably all uttered the same praise of God's wonderful works (2:11), but they did not understand what they were saying (1 Cor. 14).

➤**5-11 there were dwelling at Jerusalem Jews, devout men, out of every nation**—They probably were in Jerusalem for more than just the feast of Pentecost though they were not permanently settled there. These Jews came from many nations surrounding Israel and beyond. The listing of the various nations shows the universality of the convocation.

### 14-36 PETER, FOR THE FIRST TIME, PREACHES CHRIST PUBLICLY

➤**15 these are not drunken**—This refers to the whole group of disciples, not just the Twelve. **but the third hour**—9:00 A.M. (see Eccles. 10:16; Isa. 5:11).

➤**17, 18 in the last days**—This phrase is used in the NT to designate the entire NT period which precedes the parousia of Christ (see 2 Tim. 3:1; Heb. 1:1). **I will pour out of my Spirit**—Here begins Peter's quotation of Joel 2:28-32a. The outpouring of the Spirit contrasts with the preceding times when the Spirit was given sparingly. **upon all flesh**—The Spirit was previously given only to the Jews. **sons and . . . daughters . . . young men . . . old men . . . servants . . . handmaidens**—There is no discrimination as to sex, age, or rank. **see visions . . . dream dreams**—This refers to the way in which the Spirit previously spoke to men. In the NT, visions and dreams were more the exception than the rule. **and they shall prophesy**—This clause, though present in most of the ancient manuscripts, is not part of the Joel passage.

➤**19 I will show wonders** —This refers to signs that were to come before the destruction of Jerusalem (Luke 21:25-28).

➤**21 whosoever shall call on the name of the Lord shall be saved**—Calling on the Lord's name (audibly), accompanied by genuine belief in Christ, became the NT pattern for obtaining salvation (see Rom. 10:12, 13; 1 Cor. 1:2). It is interesting to note that Peter did not quote all of Joel 2:32. He stopped where he did because the last part of Joel 2:32 deals with a different dispensation. (Cf. Jesus' quoting Isa. 61:1, 2a in Luke 4:18, 19.)

➤**23 the determinate** [fixed] **counsel and foreknowledge of God**—Christ's death had been predetermined from before the world's foundation (see 1 Pet. 1:19, 20; Rev. 13:8).

➤**24 it was not possible that he should be holden of it**—It was impossible that the living One could remain in the tomb with the dead (Luke 24:5).

➤**25-28 For David speaketh concerning him**—That which follows is taken verbatim from Psalm 16:8-11 in the Septuagint. **thou wilt not leave my soul in hell**—Hades (see Luke 16:23). **neither wilt thou suffer thine Holy One to see corruption**—The Holy One (Christ) would not experience mortal decay. **the ways of life**—i.e., the way to resurrection via the power of the divine life. **full of joy with thy countenance** [presence]—This refers to Christ's return to the Father's presence (through ascension) and the joys that followed their reunion in glory (see John 17:5, 24).

➤**29 David . . . is both dead and buried**—Peter, filled with the Spirit, realized that Christ (and his resurrection) is the only possible fulfillment of David's words in Psalm 16:8-11. Thus, David was not speaking of himself in this Psalm (cf. Ps. 110:1) but rather of Christ.

➤**30 Therefore**—He sums up what has been said. Israel had the evidence of (1) Christ's resurrection, (2) the fulfillment of previous prophecies, and now (3) the Holy Spirit.

➤**33 received of the Father the promise of the Holy Ghost** [Spirit]—See Luke 24:49; Acts 1:4, 8.

➤**34, 35 The LORD** [God, Yahweh] **said unto my Lord** [the Son of David, the Messiah]—David addressed his descendant as

being his "Lord," thus recognizing that the Messiah would be divine (cf. Matt. 22:41-45). **Sit thou on my right hand**—a clear reference to Christ's enthronement. **until I make thy foes thy footstool**—an expression of dominion, referring to the total dominion Christ will one day have over all his enemies. The quote comes from Psalm 110:1.

➤**36 the house of Israel**—This was the kingdom of God at that time. **God hath made**—Peter's purpose was to impress upon the people that what had happened was part of God's plan for man. **Jesus, whom ye have crucified**—Peter not only wanted to prove that Jesus was the Messiah, but he wanted the people to realize their own need for a change of heart. **both Lord and Christ**—Jesus' most significant titles.

➤**37 they were pricked** [stung] **in their heart**—See Zechariah 12:10. The complete fulfillment is still to come (Rom. 11). **what shall we do?**—Realizing their guilt, they genuinely wish to be changed. (Cf. Saul, 9:6.)

➤**38 Repent**—lit., "change your thinking." A change of mind must include understanding and acceptance of Christ's death and resurrection in payment for sin. **and be baptized**—This is a visible sign of that inward change. **receive the gift of the Holy Ghost** [Spirit]—The Holy Spirit is the sign of the New Covenant.

➤**39 the promise is unto you**—the Jews, **and to all that are far off**—the Gentiles (Eph. 2:17).

➤**40 with many other words**—We have here only a summary of what he said. **Save yourselves**—lit., "be saved." **from this untoward generation**—Israel would no longer be saved as a corporate body. Change must now be made on a personal level.

## 41-47 THE BEGINNING OF THE CHRISTIAN CHURCH

➤**41 and the same day there were added unto them about three thousand souls**—cf. 4:4.

➤**42 in the apostles' doctrine** [teaching] **and fellowship**—With such a large group of new disciples, these teaching sessions were very important in maintaining a unified body. **in breaking of bread**—The early Christian community met for many common meals at which time the Lord's Supper was often taken.

➤**44 all that believed were together**—See comments on 2:47. **and had all things common**—This was not communal living, but a voluntary sharing to help those in need.

➤**46 continuing daily with one accord in the temple**—The early Christians in Jerusalem habitually met at an outer court of the temple called Solomon's porch (see 3:11; 5:12). As Jews who had become Christians, they still kept their attachment to the traditions of Judaism. It would take some time before the Christian church completely broke away from Judaism. In fact, throughout Acts Christians were considered a sect of Judaism (see 24:5). **breaking bread from house to house**—In addition to the larger meetings at the temple, the early believers met in homes for more intimate and informal fellowship. Many early churches began in homes.

➤**47 the Lord added to the church**—According to the earliest manuscripts, this should read "the Lord added to the fellowship." The Greek words for "to the fellowship" (*epi to auto*), lit., "toward the same thing (or, goal)," convey the idea of united purpose—fervent, collective unity. In the early church, it acquired a quasi-technical meaning that denoted the union of the Christian body (Metzger). (See 1:15; 2:1; 1 Cor. 11:20; 14:23 for the use of the same expression.) **such as should be saved**—actually, "those who were being saved."

Chapter **3**

## 1-26 PETER HEALS A LAME MAN LYING AT THE TEMPLE GATE; HE ADDRESSES THE CROWD OF ONLOOKERS

➤**1 Peter and John**—They were mentioned by Christ as being together first with James (Mark 1:29; 5:37; 9:2), and then by themselves (Luke 22:8; John 13:23, 24). Now they were constantly together, although the younger, John, was silent.

➤**2 man lame from his mother's womb**—He was over forty years old (4:22).

➤**6 In the name of Jesus Christ of Nazareth rise up and walk**—These words, spoken with supernatural power and authority, inspired enough faith within the lame man to heal him.

➤**7 he took him by the right hand and lifted him up**—Jesus had done this with Peter's mother-in-law (Mark 1:31). **feet and anklebones**—Med-

ical terminology supports the assumption that Luke, a doctor (Col. 4:14), is the writer here.

➤**8 he leaping up stood, and walked, and entered with them into the temple**—These descriptive phrases suggest that the healing of the lame man was both complete and instantaneous.

➤**9 And all the people saw him**—The people had assembled for public prayer; thus the miracle had immediate, wide publicity.

➤**10 they knew that it was he which sat for alms**—cf. John 9:8.

➤**11 held Peter and John**—He expressed his thanks. **the people ran together . . . greatly wondering**—Peter was again given an audience who would listen with respect to what he had to say.

➤**12 why marvel ye at this?**—Miracles seem astounding because of man's limited power and understanding. **as though by our own power or holiness** [godliness]—Nothing within man's own capabilities could have accomplished this miracle.

➤**13 The God of Abraham, etc.**—the God of the Jews' ancestors. **hath glorified his Son** [or, Servant] **Jesus**—The Greek word (*pais*) translated "Son" in KJV can also be rendered "Servant" (see Matt. 12:18; Isa. 42:1 49:6; 52:13; 53:11).

➤**14 murderer**—Barabbas.

➤**15 killed the Prince** [Author] **of life**—This paradox was meant to stir the consciences of those listening. In these verses (3:13-15), Peter boldly points out their three major sins: (1) they delivered Jesus to Pilate (who wanted to release him), (2) they denied the Holy One and Just (and chose a murderer instead), and (3) they killed the Author of life (but God raised him).

➤**17 brethren**—Though his charges were severe, Peter spoke with love.

➤**18 that Christ should suffer**—According to the earliest manuscripts this should read "that his Christ should suffer." This idea totally opposed the prevailing Jewish doctrine. It was even hard for the disciples to accept the idea that Christ would have to suffer. Peter had firmly denied the possibility when it was first announced, but here he affirms Christ's suffering as a fundamental truth of the ancient prophecy that was fulfilled by the actions of the Jews.

➤**19 Repent . . . and be converted**—or, turned around. **sins . . . blotted out**—wiped away, erased (see Col. 2:14). **when**—so as. **the times of refreshing**—seasons of refreshment. **shall come**—lit., "may come." **from the presence of** the Lord—The repentant believer receives the Lord's presence as a continual source of refreshment.

➤20 he shall send [lit., "he may send"] Jesus Christ—This does not refer to the parousia, as such, but to Jesus Christ's personal presence (through the Spirit) with each one who turns to him. which before was preached unto you— This should be translated, "who has been appointed for you." According to the Greek, the last clause reads, "that he may send the Christ appointed for you, Jesus" (see RSV).

➤21 whom the heaven must receive until the times—This refers to all the time between the ascension and the Second Coming. restitution of all things—He will heal every disorder and division caused by the fall of man.

➤22, 23 A prophet . . . like unto me—Jesus was like Moses in intimacy of communication with God (Num. 12:6-8) and as the Mediator of a new order (Heb. 3:2-6). Peter assumes that those listening to him would understand that this "Prophet" was Christ. (Acts 3:22, 23 is taken from Deut. 18:15, 16a, 19.)

➤24 all the prophets from Samuel [the next one after Moses] and those that follow after— i.e., all the prophets from Moses to Malachi, foretold of these days—All of the prophets spoke of the Messiah and the forming of a new creation (Heb. 9:10).

➤25 thy seed—See Genesis 22:18; Galatians 3:8.

➤26 God, having raised up—not from the dead, but having provided and prepared. his Son Jesus—should read, "his Servant Jesus" (see 3:13). sent him to bless you, in turning away every one of you from his iniquities—They had been looking for a Messiah who would bring outward blessings to Israel as a nation, and through her to the rest of the world. Peter says that Christ came, instead, to bring salvation from sin.

Chapter 4

## 1-13 PETER AND JOHN ARRESTED AND BROUGHT BEFORE THE JEWISH COUNCIL

➤1 the captain of the temple—The guards were disturbed by the large crowd and the excitement that was being created. and the Sadducees—These men did not believe in res-

urrection from the dead so they were angered by what Peter had been saying.

➤6 Annas . . . Caiaphas—See Luke 3:2. John, and Alexander—Nothing historical is known about them. gathered together at Jerusalem—This refers to the assembly of the Sanhedrin (Matt. 2:4).

➤7 By what power, or . . . name, have ye done this?—They do not deny that a miracle had been performed (4:16).

➤8 filled with the Holy Ghost [Spirit], said—See Mark 13:11; Luke 21:15.

➤10 Be it known unto you all, and to all the people of Israel—Peter gives a formal legal testimony to the entire nation through these representative rulers. by the name of Jesus —See 3:13. by him doth this man stand here before you whole—The healed man was present during this hearing (4:14).

➤11 This is the stone which was set at nought [set aside] of you builders, which is become the head of the corner—i.e., the chief cornerstone. Christ had already used this phrase from Psalm 118:22 in Matthew 21:42. It is particularly fitting here as Christ had been rejected by these very "builders."

➤12 Neither is there salvation in any other—person. Christ is the unique way to salvation (cf. John 14:6).

➤13 unlearned—common men who were not trained in the Jewish schools to be teachers. took knowledge of them, that they had been with Jesus—This is perhaps better interpreted to mean that the council realized that they had not gotten rid of Jesus, for he was present in these men.

➤16 What shall we do . . . we can not deny—This implies the council's unwillingness to accept the truth about Christ. They could not punish the disciples because of the people's attraction to them (4:21).

➤18-20 commanded them not to speak at all nor teach in [with respect to] the name of Jesus—The disciples had been commanded just the opposite by their risen Lord Jesus (for example, see Matt. 28:18-20), for whom they would now sacrifice their lives if need be. They had been called to be witnesses (see 1:8); so they said, we cannot but speak the things which we have seen and heard.

## 23-27 PETER AND JOHN RETURN TO THE OTHER DISCIPLES AND TELL OF THEIR EXPERIENCE. FOLLOWING THIS, THEY PRAY TOGETHER

➤**24 Lord**—Greek, *despota* ("Master," "ruler"). **thou art God**—This statement is not present in the earliest manuscripts.

➤**25, 26 Who by the mouth of thy servant David hast said**—According to the earliest manuscripts this reads, "Who by the Holy Spirit, [even by] the mouth of our father David, your servant, said." The Greek behind this reading is difficult—if not impossible—to comprehend. The thought seems to be that God spoke through the Holy Spirit and David's mouth as through a united mouthpiece. According to the Greek, David's mouth is in apposition to the Holy Spirit; this indicates that David's prophetic utterance was the same as the Holy Spirit's (GAM). The quote comes from Psalm 2:1, 2 in which David showed the conflict between the heathen nations and the Messiah, the anointed One. Here the believers see Herod, Pilate, the Gentiles, and the people of Israel rejecting the Messiah (3:13).

➤**29 behold their threatenings**—The great conflict between the church and the rest of the world is recognized.

➤**31, 32 they were all filled with the Holy Ghost [Spirit], and they spake the word of God with boldness**—The Spirit's presence was twofold: the men spoke with boldness, and their former selfishness and individuality gave way to a new spirit of unity and fellowship. The community of goods was an outward expression of this spirit.

➤**33 with great power gave the apostles witness of the resurrection**—See 1:8.

➤**34, 35 distribution was made unto every man according as he had need**—This does not suggest political communism, but the spirit of unity which characterized this body of believers (4:32).

➤**36, 37** These verses provide an example of the spirit of sharing. **Joses . . . a Levite**—Although this tribe received no inheritance, some men did individually have property (Deut. 18:8). **Barnabas**—Joses' nickname. This is the first mention of this important figure in the early church. **son of consolation**—or, "son of encouragement" (a translation of the Hebrew word for "Barnabas"). **Cyprus**—an island located in the Mediterranean.

## Chapter 5

## 1-11 ANANIAS AND SAPPHIRA

➤**1 Ananias, with Sapphira his wife**—The story of Ananias and Sapphira is the first mention of a problem within the early church. Some interpreters have suggested that rivalry grew between groups of new Christians so that each tried to outdo the other in their giving. Perhaps some, like Ananias and Sapphira, tried to appear liberal against their own nature.

➤**2 kept back part of the price**—It was not required that people with property sell it and turn all the money over to the church. Their sin was in giving only part of the money to the church while claiming to have given it all.

➤**3 why hath Satan filled thine heart?**—Satan was the source of their deception (cf. John 13:2, 27). **to lie to the Holy Ghost [Spirit]**—They directly lied to men who were the Spirit's guidance.

➤**4 after it was sold, was it not in thine own power?**—This verse (with 4:34) indicates the completely voluntary nature of the sacrifices that supported the young Christian community. **thou hast not lied unto men, but unto God**—Since the Holy Spirit is within the members of the church, one who deceives the church is in effect attempting to deceive the Holy Spirit. Peter's language implies the divinity and distinct personality of the Holy Spirit ("Holy Spirit," 5:3; "God," 5:4).

➤**5 great fear came on all**—The members of this community were awed at this demonstration of God's power within the young church.

➤**6 young men**—The younger and more active church members acted as assistants rather than as officers or leaders.

➤**9 to tempt the Spirit of the Lord**—See comments on 5:2, 3.

➤**10 buried her**—It was the Jewish practice to bury the dead before sunset on the day of death.

➤**11** Compare this incident with a similar experience in Joshua, where Achan is guilty of misusing some of the spoils of Jericho. The sin, the time, and the effect were similar in both cases.

**12-26 THE APOSTLES' CONTINUING MINISTRY LEADS TO THEIR ARREST THEY ARE MIRACULOUSLY RELEASED BY AN ANGEL AND RESUME THEIR TEACHING**

➤**12 Solomon's porch**—See John 10:23.

➤**13, 14 of the rest durst** [dared] **no man join himself**—Because of what had happened to Ananias and Sapphira, people did not come to the Lord unless they really were serious. Yet many more did become believers and were **added to the Lord**—To be added to the church (or, fellowship) was to be added to the Lord (see 2:47) because the church was one with Christ as his very own body.

➤**15 into the streets**—This means "into every street." **on beds and couches**—The soft beds belonged to the rich, the hard couches (mats) to the poor. **shadow of Peter . . . might overshadow some of them**—cf. 19:12; Luke 8:46. This verse shows how Peter had become the spiritual leader of the new church as predicted in Matthew 16:18. As people had desired the touch of Jesus upon them, they had faith that God would heal them even through the shadow of his servant, Peter.

➤**17 the Sadducees**—See 4:1, 2.

➤**19 by night**—This occurred on the same night.

➤**20 this life**—The new life in Christ, the resurrected life, was the subject of the apostles' teaching.

➤**21 senate**—This is the Sanhedrin. It seems that the senate was hastily called for the specific purpose of dealing with the apostles.

➤**23** This is the reverse of the miracle described in 16:26 (cf. Luke 5:6; John 21:11).

➤**24 they doubted**—They were both puzzled and afraid of what the crowd which supported the apostles might do.

➤**26 they feared the people**—It is ironic that they did not fear God whose power they had witnessed so clearly in the miracles that the apostles were doing.

**27-42 THE APOSTLES APPEAR BEFORE THE JEWISH COUNCIL (SANHEDRIN). EVENTUALLY THEY ARE RELEASED AND CONTINUE THEIR TEACHING**

➤**28 ye have filled Jerusalem with your doctrine** [teaching]—This indicates the success of their preaching. **intend to bring this man's**

**blood upon us**—They avoided using the name "Jesus." Perhaps they remembered their own recent curse, "His blood be on us . . . " (Matt. 27:25), and the words of Judas, "I have betrayed the innocent blood" (Matt. 27:4).

➤**29 Then Peter**—See 2:22; 3:13.

➤**31 Prince and a Saviour**—The first title expresses the royalty that Israel expected in the Messiah. They had completely lost sight of the element expressed by "Savior." Together these names represent the whole of Jesus' work (cf. 3:15; Heb. 2:10). **repentance . . . forgiveness**—Repentance is a change within man; forgiveness is experienced from God through the work of Christ (cf. 2:38; 20:21).

➤**32 we are his witnesses . . . so is also the Holy Ghost** [Spirit]—The apostles presented the facts of Christ's life, death, burial and resurrection. The Holy Spirit confirmed these facts by the miracles that he performed through them.

➤**34 Gamaliel**—This teacher was the son of Simeon and grandson and pupil of Hillel, another prominent rabbi. He was a loyal Pharisee, well known for his legal wisdom. He is best known as the teacher of Saul of Tarsus.

➤**36 Theudas**—This is not the same Theudas mentioned by Josephus (*Antiquities,* 20.5.1), but an earlier insurrectionist who led the Palestinians against the Roman rule.

➤**37 Judas of Galilee**—Feeling that taxation was an insult and a dishonor to God, Judas of Galilee led a revolt that the Romans quickly ended (Josephus' *Antiquities,* 13.1.1).

➤**38 if this counsel or this work be of men, it will come to nought**—This neutral position was wise, considering the hostility of the council. Remaining neutral as an individual before God, however, is unwise and, in fact, impossible (Luke 11:23).

➤**40 beaten them**—They had disobeyed the earlier orders from the Senate (cf. Luke 23:16).

➤**41 rejoicing that they were counted worthy to suffer shame for his name**—The apostles were victorious in their first experience of persecution. They felt privileged to suffer for the cause of Christ (Matt. 5:12; 1 Pet. 4:14, 16).

➤**42 in the temple** [court], **and in every house**—This means that they preached in public and in private (see comments on 2:46). **teach and preach Jesus Christ**—in the Greek, "teaching and preaching the Christ, namely Jesus." The apostles proclaimed Jesus to be the Christ.

*Chapter* 6

## 1-7 THE APPOINTMENT OF THE FIRST DEACONS

➤**1 the Grecians**—These may have been Greek-speaking Jews born in the provinces. **the Hebrews**—Jews born in Palestine used their native tongue and often looked down on the Greek Jews. **their widows were neglected in the daily ministration**—In each temple there were officials who collected alms on Friday morning. Later that day, this food was distributed to those with both temporary and permanent needs. The complaint here may have been true, though there is no indication of partiality on the part of those who distributed the money and/or food.

➤**2 called the multitude of the disciples**—They had some practical decisions to make. **the word of God**—Preaching the Word was regarded as their primary duty.

➤**3 full of the Holy Ghost** [Spirit]—Not necessarily to perform miracles, but to be led and guided by the Spirit in all things. **and wisdom**—practical knowledge. **whom we may appoint**—The general community was to "elect," but the "appointment" lay with the apostles.

➤**5 Stephen, . . . and Philip, and Prochorus, and Nicanor, and Timon, and Parmenas, and Nicolas**—It seems from the names listed that all seven men were Greeks. This was a wise decision as it would restore mutual confidence and help to solve the complaint.

➤**6 when they had prayed** [for them], **they laid their hands on them**—All official gifts within the community came from Christ. The laying on of hands was a commissioning service to affirm the choice of individuals for a particular task. Although the word is not specifically used here, these seven men are thought to be the first deacons. Note the following as implied by this experience; (1) misunderstandings do arise even among the most dedicated

and loving servants; (2) misunderstandings can be quickly healed where there are honest intentions, love, and wisdom; (3) even though those who were being complained against were the majority, they were confident and trusting enough to choose all seven men from among the minority; (4) the apostles are not interested in power within the community as seen by the willingness to let others make choices and assume responsibility; (5) the young community had little formal organization. When a problem arose, they were able to adopt the solution that seemed most reasonable and effective.

➤**7 word of God increased . . . disciples multiplied . . . a great company of the priests were obedient to the faith**—This was the crowning triumph of the gospel and the result of oneness among the believers (see John 17:21).

## 8-15 STEPHEN BEFORE THE JEWISH COUNCIL (SANHEDRIN)

➤**9 the Libertines**—This cult of Jewish freedmen had been expelled from Rome and were then residing in Jerusalem. They were probably arguing about whether Jesus was the Messiah. **Cyrenians**—They were from Libya, on the northern coast of Africa. **Cilicia**—Saul of Tarsus might have been one of these (7:58; 21:39). **Asia**—See 16:6.

➤**11 blasphemous words against Moses**—probably referring to the impending disappearance of the whole Mosaic system. **and against God**—This must refer to the supreme dignity and authority that Stephen claimed for Christ as the head of that new economy which was superseding the old (see 7:56-60).

➤**14 this Jesus . . . shall destroy this place**—i.e., the temple. The same false accusation was used at Jesus' trial (see John 2:19 and the twisted version of this in Matt. 26:61).

*Chapter* 7

## 1-60 STEPHEN'S DEFENSE AND MARTYRDOM

Stephen's comments are rather lengthy and circuitous. His object is to show that (1) he knows and respects the entire history of God's dealing with the Jews, but (2) they were repeating old mistakes by resisting God's Spirit and Christ's kingdom.

**➤1, 2 the high priest**—This was probably Caiaphas. **The God of glory**—A magnificent appellation, fitted at the very outset to gain the attention of his audience; denoting not that visible glory that attended many of the divine manifestations, but the glory of those manifestations themselves, of which this was regarded by every Jew as the fundamental one. It is the glory of absolutely free grace. **appeared unto our father Abraham . . . before he dwelt in Charran**—This first call of Abraham by God is not recorded in Genesis but is implied in Genesis 15:7 and Nehemiah 9:7.

**➤4 when his father was dead, he removed him into this land**—Though Abraham was in Canaan before Terah's death, his settlement in it as the land of promise is here said to be after it, as being in no way dependent on the family movement, but a transaction purely between Yahweh and Abraham himself.

**➤6 four hundred years**—These are round numbers found in Genesis 15:13, 16 (see also Gal. 3:17).

**➤7 after that shall they come forth, and serve me in this place**—This combines the promise given to Abraham (Gen. 15:16) with that given to Moses (Exod. 3:12), thus rapidly summarizing the facts.

**➤8 the covenant of circumcision**—Circumcision was the sign of a promise (Gen. 17:10; 21:4). **the twelve patriarchs**—These were the founders of the twelve tribes.

**➤9 the patriarchs, moved with envy, sold Joseph into Egypt: but God was with him**—Here is Stephen's first example of Israel's opposition to God. God's purpose was accomplished despite the people involved. Verses 9-34 briefly retell the highlights from Genesis 37 through Exodus 3.

**➤14 threescore and fifteen souls**—See Genesis 46:27, Septuagint.

**➤17 grew and multiplied**—They grew from 75 to 600,000 in number.

**➤20 In which time**—of deepest depression. **Moses**—was Israel's deliverer from Egypt. **fair**—"fair to God" or "divinely fair" according to the Greek (Heb. 11:23).

**➤22 mighty in words**—Though Moses had a speech problem (Exod. 4:10), his written words show a remarkable ability to communi-

cate. **and in deeds**—referring to unrecorded circumstances in his early life, according to Josephus.

**➤23, 30, 36** These verses represent Moses' life in three periods of forty years each. The Jewish writers used the same scheme, which is consistent with Moses' death at age 120 (Deut. 34:7).

**➤24 smote the Egyptian**—This was probably more than he intended to do.

**➤25 he supposed his brethren would have understood how that God by his hand would deliver them**—Perhaps Moses thought this the proper time to call the Israelites together under his leadership. **but they understood not**—Moses assumed that their attitude was the same as his and was humiliated to find out otherwise. This gives Stephen another example of Israel's slowness to understand and cooperate with God's plan.

**➤26 he showed himself unto them as they strove**—Moses, as an unauthorized mediator, was resented by the guilty brother.

**➤28 Wilt thou kill me, as thou diddest the Egyptian yesterday?**—Moses did not think anyone knew about that (Exod. 2:12), but he was mistaken.

**➤29 Then fled Moses**—Pharaoh was seeking to kill Moses in punishment (Exod. 2:15).

**➤30 an angel of the Lord**—The earliest manuscripts read simply, "an angel."

**➤35** See Psalm 118:22.

**➤37 A prophet shall the Lord your God raise up unto you of your brethren, like unto me**—See Deuteronomy 18:15. Stephen quotes Moses to remind his audience that Moses should not be the object of the church's devotion but only a humble forerunner of the one to whom they would completely submit.

**➤38 the church in the wilderness**—This refers to the collective body of God's chosen people. In the Septuagint (from which Stephen, a Greek, consistently quoted) the *ekklēsia* was often used to describe Israel. **the angel which spake to him**—Moses was close to God and to his people. By offering this highly respectful and valid opinion of Moses, Stephen refutes the main charge for which he had been arrested.

**➤39 whom our fathers would not obey**—Stephen pointed out that the greatest dishonor was done to Moses by the nation that was now so jealous of his honor. **and in their hearts**

turned back again into Egypt—Stephen hoped to convince his audience that they were about to make a mistake.

►42 written in the book—Amos 5:25. have ye offered to me—The emphasis is on "to me." Israel made sacrifices but not always *to God,* in the right way, or with an acceptable attitude.

►43 The Israelites are charged here with worshiping the golden calf and the heavenly bodies. I will carry you away beyond Babylon—This refers to the region of Judah's captivity. The entire verse is quoted from Amos 5:27.

►44 the tabernacle of witness in the wilderness—This was a constant reminder that God was with them, so their guilt as idolaters was even more severe.

►45 Jesus—actually, Joshua ("Jesus" is the Greek equivalent of the Hebrew name, "Joshua"). unto the days of David—Stephen mentioned David in order to make the transition from the tabernacle to Solomon's temple in Jerusalem.

►46 the God of Jacob—Other manuscripts read, "the house of Jacob."

►48-50 Stephen cited Isaiah 66:1, 2 to show that the temple—the admiration of all those Jews—is not really adequate for God's habitation. God's habitation is in man's spirit (see John 4:24; Eph. 2:22). But these Jews were hardened to God, and thus God could not penetrate them.

►51 ye stiffnecked [stubborn] and uncircumcised in heart and ears, ye do always resist the Holy Ghost [Spirit]—Stephen summarized his historical sketch of Israel. They had always been spiritually blind to God's plan for them and had continually resisted the working of the Holy Spirit to that very day.

►52 Which of the prophets have not your fathers persecuted?—The Jews had always been hostile to God's messengers, whose task was to prepare the way for Christ, the Messiah. the Just One—See Isaiah 53:11; Jeremiah 23:6. The hostility of the Jews was consummated in the betrayal and murder of Christ himself, a deed done by those same men who were now sitting in judgment on Stephen.

►53 Who have received the law by the disposition [ordination] of angels—In spite of the divine manner in which the Jews were given the laws, they disobeyed them. (See Gal. 3:19.)

►55 looked up stedfastly into heaven, and saw the glory of God—This vision was apparently witnessed by Stephen alone. Jesus standing—Jesus is usually described as "sitting." Jesus stood up to eagerly watch the scene in that council.

►56 the Son of man standing on the right hand of God—Here and in Revelation (1:13 and 14:14) are the only places where Jesus is called "the Son of man" after his ascension. Stephen, filled with the Spirit, repeats the same words that Jesus used before the same council to foretell his glorification (Matt. 26:64), thus suggesting to the council that the exaltation of the Son of man was real and had already begun.

►58 cast him out of the city—Cf. Leviticus 24:14; Numbers 15:35; 1 Kings 21:13; Hebrews 13:12. the witnesses—Those who testified against Stephen would throw the first stones. Saul of Tarsus not only consented to this death, but took part in the evil deed.

►59 Lord Jesus, receive my spirit—This is the same kind of prayer that Jesus prayed on the cross.

►60 Lord, lay not this sin to their charge—This is also similar to Christ's prayer (Luke 23:34). he fell asleep—a euphemism for, "he died" (see 1 Thess. 4:14).

# Chapter 8

## 1-4 SAUL'S PART IN THE CONTINUED PERSECUTION OF THE CHRISTIANS

►1 Saul was consenting unto his death—This does not necessarily mean that he was a member of the council. they were all scattered abroad—This could have been the beginning of the the same diaspora spoken of in James 1:1 and even 1 Peter 1:1. throughout the regions of Judaea and Samaria—As was foretold by Jesus, the gospel spread from Jerusalem to Judea and Samaria (1:8). Jesus, however, did not say that a persecution would be the impetus for the dispersion. except the apostles—They did not face less risk, but they were determined to remain to hold the new young church together.

►2 devout men—i.e., godly Jews. These men were probably impressed with Stephen's testimony and secretly leaned toward Christianity.

➤**3** See Paul's later confessions (22:4; 26:9, 10; 1 Cor. 15:9; Gal. 1:13; Phil. 3:6; 1 Tim. 1:13).

➤**4 went every where preaching**—They were commanded by Christ to do this (Luke 24:47; Acts 1:8) but probably would have remained in Jerusalem had it not been for the persecution. Thus, the result of the enemy's anger was the spread of Christianity (see Phil. 1:12, 13).

## 5-25 PHILIP'S SUCCESSFUL PREACHING IN SAMARIA AND HIS EXPERIENCE WITH SIMON MAGUS

➤**5 Philip**—This is not the apostle but the deacon, Philip (6:5), second most prominent to Stephen. The persecution may have been strongly carried out against Stephen's close associates. **the city of Samaria**—This was possibly a city in Samaria (Sebaste or Gitta, the home of Simon Magus). Jesus had said that the harvest among the Samaritans would be bountiful (John 4:4, 35, 36). The fact that the Jews were preaching the message of Christ to the Samaritans is important because Samaria was the bridge from Jerusalem to the rest of the world. In God's plan, a Greek-speaking Jew was sent to the Samaritans, who probably would not have listened to a Jew born in Judea.

➤**8 great joy**—This resulted from the miracles that Philip did and the general change that the gospel brought upon the people.

➤**9 Simon**—This was Simon Magus.

➤**10 the great power of God**—lit., "the power of God which is called great."

➤**11 to him they had regard**—He was prominent because of the magic he had done for so long. These people were open to a spiritual change and eagerly accepted Philip's message (8:12).

➤**13 Then Simon himself believed**—Left without followers, Simon was also ready to believe the gospel about Christ.

➤**14 they sent unto them Peter and John**—They were to help establish a strong community among these new Christians. Here we see Peter reaching out to people not fully Jewish—a precursor to his role in opening the gospel to the Gentiles (Acts 10).

➤**17 laid they their hands on them, and they received the Holy Ghost** [Spirit]—This act of the laying on of hands was not prerequi-

site to receiving the Holy Spirit. It was more of a confirmation to assure the new converts. The laying on of hands probably symbolized attachment between the apostles and the new believers in one fellowship, one body. "The most important aspect of God's withholding the Spirit till apostolic representatives came from the Jerusalem church was to prevent schism. Because of the natural propensity of division between Jews and Samaritans it was essential for Peter and John to welcome the Samaritan believers officially into the church" (Toussaint).

➤**18 the Holy Ghost** [Spirit]—According to the best manuscripts, this should read "the Spirit." **he offered them money**—The term "simony" usually refers now to the purchase of ecclesiastical offices.

➤**19 that on whomsoever I lay hands, he may receive the Holy Ghost** [Spirit]—Simon was interested only in adding this trick to his repertoire.

➤**20 Thy money perish with thee**—This is similar to Christ's rebuke of Peter (Matt. 16:23).

➤**22 if perhaps**—Peter's doubtful manner of speech was to impress Simon with concern for his sin.

➤**23 the gall of bitterness**—i.e., the pain or irritation of bitterness. **bond of iniquity**—he was stopped by his unrighteousness.

➤**24 Pray ye to the Lord for me**—Peter urged Simon to pray himself. Simon had no real concern for forgiveness. He was probably hoping that Peter's contact with the spiritual realm might keep these things Peter had threatened from happening. This is the last mention of Simon Magus in the Bible. Tradition describes him as continuing his career, combining Greek or Oriental philosophy with some elements of Christianity.

## 26-40 PHILIP'S EXPERIENCE WITH THE ETHIOPIAN TREASURER

➤**26 go toward the south**—The angel directs Philip to leave the scene of the great revival to go to a desert region. Philip is obedient to the Holy Spirit as he had no other purpose for such a journey.

➤**27 Ethiopia**—This was in ancient Upper Egypt, Meroe. **an eunuch**—In the East, eunuchs were generally employed for confidential offices. **Candace**—This is the name for the queens of Upper Egypt. **had come to Jerusalem for to worship**—As a Gentile converted to the Jewish faith, he had gone to keep the recent Feast of Pentecost (Isa. 56:3-8; John 12:20).

➤**28 Was returning**—He had stayed for some time past the feast days.

➤**29 the Spirit said**—cf. 10:19; 16:6, 7. **Go near, and join thyself**—Philip now expects the purpose for his journey to become clear.

➤**30 Understandest thou what thou readest?**—This sincere question on Philip's part shows that he was ready to give any insight that might help the reader.

➤**31 How can I, except some man should guide me?**—This is an expression of his humility.

➤**32, 33 The place of the scripture which he read** [out loud] **was this**—from Isaiah 53:7, 8 in the Septuagint. (Philip, a Greek, would have no problem interpreting the Greek OT.)

➤**34 of whom speaketh the prophet?**—The eunuch probably knew that some acknowledged Jesus to be the Messiah, but his question shows that he did not recognize in Jesus the fulfillment of Isaiah's prophecy.

➤**35 Philip . . . began at the same scripture**—Philip used this passage as the basis for his explanation to the eunuch. **preached unto him Jesus**—Philip showed him that Jesus was the subject of this prophecy and how it was fulfilled by his life, death, and resurrection.

➤**36 See, here is water**—He had already understood the truth about Christ and was looking for the first opportunity to become one of the visible disciples of Jesus. **what doth hinder me to be baptized?**—This is the first mention of baptism in this particular case.

➤**37** This verse does not appear in all the earliest manuscripts and was probably added later from a baptismal formula.

➤**38 into the water**—The precise *form* of his baptism is unclear and is of no consequence.

➤**39 the Spirit of the Lord caught away Philip**—Philip had been led by the Spirit to baptize a Gentile eunuch, which a strict Jew would never have done. Some view Philip's departure as a miraculous kind of rapture (cf. 1 Kings 18:12; 2 Kings 2:16; 2 Cor. 12:2, 3; and 1 Thess. 4:17). Others interpret the passage as indicating

a Spirit-led departure (cf. Mark 1:12). But to deny a physical miracle does not deny the miraculous leading of God's Spirit. **the eunuch saw him no more**—His thoughts were centered on his joy rather than on Philip. **he went on his way rejoicing**—His soul had been freed and he had sealed his Christian discipleship. Although his teacher had gone, his new life remained.

➤**40 Philip was found at Azotus**—perhaps, "Philip appeared at Azotus" (NIV, NEB). **he preached in all the cities**—He passed all the cities along the coast, traveling northward from Azotus. **Caesarea**—This city is 65 miles northwest of Jerusalem, on the Mediterranean Sea just south of Mt. Carmel. It was rebuilt by Herod in 13 B.C. and was named in honor of Caesar Augustus. Philip apparently established his home in Caesarea (21:8).

*Chapter* **9**

## 1-25 THE CONVERSION OF SAUL AND THE BEGINNING OF HIS MINISTRY

➤**1 And Saul**—This verse introduces Saul as a leader in the attempt to stifle Christianity, following Stephen's death. Saul was born in Tarsus, the capital of Cilicia. As a child, he was taught the Jewish law by his parents. As a teenager, he was sent to Jerusalem to study with Gamaliel and probably attended the temple in which Stephen debated with the freedmen (6:9). He was thus familiar with the Christian movement and its threat to Judaism.

➤**2 letters . . . to the synagogues**—These letters authorized Saul to carry out his work of persecution. **Damascus**—the capital of Syria, approximately 130 miles northeast of Jerusalem, had a large Jewish population. **men or women**—Women are mentioned three times as specific objects of cruelty (8:3; 22:4).

➤**3 he came near Damascus**—cf. 22:6; 26:12.

➤**4 he fell to the earth**—Those who were traveling with him (26:14) saw the light (22:9) and also fell. **heard a voice saying**—The voice spoke in Hebrew (26:14). **Saul, Saul**—His name was soon changed to Paul. **why persecutest thou me?**—In persecuting the Christians, Saul was persecuting Christ, for Christ and his body are one.

➤**5 Who art thou, Lord?**—Jesus knew Saul before Saul knew Jesus. That Saul saw as well as heard Jesus is specifically stated by Ananias (9:17; 22:14), by Barnabas (9:27), and by Paul himself (26:16). Later, when Paul claims his apostleship, he expressly states that he had "seen Jesus" (1 Cor. 9:1; 15:8). **I am Jesus**—the Nazarene (as in 22:8) who now speaks to you from heaven. **it is hard for thee to kick against the pricks**—This statement is not found in all the earliest manuscripts, but it is found in 26:14 (from which this was taken). (See comments on 26:14.)

➤**6** The first half of this verse (up to **the Lord said unto him**) does not appear in the earliest manuscripts. The expression was borrowed from 22:10 (see comments there).

➤**7 The men . . . stood speechless**—Having fallen to the ground at first, they had apparently gotten up while Paul remained on the ground (26:14). **hearing a** [the] **voice, but seeing no man**—They did not understand what they heard (22:9).

➤**8 he saw no man**—Saul had closed his eyes to protect them from the bright light. When he opened them, he was blind (see 22:11).

➤**9 And he was three days without sight, and neither did eat nor drink**—Such a period of abstinence from food and water, taking into account Saul's mental state, is quite believable. During those three days of dark solitude, Saul changed a great deal.

➤**10 Ananias**—See 22:12.

➤**11 the street which is called Straight**—This street was known as "the street of the bazaars." It runs through the city from the east gate to the Palace of Pacha. **he prayeth**—Ananias would find the former persecutor at prayer.

➤**12 hath seen in a vision**—Both men, as in the later case of Cornelius and Peter, are prepared for their part in the experience. There is no record of Saul's seeing Ananias except in this reference.

➤**13 Lord, I have heard . . . how much evil he hath done to thy saints at Jerusalem**—Ananias's objections were removed (9:15).

➤**14 hath authority . . . to bind all that call on thy name**—News of Saul's coming had reached the city, causing great fear to the Christians in Damascus. The early Christians were known as those who called on the name of Jesus.

➤**15 Go thy way**—Don't object any further. **chosen vessel**—This word is often employed by Paul for those used by God to carry out his plan (Rom. 9:21-23; 2 Cor. 4:7; 2 Tim. 2:20, 21; cf. Zech. 3:2).

➤**16 I will show him**—cf. 20:23, 24; 21:11. **how great things he must suffer for my name's sake**—Saul had committed many violent acts against Christ, but now Paul would suffer for Christ.

➤**17 Brother Saul**—Ananias already considered Saul a fellow brother in Christ. **be filled with the Holy Ghost** [Spirit]—Ananias probably assumed that the Spirit would come upon him before his baptism. (Cf. 10:44-48. Cornelius and his company received the Spirit prior to their baptism.)

➤**18 immediately**—His blindness and the cure were both miracles. **and was baptized**—Ananias directed that it should be so (22:16).

➤**19 Then was Saul certain days with the disciples which were at Damascus**—cf. Gal. 1:15-17.

➤**20 he preached Christ**—According to the best manuscripts, this should read "he preached Jesus." The Jews already knew about the Christ, the Messiah; Saul told them about Jesus—declaring that this Jesus was **the Son of God** and the "very Christ" (9:22).

➤**23 after . . . many days**—According to Galatians 1:17, 18, Paul indicated that he went to Arabia and returned again to Damascus during this period. The time from his baptism to his return was three years. There are several possible reasons for Paul's trip to Arabia: (1) Perhaps he felt a need for rest and seclusion after the excitement of his conversion. (2) Possibly he wanted to put off the confrontation that was sure to occur between him and his old friends and associates. (3) He may have needed the time to prepare for his eventual teaching and preaching.

➤**24 they watched the gates day and night to kill him**—See Paul's own account of this experience in 2 Corinthians 11:32.

➤**25 by the wall**—i.e., "through an opening in the wall" (TLB). Such overhanging windows in the wall were common at that time. (See 2 Cor. 11:32.)

## 26-31 SAUL'S FIRST VISIT TO JERUSALEM AFTER HIS CONVERSION

➤**26 when Saul was come to Jerusalem**— Three years after his conversion, Saul went to Jerusalem to see Peter, the leading apostle (Gal. 1:18), to discuss his coming ministry to the Gentiles. **they were all afraid of him**—They knew him only as the persecutor of the Christians. Rumors of his conversion may have reached the Christians in Jerusalem, but the work of Saul since his conversion was generally unknown to Jerusalem.

➤**27 Barnabas . . . brought him to the apostles**—He was specifically brought to Peter and James (Gal. 1:18, 19). Saul and Barnabas were both Greek Jews who were well known and respected in their hometowns. Some critics think that they may have been acquainted prior to this time. Barnabas's character is consistent with descriptions in other places (11:24; 4:36). **how he had seen the Lord . . . and that he had spoken to him**—Saul had received his commission directly from the Lord.

➤**28 he was with them**—He stayed with them for about fifteen days, lodging with Peter (see Gal. 1:18).

➤**29 spake boldly**—Saul spoke to the Greeks (see comments on 6:1) because he was of the same class and had spoken along with them against Jesus. **they went about** [attempted] **to slay**—Thus, Saul was made to experience what he had earlier made others feel—the cost of discipleship.

➤**30 they brought him down to Caesarea**—Saul left not only to escape danger but also because he had received specific instructions to leave Jerusalem (22:17-21). **sent him forth to Tarsus**—his hometown. From Galatians 1:21, it seems that he landed first at Seleucia, then traveled to Antioch, then to Cilicia, and from there to Tarsus. This was Paul's first visit home after his conversion. It is not certain whether he ever visited there again (see comments on 11:30). It was probably during this visit that Paul talked about Christ with his relatives who are mentioned in 23:16; Romans 16:7, 11, 21.

➤**31 the churches**—According to the earliest manuscripts, this should read "the church." The then existing, universal church was in Judea, Galilee, and Samaria. **had . . . rest**— from persecution; hence, "peace." Paul was no longer leading the violent persecution, and the strict Jews were busy fighting the emperor Caligula who was trying to gain control over the temple worship. **Judaea and Galilee and Samaria**—Most of Jesus' teaching took place in these locations.

## 32-43 PETER HEALS AENEAS AT LYDDA AND RESTORES DORCAS TO LIFE AT JOPPA

In order to tell about the experience of Cornelius (chapter 10), Luke now returns to Peter's activities.

➤**32 Peter passed throughout all quarters**—Peter was not attempting to avoid persecutors but to visit and encourage the young churches. **Lydda**—This was about five miles east of Joppa.

➤**34 Jesus Christ maketh thee whole**— See comments on 3:6. **arise, and make thy bed**—See John 5:8.

➤**35 Saron**—This rich plain was between Joppa and Caesarea. **turned to the Lord**—As a result of this miracle, others became Christians.

➤**36 Joppa**—the port for Jerusalem, lying about 35 miles northwest of the city on the Mediterranean Sea. **Dorcas**—This Greek name for "antelope" (signifying loveliness) was often used as a proper name for women. The Aramaic is "Tabitha" (9:40).

➤**37 an upper chamber**—Cf. 1 Kings 17:19.

➤**38 they sent unto him two men, desiring** [beseeching] **him . . . to come to them**—The disciples did not generally possess the ability to perform miracles. Peter was not only their leader but had the gift of healing.

➤**39 widows**—Dorcas had fed and clothed many helpless people. She was continually making and giving away clothes to these widows.

➤**40 Peter put them all forth, and kneeled down, and prayed**—See Luke 8:54; cf. 2 Kings 4:33.

➤**41 he gave her his hand and lifted her up**—Jesus had done this with Peter's mother-in-law (Mark 1:31).

➤**43 Simon, a tanner**—This occupation was considered disrespectful and unclean due to the contact with dead animals and blood. Tanners usually lived outside the town, so

Simon's house was by the shore (10:6). Peter's staying there suggests that he was already, to some extent, able to live above Jewish prejudice.

# Chapter 10

## 1-48 THE GENTILES ARE BROUGHT INTO THE CHURCH WHEN PETER BRINGS THE GOSPEL TO CORNELIUS

This chapter introduces an entirely new phase of the Christian work, the admission of Gentiles as equals with the Jews in the church. Paul probably acted on this principle from the very beginning of his ministry. But Peter, the apostle of the circumcision, was given the responsibility of admitting Gentiles without circumcision.

➤**1 Caesarea**—See comments on 8:40. **Italian band**—i.e., "Italian regiment" (TLB, NIV). This regiment, unlike the native soldiers, probably served as bodyguard to the Roman administrator who lived there.

➤**2 a devout man, and one that feared God**—i.e., he was a "God-fearer." Luke identifies such a category of people throughout the book of Acts (see 10:2, 22, 35; 13:16, 26 for the expression "fearing God" and 13:43, 50; 16:14; 17:4, 17; 18:7 for the expression "worshipping God"—both characterize the same category of people, the "god-fearers"). The "God-fearers" were Gentiles who were interested in Judaism but were not necessarily converts or proselytes. They would observe the same God and the same law as did the Jews, but they would not be circumcised. Many of these "God-fearers" were the first Gentiles to become Christians. Cornelius was the prototype. **which gave much alms to the people**—cf. Luke 7:5. The Jews emphasized regular giving (Matt. 6:2-4) to the poor and disabled. **prayed to God alway**—He prayed at the daily appointed times.

➤**3 saw in a vision evidently**—should be translated, "saw in a vision clearly." **ninth hour**—3:00 P.M. This was the time of the evening sacrifice.

➤**4 Thy prayers and thine alms**—"Prayers" suggest the spiritual element of his character; "alms," the practical reaching out to men around him. **are come up for a memorial before God**—i.e., ascended to God as a well-accepted sacrifice.

➤**5 send men to Joppa, and call for . . . Simon**—See 9:11.

➤**7 when the angel . . . was departed**—Cornelius did as he was told without hesitation, indicating the simplicity and sincerity of his faith. **a devout soldier**—The soldier, like Cornelius, was devout and godly. This is the way Luke characterized many of the Gentiles who first received the gospel.

➤**9, 10 upon the housetop**—This was a cool place away from other distractions in the house. **trance**—This differed from the "vision" of Cornelius (10:3). In a trance, a man stands outside himself, so the experience had not the same objective reality, though both were supernatural.

➤**12 four-footed beasts**—Both clean and unclean animals were represented.

➤**14 I have never eaten any thing that is common or unclean**—Distinctions between "clean" or "unclean" meat were established by national laws.

➤**15 What God hath cleansed . . . call not . . . common**—a clear allusion to the fact that God was about to grant cleansing to the Gentiles. Thus, the Gentiles were to be regarded as equal to the Jews in every respect.

➤**16 This was done thrice**—cf. Genesis 41:32.

➤**17-20** Both Peter and Cornelius were prepared by God for this meeting.

➤**21 I am he whom ye seek**—Peter said this before any of the others had spoken.

➤**22 Cornelius . . . a just man, and one that feareth God**—This is a good reference to Cornelius's character. **to hear words of** [from] **thee**—See 11:14.

➤**24 Cornelius . . . had called together his kinsmen and near friends**—He had been at Caesarea for some time, and had formed intimate friendships.

➤**25 fell down at his feet, and worshipped**—In the East, to prostrate oneself was a way of showing respect to one's superiors. Among the Greeks and Romans it was reserved for the gods.

➤**26** Peter therefore refused this symbolic gesture, saying **Stand up; I myself also am a man**—or, "I myself am human."

➤**28 it is an unlawful thing for a . . . Jew to keep company** [with] **. . . one of another nation**—Any form of intimate social fellowship between Jews and Greeks was thought to violate the spirit of the law and was therefore nonexistent.

➤**29 Therefore came I unto you without gainsaying**—i.e., "I came without objection" (RSV). Since Peter realized the significance of the new relationship that was to be formed, he treated these people with dignity.

➤**30 Four days ago**—The messengers were sent on the first day, reached Joppa on the second (10:9), started for Caesarea on the third, and arrived home on the fourth.

➤**33 Now therefore are we all here present before God**—This demonstrated their sincere desire to know completely what God had planned for them and to give Peter the opportunity to freely speak all that God had told him to say.

➤**34 God is no respecter of persons**—God looks at man individually with no regard for national distinctions, physical characteristics, or religious heritage (see Deut. 10:17; Rom. 2:11; Eph. 6:9; Col. 3:25).

➤**35 in every nation he that feareth him, and worketh righteousness, is accepted with him**—This is the typical way of describing godly persons in the OT. Cornelius was not just a virtuous man, but a man absorbing the Jewish faith and following the one true God. To such a Gentile, God opened the door of salvation; and many more Gentiles from all nations would walk through that opened door. Peter was not sent as the instrument of Cornelius's conversion, but simply to "show him the way of God more perfectly," just as Philip had been able to further teach the Ethiopian eunuch.

➤**36** Beginning with this verse and continuing through 10:43 there is a summary of the message that the apostles taught. **the children of Israel**—The gospel was first told to the Jews by Jesus who lived his life among them. **preaching peace by Jesus Christ**—This is the essence of the gospel (1 Cor. 1:20-22). **he is Lord of all**—Jew and Gentile alike can be brought into God's family through Jesus, now exalted Lord of all (Eph. 2:13-18).

➤**37 That word** [message or thing] **. . . was published** [spread] **throughout all Judaea**—The Greek word *rhema* can mean "message" or

"thing." In this verse, it could refer to the proclaimed message or to the total event of Jesus' ministry. **after the baptism which John preached**—See 1:22. **from Galilee**—See Luke 4:14, 37, 44; 7:17; 9:6; 23:5.

➤**38 God anointed Jesus of Nazareth with the Holy Ghost** [Spirit] **and with power**—This refers to his baptism (Luke 4:18-21), after which he came among the people for acceptance. **went about doing good**—This part of his character was predicted (Isa. 35:5, 6). **healing all that were oppressed of** [by] **the devil**—The supreme authority of Christ was thus established.

➤**39 we are witnesses**—They could give the historical facts of Christ's life. **hanged on a tree**—See 5:30; Gal. 3:13.

➤**40 showed him openly**—lit., "gave him to become visible." After his resurrection, Christ was always with his disciples through his spiritual, invisible presence. But, on occasion, he would become visible—i.e., he would make an appearance (see comments on 1:3).

➤**41 Not to all the people, but unto witnesses**—Christ's post-resurrection appearances were made in the presence of his disciples only (see the last chapters of all the Gospels.) **chosen before of God**—lit., "previously hand-picked by God." The witnesses were especially chosen for their task.

➤**42 ordained of God to be the Judge of quick** [living] **and dead**—Jesus was already named as the giver of "peace" to all. Now Peter announces that Jesus is supreme in exercising his judgment on both the Jew and the Gentile (see John 5:22, 23, 27; Acts 17:31).

➤**43 To him give all the prophets witness**—This was the point of the prophetic messages. **whosoever believeth in him**—This was said especially for the benefit of the Gentiles who were listening to Peter at this time. **shall receive remission of sins**—i.e., forgiveness of sins.

➤**44 the Holy Ghost** [Spirit] **fell on all them which heard the word**—This has been called traditionally "the Gentile Pentecost" (cf. 2:4; 15:8).

➤**46, 47 speak with tongues**—as did the first recipients of the Holy Spirit's effusion (2:4). **Can any man forbid water, that these should not be baptized, which have received the Holy Ghost** [Spirit] **as well as we**—Since they had already been marked as believers, their baptism would confirm their faith. Now Jew and Gentile were baptized by one Spirit into the one body of Christ (1 Cor. 12:13). **he commanded them to be baptized**—It is not clear whether Peter actually performed the baptism. Most critics think that he did not, just as Paul rarely baptized anyone (1 Cor. 1:14-17; cf. Acts 2:38; John 4:2). **prayed** [asked] . . . **him to tarry** [stay]—They wanted him to give them more detailed instruction and to encourage them in this new venture.

*Chapter* **11**

## 1-18 PETER SPEAKS TO THE CHURCH AT JERUSALEM ABOUT HIS DEALING WITH CORNELIUS AND THE OTHER GENTILES WITH HIM

The law was extremely important to Judaism. When Paul seemingly ignored the law, he created a great furor among the Jews.

➤**1 in Judaea**—This meant "throughout the province of Judea."

➤**2 they that were of the circumcision**—In this case, the most strict and legalistic Jewish Christians are referred to.

➤**3, 4 Thou wentest in to men uncircumcised . . . But Peter rehearsed** [explained]—Though Peter was the chief apostle, these men demanded an explanation of his actions. Peter's response does not indicate that there was any disrespect toward his authority on the part of those who were questioning him.

➤**4-11** This is a simple, factual description of the vision that Peter saw at the home of Simon the tanner (see 10:11-16).

➤**12 the Spirit**—Peter first explains that his actions were in response to instructions given by the Spirit. **entered into the man's house**—Cornelius is not mentioned by name. **nothing doubting**—This reads "making no distinction" (between Jews and Gentiles) in several early manuscripts.

➤**13, 14 Peter . . . shall tell thee words, whereby thou and all thy house**[hold] **shall** [may] **be saved**—This is stated more generally in 10:6, 22, 32. Concerning the salvation of Cornelius, see comments on 10:34, 35.

➤**16, 17 Then remembered I the word of the Lord . . . ye shall be baptized with the**

**Holy Ghost** [Spirit]—Since God had put these Gentiles on the same level with the Jews, it would have been against God's plan for Peter to have refused them fellowship as still "unclean."

➤**18 God also to the Gentiles granted repentance**—God is not only willing to pardon man upon his repentance, but he provides a way for man to repent. (Cf. Heb. 12:1; 2 Cor. 7:10.) **unto life**—i.e., resulting in life. The repentant person receives God's life (*zōe* in Gk.).

## 19-24 BARNABAS IS SENT TO WORK AMONG THE CHRISTIANS IN ANTIOCH

➤**19 Now they which were scattered abroad upon** [from] **the persecution that arose about** [concerning] **Stephen**—They preached about Jesus (8:1-4) as far away as Phoenicia and Cyprus. **and Antioch**—This city is near the northeast coast of the Mediterranean, located at the head of the Orontes River. Antioch was the former capital of the Seleucid kingdom and was at this time the seat of Roman government for the province of Syria. It was the third largest city in the world, after Rome and Alexandria. Antioch was the home of a large colony of Jews who had converted many people to their religion. Some suggest that Antioch was an oriental Rome, having all aspects of civilized life that were found in Rome. During the first two centuries after the crucifixion of Christ, Antioch was known as "the Gate of the East," a name later given to Constantinople.

➤**20 some of them were men of Cyprus and Cyrene**—See comments on Luke 23:26. Lucius (13:1) was such a man. **spake unto the Grecians**—"Greeks" in some manuscripts; "Hellenists" in others. In 6:10 and 9:29 the "Hellenists" are clearly Greek-speaking Jews. But here the term cannot mean Greek-speaking Jews because these people are contrasted with the Jews in the previous verse. These "Hellenists" are simply Greek-speaking people (Metzger).

➤**21 a great number believed**—Therefore, many uncircumcised Gentiles joined the Christian church before Cornelius (10:1ff.). The case of Cornelius served mainly as formal recognition of the principle that God wanted both Jew and Gentile to come into the fellowship through the sacrifice of Jesus.

➤**22 sent forth Barnabas [to] Antioch**—They stopped at other churches on the way. Barnabas, as a Greek from Cyprus (4:36), was probably sent to see what was happening.

➤**23 when he . . . had seen the grace of God**—Barnabas realized by the lives of the new converts that this was an act of God even though these men were uncircumcised. **with purpose of heart they would cleave unto** [remain close to] **the Lord**—He opposed hasty and shallow discipleship.

➤**24 good man**—The sense of the Greek word for "good" indicates he was liberal-minded and not concerned with narrow Jewish sectarianism. **added unto the Lord**—See comments on 5:14.

## 25, 26 BARNABAS, NEEDING MORE HELP IN ANTIOCH, GOES TO TARSUS TO GET SAUL (PAUL)

➤**25 Then departed Barnabas to Tarsus . . . to seek Saul**—Earlier, Barnabas had sent Saul to Tarsus, probably to escape the fury of the Jews in Jerusalem. Barnabas had been the first to understand Saul's mission; thus, instead of going back to Jerusalem to find a helper, he went to Tarsus specifically to find Saul. They returned to Antioch to become workers in the church there.

➤**26 the disciples were called Christians first in Antioch**—This name had its origin outside the Christian community. The Jewish enemies called them "Nazarenes" (24:5), but it was the heathen Romans of Antioch who first used the word "Christian." The term was merely descriptive in its first use; it means "of Christ," "belonging to Christ."

## 27-30 BARNABAS AND PAUL RETURN TO JERUSALEM

➤**27 came prophets from Jerusalem unto Antioch**—These were inspired teachers who sometimes foretold future events. They were classed next to the apostles (1 Cor. 12:28, 29; Eph. 4:11).

➤**28 great dearth** [famine] **throughout all the world**—i.e., the whole Roman world. This was fulfilled during the reign **of Claudius Caesar.** Four famines occurred during his reign; this one was between A.D. 41 and 45.

➤**29 the disciples . . . determined to send relief unto the brethren which dwelt in Judaea**—A spirit of love and concern for all

the believers characterized the early Christians. (See comments on next verse.)

➤**30 sent it to the elders**—This is the first time elders of a local church are mentioned in the NT. This was patterned after the synagogue rather than the temple. **by the hands of Barnabas and Saul**—It seems that the Christians at Antioch saved regularly for their relief fund. When the collection was complete, Barnabas and Saul took the money to Jerusalem. This was Saul's second visit to Jerusalem following his conversion.

## Chapter 12

## 1-19 THE CHURCH IS PERSECUTED BY HEROD AGRIPPA I

➤**1 Herod the king**—He was the grandson of Herod the Great and son of Aristobulus. At this time, he ruled over all his father's kingdoms. For 30 years prior there had been no king in Jerusalem ruling Judea, nor was there afterward, except during the last three years of Herod's life. With this new wave of persecution, the apostles became the primary objects of attack. During Herod's brief reign over Judea (A.D. 41-44), he proved to be a strong supporter of Judaism and sought to maintain friendly relations with the religious leaders.

➤**2 killed James the brother of John with the sword**—James was beheaded. This James was among the original inner circle of the Twelve.

➤**3 he saw it pleased the Jews**—The motive of his killing James was to become popular with the people. **he proceeded further to take Peter**—Peter's death at this point in the development of the church would have been irreparable. **days of unleavened bread**—during the Passover.

➤**4 four quaternions of soldiers**—i.e., 16 soldiers. Four groups of four soldiers each kept the four Roman watches. Two were with Peter in prison, and two were at the gate. **intending after Easter**—which should be rendered, "Passover"—**to bring him forth to the people**—for judgment and execution. The Jews were against putting anyone to death during the Passover.

➤**5 prayer**—Luke 22:44; Acts 26:7; 1 Pet. 4:8. **was made without ceasing of the church**

**unto God for him**—This was not a public assembly, which would have been too dangerous, but small groups in private homes, one of which was Mary's (12:12). This went on all during the seven days of Passover.

➤**6 bound with two chains**—Roman prisoners were fastened by a chain between their right hand and the soldier's left hand. For greater security, the prisoners were often chained to two guards, one on each side (see 21:23).

➤**9 thought he saw a vision**—He really didn't expect to be delivered from these circumstances (see also 12:11).

➤**12 came to the house of Mary**—Mary's house was quite large and had served as a meeting place for Jerusalem Christians. Mary must also have been known for her faith and courage to allow such a meeting under threat of persecution. It was natural that Peter would go to her house. **mother of John . . . Mark**—She is named to distinguish her from the other Marys.

➤**15 Thou art mad**—"You are crazy" (TEV). Peter's presence seemed too good to be true. **It is his angel**—They could not accept the very miracle for which they had been praying.

➤**16 Peter continued knocking**—It was dangerous for him to stand outside.

➤**17 hold their peace**—Amidst the excitement there was probably some embarrassment for their inability to believe Rhoda's announcement of Peter's presence. **show these things unto James, and to the brethren**—It is unclear whether Peter is referring to James the son of Alpheus, who was one of the Twelve, or to James, the brother of Christ; but it is most likely the latter. James is here singled out for a prominent place in the Jerusalem church (15:13ff.). **went into another place**—Once before, when Peter was miraculously released from prison, he was told to go and preach among the people (5:20). In this case, God wished to protect him from what would have been certain death had he presented himself in public.

➤**18 as soon as it was day**—dawn. Peter's release from prison must have occurred during the fourth watch (3:00-6:00 A.M.).

➤**20 Herod was highly displeased with them of Tyre and Sidon**—The reason is unknown. **their country was nourished by the king's country**—They were economically dependent upon Herod (cf. 1 Kings 5:11; Ezra 3:7; Ezek. 27:17). Perhaps the famine (11:28) made them more immediately concerned with establishing peace.

➤**21 made an oration unto them**—He spoke to the Tyrians and Sidonians.

➤**22 the voice of a god**—The people were deifying him.

➤**23 the angel of the Lord smote him . . . and he was eaten of worms**—Several cases of such deaths occurred in history (Judas, Herod the Great, Antiochus IV). See Josephus's account of Herod's death (*Antiquities,* 19.8.2). According to Josephus, he died of intense abdominal pains, knowing that he was stricken for accepting the people's deification.

➤**24 the word of God grew and multiplied**—The persecution, rather than stopping Christianity, served rather to further it.

➤**25 Barnabas and Saul returned from Jerusalem, when they had fulfilled their ministry**—Some early manuscripts read "to Jerusalem" instead of "from Jerusalem." In order to fit this in the Acts narrative thus far, this could be rendered, "Barnabas and Saul returned, having fulfilled their service in Jerusalem." After accomplishing their mission in Jerusalem, they returned to Antioch (13:1).

*Chapter* **13**

## 1-3 BARNABAS AND PAUL ARE SENT OUT BY THE CHURCH AT ANTIOCH TO WORK AMONG THE GENTILES

The first seven chapters of Acts deal with the church as it was developing among the Jewish Christians. Chapters 8–12 are concerned with the transition from the Jews to the Gentiles, and the last sixteen chapters deal with the church among the Gentiles. Christianity had by this time spread beyond the boundaries of Palestine, but the church had no organized missionary effort. It was from the church at Antioch that the first teachers were sent forth with the purpose of spreading the gospel of Christ and organizing local churches (14:23).

➤**1 church . . . at Antioch**—The church was called by the city in which it existed. All the believers in a particular locality constituted the church in this locality. **prophets**—**and**

**teachers**—It is not certain whether Luke means that there were other teachers and prophets, or only these five. **Simeon that was called Niger**—"Simeon" is the Jewish name; "Niger" (meaning "black") is a Gentile name. He was probably from Africa and possibly the same Simon from Cyrene of Luke 23:26, whose sons Alexander and Rufus were later known to be among the Christians at Rome—Romans 16:13 (Longenecker). **Lucius of Cyrene**—perhaps one of the men mentioned in 11:20. **Manaen**—was named after one of the kings of Israel (2 Kings 15:14). **brought up with Herod the tetrarch**—i.e., he was Herod Antipas's foster brother. It is interesting to note how different these two brothers became. Herod was responsible for the death of one of God's most distinguished prophets; Manaen became a devoted disciple and leader in the church at Antioch. **and Saul**—Saul's (Paul's) experiences and his effect on Christian history are the subject of the rest of the book of Acts.

➤**2 ministered to the Lord**—In the OT, this word refers to any of the priestly functions. Here it means attending to the corresponding responsibilities within the church. **and fasted**—As this was done on other special occasions (13:3, 14, 23), they may have been expecting a prophetic message. **the Holy Ghost** [Spirit] **said**—through some of the prophets mentioned in 13:1. **separate**—designate (see Rom. 1:1).

➤**3 laid their hands on them . . . sent them away**—They were "committed to God for the work" (cf. 14:26; see comments on 6:6).

### 4-12 BARNABAS AND PAUL GO TO CYPRUS

➤**4 Seleucia**—Located on the Orontes River, five miles from the Mediterranean coast, Selucia was the seaport for Antioch. **thence they sailed to Cyprus**—There were four possible reasons for their decision to go to Cyprus. (1) It was very near to the mainland. (2) It was the home of Barnabas and he may have wished to share the gospel with his family and close friends. (3) The gospel would be accepted more readily if it were brought by one of their own people. Although their mission was primarily to the Gentiles, one of the best ways to reach them was through converts and Greek Jews. (4) There were a number of Christians already

on Cyprus (11:19, 20) who would give Barnabas and Paul a good base for their work.

➤**5 Salamis**—The Greek capital of the island was located on the eastern side. There was a large Jewish population living there.

➤**6 Paphos**—The Roman capital was about 100 miles to the west of Salamis. **a certain sorcerer, a false prophet, a Jew, whose name was Bar-jesus**—Many impostors were encouraged even by the well-educated Romans.

➤**7 deputy**—lit. ,"proconsul." The name "proconsul" was reserved for those who governed settled provinces under the rule of the Roman senate. **desired to hear the word of God**—He was honestly seeking an understanding of the truth.

➤**8 But Elymas the sorcerer**—Bar-jesus was called "Elymas" (meaning sorcerer, magician). **to turn away the deputy from the faith**—He probably sensed the eagerness with which Sergius was listening and feared that the governor might put him aside (cf. 2 Tim. 3:8).

➤**9 Saul, (who is also called Paul,)**— "Saul" was his Hebrew name, "Paul" his Latin name. Since Paul's work was shifting from the Jews to the Gentiles, it was appropriate that the Latin name be used instead of the Hebrew.

➤**10 subtilty**—"trickery" (TLB). This refers to his magic. **mischief**—meaning ease in doing "recklessness, wickedness."

➤**12** Cf. Mark 1:27.

### 13-52 JOHN MARK LEAVES THE GROUP AT PERGA. PAUL AND BARNABAS CONTINUE THEIR TEACHING IN ANTIOCH OF PISIDIA

➤**13 Perga**—the largest city in Turkey, was located on the Cestrus River, about seven miles inland from Attalia. **John departing from them returned to Jerusalem**—Luke does not discuss his reasons for leaving. From this point, Paul becomes leader of the missionary group and the central figure throughout the remaining part of Acts. Whatever the reason for John's leaving, he lost Paul's respect and was later refused as part of the second missionary journey (cf. 15:37-40). John Mark later regained the respect of Paul (Col. 4:10).

➤**14 Antioch in Pisidia**—Antioch in Syria was the city from which they began their trip. Antioch in Pisidia was located directly north of Perga. The distance was short, but the road passed through mountains, along rivers, and through an area heavily inhabited by robbers. Paul may be referring to this trip in 2 Corinthians 11:26.

**►16 Paul stood . . . beckoning with his hand**—This was customary (21:40; 26:1). **ye that fear God**—This refers to those who were Gentile converts and participated in the Jewish worship.

**►18 suffered**—lit., "bore with." But other manuscripts read, "cared for" (lit., "carried them as a nurse"). The textual problem involves a one-letter difference (phi/pi) in two Greek words: *etrophophorēsen* (nourished) and *etropophorēsen* (bore with). The first word is more likely the original for two reason: (1) it comes from Deuteronomy 1:31 (LXX), the passage cited by Paul; and (2) in the context of 13:17-19, which contains a series of positive acts that God did for Israel, it would be incongruous to inject a disparaging word (as in the second reading).

**►20 judges [ruled] about . . . four hundred and fifty years**—This appears to contradict 1 Kings 6:1 (480 years). Several explanations have been proposed: (1) After approximately 450 years had passed from the time of the covenant with Abraham, God gave judges to the Israelites. (2) The period of the judges itself lasted approximately 450 years. (This seems to be historically correct if one includes the time of subjection to foreign powers and interprets it to describe the entire period from the settlement of the tribes in Canaan to the establishment of royalty.) (3) The 450 years denotes the interval between the beginning of Abraham's journey and the occupation of the land but does not cover the period of the judges.

**►21 forty years**—This agrees with Josephus (*Antiquities,* 6.14.9).

**►23 Of this man's seed [David's] hath God according to his promise raised unto Israel a Saviour, Jesus**—Two points in this statement are important: (1) Jesus came from David's family in fulfillment of a prophecy, and (2) Jesus came as a savior (note Matt. 1:21).

**►26 whosoever . . . feareth God**—See comments on 13:16.

**►27 they that dwell at Jerusalem, and their rulers**—It seems that the guilt for Christ's death lay with the rulers and the people of Jerusalem.

**►28 they found no cause of death**—They looked for a reason but could not find one (Matt. 26:59, 60).

**►29 they took him down from the tree, and laid him in a sepulchre**—The burial of Christ was an act of honor and love by the disciples who took charge of his body. His enemies oversaw the burial and placed guards to watch the tomb. Paul views this as the last act of opposition toward the Messiah.

**►30 But God raised him from the dead**—The central theme of the Christian "kerygma" (proclamation) is that God raised Jesus from the dead. This was the proclamation announced by all the early apostles.

**►31 He was seen many days**—lit., "over many days." **of them which came up with him from Galilee to Jerusalem**—This refers to the close associates of his ministry in Galilee and to those who traveled with him on his last trip to Jerusalem. Their intimacy with Jesus prior to his death made their testimony to his resurrection the more valid.

**►33 raised up**—i.e., raised up from the dead. Although many commentators say this raising up refers to establishing or positioning Christ, the context (the previous verse and the following verse) points to Christ's resurrection. **the second psalm**—according to some manuscripts, "the first psalm." The Jews may have considered our "Psalm 1" to be an introduction to the book of Psalms. **Thou art my Son, this day have I begotten thee**—Christ was "begotten" in resurrection in the sense that he was born into a new sphere of existence. The same idea is conveyed in John 16:21; Colossians 1:18; Revelation 1:18. The resurrection manifested, testified, and certified his eternal, divine sonship (see Rom. 1:4).

**►34 I will give you**—This "you" is plural in Greek, although it is applied to Christ. **the sure mercies of David**—lit., "the holy and faithful things of David." To Jesus, "the Holy One" (13:35), were promised the sure and holy things of David. David was promised an eternal kingdom, but this kingdom could only be fulfilled in Christ and by his resurrection (the quote comes from Isa. 55:3, LXX).

**►35** This is a quote from Psalm 16:10 (LXX).

**►36 For David, after he had served his own generation by the will of God**—David had placed himself completely before God as an instrument to be used in carrying out God's plan. **fell on [a]sleep** [a euphemism for death] **and was laid unto his fathers** [joined his ancestors in death], **and saw corruption**— Thus, Paul points out, David could not be the subject of his own prediction, which was fulfilled later by the resurrected Christ.

➤**38 the forgiveness of sins**—This is of the first priority for the sinner and thus is the first gift from Christ.

➤**39 could not be justified by the law of Moses**—Paul is here saying that Christ frees men from all their guilt and makes them righteous, whereas the Jewish law could do nothing for man's sinful state.

➤**41** This verse paraphrases Habakkuk 1:5. These words were originally a warning against the approaching destruction of Jerusalem by the Chaldeans and the subsequent Babylonian captivity. Here they accurately describe the disaster that awaits the generation that Paul is speaking to.

➤**42 the Gentiles**—According to the best manuscripts should read simply, "they" (the Jews and their proselytes). **besought that these words might be preached to them**—They were apparently impressed and honestly wanted to know more about the Messiah.

➤**43 many**—Many had responded favorably to Paul's teaching. **followed Paul and Barnabas**—They were drawn to the two men who had begun a change in their spiritual lives. **persuaded them to continue in the grace of God**—Paul and Barnabas continued to encourage their interest by talking about God's grace in Christ (cf. 11:23).

➤**44 the next sabbath day came almost the whole city together to hear the word of God**—They had probably spent the week teaching about Jesus. By the Sabbath day, the Gentiles had sensed the excitement and came with the usual worshipers into the synagogue.

➤**46 the word of God should first have been spoken to you**—Note the instruction of Christ in Luke 24:47. **we turn to the Gentiles**—This is the move of the Holy Spirit, which then characterizes the rest of Acts in that the narrative shows how the gospel went to the Gentiles.

➤**47 so hath the Lord commanded us**— Paul was given a good understanding of this

prediction in his presentation for work among the Gentiles. **I have set thee to be a light of the Gentiles**—from Isaiah 49:6.

➤**48 as many as were ordained** [or, appointed] **to eternal life believed**—A divine ordination to eternal life is the cause, not the effect, of man's believing (see Rom. 8:29).

➤**49 the word of the Lord was published** [carried] **throughout all the region**—Paul and Barnabas remained in Antioch for some time, teaching and preaching in and around the city.

➤**50 devout and honourable**—These were Gentiles converted to Judaism. **expelled them**—It was easier to do this than to prove that they were not speaking the truth.

➤**51 they shook off the dust of their feet against them**—See Matthew 10:14. **came unto Iconium**—This large city was about 45 miles southeast of Antioch (in Pisidia), located at the base of Mt. Tarsus at the borders of Lycaonia, Phrygia, and Pisidia.

➤**52 disciples**—Though they were not sent away, they endured suffering because of their belief (see 14:22). **were filled with joy, and with the Holy Ghost** [Spirit]—They were given strength to overcome their fears.

*Chapter* **14**

1-7 PAUL AND BARNABAS HAVE CONTINUED SUCCESS AT ICONIUM, BUT DUE TO THE OPPOSITION, THEY GO TO LYSTRA AND DERBE TO PREACH

Luke's description of their experiences there is brief, probably because their message and its consequences were similar.

➤**1 went . . . together**—Though Paul was more prominent, Barnabas accompanied him at all times. **Greeks**—or, "Greek-speaking people." The dominant language of Iconium was Greek.

➤**2 Jews**—These men were probably leaders and rulers in the synagogue.

➤**3** They stayed there a **long time . . . Speaking boldly in the Lord**—In spite of the opposition, many were coming to understand and accept their message.

➤**5, 6 when there was an assault . . . to stone them**—Paul was stoned later at Lystra (14:19), as he mentions in 2 Corinthians 11:25. Thus there was opposition here that might have ended in stoning had they not left. **fled**—See Matthew 10:23. **Lystra and Derbe**—were **cities** in the province **of Lycaonia.** Lystra was 20 miles south of Iconium and Derbe was 60 miles east.

## 8-28 THE EXPERIENCES OF PAUL AND BARNABAS IN LYSTRA AND DERBE

Since there is no mention of their preaching in the synagogue it is assumed that there were too few Jews to warrant one.

➤**9 The same heard Paul speak**—Paul was probably addressing a crowd that had gathered outside (14:11). **perceiving that he had faith to be healed**—Paul, looking at the cripple, may have been reminded of the healing that Christ had done.

➤**10 he leaped and walked**—The healing was instantaneous.

➤**11 in the speech of Lycaonia**—They may have been speaking some form of Greek or another older language. **The gods are come down to us in the likeness of men**—This is the language of uneducated people.

➤**12 they called Barnabas, Jupiter**—Greek, Zeus. The chief god of the Romans, Jupiter, corresponded to the Greek god, Zeus. **Paul, Mercurius**—Greek, Hermes.

➤**13 the priest of Jupiter . . . brought oxen and garlands**—Customary worship and celebration were about to be performed in honor of Paul and Barnabas.

➤**15 why do ye these things?**—Although the Jews had learned that idolatry was wrong and that loyalty to Yahweh was very important, Paul was speaking from something more than just that loyalty. Because of Paul's union with God through Christ, he felt great horror and grief at the dishonor that was being done to God. **We also are men of like passions**—i.e., "We are merely human beings like yourselves" (TLB). Paul was concerned that these people understood that he was God's vessel and therefore did not deserve any honor. **turn from these vanities unto the living God**—This language is typical of OT content and stands in contrast to the language of the heathen. **God . . . made heaven, and earth, and the sea, and all things that are therein**—This idea of creation, largely unknown to these people,

would give them some understanding of the nature of God (cf. 1 Thess. 1:9).

➤**16 Who . . . suffered** [allowed] **all nations to walk in their own ways**—He did not give them any knowledge of his plan or of the free gift of life which was available to them (cf. 17:30; 1 Cor. 1:21; Rom. 1:20).

➤**17 he left not himself without witness**—Though God had not revealed much of himself to the heathen, some evidences of his goodness and love were available so that they should not be entirely ignorant of his divinity.

➤**19 stoned Paul**—See comments on 14:5. Barnabas was left alone, as Paul was the speaker and object of their hate. No doubt the Jews took the lead, but it was the crowd that stoned him and dragged him out of the city (cf. 7:58).

➤**20 as the disciples stood round about him**—Timothy seems to have been greatly inspired by this event (see comments on 16:1-3). **he rose up**—He may have been miraculously healed. **the next day he departed**—He would hardly have been ready to travel had his recovery been merely natural.

➤**21 they returned again to Lystra, and to Iconium, and Antioch** [in Pisidia]—They wanted to encourage the new disciples and help strengthen the young churches.

➤**22 the kingdom of God**—This is the eternal "kingdom," not the temporary, earthly "kingdom" each local church was to be.

➤**23 ordained them elders**—The Greek word for "ordained" means "to choose by a show of hands" (cf. 2 Cor. 8:19). But the word was also used to designate direct appointment. The local churches probably selected elders, and Paul and Barnabas ordained them (cf. Titus 1:5). **prayed with fasting**—This clause supports the interpretation that they were first chosen and then ordained, for the prayer and fasting was done for the purpose of ordination (see 13:2, 3).

➤**25 went down into Attalia**—This seaport on the gulf of Pamphylia was an important trade center for both Egypt and Syria.

➤**26** See comments on 13:13.

➤**27 had gathered the church together**—As their mission had been confirmed by this church, it was only proper that they should report as to how things went. **God . . . had opened the door of faith unto the Gentiles**—Note that they give God the credit for making the Gentiles ready to hear and respond to the gospel (see 11:21; 1 Cor. 16:9; 2 Cor. 2:12; Col. 4:3).

➤**28 long time**—This was two or three years.

Chapter **15**

**1-35 THE JERUSALEM COUNCIL: ITS BACKGROUND, MEETINGS, AND DECISIONS**

➤**1 ye cannot be saved**—This was a critical attack against the truth of the gospel. Paul fought against this falsehood throughout his ministry (see Galatians). He constantly affirmed that salvation is by faith through grace, not by works of law (see 15:11).

➤**2 Paul and Barnabas**—They were the recognized leaders of the church at Antioch. **certain other of them**—Titus was among them as an uncircumcised Gentile convert who had been given the gifts of the Spirit (Gal. 2:1).

➤**3 And being brought on their way by the church**—The Antioch church assumed the financial responsibility for their trip. The church at Antioch was to the Gentile Christians what the Jerusalem church was to the Jewish Christians. **they passed through Phenice** [Phoenicia]—See comments on 11:19. **caused great joy**—Note the contrast between the spirit of the Jewish Christians and the Jewish legalists.

➤**4 Jerusalem**—This was Paul's third visit to Jerusalem following his conversion. He describes his experiences in Galatians 2:1-10. **they were received of the church, and of the apostles and elders**—Evidently a formal meeting had been arranged for the purpose of welcoming Paul and Barnabas (see comments on Gal. 2:2). **they declared all things that God had done with them**—See 14:14-27.

➤**6 the apostles and elders came together**—in the presence of the church (15:12, 22, 23).

➤**7 Peter**—This is the last time Peter is named in Acts. He supported Paul's work in explaining the relationship of the Gentiles to the Jewish law. **a good while ago**—This was probably fifteen years earlier. **the Gentiles**

**by my mouth should hear the word of the gospel**—See comments on 11:21.

➤**8 God, which knoweth the hearts**—Though the state of man's heart cannot be known by men, any other criteria for membership in the local church community would be inadequate and beside the point.

➤**9 purifying their hearts by faith**—Their hearts were purified by the sprinkling of the blood of Jesus Christ when and as they believed.

➤**10 why tempt ye God**—This is to "tempt, try, provoke" him by disrupting his plan. **to put a yoke upon the . . . disciples, which neither our fathers nor we were able to bear?**—The circumcised man had to keep the whole law (see Gal. 5:1-6), so that the obligations accompanying circumcision became impossible to fulfill (see Rom. 3:5; Gal. 2:4).

➤**11 through the grace of the Lord Jesus Christ we shall be saved, even as they**—lit., "saved in the same way." Both Jew and Gentile are saved by grace.

➤**12 Barnabas and Paul, declaring what miracles and wonders God had wrought among the Gentiles**—proved that God approved their salvation. This would silence the opposition.

➤**13 James**—was the head of the church at Jerusalem (Gal. 1:19) and was presiding over this meeting. He speaks last, bringing the debate to a close. Traditionally, he is thought to be James, the brother of Jesus.

➤**14 Simeon hath declared**—i.e., Simon Peter has just explained. **God at the first did visit the Gentiles**—referring to Cornelius's conversion.

➤**15 to this agree the words of the prophets**—This specifically refers to the prophecy in Amos 9:11, 12 but includes all of the OT prophecy addressing the inclusion of the Gentiles in God's plan.

➤**16, 17** James quoted either the Septuagint rendering of Amos 9:11, 12 or a Hebrew variant of it (found in a scroll discovered in Cave 4 at Qumran); he did not quote the traditional Hebrew text. The point of citing this passage was to show that Gentiles would be brought into God's new economy through a relationship with the Jews. When God would recover the fallen house of David, a remnant of Gentiles would be included in the restoration. This kind of speaking primarily fits end-time prophecy—when the Davidic kingdom will be established on earth with the Jews at the center and the Gentiles on the circumference, sharing in the messianic blessings but not necessarily becoming proselytes (see Longenecker). Thus, James interpreted Peter's words eschatologically.

➤**18 Known unto God are all his works from the beginning of the world**—This is the reading found in certain ancient manuscripts, but the most ancient manuscripts read "known from eternity"—a phrase joined to the last part of 15:17: ". . . these things known from eternity." The words "known from eternity" do not come from Amos; they perhaps allude to Isaiah 45:21. If the verse as stated in the KJV is genuinely Lucan, we must understand it to be added by James to affirm the eternal plan of God.

➤**19 are turned to God**—lit., "are turning to God." The present tense suggests that the work is in progress, advancing rapidly.

➤**20 pollutions of idols**—i.e., food sacrificed to idols. This was to take away all identification with idolatry. **from fornication**—This characteristic sin of the pagan indicates that they were not entirely free from idolatry. **from things strangled, and from blood**—From the Jewish viewpoint, life was present in the blood (see comments on 15:28, 29). There are varying views on these three requirements. Some say they represent a compromise between two warring parties; others see them as Mosaic restrictions, which in essence are no different from the law concerning circumcision; and others see them as moral injunctions that Gentiles should observe in order to live a godly life and be at one with their Jewish-Christian brothers. It seems they were, in fact, a compromise—and a wise one at that. But it does not appear that they were regarded as further "yokes" of the law to be put upon the Gentile believers, for Paul and Peter did not disagree, nor did anyone in the assembly.

➤**21 The laws of Moses were read in the synagogues every sabbath day**—All the Jews, knowing the requirements of the law, would be glad to see Gentile Christians observe the moral laws set forth by the council.

➤**22 Judas surnamed Barsabas**—This was not the brother of James (1:13) who was surnamed Thaddeus (Matt. 10:3), nor the brother of Joseph called Barsabas (1:23). **and Silas**—This is a contracted form of the Greek Silvanus. Silas was to become Paul's companion on his second missionary trip (15:40).

➤**23 letters**—This is the first mention of letter writing as an aid to the development of Christian community. The combination of written and oral transmission emphasized an important decision here as it did in the OT (Exod. 17:14). **unto the brethren which are of the Gentiles** [or, nations] **in Antioch and Syria and Cilicia**—Church communities existed in Cilicia as well as in Syria. These groups were most likely founded by Paul during the time between his return to Tarsus (9:30) and his leaving with Barnabas for Antioch (see 11:25, 26).

➤**24 to whom we gave no such commandment**—They may have pretended to be representatives from the Jerusalem church in an attempt to bring these Christians back into legal and judicial bondage.

➤**25, 26 Barnabas and Paul, men that have hazarded their lives**—Paul and Barnabas risked their lives to preach the gospel.

➤**28, 29 For it seemed good to the Holy Ghost** [Spirit], **and to us**—The Holy Spirit was inwardly guiding these men as they dealt with this problem. Leaders of all Christian communities must rely on the guidance of the Holy Spirit in making decisions and in dealing with problems and questions that believers encounter. **That ye abstain . . . and from fornication**—The Gentile converts were apparently deferring to the Jewish feelings, as it is not suggested that these were absolute obligations.

➤**31 they rejoiced for the consolation**—The problem of the Judaizers was solved in a wise manner.

➤**32 prophets**—These were "inspired teachers." **confirmed them**—or, strengthened them. They probably emphasized the need for unity between Jewish and Gentile believers and the principle of Christ's free love upon which that unity was based.

➤**34** Several ancient manuscripts do not include this verse. It may have been added later as an explanation of Silas's presence in Antioch (15:40). Silas was likely staying there with Paul.

## 36-41 PAUL AND BARNABAS HAVE A DISAGREEMENT. THEY SPLIT UP AND BEGIN SEPARATE MISSIONARY JOURNEYS

➤**36 Paul said unto Barnabas, Let us go again and visit our brethren in every city where we have preached the word of the Lord, and see how they do**—This is a good example to churches and missionaries of any age. Paul obviously never thought that his job was to remain in one place working within one local church. He felt concern and care for those to whom he proclaimed the gospel. This part of his character is further revealed in his personal correspondence.

➤**37 John ... Mark**—This was Barnabas's cousin (Col. 4:10).

➤**38 him ... who departed from them from Pamphylia**—See 13:13.

➤**39, 40 the contention was so sharp between them, that they departed asunder**—John Mark later proved his character, and he and Paul were reconciled (Col. 4:10, 11; 2 Tim. 4:11). It seems that both Paul and Barnabas were correct in the positions that they took. With differences in individual personalities and emotional characteristics it is very difficult to see important questions in the same light. If this happens and agreement does not come, then it is best that each individual follow his own course without judging or criticizing the other. **Barnabas took Mark ... Paul chose Silas**—They went in pairs as in Mark 6:7 and Luke 10:1. **being recommended by the brethren**—This probably involved a special ceremony of commission (see 13:13; 14:26). The fact that Luke does not mention a similar blessing for Barnabas does not mean that he was not given one, nor does it necessarily imply that the Antioch church sided with Paul in this disagreement with Barnabas—although many expositors see and affirm this implication.

➤**41 he went through Syria and Cilicia, confirming** [or, strengthening] **the churches**—It is quite possible that Paul and Barnabas split up the territory, with Paul traveling westward through the continent, and Barnabas visiting the islands. Paul's second missionary journey was undertaken for the purpose of revisiting the established churches. It took on a much wider scope, however, bringing Paul into Europe.

Paul's second missionary journey is recounted in 15:41–18:22.

*Chapter* **16**

## 1-5 PAUL VISITS THE CHURCHES THAT WERE FORMERLY ESTABLISHED

➤**1 to Derbe and Lystra ... a certain disciple was there, named Timotheus**—They met Timothy in Lystra, not in Derbe as some interpret from 20:4 (see 14:20). In 1 Timothy 1:2, Paul describes Timothy as his "son." Timothy must have become a Christian during Paul's first visit. If this is true, then Timothy would have known about Paul's previous troubles at Lystra as indicated by 2 Timothy 3:10, 11. He was encouraged and strengthened by Paul's second visit. **the son of a certain woman, which was a Jewess**—cf. 2 Timothy 1:5; 3:15. Timothy's gifts and role as a servant of Christ had already been confirmed (1 Tim. 1:18; 4:14). By the time of Paul's second visit, Timothy was well known around his hometown (16:2). **but his father was a Greek**—Such mixed marriages, although discouraged by the strict Jews in Palestine, were frequent among the Jews of the dispersion, especially in the remote areas where Jews were in the minority.

➤**3 Him would Paul have to go forth with him**—Paul had no relatives to support him in his work. He had few close friends, and though Silas would take the place of Barnabas, Paul probably wanted someone to replace Mark as his "son." This is what Timothy became (Phil. 2:19-23; 1 Cor. 4:17; 16:10, 11; 1 Thess. 3:1-6). He was particularly qualified to work with Paul as his mother was a Jew and his father a Gentile. Timothy seems to have been the first Gentile Christian to become a missionary. **circumcised him**—This implies that Timothy's father had not accepted the Jewish religion. No Jewish mother was permitted to circumcise her son against the wishes of a Gentile father. (See also 2 Tim. 1:5.) Paul's approach in the cities was to preach first to the Jews in the synagogues and then to the Gentiles. This would have been impossible if Timothy had remained uncircumcised. Paul later refused to compel Titus to be circumcised (Gal. 2:3), because circumcision was not a necessary part of salvation.

➤**4, 5 as they went through the cities . . . so were the churches established in the faith, and increased in number daily**— The membership of churches which were already formed increased in size. To be established "in the faith" was to become solid in the knowledge of the truth concerning God's NT economy and plan of salvation.

## 6-12 THE MISSIONARY JOURNEY EXPANDS INTO NEW TERRITORY

➤**6 throughout Phrygia and . . . Galatia**—They proceeded in a northwest direction. The churches at Galatia were probably started at this time (Gal. 1:2; cf. 1 Cor. 16:1); they were already in existence at the time of Paul's third missionary journey (18:23). There are several explanations for the lack of a detailed description of Paul's work at this time. Some think it was because Luke (the writer) had not yet joined the group. Others maintain that Luke was anxious to bring his written record to the time of Paul's activities in Europe. Possibly the general theme of the development of the Christian church from Jerusalem to Rome made Paul's short time in Phrygia and Galatia of relatively little importance in that context. **forbidden of the Holy Ghost** [Spirit] **to preach the word**—This is the first time the Holy Spirit directly intervenes in the apostolic course. **Asia**—This is not the continent of Asia nor Asia Minor, but rather the Roman province of Asia.

➤**7** After coming to **Mysia,** they tried to go to **Bithynia,** but were not allowed to work in this part of Roman Asia. **the Spirit**—According to the earliest manuscripts, this should read "the Spirit of Jesus." **suffered them not**— would not allow them to enter. The time was right for the gospel to be brought to Europe; God would use other individuals to bring his message to the eastern part of Asia Minor (1 Pet. 1:1). By the end of the first century, as recorded by the governor Pliny, Bithynia was filled with Christians. The Holy Spirit (16:6), who was equated with the Spirit of Jesus (16:7), steered Paul away from those regions because he was about to receive the Macedonian call (16:9ff.). This is the first and only time the NT contains the phrase "the Spirit of Jesus." Elsewhere, the Spirit is called "the Spirit of Christ" (Rom. 8:9; 1 Pet. 1:11) and

"the Spirit of Jesus Christ" (Phil. 1:19). The use of the title "Spirit of Jesus" in Acts shows the unity of action between Jesus and the Spirit that permeates this book. During the days of Jesus' earthly ministry, the disciples were directed by Jesus; now, after his resurrection and ascension, by "the Spirit of Jesus."

➤**8 came down to Troas**—This city was located on the northeast coast of the Aegean Sea, with Asia Minor on the west. This region was the scene of the Trojan war.

➤**9 there stood a man of Macedonia . . . saying, Come over into Macedonia, and help us**—This marked a significant turning point in the early history of the gospel. By going over to Macedonia, Paul would begin the gospel work in Europe.

➤**10 we endeavored to go into Macedonia**—The first person plural "we" indicates that Luke had joined Paul's missionary group (see Introduction). Perhaps Paul's bad health had made it necessary for Luke, a doctor, to join the group (Col. 4:14).

➤**11 Samothracia**—This island was on the Thracian Coast, north of Troas and slightly to the west. The wind must have been blowing from the south or southeast to bring them there so soon, since the current is usually strong in the opposite direction (cf. 20:6). **and the next day to Neapolis**—This was the seaport for the city of Philippi. Neapolis was 65 miles from Samothrace and 10 miles from Philippi.

➤**12 Philippi**—This city was named after Philip of Macedon, who rebuilt it as a fort in 350 B.C. **a colony**—Anthony and Octavian sent some of their veterans there following the battle of Philippi in 42 B.C. As a Roman colony, it had all the privileges of Roman citizenship, such as exemption from scourging and arrest, as well as the privilege of appeal from the local magistrate to the emperor.

## 13-34 THE CONVERSION OF LYDIA AND ANOTHER ARREST FOR PAUL

➤**13 on the sabbath**—This was the first Sabbath after their arrival. As their plan was to speak first to the Jews, they waited for the time when the Jews met together for worship. **we went . . . by a river side, where prayer was wont to be made**—is better translated "where we supposed there would be a place of prayer" (a reading in several ancient manuscripts). Since there was no synagogue in Philippi (due to the small Jewish population), the women in that city met by a river for prayer. This was an ancient Jewish custom (see Ezra 8:14, 21-23; Ps. 137; Ezek. 1:1; Dan. 8:2). **we . . . spake unto the women**—This was a rather informal and simple manner of beginning their ministry in Europe.

►**14 Lydia**—This was a common Greek and Roman name. **a seller of purple** [cloth]— The people of Thyatira were known for their excellent ability to dye material. Lydia probably had a store in Philippi where she sold material from her hometown. She **worshipped God**—She was among those known as "God-fearers" or "God-worshippers" (see comments on 10:2). **whose heart the Lord opened**—See 16:15; cf. Matthew 11:27; Luke 24:45.

►**15 she was baptized, and her household**—This probably happened right away. **she constrained us**—The missionary group probably did not want to impose, but at her insistence, they finally accepted her invitation to stay in her home.

►**16 a spirit of divination**—lit., "a spirit of Python." This means she was "possessed or inspired by the spirit of Pythian Apollo."

►**17 These men are the servants of the most high God**—See comments on Luke 4:4.

►**18 many days**—They met together often for worship or prayer. **Paul, being grieved**— or, troubled. He exorcised the spirit **in the name of Jesus Christ.**

►**19 Paul and Silas**—They were the leaders. **marketplace**—Greek, *agora,* the usual place for forums.

►**20 Jews**—Jews were objects of dislike, contempt, and suspicion to the Romans. **trouble our city**—See 17:6; 24:5; cf. 1 Kings 18:17.

►**21 teach customs, which are not lawful for us to receive, neither to observe, being Romans**—Although the introduction of new gods was forbidden by the laws, these men probably would not have been upset if Paul and Silas had not destroyed their source of income. They concealed their real anger under the cause of religious zeal and concern for law and order (see 17:6, 7; 19:25, 27).

►**22 the multitude rose up together against them**—See 19:28, 34; 21:30; Luke

23:18. **beat them**—They were not given any trial. This seems to have happened to Paul on three different occasions (2 Cor. 11:25).

►**23 And when they had laid many stripes upon them**—Their wounds were not washed and bandaged until much later when their jailer was converted.

►**24 the inner prison**—This prison was very likely cold and rat-infested, with no light or fresh air. **made their feet fast in the stocks**—The stocks were instruments of torture as well as of confinement. They were made of wood bound with iron, with holes stretched apart for the feet.

►**25 Paul and Silas prayed, and sang praises unto God**—The tense of both words suggests that they continued praying and singing for a long period of time. The word here used for "singing" refers to singing a hymn; the same word describes the Paschal hymn sung by Christ and his disciples after their last Passover (Matt. 26:30). In spite of their physical weakness and injuries, Paul and Silas rose above their suffering to praise God. **and the prisoners heard them**—The other prisoners were not asleep but were paying attention, in wonder and amazement, to what was going on.

►**26 suddenly there was a great earthquake**—The prayers of Paul and Silas were answered.

►**27, 28 the keeper of the prison . . . would have killed himself, supposing that the prisoners had . . . fled**—He knew that he would be killed since he was personally responsible for all prisoners (12:19; cf. 27:42). **But Paul cried with a loud voice, saying, Do thyself no harm**—Paul's concern was immediately to save the jailer. He promptly assured him that all the prisoners were still there.

►**30 Sirs, what must I do to be saved?**— The jailer was not trembling with fear for his own safety as the prisoners were all there. He had become aware of his own spiritual condition. The jailer probably had some idea of why Paul and Silas were in prison, for they had been whipped in public. The cry of the demon-possessed girl (16:17) would also have informed the public as to their mission.

►**31 Believe on the Lord Jesus Christ**— The last word is not present in the earliest manuscripts. **and thou shalt be saved**—This is a short, simple, and direct reply. It was quite enough at this moment that his need be directed simply to the Lord Jesus with the assurance that this would provide his salvation. Later he could be given a more complete explanation. **and thy house**[hold]—i.e., his family (see 16:34).

➤**32 they spake unto him the word of the Lord, and to all that were in his house**—They gave him a full explanation of the Lord's message and the meaning of salvation.

➤**33 the same hour . . .** [he] **washed their stripes**—He took them to a well or fountain near the prison. Earlier the jailer had ignored the wounds of the prisoners, but now he felt a debt to them and could not rest until he had cared for them. **was baptized, he and all his** [family]—This may have occurred at the same fountain or well where he was washing the wounds of Paul and Silas.

➤**34 believing in God with all his house**[hold]—The jailer was a converted pagan who had now come to believe in God. For accounts of other households becoming Christian, see Cornelius (11:14), Lydia (16:15), and Crispus (18:8).

➤**35 Let those men go**—The reason for this change in the magistrates' attitude is not certain.

➤**37 But Paul said unto them**—The messengers who had come in with the jailer had to report back to the magistrates. They wanted to make sure that Paul and Silas had left the jail. **they have beaten us openly** [publicly] **uncondemned**—See 1 Thessalonians 2:2. **being Romans**—Both their beatings and their jailing were illegal because they were Roman citizens (see 22:28). **now do they thrust us out privily** [secretly]?—Note the contrast between their public beatings and the privacy in which the magistrates wanted them to leave. **Let them come themselves and fetch us out**—An open and formal act equal to their public beating would, in effect, say to everyone that these two men were innocent.

➤**38 they feared, when they heard that they were Romans**—It was against the law to punish Roman citizens without trial; therefore, they feared they might be punished for what they had done. Paul was born a Roman citizen (22:27-29).

➤**39 brought them out**—Since Paul and Silas were publicly declared innocent, it was of no value to them to make further demands on the magistrates.

➤**40 entered into the house of Lydia**—They took their time and did not leave the city until they were ready to. **when they had seen the brethren**—This may have included the jailer's family as well as others who had recently accepted the gospel. This meeting constituted the first European church. **comforted**—This word can also be rendered "exhorted, encouraged." They not only taught them but encouraged and comforted them also. **and departed**—Apparently Luke and Timothy remained in Philippi (see comments on 17:14).

*Chapter* **17**

## 1-15 PAUL PREACHES AT THESSALONICA AND BEREA AND LATER GOES TO ATHENS

➤**1 they . . . passed through Amphipolis**—They traveled 30 miles southwest of Philippi on the Strymon River. Amphipolis was on the Aegean seacoast with the Via Egnatia, a Roman highway, passing through it. **and Apollonia**—Also on the Via Egnatia; this city was about 30 miles from Amphipolis and 38 miles from Thessalonica. **they came to Thessalonica**—Lying at the head of the Thermaic (Thessalonian) Gulf, this was the most important city in Macedonia. It had been made a free city by the Romans in 42 B.C., which meant there were no Roman soldiers stationed there. The importance of Paul's work in Thessalonica is seen in his statement to the Thessalonian church (1 Thess. 1:8), "And now the Word of the Lord has spread out from you to others everywhere, far beyond your boundaries, for wherever we go we find people telling us about your remarkable faith in God. We don't need to tell them about it" (TLB). **synagogue of the Jews**—There was not one in either Amphipolis of Apollonia.

➤**2 as his manner**—custom. He began by preaching to the Jews. In spite of persecution from the Jews at Philippi, he thought it best to begin, whenever possible, with the Jews (see 1 Thess. 2:2). **reasoned with them out of the scriptures**—"developed the arguments from Scripture for them" (JB).

➤**3 Opening and alleging**—i.e., opening up the Scriptures and setting them before the Jews. **that Christ must . . . have suffered, and risen again from the dead**—Paul's preaching used the OT to show that the Messiah would suffer, die, and come to life again. Then Paul showed **that this Jesus** was the Messiah.

➤**4 devout Greeks**—lit., "worshiping Greeks," who were among the "God-fearers" (see 10:2). **chief women**—"prominent women" (NIV). It seems from 1 Thessalonians that these converts were nearly all Gentiles. During Paul's stay, he supported himself by working part time (1 Thess. 2:9; 2 Thess. 3:7-9). He also received some financial support from the Philippians (Phil. 4:15, 16).

➤**5 moved with envy**—lit., "becoming jealous" because they saw that their influence was being undermined. **lewd fellows of the baser sort**—i.e., "bad characters from the marketplace" (NIV). These were derelicts who lived in the streets of the marketplace. **assaulted the house of Jason**—Paul and Silas were staying with him (17:7). Jason was a Greek Jew whose name was derived from the Greek, Joshua. He was a close friend or relative of Paul.

➤**6 rulers of the city**—lit., "politarchs." The magistrates of Thessalonica were called "politarchs." This term is not found in classical literature but is evident in the inscriptions found in many Macedonian ruins. **These that have turned the world upside down**—This refers to a subversive or revolutionary action (see 16:20).

➤**7 saying that there is another king, one Jesus**—This was an accusation of treason against Caesar.

➤**10 Paul and Silas** went to **Berea** [or, Beroea]. It would have been useless to preach any more in Thessalonica. Berea was a rather large town about 50 miles southwest of Thessalonica.

➤**11 These were more noble than those in Thessalonica**—Note the distinction that Luke makes between the Jews in Thessalonica and those in Berea. They were much more willing to listen to Paul and Silas. Most of the success in Thessalonica was among the Gentiles. **received the word with all readiness of mind**—They were not prejudiced; rather, they were eager to receive what Paul was teaching.

They **searched the scriptures daily**—They wanted to know if Paul's interpretation of the OT concerning Christ was correct. Those who sincerely study the OT Scriptures with an open mind will come to see that Jesus was the predicted Messiah.

➤**12 Therefore many of them believed**—They were convinced that Jesus of Nazareth was the Messiah promised by the OT prophets. From this experience it is seen that (1) people are entitled to study the Scriptures for themselves; (2) they are obligated to determine whether the teaching they receive from ministers agrees with the Scriptures; (3) only a belief that results from personal conviction is of any value. **honourable women**—prominent women. These upper-class people were probably better educated than those of Asia Minor.

➤**13 But when the Jews of Thessalonica . . . they came thither also, and stirred up the people**—This had been done before, from Iconium to Lystra (14:19).

➤**14 the brethren sent away Paul**—It is not recorded how long Paul stayed in Berea. He did want to return to Thessalonica in a short time (1 Thess. 2:17), so his stay was probably a matter of weeks. He gave up his desire when he realized that his life was in danger and he could not safely visit there. **but Silas and Timotheus abode there still**—They stayed to continue teaching and organizing the new Christians. Paul had originally left Timothy in Philippi to continue teaching. Timothy later returned to Paul (perhaps bringing the financial support of the Philippians) when Paul was in Thessalonica, and traveled with him to Berea.

➤**15 Silas and Timotheus . . . to come to him**—Paul probably wanted their help in preaching to the Athenians, and he waited for them before going on (17:16). Timothy did join Paul and they preached together in Athens for a while. Paul soon thought it better for Timothy to go back to Thessalonica because of the activities there, so Timothy left and later rejoined Paul in Corinth (18:5).

## 16-24 PAUL IN ATHENS

➤**16** while Paul waited for them at Athens, his spirit was stirred [provoked, agitated] **in him, when he saw the city wholly given to idolatry**—Petronius (a contemporary writer at Nero's court) said satirically that it was easier to find a god at Athens than a man. Several hundred years prior to this time, Athenian statesmen had criticized the townspeople for their attraction to novelty rather than to matters of importance (see Paul's statement in 17:21). Paul dealt with the Jews in the synagogue and went into the marketplace as well.

➤**18 Epicureans**—"The Epicureans, who followed Epicurus (341-270 B.C.), said the chief end of man was pleasure and happiness. This pleasure, they believed, is attained by avoiding excess and the fear of death, by seeking tranquility and freedom from pain, and by loving mankind. They believed that if gods exist, they do not become involved in human events" (Toussaint). **Stoicks**—These were followers of Zeno (c. 334-262 B.C.). They got their name from the Greek word *Stoa* (meaning "porch"), for Zeno taught from there in Athens. The Stoics were pantheists who thought the universe was ruled by an absolute Purpose or Will—to which a man must conform his will, unmoved by all external circumstances and changes. If a man could do such, he would reach the perfection of virtue. The by-products of such a philosophy were pride and self-sufficiency. **babbler**—lit., "seed-picker." Like a bird who picks up seed here and there—and then passes it on as if he were some great teacher. **strange gods**—lit., "foreign demons." According to the Greeks, demons were deities or divinities, not evil spirits. **he preached unto them Jesus, and the resurrection**—See 17:31, 32.

➤**19** The **Areopagus** (otherwise known as "Mars' Hill") was a very famous judicial court where the worst criminals and great religious questions were dealt with. According to Athenian tradition, the institution had been established at least 1,000 years before by the city's patron goddess, Athene. Athens had become a democracy during the fifth century B.C., so that much of the power of Mars Hill had been taken away, but it still retained great prestige which even increased under Roman rule. It seems that one of its primary responsibilities was to determine whether or not to allow public lectures. Paul was taken before the court, not to be put on trial, but to explain more fully what he had been talking about in in the marketplace.

➤**21 hear some new thing**—lit., "to hear something newer" as if that which was new was

presently becoming stale—thus, they craved something still more new (Bengel).

➤**22 Mars' hill**—lit., "Areopagus" (see comments on 17:19). **ye are too superstitious**—or, "You are very religious" (NIV). The statement could be taken as a compliment or a criticism. Paul chose it because of its dual function.

➤**23 an altar with this inscription, TO THE UNKNOWN GOD**—It was probably built to commemorate some divine occurrence that they couldn't attribute to any other god. Paul used this as the basis for speaking to them about the shallowness of their religion. **whom**—Greek, "that which." The Greeks did not revere a personal God but an abstract idea. **ye ignorantly worship**—you ignorantly revere. This was similar to his message to the idolaters of Lycaonia (14:15-17). Paul's subject was not Jesus as the Messiah; rather, he spoke about the living God as opposed to the materialistic and pantheistic religion of the Greeks. Notice the authoritative way in which Paul brings the truth to these people.

➤**24 God that made the world and all things therein**—The greatest Greek philosophers could not see any difference between God and the universe. Therefore, their religious concepts were cloudy. In order to overcome this, Paul made an authoritative statement as to the basis for all true religion. **he is Lord of heaven and earth**—Everything is subject to him, and he gives meaning to their existence. This was in contrast to the ideas of blind Force and Fate, which the Greeks believed in. **dwelleth not in temples made with hands**—This idea, which was familiar to the Jews (1 Kings 8:27; Isa. 66:1, 2; Acts 7:48) and basic to Christianity, helped to define the nature of the living God to this group of people.

➤**25 Neither is worshipped** [served] **with men's hands, as though he needed any thing**—See Job 35:6, 8; Psalms 16:2, 3; 50:12-14; Isaiah 40:14-18. God is self-sufficient and self-sustained. **he giveth to all life, and breath, and all things**—The one who gives all cannot be dependent upon those who receive all (1 Chron. 29:14).

➤**26 hath made of one blood**—According to the earliest manuscripts, this should read "has made of one"—the one substance being unnamed. Later, in the transmission of the text, scribes added "blood." **all nations of men . . . to dwell on all the face of the earth**—This agreed with OT teaching, but strongly contradicted the Athenian doctrine that man was created from their attic soil (cf. Gen. 9:4; Lev. 17:11; Deut. 12:23). **hath determined the times before appointed, and the bounds of their habitation**—Paul opposed both Stoical fate and Epicurean chance, saying that men and nations live according to God's sovereign arrangement of history (**the times**) and location (**the bounds of their habitation**).

➤**27 That they should seek the Lord**—In earlier manuscripts, the last word is "God." This is the purpose of the plan that God has for man. **might feel after him**—as men groping their way in the dark, looking for the light of God's truth. **though he be not far from every one of us**—The difficulty in finding God is not that he is far from man, but that man, because of sin, is far from God.

➤**28 For in him we live, and move, and have our being**—This quote comes from the Cretan poet Epimenides (c. 600 B.C.) in his poem called *Cretica*. Paul used it to say that God is the living and immanent principle of all existence. **as certain also of your own poets have said, For we are also his offspring**—This was quoted from *Phaenomena* by the poet Aratus, a Greek who lived about three centuries before Paul. In context, the statement affirms the fact that all men are God's creatures inasmuch as their very lives come from him. Paul elsewhere quoted the Greek poets (1 Cor. 15:33; Titus 1:12).

➤**29 the Godhead**—is better translated, "the Deity" (JB) or "the divine nature" (from the Gk. *ton theion*). "Godhead" is a translation of another Greek word, *theotetos* (Col. 2:9). See comments on Romans 1:20; 2 Peter 1:3, 4. **is like unto gold**—God's divinity, God's nature cannot be replicated by man-made images. Paul makes the same argument in Romans 1:19-25.

➤**30 the times of this ignorance God winked at**—lit., "overlooked." God overlooked this ignorance (see 14:16; Rom. 1:24). **but now**—Now men have the gospel that Christ has brought. **commandeth**—He specifically states the nature of man's responsibility. For one thing, he must put away idols and worship only him (cf. Col. 1:6, 23; Titus 1:11).

➤**31 he hath appointed a day, in the which he will judge the world**—That most serious judgment will take place at the same time for all men. **by that man whom he hath ordained** [designated]—Cf. John 5:22, 23, 27; Acts 10:42. **he hath given assurance unto all men, in that he hath raised him from the dead**—Christ's resurrection gives evidence of his judicial authority.

➤**32 when they heard of the resurrection**—The Greeks viewed the body as the prison of the soul. Once the soul was liberated from the body by death, what would be the point of a bodily resurrection?

➤**33 Paul departed from among them**—Paul might have continued if he had not been interrupted, or he may have been waiting to talk with those who were sincerely interested. In either case, his remarks end before they have been completed.

➤**34 certain men clave unto** [joined] **him, and believed**—A few received further teaching from Paul and became believers. **Dionysius**—Ancient tradition says that Paul chose Dionysius to be the leader of the small group of Christians at Athens. **and a woman named Damaris**—She was not one of those who listened to Paul on Mars' Hill. Paul was not driven away from Athens, but there is no record of further work there, nor any mention as to how long he remained. The commercial men of Thessalonica and Corinth believed Paul's message more readily than the highly educated and well-cultured Athenians. Paul apparently never found it necessary to communicate with the church at Athens, and there is no indication that he ever visited there again.

*Chapter* **18**

**1-23 PAUL TRAVELS TO CORINTH WHERE HE IS JOINED AND ASSISTED BY SILAS AND TIMOTHY AND EVENTUALLY RETURNS TO ANTIOCH OF CAESAREA**

➤**1 Paul departed from Athens, and came to Corinth**—This great trading center had a double harbor. The ancient Corinth was destroyed by the Roman Mummius in 146 B.C.; the new Corinth was rebuilt by Julius Caesar in 46 B.C. As the capital of the province, it was also the residence of the proconsul. Corinth had a rather large Jewish population, perhaps due to the recent eviction of Jews from Rome by Claudius Caesar (18:2).

➤**2, 3 a certain Jew named Aquila ... with his wife Priscilla**—From these Latin names, one might conclude that they had lived so long in Rome they had lost their Jewish family names. **born in Pontus**—This was a province in the northern part of Asia Minor, located on the southern shore of the Black Sea. It had a rather large Jewish population. It is not certain whether the couple had been converted to Christianity before meeting Paul in Corinth. They were apparently quite wealthy and eventually settled in Ephesus after much traveling. **Claudius had commanded all Jews to depart from Rome**—Suetonius, in his biography of the emperor, states that the Jews were ordered to leave because of their constant rioting at the instigation of Chrestus. **they were tentmakers**—as was Paul. All three were skilled in making goat-hair tents. Paul, like every other Jewish youth, had been taught a trade. Paul made good use of his skill to support himself so that his motives in becoming a minister would not be called into question.

➤**4 Greeks**—These were converts to Judaism.

➤**5 when Silas and Timotheus were come from Macedonia**—See 17:15. **Paul was pressed in the spirit**—According to all the earliest manuscripts, this should read, "he was pressed by the word" (lit.), which means "he was occupied with preaching" (RSV) or under pressure to preach the word. Paul had come from Athens, which was his first experience with unresponsive Gentiles. Paul apparently preached alone at Corinth, during which time he was anxious about the Christians in Thessalonica. The arrival of Silas and Timothy greatly encouraged Paul. They brought financial assistance from the Christians at Philippi, and also good news of the faith and love of the Thessalonian Christians (see 1 Thess. 3:1-10). At that time Paul wrote his first letter to the Thessalonian church.

➤**6 Your blood be upon your own heads**—see Ezekiel 33:4, 9. **from henceforth I will go unto the Gentiles**—a repetition of 13:46.

➤**7 Justus**—called Titius Justus or Titus Justus in some ancient manuscripts. Paul kept living with Aquila and Priscilla, but used Justus's house as a meeting place. **one that worshipped God**—He was among those Luke had elsewhere called "God-fearers" (see comments on 10:2). **house joined hard to the synagogue**—i.e., his house was next door to the synagogue.

➤**8 Crispus, the chief ruler of the synagogue, believed on the Lord with all his house**[hold]—This was an important event. Paul himself baptized Crispus, which was not his usual practice (1 Cor. 1:14-16). **and many of the Corinthians . . . believed**—This was the beginning of the Corinthian church.

➤**9 Be not afraid, but speak**—Paul's successes had so angered the unbelieving Jews that he probably feared being driven violently from the city. Paul was reassured by this vision.

➤**10 I have much people in this city**—cf. 13:48.

➤**11 he continued there a year and six months**—This was the entire period of his stay, during which time he wrote the second letter to the Thessalonian church (see 18:5).

➤**12 when Gallio . . . the deputy** [proconsul] **of Achaia**—See 13:7. Gallio was the brother of the famous philosopher Seneca, the teacher of Nero, who passed the death sentence on both brothers.

➤**13 persuadeth men to worship God contrary to the law**—They did not require Gentiles to be circumcised.

➤**14 If it were a matter of wrong**—should read, "If it was a crime"—then it would be punishable by the magistrate.

➤**15 But if it be a question . . . of your law**—The question was clearly beyond his legal bounds.

➤**17 Sosthenes**—It was probably the successor of Crispus who led the accusing group. He is not the same Crispus whom Paul later refers to as "brother" (1 Cor. 1:1). **Gallio cared for none of those things**—He remained indifferent to whatever was beyond his sphere of responsibility.

➤**18 Paul . . . tarried there . . . a good while**—During his long stay at Corinth, Paul also started churches in Achaia (2 Cor. 1:1). **sailed . . . into Syria**—He headed for Antioch, which was the starting point for all of Paul's missions to the Gentiles. **Priscilla and Aquila**—They were also accompanied by Silas, Timothy, Erastus, Gaius, and Aristarchus (19:22, 29). **in Cenchrea**—This was the eastern harbor of Corinth, about 10 miles away, where a small church had been formed (Rom. 16:1). **for he had a vow**—This may have been the temporary Nazarite vow (Num. 6) but was more likely a vow taken during some time of difficulty or danger. To fulfill the vow, Paul cut off his hair and hurried to Jerusalem to offer a sacrifice (see 21:24).

➤**19 he came to Ephesus**—Ephesus was the capital of the Roman province of Asia. The trip from Corinth was directly east across the Aegean Sea. In a fair wind, the trip took eight days. **he himself entered into the synagogue, and reasoned with the Jews**—The Greek tense (aorist) implies that Paul had no intention of remaining there. He was only taking advantage of their stop to say a few words in the synagogue.

➤**21 I must by all means keep this feast**—This probably refers to Pentecost. **but I will return**—His later return is recorded in 19:1. **And he sailed from Ephesus**—Leaving the ship, Paul made his fourth trip to Jerusalem following his conversion (see 16:6).

➤**22 landed at Caesarea**—northwest of Jerusalem. **gone up**—to Jerusalem. **and saluted** [greeted] **the church**—in Jerusalem. These few words speak of Paul's fourth visit to Jerusalem. **he went down to Antioch**—whence he began his missionary journeys.

➤**23 spent some time there**—This was Paul's last visit to Antioch. During this time, Paul ordained the weekly collection (1 Cor. 16:1, 2), which has been adopted in most Christian churches. Timothy, Erastus, Gaius, and Aristarchus, probably went with him (19:22, 29; 2 Cor. 1:1). **went** [to] **Galatia and Phrygia in order**—actually in the reverse order of his second missionary journey (16:6).

24-28 APOLLOS AT EPHESUS

➤**24 a certain Jew named Apollos**—This is a contracted form of Apollonius. **born at Alexandria**—This famous Egyptian city was founded by Alexander the Great on the eastern coast of the Mediterranean Sea. In this city there was a blend of Greek, Jewish, and Oriental philosophies and customs, and a Jew edu-

cated in Alexandria would possess characteristics of all three. Apollos's education enabled him to express himself clearly and made him a skillful teacher of his OT knowledge. His reason for coming to Ephesus is not known. **eloquent**—gifted in speech. **mighty in the scriptures**—He had a powerful grasp of the OT Scriptures that enabled him to expound on them with clarity and dynamism.

➤**25 This man was instructed in the way of the Lord ... knowing only the baptism of John**—He was enthusiastic about the gospel, but his knowledge was incomplete. Luke describes his character to emphasize his genuine desire to teach. Apollos was **fervent in the spirit** (cf. Rom. 12:11) and **taught** the Scripture **diligently** [i.e., accurately]. They were very happy to see his knowledge and his enthusiasm for the truth.

➤**26 Aquila and Priscilla ... expounded** [explained] **unto him the way of God more perfectly**—lit., "more accurately." Apollos's exposition was accurate but limited, for he had not known about Christ's death, resurrection, ascension, etc. He needed to know the truth more accurately.

➤**27 he was disposed** [intending] **to pass into Achaia**—He wanted to preach and teach in Corinth. **the brethren wrote, exhorting the disciples to receive him**—This "letter of recommendation" (see 15:23, 25-27; 2 Cor. 3:1) served as a form of communication and encouragement between the early churches. **when he was come, helped them much**—Apollos was a great contribution to Achaia. **believed through grace**—Luke here indicates that faith and salvation are accomplished by God's grace and not by works (cf. Eph. 2:8-10).

➤**28 he mightily convinced** [confuted, refuted] **the Jews**—The verb indicates that a large part of Apollos's ministry included debate with the Jews. **showing** [proving] **by the scriptures that Jesus was Christ**—cf. 18:25. His teaching and preaching were richer due to his more complete knowledge.

*Chapter* **19**

1-41 PAUL'S MINISTRY IN EPHESUS

➤**1 while Apollos was at Corinth**—Some of the Christians there preferred Apollos's teaching to Paul's (1 Cor. 1:12; 3:4)because it was doubtless influenced by Greek philosophy Paul consciously avoided (1 Cor. 2:1-5). **Paul . . . passed through the upper coasts came to Ephesus**—He thus fulfilled his promise (18:21). **finding certain disciples**—They were probably in the same stage of Christian understanding as Apollos had been when Priscilla and Aquila met him (18:24). Perhaps these disciples had just arrived in Ephesus and had made no contact with the Ephesian church.

➤**2 Have ye received the Holy Ghost since ye believed?**—i.e., "Did you receive the Holy Spirit when you believed" (TLB). Luke does not give the reason for this question (see comments on 8:14-17). **We have not . . . heard whether there be any Holy Ghost [Spirit]**—These Christians lacked awareness of the Holy Spirit's presence. Paul felt that another baptism was necessary, not implying that their first was incorrect but that it had been incomplete.

➤**4 John verily baptized with the baptism of repentance, saying unto the people, that they should believe on him which should come after him**—The point of contrast is not between John and Christ personally, but between the baptism of John and the baptism of the Spirit that Jesus brought. Paul is not denying the reality of their first baptism. He just defines it and suggests that they must go on to the next step.

➤**5 When they heard this**—Then they understood what Paul was talking about. **they were baptized**—Paul did not perform the baptism (1 Cor. 1:14).

➤**6 the Holy Ghost [Spirit] came on them**—See 10:44, 45.

➤**8 he went into the synagogue**—See 17:2, 3.

➤**9 he departed**—He stopped preaching in the synagogue, as he had done in Corinth (18:7). **separated the disciples**—This was done to separate the new believers from those who had rejected his message. **Tyrannus**—He was probably a converted teacher of speech or philosophy. This hall served the same purpose as did the home of Justus in Corinth.

➤**10 two years**—This was in addition to the three months that he had already spent there. Sometime during those two years Paul must have made another unmentioned trip to Corinth, since the next recorded visit is twice called

his third visit (2 Cor. 12:14; 13:1; see also 2 Cor. 1:15, 16). Toward the end of Paul's two-year stay at Ephesus, he probably wrote the first letter to the Corinthians (cf. 1 Cor. 16:8). Some scholars believe that he also wrote a letter to the Galatians at this time. **so that all they which dwelt in Asia heard the word of the Lord**—This was a great opportunity for Paul, and he decided to remain in Ephesus for a long time. The freshness and varied nature of his work are illustrated in his address to the Ephesian elders (20:17ff.). Ephesus became the Christian center for the entire region and held that position for some time. Churches grew at Colosse, Laodicea, and Hierapolis either directly through the work of Paul or by the work of his assistants, Epaphras, Archippus, and Philemon (Col. 1:7; 4:12-17; Philem. 23).

➤**11 God wrought special miracles by the hands of Paul**—implying that Paul was not accustomed to such miracles.

➤**12 So that from his body were brought unto the sick handkerchiefs or aprons . . .**—cf. 5:15, 16. The miracles that God worked through Paul were quite different from the magic practiced by others in Ephesus. The exorcists (19:13), noticing that the name of Jesus was the secret of Paul's miracles, hoped that by using it they would be equally successful.

➤**13 vagabond Jews**—They wandered from place to place practicing exorcism. Matthew 12:27 implies that this ability did exist for a time, but it also gave rise to many impostors. **We adjure you by Jesus whom Paul preacheth**—This was a good testimony to the power that was in Paul.

➤**14 Sceva, a Jew, and chief of the priests**—"a Jewish chief priest" (NIV). Since Sceva was a priest, the Jews believed that he knew the secret pronunciation of the name of Yahweh and thus had the ability to command special powers.

➤**15, 16 the evil spirit answered**—A distinction must be made between the evil spirit and the man who was possessed by the evil spirit. The spirit spoke through the man. **leaped on them**—The demon acted through the man's body.

➤**19 Many of them also which used curious arts brought their books . . . and burned**

**them**—The word for "curious" in Greek means "overworked"—significantly applied to the magic arts in which laborious but senseless incantations were practiced. **fifty-thousand pieces of silver**—At that time, books in general were expensive, and these were more valued because of their content.

**➤21 Paul purposed in the spirit**—or, resolved in his spirit.

**➤22 he sent into Macedonia . . . Timotheus and Erastus**—They were sent to speak to the Macedonians about Christ (1 Cor. 4:17; 16:10) and to advise them of Paul's opinion on specific issues (1 Cor. 16:11). This Erastus is most likely not the one mentioned in Romans 16:23. **but he himself stayed in Asia for a season**—He stayed longer in Ephesus.

**➤23 the same time**—This refers to the time of Paul's leaving.

**➤24 Demetrius**—As this was a common name, it is unclear whether he is the same man mentioned in 3 John 12. **a silversmith, which made silver shrines for Diana**—These shrines were sold to tourists and visitors as souvenirs. Diana (a Roman name) in the Greek is called *Artemis*.

**➤26 gods . . . made with hands**—Most people thought that the shrines they bought were actually gods.

**➤27 the temple of the great goddess Diana should be despised, and her magnificence should be destroyed**—This temple was one of the wonders of the ancient world. It had been made in 550 B.C. but had been burned the night that Alexander the Great was born, 356 B.C. It was rebuilt with even more splendor. It was 425 feet long, 220 feet wide, and had 127 sixty-foot columns, each the gift of a king. It housed most of western Asia's money. The building was constantly being redecorated by famous artists and craftsmen, and it inspired great admiration and superstition. The small wooden image of the goddess Diana was very primitive. Like other famous idols, it was believed to have fallen from heaven (19:35). Many copies of it were sold and set up for worship in other cities.

**➤28 Great is Diana of the Ephesians**—These people were so proud of this temple that they refused to write the name of Alexander the Great on it, even though he had offered them all of his eastern countries in return.

**➤29 having caught Gaius and Aristarchus**—Cf. 17:5, 6. These men are mentioned in 20:4; 27:2; Romans 16:23; 1 Corinthians 1:14; and perhaps 3 John 1. Paul probably went to the house of Priscilla and Aquila for safety, which explains the reference in Romans 16:3, 4.

**➤31 the chief of Asia**—Wealthy and distinguished citizens of the main Asian towns were chosen annually to preside over certain festivities. Some of these had heard Paul's teaching and were interested in the gospel. They also warned him against going into the amphitheater.

**➤33 they drew Alexander out of the multitude, the Jews putting him forward**—The Jews would naturally have been blamed for this disturbance. Thus they selected someone who could prove that they had not instigated the riot.

**➤34 But when they knew that he was a Jew, all . . . cried out**—They shouted so that no one would hear him. His appearance had the opposite effect from what was intended.

**➤35 the town clerk**—He was the scribe (secretary) of the assembly and its chief executive officer. "He came to his position within the assembly and was not appointed by Rome. As the most important native official of the city, he was responsible for disturbances within it" (Longenecker). **the city of the Ephesians is a worshipper**—The word means "temple-keeper" or "temple-guardian." Thirteen cities in Asia participated in the worship of Diana, but Ephesus held the special responsibility and honor of caring for the temple.

**➤36 these things cannot be spoken against**—As anyone with legal training would have done, he urged that the very existence of the city was based on this fact. And furthermore, these men had no power to change the facts.

**➤37 nor yet blasphemers of your goddess**—Paul's gospel was positive: he proclaimed Jesus as the Son of God; he did not speak evil against the Greek's gods or goddesses.

**➤38-41** These verses help us see what an orderly, *lawful* Greek "assembly" (*ekklēsia*—one of the few occurences in the NT in which it does not mean "church" but simply a Greek assembly) should have been like. This particular assembly was not a lawful one, so it was dismissed by the town clerk.

# Chapter 20

## 1-12 PAUL CONTINUES HIS THIRD MISSIONARY JOURNEY

Paul goes again to Macedonia and Greece, and revisits Philippi and Troas. Luke gives only a brief summary here. Paul writes of this period with more detail in his letters.

➤1 Paul . . . departed . . . to go into Macedonia—This was after the Pentecost observances (1 Cor. 16:8). Paul was beginning to carry out the plan that the Holy Spirit had given him (19:21). From Paul's letters we learn (1) that Paul stopped again in Troas (2 Cor. 2:12); (2) that he had done no missionary work the first time he was there but went this time to preach. He was quite successful and was able to establish a church there; (3) that he would have stayed there longer, but was worried about Titus who had not met him in Troas as planned. Paul had sent Titus to Corinth to collect money for the poor Christians in Jerusalem (1 Cor. 16:1, 2; 2 Cor. 8:6). Paul was also anxious to know the effect of his letter to the Corinthians. (4) Anxious that something might have happened to Titus, Paul left Troas and went to Macedonia. He may have stopped in Philippi, landing at the seaport Neapolis (see comments on 16:11, 12; cf. 2 Cor. 11:9 with Phil. 4:15). In Philippi, Paul found a united, growing church that gave him a very warm and generous welcome. (5) When Paul arrived in Philippi, Titus was not there and Paul was extremely concerned (2 Cor. 7:5). (6) After some time, Titus arrived, bringing news of the Corinthian church. The church was doing well (2 Cor. 7:6, 7, 13), but there were some who were trying to weaken their group by criticizing Paul's authority. (7) With mixed feelings, Paul wrote them another letter and sent Titus to deliver it. (8) While waiting for a reply to his letter, he probably made a short trip northwest to Ilyricum, on the coast of the Adriatic (Rom. 15:19). Paul finally arrived in Greece and began the second part of his plan (19:21).

➤2, 3 he came into Greece, and there abode [remained] three months—Though Luke mentions only the province, he undoubt-edly means Corinth. Paul anticipated a difficult situation in Corinth but was generally hopeful of success (2 Cor. 10:1-8, 11; 13:1-10). There were other churches in Greece that he could visit during his three-month stay. It was during this time that Paul wrote his letter to the Romans, which may have been delivered by Phoebe, a woman who traveled to Rome on business (see 18:3). And when the Jews laid wait for him, as he was about to sail into Syria, he purposed to return through Macedonia—He had probably planned to sail from Cenchrea (Corinth's eastern seaport) to Palestine on his way to Jerusalem, according to the third part of his plan (19:21). After discovering the plot against his life, he thought it better to take another route back through Macedonia, which would allow him to visit Berea, Thessalonica, and Philippi. This was his last visit to Corinth.

➤4 Sopater of Berea—to which the earliest manuscripts add "[son] of Pyrrhus." Some scholars believe that the father is mentioned to distinguish him from Sosipater (Rom. 16:21). It seems more likely, however, that they were the same person. Aristarchus—See 19:29. Gaius of Derbe—This is probably the same Gaius mentioned in 19:29. Tychicus and Trophimus—These Ephesian men were Paul's assistants and seem to have been a great help to him (Eph. 6:21, 22; Col. 4:7, 8; Acts 21:29; 2 Tim. 4:12, 20). Most likely each of these men had been sent by their churches to collect money at Berea, Thessalonica, and Philippi for the relief fund that was being sent to Jerusalem.

➤5 These going before—They probably went ahead to make plans for Paul's arrival.

➤6 Troas—This was Paul's third and last visit there.

➤7 the first day of the week—This reference, along with 1 Corinthians 16:8 and others, indicates that the early church groups had already begun to meet regularly on the first day of the week for worship and instruction.

➤8 there were many lights [lamps] in the upper chamber—This increased the heat and made Eutychus drowsy (20:9).

➤9 Eutychus . . . fell down from the third loft, and was taken up dead—He was probably sitting on a bay window which projected over the street.

➤**10 his life is in him**—or, his soul (*psuche̅*) is in him. Compare Paul's actions to those of Elijah (1 Kings 17:21) and Elisha (2 Kings 4:34, 35).

### 13-38 PAUL CONTINUES TOWARD JERUSALEM, STOPPING AT MILETUS

➤**14 Mitylene**—The capital and largest city of the island of Lesbos lay opposite the eastern coast of the Aegean, about 30 miles south of Assos.

➤**15 Chios**—This was another island. **Samos**—This island was near the coast where they spent the night. **Miletus**—The ancient capital of Greece was located near the mouth of the Meander River.

➤**16 Ephesus**—They were opposite Ephesus when passing Chios. **he hasted** [hurried] **. . . to be at Jerusalem the day of Pentecost**—This was a good time to deliver the relief fund that was collected for the Jerusalem church. Paul also wished to clarify his apostolic relationship with the church. As it was only a month before Pentecost, stopping at Ephesus was impossible.

➤**17 from Miletus he sent to Ephesus, and called the elders of the church**—This was a 30-mile trip for them. It would seem that Paul could have saved time by stopping at Ephesus since he was so close, but he probably did not want to risk getting stuck there due to bad sailing conditions.

➤**18 Ye know**—He appealed to the Ephesians' knowledge of Paul's sincerity in working for God.

➤**19 with many tears**—He showed concern for the many new Christians and sensitivity to the hatred of the Jews.

➤**20 taught you publickly**—in corporate meetings of the entire church. **and from house to house**—in home meetings. The church met in both ways.

➤**21 repentance toward God, and faith toward our Lord Jesus**—"Repentance" is the change that occurs in man's heart when he realizes that he has disobeyed the laws of God. "Faith" is confidence in Christ as the mediator who brings God's love and grace to all men and carries their sin so that they may be perfect before God. Thus, repentance precedes faith.

➤**22 I go bound in the spirit** [or, Spirit]— The Spirit's indwelling presence controlled all of Paul's activities.

➤**23 the Holy Ghost** [Spirit] **witnesseth**— through prophetic utterances (see 21:10, 11).

➤**24 that I might finish my course**—an allusion to the race set before Paul. He uses the same expression in 2 Timothy 4:7, declaring that he had, in fact, finished his course.

➤**25 I know that ye . . . shall see my face no more**—This was not necessarily a prediction, but it was what Paul expected.

➤**26 I am pure from the blood of all men**—cf. 1 Samuel 12:3, 5; Ezekiel 3:17-21; 33:8, 9.

➤**27 all the counsel of God**—Paul related to the Ephesians the full will of God related to salvation. Later, he would unveil the counsel concerning God's NT economy to the saints at Ephesus (see Eph. 1:4-11; 3:1-6).

➤**28 Take heed . . . unto yourselves**—Cf. 1 Timothy 3:2-7; 4:16; 6:11. **and to all the flock**—cf. Hebrews 13:17. **over the which the Holy Ghost** [Spirit] **hath made you**—Cf. John 20:22, 23; Ephesians 4:8, 11, 12; Revelation 3:1. **overseers**—often translated "bishops." The elders of a church functioned as the overseers of that church. The terms "bishops" and "elders" were interchangeable (see 20:17) until the second century. **church of God**—This reading is found in Codex Sinaiticus and Codex Vaticanus, two of the earliest extant manuscripts. Other ancient manuscripts read, "church of the Lord." Good arguments have been put forth to support both readings. Those who argue for "church of the Lord" say that this title appears nowhere else in the NT and therefore was subject to be changed to the more common title "church of God" (used by Paul nine times). But those who argue against "church of the Lord" say that it was changed from "God" to "Lord" because the following clause speaks of the one who purchased the church with his own blood. Uncomfortable with the statement that God purchased the church with his blood, scribes changed "God" to "Lord." **which he hath purchased with his own blood**—All early manuscripts read, " . . . with the blood of his own." The expression "his own" (*tou idiou*) was used in Greek papyri as a term of endearment (Moulton and Milligan). Thus, God's Son, the one dear to him, is perhaps called here "his Own"—as elsewhere he is called his "one and only" (John 1:14, 18; 3:16—see NIV). Nevertheless, the

Greek could also mean that God purchased the church with his own blood. This would, of course, mean that Paul was calling Jesus "God" for it was Jesus who shed his blood for the church.

➤**29, 30 wolves enter in among you, not sparing the flock ... also of your own selves shall men arise ... to draw away disciples after them**—Some teachers would attack the church from without and others would arise from within the church to pervert the truth (see Paul's epistles to the Ephesians, the Colossians, and to Timothy). Church leaders in every age must guard the unity of the believers.

➤**31 three years**—speaking in round numbers, for it was actually a little more than two and a half.

➤**32 the word of his grace**—See 20:24. **which is able to build you up, and to give you an inheritance ...**—The process begins with reconciliation and ends with the Christian's final inheritance. The Christian, meanwhile, is empowered by God to become more like Christ (Rom. 16:25; Eph. 3:20; Jude 24; cf. 2 Tim. 1:12). **among all them which are sanctified**—This is a composite of all who have been set apart by God for God.

➤**34 these hands have ministered unto my necessities, and to them that were with me**—Paul had labored (as a tentmaker) in Thessalonica (1 Thess. 2:9) and Corinth (Acts 18:3) to provide for himself and other co-workers.

➤**35 It is more blessed to give than to receive**—This saying is not written anywhere in the Gospels, but was certainly implied by Christ in a general sense (see Luke 6:38).

➤**36-38** These three verses are very touching, leaving an indelible impression of rare ministerial fidelity and affection on the apostle's part, and of warm admiration and attachment on the part of the Ephesian elders.

*Chapter* **21**

### 1-16 PAUL AND HIS COMPANIONS SAIL FROM EPHESUS TO PTOLEMAIS AND TRAVEL BY LAND TO JERUSALEM

➤**1 Coos**—or, Cos. This island was about six hours south of Miletus. **Rhodes**—This island city was founded in 408 B.C. **Patara**—This was a town on the mainland of Lycia,

directly east of Rhodes. The famous oracle of Apollo was located here.

➤**2 Phe[o]nicia**—See comments on 11:19.

➤**3 left it on the left**—They went to the southeast of it. **landed at Tyre**—This center of sea trade between the east and the west was about two days from Patara. **the ship was to unlade her burden**—unload the cargo. The unloading process gave Paul some time to spend there.

➤**4 he should not go up to Jerusalem**—See comments on 2:23; 21:11-14. But Paul insisted that he was doing what God wanted.

➤**7 Ptolemais**—This was the OT city, Accho, known in modern times as Akko. During Paul's time it was a Roman colony, probably named in honor of Ptolemy II (285–246 B.C.).

➤**8 Caesarea**—was about 30 miles farther south along the coast. **Philip the evangelist**—Philip, who baptized the Ethiopian eunuch (8:5ff.) and preached throughout Samaria. **one of the seven**—deacons first appointed by the church (6:5).

➤**9 four daughters, virgins, which did prophesy**—This fulfilled the prophecy of Joel 2:28 (see 2:18).

➤**10 Agabus**—See 11:27, 28.

➤**11 So shall the Jews at Jerusalem bind the man ... and deliver him into the hands of the Gentiles**—i.e., the Romans (see 28:17).

➤**15 went up to Jerusalem**—This was Paul's fifth visit to Jerusalem following his conversion and the end of his third missionary trip. Paul did get to Rome, though he went as a prisoner.

➤**16 Mnason of Cyprus, an old** [ancient, early] **disciple**—He may have been one of the 3,000 who were converted on the day of Pentecost or someone who followed Jesus before his crucifixion.

### 17-40 PAUL REPORTS THE EVENTS OF HIS THIRD MISSIONARY TRIP. HE IS ARRESTED IN THE TEMPLE

➤**17 the brethren received us gladly**—This warm welcome was very different from his official reception by the elders (21:18ff.).

➤**18 Paul went in with us unto James; and all the elders were present**—He gave a formal report of his most recent trip.

➤**19 declared** [recounted] **particularly what things God had wrought among the**

**Gentiles by his ministry**—See 14:27; Romans 15:15. No doubt he mentioned his controversy with the legalistic Jewish Christians.

➤**20 they glorified the Lord**—In spite of the Jewish influence on the Jerusalem church, they knew that Paul was following God's plan. **how many thousands of Jews there are which believe; and they are all zealous of the law**—The church at Jerusalem was composed of countless Jews who believed in Jesus as their Messiah, but they still retained their Judaism, especially their adherence to the law. Several conservative Jewish believers strove to "turn Christianity into a Jewish sect" (Conybeare and Howson).

➤**21 they are informed of thee**—Paul had a bad reputation among many believers in Jerusalem. It was said of Paul that he taught **the Gentiles to forsake Moses,** which was half truth, half lie.

➤**22 the multitude must needs come together**—There must be a meeting of the church.

➤**23, 24 four men which have a vow**—probably a Nazarite vow. **purify thyself with them**—participate in their purification. **be at charges with them**—pay for the expenses of fulfilling their purification vows. Paul's participation in their vow would show that he was not against the law—in fact, quite the contrary.

➤**25** This is a repetition of the edict formulated at the council in Acts 15.

➤**26 Then Paul took the men, and ... purifying himself with them entered into the temple, to signify the accomplishment of the days of purification, until that an offering should be offered**—The offering consisted of two pigeons and one lamb for each man (Num. 6:9-12). Should Paul have participated in this purification ceremony? Was it contrary to what he himself preached about the grace of Christ freeing us from the law? Those who defend Paul's actions say that he did all this to conciliate the Jerusalem church and thereby promote unity. Furthermore, Paul had earlier performed a Nazarite vow (18:18) but had no qualms about being a Jew for the sake of the Jews (1 Cor. 9:20, 21); he had Timothy circumcised (16:3) when it was expedient to do so for the sake of the ministry to the Jews. Perhaps Paul was above it all, living in his freedom to perform the law or not perform it (see Gal. 6:14, 15).

Or perhaps Paul succumbed to the pressure of the Jerusalem elders and thereby compromised his stand. Whatever the case, the disruption that soon followed prevented Paul from carrying out the purification rite to the end. The offerings were never made. We cannot overlook God's hand in this intervention.

➤**27 Jews which were of Asia**—probably from Ephesus (see 21:29). They had known Paul from before and had been agitated by him (see 19:9; 20:19).

➤**28-30** The Jews from Asia ignited a mob scene.

➤**31 the chief captain**—lit., "The chiliarch." **of the band**—lit., "cohort."

➤**34 commanded him to be carried into the castle**—This may have been the soldiers' barracks in the Fort of Antonia. The fort was built by Herod on a high rock at the northwest corner of the temple area and named after Mark Antony.

➤**36 Away with him**—The same shout was heard at Jesus' trial (Luke 23:18; John 19:15).

➤**38 Art not thou that Egyptian ...**—See Josephus's *Jewish Wars* (2.8.6 and 2.13.5). **murderers**—lit., "Sicarii." The Sicarii murdered Romans and Jews alike if they sympathized with the Roman government (see comments on Matt. 10:4).

➤**39 I am ... a Jew of Tarsus, a city in Cilicia**—See 16:37. Paul assured the commander that he was a Jew, not an Egyptian.

➤**40 a great silence**—The people were amazed that the commander had given Paul permission to talk and that he himself was willing to listen to Paul's defense. **in the Hebrew tongue**—which was Aramaic, the vernacular of the Jews in Palestine since the captivity.

*Chapter* **22**

1-30 PAUL'S DEFENSE

➤**1, 2 when they heard that he spake in the Hebrew tongue to them, they kept the more silence**—See comments on 21:40.

➤**3 brought up in this city at the feet of Gamaliel**—Paul's education was important to his later ministry just as Moses' education in the Egyptian dessert had been to his work. **Gamaliel**—possibly the grandson of Hillel, the most honored rabbi of the first century (*NIVSB*). (See 5:34-40.) **taught according to the perfect manner of the law of the fathers**—Paul had a very strict Jewish upbringing. **zealous toward God, as ye all are this day**—Paul's previous zeal against the early Christians is mirrored in this angry crowd.

➤**4 I persecuted this way**—See comments on 9:1, 2, 5, 7.

➤**5 the high priest doth bear me witness**—Note that Paul speaks of things that are meaningful to his audience. **all the estate of the elders**—the Sanhedrin.

➤**8 Jesus of Nazareth**—See comments on 9:5.

➤**9 they that were with me**—See comments on 9:7.

➤**12 Ananias**—Paul does not give the slightest hint that Ananias is a Christian, for he wanted to present him as an acceptable man to these strict Jews. Ananias is presented as **a devout man according to the law**—i.e., a "God-fearer"—see comments on 10:2.

➤**14 The God of our fathers hath chosen thee**—Paul carefully links the God of the past with the present and future. **see that Just One, and shouldest hear the voice of his mouth**—See 3:14; 7:52. Thus, Paul was on the same level as the other apostles who had seen Jesus following his resurrection.

➤**16 be baptised, and wash away thy sins**—Baptism was the visible sign of forgiveness from sin. **calling on the name of the Lord**—This preceded the baptism (see 8:37).

➤**17 when I was come again to Jerusalem**—This is described in 9:26-29. **while I prayed in the temple**—Even after his conversion, Paul continued in the Jewish forms of worship.

➤**18 get thee quickly out of Jerusalem**—See 9:29, 30. **for they will not receive thy testimony concerning me**—Paul's testimony to the Jews would be constantly rejected, especially in Jerusalem.

➤**19-21** The fact that Paul was known to the Jews of Jerusalem, even known as a persecutor of the Christians, did not turn out to his advantage when he was converted and made an about-face. This conversion made the Jews even more incensed; it in no way opened their hearts to seek how and why such a Jesus-hater could become a Jesus-lover. Besides, God's plan for Paul's life was for him to be a minister **unto the Gentiles.** But Paul had a difficult time giving up his zeal for his fellow countrymen (see Rom. 9:1ff.). This zeal brought him into many such difficulties.

➤**22 Away with such a fellow**—Their national prejudices would not allow them to accept such a ministry.

➤**24 examined by scourging**—This was the Roman custom.

➤**25 Is it lawful for you to scourge a man that is a Roman, and uncondemned?**—See 16:37.

➤**27 art thou a Roman?**—That Tarsus was his home did not necessarily make him a Roman citizen.

➤**28 With a great sum obtained I this freedom**—Roman citizenship was sold for a high price during the reign of Claudius. **But I was free born**—Roman citizenship could be purchased, given as an award for some outstanding service, or attained by birth into a citizen's family. No one knows how Paul received his citizenship.

➤**29 they departed from him**—See 16:38.

➤**30 the chief priests and all their council**—These men made up the Sanhedrin.

Chapter **23**

## 1-10 PAUL DEFENDS HIS BELIEFS BEFORE THE SANHEDRIN

The Roman commander had to treat Paul, a Roman citizen, according to Roman law. Therefore, the Jews' accusation against Paul was brought before an official meeting of the Sanhedrin. Paul's statement concerning the resurrection of Christ created a division in that group. The Pharisees accepted the idea of the resurrection and the spirit-world, while the Sadducees denied both. A Sadducee thus could not become a Christian without drastically changing his beliefs.

➤**1 earnestly beholding the council**—Paul was honest and courageous. He may have recognized some of his early classmates in this group. **I have lived in all good conscience before God**—The Greek word for "lived" means "behaved as a citizen." Thus, Paul was claiming good citizenship among the commonwealth of Israel (cf. Phil. 3:6).

➤**2 Ananias**—This man, the son of Nedebaeus, was a very greedy politician. Ananias was the high priest from A.D. 47 to 58. **commanded them that stood by him to smite him on the mouth**—This was a characteristic method for silencing a speaker in Eastern culture. It was common to slap a prisoner, but it was a disgrace for a judge to slap a person who was on trial.

➤**3 God shall smite thee**—Ananias was later killed by a Jewish assassin during the Jewish war. **thou whited wall**—This expression means "hypocrite" (Matt. 23:27).

➤**5** Paul said he did not know that his judge **was the high priest.** The high priesthood at that time was constantly changing. It is likely that Paul, having been away from Jerusalem for so long, really didn't know who the high priest was or what his responsibilities and roles were. (Cf. a similar response by Christ, John 18:22, 23.) Paul was quick to make up for his mistake. **Thou shalt not speak evil of the ruler of thy people**—See Exodus 22:28.

➤**6 I am a Pharisee, the son of a Pharisee**—This was a clever move to secure the support of the Pharisees, who believed in a specific resurrection. **resurrection of the dead**—His was not a general hope in immortality, but a specific expectation of resurrection.

➤**8 the Sadducees say that there is no resurrection, neither angel, nor spirit**—See comments on Luke 20:37.

➤**9 a spirit or an angel hath spoken to him**—there on the Damascus road (see 22:17). **let us not fight against God**—The Pharisees basically agreed with Paul's view of resurrection and did not think any more inquiry or disturbance was necessary.

➤**10 There arose a great dissension**—The Sanhedrin was split with one group trying to take Paul's part, and the other opposing him.

## 11-35 PAUL IS PUT IN JAIL AND TAKEN TO CAESAREA FOR A HEARING

➤**11 so must thou bear witness also at Rome**—See 11:21. This vision gave Paul encouragement and a definite sense of purpose. The Greek term that is translated "must" carries a sense of moral obligation.

➤**12 bound themselves under a curse, saying that they would neither eat nor drink till they had killed Paul**—cf. 1 Samuel 14:24; 2 Samuel 3:35.

➤**16 Paul's sister's son**—See comments on 9:30. He was probably a student in Jerusalem and may have heard from someone at school of the plan to kill Paul.

➤**17 Paul called one of the centurions**—Paul, of course, knew that God would protect him, but he assumed the responsibility of protecting his own life for the work that God still had for him to do (see 27:22-25, 31).

➤**23, 24 two hundred soldiers**—This was a large group, but the Roman officials obviously wanted to take every precaution to protect Paul and to keep peace. **Felix the governor**—He was governor of Judea from A.D. 52 to 59 (see 24:24, 25).

➤**26 Claudius**—The commander took this Roman name at the time of his citizenship. **Lysias**—This was his Greek name.

➤**29 Whom I perceived to be accused of questions of their law, but to have nothing laid to his charge worthy of death or of bonds**—A religious question was of no concern to the civil court.

➤**31 Antipatris**—This was located about halfway between Jerusalem and Caesarea. Antipatris was named by Herod in honor of his father, Antipater.

➤**34 when the governor had read the letter, he asked of what province he was**—The letter described him as a Roman citizen.

➤**35 Herod's judgment hall**—Herod's old palace, called "the Praetorium," was now occupied by the Roman governors. Paul was kept in a building adjacent to the Praetorium.

*Chapter* **24**

## 1-27 PAUL CONTINUES HIS DEFENSE BUT REMAINS IN PRISON

➤**1 after five days**—This was after he had left Jerusalem. **Ananias . . . with the elders**—This group was sent by the Sanhedrin. **orator named Tertullus**—This man was fluent in the language of the courts.

➤**2 by thee we enjoy great quietness**—Felix had been successful, to a degree, in keeping law and order.

➤**5 a mover of sedition**—"an agitator" (RSV) or one "stirring up riots" (NIV). This charge was based on incidents as recorded in 16:20. **throughout the world**—This referred to the Roman Empire. Tertullus charged Paul with sedition because this was a serious offense in Roman law. **a ringleader of the sect of the Nazarenes**—This second charge was certainly true. "To be a leader of a religious sect without Roman approval was contrary to law" (*NIVSB*). To outsiders, the Christian church was perceived as being a Jewish sect—here called "the sect of the Nazarenes." No doubt, the term "Nazarene" carried with it all the derision that Jesus experienced when he was called "the Nazarene."

➤**6 gone about** [attempted] **to profane** [defile] **the temple**—This charge was false.

➤**7, 8a But the chief captain . . . Commanding his accusers to come unto thee**—All of verse 7 and the first part of verse 8 are not found in the earliest manuscripts. According to the text in the KJV (which includes this portion), Tertullus was implying that Lysias should not have sent the case on to Felix but left it in the hands of the Sanhedrin.

➤**10 thou hast been of many years a judge unto this nation**—He had ruled for six or seven years in this particular province, and in Galilee for an even longer period. **I do the more cheerfully answer**—Paul was glad that Felix's long experience would help him understand Paul's case and make the correct judgment.

➤**11 there are yet but twelve days since I went up to Jerusalem for to worship**—cf. 21:15, 18, 26, 27; 22:30; 23:11, 12, 23, 32; 24:1. Chapters 21 and 22 of Acts record the events of those twelve days: Paul arrived in Jerusalem, met with James and the elders, and went to the temple to make a vow. There he was arrested and brought before the Sanhedrin. The Jews planned to kill Paul, but their plan was discovered, and Paul was quickly taken from Jerusalem to Caesarea. Acts 24:1 mentions the remaining days. Paul's point was that he could not have done all that he was accused of in so short a time. He had come to Jerusalem to worship, not create any disturbance.

➤**14 But this I confess**—Felix would not see Paul's confession as a crime. **after the way which they call heresy**—rather, "a sect" (see 24:5). **so worship I the God of my fathers**—Paul's argument is twofold: (1) Israel was

divided into the two religious sects of the Sadducees and the Pharisees. Paul here asserts that he simply belongs to a third sect, the Nazarenes, and that because of this he is despised. (2) The Roman law allowed every nation to worship their own God. Thus, Paul felt that he had the right to worship the same God as a member of a different sect. **believing all things which are written in the law and in the prophets**—Paul affirmed the authority and veracity of the OT.

➤**15 And have hope . . . which they themselves . . . allow, that there shall be a resurrection**—The Pharisees were now accusing him before the court. **both of the just and unjust**—This is the only time that Paul referred to the resurrection of the unrighteous.

➤**16 And herein do I exercise myself**—Paul anticipated and prepared for a day of judgment (2 Cor. 5:10). **to have always a conscience void of offence toward God, and toward men**—These guidelines of Paul's life were quite opposed to trouble making and sectarianism (cf. 23:1; 2 Cor. 1:12; 2:17).

➤**17 I came to bring alms to my nation, and offerings**—He here refers to the relief offering that had been collected in Macedonia and Greece (Rom. 15:25, 26; 1 Cor. 16:1-4; 2 Cor. 8:1-4).

➤**18 found me purified in the temple**—He had not polluted the temple as his accusers had said.

➤**21 Touching** [concerning] **the resurrection of the dead I am called in question**—He again alluded to the inconsistency of the Pharisees, who sided with him one minute and were against him the next.

➤**22 Felix . . . having more perfect** [accurate] **knowledge**—See comments on 24:10. **deferred them**—Felix could have dismissed the case because of insufficient evidence, but he wanted to consult with **Lysias.** Verse 23 indicates that he was sympathetic toward Paul.

➤**24 Drusilla**—She was the third daughter of Herod Agrippa I, who had previously been married to Azizus, king of the Emesenes. However, Festus, the governor of Judea, was attracted to Drusilla and persuaded her to leave Azizus and marry him. Apparently her marriage to Felix was her third. **he sent for Paul, and heard him concerning the faith in Christ**—Felix and his wife were probably curious to know more about this new sect of Judaism. No doubt Paul sensed this and satisfied their curiosity by presenting to them the basic features of the gospel. Verse 25 suggests, however, that Paul's teaching became more directed toward the lives of Felix and Drusilla.

➤**25 he reasoned** [discussed] **of righteousness**—This concerned Felix's public life. **temperance**—self-control. This had to do with Felix's immorality. **judgment to come**—He would be called to account for both righteousness and self-control. **Felix trembled**—"was afraid" (NIV). Tacitus, the Roman historian, writes that Felix ruled with a high degree of corruption, crime, and immorality. Paul was bold to confront this man about such matters. **I will call for thee**—Felix often called for Paul, but they never again spoke about Christianity or the judgment that was to come.

➤**26 He hoped also that money should have been given him of Paul**—i.e., Felix hoped to receive a bribe. Many of Paul's visitors were wealthy and could easily have bought Paul's release, but Paul would not allow it.

➤**27 after two years**—This was a long time for Paul to be inactive. During this period he was in constant written communication with the churches, and some scholars even think that he supervised Luke's writing of the Acts. **Porcius Festus**—When Felix was recalled to Rome in A.D. 59, Festus took his place as Roman procurator of Judea. **left Paul bound**—in chains (26:29).

*Chapter* 25

## 1-12 FESTUS REFUSES TO BRING PAUL TO JERUSALEM FOR TRIAL, BUT DECIDES TO HEAR THE PARTIES IN CAESAREA

➤**1 after three days he ascended** [went up] **from Caesarea to Jerusalem**—He wanted to become familiar with the main city of his government as soon as possible. Festus, generally regarded as more honest than Felix, ruled from A.D. 59 until his death in A.D. 62.

➤**3 send for him to Jerusalem**—cf. 25:15. **laying wait in the way to kill him**—Even after two years, their hatred for Paul was this strong.

➤**5 them . . . which . . . are able**—These were representatives from among the chief priests and Jewish leaders.

➤**7 the Jews . . . from Jerusalem**—See 25:24. **many . . . complaints** [charges] **against Paul, which they could not prove**—None of these political and religious accusations were based on any evidence. Paul's reply was a brief denial and a challenge to prove any of these charges.

➤**8 nor yet against Caesar**—Paul was also being charged with political crimes.

➤**9 Wilt thou go up to Jerusalem, and there be judged**—The Jews had said that Paul's crime took place in Jerusalem. Thus, that would be the logical place for the trial.

➤**10, 11 I stand at Caesar's judgment seat, where I ought to be judged**—Paul insisted that he was already standing before the proper judge, since Festus was the emperor's representative. Festus's proposal was to turn him over to the Sanhedrin for judgment (25:11) with a promise of protection, but Paul would have been killed as soon as he arrived in Jerusalem, no matter how strong the protection. He thus called upon Festus to remember his innocence. **I appeal unto Caesar**—Every Roman citizen had the right of appeal to the highest ruler. Paul used this power since the alternative was to be killed by an angry mob of Jews.

➤**12 Festus** didn't expect Paul to appeal, but he was obligated to respect it.

## 13-27 PAUL COMES BEFORE HEROD AGRIPPA II

➤**13 king Agrippa**—This king was the great-grandson of Herod the Great, son of Herod Agrippa I (12:1), and brother of Drusilla (see comments on 24:24). When his father died, he was considered too young to succeed, so Judea was attached to the province of Syria. When his uncle Herod died a few years later, he was made king of the northern districts of Chalcis and was later given Batanaea, Ituraea, Trachonitis, Abilene, Galilee, and Perea. He died in A.D. 100 after a reign of 51 years. **Bernice**—This was his sister. She married her uncle Herod, the king of Chalcis. When he died, she came to live with her brother, Agrippa II, and probably had an incestuous relationship with him. **came unto Caesarea to salute** [greet] **Festus**—This was probably to congratulate him on his promotion.

➤**14 Festus declared Paul's cause unto the king**—He took advantage of the king's abilities to deal with such matters.

➤**15-21** In these verses, Festus gives his description of Paul's case. **Jesus, which was dead, whom Paul affirmed to be alive**—Christ's resurrection was central to all of Paul's preaching.

➤**22 I would also hear the man myself**—No doubt the king had heard of Paul and was curious to listen to such a radical and controversial figure.

➤**23 principal** [prominent] **men of the city**—This included both Romans and Jews.

➤**25 Augustus**—Greek, *Sebastus* ("revered" or "august"), appearing here and in 25:21; 27:1.

➤**26 lord**—Caesar Nero was called "lord" (*kurios*), a title of majesty.

*Chapter* **26**

1-32 PAUL DEFENDS HIMSELF BEFORE AGRIPPA

This speech was similar to that given earlier in Jerusalem (chap. 22). He spent more time speaking about his conversion, God's protection, and his ministry than in defending himself against the charges that were made. Paul insisted that the gospel he preached was founded in history and was not his own invention.

➤**1 Agrippa said**—As king, Agrippa most likely presided over the meeting. **answered for himself**—defended himself.

➤**3 I know thee to be expert in all customs and questions which are among the Jews**—He was president of the temple and had been appointed a high priest.

➤**4 My manner of life from my youth**—See comments on 22:3.

➤**5 if they would testify**—They would not, since it would be a point in Paul's favor.

➤**6 I stand and am judged for the hope of the promise made of God unto our fathers**—Paul asserted that he was being tried for believing that God's promise of a Messiah was fulfilled in the resurrected Jesus.

➤**7 For which hope's sake**—Paul implies that the only difference between himself and the other Jews was that his hope had been fulfilled while theirs was yet to come.

➤**8 that God should raise the dead?**—He had done that and would continue to do so. Paul obviously viewed the resurrection as an accomplished fact. It is interesting that no one challenged the evidence of Christ's resurrection but rather found the whole thing to be "incredible."

➤**9-15** See comments on 9:1ff. and 22:4. **it is hard for thee to kick against the pricks** [goads]—This was a proverb speaking of the futility of resisting the master's guidance. No matter how much an ox would kick against its master's goad, it could not change its circumstance.

➤**16** Beginning with this verse and to the end of 26:18, Paul summarizes the message he had received from God regarding the work he was to do (cf. Ezek. 2:1ff. for a similar description of Ezekiel's commission). **for I have appeared unto thee for this purpose, to make thee a minister and a witness both of these things which thou hast seen, and of those things in the which I will appear unto thee**—Some ancient manuscripts have the word "me" (referring to Jesus) after the word "seen." The translation would then be as follows: " . . . witness both of the things wherein you have seen me and of the things wherein I will appear to you." According to this reading, the emphasis is on Jesus' revelation of himself to Paul. It is not just that Jesus revealed many things (or, many items) to Paul. Jesus revealed himself, the unsearchably rich Christ, to Paul so that Paul may preach him among the nations (see Eph. 3:8). The first appearance Jesus made to Paul was on the road to Damascus. It was at this time that Paul saw the resurrected Christ (see 1 Cor. 15:8). Subsequent to this appearance, Paul received more appearances, in which Jesus revealed more and more to him about his commission.

➤**17 Delivering thee from the people**—meaning, the Jews. Paul was continually the object of Jewish hatred. Although God had promised to protect him, Paul was responsible for looking after his own safety and asserting his legal rights. **the Gentiles, unto whom now I send thee**—The emphatic "I" here denotes the authority of the Sender (Bengel).

➤**18 To open their eyes**—This would happen when their eyes were opened to their true condition (Isa. 61:1; Luke 4:18). Satan's power keeps men in the dark, blind to the truth of the gospel—until God's light shines into their hearts (2 Cor. 4:4). Note the parallelism: **from darkness to light . . . from the power** [authority] **of Satan unto God**—Satan is the ruler of darkness (Eph. 2:2; 6:12); God himself is light (1 John 1:5). **that they may receive forgiveness of sins, and inheritance among them which are sanctified by faith . . . in me**—Faith is the means to salvation and results in forgiveness and God's inheritance among those who are his sanctified people. This faith is based on the death and resurrection of Christ.

►**20 Damascus, and at Jerusalem, and throughout . . . Judaea**—This is not chronological. Perhaps Paul's intent was to mention those places where Jewish hatred was best known. He mentioned the Gentiles who were so disagreeable to this audience at the last. **that they should repent and turn to God, and do works meet for** [worthy of] **repentance**—This was Paul's purpose for going to Damascus. This brief summary of conversion was probably suggested by John the Baptist's teaching (Luke 3:7, 8).

►**22, 23 Having therefore obtained help of God**—God spared him so that he could continue his teaching. **the prophets and Moses did say . . . that Christ should suffer**—See Numbers 21:7-9; Isaiah 53. **and that he should be the first that should rise from the dead**—See Psalms 2:7; 16:9, 10; Isaiah 25:8. **and should show light unto the people, and to the Gentiles**—See Isaiah 9:1, 2; 42:6; 49:6; 60:1, 3, 19, 20.

►**24 much learning doth make thee mad**—or, too much study is driving you crazy. Festus interrupted Paul's speech with this interjection. Perhaps Festus thought Paul's knowledge of the Scriptures had twisted his mind—but Agrippa knew better. So Paul, having defended himself to Festus, turned to Agrippa (26:25, 26).

►**27 believest thou the prophets?**—Anyone familiar with the prophetic writings could not deny what Paul had just said.

►**28 Almost thou persuadest me to be a Christian**—Although several ancient commentators affirmed the thought reflected in the KJV rendering—that Paul's preaching had a positive effect on Agrippa, most modern exegetes disagree with this translation, both lexically and contextually. The Greek requires a rendering as in the RSV or NIV: "Do you think that in such a short time (*en oligō*) you can persuade me to be a Christian?" Paul's response in the next verse, again accurately translated in the RSV or NIV ("Whether short [*en oligō*] or long, I would to God that not only you but also all who hear me this day might become such as I am—except for these chains"), indicates that Paul picked up on the same Greek term (*en oligō*) with the same meaning.

►**32 if he had not appealed unto Caesar**—Once such an appeal was made, it had to be carried through.

Chapter **27**

## 1-44 PAUL AND HIS COMPANIONS TRAVEL TO ITALY. AFTER A SHIPWRECK THEY ARRIVE SAFELY AT MALTA

►**1 we should sail**—Luke has once again joined Paul. **certain other prisoners**—Other prisoners of the state were going to Rome for trial. **Julius**—This man treated Paul very well (27:3, 43; 28:16). He may have been impressed by Paul's testimony before Agrippa.

►**2** They were bound for the Greek port of *Adramyttium,* located on the northeast coast of the Aegean Sea. **Aristarchus, a Macedonian from Thessalonica, being with us**—He was seized by the Ephesians as he had traveled with Paul (19:29; 20:4). He was again identified as Paul's companion in Rome (Col. 4:10; Philem. 24).

►**3 the next day**—Apparently they had a good wind, as the distance covered was about 70 miles.

►**4 the winds were contrary**—These winds would have been from the west or northwest.

►**5 Cilicia and Pamphylia**—Both were familiar to Paul. **Myra, a city of Lycia**—This seaport served as the center for cross-sea traffic and was one of the chief ports of the Egyptian grain trade. It was located slightly east of Patara.

►**6 the centurion**—This refers to Julius. **found a ship of Alexandria, sailing into Italy**—Egypt provided the grain for Italy and this ship, with its load of wheat (27:35), could easily carry around 300 men. Though it was round about for a ship going from Alexandria to Italy to be stopped at a Lycian port, this was most likely the best route due to the constant western wind and the direction of the current.

**➤7, 8 sailed slowly many days**—They had bad winds. **Cnidus**—This town, with its large harbor, was located on a peninsula with the island of Cos (see 21:1) just to the west. With a good wind they might have made the entire distance to Myra (130 miles) in one day. **Crete**—See Titus 1:5. **Salmone**—This was located on the eastern edge of the island. **fair havens**—or, Fair Havens. This small port was near the center of the south coast and slightly east of Cape Matala.

**➤9 the fast was now already past**—i.e., the fast that accompanied the Atonement observance. It was the beginning or middle of October, for it was past the Day of Atonement, which occurred at the end of September. Many writers said navigation was unsafe after this time. **Paul admonished them**—They had to decide whether to spend the winter in Fair Havens or to travel a bit farther to Phoenix.

**➤10 I perceive that this voyage will be with hurt**—This was a judgment based on Paul's knowledge and experience.

**➤12 the haven was not commodious to winter in**—It was open more than 180 degrees. **Phenice**—Phoenix, which was 40 miles on up the coast.

**➤14 Euroclydon**—"northeaster" or "Euro-aquilo" (east-northeast) wind.

**➤16 Clauda**—This was southwest of Crete. **the boat**—the lifeboat that was towed behind. It was probably filled with water.

**➤17 undergirding the ship**—The crew wrapped four or five turns of heavy rope around the hull of the ship to increase her strength for the rough waters that were ahead. This technique is seldom used today. **fall into the quicksands**—They referred to Syrtis, a gulf southwest of Crete.

**➤18 they lightened the ship**—which was probably already beginning to leak, by throwing cargo overboard.

**➤20 many days**—It was actually fourteen days (27:27). Having no stars by which to navigate due to the storm clouds, they were lost.

**➤21 Sirs, ye should have hearkened** [listened] **unto me**—This comment was not meant

to aggravate the situation, but to give authority to what Paul was about to say.

**➤23 stood by me this night the angel of God**—Cf. 16:9; 23:11. **whose I am, and whom I serve**—See 1 Corinthians 6:19, 20.

**➤24 God hath given thee all them that sail with thee**—While the crew was busy pumping water out of the ship, Paul was praying for himself and for his shipmates. God heard Paul's prayers and agreed to protect all of them.

**➤25, 26 it shall be even as it was told me**—Paul had received a strong vision of the eventual shipwreck and of everyone's survival.

**➤27 the fourteenth night**—This was fourteen days after they had left Fair Havens. **driven up and down**—They were drifting. **Adria**—the Adriatic Sea. This sea lies between Greece and Italy. **the shipmen deemed that they drew near to some country**—i.e., "the sailors suspected land was near" (TLB). They could probably tell from the sound of the waves.

**➤28 sounded**—This refers to a technique for measuring the depth of the water.

**➤29 they cast four anchors out of the stern**—Most ships today are equipped with anchors only at the bow. Since both ends of this ship were built alike, it needed anchors at both ends. Two anchors were usually used during a storm, which shows the severity of this gale. **wished**—they anxiously waited. **for the day**—At that time they could see where they were and whether there was a safe place to dock the boat.

**➤30 as the shipmen were about to flee**—They were about to abandon ship and take the lifeboat to shore.

**➤33 Paul besought them all to take meat**—With everyone working to keep the ship floating, it was impossible to cook.

**➤35 he took bread**—Paul took the lead in eating. **gave thanks to God in presence of them all**—This certainly impressed the others with his faith in God. This was not a celebration of the Lord's Supper, but simply a meal.

**➤39 a creek**—actually, a bay. This would be their only chance for finding safety.

**➤40 loosed the rudder bands**—These had been raised and fastened down while the ship was at anchor.

**➤41 a place where two seas met**—This was a mudbank formed by converging currents.

**➤42 The soldiers' counsel was to kill the prisoners, lest any of them should swim out, and escape**—The soldiers were personally responsible for the prisoners.

**➤43 But the centurion, willing to save Paul, kept them from their purpose**—Julius had been greatly influenced by Paul's previous testimony as well as by his conduct during this trip. Therefore, he determined to save Paul's life.

# Chapter 28

## 1-31 PAUL SPENDS THE WINTER IN MALTA AND FINALLY COMES TO ROME

**➤1, 2 island called Melita**—now known as Malta. For a long time critics believed that they were actually on the island of Meleda, but that theory has since been proved inaccurate. **barbarous people**—i.e., people who did not speak Greek. Originally Phoenician colonists, they spoke neither Greek nor Latin.

**➤3 viper**—The snake was lying among the sticks as a resting place for the winter months. **out of the heat**—the snake was aroused from its inactive state.

**➤4 No doubt this man is a murderer**—According to their superstition, they believed that Paul was being punished for a crime.

**➤5 he shook off the beast . . . and felt no harm**—See Mark 16:18, but note comments on the text.

**➤6 he should have swollen, or fallen . . . dead**—These were the usual effects of such a bite. **no harm come to him, they changed their minds, and said that he was a god**—A similar change occurred in the Lycaonians (14:13, 19).

**➤7 Publius**—Publius was Malta's representative to the Roman province of Sicily, to which Malta belonged. **who received us**—This refers to Paul and his friends, probably including Julius.

**➤8 laid his hands on him and healed him**—Paul was able to repay Publius for his kindness. (Note the fulfillment of two prophecies recorded in Mark 16:18—but note comments on the text.)

**➤9 others also, which had diseases in the island, came, and were healed**—The use of the imperfect tense in the Greek for both verbs indicates that this happened over the course of Paul's stay at Malta.

**➤10 they laded us with such things as were necessary**—These were gestures of appreciation. Most likely Paul's stay in Malta provided the beginning of the Christian community there.

**➤11 after three months**—i.e., around late February, a good time to set sail again. **whose sign was Castor and Pollux**—Greek, Dioscuri, referring to the two sons of Zeus. These gods, as the guardians of the sailors, were thought to bring good luck to all who sailed under them, and their images were carried on board many ships.

**➤12 Syracuse**—The capital of Sicily was located on its eastern coast, about 80 miles north of Malta. **we tarried there three days**—Paul took advantage of this wait for favorable winds to do some preaching among the people living there.

**➤13 Rhegium**—This is a seaport on Italy's southwest coast. **Puteoli**—It was located on the northern part of the bay of Naples, about 180 miles north of Rhegium.

**➤14 Where we found brethren**—Christians. This was probably a surprise for all of them. **to tarry** [stay] **with them seven days**—Julius may have had to wait for further orders from Rome. In any case, Paul was able to spend a week with the Christians there.

**➤15 when the brethren** [in Rome] **heard of us**—Julius had sent a letter from Puteoli. **Appii forum**—or, the Forum of Appius. The Appian Way was "the oldest, straightest, and most perfectly made of all the Roman roads, named after the censor Appius Claudius who started its construction in 312 B.C." (Longenecker). The Forum of Appius was a small station along the way, about 43 miles outside of Rome. **The three taverns**—another station along the Appian Way, about 33 miles from Rome. The word "tavern" meant any kind of shop (*NIVSB*). Christians came from there also to meet Paul. **thanked God**—He appreciated this welcome (Rom. 1:9). **took courage**—He knew that God's plan for him was nearly complete (19:21).

**➤16 Rome**—The capital of the ancient world was located on the Tiber River. **Paul was suffered** [permitted] **to dwell by himself** [i.e., not in prison] **with a soldier that kept him**—This privilege was given to many of the better-class prisoners who were not charged with any serious crime. Festus's letter and Julius's high recommendation probably helped Paul to secure this arrangement. His guards were changed often, which gave him a good chance to spread the gospel among the Praetorian guard (see Phil. 1:7, 13; 4:22).

➤**17 Paul called the chief of the Jews together**—The Jews had earlier been banished from Rome. Now, however, they were tolerated and had obtained considerable wealth and influence there. Prior to this time, a Christian body had formed, to which Paul had written a letter (The Epistle to the Romans).

➤**19 I was constrained to appeal unto Ceasar**—He did not wish to accuse the Jews, but to defend himself.

➤**22 But we desire to hear of thee what thou thinkest**—The Jews in Rome were apparently open-minded, probably because they did not want to be banished again. **this sect**—the sect of the Nazarenes (see comments on 24:5).

➤**23 came many to him into his lodging**—Paul was not renting a house but was staying with friends, possibly Aquila and Priscilla (Rom. 16:3). **the law of Moses, and . . . the prophets**—i.e., the OT (see Luke 24:27, 44).

➤**25 they**—This refers to the Jews. **after that Paul had spoken one word**—The language here can be misleading. The Jews did not leave until after Paul spoke what was recorded in 28:26-28.

➤**26, 27** The quote comes from Isaiah 6:9, 10. Jesus quoted this same passage on two occasions (see Matt. 13:13-15; John 12:38-40 and comments) when also speaking of the Jews' obduracy and blindness.

➤ **28 the salvation of God is sent unto the Gentiles**—See comments on 13:44-48. (Two other examples of Paul's speaking in this manner of the Gentiles are found in 13:46 and 18:6.)

➤ **29** This verse is not present in all the earliest manuscripts.

➤ **30 Paul dwelt two whole years in his own hired [rented] house, and received all that came in unto him**—He was still under guard and was not allowed to go out but could have visitors in his house.

➤ **31 Preaching the kingdom of God . . . with all confidence [boldness]**—This verse characterizes the dynamic energy with which Paul preached about God's kingdom and the Lord Jesus Christ.

BIBLIOGRAPHY
Bengel, John A. *New Testament Word Studies.* 1742. Reprint. Grand Rapids: Eerdmans, 1971.
Bruce, F. F. *The Acts of the Apostles.* Chicago: InterVarsity Press, 1952.
Conybeare, W. J., and Howson, J. S. *The Life and Epistles of St. Paul.* 1851. Reprint. Grand Rapids: Eerdmans, 1978.
Longenecker, Richard. "The Acts of the Apostles" in *The Expositor's Bible Commentary.* Grand Rapids: Zondervan, 1981.

Metzger, Bruce. *A Textual Commentary on the Greek New Testament.* New York: United Bible Societies, 1971, 1975.
———.The New Testament: Its Background, Growth, and Content. 2d ed. Nashville: Abingdon Press, 1965, 1983.
Moulton and Milligan. *The Vocabulary of the Greek New Testament.* Grand Rapids: Eerdmans, 1930.
Toussaint, Stanley. "Acts" in *The Bible Knowledge Commentary.* Wheaton: Victor Books, 1983.

# ROMANS

## Introduction

The genuineness of the Epistle to the Romans has never been questioned. It has the unbroken testimony of all antiquity, including Clement (mentioned in Phil. 4:3), who quotes from it in his Epistle to the Corinthians, written before the close of the first century. The most searching investigations of modern criticism have left it untouched.

We have the means of determining when and where this epistle was written with good precision—from the epistle itself and from Acts. Up to the date of writing, the apostle had never been at Rome (1:11, 13, 15). He was then on the eve of visiting Jerusalem with a contribution for its Christian poor from the churches of Macedonia and Achaia, after which his purpose was to visit Rome on his way to Spain (15:23-28). He carried this contribution with him from Corinth, at the close of his third visit to that city, which lasted three months (Acts 20:2, 23; 24:17). On this occasion certain persons accompanied him from Corinth, whose names are given by the historian of the Acts (Acts 20:4), and four of these are expressly mentioned in this epistle as being with the apostle when he wrote it—Timothy, Sosipater, Gaius, and Erastus (16:21, 23). Of these four, Gaius was an inhabitant of Corinth (1 Cor. 1:14), and Erastus was "chamberlain of the city" (16:23), which can hardly be supposed to be other than Corinth. Finally, Phoebe, the bearer, it appears, of this epistle, was a deaconess of the church at Cenchrea, the eastern port of Corinth (16:1). Putting these facts together, it is impossible to resist the conviction, in which nearly all critics agree, that Corinth was the place from which the epistle was written, and that it was dispatched about the close of the visit above mentioned, probably in the spring of the year 58.

The founder of this celebrated church is unknown although tradition teaches that it owed its origin to the apostle Peter and that he was its first bishop. This was taught in the church of Rome as a fact not to be doubted but is refuted by the clearest evidence. If Peter founded the church at Rome, how are we to account for so important a circumstance being passed by in silence by the historian of the Acts, not only in the narrative of Peter's labors, but in that of Paul's approach to the metropolis, of the deputations of Roman "brethren" that came as far as Appii Forum and the Three Taverns to meet him, and of his two years' labors there? And how could he express his anxious desire to come to them that he might have some fruit among them also, even as among other Gentiles (1:13), if all the while he knew that they had the apostle of the circumcision for their spiritual father? And how, if so, is there no salutation to Peter among the many in this epistle? The same considerations would seem to prove that this church owed its origin to no prominent Christian laborer; and this brings us to the much-debated question.

For what class of Christians was this epistle principally designed—Jewish or Gentile? That a large number of Jews and Jewish proselytes resided at this time at Rome is known to all who are familiar with the classical and Jewish writers of that and the immediately subsequent periods; and there can be no doubt that those of them who were at Jerusalem on the day of Pentecost (Acts 2:10) and formed probably part of the three thousand converts of that day would on their return to Rome carry the glad tidings with them. Probably some of the believers addressed in the salutations of the epistle were Christians already of long standing, if not among the earliest converts to the Christian faith. Others of them who had made the apostle's acquaintance elsewhere, and who, if not indebted to him for their first knowledge of Christ, probably owed much to his ministry, seemed to have been doing the work of the Lord in the capital. And thus it is not improbable that up to the time of the apostle's arrival the Christian community at Rome had been dependent upon its own members for the increase of its numbers, aided perhaps by occasional visits from preachers. Nonetheless, it is clear that the apostle wrote to them expressly as to a Gentile church (1:13, 15; 15:15, 16). But it is equally plain that there were Jewish Christians among them, for the whole argument presupposes an intimate acquaintance on the part of his readers with the leading principles of the OT. Perhaps the major constituency of the Gentiles were actually Jewish proselytes and/or "God-fearers" (see comments on Acts 10:2).

It remains only to speak briefly of the plan and character of this epistle. Of all the epistles of Paul, this is the most elaborate, and at the same time the most glowing. It has just as much in common with a theological treatise as with a personal, heartfelt epistle. Its first great topic is what may be termed the legal relation of man to God as a violator of his holy law, whether as merely written on the heart, as in the case of the heathen, or, as in the case of the chosen people (Israel), as further known by external revelation. It next treats that legal relation as wholly reversed through faith in the Lord Jesus Christ, resulting in the believer's justification. And its third and last great topic is the new life in Christ that accompanies this change of relation. The bearing of these wonderful truths upon the condition and destiny of the chosen people, to which the apostle next comes, is in some respects the deepest and most difficult part of the whole epistle, carrying us directly to the eternal springs of grace, sovereign love, and the inscrutable purposes of God. After this, however, we are brought back to the historical platform of the visible church, in the calling of the Gentiles, the preservation of a faithful Jewish remnant amidst the general unbelief and the fall of the nation, and the ultimate recovery of all Israel to constitute, with the Gentiles in the latter day, one universal church of God upon earth. The remainder of the epistle is devoted to the practical application (in church life) of the truths previously revealed. And then the epistle concludes with Paul's heartfelt salutations to several different believers in Rome.

Chapter **1**

## 1-17 INTRODUCTION

➤**1 Paul** (see Acts 13:9) describes himself as **a servant of Jesus Christ**—The word here translated "servant" means "a bondslave," or one subject to the will and wholly at the disposal of another. In this sense it is applied to the disciples of Christ at large (1 Cor. 7:21-23), and in the OT it refers to all the people of God (Isa. 66:14). However, in addition to this, the prophets and the kings of Israel were officially "the servants of the Lord" (Josh. 1:1; Ps. 18); the apostles also called themselves "the servants of Christ" (see James 1:1; 2 Pet. 1:1; Jude 1), expressing absolute subjection and devotion to the Lord Jesus. The salutation of this letter is typically Pauline and reflects the regular epistolary style of the first-century world. Many examples of such salutations exist in the letters written during that period, and all follow the same general pattern. First, there is the writer's name, then the reader's name follows, finally followed by the greeting of the writer. Remember that Paul has not visited Rome at this time and thus addresses a church with which he has had no personal contact. Therefore, Paul presents his credentials, first by indicating that he is a "servant," and then by noting that he is **called to be an apostle.** This occurred when he "saw the Lord," the indispensable qualification for apostleship. (See comments on Acts 9:5; 22:14; 1 Cor. 9:1.) The term "apostle" means "one sent with a message." Paul's calling was a special calling; the apostle consistently maintained his call to this position. The title had initially belonged to the Twelve who were distinguished by their association with Jesus while he ministered in Palestine. The title was later given to other church leaders and preachers (Acts 14:14). The apostle declares himself to be **separated unto the gospel of God.** This statement is reminiscent of Paul's call to the ministry, not so late as that which occurred in the Antioch church (Acts 13:2) and probably not so early as the one mentioned in Galatians 1:15. The apostle likely refers to the experience mentioned in Acts 26:16-18. **the gospel**—Greek *euaggelion,* the good news of God's salvation in Christ. It is a "gospel of God," not only belonging to God but a gospel of which

God is the author. (See 15:16; 1 Thess. 2:2, 8, 9; 1 Pet. 4:17.) When Paul wrote the term "apostle," the thought led him immediately to the "gospel," which in turn led him into a passage of great Christological value. Davidson and Martin note that "he proceeds to define the gospel of God as divine (v. 1), predicted (v. 2), and Christocentric (1:3-5)."

➤**2 promised afore by his prophets in the holy scriptures**—Even before describing the gospel fully, the apostle affirms that the gospel is no new innovation of God's message but notes the continuity that exists between the gospel and the revelation previously given to the Jewish people. Thus, it is in line with the promises given to the prophets. Rooted in the OT, the gospel describes God's liberation of exiled people (cf. Isa. 40:9; 52:7; 61:1) as "good news." Though the church in Rome was primarily Gentile by nation (see 1:13) and consisted primarily of proselytes of the Jewish faith, they are here reminded that in embracing Christ they had not cast off Moses and the prophets, but only the more profoundly yielded themselves to them (Acts 13:32, 33).

➤**3, 4** Paul emphasizes the fact that the gospel concerns **his Son,** this emphasis being the grand and central theme of "the gospel of God." Paul describes Jesus as **made of the seed of David according to the flesh.** Of course, the apostle is speaking in terms of Jesus' human nature (cf. 9:5 and John 1:14), implying that he had another nature of which the apostle immediately begins to speak. That Jesus is descended from David fulfills messianic prophecy, which anticipated that God's Deliverer would be a descendant of David's family (2 Sam. 7:12). This important messianic testimony is seen in the intertestamental Jewish literature, both that of the rabbis and of Qumran. It is also emphasized in NT writings (Heb. 1:5; 2 Tim. 2:8). **declared to be** [designated] **the Son of God with power, according to the spirit of holiness, by the resurrection from the dead**—He "was made of the seed of David according to the flesh" but he is "designated Son of God" (cf. 1:1, 14 and Isa. 9:6). Thus the sonship of Christ is in no proper sense a *born* relationship to the Father, as some conceive of it. By his birth in the flesh that sonship, which was essential and uncreated, palpably manifested itself. (See the comments on Luke 1:35

and Acts 13:32, 33.) "With power" may either be connected with "designated," and then the meaning will be "powerfully declared" (Luther, Alford), or with "Son of God," the sense being "designated to be the Son of God in possession of that 'power' belonging to him as the only begotten of the Father." He then is no longer shrouded as in the days of his flesh, but "by the resurrection from the dead" is gloriously displayed and henceforth forever exalted in this nature of ours (Calvin, Hodge). The expression, "according to the spirit of holiness," could speak of the Holy Spirit's work in raising Jesus from the dead (see 8:11) and thus designated him the Son of God. But since the expression is parallel to "according to the flesh" (i.e., according to his human nature), it probably refers to Christ's human spirit, which was a spirit of holiness. His spirit, united to the divine Spirit, was instrumental in the designation of his divine sonship. The resurrection affirmed Jesus Christ's deity and thus designated him (or, marked him out) as the Son of God. In his earthly life Jesus fulfilled the office of Messiah, since he was "descended from the seed of David." Now in resurrection he is to be recognized as the divine Son. What had been concealed in his incarnate life is now openly displayed in his position as Lord of the church (2 Cor. 13:4). One further comment on the expression "resurrection from the dead." Actually, this should read, "resurrection *of* the dead." When the Scriptures speak of Christ's resurrection, it is usually phrased, "resurrection out from among dead ones" (lit.)—i.e., Christ arose out from the midst of dead persons (see Acts 17:31; 1 Pet. 1:3). Elsewhere when Scripture speaks of the resurrection, in general, of many dead persons, it is phrased, "a resurrection of dead ones" (lit.). (For example, see 1 Cor. 15:12, 13, 42.) Here, in Romans 1:4, Christ's resurrection is spoken of as "a resurrection of dead ones." The same terminology is used in 1 Corinthians 15:21: "For since through a man death came" (lit.). This shows that Christ's resurrection included the resurrection of (many) dead persons (Alford). When he arose, many arose with him, for they were united with him in his resurrection (see Rom. 6:4, 5; Eph. 2:6; Col. 3:1).

➤5 By whom [as the ordained channel] we have received grace [the whole "grace that brings salvation"] and apostleship for the proclamation of that "grace" and the establishment of as many as receive it in the church's visible discipleship. Other commentators indicate that the Greek suggests we understand this phrase to read, "the grace of apostleship" (Bruce, Witmer). for obedience to the faith— i.e., "to bring about the obedience of faith" (RSV). Men must yield themselves to the belief of God's saving message, which is the highest of all obedience. Because Paul is the apostle chosen of God to minister to the Gentiles and consequently is interested particularly in the Romans, both as potential and actual recipients of divine grace, this "obedience to the faith" becomes the end result of his ministry to the Romans. for his name—that his name may be glorified.

➤6 among whom are ye also the called of Jesus Christ—This includes the Roman believers along with others. The apostle ascribes nothing special to the church in Rome (cf. 1 Cor. 14:36). Some have interpreted the expression "called of Jesus Christ" as meaning "called by him" (John 5:25). However, it seems that it means "called to belong to Jesus Christ" (RSV).

➤7 To all that be in Rome—Unlike many of his other epistles, Paul did not here address the church in a particular locality (Rome in this case); rather, he sent this epistle to the individual believers in Rome, many of whom he knew (see the personal greetings in chap. 16). beloved of God, called to be saints—Paul uses three terms—"beloved," "called," and "saints"—used in the OT to refer to Israel. The salutation concludes with the typical Pauline expression: Grace to you and peace from God our Father, and the Lord Jesus Christ. "Grace" is the unmerited favor of God; "peace" is the peace Christ made through the blood of his cross (Col. 1:20), which is present in the believer's mind as the peace of God that passes all understanding (Phil. 4:7). "Grace" and "peace" are from the Father and the Lord Jesus. Nothing speaks more decisively for the divinity of Christ than these juxtapositions of Christ with the eternal God, which run through the whole language of Scripture. The name of no man can be placed by the side of the Almighty. He only, who is himself God become flesh, may be named beside him (Olshausen).

►**8 your faith is spoken of throughout the whole world**—This was quite practicable through the frequent visits paid to the capital from all the provinces; and the apostle, having an eye to the influence that would exercise upon others, as well as their own blessedness, gives thanks for such faith to God who is the source of all grace in men. "The very existence of a church at Rome was something to be thankful for" (Denney).

►**9 For God . . . whom I serve**—the word denotes religious service. **with my spirit in the gospel of his Son**—Paul's entire spiritual life and activity were consecrated to the gospel. **I make mention of you always in my prayers**—so for the Ephesians (Eph. 1:15, 16); the Philippians (Phil. 1:3, 4), the Colossians (Col. 1:3, 4), and the Thessalonians (1 Thess. 1:2, 3). What all-absorbing spirituality, what impassioned devotion to the glory of Christ among men!

►**10** Verse 13 indicates that Paul had desired to visit Rome on other occasions but was unable to do so. He now informs the Romans that he requests that he **might have a prosperous journey by the will of God** to visit Rome. For a long time he had wanted to visit the capital, but he had encountered a number of difficulties. (In addition to 1:13, see 15:22 and Acts 19:21; 23:11; 28:15.) Many years elapsed before Paul was able to visit Rome, and then only as "a prisoner of Jesus Christ."

►**11, 12** These verses express Paul's longing to see the Romans and indicate that his desire was not simply a selfish motive but that rather he wished to **impart . . . some spiritual gift, to** establish them. The "spiritual gift" was not a miraculous gift, but a gift of spiritual worth, a spiritual blessing. Without question, Paul imparted his "spiritual gift" through the medium of this writing. However, what he really wished to do for the readers of this letter was to further their understanding and comprehension of the purpose of God in Christ Jesus. **that I may be comforted together with you by the mutual faith of both you and me**—i.e., Paul and the Roman believers may be mutually encouraged by each other's faith. Paul did not claim to be in a position in which all the giving came from him. When he would visit the Romans, his desire was that the exchange of gifts and encouragement might be mutual.

►**13** Paul here reiterates his desire to visit Rome; his reiteration is also expressed in 15:20-24, where Paul notes particularly that his ambition was to preach the gospel where Christ was not already known. His purpose in visiting Rome is that he might have some fruit among the Romans, as well **as among other Gentiles.** The Gentile constituency of the Roman church is explicitly stated here. However, it seems rather obvious from the Jewish strain of argument that some Jews must also have been included in the group. (See the introduction to this epistle.)

►**14, 15 debtor both to the Greeks, and to the Barbarians**—The "barbarian" was an individual who did not speak Greek. Paul felt obligated both to Greek-speakers and non-Greek speakers. This was the twofold cultural division of Paul's world. Then Paul divided men intellectually when he said that he was a debtor **both to the wise, and to the unwise.** Whatever cultural or intellectual background, Paul was eager to preach the gospel, especially to the ones in Rome. He felt himself under an all-subduing obligation to carry the gospel to all classes of mankind, as adapted to an ordained equality for all (1 Cor. 9:16). Since the Roman believers must have already heard the basic truths of the gospel, one wonders why Paul felt that he had to give them the gospel. Probably, they had not heard the gospel in full, and so Paul wrote this epistle to manifest what the full gospel includes.

►**16, 17** These verses reveal the theme of the gospel. Davidson and Martin call this "short paragraph . . . the seed plot of the subsequent chapters." Paul begins with the declaration **for I am not ashamed of the gospel.** (The words "of Christ" in the KJV do not appear in the earliest manuscripts.) The gospel (Gk. *euaggelion*) means "good news." This language implies that it required some courage to bring to the mistress of the world (Rome) what "to the Jews was a stumbling block and to the Greeks foolishness." But the gospel's inherent glory, which comes by virtue of its being God's life-giving message to a dying world, so filled his soul that he "despised the shame" as did Jesus when he endured the suffering of the cross. **for it is the power of God unto salvation to every one that believeth**—Here and in the next verse the apostle announces the great theme of his ensuing argument: salvation, the one overwhelming necessity of perishing men, and this salvation revealed in the gospel message. That message is so owned and honored of God as to carry in the proclamation of it God's own power to save every soul that embraces it, Greek and barbarian, wise and unwise alike. The power of the gospel is demonstrated by what it does, not by the argument of mere men who seek to defend it. Denney points out that "salvation is one of a class of words . . . used by Paul to denote the last result of the acceptance of the gospel." Paul says the gospel is God's power for salvation **to the Jew first, and also to the Greek.** Thus the apostle insists that the gospel is, for all men, the very same gospel given on identical terms to all without prejudice concerning the historical prerogative of the Jew. The following verse indicates how the gospel is a saving power. It is such because there is revealed in it the **righteousness of God.** The "righteousness of God" (as the whole argument of the epistle shows) is God's provision of justifying a sinner. Luther defined the "righteousness of God" as a "righteousness valid before God, which a man may possess through faith." Luther said that this righteousness is the first and last need of the sinful individual. Denney notes that Paul used "righteousness of God" to mean "a divine righteousness." Davidson and Martin note that the "righteousness" in Paul's letter to the Romans carries a double sense and may be labeled both legal and moral. These men further state that the expression is preeminently used in Scripture as describing a divine attribute that establishes a lofty standard for human behavior. This lofty standard cannot be achieved by man apart from God's provision. Thus, God had to act to bring his people into a right relationship with himself. The outworking of God's action is to make a man justified and therefore right with God. As such, righteousness can be "revealed"— i.e., brought by God within the realm of human experience and received by faith. Finally, the term "righteousness of God" may have been used by Paul to define a quality of life expected of believers in their personal relationship to God. This quality can be appropriated only by the working and energizing of the Holy Spirit (Rom. 8:2-4). **from faith to faith**—This is a difficult phrase. Although many speculate on

its meaning, it probably conveys some idea like "based on faith and addressed to faith"; or "out of faith" (lit.) speaks of eliciting faith (by the message of the gospel) and "to faith" indicates "resulting in faith." Thus, the gospel elicits faith and results in faith in those who believe. Some interpreters paraphrase the expression "from one degree of faith to another." But Paul is not discussing progressive stages of faith; rather, he is concerned solely with faith itself as the appointed way of receiving God's righteousness. Perhaps it should be understood in this manner: "The righteousness of God in the gospel message is revealed by the preacher's faith for the believer's faith." Paul appeals to Habakkuk 2:4 in the quotation, "The just [person] shall live by faith." This golden maxim of the OT is quoted three times in the NT: in this verse; Galatians 3:11; and Hebrews 10:38. These quotations show that the gospel way of "life by faith" does not disturb but rather continues and develops the ancient method. In using Habakkuk 2:4 the apostle goes directly to the heart of the prophet's message, reinterpreting faith as personal trust in God. He insists that a right relationship with God on that basis will work itself out in life. Verses 16 and 17, according to Forrester, give the theme of the epistle: A righteousness of God for unrighteous men. Griffith Thomas notes a number of things concerning the gospel as revealed in these verses. Its source is God, its nature is powerful, its purpose is salvation, its scope includes everyone, its limit is faith, and its result is righteousness.

## 18-32 CONDEMNATION OF THE GENTILES

▶**18 The wrath of God** is his holy displeasure and righteous vengeance against sin and **is revealed from heaven.** Barrett states that "wrath is God's personal reaction . . . against sin." This "wrath" is being revealed (present tense in Gk.) in the consciences of men. Therefore, both the righteousness of God (1:17) and the wrath of God (1:18) are "being revealed." God's wrath stands **against all ungodliness,** a term that refers to man's whole irreligiousness, or his living without any conscious reference to God and proper feelings toward him. This well describes the paganistic religion. His "wrath" stands also against the **unrighteous-**

**ness of men** (i.e., against heathen immorality). Man's deviations from moral rectitude in heart, speech, and behavior are included in the term "unrighteousness." God's "wrath" is standing against those **who hold** [suppress] **the truth in unrighteousness.** Although the apostle begins this verse with a comprehensive proposition regarding men in general, he is actually speaking to only one of the two great divisions of mankind—thus gently moving into his argument. But before enumerating the sins of the Gentiles, he goes back to the origin of their sin: the suppression of the truth, their stifling of the light. As darkness overspreads the mind, so impotence takes possession of the heart when the "still small voice" of conscience is regarded less and less, then thwarted, and eventually deadened. Thus, "the truth" is suppressed. God left the truth with man and in man, but man chose to obstruct its working (cf. Matt. 6:22, 23; Eph. 4:17, 18).

➤**19 Because that which may be known of God is manifest in** [to] **them; for God hath showed it unto them**—This pregnant statement begins to unfold in the next verse. Paul is not creating a naturalistic theology but is reminding the reader that God can be known from what he made, the knowledge being in the midst of man, if not in him (Barrett).

➤**20 For the invisible things of him from the creation of the world are clearly seen, being understood by the things that are made**—God's nature has been clearly perceived in the things that have been made. Therefore, the outward creation is not the parent but the interpreter of our faith in God. That faith has its primary sources within our own hearts (1:19), but it becomes an intelligible and articulate conviction only through what we observe around us in the things that have been made. And thus are the inner and outer revelations of God the complements of each other, making up between them one universal and immovable conviction that God is. **eternal power**—or, everlasting power. **Godhead**—more accurately translated "divinity." (There is another Greek word for "Godhead," used by Paul in Col. 2:9.) Since God himself is spirit, he cannot be seen by our naked eye. Therefore, God manifests himself to all men through his creation, in which is clearly reflected God's unceasing power and divine nature. Thus, **they**

**are** [i.e., all men] **without excuse;** all their degeneracy is a voluntary departure from the truth they know in their hearts and minds.

➤**21** Paul concedes that **they knew God,** meaning that they retained some genuine knowledge of him before they sank into the state which he describes in the next clause. **they glorified him not as God, neither were thankful; but became vain in their imaginations, and their foolish heart was darkened**—The expression "vain in their imaginations," better translated as "futile in their thinking" (RSV, NIV), indicates that all of their thoughts, notions, speculation, and philosophies regarding God were futile. (Cf. Matt. 15:19; Luke 2:35; 1 Cor. 3:20.) The expression "their foolish heart was darkened" reveals the downward progress of the human soul Paul here traces.

➤**22, 23** These people **changed** [exchanged] **the glory of the uncorruptible God into an image made like to corruptible man, and to birds, and fourfooted beasts** [animals], **and creeping things** [reptiles]—The word "exchanged" is a market term and means "to exchange one thing for another." The allusion here is doubtless to Greek worship, and the apostle may have had in mind those exquisite chiselings of the human form that lay so profusely beneath and around him as he stood on Mars Hill, the experience itself described in Acts 17:29. The terms birds, animals, and reptiles may well refer to Egyptian and Oriental worship. In the face of these plain declarations of the descent of man's religious belief from loftier to ever lower and more debasing conceptions of the supreme beings, some expositors of this epistle do not believe in any fall from primeval innocence. Their explanation is that the innocence was only by degrees obliterated by willful violence to the dictates of the conscience, and they maintain that man's religious history has always been a struggle to rise from the lowest forms of nature worship, suited to the childhood of our race, to that which is more rational and spiritual. But Paul's description of mankind is exactly the opposite.

➤**24 Wherefore God also gave them up**—This divine abandonment of men is here strikingly traced in three successive stages; the same word is used at each of the stages (1:24, 26, 28). They deserted God; God in turn deserted them. He permitted men to do what they pleased, even what was in the last degree vile, that those who had not honored God might dishonor themselves (Grotius). Paul apparently is drawing heavily from the Genesis account of Adam's disobedience to God rather than from Stoic philosophy or intertestamental literature. The important thing to see in 1:24 is that the apostle turns from man's sin to his punishment. It is because of his sin that God gives them up. Denney says that "to lose God is to lose everything; to lose the connection with him involved in constantly glorifying and giving him thanks, is to sink into an abyss of darkness, intellectual and moral."

➤25 Man is described as having **changed the truth of God into a lie**—i.e., they turned to idolatry, which is falsehood. **and worshipped and served the creature more** [rather] **than the Creator**—Professing merely to worship the Creator by means of the creature, man soon lost sight of the Creator in the creature. The Creator is described as **blessed for ever. Amen.** By this doxology the apostle instinctively relieves the horror that the writing of such things excited within his breast.

➤26, 27 Paul states plainly that God gave **them up unto vile** [dishonorable] **affections** [passions]—These "passions" are further described in the clause "their women exchanged natural relations for unnatural" (RSV). The practices the apostle here refers to are abundantly attested by classical authors. These vices are here seen as consuming and exhausting. When passions, scourged by violent and continued indulgence and vices, became impotent to yield the craved enjoyment, women resorted to artificial stimulants by the practice of "unnatural" and monstrous vices. The case of Sodom shows how early these were in full bloom. And because of such abominations, even centuries after that, the land of Canaan "spued out" its old inhabitants. Long before Paul penned this chapter, the Lesbians and others throughout refined Greece had been participating in such debasement. Tacitus speaks of the Emperor Tiberius's revealing that new words had then to be coined to express the newly-invented stimulants to jaded passion. No wonder, then, that poor humanity was sick and dying under even the highest earthly culture.

➤27 **Men** are described as **leaving the natural use of the woman,** and burning **in their lust one toward another.** This homosexuality, condemned by God in Leviticus 18:22, is judged by God. The offenders would bring about their own suffering under the righteous government of God.

➤28-31 But not only did the Creator give them up to "dishonorable passions," he also **gave them over to a reprobate mind.** They did not choose to keep God in their knowledge so he gave them up to "a reprobate mind," i.e., a mind disapproved by God. In the same manner in which these idolaters disapproved of God, God also abandoned them to a disapproving conscience. **to do those things which are not convenient**—i.e., "to have improper conduct." The expression in Greek indicates what "is offensive to man even according to the popular moral sense of the Gentiles, i.e., what even natural human judgment regards as vicious and wrong" (*kathekonta, TDNT*).

➤29 These Gentiles were **filled** with these vices. The expression "being filled" refers to a perfect passive participle and suggests a state of completion, meaning "filled to the point of overflowing." **fornication**—The word is not present in many ancient manuscripts. **wickedness**—may express "active wickedness" (as in Mark 7:22). **covetousness**—See Luke 12:15 and 1 Thess. 2:5. **maliciousness**— is an inward viciousness of disposition (see 1 Cor. 5:8). They are **full of envy, murder, debate, deceit, malignity,** [they are] **whisperers,**

➤30 **Backbiters, haters of God**—The last expression usually signifies "God-hated," which some commentators prefer here, in the sense of "abhorred by God." If so, the term expresses the detestableness of their character in his sight (cf. Prov. 22:14; Ps. 73:20). But the active sense of the term, which is adopted by the majority of expositors, agrees better with the context. The Gentiles are additionally **despiteful** [insolent], **proud** [arrogant], **boasters** [braggarts], **inventors of evil things** [new forms of vice].

➤31 **without understanding**—undiscerning in moral and spiritual things. **covenant breakers**—faithless.

➤32 In spite of all their sins, they know **the judgment** [decree] **of God, that they which commit such things are worthy of death.**

Their knowledge comes from the voice of conscience (2:14, 15). The expression "such things" translates a qualitative term and refers to the kind of things previously mentioned. Yet, these people **not only do** them, **but have pleasure**—i.e., consent to do (practice) them. They deliberately approve of such actions by encouraging and applauding others who do them. This is the climax of the apostle's charges against the heathen; and certainly, if the things are in themselves as black as possible, this settled and unblushing satisfaction of the practice of them must be regarded as the darkest feature of human depravity.

*Chapter* 2

## 1-16 BOTH JEWS AND GENTILES ARE CONDEMNED

Paul stresses here that the Jew is condemned as is the Gentile. From those outside the revelation of law, the apostle now turns to those within the pale of revealed religion, the self-righteous Jews. The Jews looked down upon the uncovenanted heathen as beyond the scope of God's mercies, within which they deemed themselves secure however inconsistent their lives might be. Bruce incisively states that "Paul's style is appropriate to the type of composition that the ancients called the *diatribe,* in which questions or objections are put into the mouth of an imagined critic in order to be demolished or answered." Barrett suggests that it is easier to follow Paul's arguments if the reader imagines him face-to-face with a heckler.

➤**1** Paul states bluntly that man, whoever he is, is without excuse in judging another; **for wherein thou judgest another, thou condemnest thyself; for thou that judgest doest the same things.** The Jew was constantly critical of Gentiles, but he was guilty of the same things for which he judged the Gentiles.

➤**2** The Jews do not question **the judgment of God,** recognizing that it rightly comes **against them which commit such things.** Therefore, they would surely agree with Paul's earlier condemnation of Gentiles. There could be no question concerning the righteousness of God in passing his judgment.

➤**3** The Jews so far would have agreed with Paul. However, Paul drives home the point of

his argument by the question, **thinkest thou this, O man, that judgest them which do such things, and doest the same, that thou shalt escape the judgment of God?** The Jew who is guilty of the same activity for which the Gentile stands under the judgment of God has no reason to expect anything less severe than God's acts in the case of the Gentile. Although the Jew might be prone to depend upon his national heritage, the NT abounds in evidence that this relationship to God does not exempt the Jew from divine judgment (cf. Matt. 3:9; Gal. 2:15).

➤**4** Paul warns the Jew lest he had presumed upon **the riches of** God's **goodness and forebearance and longsuffering.** Reminding the Jew that God's kindness is intended to bring him **to repentance,** he points out that the goodness could never become an escape from the reality of God's judgment. What appears to be indifference on God's part to sin is in reality due to his "long-suffering," which is intended to bring them to repentance.

➤**5 treasurest up** [storing up] . . . **wrath against the day of wrath and revelation of the righteous judgment of God**—i.e., wrath to come on the Jew in the day of wrath. What an awful idea is here expressed—that the sinner himself is amassing, like hoarded treasure, an ever-accumulating stock of divine wrath, to burst upon him in the day of revelation of the righteous judgment of God! This is not said of the reckless but of those who boasted of their purity of faith in life. (Cf. Isa. 13:6; Ezek. 30:3; Acts 2:20; 1 Cor. 1:8; 2 Cor. 1:14; 1 Thess. 5:2.)

➤**6** This verse reiterates the norm of divine judgment as defined in the NT. God judges **every man according to his deeds.**

➤**7-10** The substance of these verses is that the final judgment will be based upon character alone. **by patient continuance in well doing**—cf. Luke 8:15. This verse describes the enduring and progressive character of the new life.

➤**8 But unto them that are contentious** [factious], **and do not obey the truth**—referring to keen and determined resistance to the gospel, which Paul himself had painfully witnessed on the part of his own countrymen (see Acts 13:44-46; 17:5, 13; 18:6, 12; cf. 1 Thess. 2:15, 16). The expression "**indignation and wrath**" describes the nature of the judgment.

➤**9 Tribulation and anguish**—the effect of indignation and wrath on the sinner.

➤**11, 12** Verse 11 states that there is **no respect of persons with God**—i.e., no partiality. The term "partiality" is derived from a Greek expression translating an OT metaphor, "to lift up the face," meaning "to show favor to a person." As has been seen previously, the Jews claim favor from God inasmuch as they felt they could depend and rely upon their national heritage. **as many as have sinned**—Not "as many as have sinned at all," but "as many as are found in sin" at the judgment of the Great Day (as the entire context demonstrates). **without law**—without the advantage of a positive revelation. The Gentile is not without law although he does not possess the Mosaic Law. **shall also perish without law**—within the scope of a positive, written revelation. Therefore, Paul notes that every man is morally responsible unto God, whether he possesses the law or does not know the written law. Nonetheless, each individual is responsible to God.

➤**13-15 For not the hearers**—Concerning the Jews in whose ears the written law is continually resounding, the condemnation of as many of them as are found sinners at the last involves no difficulty. Concerning the heathen who are strangers to the law and its positive and written form: since they show how deeply it is engraven on their moral nature—which witnesses within them for righteousness and against iniquity, accusing and condemning them according as they violate or obey its stern dictates—their condemnation also for all the sin for which they live and die will carry its dreadful echo in their own conscience. Paul states that it is not enough merely to *hear* the law; an individual must also *do* the law. Paul is then insisting that all men have a standard for life; the Gentiles have the law of conscience, and the Jews have the written Torah. **their thoughts the mean while accusing or else excusing one another**—i.e., "their conflicting thoughts accuse or perhaps excuse them" (RSV). Some interpreters suggest that Paul means that at times their thoughts may accuse them, while at other times their thoughts may excuse them. However, Paul has made the point that every individual has a conscience, a moral faculty that knows the difference between right

and wrong, truth and untruth. Therefore, this "conscience" will either "accuse" or "excuse" him, depending upon his personal conduct.

➤**16** This verse resumes the thought of 2:12. Man's acquittal or condemnation will occur **in the day when God shall judge the secrets of men by Jesus Christ.** (See 1 Cor. 4:5.) The expression **"according to my gospel"** refers to Paul's teaching as a preacher of the gospel.

## 17-24 CONDEMNATION OF ISRAEL

The previous verses of this chapter have prepared the way for Paul to show that God's judgment is impartial and personal. He is now prepared to bring direct and personal charges against the Jews. It is the apostle's purpose to show that the Jews are just as guilty as the Gentiles.

➤**17 thou art called a Jew**—The apostle here emphasizes the nationality of his readers. The term "Jew" defines their race in distinction from the Gentiles; the term "Israelite" defines their relationship to God in religion; the term "Hebrew" implies their origin as well as their language. Paul points out that being called "a Jew" (the term means "one who is praised") is not enough in the sight of God. These people who relied upon **the law** (the written Mosaic system) would find that this reliance is not adequate.

➤**18** The apostle further notes that the Jews know **his will, and approvest the things that are more excellent.** Phillips translates the expression, "You are able . . . to appreciate moral values."

➤**19** Paul indicates that the Jew not only claims to have the ability of discernment between right and wrong and the shades of moral value but also claims to be **a guide of the blind, a light of them which are in darkness.** But this ability to teach "the blind" and to provide "light" to those who are in "darkness" will not suffice in the time of judgment. See Jesus' employment of the expression "a guide to the blind" in Matthew 15:14 and 23:16. The prominence of this phrase has led numerous interpreters to suggest that the phrase is proverbial in nature.

➤**20 An instructor of the foolish, a teacher of babes**—phrases that further identify the capability of the Jews as teachers. They looked upon the non-Jew as "foolish," or as "a child." But Paul drives home a penetrating argument when he reminds them that they have **the form** [embodiment] **of knowledge and of the truth in the law.** They are not left as the heathen to a vague conjecture concerning divine things, but God favored them with definite and precise information from heaven. It is important to remember that not only did the Jews have the Mosaic law, but their rabbis had taken this law and interpreted it in reference to every conceivable human situation and need. Still this minute knowledge and this interpretation did not save the Jews. The term "embodiment" is the translation of the Greek *morphosis,* implying the outline or delineation of the essential form. Bruce says that the Jew possessed "the formulation or embodiment of knowledge and truth."

➤**21, 22 Thou therefore which teachest another**—If the Jews have ability to teach others, will they not also teach themselves? **thou that abhorrest idols, dost thou commit sacrilege?**—i.e., do you rob temples? The Jews certainly abhorred idols, and it is implied in Acts 19:37 that the Jews were sometimes blamed for robbing temples. Josephus (*Antiquities,* 4.8.10ff.) records an incident occurring in A.D. 19 when some Jews of Rome, led by one who professed to be a teacher of the Jewish faith, persuaded a Roman lady, who had become a convert to Judaism, to make a significant contribution to the temple at Jerusalem. However, these Jews took the contribution for their own uses. It was because of this incident that Emperor Tiberius drove all resident Jews from the city.

➤**24** As a result of Jewish claims negated by personal conduct, **the name of God is blasphemed among the Gentiles through you.** This quote comes from Isaiah 52:5; Ezekiel 36:22. Bruce states, "Now it is not His people's misfortune, but their misconduct, that causes the Gentiles to conclude that the God of such people cannot be of much account. Members of the Qumran community were warned to be careful in their dealings with Gentiles, 'lest they blaspheme.' "

➤**25** Then speaking of the value of **circumcision,** Paul forcefully states that the rite is of value only **if thou keep the law.** The same concept is recorded in Galatians 5:3. The Gentile resented and despised the Jew for his emphasis upon this rite. But if the Jew breaks the law, then his **circumcision is made uncircumcision.** The rite revealed one's being within the covenant relationship with God, of which circumcision was the outward sign and seal. Paul meant that circumcision is of value only if the inward reality corresponds to the outward sign; otherwise, the rite is of no value.

➤**26-29** The following verses state this principle from a slightly different perspective, with reference to the Gentile. If the Gentile (the uncircumcised man) **keep**[s] **the righteousness** [righteous requirements] **of the law . . . his uncircumcision** is **counted for circumcision.** Therefore, it is not "circumcision" that matters, but man's relationship to the law, the will of God. If he keeps the law, cannot be right with God whether or not he is circumcised. Verses 27-29 logically set forth this principle. The Gentile who keeps the law condemns the Jew who breaks the law. The true Jew is not a man who is one outwardly, nor is true circumcision something external and physical. True circumcision is "a matter of the heart" (see Deut. 10:16; Jer. 4:4; 9:26; Ezek. 44:7). **in the spirit, and not in the letter**—i.e., "spiritual, not literal" (RSV). Note the experience of Cornelius (Acts 10), who though outside Judaism, yet came to the knowledge of the truth contained in it and manifested the grace of the covenant without the seal of circumcision. He thereby exemplified the character and walk of Abraham's children, though not called by the name of Abraham. Thus, this is but another way of announcing that God was about to show the insufficiency of the mere badge of the Abrahamic covenant by calling from among the Gentiles those who had never received the seal of circumcision (See Gal. 5:6). This interpretation is confirmed by 2:28, 29. In these last two verses Paul is insisting that the name "Jew" and the rite of "circumcision" were designed as outward symbols of a separation from the irreligious and ungodly world to a devotedness of heart and life to God. Where this is realized, the signs are full of significance; but where it is not, they are useless. **praise**—a word play on the term "Jew," derived from Judah, a tribal name linked with the Hebrew *yadah,* a term which means "to praise." (cf. Gen. 29:35; 49:8.)

Chapter 3

## 1-18 JEWISH OBJECTIONS ANSWERED

In this section Paul puts himself in the place of the Jew and proposes questions the Jew will likely use in objecting to Paul's statement concerning Jewish unrighteousness. The Jews would surely not permit the statements of Paul concerning condemnation of their "righteousness" to go unchallenged. The style of these verses is diatribe. Perhaps genuine debates lie behind these verses.

➤**1, 2 What advantage then hath the Jew?**—If the final judgment will turn solely on the state of the heart, and this may be as good in the Gentile *without* circumcision as in the Jew *within* the sacred enclosure of God's covenant, in what sense are we Jews better for all of our advantages? The answer is concisely stated: **Much** [in] **every way.** Paul then elaborates briefly on this major claim by noting: **chiefly** [firstly] . . . **unto them** [the Jews] **were committed the oracles of God.** The term translated "oracles" is the Greek term *logia* (cf. Acts 7:38; Heb. 5:12; 1 Pet. 4:11). This term refers to God's utterances on Sinai and his promises concerning the coming of the Messiah. The term denotes "divine communications" in general and is transferred to the Scriptures to express their oracular, divine, authoritative character. This first reason for Jewish advantage is never followed by a second reason.

➤**3** But Paul quickly proposes additional questions: **What if some did not believe? shall their unbelief make the faith of God without effect?** It is the unbelief of the great body of the nation at which the apostle points, but as it sufficed for his argument to put the supposition gently, he uses the word "some" to soften their prejudice. The answer to the question is found in 3:4.

➤**4** The expression translated "God forbid" should be rendered "May it never come to pass!" This is a favorite expression of the apostle and was used when he would not only repudiate a supposed consequence of his doctrine but express abhorrence of it. Hodge comments, "The Scriptures do not authorize such a use of God's name as must have been common among the English translators of the Bible." **every man a liar**—The faithlessness and false-

ness of man does not nullify the veracity of God (cf. 3:8; 1 Cor. 15:12, 34; Phil. 1:15). **That thou mightest be justified in thy sayings, and mightest overcome when thou art judged**—Paul used the Septuagint version of Psalm 51:4 here, instead of the Hebrew text. The Septuagint rendering changed the active voice to passive for the verb "judge." In what sense is God judged? God is questioned by men when he renders judgment. But God will overcome all the questions and accusations against him.

➤**5, 6** Still another objection is proposed, which may be paraphrased as follows: "It would appear, then, that the more faithless we are, so much the more illustrious will the fidelity of God appear; and in that case, for him to take vengeance upon us for our unfaithfulness would be (to speak as men profanely do) unrighteousness in God." A thought such as this would eliminate the possibility of all future judgment. This objection, the apostle states, is couched in the terminology of man. The Jew has asked, "Why not permit man to sin more and more in order to glorify God to a greater degree?" But Paul simply suggests that he will not argue with a man who thinks and reasons at the expense of his own conscience.

➤**7, 8** This objection is still a further illustration of the sentiment expressed in the last objection. Such reasoning amounts to this—which indeed we who preach salvation by free grace are slanderously accused of preaching—that the more evil we do, the more glory will redound to God—an unthinkable principle. The apostle, instead of refuting this principle, thinks it enough to hold it up to examination as one that shocks the moral sensitivity. Their **damnation** [judgment] **is just**—Paul declares that the man who reasons this way receives his just condemnation. In this section Paul has given the Scriptures a prominent place (3:1, 2). Moreover, he has noted that the doctrine of salvation by grace and the unchanging obligations of God's law have always been subject to the charge of inconsistency by those who do not know the truth. But in the midst of all the clouds and darkness that envelop the divine economy in this present state, as well as enveloping many of the truths of the Bible, such broad and deep principles as are here laid down and that shine in their own luster will be found in the anchor of our faith.

## 9-20 THE SCRIPTURE PROVES THAT THE JEW AS WELL AS THE GENTILE STANDS CONDEMNED

Paul's plan in this section of Romans now becomes obvious. In the section presently under consideration Paul shows that the Jews are condemned just as the Gentiles are condemned. Both groups are sinners. To establish his point, the apostle appeals to and employs the absolute authority of the Scriptures, which was universally accepted by the Jews.

➤**9 What then? are we [Jews] better than they?**—Paul's response is that the Jew was in no better condition even though he had received the oracles of God. The receiving of these oracles simply aggravated the Jewish guilt. Paul's sweeping statement is **for we have before proved both Jews and Gentiles, that they are all under sin.**

➤**10-12 As it is written**—in Psalm 14:1-3; 53:1-3. These statements of the psalmist were indeed suggested by particular manifestations of human depravity occurring under his own eye; but since this showed only what man, when unrestrained, is in his present condition, they were quite pertinent to the apostle's purpose. These verses do not admit the possibility that even one Jew or one Gentile is sinless before God.

## 13-18 MANKIND'S COMPLETE SINFULNESS

These verses reveal that the entire human personality is saturated in sin. Paul refers to the individual's **throat, tongue, lips, mouth, feet, and eyes.** In 3:10-12 the apostle has spoken in generalities, but here he directs his attention to particulars, employing different portions of Scripture passages speaking of depravity as it affects the different members of the body. His purpose seems to be to show how completely man is corrupted by sin.

➤**13 Their throat is an open sepulchre**—From Psalm 5:9. What proceeds out of their heart and finds vent in action through the throat is like the breath of an open grave. **with their tongues they have used deceit**—See Psalm 5:9. The **poison of asps is under their lips**—Psalm 140:3. "Lips," which are made by God to be useful in his kingdom (Prov. 10:21; Heb. 13:15), often are employed to secrete and to

spew deadly poison as one throws a dart toward a target.

➤**14 Even the mouth is full of cursing and bitterness.** This is reminiscent of James 3:6.

➤**15 Their feet are swift to shed blood**—See Proverbs 1:16; Isaiah 59:7. These are feet which should perform God's commandments (Ps. 119:32) but are employed to conduct man to deeds of darkest crime.

➤**16, 17** This is a supplementary statement concerning men's ways, suggested by what had been said concerning the "feet," and expresses the mischief and misery which men scattered in their path.

➤**18** The climactic accusation is found in the words: **There is no fear of God before their eyes** (from Ps. 36:1). These eyes should possess a reverential awe of God with whom man must come into relationship. How graphic is this picture of human depravity, finding its way through each organ of the body into the life! How small a part of the "desperate wickedness" that is within (Jer. 17:9) comes from the heart of man! (See Mark 7:21-23; Ps. 19:12.)

➤**19** In this verse Paul insists that the Scriptures are given for the purpose of stopping **every mouth** so that **all the world may become guilty before God.**

➤**20 by the law is the knowledge of sin**—See 4:15; 7:7; 1 John 3:4. How broad and deep does the apostle in this section lay the foundations of this great doctrine of justification by grace! In the disorder of man's whole nature, the consequent universality of human guilt, the condemnation by a breach of divine law, and the impossibility of justification before God by obedience to that violated law are emphasized. Only when these humiliating conclusions are accepted is man in a condition to appreciate and embrace the gospel of grace. "Truly, the law brings hopelessness, for it creates a consciousness of sin, a realization of what it means to God and man, to the Judge and to the judged" (Davidson and Martin).

## 21-26 GOD JUSTIFIES MEN THROUGH FAITH IN CHRIST

This section is given to a discussion of the righteousness of God and its application to the heart of man. It must be kept in mind that this is the way in which Paul himself was made right with God. Although he was a Pharisee of the Pharisees, he excelled among his contemporaries, and he had been taught by Gamaliel he could become right with God only by following God's method and conditions.

►21 the righteousness of God without the law is manifested—the "righteousness" of which Paul speaks is a righteousness that cannot be obtained by keeping the law (3:28; Gal. 2:16). Paul, here in Romans and also in Galatians, insists that the law is a tutor to bring man to God. The law reveals not only the requirements God makes of man, but likewise reveals unto man his shortcomings and his sinfulness. By the law and the prophets Paul means the OT Scriptures. Thus this justifying righteousness, though new, as only now fully disclosed, is an old righteousness predicted and foreshadowed in the OT. Thus the apostle insists that there is not a "new" way of becoming right with God, but rather it is the same way that was first revealed in the "law and the prophets."

►22, 23 the righteousness of God which is by faith of [in] Jesus Christ unto all and upon all them that believe—This explains the means whereby man appropriates this "righteousness of God." It must also be noted that this "faith" is to be placed in "Jesus Christ." Luther observes that this "righteousness" was brought nigh (near) "unto all" men and actually "upon all" believing men as their possession; however, most interpreters understand both statements as only a more emphatic way of saying that all believers, without distinction or exception, are put in possession of this gratuitous justification purely by faith placed "in Jesus Christ." The phrase "faith of (or, in) Jesus Christ" is ambiguous. The Greek case is the genitive and could be construed as either a subjective ("faith produced by Christ") or objective ("faith in Jesus Christ") genitive. there is no difference—Though men differ greatly in the nature and extent of their sinfulness, there is absolutely no difference between the best and the worst of men because all have sinned, and come short of the glory of God. Consequently, they lie under the wrath of God. To "come short of the glory of God" is to fail to earn his condemnation. The Greek term husterein, translated "come short," means "to fall behind," "to be inferior," "to suffer lack"

(cf. Matt. 19:20; 1 Cor. 8:8; 2 Cor. 11:5; Phil. 4:12). "Through sin man falls short of the idea which God had in view when he brought him into being" (Bruce). "All" come short of the praise and approval of God. The expression translated "all have sinned" is identical to the expression in Romans 5:12. The biblical background for our understanding of this verse is Genesis 1:26ff. Adam was created in the image of God, but he forfeited that honor when he disobeyed God. Davidson and Martin state, "Men generally, sprung from Adam's stock, have failed to reach their God-intended destiny and in that sense 'all fall short of the glory of God.' Only in the second Adam is the image restored. Rabbinic Judaism held that Adam, at his fall, lost the image of God." The term "glory" refers to the brightness and majesty which emanates from the character of God. This is the Shekinah glory mentioned frequently in the OT (Exod. 16:10; 24:16ff.; 29:43; 33:18, 22). This same glory was embodied in Jesus, the Word (see John 1:14; 2 Cor. 3:18; 4:6).

►24 Justification by his grace is construed by the apostle as a gift given through the redemption that is in Christ Jesus. Man does not do anything on his part to deserve justification. The clause "through the redemption that is in Christ Jesus" is most important, teaching us that though justification is quite gratuitous, it is not a mere decree of the divine will but is based on a "redemption," that is, "the payment of a ransom" accomplished by Christ's death. The Greek term for "redemption" (apolutrōsis) means "a release effected by payment of a ransom," and therefore means "redemption, emancipation, or deliverance."

►25, 26 In these verses Paul describes Jesus as a propitiation [or, expiation]; the term "expiation" (Gk. hilastērion) is the neuter adjective derived from the Greek verb hilaskomai, a term that has three meanings: (1) "to placate or appease"; (2) "to be propitious and merciful"; or (3) "to make propitiation for someone." Luke 18:13 and 1 John 2:2 reveal NT usages of the last two meanings. Therefore, the term primarily carries with it the concept of the expiation of man's sin through the mercy of God brought by the atoning death of Christ. But since Paul also speaks of God's wrath, it must also refer to the conciliation of God's anger by means of a sacrifice. Since the word *hilastērion* was used in the Septuagint to translate the Hebrew word for "mercy seat," Paul is here presenting Christ as the antitype of that place where God and man can meet because of Christ's shed blood. **through faith in his blood**—Paul again emphasizes the fact that this "expiation" is accepted by faith in the shed blood of Jesus. God has chosen to redeem man by a redemption that is once-for-all, not a redemption that must be repeated annually. **to declare** [show] **his righteousness for the remission of sins that are past, through the forbearance of God**—The sense of this statement is made clearer in the RSV: "This was to show God's righteousness, because in his divine forbearance he had passed over his former sins." God, in his forbearance, passed over the sins committed during the time of the old economy, before Christ came "to put away sin by the sacrifice of himself." The expression "because in his divine forbearance" indicates that God did not *remit sin* but rather restrained himself from punishing it. So he passed by sin, until an adequate atonement for it could be made. And thus not imputing sin, God was righteous, but he was not seen to be so; there was no manifestation of his righteousness in doing so under the old economy. But now that God can "set forth" Christ as a "propitiation [for sin] through faith in his blood," the righteousness of his procedure in passing by the sins of believers before and now remitting them is declared, brought fully out to the view of the whole world. "The death of Christ, then, is the means by which God does away with his people's sins—not symbolically, as in the ritual of Leviticus 16 in which the material mercy seat figured, but *really* and *really* in a twofold sense; the sin has been removed not only from the believer's conscience, on which it lay as an intolerable burden, but from the presence of God" (Bruce).

➤**26 that he might be just, and the justifier of him which believeth in Jesus**—Glorious paradox! "Just in punishing," and "merciful in pardoning," we can understand; but "just in justifying the guilty" startles us. Propitiation through faith in Christ's blood resolves the paradox and harmonizes the discordant elements. For in that "God hath made him to be sin for us who knew no sin," justice

has full satisfaction; and in that "we are made the righteousness of God in him," mercy has her heart's delight! Note: (1) One way of a sinner's justification is taught in the OT and the NT alike. (2) Since there is no difference in the need, so there is none in the liberty to appropriate the provided salvation. The best people need to be saved by Jesus Christ; and the worst need that same salvation. On this common ground, all saved sinners meet and will stand forever. (3) It is on the blood of Jesus Christ, as the one propitiatory sacrifice God has set forth, that the faith of the sinner fastens for deliverance from wrath. Though he knows that he is "justified freely, by God's grace," it is only because it is "through the redemption that is in Christ Jesus" that he is able to find peace and rest even in this. (4) The strictly accurate view of the believers under the OT is not that of a company of pardoned men, but of men whose sins were passed over awaiting a future expiation in the fullness of time (see Luke 9:31; Heb. 9:15; 11:39, 40).

27-31 SOME INFERENCES FROM THE FOREGOING DOCTRINES

Paul notes that boasting is excluded by these doctrines and that there is no other way to justification but by faith.

➤**27, 28 Where is boasting then? It is excluded. By what law** [principle]? **of works? Nay: but by the law** [principle] **of faith**—The unavoidable tendency to try to gain acceptance with God by our own works produces a spirit of "boasting." But the fact that our faith produces righteousness manifestly and entirely excludes boasting.

➤**29, 30 Is he the God of the Jews only?**—The way of salvation must be one equally suited to the whole family of fallen men. **is he not also of the Gentiles? Yes, of the Gentiles also: Seeing it is one God, which shall justify the circumcision by faith, and uncircumcision through faith**—This is a varied statement of the same truth for greater emphasis (see 3:22).

➤**31 Do we then make void** [destroy] **the law through faith?**—Paul means, "Does this doctrine of justification by faith then dissolve the obligation of the law? If so, it cannot be of God. But away with such a thought, for it does just the reverse." **we establish the law**—The glory of God's law, in its eternal and immutable obligations, is then only fully apprehended by the sinner and enthroned in the depths of his soul when he believes that Jesus was made sin for him and sees himself made the righteousness of God in Jesus. Thus, we do not make void the law through faith; we rather establish the law. It will be observed that as important as this objection is, and opening as it did so noble a field for the illustration of the peculiar glory of the gospel, the apostle does no more here than indignantly repel it, intending at a subsequent stage of his argument (chap. 6) to resume and discuss it at length.

*Chapter* 4

## 1-25 AN ILLUSTRATION OF THE FOREGOING DOCTRINE OF JUSTIFICATION BY FAITH

Paul calls upon illustrations from the OT Scriptures. These illustrations revolve basically around Abraham and his experiences.

➤**1 What shall we say then that Abraham our father** [some ancient manuscripts read, "forefather"], **as pertaining to the flesh, hath found?**—Abraham was selected by Paul as the outstanding OT example of justification by faith. Perhaps we are to understand here that Paul imagines that he is still confronted by an objector who rejects the concept of justification by faith. The objector quizzes the apostle, asking where Abraham fits into this discussion. Is the patriarch to be considered as a man justified by faith, or a man justified by works? The point indeed is crucial, but the apostle Paul demonstrates beyond any question that Abraham was justified by faith and not by works of law. Reverting to Genesis 15:6, Paul proceeds to show that Abraham was justified by faith. This case and particular references were chosen by Paul because the rabbis used this text as a basis for their doctrine of merit. "What then shall we say about Abraham, our forefather according to the flesh?"—This question asks, "What has Abraham gained by all his natural efforts or legal obedience?"

➤**2 For if Abraham were justified by works, he hath whereof to glory** [boast]; **but not before God**—If works were the ground of Abraham's justification, he would have ade-

quate reason for boasting; but as it is perfectly certain that he has none in the sight of God, it follows that Abraham could not have been justified by works. The words of the OT agree with this statement of Paul.

➤**3 For what saith the scripture? Abraham believed God, and it was counted** [reckoned] **unto him for righteousness**—See Genesis 15:6. Some expositors make this to mean that Abraham's act of believing was accepted by God as a substitute for complete obedience. But this is at variance with the whole spirit and letter of the apostle's teaching. Throughout this entire argument, faith is set in direct opposition to works in the matter of justification—and even in the next two verses. The meaning, therefore, cannot possibly be that the mere *act* of believing—which is as much a work as any other piece of command duty (John 6:29; 1 John 3:23)—was counted to Abraham for all obedience. The meaning is that Abraham believed in the promise which embraced Christ (Gen. 12:3; 15:5, etc.), just as we believe in Christ himself. In both cases faith is merely the instrument that puts us in the blessing gratuitously bestowed.

➤**4, 5** The wages of the laborer are not construed as a gift (of **grace**), but as his **debt** (or, reward). **But to him that worketh not, but believeth on him that justifieth the ungodly, his faith is counted** [reckoned] **for righteousness**—The man who casts himself upon the mercy of the justifying God, realizing that he deserves only condemnation, is justified by God's grace.

➤**6-8 Even as David also describes**—in Psalm 32:1, 2. In these verses, Paul quotes David's words to affirm the blessedness of being justified and forgiven by faith.

➤**9-11** Paul thus reasons in these verses that Abraham's faith was reckoned as **righteousness** prior to the patriarch's circumcision. Circumcision then is not a means of righteousness, but rather is to be seen as the **sign** or **seal of the righteousness of the faith which he had yet being uncircumcised.** The purpose was to make Abraham **the father of all them that believe, though they be not circumcised; that righteousness might be imputed** [reckoned] **unto them also.**

➤**12** But Abraham also is to be seen as **the father of circumcision to them who are not** of the circumcision only, but who also walk in the steps of that faith of our father Abraham, which he had being yet uncircumcised. Therefore, Abraham stands to every age as the parent—the model man of justification by faith. The expression "walk in the steps" in Greek means "to walk in line," "to keep in step with." The expression was used for military marching. Abraham is here depicted as leading the march; and all who believe, whether Jew or Gentile, follow his steps.

➤13 The promise . . . to Abraham—This is simply an enlargement of the foregoing reasoning, applying to the law what had just been said of circumcision. The promise given to Abraham, that he should be the heir of the world, did not come through the law, but through the righteousness of faith. In other words, this inheritance did not come by virtue of obedience to the Mosaic law but by virtue of his simple faith in the divine promise.

➤14 If the blessing is to belong to the adherents of the law, then faith is made void, and the promise made of none effect. The whole divine method is then subverted.

➤15 This verse states the ground for Paul's reasoning. the law worketh [produces] wrath; therefore, it has nothing to give to those who break it but condemnation and vengeance. for where no law is, there is no transgression— The law itself produces transgression because it cannot be kept. So, law and transgression cannot exist without each other.

➤16, 17 These two verses give a general summary of the preceding verses. Justification is by faith in order that its purely gracious character may be seen, and that all who follow in the steps of Abraham's faith—whether of his natural seed or not—may be assured of like justification with the parent-believer. It is by this faith that Abraham becomes the father of us all, both of those who are Gentiles and those who are Jews. Paul again quoted from Genesis, this time 17:5, in order to justify his calling Abraham "the father of us all." Since Abraham is "the father of us all," we may be assured that in doing as he did we shall also be treated as he was. Abraham believed a God who quickeneth the dead, and calleth those things which be not as though they were. What Abraham was required to believe was beyond the workings of nature; therefore, his faith was forced to

fasten upon God's power to surmount physical incapacity and call into being what did not exist. But since God made the promise, Abraham believed him in spite of those obstacles. This is still further illustrated in the following verses.

➤18, 19 Who against hope—when no ground for hope appeared. believed in hope— that is, he cherished the believing expectation. that he might become the father of many nations, according to that which was spoken, So shall thy seed be—See Genesis 22:17, "as the stars of heaven . . . " Abraham paid no attention to those physical obstacles and liabilities, both in himself and in Sarah, which might seem to render the fulfillment hopeless. Although he realized that he and his wife were beyond the age when husband and wife normally became parents, he did not become weak in faith, he considered not his own body now dead—According to all the earliest manuscripts, this should read, "he considered his own body now dead." Despite his deadness and the deadness of Sarah's womb, Abraham believed that God was able to make his own word good. Perhaps there was every reason for Abraham to vacillate in his attitude toward God's promises, but he refused to do so.

➤20 He staggered not at the promise of God through unbelief; but was strong in faith, giving glory to God—The glory which Abraham's faith gave to God consisted in this: No difficulties shook him because he was firm in the persuasion of God's ability to fulfill his promise.

➤22 This verse stands as a summary of this section, as if Paul is saying, "Let all then take notice that this was not because of anything meritorious in Abraham but merely because he so believed God." The patriarch's faith was imputed [reckoned] . . . for righteousness. It is readily seen that the apostle concludes the argument on the premise with which it all began, that faith was imputed to him for righteousness (4:3).

➤23, 24 These verses apply the whole argument of Abraham's faith and its results to the Christian. Paul insists that these things were not recorded as mere historical facts, but as an illustration, for all time, of God's method of justification by faith. So, the promise was effected in Abraham's case, and it will be in ours also. The requisite to this reckoning is faith. Abraham believed that God would raise up the Seed in whom all nations should be blessed; to enjoy this blessing promised to Abraham, the contemporary man simply must exercise the same quality of faith as did the patriarch.

➤**25 Who was delivered for our offences, and was raised again for our justification**— Christ's resurrection is the divine assurance that he has put away sin through his sacrifice. The resurrection is also the crowning of his whole work; our justification is fitly connected with that glorious act.

*Chapter* **5**

## 1-11 THE EFFECTS OF JUSTIFICATION BY FAITH

Paul has now established the fact that man is justified by faith, not by works. He has pointed out that Abraham was justified by his belief in God even before the rite of circumcision was given. Inasmuch as he has offered proof of this doctrine, the apostle now reaps its fruits, reserving the full consideration of this topic to another stage of the argument, contained in chapter 8. Some interpreters view chapter 5 as a devotional discussion based upon Paul's personal experience with God. However, a close examination indicates that the theme of justification by faith has been developed further in this chapter. It is significant that Paul uses the first person plural personal pronoun (*we*) in this discussion, and therefore identifies himself with all believers.

➤**1** The word "**therefore**" is always a significant term in interpretation. In Paul's usage it indicates that what he is about to write is based upon that which he has previously written. Granted that we are **justified by faith,** certain truths are evident. It is with these truths that Paul now concerns himself. **we have peace with God**—This is the reading in an early third-century manuscript (designated 0220) and in two other early manuscripts—Codex Sinaiticus and Codex Vaticanus (but both these manuscripts show this reading in the handwriting of a later corrector). Other early manuscripts read, "let us have peace with God." (These include the original text of the

Sinaiticus and the Vaticanus.) One reading could have been easily mistaken for the other because they differ by only one letter: omicron/omega. One word means "we have peace," and the other, "let us have peace." If Paul originally used the subjective form, he was calling upon the believers to realize and appropriate their peace with God. If Paul originally used the indicative form, he was asserting that the believers do in fact have peace with God. **Peace** is first the change in God's relationship to us, and next, as a consequence, a change in our relationship toward him. God, on the one hand, has "reconciled us to himself by Jesus Christ" (2 Cor. 5:18); on the other hand, we, setting our seal to this, "are reconciled to God" (2 Cor. 5:20). The "propitiation" is the meeting place. There the controversy on both sides terminates in an honorable and eternal "peace."

➤**2** It is through Jesus that **we have access by faith into this grace wherein we stand.** (The phrase "by faith" does not appear in the two earliest manuscripts.) The expression "have access" in Greek was often used in connection with introducing someone into the presence of a king. Through Christ's work we have gained his favor with God; he leads us to God (Eph. 2:18; 3:12). To that same faith that first gave us "peace with God" we owe our introduction into that permanent standing in the favor of God justified men enjoy. **we . . . rejoice**—i.e., we boast. **in** [on] **hope of the glory of God**—i.e., we boast on the basis of our hope of participating in God's glorification of his many sons (see 8:18, 19, 29, 30). Not by our own merit have we entered into this favor with God, but through the merit of our Savior.

➤**3** This verse gives still another result of being justified by faith: **we glory** [boast] **in tribulations . . . knowing that tribulation worketh patience** [or, endurance]—The Christian is able to rejoice in suffering because suffering brings endurance, "the ability to remain beneath the load" (according to the Gk.). Suffering and endurance bring many valuable Christian qualities.

➤**4 patience** [endurance], **experience** [proven worth] **. . . hope**—Endurance—the ability to remain beneath the load—is the quiet endurance of that which we cannot but wish removed. Christians need to see that trials are the required discipline of God's children, are but for a definite period, and are not sent without abundant promises of "songs in the night." If such be the "endurance" that suffering "tribulation" works, it is no wonder that endurance works proven worth (or, character—the Gk. word designates that which has been tried and found acceptable), and that proven worth produces hope. This "hope" anticipates the glory of God as that which God has prepared for us. Thus we have hope in two distinct ways and at two successive stages of the Christian life: first, immediately upon believing, along with the sense of peace and abiding access to God (5:1); next, after the reality of this faith has been "proved," particularly by the patient endurance of trials that test it. We first obtain it by looking away from ourselves to the Lamb of God, next by "looking unto Jesus, the author and perfecter of our faith."

➤5 **hope maketh not ashamed**—This hope does not put to shame, as empty hopes do, because this "hope" is a confident expectation of God's fulfilling his promises in and through Jesus Christ. Hope gives confidence **because the love of God is shed abroad** [poured] **in our hearts by the Holy Ghost** [Spirit] **which is given unto us.** The expression "love of God" (a subjective genitive) means "God's love for man"—as most expositors agree. This "love" is infused into men's hearts (cf. John 7:38; Titus 3:5, 6). This infusion comes by the working of the Spirit. That work began at the great Pentecostal effusion, which is viewed as the formal giving of the Spirit to each believer for all time. It is as if the apostle had said, "And how can this hope of glory, which as believers we cherish, put us to shame? It cannot put us to shame when we feel God himself given to us through his Spirit, drenching our hearts in sweet, all-subduing sensations of his wondrous love to us in Christ Jesus." This leads the apostle to speak exaltingly of the amazing character of that love.

➤6-8 In 5:6-11, the apostle discusses the security of the believer. The security is guaranteed by the death of Jesus and by his resurrected life. Paul speaks of God's love for the unworthy by describing the time of this love's manifestation—**when we were yet without strength.** We were powerless to deliver ourselves, and so we were on the verge of perishing. **in due time**

**Christ died for the ungodly**—The apostle underscores the fact that Christ's death was at the appointed time. Three signal properties of God's love are here given: First, "Christ died for the ungodly," whose character was far from meriting any interposition in their behalf, who were altogether repulsive in the eyes of God. Second, he did this, "while we were yet without strength," with nothing between us and perdition but that divine compassion. Third, he did this "in due time," when it was most fitting that it should take place (cf. Gal. 4:4). The apostle proceeds to illustrate the two former properties that he mentions. **For scarcely for a righteous man will one die**—i.e., one will not die for a man of unexceptionable character. **Yet peradventure for a good man some would even dare to die**—i.e., a man who is distinguished for goodness, a benefactor to society, besides being unexceptionable. It is incorrect to make the "righteous man" and the "good man" one and the same. This is the position of Calvin. But the apostle obviously is making a contrast between these two individuals. Barrett affirms this: "You would scarcely bring yourself to die for a righteous man, would you? Well, perhaps for a really good man you might . . . . But now see what Christ has done. We were neither good nor righteous, but still sinners when he died for us." **God commendeth**—He sets off and displays (in glorious contrast with all that men will do for each other) **his love toward us, in that, while we were yet sinners, Christ died for us**—We were not in a state of positive "goodness" nor even of "negative righteousness," but on the contrary, we were "sinners," a state God despises. Yet, his Son "died for us." If anyone asks how man knows that God loves him, Paul responds with this answer: it was while we were sinners that Christ gave his life for us; the cross proves God's love for lost men.

➤9 **Much more then, being now justified by his blood, we shall be saved from wrath through him**—The apostle's usage of the expression "much more" continues his declaration of the security of the Christian's righteousness. God's love toward undeserving and rebellious sinners is tested by the sacrificial death of his Son in our behalf. To be saved by him from the wrath of God denotes the whole work of Christ toward believers, beginning with the moment of justification when the wrath of God is turned away from them and continuing until the Judge on the great white throne shall discharge that wrath on them that "obey not the gospel of our Lord Jesus Christ" (2 Thess. 1:8).

➤**10 For if, when we were enemies, we were reconciled to God by the death of his Son, much more, being reconciled, we shall be saved by his life**—If the Savior shed his blood for persons who were actually God's enemies, how **much more** will he gladly give his divine life to those who are now his friends. If God achieved our reconciliation by the sacrificial offering of his Son, **much more** is he able to keep the believer in peace with himself through the resurrection of his Son. If the Father is able to justify us sinners, it is beyond question and doubt that he is also able to accomplish our sanctification—for we have not only Christ's saving death but also his saving life.

➤**11 not only so, but we also joy in God through our Lord Jesus Christ, by whom we have now received the atonement**—better translated, "reconciliation." "Reconciliation" is the translation of the Greek word *katallagē*, which means "change" or "exchange." When used in relationships between people, the term implies a change in attitude on the part of both individuals, a change from enmity to friendship. When used to describe the relationship existing between God and man, the term then implies the change of attitude on the part of both man and God. The needed change on the part of man is obvious, but some argue that the change needed on the part of God is not so obvious. But inherent in the doctrine of justification is the changed attitude of God toward the sinner. Several concepts relative to this section are worthy of notice. (1) Justification makes possible the entrance to a permanent standing in divine favor and a triumphant expectation of future glory. There is no other peace worthy of the name, and as those who are strangers to it rise not to the enjoyment of such high fellowship with God, so they have neither any taste of it nor desire after it. (2) Since only believers possess the true secret of patience under trials, and trials divinely sent afford the opportunity of evidencing their faith by the grace of patience under them, they should "count it all joy" (5:3, 4; see also James 1:2, 3). (3) As used

in the NT, the term "hope" is not a lower degree of faith or assurance, but means "the confident expectation of future good." The term itself presupposes faith, and what faith assures us will be ours, hope accordingly expects. (4) The Holy Spirit produces in the soul the full conviction and joyful consciousness of the love of God displayed in Christ Jesus toward sinners and toward ourselves in particular. (5) The justification of sinful man is not in virtue of his amendment, but rather because and through the blood of God's Son; therefore, while this is expressly affirmed in 5:9, our reconciliation to God by the "death of his Son," affirmed in 5:10, is but a variety of the same statement. In both, the result is the restoration of the sinner to a right standing in the presence of God.

## 12-21 COMPARISON AND CONTRAST BETWEEN ADAM AND CHRIST IN THEIR RELATIONSHIP TO THE HUMAN FAMILY

This profound section has occasioned an immense amount of critical and theological discussion in which almost every point and clause has been contested. The apostle basically points out that justification is the solution to the whole sin problem. Bruce, entitling this section "The old and the new solidarity," says, "The portrayal of Christ as the last Adam, the counterpart of the first Adam, is a prominent feature of Paul's Christology. It is not peculiar to him among the NT writers, and it may not even have been original with him, but he develops it more fully than any other, especially in this section of Romans and in discussion of resurrection in 1 Corinthians 15:22, 45-49." Bruce further writes, "Adam is for him a 'figure'—a counterpart or type—of Christ. As death entered the world through Adam's disobedience, so new life comes in through Christ's obedience. As Adam's sin involves his posterity and guilt, so Christ's righteousness is credited to his people." Davidson and Martin state that the typological contrast that Paul draws between Adam and Christ has a twofold objective. This typology indicates how the activities of one individual can affect the lives of others who are intimately and vitally connected with the first, and Paul employs the fall of Adam "as a foil to set forth the excellence of God's renewal of lost humanity in Christ."

These interpreters further note that two exegetical methods known in the Judaism of Paul's day are prevalent in the apostle's interpretation of this passage. (1) In the principle of solidarity Adam represents the whole of mankind. Employing this principle, Paul extends it to the conception of "the whole Christ," meaning that Christ and his people are one whole in God. (2) Paul enunciates the principle from his Jewish faith of th close connection existing between events at the beginning of time and the setting right of the world's wrongs and inconsistencies at the end of the age. This principle is known as *restitutio in integrum*. The principle allowed the apostle to teach that even as the old world had been marred by Adam's sin and subsequent fall, so the new world would be altered by Christ's obedience to God.

➤**12 Wherefore**—actually, "therefore"; it refers back to the whole preceding argument. **as by one man sin entered into the world**— Sin is viewed here as a principle, not an action. This sin is personified: it entered the world (5:12), reigned in death (5:21), can lord it over a person (6:14), spiritually mortify a person (6:14), and dwell in a person (7:17, 20). Paul uses the Greek preposition *dia* (through) to express the idea of Adam's sin serving as a channel for death to enter into mankind. Death also is depicted as a personified substance (called "the death" in Gk.). **death passed upon** [spread into] **all men, for that all have sinned**—The point Paul makes here is that "all men sinned" in that one man's first sin. Thus death reaches every individual of the human family as a penalty to man himself. Here we would have expected the apostle to finish his sentence perhaps in this manner: "Even so, by one man righteousness has entered into the world, and life by righteousness." But instead of this, we have a digression extending five verses for the purpose of illustrating the important statement of 5:12; and it is only at 5:18 that the comparison is resumed and finished. The following statement from Bruce is helpful: "It is not simply because Adam is the ancestor of mankind that all are said to have sinned in his sin (otherwise it might be argued that because Abraham believed God all his descendants are automatically involved in his belief); it is because Adam is mankind." Therefore, the apostle is stating very bluntly and overtly that all men are involved in Adam's sin, and consequently, all men sinned in him.

➤**13, 14 For until** [the time of] **the law sin was in the world**—Paul is referring to the period from Adam until the time the law was given to Moses. During this time, God continued to treat men as sinners although the law had not been given to Moses. Sin had gained an entry through Adam and death followed. The point Paul is making is that sin existed prior to the giving of the law; men continued to sin and thus died before this time. **but sin is not imputed** [reckoned] **when there is no law**— Therefore there must have been a law during that period because sin was then imputed as the apostle is to show. The thought seems to be that sin continues to manifest itself as sin and disobedience, even though there are no specific laws for man to transgress. Nonetheless, the very attitude and character of man shows that he is a sinner and proves him to be so, apart from the existence of a law. The very fact that men continued to die is indicative of the fact that they continued to sin even prior to the giving of the law. Before the giving of the Mosaic law, death reigned from the time of Adam, **even over them that had not sinned after the similitude of Adam's transgression, who is the figure** [type] **of him that was to come.** Who are these individuals over whom death reigned? This is a much-debated question. Augustine, Beza, and Hodge, for example, insist that death reigned over infants, who being guiltless of actual sin, may be said not to have sinned in the way that Adam did. But why should infants be especially connected with a period "from Adam to Moses" since they die alike in every period? And if the apostle meant to express here the death of infants, why has he done it so enigmatically? Besides, the death of infants is comprehended in the universal mortality on account of the first sin, so emphatically expressed in 5:12; what need then is there to specify it here? And why, if not necessary, should we presume it to be meant here unless the language unmistakably should point to it, which it certainly does not? The meaning then must be that "death reigned from Adam to Moses, even over those whose sins were not like the transgression of Adam." They did not transgress a specific positive commandment that threatened death to the disobedient. In this case, the particle "even" simply explains what it was that made the case for those who died from Adam to Moses worthy of particular notice—namely, that all who lived between the time of Adam and Moses had no positive threatening of death for transgression; nonetheless death reigned over them. The expression "who was a type of the one who was to come" means that Adam is a type of Christ—the first Adam being a type of the last Adam (see 1 Cor. 15:45, 47). Both Adam and Christ are here presented in their public character, as representative men.

➤**15 But not as the offence, so also is the free gift**—i.e., the two cases present points of contrast as well as resemblance. It is these points that the apostle now takes up. **For if through the offence of one many be dead, much more the grace of God, and the gift by grace, which is by one man, Jesus Christ, hath abounded unto many**—By "many" is meant the mass of mankind represented respectively by Adam and Christ, as opposed not to a few, but to "the one" who represented them. By "the free gift" is meant (as in 5:17) the glorious gift of justifying righteousness; this is expressly distinguished from "the grace of God," as the effect from the cause; and both are said to "abound" toward us in Christ—in what sense will appear in the next two verses. And the "much more" of the one case and the other does not mean that we get **much more** of good by Christ than of evil by Adam (for it is not a case of quantity at all). Rather, it means that we have much more reason to expect, or it is much more agreeable to our idea of God, that the many should be benefited by the merit of one than that they should suffer for the sin of one. And if the latter has happened, "much more" may we assure ourselves of the former. Paul has been contrasting what has happened in the human race because of Adam and what has occurred because of Christ. A single act on the part of each influenced the whole human race. The contrast now follows. Death is the end result of Adam's sin; the end result of Christ's righteousness is life. Calvin noted a natural inference from these words is that a greater gift belonged to humanity because of God's grace in Christ than our liability because of Adam's sin. Calvin's argument was that if Adam's fall produced sin in the human race, the grace of

God was much more effective in bringing benefit and blessings of salvation to many. This is true because Christ's gift is more powerful than Adam's liability.

➤**16 And not as it was by one that sinned, so is the gift**—i.e., "And the free gift is not like the effect of that one man's sin." This is another point Paul is compelled to mention. The logical statement follows: **for the judgment was by one** [offense] **to condemnation, but the free gift is of many offences unto justification.** This is a glorious point of contrast. The condemnation by Adam was for one sin; but the justification by Christ is an absolution, not only from the guilt of that first offense, mysteriously attached to every individual of the human race, but from the countless offenses which, as a germ lodged in the bosom of every child of Adam, it multiplied into all of humanity. This is the meaning of "grace abounding toward us in the abundance of the gift of righteousness." It is a grace not only rich in its character but also rich in detail. It is a "righteousness" not only rich in a complete justification of the guilty, condemned sinner but in its extensiveness, leaving not one sin of any of the justified uncancelled. This grace is so expansive that it is efficacious in redeeming man from sin though he is loaded with myriads of offenses.

➤**17 For if by one man's offence, death reigned by one** [man]—if death came into the human race because of Adam's sin—**much more they which receive abundance of grace and of the gift of righteousness shall reign in life by one, Jesus Christ**—We have here the two ideas involved in 5:15 and 16 sublimely combined into one. The apostle does this quite naturally, as if the subject had grown as he advanced in his comparison of the two cases. Here, for the first time in this section, he speaks of that life that springs out of justification in contrast with the death that springs from sin and follows condemnation. Paul is speaking in terms of life in its widest sense—life in the whole man and throughout the whole duration of human existence, the life of a blissful and loving relationship with God, and the life of Christ imparted to his believers. This is the life Christians reign in. It is worthy of note also that while he says "death reigned over" us through Adam, he does not say life "reigns over us" through Christ. This would seem to invest this new life with the very attribute of death—that of malignant tyranny over its victims. Nor does he say life reigns in us, which would obstensibly have been a scriptural idea. While freedom and might are implied in the figure of "reigning," "life" is represented as a glorious territory or atmosphere of that reign. And by reverting to the idea of 5:16, as to the "many offenses" whose complete pardon shows "the abundance of grace and the gift of righteousness," the whole statement is to this effect: "If one man's offense let loose against us the tyrant power of death to hold us as its victims in helpless bondage, much more, God's abounding grace in Christ makes possible our possessing a life divinely owned and legally secured, reigning in exultant freedom and unchallenged might, through that other matchless One, Jesus Christ!" By this "gift of righteousness" Paul means the gift of justification, the righteousness God bestows upon those who believe in him.

➤**18 Therefore**—Now at length he resumed the unfinished comparison of 5:12 in order to give his discourse a proper conclusion. **as by the offence of one judgment came upon all men to condemnation; even so by the righteousness of one the free gift came upon all men unto justification of life**—Paul here expresses the statement of 5:12 in a more concentrated and vivid form. Christ's death is the one righteous act that reversed the one disobedient act of Adam. As a result of Christ's righteousness, we get the free gift of being justified (made right) with God and receiving God's eternal life. Our justification entitles us to the rightful possession and enjoyment of the divine, eternal life.

➤**19 so by the obedience of one shall many be made** [constituted] **righteous**—The "obedience" of Christ involves the entire work of Christ in its "obedient" character—leading ultimately to death on the cross. Jesus himself represents even his death as a great act of obedience to the Father. (Cf. John 10:18, where Jesus indicates that the Father gave him the right to lay down and resume his life.) The vital word "made" does not signify "to work a change" upon a person or thing but "to constitute or ordain," as can be seen from all the places where it is used. Accordingly, it is intended here to express that judicial act which

constitutes men as sinners by virtue of their connection with Adam and constitutes believers as righteous by virtue of their connection with Christ. The change of tense from the past to the future—"shall be constituted righteous"—delightfully expresses the enduring character of the act and of the economy to which such acts belong in contrast to the forever-past ruin of believers in Adam. The "all men" of 5:18 and the "many" of 5:19 are the same party, though viewed under slightly different aspects. In the latter case, the contrast is between the **one** representative (Adam-Christ) and the **many** whom he represented; in the former case, it is between the one *head* (Adam-Christ) and the *human race,* affected for death and life respectively by the actings of that one. Only in this latter case it is the redeemed family of man that is alone in view; it is humanity that is actually lost, but also is actually saved, as ruined and recovered. But those who refuse to cooperate with the high purpose of God to constitute his Son a "second Adam," the head of a new race, have no place in this section of the epistle. Paul's sole object here is to show how God repairs in the second Adam the evil that was done by the first. Therefore, the doctrine of universal salvation has no place here or elsewhere in the NT. Surely it is true, according to the teachings of Jesus concerning the final judgment, that a part of mankind will not be saved; this is not the aspect in which the subject is here presented. It is totals that are compared and constrasted; and it is the same total in two successive conditions—namely, the human race as ruined in Adam and as recovered in Christ. This one principle must be kept in mind in the interpretation of this difficult passage.

➤**20** The Jew may object, stating, "If the whole purposes of God toward men center in Adam and Christ, where does 'the law' enter and what is its use?" Paul answers this hypothetical question by noting that **the law entered, that the offence might abound.** The word "entered" in Greek means "to enter along side," "to come into a state of things already existing." Hence, it suggests an incidental entrance. Therefore, the promulgation of the law at Sinai was no primary or essential feature of the divine plan, but it was "added" (Gal. 3:19) for a subordinate purpose—the more fully to reveal the evil occasioned by Adam, and the need and glory of the remedy brought by Christ. The expression "that the offence might abound" suggests that the "law came in" for the purpose of multiplying "the offence" (or, "trespass"). But what "trespass"? In this section "trespass" has only one meaning; it is the trespass of Adam, multiplied by his descendants. The law was given to expose men's sin and to show them their need of salvation. Denney notes that "the offense is multiplied because the law, encountering the flesh, evokes its natural antagonism to God, and so stimulates it into disobedience." **But where sin abounded** [was multiplied], **grace did much more abound**—The comparison here is between the multiplication of one trespass into countless transgressions and such an overflow of grace as more than meets that appalling case.

➤**21 as sin hath reigned unto** [in] **death, even so might grace reign**—It is interesting to note that Paul changes from the term "offense" (or, "trespass") to the more general NT word describing disobedience, "sin." In 5:14 and 17 we noted the reign of **death** over the guilty and condemned in Adam. Here it is the reign of sin that endues death with venomous power (1 Cor. 15:56) and with awful authority (6:23), and the reign of grace that originated the scheme of salvation. This is the grace that "sent the Son to be the Savior of the world" (1 John 4:14), the grace that "made him to be sin for us who knew no sin" (2 Cor. 5:21), the grace that makes us to be "the righteousness of God in him (2 Cor. 5:21)," so that "we who receive the abundance of grace and of the gift of righteousness do reign in life by One, Jesus Christ!" **through righteousness**—This does not refer to man's righteousness, but rather refers to Jesus' whole mediatorial work in the flesh. This is here represented as the righteous medium through which grace reaches its objects and obtains all its ends. It is the stable throne from which Grace as a sovereign dispenses its saving benefits to as many as are brought under its benign sway. **eternal life**— is life in its highest form, for it is the life that God possesses and dispenses to his sons. This life is brought **by Jesus Christ our Lord.**

*Chapter* **6**

## 1-12 RESULTS OF JUSTIFICATION

Justification by faith does not leave the individual in a vacuum, nor does it leave him without some specific obligations and responsibilities. To be saved by grace means that an individual is to manifest his salvation in his life (cf. Gal. 5:6). The problem which is confronted in this passage faces at least two questions: (1) Does justification by faith not simply encourage sin, whereas justification by works would not? (2) Moreover, does justification by faith result in one's ignoring the law of God?

➤**1 What shall we say then? Shall we continue in sin, that grace may abound?**—The subject of this division of Paul's letter to the Romans announces itself in the opening question. Notice the term "continue." Had the apostle's doctrine been that salvation depends in any degree upon man's good works, no such objection to it could have been made. Against the doctrine of purely gratuitous justification, the objection is plausible; nor has there ever been an age in which it has not been asked. The charge was brought against the apostles themselves according to Romans 3:8; Galatians 5:13; 1 Peter 2:16; and Jude 4. But Paul proceeds at this point to show that all such objections pervert the doctrine of grace.

➤**2 God forbid**—Paul again uses the expression which may be translated, "May it never come to pass!" **How shall we, that are dead to sin, live any longer therein?**—How can we who died to sin (as presently to be explained) live in sin any longer?

➤**3 Know ye not, that so** [as] **many of us as were baptized into Jesus Christ** [should read, Christ Jesus] **were baptized into his death?**—Since Christ was "made sin" and "a curse for us" (2 Cor. 5:21; Gal. 3:13) and rose "again for our justification" (4:25), our whole sinful case and condition have been brought to an end in his death. Paul means that the individuals who have been "baptized into Christ Jesus" have become members of his body. They have shared his crucifixion, his burial, his resurrection, and his exaltation. Therefore, the one who has been "baptized into his death" has surrendered the whole state and life of sin, as in Christ, a dead thing. He has sealed himself to be not only "righteousness of God in him" but also "a new creature." Since he cannot be in Christ to the one effect and not to the other, he has bidden farewell to his entire connection with sin. Consequently, the question "are we to continue in sin that grace may abound?" is entirely out of place. The two things are as contradictory in the fact as they are in the terms.

➤**4 Therefore we are** [were] **buried with him**—a past act, completed at once. **by baptism into death: that like as Christ was raised up from the dead by the glory of the Father, even so we also should walk in newness of life**—Paul does not mean "by baptism we are buried with him into death," but "by baptism with him into death we are buried with him." In other words, "by the same baptism that publicly enters us into his death, we are made partakers of his burial also." We have by this public act of baptism severed our last link of connection with that whole sinful condition in life that Christ brought to an end in his death. The expression "that like as Christ was raised up from the dead by the glory of the Father" means God expressed his glory in raising his Son from the dead (see John 13:31, 32). **even so we also**—as risen to a new life with him. **should walk in newness of life**—To walk in newness of life is to live in that new life Christ has given to us by virtue of our union with him in resurrection. If our old life, now dead and buried with Christ, was wholly sinful, the new must be altogether a holy life. Therefore, every time we go back to "those things whereof we are now ashamed" (6:21), we belie our resurrection with Christ to a newness of life and forget that Christ has purged us from our old sins (2 Pet. 1:9).

➤**5 if**—This introduces a first-class conditional clause that could be translated, "Since we have been united . . . " Since Christ's death and resurrection are inseparable in their efficacy, union with him in the one carries with it participation in the other, both for privilege and duty alike. **we have been planted together**—or, we have become organically united. The Greek word *sumphutoi* means "to grow in union" or "to plant in union." The word describes two organic entities, like plants, that have been planted together and are growing together, closely entwined or even united. The context speaks of union, our union with Christ

in death (6:4) and in resurrection (6:5). Our union with Christ in death was like being planted with him, the grain that was sown into the ground (John 12:24). Our union with Christ is now a loving union, in which we are growing with him **in the likeness of his resurrection.** When we have grown to complete maturity, we will have become completely like him.

➤**6, 7** The apostle now becomes more definitive and vivid in expressing the sin-destroying efficacy of the Christian's union with the crucified Savior. He notes that **our old man** has been crucified with Christ. The "old man" refers to all that we were in our old and unregenerate condition before we came to Christ by faith. (Cf. Gal. 2:20; 5:24; 6:14; Eph. 4:22-24; Col. 3:9.) This crucifixion "destroys" (annuls, abrogates) **the body of sin.** The word for "destroy" in Greek means "to annul the work of." Christ's death did not annihilate our sinful bodies; it annuled the effectiveness of sin. An additional aspect to the crucifixion of the "old man" is contained in the clause **that henceforth we should not serve sin.**

➤**7 For he that is dead is freed from sin**—lit., "justified," "acquitted," "received his discharge from sin." As death dissolves all claims, so the claim of sin has been discharged once for all by the believer's penal death in the death of Christ. No longer is he a debtor to the flesh to live after the flesh (8:12). Just as the experience of death eliminates all the monetary debts an individual has incurred, even so, the man who has died with Christ has his past record cleared and is then ready to begin the experience of the Christian life, freed from the involvements and entanglements of the past.

➤**8** This verse is constituted by a first-class conditional sentence and could well be translated, "But since we died with Christ, we believe that we shall also live with him." The first-class conditional sentence does not express doubt but rather a strong confidence. This is indicated by the insertion of the term "since" (or, "because") in the translation. Our union with Christ is in his death and in his life.

➤**9, 1 0 Knowing that Christ being raised from the dead dieth no more; death hath no more dominion over him**—Though Christ's death was a voluntary act (James 1:17, 18; Acts 2:24), that voluntary surrender gave death rightful "dominion over him." But having conquered death, Jesus no longer is subject to it. **For in that he died, he died unto sin**—i.e., he died in obedience to the claims of sins. **once** [for all]: **but in that he liveth, he liveth unto God**—Of course, there never was a time when Jesus did not "live unto God." But in the days of his flesh, he did so under the continual burden of sin "laid on him" (Isa. 53:6; 2 Cor. 5:21); whereas, now that he has "put away sin by the sacrifice of himself" (Heb. 9:26), he "lives unto God" as the acquitted and accepted Surety, unchallenged and unclouded by the claims of sin.

➤**11 Likewise reckon ye also yourselves to be dead indeed unto sin, but alive unto God through Jesus Christ**—The words "our Lord" do not appear in the best manuscripts. The Christian must consider himself to be in the same condition as is his Savior. That "we would continue in sin that grace may abound" (6:1) is abhorrent to every Christian mind as a monstrous abuse of the most glorious of all truths. Furthermore, since the death of Christ is not only the expiation of guilt but also the death of sin itself and of all who are vitally united to him, the resurrection of Christ is the resurrection of believers not only to acceptance with God but also to newness of life (6:4). Davidson and Martin write, "It is the way of justification. God not only puts us right, but keeps us right with Himself. His righteousness is first imputed, then imparted to us." But the Christian must "continue to reckon" (the tense in Gk. is present, denoting continuous action) himself to be dead to sin in order to maintain the vitality and reality of his position in Christ.

## 12-23 PRACTICAL RESULTS OF THE CHRISTIAN'S DEATH TO SIN AND LIFE WITH GOD THROUGH UNION WITH CHRIST

Prior to this section, Paul has limited himself basically to a discussion of the divine aspect of justification. In this section, no longer content with showing that his doctrine has no tendency to relax the obligations to a holy life, the apostle proceeds to enforce these obligations.

➤**12 Let not sin therefore reign in your mortal body, that ye should obey it in the lusts thereof**—The reader will observe that the words "sin," "obedience," "righteousness,"

"uncleanness," and "iniquity" are sometimes personified to represent a master of life. The Christian is not to "obey . . . lusts"; lusts are here understood to be of the body. The "body" is here viewed as the instrument by which all the sins of the heart become realities in the outward life. The "body" itself is the seat of the lower appetites and is called "mortal." Paul probably uses this term to remind us of how unsuitable this reign of sin is in those who are "alive from the dead." But the reign here meant is the unchecked dominion of sin *within* us. Its outward acts are next mentioned.

➤**13 Neither yield ye your members as instruments** [or, weapons] . . . **unto sin: but yield yourselves unto God, as those that are alive from the dead, and your members as instruments of righteousness unto God**—But what if indwelling sin should prove too strong for us? The reply is simple: it will not because it is not too strong for Christ who lives in us.

➤**14 For sin shall not have dominion over you** [as the slaves of a tyrant lord]: **for ye are not under the law, but under grace**—This is the reason for the believer not to permit the members of his body to be used as "instruments of unrighteousness." The force of this glorious assurance can only be felt by observing the grounds on which it rests. To be "under law" is, first, to be under its claim to entire obedience; second, it means to be under its curse for any breach of obedience. And as all power to obey can reach the sinner only through grace, of which the law knows nothing, it follows that to be "under law" is, finally, to be shut under an inability to keep it and consequently to be a helpless slave to sin. On the other hand, to be "under grace" is to be under the glorious canopy and saving effects of that "grace which reigns through righteousness unto eternal life through Jesus Christ our Lord" (see 5:20, 21, RSV). The curse of the law has been completely lifted from off them; they are made the righteousness of God in him; and they are alive unto God through Jesus Christ. So that, as when they were "under the law," **sin** could not but have dominion over them; so now that they are "under grace," **sin** cannot but be subdued by them. If **sin** resistlessly triumphed before, **grace** will now be more than conqueror.

➤16 Know ye not, that to whom ye yield yourselves servants [slaves] to obey [with a view toward obeying him], his servants [slaves] ye are to whom ye obey; [to whom you yield that obedience] whether of sin [which leads] unto death, or of obedience [which leads] unto righteousness?—Obedience results in a righteous character (see 1 John 2:17; John 8:34; 2 Pet. 2:19; Matt. 6:24). In these two verses the apostle makes it evident that there are only two possible masters to rule man—God or sin. Illustration of the apostle's thought is derived from contemporary slave law. A slave could buy his freedom if he was able to pay his price to the temple, meaning, that he gave his purchase money to some god or goddess and in this way claimed his freedom. However, the money actually went to the master through the temple channels. But in that way the deity ransomed the slave and the slave was set free, although the slave was still enslaved to the god or goddess who had ransomed him. The Christian is free in the sense only that he has become enslaved to God. He finds his greatest freedom under those conditions and circumstances. "Freedom in slavery" is one of the startling paradoxes of the Christian life.

➤17 But God be thanked, that ye were [once] the servants [slaves] of sin, but ye have obeyed from the heart that form of doctrine which was delivered you—According to the Greek, the verb is passive—"you were delivered," but is often translated in the active voice: "to which you were committed" (see NASB, RSV, NIV). However, the context may call for the divine passive and therefore could be rendered, "to which God has committed you" (TLB). The Romans had been given to and committed with the teaching of the apostles, and this teaching, to which they had heartily yielded themselves, had stamped its own impression upon them.

➤18 Being then made free from sin, ye became the servants of righteousness—This is the continuation and conclusion of the preceding sentence and is not to be considered a new sentence. The case is one of emancipation from entire servitude to one master to entire servitude to another (see the comments on 1:1). There is no middle state of personal independence; we were never made for personal independence, and to that we have no claim. When we would not have God reign over us, we were "sold under sin"; now we have been freed from sin to become "slaves of righteousness." This is our true freedom.

➤19 I speak after the manner of men (condescending for purposes of illustration to the level of common affairs), because of the infirmity [weakness] of your flesh—This is a reference to the weakness of the Romans' spiritual apprehension. On other occasions Paul recognized similar weaknesses and spoke in similar terms (cf. 1 Cor. 15:32; Gal. 3:15). for as ye have yielded your members servants to uncleanness (the thing being viewed is now past) and to iniquity unto iniquity; even so now yield your members servants to righteousness unto holiness—Cf. 1 Corinthians 1:30; 2 Thessalonians 2:13; 1 Peter 1:2. The apostle's argument is concluded by a reference to their past practices and an appeal to emulate that zeal in new service.

➤20 when ye were the servants [slaves] of sin, ye were free from [in regard to] righteousness—The import of the verse seems clear: Since no servant can serve "two masters" (Matt. 6:24) (much less where their interests come into deadly conflict and each master demands the service of the whole man), while we were in the service of sin, we were in no proper sense the servants of righteousness and never did it one act of real service. Whatever might be our conviction of the claims of righteousness, our real services were always given to sin. Therefore, we have full proof of the nature and advantages of sin's service. The searching question that follows this verse reveals this to be the meaning.

➤21 What fruit had ye then in those things whereof ye are now ashamed? for the end of those things is death.—What permanent advantage and what abiding satisfaction have those things yielded? The apostle answers his own question: "Abiding satisfaction, did I ask? They have left only a sense of 'shame.' " Permanent advantage? "The end of them is death." By saying they were "now ashamed," Paul makes it plain that he is not referring to that disgust of themselves and remorse of conscience of which those who are the most helplessly "sold under sin" are often stung to the quick; but he rather is referring to that pierces and weighs down the children of God as they think of the dishonor their past life did to his name, the ingratitude it displayed, the violence it did to their own conscience, its deadening and degrading effects, and the spiritual death into which it was dragging them. (On the sense of "death" here, see the comments on 5:12-21.) Denney makes the point that to be freed from sin, an individual must be able to disown it, but at the same time "own" it, in the sense of controlling and overcoming it through the power of Christ.

➤22 The expression **but now** seems to indicate that Paul now seeks to move toward a conclusion. **being made free from sin, and become servants** [slaves] **to God**—means that the Christian has been freed and enslaved in an absolute sense, as is intended throughout this passage. **ye have your fruit unto holiness, and the end everlasting life**—The term "holiness" (or, "sanctification") refers to the permanently holy state and character that is built up out of the whole "fruits of righteousness," which believers successively bring forth. They "have their fruit" unto holiness, that is, all going toward this blessed result. (The imagery of fruit-bearing builds upon that of planting in 6:5.) The expression "eternal life" is in apposition to the word "end." The expression "eternal life" refers to the final state of the justified believer. This is the beatific experience not only of complete exemption from the fall and its effects but of the perfect life of acceptance with God in conformity to his likeness, of unveiled access to him, and an ineffable fellowship with him through all eternity.

➤23 **For the wages of sin is death; but the gift of God is eternal life through Jesus Christ** ["Christ Jesus" in the best manuscripts] **our Lord**— Just as the laborer is worthy of his hire and feels it to be his due, so death is the due of sin, the wages the sinner has well wrought for his own. But "eternal life" is in no sense or degree the wages of our righteousness; we do nothing whatever to earn or become entitled to it and never can; therefore, it is in the absolute sense "the gift of God."

*Chapter* 7

Paul continues his discussion of the same general subject, noting that one of the great problems involved in the Jewish acceptance of the righteousness of God by faith was the ex-

alted position the Jews assigned to the law. For all practical purposes, they worshiped the law; therefore, it was blasphemous to believe that faith could occupy the place once occupied by the law.

## 1-6 THE VALIDITY OF THE LAW

The first illustration Paul employs is of the widow freed from her responsibilities to her deceased husband.

➤1 **I speak to them that know the law**— i.e., the law of Moses. Although Paul is not speaking to Jews only, he is speaking to people to whom the OT concept of law was familiar.

➤2, 3 If a husband dies, then his wife is **loosed** [discharged] **from the law of** [concerning] **her husband.** She is then free to be married to another, but if this second marriage should occur during her husband's lifetime, then she would be **called an adulteress.**

➤4 **ye also are become dead to the law by the body of Christ**—through his slain body. According to the Greek, the apostle here departs from his usual word "died," using a more expressive phrase "were put to death." The verb is an aorist passive, and some of the older commentators translated the word with the more vivid phrase "were slain" to assist us in seeing that the phrase refers to the definite time of their being crucified with Christ (Gal. 2:20). It has been thought that the apostle should here have written that "the law died to us," not "we died to the law," but that Paul purposely inverted the figure in order to avoid the harshness to the Jewish ears of the "death of the law." Chrysostom, Calvin, and other interpreters have taken this approach. But the apostle's design in employing this figure was merely to illustrate the general principle that "death dissolves legal obligation." It was essential to his argument that we, not the law, should be a dying party since it is we who are "crucified with Christ," and not the law. **that ye should be married to another, even to him who is raised from the dead, that we should bring forth fruit unto God**—Our death dissolves our marriage obligation to the law, leaving us at liberty to contract a new relation—to be joined to the risen One in order to produce spiritual fruitfulness to the glory of God. All the issues of this new life in Christian obedience are regarded as the "fruit" of this blessed union to the risen One.

➤**5 when we were in the flesh**—refers to our unregenerate state. (See John 3:6 and Rom. 8:5-9.) **the motions** [passions] **of sins, which were by the law** [through the law], **did work in our members to bring forth fruit unto death**—These "sinful passions" were aroused by the prohibitions of the law. These "passions" worked in the members of the body making them the instruments to carry out the sinful desires (see 6:6). The end result of such stimulation is expressed in the clause "to bring forth fruit unto [resulting in] death." This is to be understood as "death" in the sense of 6:21. Therefore, it is impossible to bear holy fruit prior to union with Christ.

➤**6 But now**—See the comments on the same expression in 6:22 and cf. James 1:15. **we are delivered** [discharged] **from the law**—In 6:6 and elsewhere the word rendered "destroyed" should be translated "discharged" (see RSV, NEB). The writer is attempting to impress upon the reader the violence of that death by which we are "discharged from the law." **that we should serve in newness of spirit, and not in the oldness of the letter**—This new service is not to be rendered in our old way of literal, mechanical obedience to the divine law as to a set of external rules of conduct, without any reference to the state of our hearts. The new service is to be rendered in that new way of spiritual obedience, which through union to the risen Savior, we have learned to render (cf. 2:29; 2 Cor. 3:6).

## 7-25 PAUL REPELS FALSE INFERENCES CONCERNING THE LAW

➤**7, 8** In these two verses Paul informs his readers that he once lived apart from any consciousness of the law; furthermore, if it had not been for the law, Paul would not have known **sin.** He pointedly emphasizes the fact that he would have **not known** the meaning of covetousness if the law had not said, **Thou shalt not covet. But sin, taking occasion** [or, "getting a point of attack," *New Translation,* Darby] by the commandment, wrought [worked] **in me all manner of concupiscence** [lust]—Paul uses the word "sin" here to describe "the principle of sin in the heart of fallen man." The sense of his statement is this: "It was by means of the

law that I came to know what a virulence and strength of sinful propensity I had within me." He did not need the law to reveal the existence of sin to him; for even the heathen recognized and wrote of it. But the dreadful nature and desperate power of it was uncovered and disclosed personally to Paul by the force of the law in the way he proceeds to describe. Paul came to understand his desire for what is forbidden as the first conscious form of sin. "The function of the law is thus propaedeutic; by revealing to men their sinfulness and inability, it reveals to them also their need of that deliverance which only God's grace can effect" (Bruce). Paul's sinfulness at the point of coveting was especially revealed by the force of the law. (Cf. Exod. 20:17 and Deut. 5:21.) It is only normal for man to desire the possession of things. Once it is brought to his attention that those things which he desires are forbidden, he has the tendency to desire them more intensely. In 7:8 Paul gives a deeper view of the tenth commandment than the mere word suggests. The apostle saw in it the prohibition not only of desire there specified but of desire after everything divinely forbidden. It was this desire that he had not known except by the specific commandment negating it. The law forbidding all such desire so stirred his fallen nature that it wrought in him all manner of lusting, all desiring of every sort after what was forbidden. Thus, sin, through the law, attacked him (see Darby's translation noted above), warred against him (7:23), deceived him and "killed him" (7:11). **For without the law sin was dead**—before its extensive demands and prohibitions came to operate upon his corrupt nature. The sinful principle of his fallen nature was so dormant, so sluggish, that its virulence and power were unknown and therefore was, to his feeling, as good as dead.

➤**9 I was alive without the law once**— This refers to the days of Paul's ignorance, when in a sense he was a stranger to the law. **but when the commandment came**—forbidding all inordinate desire. With the coming "of the commandment," **sin revived, and** the apostle **died.** The idea of sin's reviving refers to its coming to life in malignity and strength, as if it had sprung from the dead. The idea of Paul's dying refers to the apostle's seeing himself in the eye of the law never kept and not to be kept, as a dead man.

➤**10, 11** The apostle's experience with the law was that it actually brought death to him although it had been given to promote life (cf. 10:5; Lev. 18:5). **For sin, taking occasion** [or, "getting a point of attack," *New Translation,* Darby] **by the commandment, deceived me, and by it slew me**—In these words Paul explains how sin drew him into the very thing which the commandment forbade. (Cf. Gen. 3:13; 2 Cor. 11:3.) The term "deceived" is a word which means "to make me lose my way." Robertson observes that "sin here is personified as the tempter (Gen. 3:13)."

➤**12** This verse completes the inquiry the apostle began in 7:7. He concludes that the commandment is of God and consequently just in all of its requirements, for it was given for the good of men. Although some may argue that the law was unjust, Paul will have none of this argument. God gave the law for the purpose of giving life, not death.

➤**13, 14** Paul's argument may have led the unobserving reader to believe that the law brought death. But Paul says, "God forbid!" It was **sin, that it might appear sin** [that sin might be shown to be sin], **working death in me by that which is good; that sin by the commandment might become exceeding sinful**—Paul is here stating that the law functioned to show him how sinful he was because it exposed his inability to obey its decrees. Some inquire as to what period of Paul's history these circumstances relate. The scholars differ. Some believe that Paul was speaking of his experience prior to regeneration. They say that this whole description of his inward struggles and progress is probably the culmination of all his past recollections and subsequent reflections on his unregenerate state, which he threw into historical form only for greater vividness. As such, Paul was using himself as an example of the unregenerate. Other scholars argue that Paul was speaking of the experience of the Christian who has two natures to cope with— the old, unregenerated nature still living in the flesh and the new, regenerated nature now living in the spirit.

➤**14 For we know that the law is spiritual**—in its demands. But the apostle is **carnal, sold under sin.** By the expression "carnal" Paul means "fleshly" and as such, incapable of yielding spiritual obedience. Paul is enslaved

by sin. The "I" here is neither the regenerate nor the unregenerate, but the sinful principle of the renewed man, as expressly stated in 7:18. Some scholars insist that the experience Paul describes in 7:14-25 is essentially that of his pre-Christian days. However, other scholars insist that this is the case of the regenerate man who longs to do better but is unable to do so.

➤**15, 16 For that which I do I allow not**— i.e., "I do not understand my own actions" (RSV). This refers to his obeying the impulses of his carnal nature, thereby acting as the slave of a will other than his own will as a renewed man. **for what I would, that do I not; but what I hate, that do I**—i.e., "for I do not do what I want, but I do the very thing I hate" (RSV). This illustrates the inward conflict, this time from the standpoint of a negative expression.

➤**17 Now then it is no more I that do it, but sin that dwelleth in me**—These words refer to the principle of sin that still had its abode in Paul. In reference to his previous explanation, it is not the true Paul who is responsible for this line of conduct, but the sin that has its habitation in him. Those interpreters who explain this and the following statements as pertaining to the unregenerate struggling against their better convictions do painful violence to the apostle's language and also attribute to the unregenerate what is untrue. That coexistence and mutual hostility of "flesh" and "spirit" in the same renewed man (so clearly taught in 8:4 and Gal. 5:16) is the true and only key to the language of this and the following verses. (It is hardly necessary to observe that the apostle means not to disown the blame of yielding to his corruptions by saying, "It is not I that do it, but the sin that dwells in me." Early heretics thus abused his language; but the strain of the passage shows that his whole object in thus expressing himself was to bring more vividly before his readers the conflict of two opposing principles, and how entirely, as a new man—honoring from his inmost soul the law of God—he condemned and renounced his corrupt nature with its affections and lusts, its stirrings and its outgoings, root and branch.)

➤**18** Paul realized the extensiveness of his sin by admitting that **in me (that is, in my flesh,) dwelleth no good thing.** On the other hand, he insists that he "can will what is right, but . . . cannot do it" (RSV). Here again we see the double self of the renewed man, according to some interpreters. Others would say that this is the life of Paul the Pharisee as viewed through the life of Paul the Christian.

➤19-21 The conflict here graphically described between a self that desires to do good and a self that in spite of this does evil, cannot be the struggles between conscience and passion in the eyes of the unregenerate because the description given of this "desire to do good" in the verse immediately following is such as cannot be ascribed, with the least sure truth, to any but the renewed.

➤22 For I delight in the law of God after the inward man—as we would say colloquially, "from the bottom of my heart." The word here rendered "delight" is indeed stronger than "would" (or, "wish") in 7:16. But both express a state of mind and heart to which the unregenerate man is a stranger.

➤23 But Paul sees another law . . . warring against the law of [his] mind—The term translated "another" is the Greek term *heteros,* which means "another of a different kind." Here the term "law" means an inward principle of action, good or evil, operating with the fixity and regularity of the law. The apostle found two such laws within him: the one "the law of sin and its members" called "the flesh which lusts against the spirit" (Gal. 5:17, 24), that is, the sinful principle in the regenerate; the other, "the law of the mind," or the holy principle of the renewed nature. Moreover, when the apostle says he "sees" one of these principles "warring" against the other and "bringing him into captivity" to itself, he was not referring to any actual rebellion going on within him while he was writing or to any captivity to his own lusts then existing. He is simply describing the two conflicting principles and is pointing out the inherent properties of each. Furthermore, when the apostle describes himself as brought into captivity by the triumph of the sinful principle of his nature, he clearly speaks in the person of a renewed man. Men do not feel themselves to be in captivity in the territories of their own sovereign and associated with their own friends, breathing a congenial atmosphere and acting quite spontaneously. But here the apostle describes himself, when drawn under the power of his sinful nature, as forcibly seized and reluctantly dragged to his enemy's camp from which he would gladly make his escape.

➤24 O wretched man that I am! who shall deliver me from the body of this death?—The apostle speaks of the "body" here with reference to the "law of sin," which he had said was "in his members" as the instrument by which sin finds vent in action and is itself the seat of the lower appetites (see comments on 6:6 and on 7:5); and he calls it "the body of this death," feeling, at the moment when he wrote, the horrors of that death into which it dragged him down (see 6:21 and 7:5). But the language is not that of a sinner newly awakened at the sight of his lost state; it is the cry of a living but agonized believer, weighted down under a burden he longs to shake off from his renewed self. Nor does the question imply ignorance in the way of relief at the time to which the apostle refers. It was designed only to prepare the way for the outburst of thankfulness for the divinely provided remedy that immediately follows.

➤25 I thank God—the source. through Jesus Christ—the channel of deliverance. So then—to sum up the entire matter. with the mind I myself serve the law of God; but with the flesh the law of sin—Such then is the unchanging character of these two principles within me. God's holy law is dear to my renewed mind and has the willing service of my new man, although the corrupt nature that still remains in me listens to the dictates of sin. Interpreters who view chapter 7 as a reflection of the Christian's life, particularly at the point of his inability to do what God wishes, suggest that the following factors be noted: (1) This whole chapter was of essential service to the Reformers in their contendings with the Roman church. When the Roman divines denied that the sinful principle of our fallen nature (which they called "Concupiscence," and which is called "Original Sin") had the nature of sin at all, they were triumphantly answered from this chapter. The Reformers noted that the first section of the chapter speaks of sin in the unregenerate, and the latter portion of the chapter treats of sin's presence and actings in believers. (2) Here we see that inability is consistent with accountability. (See 7:18 and Gal. 5:17.) Hodge, for example, notes: "As the Scriptures constantly recognize the truth of these two things, so they are constantly united in Christian experience. Everyone feels that he cannot do the things that he would, yet is sensible that he is guilty for not doing them. Let any man test his power by the requisition to love God perfectly at all times." (3) It is unfortuate when such topics as these are handled as mere questions of biblical interpretation or systematic theology. The apostle himself could not treat them apart from personal experience. The realities of his own life and the feelings of his own being furnished him with abundant illustrations as lively as they were applicable. One cannot go far into the investigation of indwelling sin without breaking out into an "O wretched man that I am!" and exclaiming, "Thanks be to God through Jesus Christ our Lord!"

*Chapter* 8

Chapter eight serves as a conclusion to the entire argument Paul has opened in chapter 7. It reveals the completeness of the man who lives in Jesus Christ. In this supreme chapter the several streams of the preceding argument meet and flow together. The subject discussed by Paul in this chapter is life in the Spirit, which breaks the power of sin and enables the believer to live in God's purpose and way.

### 1-13 THE SANCTIFICATION OF THE BELIEVERS

➤**1 There is therefore now**—referring to the immediately preceding context. The subject with which chapter 7 concludes is still under consideration. The scope of the four opening verses is to show how "the law of sin and death" is deprived of its power to bring believers again into bondage and how the holy law of God receives in them the homage of a living obedience. **no condemnation to them which are in Christ Jesus**—As Christ, who "knew no sin," was "made sin for us," so are we who believe in him "made the righteousness of God in him" (2 Cor. 5:21). And thus, since we are one with him in the divine reckoning, there is to such "no condemnation." (Cf. John 3:18; 5:24; Rom. 5:18, 19.) This is no mere

legal arrangement; it is a union in life; believers, through the indwelling of Christ's Spirit in them, have one life with him as truly as the head and the members of the same body have one life. A very important term in the interpretation of this verse is the word "now" (*nūn*, Gk.), which is temporal and thus distinguishes between the pre-Christian and Christian period. **who walk not after the flesh, but after the Spirit**—This clause is not present in the best manuscripts. Later copyists borrowed it from 8:4b and inserted it here.

➤**2 For the law of the Spirit of life in Christ Jesus hath made me free**—lit., "freed me," referring to the time of his conversion. However, Paul does not leave the term "free" dangling, but qualifies it by the addition of the prepositional phrase **from the law of sin and death.** The Holy Spirit is here named the "Spirit of life," as he opens up in the souls of believers the fountain of spiritual life (see John 7:38, 39). The Spirit of life is the life-giving Spirit (see John 6:63; 1 Cor. 15:45; 2 Cor. 3:6). This Spirit is **in Christ Jesus**—i.e., this life-giving Spirit is in union with Christ Jesus. Thus, to experience the Spirit is to experience Christ (see 8:9-11). The term "law" has the same meaning here as in 7:23: "an inward principle of action, operating with the stability and regularity of a law." It thus appears that "the law of the Spirit of life in Christ Jesus" here means "that new principle of action which the Spirit of Christ has opened up within us— the law of our new being." This sets the Christian free as soon as it takes possession of the inner man. At the same time, the man is freed from "the law of sin and death." Paul means by this that the Christian is free from the enslaving power of the corrupt principle that produces spiritual death. Therefore, it is readily seen that the weaker principle is dethroned and expelled by the more powerful; the principle of spiritual life prevails against and overpowers the principle of spiritual death.

➤**3 For what the law could not do**—This is a very difficult and much disputed verse. The apostle has spoken of the law's inability to free the Christian from the dominion of sin. The law could arouse our sinful nature into more virulent action, as seen in 7:5, but it could not secure its own fulfillment. How that is accomplished comes now to be shown. **in that it was**

**weak through the flesh**—This partially explains what Paul had in mind. Because the law had to address itself to us through our corrupt nature, which is too strong to be influenced by mere commands and threatenings, the law utterly failed. But God did not fail. (Note: at this point in the verse, the word "did" needs to be supplied after the word "God": "For what the law could not do . . . God *did*—by sending his Son. . . .") God gained a victory by **sending his own Son in the likeness of sinful flesh, and for sin.** The sentence is somewhat difficult in its structure, which occasions a certain obscurity. The meaning is that whereas the law was powerless to secure its own fulfillment for the reason given, God took the method now to be described for obtaining that end. He gained the victory by "sending his own Son." This and similar expressions indicate that Christ was God's "own Son" before he was sent. In his own proper person and independent of his mission and appearance in the flesh, he was God's Son (see comments on 8:32; Gal. 4:4). If so, he not only has the very nature of God, even as a son of his father, but is essentially *of* the Father, though in a sense too mysterious for any language of ours properly to define. And this peculiar relationship is put forward here to enhance the greatness and define the nature of the deliverance he provided as coming, not from the precincts of sinful humanity, but immediately from the Godhead itself. "In the likeness of sinful flesh, and for sin" is a very remarkable and pregnant expression. He was made in the reality of our flesh but only in the likeness of its sinful condition. He took our nature as it is in us, compassed with infirmities, with nothing to distinguish him as man from sinful men except that he was without sin. Nor did this mean that he took on a nature with all its properties except one, sin; for sin is no property of humanity at all but only the disordered state of our souls as the fallen family of Adam. This disorder affects and overspreads our entire nature but is still purely our own. The expression "and for sin" denotes the purpose of God's "sending his own Son in the likeness of sinful flesh." The expression is purposely a general one because the design was not to speak of Christ's mission to atone for sin but in virtue of that atonement to destroy its dominion and expiate it altogether from believers. There-

fore, he **condemned sin in the flesh**—that is, in human nature. He condemned it but did not destroy it. We can still live in the flesh, but that is like living in a condemned house. From henceforth we should live in the Spirit.

►4 This verse further explains the purpose of Jesus' coming in the flesh. **That the righteousness** [righteous requirements] **of the law might be fulfilled in us**—This refers to the righteous demands, the just requirements of the law. These demands are to be "fulfilled in us," realized in us. But it is to be realized "in us," **who walk not after** [according to] **the flesh, but after** [according to] **the Spirit.** The most ancient expression of the event of one's life, whether in the direction of good or evil, is expressed by the term "walk." (See Gen. 48:15; Ps. 1:1; Isa. 2:5; Mic. 4:5; Eph. 4:17; 1 John 1:6, 7.) The man who believes in God is to walk "according to the Spirit." There is some discussion whether the term "Spirit" refers to the spirit of the renewed Christian or whether the word refers to the Holy Spirit. In this verse the word "Spirit" probably denotes the regenerated human spirit united to the divine Spirit (see 8:16). A contrast then is drawn between walking "according to the flesh" and "according to the Spirit."

►5 **For they that are after the flesh**—under the influence of the fleshly principle. **do mind the things of the flesh; but they that are after the Spirit the things of the Spirit**—Men must be under the predominant influence of one or the other of these two principles. Therefore, they live according to the dictates of the mastery of one or the other. The character and complexion of their actions will be determined by the dominant dictation in their lives. If the flesh dominates, then they live "according to the flesh"; but if the Spirit dominates, then they "set their minds on the things of the Spirit."

►6 The apostle elaborates on this idea by noting that **to be carnally minded** [i.e., to set the mind on the flesh] **is death; but to be spiritually minded** [i.e., to set the mind on the Spirit] **is life and peace.** A literal rendering of this verse could be as follows: "For the mind of the flesh [is] death, but the mind of the Spirit [is] life and peace." The mind occupied with the flesh will become a mind of death, but the mind occupied with the Spirit will become a spiritual mind full of life and peace. The pursuit of the flesh produces death, but the pursuit of the Spirit brings spiritual results. Notice that the apostle reminds the reader that the setting of "the mind on the Spirit is life and peace" in contrast to the setting of "the mind on the flesh," which brings death.

➤**7 Because the carnal mind** [the mind that is set on the flesh] **is enmity against God**—The desire and pursuit of carnal ends is a state of enmity against God, wholly incompatible with true life and peace in the spirit. **it is not subject to the law of God, neither indeed can be**—This explains what Paul means by the hostility of the mind toward God. In such a state of mind there neither is nor can be the least subjection to the law of God.

➤**8 they that are in the flesh cannot please God**—having no obediential principle, no desire to please him. They simply inhabit the world of self and make that world supreme.

➤**9 But ye are not in the flesh, but in the Spirit, if so be that the Spirit of God dwell in you**—This does not mean "that if the disposition or mind of God dwells in you," but rather "if the Holy Spirit dwells in you" (see 1 Cor. 6:11, 19; 3:16). It is possible for us to be in the Spirit if and only if we are indwelt by the Spirit of God. His indwelling us permits us to dwell and live in him. **Now if any man have not the Spirit of Christ, he is none of his** [he is not his]—Again, this does not mean "the disposition of the mind of Christ," but rather this refers to the Holy Spirit, here called, "the Spirit of Christ" just as he is called the "Spirit of life in Christ Jesus" (8:2). The Spirit is called "the Spirit of Christ" because of the Spirit's union with Christ, and vice versa. This title appears only one other time in the NT: 1 Peter 1:11. Elsewhere, the Spirit is called "the Spirit of Jesus" (Acts 16:7), and "the Spirit of Jesus Christ" (Phil. 1:19). Now if any man's heart be void of "the Spirit of Christ," that man does not belong to Christ. Even though intellectually convinced of the truth of Christianity and in a general sense influenced by its Spirit, he "who does not have the Spirit of Christ does not belong to him" (RSV). This is a solemn statement! To possess the Spirit of Christ is to be possessed of God; not to possess the Spirit of Christ is to be dispossessed of God.

➤**10 And if Christ be in you**—Earlier, Paul said that "the Spirit of God" and "the Spirit of

Christ" indwell us (8:9); now he says Christ is in us. The terms "Spirit of God," "Spirit of Christ," and "Christ" are used interchangeably. The Spirit of God is the Spirit of Christ, and the Spirit of Christ is Christ. "Being 'in Christ' and being 'in the Spirit' are the same thing; and in the thought of the apostle, 'Christ,' 'the Spirit of Christ,' and 'the Spirit of God' are practically synonymous. At the resurrection Christ became a Life-giving Spirit to mankind" (Somerville). Paul identifies the Spirit of Christ with Christ because Christ indwells his believers through his Spirit. Christian experience attests to the reality that we experience Christ by his indwelling Spirit. **the body is dead because of sin; but the Spirit is life because of righteousness**—What does Paul mean by the term "Spirit"? Is this the Holy Spirit? Or is this the spirit of the believer? Because of the contrast with the human body, it is likely that Paul was thinking of the human spirit—but not merely the human spirit, rather, the human spirit regenerated and indwelt by God's Spirit. Bruce paraphrases this statement in this manner: "If Christ dwells within you, then, while your body is still subject to that temporal death which is the consequence of sin, the Spirit who has taken up His abode in you, the living and quickening Spirit, imparts to you that eternal life which is the consequence of justification."

➤**11 But if the Spirit of him that raised up Jesus from the dead dwell in you**—i.e., if he dwells in you as the Spirit of the Christ-raising One, or, in all the resurrection power that he put forth in raising Jesus Christ. **he that raised up Christ**—Observe the change of the name from "Jesus," as the historical individual whom God raised from the dead, to "Christ," the same individual, but considered as the Lord and head of all his members of redeemed humanity. **from the dead shall also quicken your mortal bodies by his Spirit that dwelleth in you**—which is to say, "Your bodies are not exempted from the death that sin brought; but your spirits even now have in them an undying life. And if the Spirit of him that raised up Jesus from the dead dwells in you, even those bodies of yours, although they yield to the last enemy and the dust of them return to the dust, shall yet experience the same resurrection as that of your living Head, by virtue of the indwelling of the same Spirit in you that quickened him." (Cf. 1 Cor. 6:14; 2 Cor. 4:14; 1 Thess. 4:14 where the apostle also makes the resurrection of believers totally dependent upon the resurrection of Christ.)

►12, 13 These two verses constitute an aside and form an exhortation. Believers are here exhorted to live according to the direction of the Spirit, not according to the personal desires, thereby putting to death the deeds of the body. **Therefore, brethren, we are debtors, not to the flesh, to live after** [according to] **the flesh**—Formerly we were "sold under sin" (7:14); but now that we have been set free from that hard master and become servants of righteousness (6:22), we owe nothing to the flesh, we disown its unrighteous claims and are dead to its imperious demands. **For if ye live after** [according to] **the flesh, ye shall die: but if ye through the Spirit do mortify** [put to death] **the deeds of the body, ye shall live**— The apostle is not satisfied with assuring them that they are under no obligations to the flesh to hearken to its suggestions, without reminding them where it will end if they do; and he uses the words "Put to death the deeds," which is the equivalent of one's saying, "to reckon as dead." It is a kind of play upon the word "die" just before it. Thus, the apostle is saying, "If you do not kill sin, it will kill you." But he tempers this with a valid alternative; if they do crucify and overcome the deeds of the body through the Spirit, such a course will result in "life" everlasting. This leads the apostle into a new line of thought that opens into his final subject, the "glory" awaiting the justified believer.

## 14-27 THE SONSHIP OF BELIEVERS; THE BELIEVER'S FUTURE INHERITANCE; THE INTERCESSION OF THE SPIRIT FOR BELIEVERS

►14 The end of the triumph of grace is the believer's sonship with God. Until now the apostle has spoken of the Spirit simply as a power through which believers "put to death" the deeds of death; now he speaks of the Spirit as a gracious, loving guide, whose "leading" is enjoyed by all and who indwells Christians, indicating that they are **sons of God.**

►15 **For ye have not received the spirit of bondage** [slavery] **again to fear**—The time to which Paul alludes is the time of the conversion experience. At that time, the believer did not receive a spirit of bondage that brought him into "fear." Was not the individual's condition prior to faith, when he lived in legal bondage, haunted by incessant forebodings under a sense of unpardoned sin? But the believer did not receive a spirit that perpetuated that wretched state. On the contrary, the believer **received the Spirit of adoption**—which can also be translated "the spirit of sonship" (RSV). This phrase stands in sharp contrast with the "spirit of slavery." The Greek term for "adoption" or "sonship" literally means "placed as a son" or "positioned as a son." The term describes legal placement into the position and privilege of genuine sonship—an action concurrent with regeneration (see 8:16). The custom of adoption was familiar to the Greeks and the Romans, although foreign to the Jews. **whereby we cry, Abba, Father**—The word "cry" is emphatic, expressing the spontaneity, strength, and exuberance of filial emotions. In Galatians 4:6 this cry is said to proceed from the Spirit in us, drawing forth the filial exclamation in our hearts. Here, it is said to proceed from our own hearts under the vitalizing energy of the Spirit as the very element of the new life in believers (cf. Matt. 10:19, 20; and see comments on 8:4). The term "Abba" is the Aramaic word for "Father"; the Greek word for the former term is added, surely not to tell the reader that both mean the same thing, but for the same reason that drew both words from the lips of Christ himself during his agony unto God (Mark 14:36). He doubtless loved to utter his Father's name in both the accustomed forms, beginning with his cherished mother-tongue and adding that of the "lingua franca" of his day. In this view the use of both words has a charming simplicity and warmth. The phrase "Abba, Father" also occurs in Galatians 4:6. Commenting on this phrase, Luther said, "This is but a little word, and yet notwithstanding it comprehends all things. The mouth speaks not, but the affection of the heart speaks after this manner. Although I be oppressed with anguish and terror on every side and seem to be forsaken and utterly cast away from your presence, yet am I your child, and you are my Father for Christ's sake: I am beloved because of a Beloved. Wherefore, this little word, Father, conceived effectually in the heart, passes all the eloquence of Demosthenes, Cicero, and of the most eloquent rhetoricians that ever were in the world."

►**16 The Spirit itself** [or, himself] **beareth witness with our spirit, that we are the children of God**—The testimony of our own spirit is borne in that cry of conscious sonship, "Abba, Father"; but we are not therein alone. For the Holy Spirit within us, even in that very cry that is his to draw forth, sets his own distinct seal to ours. And therefore, in the mouth of "two witnesses" the thing is established. The apostle had before called us "sons of God," referring to our adoption; here he changes to "children," referring to our new birth. By this new birth the Holy Spirit regenerated our human spirit (see John 3:6) and from thenceforth became united to it. This union of Spirit with spirit shows why it is quite difficult to distinguish which spirit Paul is speaking of in several of his writings (see comments on 8:10). Nonetheless, we have become children of God by this divine regeneration. In 8:14 Paul called us "sons of God"; here we are called "children of God." The one expresses the dignity to which we are admitted; the other the new life which we receive. The latter is more suitable here because a son by adoption might not be heir of a property (although he would have been "heir" according to Roman law), whereas a son by birth certainly is, and this is what the apostle is about to state.

►**17 And if children, then heirs; heirs of God, and joint-heirs with Christ**—To be "heirs of God" is to be heirs of our Father's kingdom. To be "joint-heirs with Christ" is to be fellow-heirs with the one who is "firstborn among many brethren." The concept of inheritance is prominent both in the OT and NT. (Cf. Num. 26:56; Ps. 25:13; Isa. 60:21; Matt. 5:5; 21:38; Gal. 3:29; 4:7.) Paul teaches that the indwelling Spirit is the guarantee (or earnest) of the Christian's inheritance (cf. 2 Cor. 1:22; 5:5; Eph. 1:14). Paul is stating that the Christian has a common inheritance with Christ. This inheritance will be shared at the proper time. The clause **if so be that we suffer with him, that we may be also glorified together** may be a quotation of a familiar saying of the early church (cf. 2 Tim. 2:11-13). It seems that this quotation was prominent among the early Christians, probably because of the suffering and persecution. This reflects something of the

"better days to come" concept enunciated so often in intertestamental literature. The necessity of conformity to Christ in suffering in order to participate in his glory is taught by Christ himself and by his apostles (Matt. 16:24, 25; John 12:24-26; 2 Tim. 2:12).

►**18 I reckon that the sufferings of this present time are not worthy to be compared with the glory which shall be revealed in us**—Yes, we must suffer with Christ if we would partake of his glory; but what of that? For if such sufferings are compared against the coming glory, these sufferings sink into insignificance. The concept of suffering "with him" speaks of cross-bearing and sacrifice, experiences that within themselves are not redemptive, but experiences that complete what is lacking in Christ's afflictions (see the comments on Col. 1:24).

►**19-22** In these verses Paul confirms his confidence concerning the Christian's future glory. He begins by pointing to the organic unity of God's creation. The interpreter must remember that the apostle is stating a scientific fact viewed theologically. "Man and nature are so closely related that, as by man's sin nature suffered with him, so by free grace in putting man right with God, nature also shares the hope of righteous readjustment of perfect completion" (Davidson and Martin). Bruce writes, "The doctrine of the cosmic fall is implicit in the biblical record from Genesis 3 (where the ground is cursed for man's sake) to Revelation 22 (where there shall be no more curse); and is demanded by any world-outlook which endeavors to do justice to the biblical doctrine of creation in the facts of life as we know them. Man is part of nature, and the whole nature of which he forms part was created good, has been subjected to frustration and futility by sin, and will ultimately be redeemed. It is no accident that the redemption of nature is here seen as coinciding with the redemption of man's body—that physical part of his being which links him with the material creation." These words do not mean that the world as we know it will be annihilated, but they refer rather to a total and complete transformation of the present universe so that the world will then be able to fulfill the purpose for which God had created it.

**➤19 For the earnest expectation** [anxious watching] **of the creature** [creation] **waiteth for** [eagerly expects] **the manifestation of the sons of God**—Paul is saying that the created world (here personified) is looking for the full and final redemption of God's sons, which will reveal their sonship, now hidden (cf. Luke 20:36; Rev. 21:7). The creation's liberation is entirely dependent upon man's liberation because man is creation's deputized head (Gen. 1:26-28; Ps. 8:5-8).

**➤20 For the creature** [creation] **was made subject to vanity** [futility], **not willingly, but by reason of him who hath subjected the same in hope**—God subjected the creation to futility, even though it was not willing to be subjected thus (again, creation is personified).

**➤21 But there is the hope that the creation will be delivered from the bondage of corruption** to participate in **the glorious liberty of the children of God.** The connection between 8:20 and 21 is clearer when rendered " . . . in hope that . . . " instead of " . . . in hope, because . . . ," as in the KJV.

**➤22 For we know that the whole creation groaneth and travaileth in pain together until now**—It seems as if Paul may have been thinking in terms of the contemporary Jewish thought, which anticipated the time of distress (the birth-pangs) that would introduce the messianic age (cf. Mark 13:8). If this is the proper interpretation, the apostle then regards all of mankind, which includes creation as a whole, as sharing in this distress and in these birth-pangs. Paul seems to be saying that even the earth itself will share in man's final recovery—and, as such, to represent it as sympathizing with man's miseries and anticipating man's complete redemption, for creation's own emancipation comes with the liberation of God's children.

**➤23 And not only they, but ourselves also, which have the firstfruits of the Spirit**—In addition to the inanimate creation, man, possessing the fruits of the Spirit of personal redemption, longs for that particular day of total redemption. **groan within ourselves, waiting for the adoption . . . the redemption of our body**—Though we have so much of glory already within us, nonetheless we "groan inwardly" awaiting the "adoption of sons." The "firstfruits" is the "first installment" or the

"downpayment" of the eternal spiritual heritage of glory that awaits the believers. See 2 Corinthians 1:22; 5:5 and Ephesians 1:14 for an identical teaching concerning the Spirit as the "pledge" or "earnest" of the Christian's inheritance. The term used in these passages is the Greek word *arrabōn*, which is the term employed in Greek usage for an engagement ring. It is highly suggestive of what the Christian expects God to complete in his relationship. Anticipating God's spiritual working causes us to "groan inwardly as we wait for adoption as sons, the redemption of our bodies" (RSV). Of course, the term "adoption" suggests the believers' relationship to God as true sons of God. In the Roman world, adopted sons could not be deprived of their inheritance, being recognized as legal sons.

**➤24** Verses 24 and 25 state Paul's second witness to his confidence of future glory. **For we are saved by hope**—rather, "for in hope we are saved" (i.e., it is more a salvation in hope than as yet in actual possession). **hope that is seen is not hope**—It is the expectation that something now *future* will become the *present.* **for what a man seeth, why doth he yet hope for?**—According to the best manuscript evidence, this should read, "for who hopes for what he sees?" Hope is over when the thing for which an individual "hopes" becomes reality. Once the individual sees this, he ceases to hope for that which is already reality.

**➤25 But if we hope for that we see not, then do we with patience wait for it**—Then, patient waiting for it is the Christian's fitting attitude (cf. 2 Cor. 4:18). Although the Christian is saved, "full salvation" lies ahead.

**➤26 Likewise the Spirit also helpeth our infirmities: for we know not what we should pray for as we ought: but the Spirit itself maketh intercession for us with groanings which cannot be uttered**—By the term "infirmities" (or, "weakness") the apostle means "the general weakness of the spiritual life in its present state," of which one example is here given. Paul uses the example of prayer, noting that we do not know how to pray as "we ought." The believers do not have difficulty with how to pray, but what to pray. This difficulty arises partly from the dimness of our spiritual vision and the present veiled state, while we have to "walk by faith, not by sight" (see comments on

1 Cor. 13:9 and on 2 Cor. 5:7). Prayer is also made difficult by the large mixture of ideas and feelings in our spirits, and by the imperfection of all human language as a vehicle for expressing intricate spiritual feelings. In these circumstances, we can see how uncertainty surrounds all our spiritual exercises, and how, therefore, doubts spring up within us whether our utterance is altogether fitting and well pleasing to God. Nor do these anxieties subside, but rather deepen with the depth and brightness of spiritual experience. But we are not left to our own resources, for the Spirit himself intercedes for us. His intercession is "with sighs too deep for words" (RSV). What a sublime and affecting idea! As we struggle to express in articulate language the desires of our hearts (the deepest emotions are the most inexpressible), we "groan" under our inability. But not in vain are these groanings. For "the Spirit himself" is in them, giving to the emotions that he himself has kindled the only language capable of being understood by God; so that though on our part they are the fruit of impotence to utter what we feel, they are at the same time the intercession of the Spirit himself in our behalf. What man is unable to express, the Spirit is able to express unto God.

➤27 **And he that searcheth the hearts knoweth what is the mind of the Spirit**—As the searcher of hearts, God watches the surging emotions of them in prayer and knows perfectly what the Spirit means by the groanings he draws forth within us. **because he maketh intercession for the saints according to the will of God**—the blessed Intercessor asks for what God himself has designed.

28-39 PAUL'S TRIUMPHANT SUMMARY OF HIS ENTIRE ARGUMENT

➤28 **And we know that all things work together for good to them that love God**—According to some ancient manuscripts, this reads, "And we know that God works all things together for good to them that love him. . . ." It seems that this was a household word, a "known" thing among the early believers. This divine working of all things for good is done quite naturally to "them that love God" because such people, persuaded that he who gave his own Son for them cannot but mean them well in all his actions, learn thus to accept whatever

he sends them. **to them who are the called according to his purpose**—God called certain people in accordance with his eternal purpose (see Eph. 1:9-11; 3:9-11). All such people have been called into the fellowship of his Son Jesus Christ (1 Cor. 1:9). They are confident that the One "of whom and through whom, and to whom are all things," will not allow his purpose to be thwarted by anything, no matter what happens to us.

➤29 The conjunction **for** relates this verse to the expression "called according to his purpose." This verse states that God's eternal purpose is to conform many sons to the image of his Son. **whom he did foreknow, he also did predestinate**—or, "foreordained." In what sense are we to take the word "foreknew" here? Some commentators insist that it does not mean "advanced awareness or knowledge of someone" (Harrison), even though this use of "foreknowledge" is affirmed by Acts 26:5 and 1 Peter 1:20. But in other verses (Acts 2:23; Rom. 11:2; 1 Pet. 1:2; 2 Pet. 3:17), the word could very well indicate advanced knowledge. In this sense, God knew us before he predestinated us. But it is argued that such knowledge would invalidate the absoluteness of God's predestination and eternal election—for he would choose those whom he knew would choose him. It is difficult indeed for our limited minds to comprehend the divine mind toward men. But probably God's foreknowledge of his own people means his particular, gracious affection for them, while his "predestinating" or "foreordaining" them signifies his fixed purpose, flowing from this, to "save them and call them with an holy calling" (2 Tim. 1:9). To predestinate means "to mark out beforehand," "to establish one's boundary, one's limits beforehand." Those who have been predestinated have been marked out for a special purpose in life: **to be conformed to the image of his Son.** God desires his sons to be conformed to the pattern, the model, or the image of his Son. The process of conformation, like that of transformation (see 12:1; 2 Cor. 3:18) takes a lifetime. **that he might be the firstborn among many brethren**—The "firstborn" is a title ascribed to Jesus, elsewhere called "the firstborn from among the dead" (Col. 1:18; Rev. 1:5). As the firstborn, he was made the prototype—to whom all the other sons would be conformed. As the firstborn, he became the older brother of all the sons of God (see John 20:19; Heb. 2:11-13).

**►30 Moreover whom he did predestinate, them he also called**—The term "called" is never applied in the NT epistles to those who have only the outward invitation of the gospel (as in Matt. 20:16; 22:14). It always means called "internally, effectually, savingly." It comprises the first great step in personal salvation and answers to "conversion." Only the word "conversion" expresses the change of character that then takes place, whereas this "calling" expresses the divine authorship of the change and the saving power by which we are summoned, Matthew-like, Zaccheus-like, out of our old, wretched, perishing condition, into a new, safe, blessed life. **whom he called, them he also justified**—i.e., he made them right with himself. **and whom he justified, them he also glorified**—He brought them to final glory (see 8:17, 18). What a noble climax and so rhythmically expressed! And all this is viewed as past because starting from the past decree of "predestined to be conformed to the image of his Son"—of which the other steps are but the successive unfoldings—all is beheld in one entire, eternally completed salvation.

**►31 What shall we then say to these things?**—Bengel once noted that we can go no farther, only think, only wish. This whole passage, up to verse 34 and even to the end of the chapter, strikes all thoughtful interpreters and readers as transcending almost everything in language. Paul continues his triumphant hymn of praise with the question, **If God be for us, who can be against us?** If God be resolved and engaged to bring us through an experience, all our enemies must be his. What strong consolation has the apostle here spoken! Davidson and Martin state succinctly: "If God be in our destiny, nothing else matters. To us who are of the faith-family He gave His own Son, and with the greatest gift all else is certainly included."

**►32 He that spared not his own Son, but delivered him up for us all, how shall he not with him also freely give us all things?**—This is the pledge referred to in 8:31. God did not withhold, did not keep back his Son. This expressive phrase, as well as the whole thought, is suggested by Genesis 22:12, where Jehovah's touching commendation of Abraham's conduct regarding his son Isaac seems designed to furnish something like a glimpse into the spirit of his own act in surrendering his own Son. (Cf. Gen. 22:2.) In view of God's instruction to Abraham concerning the offering of his own son, Paul must mean to convey nothing less than this, that in "not sparing his own Son, but delivering him up," God exercised (in his paternal character) a mysterious act of self-sacrifice. This verse helps to elucidate the sense of God's love revealed in John 3:16. When Paul said that God gave him up for us all, he meant that God "gave him up" for all believers alike—as almost every interpreter admits must be the meaning here. If God was willing to give his Son for all believers, and this is the fact which Paul has emphasized, then will he not also give us all things with him? All other gifts being not only immeasurably less than this gift of all gifts, but virtually included in it—God will surely give us all things.

**►33, 34 Who shall lay any thing to the charge of God's elect?**—This is the first place in the epistle where believers are described as the "elect." In what sense this is meant will appear in chapter 9. We detect in this forensic language an echo of the similar challenge contained in Isaiah 50:8, 9: "He who vindicates me is near. Who then will bring charges against me? Let us face each other! Who is my accuser? Let him confront me! It is the Sovereign Lord who helps me. Who is he that will condemn me?" (NIV). Paul explains the inability of any man to bring charges against "God's elect" by adding further, **It is God that justifieth.** If God justifies, then the logical question follows: **Who is he that condemneth?**—It is obvious in the passage that the God who justifies will not condemn the very ones he justifies. **It is Christ that died, yea rather, that is risen again, who is even at the right hand of God, who also maketh intercession for us**—Here, as in some other cases, the apostle delightfully corrects himself (see Gal. 4:9 and the comments on Rom. 1:12), not meaning that the resurrection of Christ was of more saving value than his death, but that having "put away sin with the sacrifice of himself"—which though precious to us was bitter to him—it was incomparably more delightful to think that he was alive again and living to see the efficacy of his death in our behalf. From ancient times, the right hand of the king was the seat of honor (cf. 1 Sam. 20:2; 1 Kings 2:19; Ps. 45:9) and denoted participation in the royal power and glory (Matt. 20:21). The classical writings contain similar allusions. Accordingly, Christ's sitting at the right hand of God—predicted in Psalm 110:1 and historically referred to in Mark 16:19; Acts 2:33, 7:56; Ephesians 1:20; Colossians 3:1; 1 Peter 3:22; Revelation 3:21—signifies the glory of the exalted Son of man and the power and government over the world in which he participates. Hence he is described as "sitting on the right hand of power" (Matt. 26:64) and "sitting on the right hand of the majesty on high" (Heb. 1:3). The apostle further describes Jesus as interceding in behalf of us, using all his boundless interest with God in our behalf. This is the apex of the climax. His being seated at God's right hand denotes his power to save us; his intercession, his will to do it (Bengel). But how are we to conceive of this intercession? Calvin says, "Not certainly as of one pleading 'on bended knees' and with outstretched arms." Yet, neither is it merely a figurative intimation that the power of Christ's redemption is continually operative or merely to show the favor and vehemence of his love for us (Chrysostom). It cannot be taken to mean less than this, that the glorified Redeemer, conscious of his claims, expressly signifies his will that the efficacy of his death should be made good to the uttermost and signifies it in some such royal style as we find him employing in that wonderful intercessory prayer that he spoke as from within the veil (see John 17:11, 12).

**➤35 Who shall separate us from the love of Christ?**—This does not mean "our love to Christ," as if, "who shall hinder us from loving Christ?" The context speaks of "Christ's love to us," as is clear from the closing words of the chapter. **shall tribulation, or distress, or persecution, or famine, or nakedness, or peril, or sword?**—The term "tribulation" refers to the outside pressure; the term "distress" refers to "anxiety." The term "persecution" perhaps refers to civil or governmental persecution, while the term "famine" refers to hunger. "Nakedness" refers to one's inability to enjoy some of the usual and normal things of life, such as clothing. "Peril" then refers to danger, while "sword" may well refer to death itself. But none

of these, nor all together, regardless of how terrible to the flesh, are tokens of God's wrath, or the least ground for doubt of his love. From whom better can such an utterance come than from one who had himself for Christ's sake endured so much? (see 2 Cor. 11:11-33).

**➤36 As it is written, For thy sake we are killed** [being put to death] **all the day long**— The apostle quotes Psalm 44:22 as descriptive of what God's faithful people may expect from their enemies at any period when their hatred of righteousness is roused and there is nothing to restrain it. Historically, this psalm refers to a plea Israel made to God during a time of unusual distress.

**➤37 Nay, in all these things we are more than conquerors through him that loved us**—Hodge notes that Paul does not say: "We are so far from being conquered by them, that they do us much good"; for though this be true, the words mean simply, "We are preeminently conquerors." (See comments on 5:20.) The trials do not separate us from Christ's love, rather, "through him that loved us" we are victorious over them.

**➤38, 39** For I am persuaded, that neither death, nor life, nor angels, nor principalities, nor powers, nor things present, nor things to come—The terms "principalities" and "powers" refer to evil's forces in our world. Not even the forces of evil are able to defeat the Christian. Although commentators have debated the issue of whether Paul is speaking with reference to good "powers" and "principalities," it is obvious that "good powers" and "principalities" would have no desire in handicapping Christians. "Nor things present, nor things to come" may signify any condition of the present life, as well as any of the unknown possibilities of the life to come. The expression "nor any other creature" actually means "created things," any other thing in the whole created universe of God. Paul is suggesting that if he has omitted anything in his catalog of deterrents, then the reader can fill in the blanks with any other problem. Paul is convinced that nothing shall be able to separate us from the love of God, which is in Christ Jesus our Lord. All the terms here are to be taken in their most general sense and need no closer definition. The indefinite expressions are meant to denote all that can be thought of and are only a rhetorical paraphrase of the conception of "allness." Thus does this wonderful chapter (with which the argument of the epistle properly closes) leave us who are justified by faith in the arms of everlasting love.

# Chapter 9

The end of chapter 8 marks the conclusion of the first major section of this epistle. Paul resumes his major themes in 12:1. It seems that Paul has reached the very apex of his expression concerning the glorious experiences of the Christian in his relationship to Jesus Christ. He has discussed the doctrines of justification, sanctification, and glorification. Paul has reached the very apex of his thought, but there is another problem which troubles the apostle—the so-called "Jewish question." Paul must have faced this problem many times. But to state it simply, the problem is this: Paul has preached a gospel of righteousness by faith instead of righteousness by law. His gospel has made possible the salvation of the Gentiles without their becoming Jews. In so doing, the gospel has nullified the covenant rites of the Jewish race and has passed them by as the channels of revelation. What then is the future of the Jews? Does this mean that the Jews have been rejected entirely? Not at all! Although an apostle to the Gentiles, he himself was a Jew. Therefore, this Jewish problem presented very serious questions for him. What could be done about the Jewish problem? Does it mean that all Jews are lost forever? If they are to be saved, how will they be saved? In chapters 9 through 11 Paul attempts to resolve this problem of the Jewish question by dealing with three areas: (1) The absolute sovereignty of God (9:1-29); (2) the freedom of man (9:30-10:21); and (3) the harmonizing of the two (11:1-36). Paul knew that he was regarded as a traitor to the dearest interest of his people (Acts 21:27, 28; 22:22; 25:24); therefore, the apostle opens his discussion of the subject by giving vent to his real feelings with extraordinary vehemence of protestation.

## 1-33 GOD'S PLAN FOR THE GENTILES AND THE JEWS

➤1, 2 I say the truth in Christ—as if steeped in the Spirit of him who wept over impenitent and doomed Jerusalem (cf. 1:9; 2 Cor. 12:19). Note that Paul's solemn oath is further enhanced by the expression **I lie not, my conscience also bearing me witness in the Holy Ghost** [Spirit]—Perhaps Paul's Jewish adversaries insisted that he was not sincerely concerned for his people; if this be so, this accusation explains his dogmatic defense in this passage that reveals him to be a true friend of his people. When Paul refers to his "conscience," he means that his "conscience" is quickened, illuminated, and even now under the direct influence of the Holy Spirit. Paul has great grief and unceasing anguish in his heart—the bitter hostility of his nation to the glorious gospel and the awful consequences of their unbelief weighing heavily and incessantly upon his spirit. He reveals himself to be a true patriot.

➤3 Paul was so earnestly involved in the problem concerning his people that he **could wish** himself **accursed from Christ for** the sake of his **brethren,** his **kinsmen according to the flesh.** This is reminiscent of Moses' solemn adjuration recorded in Exodus 32:32. Paul obviously loved his people and was happy to call them "my brethren, my kinsmen." To the proportion that he felt himself severed from his nation, he seems to have realized all the more vividly the natural relationship. To explain away the wish here expressed as too strong for any Christian to utter or conceive has caused interpreters to explain the opening words ("for I could wish") as being spoken during his former unenlightened state. Others have unwarrantably diluted the sense of the word "accursed." But these suggestions violate the context.

➤4 **Israelites**—See 11:1; 2 Corinthians 11:22; Philippians 3:5. **to whom pertaineth the adoption** [sonship], **and the glory, and the covenants, and the giving of the law, and the service of God, and the promises**—It is true that the old economy was a state of tutelage and bondage (Gal. 4:1-3); yet, compared with the state of the surrounding heathen, Abraham and his seed were very special and privileged as members of God's family. God had adopted them as his own and fathered them (Exod. 4:22; Deut. 32:6; Isa. 1:2; Jer. 31:9; Hos. 11:1; Mal. 1:6). When Paul refers to the "glory," he is speaking of the "visible token of divine presence in the midst of them," which rested on the ark and filled the tabernacle during all their wanderings in the wilderness. In Jerusalem it continued to be seen in the tabernacle and temple, and only disappeared when the temple was demolished during the captivity (see Ezek. 10). This glory was what the Jews called the "shekinah glory." The term "covenants" refers to the "covenants of promise," meaning the *one covenant* of Abraham and its successive renewals (see Gal. 3:16, 17). The expression "the giving of the law" refers to the giving of the law from Mount Sinai and the possession of it thereafter, which the Jews justly deemed their peculiar honor (Deut. 26:18, 19; Ps. 147:19, 20; Rom. 2:17). "The service of God" denotes the entire system of worship and service pertaining to the temple and the God-ordained sacrifices and rituals. "The promises" refer to the great Abrahamic promises, successively unfolded, and which had their fulfillment only in Christ. (See Acts 26:6, 7; Gal. 3:16, 17; Heb. 7:6.)

➤5 **Whose are the fathers, and of whom as concerning the flesh [the] Christ came**— Here the three great fathers of the covenant— Abraham, Isaac, and Jacob—are referred to. Paul very carefully indicates the most exalted privilege of all was that Christ, according to his humanity, came from the Jewish race. (Cf. 1:3 for the affirmation of Christ's Davidic descent.) **who is over all, God blessed for ever. Amen**— Although this verse has been punctuated in many ways in different translations, the punctuation basically functions to either conjoin the expression "who is over all, God, blessed forever" with "Christ" or to separate it from "Christ." Depending upon which punctuation is employed, Christ is said to be God or not to be God. The difference is critical. One of the following two renderings represents the original thought:

(1) Whose are the fathers, and from whom is the Christ according to the flesh, who is over all, God, blessed forever. Amen. (2) Whose are the fathers, and from whom is the Christ according to the flesh. God, who is over all, be blessed forever. Amen. In the first rendering the comma

following "flesh" signals that the following words constitute appositional expressions; hence, "Christ" is (1) "over all," (2) "God," and (3) "blessed forever." In the second rendering, the period following "flesh" separates "the Christ" from these expressions—which are, instead, turned into a sentence of their own by inserting a predicate: "God, who is over all, be blessed forever!" The first rendering closely follows the syntax of the Greek; the second really strains the Greek. Nearly all the Greek fathers understood the expression "God over all" to describe Christ. And most of the early translations also joined "Christ" to "God." Little can be offered to validify the second rendering, while much can be said to support the first. The language itself provides the strongest defense ("Christ" is naturally and smoothly followed by the appositional expression "who is over all, God blessed forever.") And so does the context. Paul would not abruptly, even sporadically, insert a praise to God the Father at the end of his enumeration of the divine privileges and promises given to the Jews. To the contrary, he was culminating that list with the greatest blessing of all—i.e., the Christ, who is God over all, blessed forever, would come from the Jewish race! How could the Jews then reject him? This created anguish in Paul's heart, not joy or praise. How incongruous it would be, then, for him to praise God. Paul was grieved that the Jews rejected the greatest blessing—Christ himself, who is God *(GAM)*.

➤6 The first objection Paul confronted is the argument that God apparently has been unfaithful in the keeping of his promises. **Not as though the word of God hath taken none effect**—"had fallen (to the ground)," i.e., failed (cf. Luke 16:17). **For they are not all Israel, which are of Israel**—i.e., "For not all who are descended from Israel belong to Israel" (RSV). Here the apostle begins to discuss the profound subject of election, the treatment of which extends to the end of chapter 11. In essence, this is Paul's argument: "Do not think that I mourn over the total loss of Israel; for that would involve the failure of God's word to Abraham;

but not all that belong to the actual seed and go under the name of Israel are the Israel of God's irrevocable choice." The difficulties that encompass this subject lie not in the apostle's teaching (which is plain enough), but in the truths themselves, the evidence for which taken by themselves is overwhelming, but whose perfect harmony is beyond human comprehension in the present state. The great source of error here lies in hastily inferring from the apostle's taking up the calling of the Gentiles in connection with the rejection of Israel, and continuing this subject through the next two chapters that the election spoken about in this chapter is a national, not personal election, and consequently is election merely to religious advantages, not to salvation. In that case, the argument of 9:6 would be this: "The choice of Abraham and his seed has not failed because, though Israel has been rejected, the Gentiles have taken their place; and God has a right to choose what nation he will to the privileges of his visible kingdom." But so far from this, the Gentiles are not so much as mentioned at all until toward the close of the chapter. And the argument of this verse is that "all Israel is not rejected, but only a portion of it, the remainder of it being the 'Israel' whom God has chosen in the exercise of his solemn right." And that this is a choice not to mere external privileges but to external salvation will appear clearly from what follows.

►**7-9 Neither, because they are the seed of Abraham, are they all children**—Not in the line of mere fleshly descent from Abraham does the election run. Were this true, Ishmael, Hagar's child, and even Keturah's children, would be included, but they were not. Paul is simply asking and answering simultaneously the question, "Since the Jews were the seed of Abraham does this mean all Jews are the children of God?" In answering this question, Paul declares that God exercises his sovereignty and has decreed that faith, not heredity and blood lineage, is the only external principle of sonship. This is underscored very vividly in the expression **but, In Isaac shall thy seed be called** (see Gen. 21:12). Therefore, as Paul deals briefly with God's redemptive purposes concerning the patriarchs and their offspring, he reminds us that the promises to Sarah and Rebecca were actually fulfilled. God freely exercised his selective grace in the case of these

patriarchs. After all, it was he who was the originator of his eternal purpose.

►**10-13 And not only this; but when Rebecca also had conceived by one** [man], **even by our father Isaac**—It might be thought that there was a natural reason for preferring the child of Sarah as being Abraham's true and first wife, both to the children of Hagar, Sarah's handmaiden, and to the children of Keturah, his second wife. But there could be no such reason in the case of Rebecca, Isaac's only wife. For the choice of her son Jacob was the choice of one of two sons by the same mother, the younger in preference to the elder, and before either of them was born, and consequently before either had done **good or evil**, which could possibly be a ground of preference: and all to show that the sole ground of distinction lay in the unconditional choice of God—**not of works, but of him that calleth.** Verse 13 presents a particularly difficult statement in the words **Jacob have I loved, but Esau have I hated.** This statement must be interpreted with reference to nations, not individuals. Davidson and Martin note that this nationalistic emphasis is "the original reference in the two Old Testament quotations" (Gen. 25:33; Mal. 1:2, 3). Bruce agrees with this interpretation and calls the reader to remember the historical context of the Malachi verses. Furthermore, Bruce points out that communities of the ancient Near East were often spoken of in terms of their ancestors, illustrating the common oscillation in biblical thought and speech between individual and corporate personality.

►**14 What shall we say then? Is there unrighteousness** [injustice] **with God? God forbid**—This is the first of two objections to the foregoing doctrine that God chooses one man and rejects the other, not on the basis of their works, but purely in the exercise of his own good pleasure: "This doctrine is inconsistent with the justice of God," someone objects. The answer to this objection extends to 9:19, where we have the second objection. Paul emphatically denies the accusation by using the construction that may be translated, "May it never come to pass," and here translated, "God forbid."

►**15 For he saith to Moses, I will have mercy on whom I will have mercy, and I will have compassion on whom I will have compassion**—There can be no unrighteousness in

God's choosing whom he will, for to Moses he expressly claims the right to do so. Yet it is worthy of notice that this is expressed in the positive rather than the negative form. He does not say, "I will have mercy on *none but* whom I will," but "I will have mercy on *whomsoever* I will." Therefore, the apostle is insisting that both mercy and compassion belong entirely to God. Of course, this is no new doctrine—see Exodus 33:19.

►**16 So then it is not of him that willeth, nor of him that runneth, but of God that showeth mercy**—Cf. 1 Corinthians 9:24, 26; Philippians 2:16; 3:14. Both of these are indispensable to salvation, yet salvation is owing to neither, but is purely "of God who shows mercy." (See comments on Phil. 2:12, 13.)

►**17** Paul again quotes from Exodus (9:16), relating God's words to Pharaoh: **For the scripture saith unto Pharaoh, Even for this same purpose have I raised thee up, that I might show my power in thee, and that my name might be declared throughout all the earth.** It is important to note that instead of employing the term "God," Paul uses the term "Scripture" and personifies it as if speaking to Moses. The apostle has shown that God claims the right to choose whom he will; here he shows by an example that God punishes whom he will. God did not make Pharaoh to be the wicked, hateful individual that he was. Denney states: "The purpose Pharaoh was designed to serve, and actually did serve, on this stage, was certainly not his own; as certainly it was God's. God's power was shown in the penal miracles by which Pharaoh and Egypt were visited, and his name is proclaimed to this day wherever the story of the Exodus is told." The Pharaoh (the Egyptian ruler, Rameses II) was raised up for the purpose of showing God's power. Therefore, he is to be understood simply as a vehicle through which God displayed his power.

►**18 Therefore hath he mercy on whom he will have mercy, and whom he will he hardeneth**—He does this by judicially abandoning them to the hardening influence of sin itself (Ps. 81:11, 12; Rom. 1:24, 26, 28; Heb. 3:8, 13).

►**19** This verse introduces a second objection to the concept of divine sovereignty. The charge is namely, "If what Paul has written is true, then God is unjust in blaming man. If God is free to elect men for better or worse in the absolute sense, as Paul has just demonstrated, what then is human responsibility?" The whole point is, "This doctrine is incompatible with human responsibility." **Why doth he yet find fault? For who hath resisted his will?**—If God chooses and rejects, pardons and punishes whom he pleases, why are those blamed who if rejected by him cannot help sinning and perishing? This objection (as the former) shows quite conclusively the real nature of the doctrine to which the reader may object—that it is election and nonelection to eternal salvation prior to any difference of personal character. This is the only doctrine that can suggest the objection here stated, and to this doctrine the objection is plausible. What now is the apostle's answer? It is twofold. First: "It is irreverence and presumption in the creature to arraign the Creator."

►**20, 21 Nay but, O man, who art thou that repliest against God? Shall the thing formed say to him that formed it, Why hast thou made me thus?**—See Isaiah 45:9. **Hath not the potter power [the right] over the clay, of the same lump to make one vessel unto honour, and another unto dishonour?**—Paul is saying in essence that the argument is "out of bounds." The one created has no right to speak in this fashion to the Creator. To drive home his point, the apostle employs the illustration of the clay and the potter. The potter makes one vessel to contain flowers in the parlor, while another vessel is made from the same lump of clay to contain garbage from the kitchen. Does the clay have any right to object to the potter's action? (Cf. Isa. 29:16; 45:9, 10; 64:8; Jer. 18:6.) The objection here stated is based on ignorance and misapprehension of the relationship that exists between God and his sinful creatures. All men are sinners and have forfeited every claim to his mercy; it is therefore perfectly reasonable for God to spare one and not another, to make one vessel to honor and another to dishonor. But it is to be kept in mind that Paul here speaks not of God's right over his creatures *as creatures* but as *sinful creatures:* as he himself clearly intimates in the next verses (Hodge). But still a second objection is offered by the apostle: "There is nothing unjust in such sovereignty."

►**22, 23 What if God, willing to show his wrath and to make his power known, endured with much longsuffering the vessels**

**of wrath**—i.e., "vessels destined to wrath." "Vessels of mercy" in the next verse means "vessels destined to mercy" (cf. Eph. 2:3). The expression **fitted to destruction** creates some problems, and these problems cannot be removed merely by softening the language of the text. If God, as the apostle teaches expressly, desiring to show his wrath and make known his power, could do so by punishing some and pardoning others, then this is within the scope of his sovereignty. Moreover, if the choice between the two classes was not to be founded on their doings but on God's good pleasure, the decision ultimately stood with God. **that he might make known the riches of his glory on the vessels of mercy, which he had afore prepared unto glory**—The "vessels of mercy" were prepared beforehand while the "vessels of wrath" are "fitted for" (a perfect participle, meaning "having been fitted"). Note, God is not stated as the agent of the "fitting"; the condition is merely stated as historical fact. Therefore, some would prefer the translation "fit for destruction" (ripe and ready for destruction). Davidson and Martin write: "The mystery of predestination must remain, yet there appears here no warrant for any dogma of predestination to damnation, while the parallel of foreordination to glory is stated with no uncertainty." These commentators also observe that in the case of the "vessels of mercy" God's activity was that of preparation, but in the case of "vessels of wrath" the Creator simply "endured with much patience." Thus, the Creator is pictured as active in the case of one but passive in the case of the other. Paul's argument leaves the objector without an answer.

➤**24 Even us, whom he hath called, not of the Jews only, but also of the Gentiles?**—The definitive identification is "not from among the Jews only, but also from among the Gentiles." Here for the first time in this chapter the calling of the Gentiles is introduced. Everything prior to this point has been said in respect, not to the substitution of the called Gentiles for the rejected Jews, but to the choice of one portion in the rejection of another of the same Israel. Had Israel's rejection been total, God's promise to Abraham would not have been fulfilled by the substitution of the Gentiles in their place; but Israel's rejection was only partial, and the preservation of a "remnant," in which the

promise was made good, was but "good according to the election of grace." Now for the first time, the apostle tells us that it was God's purpose all along to take out of the Gentiles a people for his name (Acts 28:14). That subject, now introduced, continues to the conclusion of chapter 11.

➤**25** Hosea is here quoted (2:23); the passage relating immediately, not to the heathen, but to the kingdom of the ten tribes. But since they had sunk to the level of the heathen, who were "not God's people" and in that sense, "not beloved," the apostle legitimately applies it to the heathen as "aliens from the commonwealth of Israel and strangers from the covenants of promise" (Eph. 2:12). See comments on 1 Peter 2:10.

➤**26** This verse contains another quotation from Hosea (1:10). **that in the place where it was said unto them, Ye are not my people; there shall they be called the children** [sons] **of the living God**—This expression emphasizes the gracious change here announced, a change from divine exclusion to divine admission to the privileges of God.

➤**27-29** The apostle now turns to quote **Esaias** [Isaiah] **. . . concerning Israel.** The expression "Isaiah crieth" denotes a solemn testimony borne openly (John 1:15; 7:28, 37; 12:44; Acts 23:6). This quotation is from Isaiah 10:22, 23 (LXX). The sense given to these words by the apostle may seem to differ from that intended by the prophet. But the sameness and identity of sentiment in both places at once appears if we understand those words of the prophet to mean that while a **remnant** of Israel should be graciously spared to return from captivity, Paul looks beyond "the return" to ultimate deliverance (or, salvation). The "short work" seems to indicate the speedy accomplishment of his word, both in cutting off the major portion of Israel and in saving the remnant. The doctrine of the "remnant" is to be treated further in 11:1-10. **And as Esaias** [Isaiah] **said before**—referring probably to an early part of his book, namely Isaiah 1:9. **Except the Lord of Sabaoth** [hosts] **had left us a seed**—again a reference to the remnant, small at first, but in due time to become plenteous (cf. Ps. 22:30, 31; Isa. 6:12, 13). **we had been as Sodoma** [Sodom], **and been made like unto Gomorrha**—But for this precious seed, the chosen people would have resembled the cities of the plain, not only in degeneracy of character, but also in merited doom.

►**30, 31 What shall we say then?**—or, "What now is the result of the whole?" The result is this—very different from what one would have expected: **That the Gentiles, which followed not after righteousness, have attained to righteousness, even the righteousness which is of faith**—As we have seen, the "righteousness of faith" is the righteousness that justifies (see comments on 3:22). This verse must mean that "the Gentiles, who while strangers to Christ were quite indifferent about acceptance with God, having embraced the gospel as soon as it was preached to them, experienced the blessedness of a justified state." **But Israel, which followed after the law of righteousness, hath not attained to the law of righteousness**—The term "law" is used here perhaps in the same sense as in 7:23, denoting "a principle of action." Israel, though sincerely and steadily aiming at acceptance with God, nevertheless, missed it.

►**32** Israel missed that "righteousness" **Because they sought it not by faith,** the only means whereby even a Jew could be justified. The apostle notes that they rather pursued it **as [if] it were by the works of the law. For they stumbled at that stumblingstone**—meaning Christ. The "stumbling stone" may refer partially to the cross (1 Cor. 1:23), the seeming shame the Jews were unable to accept as being the destiny of their Messiah. Some interpreters, however, think that the reference refers primarily to the Jews' inability to understand that righteousness was gained by faith, not by works of law.

►**33 Behold, I lay in Sion** [Zion] **a stumblingstone and rock of offence: and whosoever believeth on him shall not be ashamed**—The apostle here quotes Isaiah 8:14 and 28:16, combining two messianic predictions, not unusual in NT writers' usage of OT quotations. The prediction brings together both the classes whom the apostle is treating: those to whom the Messiah should be only a stone of stumbling and those who were to regard him as the Cornerstone of all their hopes.

*Chapter* **10**

## 1-21 THE WAY OF SALVATION FOR BOTH GENTILES AND JEWS

In the previous chapter the apostle stressed the point of God's sovereignty. However, this has not resolved the problem on the part of the Jews, and Paul continues his discussion on this subject.

►**1 Brethren, my heart's desire**—The term "desire" here means that which would give the heart full satisfaction. It is a term that may mean "pleasure," "a perfect satisfaction connected with it." (Cf. Matt. 11:26; Eph. 1:5, 9; Phil. 1:15; 2 Thess. 1:11.) **and prayer to God for Israel is, that they might be saved**—This shows Paul's intense feeling and concern for his Jewish kinsmen. He prays for their salvation. Having before poured forth the anguish of his soul at the general unbelief of this nation and its dreadful consequences (9:1, 3), he here expresses in the most emphatic terms his desire and prayer for their salvation.

►**2 I bear them record**—as well he could from his own sad experience. **that they have a zeal of** [for] **God, but not according to knowledge**—cf. Acts 22:3; 26:9-11; Galatians 1:13, 14. Paul alludes to the zeal of his people (despite their spiritual ignorance), not to excuse their rejection of Christ and their rage against his followers, but as some ground of hope regarding them (see 1 Tim. 1:13). Their strong desire for religion is not in accordance with knowledge of God's plan and ways. Judah B. Tema (Aboth, v. 20) states: "Be strong as the leopard and swift as the eagle, fleet as the gazelle and brave as the lion to do the will of thy Father which is in heaven." But these words are characteristic of Judaism only at its best. In a measure, Israel had given herself to God, but at the same time her sins had created her undesirable relationship with God.

►**3 For they being ignorant of God's righteousness**—i.e., the righteousness that comes from God. **and going about to establish their own righteousness, have not submitted themselves unto the righteousness of God**— The apostle views the general rejection of Christ by the nation as one act. (Cf. Phil. 3:9 for a close parallel to this verse.)

➤4 For Christ is the end of the law for righteousness to every one that believeth— The first part of this verse is ambiguous; it could mean that "Christ marks the termination of law" (Goodspeed), "Christ has brought the law to an end" (*Twentieth Century New Testament*), "Christ is the . . . completion of the Law" (Berkeley), or "the consummation of the Law is Christ" (Weymouth). If we accept all these meanings as legitimate, the expression means that Christ fulfilled the law (Matt. 5:17, 18), and then paid the price through his sacrificial death to put an end to the righteous requirements of the law over sinners (8:3, 4). Thus, Christ became the end of the law. Whoever believes in him is made righteous—i.e., is made right with God.

➤5-8 Moses describeth the righteousness which is of the law, That the man which doeth those things shall live by them—This statement, taken from Leviticus 18:5, declares that once a man determines to keep the law, he must live according to every mandate of the law. But the righteousness which is of faith speaketh—Its language or import is to this effect (the apostle quotes in substance Deut. 30:13, 14). Say not in thine heart, Who shall ascend into heaven? (that is, to bring Christ down from above)—You do not have to sigh over the possibility of attaining justification; that is as if one should say, "Ah! If I could but get someone to mount up to heaven and fetch me down Christ, there might be some hope, but since that cannot be, mine is a desperate case." Who shall descend into the deep [abyss]?— another case of impossibility, suggested by Proverbs 30:4 and perhaps also by Amos 9:2; probably both of these questions are proverbial expressions of impossibility (cf. Ps. 139:7, 10; Prov. 24:7). But what saith it?—The apostle continues the quotation from Deuteronomy 30:14. The word is nigh thee, even in thy mouth, and in thy heart: that is, the word of faith, which we preach—Paul is insisting that the "word" is easily accessible. The expression "in thy mouth" relates to confessing him, while the expression "in thy heart" relates to believing him. In the Deuteronomy passage, Moses was exhorting the Israelites to keep the words of the law in their mouth and in their heart. Paul appropriates this passage because he sees Christ as the consummation of the law (10:4).

The believer will receive Christ by responding to the words of the gospel. This Christ is not far away—one does not have to go to heaven to contact him and one cannot find him in the abyss, for he has risen from the dead. He is near, as near as one's confessing mouth and believing heart.

➤9 That if thou shalt confess with thy mouth the Lord Jesus, and shalt believe in thine heart that God hath raised him from the dead, thou shalt be saved—This verse and the following verse may well indicate an early Christian form of presenting the way of salvation. (For example, see Paul's reply to the question asked by the Philippian jailer in Acts 16:31.) Paul here gives the means by which an individual is truly justified. (Cf. Matt. 10:32; 1 John 4:15.) The idea of confessing "with your mouth" is put first merely to correspond with the previous quotation from Deuteronomy "on your lips and in your heart." Actually, believing comes before confessing. Although Paul notes "belief" last in this verse, the two actions are placed in their proper order in 10:10. This confession of Christ's name, especially in time of persecution, and whenever denunciation is attached to the Christian confession, is an indispensable test of discipleship.

➤11 Paul now quotes Isaiah 28:16, a messianic passage: Whosoever believeth on him shall not be ashamed. Here, as in 9:33, the quotation is from the Septuagint, which renders the words of the original Hebrew "shall not make haste" (i.e., "not fly for escape as from conscious danger") as "will not be put to shame"—which amounts to the same thing. Thus Paul introduces the second point, that the way of salvation for all men is alike. He has earlier indicated that the way of salvation is by faith; now he says that the way of salvation is the same for both Jew and Greek.

➤12 For there is no difference between the Jew and the Greek: for the same Lord over all is rich unto all that call upon him— Calvin and Hodge take the term "Lord" to refer to God, while most other commentators take this as a reference to Christ. Paul describes the Lord as bestowing his riches upon all who call upon him. This is a favorite Pauline term used to express the exuberance of that saving grace which is in Christ Jesus. The expression "call upon him" confirms the application of the preceding words "to Christ," since calling upon the name of the Lord is a customary NT expression used with reference to Christ (see Acts 7:59, 60; 9:14, 21; 22:16; 1 Cor. 1:2; 2 Tim. 2:22). This calling, as practiced in the NT, was audible, genuine, and bold.

➤**13 For whosoever shall call upon the name of the Lord shall be saved**—The expression in Greek is emphatic, "Every one, whosoever calls . . . " The quotation is derived from Joel 2:32, quoted also by Peter in his sermon on the day of Pentecost (Acts 2:21) with its evident application to Christ. Therefore, Paul has arrived at these conclusions: (1) justification is by faith; (2) justification is by the same method for both Jew and Gentile alike; (3) the Jew is responsible for his present spiritual condition because he has not called "upon the name of the Lord."

➤**14, 15 How then shall they call on him in whom they have not believed? and how shall they believe in him of whom they have not heard? And how shall they hear without a preacher?**—The same Lord over all is rich unto all alike that call upon him (both Jew and Gentile), but this calling implies believing, and believing implies hearing, and hearing implies preaching, and preaching, an evangelist to preach. Why, then, did the Jews respond as they did when the gospel was preached among the Gentiles? (Cf. Acts 26:16-18.) Paul notes that this gospel has been preached both to Jews and to Greeks. The expression "call upon" relates to the phrase of 10:13 (from Joel 2:32). Verse 15 is a quotation of Isaiah 52:7. Careful comparison with the OT text makes it obvious that the apostle quotes freely from the Hebrew text. The picture drawn in this passage is that of a herald who is announcing the promise of Israel's restoration from the exile. However, in this passage, as elsewhere in the NT, the Isaiah passage is interpreted in accordance with the gospel age. For the apostle, this passage constitutes a picture of one who brings the good news of God's mercy and redemption for sinners.

➤**16, 17 But they have not all obeyed the gospel**—The Scripture has prepared us to expect this sad result. **For Esaias** [Isaiah] **saith, Lord, who hath believed our report?**—i.e., "Where shall one find a believer?" The prophet speaks as if next to no one would

believe. The apostle softens this by the words, "they have not all obeyed the gospel." But the apostle notes that **faith cometh by hearing, and hearing by the word of God** ["Christ" in the earliest manuscripts]. This is another confirmation of the truth that faith supposes the hearing of the word and thus a commission to preach it. The content of the hearing is defined by "the word of Christ." The Greek term for "word" here is *rhēma*, and it designates the spoken word, utterance, instant speech. The "word of Christ" is the preaching concerning Christ, the word spoken concerning Christ. In 10:6-8 this word (*rhēma*—see 10:8) is identified with Christ—because to receive this word is to receive Christ, for the living Christ is conveyed through his word. And this spoken word can produce faith in the hearer.

➤**18 But I say, Have they not heard?**— Can Israel, throughout all the Mediterranean world, plead ignorance of these glad tidings? Paul answers in the intensified expression, **Yes verily, their sound went into all the earth, and their words unto the ends of the world**— These beautiful words are derived from Psalm 19:4; whether the apostle quoted them as in their primary intention (applicable to his subject), or simply used scriptural language to define his own ideas, expositors are not agreed.

➤**19 But I say, Did not Israel know?**— Could Israel not know, from their own Scriptures, God's intention to bring the Gentiles into his kingdom? **First**—that is, first in the prophetic line. The apostle now quotes **Moses** as saying, **I will provoke you to jealousy by them that are no people, and by a foolish nation I will anger you**—This is a quotation of Deuteronomy 32:21, in which God warned his ancient people that because they had moved him to jealousy with their "no-gods" and provoked him to anger with their vanities, he in requital would move them to jealousy by receiving into his favor a "no-people" and provoke them to anger by adopting a nation void of understanding. So Paul notes that the "law giver" (Moses) had warned Israel.

➤**20** Then he quotes **Esaias** [Isaiah] as very boldly saying, **I was found of them that sought me not; I was made manifest unto them that asked not after me**—Paul used Isaiah 65:1 (from the LXX) to show that God, in reaction to Israel's disobedience, would reveal himself to the Gentiles. In this passage quoted by Paul, Isaiah speaks of the Gentiles and immediately follows with the words: " 'Here am I, here am I' to a nation that did not call on my name" (RSV).

➤21 But to Israel he saith, All day long I have stretched forth my hands unto a disobedient and gainsaying [contrary] people—taken from Isaiah 65:2 (LXX). God's graciousness is set in sharp contrast to the disobedience of Israel. These words, immediately following the announcement just quoted concerning the calling of the Gentiles, were enough to forewarn the Jews of God's purpose to eject them from their privileges and turn his favor to the Gentiles.

## Chapter 11

Paul discussed the sovereignty of God in chapter 9 and the freedom of man in chapter 10. In this chapter he seeks to harmonize the sovereignty of God and the freedom of man. He comes face to face with the historical fact of the Jews' rejection of Christ and discusses whether this rejection means the absolute and final rejection of Israel. The apostle concludes that the rejection of the Jews does not mean their final rejection but rather that there is a believing remnant. Furthermore, he is confident that just as the Jews' rejection had led to the conversion of Gentiles, God would make the Gentiles instrumental in turning the Jews back to God. Although Jews have been disobedient, God's purpose is to bring them back to him. The results of this divine purpose is that all men will be brought to God by grace, Jew and Gentile alike. Paul's argument is thrilling because he was a Jew and thereby knew that God would not finally cast his people away.

### 1-10 THE REJECTION OF THE JEWS IS ONLY PARTIAL—A REMNANT REMAINS

➤1 I say then, Hath God cast away his people?—Paul answers the question by using the expression so often employed in this epistle, God forbid (actually, "may it never come to pass"). Jesus did indeed announce that the kingdom of God would be taken from Israel (Matt. 21:41). And when he was asked by the Eleven at his resurrection if he would at that time "restore the kingdom to Israel," his reply

was a virtual admission that Israel was in some sense already out of the covenant (Acts 1:6-9). Yet, here the apostle teaches that in two respects Israel was not cast away. First, she was not cast away *totally*. Second, she was not cast away *finally*. The apostle gives his initial attention to the fact that Israel was not wholly and completely cast away. He proves this by indicating that he himself is an Israelite, of the seed of Abraham, of the tribe of Benjamin—cf. Philippians 3:5. Paul was living proof of the fact that not all Jews have been cast aside. Inasmuch as he was a descendant of Abraham, he was of pure descent from the father of the faithful. The apostle notes that he belonged to the "tribe of Benjamin," that tribe which, on the revolt of the ten tribes, constituted along with Judah the one faithful kingdom of God (1 Kings 12:21). Following the captivity, Benjamin, along with Judah, provided the kernel of the returned Jewish nation (Ezra 4:1; 10:9). Therefore, Paul uses himself as an illustration of the fact that there remains among the Jews a believing remnant. What better proof could he offer!

➤2-4 God hath not cast away his people which he foreknew—On the word "foreknew" see the comments on 8:29. The apostle then turns to the case of Elijah and uses the ancient prophet as an illustration. (Cf. 1 Kings 19.) Elijah had every good reason to condemn Israel for turning away from God, but God reminded the prophet that he still had a remnant among Israel. Although his people proved exceedingly stubborn, rebellious, and disobedient, the prophet was reminded that God had reserved to himself seven thousand men, who had not bowed the knee to . . . Baal.

➤5 Even so then at this present time also there is a remnant according to the election of grace—The apostasy of Israel was not so universal as it seemed to be in Elijah's time, or as the prophet in his despondency concluded it to be; so now the rejection of Christ by Israel is not so appalling as one would be apt to think. There is now, as there was then, a faithful remnant. This remnant did not consist of persons naturally better than the unbelieving mass, but rather it consisted of people graciously chosen to salvation (see 1 Cor. 4:7; 2 Thess. 2:13). This substantiates Paul's argument on election in chapter 9 as being an election not of

Gentiles in place of the Jews, but a sovereign choice of some of Israel itself to believe and to be saved, along with many Gentiles.

►6 Paul points out that this is an act of grace: election is no longer on the basis of works; **otherwise grace is no more grace.** The general position here laid down is of vital importance: that there are two possible sources of salvation—men's works and God's grace; and that these are so essentially distinct and opposite that salvation cannot be of any combination or mixture of both but must be wholly either of the one or of the other.

►**7-10 What then?**—How stands the fact? Israel failed to obtain what it sought. **but the election** [elect] **hath obtained it, and the rest were blinded** [hardened]—What Israel was attempting to find—justification, or acceptance with God—she found not. But the election (the elect remnant of Israel) found it, and the rest were hardened or judicially given over to the hardness of their hearts. The apostle again returns to Isaiah (29:10) and Deuteronomy (29:4) for OT support of his position. The quotation **God hath given them the spirit of slumber** [stupor or torpor] means that the people were possessed of spiritual insensibility (cf. the Isa. 29:10 reference). The apostle also quotes David (Ps. 69:22), saying, **Let their table** [feast] **be made a snare, and a trap**—i.e., let their very blessings prove a curse to them and their enjoyments only sting and take vengeance on them. **Let their eyes be darkened, that they may not see, and bow down their back alway**—This is expressive of the decreptitude or of the servile condition to come on the nation through the just judgment of God. The apostle's object in employing these particular quotations is to show that what he had been compelled to say of their present condition and the prospects of his nation was more than substantiated by the Scriptures on which Israel relied.

11-15 THE JEWISH REJECTION IS NOT FINAL, ONLY TEMPORARY

The illustration at this point extends from 11:11 to 11:31.

►**11 I say then, Have they stumbled that they should fall?**—Davidson and Martin translate the verse in this manner, "Was it the purpose of God to make the Jews stumble in order that they might fall?" Did God cause this irretrievable tragedy? **God forbid**—is the apostle's answer. This is the same expression he has used repeatedly and may also be translated, "May it never come to pass" (11:1). **but rather through their fall** [trespass] **salvation is come unto the Gentiles, . . . to provoke them to jealousy**—Here, as also in 10:19 (quoting from Deut. 32:21), we see that emulation is a legitimate stimulus to what is good.

►**12 if the fall of them** [their trespass] **be the riches of the world, and the diminishing** [defection] **of them the riches of the Gentiles; how much more their fulness?**—Paul here shows God's providential activities in reaching all men. The Jews' trespass (in failing to accept Jesus as the Messiah, and even more so in crucifying him) brought about a diminishing—i.e., the true Israel was reduced to a remnant. But whereas the Jews trespassed the will of God, their trespass meant riches for the world, riches for the Gentiles. The term "fullness" means "their full recovery" and the "making up of them to their full numbers." If an event so significant as Israel's fall was the occasion of such unspeakable good to the Gentile world, how much greater good may the world expect from an event so blessed as their full recovery!

►**13 For I speak to you Gentiles**—This is additional proof that this epistle was addressed to Gentile believers. (See 1:13.) **I magnify mine office** [ministry]—Paul wanted his readers to understand that one reason for his emphasis upon the commission God gave him as an apostle to the Gentiles was to provoke his own people to jealousy and to subsequently turn them to Christ.

►**14 If by any means I may provoke to emulation them which are my flesh** [i.e., the Jews] **and might save some of them**—Even here Paul is speaking in terms of the "remnant" because he does not speak of the salvation of "all Jews," but "some of them."

►**15 For if the casting away . . .**—In 11:2 the apostle had denied that they were cast away (or, "pushed away" according to the Gk.); here he affirms it. But both are true; they were cast away, though neither totally nor finally, and it is of this partial and temporary rejection that the apostle here speaks. **what shall the receiving of them be, but life from the dead?**—The reception of the whole family of Israel, scattered as they are among all nations under heaven and the most inveterate enemies of the Lord Jesus, will be such a stupendous manifestation of the power of God upon the spirits of men as will not only kindle devout astonishment far and wide, but so change the dormant mode of thinking and feeling on all spiritual things as to seem like a resurrection from the dead. However, it is unlikely that Paul is suggesting that every Jew will receive Christ; it seems rather he is suggesting that a "large portion" of the Jews will be saved.

➤**16 For if** [the dough offered as] **the firstfruit be holy, the lump is also holy: and if the root be holy, so are the branches**—The Israelites were required to offer to God the firstfruits of the earth, both in their raw state (in a sheaf of newly reaped grain, Lev. 23:10, 11), and in their prepared state (made into cakes of dough, Num. 15:19, 21). Therefore, the whole produce of that season was regarded as holy. The latter of these offerings is here intended, since the term "lump" (lit., "a mingling"—of flour and water, etc.) was used by Paul. The apostle's argument is that the separation unto God of Abraham, Isaac, and Jacob (the patriarchs) from the rest of mankind was as real an offering of firstfruits as that which hallowed the rest of the produce. So in the divine estimation it counted for the sanctification of the entire nation to God. The figure of the "root" and its "branches" is of like import—the consecration of the one extending to the other. If the "root" is set apart to God, so also are the "branches." In both illustrations, Paul asserts the principle that the source characterizes the whole. Thus, all of Israel must be holy because its source is holy.

➤**17, 18 And if some of the branches . . .**—The mass of the unbelieving and rejected Israelites are here called "some," not as before to pacify Jewish prejudice (see comments on 3:3, and on "not all" in 10:16), but with the opposite view of checking Gentile pride. **thou, being a wild olive tree** [shoot], **wert graffed** [grafted] **in among them, and with them partakest of the root and fatness of the olive tree**—Though it is more usual to graft a superior cutting into an inferior stem (see 11:24), the opposite method intended here is not without example. The figure of the "olive tree" warns the Gentiles against any tendency

toward boastful pride and also substantiates the apostle's optimism about the Jews. By "a wild olive shoot" the apostle means Gentile Christians who have been placed into God's NT economy. The Gentiles grafted into God's organic economy partake of the riches along with the remnant of Jews who believe (see Eph. 3:6).

➤**18** But the apostle warns the Gentiles: **Boast not against the branches. But if thou boast, thou bearest** [support] **not the root, but the root thee**—The Gentile has no reason to boast against the rejected branches. If the branches may not boast over the root that bears them, then the Gentile may not boast over the seed of Abraham; for what is the Gentile's standing in relation to Israel but that of a branch in relation to the root? From Israel has come all that the Gentiles are and possess in the family of God, for "salvation is of the Jews" (John 4:22).

➤**19 Thou wilt say then, The branches were broken off, that I might be graffed** [grafted] **in**—Though the Gentile has a tendency to despise the disobedient and faithless Jew, he should remember that he is taking the place of the Jew and that if one can be broken off, the other branch may also be broken off.

➤**20 Well; because of unbelief they were broken off, and thou standest by faith. Be not highminded, but fear**—This reminds us of Hebrews 4:2. Despite God's relationship to the "natural branches," he did not spare them. Why should the Gentile believe that he will be spared if he conducts himself as did the Jew?

➤**22, 23 Behold therefore the goodness and severity of God: on them which fell, severity; but toward thee, goodness, if thou continue in his goodness: otherwise thou also shalt be cut off**—God was good and kind to admit the Gentiles (who before were strangers to the covenant's promise—Eph. 2:12-20) into his household and economy. If the Gentile "continue in his kindness" means if the Gentile remains in believing dependence on that pure goodness that made the Gentile a Christian in the first place. Paul continues to employ the figure of the olive branches in the expression "otherwise thou also shalt be cut off." Branches may be grafted into trees, but they also may be removed from trees. **And they also, if they abide not still in unbelief, shall be graffed** [grafted] **in: for God is able to graff** [graft] **them in again**—Here a repeated emphasis is placed upon unbelief and God's ability to graft in "the branches." If the Jew does not persist in unbelief, then he will be grafted into the branches. This appeal to the power of God to effect the recovery of his ancient people implies the vast difficulty of such a recovery, which all who have ever labored for the conversion of the Jews have depressingly felt. Some expositors believe that Paul is referring to the Jewish nation as a group; others that Paul is referring to individual Jews, reintroduced from time to time in the family of God on their believing in Jesus Christ. Either way, "Paul implies a spiritual, if not a horticultural, reality; the original branches are more akin to the tree than the wild shoots and should therefore be easier to graft into the stock from which they were originally taken" (Davidson and Martin).

➤**24 For if thou wert cut out of the olive tree which is wild by nature, and wert graffed** [grafted] **contrary to nature into a good** [cultivated] **olive tree: how much more shall these, which be the natural branches, be graffed** [grafted] **into their own olive tree?**—In using the phrase "contrary to nature," Paul may be "thought to disarm criticism in advance by showing that he is aware of the unnaturalness of the particular kind of grafting here described. But he need mean no more than that the process of grafting is itself 'contrary to nature'—a view which was commonly taken by the ancients" (Bruce). Emphasis must be placed upon the "how much more." If God is able to do that which is "contrary to nature," then by what greater token will these natural branches be grafted back into their olive tree. The apostle is arguing that it is more natural and more conceivable for one to restore his own people than it is for one to restore those who are not his own.

## 25-32 PAUL'S RESOLUTION OF THE PROBLEM

➤**25 that ye should be ignorant of this mystery**—The term "mystery" (Gk., *musterion*) so often used by Paul, does not mean something incomprehensible, but "something before kept secret, either wholly, or for the most part, and now only fully disclosed" (cf. 16:25; 1 Cor. 2:7-10; Eph. 1:9, 10; 3:3-6, 9, 10). In Paul's cultural and religious environment the term was often used with reference to the mystery religions. As these peoples used the term, the word referred to a secret known only to the initiated ones. However, Paul uses the term to mean a secret that is openly revealed. Paul wishes his readers to know that the current spiritual state of Israel is not their final condition. They are to be grafted in again because God will bring about the restoration of his people. **blindness** [hardness] **in part is happened to Israel**—i.e., part of Israel has become hardened. **until the fulness of the Gentiles be come in**—The word "blindness" in the KJV should be "hardness" or "hardening." The Greek word indicates callousness, dullness. Paul does not mention the agent involved in the hardening. The suggestion in the expression "until the fulness of the Gentiles be come in" does not refer to an exact, predetermined number as such, but to the full strength, the complete totality of the Gentiles who will come to Christ. The bringing in of the full complement (*plērōma*) of the Gentiles is to be followed by the bringing in of the fullness of the Jews (11:12).

➤**26, 27 And so all Israel shall be saved**—The crux of the problem involved in the interpretation of this verse is the particle *houtos* (here translated "so"). Those who consider this a temporal particle wish to translate the expression, "and then all Israel will be saved." However, this is not a temporal article but is rather a modal concept and should be translated "in like manner all Israel will be saved," or "in this manner all Israel will be saved." What does Paul mean by the expression "all Israel"? Some interpreters understand the expression to refer to the true spiritual Israel, while others seem to interpret this as a reference to the people taken as a race. Remembering 9:6-8, where Paul stresses the spiritual nature of the true Israel, some interpreters see the words here as referring to the true and eternal seed of Abraham, which includes, of course, both Jews and Gentiles (cf. Gal. 6:10). Calvin also interprets the expression to refer to spiritual Israel. Bruce reminds us that "all Israel" is a recurring expression in the Jewish literature, where it surely does not mean "every Jew with no exception" but rather "Israel as a whole." Therefore, "all Israel" has a portion in the age to come, says the Mishnah Tractate, Sanhedrin (10.1). Other commentators say that these words should not be all-embracing, because the phrase has the same meaning in relation to the Jews as do the terms "fullness of the Gentiles" in relationship to the Gentiles, that is, all means "all those who will turn in faith to Christ." Davidson and Martin point out that interpreting the expression as a reference to universal salvation conferred upon all men in view of their physical birth irrespective of their belief would contradict all else that Paul has taught (see 2:28, 29). However, some interpreters do insist upon the meaning of the ultimate ingathering of Israel as a nation in contrast to the present "remnant." These interpreters note three confirmations of this interpretation, two from the prophets and a third from the Abrahamic covenant itself. **There shall come out of Sion [Zion] the Deliverer, and shall turn away ungodliness from Jacob**—The apostle, having drawn his illustrations of man's sinfulness chiefly from Psalm 14 and Isaiah 59, now seems to combine the language of the two places regarding Israel's salvation from it (Bengel). In the one place the psalmist longs to see the "salvation of Israel coming out of Zion" (Ps. 14:7, RSV); in the other, the prophet announces that "the redeemer shall come to Zion" (Isa. 59:20, RSV). But as all the glorious manifestations of Israel's God were regarded as issuing out of Zion, as the seat of his manifested glory (Ps. 20:2; 110:2; Isa. 31:9), the term that the apostle gives to the words merely adds to them that familiar idea. And whereas the prophet announces that "he shall come to them that turn from transgression in Jacob," Paul has him say that he shall come "to turn away ungodliness from Jacob." This is taken from the Septuagint and seems to indicate a different reading of the original text. The sense, however, is substantially the same in both.

➤27 **For this is my covenant unto them, when I shall take away their sins**—This is rather a brief summary of Jeremiah 31:31-34, than the express words of any prediction. (See also Isa. 27:9.)

➤28, 29 **As concerning the gospel, they are enemies**—i.e., they are regarded and treated as enemies (in a state of exclusion through unbelief, excluded from the family of God) for the benefit of you Gentiles; this is in

the sense of 11:11, 15. **but as touching the election** [of Abraham and his seed], **they are beloved** [even in their state of exclusion] **for the fathers' sakes. For the gifts and calling of God are without repentance** [irrevocable]—The gifts of God are not to be recalled nor to be altered. The "calling of God" in this case means the sovereign act by which God, in the exercise of his free choice, called Abraham to be the father of a peculiar people; while "the gifts . . . of God" here denote the articles of the covenant God made with Abraham, which constituted the real distinction between his and all other families of the earth. Both of these are irrevocable. And since he refers this to the final destiny of the Israelite nation, it is clear that the perpetuity through all time of the Abrahamic covenant is the thing here affirmed. The apostle is pointing out that God is immutable and changeless, that he never regrets his promises nor does he alter his purpose. This fact is corroborated from Isaiah 59:20, 21 and 27:9, and in Romans 11:26, 27. Paul reminds us that the Jews are God's enemies because they have rejected the gospel, but from the standpoint of **election** they are his **beloved.** In their activities of that time the Jews were aligned against Christ and therefore characterized by disobedience to God and to God's purpose. Paul indicates that this situation existed so that the Father could have mercy on both Jew and Gentile alike. The idea of their obtaining "mercy" is an entirely new idea. The apostle has hitherto emphasized the unbelief of the Jew and the making way for the faith of the Gentiles—the exclusion of the one occasioning the reception of the other. Then, opening a more cheerful prospect, Paul speaks of the mercy shown to the Gentiles as a means of Israel's recovery. It seems to mean that it will be by the instrumentality of believing Gentiles that Israel will at length turn to the One whom they have pierced (Zech. 12:10).

➤32 **For God hath concluded them all in unbelief** [disobedience], **that he might have mercy upon all**—The apostle here is referring to the "all" of whom he has been speaking. Salvation then is of the Gentiles first and after them the Jews. The apostle here is dealing universally, not individually. He seems to be dealing with those great divisions of mankind, Jew and Gentile, and what he says here is that

God's purpose was to shut up each of these people to the experience, first, of a humbled, condemned fate, without Christ, and then to the experience of his mercy in Christ. Barrett, at this point, reminds us that the only double predestination found in Paul's writing is that all men have been shut up under condemnation in order that salvation may be offered all. Were they not predestined to wrath, they could not be predestined to mercy.

## 33-36 PAUL'S PRAISE OF GOD'S WISDOM

Paul has concluded his argument. He has not only illustrated the justice and mercy of God, he has vindicated that justice and mercy in his election of Jews and election of Gentiles. In conclusion he eulogizes and praises God for his wisdom and his ways.

➤**33** God's way is described in the expression **the depth of the riches both of the wisdom and knowledge of God!** The apostle now yields himself to admiring and contemplating the grandeur of that divine plan he has just sketched. The expression **how unsearchable** means that God's ways are beyond tracing out! "Riches . . . of God" is a rare expression used only by the apostle. And the words immediately following limit our attention to the unsearchableness of God's **judgments,** which probably means his decrees or plans (Ps. 119:75). **his ways**—indicate the method by which he carried these plans into effect (Luther, Calvin, Hodge). All that follows to the end of the chapter seems to show that while the grace of God to guilty men in Christ Jesus is presupposed to be the theme of this chapter, that which called forth the special admiration of the apostle, after sketching at some length the divine purposes and methods in the bestowment of God's grace, was the depth of the riches and wisdom and knowledge of God in these purposes and methods. The "knowledge" probably points to the vast sweep of divine comprehension here displayed; the "wisdom" of that fitness to accomplish the ends intended, which is stamped on all this procedure.

➤**34, 35 For who hath known the mind of the Lord? or who hath been his counsellor?**—See Job. 15:8; Jeremiah 23:18; Isaiah 40:13, 14. **Or who hath first given to him, and it shall be recompensed unto him again?**— See Job 35:7 and 41:11. These questions are simply quotations from the OT, employed by the apostle as if to show how familiar to God's ancient people was the great truth the apostle himself had just uttered, namely, that God's plans and methods in the dispensation of grace have a reach of comprehension and wisdom stamped upon them that finite minds cannot fathom, much less ever imagine before they are disclosed!

➤**36 For of him, and through him, and to him, are all things: to whom be glory for ever. Amen**—In a brief but worthy manner equalled only by its sublimity, the apostle here sums up this whole matter. "From him . . . are all things" refers to their eternal source; "through him . . . are all things" inasmuch as he brings all to pass that in his eternal counsels he purposed; "to him are all things," as being his own last end. The manifestation of the glory of his own perfections are the very ultimate because they are the highest possible design of all his procedure from first to last.

## Chapter 12

In this chapter Paul discusses the believers' duties and responsibilities, both general and particular. While not all Pauline epistles can be divided into a doctrinal and a practical section, this for the sake of discussion is often done. Thus most interpreters would view the section beginning with 12:1 and continuing through 15:13 as a practical section composed of a series of exhortations. Some of these interpreters refer to this as the practice of Christianity. It is not enough for Paul to tell men that they are lost, to explain to them how they may be saved, to share with them the realities of Christian experience. He must also indicate to them the kind of life that they are to live as God's people.

## 1-2 THE TRANSFORMATION OF LIFE

The "therefore" in the very first verse of this section indicates a transition from the doctrinal to the practical.

➤**1 I beseech you therefore**—in view of all that has been advanced in the foregoing part of the epistle. (See 1 Cor. 4:16; Eph. 4:1; 1 Tim. 2:1 for a similar appeal.) **the mercies of God**— This presents the basis for his appeal. **that ye present**—The same verb was translated "yield" in 6:13. The readers are admonished to "present" their **bodies,** to "offer" them as the OT worshiper offered his offering. Paul means by this that they are to present "themselves in the body," considered as the organ of the inner life. As it is through the body that all the evil that is in the unrenewed heart comes forth into tangible manifestation and action, so it is through the body that all the gracious principles and affections of believers reveal themselves in the outward life. The sanctification extends to the whole man (1 Thess. 5:23, 24). **a living sacrifice**—stands in glorious contrast to the legal sacrifices, which were no sacrifices at all except as they were slain. Paul insists that his readers present themselves as "living sacrifices." These are the kind of people God can use. The sacrifices in the levitical system were offered without blemish to God; they were regarded as holy. Even so believers are to present themselves as dedicated, sanctified unto God's service. They are to become instruments of righteousness unto God. **acceptable**—lit., "well-pleasing." **reasonable**—from the Greek word *logikos,* meaning "logical, reasonable, and spiritual" (see *BAG*). This stands in sharp contrast to the sacrifice of irrational beasts, though the beasts may have been specified by the Mosaic law. Our service to God is the most rational and spiritual occupation of God's reasonable creatures.

▶**2 And be not conformed to this world**— or do not appropriate the same fashion as the world's. (Cf. Eph. 2:2; Gal. 1:4.) Thomas says, "Do not make the world your fashionplate." **be ye transformed by the renewing of your mind**—The Greek word for "be ye transformed" is *metamorphousthe;* it means "to change the form," "to change the expression." The greatest of all miracles is the transformation of one's conduct and the renewing of one's "mind." This transformation is not by mere outward disconformity to the ungodly world. Many of those actions in themselves may be virtuous and praiseworthy, but by such an inward spiritual transformation as makes the whole life new—new in its motives and ends, even where the actions differ in nothing from those of the world—new, considered as a whole and in such a sense as to be wholly unattainable except through the constraining power of the love of Christ. The term that suggests unconformity ("do not be conformed") is from the

Greek term *schēma*, which implies an "external semblance." The word that means "transformed" is derived from the Greek term *morphē*, a term meaning "an essential and a radical likeness." The purpose of this admonition is stated in the clause **that ye may prove what is . . .** [the] **will of God.** Paul means that the Romans will prove this "will" experientially. (Cf. 1 Thess. 5:10, where the sentiment is essentially the same.) **what is that good, and acceptable, and perfect**—His will is "good," as it demands only what is essentially and unchangeably good (7:10); it is "well-pleasing" in contrast with all that is arbitrary, as demanding only what God finds eternal salvation in; it is "perfect" in that God requires his perfection to be reflected in the perfection of his children. Such then is the general duty of the redeemed: consecration of our whole spirit and soul and body to God, who has called us into the fellowship of his Son, Jesus Christ.

## 3-8 THE USE OF SPIRITUAL GIFTS

This is the first area of exhortation. The apostle now applies the law in several main ideas of exhortation. The apostle begins with humility, the chiefest of all the graces—but here with special reference to spiritual gifts.

▶**3 through the grace given unto me**—As an apostle of Jesus Christ, thus exemplifying his own precept by modestly falling back on that office which both warranted and required such plainness toward all classes. **not to think of himself more highly than he ought to think; but to think soberly**—It is impossible to convey in good English the emphatic word play in the Greek. Calvin notes: "Not to be high-minded above what he ought to be minded, but so to be minded as to be soberminded." This is merely a strong way of characterizing all undue self-elevation. **according as God hath dealt to every man the measure of faith**—Faith is here viewed as the inlet to all the other graces and as the receptive faculty of the renewed soul. God has given to each his particular capacity to take in the gifts and graces which he designs for the general good.

▶**4, 5 as we have many members in one body**—The same diversity and unity prevails in the body of Christ, whereof all believers are members, as in the natural body. This is the first mention of Christ's body, the church, in the NT.

The body of Christ is comprised of all the many members constituting one organic unit. All the members belong to one another and function for the benefit of the entire body. Paul uses the figure of the body elsewhere in his writings, and with greater detail (see 1 Cor. 12:12ff.; Eph. 4:16; Col. 2:19).

**➤6-8 Having then gifts differing according to the grace that is given to us**— All the gifts of the believers alike are viewed as coming from grace. **prophecy**—This indicates speaking for God, whether with reference to the past, the present, or the future. **let us prophesy according to the proportion of faith**—Some expositors (Calvin and Hodge, for example) call this "the analogy of faith," understanding by it "the general tenor" or "rule of faith," divinely delivered to men for their guidance. But this is against the context, whose object is to show that as all the gifts of believers are according to their respective capacity for them, they are not to be puffed up on account of them, but rather to use them purely for their proper ends. This is the principle upon which Paul insists in all of his words concerning the spiritual gifts God grants for the edification of his body. **ministry**—or, service. The word here used indicates any kind of service, from the dispensing of the word of life (Acts 6:4) to the administering of the temporal affairs of the church (Acts 6:1, 3). **he that teacheth**— Teachers are expressly distinguished from the prophets and placed beneath them as exercising a lower function (Acts 13:1; 1 Cor. 12:28, 29). Probably it consisted mainly in opening up the evangelical and Christological passages of the OT Scriptures, and it was in this department apparently that Apollos showed his power and eloquence (Acts 18:24). **he that exhorteth, on** [in] **exhortation**—Since all preaching, whether by apostles, prophets or teachers, was followed by exhortation (Acts 11:23; 14:22; 15:32), many think that no specific class is here in view. But this may refer to those whose teaching was more practical and life-applicable than expository. **that giveth** [or, shares]—in the exercise of private benevolence, rather than in the discharge of a deacon's duty. **with simplicity**—or, "with generosity," as it is used in 2 Corinthians 8:2; 9:11. **he that ruleth**—or, "he who takes the

lead." This probably refers to an elder of a local church (see 1 Tim. 3:4, 5). **he that showeth mercy, with cheerfulness**—The Christian who shows mercy is to do so "with cheerfulness." Not only without grudging either the inconvenience or monetary relief, but feeling it to be "more blessed to give than to receive" and to help than to be helped.

## 9-13 THE EXPRESSION OF LOVE IN CHRISTIAN ACTIVITIES

**➤9** Christian **love** is to **be without dissimulation**—lit., "unhypocritical." (See 2 Cor. 6:6; 1 Pet. 2:22; and 1 John 3:18.) Paul, as did the Savior before him, stressed the fact that love is not only the norm of the Christian life, it is the motivation and ruling principle of the Christian life. The love of which he speaks is no mere emotionalism or sentimentality. The Greek term here translated "love" is $agap\bar{e}$ and implies an unselfish love, because $agap\bar{e}$-love is a love willfully exercised and expressed to those who would not be naturally appealing or would not automatically reciprocate. It has been defined as "loving for love's sake, loving without expecting anything in return." It is a term that emphasizes "giving, not receiving." **Abhor that which is evil; cleave** [hold fast] **to that which is good**—What a lofty tone of moral principle in feeling is here imparted! It is not "abstain from the one and do the other," nor "turn away from the one and draw to the other"; it is "abhor the one, and cling with deep sympathy to the other." Love is to be "genuine," void of all hypocrisy; then that love will express itself in varying forms as the outline indicates. One form of its expression will be the clinging to what is good.

**➤10 Be kindly affected** [show tender affection] **one to another with brotherly love; in honour preferring one another**—The Greek term translated "brotherly love" differs from the word translated "love" in 12:9. The term in this verse designates affection among family members. (Cf. 1 Thess. 4:9; Heb. 13:1; 1 Pet. 1:22; 3:8.) The clause "in honour preferring one another" means to take the lead in giving honor to others.

**➤11 Not slothful in business** [zeal]—This seems to be a strange command, but it is a command that charges the believer not to flag in his energetic zeal for the Lord. The remainder of this sentence would lead the interpreter to believe that the love and service of the brother is linked to the love and service of the Lord because the apostle says, **fervent in spirit; serving the Lord.** The same expression, "fervent in spirit" (or "aglow with the Spirit," RSV), is used to describe Apollos in Acts 18:25. One may debate whether it carries the same force in both places. The RSV is probably correct in taking the reference to be to the Holy Spirit and thus translating it, "Be aglow with the Spirit." Calvin, Bruce, and Cranfield, among others, relate this fervency to the Holy Spirit's action in the believer. The expression "serving the Lord" refers, of course, to Jesus. Some manuscripts read, "serving the opportunity," a reading of the Western textual tradition; but this is a case in which the Greek word *kairō* (opportunity) was mistaken for the word *kurío* (Lord).

➤**12 Rejoicing in hope**—Here it is more lively to retain the order of the original: "in hope, rejoicing; in tribulation, enduring; in prayer, persevering." Each of these exercises assists the other. If our "hope" of glory is so assured that it is a rejoicing hope, we shall find the spirit of endurance and tribulation natural and easy; but since it is "prayer" that strengthens the faith that begets hope and lifts it up into an assured and joyful expectancy and since our patience and tribulation is fed by this, it will be seen that all depends upon our perseverance in prayer.

➤**13 Distributing to the necessity of saints; given to hospitality**—The word "hospitality" refers to the entertainment of strangers. It must be remembered that there were no hotels and inns for the Christians traveling from place to place. Therefore, it was significant and important that fellow Christians cared for the need of these travelers; this was especially necessary in the times of persecution. Perhaps there is a greater emphasis today placed upon hospitality in the Eastern world than in the Western world. Hospitality in the East is considered a sacred duty.

## 14-21 SOME ADDITIONAL INSTRUCTIONS IN THE APPLICATION OF CHRISTIAN PRINCIPLES

➤**14 Bless them which persecute you: bless, and curse not**—This is reminiscent of Jesus' teaching recorded in the Sermon on the Mount, which from the allusions made to it, seems to have been the storehouse of Christian morality among the churches (cf. Matt. 5:44).

➤**15 Rejoice with them that do rejoice, and weep with them that weep**—What a beautiful spirit of sympathy with the joys and sorrows of others is here expressed! What a world ours would be if this would become its reigning spirit! Of the two, however, it is more easy to sympathize with another's sorrows than with his joys because in the one case he needs us, in the other case he does not need us. Just for this reason the latter is the more disinterested and so the much nobler.

➤**16 Be of the same mind one toward another**—The feeling of the common bond that binds all Christians to each other, whatever diversity of station, cultivation, temperament, or gifts may characterize them, is the thing here enjoined. This is next taken up in detail. **Mind not high things**—negates any inclination to cherish ambitious or aspiring purposes and desires. As this springs from selfish severance of our own interests and objects from those of our brethren, so it is quite incompatible with the spirit inculcated in the preceding clause. **but condescend to men of low estate**—or, "but be willing to do menial work [or, things]" (NIV mg.). **Be not wise in your own conceits**—This is a check against high-mindedness. Note similar statements of the apostle in 2 Corinthians 13:11 and Philippians 2:2; 4:2. (See also Prov. 3:7 with reference to the matter of conceit.)

➤**17 Recompense to no man evil for evil. Provide things honest in the sight of all men**—The idea (which is from Prov. 3:4) is that Christians should take care how they conduct themselves so as to gain the respect of all men. The Christian is not to be guilty of returning "evil for evil." (Cf. Jesus' teaching in Matt. 5:43, 44 and that of the apostle Paul in 1 Cor. 13:5, 6, as well as that of Peter in 1 Pet. 3:9.)

➤**18 If it be possible, as much as lieth in you, live peaceably with all men**—The impossibility of this in some cases is hinted at, but it encourages those, who having done their best to live in peace, and failed, might be tempted to think that failure was necessarily their fault. But how emphatically expressed is the injunction that nothing on our part prevent it! Would that all Christians were guiltless in this respect!

➤19 avenge not—See comments on 12:14. The idea of revenge and vindication occupies an important place in Pauline thought. Instead of avenging self, the Christian is to leave it to God's wrath: for it is written, Vengeance is mine; I will repay, saith the Lord—As the context shows in this injunction, vengeance is to be left to God, and "wrath" here seems to mean, not the *offence* which we are tempted to avenge, but the *avenging wrath* of God (see 2 Chron. 24:18), which we are enjoined to await. (Cf. Deut. 32:35 for an OT expression of this principle.) The Christian is to permit "retribution inherent in the moral universe to pursue its course" (Davidson and Martin).

➤20 if thine enemy hunger, feed him— This is taken from Proverbs 25:21, 22, which without doubt supplied the basis for those lofty precepts on that subject that form the culminating point of the Sermon on the Mount. The attitude of Christians is to be that of love, not retaliation. if he thirst, give him drink: for in so doing thou shalt heap coals of fire on his head—The heaping of "coals of fire" is an OT figurative expression of vengeance (Ps. 140:10; 11:6; etc.); thus, the true sense of these words seems to be, "that will be the most effectual vengeance." (See Alford and Hodge.) The next verse obviously confirms this interpretation. The verse suggests giving the "enemy" a sense of shame. Some interpreters wish to find a specific historical background and refer to the Egyptian ritual in which a man sought to purge his body of a particular offense by carrying on his head a dish that contained burning charcoal. However, inasmuch as the quotation is derived from the OT, it seems that the reference is not to the Egyptian practice but rather to a spiritual response. Bruce notes that "the best way to get rid of an enemy is to turn him into a friend and so 'overcome evil with good.' " In this manner the victory belongs to the Christian. He has subdued his enemy in the noblest sense.

*Chapter* **13**

This chapter introduces the second section of exhortations, and the apostle moves directly from personal matters to the realm of the Christian's responsibility in politics. In this section Paul notes that the Christian is responsible to the state because the government is an institution of God and is blessed of God. Most commentators divide this chapter into two basic sections: political ethics (13:1-7) and personal ethics (13:8-14).

1-7 POLITICAL ETHICS

➤1, 2 In these verses the apostle notes that civil government is an institution of God. The command to be subject to the higher powers [the superior authorities] involves every soul [person]. The apostle uses the imperative verb form, which may be translated "let every one continue to be in subjection (or subjected)." It will be remembered that Paul's relationship to the Roman officials had been on the highest level of respect and that he had obviously found this relationship extremely helpful in his missionary activities. For there is no power [authority] but of God: the powers [authorities] that be are ordained of God—Paul notes that all "authority" is derived from God and that the Christian has a responsibility to subject himself to this authority. Bruce has suggested that these are the most important words ever written for "the history of political thought." To resist the power [authority] is to resist the ordinance of God—In other words, the apostle is indicating that disobedience toward the authorities is in essence disobedience toward God because God has ordained this civil authority. A Christian is to follow the instructions of the state so long as this obedience does not conflict with God's will or Christ's authority. The word translated "resisteth" is an extremely suggestive word and could be translated "the one who continues lining himself up against." To remember that in "lining one's self up against" the state one also "lines himself up against God" is of greatest significance for an understanding of these verses. Paul notes that this resistance can bring on one thing: damnation (lit., "judgment"). Cullmann states, "Few sayings in the NT have suffered as much misuse as this one." Cullmann is thinking particularly of its misuse in the justification of total submission to totalitarian powers. However, this context, as well as the general context of the NT, affirms that the state has a right to command obedience only within the limitation of the purposes for which God has divinely instituted the state. It follows, then, that the state must be resisted when she demands an allegiance due rightfully only unto God.

➤**3, 4** These two verses state that government ordained of God is for the purpose of promoting social good and preventing social evil. **For rulers are not a terror to good works, but to the evil**—Governmental authorities hold terror only for the individual who resists the law of the state. Of course, Paul is speaking in terms of governmental officials who conduct themselves according to the basic premise he has laid down, namely, that the government is ordained for the benefit of mankind, not for the curse of mankind. **Wilt thou then not be afraid of the power** [authority]? **do that which is good, and thou shalt have praise of the same**—See Peter's similar teaching in 1 Peter 3:13. **For he is the minister of God to thee for good. But if thou do that which is evil, be afraid; for he beareth not the sword in vain: for he is the minister of God, a revenger to execute wrath upon him that doeth evil**—It is interesting to observe that on two occasions in this brief verse Paul calls civil government "God's minister." This term continues the same line the apostle has previously noted—i.e., government is ordained of God and consequently is a "servant" of God. But the disobedient servant has every right to fear government because "he (the government or governmental official) is the servant of God to execute his wrath on the wrong doer" (RSV). It is obvious from these words that God has charged governmental authority with this responsibility. How can social evil be avoided if governmental authority is lax in its responsibility toward God? These last words, spoken with respect to magistracy in general, are considered as a divine ordinance. The statement applies equally to all forms of government, from an unchecked despotism—such as flourished when this was written under the Emperor Nero—to a democracy. The inalienable right of all subjects to endeavor to alter or improve the form of government under which they live is

left untouched here. But since Christians were constantly accused of turning the world upside down and since there certainly were elements enough in Christianity of moral and social revolution to give plausibility to the charge, it was of special importance that the specific, submissive, loyal spirit of those Christians who resided at the great seat of political power (Rome) should furnish a visible refutation of this charge. To summarize these words, Paul teaches that civil government has the authority to check civil evil. In so doing, government functions as God's minister.

➤**5 Wherefore ye must needs be subject, not only for** [to avoid God's] **wrath, but also for conscience sake**—The comments on 13:1-4 also apply to this verse. The latter portion of this verse and the next two verses remind us of the fact that our consciences approve governmental authority. "It is because conscience recognizes the moral value of the state as an ordinance of God that we pay taxes" (Denney).

➤**6, 7** This is the reason why we **pay . . . tribute** [taxes] necessary for maintaining the civil government. **for they are God's ministers, attending continually upon this very thing. Render therefore to all their dues: tribute** [taxes] **to whom tribute** [taxes] **is due . . . honour to whom honour**—The term which describes governmental authorities as "ministers" is the Greek word *leitourgos* (lit., "public worker"). The word was used in Greek literature to describe a man who performed some public service at his own expense. In general, it means a public servant, or administrator. Verse 7 seems reminiscent of Jesus' teachings concerning the payment of taxes to Caesar (Mark 12:17). The apostle summarizes the question of the Christian's relationship to governmental authority by noting that the Christian is not to shirk the payment of taxes, neither is he to shirk the payment of "fear" (or, "respect") and "honor" to whom fear and honor are due.

## 8-14 PAUL'S TEACHING CONCERNING SOCIAL RELATIONS

➤**8** The first clause of 13:7 leads Paul to the concept in 13:8. **Owe no man any thing, but to love one another**—"Acquit yourselves of all obligations except love, which is a debt that must remain ever due" (Hodge). This indebtedness of which Paul speaks is an indebtedness that can never be paid. Bengel refers to it as "the Christian's immortal debt." Origen writes, "It is our duty always to pay and always owe this debt of love." The word Paul uses for "love" (Gk., *agapē* is the "love of intelligent principle, it is the giving of one's self to the object of love, it is loving unselfishly." The clause **for he that loveth another hath fulfilled the law** explains why an individual is obligated to love his fellowman. The law itself mandates nothing but love in manifold action. Paul's quotation of Leviticus 19:18 places the apostle in the same tradition as Jesus (Bruce).

►**9** The commandments cited here are taken from the sixth to the tenth of the Ten Commandments. The ninth commandment ("Thou shalt not bear false witness") is not present in the earliest manuscripts. All these commandments are fulfilled in the law given in Leviticus 19:18. The apostle refers here only to the second table of the law since love to the neighbor is the thing he is actually discussing.

►**10 Love worketh no ill to his neighbour: therefore love is the fulfilling of the law**—Love of neighbor is the "filling" or "complementing" of the law. Paul is not referring to that attitude when an individual expresses a shallow emotionalism and then proceeds to treat or disregard a person as he pleases. The apostle is rather stating that this love is the true fulfillment of the will of God as expressed in the law. Love delights in the happiness of its object and leads men to fulfill all that the law requires because the law provides for that which is conducive to the best interest of one's fellowman. "Love can never be 'fulfilled,' but it is itself 'the fulfillment of the law' " (Nygren). Even when an individual has paid all of his other debts, one debt will still remain—the law of love.

►**11 knowing the time, that now it is high time to awake out of sleep: for now is our salvation nearer than when we believed**— Paul reinforces his statements concerning the obligation to love by noting that the coming of the Lord is nearer to us now than when we first believed. Numerous NT references cite this imminence as a strong motivation to Christian responsibility and living (Matt. 25:31-46; Mark 13:33-37; Phil. 4:4-7; 1 Thess. 5; Heb. 10:24ff.; James 5:7-11). This "time" (Gk.,

kairos) is the time of crisis and challenge; the apostle's words must not go unheeded.

►**12 The night is far spent, the day is at hand: let us therefore cast off the works of darkness, and let us put on the armour of light**—This "armor of light" is described in Ephesians 6. The Christian is to "wake from sleep" (13:11). This is no time for inactivity on the part of the Christian; he must intently express this love that is so characteristic of his Savior. The terms "night" and "day" are reflective of the dualism of the time in which moral goodness was described by "day" and immorality was described by "night." (Cf. Ps. 43:3; Isa. 2:5; 9:2; 42:6ff.; Acts 26:18; 2 Cor. 6:14; Eph. 5:8.) The people of the Qumran community described themselves as "sons of light" in opposition to the "sons of darkness," against whom they envisioned themselves pitted in an eschatological battle. Note that "darkness" has its "works" while the Christian has his "armor of light." The NEB translates this portion, "Let us therefore throw off the deeds of darkness and put on our armour as soldiers of the light."

►**13 let us walk honestly, as in the day**— Men choose the night for their rebelling, but our night is past, for we are all the children of the "light and of the day" (1 Thess. 5:5). Let us therefore only do what is fit to be exposed to the light of such a day. **not in rioting** [reveling] **and drunkenness**—varied forms of intemperance, denoting revels in general, usually ending in intoxication. **not in chambering** [lit., "in beds"] **and wantonness** [excesses]—The first term points to illicit sexual intercourse, the second to general licentiousness. **not in strife and envying**—varied forms of that venomous feeling between men who reverse the law of love.

►**14 But put ye on the Lord Jesus Christ**—To sum up all in one word, "put on the Lord Jesus Christ." Thus, Christ alone would be seen as the Christian's expression (see 2 Cor. 3:3; Gal. 3:27; Eph. 4:24). Moreover, Paul commands the Christian to **make** [no] **provision for the flesh,** which means to take no forethought about how to **fulfil** its **lusts.** Paul is saying that the Christian is to direct none of his attention to the craving of the corrupt nature or to the methods by which he may provide for their gratification.

## Chapter 14

This chapter continues the same basic discussion as the latter half of chapter 13—i.e., Christian love and forbearance. The material from this point to chapter 15:13 focuses on the responsibility of the stronger Christian toward the weaker one. This, of course, is a true expression of the law of love manifested in one particular form. How is the Christian to react toward the individual who disagrees with him concerning matters of Christian fellowship? Is he to "browbeat" the weaker Christian into submission? Is the conscience of the weaker Christian to be honored by the conscience of the stronger individual? Two dogged questions that occasioned sincere and serious doubts among the Christians of Paul's time were the eating of flesh and the keeping of the Sabbath.

## 1-12 THE WEAK CHRISTIAN IS RESPONSIBLE TO GOD, NOT TO THE STRONGER CHRISTIAN

➤1 The strong Christian is commanded by the apostle to welcome the man who **is weak in the faith** and not to be involved with him in **doubtful disputations** [i.e., disputes over opinions]. The man who is "weak in the faith" is the individual whose faith lacks that firmness and breadth that would raise him up above small scruples. The word which is translated "receive" is suggestive of "genuine cordiality." But this one is not to be welcomed for the purpose of arguing him out of his opinions. He rather is to be received to full brotherly confidence and cordial interchange of Christian affection. Two examples of such scruples are here specified: the observance of days and the eating of meats. The strong believers are those who know that these practices were abolished by Christ; the weak believers are those who have convictions on one or both of these points. The NEB's translation, "attempting to settle doubtful points," conveys precisely the idea.

➤2 The problem is delineated in this verse. A Christian possessing the strong conscience **believeth that he may eat all things,** while the Christian possessing the weak conscience eats only vegetables. The latter restricts himself with the vegetable diet because he fears that he might eat some meat, a portion of which may have been offered to idols and therefore would

be unclean (see 1 Cor. 8). The weaker individual felt himself restricted by the Jewish dietary laws, but the stronger individual believed himself to be totally freed from those laws.

➤3 **Let not him that eateth despise him that eateth not; and let not him which eateth not judge him that eateth: for God hath received him**—The commands of this verse eliminate any judgment on the part of either individual. Both individuals belong to God, both have been "received" or "welcomed" by God.

➤4 How can a Christian pass judgment on **another man's servant?** The weaker individual **to his own master ... standeth or falleth.** Even though he be weak, he **shall be holden up: for God** [the Lord] **is able to make him stand.** The Christian is either condemned by Christ or acquitted by Christ, not by this "strong" individual.

➤5 This verse introduces the second problem, that of the observance of days. Paul delineates the problem very succinctly in stating that **One man esteemeth one day above another: another esteemeth every day alike.** It seems that Paul is referring to one person who reflects upon the particular sanctity of given days while being fully aware of the fact that to another individual every day is just as the other days. To him there are no "holy days."

➤6 The individual who believes in holy days is convinced that he **regardeth it** [the holy day] **unto the Lord.... He that eateth, eateth to the Lord, for he giveth God thanks**—The one gives thanks to God for the flesh that the other refuses to eat; the other does the same for the herbs. Relative to the observance of days, Alford infers that such language could not have been used if the Sabbath-law had been enforced during the early days of the church: "If any one day of the week were invested with the sacred character of the Sabbath, it would have been wholly impossible for the apostle to commend or uphold the man who judged all days worthy of equal honor." However, some of the early Christians, given their Jewish background, still observed the Sabbath. These were considered by Paul to be the weaker Christians. Those Christians who had more light ought, out of love, merely to bear this practice of the weaker Christian. Paul's concept here is that the observing of days, or failure to observe days is not the common denominator dictating Christian fellowship.

➤**7 For none of us liveth to himself, and no man dieth to himself**—No Christian is free to dispose of himself or shape his own conduct after his own ideas and inclinations (see 2 Cor. 5:14, 15).

➤**8 we live unto the Lord; ... we die unto the Lord; whether we live therefore, or die, we are the Lord's**—No one would utter these words if Christ were a mere creature. For Christ is here held up as the supreme object of the Christian's life and death. Paul appeals to this as a well-known and recognized fact, and therefore, he felt it was essential only to remind his readers of this fact. And since the apostle had never been in Rome, he could only know that the Roman Christians would assent to this view of Christ because it was the common teaching of all the accredited ministers of Christ and the common faith of all Christians.

➤**9 For to this end Christ both died, and rose, and revived**—This should read, "Christ died and lived again." **that he might be Lord both of the dead and living**—One object of his death was to acquire this absolute lordship over his redeemed people, both in their living and in their dying. Note the apostle's continued emphasis upon the slave-lord relationship.

➤**10 why dost thou judge thy brother?**—Does the stronger Christian have any inherent right to condemn the weaker brother? Does the stronger brother have any right to **set at nought** [despise] the weaker **brother?** Paul's reasoning for his position at this point is very simple: **all** Christians will **stand before the judgment seat of Christ.** The earliest manuscripts read, "the judgment seat of God." The reading represented in the KJV was probably borrowed from 2 Corinthians 5:10 and inserted by later scribes.

➤**11, 12 For it is written**—in Isaiah 45:23. **As I live, saith the Lord, every knee shall bow to me, and every tongue shall confess to God**—as a consequence of God's judgment on every man's character and actions. **So then every one of us shall give account of himself to God**—Now if it be remembered that all this was adduced quite incidentally to show that *Christ* is the absolute master of all Christians and ruler of their judgments and feelings toward each other while "living," the testimony

it bears to the absolute divinity of Christ will appear remarkable.

## 13-23 PAUL TEACHES THAT CONCERN FOR OTHERS IS MORE IMPORTANT THAN THE ASSERTION OF ONE'S OWN LIBERTY

In the previous verses Paul has advised the Romans not to judge one another, whether one is weak or strong, but to be kind and sympathetic in their understandings of the needs of each. It is their responsibility not to place any temptation in the path of the weaker brother, but rather as the stronger Christian they are to support the weaker.

➤**13 Let us not therefore judge one another any more: but judge this rather, that no man put a stumblingblock or an occasion to fall** [a snare] **in his brother's way**—Paul is indicating that the strong mature Christian is never to look upon himself as being so sure and confident of his position that he is to become a stumbling block in the pathway of the weaker brother. Paul's wording turns on the term "judge" (Gk., *krinō*). The expression could be translated "therefore let us no longer judge one another, but rather judge this ... " The stronger Christian is to pass judgment on the possibility of his becoming a stumbling block to the weaker Christian.

➤**14, 15 I know, and am persuaded by the Lord Jesus**—as one who has the mind of Christ (1 Cor. 2:16). The expression that **nothing is unclean of** [in] **itself** serves as the object of the verbs "know" and "am persuaded," thereby defining the content of his knowledge and conviction. Those whom Paul considers the stronger brothers are those who, like himself, believe in the abolition of all ritual distinctions. (See Acts 10:15.) **but to him that esteemeth any thing to be unclean, to him it is unclean**—and therefore, though you can eat of it without sin, he cannot. The expression "unclean in itself" is speaking of edible food with respect to the ceremonial law. Some obviously disagreed with the apostle, and for them, their conviction had to determine their conduct. **if thy brother be grieved with thy meat, now walkest thou not charitably**—If the brother has his weak conscience hurt because of what you choose to eat, then the principle of love no longer determines your conduct. This ruling principle of love has been explained by Paul in 12:9-13. He now stresses that this weak brother is loved of God and also has shared in the scope of his redeeming work. Therefore, **Destroy not him with thy meat, for whom Christ died.** The "worth of even the poorest and weakest brother cannot be more emphatically expressed than by the words 'for whom Christ died'!" (Olshausen). The same sentiment is expressed with equal sharpness in 1 Corinthians 8:11.

►**16, 17 Let not then your good be evil spoken of**—This liberty of yours concerning Jewish meats and Jewish holidays, well founded though it may be, is never to be used in such fashion as to become evil to others. By the expression, **the kingdom of God,** Paul probably means approximately what we would mean by the term "the Christian community," the proper business and blessedness for which Christians are formed into a community of renewed men in thorough subjection to God (cf. 1 Cor. 4:20). The kingdom of God is not to be identified with **meat and drink** but rather with **righteousness, and peace, and joy in the Holy Ghost** [Spirit]. This is a beautiful and comprehensive division of living Christianity. The term "righteousness" has respect to God, denoting here "rectitude" in its widest sense (as in Matt. 6:33). The second term "peace," relates to our neighbors, denoting "concord" among brethren (as is plain from 14:19; cf. Eph. 4:3; Col. 3:14, 15); the third, "joy in the Holy Spirit," has reference to ourselves. This phrase represents Christians as so thinking and feeling under the workings of the Holy Spirit that their joy may express the One who inspires it (cf. 1 Thess. 1:6).

►**18 he that in these things serveth Christ is acceptable to God, and approved of men**— The expression "these things" refers to the threefold Christian life described in the previous verse. The expression "serveth Christ" reminds us that it is Christ we serve in doing these things. The apostle passes here from God to Christ as naturally as before from Christ to God, and in a way that is inconceivable if Christ had been viewed as a mere creature (cf. 2 Cor. 8:21). Serving Christ in this manner means that we become "acceptable to God and approved of men" because we do the things in which God delights, and consequently men are constrained

to approve. (Cf. Prov. 3:4; Luke 2:52; Acts 2:47.)

►**19 Let us therefore follow after the things which make for peace, and things wherewith one may edify another**—The obvious conclusion, to be expected from the apostle in view of the foregoing statements.

►**20 For meat destroy not the work of God**—See the comments on 14:15. The apostle asserts that whatever violates a brother's conscience brings destruction to God's work (for every converted man is God's work)—on the same principle as "whosoever hateth his brother is a murderer" (1 John 3:15). "Destroy" means to "pull down" and was used in secular literature to describe the unloading of a camel's pack. **All things** [food] **indeed are pure** [clean]; **but it is evil for that man who eateth with offence**—Ritual distinctions have been brought to an end, but there is criminality in the individual who causes the weak brother to stumble.

►**21 It is good neither to eat flesh, nor to drink wine, nor any thing, whereby thy brother stumbleth**—Because what we eat or what we do may influence other Christians, it is necessary that we be extremely careful not to cause the brother to stumble by our inadequacies and misunderstandings of their weakness. That it may be senseless and needless for them to be offended by what we eat or when we do or do not observe a particular day is quite beside the point. The point is that the stronger Christian has the responsibility toward the weaker brother. It is his responsibility not to become a stumbling block before the weaker brother. This injunction to abstain from meat, wine, or anything that makes your brother stumble must be properly understood. Manifestly, the apostle is treating the regulation of the Christian's conduct simply with reference to the condition of the weak in faith; and his directions are to be considered not as prescriptions for one's entire lifetime, even to promote the good of men on a large scale, but simply as cautions against the undisciplined and free use of Christian liberty in matters where other Christians, through weakness, are not persuaded that such liberty is divinely allowed.

►**22 Hast thou faith? have it to thyself before God**—an important truth. It is not mere sincerity, nor private opinion, of which the apostle speaks; it is conviction as to what is the truth and will of God. If you have formed this conviction in the sight of God, keep yourself in this frame of mind before him. Of course, this is not to be over-pressed, as if it were wrong to discuss such points at all with our weaker brethren. All that is here condemned is such a zeal for small points as endangers Christian love. **Happy is he that condemneth not himself in that thing which he alloweth** [approves]—The apostle notes that the "happy" individual is he who has no reason to judge himself for what he approves. The Christian who acts against his conscience merely condemns himself, not the conscience of the other individual.

➤**23 And he that doubteth is damned** [condemned] **if he eat, because he eateth not of faith**—because he does not act on the basis of his faith. **for whatsoever is not of faith is sin**—a maxim of unspeakable importance in the Christian life. Note the following important facts: (1) Some factors in Christianity are unessential to Christian fellowship, so that though one may be in error concerning them, he is not on that account to be excluded either from the communion of the church or from the full confidence of those who have more light. This distinction between the essential and nonessential truths is denied by some who affect more than ordinary zeal for the honor and truth of God. But they must settle the question with Paul. (2) Acceptance with God is the only proper criterion of a right to Christian fellowship. Whom God receives, men cannot lawfully reject. (3) Since there is much self-pleasing in setting up narrow standards of Christian fellowship, one of the best preservatives against the temptation to do this will be found in the continual remembrance that Christ is the one object for whom all Christians live and to whom all Christians die; this will be such a living and exalted bond of union between the strong and weak as will overshadow all their lesser differences and gradually absorb them. The consideration of the common judgment-seat at which the strong and the weak shall stand together will be found another preservative against the unlovely disposition to sit in judgment one on another.

*Chapter* **15**

This chapter continues the apostle's discussion of the same subject: the responsibility of the stronger Christian toward the weaker one. The conclusion to this subject is found in 14:1-13. Unless the more mature Christians are able to arrive at a proper understanding of their relationship to the weak and the problems confronted by the weak Christian, there is likely to be division within the church. Paul here sounds a warning against the dangers and problems of divisions.

1-13 PAUL CONTINUES TO ENCOURAGE FORBEARANCE AND UNITY

➤**1** Paul's forceful thrust of the argument is found in the expression **We then that are strong.** The "strong" are those who have seen that the Jewish laws have been abolished in the NT economy. (See comments on 14:14, 20.) **ought to bear the infirmities of the weak, and not to please ourselves**—Paul is simply stating the fact that two groups of people do exist: those who are "strong spiritually" and those who are "weak spiritually." The apostle then stresses that those who are strong have a responsibility not to assert their strength and liberty if this assertion means the downfall and degradation of the weak.

➤**2, 3 Let every one of us please his neighbour**—not indeed for his mere gratification, but—**for his good**—and with a view—**to edification** [building up]. **For even Christ pleased not himself: but, as it is written, The reproaches of them that reproached thee fell on me**—This is taken from Psalm 69:9. Paul could well point out that Jesus' act of sacrifice that culminated in his death on the cross was not an experience in which Jesus sought to please himself. Had this been his desire, then surely he would have never yielded himself to the way of God, which culminated in death by crucifixion.

➤**4 For whatsoever things were written aforetime were written for our learning, that we through patience and comfort** [encouragement] **of the scriptures might have hope**—Think not that because such portions of the Scripture relate immediately to Christ, they are inapplicable to you; for though Christ's sufferings were exclusively his own, the motives that prompted them, the spirit in which they were endured, and the general principle involved in the whole work—self-sacrifice for the good of others—furnish our most perfect and beautiful model. And so all Scripture relating to these is for our instruction. Since the duty of forbearance, the strong with the weak, requires "patience," and this again needs "comfort," all those Scriptures that speak of patience and consolation are our appointed and appropriate nutriment, ministering to us "hope" of that blessed day when these shall no more be needed. (For this connection between "patience" and "hope" see 12:12 and 1 Thess. 1:3.)

➤5, 6 **the God of patience and consolation**—Such beautiful names of God are taken from the graces he inspires: as "the God of hope" (15:13) and "the God of peace" (15:33). **grant you to be likeminded one toward another according to Christ Jesus**—It is not mere unanimity the apostle seeks for them, for unanimity in evil is to be deprecated; but it is likemindedness "according to Christ Jesus"— after the model of him whose only desire was to do not his own will, but the will of him that sent him (John 6:38).

➤6 **That ye may with one mind and one mouth glorify God**—The prayer is a prayer for the unity that expresses God's glory (cf. Jesus' prayer in John 17).

➤7 **Wherefore receive ye one another, as Christ also received us to the glory of God**—If Christ received us and bears all our weaknesses, well may we receive each other and show compassion one to another, and by so doing, God will be glorified. This is the second way to achieve unity.

➤8-12 "Having pointed to the Lord Jesus as the model for Christians, Paul proceed[s] to discuss Jesus' ministry and its objectives" (Witmer). **Christ was** [became] **a minister of the circumcision**—a remarkable expression, meaning "Christ became the Father's servant for the salvation of the circumcision (the Jews)." **for the truth of God**—to make good the veracity of God toward his ancient people. **to confirm the** [messianic] **promises made unto the fathers**—Paul wrote this to cheer the Jewish believers, whom he might seem to have been disparaging, and to keep down Gentile pride. The apostle holds up Israel's salvation as the primary end of Christ's mission. Barrett

suggests that Paul probably means, "I am telling you 'strong' Christians to put up with the religious oddness of the 'weak,' and this is precisely what Christ did; for He made Himself the servant of the oddest of all religious people—the Jews." But next after this, it says Christ was sent **that the Gentiles might glorify God for his mercy**. A number of quotations from the OT follow for the purpose of showing that God's plan of mercy embraced Gentiles along with the Jews from the very first. **as it is written**—in Psalm 18:49. **For this cause I will confess to thee** [or, give thee praise] **among the Gentiles, . . . And again he saith** [Deut. 32:43, LXX], **Rejoice, ye Gentiles, with his people** [Israel]. **And again** [Ps. 117:1, LXX], **Praise the Lord, all ye Gentiles; and laud him, all ye people**—a reference to the various nations outside the pale of Judaism. **And again, Esaias** [Isaiah] **saith** [Isa. 11:10, LXX], **There shall be a root of Jesse, and he that shall rise to reign over the Gentiles; in him shall the Gentiles trust** [hope]—The expression "root of Jesse" is a messianic title. As the root of Jesse, Jesus Christ is David's Lord (see Matt. 22:42-45); as the offspring of Jesse (see Rev. 22:16 where Jesus calls himself "the root and the offspring of David"), Jesus is David's son.

➤13 This verse seems to constitute a concluding prayer, suggested by the whole preceding subject matter of the epistle. God is described as **the God of hope** (see comments on 15:5). Paul's prayer is that this God may **fill** the Romans **with all joy and peace in believing**—the practical appropriation of that **faith**, which is the great theme of this epistle. **that ye may abound in hope, through the power of the Holy Ghost** [Spirit]—The reference to "hope" seemingly connects this prayer with the promise that is derived from Isaiah 11:10, a prayer that will prompt the Gentiles to place their "hope" in the mercies of God.

## 14-21 PAUL'S EXPLANATION FOR WRITING TO THE ROMAN CHRISTIANS

Paul has concluded his doctrinal section of the letter and likewise comes to the point of concluding the practical section of exhortation based upon the doctrinal concepts. He now considers his own plans.

➤14 I myself also am persuaded of you— Paul has no question concerning their intelligence or their love. **ye also are full of goodness**—We are not to understand that Paul is speaking in generalities with reference to "goodness," but he is referring to the principle of love, which he has stressed in chapter 14 as the basic and primary rule of Christian conduct. Moreover, the Romans stand **filled** (a perfect participle meaning "to fill to the point of overflowing") **with all knowledge.** The apostle probably means that the Romans have comprehended the essence of Christian truth, or possibly it may be an apology for the strong doctrinal emphasis and character of the letter.

➤15 I have written the more boldly unto you in some sort [on some points], as putting you in mind, because of the grace that is given to me of God—The NEB translates, "I have written to refresh your memory, and written somewhat boldly at times."

➤16 Paul explains that by God's grace he is a **minister of Jesus Christ** ["Christ Jesus" according to the Gk.] **to the Gentiles, ministering the gospel of God**—The term translated "ministering" was commonly employed to express the office of the priesthood, from which accordingly the figurative language of the remainder of the verse is taken. Paul viewed himself as a "minister [*leitourgos*] to the Gentiles"; this is additional proof that the epistle was addressed to a Gentile church (see 1:13). God's purpose in making Paul a minister to the Gentiles is seen in the clause, **that the offering up of the Gentiles might be acceptable, being sanctified by the Holy Ghost** [Spirit]. It is interesting to note that Paul here views the Gentiles as his oblation to God, but he knew that they were "acceptable" only when "sanctified by the Holy Spirit." Without question the Jews would have insisted that these Gentiles were "unclean" because they had not undergone circumcision. Paul responded to these hypothetical objections by indicating that they were cleansed by the working of God's Spirit (cf. Acts 15:8ff.; Rom. 8:8, 9; Phil. 3:3).

➤17 Paul's only ground for boasting of his work is that it was done **through Jesus Christ.** Note that he does not describe his "work" as being solely his, but rather he has done **those things which pertain to God.**

➤18 For I will not dare to speak of any of those things which Christ hath not wrought by [through] me—a modest, though somewhat obscure form of expression meaning, "I will not venture to go beyond what Christ has worked through me." This statement provides a preface for what follows. Observe here how Paul ascribes all the success of his labors to the activity of the living Redeemer, working in and by him. Paul's success in Gentile ministry is explicable only on the basis of Christ's performing the ministry through Paul. All of the glory consequently belongs to Christ. Paul refers to **word and deed,** a likely reference to preaching and working. The latter term is explained in the next clause.

➤19 Through mighty signs and wonders—"Signs" and "wonders" are generally employed in the NT to define what we know as "miracles." "Powers" is often used synonymously (cf. Mark 6:2). These three terms are applied to Paul's miracles in 2 Corinthians 12:12; to similar works in Hebrews 2:4; and in 2 Thessalonians 2:9 the terms are used to describe the works of "the man of lawlessness." The term "wonders" emphasizes the "awesomeness" and "wonderfulness" of the miracle, while the term "sign" stresses the import or significance of the miracle. **power**—In this passage "power" probably refers to the power with which these works impressed the observers. **the Spirit of God**—This reading is supported by several early manuscripts (including the Chester Beatty Papyrus, P46, and Codex Sinaiticus). Codex Vaticanus, however, reads simply, "the Spirit." **from Jerusalem, and round about unto Illyricum**—This encompasses the field of Paul's labor. (Cf. Acts 9:19 and Galatians 1:17 for descriptions of the apostle's early ministry. Acts 11:25ff. and 13:1ff. record his later ministry to the Gentiles.) It cannot be determined why Paul referred to Jerusalem as the point of origin of his ministry. He was possibly referring to some particular historical occasion, but more likely he identified Jerusalem because this was the center of the Christian movement as a whole (cf. Luke 24:47; Acts 1:4, 8; 8:14, etc.) "Illyricum" is the Roman province that bordered the eastern shore of the Adriatic Sea. The province is not mentioned in Acts or in any of the Pauline epistles up to this point. The period of time between the conclusion of Paul's ministry in Ephesus and the initiation of his last journey to Jerusalem may well have been much more extensive than Acts seems to indicate. Scholars are generally agreed that Paul journeyed from Ephesus to Macedonia for a so-called "third journey" (cf. 2 Cor. 2:12 ff.). Perhaps within this time he traveled to the frontier of Illyricum. The point which he wishes to make is that from Jerusalem to Illyricum he had **fully preached the gospel of Christ.** The NEB translation helps clarify the statement: "I have completed . . . the gospel of Christ." Paul had preached the gospel in the Gentile regions from Jerusalem to Illyricum, and in this sense, had completed his apostolic commission, at least in that portion of the Gentile world.

➤**20 so have I strived to preach the gospel, not where Christ was named, lest I should build upon another man's foundation**—Paul's methodology comes immediately to the surface. His desire was to preach the gospel where others had not already preached it. The true heart of this missionary is immediately seen. Paul wished to preach in virgin territory. His comment in 1 Corinthians 3:10 concerning the fact that he "laid the foundation, and another built thereon" reveals this missionary zeal. "This noble ambition of Paul's is not within the range of some ministers who can only build on another's foundation as Apollos did in Corinth. But the pioneer and missionary has a dignity and glory all his own" (Robertson).

➤**21 But as it is written**—This introduces a quotation from Isaiah 52:15, LXX. **To whom he was not spoken of, they shall see: and they that have not heard shall understand**—The Isaiah passage refers historically to the surprise of nations and kings alike upon seeing the suffering Servant exalted. His exaltation would occur in spite of the fact that they had despised the Servant. Paul's gospel would convey to the nations that God's Servant had suffered at the hands of men and then been exalted by the hand of God.

➤**22 I have been much hindered from coming to you**—This verse explains Paul's delay in visiting Rome. He had been so preoccupied in his missionary responsibilities toward the Gentiles that he simply had not been

able to visit Rome, although he sincerely desired to do so.

➤**23 But now having no more place**—"no longer having place," i.e., unbroken ground, where Christ had not been preached. **and having a great desire these many years to come unto you**—See 1:9-11.

➤**24 Whensoever I take my journey into Spain, I will come to you**—Whether this purpose was ever accomplished has been much disputed, since no record of it or allusion to it appears elsewhere. Some interpreters who believe the apostle was never released following his first imprisonment at Rome will hold, of course, that Paul never visited Spain. Others who are persuaded that Paul was imprisoned in Rome and then released believe that he visited Spain prior to the second imprisonment. The verse not only expresses his intention to visit Spain but also indicates that he hopes to be sped on his **journey** there by the Romans, once he has enjoyed their **company** for a little. Paul had previously expressed the desire to enjoy their fellowship and to share spiritual gifts mutually (1:11-13).

➤**25 But now I go unto Jerusalem to minister unto the saints**—This ministry was actually a relief offering Paul would take from Macedonia and Achaia to the poor Christians in Jerusalem. Paul had pointed out that Jerusalem Christians had shared their spiritual inheritances with the Gentiles; therefore, it was the spiritual and moral responsibility of the new Christians among the Gentiles to share their material possessions with the Christians in Jerusalem. (See 1 Cor. 16:1-4 and 2 Cor. 8, 9 for additional information on the relief offering.) Bruce has an excellent discussion of this relief offering. Among other interesting observations, he notes: (1) that Paul explained to the Romans that the relief offering was a means for the Gentile Christians to show their indebtedness to Jerusalem, for the gospel had spread from Jerusalem. (2) that Paul envisioned it as a means of strengthening the fellowship that ought to be maintained between Jerusalem and the Gentile Christians. (3) that this was the climax of Paul's Aegean ministry and was an act of worship and dedication prior to his journeying to the west.

➤**26 Paul used Macedonia and Achaia as** an illustration of those who had been pleased to make a certain contribution for the poor [among the] **saints which are at Jerusalem.** The term translated "hath pleased them" expresses "the formal resolution of the churches in question, but here as in many places with the idea that it was a spontaneous and cordial resolution" (Denney).

➤**27 It hath pleased them verily; and their debtors they are. For if the Gentiles have been made partakers of their spiritual things, their duty is also to minister unto them in carnal things**—i.e., material goods. This verse reiterates what has been noted earlier concerning the responsibility of the individual who has received the gospel. This principle is enunciated throughout the NT. An outstanding illustration is 1 John 3:17ff. The Gentiles' resolution to assist the poor of Jerusalem was not without motivation. In a sense, the term translated "their duty is" (lit., "they are debtors") tells us that the Gentiles were paying a debt that they owed. To be indebted spiritually means that one may relieve this indebtedness by sharing material blessings with people who already possess spiritual blessings. The source of the Gentiles' spiritual blessings had been the Jerusalem church. Inasmuch as the Jerusalem church already possessed spiritual blessings, it was only logical that the Gentiles should repay them from their materialism.

➤**28 When therefore I have performed this, and have sealed to them this fruit, I will come by you into Spain**—The NEB translates, "And delivered the proceeds under my own seal. . . ." This expression was used in the business world of Paul's day to speak of guaranteeing a delivery. The "fruit" he was "sealing" (guaranteeing) was "the contribution from the Gentile churches" (*NIVSB*).

➤**29 and I am sure that, when I come unto you, I shall come in the fulness of the blessing of the gospel of Christ**—The words "of the gospel" do not appear in any of the earliest manuscripts. Paul had such confidence—even though his visit to Rome was under extremely different circumstances from what he had anticipated. His planned visit to Spain is not substantiated in the NT but 1 Clement (5: 6, 7) describes a wider ministry than that described in Acts. Clement states: "He was a herald both in the east and in the west . . . he taught righteousness to all the world, and when he had

reached the limits of the west, he gave his testimony before the rulers."

➤**30 Now I beseech you, brethren, for the Lord Jesus Christ's sake, and for the love of the Spirit**—not the love that the Spirit bears to us, but the love we have for the Spirit because he kindles in the hearts of believers love for one another (see Col. 1:18). Paul besought the Roman believers by the Savior who is dear to all the believers and whose unsearchable riches Paul lived to proclaim, and by that love which the blessed Spirit diffuses through all the brotherhood, making the labors of Christ's servants the matter of common interest to all. **that ye strive together with me**—lit., "wrestle together with me"; see comments on Philippians 1:27. **in your prayers to God for me** [on my behalf]—This statement implies that he had some anxiety about going to Judea.

➤**31 That I may be delivered from them that do not believe in Judaea**—Actually, the text reads " . . . from those disobeying," i.e., the disobedient. Many of the Jews disobeyed the demands of the gospel (cf. 1:5). This is his first petition. He saw the storm that was gathering over him in Judea and realized that this storm would surely burst upon his head when he reached Jerusalem. The event there shows all too clearly the correctness of these apprehensions. The second petition is that **my service which I have for Jerusalem may be accepted of the saints.** This is a reference to the relief offering. Paul wanted the Romans to join him in the prayer that this relief offering would be acceptable to the Christians in Jerusalem. He was not without apprehension lest the opposition of many Jewish converts against the free reception of the Gentile brethren into the church should make this gift of theirs less welcome than it ought to be. He would have the Romans therefore join him in wrestling in prayer that this gift might be gratefully received and prove a uniting force between the two parties.

➤**32 He further enjoins the Romans to pray That I may come unto you with joy by the will of God, and may with you be refreshed**—The will of God was never far removed from the mind of Paul (see Acts 18:21; 1 Cor. 4:19; 16:7; Heb. 6:3; James 4:15). He prayed that they would enjoy spiritual refreshment in one another's company.

➤**33 Now the God of peace be with you
all. Amen.** The word "peace" here is to be
understood in its widest sense: the peace of
reconciliation to God, first, through the blood
of the everlasting covenant (see Heb. 13:20; cf.
1 Thess. 5:23; 2 Thess. 3:16); then the peace
which that reconciliation gives to all the partakers of it (1 Cor. 14:33; 2 Cor. 13:11; see also
comments on Rom. 16:20); finally, that peace
which the children of God, in beautiful imitation of their Father in heaven, are called and
privileged to spread far and wide through this
sin-distracted and divided world (Matt. 5:9;
Heb. 12:14; James 3:18). After 15:33, the oldest extant manuscript (the Chester Beatty Papyrus, P46, third century) has the doxology that
appears at the end of the book, namely Romans
16:25-27. See introductory comments on chapter 16.

*Chapter* **16**

## 1-16 PAUL SENDS HIS GREETINGS TO NUMEROUS ROMAN CHRISTIANS

By Paul's own admission in the previous
chapter, the apostle had never been to Rome.
Therefore, the question of his having so many
friends in a city he had not visited has created
a problem for many interpreters. Consequently
some reject this chapter as a portion of the
initial Roman letter, suggesting that it is a mere
fragment of a letter the apostle addressed to the
Ephesian church. Prior to 1935, this hypothesis
remained a conjecture; but with the publication
of the Chester Beatty Papyrus containing the
Pauline Epistles (designated P46, dated early
third century), it became evident that the oldest
known manuscript of Romans concluded with
the doxology of the previous chapter. In spite
of this evidence for a separate origin of chapter
16, F. F. Bruce opts for the position that retains
this chapter as a portion of the original letter.
His arguments are based chiefly on the large
number of inscriptions discovered that contain
personal names connected with Rome, and on
the swiftness of travel because of the Roman
roads and the *pax Romana*. The Babylonian
exile had taken the Jews from the realm of a
meager agricultural activity to that of extensive
commercialism. Surely the Jew of the first-
century world was interested in commerce

and trade; consequently he traveled along the
well-used trade routes of his day. Paul, in this
chapter, either commends or greets Christians
who are living at Rome, or else are journeying
to Rome. Approximately one-third of the
names are those of women, and this fact
within itself reveals the prominent positions occupied by women in the Roman
church. Brunner writes: "A dry list of names—
so it appears at first sight. Yet it is one of the
most instructive chapters of the New Testament. . . .This conclusion of the letter is particularly significant for the reason that it
comes at the end of the 'letter to the Romans,'
the greatest, the richest and hardest piece of
doctrine writing in the Bible. It is the one and
the same Paul who penned the 15 preceding
chapters and this 16th chapter, and the one is
as important to him as the others." (For a
well-balanced discussion of the nature and
origin of this chapter see Davidson and
Martin, and Bruce.)

➤**1** Paul introduces this chapter of greetings
by commending **Phebe** [Phoebe] **our sister,
which is a servant**—lit., "deacon" (masculine
in Gk.), although it is translated "deaconess" in
RSV and other versions. Such commendatory
letters were well known in the ancient world
(see 2 Cor. 3:1). It seems rather obvious that
Phoebe is the bearer of the letter to the Roman
church and that she was prepared to begin her
journey at the time Paul was completing the
writing of this letter. **the church which is at
Cenchrea**—"Cenchreae" was one of two seaports of the city of Corinth (Acts 18:18). It was
located on the Saronic Gulf. Bruce conjectures
that the "church" there may well have been
planted by the city church of Corinth. That
there were deaconesses in the earliest churches
is evident; there is no reason to doubt this fact.
So early at least as the reign of Trajan, we learn
from Pliny's celebrated letter to that emperor
(A.D. 110-111) that they existed in the Eastern
churches. Indeed from the relation in which the
sexes then stood to each other, something of
this sort would seem to be a necessity.

➤**2 That ye receive her in the Lord, as
becometh saints**—This states that the Roman
Christians were to accept her into their fellowship as a fellow-Christian. **and that ye assist
her in whatsoever business she hath need of
you: for she hath been a succourer of many,**

**and of myself also**—Paul's instructions at this point are reminiscent of what he had stated in the last chapter concerning the mutual responsibility of Christians toward one another. Paul was indebted to Phoebe, as were many other people to whom she had ministered. She was a "succourer of many"—i.e., she was a helper of many, a protector of many. The Greek word literally means "one who stands for you"; hence, it was used as a legal representative and/or a wealthy patron. Here, it is used generally, to speak of one who helped and succored many of the believers, including Paul.

➤**3 Greet Priscilla** [Prisca] **and Aquila, my helpers** [fellow workers] **in Christ Jesus**—Paul uses the name "Prisca" (1 Cor. 16:19; 2 Tim. 4:19), but Luke calls her "Priscilla," a more familiar form of the name (Acts 18:2, 18, 26). It is interesting to note that Paul mentions her before her husband, probably because she was the more prominent and helpful to the church. However, it must be observed that some interpreters infer from this fact that her social rank was superior to that of her husband. Following that thesis, these interpreters suggest that she may have belonged by birth or manumission to the clan **Prisca**, a Roman family of great nobility. On the other hand, Aquila was a Jew from Pontus (Northern Asia Minor).

➤**4 Who have for my life laid down their own**—This clause explains the extent to which this couple was willing to be sacrificed for Paul. Just *when* the couple willingly risked their lives for Paul, we are left only to conjecture. It has been suggested that such an experience may well have occurred during Paul's Ephesian ministry (see Acts 19:30, 31; 1 Cor. 15:32 and Acts 18:6, 9, 10 for the possibility of the events occurring in Corinth). They must have returned from Ephesus (where we last find them in the history of Acts to Rome, from which the edict of Claudius had banished them (Acts 18:2). If they were not the principal members of that Christian community, they were at least the most endeared to the apostle Paul. **unto whom not only I give thanks, but also all the churches of the Gentiles**—whose special apostle this dear couple had rescued from imminent danger.

➤**5 Likewise greet the church that is in their house**—This statement is important to

our understanding the structure of the early church. Other scriptures speak of there being a "church" (*ecclēsia*)—which could also be rendered "assembly," or "meeting") in a house (see 1 Cor. 16:19; Col. 4:15; Philem. 2). But there has been some debate about whether the house church constitutes the smallest unit for an *ecclēsia* or the local church (i.e., the church in the locality). According to the overall pattern of the NT, it appears that there was only one church proper per city—i.e., in each city there was one unified group of Christians under one eldership (see Acts 14:23; 15:2, 4; 20;17, 18; Titus 1:5). Thus, the church was called by the name of the city in which it existed (e.g., the church in Jerusalem, Acts 8:1; the church in Antioch, Acts 13:1; the church in Cenchrea, Rom. 16:1; the church in Corinth, 1 Cor. 1:2 and 2 Cor. 1:1; the church of the Thessalonians, 1 Thess. 1:1 and 2 Thess. 1:1; and the seven local churches mentioned in Rev. 2 and 3). However, within the local church proper there must have been several "assemblies" or "meetings" of the believers, held in various homes. (This is evident from passages like Acts 2:46; 5:42; 12:12; 20:20; Titus 1:11.) Each one of these meetings had every right to be called an *ecclēsia*—for the word at its very root means nothing more than an "assembly" or "meeting." (This is the usage and meaning of the word in 1 Cor. 4:17; 11:18; 14:4, 19, 28, 35; Heb. 2:12; 12:23.) Therefore, within one local church proper, there could be several home meetings—or, if the church were small, only one home meeting. A church like Jerusalem would have many home meetings, whereas a church like Colossae had only one (see comments on Philem. 2). But no one knows for sure how many believers there were in Rome at the time Paul wrote this epistle. Some commentators suggest a large number, others think the assembly was rather small. The church at Rome could have had several home meetings, several home "churches"—one of which was at Aquila and Priscilla's house, or the entire church, if small enough, could have met at their house. (When Aquila and Priscilla lived in Ephesus, an *ecclēsia* met in their home [see 1 Cor. 16:19]; but whether or not it was the entire church is still debatable [see comments on 1 Cor. 16:19, 20].) But it is much more likely that the *ecclēsia* in Aquila and Priscilla's house was not the entire church at Rome. If it were, why would Paul ask the church at Rome (which equals "all that be in Rome," 1:7) to greet the church at Rome? Later in this chapter, Paul exhorts all the Roman believers to greet one another (16:16). This is natural. But it is unnatural and illogical for Paul to ask the church in Rome to greet itself. Thus, the church in Priscilla and Aquila's house was not the entire church in Rome but simply a house meeting. Several believers in Rome met with this couple, while other believers met with the saints mentioned in 16:14 and likewise in 16:15. (Again, see comments on 1 Cor. 16:19, 20; Col. 4:15; Philem. 2.) Several such home meetings would comprise the church proper in Rome, which in itself was a governmental unit. Each home meeting was not to become a separate church entity within a locality, for that would lead to division (see 16:17; 1 Cor. 1:10-14) (Comfort). **Salute my well-beloved Epaenetus, who is the first fruits of Achaia unto Christ**—The best manuscripts read "Asia" instead of "Achaia." And besides, 1 Corinthians 16:15 says that the household of Stephanas was the firstfruits of Achaia. Epaenetus was the first believer in that region called Proconsular Asia and was dear to the apostle. None of the names mentioned from 16:5-15 are otherwise known. One wonders at the number of them, since the writer had never been in Rome. But as Rome was then the center of the civilized world, to and from which journeys were continually taken to the remotest parts, there is no great difficulty in supposing that so active a traveling missionary as Paul would make the acquaintance of a considerable number of Christians then residing at Rome. His missionary journeys had already stretched over many years.

➤**6 Greet Mary**—Who is this **Mary?** There are six women in the NT bearing the name "Mary," but this is the only reference to this particular Mary. She is mentioned because of her conspicuous service. Perhaps Paul had learned of this service from Prisca.

➤**7 Salute Andronicus and Junia** [Junias] **my kinsmen, and my fellow prisoners**—There has been much discussion concerning the gender of "Junias." If the name is feminine, then perhaps the woman was either the sister or wife of Adronicus. The expression "my kinsmen" does not mean "relatives" but rather "fel-low countrymen," as well as his "fellow prisoners." We do not know on what occasion these had been in prison with Paul. However, in 2 Corinthians 11:23 Paul notes that he was frequently in prison. **who are of note among the apostles, who also were in Christ before me**—Those who think there were only a select group of apostles (i.e., the Twelve plus Paul), explain this apostleship as a general missionary office or function. Others, who think the term "apostle" extends beyond just the Twelve and Paul, say that Adronicus and Junias ranked among the genuine apostles (see Phil. 2:25, in which Epaphroditus is called an apostle). The phrase "in Christ before me" must mean that these had become Christians prior to Paul's Damascus road experience.

➤**8 Greet Amplias** [Ampliatus] **my beloved in the Lord**—This name is a slave name, but this particular "Ampliatus" is unknown. It was a common Roman name and is found on numerous Roman inscriptions from the period. The cemetery of Domitilla, the oldest cemetery in Rome, can be traced to the first century. On one particular tomb in that cemetery the inscription Ampliat is carved in uncials (Bruce).

➤**9 Salute Urbane** [Urbanus]—He is described as **our helper** [fellow worker] **in Christ.** His name is also a common Roman name. The name itself suggests "belonging to the *urbs* or city" (see Bruce). **Stachys** is also unknown. the name means "ear" and was an uncommon name.

➤**10 Apelles approved in Christ**—He also earns Paul's greeting. The name itself was fairly common among the Jews and is found in numerous Roman inscriptions. Some of these inscriptions relate to the imperial household and some to the common people. Apelles is identified as a distinguished Christian. **them which are of Aristobulus' household**—We are not sure of the identity of this Aristobulus. J. B. Lightfoot thinks that he is to be identified as a brother of Herod Agrippa I. The name itself was a very popular name during the intertestamental period. If Lightfoot is correct in his conjecture, then this man was a grandson of Herod the Great. This "family" would obviously include his relatives, as well as his officials and slaves.

►**11 Salute Herodion my kinsman**—Perhaps this person belonged to the household of Aristobulus. **Greet them that be of the household of Narcissus, which are in the Lord**—Calvin, among others, identified Narcissus with Tiberius Claudius Narcissus, who was a wealthy freedman of the emperor Tiberius; this man was executed by an order issued by Nero's mother, Agrippina, soon after Nero ascended the throne in A.D. 54. Of course, his goods would have been confiscated under those conditions, and his slaves would have immediately become the property of the emperor. They would have been distinguished from other groups in the emperor's household by the designation "Narcissini." If this identification can be established, then Paul is greeting Christians among those "Narcissini" (see Bruce).

►**12 Salute Tryphena and Tryphosa, who labour in the Lord**—Perhaps these were sisters. We know only that they were very active in the Lord's service. **Salute the beloved Persis, which labored much in the Lord**—This name is a feminine name. She also is described as expending much energetic labor in the service of the Lord.

►**13 Salute Rufus chosen in the Lord**—It is conjectured that "Rufus" is the Cyrenian referred to in Mark 15:21. The term "chosen" could also simply mean "eminence." Being the son of Simon the Cyrenian (the man who helped carry Jesus' cross) would have given him honor among the Christians. **and his mother and mine**—We are not to understand that Paul's mother was in Rome, but rather that Rufus's mother at one time or the other served Paul as his own mother would have ministered to his needs. Therefore, she is included in this greeting.

►**14, 15** These have been thought to be the names of ten less notable Christians than those already named. But this will hardly be supposed if it be observed that they are divided into two pairs of five each and that after the first of each pair, it is added **and the brethren which are with them.** After the second pair are the words **and all the saints which are with them** added. Many commentators have thought that Paul's words here imply church meetings in the homes of each group thus mentioned. Since Rome was a large city, several such small gatherings could have existed throughout the city. Each gathering (or assembly), however, did not constitute a separate local church, for the NT principle was that there was only one church in each city. Each local church, however, could have several home meetings or just one home meeting. (See comments on 16:5.) These meetings may have been for further instruction, for prayer, for missionary purposes, or some other Christian objects. These little glimpses into the rudimental forms that Christian fellowship first took in the Greek cities are too indistinct for anything more than conjecture, but nonetheless they are singularly interesting. Our apostle would seem to have been kept minutely informed as to the state of the church at Rome, both as to its membership and its varied activities, probably by Prisca and Aquila. **Hermas**—better rendered, "Hermes," may well be an abbreviation of Hermagoras, Hermogenes, or Hermodorus. It obviously was a very common name. Later a Roman slave by this name wrote "The Shepherd." **Patrobas** is the abbreviated form of "Patrobius." A wealthy freedman of Nero was named Patrobius. Lightfoot conjectures that possibly the man Paul mentions may have been a dependent of the freedman. **Hermes**—better rendered, "Hermas," was a slave's name, very commonly used. **Philologus** and **Julia** were possibly husband and wife. Some conjecture that they were brother and sister. The name "Julia" does connote some association with the emperor's household. **Nereus**—in Roman ecclesiastic tradition was associated with Flavia Domitilla by a Christian of the imperial household who was deported to the island of Pandateria by Domitian in A.D. 95. However, he was released following his death. It is her name that is perpetuated in the cemetery of Domitilla. (See Bruce.) The name **Olympas** is an abbreviation of Olympiodorus.

►**16 Salute one another with an holy kiss**—See 1 Corinthians 16:20; 1 Thessalonians 5:26; 1 Peter 5:14. The custom of greeting "one another with a holy kiss" prevailed among the Jews, and the custom itself probably came from the East. Its adoption into the Christian churches, as a symbol of higher fellowship than it had ever expressed before, was probably as immediate as it was natural. In this case the apostle's desire seems to be that upon receiving his epistle the Romans should in this manner expressly manifest their Christian affection. Later the kiss came to have an established place in the church service—immediately after the celebration of the Supper; and the practice continued for many years. In such matters, however, the state of society and the peculiarity of different places must be studied. **The churches of Christ salute you**—According to the best manuscripts, this should read "all the churches of Christ greet you." This assures the Romans in what affection of esteem they were held by all the churches. Apparently all the churches that knew Paul was writing to Rome had expressed themselves so, asking that their own salutations be sent to them.

## 17-20 A CONCLUDING ADMONITION

**➤17 Now I beseech you, brethren, mark them which cause divisions and offences contrary to the doctrine which ye have learned; and avoid them**—The fomentors of "divisions" here referred to are probably those who are unfriendly to the truths taught in this epistle, while those who cause offenses were probably those referred to in 14:15 as wholly disregarding the prejudices of the weak. The action concerning both groups is, first, to mark such, lest the evil should be done before it was fully discovered; and second, to "avoid" them (cf. 2 Thess. 3:6, 14), so as neither to bear any responsibility for their procedure nor seem to give them the least confidence.

**➤18 For they that are such serve not our Lord Jesus Christ**—"Our Lord Christ" is the proper reading. Instead of serving him, they serve **their own belly** [appetites]. In Philippians 3:19 Paul warns the Christians against people "whose God is their belly." It seems that here, as well as in that reference, Paul is probably referring to those antinomians who used the gospel as pretext for the indulgence of their own appetites. **and by good words and fair speeches deceive the hearts of the simple**—the unwary, the unsuspecting. (See Prov. 14:15.)

**➤19 For your obedience is come abroad unto all men. I am glad therefore on your behalf: but yet I would have you wise unto that which is good, and simple concerning evil**—The readers need to employ wisdom to discriminate between apparent truth and possible error with that guileless simplicity that instinctively *cleaves to the one and rejects the other.*

**➤20 the God of peace shall bruise Satan under your feet shortly**—The apostle encouraged the Romans to persevere in resisting the wiles of the devil with the assurance that as good soldiers of Jesus Christ they would "shortly" receive their discharge and would have the satisfaction of putting their feet upon the neck of that formidable enemy—a symbol familiar in all languages to express not only the completeness of defeat but the abject humiliation of a conquered foe. (See Josh. 10:24; 2 Sam. 22:41; Ps. 91:13; Ezek. 21:29.) Though the apostle here describes him who is thus to bruise Satan as "the God of peace" with special reference to the "divisions" (16:17) by which the Roman church was in danger of being disturbed, this sublime appellation of God has here a wider sense. It points to the whole purpose for which the Son of God was manifested, i.e., to destroy the works of the devil (1 John 3:18). Indeed this assurance is but a reproduction of the first great promise that the seed of the woman should bruise the serpent's head (Gen. 3:15). **The grace of our Lord Jesus Christ be with you**—This concludes Paul's admonition. What comes after this has its parallel in Philippians 4:20. It is very common in epistolary writings; it marks the epistle's genuineness.

## 21-23 GREETINGS FROM CORINTH

**➤21** Paul describes **Timotheus** [Timothy] as his **workfellow** [fellow worker]. Timothy also joins in greeting the Romans (see Acts 16:1-5 for a discussion of Timothy's relationship to Paul). The apostle mentions him here rather than in the opening address to his church, since he had not been at Rome (Bengel). **and Lucius, and Jason, and Sosipater, my kinsmen, salute you**—"Lucius" is not Luke because the fuller term of "Lukus" is not "Lucius" but "Lucanus." The person meant by Paul seems to be Lucius of Cyrene, who was among the "prophets and teachers" at Antioch with Paul before the apostle was summoned into the missionary field (Acts 13:1). See Acts 17:5 for Luke's statements concerning Jason. Jason had probably accompanied, or followed, the apostle from Thessalonica to Corinth. For his reference to **Sosipater,** see Acts 20:4.

**➤22 I Tertius, who wrote this epistle, salute you in the Lord**—Tertius was the apostle's amanuensis or secretary. He too joins in saluting the Romans "in the Lord." So routinely did the apostle dictate his epistles that he calls special attention in Galatians to the fact that he wrote to the Galatians with his own hand (Gal. 6:11). But this "Tertius" wanted the Romans to know that his own heart went out to them in Christian affection.

►23 Gaius, the apostle's host, and of the whole church, also sent his greeting to the Roman church. The church in Corinth (whence Paul wrote this epistle) met in Gaius's home, and Gaius had been baptized by Paul (1 Cor. 1:14). It is doubtful that the man named Gaius in John's third epistle was the same Gaius here. Erastus, the chamberlain [city treasurer] . . . saluteth you, and Quartus a brother [or, his brother]—Erastus was doubtless the treasurer of the city of Corinth (see Acts 19:22; 2 Tim. 4:20). Nothing more is known of Quartus, but we assume that he was a brother in the same sense as Sosthenes and Timothy. Erastus can be identified because the name has been found in a Latin inscription on a marble paving-block discovered at Corinth in 1929 by members of the American School of Classical Studies (Bruce). The name "Tertius" is the Latin word for "third" and "Quartus" is the Latin word for "fourth." Bruce simply asks, "Would it be excessively far-fetched to think of him as Tertius's brother, born next after him?"

►24 This verse, a repetition of 16:20b, is not present in any of the earliest manuscripts.

## 25-27 A CONCLUDING DOXOLOGY

The doxology (16:25-27) has been positioned in various places in the book of Romans in various manuscripts: (1) after 16:23 (possibly one early papyrus manuscript—P61, Codex Sinaiticus, Codex Vaticanus, Codex Ephraemi, Rescriptus, Codex Bezae, etc.); (2) after 14:23 and 16:23 (Codex Alexandrinus and other late manuscripts); (3) after 14:23 (Codex Regius and other later manuscripts); and (4) after 15:23 (the third-century Chester Beatty Papyrus—P46). Scholars have entertained many opinions and conjectures concerning this textual problem, one too involved to recount here. The simplest solution is to adhere to the best attestation among the manuscripts; far and away, the first position indicated above has the best testimony (*GAM*).

►25 Now to him that is of power to stablish you according to my gospel, and the preaching of Jesus Christ—The power of God is still underscored, just as Paul stressed it in 1:16 and 14:4. "God's omnipotence is redemptive through the gospel for it is 'the power of God unto salvation.' This conception, which was earlier emphasized in the Epistle, is now, at its close, proclaimed after the inspired exposition of the gospel entrusted to the apostle" (Davidson and Martin). Notice that the "gospel" is here described as "the preaching of Jesus Christ." Thus the gospel is the announcement of God's good news in the person of Christ. according to the revelation of the mystery, which was kept secret since the world began—lit., "kept silent during times eternal." (Cf. 1 Cor. 2:7; Eph. 1:9.) The mystery (or, secret) of God's eternal plan to unite Jews and Gentiles in one body under Christ's leadership was revealed to Paul for him to reveal to others.

►26 But now is made manifest—This mystery had been concealed in times past but was revealed by God to Paul and by Paul to us. (Cf. Colossians 1:26ff. and Ephesians 3:3ff. In these passages the mystery refers particularly to Paul's apostleship to the Gentiles.) by the scriptures of the prophets [lit., "prophetic writings"]. according to the commandment of the everlasting God, made known to all nations for the obedience of faith—The gospel had been foretold by the OT prophets. These prophets were commissioned by Yahweh to declare the offering of his salvation to all men. Thus they "bring about the obedience of faith" (RSV). "Although the prophets had formally taught all that Christ and the apostles have explained, they taught with so much obscurity, when compared with the shining clarity of the light of the gospel, that we need not be surprised if these things which are now revealed are said to be hidden" (Calvin). The NT evangelists frequently employed the OT Scriptures in their preaching (cf. 1 Pet. 1:10-12).

►27 To God only wise, be glory through Jesus Christ for ever. Amen.—The doxology (as with the introduction to Romans) begins with an ascription of praise to the divine power that could do all of this for sinful man; it closes with praise to the divine wisdom that planned and presides over the gathering of the redeemed people of all nations. The apostle adds his devout "Amen," to which the reader cannot but also echo, "Amen."

BIBLIOGRAPHY

Alford, Henry. *The Greek New Testament*. Vol. 3. 1852. Reprint. Grand Rapids: Guardian Press, 1973.

Barrett, C. K. *A Commentary on the Epistle to the Romans*. New York: Harper & Brothers, 1957.

Bruce, F. F. *The Epistle of Paul to the Romans* in the Tyndale New Testament Commentaries. Grand Rapids: Eerdmans, 1963.

Brunner, Emil. *The Letter to the Romans, A Commentary*. London: Lutterworth, 1959.

Calvin, John. *Commentary on the Epistle of Paul the Apostle to the Romans*. 1583. Reprint. Grand Rapids: Eerdmans, 1947.

Cullman, Oscar. *The State in the New Testament*. New York: Scribner, 1956.

Darby, J. N. *New Translation*. 1871. Reprint. Addison, Ill.: Bible Truth Publishers, n.d.

Davidson, F. and Ralph Martin. "Romans" in *The New Bible Commentary*. Edited by Guthrie and Motyer. London: InterVarsity Press, 1953, 1970.

Denney, James. "St. Paul's Epistle to the Romans" in *The Expositor's Greek Testament*. London: Hodder & Stoughton, 1917.

Forrester, E. J. *A Righteousness of God for Unrighteous Men*. New York: Doran Co., 1929.

Grotius, Hugo. *The Truth of the Christian Religion*. 1632. Reprint. London: Baynes & Son, 1854.

Hodge, Charles. *A Commentary on the Epistle to the Romans*. New York: Armstrong, 1896.

Lightfoot, J. B. *St. Paul's Epistle to the Romans*. London: Macmillan & Company, 1913.

Luther, Martin. *Commentary on the Epistle to the Romans*. 1522. Reprint. Grand Rapids: Zondervan, 1954.

Nygren, Anders. *Commentary on Romans*. Philadelphia: Muhlenberg Press, 1949.

Olshausen, Hermann. *Biblical Commentary on the New Testament*. New York: Sheldon, 1858.

Philippi, Friedrich A. *Commentary on St. Paul's Epistle to the Romans*. Edinburgh: T. & T. Clark, 1878.

Robertson, A. T. *Word Pictures in the Greek New Testament*. Nashville: Broadman Press, 1932.

Schlier. *"kathekonta"* in *Theological Dictionary of the New Testament*. Edited by Kittel. Grand Rapids: Eerdmans, 1964.

Somerville, David. *St. Paul's Conception of Christ*. Edinburgh: T. & T. Clark, 1897.

Tholuck, August. *Exposition on St. Paul's Epistle to the Romans*. Edinburgh: T. & T. Clark, 1842.

Thomas, W. H. Griffith. *St. Paul's Epistle to the Romans*. 3 vols. London: The Religious Tract Society, 1911/1912.

Witmer, John. "Romans" in *The Bible Knowledge Commentary*. Wheaton: Victor Books, 1983.

# 1 CORINTHIANS

## Introduction

The authenticity of this epistle is attested by Clement of Rome (*Epistle to the Corinthians*, 47), Polycarp (*Epistle to the Philippians*, 11), Irenaeus (*Against Heresies*, 4.27.45), Clement of Alexandria (*Paidagogos*, 1.6.33), and Tertullian (*Prescription of Heretics*, 33). The city to which it was sent was famed for its wealth and commerce, which were chiefly due to its situation between the Ionian and Aegean Seas on the isthmus connecting the Peloponnese with Greece. In Paul's time it was the capital of the province Achaia and the seat of the Roman proconsul (Acts 18:12). The state of morals in it was notorious for debauchery, even in the profligate heathen world; so much so that "to Corinthianize" was a proverbial phrase for "to live like a Corinthian in the practice of sexual immorality" (Mare); hence, arose dangers to the purity of the church at Corinth, which was founded by Paul on his first visit (Acts 18:1-17).

Paul had been the instrument of converting many Gentiles (12:2) and some Jews (Acts 18:8), notwithstanding the vehement opposition of the countrymen of the latter (Acts 18:6), during the year and a half in which he lived in Corinth. The converts were chiefly of the humbler classes (1:26). Crispus (1:14; Acts 18:8), Erastus, and Gaius were, however, men of rank (Rom. 16:23). A variety of classes is also implied in 11:22. The risk of contamination by contact with the surrounding corruptions and the temptation to a craving for Greek philosophy and rhetoric (which Apollos's eloquent style rather tended to foster, Acts 18:24, etc.) in contrast to Paul's simple preaching of Christ crucified (2:1, etc.), as well as the opposition of certain teachers to him, naturally caused him anxiety. Emissaries from the Judaizers of Palestine boasted of "letters of commendation" from Jerusalem, the metropolis of the faith. They did not, it is true, insist on circumcision in refined Corinth, where the attempt would have been hopeless, as they did among the simpler people of Galatia; but they attacked the apostolic authority of Paul (9:1, 2; 2 Cor. 10:1, 7, 8), some of them declaring themselves followers of Cephas (Peter), the chief apostle, others boasting that they belonged to Christ himself (1:12; 2 Cor. 10:7), while they haughtily repudiated all subordinate teaching. Those persons considered themselves apostles (2 Cor. 11:5, 13). The ground taken by them was that Paul was not one of the Twelve, and therefore not an eyewitness of the gospel facts. Another group avowed themselves followers of Paul himself, but did so in a party spirit, exalting the minister rather than Christ. The followers of Apollos, again, unduly prized his Alexandrian learning and eloquence, to the disparagement of the apostle, who studiously avoided any deviation from Christian simplicity (2:1-5). Among some of this last philosophizing party there may have arisen the Antinomian ("against law") tendency which tried to defend theoretically their own practical immorality; hence their denial of the future resurrection, and their adoption of the Epicurean motto, prevalent in heathen Corinth, "Let us eat and drink, for tomorrow we die" (15:32)—and hence perhaps arose their connivance at the incestuous intercourse kept up by one of the so-called Christian body with his stepmother during his father's life. The household of Chloe informed Paul of many other evils, such as contentions, division, and lawsuits brought against brethren in heathen law courts by professing Christians; the abuse of their spiritual gifts into occasions of display and fanaticism; the interruption of public worship by simultaneous and disorderly ministrations; decorum violated by women speaking unveiled, and so usurping the office of men; and even the Lord's Supper desecrated by greediness and reveling on the part of the participants. Other messengers, also, came from Corinth, consulting him on the subjects of (1) the controversy about meats offered to idols; (2) the disputes about celibacy and marriage; (3) the due exercise of spiritual gifts in public worship; (4) the best mode of making the collection that he had requested for the saints at Jerusalem (16:1, etc.). Such were the circumstances which called for the First Epistle to the Corinthians, the most varied in its topic of all the Epistles.

In 5:9 ("I wrote unto you in an epistle not to company with fornicators") it is implied that Paul had written a previous letter (now lost) to the Corinthians. Probably in it he had also enjoined them to make a contribution for the poor saints at Jerusalem, whereupon they seem to have asked directions as to the mode of doing so, to which he now replies (16:2). It also probably announced his intention of visiting them on his way to Macedonia, and again on his return from Macedonia (2 Cor. 1:15, 16), which purpose he changed on hearing the unfavorable report from Chloe's household (16:5-7), for which he was charged with fickleness (2 Cor. 1:17). In the first epistle which we have, the subject of fornication is alluded to only in a summary way, as if he were rather replying to an excuse set up after rebuke in the matter, than introducing it for the first time (Alford). Preceding this former letter, he seems to have paid a second visit to Corinth, for in 2 Corinthians 12:14; 13:1, he speaks of his intention of paying them a third visit, implying he had already visited them twice. (See comments on 2 Cor. 2:1; 13:2; also 1:15, 16.) It is hardly likely that during his three years' sojourn at Ephesus he would have failed to revisit his Corinthian converts, which he could so readily do by sea, there being constant maritime access between the two cities. This second visit was probably a short one (16:7) and attended with pain and humiliation (2 Cor. 2:1; 12:21), occasioned by the scandalous conduct of so many of his own converts. His milder censure having then failed to produce reformation, he wrote briefly directing them "not to company with fornicators." On their misapprehending this injunction, he explained it more fully in the epistle, the first of the two extant (5:9, 12). See the Introduction to Second Corinthians for comments on the possibility of there having been four epistles: (1) one now lost (referred to in 1 Cor. 5:9); (2) the epistle called "First Corinthians"; (3) another epistle written before "Second Corinthians" and now lost; and (4) the epistle called "Second Corinthians."

The place of writing was Ephesus (16:8). At the time of writing, Paul implies (16:8) that he intended to leave Ephesus after Pentecost of that year. He really did leave it about Pentecost (A.D. 55 or 56). Cf. Acts 19:29. The allusion to Passover imagery in connection with our Christian Passover (5:7) makes it likely that the season was around the Passover. Thus the date of the epistle is fixed with tolerable accuracy about Passover, certainly before Pentecost in the third year of his residence at Ephesus, A.D. 55 or 56. (For other arguments, see Conybeare and Howson's *The Life and the Epistles of St. Paul.*)

The epistle is written in the name of Sosthenes "[our] brother" (1:1). Perhaps he is the same as the Sosthenes in Acts 18:17, who, after the incident recorded there, must have become a Christian and joined Paul. He took no part in writing the epistle itself, for the apostle in the very next verses (1:4ff.) uses the first person. The bearers of the epistle were probably Stephanas, Fortunatas, and Achaicus, whom he mentions (16:17, 18) as being with him then, but who he implies are about to return to Corinth; and therefore he commends them to the Corinthians.

*Chapter* 1

1-31 THE INTRODUCTION THANKS-
GIVING FOR THE SPIRITUAL CONDITION
OF THE CORINTHIAN CHURCH.
REPROOF OF DIVISIONS. PAUL'S
METHOD OF PREACHING ONLY CHRIST

➤1 **Paul**—Paul here uses the usual Greek greeting, first giving his own name, followed by the credentials which have a bearing on the particular message. **called to be an apostle** [a called apostle] **of Jesus Christ through the will of God**—By mentioning his calling, Paul acknowledges that he is an apostle only because God intervened directly in his life; he also reminds the Corinthians that it was by God's choice, and not by his decision or theirs, that he functions as an authority among them. (See Gal. 1:1, 2.) **Sosthenes our brother**—This man is believed to be the same Sosthenes mentioned in Acts 18:17. If so, he had recently been appointed a high official in the Jewish synagogue at Corinth at a time when Paul was brought to trial by other Jews in the city. Gallio, the governor, refused to hear the case and had all the Jews thrown from the judgment hall. This act precipitated widespread punishment of the local Jews by the Romans, and Sosthenes was among those who were flogged. There is no record of direct contact between Paul and Sosthenes, but in the intervening time Sosthenes had been converted. Paul could be mentioning Sosthenes here to add weight to his own authority, or he could simply be documenting his acceptance of Sosthenes as a believer. ➤2 **the church of God which is at Corinth**—The events surrounding the beginning of this church are recounted in Acts 18:1-18.

The city itself was wealthy, its location making it important both commercially and politically. Its popular reputation, however, arose from the extreme debauchery of its citizens, so that the term "to Corinthianize" meant, to most hearers, "to be a libertine." **to them that are sanctified in Christ Jesus**—i.e., consecrated or set apart as holy to God by union with Christ Jesus. **called to be saints**—i.e., saints by calling, a designation applied by Paul to all professing members of the church. **with all that in every place call upon the name of Jesus Christ our Lord, both theirs and ours**—This epistle was addressed to **all** believers in Christ, not just the Corinthians. This form of speech stresses the catholicity and unity of all those who call upon Jesus Christ as Lord (see 2 Tim. 2:22). The Corinthians were to recognize their essential unity with all believers; this would help them see the error of division (see 1:10ff. and comments).

➤3 **Grace be unto you, and peace**—Of all of God's blessings which Paul desires for the Corinthian church, grace and peace are the gifts which he specifies. These seem particularly appropriate in view of the dissension among the church members at the time.

➤4 Paul expresses praise and gratitude for progress in the church before he reproves them for their shortcomings. That this was a common strategy for Paul can be seen in Romans 1:8 and Philippians 1:3. **by Jesus Christ**—should read "in Christ Jesus."

➤5 **That in everything ye are enriched by him, in all utterance, and in all knowledge**—Members of the church at Corinth were particularly gifted both in the understanding of truth as revealed in Christ, and in its communication. Paul appealed to the pride the Corinthians took in these abilities, though he would later have to deal with abuses of these very gifts.

➤**6, 7 the testimony of** [concerning] **Christ**—Cf. 2:1; 1 Timothy 2:6; 2 Timothy 1:8. **confirmed**—God confirmed the gospel in the Corinthians by their accepting it and setting their seal to its truth, through the inward power of the Holy Spirit, and the outward gifts and miracles accompanying it (Calvin). **waiting for the coming of our Lord Jesus Christ**—The Greek participle expresses anticipation ("awaiting" or "expecting") which does not cease until the expected event has occurred.

➤**7 So that ye come behind**—lit., "you are lacking"—**in no gift.**

➤**8 Who shall also confirm** [establish] **you unto the end**—God guarantees his workmanship right up to the moment of Christ's return, after which we will no longer be subject to Satan's attacks.

➤**9 called unto the fellowship of his Son**—i.e., called to participate in the Son's communion with the Father, as joint-heirs together with Christ. The fellowship between the Son and the Father has now been extended to include all the believers (see Rom. 8:17, 28-30; 1 John 1:3). **Jesus Christ our Lord**—Paul mentions Christ's name more often in this epistle than in any other. The Corinthians needed these persistent reminders that their primary loyalty should be to Christ, and not to their party leaders.

➤**10** Paul has already acknowledged that the Corinthians have knowledge of God, the ability to communicate what they know, and hope for the future return of Christ. He now urges loving unity in the church, as among family members. **by the name of our Lord Jesus Christ**—Paul claims authority of Christ as he earlier has of God, and sets him forth again as a rallying point for the divided church. **that ye all speak the same thing**—Paul urges harmony in contrast to the divisive attitude prevalent in the church. **no divisions**—The word here carries the same connotation as of a split or a tear. **joined together in the same mind and in the same judgment** [opinion]—Paul wanted the Corinthians to be unified both in their inward beliefs and attitudes, and in the outworking of these convictions in practical opinions and decisions.

➤**11 the house of Chloe**—Although the Corinthians had written Paul for advice on matters such as marriage, the eating of food offered to idols, and the role of women in the church, they had apparently not mentioned the divisions among them (see 1 Cor. 7:1). Paul had this information from Chloe's household, and from common report (1 Cor. 5:1, 2 and 11:18). Paul prudently named the family to show that he did not confront the church without a reliable source of information, yet he did not identify the individuals concerned. **contentions**—or, strifes. This word is milder than the word "splits," as used in 1:10.

➤**12 every** [each] **one of you saith, I am of Paul**—Though no actual party divisions were made, the spirit of competing factions was certainly being displayed. Paul did not succumb to the flattery of a following, and refused to dishonor Christ by claiming any special glory for the conversion of persons by means of his preaching. **I of Apollos**—Apollos was Paul's successor at Corinth (Acts 18:24ff.), who had been trained in rhetoric at Alexandria. His speaking was not like Paul's plain style of speech (1:17). But it does not seem that Apollos, any more than Paul, was intentionally fostering a spirit of favoritism among the Corinthians. **I of Cephas**—i.e., of Peter. These were probably Judaizers, or Christians who adhered legalistically to points of Jewish law, such as that of circumcision. Quite likely those who called themselves "of Paul," on the other hand, were inclined to overemphasize freedom from the Jewish law. **I of Christ**—Apparently this group was claiming Christ's name in an exclusive manner, so as to slight the ministry of Paul and their other teachers (see 1 Cor. 4:8). This passage can be compared with 2 Cor. 10:7-18.

➤**13 Is Christ divided?**—into various parts—one under one leader, another under another (Alford). The unity of Christ's body is not to be cut in pieces, because all the members belong to him, the one head. **was Paul crucified for you?**—In the Greek, this question mandates a strong negative answer; i.e., "Was it Paul (surely you will say no) that was crucified for you?" Although Paul was the founder of the Corinthian church, he made a clear distinction between himself and Christ, the Redeemer. By implication, the distinction should be at least as clear between Christ and the other church leaders, since they were relative newcomers to the local scene. **were ye baptized in the name of Paul?**—Galatians 3:27 explains clearly that the Christian is baptized into union with Christ, and thereby incorporated into him.

►**14 I baptized none of you but Crispus and Gaius**—Crispus was the former ruler of the synagogue (Acts 18:8), and Gaius was a wealthy man who was Paul's host and in whose home the church had its meetings (Rom. 16:23). Although baptism was generally the responsibility of the deacons rather than the apostles, these two men were among the first converts in Corinth, and thus were baptized by Paul.

►**15 Lest any should say that I had baptized in mine own name**—Paul didn't anticipate this problem at the time when the church was founded, but God had arranged things so that no one could accuse Paul of trying to baptize in his own name.

►**16 the household of Stephanas**—These again were early converts (Acts 16:15). Infant baptism is often supported from such passages as this one (cf. Acts 16:33), which indicate that entire households were baptized.

►**17 For Christ sent me not to baptize**—Paul in no way denigrates the act of baptism here; he is simply reminding the Corinthians that his particular mission as an apostle was **to preach the gospel,** found new churches, and then supervise and oversee these churches. **not with wisdom of words**—The Corinthians had come to set a high value on philosophical reasoning and oratorical language because of Apollos's training in these areas. **lest the cross of Christ should be made of none effect** [void]—Paul did not want his hearers to be distracted from the main thrust of his message, which was the message of the crucified Christ, by a preoccupation with either the method or the form of his delivery.

►**18 For the preaching** [message] **of the cross . . . is the power of God**—Paul draws a contrast between the power of the message of redemption, which is of God, and the power of the "profound words" themselves (1:17), which, though limited, can actually hinder or dilute the message. **them that perish . . . us which are saved**—These phrases in the Greek do not indicate the final state of the persons described, but rather put a person in the class of those who "are perishing" (lit.), or alterna-

tively, in the category of those who "are being saved" (lit.). The implication is that those who are being saved are those who recognize the message as being from God.

►**19** This verse is a slightly altered rendition of the prophecy in Isaiah 29:14 (LXX). The Hebrew text reads: "The wisdom of the wise shall perish, and the understanding of their prudent men shall be hid." Paul by inspiration gives the spiritual sense by making God the subject of the sentence.

►**20 the wise**—This general term refers to all self-styled sages. **the scribe . . . the disputer**—The first term refers to the Jewish scribes, the second to the Greek philosophers. **of this world**—The term "world" here means "this age" or "this earthly order of things" in a moral sense, as contrasted with the Christian's scheme of values and priorities. The Greek word for "world" in this verse is different from "the world" as it is referred to in 1:21, where the earth is viewed as a cosmic entity, from God's perspective, outside the world-system.

►**21 in the wisdom of God**—This phrase could also be read "according to God's wise arrangement." **the world by wisdom knew not God**—God has arranged things so that whatever other knowledge man may be capable of by his own intelligence, man is not able to prove God or determine the proper relationship between himself and God by means of reason alone. This statement runs directly counter to the deistic theory that man can discover his duty to God through the revelation of nature alone, rather than by the direct revelation of God to man through Christ. Even the Jews, with their long history of dealings with God, missed this revelation insofar as they approached God with only their finite understanding of the situation.

►**22 a sign**—should read, "signs." What the Jews wanted here were not simply miracles, but direct demonstrations from heaven to attest to Jesus' identity as the Messiah. Such manifestations of authority would have provided for the Jews the same sort of comfortable assurance that a logical proof would have provided for the Greeks. **the Greeks seek after wisdom**—God does not offer demonstrative proof that Christianity is a philosophically tenable position. Once a person has a reasonable amount of evidence that the alleged revelation is indeed the Word of God, then a leap of faith is necessary on the basis of this revelation. Christianity does not begin with the solution of intellectual problems, but rather with the rectification of the human condition. Athens, the intellectual hub of Greece, found it more difficult to accept the gospel than did the wealthy but dissolute Corinth (see Acts 17:18-21).

➤**23 we preach**—"We" refers to Paul and Apollos. **Christ crucified**—lit., "having been crucified." The Greek participle expresses not only the fact of Christ's crucifixion, but also the permanent character which this transaction gave to Christ as the Redeemer, or Savior. The very idea that their Messiah should be crucified was highly offensive to the Jews, and the seeming absurdity of the whole plan made Christianity appear contemptible to the Greeks. This basic and wholesale opposition on the part of both Jew and Gentile suggests that Christianity could never have gained a large hearing had it not been of divine origin.

➤**24 But unto them which are called**—This phrase carries the same meaning as "those who are being saved" in 1:18. **Christ the power of God**—To the Jew who, by faith, was able to see beyond the offensiveness of Christ as crucified, the cross itself became the "sign" of God's power. **and the wisdom of God**—To the Greek who, by faith, could set aside the limitations of his own reasoning, God's plan was seen to exhibit the highest degree of the very wisdom which he sought.

➤**25 foolishness of God**—i.e., God's plan of salvation, which men deem "foolishness." **weakness of God**—Cf. 2 Corinthians 13:4, which says that Christ was "crucified through weakness."

➤**26 For ye see your calling, brethren**—or, consider "what you were when you were called" (NIV). God called those who, according to human standards, were not the wise, powerful, or noble (well-born).

➤**27 But God hath chosen the foolish things**—a general phrase for "all persons and things foolish." **to confound** [shame] **the wise**—Not only do ignorant and weak people triumph over the learned and powerful when they accept Christ as Redeemer, but God is able to use even foolish things to shame the worldly-wise. **chosen . . . chosen**—The repetition underscores the gracious purposiveness of God's plan to redeem mankind.

➤**28 yea, and**—These words are not present in most of the earliest manuscripts. Thus, the phrase **things which are not** is in apposition to "foolish," "weak," "base" (low-born), and "despised." God has chosen all four, though regarded as nothing, to bring to nothing the things that are.

➤**29 no flesh**—i.e., no mortal. **glory**—boast.

➤**30 But**—in contrast to those that boast in worldly greatness. **of him**—not of yourselves, but of God (cf. Eph. 2:8). **are ye in Christ Jesus**—living in union with him. **who of God is made unto us wisdom**—lit., "who became wisdom to us from God" because our union with Christ provides us with **righteousness, and sanctification, and redemption. righteousness**—the basis of our justification (Jer. 23:5, 6; Rom. 4:25; 2 Cor. 5:21). **sanctification**—made holy by the Holy Spirit. The Greek word refers to a process which is perfect in principle though not yet in attainment. Though we are not yet completely holy, we stand in relation to God as though we were. The Greek fuses this process of becoming and this state of relationship into a single concept. **redemption**—in this position (last of the three) probably refers to the final stage of our salvation, the deliverance of our body from mortality and corruption (see Luke 21:28; Rom. 8:23; Eph. 1:4; 4:30).

➤**31 as it is written**—See Jeremiah 9:23, 24. **glory** [boast] **in the Lord**—Paul does not advocate morbid self-effacement, but reminds the Corinthians that human dignity and achievement derive from God's actions on man's behalf.

*Chapter* **2**

## 1-16 PAUL PREACHES CHRIST CRUCIFIED, ACCORDING TO THE DIVINE WISDOM

➤**1 when I came to you**—See Acts 18 for an account of this first visit. **came not with excellency of speech or of wisdom**—Paul's preaching could easily have exceeded the Corinthians' expectations with respect to style or content that could be achieved through human wisdom. His educational background was impressive, including as it did the secular knowledge available at Tarsus, and a course in Hebrew law under the rabbis at Jerusalem. The schools of Tarsus were preferred by some to those of Athens and Alexandria, and would have exposed Paul to such Greek thinkers as Aratus, Epimenides, and Menander (see Acts 17:28; Titus 1:12; 1 Cor. 15:33). Paul was also a Roman citizen. **the testimony of God**—This reading is supported by some reliable, early manuscripts. However, another reading, "the mystery of God," is also supported by other reliable, early manuscripts. In the Greek, the two words can easily be confounded because they look so much alike. Either word is defensible by the context.

**➤2 For I determined not to know any thing among you, save** [except] **Jesus Christ, and him crucified**—As one translator states it, the person of Christ as crucified was "the only definite thing that I [Paul] made it my business to know among you."

**➤3 I was with you in weakness**—Paul was weak physically, as well as in the method he used for preaching the gospel (see 2 Cor. 10:10; 12:7, 9). **in fear, and in much trembling**—The word "trembling" does not simply reinforce the notion of timidity, but adds the concept of being conscientiously anxious to perform a duty.

**➤4 enticing words of . . . wisdom**—To Paul's audience, this would have meant a form of persuasive speech used by a rhetorician to prove a point or to win people to his side in an argument. Since Paul refused to engage in this sort of argument, that persuasion which occurred was by the power of God's Spirit.

**➤5 stand in the wisdom of men**—This statement carries the connotations of resting upon something, as well as of being dependent upon it for one's origin and continued existence.

**➤6 Howbeit we speak wisdom among them that are perfect** [mature]—Paul had been discussing his method of preaching in public. Here he reflects on more intimate conversations concerning Christian truths which he felt free to discuss only with Christians who have accrued a great deal of knowledge and experience. These mature men were distinguished not only from great men of the world who do not acknowledge Christ, but also from

young Christians whose understanding and experience were still very limited. **the princes of this world, that come to nought**—These men are "being brought to nothingness" and their great ideas with them.

**➤7 But we speak the wisdom of God in a mystery**—This does not refer to some ancient tradition distinct from the gospel. Rather, this means that God reveals his plan gradually to men as their spiritual comprehension increases. Paul is here discussing "mysteries" of the Christian faith, which does not mean that such things cannot be understood, but rather that they are only disclosed to the initiate members of a new order. Whereas pagan mysteries were revealed only to a select few, God's plan in its entirety is available to the person who will believe and obey God's instructions (see 2 Cor. 4:3). Paul had not been able to touch on these areas in his earlier visits to Corinth. **ordained**—lit., "foreordained." **before the world**—rather, "before the ages" (of time); i.e., from eternity. This infinitely antedates worldly wisdom in antiquity. **unto our glory**—both now and hereafter, from "the Lord of glory" (2:8).

**➤8 crucified the Lord of glory**—This phrase implies the inseparable connection between Christ's humanity and his divinity.

**➤9** This verse is an inspired exposition of the idea expressed in Isaiah 64:4. Whereas the Isaiah passage speaks to those who *wait* for the coming Messiah, Paul speaks to those who **love** the Messiah as having already appeared. **entered**—lit., "come up into the heart," a Hebraism (see Jer. 3:16).

**➤10 But**—rather, "for." **God hath revealed them unto us by his Spirit**—Whereas the OT primarily shows the dealings of God the Father with his people, and the Gospels show us God the Son living on earth, the epistles deal predominately with the ministry of God the Spirit in the lives of those who love God. Before Jesus left this earth, he told the believers how the Spirit would come to reveal the riches of God in Christ (see John 14:26; 15:26; 16:13-15). The NT epistles are a testimony to that spiritual unveiling. **the Spirit searcheth all things, . . . the deep things of God**—According to a parallel NT passage (John 16:13-15, see comments there), these "things" are all the things of God given to Christ for the believers' enjoyment and participation. All that the Father possesses has been given to the Son, and all that the Son is and has is continually revealed to us by the Spirit.

➤**11 For what man knoweth**—This phrase in the original reads "who can know," which may imply that angels as well as men are unable to know God's thought unless they are specifically revealed by his Spirit. **the things of a man . . . the spirit of man . . . the things of God . . . the Spirit of God**—What is in man can be known only by the human spirit; likewise, what is in God can be known only by the divine Spirit.

➤**12 the spirit of the world**—The "spirit" here mentioned is not the human spirit of an individual (as in 2:11), but is, rather, the spirit of the evil one who rules this world, and is in direct conflict with the Spirit of God (see Eph. 2:2).

➤**13 which the Holy Ghost** [Spirit] **teacheth**—The earliest manuscripts read simply "the Spirit," without "Holy." **comparing spiritual things with spiritual**—This expression can mean: (1) "explaining [as the word is translated in Gen. 40:8, LXX] spiritual things to spiritual men," or (2) "matching spiritual things with spiritual words"—i.e., each spiritual truth was matched by corresponding words. The context seems to indicate that Paul was speaking about how he (as with the other apostles) was given the utterance by the Spirit to express spiritual truths. This affirms the divine inspiration of NT Scripture, for the apostles were given their words by the Spirit. These words of the Spirit can be understood by other believers in whom the Spirit is also working.

➤**14 the natural man**—lit., "the soulical man" (see Rotherham's *Emphasized Bible*), the man governed by his rational mind and intellect. The non-Christian has at best only the aid of his human intellect and emotions, and at worst is actively beset by the evil spirit, which runs counter to the Spirit of God. **they are foolishness unto him**—The words of the Spirit are as incomprehensible to the natural man as a foreign language without an interpreter. Since the non-Christian thinks he is seeking wisdom, and God's plan sounds so foolish, he will naturally shun it. **neither can he know them, because they are spiritually discerned**—Just as the mysteries of God's plan are made available to all believers, so is God's message transmitted to all mankind. The natural man, however, simply lacks the necessary equipment for receiving the message.

➤**15 he that is spiritual**—lit., "the spiritual man," the man in whom the Spirit rules. In the unregenerate, the spirit which ought to be the organ of the Holy Spirit (and which is so in the regenerate), is overridden by the animal soul, and is in abeyance, so that such a one is never called "spiritual." **judgeth all things, yet he himself is judged of no man**—It is more accurate to use the word "discern" than "judge" (the same Greek word has been rendered "discerned" in 2:14). The spiritual man, under the influence of the Holy Spirit, has practical insight into the realities of the spiritual realm and Christian life (cf. 1 John 2:27; 4:1). But those who do not have the Spirit are not qualified to discern the internal workings of the Spirit in the Christian's life.

➤**16 For**—what follows substantiates the last assertion of 2:15, that the spiritual man "is judged [discerned] of no man." In order to judge the spiritual man, the ordinary man must know **the mind of the Lord.** But who among ordinary men knows that? **that he may instruct him**—so as to be able to set God right through counseling him (quoted from Isa. 40:13, LXX). **we have the mind of Christ**—Through our union with Christ, we have access to Christ's mind, Christ's divine thoughts, Christ's counsel. In the Isaiah passage quoted by Paul, the subject is Yahweh (translated "LORD"); but here the subject is "Christ." This affirms Christ's deity and unity with the Godhead.

*Chapter* **3**

## 1-23 PAUL'S REPROOF FOR DIVISIONS IN THE CHURCH AND DIRECTION CONCERNING THE MANNER OF BUILDING GOD'S HOUSE

➤**1 I, brethren, could not speak unto you as unto spiritual** [men]—Paul regretted that he could not interact with the Corinthians as with mature, spiritual Christians. These men lived a mixed life—living according to natural desires *and* living in harmony with the Spirit of God. Although this problem is common to all

Christians, Paul reproved the Corinthians because they had not chosen to give the Spirit precedence over their own inclinations. The primary issue was that of party divisions, expressing favoritism for certain Christian teachers. **babes in Christ**—contrasted with those mature in Christ (Col. 1:28). They were not completely natural or carnal; they had a life in Christ, but it was young.

➤**2 milk**—Paul had to continually review the elementary principles of Christian doctrine, which prevented him from moving on to more complex truths (see Heb. 5:13, 14).

➤**3 envying** [jealousy], **and strife, and divisions**—The feelings, words, and actions of the Corinthians were all awry: jealousy had provoked quarrels which caused divisions among them (see Gal. 5:19, 20). Paul's censure is more stern now than in his opening statements, and will become yet more severe before he has finished. (The word "divisions" appears in some ancient manuscripts but is absent in several other very early, reliable manuscripts.) **are ye not carnal, and walk as men?**—Divisiveness is the work of the flesh (Gal. 5:20) and a manifestation of activity characteristic of unregenerate men. Quarreling and divisiveness are self-seeking rather than God-seeking activities. God's Spirit motivates a concern for other men which is at least on a par with one's personal desires (see Matt. 16:23; Rom. 8:4; Gal. 5:25, 26).

➤**5 Who then is Paul, and who is Apollos?**—What intrinsic worth has any leader that the Corinthians should show him such favoritism? The oldest manuscripts have the names in reverse order, indicating further humility on Paul's part. **but ministers by whom ye believed**—The Corinthians believed in Christ by the help of these ministers, but they were not to believe *in* the ministers as ends in themselves.

➤**6 I have planted**—Paul started the church. **Apollos watered**—Apollos was sent to Corinth at his own request to further Paul's early work (Acts 18:27, 28). It is interesting to note that the Greek verbs describing the work of both Paul and Apollos (i.e., planting and watering) denote completed actions, whereas the verb concerning God's work with the church (i.e., growth) is in the imperfect tense to indicate continuing activity. **God gave the increase** [was making to grow]—Granted that no work of man can succeed unless God prospers it, still God has promised to work through men as his vessels, and to multiply their efforts on God's behalf.

➤**7 God that giveth the increase** [growth]—In the Greek, the word "God" occupies an emphatic position in the sentence: "He that gives the growth, (namely) God." The following section (3:8-21) contains a parenthetical idea, "Let's have no boasting about what men can do," which underscores the idea that all true accomplishment comes by God's power.

➤**8 one**—engaged in one and the same ministry. Since these two men were working toward the same goal, it was foolish for the Corinthians to try to divert their energies into different channels, assuming, of course, that the Corinthians had the same goals as their teachers. **every man shall receive his own reward according to his own labour**—Though the aim of all Christians is the same, personal responsibility for assigned tasks is most emphatically maintained. Each minister will receive **his own** reward (over and above his salvation) according to **his own** labor (2 John 8). The reward will not be based on the success or the amount of work involved, but rather on the faithfulness of the worker to his own assignment (Matt. 25:23).

➤**9 For we are labourers together with God**—Though Christians are working *with* God, still they are *under* him and *belong to* him, as servants (2 Cor. 5:20; 6:1). **ye are God's husbandry** [farm, garden, tillage], **ye are God's building**—The metaphor of the garden shifts here to that of a building, which better suits Paul's following discussion of various kinds of teaching and their outcomes.

➤**10 According to the grace of God which is given unto me**—Paul does not deprecate his own abilities, but he always acknowledges God as their source. God teaches any Christian just what he needs to know to accomplish the work given him to do. **as a wise masterbuilder, I have laid the foundation**—A proper foundation is the mark of an expert builder; the novice will often not lay a foundation at all. Christ is the only adequate foundation to the building of the faith (3:11). **and another buildeth thereon. But let every man take heed how he**

**buildeth thereupon**—Paul here refers to anyone who should "build" after him, and not to Apollos specifically. From all indications, Paul found Apollos's work quite satisfactory. Paul was, in effect, serving notice that he had done his part, and that his followers should take care to do the same (1 Pet. 4:10, 11). The superstructure to be built here is not the church as made up of believers (as in Eph. 2:20 and 1 Pet. 2:5), but rather the practical and doctrinal teaching which will be based on such foundational truths as redemption through Christ's crucifixion. Paul's complaint is not that this further teaching had been false, but that it was subtle and speculative in nature, rather than clear and substantial.

►**11** See Isaiah 28:16 for an OT reference to Christ as the **foundation.** Paul's concern was with men's additions to the foundation, never with the foundation itself. As this true foundation had already been laid, no one could possibly lay another in its place. **Jesus Christ**—The name "Jesus" expresses the character of God as Savior; "Christ" is the Messiah or anointed One. Paul's use of both names here shows that concepts of the redemption and the sovereignty of Christ are both foundational to sound Christian doctrine.

►**12** The image here is of a building laid on a solid foundation, but composed partially of durable materials and partially of perishable ones. These materials will be tested by fire as to their value. The gold, silver, and jewels represent teachings which can survive testing, whereas the sticks, hay, and straw represent teachings of no lasting value. These worthless teachings aren't strictly heretical, but are mixed with so much speculation and legalism as to render them useless. The building represents not only doctrines and rules, but also persons added to the church by means of these teachings, the quality of whose conversions will likewise be tested. Though the least grain of gold will never be lost (1 Pet. 1:7), the lightest straw will feed the fire (Matt. 5:19).

►**13 the day**—i.e., the day of the Lord (see 1 Thess. 5:14; 2 Thess. 1:7 8; Heb. 10:25). **it shall be revealed by fire**—Translated literally, this phrase would read "is being revealed by fire." The present tense in Greek implies the certainty and the nearness of the event (Rev. 22:10, 20). The "fire" may be merely figurative

here, as are the jewels and the straw. In any case, the fire is not a "purgatory" (see explanation that follows) for punishment and purification, but rather a universal judgment on believers and unbelievers alike (2 Cor. 5:10). This fire is not present until the "last day," whereas the fire of purgatory is thought to begin on the day of an individual's death. The fire Paul refers to tests a person's works and causes loss to the person by burning away unworthy accomplishments; Purgatory is believed to test the person himself, and to bring heaven at last to those who are purified by its flames. Thus this passage, often used in support of the notion of purgatory, actually contradicts the idea. This erroneous doctrine grew out of the well-intentioned but misguided practice of praying for the dead.

►**14 he shall receive a reward**—The Christian whose work still stands after the testing by fire will receive his wages (Phil. 2:16). The best reward for Christian workers is to see their converts mature in Christ (2 Cor. 1:14; 1 Thess. 2:19).

►**15 he shall suffer loss**—If the Christian's work is of materials which are consumed by the fire, he will not lose his salvation, which is a free gift, but he will forfeit the special reward promised for work well done. The foundation will remain, and the man himself will be spared, but he will escape as from a burning building (see Zech. 3:2; Amos 4:11; Mal. 3:2; Jude 23).

►**16 Know ye not**—It was apparently nothing new for the believers to be described as God's building; the statement implies, "You know and ought to remember." **ye are the temple of God**—Here Paul describes God's building as composed of believers themselves, who together make up the house of God. He does not say, "you are each a temple" but "you [plural] are *the* temple," with each person participating as one of the building-stones (1 Pet. 2:5). **and that the Spirit of God dwelleth in you**—The NT does not recognize any specific church building as God's house, but only the spiritual building made up of believers, in and among whom the Holy Spirit lives (John 4:21-24; Eph. 2:21, 22). The synagogue, rather than the temple, provides a model for Christian worship. The temple was a place of sacrifice, of silent, individual prayer (Luke 18:10-13), and was the earthly dwelling place of God. The synagogue, on the other hand, was a place for men to gather for joint public prayer and Scripture reading. God now has a temple not built of wood and stone, but of the congregation of believers themselves. Christ is the High Priest in this temple, and each believer likewise functions as a spiritual priest within God's group of believers (Mal. 1:11; Matt. 18:20; 1 Pet. 2:5).

➤17 **If any man defile the temple of God, him shall God destroy**—The two verbs have come from the same Greek word, which in this context could mean "desecrate." God desecrates the desecrating individual. As physical death was the penalty for intrusion in the material temple (Exod. 28:43; Lev. 16:2; Dan. 5), so eternal death is the penalty for defacing the spiritual temple, which is the body of believers (Heb. 12:14; 10:26, 31). These destroyers are distinct from the unskillful and unwise builders mentioned in 3:11-15. Though these builders were unwise in their choice of materials, still they will be saved because they maintained the foundation. The destroyers seek to subvert the temple itself, and will themselves be destroyed. In this discussion, Paul includes all the members of the church who serve as priests of God (Exod. 19:6; 1 Pet. 2:9; Rev. 1:6), rather than just the teacher-builders. **the temple of God is holy**—See Habakkuk 2:20. Since believers make up this house, any impurity on their part will defile it. **which temple ye are**—or, "the which are ye," i.e., ye are holy (Alford).

➤18 **let him become a fool**—By receiving the gospel in its unworldly simplicity, the Christian becomes a fool in the world's estimation. It is better to desire God's wisdom than to consider oneself already wise.

➤19 **For it is written**—See Job 5:13. This is the only place in the NT where Job is directly quoted, and lends authenticity to the book as part of the OT canon. **He taketh** [catches] **the wise in their own craftiness**—The foolishness of human wisdom is shown as these "wise" men are caught in their own traps.

➤20 This verse is a paraphrase of Psalm 94:11. The psalmist speaks of the thoughts of men; Paul makes the comment apply more specifically to the reasoning process.

➤21, 22 **Therefore let no man glory in men**—Paul here resumes the topic from which he digressed in 3:4 (see also 1 Cor. 1:31). **For all things are yours**—Not only all men. For the Corinthians to boast in men was to lower themselves from their high position as heirs of all things. All men (including the Corinthians' teachers) belonged to Christ and therefore to them, by their union with him. **Whether Paul, or Apollos, or Cephas** [Peter]—Having just reminded the Corinthians that God had already given them everything they needed, Paul enumerated some of the things included, listing first the help of their Christian leaders. He did not say, "and Christ" after Peter (though some of the Corinthians had claimed to belong exclusively to Christ), as though he were merely another human leader, but rather he reminded them (in the following verse) that they all belonged to Christ.

➤23 **And ye are Christ's**—Paul here reminds the Corinthians that their ultimate allegiance is not to any finite leader, but that they and their teachers alike belong to Christ (cf. Matt. 23:8-10). **and Christ is God's**—God is the ultimate end of all things, including his Son, Christ, who is co-equal with the Father (see 15:28; Phil. 2:5-11).

*Chapter* 4

## 1-21 PAUL'S DEFENSE OF HIS APOSTOLIC MINISTRY AND FATHERHOOD OF THE CORINTHIANS

### 1-4 PAUL EXPLAINS THE ROLE AND FUNCTION OF CHRISTIAN MINISTERS OR STEWARDS

➤1 **ministers of Christ**—lit., "attendants of Christ." Paul did not want teachers in the church to be regarded as high officials, but as servants (attendants) sent to attend to Christians' needs. **stewards**—lit., "household managers," one who manages the master's household and takes care of distributing the master's goods. Paul saw himself as a steward entrusted with God's mysteries, which he had to dispense to all the members of God's household. **of the mysteries of God**—God instructed Paul and Apollos as to the distribution of his divine secrets (see Eph. 3:1-7). The minister must share those truths which God has revealed to him with any who will listen.

➤2 **Moreover**—to which we should add "here," according to the earliest manuscripts. "Here" means here on earth. **it is required in**

**stewards, that a man be found faithful**—The Corinthians were showing partiality toward one teacher or another because of their particular *gifts*. But it is "faithfulness," not "giftedness," that is required of God's stewards.

➤**3 with me it is a very small thing that I should be judged of you**—not that Paul discounted the opinion of the Corinthians, but that next to God's opinion, it simply did not matter. **man's judgment**—lit., "human day." "Just as the term 'day of the Lord' (1 Cor. 1:8; 5:5) involves God's judgment in that eschatological day, so in this context a 'human day' means man's judgment in the day when his (man's) courts are in session" (Mare). **I judge not mine own self**—For this reason, Paul did not even trust his own judgment as to how well he was doing.

➤**4 For I know nothing by myself**—This actually should read, "For I know nothing against myself" (ASV), which means "I am conscious to myself of no (ministerial) unfaithfulness." **yet am I not hereby justified**—Conscience is not considered by Paul to be an infallible guide, nor are his personal feelings given the last word. **he that judgeth me is the Lord**—The Lord himself must decide whether or not Paul was doing acceptable work.

➤**5 judge nothing before the time**—In 4:3, 4 Paul referred in passing to other people's opinions concerning his personal merit. In this verse, passing judgment on others is taken much more seriously, in the sense of presumptuously assuming a role that belongs to God alone. **until the Lord come**—The title "Lord" fits the analogy of the master of the household for whom the servants work; for the Christian, the master is Jesus Christ, who will reward his workers as they deserve when he comes again.

➤**6** Paul changes his approach here to make general principles apply specifically to the Corinthian situation. **I have in a figure transferred** [I have adopted, applied] **to myself and to Apollos**—Though Paul had mentioned himself and Apollos by name, he intended that his comments should apply to *any* minister or teacher. He did not want to embarrass individual members of the Corinthian church, but he did want them to get the point of his remarks. **that ye might learn in us not to think of men above that which is written**—lit., "that ye might learn the (i.e., the rule) 'not beyond what

things have been written.' " "The saying appears to be proverbial, perhaps a Rabbinical adage" (Vine). The adage essentially means, "keep to the rule of Scripture, not a step beyond the written word!" (see Findlay).

➤**7** Since God is the only one who can tell what is worthwhile in an individual, it was foolish of the Corinthians to believe themselves capable of making such distinctions between one teacher and another.

➤**8** Paul here speaks ironically of the Corinthians who think they have already arrived at a goal toward which their leaders are still struggling. The contrast will be reinforced at both the material and spiritual levels. The Corinthians enjoyed wealth and prestige, while the apostles remained in great physical discomfort; these Christians were also very complacent spiritually, whereas Paul and Apollos "hungered and thirsted after righteousness" (see also Rev. 3:17; Hos. 12:8). **I would** [indeed] **. . . ye did reign, that we also might reign with you**—Paul certainly wished that the Corinthians were already reigning with Christ, for Paul and Apollos, as their spiritual leaders, would therefore have their reward from Christ, the righteous judge (1 Thess. 2:19).

➤**9 For I think that God hath set forth** [exhibited] **us the apostles last**—Whereas the Corinthians considered themselves above average in intelligence (3:18), Paul felt that God had *exhibited* (a more accurate rendering than "set forth") the apostles at the end of the show, in the last place. "One imagines a grand procession, on some day of public festival; in its rear march the criminals on their way to the arena, where the populace will be regaled with their sufferings" (Findlay). (Paul uses the term "apostles" in a broad sense here to include Apollos as one of God's messengers—see Rom. 16:7; 2 Cor. 8:23.) **as it were appointed to death**—as criminals condemned to die. **made a spectacle**—Condemned criminals in Paul's time were displayed in the amphitheater for the amusement of the public. This is one of several images Paul uses to convey a sense of being on stage before a hostile audience. (The same image is used in 2 Cor. 2:14.) **unto the world, and to angels, and to men**—The activities of God's messengers are apparently of intense interest not only to their contemporaries, but also to unseen opponents who are pleased to see them suffer.

➤10 Paul here reiterates the ironic contrast between his perspective and that of the Corinthians as he begins to list specific difficulties which he encounters.

➤11 Paul then relates his current experience which was similar in many respects to the treatment Christ received during his ministry on earth (see 2 Cor. 11:23-27)—but was very different from the circumstances enjoyed by the Corinthians.

➤12 working with our own hands—See Acts 18:3; 20:34.

➤13 defamed, we intreat—The Greeks thought it cowardly to respond kindly to abuse. filth—"the refuse" (Conybeare and Howson), the sweepings or rubbish thrown out after a cleaning. offscouring—scrapings.

➤14 as my beloved sons [children] I warn you—The imagery changes now from that of master and servants to that of father and children. Paul instructs the Corinthians as his spiritual children.

➤15 ten thousand instructors in Christ—The number is exaggerated for effect. The word translated "instructors" could as easily be translated "tutors" or "trainers" (lit., "pedagogues"). A tutor had the responsibility for instructing a child, but he did not have the authority or the affection of the real father. yet have ye not many fathers: for in Christ Jesus I have begotten you through the gospel—Paul claims the intimacy and the authority of the father's position with respect to the Corinthians, whereas their other teachers are to be regarded as tutors who will instruct them.

➤16 be ye followers of me—Paul urges the Corinthians to learn by imitating him as all children learn by imitating their parents. There seems to have been no discrepancy between Paul's preaching and his personal conduct (see also Acts 26:29).

➤17 I sent unto you Timotheus—Paul sent Timothy to Corinth so that he could serve as an example for the Christians to imitate in Paul's absence. Furthermore, through long and close association with Paul, Timothy was familiar with his instructions and suggestions to other churches and could continue to teach them in Paul's place. Paul had a great deal of confidence and affection vested in Timothy (see 1 Cor. 16:10; 2 Tim. 1:2).

➤18 Now some are puffed up, as though I would not come to you—There were those in the church who would assume that Paul, in sending Timothy, was afraid to come himself, and who therefore would not change their behavior.

➤19 But I will come to you shortly—Paul hoped to visit Corinth shortly after Pentecost, though he seems to have been delayed (Acts 16:7, 8). Some translate the first phrase more emphatically, to read "But come I will." [I] will know, not the speech of them which are puffed up, but the power—This refers back to a point made earlier about the emptiness of rhetorical ability as compared with the power of God's Spirit.

➤20 not in word [speech], but in power—Paul was not interested in the natural abilities of these men; he wanted to see evidence that God was changing their lives (1 Thess. 1:5).

➤21 Paul, speaking again as a father, asserted that their behavior would set the tone for his next visit.

# 5

*Chapter*

## 1-13 PAUL'S DEALINGS WITH AN IMMORAL BROTHER

➤1 It is reported commonly [actually] that there is fornication among you—Though the Corinthians had written to ask Paul's advice on several problems, they never even mentioned the incestuous affair of one of their own church members, news of which reached Paul indirectly. and such fornication as is not so much as named among the Gentiles, that one should have his father's wife—This kind of fornication (or possibly marriage by the two in question) was expressly forbidden by Jewish, Greek, and Roman law (for the Jewish statement see Lev. 18:8 and Deut. 22:30). The relationship was the more disturbing because the man's father was still living (2 Cor. 7:12). It is significant that this situation made such a stir in Corinth, where sexual immorality was tolerated on such a grand scale. That Paul did not rebuke the woman involved suggests that she was not among the Christians in Corinth (see 5:12 and 13).

➤**2 ye are puffed up**—i.e., conceited. The Corinthians were too preoccupied with their supposed wisdom and knowledge to make the proper response to this critical situation. **taken away from among you**—The Christians practiced two forms of excommunication: a lighter one and a heavier one (following the practice of the Jewish synagogue). In the lighter case, the offender was not allowed to participate in the Lord's Supper. A more serious fault required complete separation from the group of believers. Paul recommended the more severe punishment, which in this case did prove effective (2 Cor. 2:5-10).

➤**3 I . . . have judged already**—The perfect tense in Greek designates a past action with a present, abiding result. **as though I were present**—Although he was not physically present, he was as involved in the situation as though he were there in person.

➤**4 In the name of our Lord Jesus Christ**—Paul acts on the authority of Christ himself in this recommendation. He will be with the Corinthians in spirit, and they will be given power by God's Spirit as they meet to expel the incestuous man from the church fellowship.

➤**5 to deliver such an one unto Satan**—The only other NT use of this phrase occurs in 1 Timothy 1:20. The expression seems to refer to the process of excommunication. Since Satan rules all aspects of the world outside of the church body, being turned out of the church involves being sent defenseless into Satan's territory. **day of the Lord Jesus**—The two earliest manuscripts read, "day of the Lord."

➤**6 a little leaven leaveneth the whole lump**—The Corinthians' complicity in the one man's guilt could lead to future contagion. Paul's concern was that if the Christians could excuse such evil behavior in a fellow believer, they might soon be excusing themselves for similar conduct (cf. Gal. 5:9).

➤**7 Purge out therefore the old leaven**—The imagery is drawn from the extreme care the Jews took in extracting every bit of leaven from their homes in preparation for the Passover celebration (see Deut. 16:3, 4). The analogy is between the forbidden leaven and the evil practice within the Corinthian congregation, and extends to an identification of Christ with the sacrificial lamb. (Verses 6-8 assume

familiarity with the Jewish Passover celebration, described in Deut. 16:1-8.) **that ye may be a new lump, as ye are unleavened**—The Corinthians are asked to practically maintain their spiritual position of being a new, unleavened lump (i.e., a new creation) by rejecting the leaven (i.e., the evil influence). **Christ our passover** [lamb] **is** [was] **sacrificed for us**—"In his death on the cross, Christ fulfilled the true meaning of the Jewish sacrifice of the Passover lamb (Isa. 53:7; John 1:29). Christ, the Lamb of God, was crucified on Passover day" (*NIVSB*).

➤**8 let us keep the feast**—The present tense indicates that the Christian experience is a festival to be observed continuously. **not with old leaven**—The Corinthian church is instructed to dismiss the remaining portions of its unregenerate nature (as represented by the leavened bread), and to concentrate instead on Christ (the Passover Lamb) and its new life in Christ (pure, or unleavened bread of sincerity and truth). **neither with the leaven of malice and wickedness**—"Malice" refers to malicious motives, whereas "wickedness" denotes the evil acts which follow these vicious inclinations. **sincerity and truth**—Similarly, the "sincerity" to be desired refers to purity of motive, and "truth" to purity of action.

➤**9 I wrote unto you in an** [the] **epistle not to company with fornicators**—As there is no warning against contact with immoral persons in the opening part of 1 Corinthians, Paul must have written an earlier letter to the Corinthians which has not been preserved.

➤**10 Yet not altogether . . . for then must ye needs go out of the world**—In Corinth, to avoid people who were immoral would have meant virtually no contact at all with unbelievers. The Christian is supposed to live among the non-Christian people of the world without copying behavior patterns which are contrary to God's nature (John 17:15; 1 Cor. 10:27; 1 John 5:18, 19).

➤**11 not to keep company . . .** —Rather than avoid contact with the "outside world," the Christian is forbidden to socialize with people who call themselves Christians but behave like unbelievers (Matt. 5:13-16; 2 John 1:10, 11). **an idolater**—Paul had already discussed the problem of fornication within the Corinthian church, and he would soon be dealing with other problems, such as the questions concerning food offered to idols (chpt. 8).

➤12 This verse is better stated in the RSV: "For what have I to do with judging outsiders? Is it not those inside the church whom you are to judge?" This anticipates Paul's next topic concerning lawsuits by Christian against Christian.

➤13 **Therefore put away from among yourselves that wicked person**—This restates the sentence of excommunication in language borrowed from Deuteronomy 24:7. Paul's use of a plural verb and pronoun (in Greek) indicates that it was the responsibility of the entire church to discipline this offender.

# Chapter 6

## 1-11 PAUL'S TREATMENT OF LAWSUITS AMONG THE BROTHERS

➤1 **Dare any of you, having a matter against another, go to law before the unjust, and not before the saints?**—One of the many causes for scandal concerning the Corinthian church was that one Christian was suing another in the pagan law courts. Paul takes up this topic in 6:1-11. The problem was not simply that the Christians should have been able to resolve their differences in a spirit of love, but that it was considered a disgrace for Christians to bring lawsuits before heathen courts. As with the Jews, who referred their disputes to Jewish arbitrators, Christians should have settled their own differences among themselves.

➤2 **Do ye not know that the saints shall judge the world?**—Paul considered it a commonly known fact that Christians would one day be ruling the world with Christ, according to their abilities and the positions they have earned through faithfulness to earthly tasks (see Ps. 49:14; Dan. 7:22, 27; Matt. 19:28; Rev. 2:26; 3:21; 20:4). It is ironic that these Corinthians who boasted of so much knowledge concerning the things of God should not act in accordance with their knowledge. Furthermore, the petty issues which concerned them were trivial by comparison with the situations these same people would confront if they were to become rulers over nations.

➤3 **Know ye not that we shall judge angels?**—Though it is often speculated that fallen angels are referred to here, Paul did not identify the group. He simply indicated that a person who is destined to rule over angels should be able to cope with the disputes of this life.

➤4 Even the **least esteemed** among the Christians should be capable of judging disputes concerning such secondary concerns as property rights and the like.

➤5 **I speak to your shame**—Paul directs his rebuke at two aspects of the Corinthians' behavior: their conceited sense of spirituality, and their pride in their wisdom (see 5:2). **Is it so, that there is not a wise man among you?**—The Jews called each rabbi in the Jewish councils a "wise man." The Christians demeaned themselves before both Jew and Gentile because they took their quarrels to the heathen courts to be settled, and did not consider that any Christian was as capable as one of the Jewish arbitrators. This shows what their "wisdom" really amounted to.

➤6 **But brother goeth to law with brother**—The "but" in this sentence indicates a strong negative response to the question asked in the previous verse, and could as well be stated, "No! Instead one Christian sues another. . . . "

➤7 **fault**—This term is not as strong as that usually translated "sin," but represents a "shortcoming," or "failure" to live up to a position of great privilege. **take wrong**—See Proverbs 20:22; Matthew 5:39-42.

➤8 **ye do wrong**—The Corinthians not only failed to be patient when they were abused, but were actually engaging in unjust practices, even against their fellow Christians.

➤9, 10 **shall not inherit the kingdom of God**—Those who do wrong will have no part in God's righteous kingdom. The list of various kinds of sinners here is not exhaustive, but does cover areas to which the Corinthians were particularly vulnerable. (Cf. Gal. 5:19-21.)

➤11 **And such were some of you**—After listing various kinds of sinners, Paul reminds his readers that many of them have come from backgrounds such as these. However, he quickly moves on to remind the Corinthians also of the effects which their redemption has had on their lives. **ye are washed**—The Greek middle voice expresses, "You have had yourselves washed," referring to the act of baptism (see Acts 22:16) as well as perhaps to the washing of regeneration (Tit. 3:5). **ye are sanctified**—set apart to God, made holy (see 1 Pet. 1:2). **ye are justified**—made right with God by faith in Christ (see Rom. 1:17). **in the name of the Lord Jesus** [add "Christ" according to the best manuscripts], **and by the Spirit**—rather, "in the Spirit," i.e., by his indwelling. Both phrases belong to the three actions—"washed, sanctified, and justified." **our God**—In using the phrase "our God," Paul reminded the Corinthians that for all his reproofs, God was still both theirs and his (see 1:2).

►**12** In verses 12-20, Paul deals with the abuse of Christian freedom. Since the gospel of Christ had released some of the Corinthians from many petty Jewish rules, they had adopted an "anything goes" type of attitude. **All things are lawful unto me**—This statement is similar to Paul's words on other occasions when Christians were using this line as an excuse for wrong behavior (see 10:23). The particular issue in question is fornication, especially as connected with idol worship (see Acts 15:29). The practices of idol worship were closely connected with both feasting and sexual immorality. Some of the Corinthians were defending their immoral practices by arguing that both hunger and sex were natural bodily instincts and had equal right to satisfaction. Others who felt no qualms about eating food offered to idols were tempted to claim "freedom" in fornication as well, even though sexual immorality had been explicitly forbidden, when eating the food had not been. **all things are lawful for me, but I will not be brought under the power of any**—The Greek text contains a play on words which is not evident in the English translation: "All things are *in* my power, but I will not be brought *under* the power of any" or "all things are lawful for me but I will not be put under the law by anyone." Fornicators forfeit their rightful liberty, and are brought under the power of the seducer. The same principle, of course, applies to any activity which gains control over the believer, who should be subject to the Spirit's direction (see John 8:34-36; Gal. 5:13; 1 Pet. 2:16; 2 Pet. 2:19).

►**13 Meats for the belly, and the belly for meats: but God shall destroy both it and them**—Paul used this example to make two important points. First, the matter of eating or not eating certain foods is of no eternal significance, and is not in itself a moral issue (Mark 7:18, 19; Rom. 14:14-17; 1 Cor. 8:8; Col. 2:20-22). Second, even in such a casual matter as eating, the Christian must be careful not to overindulge, or eat in ways that offend other Christians. **Now the body is not for fornication, but for the Lord; and the Lord for the body**—Paul shows that whereas eating is the proper satisfaction of bodily hunger, and is relatively unimportant, fornication is *not* the intended way to satisfy the sexual instinct, nor is it of casual significance. Paul continues to deal with sexual relations in this chapter and the next; he later takes up in more detail the issue of meat offered to idols, and the resurrection of the body, which he mentions here in passing.

►**14 God hath both raised up the Lord, and will also raise up us by his own power**—In the Greek there is a play on the words "raised" and "will raise." The compound form used in the second expression may be translated "will be raised up out of" the rest of the dead. Paul did not know whether he would be dead or alive when Christ returned (see 1 Thess. 4:17). In either case, the Christian's focus is on the Lord's return rather than on physical death. The Christian is assured of bodily resurrection from death because of Christ's resurrection (Rom. 8:11; 1 Cor. 15:20; Phil. 3:21).

►**15** Paul returns to the idea expressed in 6:13 to say that our bodies are not only made *for* the Lord; they are actually a *part* of Christ's body through union with him (1 Cor. 12:27; Eph. 4:15, 16). Thus, for a Christian to have sexual relations with a prostitute is actually to defile Christ's body.

►**16 he which is joined** [joins himself] **to an harlot is one body**—The expression "joins himself" (middle voice in Gk.), referring to sexual intercourse, literally means "giving oneself to" or "sticking one's self to." Thus, the two persons become as one, **for two, saith he, shall be one flesh**—See Genesis 2:24; cf. Matthew 19:5, 6; Ephesians 5:31, 32.

►**17 he that is joined** [joining himself—middle voice in Gk.] **unto the Lord is one Spirit**—Union with Christ is a spiritual union: our spirit joins with his Spirit to form an inseparable union. This same thought is expressed in

John 3:6 and Romans 8:16. At the time of regeneration, Christ *as* Spirit (see 1 Cor. 15:45; 2 Cor. 3:17, 18) and *by* the Spirit is united, by our faith, to our spirit.

➤**18 Flee fornication**—Flight is apparently the only safeguard against this temptation (cf. Gen. 39:12; Job. 31:1-4, 9-12). **Every sin that a man doeth is without** [outside] **the body**—The Greek is very forceful here: "Any other sin whatsoever that a man might commit" is comparatively external to the body. **but he that commiteth fornication sinneth against his own body**—Even though many other misdeeds cause injury to the body, none of them runs counter to the essential nature of the body as fornication does.

➤**19 your body is the temple of the Holy Ghost** [Spirit]—In 3:17 Paul used a plural expression ("which temple ye are") to make the point that all Christians together make up the temple of God. Here the singular is used to show that the individual Christian's body is in microcosm the temple of God as well as being a part of the collective "body of Christ." The word here translated "temple" is the Greek word *naos,* which represents the most sacred portion of the Jewish temple enclosure, i.e., the sanctuary. **which is in you**—In the Jewish temple, the Shekinah glory served as a visible reminder of God's presence among his people. Each Christian now has God's Spirit living in him individually. **ye are not your own**—Christ has paid the purchase price for our bodies. If we acknowledge that we belong to Christ, then we are not free to give our bodies to another, as the fornicator does. This analogy was more meaningful to a culture where slavery was commonplace (cf. Rom. 6:16-23).

➤**20 For ye are bought with a price**—See Matthew 20:28; Galatians 3:13; 1 Peter 1:18, 19. The verb "bought" is in the aorist tense in Greek, referring to the specific action of Jesus' death on the cross. This language would bring to the Corinthians' minds a local custom whereby a slave paid the price for his freedom to a particular god's temple, thus becoming a slave to that god, even though society considered him a free man. **therefore glorify God in your body**—Though the main purpose of this passage has been to argue against sexual immorality, Paul ends with a positive reminder that we are not merely to avoid certain wrong activ-

ities, but to do all in our power to bring honor to God, who has paid the ransom money for our release from sin. **and in your spirit, which are God's**—These words are not present in all the earliest manuscripts: they were added later based on the mention of the spirit in 6:17.

**Chapter 7**

1-40 PAUL'S REPLY CONCERNING THE CORINTHIANS' INQUIRIES ABOUT SEX AND MARRIAGE

➤**1 Now concerning the things whereof ye wrote unto me**—Although several earlier comments in Paul's letter have seemed to be answers to specific questions from the Corinthians, this is the first occasion where Paul makes direct reference to a letter from them. This chapter answers several specific questions about marriage which grew out of the diverse and complicated culture of Corinth. There were church members with Jewish, Roman, and Greek backgrounds, each with their own marriage customs. **It is good for a man not to touch a woman**—"Good" here may simply mean "expedient" in view of the unsettled state of the world, and the persecution of Christians in particular. The statement might also have reference to a difference in perspective between Jewish Christians and those of Greek backgrounds. The Jews placed a high value on marriage, whereas many Greeks, the Gnostics in particular, tended to disparage it. While not degrading marriage, Paul may be reassuring a certain group of the Corinthians that celibacy is an acceptable life-style for a Christian, and even to be preferred under some circumstances.

➤**2 to avoid fornication**—lit., "because of fornications, to which as being very prevalent at Corinth, and not even counted sins among the heathen, unmarried persons might be tempted." **let every man have his own wife, and let every woman have her own husband**—The Greek construction "let every man have" is in the present imperative tense, and thus suggests that men and women are to "continue having and keeping" their spouses. Most people find it natural and desirable to marry, and would be continually tempted to sexual sin if they did not, as they would have no acceptable outlet for their natural desires.

In Ephesians 5, Paul affirms the dignity of marriage.

➤**3** In verses 3-11, Paul discusses aspects of a marriage relationship where both partners are Christians. Verses 3 and 4 establish the duty of mutual conjugal rights. Paul's concept of equal sexual rights between husband and wife was unheard of in the Graeco-Roman world.

➤**5 Defraud ye not one the other**—The term "defraud" is a strong one, meaning "to deprive" or "to rob." (See Exod. 21:10, 11; 19:15.) Paul knows nothing of a "spiritual" marriage, where a couple lives together but never consummates the marriage physically. God views the married couple as one in body, with the husband and wife completing one another. Sexual intercourse is one of the more significant ways in which this oneness can be enacted and reinforced. Neither partner has the right to arbitrarily withdraw from this aspect of the marriage union. **except it be with consent for a time, that ye may give yourselves to fasting and prayer**—The Greek literally means "so that they can be at leisure for" or "be free from interruptions" for some specific occasion or agreed-upon length of time. There must be mutual agreement for such abstinence, and it must be temporary. The words "fasting and" are not present in the earliest manuscripts. (See comments on Mark 9:29.) **that Satan tempt you not for your incontinency** [lack of self-control]—This indicates that there is a danger of temptation to adultery even when a couple has agreed to abstain from sexual relations for the purpose of prayer.

➤**6 by permission**—or by allowance. **not of commandment**—What Paul spoke in 7:1-5 was not a command but an allowance, a concession to the Corinthians.

➤**7 even as I**—having the gift of continence (see Matt. 19:11, 12).

➤**8 the unmarried and widows**—In the first part of this chapter, Paul recognizes marriage as a normal relationship even though he indicates a personal preference for celibacy. Whereas he has been dealing with general rules governing married couples, he now begins to deal with specific cases, such as whether or not a widow should remarry.

➤**9** Paul treated widows just as he did any other unmarried person. He thought they would be happier to remain single if they could do it, but that there was nothing wrong with marriage if they felt they would be more content that way.

➤**10 unto the married I command**—Some of the married Christians were wondering if it would be preferable for them to dissolve their marriages to gain the advantages of celibacy. Paul responded to this question most emphatically on the direct authority of Christ himself (see Mark 10:1-12). **Let not the wife depart from her husband**—This literally means that a wife is not to be separated from her husband.

➤**11** The marriage relationship is to be seen as a permanent one, not to be dissolved by either husband or wife. However, if the sin of separation has been committed, it is not to be compounded by that of marrying another person (Matt. 5:32). **let not the husband put away** [divorce] **his wife**—Here again the rights of husband and wife are shown to be equal, and not to the advantage of the husband, as they were in the old Jewish laws.

➤**12** Concerning a marriage where one partner is a Christian and the other an unbeliever, Paul, in the following verses, offers suggestions which seem sensible to him. There are no gospel accounts of Christ's dealing with particular situations. **speak I, not the Lord**—by any direct command spoken from him. **If any brother hath a wife that believeth not, and she be pleased to dwell with him**—The Greek word for "be pleased" actually means "consents." This seems to imply that the husband has requested that she stay, and that she has agreed. If the wife wishes to stay, the husband may not leave or divorce his non-Christian wife any more than he should if she were a believer.

➤**13** This verse simply gives the converse of the situation presented in 7:12. Since Paul was writing to people who were governed by Roman law, he considered the wife's wishes as well as the husband's, which is of course consistent with the equality of all men before God. Greek and Roman law permitted a wife to gain a divorce as readily as a husband could, whereas the Jews permitted a wife to divorce her husband only in highly restricted cases. In any case the marriage relationship between a Christian and an unbelieving mate was still proper, and a decision to dissolve the marriage must come only from the unbeliever.

►**14 the unbelieving husband is sanctified by the wife . . .** —Paul was not only saying that marriage to an unbeliever is proper and not necessarily contradictory to Christian holiness, but that the influence of the Christian may be beneficial both to the mate and to the children of the union (1 Pet. 3:1). This presupposes a situation where marriage precedes the conversion of husband or wife. Paul was not encouraging single Christians to marry unbelievers.

►**15 If the unbelieving depart, let him depart**—If a man or woman is offended because his mate has become a Christian, the Christian is to let the unbeliever go. He is not obliged to renounce his belief for the sake of preserving his marriage (see also Luke 14:26). Some interpreters believe that this gives the believer the right to remarry, though only to another Christian. **God hath called us to peace**—It is better to break up a mixed marriage of this kind than to try to perpetuate it with continual discord. Two Christians are expected to work out their differences in marriage so that peace and harmony will result (Rom. 12:18).

►**16** This verse gives the reason for allowing the unbelieving husband or wife to leave if they so desire. There is no guarantee that the unbeliever will become a Christian even if the couple undergoes the difficulty of trying to preserve an incompatible relationship.

►**17 as the Lord hath called everyone, so let him walk**—The general principle behind Paul's suggestions is that when a person becomes a Christian, he should always continue to live and work in the same manner as before his conversion, unless his circumstances create direct conflicts with his obligations as a Christian. This is a rule which Paul has laid down for all the churches, and in the next few verses he gives specific examples as to its practical implications in other areas besides that of marriage.

►**18** Circumcision is no longer an issue before God, and a person should not try to alter his status by this practice (Gal. 5:1-4). Many uncircumcised men felt pressured by the Jews to be circumcised as a sign of their salvation (Acts 15). Other men actually tried to undo a previous circumcision through surgical procedures, as many historical accounts illustrate

(e.g., 1 Macc. 1:15; Josephus's *Antiquities,* 12.5.1.).

►**19** See Galatians 5:5, 6.

►**21 a servant**—lit., "a slave." The spirit of the gospel does not favor slavery. The point Paul is making here is that the Christian needs to be content and serve God in whatever circumstances he finds himself, even though that may be difficult. If the opportunity arises lawfully to better one's condition, such as the slave's gaining his freedom, the Christian should make use of it. God can be served equally well, however, in either capacity.

►**22** This verse emphasizes the truth that all believers are equal before God except as it concerns their obedience and faithfulness to him. There are not external circumstances, such as race, rituals, occupations, etc., which can give a person superior or inferior status among his fellow Christians.

►**23 Ye are bought with a price**—our redemption was secured with the price of Christ's blood (see 6:20; 1 Pet. 1:18, 19). **be not ye the servants of men**—Free men and slave alike are subject to the tendency to become enslaved to other men's ideas and to their own emotions and ambitions.

►**24** This verse restates the principles given in 7:17, with the added assurance that the Christian will have God's presence.

►**25 concerning virgins**—This question would have been particularly pertinent to the father of a marriageable daughter, as it was his responsibility to arrange her marriage or to refuse consent to what he considered an unwise match. **I have no commandment of the Lord: yet I give my judgment** [opinion]—i.e., I have no express revelation from the Lord commanding it, but I give my opinion—under the ordinary inspiration which accompanied the apostles in all their writings.

►**26 the present distress**—Since Paul did not specify the dangers or distresses, this phrase has been interpreted in many ways. Certainly the Christians at that time suffered a great deal from persecution by those in political power. Others think Paul was speaking of the distresses Christ had warned would come to Christians just prior to his return to earth (Matt. 24).

►**27** The Christian is advised to retain the same marital state as he had when he became a believer, just as he should maintain his vocation, location, and so on.

➤**28 if thou marry, thou hast not sinned**— Paul repeatedly told the Corinthians that it is no sin to marry. **such shall have trouble**—On the other hand, he was aware that married couples face many problems and adjustments which single people simply do not have to worry about, and that these normal adjustments of marriage would be complicated by the dangers confronting Christians at that time.

➤**29 the time is short**—Cf. Rom. 13:11. In the Greek, the expression Paul uses to refer to the "time" is the same as the one used by Christ when he spoke of his return to earth in Luke 21:8 and Mark 13:33. "Short" in this verse literally means "contracted" or shortened, as though a previous plan had been altered. **they that have wives be as though they had none**—Since it would not be long until Christ's return, Christians should keep that fact firmly in mind, and not live as though their earthly arrangements were permanent or ends in themselves.

➤**30 weep . . . wept not . . . rejoice. . . rejoiced not**—See Hebrews 10:34. **buy . . . possessed not**—lit., "buy . . . as not holding fast."

➤**31 not abusing it**—The opportunities the world offers may actually help the Christian in his work for God. The warning here is not that the Christian will be perverted by earthly pleasures, but that he may easily be distracted from his main goal by getting caught up in them for their own sakes. **for the fashion of this world passeth away**—See 1 John 2:17. Paul does not say that the world *will* pass away, but that it is *now passing* away. The image in the Greek is drawn from a stage play in which the scenery is shifting from one act to the next.

➤**32 I would have you without carefulness**—i.e., "I want you to be free from worry" (TLB). Paul cannot promise the Christians a life free of trouble, but he does want to spare them as much anxiety and distraction as possible.

➤**33 he that is married careth for the things that are of the world, how he may please his wife.**—The married man is not free of anxiety, especially in a time of stress. He is not only interested in pleasing his wife, but is particularly concerned for her safety in a time of persecution.

➤**34** The wife, as well as the husband, faces a conflict of interest when she marries. In fact, the changes a woman makes in going from single to married life are usually much greater than those of the husband.

➤**35 And this I speak for your own profit**—Paul was not trying to flaunt his authority as an apostle in saying these things, nor was he trying to make the Corinthians feel guilty for doing things which are not sinful. (The image behind the words "not that I may cast a snare" is that of throwing a noose over an animal in hunting.) Paul was rather trying to make practical suggestions which would make their lives easier. **that ye may attend upon the Lord**—The idea of service is that of attentively waiting on someone. (See Luke 2:36, 37 for one example.) **without distraction**—A "distraction" is a burden or an encumbrance. The language used here to draw the contrast between service and distraction is very similar to Christ's comments concerning Mary and Martha in Luke 10:38-41.

➤**36-40** From this point to the end of the chapter, Paul is summarizing or restating his basic approach to marriage, which he has spent most of the chapter discussing in some detail. Verses 36-38 contain general suggestions to single men and women; verses 39 and 40 restate Paul's directions concerning Christian widows. There are some textual and exegetical problems in these verses. First and foremost, there is disagreement as to whether the subject of 7:36-38 is the father of the virgin or the bridegroom. The bridegroom is much more suitable to the context. Thus, this passage is translated so in the NIV: "If anyone thinks he is acting improperly toward the virgin he is engaged to, and if she is getting along in years and he feels he ought to marry, he should do as he wants. He is not sinning. They should get married. But the man who has settled the matter in his own mind, who is under no compulsion but has control over his own will, and who has made up his mind not to marry the virgin—this man also does the right thing. So then, he who marries the virgin does right, but he who does not marry her does even better." (But see NIV mg. for alternate translation reflecting the other interpretation.) In the KJV text, the words "by the law" in 7:39 are not supported by the earliest manuscripts, and in 7:40 the expression "the Spirit of God" (supported by several ancient manuscripts) is "the Spirit of Christ" in two ancient manuscripts.

Chapter 8

## 1-13 EATING MEAT OFFERED TO IDOLS

➤1 **things offered unto idols**—Paul here turns to the next question in the Corinthians' letter (see 7:1): whether or not Christians should eat meat that had been offered to idols in the heathen temples. The problem arose because generally only a small portion of the animal was burned on the altar. The remainder was divided between the priest and the worshiper, who often invited friends to a feast either in his home or in the temple. When large religious celebrations or state sacrifices were held, thousands of animals would be offered, and the greater part of the meat would be sold to the butcher shops to be bought by the public. Thus the Christian was constantly exposed to the possibility of buying or eating this meat, which had been forbidden by Jewish law (Num. 25:2; Ps. 106:28). The apostles had also banned it in their decree from Jerusalem (Acts 15:20, 29; 21:25), but Paul does not refer here to that decision. Rather, he bases his instructions on his own apostolic authority. **we know that we all have knowledge**—No doubt the Corinthians had written that they *knew* there was only one God, and that eating or not eating meat had no moral significance. Despite this claim to knowledge, however, there was apparently enough uncertainty and difference of opinion to create a problem. **Knowledge puffeth up, but charity edifieth** [love builds up]—Paul here pauses for a moment to remind the Corinthians that love, rather than their so-called "knowledge," was what the church needed. The "know-it-all" attitude is selfish, while love aims to please others. It is not enough merely to ask whether or not something is permissible. Love goes on to consider, "Is it helpful and best for others?" (See 10:23, 24; Rom. 14:15.) He returns in 8:4 to the main subject of meat offered to idols.

➤2 **if any man think that he knoweth any thing, he knoweth nothing yet as he ought to know**—The first step to true knowledge is to know our own ignorance, and without love we can only seem to have knowledge. The Greek

word for "know" here is different from the expression in 1:1, which means merely "knowing a fact." Here it means "know personally from experience." Paul was pointing out that merely knowing something intellectually, as the Corinthians claimed to do, was different from practical experience of that knowledge in their lives.

➤3 **love God**—the source of love to our neighbor (1 John 4:11, 12, 21; 5:2). **the same is known of him**—Love leads naturally to true knowledge, knowledge by experience. To love God is to know God, who first knew us (13:12; 1 Pet. 1:2).

➤4 Here Paul gets back to the original question **concerning . . . the eating of those things that are offered in sacrifice unto idols**—This is a very practical question, and the answer requires that we apply both theoretical knowledge and love. **an idol is nothing**—The god it represents is not a living reality. In 10:19, 20 Paul distinguishes carefully between the non-existent gods the worshipers believe in, and the real, living demons who deceive people, using the idols to turn them from worshiping the one true God. **none other God but one**—The earliest manuscripts read "no God but one."

➤5 **in heaven**—the sun, moon, and stars. **in earth**—animals or kings. **gods many, and lords many**—Besides these false objects of worship, angels and men in positions of authority are sometimes called "gods" (Ps. 82:1, 6; John 10:34-36), but even these derive their power only from the one true God.

➤6 **one God, the Father, of whom are all things, and we in him; and one Lord Jesus Christ, by whom are all things**—As our Creator, God has a complete claim on our lives, and we exist entirely to glorify him (Rom. 11:36). This one God is in sharp contrast to the many gods of 8:5. Furthermore, the Father and the Son are one because both are called Creator—with this fine distinction: the Father is the source of all creation (indicated by the Gk. preposition *ek*—"out from") and the Son is the medium of all creation (indicated by the Gk. preposition *dia*—"through"). **and we by him**—Christ gave us life once by creating us, and he created a new life in us through regeneration.

➤7 **Howbeit there is not in every man that knowledge**—Even though a person claims to know that there is only one God, he may have not applied this knowledge to his life; it has not become real or true for him in experience. **with conscience of the idol**—This reading is found in some ancient manuscripts, but the reading "being accustomed to idols" has slightly better testimony among the ancient witnesses. The two Greek words, very similar in appearance, could have easily been confounded: *sunētheia* (accustomed) and *suneidēsis* (conscience). **unto this hour**—now, even though they are Christians and believe in the one true God. The implication is that they have not grown in knowledge as they should have. **their conscience being weak is defiled**—Paul insisted that eating meat is neither right nor wrong *in itself* (8:8), but in 8:9 and 13 we see that it is a sin against a man's conscience to do what he *believes* is wrong (cf. Rom. 14:14, 23). The apostles in Jerusalem forbade eating meat offered to idols, not for its own sake, but because it could offend weak Christians or cause them to sin (Acts 15). Here the rule of love applies: not only "Is it allowed?" but also "Is it good for my Christian brother?"

▶**8 meat commendeth us not to God**—This puts the question in perspective as something peripheral and unimportant next to the really significant concerns such as love for our Christian brothers.

▶**9 this liberty of yours**—Paul was not forbidding them to eat offered meat, but he reminded the Corinthians that their very freedom involves responsibility. He warned them not to insist on their "right" without regard for the effect of their behavior on others.

▶**10 if any man see thee which hast knowledge**—The very knowledge the Corinthians boasted of could lead the weak to do something against their own conscience, which the Corinthians had no problem doing—i.e., eating meat sacrificed to idols. **be emboldened**—lit., "be built up." We should build up a brother to do good, not build him up by our example to violate his conscience.

▶**11 shall the weak brother perish**—One apparently unimportant action can have serious consequences in terms of a brother's conscience and faith; it can ruin his spiritual life. **for whom Christ died**—If Christ died for him, we should be willing to die for him too (1 John 3:16). Yet Christians at Corinth, far from sacri-

ficing anything for the spiritual well-being of others, actually tempted them to sin.

▶**12 when ye sin so against the brethren, . . . ye sin against Christ**—Matt. 25:34-46 and Acts 9:4, 5 amplify the idea that Christ accepts our behavior toward others, whether good or bad, as done to him, the head of his body, the church. In the same way, we as members of the body are to care and feel for one another (12:25, 26).

▶**13** If food (unimportant as it is) would make Paul's brother stumble, Paul would not eat *any* meat at all. Paul would bend over backward to avoid causing harm to a brother. What a contrast between his attitude and the pride and selfishness of the Corinthians! Yet Paul's statement is conditional; he did not say he would never eat meat, but only if and when it would hurt a brother would he refrain from eating it.

*Chapter* **9**

## 1-27 PAUL'S DECLARATION OF HIS APOSTOLIC RIGHTS

▶**1 Am I not an apostle? am I not free?**— If the Corinthians could claim to be free from human restrictions (8:9), how much more Paul, in his position of apostle! **have I not seen Jesus Christ our Lord?**—Jesus' appearance to Paul was not a mere vision, but an actual bodily presence, so that Paul saw Jesus in the flesh just as did the other apostles (see Acts 9:7, 17). Paul refers to this experience as personal confirmation that Jesus did indeed rise from the dead (15:8). To witness to Jesus' resurrection was a major responsibility of an apostle. **are not ye my work in the Lord?**—While only God can change lives, he uses the faith, work, and testimony of men.

▶**2, 3 the seal [proof] of mine apostleship**—The proof that Paul was really an apostle, chosen and sent by God, was that he had brought men to Christ. Even if others were to ignore the evidence of God's power working through Paul in miracles (Rom. 15:19; 2 Cor. 12:12) and his preaching that brought men to repentance, surely those who had been saved through his ministry could have no doubts that God had called him.

**➤5 Have we not power** [right] **to lead about a sister, a wife**—Paul had every right, just as did the other apostles, to be accompanied by a Christian wife. No doubt he did not exercise this right in order to save the Church expense, and in order to devote himself completely, without distractions, to his task of building up the church of Christ (7:26, 32, 35). **as other apostles, and as the brethren of the Lord, and Cephas** [Peter]—Some of the apostles had exercised their right to bring along a Christian wife, among whom were the Lord's brothers and Peter, all highly respected church leaders. James, Joses, Simon, and Judas may have been cousins of Jesus, since the Jews often referred to cousins as brothers, or they may have been his half-brothers by Mary and Joseph. Either way, they were held in special esteem because of their relationship to Jesus (Acts 1:14; Gal. 1:19). We know from Matthew 8:14 that Peter was married. Paul probably mentioned Peter in particular because he had a group of followers in the Corinthian church (1:12).

**➤6 Or I only and Barnabas, have not we power** [right] **to forbear working?**—In addition to their arduous travels, and continual ministry day and night to the churches, Paul and his old associate Barnabas worked to support themselves. Paul's trade was tentmaking (Acts 18:3; 20:34; 1 Thess. 2:9; 2 Thess. 3:8). It would have been only right for the churches to support Paul as he ministered to them, but he did not want to be a burden to them or allow anyone to cast aspersions on the gospel by insinuating that he preached only for his own gain or comfort.

**➤7** Here Paul illustrates the principle that churches should support their ministers: a soldier is paid by the government, a farmer lives on his crops, and a shepherd shares in what his flock produces. A minister is a spiritual soldier (2 Tim. 2:3), a farmer (3:6-8), and shepherd (1 Pet. 5:2).

**➤9, 10 it is written in the law of Moses, Thou shalt not muzzle . . . the ox that treadeth**—Paul further supports his argument from the OT law (Deut. 25:4). **Doth God take care for** [of] **oxen?**—God does care for animals (Ps. 36:6; Matt. 10:29), but still more for man, the head of the animal creation. If we show consideration for the needs of animals

that serve us, how much more should we care for men who devote their lives to ministering to us? It is a church's responsibility to see that their minister is adequately paid for his work. **For our sakes . . . this is written**—Because what follows has no OT reference, this expression could refer back to the OT quotation cited by Paul in 9:9. Because it was written that the treading ox should not be muzzled, the plower and thresher could plow and thresh in hope of partaking of the produce. **he that thresheth in hope should be partaker of his hope**—The true reading is, "he that thresheth [ought to thresh] in the hope of partaking" (viz., of the fruit of his threshing).

**➤11 we**—in emphatic contrast with "others" (9:12). **we shall reap your carnal** [physical] **things**—Mere physical necessities, which were all the Corinthians had to offer, would have been small enough return for the infinitely more precious spiritual treasures they had received.

**➤12 If others be partakers of this power over you, are not we rather?**—because of Paul's far greater sacrifice and service for them (2 Cor. 11:20-29). **Nevertheless we have not used this power; but suffer all things**—Paul is saying, "We endure anything, and, far from complaining, we try to conceal any distress we suffer because of our poverty." **lest we should hinder the gospel of Christ**—Paul was so completely devoted to the cause of the gospel that he saw everything else only in light of its contribution or hindrance to his ministry.

**➤13 they which minister about holy things**—Jewish priests and Levites. They were given a portion of the meat, grain, oil, or wine for their own needs from the gifts or sacrifices to God (Lev. 7:6; Deut. 18:1-4).

**➤14 Even so**—Paul here applies the OT teaching to the Christian ministry, although of course the duty of the minister is not to offer sacrifices but to "preach the Gospel." Tertullian wrote (*Apology*, chap. 39) that it was the custom to take voluntary offerings from the people. After the expenses of the Lord's Supper had been met, the bishop allotted stipends for the various ministers of the church (bishops, presbyters, and deacons) in proportion to their service. The remainder was given to the poor, especially to orphans and widows. (See Matt. 10:10; Luke 10:7.)

►**15** This verse eliminates any possible suspicion of Paul's motives: he would die of hunger rather than hinder the gospel. Paul took satisfaction in his ability to minister without pay, since he did not have a family to support. Note Abraham's similar attitude in Genesis 14:22, 23.

►**16** Paul explains why it was a satisfaction to him to preach without charge. He could take no special credit for preaching, because it was only the service he owed God, the responsibility God as his Master had given him. Compare Luke 17:10, "if you merely obey me, you should not consider yourselves worthy of praise. For you have simply done your duty!" (TLB). But it was not Paul's duty to minister without pay; on the contrary, he had every right to be supported by the churches. Serving without charge was Paul's way of freely offering to God more than had been demanded of him, and his joy came from seeing that through such sacrifice his ministry became even more effective in winning men to Christ.

►**17** This verse is made clearer in the NIV: "If I preach voluntarily, I have a reward; if not voluntarily, I am simply discharging the trust committed to me." **dispensation of the gospel**—Greek *oikonomia* ("stewardship" or "household management"). Paul was committed with the stewardship of God's NT economy of dispensing the riches of Christ to God's household members (cf. 4:2; Eph. 3:2-11).

►**18 What is my reward then?**—The answer is in the next verse: Paul would **gain the more** by giving the gospel free of charge. **the gospel of Christ**—The earliest manuscripts do not have the phrase "of Christ."

►**19** Paul now turns from discussing his sacrifices for the gospel's sake to his adaptability in his relationships to others. Just as he did not allow material things to hinder his ministry, so he did not let narrow attitudes or rigid approaches become obstacles to his testimony. **gain the more**—Paul saw his reward in any and all who came to Christ through his efforts (see 1 Thess. 2:19, 20).

►**20 I became as a Jew**—While Paul did not consider himself bound by Jewish law, he was willing to conform to Jewish customs whenever this did not involve compromising his Christian principles (Acts 16:3; 21:20-26). **to them that are under the law, as under the law**—Perhaps the reason for distinguishing this class from the former was that, while Paul was a Jew nationally by birth, he was no longer a Jew by creed or observance of the law.

►**21 To them that are without law**—i.e., Gentiles who did not know or follow the Jewish law given by God, although their consciences were a law to them (Rom. 2:12-15). **as without law**—Paul did not urge the Gentiles to keep the customs and obey the regulations of the Jewish law. Rather, he emphasized the necessity of faith in Christ (Gal. 3:2). An example of Paul's adaptation to others is seen at Athens, where he copied the Greek manner of speaking, and quoted Greek poets to support his argument (Acts 17:28). **being not without law to God, but under the law to Christ**—While Paul was free from the outward, ceremonial law, he was subject to a new, inward principle which governed his life. Since Christ fulfilled the law for us, we are responsible not to the law but to Christ, like parts of the body controlled by the head (7:22; Rom. 8:1-4; 1 Pet. 2:16). The law of Christ is the law of love, which fulfills the kernel of the old, outward law: love for God and neighbor.

►**22** Paul here applies the argument of 9:19-21 to the problem of chapter 8. **To the weak**—weak and inexperienced Christians who have not practically applied their freedom in Christ to their lives, and who allow insignificant questions, such as whether to eat meat offered to idols, to become major obstacles to their growth in faith. **became I as weak**—Paul did not argue with weak Christians; on the contrary, he was careful to do nothing that would damage their faith or conscience, even if he knew it was not in itself wrong. **that I might gain the weak**—Paul's overriding concern was the spiritual welfare of others, and it was this concern that governed all his behavior. He sought to bring men to faith in Christ, and then to continually strengthen them and help them mature in that faith. This attitude, rather than one of self-righteous complacency, made people willing to learn from him.

►**23 that I might be partaker thereof with you**—rather, "with them." The Greek text emphasizes that Paul shared together with those he brought to Christ in the blessings of the gospel. These blessings included both the present reward referred to in 9:18, and also the future reward Paul was determined to win, which he discusses in 9:24-27.

➤**24 run in a race** [Gk., "racecourse"]— Paul illustrated his earnest striving by referring to the Isthmian games held near Corinth every three years. The footrace was one of the major events, and was taken very seriously by the contestants, who trained for at least ten months and had to pledge to violate none of the regulations of the contest. **one receiveth the prize**—If so many athletes struggled to excel, knowing that only one could win, how much more should we be willing to strive for a far more valuable reward (see comments on 9:25)? In 10:1-5 Paul warns that even in the spiritual race, not everyone wins who runs. **So run, that ye may obtain**—Paul interjected this like a coach or spectator urging a runner on to victory.

➤**25 every man that striveth**—actually, "every man who wrestles." Wrestling was another event in the Isthmian games; it was more rigorous than running. **is temperate in all things**—The athletes disciplined themselves with a strict diet and rigorous exercise even in cold or heat. **to obtain**—There is no point in beginning the Christian race unless we are willing to "go all the way," to endure to the end (Matt. 24:13; Rev. 2:10) to obtain the reward. **a corruptible crown**—a wreath or garland of green leaves which was placed on the head of the winner. It soon withered away. **but we an incorruptible**—in contrast to the quickly-withering garland of leaves. An incorruptible crown is a special reward given to faithful runners—much like the "crown of glory" will be given to faithful elders (1 Pet. 5:4) and the "crown of life" to faithful martyrs (Rev. 2:10).

➤**26 I therefore so run**—Paul's point is the purpose of his own self-denial and hard work. **not as uncertainly**—not as a runner uncertain of the goal. Whether in conforming as much as possible to the life-style of anyone he was with, or in not demanding support from his converts, or in anything he did, Paul had a definite aim. He would not allow anything to hold him back from his goal (Heb. 12:1, 2). Paul was indifferent to what others thought of him, and obstacles or failures only spurred him on to greater efforts. **so fight I**—actually, "so I box." **not as one that beateth the air**—instead of beating the opponent—alluding to the *scia machia* (shadow boxing).

➤**27 keep under**—lit., "bruise the face under the eyes"; buffet. Paul was not recommending ascetic neglect or mistreatment of our bodies (see Col. 2:23). **my body**—i.e., the old sinful nature embodied in the flesh, with its selfishness and evil desire that are contrary to the new life in Christ (see Rom. 8:13). **bring it into subjection**—The Greek means "making it my slave." We must control our bodies and make them serve us, not let them control us. **lest that by any means, when I have preached to others, I myself should be a castaway**—disqualified, rejected (Jer. 6:30). A Christian is both a contestant and an official who calls athletes to the race. Paul was aware that even though he had preached to others, his own running of the race would be judged by God. Paul never claimed to be perfect (Phil. 3:12), but he was constantly aware of his own weaknesses, determined not to let them betray him into failure, into being disqualified. The implication is that if such earnest, self-denying effort was necessary for Paul, how much more for the Corinthians, who were carelessly taking advantage of their Christian freedom.

*Chapter* **10**

## 1-33 DANGER OF FELLOWSHIP WITH IDOLATRY ILLUSTRATED BY THE HISTORY OF ISRAEL

Fellowship with idolatry incompatible with fellowship in the Lord's Supper.

➤**1 Moreover**—actually, "For." This word indicates the connection between these verses and the preceding chapter. The experiences of Israel illustrate the Christian's danger and need for constant self-discipline. **brethren**—Paul did not impose his apostolic authority on the Corinthians; he spoke to them as brothers in Christ. **I would not that ye should be ignorant**—despite the Corinthians' boast of "knowledge." **all**—The Greek emphasizes that God guided them *all,* and this "all" is repeated four more times: **all** of the Israelites were miraculously guided, protected, and fed (10:1-4)—yet most of them disobeyed and were destroyed (10:5). Paul was warning the Christians at Corinth, "Be careful that you, who have been given greater spiritual privileges and blessings than Israel had, do not suffer the same fate through a similar sin." It is the same warning as in 9:24. **our fathers**—The Israelites are here viewed as the forefathers of the Christian church. **under the cloud**—This cloud (or, pillar of cloud) was for guidance and protection, and was a symbol of God's presence with them (Exod. 13:21, 22; Ps. 105:39; Isa. 4:5, 6). **and all passed through the sea**—the Red Sea. The miracle is described in Exodus 14:21-31 (see comments there).

**➤2 And were all baptized unto Moses**—lit., "into Moses," as united to him. **in the cloud and in the sea**—The sea and the cloud, both composed of water, covered the Israelites like the water of baptism. (Some commentators, however, liken the image to the two baptisms: the cloud depicting the Spirit baptism, and the water, water baptism. See Olshausen.) Baptism here means initiation into a new relationship with Moses, God's servant, who represented the OT covenant of the law, just as Christ, God's Son, represents the new covenant of the gospel (John 1:17; Heb. 3:5, 6). The miracles of the sea and the cloud led the people to believe and follow Moses as their leader chosen by God. Thus, the Israelites were united to Moses, just as Christians are united to Christ (through baptism). But as the Israelites' figurative baptism did not keep them from disobedience and evil desires, with their inevitable punishment, neither would the Corinthians' baptism into Christ save them from the consequences of continuing sin.

**➤3 spiritual meat**—i.e., manna. It is called "spiritual" because it was given by the power of the Spirit, not by human effort. This manna was God's miraculous provision to the Israelites in the wilderness (see Exod. 16:11-35; Ps. 105:40) and typified Christ, the true bread from heaven (see John 6:31-58).

**➤4 spiritual drink**—In the desert he gave them water from a rock (Exod. 17:5-6; Num. 20:8). Paul called it "spiritual drink" because it was given to them by the power of God's Spirit, not by human effort. The OT often speaks of the Rock of Israel, referring to both his protection and provision (Deut. 32:4, 15, 18, 30-31; Ps. 78:20-35). That Rock was Christ. The same Christ who supplies all our physical and spiritual needs accompanied Israel, and his provision for them never failed.

**➤5 But**—in spite of all God's blessings, given freely to all of them. **with many of them**—lit., "with the majority," i.e., the whole first generation, except for Joshua and Caleb. **God was not well pleased**—God alone is the only valid judge, whose punishment of Israel was therefore just. **they were overthrown**—lit., "they were strewn in heaps," a graphic description of the disastrous consequences of their sin. **in the wilderness**—far from their goal, the land God had promised them, which they had refused to enter due to unbelief:

**➤6 our examples**—samples, object lessons. The lesson from Israel's history warns Christians of what will happen to us if we also, with all our privileges, live carelessly. **we should not lust after evil things**—Evil desires are mentioned first, since they are the cause of the other sins listed in 10:7-10 (cf. James 1:14, 15). One example of Israel's evil desires is described in Numbers 11:4-6; 33, 34. The Egyptian food they wanted was not in itself bad, but the Israelites were wrong to demand what God had not given them, and to be discontented with the manna God had provided.

**➤7 Neither be ye idolaters**—a specific outgrowth of their evil desires. The Israelites sat down (a deliberate act), ate, and drank at the feast to the golden calf idol in Horeb (Exod. 32:6). Although the Corinthians were not deliberately worshiping idols, they were exposing themselves to the danger of slipping back into idolatry by joining in the pagan temple feasts.

**➤8** This case is recounted in Numbers 25. Fornication was a natural outgrowth of spiritual unfaithfulness, since sexual immorality was closely associated with pagan idol feasts (see Rev. 2:14). The temple prostitutes may have been a temptation to some of the Corinthian Christians who may have continued to go to the temple of Aphrodite. **three and twenty thousand**—Numbers 25:9 lists 24,000. The discrepancy may be explained by saying that each writer simply used round numbers—i.e., the actual number may have been somewhere between 23,000 and 24,000. Or, since 23,000 was the death toll for one day, perhaps another 1,000 died the next day to reach 24,000, the total number of deaths due to the plague.

**➤9 Christ**—This is the reading in the earliest extant manuscript (the Beatty Papyrus, P46), and in several other early witnesses

(Marcion, Theotecnus, Irenaeus, Clement, Origen, and several early Latin, Syriac, and Coptic versions), as well as several other good manuscripts. Other ancient manuscripts (Codex Sinaiticus, Codex Vaticanus, Codex Ephraemi Rescriptus) read "Lord," and a few read "God." "Christ" is the preferred reading; and even if "Lord" were original, "Lord" would refer to the Lord Jesus Christ. But it is far more likely that "Christ" was changed to "Lord" or "God" than that either of these two titles were changed to "Christ." In the context of 1 Corinthians 10 it was very natural for Paul to say, "let us not tempt Christ, as some of them did" because he saw the Lord God of the OT as equal to Christ, and he viewed Christ as being present with the Israelites in the wilderness. Since Christ was the spiritual Rock that accompanied them in their journeys (10:4), he was also the One that the Israelites were taunting. Furthermore, it was not uncommon for NT writers to name the Old Testament God according to NT parlance and thus call him (as here and Heb. 11:26) "Christ," or even "Jesus"—see comments on Jude 4 (*GAM*). Furthermore, when the Israelites tempted Christ and were bitten by the serpents, God's provision for their malady was the brass serpent on the pole, a symbol of the crucified Christ (John 3:14). Thus, the one they tempted became their Savior.

➤**10 Neither murmur ye, as some of them also murmured**—By complaining against Moses and Aaron, the people were complaining against God (Num. 16:28-35; 41-50). This may be an oblique warning to those who had been challenging Paul, Christ's apostle. **and were destroyed of the destroyer**— This is the same destroying angel seen in Exodus 12:23 and 2 Samuel 24:16.

➤**11 Now all these things happened unto them for ensamples** [by way of example]: **and they are written for our admonition**—This verse amplifies the phrases in 10:6 and 8. The OT was written to instruct us (2 Tim. 3:16); the history of Israel tells us of God's faithfulness while warning of the consequences of sin. Our God is the same as Israel's God, and neither he nor his standards have changed. **upon whom the ends of the world** [ages] **are come**—The NT dispensation in its successive phases (plural, "ends") is the winding up of all former ages. No new dispensation shall appear until Christ

comes as the Judge. The thought of Christ's return should intensify our awareness of our privileges and responsibility as his people (1 Pet. 2:9). At the peak of world history, with the record open to us, we have great responsibility to live lives of holiness and obedience.

➤**12 thinketh he standeth**—i.e., think, assume, that he in himself is in a right standing with God. Confidence in our own ability to please God and withstand temptation can only betray us into sin. Our faith must cling not to ourselves but to him; our security depends on his faithfulness, not our own. **take heed lest he fall**—from his place in the church (cf. Rom. 14:4).

➤**13 no temptation taken you . . . as is common to man: but God is faithful**—After such stern warnings, Paul encouraged the Corinthians by reminding them of God's faithfulness: he would protect and provide for them just as he did for Israel. Paul was also refuting any complaint that they "couldn't help" sinning. **who will not suffer** [allow] **you to be tempted above that ye are able; but will with the temptation also make a way to escape**— God has not promised to remove the temptation, since we need such experiences to grow in faith and patience (James 1:2-4; 12), but he guarantees that it will never be too strong for us to resist. **bear it**—Greek, "bear up under it" or "bear against it."

➤**14 flee from idolatry**—Paul returns to the central problem. He has already pointed out the danger and the need for watchfulness. Here he makes clear that while God will strengthen them against temptation, they must not "ask for trouble" by participation in the pagan temple feasts. To be safe they must flee from any association with idolatry (2 Cor. 6:16, 17; 1 Thess. 5:22).

➤**15 I speak as to wise** [prudent] **men**— Paul was perhaps referring ironically to the Corinthians' claim to wisdom (8:1). **judge ye what I say**—Paul is asking them to judge for themselves whether his argument is reasonable: just as partaking of the Lord's Supper involved partaking of the Lord himself, and partaking in the Jewish sacrifices involved partaking in the altar of God, so partaking of an idol feast involved fellowship with idols. This command to judge what is said is the responsbility of every Christian. If the apostle Paul urged men to examine his own teachings, how much more are we responsible to carefully examine all teaching in the light of Scripture, praying humbly for the illumination of the Holy Spirit.

►16 The cup of blessing—This corresponds to the "cup of blessing" in the Jewish Passover feast. It was while sharing the Passover with his disciples that Jesus instituted the Christian observance of the Lord's Supper (Matt. 26:26-28; Luke 22:14-20). is it not the communion [fellowship] of the blood of Christ?—As Christians share together both in asking God's blessing and in partaking of the bread and the cup, they are sharing spiritually in Christ's body and blood (cf. Eph. 5:30, 32), and in the many spiritual blessings which Christ's death brought. This communion, this fellowship with Christ, includes fellowship with other Christians, with various members of the body of Christ joining to share his blessings. Note that the text does not say "drinking Christ's blood," but rather "the fellowship of Christ's blood." It is unnecessary to demand that the bread and wine must actually become Christ's body and blood.

►17 For we being many are one bread, and one body: for we are all partakers of that one bread—Paul merged the image of the one loaf with that of the one body. The one loaf broken into many pieces for the participation of all is still one, even though consumed by many. So also the one body, though composed of many members, is still one entity (see 12:12). Sharing together in the one loaf is an expression of the unity of Christ's body, which experiences communion both with Christ and with other members.

►18 Israel after the flesh—the literal, as distinguished from the spiritual, Israel (Rom. 2:29; 4:1; 9:3; Gal. 4:29). partakers of the altar—Since the Jews' worship of God centered around the altar sacrifices, eating the prescribed portions of the offerings involved a distinct consciousness of their relation to God, and to one another as God's people.

►19, 20 What say I then?—Paul has compared the Christians' and the Jews' worship of God with the heathen worship of idols. He is now quick to add that the analogy is not complete, since the idols worshiped by the heathen have no real existence in the sense that they imagine. However (here Paul introduces a new fact), they are in reality sacrificing to demons, since Satan as prince of this world controls and appropriates the acts of worship which are not directed to the true God (Lev. 17:7; Ps. 106:37; Rev. 9:20). Fear, rather than love, motivates heathen worship, since fear is the spirit of Satan and his demons (James 2:19).

►21 Ye cannot—spiritually and in reality. It is impossible to have fellowship both with God and with Satan, so why appear outwardly to do so? cup of devils [demons]—At idol feasts libations were usually made from the cup to the idol first, and then the guests drank; so that in drinking they had fellowship with the idol. the Lord's table—The Lord's Supper is a feast on a table, not a sacrifice on an altar. Christ's sacrifice on the cross is the only sacrifice for Christians, and the celebration of the Lord's Supper has the same relation to his ultimate sacrifice as the Jews' feasts had to their repeated sacrifices on the altar, and the heathen idol feasts to their sacrifices. The heathen sacrifices were offered to idol nonentities, behind which Satan lurked. The Jewish sacrifices were only a symbol looking forward to the reality of Christ's death. But the Christian taking part in the Lord's Supper has communion or fellowship with the body of Christ, the Son of God himself, once sacrificed and now exalted as the head of the church.

►22 Do we provoke the Lord to jealousy?—by outwardly dividing fellowship between him and idols (Exod. 20:5; Ezek. 20:39). are we stronger than he?—How could they dare oppose God and provoke him to exert his great power?

►23 All things are lawful for me—Paul now goes back to the Corinthian claim to freedom (6:12), but he repeats his qualification: but they may not build up the church of God in faith and love. Again, Paul did not appeal to the apostles' decision in Jerusalem (Acts 15:28, 29), but rather to the basic principle which applies to Christians everywhere.

►24 Let no man seek his own, but every man another's—This principle is also found in 10:33 and in Romans 15:1, 2.

►25 shambles—the meat market. asking no question for conscience sake—If you ask and hear that it was offered to idols, you have created a problem that was unnecessary and would not have existed if you had asked no questions.

**►26** This eating without questioning is right, since everything in the world, including food, was given to us by God, and is to be gratefully received and enjoyed.

**►27 If any of them that believe not bid** [invite] **you to a feast**—This is not an idol feast, but a general entertainment at which there might be meat that had been offered to an idol (see note on 8:1).

**►28 if any man**—probably a weak and immature Christian at the table. **unto idols**—a later addition, not found in the earliest manuscripts. **for the earth is the Lord's, and the fulness thereof**—These words, taken from 10:26, are not found in the earliest manuscripts.

**►29 for why is my liberty judged of another man's conscience?**—Paul may be quoting an objection in the Corinthians' letter. The desire to be subject only to one's own conscience is a further reason not to ask questions (10:27). If you are warned, however, there is a good reason why the other man's conscience must determine your behavior, and Paul gives this reason in 10:31.

**►30 For if I by grace be a partaker**—of the food served for dinner by the non-Christian friend. A Christian should, by thankfulness, consecrate all his actions to God (1 Tim. 4:3, 4). **why am I evil spoken of for that for which I give thanks**—i.e., spoken against by a Christian who does not use his Christian liberty, but is careful to ask where the meat comes from.

**►31 do all to the glory of God**—The glory of God is to be the Christian's primary motive in everything he does, and this breaks down the barrier between so-called "sacred" or "secular" actions or occupations (Jer. 22:15, 16; Col. 3:17; 1 Pet. 4:11). In contrast, going through the motions of worship has no value if the worship does not come from the heart (Zech. 7:5, 6). Concern for the glory of God involves concern for building up other Christians.

**►32 Give none offence**—in things that do not have any moral significance. We are likely enough to offend people by standing true to Christian principles, so we must be careful not to cause problems where there is no need,

where no compromise of character is involved (Rom. 14:13; 2 Cor. 6:3).

**►33** This verse sums up the central teaching of chapters 8-10. Paul practiced what he preached, so that he could point to his own life as an example for the Corinthians to follow (9:19-27; 11:1).

*Chapter* 11

## 1-34 CRITICISM OF DISORDERLY MEETINGS: WOMEN NOT BEING VEILED, AND ABUSES AT THE LOVE FEASTS AND LORD'S TABLE

**►1** This verse should be at the end of chapter 10, since it continues Paul's illustration of his teaching with his own life. **Be ye followers of me**—imitate me. **even as I also am of Christ**—Christ did not live to please himself (Rom. 15:3), but gave himself to us by laying aside his divine glory to become a man and die for us (Eph. 5:2; Phil. 2:5-8). We are all to follow Christ first, and to imitate earthly teachers only so far as they follow Christ.

**►2** Here the chapter ought to begin, as a new subject is introduced. **that ye remember me in all things**—Paul was praising them for obeying him *in general,* since he went on to mention specific matters in which they had failed to follow his instructions. **ordinances**—Greek, "traditions," i.e., apostolic directions given by word of mouth or in writing (see 15:3; 2 Thess. 2:15). In this verse he specifically has in mind his recommendations as to procedures they should follow regarding the Lord's Supper, which he insists he received directly from the Lord (11:23).

**►3** By declaring that in Christ there are no distinctions of sex, race, or social standing (Gal. 3:28), the gospel had raised women from their degraded position (especially in the Middle East). But some Corinthian women had then discarded the customary dress and behavior of women in Greek culture. In Corinth, only the prostitutes went without veils, so for a woman not to wear a veil was a sign of loose morals or low character. **the head of every man is Christ**—Christ is not the head *merely* of husbands, but of the entire church, his body, male and female (Eph. 5:22-24). Wives as well as husbands are responsible to Christ, submitting to him and to one another. However, Paul emphasizes particularly that Christ is the head of every *man*. The husband has a special responsibility before God not only for himself, but also for his wife and children, and he is to love his wife as Christ loved the church (Eph. 5:23, 25). **the head of the woman is the man**—See Genesis 3:16; 1 Timothy 2:11, 12; 1 Peter 3:1, 5, 6. **and the head of Christ is God**—See 15:27, 28. The relationship between man and woman is compared to the relationship between God the Father and God the Son. Scripture teaches that while Christ was fully God, equal with the Father (Phil. 2:5; Col. 2:9, 10), he willingly submitted himself to the Father (John 8:28, 29; 14:28, 31). In the same way, even though man and woman are equal before God in Christ, a wife must willingly submit to her husband as to the Lord (Eph. 5:24; 1 Pet. 3:1, 5, 6).

➤**4 praying or prophesying**—in public, in the church meeting. **having his head covered**—It was the Greek custom for men to worship with their heads uncovered. **dishonoureth his head**—the principal part of his body. Since a covered head was in the Greek culture a sign of subjection to men, a man would dishonor himself by wearing a veil or hat.

➤**5 every woman that prayeth or prophesieth**—Examples of women who participated publicly in the worship services or had positions of leadership are Anna the prophetess; Priscilla, who worked along with Paul and her husband Aquila and instructed Apollos (Acts 18:26); Phoebe (Rom. 16:1, 2); and the daughters of Philip (Acts 21:9). See also Acts 2:18. Paul has more to say about the conduct of women in the public meetings in 14:34, 35 and 1 Timothy 2:11, 12. **with her head uncovered dishonoureth her head**—Since the veil was a sign of modesty and chastity, a woman who removed her veil was publicly declaring independence from her husband, and rejection of his claims on her. Compare the Jewish custom of uncovering the head of a wife suspected of adultery (Num. 5:18).

➤**6** Among the Jews and Greeks, long hair was a woman's glory, while a shaved head was a punishment for adultery. Paul was saying to the Corinthian women, "You are carelessly flouting the customs of your society, with no concern for the impression of loose character

you are giving. If you are going without veils, you might as well be consistent and have your heads shaved, which is considered even more disgraceful." By carrying the matter a step further to something they would never consider doing, Paul was showing them the impropriety of their behavior.

➤**7, 8 For a man . . . is the image and glory of God**—Man was created in the image or likeness of God; he is a small, finite reflection of God's infinite glory (Gen. 1:26, 27; James 3:9). Jesus Christ, the Son of man, was the perfect man, man as God created him to be. Thus he was also the perfect likeness of God; he revealed God's glory not through a dim and imperfect reflection, but as the very Word, God's own self-revelation (John 1:14; Col. 1:15; Heb. 1:3). **the woman is the glory of the man**—Notice that the woman is not said to be the image of man, since both male and female were created in the image of God. However, as Paul goes on to note, the woman was formed out of the man; thus, although created directly by God, she derived existence and glory from God through man: **For the man is not of** [out from] **the woman; but the woman of** [out from] **the man.**

➤**9 the woman for the man**—We can hardly suppose that Eve was simply an afterthought on God's part; rather, woman was an integral part of God's total plan for the creation which he pronounced "very good." But God did create Adam first, and Genesis emphasizes his incompleteness, his need for someone suited to his needs, a companion, by saying that it was not good for him to be alone (Gen. 2:18); woman was created to supply this lack. Although both man and woman were created equally in God's image, to glorify God and have dominion over the earth, woman was created under the headship of man. In the Greek culture, a woman's head covering was a sign of her submission to her husband's authority.

➤**10 For this cause ought the woman to have power** [authority] **on her head because of the angels**—The meaning of this phrase is unclear, but perhaps just as man is ranked "a little lower than the angels" (Ps. 8:5), so woman should take her place in submission to man. The angels, present at the church meetings, would respect this sign of submission. Bengel said, "As the angels are in relation to God, so the woman is in relation to man. God's face is uncovered; angels in his presence are veiled (Isa. 6:2). Man's face is uncovered; woman in his [God's] presence is to be veiled. For her not to be so, would, by its indecorousness, offend the angels (Matt. 18:10)."

➤11, 12 **Nevertheless neither is the man without the woman**—Paul was quick to warn that men must not abuse their authority by showing contempt to women or by displaying a domineering spirit toward women. He reminded them that men and women are dependent upon one another, and that both depend on God (Rom. 11:36; 2 Cor. 5:18). Together they fulfill God's plan for the church, the bride of Christ.

➤13 **Judge in yourselves**—Paul now appeals to the Corinthians' own sense of what is right or appropriate.

➤14, 15 **if a man have long hair, it is a shame unto him . . . if a woman have long hair, it is a glory to her**—As in 11:6, Paul compares the natural head covering of hair with the artificial covering of a kerchief or veil. Since the women took pride in their covering of hair, they ought to be willing to wear the additional covering expected by society. A man customarily wore his hair short, except for Nazarites, who grew their hair long as a sign of their consecration to God (Num. 6:5).

➤16 **if any man seem to be contentious**—The Corinthians were apparently fond of arguing, each claiming to have the last word or the ultimate answer (8:1). **we**—the apostles. **have no such custom**—as that of women praying uncovered. **neither the churches of God**—Paul closed his argument by appealing to the universal custom of the churches. While custom does not determine correct doctrine (since doctrine has been authoritatively revealed in Scripture), custom is a helpful guide in practical questions of what is proper or appropriate. This phrase, then, supports the conclusion that the specific instructions regarding veils, etc., depend on cultural expectations and would not always apply. Paul's teaching, however, is based on underlying principles that should always be observed.

➤17 **I praise you not**—Paul now qualifies his praise mentioned in 11:2, where he said that in general they had followed his teachings. The first exception to his praise had been the dis-

tracting behavior of women at their meetings; now he turns to their improper handling of the love feasts and the Lord's Supper.

➤18 **when ye come together in the church**—lit., "when you come together in an assembly." Paul is speaking here of a church meeting or an assembling together; he is not talking about going to a church building—a concept found nowhere in the NT. **divisions**—The Greek word is "schisms": divisions both of opinion (1:10; 8:1) and thoughtless behavior (11:21). **I partly believe it**—Paul did not want to unjustly criticize any who may have been innocent of quarreling. In essence, he was saying, "I am unwilling to believe all I hear, but some things I cannot help believing."

➤19 **For there must be also heresies** [sects] **among you**—The Greek word underlying "heresies" designates party division, factions, sects. At the time of this writing the word "heresy" had not yet acquired its technical sense of indicating doctrinal error. Knowing that divisiveness existed among the Corinthians, Paul affirmed that there **must be** also factions among them. Paul may have been echoing Jesus' prediction (Matt. 24:10, 12) that sin would lead to such quarrels. **that they which are approved may be made manifest**—See 1 John 2:19. In attempting to preserve unity among the believers we should adhere to Augustine's rule: "In doubtful questions, liberty; in essentials, unity; in all things, charity."

➤20, 21 From the beginning, Christians had observed the Lord's Supper in connection with a "love feast" or meal together, for which each person brought his own food (Acts 2:46; Jude 12). Instead of a time of joyful fellowship, this had come to cause more harm than good, since the rich greedily ate and drank too much, while the poor were shamed and went hungry (11:22). The disorder and selfishness made it impossible to properly celebrate the Lord's Supper with a sense of its spiritual meaning.

➤22 **despise ye the church of God, and shame them that have not?**—The congregation was largely made up of the poor, whom "God has chosen" (James 2:5). By despising the poor (cf. James 2:6) and making the assemblies disruptive, they were also disgracing the church in the eyes of unbelievers.

➤23 Paul here shows how wrong their conduct was by contrasting it with the solemnity of the Lord's Supper. **I have received of the Lord that which also I delivered unto you**— Paul was emphatic that these were not his own ideas, but instructions from Jesus Christ about *his* Table. Paul received this teaching by direct revelation from God (cf. 2 Cor. 12:1-4; Gal. 1:12). Luke's description of the night when Christ instituted the Supper with his disciples is similar to Paul's account, and it is likely that Luke learned the details from Paul on their travels together. **the . . . night in which he was betrayed**—With the traitor at the table, and death just ahead, Christ left this ordinance as a symbol of his amazing love for us shown by his death.

➤**24 he brake it, and said, Take, eat**—The distribution of the bread is in contrast with the selfish eating of the Corinthians. **this is my body, which is broken for you**—Since Christ was physically present with his disciples, he could not have meant that the bread actually was his body, but rather a symbol. As bread is to physical health, so Christ's body is to the spiritual health of the believer. "For" means literally "in behalf of." **in remembrance of me**—The Lord's Supper brings to remembrance Christ's once-and-for-all sacrifice for the full and final remission of sins.

➤**25 when** [after] **he had supped**—Since the communion celebration followed the Passover supper, the Corinthians should have separated common meals from the Lord's Supper. **the new testament** [or, covenant] **in my blood**—Like a will (or, testament) which goes into effect when a person dies, Christ's death made possible a new relationship with God, and gave us all his blessings, both now and in eternity (Heb. 9:12). **as oft as ye drink it**—lit., "however many times," implying that it was to be done often. **in remembrance of me**—Matthew and Mark left this to be understood, but Luke mentions it, and Paul says it twice (here and in 11:24). The Jewish sacrifices constantly reminded Jews of their sin (Heb. 10:1-3), but the Lord's Supper brings to mind Christ and his sacrifice that paid for our sins once for all.

➤**26 show**—declare, announce publicly. **the Lord's death**—By the Lord's Supper we identify ourselves with Christ, as members of his body, appropriating for ourselves the benefits of his death. **till he come**—The Greek verb leaves no doubt that he is certainly coming. When Christ is physically present with us, we

will no longer need the symbols of his body. The Lord's Supper is a foretaste of the time when we will eat and drink with him in the Father's kingdom (Matt. 26:29). Just as the bread was placed before the Lord every Sabbath (Lev. 24:5-8), so the early church celebrated the Lord's Supper every Sunday. Like priests in the Holy Place of the temple, we worship in Christ's spiritual temple, but so far he, like the High Priest in the Holy of Holies, is the only one who has physically entered (Heb. 9:1-3, 6, 7). When he comes again, however, we too will enter (Rev. 7:15; 21:22).

➤**27 unworthily**—This does not refer to how worthy we are, since no one is ever worthy in himself. It refers to participating in the supper in an unworthy manner, a manner spoken against by Paul in 11:20-22. **guilty of the body and blood of the Lord**—Cf. Hebrews 6:6.

➤**28 let a man examine himself**—This self-examination is not meant to keep him away from the Lord's Table, but to allow him to partake of the bread and cup in the right way.

➤**29 unworthily**—This word is not present in the earliest manuscripts. **damnation**— should read, "judgment." This is not "the judgment"; rather, judgment in general. **not discerning the Lord's body**—his actual body, not the body of Christ. The word "Lord's" is not present in the earliest manuscripts.

➤**30-32 many are weak and sickly among you, and many sleep** [i.e., die]—This verse defines the "judgment" of 11:29 as physical illness or death, which is intended to restore the sinning Christian to save him from ultimate condemnation (11:32; see also Heb. 12:8; Rev. 3:19).

➤**33 tarry** [wait] **one for another**—in contrast to the greedy haste spoken of in 11:21.

➤**34 the rest will I set in order when I come**—"the rest" means "the other questions you asked about how to properly celebrate the Lord's Supper," not other questions in general, since he does go on to deal with other matters in this letter.

*Chapter* **12**

1-31 THE USE AND ABUSE
OF SPIRITUAL GIFTS

➤**1 spiritual gifts**—These are signs that the Holy Spirit is still present, working in Christ's body, the church. Whether these gifts are ordinary and permanent or extraordinary, they all come from the power of the Holy Spirit, and they complement each other to supply all the needs of Christ's body. The extraordinary gifts, such as miracles and speaking in strange languages, do not mean that the person is especially holy, since a person might have them without even knowing the Lord (Matt. 7:22). But these miraculous abilities were needed in the early Church as signs that Christians were really the people of God. In the following verses, Paul discusses: (1) the unity of the body (12:1-27); (2) the variety of its members and functions (12:28-30); (3) love, which should always govern the use of the gifts (12:31 and chapter 13); and (4) a comparison of the gifts (chapter 14).

➤**2 that** [when] **ye were Gentiles,** [you were] **carried away unto these dumb idols**—The Gentiles' condition without Christ is also described in Eph. 2:11ff. Paul here contrasts the idols, which cannot speak, to the living God, who "speaks" in the believer by his Spirit (12:3). Since the Corinthians were not experienced in discerning between God's voice and false teachings, they needed instruction.

➤**3 calleth Jesus accursed**—as the Jews and Gentiles did when they crucified him (Gal. 3:13). **no man can say that Jesus is the Lord**—or, no man can say, "Lord Jesus." The one test of whether or not a teacher is inspired by God is whether or not he confesses Jesus as Lord (cf. 1 John 4:2; 5:1). Jesus is not an abstract dogma, but a genuine person, the historical, living God-man (Rom. 10:9). Confession involves placing oneself under Christ's authority as his servant. **by the Holy Ghost** [Spirit]—The Spirit of God is also called the Holy Spirit, since only God is holy. The Holy Spirit is the source of all truth (John 15:26).

➤**4-6** Notice that here are mentioned all three "Persons" of the Trinity. The Holy **Spirit** gives us the gifts (12:4) to serve Christ our **Lord** (12:5), and this shows **God** the Father's operation at work in all the members of Christ's body. The word "administrations" in 12:5 is the same word usually translated "ministries." The expression "all in all" in 12:6 means "all the gifts in all the persons who possess them."

➤**7** Though all the gifts or abilities flow from the *one* God, Lord, and Spirit, the mani-

festation of the Spirit is expressed in different ways in different individuals. The purpose of our different gifts is not to benefit ourselves alone, but to help the entire church.

## 8-10 PAUL LISTS VARIOUS ABILITIES GIVEN BY THE SPIRIT

The gifts can be divided into three groups: (1) gifts of intellect—wisdom and knowledge; (2) gifts of miracles that depend on a special faith—healing, miracles, prophecy, and the ability to discern spirits (i.e., to distinguish between those who are really inspired by God and those who only pretend to inspiration); and (3) gifts related to speaking in unknown languages—speaking them and interpreting what others speak. Some additional abilities are listed in 12:28.

➤**8 word of wisdom**—the ready utterance of wisdom (Eph. 6:19). This wisdom concerns new revelations of the divine wisdom of God's purposes, as contrasted with human philosophy (see 1:24; 2:6, 7; Eph. 1:8; 3:10; Col. 2:3). **word of knowledge**—ready utterance of truths already revealed. Wisdom or revelation belongs to the prophets; knowledge to the teacher.

➤**9 faith**—This is faith that God will use them to perform any required miracle (Mark 11:23; James 5:15). Like the faith which leads to salvation, this faith is relying on God and his supernatural power (Eph. 1:19, 20). Note that it is never the faith itself which saves a man or performs miracles, but rather God to whom the faith is directed. **healing**—lit., "healings," referring to different kinds of diseases which need different kinds of healing (cf. Matt. 10:1).

➤**10 working of miracles**—Since "healings" are miracles, those meant here must refer to miracles of special and extraordinary power. **prophecy**—In its wider sense, "prophecy" is proclaiming God's message to man, but here, in the context of other miraculous abilities, Paul probably specifically means predicting the future by God's power (Acts 11:27, 28; 1 Tim. 1:18). Like the other miracles, it depends on faith (Rom. 12:6). **discerning of spirits**—See comments on 12:8. **kinds of tongues**—the power of speaking various languages. **interpretation of tongues**—Cf. 14:13, 26, 27.

➤**12 For as the body is one, and hath many members, and all the members of that**

**one** [this word is not present in the earliest manuscripts] **body, being many, are one body**—As the many members of the body compose an organic whole and none can be dispensed with as needless, so those believers variously gifted by the Spirit compose a spiritual organic whole, the body of Christ. In this body there is unity of life and nature among the many members, but not unvarying uniformity in gifts, function, and expression. **so also is Christ**—lit., "the Christ," i.e., the whole Christ, the head and the body. The head and body comprise one person, here called "the Christ." As such, the church (as body and head) is the corporate Christ, the composite Christ.

➤**13 For by one Spirit are we all baptized into one body**—"Baptize" means literally "to place into," so that the Spirit has placed us into the church, making us a part of Christ's body. We are to be baptized in water as a sign that we have experienced this inner, spiritual baptism. **have been all made to drink into** [of] **one Spirit**—lit., "were all given to drink of one Spirit." To drink the Spirit (see John 7:37-39) is to receive the Spirit; and this Spirit is the common supply of life for all the members of Christ's body.

➤**14-18** Paul was probably thinking of a well-known fable spoken by Menenius Agrippa (*Livy,* 2.32), in which the rest of the body thinks it is unfair that they have to work so hard to feed the stomach, which did nothing but enjoy what they gave it. When they stopped feeding it, however, the other parts became weak, and they realized that the stomach fed them all as well as itself. Paul teaches that just as each part in the body has its own specific function, so every Christian should realize that he is needed to take his place and make his contribution to the body of Christ. Leaders should not ignore or look down on humbler members whose abilities may not be as obvious or as impressive, and no one should feel that he is unimportant or dispensable.

➤**19, 20 And if they were all one member, where were the body? But now are they many members, yet but one body**—By its very nature, a body is one harmonious unit, made up of many different parts, all dependent on one another.

➤**22 which seem to be more feeble**—more susceptible to injury: e.g., the brain, the extremeties, the eyes. Their susceptibility calls for greater care.

➤**23 less honourable . . . uncomely**—refers to the parts of the body that should not be exposed. **upon these we bestow more abundant honour**—i.e., we cover them with clothing.

➤**24 God hath tempered the body together**—so that each part compensates for the weaknesses of the other parts.

➤**25 no schism** [division] **in the body**—The harmony that God designed for the body is here contrasted with the quarreling and "division" in the Corinthian church (1:10-13; 11:18).

➤**26** The principle of sharing in one another's sufferings and joys is also found in Romans 12:15.

➤**27 ye are the body of Christ**—This could be addressed to just the church at Corinth or to the church at Corinth together with all that believe in Christ (see 1:2)—i.e., the entire body of Christ. If it is the former, Paul was indicating that the church at Corinth was the body of Christ. While the body of Christ is made up of all Christians everywhere throughout history, each local church is the body of Christ in miniature, with individual members filling their different roles to make it a balanced and harmonious unit.

➤**28 apostles**—In addition to the Twelve chosen by Christ, others were called "apostles": Paul (1:1), Barnabas (Acts 14:14), Andronicus and Junia (Rom. 16:7), Titus (2 Cor. 8:23, Gk.), Epaphroditus (Phil. 2:25, Gk.). **prophets . . . teachers**—While the prophets received new revelations by the Holy Spirit, the teachers taught what was already revealed. The teachers include evangelists and pastors (shepherds). **miracles**—or, miracle-workers. These are ranked after the prophets and teachers, since teaching is more important in building up the church, though it is not as spectacular as miracles. **gifts of healings**—See comments on 12:9. **helps**—or, helpers. Examples of helpers are deacons who help to supply the needs of the poor (Acts 6:1-10), those who help the teachers in baptizing and preaching, and those who give time or money to help in the Lord's works. **governments**—lit., "governings." This refers to elders whose function was to govern the local church (see 1 Tim. 5:17; Heb. 13:17, 24).

**diversities of tongues**—refers to those who were given the ability to speak in different languages.

➤**29-30** According to the Greek, the answer expected from all these questions is "no."

➤**31 covet [desire] earnestly the best gifts**—Paul was not urging them to be dissatisfied with their abilities or their place in the body, since he had just explained that the Holy Spirit determines this, and that all parts are equally necessary. He wanted them, however, to hold the best gifts in the highest estimation by recognizing that the value of an ability does not depend on how spectacular it is but on how much it strengthens the church. Paul also wanted them to develop and use their abilities to the fullest for God, and to be available to the Holy Spirit. He implied that if we do not take full advantage of our present abilities and opportunities to glorify God and strengthen the church, then we cannot expect the Spirit to give us anything more. **and yet show I unto you a more excellent way**—the more excellent way is the way of love. Paul devotes the whole next chapter to love, which includes not only faith and hope (13:7), but all of the fruits of the Spirit (cf. Gal. 5:22, 23): patience (13:4), faithfulness (13:7), joy (13:6), gentleness (13:5), goodness (13:5), and kindness (13:4). This love is produced in us as a response to God's love for us shown in Christ. Love for God overflows in love for men, especially to our brothers in Christ.

*Chapter* **13**

## 1-13 LOVE IS BETTER THAN ANY OF THE GIFTS

➤**1 Though I**—Paul now shifts to the first person. **speak with the tongues**—The Corinthians were very impressed with Apollos's eloquence (Acts 18:24; 1 Cor. 1:12) and with the miraculous ability to speak in unknown languages, but Paul here shows that tongues-speaking is nothing by comparison with love. He then moves on to prophecy, knowledge, faith, and even self-sacrifice; without love, all are worthless.

➤**2 all mysteries, and all knowledge**—This includes knowledge both of what God had revealed long ago, and of secrets God was just then making known to his people (see Rom. 16:25; Eph. 3:3-6). **faith . . . [to] remove mountains**—Paul illustrated the great power of faith the same way Jesus did (Matt. 17:20). **charity**—a good attempt by the KJV translators to render the Greek, *agapē*. This Greek word was rarely used in Greek literature prior to the NT. In the NT, the word *agapē* took on a special meaning; it was used by the NT writers to designated a volitional love (as opposed to a purely emotional love), a self-sacrificial love, a love naturally expressed by divinity but not so easily by humanity. In this chapter, Paul displays the divine characteristics of this most excellent virtue, *agapē*.

➤**3 I give my body to be burned**—This is the reading in some ancient manuscripts. But the three earliest manuscripts read, "I give my body that I may boast." According to the Greek, there is but a one-letter difference between the first reading and the second: *kauchēsomai* (I may boast) and *kauthēsomai* (I may be burned). Good arguments have been advanced by scholars in support of each reading. But those who support the second reading point to the earlier attestation and to the fact that martyrdom by burning was a phenomenon yet unknown to the original readers of this epistle. Gordon Fee pointed out that in Clement of Rome's letter to the church in Corinth (c. A.D. 96), Clement spoke of those who delivered themselves to bondage in order to ransom others. This could very well be what Paul was referring to—unless Paul was thinking about the fiery ordeal of Shadrach, Meschach, and Abednego (see Dan. 3), in which case the first reading would be the one he wrote. Whatever the reading, the verse says that love produces willingness to give sacrificially and to suffer, but this giving and suffering can exist without love, in which case even they have no value.

➤**4** After emphasizing how essential love is, Paul begins not by defining it but by describing what love in action is like. **suffereth long**—under provocations of evil from others. **is kind**—in its goodness toward others (cf. James 3:17). **envieth not**—is not jealous. **vaunteth not itself, is not puffed up**—like the Corinthians, who liked to show off their spiritual gifts.

➤**5 not . . . unseemly**—is not discourteous, or inattentive to civility and propriety. **thinketh no evil**—Love, far from plotting evil against others, overlooks insults (Prov. 10:12) and makes allowances whenever possible for the evil others do to it.

►**6 rejoiceth in the truth**—The truth is the gospel truth, the inseparable ally of love (see Eph. 4:15; 2 John 12).

►**7 beareth all things**—The Greek verb *(stegei)*, here translated "beareth," literally means "to cover" or "to hold fast" like a watertight ship, without leaking. Hence, the word means "to hold out against," "to endure patiently," "to contain one's self" (see 1 Thess. 3:1, 5). The believer who possesses this characteristic of love restrains himself from giving vent to what selfishness would prompt under personal hardship.

►**8-10 never faileth**—Love will never be obsolete; it will always have its place. **shall fail . . . vanish away**—The same Greek verb is used for both; it means "to be abolished." In contrast to love, prophecy, tongues (speaking in unknown languages), and special knowledge will one day cease. They will no longer be necessary when "that which is perfect [or, complete] is come." Some take this expression to mean the completion of the NT canon, and thus they say that the gifts existed during the apostolic era. Others take this expression to designate Christ's coming, with which come perfection and completion. (For the arguments on both sides, see Mare.) **in part**—partially, imperfectly.

►**11 childish things**—These things correspond to tongues, prophecy, and knowledge.

►**12 we see through a glass**—lit., "mirror." Mirrors in Paul's time were made of polished brass or other metals; they gave a hazy or blurred reflection, which is expressed by the word *darkly* (lit. "enigma"). Even God's word, which is also likened to a mirror (James 1:23-25), makes us understand Christ only dimly in comparison with how we will see and know him when he returns and we are with him face to face. (Paul's language here echoes Num. 12:8 in the Septuagint.)

►**13 And now abideth** [remains] **faith, hope, charity** [love]—Faith, hope, and love, in contrast to the gifts and powers from God that will come to an end, will remain. In a sense even faith will be superseded by sight, and hope will give way to actual experience, but they certainly remain necessary as long as we are on earth, while the gifts have already played their part. Only a Christian experiences these three things; for without Christ we would have only unbelief, despair, and hatred. Faith is directed toward God; hope is for our benefit; and love flows first to God and then to our neighbors. Love is the "greatest" of these because it sums up or includes both faith and hope.

Chapter **14**

## 1-25 THE SUPERIORITY OF PROPHECY OVER TONGUES

►**1 Follow after charity**—"let love be your greatest aim" (TLB), because love is the greatest quality and will always remain (13:13). **and desire spiritual gifts, but rather that ye may prophesy**—Prophecy, which could be defined as speaking for God under the inspiration of the Spirit, included foretelling the future, explaining difficult parts of Scripture, and teaching Christian belief and behavior. Preaching and teaching today correspond to this prophecy, but without the direct divine inspiration, since the Bible contains God's complete message to his church. Paul was telling the Corinthians to desire the gift of prophecy more than any other gift, especially more than speaking in tongues.

►**2 speaketh . . . unto God**—since he is the only one who understands all languages. **for no man understandeth him**—except those who can interpret. **in the spirit**—as opposed to "the understanding" (14:14). **mysteries**—unintelligible to the hearers, exciting their wonder, rather than instructing them. Corinth was a trade center, and its mixed population of merchants from Asia, Africa, and Europe made the ability to speak in other languages an advantage in preaching the gospel (compare Acts 2:5-11), but the Corinthian Christians were apparently more interested in showing off their ability in the worship services, where it was no help to the others.

►**3 edification, and exhortation** [encouragement], **and comfort** [consolation]—Along with worshiping God together, the main purpose of meeting together as a church is to build each other up and strengthen each other. Two aspects of this are "encouraging," or urging each other to continue to obey Christ and live as he wants us to, and "comforting" each other with prayerful concern—"bearing one another's burdens."

➤**4** Paul here makes clear the self-centeredness of the Corinthians' preoccupation with "tongues." In 14:20 he adds that they were behaving childishly and foolishly.

➤**5 I would** [desire] **that ye all spake with tongues**—Paul had no objection to tongues-speaking—it is a good and desirable gift—but he continually asserted that prophecy is so much more valuable and useful to the church. **he interpret**—i.e., he translate.

➤**6** Paul now turns the situation around by putting the Corinthians in the hypothetical position of having to listen to words they could not understand. Since they would not like for Paul, great teacher and apostle as he was, to speak to them in "tongues," why should they insist on doing it to others?

➤**7-9** Paul illustrates his point with musical instruments. Their music consists of distinct notes which make up a recognizable melody. In addition, specific meanings can be attached to particular tunes: a soldier can be ordered to attack or retreat by a few notes on a bugle. In the same way, Paul says, the human voice was not made merely to produce a babble of meaningless noise: it was made for communication.

➤**10 many kinds of voices in the world**—There are, in fact, over 5,000 different languages in the world today. **none . . . without signification**—none without articulate voice (i.e., distinct meaning).

➤**11 a barbarian**—a foreigner, one speaking a foreign language.

➤**12** Spiritual gifts should be exercised to edify or build up the church.

➤**13 let him that speaketh in an unknown tongue**—i.e., "If someone while praying speaks in an unknown language" (Alford), since the passage (through 14:17) is about prayer (see the connection with the next verse).

➤**14 my spirit**—my higher being, the passive instrument of the Spirit's operation. When speaking in tongues, a Christian was merely the passive instrument of the Holy Spirit; he did not have any control over what he said and did not understand what he was saying. **my understanding is unfruitful**—i.e., nonproductive, of no benefit.

➤**15 I will pray with the spirit, and I will pray with the understanding also**—The implication is that if he cannot make himself understood by others, he will keep silent.

➤**16 Else when thou shalt bless with the spirit, how shall he that occupieth the room of the unlearned say Amen**—Prayer is not a duty someone else can perform for us. Rather, we must join with one who leads in prayer and praise, agreeing with his words, praying them from our own hearts, and saying aloud our responsive "Amen" in assent, as was practiced among the Jews (Deut. 27:15-16; Neh. 8:6) and the early church (Justin Martyr's *Apology,* 2.97).

➤**17 givest thanks**—The prayers of the Christians are called "thanksgivings" (see Col. 4:2; 1 Thess. 5:17, 18).

➤**18 tongues**—singular "tongue," "language," according to the earliest manuscripts.

➤**19 in the church**—lit., "in an assembly" or "in a meeting." **I had rather speak**—lit., "I want to speak."

➤**20 Brethren**—This phrase was used by Paul to show that he loved the Corinthians, and that he was pleading with them for their own good. **be not children in understanding: howbeit in malice be ye children**—This same idea is expressed in Matthew 10:16; Romans 16:19.

➤**21 In the law**—an expression encompassing the whole OT (cf. John 10:34). Paul was specifically referring to Isaiah 28:11, 12. "The point of the quotation is that if Israel would not hear the Lord through the prophets, they would not hear even when he spoke in foreign languages to them through foreign people. So, Paul is saying, why put so much stress on tongues?" (Mare).

➤**22 tongues are for a sign . . . to them that believe not**—Tongues show the power of God to the unbeliever. But the believer does not need such a demonstration.

➤**23, 24 the whole church be come together**—Contrary to modern idiom the NT does not speak of "going to church" but of the church coming together to meet. **all speak with tongues**—Even for unbelievers, "tongues" have very little use. The speaking forth of God's word ("prophesying") is more likely to bring them to repentance, while if everyone talks at once in unknown languages, they will only think they are mad (lit., "rave")—like the

Greek saying about two deaf men arguing their cases before a deaf judge.

➤**25 secrets of his heart made manifest**— This is the work of the powerful Word of God (Heb. 4:12) as it is preached and taught. The Holy Spirit always works in connection with the Word. Like the woman of Samaria (John 4:19, 29), when one's sinful character is exposed, he or she will be convinced that the gospel is true, and that "God is really there among you" (TLB).

## 26-40 GUIDELINES FOR CHRISTIAN MEETINGS

➤ **26 How is it then, brethren? when ye come together**—Paul has shown the Corinthians the true purposes for "tongues" and prophecy. He now gives practical guidelines for ordering their meetings. These guidelines are based on the principle that everything that is done must be useful to all, and build them up; and that to accomplish this, everything must be done properly and in order (14:40). **a psalm**—extemporary praise, inspired by the Spirit, as that of Mary, Zechariah, Simeon, and Anna (Luke 1 and 2). **a doctrine**—lit., "a teaching," to impart and set forth before the congregation. **tongue . . . revelation**—The order is transposed in the earliest manuscripts.

➤**27 let it be by two**—at each time, in one meeting; not more than two or three might speak with tongues at each meeting. **let one interpret**—only one. God would not give differing interpretations to different people, but just as he gave a person the miraculous ability to speak in a foreign language, so he often gave a person the ability to interpret it.

➤**29, 30** Prophesying, like speaking in tongues, must be done in an orderly way so that everyone can profit. **judge**—carefully examine what is said to see whether it accords with the gospel and is truly a message from God.

➤**31 For ye may** [can] **all prophesy one by one**—by taking turns, and by allowing those who receive sudden revelations from the Spirit to speak immediately. To prophesy can mean "to foretell" or "forthtell" (i.e., to speak forth for God). In this context, it seems that Paul's comments refer to both kinds of prophecy.

➤**32, 33** Apparently, anyone who had a message from God demanded to speak, and

monopolized the time, claiming that he had no control over himself, and that it was simply the Spirit speaking through him. Thus they were blaming God for the noise and disorder of their meetings. But Paul emphatically denied this, for he asserted that the prophet's spirit (through which the Holy Spirit acted) is subject to his control.

➤**34 Let your women keep silence in the churches** [meetings]—This statement is difficult because Paul had previously spoken about women praying and prophesying (11:5ff.). It could be that the praying and prophesying of chapter 11 was done outside the meeting, but the context of that chapter argues against this (see 11:16, 17). Then what kind of speaking by women was Paul prohibiting? According to 1 Timothy 2:11, 12, it is very clear that a woman should not teach a man in a Christian gathering. The same passage exhorts women to "learn in silence," which is also the teaching of 1 Corinthians 14:34, 35. What is clear is that women should not teach or speak in any way that causes disturbance in a church meeting. But we cannot dogmatically say that women did not and could not pray and/or prophesy in church meetings. **to be under obedience**— The Greek word does not indicate subordination, but submission (see 11:3; Eph. 5:22; Tit. 2:5; 1 Pet. 3:1). **the law**—referring to the OT, specifically Genesis 3:16.

➤**35, 36** As in 11:6, 16, Paul is talking about what is proper in the church meetings, and he appeals to the practices of the other churches for support. He is also rebuking the Corinthians for their pride and independence, as if they alone had received the gospel, and were able to teach everyone else.

➤**37 or spiritual**—Paul is referring especially to the ability to discern spirits. (12:3, 10). **the things that I write unto you are the commandments of the Lord**—Paul claims direct inspiration for his teaching; a prophet himself, he was passing on to them God's own instructions.

➤**38 if any man be ignorant**—deliberately rejecting the authority of Paul's instructions. **let him be ignorant**—It would be a waste of words to try to convince him when he was determined to ignore Paul's teaching.

➤**39 covet** [be eager] **to prophesy**—This, Paul says, is important; it is a goal worth wanting and working for. He does not urge them to "long to speak in tongues," but only cautions them not to over-react and forbid "tongues."

➤**40 Let all things be done decently and in order**—"all things" would include both prophesying and speaking in tongues, as well as the celebration of the Lord's Supper, the conduct of women, and anything else involved in their meetings. An orderly procedure is the only way to have true Christian freedom.

# Chapter 15

## 1-58 THE REALITY AND IMPORTANCE OF CHRIST'S RESURRECTION

➤**1 I declare**—"I make known." This phrase is somewhat reproachful, for it should not have been necessary for Paul to remind the Corinthians, who thought they were so spiritual, of the basic facts of the gospel on which their faith rested (Gal. 1:11, Gk.).

➤**2 By which also ye are saved**—lit., "are being saved," a present, actual reality based on their continuing faith. Paul was reminding them not only of the gospel, but also of the very words and arguments he used in preaching it to them. **unless ye have believed in vain**— "unless of course you never really believed it in the first place" (TLB).

➤**3 I delivered unto you**—"I handed on to you" (NEB). Even in Paul's time there was probably a short creed or confession of faith stating the essentials of the gospel, such as he goes on to list. Before being baptized a person declared that he believed this gospel, and claimed for himself salvation through Christ. **that which I also received**—by Christ himself through special revelation (Gal. 1:12). **Christ died for our sins**—Christ died to pay the penalty for our sins, and thus to take them away completely (2 Cor. 5:15; Tit. 2:14; 1 Pet. 2:24; 1 John 3:5). **according to the scriptures**—To prove Christ's death and resurrection, Paul points to the OT Scriptures even before pointing to the eyewitnesses. For example, see Isaiah 53:12 (which Christ quoted as referring to himself in Luke 22:37) and Psalm 16:8-11 (which Peter quoted as referring to Christ in Acts 2:25-28).

➤**4 buried . . . rose again**—His burial is more closely connected with his resurrection

than his death. Even at the moment when Christ died, the power of his inextinguishable life exerted itself (Matt. 27:52). For Christ, the grave was not a place where his body would decay, but the place from which he would come with new life—Acts 2:26-28 (Bengel). "Rose again" is literally "has risen"; it was the beginning of a life which still continues and will never end. **according to the scriptures**—See Ps. 16:10, 11; Ps. 110:1.

➤**5 seen of Cephas**—Peter (Luke 24:34). **the twelve**—This was their ordinary appellation, even when their number was not full. However, it was very possible that Matthias was present (Acts 1:22, 23).

➤**6 five hundred**—This was probably on the mountain in Galilee where Christ had promised to meet his disciples after his resurrection (Matt. 26:32; 28:7, 10, 16). It would have been dangerous for such a large number to meet in Jerusalem after Christ's crucifixion. **remain unto this present**—and therefore could be found out for giving testimony. **some are fallen asleep**—a euphemism for death.

➤**7 James**—the brother of Jesus our Lord (Gal. 1:19). **all the apostles**—i.e., many others besides "the twelve" already enumerated (15:5).

➤**8 last of all he was seen of me also, as of one born out of due time**—more literally, "as one aborted," referring to one born abortively and therefore prematurely. In other words, Paul was saying that he was puny among the apostles, scarcely justified to be called an apostle. Moffatt translated this expression, "by this so-called abortion of an apostle." Paul normally would never have seen Jesus after his resurrection, because he had not been Christ's disciple during his life on earth. Paul humbly declared that it was only by the special grace of God that he was made an apostle—certainly not because of his own merits, since he was persecuting the church when Jesus Christ met him (Acts 9).

➤**9 For I am the least of the apostles**— Paul's name in Latin ("Paulus") means "least." **I persecuted the church**—Though God had forgiven him, Paul could not forget his most grievous sin.

➤**10 by the grace of God**—God's grace had not only saved him, but also made him, the least worthy apostle, the apostle whom God used powerfully to bring the gospel to so many.

What a contrast between Paul's gratitude and humility, and the self-righteous prayer of another Pharisee (Luke 18:10-12). **I laboured more abundantly than they all**—his missionary efforts prove this. **yet not I, but the grace of God . . . with me**—cf. "the Lord working with them" (Mark 16:20). Paul saw himself as merely cooperating with God's grace in all of his work (cf. 2 Cor. 6:1; Phil. 2:12, 13).

➤**12 some among you**—These would not believe in the resurrection because they could not understand *how* it could happen (see 15:35, 36; see also Acts 17:32; 26:8).

➤**13** Christ's resurrection and the future resurrection of all the dead cannot be separated; you cannot deny one without denying the other. The *fact* of Christ's resurrection is the basis for our expectation that we too will rise some day (15:20).

➤**14 if Christ be not risen, then is our preaching vain, and your faith is also vain**—Without the solid fact of the resurrection, the whole gospel becomes empty and unreal. If Christ had remained dead, we would have no reason to be sure our sins have been forgiven, for it is the same power of God which raised Jesus Christ and which forgave our sins. Our faith then would be empty and worthless.

➤**15 and we are found false witnesses**—The early preachers based their whole message on the miracle of the resurrection (Acts 1:22; 2:32; 4:10, 33; 13:37; Rom. 1:4).

➤**17 your faith is vain**—useless. **ye are yet in your sins**—since it is Christ's resurrection that made us "right with God" (Rom. 4:25).

➤**18 fallen asleep in Christ**—a euphemism for "Christians who have died." **perished**—They would be lost eternally.

➤**19 we are of all men most miserable**—Christians from the early church on have suffered hardship and persecution for the sake of their faith in Christ and their confidence in the resurrection and eternal life. If this hope is false, they have lost many present enjoyments for nothing. The salvation of our souls as well as our bodies depends on the resurrection of Christ, without which his death could do us no good (Eph. 1:19, 20; 1 Pet. 1:3). We would be worse off than unbelievers who are "without hope" (Eph. 2:12; 1 Thess. 4:13).

➤**20 But now is Christ risen from the dead**—After painting the dark picture in 15:13-19 of how hopeless our condition would be without Christ's resurrection, Paul joyfully proclaims the unshakable fact: "Christ rose from the dead!" **the firstfruits of them that slept** [died]—Paul used the metaphor of the firstfruits of a harvest. The "firstfruits" was the first of the crop that was harvested, and the Jews offered it in thanksgiving to God (see Lev. 23:10, 11) the day after the Passover sabbath (which was also the day Christ arose). The "firstfruits" was a promise that the whole harvest was coming.

➤**21 by man . . . by man**—The "firstfruits" were always the same as the rest of the crop. In the same way, Adam had the same nature as the man to whom he brought death, and Christ, who brings life to men, was also a man.

➤**22 in Adam all die**—When Adam died he represented the whole human race, which shares his nature. In his death, all men die. **in Christ shall all be made alive**—Christ represented the human race when he conquered sin and death. Those who by faith in him become children of God share his life, and will surely rise just as he did.

➤**23** In this portion (15:23-28) Paul lists the order of events of Christ's second coming, which is treated as a period of time, beginning with the resurrection of his people when he returns, and ending with the final judgment. **But every man in his own order**—rather, "rank"; the Greek is not in the abstract, but concrete, drawing upon an image from troops, "each in his own regiment." Though all shall rise again, let not any think all shall be saved; rather, each shall have his proper place: Christ first (Col. 1:18); and after him the godly who die in Christ (1 Thess. 4:16), in a separate group from the ungodly; and then "the end," i.e., the resurrection of the rest of the dead. Christians will be judged first "at his coming" (Matt. 25:1-30); then "all the nations" (Matt. 25:31-46). Christ's own flock shall share his glory "at his coming," which is not to be confounded with "the end," or general judgment (Rev. 20:4-6, 11-15). The latter is not in this chapter specially discussed, but only the first resurrection, viz., that of the saints. The second coming of Christ is not a mere point of time, but a period beginning with the resurrection of the just at his appearing and ending with the general judgment. The ground of the universal resurrection is the union of all mankind in nature with Christ, their representative head, who has done away with death by his own death in their stead; the ground of the resurrection of believers is not merely this, but their personal union with him as their "life" (Col. 3:4), effected causatively by the Holy Spirit, and instrumentally by faith as the subjective, and by ordinances as the objective means.

➤**24 Then cometh the end, when he shall have delivered** [according to some early manuscripts, "when he delivers"] **up the kingdom to God, even the Father**—This does not contradict Daniel's prophecy that Christ's "dominion is an everlasting dominion which shall not pass away" (Dan. 7:14). Christ's kingdom will not come to an end, but he will have finished his work as the mediator between God and sinful man when he has conquered all enemies and removed all evil from the world. He will then continue to reign, co-equal with God, though in his manhood he will be subordinate to the Father. Both the throne of God and the throne of the Lamb will be in heaven (Rev. 22:3). Thus when Christ returns, the unity of the Godhead will be shown (Zech. 14:9). **shall have put down all rule**—Paul is referring to Psalm 110:1, 2; 8:6; and 2:6-9 (see also Eph. 1:22). This will be realized in the millenial kingdom.

➤**25 all enemies under his feet**—"An OT figure for complete conquest. Verse 25 is an allusion to Ps. 110:1" (*NIVSB*).

➤**26 shall be destroyed**—lit., "is destroyed." The present tense indicates "what is true now in God's determination, in the fixed succession of things" (Findlay). Death is here personified, as in 15:55, Isaiah 25:8; Revelation 20:14 (cf. Heb. 2:14).

➤**28 the Son also himself be subject unto him that put all things under him**—Christ's position will not be the same as that of created beings, for he will be voluntarily subordinate to the Father, although co-equal with

him. When he has conquered all enemies, Christ's kingdom will merge with the Father's, with whom he is One. This does not detract from Christ's honor, for the Father wills that everyone should honor the Son, just as they honor the Father (John 5:23). In beautiful harmony, the Father makes the Son ruler over all things; and the Son freely puts himself under the Father's authority "so that God who has given him the victory over everything else will be utterly supreme" (TLB). Christians who desire and struggle to make God supreme in their lives (Ps. 73:25) will find glorious fulfillment when all resistance and evil, whether human or demonic, will be gone, and God truly will be "utterly supreme."

➤**29 Else what shall they do which are baptized for the dead**—The original makes clear that Paul did not include himself among the "people" being baptized for the dead. Without approving of the practice, he may be merely pointing out that even it depended for what meaning practicioners might give it on the assumption that the dead will rise again. If there was any practice of baptism for the dead at Corinth, it was very limited, and was generally unknown in the church at large. "Baptized on behalf of the dead is possibly proxy-baptism on behalf of friends who had died unbaptized. The Greek can also mean 'baptized because of the dead', i.e., the reference is to the baptism of those influenced by the testimony of a Christian who had recently died, and in the hope of being reunited with him at the resurrection. In either case, if death is the end, the future is hopeless" (Hillyer).

➤**30 And why stand we in jeopardy every hour?**—Paul and his fellow-workers were risking death for the sake of the gospel because they believed they possessed eternal life.

➤**31 I die daily**—See 2 Corinthians 1:8, 9; 4:11, 12; 11:23-27. Paul suffered and faced death so that the Corinthians and other Christians would enjoy spiritual life and growth in the Lord.

➤**32 I have fought with beasts at Ephesus**—This should be understood as a metaphor, since there is no record of Paul having been subjected to the torturous attack of wild beasts—a punishment not inflicted on Roman citizens. There is a parallel passage to this in Ignatius's epistle to the Romans, wherein he spoke of his captors as wild beasts: "From Syria to Rome I am fighting with wild beasts, by land and sea" (5:1). Paul was writing from Ephesus (16:8), where his life was in danger every day from many enemies (16:10). It was very soon after he wrote this letter that the riot occurred (Acts 19:29-20:1), and Paul had to leave immediately for Macedonia (northern Greece). **let us eat and drink; for tomorrow we die**—Paul here quotes from Isaiah 22:13 (LXX). South commented, "If men persuade themselves that they will die like beasts, they soon will live like beasts too."

➤**33 evil communications corrupt good manners**—This is an iambic line (in Gk.) from Menander's comedy *Thais* (see Vincent, Hillyer). Not only did a false view of man's eternal destiny lead to careless and sinful living (15:32), but keeping company with such people had also corrupted the Corinthian Christians. In turn, those who lived in sinful pleasures did not like the idea of being raised to face God's judgment, so they quickly persuaded themselves that there would be no resurrection.

➤**34 Awake to righteousness, and sin not**—Paul minced no words in scolding the Corinthians; he told them literally to "wake up" and realize how sinful they were (not spiritual as they considered themselves) and how empty they were of real wisdom. **some have not the knowledge of God**—This phrase is a strong one in the Greek. Some of the Corinthians had deliberately chosen to be ignorant of God so that they could hold on to their sins (John 7:17; 1 Pet. 2:15). **I speak this to your shame**—The Corinthians should have been ashamed of allowing in their fellowship those who were so ignorant that they denied the resurrection and thus were a harmful influence on the Christians (15:33).

➤**35 How are the dead raised up?**—It is a sign of foolishness to refuse to believe something God tells us just because our limited minds cannot completely understand it. Contrast Ezekiel's answer of faith (Ezek. 37:3; see also Mark 10:27). **with what body do they come?**—How could they be the same bodies, since they will have completely decomposed, and since the new bodies will not eat or drink or reproduce as our present bodies do? If they are different bodies, then how can our personal identities be preserved? Paul answers that in a sense they will be the same bodies, and at the same time they will be new and different.

➤**36 that which thou sowest is not quickened, except it die**—Paul illustrated his theological point with a natural phenomenon: that of the growth of a seed. He turned the very objection, the death of the natural body, into an argument for his case. A plant begins to grow through the disintegration of the seed. Christ's resurrection did not eliminate physical death for us; rather, he allows it to take its course so that out of death he can create for us a new and heavenly life.

➤**37 thou sowest not that body that shall be, but bare grain**—Our new bodies will be different from our present ones, but our identity will remain; i.e., we will still be recognizably ourselves, just as a particular kind of seed always turns into the same kind of plant (Phil. 3:21). Jesus had used the same example of a seed being sown in death and then coming forth in resurrection, to tell his disciples that it was necessary for him to die before he could put on his glorified body and reproduce his new life in many (John 12:24). Thus, death is the entranceway not merely to revivification or reanimation but to resurrection, regeneration, and spiritual reproduction.

➤**38 God giveth it a body . . . to every seed his own body**—Just as God created the different species of plants and arranged for each plant to produce new plants of the same kinds, God will give each of us individual bodies, appropriate and suitable to us, substantially the same as our present bodies, but completely glorious and beautiful.

➤**39 All flesh is not the same flesh**—The implication is that in some sense our resurrection bodies will be really flesh, not just spirit. Verses 39-41 make the point, first, that our new bodies will be different from one another and will be suitable to us. Second, they emphasize that our new bodies will be different from our present bodies, but they will still be bodies. All this is to illustrate the difference of the new celestial body from its terrestrial seed, while retaining a substantial identity.

►**40, 41 celestial bodies**—not the sun, moon, and stars, which are first introduced in 15:41, but the bodies of angels, as distinguished from the bodies of earthly creatures. **terrestrial**—"The differences in splendor between the earthly bodies and the heavenly bodies suggested to Paul the differences between a natural and a spiritual body" (Lowery). Daniel 12:3 describes God's people as shining like the sun and stars, and Jesus repeated the idea (Matt. 13:43) in the parable about the wheat and tares.

►**42 sown**—The Greek continues the comparison by speaking of our bodies as being liable to corruption. **in corruption**—liable to incorruption.

►**43 dishonour**—corresponding to our "body of humiliation" (lit.). (See Phil. 3:21.) **glory**—like Christ's glorious body (2 Cor. 5:2-4). **in weakness**—liable to weakness (2 Cor. 13:4) **in power**—the power of resurrection.

►**44 a natural body**—lit., "a soulical body" (see Rotherham's *Emphasized Bible*), a body shaped in its organism of flesh and blood to suit the human soul. The Holy Spirit in the spirit of the believers is an earnest (or, token) of a superior state of being, but meanwhile in the body the human soul predominates. Hereafter the spirit shall predominate, and the human soul be subordinate. **spiritual body**—a body wholly moulded by the Spirit and suitable to the Spirit. This body will meet the needs of man's spirit and be its faculty for life and expression, just as the natural (soulical) body met the needs of man's soul (or, personality) and provided man a faculty for living and expression.

►**45 it is written, The first man Adam was made** [became] **a living soul**—This is written in Genesis 2:7, which speaks of the result of God's creation of man. **the last Adam**—Jesus Christ (cf. Rom. 5:14). **was made** [became] **a quickening spirit**—lit., "life-giving spirit," not just a living spirit but a spirit who makes [others] alive (cf. John 5:21; 6:57; Rom. 8:2, 11). When Christ was resurrected, he was glorified *and* he became spirit (*pneuma*). It appears that when he arose the indwelling Spirit

penetrated and saturated his body so as to constitute his entire being with spirit. William Milligan, the author of a great English classic on Christ's resurrection, said that the risen Christ is spirit (*pneuma*). In that classic, called *The Resurrection of Our Lord*, he wrote:

> [T]he condition of our Lord after His Resurrection was viewed by the sacred writers as essentially a state of *pneuma* (spirit). Not indeed that our Lord had then no body, for it is the constant lesson of Scripture that a body was possessed by Him; but that the deepest, the fundamental characteristic of His state, interpenetrating even the body, and moulding it into a complete adaptation to and harmony with His spirit, was *pneuma*. In other words, it is proposed to inquire whether the word *pneuma* in the New Testament is not used as a short description of what our Lord was after His Resurrection, in contrast with what He was during the days of His humiliation upon earth.

In other writings Paul identified the risen Christ with the Spirit (see Rom. 1:3, 4; 8:2, 9-11; 2 Cor. 3:17, 18). This is not to say that the second person of the Trinity became the third (as in the heresy of Modalism), but that Christ, through resurrection, became identified with the Spirit. Speaking of Christ's resurrection and the change it brought about in him, Gaffin wrote:

> Christ (as incarnate) experiences a spiritual qualification and transformation so thorough, and endowment with the Spirit so complete that as a result they can now be equated. This unprecedented possession of the Spirit and the accompanying change in Christ result in a unity so close that not only can it be said simply that the Spirit makes alive, but also that Christ as Spirit makes alive.

►**46 and afterward that which is spiritual**—We have natural bodies before we receive our new resurrection bodies, just as Adam came before Christ. Although

Adam was created to live forever (if he had eaten of the tree of life), he became mortal because of sin. Yet his created body was not the glorious spiritual body we will receive. Adam received his life to become "a living soul"; he was not "life-giving Spirit."

➤47 **The first man is of the earth**—Adam's name means "red earth"; he was not merely born on the earth, but his body was actually made from it, in contrast to Christ, who came from heaven (John 3:13, 31). (The words "the Lord" are not present in the earliest manuscripts.)

➤48, 49 Since we have descended naturally from Adam, we belong to his race, and have not only the same kind of body but the same nature. **bear the image of the heavenly**—the heavenly One, Christ. In the same way, when we belong to Christ and draw our life from him, we receive his nature, and even now we are starting to become like him. At the resurrection we will be made completely like him, both in spirit and body (see Phil. 3:20, 21).

➤50 Because our present bodies become sick and weak and old, and give us much trouble, a Christian should be glad that we are doomed to die, so that we can receive the glorious new bodies that will last forever. Although these new bodies will have no pain or decay or death, they will still keep our personal identities, just as Christ's did when he arose (see Luke 24:39; John 20:27). And furthermore, it is impossible for our present, natural bodies, made of flesh and blood, to inherit God's kingdom.

➤51 **a mystery**—a secret the Corinthians, for all their "wisdom," could never have discovered. Even those who are still alive when Christ returns will be miraculously transfigured, as well as those who have died (1 Thess. 4:15-17). Elijah and Enoch are types and forerunners. Paul says "*we* shall not all die" because we do not know when Christ will return, but we should be expecting him at any time just as Paul did.

➤52 **the last trump**—the trumpet sounding on the last day (Matt. 24:31). Perhaps this trumpet will be the last one to blow following the others mentioned in Revelation 8:6–11:15 (see also Isa. 27:13). A trumpet was used to call people together for solemn celebrations and worship. This last trumpet will call *all* God's people to his presence, even those who have died.

➤53 **this corruptible** [body] **must put on incorruption**—This is explained in 2 Corinthians 5:1-4. **this mortal must put on immortality**—The only other place the word "immortality" is used in the NT is 1 Timothy 6:16, which speaks of God himself. The Bible never teaches that our spirits and souls will live forever without bodies; it teaches the immortality of our souls (or, spirits) and bodies together.

➤54 **then shall be brought to pass the saying that is written**—Although death still has power over our bodies, Christ has already defeated death for us so that we need no longer fear it. Paul quotes from Isaiah 25:8 to express the triumph we can experience even now, and the glorious fulfillment we are looking forward to when at the resurrection we have complete victory over death. The expression **Death is swallowed up in victory** in Hebrew means "Yahweh will swallow up death for ever" (cf. Jer. 3:5; Lam. 5:20). Christ has conquered death so that it shall never more regain its power (2 Cor. 5:4; Heb. 2:14, 15; Rev. 20:14; 21:4).

➤55 **O death, where is thy sting? O grave** [death], **where is thy victory?**—from Hosea 13:14, not quoted verbatim, but substantially captured by Paul for its use in this context.

➤56 **The sting of death is sin**—It is our sin that gives death its rightful power over us. If there were no sin, there would be no death. In fact, death entered the world through sin (Rom. 5:12). **the strength** [or, power] **of sin is the law**—the law points out our guilt, contrasting it vividly with God's own character, and his perfect will for us (Rom. 3:20; 7:8-10). Because of Christ, the law is no longer our judge (Rom. 6:14).

➤57 **thanks be to God**—We were helplessly bound by sin and death, and our victory is due only to God. **which giveth us the victory**—which death had aimed at, but now we have gained. This victory is our present experience, day by day.

➤58 **the work of the Lord**—spreading the gospel to others and building them up in their faith.

*Chapter* **16**

## 1-24 DIRECTIONS ABOUT GIVING

Paul's plans. Closing greetings.

➤**1 collection for the saints**—at Jerusalem (see Acts 11:28-30; Rom. 15:26; 2 Cor. 8:1-4). Paul says "saints" rather than "the poor," reminding the Corinthians that these Jews were their brothers in the faith. Toward the close of the national existence of the Jews, Judea and Jerusalem were harassed with various troubles. Jewish Christians were the targets of added persecution, and their sufferings were increased by famine. Paul, who had once hounded the Jewish Christians to death (Acts 22:14), was now just as energetic in his efforts to help them. **as I have given order to the churches of Galatia**—Paul had visited the churches of Galatia and Phrygia just before writing this letter (Acts 18:23). In urging the churches to give generously, Paul used the Galatians as an example to the Corinthians, and the Corinthians and Macedonians to the Romans (Rom. 15:26, 27).

➤**2 the first day of the week**—or Sunday, the day of Christ's resurrection. Christians gradually made Sunday their day of rest and of joining together for worship and fellowship, instead of Saturday, the Jewish sabbath. The command to keep one day of the week as a holy day of rest was not merely a part of the Jewish law, for it was given at creation, and is still needed today. **every one of you**—not just the rich, but even those with limited resources. **lay by him in store**—Although there was not a public collection every week, each individual was to set apart a definite proportion of his weekly income, to be given when the collection was taken. **that there be no gatherings** [collections] **when I come**—On Paul's visit, he wanted to spend the time teaching rather than collecting money.

➤**3 approve by your letters**—i.e., whomsoever you approve, them will I send with letters: viz., letters from Paul to the leaders of the Jerusalem church, explaining the purpose of their visit, and asking them to welcome these Gentile strangers as brothers in Christ.

➤**5-8** Paul was writing from Ephesus. His original plan had been to visit Corinth on his way to Macedonia, and again on his way back to Jerusalem. He changed his mind and went directly to Macedonia, where he wrote the second letter to the Corinthians. He then spent the winter (three months) at Corinth. (See 15:32; see also Acts 20:1-6; 2 Corinthians 1:15-18; 2:1-3, 12, 13.)

➤**9 a great door and effectual** ["for effective work," RSV, NIV] **is opened**—Paul was always alert, ready to take advantage of any chances to preach the gospel as opportunities given him by God, who controls circumstances. (Cf. Acts 14:27; 2 Cor. 2:12; Col. 4:3.) **many adversaries**—Wherever God blessed Paul's work, so that people believed in Christ and churches were established, Satan raised up opposition, trying to keep Paul from entering the wide-open door.

➤**10 Now if Timotheus** [Timothy] **come**—Paul had sent Timothy ahead to Macedonia, with the possibility that on his return he would visit Corinth. This was not certain, but Paul told the Corinthians to welcome and respect him if he did arrive. **that he may be with you without fear**—Timothy was young (1 Tim. 4:12), and Corinth was a large and sophisticated city compared to his hometown of Lystra; so he might easily feel timid when alone among all the strangers.

➤**11 Let no man therefore despise him**—This is reiterated, to Timothy, in 1 Timothy 4:12. **I look for him**—Timothy and Titus were appointed to meet Paul in Troas, whither the apostle purposed proceeding from Ephesus (2 Cor. 2:12, 13). **with the brethren**—Others besides Erastus accompanied Timothy to Macedonia (Acts 19:22).

➤**12 our brother Apollos, I greatly desired him to come unto you**—Apollos had ministered to the Corinthians, and was very popular with them (Acts 18:27; 1 Cor. 1:12), so Paul probably said this to make clear that there was no jealousy or competition between them. **but his will was not at all to come at this time**—This was probably because Apollos was aware of the divisions in the Corinthian church among those who liked Paul and those who liked Peter or Apollos (1:11-13), and he deplored this as much as Paul did.

➤**13** Paul gave several sharp commands for the Corinthians as he closed the letter, to prod them out of their carelessness, pride, and selfishness.

**➤14 charity**—*agapē*-love (see chap. 13).

**➤15 house of Stephanas**—Paul had baptized this household himself (1:16). **firstfruits of Achaia**—the first converts in Achaia (cf. Rom. 16:5). As the first Christians in Greece, their faith and dedicated work for the Lord were no doubt a special joy to Paul. **addicted themselves to the ministry of the saints**—i.e., "devoted themselves to the service of the saints" (NIV).

**➤17** After visiting Paul, **Stephanas, Fortunatus, and Achaicus** probably returned to Corinth, taking with them this letter from Paul.

**➤18 acknowledge**—render them due honor (cf. 1 Thess. 5:12).

**➤19 Asia**—This was not the whole continent which is now called Asia, nor all of Asia Minor, but rather the province of Asia of which Ephesus was the capital. **Aquila and Priscilla salute you much in the Lord**— When the Jews were driven out of Italy, Aquila and Priscilla settled in Corinth, Paul stayed in their home and they all worked together, both in tentmaking and in preaching the gospel in Corinth. Aquila and Priscilla would want to send greetings to their Corinthian friends. **the church that is in their house**—lit., "an assembly in their house." Because the next verse says "all the brethren" (i.e., the whole church in Ephesus), it seems likely that the assembly (*ecclēsia*) in Aquila and Priscilla's house was an assembly of a certain number of believers in Ephesus, but not the entire number. When this couple was in Rome, a group of believers (also called an *ecclēsia*) met in their home. (See Rom. 16:3-5 and com-

ments for a discussion on the "home church" in relationship to the local church.) In the early period of the NT church, the believers in a locality could meet in one home (if their number was small enough) or in several. According to Neander, the entire church at Corinth met at Gaius's home (see Rom. 16:23 and cf. 1 Cor. 14:23), and perhaps the entire church at Laodicea met at Nymphas's home (see Col. 4:15 and comments).

**➤20 holy kiss**—the token of the mutual love of Christians, especially at the Lord's Supper (cf. Rom. 16:16; 1 Thess. 5:26).

**➤21 salutation . . . with mine own hand**—Paul had dictated the rest of the letter, but this solemn warning he wrote himself for emphasis, adding to it the weight of his authority as an apostle (cf. Col. 4:18).

**➤22 If any man love not the Lord**—Christ alone is worthy of our first and highest love. Love for human teachers, like Paul or Apollos, comes second, growing out of our love for Christ. **Jesus Christ**—These words are not present in the earliest manuscripts. **let him be Anathema**—let him be a curse. The Greek word for curse is *anathema*. After "Anathema" in the KJV there is no period. There should be; otherwise, the reader will think "Anathema maranatha" constitutes one expression, which it does not. **Maranatha**—Aramaic (*Marana tha*) for "Come, Lord." This was a motto in the early church, urging Christians to be always ready for Christ's return (Phil. 4:5).

**➤23, 24 grace . . . love**—After administering some severe rebukes, he closes with grace and love, for the Corinthians needed grace and the assurance that love had motivated Paul's words to them.

BIBLIOGRAPHY

Alford, Henry. *The Greek New Testament*. Vol. 3. 1852. Reprint. Grand Rapids: Guardian Press, 1973.

Bengel, John A. *New Testament Word Studies*. 1742. Reprint. Grand Rapids: Eerdmans, 1971.

Fee, Gordon. "The First Epistle to the Corinthians" in *The New International Commentary on the New Testament*. Grand Rapids: Eerdmans, 1987.

Findlay, G. G. "St. Paul's First Epistle to the Corinthians" in *The Expositor's Greek Testament*. London: Hodder & Stoughton, 1917.

Gaffin, Richard. *The Centrality of the Resurrection*. Grand Rapids: Baker Book House, 1978.

Hillyer, Norman. "1 and 2 Corinthians" in *The New Bible Commentary, Revised*. London: InterVarsity Press, 1970.

Lowery, David K. "1 Corinthians" in *The Bible Knowledge Commentary*. Wheaton: Victor Books, 1983.

Mare, W. Harold. "First Corinthians" in *The Expositor's Bible Commentary*. Grand Rapids: Zondervan, 1978.

Milligan, William. *The Resurrection of Our Lord*. London: Macmillan and Co., 1884.

Neander, Johann A. *A General History of the Christian Religion and Church*. 9 vols. Edinburgh: T. & T. Clark, 1849-52.

South, Robert. *Sermons Preached on Various Occasions*. 8 vols. 1842. Reprint. New York: AMS Press, n.d.

Vine, W. E. *Expository Dictionary of New Testament Words*. London: Oliphants, 1940.

# 2 CORINTHIANS

## Introduction

Prior to this century, most commentators believed that the epistle we call "Second Corinthians" was actually Paul's third epistle to the Corinthians. According to these commentators, the first epistle, referred to in 1 Corinthians 5:9, is now lost; the second epistle is now called "First Corinthians"; and the third is called "Second Corinthians." But most contemporary commentators believe that there were four epistles written to the Corinthian church. In addition to those just mentioned, another was written between First and Second Corinthians. This would make "Second Corinthians," in actual fact, the fourth epistle to Corinth.

The scholars of the past saw every reference in Second Corinthians to Paul's previous stern actions and "sorrowful letter" as pointing to First Corinthians, especially in chapter five, in which Paul dealt severely with an incestuous brother. Scholars thought this was the epistle written "with many tears" (2:4). There is much to support this view. Paul, in Second Corinthians, refers to a brother who has been severely punished (2 Cor. 2:4ff.), and his words there closely parallel his words in 1 Corinthians 5:1-5 (see comments on 2 Cor. 2:4ff.). Scholars in the past had thought that the epistle which Paul regretted writing (and then again did not regret when he saw the positive effect it had on the Corinthians—see 2 Cor. 7:8ff.) was none other than First Corinthians. But there is a problem with this interpretation. Paul, in 2 Corinthians 7:12, speaks of a man who caused an offense and of another man who was offended (see comments on 7:12). Since there is no mention of an offended man in 1 Corinthians 5:1ff., modern scholars have thought that Paul must have been referring to another incident, one that occurred during a painful visit which took place after the writing of First Corinthians, and that prompted a third, "sorrowful letter," which is now lost.

Modern scholars have attempted to reconstruct the circumstances that led to the writing of Paul's third letter (now lost). In brief, scholars have proposed that Paul wrote this epistle because First Corinthians failed to remedy the problems at Corinth and an ensuing visit also failed to pacify the troubled church (Lindsell). The church at Corinth was troubled by Judaizers (called "false apostles" by Paul), who were attempting to undermine Paul's authority (see chapter 11). Some of the Corinthians must have been affected, for Paul had to deal very severely with them during this painful visit (2:1; 12:14; 13:1). But still there was turmoil. Therefore, some time later (c. A.D. 56 or 57), while Paul was in Macedonia, he wrote this epistle, which he sent with Titus to Corinth. Second Corinthians bears witness to the anxiety Paul experienced in waiting to see how the Corinthians would respond to his third epistle (see 7:5ff.). When Titus brought good news of the Corinthians' response to Paul's stern letter, he penned the epistle now called "Second Corinthians." This was his fourth letter to the Corinthian Church.

This epistle is very emotional, personal, and autobiographical. Paul's emotions are displayed before us: both his depression and his elation. Paul's personal feelings and thoughts are time and again revealed unguardedly. Because he was speaking as a father to his beloved children, he forewent formality and even politeness. Here we see Paul as Paul, in his heights and in his depths. And because of the Judaizers who were undermining his apostolic authority, Paul was forced to present his apostolic biography—and with much detail. Acting as the Corinthians' spiritual father, he reproved them, encouraged them, disciplined them, and loved them. As a father jealous over his daughter, Paul wanted to preserve the Corinthians' spiritual purity and so present them as a chaste virgin to Christ (11:2).

Chapter 1

1-24 INTRODUCTION

➤1 Timothy our brother—When Paul wrote directly to Timothy, he called him "my son" (1 Tim. 1:18). Writing of him, Paul called him "brother" and "my beloved son" (1 Cor. 4:17). Timothy had previously been sent to Macedonia and later met Paul in Philippi during Paul's trip from Troas to Macedonia (cf. 2:12, 13). in all Achaia—This refers to Hellas and the Peloponnese. The Gentiles and the proconsul, Gallio, disapproved strongly of the Jews' accusation against Paul. Hence, Paul was able to labor in Achaia and successfully bring the gospel to Greece. Several churches were established as a result of his teaching (see 1 Thess. 1:8; 2 Thess. 1:4). In Paul's letters written from Corinth, he speaks of the "churches" as including groups of Christians at Athens, Cenchrea, Sicyon, and perhaps Argos, in addition to Corinth. Here he addresses the church of Corinth directly, and all the "saints" in the country indirectly.

➤3 After his introduction Paul explained why he had not visited the Corinthians as he had promised (1:15-24). the Father of mercies—i.e., the source of all mercies (cf. James 1:17; Rom. 12:1). comfort—or, encouragement. Our comfort comes from our experience of God's mercy. The troubles that Christians have are not beyond the reach of God's mercy, since God is their comforter and encourager in every situation (Ps. 146:3, 5, 8; James 5:11).

➤4 that we may be able to comfort them

which are in any trouble—Paul lived, not for himself, but for the church. Whenever he experienced God's help he shared this experience for the benefit of other believers. In this he imitated Jesus who, by participating in all our hardships and troubles, was particularly qualified to be our comforter and encourager in all situations (Isa. 50:4-6; Heb. 4:15).

➤5 sufferings—This term is contrasted with "salvation" (1:6), as "tribulation" is with "consolation" (1:6). of Christ—Cf. Colossians 1:24. This refers to sufferings endured either by Christ or by his body, the church (Matt. 25:40; Acts 9:4; 1 John 4:17-21). Christ identifies with the sufferings of his people as his own (1) because of the mystical union between Christ and the church (Rom. 8:17; 1 Cor. 4:10); (2) because the suffering is endured for his sake; and (3) because the Christian's patience in suffering brings glory to him (Eph. 4:1; 1 Pet. 4:14, 16). aboundeth by Christ—The sufferings are more than made up for by his comfort. Comfort is a predominant message in this letter.

➤6 whether we be afflicted, it is for your consolation and salvation—This is an example of the kind of concern that Christians have for one another (Phil. 2:26, 27). The trouble and comfort of Paul brought comfort to the rest (1:4; 4:15). which is effectual in the enduring—in enabling one to endure. Paul's example would enable other Christians to endure when similar troubles faced them. The last clause in the KJV ("or whether we be comforted, it is for your consolation and salvation") is not present in the earliest manuscripts. (See

RSV, NASB, NIV for good renderings of the shorter text.)

➤**7 stedfast**—firm, guaranteed. **partakers**—participants. **consolation**—or, encouragement, comfort.

➤**8 trouble**—affliction. This may be a reference to a serious illness under which Paul worked, or to the threat of death which he encountered in Ephesus (Acts 19:23-41). (See also Acts 20:19; 1 Cor. 15:32; 16:9.) Paul's weak health, combined with this strain, had all but killed him (see 11:29; 12:10). **pressed out of measure**—He was overpowered by human opposition. **despaired even of life**—There was no human hope of help, but God enabled them to survive (4:8, 9).

➤**9 we had the sentence of death in ourselves**—They looked upon themselves as men condemned to die (Paley). **trust . . . in God which raiseth the dead**—Since they were certain to be killed, their attention was focused on the hope of resurrection from the dead (cf. 1 Cor. 15:32).

➤**10 delivered us . . . doth deliver** [actually, "will deliver," with respect to immediately imminent dangers] **. . . will yet deliver**—This hope of God's deliverance (or, rescue) covers past, present, and future dangers.

➤**11 helping together by prayer for us**—According to the Greek, this should read "cooperating on our behalf with petition," or as it reads in the RSV, "help us by prayer." The NIV makes the next part of the verse clearer than in the KJV, for the NIV reads, "Then many will give thanks on our behalf for the gracious favor granted us in answer to the prayers of many."

➤**12 simplicity**—This is the reading in a few ancient manuscripts; but the earliest manuscripts read "holiness." One word could have easily been confused with the other because the two words differ in only a few letters in Greek: *hagioteti* (holiness) and *haploteti* (simplicity). **godly sincerity**—lit., "sincerity of God." It indicates divine purity. "Sincerity" in the Greek implies the absence of any foreign element. Thus Paul had no impure or selfish motives in not visiting the Corinthians as he promised. **fleshly wisdom**—which is self-serving and relies on human means, suggests insincere motives and dealings. **the grace of God**—which influenced Paul (Rom. 12:3;

15:15), suggests straightforwardness and sincere faithfulness to promises (1:17-20), just as God is faithful to his promises. **we have had our conversation** [conduct of life] **. . . to you-ward**—Paul's great love for the Corinthians would cause him to be even more sincere in his dealings with them (see 2:4).

➤**13 For we write none other things unto you, than what ye read**—Some of the Corinthians thought that Paul had been writing privately to individuals in the church, and expressing views which contradicted his public letters (Conybeare and Howson). Paul replies that his letters were all for everyone to read, and that they were consistent with things he had told them before, as well as with the way he lived (1 Thess. 5:27).

➤**14 ye have acknowledged us in part**—This can mean two things: (1) The Corinthians must have acknowledged Paul's ministry and sincere character at least in some degree (partially); or (2) only part of the Corinthians acknowledged Paul's ministry and responded to the First Epistle. **rejoicing**—boast.

➤**15 in this confidence**—of Paul's sincerity being acknowledged by the Corinthians. **was minded**—He had intended to visit them earlier. **to come unto you before, that ye might have a second benefit**—He had planned to stop both going to and coming from Macedonia. Paul's visits were always an encouragement to the young churches (see Rom. 1:11, 12; 1 Cor. 4:18; 5:9).

➤**16 Macedonia**—This is where he was writing from (see 1 Cor. 16:5; also 4:18, which, combined with these words, imply that some of the Corinthians thought that he would not come at all). His change of plans had taken place before his first letter to the Corinthians (1 Cor. 4:17; see also Acts 19:21, 22; 20:1, 2).

➤**17 did I use lightness?**—The Greek expression indicates vacillation and fickleness. **or**—He suggests another alternative. **do I purpose according to the flesh, that with me there should be yea yea . . . nay nay**—i.e., "do I make my plans in a worldly manner so that in the same breath I say, 'Yes, yes' and 'No, no'?" (NIV). (See Matt. 5:37; James 5:12.)

➤**18 true**—This means "faithful" (1 Cor. 1:9). **our word toward you was not yea and nay**—The doctrines and beliefs that Paul preached were true and self-consistent.

Furthermore, this statement assures the Corinthians that although Paul's plans might change, his teaching would not.

➤**19 the Son of God, Jesus Christ**—The teachings are unchangeable as to their subject, Jesus Christ, who is identified with the God who does not change (cf. 1 Sam. 15:29; Mal. 3:6). **by me and Silvanus and Timotheus** [Timothy]—Although the gospel was told by different men, the message was the same. "Silvanus" was shortened to "Silas" (Acts 15:22; cf. 1 Pet. 5:12).

➤**20 For all the promises** [or, however so many promises] **of God in him are yea**—All of God's promises are affirmatively fulfilled and realized in Christ. **in** [through] **him Amen**—All the OT and NT promises are verified and actualized in Christ (see Heb. 6:18; Rev. 3:14). **unto the glory of God by us**—according to the Greek, "for glory unto God by us [the apostles]."

➤**21 Now he which stablisheth**—secures, makes firm, guarantees. **us with you in Christ**—lit., "the anointed One." **and hath anointed us**—with the Spirit (1 John 2:27). Both Paul and the believers have been securely united with Christ, the anointed One, by receiving the anointing of the Spirit.

➤**22 sealed us**—or, marked us as his possession. This happens at the time of regeneration through the operation of the Holy Spirit (Eph. 1:13; 4:30). **given the earnest of the Spirit**—i.e., the Spirit is given to believers as a first installment, guarantee, and foretaste of the full inheritance yet to be given (Eph. 1:13, 14). Paul's images were very familiar to his readers. The Greek word for "stablishes" (in 1:21) was used as a technical term "denoting a seller's guaranteeing of the validity of a purchase" (Harris, citing Deissman). As such, God's gift of the Holy Spirit is our guarantee. The word "sealed" was commonly used in connection with people branding or marking personal possessions and/or letters with their personal seal. God's people have been marked as his possession with the seal of the Holy Spirit—and this seal will remain until we, as God's possession, are fully redeemed (see Eph. 1:13, 14; 4:30). And finally, the term "earnest" or "guarantee" (*arrabōna*) was commonly used in connection with providing a promissory first installment that guaranteed a full, final pay-

ment. The Greek word *arrabōna* was even used to describe an engagement ring (Moulton and Milligan). As Christians, we have received the Spirit as a guarantee that we will one day obtain our full inheritance.

➤**23 for a record upon my soul**—as a witness as to the secret purposes of my soul, and a witness against it, if I lie (see Mal. 3:5). **that to spare you I came not as yet unto Corinth**—Paul wished to give them time for repentance, so that he would not have to be stern with them when he saw them. He sent Titus ahead to prepare them. Those who were attacking Paul portrayed him as threatening what he was actually afraid to do (1 Cor. 4:17, 19; 2 Cor. 10:10, 11).

➤**24 Not for that we have dominion over your faith**—lit., "not that we lord it over your faith." Jesus is the Lord of the believers, not any Christian worker, even one as great as the apostle Paul. No apostle or Christian worker can control the faith of the believers. **helpers of your joy**—Paul's function was to help the Corinthians enjoy Christ, to be a fellow helper of their joy (Rom. 15:13; Phil. 1:25). This verse softens the authoritarian tone of 1:23.

*Chapter* **2**

1-17 THE REASONS WHY PAUL DID NOT VISIT THEM. THE MAN GUILTY OF INCEST SHOULD BE FORGIVEN. PAUL'S ANXIETY TO HEAR ABOUT THEIR STATE FROM TITUS, AND HIS JOY WHEN, AT LAST, GOOD NEWS REACHES HIM

➤**1** Following from 1:23, Paul accounts for his not visiting them. **that I would not come again to you in heaviness**—This implies that he had already paid them a painful visit, at which time he had warned some of the Corinthians that they would be punished if their behavior did not change (12:13; 13:1, 2). (See Introductions to First Corinthians and Second Corinthians.)

➤**2 For**—Paul will give proof that he does not want to cause them pain. **if I**—The "I" is emphatic here. Those who were attacking Paul may say that this was not his reason for not coming, since he certainly caused pain in his first letter to the Corinthians. But he answers, "If I am the one who causes you pain, it is not because I receive any pleasure in doing so. My object was that the one whom I made sorry should turn from evil, thus making me glad."

**➤3 I wrote this same unto you**—that I would not come to you then; for if I did, I would come in heaviness. This was written in 1 Corinthians 4:19, 21; 16:7. **lest . . . I should have sorrow from them of whom I ought to rejoice**—Had he visited the Corinthians when he intended to, there would have been unhappiness on all sides because of their behavior. By waiting, he hoped it could be a pleasant visit. **having confidence in you all**—He trusted that they would understand the need for postponing his visit. Since they were equal members of a community, they should have been able to identify with Paul's feelings.

**➤4 I wrote unto you with many tears**—Throughout church history, commentators have identified this tearful letter as First Corinthians because that epistle contains material about the incestuous brother (1 Cor. 5:1ff.), which seems to match what Paul says here (2:4-11) about a brother who has been punished and now needs to be restored. First Corinthians was, in fact, a very stern letter which could have caused Paul great anguish as to how the Corinthians would respond to it. But in the last century, more and more commentators have proposed the theory that the tearful letter was another letter written before Second Corinthians. This non-extant letter, they believe, was more severe than First Corinthians and therefore really caused Paul anguish, anxiety, and even regret for having written it (see Introduction). The commentary that follows (on 2:5-11) tends to favor the traditional interpretation. **not that ye should be grieved**—Paul's main objective was not to bring you pain, but rather that through your pain, you might turn from your evil. **but that ye might know the love**—Paul wanted the Corinthians to recognize that sincere criticism and rebuke come from love (Ps. 141:5; Prov. 27:6). **unto you**—The Corinthians had been particularly committed to Paul by God (Acts 18:10; 1 Cor. 4:15; 9:2).

**➤5 any**—anyone, referring to the incestuous man (1 Cor. 5) or to the brother who offended Paul (see comments on 7:5-12). **that I may not overcharge you all**—i.e., "that I may not press too harshly upon all" (Conybeare).

**➤6 Sufficient . . . is this punishment**—Any more would cause him to despair (2:7), for the object of the punishment was to help him turn from his evil practice (see Acts 22:22; 1 Cor. 5:5). **inflicted of many**—rather, "by the majority." The word "inflicted" is a supplied word; there is no verb in the Greek.

**➤7** If this verse is speaking about the incestuous brother (see comments on 2:4), Paul has changed his directive from judgment (1 Cor. 5:3-5) to forgiveness. If it is speaking about a brother who offended Paul, then Paul's words direct the Corinthians to extend forgiveness to this one.

**➤8 confirm your love toward him**—restore him to good standing in the church, and support him by being loving and kind to him personally.

**➤9** As another reason for postponing his visit, Paul wanted to test their obedience. Now he fully states his motives, since he has seen the success of his experiment.

**➤10 To whom ye forgive . . . I forgive**—This is the reversal of Paul's words in 1 Cor. 5:4, in which he, joined in Spirit with the Corinthians, judged the incestuous brother in the name of Christ. Here, he joins them in extending forgiveness to him **in the person of Christ** (i.e., representing Christ and acting by his authority), so that the church would not suffer the loss of one of its members.

**➤11 Lest Satan should get an advantage of us**—"lest we are taken advantage of by Satan," viz., by letting one of our members be lost to us through despair. (Compare Paul's directive concerning the incestuous brother and Satan in 1 Cor. 5:5.)

**➤12 when I came to Troas**—Paul planned to meet Titus in Troas to hear how his first letter had affected the Corinthians. Disappointed that Titus did not meet him, Paul went on to Macedonia and found that Titus was there (7:5-7). Acts does not record Paul's trip from Ephesus to Macedonia, but it does mention his coming from that country (Acts 20:6) and that he had disciples with him (Acts 20:7). Paul had undoubtedly planned to meet Titus in Philippi if he were unable to get to Troas.

**➤13 I had no rest in my spirit**—Cf. 7:5, where his "flesh" had no rest. His "spirit," guided by the Holy Spirit, determined that it was not right for him to stay at Troas beyond the time agreed upon for meeting Titus. **taking my leave of them**—This refers to his departure from the disciples at Troas.

➤**14** Even though Paul had to leave such a good opportunity for preaching at Troas, God blessed him, because Titus brought good news concerning the Corinthians and others who had heard the gospel. **God . . . causeth us to triumph in Christ**—According to the Greek, this should read, "leads us in [his] triumph." God was triumphantly leading Paul through the Greek and Roman world as a part of his processional display of his power to both subdue and save. The foe of Christ now becomes the servant of Christ. The image is taken from the triumphal procession of a victorious general. Unlike most captives, however, the idea of willful obedience (10:5) on the part of the captive to the conqueror (Christ) is included. Thus, God's captive is not only an example of his triumph over Satan, but is a conqueror himself, working to defeat Satan with God. **savour of his knowledge**—This is also from the image of a triumphal procession. As the approach of a procession was made known by the incense-bearers, so God makes known through us the sweet knowledge of Christ, the triumphant Conqueror, to everyone in every place. (See Col. 2:15 for the use of the same image.)

➤**15** The order in the Greek is "For (it is) of God (that) we are a sweet savour unto God" (cf. Eph. 5:2). **in them that are saved, and in them that perish**—Since some of the conquered foes were led in the triumphal procession to their death, the smell of the incense was the smell of death. But to those who were spared, it was the smell of life. So the sweet fragrance of the gospel that the Christians brought to all was the smell of death to those who did not believe and the aroma of life to those who did.

➤**16 savour of death unto death**—The message of Christ's death disbelieved by those who heard would eventually result in their spiritual death. **the savour of life unto life**—The message of Christ's resurrection life believed by those who heard would result in their reception of life (Matt. 21:44; Luke 2:34; John 9:39). **who is sufficient** [qualified] **for these things?**—Some of the Corinthians had accused Paul of inadequately fulfilling his task of spreading God's message. He replied by agree-

ing that no one was able to do anything adequately in his own strength (3:5,6), but God gave men the ability to fulfill what he had for them to do.

➤**17 For we are not as many**—This refers to false teachers (see chpts. 10-12; 11:13; 1 Thess. 2:3). **corrupt**—Greek, "adulterate," "hawk," "peddle." Certain men used the gospel only to make a living for themselves. **as of sincerity . . . as of God**—as one speaking from sincerity and from the command of God. **speak we in Christ**—united with Christ, doing what he had planned for them.

*Chapter* **3**

## 1-18 THE ONLY LETTER OF RECOMMENDATION THAT PAUL NEEDS IS THE ONE WRITTEN IN THE HEARTS OF THE CORINTHIANS

Paul's ministry of spirit and life is far more glorious than the old law of condemnation.

➤**1 Do we begin again to commend ourselves?**—This accusation was made by some of the Corinthians against Paul, but it was other teachers who opposed Paul that were doing this very thing (cf. 10:18). **epistles of commendation**—It was the practice for teachers who traveled from church to church to obtain letters of recommendation from the various churches they visited, so that they could present them as credentials to churches where they were strangers. For example, the thirteenth canon of the Council of Chalcedon (A.D. 451) ordered that "clergymen coming to a city where they were unknown, should not be allowed to officiate without letters commendatory from their own bishop." In Acts 18:27, the same custom is mentioned. As this occurred about two years before Paul wrote this letter, it is probably one of the instances to which he refers (1 Cor. 1:2).

➤**2 our epistle**—The Corinthian church was an epistle (a letter of commendation) written (1) on the hearts of Paul and his coworkers and (2) on the hearts of the Corinthians (3:3). This one epistle on all their hearts expressed Paul's loving care and effectual ministry to the Corinthians. The church in Corinth was known to be Paul's offspring and product—Paul carried them in his heart and they, he felt, carried him in their hearts.

➤**3 ye are manifestly declared to be the epistle of Christ ministered by us**—It was a letter declaring Christ's authorship carried about and presented by its ministers to the world for whom it was intended. **written not with ink, but with the Spirit of the living God**—Paul was the writing instrument used by God, as well as the carrier of the letter. "Not with ink" stands in contrast to the letters of recommendation which other teachers used (3:1). "Ink" also represents any physical material used for writing, such as the stone on which the Ten Commandments were written. These were made by the "finger of God" (Exod. 31:18; 32:16). Christ's letter is written by the Spirit of the living God, which Spirit gives life (3:6), as opposed to the ministry of death inherent in the law (3:6). **not in tables** [tablets] **of stone**—as the Ten Commandments were so written (3:7). **fleshy tables** [tablets] **of the heart**—lit., "in tablets (which are) fleshly hearts." This alludes to the new covenant predicted in the OT (Jer. 31:31-34; Ezek. 36:26, 27). God said that he would take away the heart of stone and give his believers a heart of flesh; at the same time he would give them his Spirit. On such a heart, God, by his Spirit, would inscribe his law.

➤**4 and such trust have we through Christ to God-ward** [God]—This refers to the apostles' relationship with God through Christ and to their reliance on God for the work he had assigned them.

➤**5 we**—This refers to "ministers." **our sufficiency is of God**—Greek, "out from God," indicating God as their source.

➤**6 able ministers**—competent ministers, sufficient ministers (cf. Eph. 3:7; Col. 1:23). **new testament**—or, new covenant, as contrasted with the old testament or covenant (1 Cor. 11:25; Gal. 4:24). Paul continues the contrast (from 3:3) between that which is written on the tablets of stone and that which is written by the Spirit. **not of the letter**—i.e., the written code, the law as written. To avoid punishment, the person who followed the old Jewish laws had to adhere to every detail that was written to instruct his behavior. **but of the spirit**—or, the Spirit. The Christian, since Christ's death and the coming of the Holy Spirit, will still fulfill the moral requirements of the old covenant, but his method of doing so

has changed. The believer is motivated more by the love of God than by the fear of punishment. He also has the indwelling Spirit in his life to replace a written code, which attempted to dictate appropriate behavior under every possible circumstance, but failed. **for the letter killeth**—by exposing one's guilt and giving knowledge of the consequential punishment: death (see Rom. 7:9-11). **the spirit** [or, Spirit] **giveth life**—This Spirit of life is in Christ Jesus (Rom. 8:2, 10), who through resurrection became "life-giving Spirit" (1 Cor. 15:45). The Spirit gives life to the word (see John 6:63). The letter, or written word, is nothing without the Spirit, since its subject is essentially spiritual.

➤**7 the ministration of death, written and engraven in stones**—lit., "the ministry of death in letters engraved in stone." This refers to the OT law (summed up in the Ten Commandments), which only brought knowledge of sin and death, in contrast to the spirit of the gospel, which brings life (3:6). **was glorious**—lit., "was made in glory." God's glory accompanied the giving of the law (Exod. 34:29). **the children of Israel could not stedfastly behold the face of Moses**—See Exodus 34:30. Moses' appearance was so unusual that the Israelites were afraid to look at him, but this "glory" soon disappeared when the occasion was over. Note the contrast between the transitory character of the old system and the permanence of the new (3:11).

➤**8 the ministration** [ministry] **of the spirit** [Spirit]—which characterizes the NT ministry. **be rather glorious**—"be even more glorious" (NIV), both now and when Christ returns.

➤**9 ministration** [ministry] **of** [producing] **condemnation be glory**—The best manuscript evidence supports another reading: "with [accompanying] the ministry of condemnation [there was] glory." God's glory accompanied the giving of the law, even though this law produced condemnation (Rom. 7:9-11). **the ministration** [ministry] **of righteousness**—the gospel, which reveals the righteousness of God (Rom. 1:17), imputes righteousness to men through faith in Christ (Rom. 3:21-28; 4:3, 22-25) and imparts righteousness by the Holy Spirit (Rom. 8:1-4).

➤**10** The glory of the gospel of Christ surpasses the glory that was on Moses at Mt. Sinai, as the glory of the rising sun causes the glory of the moon and stars to fade into nothingness.

➤**11 was glorious**—The Greek reads "was by [or, through] glory," indicating that which is transient. **is glorious**—The Greek reads, "in glory," indicating that which is permanent. The constant contrast of the OT with the NT suggests that Paul's opponents at Corinth were Judaizers.

➤**12 plainness**—boldness, openness (2:17; 4:1).

➤**13 Moses . . . put a vail over his face**—Some interpret Paul's allusion to Moses (Exod. 34:30-35) to mean that Moses removed his veil while speaking to God, but put it back on so that the people would not see the glory fade. The veil was thus a symbol of concealment. Others maintain that Moses put the veil on because the people were unable to look at him. Paul's use of the example, in either case, serves to illustrate the blindness of the Jews to the ultimate end of the law. The glory of Moses behind the veil of legal ordinances foreshadows Christ's glory. The veil has been removed for the Christian but is still interfering with the view of the unbelieving Jew (Isa. 6:10; Acts 28:26, 27), who cannot see beyond the law (see 3:14-17). **the end of that which is abolished** [being done away]—i.e., the law. Christ is the end of the law (Rom. 10:4).

➤**14 blinded**—lit., "hardened." **the same vail**—the same kind of veil that covered Moses' face. **untaken away in the reading of the old testament** [covenant]—The Jews could not see Christ when they read the OT. **which vail is done away in Christ**—The old testament, or legal covenant, can be removed (3:7, 11, 13) when a person comes to Christ.

➤**15 even unto this day, when Moses is read**—This reading of Moses (i.e., of Moses' writings) was reading done out loud, in the synagogues (Acts 15:21). **the vail is upon their heart**—blocking their understanding (John 8:43; 1 Cor. 2:14).

➤**16 it**—the heart. **the vail shall be taken away**—This is an allusion to Exodus 34:34. As Moses took off the veil when he was in God's presence, so the Israelites who turn to Christ have the veil taken off their hearts and minds.

➤**17 the Lord**—Christ (see 1:2; 3:14, 16, 18), not Yahweh (as some commentators suggest). **is that** [the] **Spirit**—the life-giving Spirit mentioned in 3:6. Actually, this statement in 3:17 continues the thought of 3:6, for 3:7-16 is parenthetical. Although some commentators have argued that the "Lord" here is Yahweh and therefore this is an affirmation about the Spirit of the living God, not Christ (see Harris), other commentators insist that the language and context unmistakenly declare that Christ is the Spirit. Berkhof argued for this when he said,

> Now the Lord is the Spirit (2 Cor. 3:17a). Some think we have to reverse subject and predicate, and to translate: "Now the spirit is Lord," the Spirit wields lordship; but the word "Lord" in 17 and 18 always means Christ. He Himself is the Spirit; as the close of verse 18 repeats: "this comes from the Lord who is the Spirit." If the Lord was not the Spirit abiding in us, how could we turn our hearts to Him? And how could we be transformed into His image? As far as practical experience is concerned, there is no difference between the indwelling Spirit and the indwelling Christ."

And so did Roehrs and Franzmann:

> *The Lord is the Spirit*—Cf. 6. Since the Lord (Christ) is present among His people, known and operative by the power of the Spirit, the two are so closely associated in God's working and in the church's experience that Paul can simply identify them in order to emphasize the fact that God's new order of things . . . is experienced by man IN CHRIST.

**where the Spirit of the Lord is**—in a man's heart (3:15) or human spirit (Rom. 8:16). **there is liberty**—Cf. John 8:36. Men stop being slaves to the law when they experience the freedom of the Spirit and the joy of Christ (Phil. 3:3). They no longer feel like slaves because they are God's own sons, possessing the Spirit of the Son (Rom. 8:15, 16; Gal. 4:6, 7). Freedom stands in opposition to the law, to the veil, and to the fear which the Israelites felt in seeing the glory of Moses unveiled (Exod. 34:30).

➤18 This verse could be translated, "But we all, with unveiled face mirroring the glory of the Lord, are being transformed into the same image from glory to glory, just as from the Lord, namely the Spirit." According to the Greek, the last phrase of this verse could also be rendered "the Lord, the Spirit" (see NASB, Coneybeare, Centenary, Weymouth) or, "the Lord who is the Spirit" (see RSV, NIV, Berkeley, Williams, Phillips) because the expression "the Spirit" is in direct apposition to "the Lord" (i.e., it is a further description of the Lord). Thus, the Lord is the Spirit. He is near to us, as near as a turn of our heart. Whenever we turn our hearts to him, he is unveiled to us. And as we gaze at him, we mirror him and are gradually transformed into the same image that we behold (see Rom. 8:29; 1 John 3:2). The expression, "from glory to glory," could mean that we will be transformed from one degree of glory to another, or it could mean that we will reflect the same glory we behold—**from** Christ's glory **to** our glory.

## Chapter 4

### 1-18 PAUL'S SINCERE PREACHING, AND PAUL'S HUMAN SUFFERINGS: AN EARTHEN VESSEL CONTAINING A TREASURE

➤1 **this ministry**—The ministry of the Spirit. The topic is resumed from 3:6, 17 and 18. **mercy**—Cf. 3:5. The sense of mercy received from God makes men active in spreading the gospel (1 Tim. 1:11-13). **we faint not**—We are bold in our speech and actions, and patient in our troubles (4:2, 8-16). Shame would lead to hiding (4:3).

➤2 **But have renounced the hidden things of dishonesty**—Paul is referring to the practices of the false teachers at Corinth (2:17; 3:1; 11:13-15). **nor handling the word of God deceitfully**—i.e., not adulterating God's word (2:17; cf. 1 Thess. 2:3, 4).

➤3 **hid**—hidden. This continues the idea of "veiled" in 3:13-18. "Hidden," in the Greek (Col. 3:3), is used for something that is completely out of view. "Veiled" suggests that a thing could be seen if it were not for the cover.

to them that are lost—rather, "to them that are perishing" (1 Cor. 1:18). The same cloud that was "light" to the people of God was "darkness" to their Egyptian foes (Exod. 14:20).

➤4 **the god of this world**—The worldly make him their god (Phil. 3:19). He is, in fact, "the prince of the power of the air, the spirit that now worketh in the children of disobedience" (Eph. 2:2). **hath blinded the minds**—This refers to a mental block, as in 3:14. The truth is not only veiled from him, but his attitudes prevent him from seeing it (2 Thess. 2:10-12). **light of the glorious gospel of Christ**—Light comes from those who are already enlightened. "Glorious" is not a mere quality of the gospel, but is the essence of the subject matter. **who is the image of God**—Christ, the "image of God," has the same nature and essence as God (John 1:18; Col. 1:15; Heb. 1:3). By beholding Christ, we are changed by the Spirit so that we can reflect God's glory (3:18).

➤5 **For we preach not ourselves**—Their blindness is not our fault, for we have no selfish motives in our preaching. **Christ Jesus the Lord**—rather, "Christ Jesus as Lord." **ourselves . . . servants** [slaves]—"Lord" (or master) is the correlative of "slave."

➤6 **For**—Paul will now show that he is a slave of Jesus, working for the Corinthians. **God, who commanded the light**—From Genesis 1:3. **hath shined**—Greek, "he who shined." **to give the light of the knowledge**—Paul used the same image from both the physical and spiritual worlds. God, the creator of light and dark (Job 37:15; Mal. 4:2; John 8:12), brings light to our hearts and minds which we then pass on to others. **the glory of God**—God's glory and the glory of Christ are equivalent (4:4). **in the face of Jesus Christ**—Christ, as God's image, is the full manifestation of his glory (John 1:14, 18; 14:9). Paul is still alluding to the brightness on Moses' face, while pointing out that the only true manifestation of God's brightness and glory is "in the face of Jesus" (cf. Heb. 1:3).

➤7 **this treasure**—This refers to the knowledge of God's glory described in 4:6. **earthen vessels**—This is the body, or the "outward man" (4:16; cf. 4:10), which is susceptible to illness and death. In ancient times, people often kept their treasures in earthenware jars or vessels. **the excellency of the power**—This refers to the Holy Spirit's power exhibited in the ministry of bringing the gospel to others (1 Cor. 2:4) and in sustaining Paul and his coworkers. **may be of God, and not of us**—This power continually comes from God.

➤**8 on every side**—This means "in all respects" (cf. 4:10; 7:5). This verse expresses inward troubles, and the next verse outward difficulties (cf. 7:5). Note the contrast in both verses between the fragility of the vessels and the strength of the power. **perplexed, but not in despair**—perplexed, but not utterly perplexed.

➤**9 not forsaken**—Jesus was forsaken both by God and his people (Matt. 27:46). **Persecuted**—chased, pursued. **cast down**—or, struck down. They were not only "chased" as a deer or bird (1 Sam. 26:20), but actually struck down as with a dart (cf. Heb. 11:35-38). The Greek tense (present) indicates that the Christian will continually experience the sufferings mentioned in 4:8-11.

➤**10 Always bearing about in the body the dying of the Lord Jesus**—"Lord" is not found in the oldest manuscripts. Paul was constantly exposed to death for preaching about Christ, and had the marks of his sufferings on his body (see 1:5; 4:11; Gal. 6:17; cf. 1 Cor. 15:31). **that the life also of Jesus might be made manifest in our body**—The name "Jesus" by itself is often repeated here by Paul amidst sufferings, for he must have tasted the sweetness of that name in his sufferings. The fact that a dying body can be upheld under such troubles suggests that both the resurrection life and death of Jesus are sources of power to us. Paul thus carried with him an image of the risen, living Jesus as well as of the suffering Jesus.

➤**11 we which live**—by the power of Christ's life manifested in our bodies, souls, and spirits (Rom. 8:10, 11; cf. 5:15). Paul regarded it as a miracle that he was still alive, following the many trials and dangers to which he had been exposed (11:23). **delivered unto death**—not by chance, but by the ordering of Providence. God delivers his saints unto death, so that they can manifest Jesus' life in their mortal bodies.

➤**12 death . . . in us**—The death of Christ is continually seen in the dying of the outward man (4:16). **life in you**—operating according to the same principle of Jesus' pattern, i.e., his death brought life to others.

➤**13 We having the same spirit of faith**—We have the same faith as the psalmist. **I believed, and therefore have I spoken**—Psalm 116:10. We believe and speak without fear, even in the midst of trouble and suffering (4:17).

➤**14 Knowing**—This knowledge comes by faith (5:1). **shall raise up us also**—This will occur at the resurrection (1 Cor. 6:13, 14). **by Jesus**—The earliest manuscripts read, "with Jesus." **present us**—See Jude 24. **with you**—See 1:14; 1 Thessalonians 2:19, 20; 3:13.

➤**15** This verse confirms 4:12, 14. **for your sakes**—2 Timothy 2:10. **that the abundant grace might through the thanksgiving of many redound to the glory of God**—i.e., "that as grace extends to more and more people, it may increase thanksgiving, to the glory of God" (RSV).

➤**16** This verse resumes the thought of 4:1. **our outward man perish**—Their bodies were being wasted away by hardship. **the inward man**—Their inner persons were still full of life in Christ through the Spirit. **is renewed**—"is being renewed," with fresh grace (4:15), faith (4:13), and hope (4:17, 18).

➤**17 For our light affliction, which is but for a moment**—lit., "the present lightness of affliction," which contrasts with the **eternal weight of glory.** Our present troubles are insignificant as compared with our future glory. The future reward will exceed any trouble or suffering that we could have in this life.

➤**18 we look not at**—This is not our aim. **the things which are seen**—We can only really see things that pertain to this world (Phil. 3:19). **the things which are not seen**—These are not the "invisible things" mentioned in Romans 1:20, but things that, though not seen now, will be seen hereafter. **temporal**—or, temporary, in contrast to what is **eternal.**

*Chapter* 5

5:1–6:2 THE HOPE OF ETERNAL GLORY IN THE RESURRECTION BODY, AND THE MINISTRY OF RECONCILIATION.

➤**1 For**—This is the reason for the statement of 4:17, that our troubles will lead to glory. **we know**—This is a certainty (4:14; cf. Job 19:25). **earthly house of this tabernacle**—implying a temporary, tent-like structure (cf. Job 4:19; 2 Pet. 1:13, 14). The wooden frame and curtains of the tabernacle wore out when Israel was in Canaan, and a permanent temple was built in its place. And as the temple and the tabernacle were identical in all essential characteristics, so will our resurrection bodies be like our bodies now—except our new bodies will be permanent and eternal. **we have**—The present tense in the Greek shows the certainty of our future possession. **a building of** [from] **God**—It will be solid and everlasting, as contrasted with the temporary structure of the tabernacle. **not made with hands**—This is an allusion to Christ's statements about his own resurrected body, which was made by God (Mark 14:58; John 2:19-22). The permanent house represents our resurrected bodies, while the earthly tabernacle represents our present, earthly bodies.

►**2 For in this** [tabernacle] **we groan**—Cf. Romans 8:23. We grow weary because of our weakness and liability to death. **earnestly desiring to be clothed upon**—Our longing for glory and for a new body are desires motivated by God; they will be fully satisfied. If God had not intended for the desires to be satisfied, he would not have created them in us. **our house which is from heaven**—Our new dwelling place will originate from heaven and will be brought to us when Christ returns (1 Thess. 4:16).

►**3 being clothed we shall not be found naked**—The new, eternal dwelling is pictured as clothing to be put on. When we put off our old bodies, we will not be without a body ("naked"), in a pure spiritual existence forever; eventually we will be clothed with a new body.

►**4 not for that we would be unclothed, but clothed upon**—It is not that we want to lose our present bodies, but rather that we want to have our new, heavenly eternal bodies. **that mortality might be swallowed up of** [by] **life**—Our mortal parts will be absorbed and transformed into life. Faith does not remove our natural unwillingness to experience the act of dying, but it does subordinate our fears to a higher hope—that of having our mortal bodies absorbed into the immortal (1 Thess. 4:15). The Bible does not teach us to neglect our bodies or ignore our emotions, but neither has it to rule us.

►**5 wrought us**—constituted us by redemption, justification, and sanctification. **for the selfsame thing**—of having our mortality swallowed up by life. **the earnest token of the Spirit**—See comments on 1:22.

►**6 we are always confident**—Paul here asserts the certainty of our future life in our new bodies. **whilst we are at home in the body, we are absent from the Lord**—lit., "being at home in the body we are away from home from the Lord." Paul continues the image of a house (cf. Phil. 3:20; Heb. 11:13-16; 13:14).

►**7 faith, not by sight**—Our life is governed by faith, and not by the outward appearance of things (4:18; cf. Rom. 8:24; 1 Cor. 13:12, 13). Our duty in this life is to be faithful to God; our reward will be to see his glory (1 Pet. 1:8).

►**8 confident**—or, "content." A literal translation of the rest of the verse would be, "to go from our home in our body, and to come to our home with the Lord." Christians would prefer to be alive at Christ's return and be given a new body without having to die, but death still means being with Christ in spirit (Acts 7:59; Phil. 1:23) until he returns to earth to resurrect our bodies (1 Cor. 15:51, 52). There may be full communion between Christ and the spirits of those without bodies, but their mutual recognition will not take place until the resurrection (1 Thess. 4:13-17), when the perfect image of Christ will be seen and recognized by all.

►**9 Wherefore**—with such a sure confidence of being blessed, whether we die or are alive at Christ's return. **whether present or absent**—lit., "whether at home, or away from home." **accepted of him**—or, well-pleasing to him. We want to be acceptable to God regardless of the circumstances.

►**10 we must all appear before the judgment seat of Christ**—Our true character will then be revealed (Col. 3:4; cf. 1 Cor. 4:5). Now we are completely known to God; at the judgment we shall be known to ourselves. Since this judgment is exclusively for believers, it is not for the purpose of determining eternal punishments or rewards. Commenting on this judgment of Christians, Harris wrote:

Appearance before Christ's tribunal is the privilege of Christians. It is concerned with the assessment of works and, indirectly, of character, not with the determination of destiny; with reward, not status. Judgment on the basis of works is not opposed to justification on the basis of faith. Delivered from "the works of the law" (Rom. 3:28), the Christian is presently committed to "the work of faith," "action stemming from faith" (1 Thess. 1:3), that will be assessed and rewarded at the bēma ("tribunal"). Yet not all verdicts will be comforting. The believer may "suffer loss" (1 Cor. 3:15) by forfeiting Christ's praise or losing a reward that might have been his. [All Scripture quotations from the NIV.]

**receive the things done in his body**—The Christian's reward will be according to the things he has done while in his earthly body (9:6-9; 2 John 8). Our salvation does not depend upon anything we do, but Christians will receive a greater or lesser reward, depending on the quality of the work that they have done for Christ (Heb. 6:10).

➤**11 the terror** [fear] **of the Lord**—We fear the Lord in the sense that he holds the power of judgment over us (5:10; 7:1; cf. Eccl. 12:13; Acts 9:31; Rom. 3:18; Eph. 5:21). **we persuade men**—Preachers and teachers should use the fear of the Lord to win others, but not to arouse their hostility (Jude 23). Paul had probably been accused of trying to influence men for his own benefit. He said (cf. Gal. 1:10) that it was the fear of the Lord that motivated him to try to win men, and that God would recognize that motive at judgment time, whether men responded to Paul's message or not.

➤**12 them which glory in appearance, and not in heart**—The false teachers were proud of their outward appearance, their recommendations (11:18), their education, manner of speech, wisdom, and riches, but not of the convictions which they held. Their consciences did not affirm their inward sincerity as Paul's did (1:12).

➤**13 beside ourselves**—crazy. This accusation was brought against Paul by Festus (Acts 26:24) because of the enthusiasm with which Paul taught. **it is to God**—Paul's excitement as an apostle was not for his own benefits but for God's glory. **sober . . . for your cause**—He adapted himself to men's weaknesses in order to win them to Christ (1 Cor. 9:22).

➤**14 the love of Christ**—Christ's love aroused the love and awe for God which produced his "insane" enthusiasm (Rom. 5:6-8). **constraineth**—The Greek word implies that it forcibly compresses all our energies into one effort or path. God's love is jealous of any rival which tries to win our soul (11:1-3). **that if**—The word "if" is not present in the earliest manuscripts. **one died for all**—Christ died so that his followers could live; they die to sin and self that they might live for God to whom they belong (Rom. 6:2-11; Gal. 2:20; Col. 3:3; 1 Pet. 4:1-3). **then were all dead**—This should read, "then all died."

➤**15 he died for all**—Christ died in their place, for their justification (Rom. 4:25), and so that he would be their Lord (Rom. 14:7-9). **they which live**—See 4:11. Everyone is indebted to Christ for life of body and soul (Menochius). **not henceforth live unto themselves**—Now that his death for them has taken place, they know that his death saves them from eternal death and his resurrection brings them spiritual, eternal life.

➤**16 Wherefore**—This follows from 5:14. **know we no man after the flesh**—i.e., according to his worldly position and social stature (11:18; John 8:15; Phil. 3:4). The outward distinctions of Jew or Gentile, rich or poor, slave or free, educated or uneducated, have no bearing or importance on those who are dead to the worldly system and alive with Christ (Gal. 2:6; 3:28). **though we have known Christ after the flesh**—Paul, as a Jew, had looked for a Messiah who would be a political ruler rather than a spiritual king. When he was converted, he realized that Christ was God's Son (Gal. 1:16). Furthermore, he began to know Christ as the life-giving Spirit (1 Cor. 15:45; 2 Cor. 3:17, 18). In this, he had an advantage over the Twelve who had known the physical presence of Jesus and then had to make the transition to live by his spiritual presence. The Christian Jews at Corinth were proud of their natural heritage and perhaps of actually having seen Christ. They may have claimed superiority over others by virtue of their close connection with him (10:7). Paul pointed out that their true aim should be to know Christ spiritually.

➤**17** As Christ entered his new heavenly life at the time of his resurrection and ascension, so all who are united with him are **new creature[s]** (see Rom. 6:9-11). "New," in the Greek, implies a nature quite different from anything that existed previously. **creature**—lit., "creation" (cf. John 3:3, 5; Eph. 2:10; 4:23; Col. 3:10, 11). **all things are become new**—an allusion to Isaiah 43:19; 65:17.

➤**18 all things**—This refers to the Christians' privileges as new creatures (5:14, 15). **God . . . hath reconciled us to himself by Jesus Christ**—God brought man back into his favor by sending his Son to die on the cross and thus satisfy the price that his justice demanded. Our position before his law was changed, but Christ did not change God's character, nor was God's love for us produced by Christ's act (Rom. 8:32). Christ's death was the price paid at the expense of God himself to satisfy the charges against us (Rom. 3:25-56). While the use of the term "reconciled" in Matthew 5:24 implies mutual satisfaction, the term here refers to a change brought about in one of the two parties involved (cf. 1 Sam. 29:4). **us**—This refers to his ministers (5:19, 20).

➤**19 God was in Christ, reconciling the world unto himself**—God accomplished this reconciliation through Christ's death on the cross (Col. 1:20). The word "reconciling" denotes the time when the reconciliation was being made (i.e., while Christ was on the cross), as well as the continuous purpose of God, from before the beginning of the world, to reconcile man to himself. Since God was in Christ, God was a participant in the conciliation (John 10:38; 14:10). God made the first step in the conciliation process (John 3:16); now man must accept this gracious offer and be reconciled to God. **the world**—This refers to all men (Col. 1:20; 1 John 2:2). **not imputing their trespasses unto them**—because God put them in Christ, the Sin-bearer (John 1:29). **us**—the NT ministers.

➤**20 ambassadors for Christ**—Christ's designated representatives. **As though God did beseech you by [through] us**—God's message of reconciliation is sent to the world through his ambassadors. **be ye reconciled to God**—Paul is urging the Corinthians to let

God's act of reconciliation have its proper effect in their lives.

➤**21 For**—not present in the earliest manuscripts. **he**—God. **made him**—Christ. **to be sin**—not a sinful person, which would be contrary to truth; nor just a sin-offering or a sacrifice for sin (although this idea is implied here); but "sin" in the sense that he was the Sin-bearer (vicariously) of the aggregate sin of all men past, present, and future. The sin of the world is one; therefore, the singular not the plural is used (see John 1:29)—though its manifestations are many. **for us**—on our behalf. **knew no sin**—by personal experience (John 8:46) (Alford). See also Hebrews 7:26; 1 Peter 2:22; 1 John 3:5 and compare John 3:14—Christ being represented by the brazen serpent, having the form, but not the substance, of the serpent. **might be made**—lit., "might become." **the righteousness of God**—not merely righteous, but righteousness itself, even the **righteousness of God**. Christ, who is God, has become our righteousness (1 Cor. 1:30). Now we stand before God the Father as righteous as his Son (Hooker). **in him**—by virtue of our position in him, and in union with him (Alford).

# Chapter 6

➤**1 workers together**—This refers to those who work together with God (Acts 15:4; 1 Cor. 3:9). **that ye receive not the grace of God in vain**—Since God's grace provided reconciliation for men (5:18, 19; cf. Gal. 2:2), do not discount this grace.

➤**2 For**—God's promise is the basis for what we, as his ministers, say to others. **he saith**—God the Father speaks to his Son and thus to all who are united with him. **I have heard thee in a time accepted, and in the day of salvation have I succoured thee**—This is a quotation of Isaiah 49:8, in which Yahweh speaks to his Servant (his Son), assuring him that he will answer his Son's prayer for the salvation of his people (see John 17) in an acceptable time (cf. Ps. 69:13). Paul takes this passage to show how important it is for the Corinthians to be reconciled to God (5:20) and receive God's salvation **now**.

## 3-18 PAUL'S APOSTOLIC MINISTRY IS APPROVED BY FAITHFULNESS IN EXHORTATION, BY SUFFERINGS, AND BY LOVE TO THE CORINTHIANS

➤3 The thought of 6:1 is resumed. **Giving no offence**—1 Corinthians 10:33. Paul made a great effort to enforce his words by his own example.

➤4 **approving** [commending] **ourselves as the ministers of God**—living consistently faithful lives before God so that others will like what they see and come to hear the gospel from us. The false teachers tried to recommend themselves by words rather than by actions (3:1). **patience**—See 12:12. Paul recounts his patience in the face of three types of trouble and suffering (6:5). The first is general hardship. The second is that which resulted from the physical violence of men. The third is that which Paul brought on himself directly or indirectly, such as exhaustion or hunger.

➤5 **stripes**—See 11:23, 24; Acts 16:23. **imprisonments**—See 11:23. Paul had been in prison in cities other than Philippi, where this letter was written. **tumults**—See Acts 13:50; 14:5, 19; 16:22; 19:23-41. **labours**—in the cause of Christ (11:23). **watchings**—See 11:27. **fastings**—This was not done out of devotional practice, but because he had no food (cf. 11:27; Acts 10:30; 14:23; 1 Cor. 4:11; Phil. 4:12).

➤6 **pureness**—or purity. **knowledge**—refers to knowledge of spiritual mysteries that are beyond reason (1 Cor. 2:6-16; 2 Cor. 3:6, 17, 18). **longsuffering . . . kindness**—These are associated with "love" (1 Cor. 13:4). **the Holy Ghost** [Spirit]—The Spirit creates these characteristics and other gifts in us.

➤7 **word of truth**—Cf. 4:2; Colossians 1:5. **power of God**—See 4:7; 1 Corinthians 2:4. **armour of righteousness**—which in Ephesians 6:14 is only the breastplate, but here is the complete suit of armor.

➤8 **honour and dishonour**—glory and disgrace. **evil report . . . good report**—Paul was alluding to actual words for him and against him.

➤9 **unknown . . . yet well known**—Unknown is our true character to those who report evil about us, well known to those who report well of us. **dying . . . we live**—See 1:9; 4:10, 11;

➤11:23. **chastened, and not killed**—See Psalm 118:18.

➤10 **making many rich**—spiritually (1 Cor. 1:5), after the example of Christ, who by his poverty, made many rich (8:9). **having nothing**—This means not claiming possession of any earthly goods (1 Cor. 7:30). **possessing all things**—The Greek implies firm possession, holding fast in possession (cf. 1 Cor. 3:21, 22). Things both of the present and of the future belong to the Christian as he possesses Christ.

➤11 **our mouth is open unto you, our heart is enlarged**—Paul was not holding back anything from the Corinthians as they had accused him of doing (4:2). The enlargement of his heart toward them (7:3) produced his openness of mouth, i.e., his unreserved expression of his inmost feelings. Because of his great love for them, he overlooked their many faults (cf. 1 Kings 4:29; Ps. 119:32; Isa. 60:5).

➤12 Anything left unfulfilled in their love was not Paul's fault but theirs (cf. 12:15). **bowels**—affections. The Greek considered "bowels" as the place of deepest emotions.

➤13 This verse could be translated, "As a recompense in the same kind . . . be enlarged also yourselves" (Ellicott).

➤14 **Be ye not unequally yoked**—The image is from the law (Lev. 19:19: "Do not mate your cattle with a different kind," or Deut. 22:10: "Don't plow with an ox and a donkey harnessed together," TLB). **with unbelievers**—The Christian and the non-Christian are so different that close relationships between them are warned against (6:16; 1 Cor. 8:10; 10:14). Cf. Deuteronomy 7:3, forbidding marriages with the heathen; also 1 Corinthians 7:39. **fellowship**—participation, share (Gk., *metochē*). **righteousness with unrighteousness**—lit., "lawlessness." **communion**—fellowship (Gk., *koinōnia*). **light with darkness**—Cf. John 1:4, 5; 1 John 1:5-7.

➤15 **Belial**—The word means "worthlessness" or "the place from which there is no ascent" (i.e., the abyss or Sheol). The name was used in Jewish literature as an appellation of the devil (Harris). Thus, Paul was saying that there is no **concord** (lit., "symphony") between Christ and the devil.

➤16 **agreement**—Cf. 1 Kings 18:21; Ephesians 5:7, 11. **the temple of God**—This is composed of Christians (1 Cor. 3:16; 6:19). **I** will dwell in them, and walk in [among] them—This is taken from Leviticus 26:11, 12. and I will be their God, and they shall be my people—An oft-repeated statement in Scripture (Exod. 6:7; Lev. 26:12; Jer. 32:38; Ezek. 37:27).

➤17 This verse is taken from Isaiah 52:11, adapted by Paul to the Corinthians' situation. The Isaiah passage speaks of separation from Babylon and its pagan idolatry; this passage calls for separation from unbelievers and pagan idolatry (see Harris). be ye separate—Cf. Hosea 4:17. touch not the unclean thing—This was anything impure according to law (7:1; Mic. 2:10). "Touching" implies more participation than does "seeing." I will receive you—Persons who have been shut out are now admitted within (5:1-10; cf. Ezek. 20:41; Zeph. 3:19).

➤18 And will be a Father unto you, and ye shall be my sons and daughters—This is adapted from 2 Samuel 7:14 (with changes from the singular to the plural and the addition of "and daughters"). The expression "sons and daughters" could have been drawn from Isaiah 43:6. The quotation in 2 Samuel 7:14, usually applied to Christ, is here applied to those united to Christ. saith the Lord Almighty—See 2 Samuel 7:27 (LXX). The relationship here described between God and his people (as Father and children) is more intimate than that described in 6:16.

Chapter 7

1-16 PAUL'S ENCOURAGEMENT CONCERNING THE CORINTHIANS WHEN HE HEARD THE GOOD NEWS FROM TITUS

➤1 cleanse ourselves—This is the conclusion of the exhortation begun in 6:1. filthiness—pollution (cf. 6:17). of the flesh—Fornication, for example, was prevalent in Corinth (1 Cor. 6:15-18). and spirit—This may refer to direct or indirect idolatry (1 Cor. 6:9; 8:1, 7, 21). The spirit becomes unclean by means of the flesh. perfecting holiness—bringing holiness to its proper completion in our lives (see 1 John 3:3; Rev. 22:11). fear of God—This is often associated with the most glorious promises (see 5:11; Heb. 4:1).

➤2 Receive us—with enlarged hearts (6:13). we have wronged . . . corrupted . . . defrauded no man—Cf. 7:9. Paul can thus ask the Corinthians to open their hearts to him. No one has been wronged by any unnecessary exercise of his apostolic authority (7:13), nor been led astray by a false gospel (11:3, 4); no one has been cheated or taken advantage of (12:17). Paul had suffered a great deal on behalf of the Corinthians (7:9, 12; 12:13).

➤3 I speak not this to condemn you—Paul was not excusing himself by accusing the Corinthians. I have said before—See 6:11, 12; cf. Philippians 1:7. die and live with you—This implies the deepest friendship (Phil. 1:7, 20, 24; 2:17, 18; cf. John 10:11).

➤4 boldness of speech—See 6:11. glorying [boasting] of you—Paul was proud to speak openly about the Corinthians to others. filled with comfort—or, encouragements. Paul was encouraged by the report he heard from Titus as to how they were getting along (7:6, 7, 9, 13). exceeding joyful—See 7:7, 9, 16. tribulation—described in 7:5; also in 4:7, 8; 6:4, 5.

➤5 This relates to 2:12, 13 where Paul had no rest in his spirit. Paul had no rest from his circumstances (1 Cor. 5:12), nor from his fears concerning the Corinthians and the false apostles (11:26; cf. 4:8 and Deut. 32:25, to which Paul seems to allude).

➤6, 7 Titus was happy to tell about the Corinthians (7:13), and Paul was glad to hear. earnest desire—Greek, longing desire, viz., to see Paul (Grotius). mourning—over the sin which led to my rebuke (cf. 1 Cor. 5:1ff.). fervent mind—zeal (see 7:11). toward me—On his behalf, they were zealous against the sin for which Paul had rebuked them.

➤8 a letter—This refers to 1 Corinthians, or perhaps another letter which is now lost (see Introduction and comments on 2:4). repent—actually, "regret." The Greek words for "repent" and "regret" are distinct. Paul, with parental tenderness, regretted having used rebukes calculated to grieve the Corinthians; but once he had learned the good effects it produced in them, he no longer regretted it.

➤9 ye sorrowed—or, ye were made sorry. after a godly manner—lit., "according to God." Regard for God makes us conform to his will (Rom. 14:22; 1 Pet. 4:6). Fortunately, no damage was done.

➤**10 godly sorrow worketh repentance to salvation not to be repented of**—i.e., "a salvation that leads to repentance and brings no regret" (RSV). Repentance implies making things right; regret merely makes a person feel uneasy. Repentance involves regret, but regret is not always accompanied by repentance. It is natural to regret the consequences of evil, without repenting of the deed itself, so that no sooner is the pain gone than the evil is once again being enjoyed (Exod. 9:27, 28-30; 1 Sam. 15:23-30; cf. Isa. 9:13; Matt. 26:75; Rev. 16:10, 11). In the end, the sorrow of the world just leads to death (see Matt. 27:3-5. TLB).

➤**11** The Corinthians can confirm 7:10 by their own experience. **carefulness**—This implies diligence in settling a matter which has been neglected. **indignation**—against the offender. **fear**—of God's anger, of sin, and of Paul (1 Cor. 4:19-21). **vehement desire** [longing]—Their longing was a natural result of their deep love. They wanted to restore Paul's approval and enjoy his presence among them again (1 Cor. 4:19; 16:5). **revenge**—in exacting punishment (1 Cor. 5:2, 3). **ye have approved** [proved] **yourselves to be clear in this matter**—whatever suspicion was on you before, you have completely removed by making things right (1 Cor. 5:2, 6).

➤**12 I wrote unto you**—See note on 2:4. **not for his cause that had done the wrong, nor for his cause that suffered wrong**—It used to be thought that this referred to the incestuous brother and the one he wronged. But who was the one he wronged? It could not be the stepmother, who was the adulteress, because the participle here is masculine, not feminine. It was probably not Paul, although some have argued for this. It was more likely the father, but some have said that he was deceased (see Alford). If, in fact, the letter mentioned here was not First Corinthians, we could imagine that Paul's letter must have dealt with two men, one an offender and the other, offended. **our care for you**—This is the reading in the earliest manuscripts (the Chester Beatty Papyrus, P46, and Codex Vaticanus); other early manuscripts read, "your care for us."

➤**13** This verse should be constructed as in most modern versions (see RSV, TEV, NIV)—

with a new paragraph beginning after, "Therefore we are comforted." The next statement begins a new thought: "And besides our own comfort we rejoiced still more at the joy of Titus, because his mind has been set at rest by you all" (RSV).

➤**14 I am not ashamed**—They treated Titus just as Paul had told him they would. **we spake all things to you in truth**—As my speaking in general to you was true (1:18), so what I told Titus about you was proved true by his report (9:2).

➤**15 his inward affection is more abundant toward you**—Cf. 6:12; Philippians 1:8; 2:1; Colossians 3:12. **obedience**—See 2:9. **with fear and trembling ye received him**—They were anxious to obey Paul's wishes and concerned that they not offend Paul or Titus (7:11; cf. 1 Cor. 2:3).

➤**16 I have confidence in you in all things**—This report healed his former doubts.

*Chapter* **8**

1-24 THE COLLECTION FOR THE SAINTS

➤**1 the grace of God bestowed on the churches of Macedonia**—The liberal giving of the Macedonians was not from their natural inclinations but God's blessing, enabling them to share with others (8:6, 9). Paul hoped that a gift from the Corinthians for the Jewish Christians in Jerusalem might reconcile him to the Judaizing Christians.

➤**2 trial of affliction**—The Greek expresses, "affliction which tested them." **the abundance of their joy and their deep poverty abounded unto the riches of their liberality**—The greater the depth of their poverty, the greater the abundance of their joy. Their poverty did not produce less giving, but rather more—a triumph of spirit over flesh.

➤**3, 4** The Macedonian contribution must have included the church at Philippi, because that was the only church that contributed to Paul's support (Phil. 4:10, 15, 16). Verse four is made clearer in modern versions: "they urgently pleaded with us for the privilege of sharing in this service to the saints" (NIV).

➤**5 first**—This act was not "first" in time but in importance. The giving of themselves to the Lord and to the apostles took precedence and motivated their other gifts (Rom. 15:16).

➤**6 Insomuch that**—Paul urged the Corinthians not to be outdone by the Macedonians' liberality. **Titus, that as he had** [previously] **begun**—Titus had begun to collect gifts from the Corinthians on his recent trip. **finish in you the same grace**—complete among you this act of grace.

➤**7 faith**—See 1:24. **utterance**—See 1 Corinthians 1:5. **knowledge**—See 1 Corinthians 8:1.

➤**9 ye know the grace of our Lord Jesus Christ**—the act of gratuitous love whereby the Lord emptied himself of his previous heavenly glory (Phil. 2:6, 7). **he became poor**—Compared to the sacrifice that Christ made, any gift of ours is a small sacrifice. **might be rich**—enriched with the unsearchable riches of Christ (Eph. 3:8).

➤**10 I give my advice**—Paul wanted to avoid making a command so that their giving could be free and spontaneous. **who have begun before . . . a year ago**—The Corinthians had the idea of making a contribution almost a year before the Macedonians made their contribution. Probably the Corinthians wanted to save for a year before making a contribution (1 Cor. 16:2).

➤**11** Christians should, in their projects, show the same zeal to begin and finish well, as the worldly do (Jer. 44:25).

➤**12 a willing mind**—lit., "readiness." Paul is testing their willing readiness (8:11). **according to that a man hath**—Give according to what you have. We are judged according to what we do when we have the opportunity (9:7; 1 Kings 8:18; Mark 14:8; Luke 21:3).

➤**13** The golden rule is to love our neighbor as we love ourselves, not more than we love ourselves.

➤**14** The reference here is only to physical needs and supplies (see Rom. 15:27).

➤**15** This verse comes from Exodus 16:18 (LXX). God gave an equal portion to all of the Israelites, whether they could gather much or little. No one should be in need while others have more than they need.

➤**16** This verse returns to the subject of 8:6. Titus had the same concern for the Corinthians as Paul had. Paul had asked Titus to visit them again, and he had readily agreed (8:6, 17).

➤**18 the brother, whose praise is in the gospel**—Paul may be speaking of Luke, for he was well known throughout the churches at that time (Acts 20:6). 2 Corinthians 9:4 implies that he was not a Macedonian. Luke was prominent because he had been with Paul when he first preached in Europe (Acts 16:10). The man referred to was elected by the churches (8:19) to travel with Paul in bringing the gifts to Jerusalem, which implies that he had lived there for some time. This was true of Luke, who, after leaving Paul six years earlier in Philippi (Acts 16), was now with him again in Macedonia (cf. 12:18; Philem. 24).

➤**19 not that only**—He was not only praised by the churches, but was elected by them. **chosen**—This was done by a show of hands (as indicated by the Greek word *cheirotoneō*—lit., "to stretch out the hand"; the same word appears in Acts 14:23). **of the churches**—Paul's companions were messengers or representatives of the churches (8:23). **to travel**—to Jerusalem. **your ready mind**—should read, "our ready mind." Paul was given a companion in this collection to guard against suspicions which would injure his reputation as a Christian. Any one person would have been hesitant to undertake this task for fear of suspicion (8:20), but together they were willing and ready.

➤**21** This verse is taken from Proverbs 3:4 in the Septuagint (quoted also in Rom. 12:17).

➤**22 we have sent with them our brother**—This was probably Trophimus, an Ephesian who went with Titus on his first trip there.

➤**23 brethren**—the two mentioned in 8:18, 22. **messengers**—In Greek this is "apostles" ("sent ones"). See note on Acts 14:14. **of the churches**—They represented the churches (cf. Phil. 2:25). The title seems to be derived from an officer in the synagogue known as the "angel of the church" (Rev. 2:1).

➤**24 show ye to them**—This is the reading in some early manuscripts; others read, "continue showing to them . . . "

# 9
*Chapter*

## 1-15 REASONS WHY TITUS WAS SENT
The reward of giving generously.

➤**1 For**—This verse relates to 8:16.

➤**2 a year ago**—They sent money in

response to Paul's former request (1 Cor. 16:1, 2). **your zeal**—This was generated for the good of others. **provoked**—or, stimulated.

►**3 the brethren**—Titus and the two others (8:18, 22). **our boasting . . . in vain**—an empty boast.

►**4 unprepared**—with their collections and gifts (9:2). **confident boasting**—According to the earliest manuscripts, it reads, "confidence." NEB reads, " . . . after all the confidence we have shown."

►**5 had notice before**—had promised before.

►**6 bountifully**—lit., "for blessings." This saying has the ring of being a well-known proverb or adage, but its OT source cannot be found.

►**7 Every man . . . as he purposeth** [chooses] **in his heart**—A gift should be freely given, and not made under pressure (Prov. 22:9; 11:25; Isa. 32:8).

►**8 all grace**—This includes external goods, as one gives to others (Bengel). God gives to us so that we can give to others. **having all sufficiency**—They should not need the help of others. **may abound to every good work**—This would be their "seed sown" (9:10).

►**9 it is written**—See Psalm 112:9. **He**—the good man (Ps. 112:5). **dispersed**—He gives openly and is not concerned with whom he is giving to. **the poor**—By this word the Greek usually means one so poor as to live by begging. **his righteousness**—or, beneficience: the evidence of his righteousness before God and man (cf. Deut. 24:13; Matt. 6:1).

►**10** This verse is clearer when translated, as in Isaiah 55:10, "He that ministereth [supplies] seed to the sower and bread for food [lit., 'bread for eating']." **minister**—rather, future tense ("will minister"). **seed**—This is the means for liberal giving. **fruits of your righteousness**—This is the reward for goodness and love (Matt. 10:42; see also Hos. 10:12; Matt. 5:6; 6:33).

►**11 through us**—They would serve as ministers of the Corinthians' gifts.

►**12** This verse is better translated: "for the rendering of this service not only supplies the wants of the saints but also overflows in many thanksgivings to God" (RSV).

►**13 experiment**—actually, "experimental proof." Your giving is experimental proof of

your professed Christian character. **your professed subjection**—lit., "the submission of your confession"—to Christ's gospel. This refers to the Corinthians' beliefs which were based on the gospel which Paul had brought to them, and on their independent study of Scripture. **liberal distribution**—liberal contribution.

►**14** This verse is better translated: "while they long for you and pray for you, because of the surpassing grace of God in you" (RSV).

►**15 unspeakable** [indescribable] **gift**—This includes all other inferior gifts (8:9; Rom. 8:32). If we receive from God an indescribably wonderful gift, then we should be willing to give a few temporal gifts for his sake.

# Chapter 10

## 1-18 PAUL'S DEFENSE OF HIS APOSTOLIC MINISTRY AND AUTHORITY

►**1 I Paul**—He no longer refers to "us" or "our" (cf. 9:11). **beseech you by the meekness and gentleness of Christ**—Paul mentions "gentleness" (Ps. 18:35; Matt. 11:29), as he was particularly hated for having that quality (Grotius). Although his natural inclination was to be gentle, he would become more severe if necessary. "Meekness" is more in the mind internally; "gentleness" in the external behavior, and in relation to others (Trench). Paul attributes these qualities to Christ; therefore, his expression of them is the issue of his appropriating Christ's gentleness and meekness.

►**2 bold against some**—He could and did use his authority in this manner. **walked according to the flesh**—"acting in worldly fashion" (RSV). Those at Corinth who were against Paul judged him as though he were influenced by worldly motives, the desire for favor, or the fear of offending someone.

►**3** They should listen to Paul's gentle request (10:2) so that he would not have to be harsh and rough.

►**4** Paul spoke against those who tried to further their cause by force and persecution (Luke 9:54-56). **weapons**—Paul could punish offenders (10:6; 1 Cor. 4:21; 5:5, 13); his weapons were bold speech, discipline (10:8; 13:10), the gifts of the Spirit, and the power of the Word. **mighty through God**—God is divinely powerful and sometimes directs this power through the life of an individual. **pulling down**—10:5; cf. Jeremiah 1:10. **strong holds**—Cf. Proverbs 21:22. Evil men shield themselves from the knowledge that they are wrong. Their learning, their eloquence, and their philosophical and psychological subtleties could all operate as defenses, or as tools for winning others to their position.

➤**5 Casting down imaginations**—overthrowing reasonings. Judaic self-righteousness, philosophic speculations and theories, and rhetorical sophistries were valued by many and threatened the Corinthian church. Paul needed to cast them down. **high thing**—not "height," but "something that makes itself high." The thought is captured well in the NIV: "every pretension that sets itself up against the knowledge of God." **exalteth itself against the knowledge of God**—This was also spoken of "the lawless one" (2 Thess. 2:4). **bringing into captivity every thought to the obedience of Christ**—True knowledge of God makes men humble; false knowledge makes them proud. Thus it is necessary to obey Christ in both thought and action. The three steps to the warfare that Paul was fighting were: (1) to destroy what was opposed to Christ; (2) to take captive those who were instruments of that opposition; and (3) to bring them into obedience to Christ (Rom. 1:5; 16:26).

➤**6 when your obedience is fulfilled**—Paul assumed that most of the Corinthian church would be obedient, but that some might choose to act otherwise. In order to give them all a fair chance, he would wait before punishing them (see Acts 18:6-11; cf. Exod. 32:34; Matt. 13:28-30).

➤**7 Do ye look on things after the outward appearance**—You look only at such things as letters of recommendation, personal appearance, voice, manners, and speaking ability. The false apostles had all these qualities, and they were admired by the people for them (10:10; cf. 5:12). **as he is Christ's**—referring perhaps to a particular Judaizer (see 11:22). **even so are we Christ's**—Paul modestly demanded for himself only an equal place with those whom he had begotten in the gospel (Bengel).

➤**8 though I should boast somewhat more of our authority**—He had authority as an apostle (10:6; 13:10). **for edification, and**

**not for your destruction**—Paul continues the image from 10:4, 5. He did not want to knock down false arguments simply for the sake of destruction, but to *really* build up ("edify") by removing those things which are hindrances to edification, and testing what is sound, and putting together all that is true in the building (Chrysostom).

➤**9** Paul could have used empty threats to frighten the Corinthians into obedience as though they were children (see 10:10, 11).

➤**10 letters**—The plural implies that more than one critical letter (1 Corinthians) had already been sent to the Corinthians. **say they**—actually, "he says." The Greek suggests that Paul was referring to a particular individual (cf. 10:7; Gal. 5:10). **his bodily presence is weak**—See 12:7; 1 Corinthians 2:3. Paul was rather humble and at times was timid among them; there was nothing to suggest majesty or authority in his manner. The false apostles, however, were quite authoritative and eloquent.

➤**12** The false charge that Paul recommends himself (3:1; 5:12) does apply to the false apostles. **compare ourselves with some that commend themselves . . . measuring themselves by themselves**—They do not measure themselves by a common standard, but only by each other. Thus, they all have high self-esteem. **are not wise**—They boasted of their "wisdom" (1 Cor. 1:19-26), but in reality they were anything but wise.

➤**13 not boast . . . without . . . measure**—There is no limit to a man's high opinion of himself, as long as he compares himself only with himself (10:13) or his fellows, none of which is superior. It is interesting to note that the word "boast" occurs 29 times in this letter and only 26 times in all of Paul's other letters combined. Paul wanted to support his authority with facts (10:15). **according to the measure of the rule . . . a measure to reach even unto you**—Paul's measure was the apportionment of his sphere of gospel labors ruled (or, measured) for him by God. For Paul, this included working with the Corinthians, but did not end there (10:16; Rom. 15:20-24). God had appointed Paul as the apostle for Corinth, and he was also responsible for approving and disciplining all ministers in the various local churches that were under his guidance.

►14 This verse is better translated: "For we are not overextending ourselves, as though we did not reach you . . . " (RSV). Paul had not over-used his authority. Had he not brought the gospel to them, he would not have had this authority.

►15 when your faith is increased . . . we shall be enlarged—Paul could not travel beyond Corinth at that time because of their immature faith. As he did not want to postpone further preaching for very long, his success in building up their faith was an important step in taking the gospel to areas beyond them. according to our rule—"within the limits set for us" (TLB). Paul would operate only according to God's plan and the authority that God had given him (10:14).

►16 another man's line of things— "another man's territory" (NIV). Paul was speaking of overstepping the boundaries for which God had made him responsible (10:4).

►17 he that glorieth [boasts], let him glory in the Lord—The false apostles boasted instead about what they had accomplished (1 Cor. 1:31; 15:10).

►18 whom the Lord commendeth—See Proverbs 27:2. is approved—can stand the test of the final trial, a metaphor from testing metals (Rom. 16:10; 1 Cor. 11:19).

## Chapter 11

### 1-33 PAUL AND THE FALSE APOSTLES

►1 bear with me—i.e., I hope that I am not unreasonable in asking you to put up with me (11:4, 20). folly—The Greek is a milder term than that for "foolishness" in Matthew 5:22; 1 Corinthians 3:19. The Greek for "folly" here implies "imprudence"; the Greek for "foolishness" includes the idea of perversity and wickedness.

►2 I am jealous over you—Paul's concern was that the Corinthians should not be drawn away from Christ. In order to dissuade them from the teachings of the false apostles, it was necessary for him to boast in a way which would have been foolish under any circumstances. godly jealousy—Cf. 1:12. This was a jealousy which had God's honor at heart (1 Kings 19:10). I have espoused [promised in marriage] you to one husband—used an anal-

ogy of a Father giving his daughter to a husband in marriage to show his fatherly care for the Corinthians. present you as a chaste virgin to Christ—This speaks of the marriage of Christ and his church (Matt. 25:6; Rev. 19:7, 9). The singular, "virgin", was used because the whole body of Christians constitutes the bride. Paul wanted to present a blameless church to Christ (Eph. 5:27-32).

►3 I fear—Cf. 12:20. Fear is not inconsistent with love. Paul was afraid that the Christians would be taken in by the false apostles. subtilty—This means some complex and clever way, as opposed to the "simplicity and purity" of devotion to Jesus alone. Eve was seduced by the serpent's cleverness (Gen. 3:1ff.). corrupted—so as to lose one's purity to a seducer (11:4). After "simplicity," the three earliest manuscripts add, "and purity."

►4 if—According to the Greek, this introduces a situation assumed to be true. he that cometh—in the pretense of being an apostle (see note on John 10:8). preacheth another Jesus—"Another" in Greek (*allon*) implies another of the same kind; hence, another Jesus would be the same Jesus "cast in the mold of Judaistic teachings" (NIVSB). another spirit— The Greek word for "another" (*heteron*) means "different." A "different spirit" would be one other than the Holy Spirit (cf. 1 John 4:1-3). another gospel—a gospel different from the one Paul preached. The Corinthians had little excuse for listening to a different gospel from the one Paul had taught them (Gal. 1:6ff.), because the false apostles didn't even pretend to be teaching the same things. They merely sought leadership and recognition among the people who were actually preferring them to Paul.

►5 chiefest apostles—lit., "super apostles." This sarcasm was directed at the false apostles, not the true apostles of God.

►6 rude [unskilled] in speech—Paul was not trained in rhetoric or skilled in diction (1 Cor. 2:1-4, 13; 2 Cor. 10:10, 11), yet he possessed special knowledge (see 12:1-5; Eph. 3:1-5). we have been throughly [thoroughly] made manifest among you in all things— They had made the truth of the gospel clear, thus proving their knowledge. Paul had not withheld any of his spiritual knowledge from them (2:17; 4:2; cf. Acts 20:20, 27).

➤**7 Have I committed an offence in abasing myself**—continuing the thought of the previous verse. The Corinthians could not object to his self-abasing, for it was proof of his superiority over the false apostles (see 1 Cor. 9:6-15). **freely**—without charge.

➤**8 I robbed**—Paul took from other churches in order to spare the Corinthians their share in his support. **other churches**—The church at Philippi was one example (Phil. 4:15, 16). Paul brought supplies with him for use while he ministered at Corinth, and when those supplies ran out he received more from the Philippians.

➤**9 chargeable**—lit., "to grow torpid," to be a dead weight upon, to be burdensome. **the brethren which came from Macedonia supplied**—Probably Timothy and Silas (Acts 18:1, 5) came with more supplies and donations from the Philippian churches.

➤**10 no man shall stop me of this boasting**—actually, "this boasting shall not be stopped."

➤**12** This verse should be translated: "And I will keep on doing what I am doing in order to cut the ground from under those who want an opportunity to be considered equal with us in the things they boast about" (NIV). Paul would continue preaching the gospel without charge, for, in fact, this made his adversaries look bad and took away their accusations in this matter. Had Paul preached for money he would be on the same level as they.

➤**13** Paul did not want to be thought of in the same way as the false apostles. **false apostles**—the "super apostles" mentioned in 11:5. **deceitful workers**—They pretended to be working for Christ, but were really working for themselves.

➤**14 Satan himself is transformed** [transforms himself] **into an angel of light**—Cf. Job 1:16. Satan can easily wear an attractive front, as he did with Eve in the garden of Eden. If Satan, the master of darkness and of all evil men, can change himself so drastically, then it is not surprising that his servants would do so also (Luke 22:53; Eph. 6:12).

➤**15 also**—as Satan. **be transformed**—transform themselves. **ministers of righteousness**—counterfeiting the true righteousness which is realized by faith in Christ. **end**—In the end, all things will be tested. Superficial forms

will be taken away and everything will be seen for what it really is (cf. Phil. 3:19, 21). **according to their works**—Their punishment will be based on their deeds and not on their present pretenses.

➤**16 I say again**—Paul now apologizes for his boasting. **if otherwise**—The Corinthians may think that Paul is a fool. **yet as a fool**—The Greek suggests one who does not properly use his mental abilities, and yet is not necessarily to blame for this condition.

➤**17 I speak it not after** [according to] **the Lord**—Even this boasting of Paul's, though undesirable, was permitted by the Spirit, for Paul's motive was to draw the Corinthians away from the false apostles.

➤**18 many glory** [boast] **after the flesh**—They boast of themselves. **I will glory also**—Paul was also boasting of such worldly advantages, to show that even in these things he was not inferior to the false apostles, but deserved the Corinthians' respect. However, these were not the things that Paul really wanted to boast about (cf. 10:17).

➤**19 gladly**—This means "willingly." This was a plea for the Corinthians to bear with Paul in his foolishness.

➤**20 suffer**—bear with. **bring you into bondage**—This was not a hypothetical case, but what was actually happening. The Judaizers were enslaving the Corinthians to the legalities of Judaism (cf. Gal. 4:1-10). **exalt himself**—They pretended to be dignified and to deserve respect as teachers. **smite you on the face**—This was the height of disrespect on their part and of submission and endurance on the Corinthians' part (see 1 Kings 22:24; Neh. 13:25; Luke 22:64; Acts 23:2; 1 Tim. 3:3).

➤**21 reproach**—He is referring to the reproachful acts mentioned in 11:20. **as though we had been weak**—Paul is saying that he can only be strong and daring by abstaining from such selfish acts.

➤**22 Hebrews**—This refers to both the language and the nationality. **Israelites**—This refers to the government and the descent from Israel. **seed of Abraham**—This refers to the people who had a share in the messianic promises (Rom. 9:7; 11:1). (Cf. Phil. 3:5.) This verse shows that the false apostles were Jews, elsewhere called Judaizers.

➤**23 as a fool**—According to the Greek, "as beside myself." This term is stronger than "fool." Paul had more to show for his ministry than the false apostles did. **in stripes . . . in prisons**—See Acts 16:23-40 for one such example. Clement, an early writer, recorded that Paul was in prison seven times. **deaths**—frequent encounters with death (see 4:10; Acts 9:23; 13:50; 14:5, 6, 19; 17:5).

➤**24 forty stripes save** [less] **one**—According to law, not more than 40 stripes were to be inflicted (Deut. 25:3). To avoid exceeding this number, they stopped one short of it. They used a whip with three lashes on its head.

➤**25 beaten with rods**—This was done by the Roman officials. An incident of beating by the Roman officials is recorded in Acts 16:23. **stoned**—cf. Acts 14:19. **shipwreck**—This was prior to the shipwreck at Melita (Acts 27). This probably refers to some of his voyages to and from Tarsus (Acts 9:30; 11:25; Gal. 1:21).

➤**26 waters**—Greek, "rivers," probably referring to flooded rivers. The road between Jerusalem and Antioch, which Paul traveled frequently, was often flooded with waters coming down from Lebanon. **robbers**—This may refer to Paul's trip from Perga to Antioch in Pisidia. Pisidia, like all the mountain lands dividing Asia from the sea, was infested with robbers. **in the city**—Damascus, Acts 9:24, 25; Jerusalem, Acts 9:29; Ephesus, Acts 19:23. **false brethren**—See Gal. 2:4.

➤**27 fastings**—This context refers only to going without food because there was none. In other places fasting is mentioned as a means of devotion (Acts 13:2, 3; 14:23; 1 Cor. 9:27), but here Paul is solely concerned with the hardships of his work. **in cold and nakedness**—This resulted from insufficient clothing (Acts 28:2; Rom. 8:35; 2 Tim. 4:13). Paul was also constantly suffering from poor health (4:7-12; 12:7-10; Gal. 4:13, 14).

➤**28 that which cometh upon me daily**—the daily pressures. **the care of all the churches**—In addition to these external hardships, Paul was heavily burdened with concern for the churches in his care.

➤**29 Who is weak, and I am not weak?**—"Care generates sympathy, which causes the minister of Christ personally to enter into the feelings of all his people, as if he stood in their position, so as to accommodate himself to all"

(Calvin). **who is offended, and I burn not?**—Paul took up a brother's cause as though it were his own.

➤**30 I will glory** [boast] **of . . . mine infirmities** [weakness]—Paul preferred to boast about what others would consider his weak points. This character was completely incompatible with the zealous enthusiasm of the false apostles (12:5, 9, 10).

➤**31 God . . . knoweth that I lie not**—This solemn assertion refers to what follows, for Paul's escape from Damascus was done in secret (Acts 9:25). Only God could witness to the veracity of what Paul now says (in 11:32, 33).

➤**32** See Acts 9:24. **governor**—Greek "ethnarch," a Jewish officer to whom Gentile rulers gave authority over Jews in large cities where they were numerous. In this case he was under Aretas, king of the Nabatean Arabs from 9 B.C. to A.D. 40. King Aretas was father-in-law of Herod Antipas. "The Roman emperor Caligula may have given Damascus to Aretas since it was once part of his territory" (*NIVSB*).

➤**33** See Acts 9:25.

*Chapter* **12**

## 1-10 PAUL'S VISIONS AND THORN IN THE FLESH

➤**1** Paul proceeds to talk about his weaknesses (11:30). He had given one example for which he might be called a fool (11:33). He then gives another example which is connected with a revelation from God. He doesn't talk about the glory of the vision, but about his weakness following the experience. **visions . . . revelations**—"Visions" refer to things which are seen; "revelations" may be heard or revealed in any way (1 Sam. 9:15). The significance of visions was not always clear; in revelations, some truth that had been hidden was revealed (Dan. 2:19, 31).

➤**2 a man**—Paul purposely used this less personal term to imply that there was a great difference between the weak, sick person that he was in the flesh and the glorified person that he was in his revelation. He realized that his body with all its weakness was temporary, whereas his spiritual self would endure (Rom. 7:25). **in Christ**—a Christian. **above** [before] **fourteen years ago**—This letter was written around A.D. 56. The time of Paul's vision was earlier than A.D. 42, perhaps during his second visit to Jerusalem (Acts 22:17). He had known the Corinthians closely for a long time, yet had never mentioned this revelation, which was not something to be taken lightly. **caught up to the third heaven**—Paul was taken "to the third heaven" first, and from there to paradise (12:4). The first heaven refers to the clouds or the air; the second to the stars and the sky, and the third to a spiritual realm (Eph. 4:10). Christ himself had passed through the heavens (Heb. 4:14) and been exalted higher than the heavens (Eph. 4:10; Heb. 7:26). Paul was permitted to hear and see some of the things in the third heaven. **whether in the body, . . . I cannot tell**—I do not know. Paul seemed to think that his spirit was taken up to heaven, apart from his body.

➤**4 he was caught up into paradise**—Most commentators say that "paradise" here is synonymous with "the third heaven" of 12:2. Both the verbs in 12:2 and 12:4 are identical in the Greek, and usually reflect the idea of being "caught away," not necessarily "caught up." Of course, Paul was "caught up" to the third heaven. But was he caught up to paradise? It all depends on where we locate paradise, which is difficult, if not impossible, to do. The word itself means "garden" or "park," and was used as such in Nehemiah 2:8; Ecclesiastes 2:5; and Song of Songs 4:13. The garden of Eden in the Septuagint is called *paradeisos* (Gen. 2:8). In later Jewish thought, writers would speak of paradise as the place of the righteous, departed dead in Sheol. Jesus perhaps alluded to this in his story of Lazarus going to Abraham in Luke 16:19-31. And when Jesus spoke to the thief on the cross, he promised him that he would, that day, be with him in paradise (Luke 23:43). This again seems to indicate a pleasant place among the dead. But the promise of paradise in Revelation 2:7 speaks of the restitution of an Edenic paradise (cf. Gen. 2 and Rev. 22) (*NBD*). Here, the paradise Paul spoke of was either the place of the departed, righteous dead (to which he was *caught away*) or the third heaven (to which he was *caught up*). If we accept the former, 12:3, 4 describes a different experience from that in 12:2; if we accept the latter, 12:3, 4 redescribes the same experience as 12:2. **heard unspeakable words**—Paul was able to understand what he saw and heard, so they were not beyond man's comprehension. They were for

Paul's own benefit, however, and were not to be communicated to others. Some heavenly words are communicable (Exod. 34:6; Isa. 6:3), but others are strictly private (John 3:12; 1 Cor. 2:9). We may know and hear more than we are able to speak.

➤**5** Paul's boasting about the spiritual, glorified self in his visions was done to show by contrast the weakness of his earthly body so that Christ would receive all the glory.

➤**6 I shall not be a fool**—If Paul wanted to boast about himself, he had plenty to boast about and would be fooling no one with false stories. **think**—"form an estimate of me." Paul wanted the Corinthians to evaluate him on the basis of what they had seen him do and heard him say, rather than on past achievements (cf. John 5:44; 12:43).

➤**7 exalted above measure**—Self-praise is a dangerous sin; great precautions were taken especially by the apostles to avoid it. **a thorn in the flesh**—The same expression was used in the OT (Num. 33:55; Ezek. 28:24). This may be the same sickness that Paul mentions in Galatians 4:13, 14 (Alford). It certainly was something that affected him personally and not just as an apostle. **the messenger of Satan**—God permits Satan to bring pain upon his saints (Job 2:7; Luke 13:16). Paul received a message from a heavenly angel, but was also subject to distress from an evil angel. **to buffet me**—present tense in Greek: "to continually buffet me."

➤**8** There was no answer to his first and second prayers, but after his third prayer he was answered and completely submitted his will to God's. The sickness seems to have been continually with Paul as a reminder of his mortality.

➤**9 My grace is sufficient for thee**—Paul had to endure suffering, but he also experienced God's limitless grace (cf. Deut. 33:25). **strength**—or, power. **made perfect**—has its most perfect manifestation. **in weakness**—God's power is best seen through man's weakness. Paul's sickness was the circumstance which caused him to draw the most on Christ's power. Christ's assurance to him appears in 4:7; 1 Cor. 2:3, 4; cf. 1 Pet. 4:14. Paul often repeats the word "weakness" in chapters 11, 12, and 13, suggesting that Christ can use our weaknesses as well as our strengths. God's way is not to take us out of every trial but to give us the strength to endure (Ps. 88:7; John 17:15). **the power of Christ may rest upon me**—lit.,

Christ's power may "tabernacle over me," i.e., cover my infirmities as with a tabernacle.

➤**10 when I am weak, then am I strong**— See 13:4; Heb. 11:34.

### 11-34 PAUL'S CONCERN FOR THE CORINTHIANS

➤**11 I ought to have been commended of you**—The Corinthians should have been recommending Paul rather than forcing him to recommend himself. **though I be nothing**— See 1 Corinthians 15:9, 10.

➤**12 the signs of an apostle were wrought among you in** [with] **all patience**—Paul endured opposition and did not leave his work on account of it. Paul was the instrument of signs and wonders, but he did not do them by himself. **signs . . . wonders . . . mighty deeds**—This is one of the few instances in the apostle's letters where miracles are mentioned. The apostles generally regarded doctrine as more important than the mighty works which they did. The purpose of the apostolic epistles was not to cause controversy or to make impressions, but to be instructional and encouraging. When miracles were mentioned by the apostles, they were given as common knowledge which did not require further explanation.

➤**13 I myself was not burdensome to you**— Paul may have been denying the Corinthians a privilege by not asking them for support. It may have been a mark of their spiritual inferiority or of Paul's lack of confidence in them (11:9, 11).

➤**14 the third time**—His second visit was probably a short one (1 Cor. 16:7), during which time he was humiliated by the conduct of some of the church members (cf. 12:21). **I seek not yours, but you**—See Phil. 4:17. **children . . . parents**—Paul was their spiritual father (1 Cor. 4:14, 15). He did not want earthly treasures from them, but was concerned with laying up spiritual treasures for them (12:15).

➤**15 I will very gladly spend**—all that I have. **be spent**—all that I am. Most parents will exert effort to acquire things for their children, but Paul was also ready to give up himself.

➤**16** Some of the Corinthians thought that although Paul had not taken their money, he had taken advantage of them in some other way (1 Thess. 2:3).

➤**17** This is Paul's reply to 12:16. Neither Paul nor his associates were at all interested in taking advantage of the Corinthians.

➤**18 I desired** [urged] **Titus**—to visit you. Paul was referring to a visit made before this letter was written (8:6, 17, 22). It was probably from this trip that Titus had just returned with the good news of their change (7:6-16). **a brother**—This is probably the man mentioned in 8:18, 22 (see notes).

➤**20 For**—This is the reason that Paul had to speak to them in the way he did. **debates**—contentions. **envyings**—singular in Greek. **strifes**—factions. The Corinthians were self-seeking, contentious and scheming against one another. **backbitings, whisperings**—Cf. Galatians 5:20. **swellings**—arrogant elation (cf. Jude 16; 2 Pet. 2:18). **tumults**—disturbances.

➤**21 humble me**—The faithful leader is humbled by the sins of his people as though they were his own. **many which have sinned**—This was before his last visit to Corinth. **uncleanness**—impurity, perhaps referring to adultery (see 1 Thess. 4:6, 7). **fornication**—See 1 Corinthians 5:1. **lasciviousness**—lewdness.

*Chapter* **13**

### 1-10 PAUL CHARGES THE CORINTHIANS TO EXAMINE THEMSELVES

➤**1 This is the third time I am coming to** [visit] **you**—He was actually coming, not merely preparing to come. This proves that there was an intermediate visit between the two recorded in Acts 18:1 and 20:2. **In the mouth of two or three witnesses shall every word be established**—quoted from Deuteronomy 19:15 (LXX). Some interpret "two or three" as referring to Paul's two or three visits made to establish either (1) the truth of the charges made against the offenders, or (2) the reality of Paul's warnings to them.

➤**2 all other**[s]—This refers to persons who had sinned since Paul's second visit or who were in danger of sinning.

➤**3** It would be better for the Corinthians to prove themselves (13:5) than to ask for proof of Paul's power in miracles or in punishment (cf. 5:11, 20, 21). It is Christ whose patience was tried when Paul's authority was disregarded.

➤**4 crucified through weakness**—Greek, "crucified out of weakness." His assumption of our weakness was the source, or necessary condition, from which the crucifixion came

(Phil. 2:7, 8; Heb. 2:14). **by the power of God**—This refers to God, the Father (Rom. 1:4; 6:4; Eph. 1:20). **weak in him**—by our union with Christ, we share his weakness (see 1 Cor. 2:3; 2 Cor. 13:9). **we shall live with him**—Our union with Christ grants us participation in his resurrection life, both now and in eternity.

➤**5 Examine yourselves**—Put yourself on trial. The Christian should be more concerned about his own condition than with trying to incriminate another believer (13:3). **Jesus Christ is in you**—If a person is not indwelt by Jesus Christ, he or she is not a Christian (see Rom. 8:9,10). **except ye be reprobates**—disapproved, disqualified. The image in the Greek is of metal that has been tried and found impure (Jer. 6:30; Rom. 1:28).

➤**6 reprobates**—disapproved. The Corinthians' self-examination would, in turn, prove that their apostle was not disapproved, for they were his product, his workmanship.

➤**7 not that we should appear approved**—This was not an attempt to gain credit for themselves. **though we be as reprobates**—spoken ironically.

➤**8** Their power as God's apostles was not given for use against the truth, but to further the truth. When churches were functioning properly there was no need to exercise this power.

➤**9 glad**—"rejoice" in the Greek. **when we are weak**—They would prefer to have no occasion for using this power and thus appear weak to the power-seekers (10:10; 11:29, 30). **ye are strong**—They had faith and were doing good work. **perfection**—actually, "restoration." The Greek word indicates perfection or completion

through uniting together (1 Cor. 1:10), and fitting together (Eph. 4:12). The Corinthians needed this kind of restoration.

➤**10 to edification, and not to destruction**—See 10:8. Paul wanted to build them up, not to knock them down.

## 11-14 PAUL'S GREETINGS AND BENEDICTION

➤**11 Be perfect**—"be restored" (see comments on 13:9). The Christian grows toward perfection by filling up that which is lacking (Eph. 4:13).

➤**12** See 1 Corinthians 16:20.

➤**13 All the saints salute you**—The saints in Macedonia (the location from which Paul wrote this epistle) sent their greetings to the Corinthians.

➤**14 The grace of the Lord Jesus Christ, and the love of God, and the communion of the Holy Ghost [Spirit], be with you all**—This benediction proves the reality of the Trinity. The "grace of the Lord Jesus Christ" comes first, for this is the only way that we can come to the love of the Father (John 14:6). **communion**—fellowship. The fellowship of the Holy Spirit unites all the believers, regardless of their earthly distinctions, into one body, the church. Anyone who has the fellowship of the Holy Spirit also has the grace of Christ and the love of God, for the three cannot be separated. The Holy Spirit conveys the Father's love to us (see John 14:16-26) and brings Christ's grace to us (see Phil. 4:23, NIV; Heb. 10:29). The doctrine of the Holy Trinity was not completely revealed until Christ came. Even now we know the Three in One more in their relation to us than in their mutual relation to one another.

BIBLIOGRAPHY

Alford, Henry. *The Greek New Testament.* 1852. Reprint. Grand Rapids: Guardian Press, 1973.

Bengel, John A. *New Testament Word Studies.* 1742. Reprint. Grand Rapids: Eerdmans, 1971.

Berkhof, Hendrikus. *Doctrine of the Holy Spirit.* Atlanta: John Knox Press, 1976.

Calvin, John. *Commentary on the Epistles of Paul the Apostle to the Corinthians.* 1577. Reprint. Edinburgh: Calvin Translation Society, 1848-49.

Conybeare and Howson. *The Life and Epistles of St. Paul.* Grand Rapids: Eerdmans, 1978 (15th printing).

Ellicott, Charles J. *Commentaries, Critical and Grammatical, on the Epistles of St. Paul.* Boston: Draper, 1866.

Fensham, F. C. "Paradise" in *New Bible Dictionary.* Edited by J. D. Douglas. Wheaton: Tyndale House Publishers, 1982 (with InterVarsity Press).

Grotius, Hugo. *The Truth of the Christian Religion.* 1632.

Reprint. London: Baynes and Son, 1854.

Harris, Murray J. "Second Corinthians" in *The Expositor's Bible Commentary.* Grand Rapids: Zondervan, 1978.

Harrison, Everett. New Testament Editor, *Wycliffe Bible Commentary.* Chicago: Moody Press, 1962.

Lindsell, Harold. General Editor, *KJV Study Bible.* Wheaton: Tyndale House Publishers, 1986, 1989.

Menochius, Giovanni Steffano. *Brevis Expositio sensus litteralis totius Scripturae.* Cologne, 1630.

Moulton and Milligan. *The Vocabulary of the Greek New Testament.* Grand Rapids: Eerdmans, 1930.

Paley, William. *Horae Paulinae* (or, *The Truth of Scripture History of St. Paul*). Dublin: Printed for M'Kenzie, 1790.

Roehrs and Franzmann. *Concordia Self-Study Commentary.* St. Louis: Concordia Publishing House, 1971.

Trench, Richard. *Synonyms of the New Testament.* London: Macmillan Co., 1876.

# GALATIANS

## Introduction

The internal and external evidence for Paul's authorship is conclusive. The style is characteristically Pauline. The superscription and allusions to the apostle of the Gentiles in the first person, throughout the epistle, establish the same truth (1:1, 13-24; 2:1-14). His authorship is also upheld by the unanimous testimony of the ancient church: see Irenaeus, *Against Heresies,* 3.7.2 (cf. Gal. 3:19); Polycarp quotes 4:26 and 6:7; Justin Martyr, or whoever wrote the *Oratio and Graecos,* alludes to 4:12 and 5:20.

The epistle was written "to the churches of Galatia" (1:2), a district of Asia Minor bordering on Phrygia, Pontus, Bithynia, Cappadocia, and Paphlagonia. Most modern scholars, however, limit the area to Southern Galatia (in which were the cities Lystra, Iconium, and Derbe—visited by Paul on his second missionary journey). Other scholars (e.g., Lightfoot) have limited the area to Northern Galatia. In either case, the inhabitants (Gallo-gaerci, contracted into Galati, another form of the name Celts) were Gauls in origin, the latter having overrun Asia Minor after they had pillaged Delphi, about 280 B.C. and at last permanently settled in the central parts, thence called Gallo-gaerci or Galatia.

The Galatians received Paul at first with all joy and kindness; but soon wavered in their allegiance to the gospel and to him, and hearkened as eagerly to Judaizing teachers as they had before to him (4:14-16). The apostle himself had been the first preacher among them (Acts 16:6; Gal. 1:8; 4:13) and had then probably founded churches, which at his subsequent visit he "strengthened" in the faith (Acts 18:23). His first visit was about A.D. 51, during his second missionary journey. Josephus (*Antiquities,* 16.62) testifies that many Jews resided in Ancyra in Galatia. Among these and their brethren, doubtless, as elsewhere, he began his preaching. And though subsequently the majority in the Galatian churches were Gentiles (4:8, 9), they were soon infected by Judaizing teachers, and almost allowed themselves to be persuaded to undergo circumcision (1:6; 3:1, 3; 5:2, 3; 6:12, 13). Accustomed as the Galatians had been to the mystic worship of Cybele (prevalent in the neighboring region of Phyrgia) and the theosophical doctrines connected with that worship, they were the more readily led to believe that the full privileges of Christianity could only be attained through an elaborate system of ceremonial symbolism (4:9-11; 5:7-12). They even gave ear to the insinuation that Paul himself observed the law among the Jews, though he persuaded the Gentiles to renounce it, and that his motive was to keep his converts in a subordinate state, excluded from the full privileges of Christianity, which were enjoyed by the circumcised alone (5:11; 4:16; cf. with 2:17); and that in "becoming all things to all men," he was a flatterer (1:10), aiming at forming a party for himself; moreover, that he falsely represented himself as an apostle divinely commissioned by Christ, whereas he was but a messenger sent by the Twelve and the church at Jerusalem; and that his teaching was now at variance with that of Peter and James, "pillars" of the church, and therefore ought not to be accepted.

His purpose, then, in writing this epistle was (1) to defend his apostolic authority (1:11-19; 2:1-14); (2) to counteract the evil influence of the Judaizers in Galatia (chaps. 3 and 4), and to show that their doctrine destroyed the very *essence* of Christianity by lowering its spirituality to an outward ceremonial system; (3) to give exhortation for the strengthening of Galatian believers in faith toward Christ and in the fruits of the Spirit (chpts. 5 and 6). He had already, face to face, testified against the Judaizing teachers (1:9; 4:16; Acts 18:23); and now that he had heard of the continued and increasing prevalence of the evil, he wrote *with his own hand* (6:11; a labor which he usually delegated to an amanuensis) this epistle to oppose it. The sketch he gives in it of his apostolic career confirms and expands the account in Acts and shows his independence of human authority, however exalted.

The Epistle to the Galatians has been called "the Magna Carta of spiritual emancipation." Martin Luther called it "my own little epistle"; he said, "I have betrothed myself to it." There is much in common between this epistle and that to the Romans on the subject of justification by faith only, and not by the law. But the Epistle to the Romans handles the subject in a didactic and logical mode, without any special reference; this epistle does so in a controversial manner, and with special reference to the Judaizers in Galatia.

The style of this epistle combines the two extremes: sternness (chapter 1; 3:1-5) and tenderness (4:19, 20), the characteristics of a man of strong emotions, and both alike well suited for acting on an impressionable people such as the Galatians were. The beginning is abrupt, as was suited to the urgency of the question and the greatness of the danger. A tone of sadness, too, is apparent, such as might be expected in the letter of a warm-hearted teacher who had just learned that those whom he loved were forsaking his teachings for those of perverters of the truth, as well as giving ear to calumnies against himself.

The time of writing has been debated and is, as yet, unresolved. Much depends on whether or not the account in Gal. 2:1ff. is identical with the Jerusalem council recorded in Acts 15:1ff. If the two were the same, then Paul probably wrote this epistle in A.D. 55 or 56. If this epistle was written before the Jerusalem council (which occurred c. A.D. 50), it could well have been in A.D. 49. If so, this would have been Paul's first epistle. But the majority of modern scholars prefer the later date.

*Chapter* **1**

## 1-24 PAUL AFFIRMS THE TRUE GOSPEL, WHICH HE RECEIVED BY DIVINE REVELATION

Judaizing teachers (Jewish Christians— including both genuine and false believers— who glorified the Mosaic law above and beyond the gospel of grace) had come to the churches in Galatia and persuaded many of the people that Paul did not himself have authority to found churches, and that his teachings were in some respects limited or faulty. The real seat of authority, according to these men, was the church at Jerusalem, which had given to Paul the assignment of preaching. They further argued that regardless of what he had told them, Paul had supported circumcision upon other occasions. In order to refute these charges, Paul appealed first to his conversion, and then to his relationship with the apostles in Jerusalem. He affirmed that he did not receive his teaching from them, nor did they act as his superiors;

rather, they had simply agreed with his teaching. Since the issues dealt with are complex and specific, the letter is not a forgery, as some claim.

## 1-5 SALUTATION

➤**1 Paul, an apostle**—In the earlier letters (see Introduction for a discussion on time of writing) written to the church at Thessalonica, Paul used no such title of authority. In those letters, he mentioned the names of Silas and Timothy in connection with his own, while in this letter he only mentions "all the brethren which are with me." This has the effect of making Paul more prominent, and seems to have been done intentionally, since the letter explicitly defends Paul's missionary commission. **not of** [from] **men**—The origin of his apostleship did not come from the commission of any men. **neither by man**—neither by a human commission (see NEB). Paul's apostleship emanated from a divine source, not a human. God commissioned Paul, not the apostles in Jerusalem. **but by Jesus Christ, and God the Father**—After noting that he was not commissioned by men, Paul asserted that he had been called by God. When Ananias laid hands on Paul (Acts 9:17), he did not act as the agent for God, but merely as a sign that Paul had already been called (Acts 13:2, 3), a fact which the Holy Spirit was merely confirming to the other Christians. **who raised him from the dead**—Even though Paul had not seen Jesus Christ in his humiliation and crucifixion, a point raised against the authenticity of his authority by opponents, he had seen the risen Christ and been made an apostle by him (1 Cor. 9:1, 2; 15:8, 9). Against this background, Paul focuses on his subject: that justification comes by faith in Christ, and not by following the law.

➤**2 all the brethren which are with me**—This emphasizes the fact that Paul was not alone, but supported by a number of people traveling with him (Acts 19:29; 20:4). They were not co-authors of the letter, but did share the feelings Paul was expressing. **the churches of Galatia**—In letters to other churches, Paul had some words of commendation (1 Cor. 1:2; 1 Thess. 1:1); he has none here. He was concerned at the extent to which they had succumbed to the influence of the Judaizers. 1 Peter 1:1 has a reference to Christians living in Galatia. It is interesting to find Peter and Paul, who had been at odds (Gal. 2:7-15), in a cooperative effort to strengthen the same churches.

➤**3** According to some early manuscripts the second part of this verse should read "from God our Father and Lord Jesus Christ," but the earliest manuscripts read, "from God [the] Father and our Lord Jesus Christ." In either case, one preposition governs both nouns and thereby shows the essential unity of Father and Son.

➤**4 Who gave himself for our sins**—as an offering unto death, on our behalf, to provide for our salvation. **deliver us from this . . . evil world**—The result of the salvation provided by Christ's sacrifice is freedom from the world (cf. Col. 1:13). Paul implied that the Galatians, in returning to the requirements of the law, were rejecting their God-given liberty. The Greek word for "world" (or, "age") indicates the present course of this world. God has delivered us from having to live in bondage to whatever "age" (or, "era") we live in. **according to the will of God and our Father**—Christ died in obedience to the plan of God (John 6:38, 39), not because we deserved it. The fact that this was in the will of God, the Creator of the universe and the Father of all Christians, should have kept the Galatians from putting legal requirements in the way of that plan.

➤**5 To whom be glory**—God is the one who rightly deserves all glory, now and forever (Eph. 3:21; Rom. 9:5; 16:27; 1 Tim. 1:17).

## 6-10 PAUL'S DENOUNCEMENT OF A DIFFERENT GOSPEL

Paul usually expressed thanks for the faith of his readers, but in this letter he plunged directly into his reason for writing. He was upset because the Galatians had fallen away from the message which he had given them and abandoned the "pure" gospel of the grace of God by accepting the perversion preached by the Judaizers. The true gospel, Paul said, was what he preached.

➤**6 I marvel**—Paul was surprised that the Galatians, whom he had thought to be doctrinally sound, had so quickly deserted his teachings, especially since he had spent so much time with them. The Greek verb is in the present tense, implying continuous amazement. If the letter was written from Corinth, only three years would have passed since Paul had been with them. If it was written from Ephesus, the interval would have been about one year. **ye are so soon removed**—lit., "are being removed." They were in the process of turning away from the gospel as Paul had presented it, but had not yet completely divorced themselves. The term Paul employs has the connotation of military desertion, yet he does not allow the full force of the word to hit them. He implies (by using the passive voice) that they have been tempted by others, and that the chief guilt belonged to these intruders. (Note, however, that the verb could also be in the middle voice, and thus state the Galatians were removing themselves from the original gospel—see Wahl, Alford.) The spiritual lives of the Galatian Christians were at an early and crucial stage of development, and Paul was concerned that they might suffer complete spiritual disaster. **called you into the grace of Christ**—lit., "in (or, by) the grace of Christ," as the instrumentality *by* which God calls us to salvation. Salvation through Christ includes justification, reconciliation, and eternal life, access to which was provided through the plan of God the Father (Rom. 8:30; 1 Cor. 1:9; 1 Thess. 2:12; 5:24). **another gospel**—The Greek word for "another" (*heteros*) means "a different gospel."

➤**7 Which is not another**—The Greek word for "another" (*allos* means "another of the same kind." By using these two words (*heteros*—1:6; and *allos*—1:7), Paul was saying that the Galatians had listened to a totally different gospel, though there is really no other gospel than the one he preached. The gospel Paul had preached to the Galatians was the only true gospel; there was no other way to obtain eternal life. **would pervert**—lit., "wish to pervert." Although these men wished to change (or, distort) the truth, the Greek text makes it clear that they could only wish to do so—even though they could cause much trouble for new converts (4:9, 17, 21; 6:12, 13). These men acknowledged Christ, but insisted on keeping many elements of the Jewish law, primarily circumcision. Paul, however, would not recognize any gospel except the pure gospel of the grace of God, unmixed with legalistic attachments.

➤**8 But though we, or an angel from heaven**—Any new message, even if backed by the performance of miracles, should not be accepted if it was in any way contrary to the message they had already received. The message they had believed came from God, and God cannot contradict himself (1 Kings 13:18; Matt. 24:24; 2 Thess. 2:9). The Judaizing teachers had claims that their authority came from the apostles at Jerusalem, but Paul was saying that when the truth was in question, no one should be respected above it, not even angels. **preach any other gospel**—This means any gospel other than that which Paul preached. **let him be accursed**—lit., "let him be a curse [an anathema]." Anyone who distorted and perverted the pure gospel should be cursed, condemned by God. In the other passages where Paul uses this Greek word, it is connected with the idea of spiritual death.

➤**9 so say I now again**—In restating the warning of 1:8, Paul assumed that these teachers had already been preaching to the Galatians, and had swayed many of them to their viewpoint. He wished to make sure that the people understood the consequences of following this "other gospel." The gospel he preached, Paul reminded them, was the one they initially received.

➤**10 do I now persuade men**—The Judaizers had evidently accused Paul of trying to win the hearts of the Gentiles by flattering them, "becoming all things to all men," so that he could make a following for himself. They further accused him of inconsistency in his actions and teachings by observing the law when he was among the Jews (in his circumcision of Timothy, Acts 16:3) while persuading the Gentiles to renounce the law (5:11). They said that Paul did this in order to keep the Gentiles in a subordinate state, away from the full privileges available only to those who had been circumcised. **or God**—Paul had been a Pharisee, a sect known by its desire to please men (Luke 16:15); now he was a servant of God, responsible to him alone (1 Cor. 4:3). **servant of Christ**—A servant tries to please his master in every way he can (Col. 3:22; Tit. 2:9).

## 11-22 PAUL'S CALLING CAME FROM GOD

➤**11 brethren**—Up to this point, the letter is stern; now Paul attempts to reason more gently. Earlier, he emphasized the integrity of the gospel; now he gives them a personal word as to the source of that message. **is not after man**—"not something that man made up" (NIV). The message was not influenced by mere human considerations, as would have been the case if it were a human invention.

➤**12 by the revelation of Jesus Christ**— According to the Greek this could be an objective genitive (a revelation concerning Jesus Christ—Jesus Christ being the object of the revelation) or a subjective genitive (a revelation from Jesus Christ—Jesus Christ giving the revelation). Both thoughts are consistent with the context (see Boice). Paul's "revelation of Jesus Christ" enabled him to see that Christ was God's Son (1:16), the sole object of our faith (2:16), and the unique source of oneness of all believers, whether Jew or Gentile, bond or free, male or female (see 3:27, 28; Eph. 3:1-11). Paul received his knowledge by special revelation (1 Cor. 11:23; 15:3; Eph. 3:3; 1 Thess. 4:15). Paul was thus an independent witness to the gospel, and although he had received no instructions directly from the apostles, only from the Holy Spirit, his teachings agreed with theirs.

➤**13 I persecuted the church of God**— Paul had been a real zealot, trying to keep Judaism pure from contamination by the Christians. Here his former activity—tearing down the church—is contrasted with his present one—building up the church.

➤**14 profited** [progressed] **in the Jews' religion**—Paul was a Pharisee just as his father had been (cf. Acts 23:6; 26:5). This sect was rather small, having only about six thousand members, but they exerted a tremendous influence on the entire nation because their members were usually in positions of authority. They were noted for their fanatical desire to keep all the minute parts of the law, and to stay away from everything ceremonially unclean.

➤**15 separated me**—set me apart. The Greek word shares the same root as the word usually translated "predestinate." Here the word means "marked out," "designated." **from my mother's womb**—Since Paul had been chosen before he was born, he did not have any merit of his own (Rom. 9:11). **called me**—on the way to Damascus (Acts 9). **by his grace**— The grace of God was the sole factor in his calling (cf. Ps. 22:9; 71:6; Isa. 49:1; Jer. 1:5; Luke 1:15).

➤**16 To reveal his Son in me**—God revealed his Son *within* Paul (see 2:20) by means of the Holy Spirit (4:6). The ministry of Paul emanated from the indwelling Christ. It would have been impossible for Paul to reveal Jesus to the Gentiles unless God had first revealed Jesus to Paul. **preach him among the heathen**—This was the main part of the commission that Paul received (2:7, 9; Eph. 3:8). There was no consultation between him and the other apostles. After he received divine revelation, he was set to preach the gospel to the Gentiles. The revelation was sufficient to spur Paul on to his work. **I conferred not with flesh and blood**—"I did not consult any man" (NIV).

➤**17 Neither went I up to Jerusalem**— The twelve apostles had remained in the church at Jerusalem. **but I went into Arabia**—His apostolic mission was completely independent of the other apostles, whom he did not consult. This retreat into the wilderness of Arabia (not recorded in Acts) probably gave him, like Moses, the needed time alone to prepare for his great work.

➤**18 after three years**—The three years probably dates from Paul's conversion; it does not mean necessarily that Paul spent three years in Arabia. This three-year period was probably concurrent with the period called "many (considerable) days" in Acts 9:23. **I went up to Jerusalem**—This is the same visit mentioned in Acts 9:26, during which he saw the vision mentioned in Acts 22:17, 18. **to see Peter**— The Greek word for "see" (*historeō*) is the root word for our English term, "history." According to the Greek, Paul and Peter would have told each other their stories, their histories (see Boice). **fifteen days**—This is a very short time in comparison with the three-year period mentioned before; it seems to underscore Paul's assertion that he did not get his commission to preach from the church at Jerusalem. He left the city for two reasons. First, the Jews there were plotting his murder (Acts 9:29). Second, the vision he received ordered him to leave, since the people in Jerusalem would not listen to his message (Acts 22:17, 18).

➤**19 apostles**—In Acts 9:27, 28, "apostles" are mentioned. This verse shows that these apostles were Peter and James, the others probably having fled after the martyrdom of Stephen. Peter himself soon left on a preaching tour of Judea (Acts 9:32). **James the Lord's brother**—This name was given to him as a means of differentiating him from James (the son of Zebedee) who was also an apostle who had been killed by Herod. Later (2:9, 12), Paul refers to him only as "James." This James was the leader of the church of Jerusalem, and the probable author of the NT epistle.

➤**20** Apparently the Judaizers had told Christians in Galatia that Paul had been given both his authority and a long course of instruction by the apostles in Jerusalem. Thus Paul was careful to emphasize that he had spent only fifteen days in Jerusalem, seeing only Peter and James.

➤**21 Afterwards I came into the regions of Syria and Cilicia**—This trip was made as a preaching journey (1:23), during which he founded and revisited the churches in Syria and Cilicia (Acts 15:23, 40, 41). Paul probably went first to the main seaport, Caesarea, and sailed from there to Tarsus, his birthplace (Acts 9:30). He probably then went from Tarsus, in the region of Cilicia, to Syria. Cilicia was cut off from the rest of Asia Minor by the Tarsus Mountains. Syria is probably mentioned before Cilicia because Antioch, the major city of Syria, was more important than Tarsus, the chief city of Cilicia. Paul also spent far more time at Antioch than he did at Tarsus. There possibly was a second visit to the church at Jerusalem which Paul does not mention here, but which Luke records in Acts 11:30. There is a great deal of disagreement at this point, but even if such a visit took place, Paul did not have the time to receive instruction from the apostles, since there was much persecution at this time, and since only James was present.

➤**22 unknown by face unto the churches of Judea**—Paul now strengthens his argument by stating that he was not even known by sight in the churches of Judea, where the apostles had done most of their missionary work. The only Judean church where he was known was the one at Jerusalem (Acts 9:26-29).

➤**23** The only thing that the Judean Christians knew about Paul was that he had been converted and changed from being the chief persecutor to being a chief evangelist.

➤**24 And they glorified God in me**—"in my case" or "because of me." Paul used this as a small needle to prick the Galatians. These churches, which had never seen Paul, rejoiced because of his conversion, while the Galatians, who had been converted under Paul's ministry, questioned his authority.

*Chapter* 2

## 1-10 PAUL'S APOSTLESHIP TO THE GENTILES RECOGNIZED BY THE JERUSALEM APOSTLES

➤**1 Then fourteen years after I went up again to Jerusalem**—There is disagreement as to when this took place. Some commentators (e.g., Alford) take it as referring to fourteen years after the conversion of Paul, while others (e.g., Lightfoot) feel that it refers to fourteen years after the first visit to Jerusalem, mentioned in Galatians 1:18. As a result, some believe this visit to be the one mentioned in Acts 11, while others believe it to be the visit for the Jerusalem council, set forth in Acts 15. The view that this visit was connected with the Jerusalem council, however, has some difficulty because it can be argued that Paul would have mentioned the decision of the council regarding the topic of circumcision, which was one of the main reasons he wrote to the Galatians. But in support of the view that this visit was the occasion of the council, it may be stated first that Paul had a desire to show the Galatians that his authority was independent of the other apostles—so the decision of the council was not to be taken into consideration by the Galatians when they were to obey his teaching. His authority was above that of a council, because he was an accredited apostle. Second, Paul was arguing his point on the grounds of principle rather than authoritative decisions. It would have been pointless for the Galatians to disregard one set of laws only to be bound by another. Third, the decree of the council of Jerusalem did not go as far as Paul did in this instance. All that was decided at Jerusalem was that the mosaic law would not be imposed on Gentiles, while Paul here asserts that the mosaic law has to be transcended. Finally, the Galatians were obeying the mosaic law of circumcision not merely as a means of salvation but as a means of furthering the perfection of their spiritual lives (3:3; 4:21). This view would have been supported by the Jerusalem council's decree and thus be of no value to Paul in his presentation. Paul dealt with the Galatians much more directly, stating that Christ would be useless to them if they tried to be justified by the law (5:4). **took Titus with me also**—Paul and Barnabas, along with others, had been sent by the church at Antioch to consult with the elders at Jerusalem on the question of the circumcision of the Gentiles (Acts 15:2). In this connection, Titus was especially noted, since he was a Gentile and was not required to undergo circumcision by the elders and apostles at Jerusalem (2:3).

➤**2 I went up by revelation**—i.e., "in response to a revelation" (NIV). Paul was not dependent on the revelation of the other disciples, but claimed that he received his revelation directly from God. The fact that he was a delegate from Antioch in no way affects the fact that he went there in response to a revelation he received from God, since it is possible that the revelation he received, which probably was in the form of a vision, may have led him to put forth the idea of a delegation to the other people in the church at Antioch (Acts 15:2). **privately to them which were of reputation**—A private meeting was arranged so that Paul and the other apostles could arrive at an agreement before they came before the rest of the council, and so that the other apostles could determine that the gospel which Paul had been preaching was the same as the gospel they had received from Jesus. When Paul and Barnabas spoke to the council as a whole, they did not defend the doctrine that they had been teaching because they had already been examined by the rest of the apostles. They spoke only about the miracles that had been done through them, using them as a proof that God himself had approved of their preaching to the Gentiles (Acts 15:12). The leaders "of reputation" mentioned here must have been Peter, James, and John (2:7-9). **I should run, or had run, in vain**—His running (i.e., his proclamation of the gospel) would have been in vain had circumcision been necessary, since he did not require it of his converts.

➤**3** So far were they from regarding that Paul had run in vain, that not even **Titus . . . a Greek, was compelled to be circumcised**— By their action in the case of Titus, the apostles at Jerusalem showed that they accepted Paul's authority as equal to their own, and that they approved of his course of action in preaching the gospel of liberty to the Gentiles. This was the point that Paul was trying to make with the Galatians. But although Titus was not forced to accept circumcision, Timothy was circumcised. The difference was that Titus was a Gentile, while Timothy was a proselyte, the son of a Jewish mother, who needed to be confirmed into his own nation. Christianity did not interfere with the customs and practices of Judaism while the temple, the symbol of the Jewish nation, still stood. After the destruction of the temple, these customs and practices lost their importance. While Christianity did not interfere with Jewish customs, Paul demanded that the Gentile Christians not be required to conform to these customs, since such conformity would have been inconsistent with grace and freedom in Christ. Paul used Titus as an example of the grace of God working in a Gentile.

➤**4 And that**—referring to Titus's uncircumcision. Paul refrained from circumcising Titus, not out of disrespect for the rite of circumcision, but because legalistic Jews would have seen such an act as Paul's admission that circumcision was necessary for all believers. **false brethren**—Judaizers, who in this case were not genuine believers in Jesus Christ. The Judaizers forced Jewish customs and laws upon Gentile Christians. **to spy**—They were actually enemies in the disguise of friends, who wanted to deprive the Gentile Christians of their freedom in the Lord. **our liberty**—The Gentiles were free from the responsibility of the Jewish ceremonial laws. **might** [will] **bring us into bondage**—The Greek verb (future tense) implies the certainty and continuance of the bondage.

➤**5 To whom we gave place by subjection, no, not for an hour**—"We did not give in to them for a moment" (NIV). The "we" is a reference to both Barnabas and Paul, since both resisted all of the efforts of the Judaizers to impose the Jewish laws on the Gentile Christians. **that the truth of the gospel might continue with you**—The question not only concerned Titus, but the truth of the unencumbered gospel which Paul had been preaching.

He did not yield on this point, insisting that he defended the true faith.

➤6 these who seemed to be somewhat [something]—i.e., the people of importance, the apostles to the circumcision. **God accepteth no man's person**—Paul admits that the apostles were great leaders, but says that this makes no difference to God, and thus no difference to him (Eph. 6:9). **in conference added**—imported (the same Greek word for "conferred" in 1:16). Paul was suggesting that just as he had not added anything to the gospel at the time of his conversion, so the leaders of the church had not added anything to his message.

➤7 But contrariwise—This prepares the way for Paul's next statement, which would show that the other apostles acted in a manner directly opposite to the way the Judaizers would have liked them to act. They approved of Paul and his commission. **the gospel of the uncircumcision was committed unto me**—Greek, "I have been entrusted with the gospel of the uncircumcision." Paul's ministry was to the Gentiles. **the gospel of the circumcision was unto Peter**—Peter had originally opened the door of the gospel to the Gentiles (Acts 10; 15:7); but in the ultimate apportionment of the spheres of labor, the Jews were assigned to him (see 1 Pet. 1:1 and comments).

➤8 he—God. **wrought effectually**—made the preached word efficacious to conversion. **in Peter**—or, for Peter. **was mighty**—same Greek word translated above as "wrought effectually," which could also be rendered "operated," "worked," or "energized" (from the Gk. $energe\bar{o}$). **in me**—or, for me.

➤9 James—is placed first in order, since he was the leading elder of Jerusalem and presided at the council (Acts 15). He was called "the Just" because of his strict adherence to the law, and was especially popular among the Judaizers, even though he did not represent as extreme a viewpoint as they did. **Cephas**—Peter was not thought of so highly by the extremists because of his dealings with the Gentile Christians. Each of the apostles was thus given a separate group as a special ministry. James, who was careful to observe the letter of the law, ministered to the Jews of Jerusalem, who would appreciate him. Peter, who had opened the door to the Gentiles but was nevertheless favorable to the Jewish Christians, min-

istered to the Jews of the dispersion. Paul, who had been an example of Judaism at its peak, had been converted suddenly and found his ministry among the Gentiles. **John**—had received an intimation in Jesus' lifetime of the admission of Gentiles into the church (John 12:20-24). **seemed to be pillars**—The pillars of the church held the superstructure in place and rested on the foundation, who is identified by Paul as Jesus Christ (1 Cor. 3:11). **perceived the grace that was given unto me**—in bringing the gospel to the Gentiles. Paul convinced the apostles that his ministry was valid by presenting the things which God had done through him. One graphic example was Titus, who had come to Jerusalem with Paul and Barnabas. **gave to me and Barnabas the right hands of fellowship**—Barnabas and Paul were recognized as colleagues in the apostleship. **we should go unto the heathen** [Gentiles]—Paul and Barnabas had the ministry to the Gentiles, whereas the Jerusalem apostles had the ministry to **the circumcision** [the Jews].

➤10 we should remember the poor—The only requirement placed on Paul's ministry was that he teach his converts the necessity of helping the poor, who at that time were centered in the churches in and around Jerusalem. This situation had arisen because the Jews who became Christians were socially and economically ostracized. Because they had a hard time earning a living, they tried an experiment in communal living (Acts 2:44-47; 4:32-37), but this only aggravated the problem. A series of famines between A.D. 30 and 50 made food prices rise. Furthermore, the church at Jerusalem supported a large number of teachers, and they provided hospitality to all of the Christian pilgrims who came to Jerusalem. **the same which I also was forward to do**—"I, too, was eager for that" (TLB). Although Paul denied that justification could come through good works, he was careful to teach that they were expected of all Christians. Paul and Barnabas had already begun their campaign to get some relief money for Jerusalem (Acts 11:23-30; 24:17; Rom. 15:25; 1 Cor. 16:1; 2 Cor. 8 and 9).

## 11-21 PAUL'S STAND AGAINST PETER'S ERROR

➤11 Peter—In the earliest manuscripts, he is named "Cephas." The fact that Paul stood up against Peter is the strongest proof offered as to his independence in relation to the other apostles. **was come to Antioch**—At this time, Antioch was the chief center of the Gentile church. It was the place where the gospel had first been given to Gentiles, and the place where the name "Christians" was first employed (Acts 11:20, 26). The issue at Antioch was not whether Gentiles could become Christians without being circumcised, since that question had been settled in the Jerusalem council; it was, rather, whether uncircumcised Gentile Christians could sit at the table of fellowship with Jewish Christians. Soon after the Jerusalem council made its decision, the Judaizers visited Antioch, and were amazed that men were being received into the fellowship of the church without being circumcised. They explained away the decision of the council, and probably wanted to see if any of the Jewish Christians were violating the law, since the Jerusalem decision had not given them this privilege (Acts 15:19). **because he was to be blamed** [condemned]—Peter's actions at this time contradicted his actions at another.

➤**12 For before . . . certain** [men] **came from James**—James leaned toward a legalistic interpretation of Christianity; and even if these men were not actually representing him (as can be inferred from Acts 15:24), they would no doubt have been a part of the Jerusalem church which had James as leader. **he did eat with the Gentiles**—The vision which Peter had received (Acts 10:10-20) and the commands he had been given (Acts 11:3-17) were consistent with this action. **he withdrew**—imperfect tense in Greek: "began to withdraw" or "continued to withdraw." Peter, through fear of these men, was unfaithful to his own principles (Acts 15:7-11).

➤**13 the other Jews dissembled likewise**—lit., "the other Jews joined [with him] in hypocrisy." They acted as though obedience to the ceremonial law was necessary for salvation, even though they knew that they were free from the law to eat with the Gentiles, having already done it (Acts 11:2-17). This was not the same problem of Christian liberty as that which Paul later faced in Corinth and Rome (1 Cor. 8–10; Rom. 14). It was a question which affected the essence of the gospel which Paul was preaching; whether the Gentiles were going to be forced to live like the Jews in order to be saved. **Barnabas also was carried away**—Barnabas was the one Paul would have least expected to be caught in this hypocrisy, since

he was present with Paul when the gospel was first preached to the Gentiles.

➤**14 they walked not uprightly**—lit., "they did not walk straight." The NIV translates, "they were not acting in line with the truth of the gospel." **the truth of the gospel**—The gospel teaches that justification by following the law is inconsistent with faith in Christ's redemption. This was the stand taken by Paul. Here he stood alone against Judaism. **I said unto Peter before them all**—Peter had to be rebuked in the presence of the Gentile believers because his high authority would lead the Gentiles to believe that since he followed the rules of the Judaizers, it was necessary for them to do the same. What Paul said is made clearer in the RSV: "If you, though a Jew, live like a Gentile and not like a Jew, how can you compel the Gentiles to live like Jews [lit., 'to Judaize']?" Peter had abandoned the Jewish dietary laws and eaten like a Gentile. How could he now switch? That would encourage the Gentiles to adhere to Jewish customs.

➤**15 We who are Jews by nature**—Since both Peter and Paul were Jews by birth, they could understand the position maintained by the Jewish Christians. Paul was contending, however, that both knew that it was wrong.

➤**16 Knowing that a man is not justified by the works of the law**—The basis of justification cannot be the law, since the only thing obedience to the law can do is to fulfill the requirements of the law (Alford). **but by the faith of** [in] **Jesus Christ**—In coupling the name of "Jesus" to the title of "Christ," Paul was affirming the Messiahship of Jesus, since "Christ" is Greek for "Messiah." **justified by the faith of Christ**—made righteous by faith in Christ. **and not by the works of the law**—No one could be justified by keeping the law, since everyone would break some part of it. And the moral law was even more demanding than the ceremonial law. **for by the works of the law shall no flesh be justified**—This is a paraphrase of Psalm 143:2. Paul rests his argument on this as an axiom of his theology. In all of Paul's writings there is hardly any other verse that so dogmatically and dynamically pronounces the core of his theology. Thrice he says that a man is not justified by the works of the law, and thrice he says that a man is justified by faith in Christ Jesus. Luther (and the Reformers) recaptured this spirit and reiterated this message with renewed fervency.

➤**17 But if, while we seek to be justified by Christ, we ourselves also are found sinners, is therefore Christ the minister of sin?**—This verse is difficult to interpret. But among the several interpretations that have been offered by various commentators, the following explanation by Boice seems the most satisfactory:

A final interpretation is that Paul refers to the standard antinomian [against the law] objection to the doctrine of justification by faith, which, significantly enough, he also deals with elsewhere. . . . According to this interpretation, Paul would be answering the objection that to eliminate the law entirely as he is doing is to encourage godless living, living without norms. The argument would go "Your doctrine of justification by faith is dangerous, for by eliminating the law you also eliminate a man's sense of moral responsibility. If a person can be accounted righteous simply by believing that Christ died for him, why then should he bother to keep the law or, for that matter, why should he bother to live by any standard of morality? There is no need to be good. The result of your doctrine is that men will believe in Christ but thereafter do as they desire." Paul's reply is abrupt. The form of his expression suggests that he was aware of the possibility that a Christian can (and that all Christians do) sin. But this is not the result of the doctrine of justification by faith, and therefore Christ is not responsible for it. Such a thought is abhorrent. "Absolutely not!" "God forbid!" If there is sin, as Paul acknowledges indirectly in the next verse, man himself is responsible ("I am a lawbreaker").

➤**18 if I build again the things which I destroyed, I make myself a transgressor**—Paul, speaking as if he were Peter, was trying to make Peter see that by allowing the law to be necessary, he was making himself a sinner, since he had sat down with Gentiles and even lived with them. He was unable to be justified by the law since he had broken it, and he was unable to be justified by Christ because he had made him to seem as the one who brought sin rather than righteousness.

➤**19 I**—Paul himself, not Peter (as in 2:18). **through the law**—The law was Paul's teacher and guide, leading him to Christ (3:24). It did this in two ways. First, the law as contained in Scripture pointed out the way that Paul failed to keep the law, as well as the punishment for that failure (Rom. 3:20; Gal. 3:13). This drove him to Christ as the refuge from God's anger, since the law itself taught that it was not permanent, but would give place to Christ (Rom. 10:4). Second, the OT Scriptures drew him to Christ through the promises in the prophets of a better righteousness, and of God's law written on the hearts of men (Deut. 18:15-19; Jer. 31:33; Acts 10:43). **am dead to the law**—lit., "died to the law." Paul became dead to the law and thereby passed from being under its power with respect to its demands (Rom. 6:14; 7:4-6; Col. 2:20). Just as a woman, once married and bound to a man, ceases to be bound to him when he dies, and is free to marry another husband, so by our union with Christ in his death, we are freed from the past power of the law over us (Rom. 6:6-11).

➤**20 I am crucified with Christ**—In the Greek, the verb is in the perfect tense, indicating the present effect of a past action: "I was crucified with Christ [at the time he was crucified] with the present result that I am now still crucified." **nevertheless I live; yet not I**—lit., "and I live no more." The "I" here is the old man, Paul's old ego; such had been crucified with Christ. **but Christ liveth in me**—in the place of Paul's old life, Christ lives—and that in Paul. Thus Paul was saying, "it is no longer I who live, but Christ who lives in me" (RSV). **the life which I now live**—the Christian life, now lived by the new "I," the new regenerated man. **in the flesh**—referring to his human existence or to his body. **I live by the faith of the Son of God**—i.e., "I live by faith in the Son of God" or "I live by the faith the Son of God gives me." Paul lived by Christ's life and by the faith Christ gave him. The phrase "Son of God" is a reminder that his divine Sonship is the source of life-giving power. **loved me, and gave himself** [over to death] **for me** [on my behalf]—referring to Christ's death on the cross. The love which motivated that giving is the link which united Paul with

Christ. Paul carefully notes that the death of Jesus was not merely an act of violence, or an accident which took place in history, but rather a self-giving on behalf of sinners (3:13; cf. Mark 10:45; Rom. 5:6; 1 John 4:10).

**➤21 I do not frustrate** [set aside] **the grace of God**—Paul did not annul God's grace, as Peter did, by turning to the law. **Christ is dead in vain**—"Christ died for nothing" (see NIV). Paul argues strongly against the practices of the Judaizers, saying that Christ's death shows that the law had no power to justify anyone. If it could have justified men, then the death of Christ would have been useless (Chrysostom).

*Chapter* 3

1-29 FAITH VERSUS LAW

**➤1 O foolish** [lit., "unthinking"] **Galatians, who hath bewitched you**—The Galatians were not thinking straight. How could they have been so easily misled? They had become "bewitched" or "charmed" by the Judaizers. **evidently set forth**—actually, "portrayed" or "placarded" (as in a public display or poster). The vivid picture Paul had painted depicting the death of Christ before their eyes should have been enough to counteract all fascination.

**➤2 Received ye the Spirit by the works of the law, or by the hearing of faith?**—The impartation of the Spirit is a divine act (see John 20:22), not based on any human effort aside from faith—and this faith is given by God when one hears the gospel (Rom. 10:16, 17). From here on in Paul will speak of the Spirit (or, spirit) seventeen times.

**➤3 begun in the Spirit . . . now made perfect by the flesh?**—The Galatians probably thought they were becoming better Christians by trying to keep the law. But the works of the law can be misunderstood easily as evidence of spirituality, when in truth they are nothing but ceremonial acts. A life begun in the Spirit must continue in the Spirit; there is nothing higher, no other way to advance in the spiritual life.

**➤4 Have ye suffered so many things**— The Christians in many of the Galatian cities had been persecuted by the Jews as well as by unbelieving fellow countrymen who had been incited by the Jews. **in vain**—fruitlessly, needlessly. By adopting the legalism of the Judaizers, the Galatians might lose the reward they had been promised for their sufferings (4:11; cf. 1 Cor. 15:2, 17-19, 29-32; 2 Thess. 1:5-7; 2 John 8). **if it be yet in vain**—Paul hoped that the Galatians would turn from legalism to the grace of God and receive the reward they had coming to them for their sufferings.

**➤5 He . . . that ministereth**—supplies. God is the supplier of **the Spirit, and worketh miracles among you**—God was the one doing the miracles which the Galatians saw all around them. The fact that Paul did not have to defend the authenticity of such miracles indicates that the Galatians considered them genuine. **by the works of the law, or by the hearing of faith?**—See comments on 3:2.

**➤6 Even as Abraham believed God**— God gave the Holy Spirit to the Galatians as a result of their faith, not because of their works, much as he had justified Abraham by his faith (Gen. 15:4-5; Rom. 4:3), and not by his works. If justification comes by faith, the gift of the Holy Spirit must come by faith as well.

**➤7 they which are of faith**—This is a reference to all of the people whose faith has served as the starting point and continuing source of their spiritual lives. **children**—sons. **of Abraham**—All believers, whether Jews or Gentiles, are the sons of Abraham, the father of faith (see Rom. 4).

**➤8 the scripture, foreseeing that God would justify the heathen through faith, preached . . . the gospel**—The Scripture is here personified and functions in unity with God to preach the gospel **unto Abraham.** Paul spoke of Scripture in the same way in Romans 9:17. Of these two passages J. I. Packer said, "Paul refers to God's promise to Abraham and his threat to Pharaoh, both spoken long before the biblical record of them was written, as words which *Scripture* spoke to these two men (Gal. 3:8; Rom. 9:17); which shows how completely he equated the statements of Scripture with the utterance of God." The gospel preached by

Scripture is contained in these words: "In thee shall all nations be blessed" (Gen. 22:18). Thus, the gospel in its most basic form is older than the law, although the law was fully developed before the gospel.

►**9 they which be of faith are blessed with faithful** [believing] **Abraham**—Abraham was saved because of his faith in the promise which God had given to him, and all who follow in his footsteps have faith. All who have this same characteristic of faith will receive the same blessing of salvation.

►**10 under the curse**—This verse confirms what Paul had just said. Those who depend on the law for their salvation cannot share the blessings of God because they are under a curse (Deut. 27:26, LXX). Perfect obedience to every part of the law is required, and no one is able to carry this out (Rom. 3:19-20).

►**11 no man is justified by the law**—The law only condemns and judges the guilty sinner; it does not acquit him. The promise, if accepted by faith, leads to salvation. Thus the contrast is evident between living by faith and living by works. **The just shall live by faith**—a quotation of Habakkuk 2:4 (also cited in Rom. 1:17).

►**12 the law is not of faith**—Many of the people depended on the law for their salvation, but they did not keep all of it. Paul pointed out that unless it is kept fully and without violation it is worthless (cf. Rom. 2:13, 17, 23; 10:5).

►**13 Christ hath redeemed us from the curse of the law**—Although Paul was probably referring mainly to the Jews as being under the curse of the law, he was also including the Gentiles. The law which was given to the Jews represents a universal standard which God demands of all men. Since the Jews, who understood the law and its requirements, were unable to keep it, and stood thus condemned before God, the Gentiles, who would be equally unable to keep the law, were also condemned by it, even though they did not realize it. They were responsible for what they did understand through their consciences, so that their curse had to be removed by the work of Christ as well. **redeemed us . . . made a curse for us**—By putting himself under the curse which lay upon all who trusted in the law for salvation, Christ bought freedom for all who would believe in him. The ransom price he paid

was his own blood (1 Pet. 1:18, 19, cf. Matt. 20:28; Acts 20:28; 1 Cor. 6:20; 7:23; 1 Tim. 2:6; 2 Pet. 2:1; Rev. 5:9). The Galatians, by putting themselves back under the law, were taking upon themselves the curse which Christ had lifted from them. **for it is written, Cursed is every one that hangeth on a tree**—The quotation is from Deuteronomy 21:23. Christ bore the specific curse of being hung on the cross, or "tree" (Acts 5:30; 10:39), as a symbol of the general curse of sin he bore for all mankind. The Jews did not actually put anyone to death by hanging or crucifixion, but in order to brand them with a certain display they would hang the corpse on a tree after the person had been put to death in some other way as a lesson to others who might be tempted to follow his evil ways. The providence of God allowed Jesus to be crucified so that this prophecy could be fulfilled completely. The Jews, in contempt, called Jesus "the hanged one" and referred to Christians as the "worshippers of the hanged one." Their greatest objection to him came because he died in a way that was accursed (1 Pet. 2:24), hung between heaven and earth as though unworthy of either.

►**14** This verse expresses the two purposes that Christ had in becoming a curse for our sake and accomplishing redemption (3:13). Each purpose is introduced with the word "that" (Gk., *hina*), and is distinctly dependent on 3:13. **That the blessing of Abraham might come on the Gentiles through Jesus Christ**—The blessing of Abraham was that of being justified by faith; that blessing is now available to the Gentiles through their faith in Christ Jesus. **that we might receive the promise of the Spirit**—lit., "the Spirit of promise" or "the promised Spirit" (see Eph. 1:13). The Holy Spirit did not come as a result of receiving the blessing promised to Abraham, but because of Christ's redemption. Redemption opens the way for regeneration by the Spirit. **through faith**—The Spirit, working from outside of the believer, kindles some spark of faith within the individual that allows him to lay hold of Christ, so that the Spirit can live within him (Flacius).

►**15 I speak after the manner of men**—I take an illustration from human affairs. **Though it be . . . a man's covenant**—In an agreement (or, covenant) between men, none of the provisions in the contract can be changed. It can hardly be expected, then, that God, who is righteous, would honor any of his agreements with men any less strictly. Paul here regards the promise God made to Abraham as being more important than the law which he gave to Moses. The promise was given first, and the law was understood as being both exceptional and temporary (3:17-24). **confirmed**—ratified. **disannulleth**—abrogates. **addeth thereto**—make additions. After a contract is ratified, none of the terms can be abrogated and no new terms can be added to it, or the original terms would be broken. In this same way, legalistic Judaism could make no change in the terms of the promise as God gave it to Abraham, which had at its foundation the idea of justification through faith. They could not add the condition of observance of the law, for this would mean that God's promise would depend on something which men could not do. God, by his grace, made Abraham righteous through the faith which Abraham had. These are the only conditions which are carried into the gospel and the only conditions which any believer must meet.

➤**16** This verse was inserted by Paul to give an interpretation of the relationship between God and Abraham and Christ. Since Christ had not come by the time the law was given, the promise to Abraham could not have been fulfilled by the law. The promise waited for fulfillment until the coming of Christ, who was the seed promised to Abraham. Paul carefully noted that the "seed" does not refer to "offspring," or "children," but to one "seed," namely Christ. **promises**—Paul used the plural because the same promise was repeated several times (Gen. 12:1-3, 7; 15:1-5, 18; 17:1-8; 22:16-18), and because the promise had several parts to it. God promised both temporal and spiritual blessings for the descendants of Abraham. In the spiritual seed, there is no difference between Jew or Gentile, but in the temporal seed, there are still some parts of the promise which have not yet been fulfilled. That part of the promise which says, "all the families of the earth shall be blessed" (Gen. 12:3) points to Christ. The promise was not that some would be blessed through the law while others would be blessed by faith, but that all would be blessed by the seed of Abraham (Rom. 4:16), which was Christ. Thus the promise did not

make any distinction between Jew and Gentile, while the law did. **He saith not, And to seeds, as of many; but as of one, And to thy seed, which is Christ**—God did not make his covenant of promise with many seeds, only with one—Christ. As Christ, the one seed, is the sole recipient (or, heir) of God's promise, the only way for anyone to participate in the covenant of promise is to be joined to Christ. According to 3:27-29, when we believe in Christ and are baptized into him, we become united to him and are therefore also "Abraham's seed, and heirs according to the promise."

➤**17 the covenant**—continues the thought of 3:15. **confirmed . . . of God**—ratified by God. **in Christ**—This phrase is not present in the earliest manuscripts. **four hundred and thirty years after**—i.e., the time when God gave the Ten Commandments. The length of time that Israel was in Egypt is here given by Paul as the period which existed between the giving of the promise and the giving of the Ten Commandments. Since the law came so much later, it cannot replace the promise by which God justifies Abraham. It was his faith that God took into account in pronouncing him righteous, not any fulfilling of the ceremonial laws. **cannot disannul**—The promise God made to Abraham would have been invalidated if the law had been able to take its place. Paul is here arguing that this promise could not have been replaced by the law (see Rom. 4:14).

➤**18 the inheritance**—God had promised to Abraham certain blessings which were going to be inherited by his actual (physical) and spiritual children. This inheritance includes justification, sanctification, and glorification (Rom. 8:17, 28-30).

➤**19 Wherefore then serveth the law?**—since it is of no use in justifying a man. Is it contrary to the promise which God had given to Abraham? **it was added because of transgressions**—This would not make a change in the original promise, since that would have made the promise invalid (3:15). This was an addition that brought into clearer focus the fact that men constantly broke the conditions of the promise (Rom. 7:7-9) when they were more conscious of their sins. In fact, it sometimes stimulates men to sin more (Rom. 5:20; 7:13). **till the seed should come**—i.e., until Christ should come. The period of time when the law was in force lasted from the giving of the law until the fulfillment of the promise in Christ. It was intended as a means of preparing the Jews for the coming of Christ. **ordained by angels**—or, "handed down by angels" (TEV). God had the angels give his laws, because such laws were severe and alien to his character (Ps. 68:17; Acts 7:53; Heb. 2:2, 3). **a mediator**—Moses. In the giving of the law, the angels were the representatives of God and the people were represented by Moses (Deut. 5:5).

➤**20 Now a mediator is not a mediator of** [between] **one**—a mediator acts between two parties. **but God is one**—not two, owing to his essential unity. God is his own representative, giving the blessing directly to Abraham, and, in its fulfillment, to Christ ("the seed") without a mediator. God normally dealt directly with men, as he did when he gave the promise to Abraham. Thus the law, with its mediators (Moses and the angels) was not God's normal pattern (Exod. 19:12, 13, 17, 21-24; Heb. 12:19-24). The law, which interposed conditions and a mediatorial priesthood between God and man, was an exceptional condition limited to the Jews. (See John 1:17 for a contrast between Moses, the severing mediator of legal conditions, and Christ, the uniting mediator of grace.)

➤**21 Is the law then against the promises of God?**—The law, which required a mediator, and the promise, which did not require a mediator, but only the action of God, seem at first to be completely at odds with each other, but Paul rejects this. **a law . . . which could have given life**—The law, since it is an externally imposed rule, can never affect the internal spiritual life of men, who are naturally dead in their sins. Since the law never claims to give men spiritual life, there is no opposition between law and promise. Righteousness and life can come only through the promise which was given to Abraham, and fulfilled in Christ.

➤**22 the scripture hath concluded** [shut up] **all under sin**—"the Scripture declares that the whole world is a prisoner of sin" (NIV, see also TLB). The Scriptures began to be written about the time the law was given and are a means of permanently convicting men that they are disobedient to the commands of God. The fact that men are all prisoners to sin contrasts with the fact that Christ has made all men free

(5:1; cf. Isa. 61:1). **the promise**—See 3:18. **by faith of** [in] **Jesus Christ**—This is the only way men can escape their imprisonment.

➤**23 before faith came**—lit., "before the faith came" (i.e., the faith in Christ Jesus mentioned in 3:22). **kept**—guarded, kept in ward, held prisoner. **shut up**—locked up. The thought of this verse is well stated in the NIV: "Before this faith came, we were held prisoners by the law, locked up until faith should be revealed."

➤**24 the law was our schoolmaster**—lit., "child-conductor" or "pedagogue." The word means a "child-custodian" or "child-attendant" (Boice). The Greeks gave a faithful servant the responsibility of taking care of a boy from childhood to puberty. The servant kept him from both physical and moral evil, and went with him to his amusements and to school, but he did not teach him. **to bring us unto Christ, that we might be justified by faith**—Until Christ was able to come as the object of faith, the law had to act as a child-custodian. The law acted as an outward check on desires, thus making the consciousness of sin more acute. It further emphasized that man is himself unable to deal with sin, thus guiding him to Christ. The moral law shows what man ought to do, and thus he learns his inability to do it. The ceremonial law tried, by the use of animal sacrifices, to compensate for this inability. Dead animals, however, did not satisfy the needs of living men for forgiveness. They thus pointed to a perfect sacrifice, the fulfillment of all sacrifices which had been offered. The judicial law shows the doom man deserves, and leads him to righteousness and peace in Christ. The message of the OT, that men are doomed for their sin, is important because without it the NT message of grace and salvation would have no meaning.

➤**25 after that faith is come**—When Christ came, faith came (cf. John 1:17). In the Greek, it is called "the faith" (see comments on 3:23). **no longer under a schoolmaster**—"child-attendant" (see comments on 3:24).

➤**26 children of God**—The Greek text says "sons of God," indicating that Christians have been granted adult status (see comments on 3:24) and no longer need the law to guide them.

➤**27 baptized into Christ**—See Romans 6:3. **have put on Christ**—This continues the idea of having reached puberty, referring to the *toga virilis,* the garment worn by full-grown men when they ceased to be children (Bengel). A Christian may thus be understood as being one who wears Christ as an emblem of his sonship. In the early church, believers were baptized immediately after they professed faith in Christ. Thus baptism, as it is used in the sense of union with Christ, symbolizes the spiritual transfer from legal condemnation to divine sonship.

➤**28 neither Jew nor Greek**—In this new relationship to Christ, there is no race privileged above any other, as the Jews had been privileged over the Gentiles under the law (Rom. 10:12; 1 Cor. 12:13; Col. 3:11). **bond nor free**—Christ belongs to both slaves and free men, and they belong to him. **male nor female**—Differences of sex are not to be regarded in Christ, while under the law the male had many more privileges. Males alone were circumcised, while baptism is now applied to both men and women alike. Under the law, men alone could be kings and priests, while now all believers, no matter what their sex, are able to be kings and priests unto God (Rev. 1:6). **ye are all one in Christ Jesus**—The Greek word for "one" is masculine and therefore designates "one man." The "one man in Christ Jesus" is "the one new man" composed of Christ, the head, and the many members of his body, united into one entity (Eph. 2:15).

➤**29 if ye be Christ's, then are ye Abraham's seed**—Christ is "Abraham's seed" (3:16) and the believers have been united to Christ through baptism (3:27, 28); therefore, the believers are also "Abraham's seed," which is tantamount to saying that they are **heirs according to the promise** because it was to Abraham's seed that the inheritance was promised (3:16). The one seed, Christ (Gen. 3:15), called a grain of wheat in John 12:24, multiplied and so produced many offspring, who are now God's sons and heirs.

*Chapter* 4

1-31 SONSHIP VERSUS SLAVERY

➤**1 the heir**—In earthly inheritances a definite blood relationship is needed. In the relationship of the believer to Christ, the sovereign will of God determines the inheritance. **as long as he is a child, differeth nothing from a servant** [slave]—Since an heir under legal age does not have all of his inheritance at his disposal, he has little more control of his destiny than does a slave. **though he be lord of all**—In an earthly inheritance, the heir is the actual owner ("lord"), but can take advantage of little of his wealth until he reaches the legal age.

➤**2 tutors and governors**—rather, "guardians and stewards." The guardians were put in charge of the person of the heir. The stewards controlled his property to make sure that it did not decrease in value. (Compare these titles with "child-attendant" in 3:24, 25.) **until the time** [previously] **appointed of the father**—The Greek word for "previously appointed" expresses a time which is defined by law or by the terms of a will. Christians were made heirs at the time God chose them (Eph. 1:9-11).

➤**3 we, when we were children, were in bondage**—Paul, a Jew, included himself with the Gentiles as having a limited amount of freedom prior to the coming of Christ. The Jews were in bondage to the law of Moses, and as representative people of the rest of the world, their bondage represents that of all men trying by good works to be reconciled to God (Rom. 2:14, 15). The Gentiles were in bondage to their own sins. No one was free to do anything until Christ, the emancipator, came. **elements of the world**—The Greek word for "elements" (*stoicheia*) can mean (1) "elementary or rudimentary principles" or (2) "elemental spirits." The word itself means things placed in line (or, in a row)—like an alphabet. It was used to speak of rudimentary principles or basic elements. If Paul was thinking of the first definition, he meant that men were in bondage to the basic elements of religion (cf. Col. 2:20); if he meant the second, he was saying that men were in bondage to the "elemental spirits," an appellation for the gods or demons. The first definition suits the overall context of Galatians, whereas the second accords with 4:8-10 (see comments there). In either case, Paul said that men were in bondage to the *stoicheia* until Christ came.

➤**4 when the fulness of time was come**—This refers to 4:2, the "time appointed of the father." The inability of man to obey all of the requirements of the law, whether the law of

Moses or the law of conscience, had been clearly evidenced by the time of Christ. All the prophecies of various ages had been focused at the time in history when Christ came. God used the course of history to further prepare the way for the Redeemer. He permitted evil to control the earth for a long time before he revealed the full remedy for it. By so doing he sharpened the contrast between his holiness and the sin of the world. God does nothing prematurely, but acts at the most opportune times for the accomplishment of his purposes (Ps. 102:13; Eph. 1:10). **God sent forth his Son**—This same concept is continued in 4:6, where God sends forth his Spirit (Acts 7:12). The Greek emphatically declares that God sent "his own Son," making a distinction between Christ, who is his own Son, and the believers, who are sons by adoption (4:5). **made of a woman**—or, born of a woman. God intervened in a special way in the birth of Christ, in that he was conceived by the Holy Spirit and born of a virgin (Matt. 1:20). **made [born] under the law**—Christ was not merely born as a member of the Jewish nation; he was born into subjection to the entire moral and ceremonial law, which he kept perfectly for all mankind. As the representative of the entire human race, he suffered its entire penalty. Hence the significance of his circumcision, his being presented in the temple (Luke 2:21-27), and his baptism by John, when he said that he must do this to fulfill righteousness (Matt. 3:15).

➤**5 To redeem them that were under the law**—Redemption involves purchasing someone from slavery. All men were enslaved to the legal demands of the law, but no one could meet those demands or secure freedom. Christ paid the price for our redemption (see 3:13). **that**—for the purpose that. **we might receive the adoption of sons**—or, sonship. The Greek word means "placement into sonship." It is a legal term that in this context indicates that we have been given the full privileges of sonship. Concurrent with this placement into sonship, God places the Spirit of his Son into our hearts so that we become his natural-born children. As such, we are not just "adopted" (in the sense the word now conveys) but genuinely "begotten" by God. God makes sons of men into sons of God, just the reverse of what happened to

Christ, who, as the Son of God, became the Son of man.

➤**6 because ye are sons**—The Gentile Christians might have thought that since the Jews were at first under the law before they were placed into the sonship of God, they (the Gentiles) must also live under law as a prerequisite for grace. Paul met this objection head-on, saying that the Gentiles were *already* sons. They were no longer underage, but had already come into their inheritance. **God hath sent forth the Spirit of his Son into your hearts**—The expression "the Spirit of his Son" (unique in the NT) suggests that his Spirit insures for the Galatians a share in the sonship. By faith they are one with the Son, so what is his belongs to the Galatians as well (cf. Rom. 8:9). **Abba, Father**—The first word is Aramaic for "father"; the second word is a translation of the Greek word *patēr*, which also means "father." The full expression is analogous to the English "Daddy, Daddy"; it implies closeness and intimacy. It is the same term that Christ used in the garden (Mark 14:36). (Cf. Rom. 8:15, which says that the Spirit cries "Abba, Father"; here, the believer cries—because the two are united in spirit.)

➤**7 no more a servant, but a son**—Men are saved and made sons of God by the action of each of the members of the Trinity. The Father sent the Son and the Spirit. The Son freed mankind from the law. The Spirit assures man of his sonship. **heir of God through Christ**—In the earliest manuscripts, this reads "heir through God." Redeemed men are the sons and heirs of God, not through the law, nor through the fact that we were born into a certain nation, but through God. The fact that God sent his Son to redeem us who were under the law (4:5), and that he sent the Spirit of his Son into our hearts (4:6), confirms the conclusion reached that we are "heirs according to the promise" (3:29).

➤**8 when ye knew not God**—The Gentiles originally knew God (Rom. 1:21), but did not choose to retain God in their knowledge, and thus corrupted their original understanding. Some still might have known about him from his creation, but they did not know him in regard to his eternity, power, or holiness. **ye did service [served as slaves] unto them which by nature are no [not] gods**—The gods of the Gentiles existed only in the minds of those who worshiped them (2 Chron. 13:8, 9; 1 Cor. 8:4; 10:19, 20). The worship they offered to these gods was a different type of bondage from that of the Jews, who worshiped the true God, yet both were burdensome yokes. Paul asked the Galatians why they wished to trade one yoke for another, when they have been made free from all yokes.

➤9 **But now, after that ye have known God, or rather are known of God**—They did not first know and love God; God first knew and loved them (Exod. 33:12, 17; John 15:16; 1 Cor. 8:3; 2 Tim. 2:19). The grace God had extended in saving them n̠ ᵈe their rejection of freedom offensive. **how**—This expresses Paul's indignant wonder at their rejection of freedom. **turn ye again to the weak and beggarly** [poor] **elements**—The same Greek word for "elements" (*stoicheia*) is used here as in 4:3 (see comments there). In this context, the word could refer to the "elemental spirits" (i.e., the "gods" mentioned in 4:8) or to the "rudimentary principles" of Judaism (see 4:10). Although the Galatians had never been under the Mosaic law, they had followed their own system of ceremonial law (in the worship of their gods) which had much in common with the Jewish law. Both systems consisted of fixed outward forms of worship, and both held that the fulfillment of the requirements of the law were sufficient for the salvation of the worshipers. Neither realized that their religion could not give salvation. All religious systems were poverty-stricken ("poor") when contrasted with the riches belonging to those who are Christ's (Eph. 1:18; 3:8). And all religious systems are powerless ("weak") to make right the sins of their adherents. This is in contrast to the power of the gospel which justifies men through faith (Heb. 7:18). Thus all other religions are immature when compared with Christianity. If the Galatians were to try to gain salvation through keeping the rules of any religious system, it would be like a college graduate going back to kindergarten to learn his ABCs.

➤10 **days**—such as the sabbath or day of Atonement (Lev. 16:29-34). **months**—perhaps referring to the first and seventh months, which were sacred. **times**—seasons of the great festivals: Passover, Pentecost, and Tabernacles. **years**—the Sabbatical year. To think that the

keeping of certain days contributes to obtaining salvation is alien to the spirit of Christianity. The Lord's Day should be kept not as a means to salvation, but as a means of making life holy. Although the entire life of the true believer has been sacrificed to God and is at his command, it is necessary that a certain portion of time be dedicated specially so that the Christian can more entirely free himself from secular pursuits and concentrate on worshiping God.

➤11 **I am afraid of you**—I fear for you. Paul was concerned for his converts.

➤12 **be as I am**—in casting off Judaism. **for I am as ye are**—I now live (like a Gentile) in non-observance of legal ordinances. When Paul visited the Gentiles, he did not practice the ordinances of the Jewish religion, since he did not regard them as contributing anything to salvation. When he was among the Jews, he did observe the law. This was not an inconsistency, since he was attempting to become "all things to all men." The Gentiles in Galatia, however, by adopting the legal ordinances of the Jews, betrayed a conviction that these laws were necessary to salvation. **ye have not injured me at all**—actually, "you did not wrong me" (the aorist tense in Gk. points to a completed past action). When Paul first came to the Galatians, he did not act as a Jew, but rather lived as a Gentile, and the Galatians did not fault the apostle and his message. Therefore, he could not understand why they were now rejecting his message and taking upon themselves the burden of the law.

➤13 **infirmity**—It is quite possible that some bodily sickness made Paul stay among the Galatians longer than he had planned. This gave him an opportunity to preach the gospel to them. **at the first**—Greek, *proteron*. According to classical Greek usage, this means "the first of two" and thus points to the *first* of two visits. Therefore at the time of this writing Paul had been to Galatia twice. (See Introduction and see Boice's note.)

➤14 **my temptation**—This is the reading in a few early manuscripts, but more of the early manuscripts read "your temptation [trial]." Paul's illness was a trial to the Galatians. **ye despised not, nor rejected**—The normal response to a sick man would have been to reject him and his message, but the Galatians did not throw Paul out. They accepted both the message and the messenger. **an angel of God**—The Greek word here used for "angel" can also mean "messenger." This phrase was also used in the Middle East of one who is to be received with highest respect (see Zech. 12:8). The contrast is heightened when one realizes that Paul, who was sick, was received as an angel, who is not subject to the limitations of the flesh, sickness, or temptation. **even as Christ Jesus**—Paul was accepted not only as an angel, but also as the representative of Jesus Christ.

➤**15 ye would have plucked out your own eyes, and have given them to me**—This was a proverbial phrase which implied the greatest self-sacrifice (Matt. 5:29). What Paul seems to be pointing out was that the Galatians, when he had first preached to them, held him in such high regard that they would have made tremendous sacrifices for him. His spiritual power and the way that it was expressed in word and action at first impressed the Galatians. They were, however, a fickle bunch. Some interpreters think that this is a hint as to Paul's physical problems, speculating that he had a defect in his eyes, perhaps resulting from his experience on the road to Damascus (Acts 22:11).

➤**16 because I tell you the truth**—The fool and the sinner hate to be reprimanded, but the righteous man does not mind being corrected by the truth (Ps. 141:5; Prov. 9:8).

➤**17 They zealously affect you, but not well**—"Those people are zealous to win you over, but for no good" (NIV). Zeal in proselytism was characteristic of the Jews, and so of the Judaizers (1:13; cf. Matt. 23:15). But the motives of the Judaizers and their methods were for the wrong purposes. **they would exclude you**—The Judaizers apparently were trying to separate the Galatians from the rest of the churches, and then to make them a part of their own party. **that ye might affect them**—lit., "that ye may be zealous of them."

➤**18 it is good to be zealously affected**—it is good to be zealous—but only for what is good. Zeal must be directed to good and positive purposes.

➤**19 My little children**—Paul here emphasizes that his relation to the Galatians was much closer than the relation of the Judaizers to the Galatians. **of** [for] **whom I travail in birth**—Paul was not only in the same relation to the Galatians as a father to his children, but he also suffered for

them the same as a mother waiting for the birth of a child. **again**—He had begotten them by the gospel during his first visit with them; now again he labors for them—not for their birth (which has already happened) but for their maturity, which he calls the formation of Christ within them. **Christ be formed in you**—The formation of Christ in a believer is the converse of a believer being conformed to the image of Christ (Rom. 8:29). As a Christian is conformed and transformed (Rom. 12:1; 2 Cor. 3:18) to Christ, Christ is formed in him or her.

➤**20 I desire to be present with you**—Since Paul could not be with them to help them, he had to write this letter. He knew that if he were to speak to them face to face it would have more effect than his writing the letter. He would be able to put forth much more loving persuasion in person than he could in a letter (cf. 2 John 12; 3 John 13, 14). **I stand in doubt of you**—Paul wanted to do whatever was necessary to bring the Galatians back to a realization of the gospel which he had preached to them, but he was unsure whether it would be more effective for him to be stern or gentle. He felt that, had he been with them, he could better judge what kind of approach to take.

➤**21 do ye not hear the law?**—The Galatians were blindly trying to follow the law, which would not lead them to salvation, but rather to condemnation. In order to point them back to the right way, Paul adopted the same method of arguing that the Judaizers had so successfully used. They loved to employ subtle, mystical, allegorical interpretations of Scripture which were often contrary to what the Scripture actually said. Paul countered their arguments with an allegory of his own, but one based solidly on history and Scripture. He recognized that biblical history could have, besides the literal, a typical meaning (cf. Rom. 5:14; 1 Cor. 10:1-4; Heb. 7:1-3; Rev. 11:8). Just as Isaac, whose birth was in some measure miraculous, took the place of Ishmael, who was naturally born, so the new children of God were going to replace the natural children of God, the Jews.

➤**22 Abraham had two sons, the one by a bondmaid, the other by a freewoman**—The Galatians would wish to be called the children of Abraham (Rom. 9:7-9). The main part of this story is related in Genesis 16:3-16.

►**23 born after the flesh**—The birth of Ishmael was natural, while the birth of Isaac took place only after God let Sarah have a child in her old age (Rom. 4:19). For Isaac's birth, Abraham had to lay aside all of his confidence in the flesh and live by faith in the promise of God.

►**24 are an allegory**—lit., "are allegorical." **these** [women] **are the** [the article is not present in the Gk.] **two covenants**—Among the Jews, the status of the mother determines the status of the child. The children of the legal bondage, analogous to those born to Hagar, are in legal bondage. Children of the covenant of promise, analogous to Sarah's child, are free. **one from the mount Sinai**—the site where the law was given and the old covenant enacted (Exod. 19:2; 20:1-17). **gendereth to bondage**—i.e., brings forth children born into slavery. **Agar**—is Hagar.

►**25 this Agar** [Hagar] **is mount Sinai in Arabia**—Some commentators have said that Mount Sinai was actually called Hagar by people in this region (so Chrysostom). But this has not been proven. Paul simply may have been carrying forward his allegory without drawing upon any natural associations between Sinai and Hagar. **answereth**—lit., "lines up with," frequently translated "corresponds" (see RSV, NIV). This verb suggests that the reader should line up all the elements of the allegory, one corresponding element against another (Lightfoot). **to Jerusalem which now is**—the present Jerusalem. Just as Hagar was in bondage to Sarah, so Jerusalem was in bondage to the law. Paul used Jerusalem because at that time it represented the center of Judaism and the Judaic law. The Galatian leaders, having been negatively influenced by the Judaizers, would have more keenly felt the impact of calling Jerusalem a city of bondage.

►**26 Jerusalem which is above**—This is a reference to the messianic theocracy, which before the second coming of Christ is the church, and after the second coming will be Christ's kingdom of glory (Meyer). It is elsewhere called "the heavenly Jerusalem" (Heb. 12:22) and "the new Jerusalem" (Rev. 3:12; 21:2), which comes down from heaven, from God. But the Jerusalem Paul talked about here is present, not future. "This Jerusalem is now present in those born again by God's Spirit" (Boice). **free**—as Sarah was. **the mother of us all**—should read, "our mother," as Sarah was the mother of Isaac. "As citizens of the heavenly Jerusalem, Christians are her children" (*NIVSB*).

►**27 it is written**—The quotation is from Isaiah 54:1. **thou barren**—The heavenly Jerusalem is compared to Sarah, who had no children by Abraham until God intervened to give her a child by the promise, as opposed to Hagar, who was able to have children in the natural way. Paul drew upon Isaiah's quote because it spoke of Jerusalem's exiled state as being barren and its recovery as being fertile. The image fits well with Paul's contrast between the two Jerusalems. **for the desolate hath many more children than she which hath a husband**—This should be translated, "for the children of the desolate one are many more than the children of her that is married" (RSV). Numerous as the children under the law were, they were few in comparison to the multitude born under the promise.

►**28 we . . . as Isaac was, are the children of promise**—Therefore, we are not under the law, and we should not wish to become under the law.

►**29 persecuted**—Ishmael mocked Isaac (Gen. 21:9). Since Ishmael was older than Isaac, he probably considered himself better than Isaac, who actually was the legitimate heir. **born after the Spirit**—lit., "born according to the spirit." With reference to Isaac, this means a spiritual or miraculous birth; with reference to those who are like Isaac (i.e., the Christians), this refers to their rebirth by the Spirit. **even so it is now**—The Jews persecuted Paul, not for preaching Christianity, but for preaching it as distinct from Judaism. Paul was attacked by Gentiles only at Philippi and Ephesus, after the Jews had stirred them up. Both Paul's epistles and the history recorded by Luke in Acts agree on this point (5:11; 6:12; Acts 9:29; 13:45-50; 14:1, 2, 19; 17:5, 13; 18:5, 6).

►**30 what saith the scripture?**—See Genesis 21:10, which Paul here uses as the basis for his allegory. Jesus spoke on the same matter in John 8:35, 36. **Cast out the bondwoman and her son**—In a literal sense, Ishmael was sent away from the house of Abraham and not allowed to share in the inheritance. In a spiritual sense, Paul was indicating that the carnal and legal men were to be removed. **shall not**

**be heir with**—The Greek carries the idea that there was *no way* they could be heirs.

➤**31 we are not children of the bond-woman, but of the free**—This verse is the conclusion that Paul reaches from his allegorical treatment of the story of Ishmael and Isaac. Those who accept the promise by faith are not sons of the slave-woman, but are sons of the free woman, and are not subject any longer to the laws of the Jews.

Chapter **5**

## 1-26 FREEDOM IN CHRIST AND LIFE IN THE SPIRIT

➤**1** This verse is important because it forms the link between the previous argument concerning Christian freedom and the following passage, which is concerned with a practical application of the concept of Christian liberty. **Stand fast therefore in the liberty wherewith Christ has made us free**—lit., "For freedom Christ freed us; stand firm therefore." The freedom which Christ has given to those who accept him by faith is based on the grace of God, not on any obedience to the requirements of the law. **be not entangled again with the yoke of bondage**—Paul exhorted the Galatians not to become entangled with the yoke of slavery (the law—see Acts 15:10), knowing that unless they were careful, people who have been freed by grace can fall into slavery again.

➤**2 Behold, I Paul say unto you**—Even though the Galatians had stopped thinking as highly of Paul as they had at one time (Acts 14:11-13), and had begun to question his authority, he demanded that they pay attention. **if ye be circumcised**—If the rites of circumcision and the keeping of the ceremonial laws are necessary for justification, then there is no way that grace can be seen as having a part in justification. **Christ shall profit you nothing**—If a man is justified by works, he is not justified by his faith; if a man is justified by faith, he is not justified by his works. Circumcision was necessary for total obedience to the law by devout Jews. Paul pointed out, however, that it was not necessary for an individual to become a Jew outwardly in order to become a Jew inwardly (cf. 1 Cor. 7:17-20). Outward circumcision has no relationship to inward faith.

➤**3 he is a debtor to do the whole law**—Paul here declares that the man who submits to circumcision is responsible for keeping all of the law. It is impossible for anyone to keep even a part of the law perfectly, much less the entire law (James 2:10). But no one can be justified by the law unless he keeps every part of it.

➤**4 Christ is become of no effect unto you**—Actually, the Greek verb here means "separated," "cut off from," "severed." The clause should be translated: "You are severed from Christ" (RSV; see also TEV, NIV, JB). Submission to the Jewish laws cuts an individual off from Christ. **ye are fallen from grace**—This means that the individual no longer "stands" in the relationship with God which is characterized by grace (Rom. 5:2), since grace and legalism cannot co-exist (Rom. 4:4, 5; 11:6). Christ not only undertook to fulfill all the law and its righteousness, but succeeded in doing it (Matt. 5:17). Any man who now tries to fulfill the law by himself, in order to be justified by God, cuts himself off from the grace which comes from Christ's fulfillment of the law and subjects himself to the punishment which comes to all who break the law. The decree of the Jerusalem council had not said anything as strong as this (Acts 15). It had only decided that Gentile Christians were not bound to subject themselves to the ordinances of the Jewish laws. The Galatians did not think that they were bound to the law for justification as much as they felt that the keeping of the law would result in their becoming more perfect (3:3).

➤**5 we through the Spirit** [in spirit]—Paul here includes himself with those who are opposed to seeking justification through keeping the law, in contrast to those who are counting on the law to justify them or perfect them (5:4). The Spirit is mentioned in contrast to the legal and fleshly requirements of the law. **wait**—eagerly expect. **the hope of righteousness**—In one sense, believers have been made right with God by the death of Christ; but in another sense, believers are still in the process of hoping for the future realization of that righteousness (Col. 1:5; 2 Tim. 4:8; 1 Pet. 1:3). **by faith**—This phrase belongs with "in spirit."

➤**6 faith which worketh by love**—In 5:5, 6, the elements of faith, hope and love are found (cf. 1 Cor. 13:13). Love is not included with faith in justification, but is shown as the guiding principle of the believer's life. The legalists supposed that the essence of the law was going to be overthrown by the doctrine of justification by faith alone, but this supposition was not valid. The law was fulfilled in one word—love—and this is the principle that faith works on (5:14). It is only the element of faith which would allow a man to fulfill the law at all. Those who had not been circumcised might have believed that because the law was not necessary to justification, they could disregard all of its provisions, but this contention, too, is invalid. Christians should seek after "love" expressed in works—which fulfills the law and is inseparable from true faith (James 2:8, 12-22). The Spirit (5:5) is a Spirit of "faith" and "love" (Rom. 14:17; 1 Cor. 7:19).

➤7 Paul again showed his concern by interrupting his argument with a parenthetical statement of disbelief that the Galatians could be so easily persuaded by the Judaizers. **who did hinder you**—The Greek word carries the idea of "hinder by breaking up a road" (the road of grace they had been running on). The Galatians found the path of the true grace so difficult to follow that they were forced away from it by the arguments of the Judaizers.

➤8 **This persuasion**—to which they were yielding. **him that calleth**—God.

➤9 **A little leaven**—This seems to be saying that only a little bit of legalism in the midst of the Galatian church would be enough to subvert its purpose and purity. If legalism and works were added to the message of the gospel, the entire thing would be undermined (cf. 1 Cor. 5:6).

➤10 **I have confidence in you through the Lord**—Paul believed that God would be able to convince the Galatians, through the Lord, of the correctness of his viewpoint. **he that troubleth you shall bear his judgment**—Not only would God convince the Galatians of the truth, but he would punish the one who was leading them astray. Paul was careful to distinguish between the people who were led astray through their own thoughtlessness and those who did the leading. Paul hoped that those who were led astray would return to the right path, while those who led the others would be doomed to the judgment of God.

➤11 **if I yet preach circumcision**—The Judaizers claimed that Paul himself taught that it was necessary to be circumcised, perhaps pointing to the fact that he had circumcised

Timothy (Acts 16:3; 20:6; 21:24). **why do I yet suffer persecution**—Paul replied that his persecution by the Jews indicated he was not preaching the doctrine of circumcision. It was precisely because he preached the crucified and risen Jesus as the sole basis for justification that the Jews were still against him. Only for conciliation did he live as a Jew when among the Jews (1 Cor. 7:18-20; 9:20). The question as to the importance of circumcision depends on the way the individual regards it. The Galatians were looking at circumcision as a way of gaining favor with God. Paul conformed to the culture of those he was with so that he would give no offense. The Jews became upset with Stephen, not just because he was preaching Christ crucified, but because he was speaking against their laws and customs. They may have been able to accept the gospel of Christ if he had mixed it with the idea that justification comes by means of keeping the laws, and if he had brought into Judaism his new converts. But if the Christian message had allowed that any of this was necessary for justification, then the death of Christ would have been unnecessary, and would have profited nothing (5:2, 4).

➤12 **I would they were even cut off**—The true reflection of the Greek phrase is captured by TLB mg.: "go and castrate themselves." The NIV reads, "I wish they would . . . emasculate themselves." The worship of Cybele included the mutilation of the pagan priests in this way. Paul probably was referring to this as one of the acts which would benefit nothing, since it was an act of devotion to a false god. He was comparing it to the legalistic acts which the Judaizers were requiring the Galatians to do. Neither would help them become right with God. Verses 9 and 10 point to the threat of excommunication of those who were involved in the practice of Judaizing. Thus Paul's statement can be understood as a play on words having both the meaning of the literal act of castration as well as the symbolic "cutting off" of excommunication. (See comments on Phil. 3:2.)

➤13 **called unto liberty**—This liberty consists of three things: freedom from the mosaic law, freedom from sin, and freedom from slavish fear. **use not liberty for an occasion to the flesh**—Even though they had been made free from the law, they were not to let their freedom become the grounds for indulgence in sensual pleasures (cf. 1 Pet. 2:16; 2 Pet. 2:19; Jude 4). **by love serve one another**—If they were going to enslave themselves, Paul suggests, why not bind themselves in love to one another? This is a hint that the legalism he had seen developing among the Galatians had come about as a result of unloving bitterness and lust for power (see 5:15).

►**14 all the law**—Love for God is presupposed as the root from which love for one's neighbor springs. This love would fulfill all of the law (Lev. 19:18). Love is the command of Christ (6:2; Matt. 7:12; 22:39, 40: Rom. 13:9, 10). **is fulfilled**—lit., "has been summed up."

►**15 be not consumed one of another**—Excessive criticism results in the destruction of the strength of the soul, the health of the body, and the character and resources of one another (see Matt. 23:14; 2 Cor. 11:20). The mutual love and respect of Christians for one another will keep this from happening.

►**16 Walk in the Spirit**—which means, "conduct your life in spirit (or, by the Spirit)." The word "spirit" in this verse and the next two could refer to the regenerated human spirit, or the Holy Spirit indwelling the believer, or both. The only way to live a fruitful Christian life is to "walk in the Spirit." **and ye shall not fulfil** [perform] **the lust of the flesh**—The Spirit is in direct contrast to the evil nature, since it is good, while human nature is fallen. The promise is not that Christians will have no evil desires or thoughts, but that they will not carry through on such desires or thoughts. If the spirit that is within a Christian can bear to countenance sin, that spirit is not from God.

►**17 For the flesh lusteth** [has desires] **against the Spirit, and the Spirit against the flesh**—All of the intentions and actions which an individual has can be traced either to the Holy Spirit and his good influence or to man's sinful nature and its bad influence. **these are contrary the one to the other: so that ye cannot do the things that ye would**—A Christian is not able to do fully all that the Spirit directs him to do; conversely, he is unable to carry out all of his evil intentions due to the influence of the Holy Spirit.

►**18 if ye be led of the Spirit, ye are not under the law**—Paul concludes that the man who is under the leading (or, guidance) of the Holy Spirit is not under the law. The law was devised

for those following their evil natures (1 Tim. 1:9) and not for men saved by God's grace (Rom. 6:14, 15).

►**19 the works of the flesh are manifest**—The fallen human nature (called "flesh") betrays itself by the works which a man does. These demonstrate that he is not living under the influence of the Holy Spirit. Paul enumerated seventeen sins, while he listed only nine fruits of the Spirit. Neither list is exhaustive, but both are representative. The Galatian Christians had come out of a pagan background where sensual sins were not only tolerated but encouraged by the pagan priests and rituals. **Adultery**—not present in earliest manuscripts. **lasciviousness**—indecency or debauchery.

►**20 witchcraft**—sorcery. **hatred**—personal animosities, variance of strife. **emulations, wrath**—jealousy, anger. These are tied together, since the emotions must first be stirred before they can explode. **strife**—rivalries, factions. **seditions**—divisions. **heresies**—This word is better translated, "sects." Divisions, unchecked, eventually become sects. Divisiveness and sectarianism is the work of the flesh.

►**21 Envyings, murders**—Envy leads to murder, even if the physical act is not carried out. **drunkenness**—is used in the sense of drunken excesses (Luke 21:34; Rom. 13:13). **revellings**—were feasts held in honor of the god Bacchus. **and such like**—This reinforces the idea that the list which is presented here is not exhaustive. **as I have also told you in time past**—Paul probably warned them about their behavior when he was with them. **shall not inherit the kingdom of God**—See 1 Corinthians 6:9, 10; Ephesians 5:5.

►**22 the fruit of the Spirit**—is the natural growth and result of the Spirit working in a Christian's life. **love**—The virtue is placed first in the list (see 1 Cor. 13). **joy**—This is the deep satisfaction which comes as a result of one's personal relationship with God. This relationship includes a desire to fulfill his will, which results in the element of joy being given to the believer. **peace**—This does not refer to a sense of physical well-being, or to the absence of conflict with another person, but to tranquility of mind and a sense of spiritual well-being. This is peace with God, not simply peace with the world. **gentleness**—kindness. **goodness**—Paul used this term in Romans 15:14, Ephesians

5:9 and 2 Thessalonians 1:11. **faith**—faithfulness. This carries with it the concept of trustfulness.

➤**23 Meekness**—When a man is able to harness his evil nature, this quality reveals itself. **temperance**—self-control. This involves every type of temperance, and implies self-restraint with regard to one's lusts and desires. **against such there is no law**—See 5:18.

➤**24 Christ's**—Some of the earliest manuscripts read, "Christ Jesus.' " **have crucified the flesh**—This was done once and for all when they became Christians (Rom. 6:3, 4), and it is done continuously (Rom. 6:6) so that the Holy Spirit will be able to produce in them the fruits just listed (5:22, 23). By faith in Christ a man becomes dead to a sinful life and rises to a new life of fellowship with Christ (Col. 3:3). The act by which Christ destroyed the old nature took place once, but the life of the believer must harmonize with what Christ has accomplished.

➤**25 If we live in the Spirit**—if our Christian life finds its only source in the Spirit, as in fact, it does. **let us also walk in the Spirit**—i.e., let us conduct our daily living in the Spirit. In other words, the outward life of a Christian should be consistent with his inward experience. This verse emphasizes that life by the power of the Holy Spirit does not indicate an occasional influence here and there from the Holy Spirit, but a continual state of living in union with the Spirit.

➤**26 Let us not be desirous of vain glory**—This type of action would obviously be contrary to the Spirit-directed life. Vainglory leads to the following: **provoking one another, envying one another**—Paul concluded his discussion of life in the Spirit by noting that conceit, provocation and envy have no place in the Christian experience.

Chapter **6**

1-18 CONCLUSION AND BENEDICTION

➤**1 Brethren**—Paul now tries to reach the Galatians with this friendly means of address. Furthermore, this shows that he did not view himself as superior, but saw them as his brothers in Christ. **overtaken in a fault**—Although Paul does not specifically mention the fault (or, trespass), the rest of the book might hint that this is the sin of falling back into legalism. **ye which are**

**spiritual**—i.e., you who live in the Spirit. Paul is here speaking to those who have not fallen into this sin. **restore**—The Greek is used of a dislocated limb put back into place. **in the spirit of meekness**—in a spirit of meekness. The stronger Christians are told that they are to conduct themselves in a spirit of meekness, which thus evidences the Holy Spirit working in their lives (5:22, 25). To be meek is to be one who "endures injury with patience and without resentment" (*Webster's Ninth New Collegiate Dictionary*). **considering thyself, lest thou also be tempted**—It is important for Christians to have the right motives and attitudes as they try to correct or help their fellow believers. Those who correct others without meekness are likely to need correction themselves at a future date (Matt. 7:2-5; 2 Tim. 2:25; James 2:13).

➤**2 Bear ye one another's burdens**—Paul seemed to be saying to the Christians who wanted to pick up the burden of the law that they should instead pick up the burdens which were being carried by their fellow believers, which in many instances would be more than their fellow believers could bear. **so fulfil**—The Greek gives the idea that such an action would show the believer's complete obedience to Christ. **the law of Christ**—Paul seems to be saying that since they wanted to follow law, they ought to put themselves under the law of Christ, not the law of Moses. The law of Christ demands only love (5:14) and was the embodiment of the entire mosaic law. Although the law of Moses was made up of many minute observances, and thus was difficult to fulfill, the law of Christ was more possible to fulfill, having only one commandment, namely, to love (John 13:34; 15:12). In Romans 15:1-3, Christ is presented as the one who is the best example of someone who bore the "burdens" of others.

➤**3** This verse stresses that self-conceit, the chief hindrance to helping others, must be put aside. **if a man think himself to be something, when he is nothing**—Paul was speaking to those who thought that they were so spiritually superior to others that they did not have any defects. **deceiveth himself**—lit., "mentally deceives himself."

➤**4** This verse continues the idea of 6:3, that a man should not think of himself too highly. **let every man prove his own work**—If a man is concerned with his own work, he will not have time to compare what he has done with what anyone else has done, because the flaws in his work will provide him with enough to think about, even if they are not apparent to others.

**➤5 For every man shall bear his own burden**—At first glance this verse seems to contradict what Paul says in 6:2, which declares that men are to share each other's troubles and infirmities. The main idea however, is that each man, by self-examination, will feel that he has enough to worry about with his own faults without comparing himself boastfully with his neighbor. Since he recognizes that he is not superior to his neighbor, he will better be able to help bear with his neighbor's faults.

**➤6 him that is taught** [instructed] **in the word**—The Christian who receives the instruction. **communicate**—share (financially). **unto him that teacheth**—the teacher. **in all good things**—material benefits. There was a great deal of teaching that went on in the early church. The teachers who shared the word with the believers were entitled to a share of beneficence from those they taught.

**➤7** Verses 7 to 10 return to the thoughts of 5:22, with emphasis on the fruits of the Spirit. **Be not deceived**—This might better be understood as meaning "Stop being misled." **God is not mocked**—Excuses which may seem valid before men will not be valid before God (Ps. 50:21). Although this verse is often quoted with reference to unbelievers, it is significant to remember that Paul applied it to Christians. God's children, especially, must live their lives with him in mind. **whatsoever a man soweth, that shall he also reap**—whatever works a man does during his lifetime he will get back in judgment from God at the end of time.

**➤8 he that soweth to his flesh**—Men naturally try to get what will be to their own advantage, since they are naturally selfish. **shall of the flesh reap corruption**—This is presented as a normal result of sowing to the natural desires, not as a special punishment for it. The idea is that the future life is but the outgrowth and result of what is sown in this life. **he that soweth to the Spirit shall of the Spirit reap life everlasting**—Only those who sow to the Spirit will reap eternal life, both now and in the future. Since the Spirit is the Spirit of life (Rom. 8:2), to invest our being to the Spirit yields life, i.e., God's life manifests in our lives. Note that in both cases the text says "*of* the flesh" and "*of* the Spirit." Both flesh and Spirit produce their own nature: flesh yields corruption,

for flesh is itself corrupt (and corrupting); Spirit yields life, for Spirit is itself life (see Rom. 8:2, 10; 1 Cor. 15:45; 2 Cor. 3:6).

**➤9 let us not be weary in well doing**—See 2 Thess. 3:13. **in due season**—When the harvest time has come and the grain is ripe, we will get our reward (1 Tim. 6:15). **if we faint not**—Paul tried to have the Galatians understand the importance of persevering in their faith. If they wanted to receive their deserved reward, they would have to keep on working.

**➤10** This is the conclusion Paul drew from his illustration of the harvest. **As we have therefore opportunity, let us do good unto all men**—Our lives are so short that it is important to take advantage of each opportunity available to be good to others. **especially unto them who are of the household of faith**—Every man naturally wants to do as much as he can to help along his own family (1 Tim. 5:8), so believers should do as much as they can to help their brothers in the faith. Christians have a special obligation in relationship to one another. Some interpreters suggest that this verse was written with the need of the Christians who were in Palestine in the back of Paul's mind. He was organizing relief projects to help them, and the Galatians would have a particular opportunity to apply the teaching Paul was stating here (Rom. 15:24-27; 1 Cor. 16:1-4; 2 Cor. 8:9).

**➤11 Ye see how large a letter** [in large letters] **I have written unto you with mine own hand**—It is probable that Paul dictated the letter to the Galatians up to this point, but finished it in his own handwriting. This was something he seems to have done in several of his letters (Rom. 16:22; 1 Cor. 16:21). The large letters suggest to some interpreters that Paul's eyesight was weak. This was an early tradition in the church, and it was specifically mentioned by Jerome. The oldest manuscripts were written entirely in capital letters. He made his letters larger than the person who had written the rest of the letter. The mention of these large letters seems to be a sign to the readers that this letter was really from Paul.

**➤12 they constrain you to be circumcised . . . lest they should suffer persecution**—The message which Paul preached, that justification was through faith alone, was not popular with the Jews, for it did not keep the mosaic law as a part of justification. The Judaizers wished to have the Galatians submit to circumcision so that they would be able to remain popular with the Jews, since the mosaic law would then be a prerequisite for becoming a Christian. Christian converts would thus first be Jewish proselytes.

➤**13** This verse is better translated as follows: "For not even they who submit to circumcision keep the law themselves, but they wish *you* to be circumcised." The Judaizers had arbitrarily selected the rite of circumcision from the entire law, as though by keeping that one part they would be excused from the rest of the law. Their insincerity was obvious to Paul. Their demand that the Gentiles should be circumcised was only so that they could point to this outward mark of "religious legalism."

➤**14 But**—The Judaizers were proud of their outward fulfillment of the rite of circumcision, but Paul put himself in a separate camp altogether from them. **God forbid that I should glory** [boast], **save** [except] **in the cross**—The cross was a great object of pride for Paul. By it, the worst of deaths, Christ destroyed all kinds of death (Augustine). We are to testify to the power of Christ's death working in us after the manner of the crucifixion (5:24; Rom. 6:5, 6). **our Lord Jesus Christ**—Paul reminded the Galatians that Jesus belonged to each of them personally, as he used the word "our" in referring to Jesus Christ. They should therefore follow Paul's example and boast only in the cross, which was God's method of redeeming mankind.

➤**15 neither circumcision . . . nor uncircumcision**—Paul here makes a final statement about the circumcision/uncircumcision issue; to him, this was not even worthy of a Christian's attention. What matters is the new creation in Christ. **new creature**—actually, new creation. The difference is not external, as it is with circumcision, but rather internal. The important thing is the transformation of the individual (Rom. 12:2; 2 Cor. 3:18).

➤**16 walk according to this rule**—In the Greek this means "line up with this principle"

(i.e., the principle [or, rule] of caring only for one's new position and disposition in Christ). **peace be on them, and mercy, and upon the Israel of God**—Peace comes from God (Eph. 2:14-17; 6:23) and is the spiritual condition resulting when grace has done its work. Mercy is defined as the grace which God promised to his people, and which his people can thus expect to receive from him. The people of this promise (the Israel of God) are not the literal descendants of Abraham, but rather the spiritual seed of Abraham who have become his children by faith (see 3:9, 29; cf. Rom. 2:28, 29; Phil. 3:3), whether Jews or Gentiles.

➤**17 let no man trouble me**—by opposing my apostolic authority. **I bear in my body the marks of the Lord Jesus**—Marks that were branded on slaves indicated their owners' names. So Paul's scars or wounds received for Christ's sake indicate to whom he belonged and in whose free and glorious service he was involved (2 Cor. 11:23-25). The Judaizing teachers gloried in the circumcision mark in the flesh of their followers; Paul gloried in the marks of suffering for Christ on his body (see 6:14; cf. Phil. 3:10; Col. 1:24). Paul's intense emotions are vividly conveyed in this verse.

➤**18 Brethren**—Paul began this chapter with an appeal to Christian brotherhood, and he ended it with the same. **the grace of our Lord Jesus Christ be with your spirit**—After having written so much scolding and rebuke, he ends this letter with kindness and encouragement, and a prayer that God's grace would be with their spirit to help them defeat the desires and temptations of the flesh (cf. 1 Thess. 5:23; 2 Tim. 4:22; Philem. 25). This grace is with the Christian's regenerated spirit. The second half of this epistle (3:1ff.) began with a call for the Galatians to return to the Spirit, a call that was resounded again and again in the following chapters (3:1-3, 5, 14; 4:6, 29; 5:16-18, 22, 25; 6:1, 8, 18). How fitting to conclude on the same note: **grace** is with **your** [plural] **spirit.**

BIBLIOGRAPHY

Alford, Henry. *The Greek New Testament.* Vol. 4. 1852. Reprint. Grand Rapids: Guardian Press, 1973.

Boice, James M. "Galatians" in *The Expositor's Bible Commentary.* Grand Rapids: Zondervan, 1978.

Conybeare and Howson. *The Life and Epistles of St. Paul.* 1851. Reprint. Grand Rapids: Eerdmans, 1978 (15th printing).

Lightfoot, J. B. *The Epistle of St. Paul to the Galatians.* 1865. Reprint. Grand Rapids: Zondervan, 1957.

Luther, Martin. *A Commentary on St. Paul's Epistle to the*

*Galatians.* 1535. Reprint. Westwood, N.J.: Revell, 1953.

Meyer, Heinrich A. W. *Commentary on the New Testament.* Edinburgh: T & T Clark, 1877.

Packer, J. I. "Inspiration" in *New Bible Dictionary.* Edited by J. D. Douglas et al. Grand Rapids: Eerdmans, 1962.

Trench, Richard. *Synonyms of the New Testament.* London: Macmillan Co., 1876.

Wahl, Christian Abraham. *A Greek-English Lexicon of the New Testament.* Abridged by Edward Robinson. Andover: Flogg and Gould, 1825.

# EPHESIANS
## *Introduction*

The headings (1:1 and 3:1) show that this epistle claims to be that of Paul. This claim is confirmed by the testimonies of Irenaeus, *Against Heresies,* 5.2.3 and 1.8.5; Clement of Alexandria, *Stromata,* 4.65, and *Paidagogos,* 1.8; Origen, *Against Celsus,* 4, 211. It is quoted (3:14-18) by Valentinus (A.D. 120), as we know from Hippolytus's *Refutation of Heresies.* Polycarp, in his *Epistle to the Philippians,* chapter 12, testifies to its canonicity. So does Tertullian, *Against Marcion,* 5.17. Ignatius, in *Ephesians,* 12, alludes to the frequent and affectionate mention made by Paul of the Christian state, privileges, and persons of the Ephesians in his epistle.

This epistle was addressed, most probably, to several churches in the district around Ephesus—namely, Asia. The Epistle to the Ephesians, so-called, was not really intended to be only for the church at Ephesus. Most modern scholars are convinced that it was an encyclical that went to several churches in Asia, including Ephesus. There are several reasons to affirm this. First, the earliest manuscripts (the Chester Beatty Papyrus—P46, Codex Sinaiticus, Codex Vaticanus) do not contain the words "in Ephesus" in Ephesians 1:1. It appears that Paul purposely left the name of the locality out, so as to be filled in later as the letter circulated to each locality. (The Greek construction in 1:1 calls for a prepositional phrase designating a locality to be present in the sentence.) Since Ephesus was the leading city of Asia, it was quite natural for scribes to assign this epistle to the church at Ephesus. Second, the Epistle to the Ephesians has all the marks of being a general treatise rather than an epistle to a specific local church. Paul had lived with the saints at Ephesus for three years (Acts 20:31). He knew them intimately. And yet in this epistle there are no personal greetings or specific exhortations. When we consider Paul's manner in many of his other epistles, it would be quite unlike him to have excluded these personal expressions. Quite the contrary, Paul speaks to the saints whom he has only heard about and who have only heard about him (see 1:15; 3:1). It is possible that this epistle was the one sent to Laodicea, and several scholars since have affirmed the same (including Conybeare and Howson). But in all fairness it must be said that the encyclical theory has been opposed by some scholars. For example, Alford makes the following objections to this theory: (1) It is at variance with the spirit of the epistle, which is clearly addressed to one set of persons throughout, coexisting in one place, and as one body, and under the same circumstances. (2) The improbability that the apostle, who in two of his epistles

(2 Corinthians and Galatians) has so plainly specified their encyclical character, should have here omitted such specification. (3) The absence of personal greetings is not an argument for either of the two theories; for similarly there are none in Galatians, Philippians, 1 and 2 Thessalonians, and 1 Timothy. The better he knows the parties addressed, and the more general and solemn the subject, the less he seems to give of these individual notices.

Paul's first visit to Ephesus (on the seacoast of Lydia, near the River Cayster) is related in Acts 18:19-21. The work, begun by his disputations with the Jews in his short visit, was carried on by Apollos (Acts 18:24-26) and Aquila and Priscilla (Acts 18:26). At his second visit, after his journey to Jerusalem, and thence to the east regions of Asia Minor, he remained at Ephesus "three years" (Acts 19:10—the "two years" in this verse are only *part* of the time—and Acts 20:31); so that the founding and rearing of this church occupied an unusually large portion of the apostle's time and care. Therefore, the language in the epistle shows a warmth of feeling and a free outpouring of thought, and a union in spiritual privileges and hope between him and them such as are natural from one so long and so intimately associated with those whom he addresses. On his last journey to Jerusalem, he sailed by Ephesus and summoned the elders of the Ephesian church to meet him at Miletus, where he delivered his remarkable farewell charge (Acts 20:18-35).

This epistle was addressed to the Ephesians during the early part of Paul's imprisonment at Rome. It was written immediately after the one to the Colossians, to which it bears a close resemblance in many passages, the apostle having in his mind generally the same great truths in writing both. It is an undesigned proof of genuineness that the two epistles, written about the same date, and under the same circumstances, bear a closer mutual resemblance than those written at distant dates and on different occasions. (Cf. 1:7 with Col. 1:14; 1:10 with Col. 1:20; 3:2 with Col. 1:25; 5:19 with Col. 3:16; 6:22 with Col. 4:8; 1:19 and 2:5 with Col. 2:12, 13; 4:2-4 with Col. 3:12-15; 4:16 with Col. 2:19; 4:32 with Col. 3:13; 4:22-24 with Col. 3:9, 10; 5:6-8 with Col. 3:6-8; 5:15, 16 with Col. 4:5; 6:19, 20 with Col. 4:3, 4; 5:22-33 and 6:1-9 with Col. 3:18; 4:24, 25 with Col. 3:9; 5:20-22 with Col. 3:17, 18.) Tychicus and Onesimus were being sent to Colosse, the former bearing the two epistles to the two churches respectively, the latter furnished with a letter of recommendation to Philemon, his former master, residing at Colosse. The date was probably about four years after his parting with the Ephesian elders at Miletus (Acts 20), about A.D. 61, before his imprisonment had become of the more severe kind, which he mentions in his Epistle to the Philippians. From 6:19, 20 it is plain he had at the time, though a prisoner, some degree of freedom in preaching, which agrees with Acts 28:23, 30, 31, where he is represented as receiving at his lodgings all inquirers. His imprisonment began in A.D. 60 or 61 and lasted "two whole years" (Acts 28:30) at least, and perhaps longer.

The church at Ephesus (and surrounding churches) was made up of converts partly from the Jews and partly from the Gentiles (Acts 19:8-10). Accordingly, the epistle addresses a church so constituted (2:14-22). Ephesus was famed for its idol temple of Artemis or Diana which, after its having been burnt down by Herostratus on the night that Alexander the Great was born (356 B.C.), was rebuilt at enormous cost and was one of the wonders of the world. Hence, perhaps, have arisen his images in this epistle drawn from a beautiful temple: the church being in true inner beauty that which the temple of the idol tried to realize in outward show (2:19-22). The epistle (4:17; 5:1-13) implies the profligacy for which the Ephesian heathen were notorious. Many of the same expressions occur in the epistle as in Paul's address to the Ephesian elders. (Cf. 1:6, 7 and 2:7, as to "grace," with Acts 20:24, 32—this may well be called "the Epistle of the grace of God" [Alford]. Also, as to his "bonds," 3:1, and 4:1 with Acts 20:22, 23. Also 1:11, as to "the counsel of God," with Acts 20:27. Also 1:14, as to "the redemption of the purchased possession," with Acts 20:28. Also 1:14, 18; 2:20, and 5:5, as to the "inheritance," with Acts 20:32.)

Finally, the Epistle to the Ephesians is Paul's treatise on the universal church, the body of Christ. As such, it is not encumbered with local problems. It soars high above any mundane affairs and takes us into heaven, where we are presented with a heavenly view of the church as it fits into God's eternal plan. In this epistle Paul paints the church with multifarious splendor. He depicts her as God's inheritance (1:11), Christ's body, his fullness (1:22, 23), God's masterpiece (2:10), the one new man (2:15), the household of God (2:19), the habitation of God (2:21, 22), the joint-body comprised of Jewish and Gentile believers (3:6), the vessel for God to display his multifarious wisdom (3:10), the body equaling Christ's full stature (4:12, 13), the full-grown, perfect man (4:13), the body growing into a building (4:16), the bride of Christ (5:23-32), the object of Christ's love (5:25), the very members of Christ's body (5:30), and God's warrior against Satan (6:11-18). Paul's presentation of the church reached its pinnacle in this epistle. The church he pictured with words was the church in ideal perfection, the church as seen from heaven—but not yet manifested on earth in fullness. There have been real expressions of this church throughout history, but most would agree that the church has not yet reached "the measure of the stature of the fullness of Christ"—nor is it yet the glorious church without spot or blemish. But there is the expectation that the church will grow and grow until its manifestation matches the image.

## Chapter 1

### 1-14 GOD'S ETERNAL PURPOSE FOR THE CHURCH; PLANNED BY THE FATHER, SECURED BY THE SON, AND PUT INTO EFFECT BY THE HOLY SPIRIT

**➤1 by the will of God**—through God's will. Paul was called to the apostleship through the same "will" that originated the church (1:5, 9, 11; Gal. 1:4). **saints**—sanctified ones, set apart by God and for God. **at Ephesus**—This phrase is not present in the three earliest manuscripts (Chester Beatty Papyrus, P46; Codex Vaticanus; Codex Sinaiticus), which could very well indicate that this epistle was an encyclical letter, whereby the name of each local church would be filled in as the encyclical circulated from church to church. Ephesus, the leading church in the region of Asia Minor, was probably the first destination for this epistle. (See Introduction for more discussion on this;

see also *GAM*.) **and . . . faithful**—is not a different category from "the saints"; rather, it is a further description of the same Christians.

**➤2** See Romans 1:7; 1 Corinthians 1:3; 2 Corinthians 1:2; Galatians 1:3.

**➤3** The initial praise to God in almost all the Epistles overflows with a real sense of God's grace as experienced by the writers and their readers (cf. 1 Pet. 1:3). In 1:3-14, Paul summarizes the triune God's plan for the church: (1) the *Father's* work of love (1:3) in choosing us to holiness (1:4), sonship (1:5), acceptance (1:6), to receive the knowledge of his will (1:8, 9), to participate in his heading up all things in Christ (1:10), to be his inheritance (1:11), and to be his glory (1:12); (2) the *Son's* act of redemption (1:7) and head of God's ultimate summation (1:10); and (3) the *Holy Spirit's* work of sealing us (1:13) and becoming the earnest (or, token) of our eternal inheritance (1:14). **the God and Father of our Lord Jesus Christ**—speaking of Christ in his humanity. **hath blessed us**—God has blessed us by allowing us to receive the benefits of Christ's redemption (1:7) and resurrection (1:19, 20). **all spiritual blessings**—We are already heirs to every possible spiritual blessing both now and for eternity. **in heavenly places**—This is the realm in which the spiritual blessings were secured for us and then given to us. Our blessings come from heaven where Christ now lives (1:20), and Christ's gift of the Holy Spirit, the source of all spiritual blessings, came as a result of his ascension to heaven (4:8). **in Christ**—by virtue of our union with Christ. Christ is the source and center of all good things given to us.

➤**4 hath chosen us**—or, elected us. The past tense refers to God's original election. **in him**—This phrase emphasizes the idea from the previous verse that it is because of our oneness with Christ, the Reconciler and Head of the church, that we were chosen. The Father's choice of each of his sons was determined by our eventual union with his Son. **before the foundation of the world**—This assumes the eternity of Christ (John 17:5, 24), and of God's plan for those who believe (2 Thess. 2:13; 2 Tim. 1:9). **holy**—See Deuteronomy 14:2. **without blame**—faultless, blemishless (5:27; 1 Thess. 3:13). **before him**—Though we stand before God the Judge, we are assured of our acceptance because of Christ's sacrifice (Col. 1:22, Rev. 7:15). **in love**—Love is both the basis for and the end product of our holiness (5:2; 1 Thess. 3:12, 13). Many commentators and translators prefer to join "in love" with 1:5. Kept at the end of 1:4, it characterizes the believers' position before God; placed at the beginning of 1:5, it describes the motivation of God's predestination.

➤**5 predestinated**—lit., "marked out beforehand"; according to the Greek, the action is concurrent with "hath chosen" (1:4). **unto the adoption of children**—lit., "unto sonship." The Greek word indicates legal placement into the position and privileges of sonship. This "outward" placement is complemented by an implantation of the Spirit of God's Son in our hearts (see Gal. 4:5 and comments). **by** [through] **Jesus Christ**—our sonship is activated by Jesus Christ and our union with him. **according to the good pleasure of his will**—joins with "predestinated"; it describes the good pleasure God enjoyed in predestinating us to become his sons. The word for "will" in Greek (*thelēma*) is more emotive than volitional; thus, God's will is God's heart's desire.

➤**6 To the praise of the glory of his grace**—See 1:7, 17, 18. The end of God's plan is that all his creatures, men and angels, will praise him for his grace. **he hath made us accepted**—he favored us; he graced us. Having been accepted through Christ, we are the recipients of God's grace (Rom. 3:24; 5:15). **in the beloved**—cf. Matthew 3:17; 17:5; John 3:35; Colossians 1:13. God's favor to us is realized by virtue of our union with his beloved Son. We could say that God's love for his only Son motivated him to have many more sons—each of which would be like his Son (Rom. 8:28-30) by being in his Son and by being conformed to his image.

➤**7 In whom**—in the beloved Son. **we have redemption**—This includes release from the guilt and the deserved punishment for sin. By Jewish law (Lev. 25:48), a slave unable to free himself could be freed by a relative. Christ became human, like us, so that he could free us from slavery to sin (Matt. 20:28). **through his blood**—Christ is the instrument through which God, being justly angry with man (Isa. 12:1), showed his kindness and favor to man. Christ's life was the price paid for man's sin (Acts 20:28; Rom. 3:25; 1 Cor. 6:20; Col. 1:20; 1 Pet. 1:18, 19). **the forgiveness of sins**—Greek, "the remission of trespasses," which follows as a consequence of redemption. **the riches of his grace**—i.e., the wealth of God's favor (cf. 1:18; 3:16).

➤**8 Wherein**—actually, "which," referring to "grace" (1:7). **wisdom and prudence** [understanding]—could be joined with the preceding phrase or the following. If it goes with the following, it can be understood that wisdom and understanding are given to the saints for them to know the mystery of God's will. If it goes with the preceding, it speaks of God's wisdom and intelligence. God's perfect wisdom and knowledge is evident in his planning of our redemption and sonship, and in carrying out that plan in history (cf. 3:10).

➤**9 Having made known**—or, "making known," an action concurrent with "hath abounded" (1:8). **the mystery**—a secret now revealed to Christian initiates. What was formerly hidden is now made clear (6:19; Rom. 16:25; Col. 1:26, 27). This secret is not like the "mysteries" of the heathen, given only to the initiated few, but is for all who love Christ.

his will—See comments on 1:5, 6. **according to his good pleasure**—joins with "making known to us" (i.e., it is God's good pleasure to make known to us the mystery of his will). **purposed**—See 1:11. **in himself**—God the Father.

**►10 That in the dispensation**—This should be rendered "unto [for] a stewardship [or, economy]." The mystery that God purposed was for (or, would result in) a stewardship. This Greek is *oikonomia;* it means "household management," here to be understood on a very large scale—hence, it could be rendered "administration" or "economy." **the fulness of times**—more comprehensive than the "fulness of time" in Galatians 4:4; the Ephesian phrase includes the entire time during which the gospel is available to men, and the church, as God's household, is involved with God's administration and economy. (Cf. other expressions dealing with time periods in Luke 21:24; Acts 1:7; 3:20, 21; 1 Cor. 10:11.) This verse refers to Christ's return to earth; other examples of such epochal events have been Christ's first coming, the descent of the Holy Spirit "when Pentecost was fully come" (Acts 2:1), and the witness of the apostles to Christ's ministry "in due time" (1 Tim. 2:6). The conversion of the Jews, Christ's return, the thousand-year kingdom, and the new heaven and earth are other specific "times" that will occur in the future when it pleases God. **gather together in one**—Greek, "to sum up," "to gather up under one head." God's purpose is to bring all of creation (angels and men, Jews and Gentiles, living and dead, animate and inanimate) under one head, Christ. Sin has caused disorder in the relationship of all creation to God, but Christ has provided the means (Col. 1:20) by which that order may be restored. Subjectively, the community of all Christians to whom Paul was writing was subordinated to God in conscious and joyful unity. Objectively, all of creation is subordinated to him.

**►11 In whom**—in union with whom. **we have obtained an inheritance**—Actually, this should read, "we were chosen as his inheritance." **predestinated**—lit., "marked out beforehand." See comments on 1:5. **purpose**—plan or design (lit., "that which is laid out beforehand"—like a blueprint). We were marked out beforehand to fit into God's design.

As Israel was foreordained to be the elect nation, so the spiritual Israelites, the believers in Christ, were chosen or foreordained to be an eternal gift to God. **counsel of his . . . will**—God's eternal plan emanated from his heart's desire (will) to have many sons in union with his beloved Son. Then this plan was to be carried out according to a counsel in which God purposed, planned, designed, predestinated, and elected.

**►12 who first trusted in Christ**—actually, "who were the first to trust in [the] Christ" (TLB). This refers to the Jewish Christians, who were given the promise of Christ in which to hope, and who looked forward to his actual coming, waiting for the deliverance of Israel (cf. Acts 26:6, 7; 28:20; Eph. 1:18; 2:12; 4:4).

**►13 ye also**—referring to the Gentiles. The priority of the Jews does not exclude the Gentiles from God's goodness given through Christ (cf. Acts 13:46). **the word of truth, the gospel**—The gospel conveys the word of truth, which sanctifies the believer through regeneration (John 17:17; 2 Tim. 2:15; James 1:18). **sealed**—Whether Jew or Gentile, the Christian is confirmed as God's adopted child by the seal of the Holy Spirit (Acts 19:1-6; Rom. 8:16, 23; 2 Cor. 1:22; 1 John 3:24). In ancient times, a seal affixed to a document gave validity to its contents (John 3:33; 6:27; 2 Cor. 3:3) and also marked its ownership. So, the Holy Spirit, filling us with the sense of God's love (Rom. 5:5), assuring us that God has adopted us as his children (Rom. 8:15, 16), and helping us to manifest our likeness to Christ, serves as a mark or seal of God's acceptance. The sealing by the Spirit is a once-and-for-all act that gives us continued assurance that we are God's children, entitled to his riches and goodness, now as well as in eternity. **that holy Spirit of promise**—actually, the promised Holy Spirit. The Holy Spirit was promised in both the OT and NT (Joel 2:28; Zech. 12:10; John 7:37-39; Acts 1:4, 5; 2:38, 39). Those who believe God's Word are sealed by the promised Spirit.

**►14 Which**—refers to the Spirit (1:13). **earnest**—downpayment, guarantee. Like earnest money in the purchase of real estate, God's Spirit provides us with his guarantee that the rest of his promises to us will materialize (Rom. 8:23; 2 Cor. 1:22). **our inheritance**—cf. 1:11, which states that we were chosen as God's inheritance. Here, God gives us an inheritance. But we will not yet receive that inheritance **until the redemption of the purchased possession**—i.e., until we have received our full and final redemption, which includes the transformation of our bodies (Rom. 8:21-23; 2 Pet. 3:13). Christ purchased us to be God's possession. As we highly value that for which we pay a high price, God valued his church so much that he sacrificed his Son to gain it (5:25, 26; 1 Pet. 1:18; 2:9).

## 15-23 PAUL'S PRAYER THAT THE BELIEVERS MAY KNOW GOD'S PURPOSE FOR THE CHURCH AND GOD'S POWER IN CHRIST TO THE CHURCH

➤**15 Wherefore**—therefore, because. **after I heard of your faith**—This could support the view that this epistle was an encyclical because it is unlikely that Paul would say this about the Ephesians to whom he had brought the gospel. (But compare Philem. 4, 5.) **love unto all the saints**—Love among Christians is one of the distinguishing traits (6:24).

➤**16 of you**—This phrase is not present in the earliest manuscripts. The words have been supplied.

➤**17 the God of our Lord Jesus Christ**—See comments on 1:3. "Lord" is an appropriate title for the Christ whom God raised from the dead to become the Head of his church (1:20, 22). Christ refers to his Father as "my God" in Matthew 27:46; John 20:17. **the Father of glory**—The Father of that infinite glory which shines in the face of Christ, who is the true Shekinah glory (see John 1:14; 17:24; Acts 7:2; 2 Cor. 3:7–4:6). **the spirit of wisdom**—either means "a spirit endued with wisdom" or "the Spirit that gives wisdom" (see Isa. 11:2). **and revelation**—enlightened understanding. **in the knowledge of him**—lit., "a fuller knowledge of him" (a more complete, progressive knowledge of God the Father). One of the functions of the Spirit is to help the Christian see God as he really is (John 16:14, 15; 1 Cor. 2:10).

➤**18 The eyes of your understanding being enlightened**—lit., "having the eyes of your heart enlightened," as a result of the Spirit giving wisdom and revelation. The eye is the symbol of intelligence; the heart is the source of life (Matt. 5:8; 6:22, 23). Just as God's first act with respect to our physical world was to create light where there had been only darkness (Gen. 1:3; 2 Cor. 4:6), so he gives light to the recreated individual (John 1:4) by means of the Spirit's wisdom and revelation. **the hope of his calling**—i.e., the hope to which he has called you. **the riches of the glory**—or, the glorious wealth. **his inheritance in the saints**—God's wealth deposited in the believers is his inheritance, his precious possession.

➤**19 the exceeding greatness of his power to usward who believe**—The same power that caused Christ to be raised after his death is available to the believers (1:20); it is now transmitted through the Head (Christ) to the body. **according**—in accordance with. **working**—Greek, "energizing." **his mighty power**—lit., "the might of his strength."

➤**20 when he raised him from the dead**—Christ's resurrection not only assures us that our bodies will, like Christ's, be raised incorruptible (Rom. 6:8-11; 8:11), it unites us to our living Head—by virtue of the resurrected life given to us (John 11:25). Christ, as God, had a part in raising himself (John 2:19; 10:17, 18), and the Holy Spirit also participated (Rom. 1:4; 1 Pet. 3:18). **and set** [seated] **him**—The angels do not sit at God's right hand; rather, they stand about the throne (Heb. 1:13). **at his own** [God's] **right hand**—See Psalm 110:1. Christ will remain there until all his enemies have been overcome (1 Cor. 15:25). He was appointed to rule during the rebellion caused by God's enemies (Ps. 110:2), and will retain this position until they have been subjected (Mark 16:19; Heb. 1:3; 10:12). According to ancient practice, the seat at the right hand signified a position of equality and/or superiority (cf. Phil. 2:9). **in the heavenly places**—See 1:3. Since Christ entered heaven with a physical body, heaven is not a mere state, but a place.

➤**21 principality**—or, rule. **power**—authority. **might**—power. **dominion**—lordship. Christ occupies a position of power and authority far greater than anyone can imagine (Matt. 28:18; 1 Cor. 15:24; cf. Phil. 2:9, Col. 1:16; Heb. 7:26; 1 Pet. 3:22). The hierarchy of good and evil spirits (6:12), as well as of earthly rulers, is included under Christ's dominion (Rom. 8:38). Christ is "King of kings, and Lord of lords" (Rev. 19:16). The higher the honor of Christ, the Head, the higher is that of his people. Some early Asian philosophers taught the names of the ranks of the angels, but Paul shows here that the truest wisdom is to understand that Christ is supreme above all other beings. **every name**—Christ's honor is greater than that of all other created beings (Rom. 8:39). **in this world**—This refers to the world as we now know it (Rom. 8:38). **that which is to come**—Christ is above all, including beings of whom we are presently unaware, but who will be made known to us in the future (Bengel).

➤**22 put . . . under**—lit., "subjected under" (Ps. 8:6; 1 Cor. 15:27). **gave him to be the head over all things to the church**—"God, in giving Christ to the Church, gave him the capacity of Head over all things" (Salmond). Christ (supreme over all creation), as Head of the church, also gives the church a share in his dominion. "Head" also implies the unity between Christ and the Christian body; thus through his being at God's right hand, we are there also (Rev. 3:21).

➤**23 Which is his body**—This is his mystical and spiritual body, the church. **the fulness of him**—The church is the receptacle for God's gifts and graces. As Christ is filled with all of God (John 1:16; Col. 1:19; 2:9), so the church becomes Christ's fullness as he imparts God to her (Col. 2:10). The expression could also mean, "his completeness," in the sense that Christ's body completes the head and thus gives him fullness of expression. **that** [who] **filleth all in all**—Christ, the Creator, Ruler, and Sustainer of the universe (Col. 1:16-19) fills all of creation.

# Chapter 2

## 1-10 SAVED BY GRACE
## TO BE GOD'S MASTERPIECE

➤**1 And you hath he quickened** [made alive]—The predicate, not present in Greek, has to be supplied from 2:5 (where it finally appears in the Gk.). This verse is definitely a continuation of 1:19-23, which speaks of the resurrection power imparted to Christ's body. Here, it is the resurrection life (2:5, 6) imparted to his body. **who were dead**—spiritually dead (Col. 2:13). **in trespasses and sins**—Sin involves alienation from God, which results in the death of the spirit (Isa. 9:2; John 5:25; 1 Tim. 5:6). "Sin" implies an

innate state of corruption; "trespass," in Greek, expresses a fall or lapse. Paul may have been applying the word "trespass" to the Jews who had the law yet ignored it, and "sins" to the Gentiles who had not known God.

➤**2 ye walked**—which means, "you conducted your life." **according to the course of this world**—lit., "according to this world's age," referring to the present and prevalent milieu that controls those who live in it (cf. 1 Cor. 2:6, 12; 3:18, 19; Gal. 1:4). This "age" is alienated from God and subject to evil powers (1 John 5:19). **prince of the power of the air**—or, the ruler of the aerial authority. Satan and his demons presently control this world (cf. John 12:31; 2 Cor. 4:4; 6:12). Christ's ascension seems to have cast Satan out of heaven (Rev. 12:5, 9, 10, 12, 13), where he had until that time been pleading his case against man before God (Job 1). No longer able to accuse those for whom Christ had removed the charges (Rom. 8:33, 34), Satan corrupts the earth. The term "power" (Gk. "authority") is here used as a plural, implying all the various singular powers of the air, or "the totality of evil powers" (Plummer). **the spirit**—is in apposition to "the power"; it is also used here collectively. Hence, the totality of evil powers is the spirit (collectively speaking) that works in the disobedient. **now worketh in**—Paul wanted the Ephesians to recognize Satan's work as a present threat rather than just a past occurrence. In other words, the Greek does not allow "the spirit" to refer to Satan, "the prince" himself, but to "the power of the air" (of which he is prince). The aerial power is the embodiment of that evil spirit, which is the ruling principle of unbelievers. **the children of disobedience**—This is a Hebraism describing men who are not ignorantly disobeying God but rather are consciously refusing to obey (Matt. 3:7). The force of the evil spirit is seen in those who actively disobey God both in faith and action (Isa. 30:9; 57:4; 2 Cor. 2:12; 2 Thess. 1:8).

➤**3 Among whom also we**—Paul included himself with the Ephesian Jews and Gentiles, switching from the second person (2:1, 2) to the first person in this verse. **had our conversation**—conducted ourselves (2 Cor. 1:12; 1 Pet. 1:18). This phrase implies an outwardly more decorous life-style than the flagrantly sinful past lives of most of the Ephesian Gentiles. Paul and his fellow Jews, though outwardly more proper than the Gentiles (Acts 26:4, 5, 18), had been just like them in living unregenerate and unreconciled lives. **fulfilling**—doing. **the desires of the flesh and of the mind**—The two concepts are distinct, with "desires of the flesh" representing blind impulses from the flesh and "desires of the mind" being mental suggestions and intentions that are independent of God. **and were by nature the children of wrath**—Men have not simply chosen to sin, thus becoming children of evil under God's anger; rather, man's original state from birth is evil, and thus all men's lives are innately corrupt. The word "nature" in Greek refers to a particular characteristic of our being which has grown in us and has been strengthened by our efforts, as distinguished from that which is placed upon us by external influences (Job 14:4; Ps. 51:5). This is an incidental proof for the doctrine of original sin. Cf. this statement from the Church of England Common Prayer Book: "Original sin (birth-sin) standeth not in the following of Adam, but is the fault and corruption of the nature of every man, naturally descended from Adam (Christ being supernaturally conceived), whereby man is very far gone from original righteousness, and is of his own nature, inclined to evil; and therefore, in every person born into this world, it deserves God's anger and damnation." **we . . . even as others**—Paul pointed out that even the Jews who descended from Abraham were by natural birth children of anger, as were the Gentiles (Rom. 3:9; 5:12-14; John 3:36). The phrase "children of wrath" is a Hebraism that conveys the principle of innate evil in man and God's consequent displeasure.

➤**4** God's rich mercy is the basis of our salvation. **for** [because of] **his great love**—joins with "hath quickened us" in 1:5 (cf. 1:7; 2:7; Rom. 2:4; 10:12).

➤**5 dead in sins** [trespasses]—Because of our innate sin we were dead to God. **hath quickened us**—vivified us, made us alive. This verse resumes the direct grammatical thought of 2:5 and finally provides the predicate: "were dead" in 2:1 is repeated here and then it says "made alive." As was noted in 2:1, the first part of chapter 2 is actually a continuation of 1:19-23, in which Paul describes Christ's resurrection and the dynamic effect it

continues to have in the church. What Paul started to say in 2:1 is now completed—when Christ was vivified from the dead, so were the members of his body, by virtue of God uniting them with him. **together with Christ**—in union with Christ. Christians were united with Christ in his resurrection (see Rom. 6:5; Col. 3:1). **by grace ye are saved**—lit., "you are [in a state of] having been saved." The perfect tense assures us that we have already passed from death to life (John 5:24). Salvation is not something to be waited for, but something that has already been delivered (1 John 3:14). Paul inserts this parenthetic clause to emphasize that it is only because of God's grace that we are saved.

➤**6 And hath raised us up together**—with Christ. Being raised up with Christ presupposes the quickening of Jesus in the tomb and of us in the grave of our sins. **made us sit together**—with Christ. The Head of the church is seated at God's right hand; thus as members of his (spiritual) body, we are already there with him, and in eternity shall be with him bodily. **in heavenly places**—lit., "in the heavenlies." See 1:3. **in Christ Jesus**—Our union with Christ is the basis for our present regeneration and future resurrection. The phrase "in Christ Jesus," which is commonly used in this letter, refers to Christ's office as Prophet, Priest, and King. When the person of Christ is the prominent concern, "Jesus Christ" is used.

➤**7 in the ages to come**—Members of Christ's church are to display God's grace during the time in which God's secret plan is revealed. These ages, though beginning with the first telling of the gospel, will not be completed until Christ returns (cf. 1:21; Heb. 6:5). **might show**—might show forth for himself (middle, reflexive in Greek). **exceeding riches**—or, surpassing wealth. **through Christ Jesus**—actually, through Jesus Christ. This same expression is often repeated to show that our blessings center in Christ.

➤**8 are ye saved**—or you have been saved (the perfect tense in Gk. emphasizes the abiding effect of our initial salvation). **through faith**—By faith we receive the effect of the power of Christ's resurrection (1:19, 20; Phil. 3:10), raising us along with him (2:6; Col. 2:12). Faith is the means to regeneration and reconciliation on the part of the believer; Christ alone is the agent of that means. **not of your-**

selves—Even our trust is a gift (Phil. 1:29). The initiation, as well as the increase of faith, is from the Spirit of God, not only by an external proposal of the word, but by an internal illumination in the soul (Pearson). Faith comes both from hearing the gospel (Rom. 10:17) and from prayer (Luke 11:13), though in both cases it is God who allows our faith to grow (1 Cor. 3:6, 7).

➤9 Not of works—This verse reinforces the truth that our salvation is a gift, since there is no way we could earn it (Rom. 4:4, 5; 11:6). lest any man should boast—See Rom. 3:27; 4:2.

➤10 workmanship—Greek, *poïema* (lit., "a thing made"; transliterated into English, "poem.") The word indicates a handiwork, a masterpiece. God's church is his "poem," his masterpiece, his workmanship. As he is the author of his handiwork, he should get all the credit. created—a completed action. in Christ Jesus—God accomplished his workmanship in the believers by virtue of their having been united with Christ. unto good works—for good works. which God hath before ordained that we should walk [conduct our lives] in them. God determines beforehand a path for each of us. God both makes ready the opportunities for our good works and makes us ready to do them (John 15:16; 2 Tim. 2:21). We cannot expect to help others unless our own lives have first been newly created. We were not saved by our good works, but rather we have been recreated to do them (Gal. 5:22-25).

## 11-22 THE CREATION OF THE ONE NEW MAN AND GOD'S SPIRITUAL HABITATION

➤11 Wherefore remember—Remembering our former state helps strengthen our thanksgiving and faith (2:19). Gentiles—The Gentiles were called unclean by the Jews because they lacked circumcision. The Jews were circumcised and thus considered themselves clean and godly. called the Circumcision in the flesh made by hands—The Jews mistakenly believed that circumcision was sufficient to mark them as godly men without the necessity of inner renewal (see Rom. 2:29 and Col. 2:11).

➤12 without Christ ... aliens—The Gentiles were not merely separated from God, but were aliens or strangers to him. The Israelites were also separated from God, but it was because they were failing to take advantage of the position God had offered them as his people. commonwealth—or, citizenship. strangers from the covenants of promise—The plural indicates the several renewals of the covenant with Abraham, Isaac, and Jacob, and later with all the Israelites at Sinai (Rom. 9:4; Gal. 3:16. no hope—of afterlife (1 Cor. 15:19). The heathen philosophers' theories about life after death were at best vague and supplied no way to atone for evil committed during a person's life. They had no "divine promise" and therefore no basis for hope. Epicurus and Aristotle did not believe in life beyond death. The Platonists believed that the soul was constantly in a state of change; the Stoics held that it existed only until everything else was destroyed. without God—lit., "atheists." The Gentiles had no knowledge of God (Acts 14:15), whereas the Jews had distinct ideas concerning God and immortality (cf. Gal. 4:8; 1 Thess. 4:5). in the world—The Gentiles were not participants in Israel's citizenship. They lived entirely and only in this evil world (Ps. 17:14), from which God rescues his people (John 15:19; 17:14; Gal. 1:4).

➤13 now—This contrasts with "at that time" (2:12). Christ Jesus—"Jesus" is added to the title "Christ" used in 2:12, implying that the relationship is personal. sometimes—at one time. far off—This is a Jewish description of the Gentiles (2:17; Isa. 57:19; Acts 2:39). are made nigh by [in] the blood of Christ—The promise of man's being brought near to God is thus fulfilled. (Cf. 1:7, where Christ's blood is referred to as the instrument of our being brought close to God.)

➤14 he—himself. The Greek form is emphatic here. is our peace—Christ made peace with God on behalf of both Jews and Gentiles which, in turn, made the way for peace between them (2:15; cf. Isa. 9:5, 6; 53:5; Mic. 5:5; Col. 1:20). made both one—Christ took both into himself and reconciled them to God and then united them. the middle wall of partition—This alludes to the wall in the Jewish temple that separated the court of the Gentiles from the holy place occupied by the Jews. A Gentile who was caught going beyond this wall was killed (see Acts 21:28, 29). Although this wall separated Jew from Gentile, it also symbolized the opposition of both to God (2:15). Hence, there was also an inner wall separating the Jewish people from the most holy part of the temple where the priests officiated (Ezek. 44:7; Acts 21:28). This twofold wall represented the Sinaitic law, which separated all men from God (through sin, a violation of the law). Christ broke down this separation by his death on the cross.

➤15 **Having abolished in his flesh the enmity**—In the Greek, "enmity" is in direct apposition to "the middle wall." To destroy the middle wall was to annihilate the enmity. God healed the breach between Jews and Gentiles, as well as between all men and himself. **the law of commandments contained** [consisting] **in ordinances**—The law was the means by which the Jew justified himself and excluded the Gentile (Rom. 4:15; 5:20; 7:10, 11; 8:7). Christ, by his death, has destroyed the wall, substituting for it the "law of love," which is the real spirit of the law and comes from realizing the sacrifice that was made out of love. **for to make** [create] **in himself of twain** [two] **one new man**—Christ created the one new man by reconciling the two parties and incorporating them, in himself, into one new humanity, thereby making them one person in him. **making peace**—between all men and God and between Jews and Gentiles. This peacemaking came as a result of Christ's annihilation of the enmity.

➤16 **reconcile both unto God**—Paul uses this Greek word for "reconcile" only here and in Colossians 1:20. It expresses not only a return to favor, but also the discarding of all hatred and opposition so that complete harmony can exist. **in one body**—This is the same image as that used for Christ's church (Col. 3:15). **by the cross, having slain the enmity thereby**—Christ had to become human and die as a human to break the power of evil and death (Heb. 2:14; Col. 2:15).

➤17 **came and preached peace**—According to the sequence of the previous verses, this coming to preach peace was (1) Jesus' coming after the resurrection to preach to the apostles directly (see Luke 24:36; John 20:19, 21, 26) and (2) Jesus' coming through the Spirit to preach to all men far off and near. **you which were afar off**—the Gentiles (2:12). **them that were nigh**—the Jews.

➤18 It is through Christ (John 14:6; Heb. 10:19) that we have access to God (3:12; Rom. 5:2). Both the Jews and the Gentiles, united in

one Spirit, are reconciled to the Father. The unity in the Spirit, through which we are able to come to God, is necessarily followed by a unity in Christ's body, the church (2:16). Note the three distinct "persons" of the Trinity mentioned in this verse. As all people have direct access to God through Christ by means of the Spirit, any intermediate priest is unnecessary.

➤19 **strangers**—are in opposition to **household** members, and **foreigners** to fellow **citizens** (cf. Phil. 3:20). **household of God**—This "spiritual" Israel (see 2:12) includes both Jews and Gentiles who have been reconciled to God and made into his household.

➤20 **are built**—actually, "having been built" (cf. 1 Cor. 3:11, 12.) The architectural image also occurs in 3:18, in Paul's letter to the Ephesian elders (Acts 20:32), and in his writing to Timothy at Ephesus (1 Tim. 3:15; 2 Tim. 2:19). The image is quite appropriate as the Jewish temple and Diana's temple (the pagan stronghold) were both splendid examples of early architecture. The "Christian temple," however, is spiritual and eternal. **the foundation of the apostles and prophets**—i.e., the foundation originated (or, laid) by the apostles and prophets (see Alford). Their life and ministry provided the new Christian church with a foundation to build on, for Christ himself, the only true foundation, was the subject and purpose of their lives (Rev. 21:14). The "prophets" here are probably the NT prophets (see 4:11). **corner stone**—or capstone (the stone that holds the structure together).

➤21 **In whom**—Christ, the one who brought the church together and continues to hold it together. **all the building**—This is the reading in some ancient manuscripts, but the most ancient read, "the whole building." In either case, Paul was probably describing the universal habitation of God. **fitly framed together**—lit., "being joined together." This assumes the function of the cornerstone. **groweth**—the building is here depicted as a living organism (cf. 4:15, 16). The church as the growth of a living body, not mere increase as by additions to a building (cf. 1 Pet. 2:5). **holy**—because it is the habitation of the holy God. **in the Lord**—"Christ is the inclusive Head of all the building, the element in which it has its being and now its growth" (Alford).

➤**22 ye also**—the Gentile believers. **are builded together**—lit., "are being built together" (indicating a process). **for** [into] **an habitation of God**—another description of the same building in 2:21. **through the Spirit**—Greek, "in spirit" (taken as a locative) or "by [the] Spirit" (taken as an instrumental). Both are appropriate here, for God's dwelling place is in man's spirit (see Isa. 57:15; 66:1, 2; John 4:24) and God makes his dwelling place in men by his spirit (1 Cor. 3:16, 17).

Chapter **3**

## 1-13 THE MYSTERY OF CHRIST REVEALED TO PAUL AND PREACHED BY PAUL

➤**1 Jesus Christ**—should read, "Christ Jesus." Paul here identifies Jesus as the Messiah or Deliverer of the Jews. The Jews were resentful of Paul's teaching that the Messiah was for the Gentiles as well, and thus imprisoned him (3:13; 2 Tim. 2:10). He digresses at "For this cause" and does not complete the sentence until 3:14.

➤**2 If**—The Greek does not imply any doubt: "Assuming that you have heard . . . " **the dispensation of the grace of God**—i.e., the stewardship of God's grace. The office of dispensing, as a steward, the grace of God to the Gentiles, was given to Paul. The Greek word for "stewardship" (*oikonomia*—household management) continues the images pertaining to God's house or household in 2:19-22.

➤**3 the mystery**—is the secret plan unveiled (**revealed**) to the initiates. **as I wrote afore in few words**—This could refer to a separate letter, but more probably to the first part of this letter (especially 1:9, 10) where he speaks on the same theme.

➤**4 read**—by reading the previous chapters, the Ephesians could **understand** (or, perceive) Paul's **knowledge in the mystery of Christ**—This phrase can be understood in three ways: (1) "Christ's mystery" (i.e., Christ has a mystery, which is the church composed of Jewish and Gentile believers—3:6); (2) "the mystery which is Christ himself" (see Col. 1:27); or (3) "the mystery pertaining to Christ" (i.e., God's secret plan, as described in chapters

1 and 2, is intricately related to Christ). All three interpretations are defensible.

➤**5 now revealed unto his holy apostles and prophets**—God's method of communicating with the Israelites was to reveal things to a chosen prophet, who would in turn teach the people. The OT prophets had some knowledge of God's plan to include the Gentiles as his children (Isa. 56:6, 7; 49:6), but they did not clearly understand the secret that was now being revealed (Acts 10:19, 20; 11:18-21). The OT does not show, for example, that the Gentiles would share equally with the Jews in God's acceptance, or that tokens such as circumcision could be omitted. The gift of the Holy Spirit to all believers is also reserved for the NT Christians. The "prophets" mentioned here are the NT prophets (see 4:11).

➤**6 fellow heirs . . . same body . . . partakers**—The idea in Greek is something like this: "joint heirs . . . joint body [united body] . . . joint partakers." This verse continues the thought of 3:3. The mystery (secret) of Christ is that the Gentiles with the Jews were to become a united body in Christ. No man ever knew this, until God revealed it to Paul and the other NT apostles and prophets. The OT foretold the salvation of the Gentiles through the Jews, but it never spoke of the Jews and Gentiles becoming one body under Christ's headship.

➤**7 Whereof**—of which, referring to "the gospel" (3:6). **according to**—in consequence of, and in accordance with **the gift of the grace of God. effectual working**—lit., "inworking."

➤**8 am**—The present tense shows that this is Paul's current evaluation of himself (1 Tim. 1:15). **less than the least**—lit., "leaster," an expression coined by Paul to express his self-deprecation. **of all saints**—Paul set himself below not only other apostles but all Christians (cf. 1 Cor. 15:9, 10). **preach**—as the gospel. **unsearchable** [untrackable] **riches** [wealth] **of Christ**—The riches of Christ are the capital of God's NT economy.

➤**9 to make all men see**—"to bring to light" (see 1:18). This indicates that all people were to know that it pleased God at this time to make known his secret plan by means of Paul and other Christians. **the fellowship of the mystery**—According to all the earliest manuscripts, this should read "the stewardship of the mystery." This stewardship is the administration that carries out God's secret plan. **from the beginning**—Greek, "from the ages," referring to vast periods of time, marked by successive stages of creation and orders of beings. **hid in God**—God kept his plan (to have one body in Christ) a secret. **who created all things**—Having created everything (physical and spiritual), God has an absolute right to order and plan things according to his will. Hence, he had complete right to keep the mystery of the church a secret until the time he chose to make it known. **by Jesus Christ**—This phrase is not present in the earliest manuscripts.

►**10 unto the principalities and powers . . . might be known**—God first shows his plan to the various orders of good angels, to which they respond joyfully (1 Tim. 3:16; 1 Pet. 1:12). He secondly shows his wisdom to the evil angels (residing in heaven in the lower sense, i.e., "the air"; cf. 2:2 with 6:12), who then understand their hopelessness (1 Cor. 15:24; Col. 2:15). **by [through] the church**—Through the church, God displays his wisdom (Luke 15:10; 1 Cor. 4:9) to the angels, who are man's fellow servants (Rev. 19:10). **manifold wisdom**—multifarious wisdom. God's wisdom, though it has unity, is seen in many different ways (Isa. 55:8, 9; Heb. 1:1). The church, though seen by us as a collection of single Christians doing singular acts, is really a unified whole, complete in Christ.

►**11 According to the eternal purpose**—joins with "might be known" in 3:10. **purposed**—actually, "made."

►**12 access**—to God (2:18). The Greek implies a formal introduction into the presence of a king.

►**13** It is because of God's love that he gave his Son, and that he allows his servants to suffer (i.e., Paul's imprisonment). Paul's suffering was the Gentile's glory, as their trust was strengthened (1 Cor. 4:10).

14-21 PAUL'S PRAYER FOR THE EPHESIANS TO BE STRENGTHENED BY THE SPIRIT, INDWELT BY CHRIST, AND FILLED WITH ALL THE FULLNESS OF GOD

►**14** This verse resumes the thought begun in 3:1. **I bow my knees**—Since our posture has some bearing on our mind, our physical attitude in prayer is not unimport-

ant. Both Paul (Acts 20:36) and Christ (Luke 22:41) sometimes prayed on their knees. **Father**—The ground for our being children in God's family is in Jesus.

►**15 Of whom the whole family in heaven and earth is named**—Some translate this as "all families" or "every family," referring to the several families of heaven and earth. Paul would thus be implying that God, in relation to his children, is the archetypal father. The idea that the angels are in distinct spiritual families is not found anywhere else in the Bible. Acts 2:36 tends to support the translation, as here, of "the whole family," in which both men and angels make up one family under God the Father through Christ (1:10; Phil. 2:10). Angels, then, are called our brothers (Rev. 19:10), and "sons of God" (Job 38:7) by their natural creation, as we are by regeneration. The church is part of this great family which includes, besides men, the higher spiritual creation, where the archetypes that man now strives for are already perfectly known. The Lord's Prayer includes the idea that this family is one universal community. Our sin, which separated us from God, also separated us from the higher spiritual world where his kingdom already exists. Thus, as Christ reconciles man to God and unites them (Jew and Gentile) together, so he also joins man to those beings who are already included in the perfect kingdom for which the church on earth hopes.

►**16 according to the riches of his glory**—or, according to his glorious wealth (cf. 1:18; 3:8). **to be strengthened with might**—cf. 1:19-22. **by his Spirit in the inner man**—Unbelievers have the same worldly nature inside and out. In Christians, "the inner man is one's inner regenerated being, in contrast to the old body." (See 1 Pet. 3:4.)

►**17 dwell**—The Greek conveys the idea, "settle down." Christ settles down in our hearts by faith. **by faith**—As we trust him, Christ changes our hearts, and consequently our words and thoughts. **being rooted and grounded in love**—both perfect participles in Greek: "having been rooted and having been founded" (emphasizing the present result of a past action). In the Greek, this clause is connected with 3:18, suggesting that by being "rooted" we will then be able to understand the magnitude of God's love. "Rooted" brings to mind the image of a tree; "grounded,"a building (see comments on 2:21, 22; Col. 2:7). Love, resulting from the Spirit's presence within us, is the basis for our understanding of the vastness of God's love.

➤**18 May be able**—Greek, "may be extra-strong." **to comprehend**—to grasp, to lay hold of. **with all saints**—This is a corporate endeavor. **breadth . . . length . . . depth . . . height**—For whatever reason, the prepositional phrase after these four nouns was not written. The most natural choice would be "of Christ's love," supplied from 3:19. Breadth might symbolize Christ's love reaching horizontally to men all over the world; length, his love extended to all ages (3:21); depth, the perfect wisdom of his love that no creature can completely comprehend (Rom. 11:33); and height, his love as triumphant and beyond the reach of any adversary (4:8) (Bengel). Breadth could also refer to the free gift of God's love to all (Jew and Gentile) that Paul has been writing about (3:3-9) and which he now prays that the Ephesians might understand more fully. Depth and height might express God's bringing us from the lower state (sin) to the highest (being with him).

➤**19 to know the love of Christ, which passeth knowledge**—The paradox in this verse implies that when Paul says "know," he does not mean that we can "rationally explain" God's love completely or even adequately. Rather, we are to know Christ's love by experiencing it. **ye might be filled with** [unto] **all the fulness of God**—Note the plural; no single believer could be filled to all God's fullness (which is the totality and completeness of God). Christ's body, his fullness (1:23), is the receptacle for all God's fullness.

➤**20 above all that we ask or think**—Our thoughts include more than we dare to ask in our prayers; our dreams exceed what we consciously desire. **according to the power**—God is willing to give more than we are capable of asking for (Rom. 8:26).

➤**21 glory**—When God's whole plan is known, all will glorify him. **in the church**—The plan of God is for the church, which is the means of showing God's glory (3:10), **by**

**Christ Jesus. throughout all ages, world without end**—lit., "unto all the generations of the age of the ages" (an expression designating eternity).

*Chapter* **4**

## 1-16 UNITY IN CHRIST'S BODY

➤**1 I . . . beseech you**—Paul now pleads with the Ephesians to follow God's plan. **the prisoner of the Lord**—Paul was imprisoned for telling the gospel to the Gentiles. Though suffering ignominy, Paul was honored by the work that God had given him and thus could rejoice even in captivity. **ye walk**—conduct your living. **vocation**—calling. **called**—Christians are called to the purposes discussed in chapters 1-3, which form the basis of their Christian duties (cf. 4:4; Rom. 8:28, 30). Paul's advice in this section of the letter is based on the conscious enjoyment of the divine privileges mentioned in chapters 1-3 (cf. 4:32 with 1:7; 5:1 with 1:5; 4:30 with 1:13; 5:15 with 1:8).

➤**2 lowliness**—The Greek means "low or humble in mind." Paul used it to mean "thinking of ourselves as small," for that in fact, is what we are. **meekness**—This is the spirit in which we should accept God's dealing with us, without arguing or resisting. **longsuffering, forbearing**—This is also how we are to deal with differences and problems between ourselves and others (2 Sam. 16:11; cf. to Gal. 6:1; 2 Tim. 2:25; Titus 3:2). It is only by becoming humble that we can be long-suffering and for-bearing (Col. 3:12).

➤**3 keep**—or, maintain. Spiritual oneness is not to be attained, but maintained (cf. 4:13). **the unity of the Spirit**—i.e., the oneness between the believers originated and sustained by the Spirit. **bond of peace**—Love for each other, which the presence of the Spirit causes, is what makes peace possible (Col. 3:14, 15). The term "peace" here includes the idea of uniting the members into one body.

➤**4 There is**—better, "Because there is," for this shows the connection between 4:3 and 4:4. We should keep the unity of the Spirit because there is one body, one Spirit, etc. **one body, and one Spirit**—The two are conjoined because the oneness of the body is based upon the reality of being indwelt by the one Spirit.

Note the Trinity in this passage: the Spirit in this verse, Christ in 4:5, and the Father in 4:6. The Holy Spirit is the common portion of all Christians (2:18, 20) and gives to the church its true oneness. Through the Spirit, we are now united in one universal body. Christ's true body (all Christians from all ages) is already united under one Head (Christ), but that unity is not yet visible. After Christ returns, the unity of his church will be fully visible (John 17:21-23; Col. 3:4). **called in one hope of your calling**—Instead of class privilege, as the Jews had it under the law, a common privilege (hope) is given to both Jewish and Gentile believers. The hope is associated with the Spirit because the Spirit is now the earnest of our future hope (1:13, 14).

➤**5 One Lord**—Jesus Christ. **one faith, one baptism**—Faith and baptism (the symbol displaying our faith) are similarly connected in Mark 16:16 and Colossians 2:12. Faith here is not *what we believe, but rather the act* of believing. Baptism is the symbol or sacrament of our being brought into "one body" (4:4). The Christian church is one in unity of faith (4:5; Jude 3), unity of being built upon Christ (2:19-21), unity of hope (4:4; Titus 1:2), unity of love (4:2), unity of lordship (4:5), and unity of divine patrimony (4:6).

➤**6 above all**—pertaining to God's supremacy. **through all**—pertaining to God's pervasiveness. **in you all**—pertaining to God's immanence. The pronoun "you" is not found in any ancient manuscripts; whereas, some read, "us." But the most ancient manuscripts do not have any pronoun. At any rate, it must be understood that the Spirit is not in all men but only in those who believe (Rom. 8:9, 14).

➤**7 every one of us**—Though the church is one body, each of its members has a special ability to be used for the good and growth of all. No one is overlooked; so everyone is important to building up the community. (See also Rom. 12:3, 6.) **according to the measure of the gift of Christ**—Each member receives a certain measure of grace in accordance with Christ's apportionment.

➤**8 he saith**—the psalmist in Psalm 68:18. God is referred to in this psalm as represented by the ark, which was being brought up to Zion in triumph by David (2 Sam. 6; 7:1; 1 Chron. 15). Paul referred to Christ's ascent to heaven. In the psalm, the victory is over the foes of David. In Paul's reference, Christ, the son of David, is triumphant in destroying his foe, Satan (Col. 2:15; 2 Pet. 2:4). In the psalm, gifts are given to men as the conqueror distributes a portion of the spoils to his people. God began to give special gifts to men following Christ's return to heaven. Paul, having made this point, does not refer to the rest of the psalm. The statement **he led captivity captive** has one of two meanings: (1) he led the captured ones (as one leads a train of vanquished foes) into their captivity, or (2) he captured the captors (i.e., he reversed the captivity; he enslaved the enslavers). Whichever meaning Paul intended, they both imply that Christ vanquished our enemies (such as death, the devil, and sin) and captivated them. **gave gifts unto men**—Instead of quoting from Psalm 68:18 verbatim, Paul adapted the thought of the OT text to this particular NT concept. The conqueror who "receives gifts" (the wording in Ps. 68:18) will, in turn, give gifts to men.

➤**9 ascended . . . descended**—Paul reasons that Christ's ascent implies a previous descent. **lower parts of the earth**—This phrase represents the farthest extreme from the heights of heaven. This phrase could also be rendered the lower parts, the earth (i.e., the lower parts so mentioned are one and the same as the earth). This, of course, would make this descent Christ's advent to earth. But it is probably more likely that Paul was thinking of Christ's descent into hades (see Acts 2:27, 28). This interpretation is further supported by God's plan to "fill all things" (4:10), from the highest height to the lowest depth.

➤**10 descended**—See comments on 4:9. **fill all things**—As a result of his descension and ascension Christ can fill the universe. "Christ, as God, is present everywhere; as glorified man, He can be present anywhere" (Ellicott).

➤**11 he gave some, apostles**—According to the Greek, "apostles" (and the other offices next mentioned) is a direct object of "gave." This indicates that God gave the apostles, etc., to the church as gifts. This concurs with the statement in 4:8, "he gave gifts" (i.e., apostles, prophets, evangelists, shepherds and teachers) "to men" i.e., to the church. Thus, the apostles, prophets, etc., are themselves the gifts given to the church. "The men who filled the office, no less than the office itself, were a divine gift" (Eadie). Apostles, like prophets, were ministers with a special vision. Pastors (shepherds) and teachers represent those who minister to a particular local church group. (According to the Greek, "shepherds and teachers" identify two functions of one person.) Evangelists were traveling ministers, similar to the missionaries of today. Usually, the evangelist founded the local church; the teacher built up the trust and belief of the members; and the pastor (or shepherd) provided the outward organization and guidance to the local community. Concerning God's revelation, evangelists usually speak of the past, and prophets of the future, both under the guidance of the Holy Spirit. Though the Jews had been strictly bound to a rigid order and ceremony as detailed in the law, no strict form for church hierarchy is given in the NT. **shepherd**—The analogy refers to the guiding and governing role of the shepherd. The elders are also given a pastoral role (Acts 20:28; 1 Pet. 5:1).

➤**12 For**—with a view to the ultimate goal. **perfecting**—i.e., equipping, furnishing, filling up the lack, restoring—so as to bring to perfection (cf. the word "perfect" in 4:13). **for the work of the ministry**—The gifted members equip the saints so that the saints can carry on the ministry's work, which, in turn, produces **the edifying** [building up] **of the body of Christ.**

➤**13 Till**—This indicates that the process described in 4:12 must go on until a certain end is achieved. **come in**—come into, arrive at. **the unity of the faith**—Whereas the unity of the Spirit must be maintained, the unity of the faith must be attained. The unity of faith is a unity of belief in Christ himself, and this belief is intrinsically related to our knowledge of him. DeWette said, "Full unity of faith is then found, when all alike thoroughly know Christ, the object of faith, and that in His highest dignity as 'the Son of God.'" **knowledge**—Greek, "fuller knowledge" or "more complete, experiential knowledge." **perfect man**—full-grown man, a man of complete maturity. The church, as a corporate man, must match Christ's stature, just as a man's physical body must be comparable to his head (see 4:15, 16). Christ's body, his fullness (1:23; 3:19), must match Christ, the fullness of God (Col. 2:9).

➤**14 no more children**—Paul gave a negative example to show the Ephesians what they were to avoid. **tossed to and fro**—A boat on a lake, blown by winds from all directions, is unable to follow a course; it is thus with the Christian who is knocked about with various doctrines or teachings. Uncritical acceptance of new teachings keeps his mind in a constant state of turmoil (Matt. 11:7; Heb. 13:9; James 1:6). The last part of the verse could be rendered, "by the cunning of men, with craftiness, leading to systematic error."

➤**15 speaking the truth**—lit., "truthing it" or "holding to truth." **in love**—Truth and love should govern our words and influence our actions (4:21, 24). **may grow up into him in all things**—It is a continuous objective of the Christian to become more like Christ.

➤**16 from whom**—lit., "out from whom," referring to the head, Christ, as the source. **the whole body fitly joined together**—lit., "of from whom," referring to the head, Christ, as the source. See 2:21. **and compacted**—or, coupled together. **by that which every joint supplieth**—The joints (in Gk. the root of this word means "to fasten, to touch") unite the body, keeping each member in touch with the other members so that all the body can receive the continual supply from the head. **according to the effectual working in the measure of every part**—This describes the "whole instrumentality and modality . . . belonging to the growth [of the body]" (Alford). **maketh increase**—makes growth. **edifying**—building up.

## 17-32 NEW LIFE IN CHRIST

➤**17** Paul now resumes his advice from 4:1. **ye henceforth walk not as other** [also] **Gentiles**—conduct not your lives as do the Gentiles. This thought carries over from 4:14. **in the vanity of their mind**—As they do not understand the truth about God, their minds are being wasted on worthless objects (idolatry) and untrue teachings (4:18, 19; Rom 1:21; 1 Thess. 4:5).

➤**18 darkened**—actually, "being darkened" (an ongoing process). **being alienated from the life of God**—"The life of God" is a unique expression, characterizing the divine life. The darkness and alienation imply that before the fall God was the life and light of unfallen man, as he is now the life and light of the regenerated man (see Gal. 2:20). **through the ignorance . . . in them**—See Acts 17:30; Romans 1:21, 23, 28; 1 Peter 1:14. **blindness**—actually, "hardness"—Paul is speaking of the unbeliever who has consciously rejected Christ to the point where he is no longer sensitive to his claims (Mark 3:5).

➤**19 being past feeling**—should read, "having put away remorse" or "having ceased from feeling sorrow," which means "having no more feeling about their degenerate condition." Such people are beyond feeling either shame or hope concerning their condition before God (Jer. 2:25; 18:12). **given themselves over**—God had given them up to their evil ways (Rom. 1:24). It is a serious punishment to have to suffer the consequences of one's own evil choices, without the benefit of corrective guidance. **to work**—The Greek implies a deliberate view to the working (as if it were their work or business). **greediness**—which includes all kinds of self-seeking (5:3, 5; Col. 3:5).

➤**20 learned Christ**—To know Christ himself is the greatest knowledge that the Christian can have (Phil. 3:10). The Ephesians began to understand this knowledge when their hearts were changed and they became participants in the new creation.

➤**21 If . . . ye have heard him**—not just heard *about* him, but heard him. **taught by him**—not just taught *about* him, but taught by him. **the truth is in Jesus**—All truth is perfect and complete in Jesus. He embodies truth (see John 1:14, 17; 8:44; 18:37).

➤**22 That ye put off**—lit., "to put off," following the verb "taught" in 4:21. **former conversation**—a person's conduct (or, way of life). **the old man**—the old, unregenerated self. **corrupt**—lit., "being corrupt" (an ongoing process of destruction and decay). Corruption and destruction are inseparably connected. **deceitful lusts**—A man's old nature with its lusts is his own executioner, bringing him closer and closer to eternal death and corruption.

➤**23 be renewed**—The Greek means "be constantly renewed, continually made young." **in** [by] **the spirit** [Spirit] **of your mind**—i.e., by the Spirit controlling your mind. In other words, this describes the regenerated man's new spiritual makeup. The spirit of a Christian (in the NT) is the human spirit regenerated by the divine Spirit (John 3:6; Rom. 8:16), now guiding and dominating the mind. The natural man is described as not having the spirit (Jude 19); thus, "spirit" (in this sense) is not a characteristic of the unregenerated man (1 Thess. 5:23).

➤**24 put on the new man**—The new man is the new humanity created in Christ, of which all believers partake, both individually and corpo-

rately. Since Paul already spoke of the new man created in Christ in terms of a new unified corporate humanity (2:14, 15), the new man in this verse must also be thought of corporately (cf. Col. 3:9-11). Of course, the immediate context points to each believer's responsibility in putting on this new nature. **which after God**—actually, "according to God," which means "in accordance with God," "like God," or "in God's likeness." **is created**—an aorist participle in Greek, indicating a complete act. The creation of the new man occurred once and for all (see 2:14, 15), but each saint needs to appropriate his image through spiritual renewal of the mind (see Col. 3:9-11). The image of God, in which Adam was originally created, is restored in Christ, the second Adam (1 Cor. 15:45-49; 2 Cor. 4:4; Col. 1:15), and then also in his church. **holiness**—lit., "sanctity of the truth" or "true sanctity." As we honestly follow the truth of God (Rom. 1:25; 3:7; 15:8), we become holy in our relationship to God, good in our relationships with men (Luke 1:75).

➤**25** From the general character of the new man, there will result specific ways of acting which Paul now lists. **speak every man truth with his neighbour**—This is a quote from Zechariah 8:16 (LXX). **for we are members one of another**—Since we are members of one another in Christ's body, our union with one another prompts us to exchange words and actions that are not destructive to the body.

➤**26 Be ye angry, and sin not**—derived from Psalm 4:4. If one is to get angry, he must do so without sinning. In fact, anger, if not directed against dishonor to God or wrongs committed by men, is illegitimate. **let not the sun go down upon your wrath**—A quarrel that is not quickly aired and resolved easily turns into sin as the individuals involved harbor resentments and seek vengeance. The Christian is advised to get rid of his anger before another day begins (Deut. 24:15) and before he parts with his brother for the night.

➤**27 Neither give place to the devil**—cf. 2 Corinthians 2:11.

➤**28 Let him that stole**—lit., "let the one stealing." **steal no more**—In most cases, a reference to stealing or "thieves" in the NT concerns a bandit or a person who engages in stealing as a livelihood. **rather let him labour**—Stealing and idleness go together; thus, Paul's charge is to not only stop stealing, but to begin honest work. **that he may have to give to him that needeth**—All

Christians should be interested not in selfish gain, but in means for being helpful to their fellowmen. See Paul's own example in Acts 20:35; 2 Thessalonians 3:8.

➤ **29 corrupt**—This term literally means "insipid," "without salt" (Col. 4:6), "worthless." Included is foul talk (5:4). We must be sensitive to the situation and the needs of anyone we talk to, and wise in choosing our words, for even good words, unless used appropriately, will be destructive instead of useful. We should not speak vaguely in words that would fit a thousand different occasions. Rather, our words should be genuine and specifically suited to the present person, time, and place. **good to the use of edifying, that it may minister grace**—God can use our words as a means of giving his grace to another person.

➤ **30 grieve not the holy Spirit of God**—cf. Psalm 78:40; Isaiah 63:10; Acts 7:51. **whereby ye are sealed**—See comments on 1:13. **unto the day of redemption**—or, with a view to the day of redemption. The seal of the Holy Spirit upon a believer marks that believer as God's property until the day he is completely redeemed (see Rom. 8:23).

➤ **31 bitterness . . . wrath . . . anger . . . clamour . . . evil speaking**—These traits are the opposite of those listed in the next verse. They are the fruits of the old man (4:22).

➤ **32 forgiving one another, even as God for Christ's sake hath forgiven you**—Though Christ has bridged the gap between us and God, so that we are forgiven once and for all in that sense, we only experience God's forgiveness in personal, practical ways as we learn to forgive others from day to day. None of us has experienced as great a wrong against ourselves as that which we have all done to God (Matt. 18:33). God had to give up his only Son to forgive us (2 Cor. 5:19); we have to give up nothing but our selfish natures to forgive our brother.

**Chapter 5**

## 1-21 LIVING AS CHILDREN OF LIGHT AND BEING FILLED WITH THE SPIRIT

➤ **1 Be ye therefore followers of God**—The Greek shows that we imitate God with respect to his love (5:2). See 1 John 4:16. **dear children**—cf. 1 John 4:19. As our sonship is by adoption, we rely all the more on the childlike process of imitation to acquire the characteristics of our Father (Matt. 5:44, 45, 48).

➤ **2 walk**—This verb continues the thought from 4:1. **as Christ also hath loved us**—From a discussion of the Father's love (5:1), Paul moves to the love of the Son, in whom God makes his love most clearly known to us. **hath given himself for us** [on our behalf]—Christ gave himself in death as a vicarious sacrifice on our behalf (John 15:13; Rom. 5:8; Gal. 2:20). **an offering and a sacrifice to God**—Although "offering" and "sacrifice" are really synonymous, the first word generally indicates a gift and the second always designates a slain sacrifice. **a sweetsmelling savour**—lit., "an odour of a sweet smell." God was well-pleased with his Son's sacrifice (see 1:6; Matt. 3:17; 2 Cor. 5:18, 19; Heb. 10:6-17).

➤ **3 uncleanness . . . covetousness**—The Greek for "uncleanness" is so close to the word for "greediness" that they are sometimes used interchangeably. The basic motivation in both cases is the desire to satisfy oneself materially in a way that excludes God.

➤ **4** Cf. Colossians 3:8. **jesting**—This use of language usually stems from a desire to remain inconspicuous by sounding like the people who surround oneself. Principle is sacrificed to the convenience of the particular occasion. Implied is a frivolous playful style of treating any subject, for which Ephesus was famous (Plautus's *Miles Gloriosus*, 3.1.42-52). **but rather giving of thanks**—Giving of thanks brings about the real joy of the spirit that the worldly try to achieve with their style of humor and communication (5:19, 20; James 5:13).

➤ **5 unclean . . . covetous** [greedy]—See Colossians 3:5. **who is an idolater**—Greed and idol worship are both forms of worshiping the creation of God rather than God as the Creator. Material things are not themselves evil, but are put to evil use when man regards them as objects of worship in place of God (1 Sam. 15:3; Matt. 6:24; Phil. 3:19; 1 John 2:15). Paul had given up worshiping and seeking material things (2 Cor. 6:10; 11:27). **the kingdom of Christ and of God**—In the Greek, "of Christ and God," emphasizes their complete unity, consistent with the doctrine that Christ is completely God (cf. 2 Thess. 1:12; 1 Tim. 5:21; 6:13).

➤ **6 Let no man deceive you with vain words**—Some try to make their evil less serious by saying that it is natural to indulge in love (impurity); it is useful to society that men should pursue gain (greed); and that God will not punish such clever wit (coarse jokes). **cometh the wrath of God**—The tense is present; God's wrath already is aroused against them.

➤**7** Close association with those who excuse or deny their own wickedness is discouraged (cf. 5:11).

➤**8 For ye were sometimes** [at one time] **darkness**—cf. 1 Thessalonians 5:4. This darkness, though part of every Christian's past, is no longer with them. **are ye light in the Lord**—The Christian is not merely enlightened, but filled with light which helps others to see (5:13). We are not "in" or "under" the light but are actually the light (see Matt. 5:14).

➤**9 fruit of the Spirit**—This reading is present in one very ancient manuscript (the Chester Beatty Papyrus, P46) and in many other late manuscripts. All the other most ancient manuscripts read, "fruit of the light." Owing to its uniqueness, the latter reading was probably changed to the former, a more familiar expression (taken from Gal. 5:22). The "fruit of the light" is the natural outcome of living in the light, for such a living produces goodness, righteousness, and truth.

➤**10 Proving**—The Christian must learn what will please God (5:8; Rom. 12:1, 2) by conscious and accurate study, and by practical attempts to put his knowledge into daily use.

➤**11 unfruitful works of darkness**—deeds done in darkness are unproductive (see Gal. 5:19, 22); their only fruit is death and decay (Rom. 6:21; Gal. 6:8). **reprove** [or, expose]—cf. Matthew 5:14-16. We should not only have no association with such evil practices; we must also take an active, vocal stance against them (5:13; John 3:19-21). This does not mean that we should avoid contact with worldly men (1 Cor. 5:10), but we should not participate in activities that would destroy or endanger our light.

➤**13 reproved**—or, exposed. **made manifest**—become visible. **For whatsoever doth make manifest is light**—or, "for everything made visible is light." This could mean that those who are exposed by the light could come to participate in the light and thus be transformed from darkness to light. Vincent said, "Whatever is revealed in its true essence by the light is of the nature of light. It no longer belongs to the category of darkness."

➤**14 Wherefore**—This refers to the whole foregoing argument (5:8, 11, 13). Since light

will expose the darkness, God says, **Awake thou that sleepest, and arise from the dead, and Christ shall give thee light**—which is a paraphrase of Isaiah 60:1 and/or Isaiah 26:19. As Israel was called to waken from its state of darkness and death (Isa. 59:10; 60:2), so each man in the church is called to alertness. Christians are called to awake out of sleep; non-Christians are called to awake from the dead (cf. Matt. 25:5; Rom. 13:11; 1 Thess. 5:6).

➤**15 walk circumspectly**—i.e., be careful how you conduct your life. Two ideas are included here. First, the Christian is to please God by his behavior. Second, he must be discreet in his actions before unbelievers so that neither party is misled or deceived by the other (Col. 4:5). **not as fools**—actually "not as unwise."

➤**16 Redeeming** [Buying up] **the time**—All the time at one's disposal following spiritual regeneration is to be used for doing good. Specific opportunities for doing good should not be wasted. This implies that we should not allow ourselves to be controlled by our circumstances, but rather should make use of time as a valuable commodity or resource, as a master does with his servant, or a merchant with an opportunity to acquire the best goods. (Cf. 6:13; Gen. 47:9; Ps. 49:5; Eccles. 11:2; 12:1; Amos 5:13; John 12:35.)

➤**17 unwise**—The Greek word is different from that for "unwise" in 5:15 (see comments) and can be translated "foolishly," "senselessly." **but understanding what the will of the Lord is**—The Christian should not know God's will merely as a matter of fact, but with understanding and action as well (Luke 12:47). The Lord's will, ultimately, is our sanctification (1 Thess. 4:3).

➤**18 be not drunk with wine**—The outward effects of drinking wine and being filled with the Spirit are sufficiently similar that Paul connects them (see Acts 2:13-18). The Spirit gives true expression; the wine, unreliable exhilaration. **wherein is excess**—i.e., dissipation. Wasteful spending and detriment to one's desire and ability to follow God can result from too much drinking. **but be filled with the Spirit**—or "filled by the Spirit" or, "filled in spirit." According to the Greek, the word "Spirit" here indicates the instrument for the filling not the content. The content is left unspecified. According to the next verse, the content is psalms, hymns, and spiritual songs. In the NT the filling of the Spirit is usually associated with the prophetic ministry—i.e., speaking for the Lord (Crater). The (speaking in) psalms, hymns, and spiritual songs are associated with this kind of prophetic ministry.

➤**19** Cf. Colossians 3:16. From this exhortation came much of the style of corporate Christian worship that is still a part of our worship today. Concerning the early Christians, Pliny wrote to Trajan, "They are wont on a fixed day to meet before daylight [to avoid persecution] and to recite a hymn among themselves by turns, to Christ, as if being God." **Speaking to yourselves** [one another] **in psalms and hymns and spiritual songs**—Psalm-singing was usually accompanied by an instrument. Hymns are in direct praise to God (Acts 16:25; 1 Cor. 14:26; James 5:13), whereas "songs" is a general term for lyric pieces. "Spiritual" indicates that they are such songs that are restricted to Christian themes, although not necessarily in direct praise to God (cf. Amos 8:10). **singing and making melody**—To the Greeks this meant "singing and playing an instrument." **in your heart**—The verbal singing and playing should be a genuine representation of the beliefs and feelings of the performer (cf. Ps. 47:7; 1 Cor. 14:15). This makes a contrast between the music of Christians, sung together in praise to God, and of the heathen, sung merely for entertainment and self-praise.

➤**20 Giving thanks always for all things**—See Colossians 3:17; 1 Thessalonians 5:18. **unto God and the Father**—God is the one who gives us all good things. **our Lord Jesus Christ**—It is because of Christ that we can accept God's gifts to us, even our sufferings (Rom. 8:35, 37; 1 Cor. 3:20-23).

➤**21** Cf. Philippians 2:3; 1 Peter 5:5. **fear of God**—According to the earliest manuscripts this should read, "fear of Christ." The Christian is to be the slave of Christ (1 Cor. 7:22); it is Christ, not God, who will be our judge (John 5:22). Thus, fear of displeasing him motivates us to honor Christ and to serve him willingly and joyfully (1 Cor. 10:22; 2 Cor. 5:11; 1 Pet. 2:13). Paul now moves from our relationship with God to our relationships with each other.

## 22-33 THE RELATIONSHIP BETWEEN HUSBAND AND WIFE: A TYPE OF CHRIST AND THE CHURCH

The relationship between Christ and his church is typified by three primary earthly relationships: those of husband and wife (5:22-33), parent and child (6:1-4), and master and servant (6:4-9).

➤**23 Wives, submit yourselves unto your own husbands**—cf. Genesis 3:16; 1 Corinthians 7:2; 14:34; Colossians 3:18; Titus 2:5; 1 Peter 3:1-7. The wife is told to "submit" in the husband-wife relationship, whereas children are taught to "obey," for there is greater equality between spouses than between parents and children (6:1). In either case, submission or obedience is required regardless of what the husband or parent is like. **as unto the Lord**—Submission to her husband is one way in which a wife can demonstrate her submission to Christ (5:24), for the husband's relationship to his wife is the same as Christ's to the church and calls for a similar response.

➤**23 he** [himself] **is the saviour of the body**—In contrast to a husband who is head of his wife by creation, Christ is the head of the church by being its Savior.

➤**24** Though there are obvious differences of headship (5:23), the act of submission (5:21, 22) is the same in both relationships. Husbands are to be obeyed in anything that is not directly contrary to God's instructions (Col. 3:18).

➤**25 gave himself** [up] **for** [on behalf of] **it** [her]—This indicates a sacrificial, substitutionary surrendering of himself to death. Christ sacrificed himself for the church because of his love for her. Husbands, then, should be ready to make whatever sacrifices are necessary for their wives. These sacrifices will never be as great as Christ's sacrifice, for the husband is already united in love to his wife, whereas Christ died for those who opposed and hated him. Love is the basis for the husband-wife relationship, whereas a servant often obeys because he fears his master.

➤**26 he might sanctify**—In the Greek, the subjunctive *hagiasē* could mean "he might begin to sanctify" or "he might have already sanctified"—most probably, the former. The context does not allow us to think of the sanctification as having been completed. Alford said, "The sanctifying is clearly a gradual process, carried on till the spotless presentation (v. 27)." **cleanse**—or, having cleansed. This aorist participle in Greek can be understood in two ways: (1) it signals action prior to the sanctification process, or (2) it signals action concurrent with the sanctification process. Many favor the first use because they believe the "cleansing of the bath with the word" is an instantaneous absolution, which occurs via regeneration (cf. Titus 3:5) and/or baptism. But others support the second use because they see the cleansing as being the mode by which the bride is continually sanctified. For example, Wuest said, " 'Cleanse' is a modal participle, showing how or in what manner the sanctification takes place." The second view seems better because the aorist participle with an aorist verb usually conveys simultaneous action in the NT (see Alford) and the context points to an ongoing process. **washing**—bath or laver. The word is used in Titus 3:5 in connection with the bath of regeneration through the Holy Spirit. Here, the bath is the pre-marriage cleansing of the bride to be. **of water by** [with] **the word**—taken instrumentally, indicates how the bath is administered.

➤**27 That he might present it** [her] **to himself**—as a bride at the wedding day (2 Cor. 11:2). **a glorious church, not having spot, or wrinkle, or any such thing**—It was traditional for a bride to take a ritual bath just before her wedding as a symbol of her chastity. Similarly, the sacrament of baptism demonstrates the Christian's desire that God should find him pure and faithful when Christ returns to claim his bride, the church.

➤**28** There exists between the husband and the wife the same union as between Christ and the church (5:30, 32). This unity is expressed in terms of conjugal union, for as husband and wife become one flesh (one body) through marriage, so Christ and his church have become one body through spiritual union. As such, the church is Christ's very own body.

➤**29 nourisheth**—speaks of providing food and internal sustenance. **cherisheth**—"warms," which speaks of providing clothing and external care (see Exod. 21:10).

➤**30 For we are members of his body**—See 1 Corinthians 12:12. **of his flesh, and of his bones**—These words are not present in the earliest manuscripts; they were added by copyists who wanted to fill out the quote from Genesis 2:23.

➤**31** The creation of the church from the single man, Christ (as Eve was produced from Adam), is the foundation of the spiritual marriage. The natural marriage where "a man must leave . . . and the two shall be one," is not the principal idea in this verse. Rather, Paul is talking about spiritual marriage as represented by natural marriage, in which Christ leaves his father to seek his own love, the church, which is lost in the world. **they two shall be one flesh**—taken from Genesis 2:24 (LXX). In a natural marriage, the husband and wife complement one another. So Christ and the church are incomplete without each other, with Christ needing the church in order to assume his position as its Head. Christ is the Head of the church, as the husband is the head of the wife (Rom. 6:5; 1 Cor. 11:3; 15:45). Christ and his church are indissolubly joined (Matt. 19:6; John 10:28, 29).

➤**32 This is a great mystery**—The union of Christ with his church is beyond man's comprehension, and can best be understood by analogy to human marriages.

➤**33** This verse returns to the human marriage, giving in summary the attitudes that are to be shown by both husband and wife.

Chapter **6**

## 1-9 PAUL'S ADVICE TO CHILDREN AND PARENTS, SLAVES AND MASTERS

➤**1 obey**—This is a stronger demand than the submission required of wives in 5:21. Submission is willing subjection to another; obedience is less rational and more implicit. **in the Lord**—This characterizes the parent-child relationship as being Christian. **for this is right**—When both parents and children love God, all of them will seek to obey and please him (see also Col. 3:20; cf. Mark 7:11-14; Acts 5:29). Furthermore, it is a natural law that children should obey their parents, the source of their lives.

➤**2** In this verse, the authority of the revealed law is added to the natural law of 6:1. **which is the first commandment with promise**—i.e., the first of the Ten Commandments that contains a promise (that of prolonged life).

See Exodus 20:12. The promise is not the main motive of our obedience. Rather, it is to do God's will (Deut. 5:16), and the promise that accompanies the command indicates this. This verse shows that the OT law has not been altogether abolished.

➤3 **thou mayest live long**—Paul adapted Exodus 20:12, in which he took away the local and limited reference to the Jews in Canaan and applied it to the godly, everywhere. The promise is always fulfilled, either literally on this earth, or by substituting a higher, spiritual blessing (Job 5:26; Prov. 10:27). The essence and true meaning of the law is eternally valid and in force.

➤4 **provoke not your children to wrath**—for they might become discouraged and quit trying (Col. 3:21). **bring them up**—Children are to be nurtured, disciplined, or trained by the placing of judicious restraints on their activities (Job 5:17; Heb. 12:7). **in the nurture and admonition of the Lord**—The word "nurture" should read "discipline" or "educational training" (Deut. 6:7; Prov. 22:6), whether as encouragement, or as pointing out errors and wrongdoing. The expression "of the Lord" means "concerning the Lord." All of the parents' efforts in raising their children should bring them to an experiential knowledge of the Lord.

➤5 **Servants**—lit., "slaves." **masters**—The service to our earthly masters is only for a short time. Our real freedom, which Christ brings, is present now and will last forever (1 Cor. 7:22). **fear and trembling**—Slaves are instructed to do their jobs carefully and to avoid displeasing their masters. They are to do as well without prompting as they would under threat of punishment. **singleness of your heart**—The slave should not try to satisfy his master with the outward appearance of his work, without the inward desire to make the master's work first in importance and consideration (1 Chron. 29:17; Matt. 6:22, 23; Luke 11:34).

➤6 **eyeservice**—seeking to please one's master only so long as one is watched by him. **menpleasers**—cf. Galatians 1:10; 1 Thessalonians 2:4.

➤7 **good will**—This good will of the slave is a genuine concern for the master's work as though it were his own. **to the Lord**—The Lord Jesus, our true Master, is not seen, but he is always aware of the state of our hearts and knows if we are shirking the job that we, as his slaves, have been given to do. This manner is also the best way to faithfully serve our earthly masters.

➤8 **the same shall he receive**—cf. 2 Corinthians 5:10; Colossians 3:25. **whether he be bond or free**—Cf. 1 Corinthians 7:22; 12:13; Galatians 3:28; Col. 3:11. Christ does not regard these distinctions in giving his love and new life to us now, nor will he in his future judgment (cf. Prov. 19:17).

➤9 **masters, do the same things unto them**—The master should have the same concern for God's will and for the slaves' well-being as they should show toward their master. Love is the guideline for the duties of both, and their equality in God supersedes distinctions of rank. (See Lev. 25:42, 43; Deut. 15:12; Jer. 34:14 as examples of how the Hebrews were to treat their brothers.) **forbearing threatening**—Threats were commonly used by slave masters to keep their slaves working hard. **knowing that your Master also is in heaven**—This emphasizes the equality of the slave and the slaveowner before Christ. **neither is there respect of persons with him**—Christ will not, in judging, condemn one man because he was a slave on earth nor accept another because he was a master (see Acts 10:34; Rom. 2:11; Gal. 2:6; Col. 3:25; 1 Pet. 1:17; cf. Deut. 10:17; 2 Chron. 19:7).

## 10-20 FIGHTING THE SPIRITUAL WARFARE

➤10 **my brethren**—These words are not present in the earliest manuscripts. **be strong**—lit., "be continually empowered." The present, plural participle indicates continual empowering to the corporate Christian community. The following verses (all in the plural) are addressed to the church as a corporate warrior, who needs to put on the complete armor of God. Of course, this corporate effort calls for each member's participation. **power of his might**—or, might of his strength (see 1:19; 3:16).

➤11 **whole armour** [panoply]—cf. Romans 13:12. The complete armor of God is both defensive and offensive (2 Cor. 6:7). The image extends throughout the following six verses. In Romans 13:14 we are told to "put on the Lord

Jesus Christ." In thus becoming new in him, we are putting on all the armor of God, so that there is no loophole for Satan. He was defeated once and for all by Christ, but we will continually battle the powers of evil until Christ's return (Rom. 6:2-14; Col. 3:3-5). **of God**—i.e., provided by God. This armor is not our own but rather is given to us by God (Ps. 35:1-3). It is therefore as strong as his mighty power (2 Cor. 10:4). **wiles**—stratagems or schemes. **of the devil**—The ruler of the enemy (6:12) has organized the kingdom of darkness against the kingdom of light (Matt. 12:26).

➤**12 For we wrestle not against flesh and blood**—Flesh and blood enemies (i.e., human enemies) are mere tools of Satan, who is our real enemy. **principalities . . . powers** [authorities]—See 1:21; cf. Romans 8:38; 1 Corinthians 15:24; Colossians 2:15. The Ephesians had practiced magic and witchcraft (Acts 19:19), so Paul's mention of evil spirits is quite appropriate. As the Bible explains the kingdom of light, the kingdom of darkness is exposed. Thus, nowhere does the kingdom of Satan come more clearly into view than in the Gospels that deal with Christ, the light. **rulers of the darkness of this world**—lit., "world-rulers of the darkness of this age" (cf. 2:2; 5:8; Luke 22:53; Col. 1:13; see also John 12:31; 14:30; 16:11; 2 Cor. 4:4; 1 John 5:19). Though Satan and his demons rule the world, they do not rule the universe; their stolen kingdom will be regained by Christ, the rightful ruler, when he appears. **spiritual wickedness in high places**—The spirits have a higher range of powers than man, since they had been (until Christ's ascension, Rev. 12:5, 9, 10) dwelling in heavenly places (Job. 1:7). They now occupy the regions of the air (see 2:2).

➤**13 take**—God's armor is already made; all we have to do is to put it on (6:11). Paul's use of this image was easily grasped by the Ephesians, whose mythical heroes were given armor by their gods. **having done all**—with respect to the total preparation for warfare. **to stand**—Repeated from 6:11, this phrase implies that the Christian soldier is to hold his ground and not flee or surrender under Satan's attack.

➤**14 having your loins girt about with truth**—cf. 2 Corinthians 1:12; 1 Timothy 1:5, 18; 3:9. The belt of truth keeps the rest of the armor together. This girding was also a sign of alertness and readiness (see Exod. 12:11; cf. Isa. 5:27; 11:5; Luke 12:35). **breastplate of righteousness**—See Isaiah 59:17; 1 Thessalonians 5:8. Our most significant defense is the evidence that we have been made right with God, and that this righteousness has been inwrought in us by the Spirit.

➤**15 feet shod**—A special sandal or military shoe was worn by the soldier that protected his feet without slowing him down. **preparation**—or, firm shooting, readiness. **of the gospel of peace**—See Luke 1:79; Romans 10:15. It is fitting that gospel preaching is typified by the feet because in Greek the word for "gospel" was used in ancient times in connection with a runner (or messenger) returning from the battle site with news of victory. (See Isa. 52:7; Rom. 10:15.)

➤**16 Above all**—rather, over all, so as to cover all the parts of armor mentioned thus far. The shield is the most important and must always be carried. **shield of faith**—The image is taken from the Roman shield, which was a large oblong or oval, approximately four feet high by two feet wide. **to quench all the fiery darts**—The ancient fire-dart was an arrow made of cane with a flammable head that was lighted and used to set fire to wood, tents, etc. **of the wicked**—Faith conquers Satan's temptations to wrath, lust, despair, vengeance, and so on (see 1 Pet. 5:9). Faith overcomes sin and evil in the world (1 John 5:4), and will likewise overcome Satan, the ruler of this world (1 John 5:18).

➤**17 And take the helmet of salvation**—given by Christ, we must put it on (1 Thess. 5:8). The helmet represents a certain hope, with no chance of disappointment (Rom. 5:5). It is added to the shield of faith (Rom. 5:1) to protect the head of the soldier. The head is the most fragile and the most important part of the body. **the sword of the Spirit**—the only offensive weapon mentioned. **which**—In the Greek, this refers to "the Spirit," not "the sword." The Spirit is the word of God (see comments on John 3:34; 6:63). God's word, as Spirit, is our only offensive weapon. Christ's use of God's word in his temptation guides our use of it against Satan (Matt. 4:4, 7, 10). As there is no armor specified for the back, we are never to turn our backs on our enemy.

Our only safety lies in constantly resisting the attack (Matt. 4:11; James 4:7).

➤**18 Praying**—This joins with 6:17; taking the Word of God should be accompanied by prayer. **always**—The Greek, "in every season," implies that we should pray at every opportunity (Col. 4:2). Paul here alludes to Christ's words from Luke 21:36. (Luke was Paul's traveling companion and is quoted elsewhere in the Epistles: see 1 Cor. 11:23; 1 Tim. 5:18; see also Luke 18:1; Rom. 12:12; 1 Thess. 5:17.) It is the Spirit in us who prays and enables us to pray (Rom. 8:15, 26; Gal. 4:6; Jude 20). **with all prayer and supplication**—Sometimes the need for prayer supersedes the need for sleep (5:14; Ps. 88:13; Matt. 26:41), as when Anna kept a perpetual watch in the temple (Luke 2:37).

➤**19 that I may open my mouth boldly, to make known the mystery of the gospel**—Since the gospel is understood not by men's powers of reason and understanding, but by God's revelation, bold, plain speech is needed. Paul did not depend upon his natural speaking ability, but relied on the Spirit for words to be given to him. Thus he asked for the prayers of his brothers that

he might be given the words to speak the mystery (see 3:2-6) of the gospel.

➤**20 in bonds**—In the Greek, the singular, "chain," is used. The Romans would bind a prisoner to a soldier by a single chain, in a kind of free custody. The term "bonds" was used when the prisoner's hands and feet were bound together (Acts 26:29).

## 21-24 CONCLUSION

➤**21** See Colossians 4:7, 8. **Tychicus**—This messenger brought this letter to the Ephesians, as well as one to the Colossians (see Introduction).

➤**22** Cf. Colossians 4:8. **our**—Paul was accompanied by Aristarchus and Mark (Col. 4:10).

➤**23 love with faith**—Paul assumed that they already had faith; he prayed that love might accompany it (Gal. 5:6).

➤**24 in sincerity**—The Greek text reads, "in incorruptibility." The phrase should be connected with the words "all them that love our Lord Jesus Christ"; it describes the realm in which the believers love Jesus—a realm of immortality and incorruption, and it also describes the way in which the believers love Jesus—"with an undying love" (NIV).

BIBLIOGRAPHY

Alford, Henry. *The Greek New Testament.* Vol. 4. 1852. Reprint. Grand Rapids: Guardian Press, 1973.

Bengel, John A. *New Testament Word Studies.* 1742. Reprint. Grand Rapids: Eerdmans, 1971.

Conybeare and Howson. *The Life and Epistles of St. Paul.* 1851. Reprint. Grand Rapids: Eerdmans, 1978 (15th printing).

Crater, Timothy. "The Fillings of the Spirit," an unpublished thesis, 1984.

Dewette, Wilhelm. *Kurzgefasstes Exegetisches Handbuch Zum Neuen Testament.* Leipzig: Weidmann, 1847.

Eadie, John. *A Commentary on the Greek Text of the Epistle of Paul to the Ephesians.* London: Griffin, 1854.

Ellicott, Charles J. *A Commentary, Critical and Grammatical, on St. Paul's Epistle to the Ephesians.* Boston: Gould, 1862.

Plummer, Alfred. *Commentary on St. Paul's Epistle to the Ephesians.* London: Robert Scott, 1918.

Salmond, S. D. F. "Ephesians" in the *Expositor's Greek Testament.* London: Hodder & Stoughton, 1917.

Vincent, M. R. *Word Studies in the New Testament.* 1886. Reprint. Grand Rapids: Eerdmans, 1946.

Wuest, Kenneth. *Ephesians and Colossians in the Greek New Testament.* Grand Rapids: Eerdmans, 1953.

Note: Certain portions of this commentary on Ephesians were adapted from a work written by the New Testament Editor, Philip W. Comfort, entitled *From Text to Translation,* "Translating Ephesians and Colossians Phrase by Phrase"; Vol. 3 in "Studies in the Greek New Testament for English Readers," Wheaton, Il., 1986.

# PHILIPPIANS
## Introduction

The internal evidence for the authenticity of this epistle is strong. The style, manner of thought, and doctrine, accord with Paul's. The incidental allusions also establish his authorship. Paley notes the mention of the object of Epaphroditus's journey to Rome, the Philippian contribution to Paul's wants, Epaphroditus's sickness (1:7; 2:25-30; 4:10-18), the fact that Timothy had been long with Paul at Philippi (1:1; 2:19), the reference to his being a prisoner at Rome now for a long time (1:12-14; 2:17-28), his willingness to die (cf. 1:23 with 2 Cor. 5:8), and the reference to the Philippians having seen his maltreatment at Philippi (1:29, 30; 2:1, 2).

The external evidence is equally decisive: Polycarp, *Epistle to the Philippians,* 3 and 11; Irenaeus, *Against Heresies,* 4.18.4; Clement of Alexandria, *Paidagogos;* Eusebius's *Ecclesiastical History,* 5.2; Origen, *Against Celsus;* Cyprian, *Testimonies against the Jews,* 3.39.

Philippi was the first (i.e., the farthest from Rome, and the first which Paul ecounterd upon entering Macedonia) Macedonian city of the district, called *Macedonia Prima* (so called as lying farthest eastward). The Greek (Acts 16:12) could also be translated "the chief city" (as in KJV, NIV, JB). But it has been argued that Thessalonica was the chief city of the province, and Amphipolis, of the district called *Macedonia Prima.* Philippi was a Roman "colony" (Acts 16:12), made so by Augustus, to commemorate his famous victory over Brutus and Cassius. A colony was, in fact, a portion of Rome itself transplanted to the provinces, an offshoot from Rome, and, as it were, a portrait of the mother city on a small scale (Aulius Gellius, 16.13). Its inhabitants were Rome citizens, having the right of voting in the Roman tribes, governed by their own senate and magistrates and not by the governor of the province, with the Roman law and Latin language.

Paul, with Silas and Timothy, planted the gospel there (Acts 16:12) on his second missionary journey. Doubtless he visited it again on his journey from Ephesus into Macedonia (Acts 20:1); and Acts 20:3 and 6 expressly mention his third visit on his return from Greece (Corinth) to Syria by way of Macedonia. His sufferings at Philippi (Acts 16:19, etc.) strengthened the Christian bond of union between him and his Philippian converts, who also, like him, were exposed to trials for the gospel's sake (1 Thess. 2:2). They alone sent supplies for his temporal wants, twice shortly after he had left them (Phil. 4:15, 16), and again a third time shortly before writing this epistle (Phil. 4:10, 18; 2 Cor. 11:9). This fervent attachment on their part was, perhaps, in part due to the fact that few Jews were in Philippi, as in other scenes of his labors, to sow the seeds of distrust and suspicion. There was no synagogue but merely a Jewish *Proseucha,* or oratory, by the riverside. There only do we read of his meeting no opposition from Jews but only from the masters of the divining damsel, whose gains had been depleted by her being dispossessed.

Though the Philippian church was as yet free from Judaizing influence, it needed to be forewarned of that danger that might at any time assail it from without (3:2), even as such evil influences had crept into the Galatian churches. In 4:2, 3 we find a trace of the fact recorded in the history (Acts 16:13, 14), that female converts were among the first to receive the gospel at Philippi.

As to the state of the church, we gather from 2 Corinthians 8:1, 2 that its members were poor, yet most liberal; and from 1:28-30, that they were undergoing persecution. The only blemish referred to in their character was a tendency to dissension on the part of some members,—hence his admonitions against disunity (1:27; 2:1-4, 12, 14; 4:2).

The object of the epistle is general: not only to thank the Philippians for their contribution sent by Epaphroditus (who was returning to take back the apostle's letter), but to express his Christian love and sympathy, and to exhort them to a life consonant with that of Christ, and to warn them against existing dissensions and future possible assaults of Judaizers from without. It is remarkable that in this epistle alone, amidst many commendations, there are no express censures of those to whom it is addressed. No doctrinal error, or schism, had as yet sprung up; the only blemish hinted at is that some of the Philippian church were somewhat lacking in lowliness of mind, the result of which lack was disputation. Two women, Euodias and Syntyche, are mentioned as having erred in this respect. The epistle may be divided into three parts: (1) Affectionate address to the Philippians; reference to his own state as a prisoner at Rome, and to theirs, and to his mission of Epaphroditus to them (chaps. 1 and 2). Epaphroditus probably held a leading office in the Philippian church, perhaps as an elder. After Tychicus and Onesimus had departed (c. A.D. 62), carrying the Epistles to the Ephesians, Colossians, and Philemon, Paul was cheered in his imprisonment by the arrival of Epaphroditus with the Philippian contribution. That faithful "brother, companion in labor, and fellow soldier" (2:25), had brought on himself by the fatigues of the journey a dangerous sickness (2:26, 30). But now that he was recovered, he "longed" (2:26) to return to his Philippian church and to relieve their anxiety on his behalf, in respect to his sickness; and the apostle gladly took the opportunity to write to them a letter of grateful acknowledgments and Christian exhortations. (2) Caution against Judaizing teachers, supported by reference to his own former and present feeling toward Jewish legalism (chap. 3). (3) Admonitions to individuals and to the church in general, thanks for their seasonable aid, and concluding benedictions and salutations.

Although some scholars have argued for Caesarea or Ephesus as the place from which Paul wrote this epistle (see arguments presented by Hawthorne, even though he favors Rome), Philippians was probably written from Rome during the imprisonment related in Acts 28:16, 20, 30, 31. The reference to "Caesar's household" (4:22), and to the "palace" (1:13, Gk.*Praetorium,* probably the barrack of the Praetorian bodyguard, attached to the palace of Nero) confirms this. It must have been during his first imprisonment at Rome, for the mention of the Praetorium agrees with the fact that it was during his first imprisonment that he was in the custody of the Praetorian Prefect, and his situation, described in 1:12-21, agrees with his situation in the first two years of his imprisonment (Acts 28:30, 31). The following reasons show, moreover, that it may have been written toward the close of that imprisonment: (1) He expresses his expectation of the immediate decision of his cause (2:23). (2) Enough time had elapsed for the Philippians to hear of his imprisonment, to send Epaphroditus to him, to hear of Epaphroditus's arrival and sickness, and send back word to Rome of their distress (2:26). (But some scholars cannot imagine that there was enough time for all this travel to have occurred between Rome and Philippi and therefore have proposed Caesarea or Ephesus instead of Rome, as the place of origin.) (3) Philippians must have been written after the other epistles sent from Rome, viz., Colossians, Ephesians, and Philemon; for Luke was no longer with him (2:20); otherwise Paul would have been specific in saluting them, having formerly labored among them, whereas Luke is mentioned as with Paul in Colossians 4:14; Philemon 24. Again, in Ephesians 6:19, 20, Paul's freedom to preach is implied; but in Philippians 1:13-18 his bondage is dwelt on, and it is implied that, not himself, but others preached and made his imprisonment known. Again, in Philemon 22, he confidently anticipates his release, which contrasts with the more depressed anticipations of this epistle. (4) A considerable time had elapsed since the beginning of his imprisonment for "his bonds" to have become so widely known that they produced good effects for the gospel (1:13). Paul had arrived in Rome c. 59/60 and spent two whole years in house arrest, so that the date of writing must have been c. 61/62.

The style of Philippians is abrupt and discontinuous—Paul's fervor of affection leading him to pass rapidly from one theme to another (2:18, 19-24, 25-30; 3:1-3, 4:14-15). In no other epistle does he use such warm expressions of love. In 4:1 he seems at a loss for words sufficient to express all the extent and ardor of his affection for the Philippians: "My brethren dearly beloved and longed for, my joy and crown, so stand fast in the Lord, my dearly beloved." The mention of overseers and deacons in 1:1 is due to the late date of the epistle, at a time when the church had begun to assume the order that is laid down in the Pastoral Epistles, which was prevalent in the first and purest age of the church.

*Chapter* 1

## 1-12 INTRODUCTION. PRAYER FOR THE GROWING CHURCH AT PHILIPPI

►**1 Timotheus** [Timothy]—Timothy was well known among the Philippians (Acts 16:3, 10-12) and was with Paul in Rome at the time of his writing this letter. Timothy's name is mentioned to include his greeting to the Philippians; it does not suggest that he wrote part of the letter. **servants** [slaves] **of Jesus Christ**—Paul called himself a "slave" in this letter rather than an apostle as in his other letters. This suggests that Paul felt close to the church at Philippi and did not need to remind them of his authority as an apostle. **all the saints . . . bish-**

ops and deacons—"All the saints" constitute the entire church at Philippi. The "bishops" were actually "overseers" (Gk., *episkopoi*). An overseer was a different title for an elder (see Acts 20:17, 28). One of the elder's functions was to oversee the church. Later, in the second century, the church promoted one of the elders above the others and called him a bishop. This is the first of Paul's letters in which they are greeted separately. As long as the apostles were constantly visiting the new churches, regular elders were not needed. These visits were becoming less frequent however, and as some of the apostles died or were unable to travel, the need for regular, permanent elders arose. Thus, the three pastoral letters following this one gave instructions for the appointment of elders and deacons. This implies that the elders and deacons were to take over the job that the apostles had been doing to this point. Note that the apostles spoke to the church more directly than did the presiding elders (Col. 4:17; 1 Thess. 5:12; Heb. 13:24; Rev. 1:4, 11). The elders were responsible for internal affairs of the church body, and the deacons for external concerns. The plural in both cases indicates that there were more than one overseer and one deacon at the Philippian church.

►2 This greeting is actually a combination of the common greetings of the Jews, the Greeks, and the Romans. The Greek salutation was "joy" (*chairein*), akin to "grace" (*charis*); the Hebrew was "peace"; and the Roman was "health" (the intermediate term between "grace" and "peace").

►3 **upon every remembrance of you**—i.e., every time I remember you.

►4 **for you all**—The word "all" following "you" suggests that Paul, by his frequent repetition of the word in this letter, was sending his love and prayers to each of the Philippians alike and was not recognizing any divisions among them. **joy**—Joy is the dominant quality expressed in this letter (cf. 1:18; 2:2, 28; 3:1; 4:1, 4), whereas "love" is the keynote of the letter to the Ephesians. Love and joy are the first two visible signs of the Spirit's presence. Paul's joy indicates his high opinion of the Philippians; they offered him much happiness and little pain.

►5 This is the reason for Paul's prayer (1:3). **fellowship**—or, participation. Paul enjoyed the Philippians' fellowship or real spiritual participation. Christians have the fellowship of the Son of God (1 Cor. 1:9) and of the Father (1 John 1:3) by sharing in the Holy Spirit (2 Cor. 13:14). This fellowship is practiced through acts of communion, not only at the Lord's Supper, but in liberal giving and receiving among one another (4:10, 15; cf. 2 Cor. 9:13; Gal. 6:6; Heb. 13:16). The Philippians' gift to Paul (4:10, 15ff.) showed their eagerness to participate with Paul in the cause of the gospel.

►6 **Being confident**—Paul's confidence strengthened his prayer (1:3, 4), and the thing that he prays for (1:4) is what gives him the confidence (Mark 11:24; 1 John 5:14, 15). **that he which hath begun a good work in you**—One very seldom begins something with no thought to finish it. Whatever God begins, he will surely finish. This verse speaks of the

particular work of perfecting the Christians (see Rom. 8:28-30). As God never left Israel, neither will he desert the spiritual Israel (Deut. 33:3; Isa. 27:3; 1 Pet. 1:5). **will perform it until**—i.e., will complete (or perfect) it up until the time Christ returns. As the Christian matures, God perfects him or her. **the day of Jesus Christ**—The day of Christ's return. The Christian can anticipate Christ's return rather than dwell on the inevitability of his own death.

►7 **meet**—The Greek word means "just" or "appropriate." **to think this of you all**—This refers to the confidence Paul had for them as expressed in 1:6. **because I have you in my heart**—or it could be translated, "because you have me in your heart . . . being partakers of my grace." Either way, Paul and the Philippians had tender feelings toward one another because they suffered and worked together for the gospel (1:28-30; 4:15).

►8 **how greatly I long after you all in the bowels** [tender affections] **of Jesus Christ**—Since Jesus Christ lived in Paul, Paul shared in Jesus Christ's love for the believers at Philippi. All real spiritual love is but a portion of Christ's love which yearns in all who are united to him (Alford).

►9 **love may abound yet more and more**—for Christ and for one another (see 2:2; 4:2). **knowledge**—more accurate knowledge, fuller knowledge, personal knowledge. **judgment**—actually, "perception." "Knowledge" and "perception" enlarge the Christian's capacities and keep his love in proper perspective.

►10 **That ye may approve** [with a view to your proving] **things that are excellent**—The Christian should not only be knowledgeable and sensitive but should develop his critical capacities so that he can discern what makes the difference in excellence. **sincere**—The Greek word means "examined under sunlight and found to be pure." **and without offence**—lit., "unoffending." **till the day of Christ**—or, in the day of Christ.

►11 **Being filled** [having been filled] **with the fruits** [fruit] **of righteousness**—The fruit produced by the Holy Spirit in us (Gal. 5:22) contains a divinely-given, divinely-wrought righteousness (see 3:9). **which are by Jesus Christ**—lit., "through Jesus Christ" (see 3:9ff.).

## 12-30 ADVANCING THE GOSPEL

**►12 ye should understand**—know. The Philippians probably thought that Paul's imprisonment would keep him from spreading the gospel; thus, he wanted to assure them that their fears were unnecessary (1:19, 28; 2:17). **fallen out rather**—rather than hindering the gospel, Paul's imprisonment advanced it. **furtherance**—According to the Greek, this indicates a pioneering advance in a cutting of a new way. (The Greek word literally means "to cut the way before," which was the work of pioneers in ancient times.) Paul was pioneering the way for the gospel in new territory, Rome.

**►13** Paul by then had been in a Roman prison for two years. In this time his cause and his message had become widely known in Rome. **palace**—praetorium. The Praetorian guards (belonging to the emperor who was called "Praetor" or "Commander-in-chief") were stationed at the palace of Nero in special barracks apart from the general Praetorian camp outside the city. Paul seemed to be in stricter custody here than in the place indicated in Acts (28:16, 20, 30, 31), where he was chained to a soldier but lived in his own rented house. He was now apparently held at the Praetorium barracks.

**►14 waxing confident by my bonds**—i.e., being encouraged by my imprisonment.

**►15 preach Christ even of envy and strife**—Due to Paul's cheerful, patient endurance in prison, the gospel was spreading successfully throughout Rome. Some preachers (probably Judaizers, cf. 2 Cor. 11:1-4) were jealously trying to attract to themselves the kind of attention that Paul was receiving. **some also of good will**—This refers to the Christians mentioned in 1:14.

**►16-17** These two verses are transposed in the earliest manuscripts. **preach Christ of contention**—These preachers were less interested in their message than in their own reputations (Gal. 6:12, 13) and attempted to take advantage of Paul's absence to gain a hearing for themselves. Some assumed that because Paul could not preach, he would be humiliated by their success, not understanding that Paul's success was not staked on his own reputation.

**►18** Despite their motives, the end result of this preaching was the same as that of Paul's as Christ was still being announced. Apparently the content of these sermons was similar to Paul's preaching and did not contain such false teaching as Judaizers were bringing to Galatia (Gal. 1:6-8). Their basic error was in motive and not in doctrine. Drawing attention to Christ, for whatever reason, was doing some good. Thus, Paul was able to appreciate the good result of their bad motives.

**►19 this shall turn** [out] **to my salvation**—The proclamation of Christ, even from wrong motives, was helping to develop and complete God's kingdom and in so doing glorify God. Thus, Paul's own salvation as part of the kingdom, was furthered (Heb. 9:28), so that their preaching, contrary to their intentions, worked to Paul's benefit. (Paul quoted Job 13:16, LXX, and applied Job's words to himself.) **through your prayer, and the supply of the Spirit of Jesus Christ**—The Philippians' prayer would generate the Spirit's supply. The Greek word for "supply" (*epichorēgia*) was used to describe the supply a choir manager would provide all the members of a Greek choir (who performed in the Greek plays). In short, he took care of all their living expenses. The word then came to mean a full supply of any kind. Paul was looking forward to getting a full supply of Jesus Christ's Spirit as a result of the Philippians' prayer. The term "Spirit of Jesus Christ" is unique in the NT (cf. "Spirit of Jesus" in Acts 16:7 and "Spirit of Christ" in Rom. 8:9 and 1 Pet. 1:11).

**►20 earnest expectation**—The Greek image conveys the idea of someone craning his neck to catch a glimpse of something very important to him. (The word is used only one other time in the NT: Rom. 8:19.) **in nothing I shall be ashamed**—Paul was determined not to have any regrets about his participation in God's work (cf. Rom. 9:33). **Christ shall be magnified in my body**—The indwelling Christ (called "the Spirit of Jesus Christ" in the previous verse) would be made visible in Paul's being and living. **whether . . . by life, or by death**—Paul, lacking foreknowledge as to his death, would nonetheless gain in either circumstance.

**►21 For to me to live is Christ**—i.e., whatever life I have to live, that life is Christ's, for Christ is the sole object for whom I live and the unique source of my life (Gal. 2:20). **to die is gain**—The Greek "to have died," expresses the state after death rather than the act of dying. In either case, God would be honored. Death, for Paul, would simply bring him closer to the God he loved and would not carry the shame or fear his enemies might wish to inflict.

➤**22** This verse could better translated, "If I am to go on living in the body, this will mean fruitful labor for me. Yet, what shall I choose? I do not know!" (NIV).

➤**23 For I am in a strait betwixt two**—i.e., I am constrained by two equally compelling forces: (1) death and departure to Christ; (2) life and service to the believers. In actuality, however, death was by far the more preferable of the two options because death would usher Paul into the presence of Christ.

➤**24 is more needful for you**—meaning "on your account." Paul was willing to give up his death wish in order to be of help to the Philippians.

➤**25** Paul had a spiritual certainty that God had more work for him to do, even though he was unaware of what his earthly circumstances would be (2:23). He planned to return to Philippi after his imprisonment (Philem. 22).

➤**26 That your rejoicing may be more abundant in Jesus Christ for me**—This would partly reassure the Philippians as they saw God answering their prayers on Paul's behalf (1:19). **by my coming to you again**—They would glorify Christ for bringing Paul to them and for the additional instruction and encouragement he would give them. The joy of the Philippians here is paralleled by Paul's joy (2:16).

➤**27** Paul here cautions them to do the tasks that God has called them to regardless of whether or not he is able to visit them. **conversation**—conduct of life (cf. Eph. 2:19). **whether I come and see you, or else be absent, I may hear of your affairs**—Paul obviously had ways of keeping in touch with the Philippians, even while in prison. His continued interest would in itself be of considerable support to them. **stand fast in one spirit**—The Spirit unites a group of Christians into one body, enabling them to overcome small differences among individual members and thus to work forcefully toward a common goal. **with one mind** [soul] **striving together for the faith of the gospel**—The image in Greek is

drawn from the athletic contests. Usually, athletes competed against one another; here Paul asks the church at Philippi to compete together as a team of athletes to help advance the faith that comes through the preaching of the gospel.

➤**28 adversaries**—opposers. **which**—refers to them not being terrified. **evident token of perdition**—i.e., "a sign to them that they will be destroyed" (NIV).

➤**29 it is given . . . to believe on** [in] **him**—Faith is a gift of God (Eph. 2:8) and comes not by man's will but by the Holy Spirit (John 1:12, 13). **to suffer for his sake**—See 2 Tim. 2:12.

➤**30 the same conflict**—or, struggle (see Acts 16:12, 19; 1 Thess. 2:2). Again, this word alludes to the Greek athletic games, for it was used to describe wrestling. Paul's life was a struggle, a wrestling match.

*Chapter* 2

## 1-11 AN EXHORTATION TO UNITY AND TO HUMILITY, FOLLOWING CHRIST'S EXAMPLE

➤**1** Paul now expands upon his statement in 1:27, "stand fast in one spirit, striving together with one mind [soul]." The four clauses in this verse are conditional; their substance will be fulfilled if and when the conditions stated in 2:2 are fulfilled. **consolation in Christ**—i.e., consolation of which Christ is the source. **comfort of love**—comfort or encouragement flowing from love. **fellowship of the Spirit**—communion together as Christians, flowing from joint-participation in the Spirit (see 1 Cor. 12:4, 13, 14). **bowels** [tender affections] **and mercies**—as the issues of fellowship in the Spirit. The opposites of these rhetorical questions are denounced in 2:3, 4, to which the four demands mentioned in 2:2 also correspond.

➤**2 Fulfil ye my joy**—Paul had experienced joy because of the Philippians. He now asks that he might have this joy completed by seeing full unity and harmony among them. **likeminded**—lit., "that you think the same thing" (see 2:5). **being of one accord**—In Greek this is a noun meaning "co-souled ones" or "united souls." **of one mind**—lit., "thinking one thing." If their thinking was focused on Christ, they would be united in thought.

➤3 The KJV supplies the words **Let nothing be done,** but it could just as well read, "Let nothing be thought." Not only our actions but our thoughts need to be guarded from selfishness. God takes our attitudes as well as our actions into account. **lowliness of mind**—actually, "humility." Humility is the realization that we are creatures who are totally dependent on God, the Creator. If we are really humble before God, we are totally relying on God. This affects our attitudes toward others, for as equally dependent creatures, we cannot take pride in accomplishments that put other men down (see Eph. 4:2; Col. 3:12). **let each esteem other better than themselves**—Instead of looking for good points in ourselves, we should look for the good in others.

➤4 This verse is better translated, "Let each of you look not only to his own interests, but also to the interests of others" (RSV).

➤5 **Let this mind be in you**—Let this kind of thinking be in you, i.e., the kind of thinking that existed in Christ Jesus. We should follow Christ's example, rather than put ourselves first. He did not think too highly of his own status to take on our humanity (2:8) with its complement of suffering and humiliation (Rom. 15:3).

➤6 Here begins what many have called an early Christian hymn (see 2:6-11). This hymn is remarkably parallel to the pericope in John 13:1-17 (see comments there). **Who, being**—Greek, "who subsisting" (*huparchōn*), a present participle indicating an existence from the beginning (from the Gk. *archōn*, "beginning"). As such the expression points to Christ's eternal preexistent state. **in the form of God**—The Greek word for "form" (*morphe*) was generally used "to express the way in which a thing, being what it is in itself, appears to our senses. . . . Thus when this word is applied to God, his *morphē* must refer to his deepest being, to what he is in himself . . . " (Hawthorne). The expression "form of God" may be correctly understood as the "essential nature and character of God" (Vincent; cf. also Lightfoot). Hawthorne elaborates:

To say, therefore, that Christ existed *in morphē theou* [in the form of God] is to say

that outside his human nature Christ had no other manner of existing apart from existing "in the form of God," that is, apart from being in possession of all the characteristics and qualities belonging to God. This somewhat enigmatic expression, then, appears to be a cautious, hidden way for the author to say that Christ was God, possessed of the very nature of God (GNB [i.e., TEV], NIV, Goodspeed, Knox, Moffatt, Phillips), without employing these exact words.

The following expression, "equal with God," corroborates this interpretation. In the Greek, there is a definite article before the expression "to be equal with God" whose function is to point back to the expression "in the form of God" and in so doing connects the thought of being in God's form with that of being equal with God. **thought it not robbery to be equal with God**—This expression has been exegeted and translated in numerous ways. But there are two basic thoughts inherent in these words: (1) Christ did not consider his equality with God as something which he had to hold on to, or (2) Christ did not think it robbery to be on an equality with God. Both ideas are defensible and true. The first idea is captured well in a translation by Lightfoot: "Though He preexisted in the form of God, yet He did not look upon equality with God as a prize which must not slip from His grasp." The expression "equal with God" in Greek is "equal things with God." Everything God is, Christ is; the equality is in essential characteristics and divine attributes.

➤7 **made himself of no reputation**—rather as the Greek, "emptied himself, taking upon him the form of a servant, being made in the likeness of men." The two latter clauses (there being no conjunctions, "and . . . and," in the Gk.) expresses in what Christ's "emptying of himself" consists, viz., in "taking the form of a servant." (See Heb. 10:5-7, which implies that it was at the time when he assumed a body, that he took "the form of a servant.") And in order to explain how he took the form of a servant, there is added, by "being made in the likeness of men." His subjection to the law (Luke 2:21; Gal. 4:4) and to his parents (Luke 2:51), his low state as a carpenter and a carpenter's reputed son (Matt. 13:55; Mark 6:3), his betrayal for the price of a bond-servant (Exod. 21:32), his slave-like death to relieve us from the slavery of sin and death, and finally and chiefly, his servant-like dependence as man on God, while his divinity was not outwardly manifested (Isa. 49:3, 7) are all marks of his "form as a servant." This proves: (1) He was in the form of a servant as soon as he was made man. (2) He was "in the form of God" before he was "in the form of a servant." (3) He was as much "in the form of God" as "in the form of a servant" and was so in the form of God as "to be on an equality with God"; he therefore could have been none other than God. The expression "he emptied himself" is so profound that scholars have tried in vain to plumb its depths. Who knows what this "emptying out" (called *kenosis* in Gk.) really involved? At best, we can say it means that Christ divested himself of his divine state (or, mode) of existence when he relinquished his *position* (but not his *disposition*) of equality with God to take on a subservient role to the Father, which would result in his being sent to earth to assume a new form of being as a man. In this form, he would accomplish redemption by death on the cross (2:8).

➤**8 being found in fashion as a man**—Due to his emptying of himself, Christ took on the likeness of men and was found (or, discovered) by men to be as they were—a genuine man. **humbled himself**—Christ humbled himself in becoming a man. **became obedient unto death**—He not only gave up his position of equality with God but became obedient to God as his slave (Rom. 5:19; Heb. 5:8). This obedience eventually brought him to his death, for his death was the climax of his obedience (John 10:18). **even the death of the cross**—Christ did not just suffer death, but the worst kind of death, death by crucifixion.

➤**9 God also hath highly exalted him**—This glorification came as the result of Christ's self-humiliation and obedience (Ps. 8:5, 6; 110:1, 7; Matt. 28:18; Luke 24:26; John 5:27; 10:17; Rom. 14:9; Eph. 1:20-22; Heb. 2:9). Christ is our example, teaching us first to humble ourselves and submit to God's will before we expect to be exalted (2:3, 5; 3:21; 1 Pet. 5:5, 6). **a name . . . above every name**—The name "Jesus" (2:10) is a name of honor (Acts 9:15, 16), a name above both men and angels (Eph. 1:21).

➤**10 at [in] the name of Jesus**—To worship in the "name of Jesus" is to worship Jesus himself (2:11). (Cf. Acts 7:59; Acts 9:14, 21; 22:16; Rom. 10:13; 1 Cor. 1:2; 2 Tim. 2:22, where people called on the name of Jesus.) **every knee should bow**—referring to Isaiah 45:23; also quoted in Romans 14:11. **in heaven . . . in earth . . . under the earth**—The angels, as well as the living and the dead will acknowledge Christ as Lord (Rom. 14:9, 11; Eph. 4:9, 10; Rev. 5:13). The demons and the dead who are unsaved may also be included here though they worship out of fear, not love (Mark 3:11; Luke 8:31; James 2:19).

➤**11 every tongue**—cf. "every knee" (2:10). **Lord**—In every way Christ will be acknowledged as Lord and no longer as servant (2:7). **to the glory of God the Father**—the grand end of Christ's mediatorial office and kingdom, which shall cease when this end shall have been fully realized (John 5:19-23, 30; 17:1, 4-7; 1 Cor. 15:24-28).

## 12-18 LIGHTS IN THE WORLD

➤**12 Wherefore . . . as ye have always obeyed**—Paul was referring to their Christ-like obedience to God (2:8), regardless of whether Paul was with them or not. **work out your own salvation**—Paul cautioned the Philippians to be all the more careful, in his absence, to "work out" their salvation in appropriate ways (2:13; Eph. 1:11). Although believers are justified once and for all, the Spirit helps us to constantly, progressively live out the implications of our conversion in daily life (2:13; Eph. 1:11). The Christian all too easily forgets the primary goals of his commitment to God, as well as the resources available to him for fulfilling his obligations (2 Pet. 1:5-8). The Philippians needed to realize that in the end they were responsible to God and not to Paul, and that everything they had received from Paul was actually from God as well. **with fear and trembling**—The same advice is given to servants concerning their attitudes in obeying their masters (Eph. 6:5). Christ should not be served through menial fear, but rather through a desire to thoroughly accomplish each assignment (1 Cor. 9:26, 27; Heb. 4:1). As we sense our complete inadequacy as humans to do what God requires, we learn to rely on God for whatever we need (Rom. 11:20).

➤**13 For** [Because] **it is God which** [who] **worketh in you**—It is not said, "Work out your own salvation, though it is God . . . ," but, "*because* it is God. . . . " The will and power to work, being first installments of his grace, encourage us to make full proof of, and carry out to the end, the "salvation" that he first "worked," and is still "working" in us, enabling us to "work it out." "Our will does nothing thereunto without grace; but grace is inactive without our will" (St. Bernard). Man is, in a different sense, entirely active, and entirely passive: God producing all, and we acting all. What he produced is our own acts. It is not that God does some, and we the rest. God does all, and we do all. God is the only proper author, we the only proper actors. Thus the same things in Scripture are represented as from God and from us. **worketh**—rather as Greek "worketh effectually." We cannot of ourselves embrace the gospel of grace: "the will" (Ps. 110:3; 2 Cor. 3:5) comes solely of God's gift (John 6:44, 65); so also the power "to do" (rather, "to work effectually," as the Gk., is the same as that for "worketh in"). **of his good pleasure**—rather, "for his good pleasure," in carrying out his eternal purpose (Eph. 1:5, 9).

➤**14 Do all things without murmurings and disputings**—Selfish complaints run counter to the example of Jesus mentioned in 2:5-8 (cf. John 7:12, 13; Acts 6:1; 1 Pet. 4:9; Jude 16). Pointless bickering among believers gives the non-Christian justifiable grounds for criticizing "Christian" behavior (2:15). These arguments stemmed from the Philippians' pride in their achievements, which Paul denounced in 2:3. It was popular among the Aristotelian philosophers around Philippi to impress others with their accomplishments; the Christians were not to take up this pastime.

➤**15 harmless**—lit., "unmixed" or "pure." **sons of God**—should read, "children of God" (Rom. 8:14-16). The Father, rather than an external law, is to guide our behavior (Matt. 5:44, 45, 48). **without rebuke**—without fault. The whole verse stands in contrast to what is said in Deuteronomy 32:5. (See also 1 Pet. 2:12.) **ye shine as lights** [luminaries] **in the world**—As the sun and the moon are "luminaries" in the physical world (see Gen. 1:14, 16, LXX; cf. Rev. 21:11), the Christians are luminaries among men (cf. Matt. 5:14-16; Eph. 5:8-13).

➤**16 Holding forth the word of life**— "Holding forth" in the Greek conveys the idea that the Christian will make God's light continuously available to the unbeliever; i.e., he will hold out the light, offering it to the unbeliever. For Christ is the "light of the world" (John 8:12), and Christians are the lightbearers, emanating his light. **that I may rejoice in the day of Christ**—because the Philippians would give him a cause for rejoicing (see 1 Thess. 2:19).

➤**17 Yea, and if**—The Greek reads "even if," suggesting that Paul regarded this as probable. Paul took into account the possibility of still being alive when Christ returned (as should every Christian), but he supposed that his death would more likely occur first. **if I be offered upon the sacrifice**—Greek, "If I am poured out [as a drink offering]." In some of the Jewish offerings wine was poured upon the sacrifice. Paul presented the Philippians' faith as the sacrifice and his blood as the wine poured upon it. (The same expression appears in 2 Tim. 4:6). Paul was less optimistic as to his release from prison in this letter than he was in letters written earlier to the Ephesians, the Colossians, and to Philemon (see Introduction). **the sacrifice and service of your faith**—"The sacrifice and service" employs one article with the two nouns and probably is a hendiadys meaning "sacrificial service" (two words connected by "and" expressing one idea). The apostle was thinking of their various Christian ministries performed as a spiritual sacrifice to God, springing from their faith (Kent). **I joy, and rejoice with you all**—Paul regarded it an honor to die for the Philippians in this way, and he expected them to take this attitude as well.

## 19-30 TIMOTHY AND EPAPHRODITUS

➤**19 to send Timotheus shortly**—Philippians 2:22 implies that Timothy had been with Paul for quite some time. In Acts 16:1-4; 17:10, 14, it is recorded that they went together from Derbe in Lycaonia and were together again toward the end of Paul's travels at Berea in Macedonia. Philippians 2:25 indicates that Epaphroditus was to leave at once for Philippi to relieve their anxiety about his illness and to deliver Paul's letter. Timothy was to follow when Paul learned what would be done with him. Paul planned to stop at Philippi as part of a longer trip, which meant that he could not arrive for quite some time yet. He wanted to send Timothy to reassure them and to give them practical and spiritual support as they were undergoing persecutions at the time (1:28-30).

➤**20 I have no man likeminded**—Paul wanted to send Timothy to Philippi because they agreed on so many issues (cf. Deut. 13:6; Ps. 55:14). **naturally**—The Greek word means "genuinely" or "sincerely." The Spirit of God can so change a man's interests that he can be naturally spiritual.

➤**21 all seek their own** [interests], **not the things which are Jesus Christ's**—Paul may have been referring to some other Christians who were with him at the time (1:14, 17; 4:21; Col. 4:14; cf. 2 Tim. 4:10; Philem. 24). Although 1:16, 17 implies that many genuine Christians were with Paul, none of them answered to Paul's needs quite like Timothy did (2:4; cf. 1 Cor. 10:24, 33; 13:5).

➤**22 proof**—proven worth. **a son with a father**—actually, "a child with a father." Paul's praise of Timothy is rare and quite touching.

➤**23 so soon as I shall see how it will go with me**—Paul still did not know when or whether he would be released.

➤**25 I supposed** [thought] **it necessary to send to you Epaphroditus**—Epaphroditus had been sent (as the Philippians' **messenger**) to convey the Philippians' current news to Paul and to do anything he could to help Paul in prison. Now Paul wanted to send him back. **messenger**—lit., "apostle," used in a general sense to denote "one sent on a mission" (cf. Rom. 16:7; 2 Cor. 8:23). **ministered**—In Greek this word carries the idea of priestly or spiritual ministry. Epaphroditus ministered to Paul's spiritual needs.

➤**26 full of heaviness**—distressed. Epaphroditus was worried because he knew that his friends were concerned about him, having heard that he was ill.

➤**27** The apostles were not given the permanent gift of miracles and healing, or Paul surely would have healed Epaphroditus. Rather, they were made instruments of the Holy Spirit to minister in whatever way was indicated. **lest I should have sorrow upon sorrow**—the sorrow of losing him by death, in addition to the sorrow of imprisonment. This is the only place in his letter where Paul mentioned his hardship in a sorrowful tone.

➤**29 in reputation**—in honor.

➤**30 for the work of Christ**—i.e., in coming to Paul to minister to him (2:25). **he was nigh unto death**—Epaphroditus was probably sick when he left Philippi and nearly died in his attempts to relieve Paul's hardships. **to supply your lack of service toward me**—Paul did not mean that the Philippians were unwilling to help him, but only that they lacked the opportunity (see 4:10). Epaphroditus did what they would have done had they been there. Therefore, they were to welcome Epaphroditus and show their appreciation for his work on their behalf. The Greek word for "service" shares the same root as that which is translated "ministered" in 2:25; it means priestly service or spiritual ministry (see Rom. 15:16; Heb. 1:7; 8:2).

# Chapter 3

**1-21 FORGETTING THE PAST; PURSUING CHRIST; STRETCHING FORWARD TO REACH THE GOAL**

➤**1 Finally**—lit., "as to what remains." Paul now makes a transition to another general subject. The word "finally" is often used to conclude a letter (2 Thess. 3:1; Eph. 6:10), but is not restricted to that usage (cf. 1 Thess. 4:1, Gk.). Paul might have intended to end his letter here and decided to comment at greater length on the problem of false teaching. **rejoice**—Joy is the prevailing feature of this letter (see 1:18, 25; 2:17; 4:4). **in the Lord**—Jesus is the source of our joy (3:3). **grievous**—irksome or burdensome. **for you it is safe**—i.e., Paul's repetition provided a safeguard against error.

➤**2 dogs**—Numerous Bible passages use the name "dog" to connote filth and impurity (cf. Deut. 23:18; Ps. 59:6, 14, 15; Matt. 7:6; Titus 1:15, 16; 2 Pet. 2:22; Rev. 21:8; 22:15). The Jews referred to the Gentiles as dogs (Matt. 15:26) but had themselves become as dogs by refusing to believe in the gospel of Christ and insisting on legalistic regulations instead (cf. Isa. 56:10, 11). **evil workers**—See 2 Corinthians 11:13. These men worked for evil as the Christian works for good and were to be avoided (3:19; cf. Rom. 16:18; 2 Tim. 2:15). **concision**—indicating mutilation. Circumcision had by this time lost its spiritual significance. For those who found justification through belief in Christ's sacrifice, circumcision was just a senseless mutilation. Christians have fulfilled God's requirements inwardly, and do not need this physical ritual. To make cuttings in the flesh was prohibited by law (Lev. 21:5) as a heathen practice (1 Kings 18:28); yet the legalists, writes Paul, were violating the law by insisting on circumcision. It is interesting to note Paul's gradual change in tone as he wrote about circumcision. In Acts 13:39, Paul did not mention circumcision, but it is implied as part of the law of Moses which is not valid as a means to salvation. Several years later Paul specifically mentioned circumcision in his letter to the Galatians (Gal. 3:3), maintaining that the practice has no spiritual value. In his letter to the Romans (Rom. 2:28, 29), he said that it is the inward circumcision of a changed heart and life, rather than outward circumcision, which is the mark of the Christian. In the letter to the Colossians, still later, Paul elaborated on spiritual circumcision (Col. 2:11; 3:11). Finally, in writing to the Philippians, Paul substituted the word "concision" for "circumcision," indicating that the practice had lost all spiritual significance. Concision refers to flesh-cutting rituals, which carried connotations of disgrace and disapproval. Though necessary for all people under the old covenant, circumcision became more and more associated in the apostle's experience with the open hostility of the NT Jews and with the warped teachings of the false brethren.

➤3 **worship God in the spirit**—Several of the earliest manuscripts read "worship by [or, in] the Spirit of God." Thus our worship is by means of God's Spirit and in God's Spirit (cf. John 4:23, 24). Legal worship was basically external, consisting of certain acts done at certain times in certain places. The worship of the Christian should flow from his inner being and embrace every aspect of his life (Rom. 12:1). **rejoice** [boast] **in Christ Jesus**—Christ's work, not the law, is our only true foundation for boasting. **no confidence in the flesh**—but in the Spirit.

➤5 Paul here lists some of his credentials: (1) his pure Jewish heritage, (2) his Jewish initiation (circumcision), and (3) his strictness in following Jewish law and custom. **Circumcised the eighth day**—This was the custom for a pure Jew; a proselyte would be circumcised later in life. **of the tribe of Benjamin**—Thus,

a son of Rachel. **Hebrew of the Hebrews**—A Hebrew-speaking Jew, as opposed to a Hellenist (a Greek-speaking Jew). **as touching the law**—i.e., as to legality and strictness. **a Pharisee**—the strictest sect (Acts 26:5).

➤6 **Concerning zeal, persecuting the church**—Paul demonstrated his religious zeal (prior to becoming a Christian) by persecuting Christians (see Acts 22:3; 26:9). **blameless**—as to ceremonial righteousness and legal perfection. Paul tried to appear perfect before men. But as to appearing perfect before God, Paul stated that he was still not all that he should be (3:12-14).

➤7 **gain**—The Greek is "gains" or "profits"—anything of apparent advantage (Matt. 16:26; Luke 9:25).

➤8 **the excellency of the knowledge of Christ**—i.e., "the surpassing greatness of knowing Christ" (NIV). The Greek word for "knowledge" here speaks of a personal, experiential, and progressive knowledge. Paul pursued this kind of knowing of Christ, and so should we. **for whom I have suffered the loss of all things**—Not only is everything else worth much less by comparison, but I have actually given up or lost everything for Christ. **count them but dung**—The word "dung" means "refuse" or "waste." **that I may win Christ**—lit., "that I may gain Christ." A man cannot make other things his gain and at the same time gain Christ. He who loses all things, and even himself, on account of Christ, gains Christ (cf. Luke 9:23, 24).

➤9 **be found**—at his coming. **in him**—living in union with him. **mine own righteousness . . . of the law**—See 3:6; Romans 10:3, 5. **righteousness . . . of** [from] **God by** [based upon] **faith**—Paul was brought from legal slavery into the freedom of Christ immediately, with no gradual transition. Hence, his Pharisaism was dropped once and for all, and opposition to Pharisaic Judaism took the place of opposition to the gospel of Christ. God's planning had perfectly prepared Paul for the work of combating legalistic justification. "The righteousness of faith," in Paul's sense, is the righteousness or perfect holiness of Christ appropriated by faith, as the *objective* ground of confidence for the believer, and also as a new *subjective* principle of life. Hence it includes the essence of a new disposition and may easily pass into the idea of sanctification, though the two ideas are originally distinct. Holiness through Christ shall be realized in all who are one with him by faith and are the vessels of his Spirit. The seed of holiness is imparted into Christians at the moment they believe, but the fruit of a life perfectly conformed to the Redeemer can only be gradually developed in this life (Neander).

➤**10 that I may know him**—experientially (the same Gk. word as in 3:8). To know Christ is more than merely to know facts or doctrine about him. Christians are those who have personally, experientially been brought into a relationship with Christ that has changed the very basis of their lives. **the power of his resurrection**—This power assures Christians of their justification (Rom. 4:25; 1 Cor. 15:7) and regeneration by virtue of their identification with Christ in resurrection (Rom. 6:4; Col. 2:12; 3:1). The power of the Holy Spirit that raised Christ from the dead is available to all men to raise them from their spiritual death now (Eph. 1:19, 20) and from their physical death in the future (Rom. 8:11). **the fellowship of his sufferings**—"These sufferings were not Christ's substitutionary sufferings on the cross. Paul knew that those could not be shared. But he desired to participate with Christ, since he was one of His, in suffering for the sake of righteousness" (Lightner). **being made conformable unto his death**—i.e., being conformed to the likeness of Christ's death (cf. Rom. 8:29) by continued sufferings for his sake and the mortification of the carnal self (2 Cor. 4:10-12).

➤**11 If by any means**—not implying uncertainty, as is clear in the NIV's rendering: "and so, somehow." **attain unto the resurrection of the dead**—This probably refers to the resurrection of Christians at the time of Christ's return (1 Cor. 15:23; 1 Thess. 4:15; Rev. 20:5, 6). Paul's wanting to attain this resurrection is in line with what Jesus said of the resurrection in Luke 20:35.

➤**12 attained**—or, "appropriated," viz., a perfect knowledge of Christ, the power of his resurrection, fellowship of his suffering, and conformity to his death (see 1 Cor. 9:24; Heb. 12:23). **apprehend that for which also I am apprehended of Christ Jesus**—i.e., I may lay hold on that (prize—3:14) for which also I was laid hold of by Christ. Christ laid hold of Paul

for Paul to lay hold of the prize, which is knowing Christ. Paul was close to gaining the prize (see 2 Tim. 4:7, 8).

➤**13** Christians must have perfection as their goal (Matt. 5:48) but should not pretend that sin does not exist (1 John 1:8). **forgetting those things which are behind**—Dwelling on the past absorbs time and energy that should be devoted to God in the present (Luke 9:62; 17:32). We are to go forward. Paul determined to forget his past religious background so as to press on toward the mark (3:14). **reaching forth**—stretching forward, like a runner in a race with body bent forward.

➤**14 I press toward the mark**—of finishing the race. **for the prize**—In the Grecian games the winner's prize was a garland wreath; in the Christian race the prize is full appropriation of Christ (see 3:10-12). The prize is spoken of elsewhere in Scripture (1 Cor. 9:24; 2 Tim. 4:8). **high calling**—a heavenly calling (as in Heb. 3:1). This calling was not just for Paul and the other apostles but is a call of encouragement for every Christian.

➤**15 therefore**—This verse refers back to circumcision (3:3). **perfect**—or complete, mature. The perfection spoken of in 3:12 had not yet been realized by Paul, for he had not yet completed his course. This perfection, however, speaks of being complete or fully fit. Bengel thought it meant "fully fit for running." **otherwise minded**—lit., "think otherwise." Paul's goals (to gain Christ, etc.) should be the same goals for all Christians. If anyone thinks differently, God will reveal to him his error.

➤**16 whereto we have already attained**—Expecting that God will reveal new things to us does not excuse us for taking lightly the things that we already know. We should be careful that we are living according to the truth that we already have before we ever hope for more (Hos. 6:3). **let us walk**—The Greek word means "let us keep in step with" (see comments on Gal. 6:16). Our lives need to be in step (or, in keeping) with the knowledge we already have. The last words of this verse **rule, let us mind the same thing** are not present in all the earliest manuscripts. They were added later, from Galations 6:16.

➤**17 be followers together of me**—lit., "be my fellow imitators." As I am an imitator of

Christ (1 Cor. 11:1), you can imitate Christ by following my example (Eph. 5:1).

➤**18 many**—The number of non-Christians is large as compared with the "little flock" (Luke 12:32) of those who truly follow Christ. **often**—There is a constant need to be aware of this problem. **even weeping**—Paul's tone was not harsh and critical. He spoke more strongly against false teachers than against those who openly rejected Christianity. **enemies of the cross of Christ**—These enemies were either the Judaizers who denied the efficacy of the cross and substituted obedience to a formal code in its place or to the Antinomians (those against law) who refused to conform to the Christ and instead lived a life of self-indulgence (Lightfoot).

➤**19 destruction**—translated "perdition" in 1:28. **whose God [god] is their belly [appetite]**—Such people are absorbed with the things which will be destroyed (1 Cor. 6:13). The Christian, in contrast, has a body which will be made like Jesus' body (3:21). **whose glory is in their shame**—Paul was probably alluding to Hosea 4:7 (cf. Rom. 1:32). There seems to be no allusion to circumcision here but rather to sensuality and carnality in general. **who mind earthly things**—cf. 3:20; Colossians 3:2.

➤**20 conversation**—rather, "citizenship." **is in heaven**—lit., "has its existence in heaven" (see Heb. 11:16). Roman citizenship was highly prized during Paul's time; how much more our citizenship in heaven should be valued (Acts 22:28; Luke 10:20). **from whence also we look for the Saviour, the Lord Jesus Christ**—We wait (Rom. 8:29) for the return of Christ as Savior (Heb. 9:28).

➤**21 change**—actually, "transfigure." **our vile body**—lit., "the body of our humiliation," or "lowly body" (RSV). **that it may be fashioned**—actually, "conformed" (see Rom. 8:29). Christ will come not only as our Savior (3:20) but will also give us new physical bodies. Following the pattern of Jesus' resurrection, our identities will not change, but our form and mode of existence certainly will (see Ps. 17:15; 1 Cor. 15:51). Christ, as life-giving Spirit (1 Cor. 15:45), indwelling the believer, will change the believer's body so as to be like his own (Kennedy). The transformation of the soul is a lifelong process; the transfiguration of the body is instantaneous (1 Cor. 15:52) and

will be performed through the Spirit dwelling in the believer (Rom. 8:11).

*Chapter* 4

## 1-9 EXHORTATION TO UNITY AND PEACE

➤**1 dearly beloved**—This phrase, repeated later in the verse, underscores Paul's love for the Philippians. **and longed for**—due to Paul's separation from them. **my joy and crown**—in the day of the Lord. **stand fast**—cf. 1:27.

➤**2 Euodias and Syntyche**—These two women, perhaps deaconesses and probably teachers (see comments on 4:3), had a difference of opinion over some matter. **be of the same mind in the Lord**—Unity of thought cannot come from a human resource; it must originate from a divine source, the Lord himself. "Be of the same mind" in Greek is "think the same thing" (see 2:2; 3:15 and comments).

➤**3 I entreat thee, also, true yokefellow**—The image is that of a yokemate, as with a pair of oxen pulling a heavy load (Matt. 11:29, 30; cf. 1 Tim. 5:17, 18). Note that the pronoun and noun are singular. Paul may have been referring to Timothy, to Silas (Acts 15:40; 16:19), or to an elder of the church at Philippi. **help those women which laboured with me**—According to the Greek, the pronoun here ("them") refers to Euodias and Syntyche. At Philippi, women were the first to hear the gospel, and Lydia was the first convert. In selecting the first teachers, those who were among the first to understand the gospel would be asked to teach. Thus Euodias and Syntyche were to take an active part in teaching, if not in public preaching (1 Tim. 2:11, 12). **Clement**—A man by this name became bishop of Rome after the deaths of Peter and Paul. His epistle to the Corinthians written from Rome is still extant. He was an eminent apostolic father and was identified by Origen as the same Clement here. **the book of life**—This account contains the name of all believers (Luke 10:20; Phil. 3:20), similar to the roll books of the ancient free cities that contained the names of all who had a right to citizenship (cf. Exod. 32:32; Ps. 69:28; Ezek. 13:9; Dan. 12:1; Rev. 20:12; 21:27).

➤**4 Rejoice**—Joy is a major feature of this epistle.

➤**5 Let your moderation be known**—or, "let your forbearance be known." Paul is here urging Christians to live openly in a Christ-like way among the other people whom they encounter every day. We are motivated to this kind of behavior by remembering that **the Lord is at hand**—i.e., his coming is near. The promise of the Lord's second coming encourages careful conduct in every age (James 5:8, 9). Harsh and inconsiderate treatment of others would be taking into one's own hands a judgment that belongs only to Christ (1 Cor. 4:5). When this occurs, God is provoked to judge us strictly by the law (James 2:12, 13).

➤**6 prayer and supplication**—"Prayer" here is a general term. Supplication refers to specific petitions. **thanksgiving**—for every event, prosperity and affliction alike (1 Thess. 5:18; James 5:13). Thanksgiving makes prayer effective (2 Chron. 20:21) by removing anxiety. All God's answers are a matter for praise. Peace is the companion to thankfulness (4:7; Col. 3:15).

➤**7 the peace of God**—Peace is God's gift, displacing worry (John 14:27; 16:33; Col. 3:15). **which passeth** [surpasses] **all understanding**—cf. 1 Corinthians 2:9, 10; Ephesians 3:20. **shall keep your hearts and minds**—God's peace will guard or secure our minds from detrimental outside forces (Isa. 26:1, 3; and 1 Pet. 1:5). **through Christ Jesus**—actually, "in Christ Jesus."

➤**8** The advice in this verse is for everyone: children and parents, husbands and wives, friends and neighbors; and it furnishes a positive example of the influence our thought life has on our outward behavior (cf. Mark 10:21; Luke 7:4, 5). **honest**—grave, dignified. **virtue**—"Virtue" was prominent in heathen ethics and is found only once in Paul's letters and three times in Peter's (1 Pet. 2:9; 2 Pet. 1:3, 5). This is the most comprehensive Greek for moral excellence (Rienecker).

➤**9 Those things, which ye have both learned, and received, and heard, and seen in me, do**—Paul did not just tell them how to behave; he recommended that they follow his living example.

10-19 PAUL'S THANKSGIVING
FOR THE PHILIPPIANS' GIFT

➤**10** Paul changes the subject here. **your care of** [for] **me hath flourished again**—Paul

knew that the Philippians were anxious to help him but had lacked a way to do so. Possibly their gift was delayed because of Epaphroditus's illness.

➤**11 I have learned**—cf. Hebrews 5:8. **to be content**—The Greek means self-sufficiency and independence from others. Paul used the term to indicate his independence, if need be, of everything but Christ, as he was the sole source of his life (see 4:13; 2 Cor. 3:5; 1 Tim. 6:6, 8).

➤**12** Cf. 2 Corinthians 4:8; 6:9, 10.

➤**13 I can do all things through Christ which strengtheneth me**—According to the earliest manuscripts, this reads, "I can do all things in the One empowering me." We do not need to worry about being given more than we can handle, as Christ supplies resources sufficient to complete what he asks us to do (Gal. 2:20; cf. 1 Tim. 1:12).

➤**14 did communicate with my affliction**—i.e., made yourselves sharers with me in my affliction. They showed their sympathy with Paul in his imprisonment by sending him gifts.

➤**15 I departed from Macedonia**—See Acts 17:14. The Philippians sent gifts to Paul after he had left Philippi and gone to Corinth (2 Cor. 11:8, 9). The gifts referred to here are those sent to Paul on two occasions while he was in Thessalonica (4:16) (Alford).

➤**16 even in Thessalonica**—The Philippians' care for Paul began when Paul was in Thessalonica (Acts 17:1-9). The church in Philippi (one of the churches of Macedonia) was known for its generosity (see 2 Cor. 8:1-5).

➤**17 a gift**—lit., "the gift." **fruit that may abound to your account**—Paul viewed gift-giving as a kind of spiritual sowing that would eventually bear fruit (see 2 Cor. 9:6-10). Here, that fruit (or, produce) would go into the believers' heavenly account, which would be given to him as a reward in that day (cf. Heb. 6:10).

➤**18 I have all . . . I am full**—Even though the gift is not what Paul sought, he was well taken care of, thanks to their generosity. **an odour of a sweet smell, a sacrifice acceptable, well pleasing to God**—is taken from the sweet-smelling incense which was burnt along with the Jewish sacrifices. Their gift was made in faith, not so much to Paul as to God (cf. Heb. 13:16).

➤**19 my God shall supply all your need**—See 2 Cor. 9:8. Just as they have supplied Paul's needs, God will supply theirs (4:16, 18). **according to his riches**—As God's assets are unlimited, the Christian will never lack anything that he needs (Eph. 1:7). **in glory**—These words modify the entire sentence. (See comments on Eph. 3:18.) **by [in] Christ Jesus**—by virtue of our being in him, the giver and mediator of all spiritual blessings.

## 20-23 CONCLUSION

➤**20 unto God and our Father be glory**—Not to us, but to him be the glory in all things.

➤**21 Salute every saint**—Paul sent individual greetings to each of the believers. **The brethren . . . with me**—Paul was referring to his coworkers, especially Timothy (1:1).

➤**22 they that are of Caesar's household**—The slaves of Nero had probably heard about Christ from Paul while he was a prisoner in the Praetorian barracks. Philippi was a Roman colony, so there may have been a tie between the citizens of the mother city and those of the colony, especially between those of the two cities who had become Christians through Paul's ministry. Paul had also been imprisoned at Philippi as he now was at Rome.

➤**23** All the earliest manuscripts read, "The grace of our Lord Jesus Christ be with your spirit." (Cf. Gal. 6:18 and see comments there.)

BIBLIOGRAPHY

Alford, Henry. *The Greek New Testament. Vol. 3. 1852. Reprint. Grand Rapids: Guardian Press, 1973.*

Bengel, John A. *New Testament Word Studies.* 1742. Reprint. Grand Rapids: Eerdmans, 1971.

Hawthorne, Gerald. *Philippians, Word Biblical Commentary.* Vol. 43. Waco, Tex.: Word, Inc., 1983.

Kennedy, H. A. A. "Philippians" in the *Expositor's Greek Testament.* London: Hodder & Stoughton, 1917.

Kent, Homer. "Philippians" in *The Expositor's Bible Commentary.* Grand Rapids: Eerdmans, 1978.

Lightfoot, J. B. *Saint Paul's Epistle to the Philippians.* 1868.

Reprint. Grand Rapids: Zondervan, 1957.

Lightner, Robert. "Philippians" in *The Bible Knowledge Commentary.* Wheaton: Victor Books, 1983.

Neander, Johann A. *A General History of the Christian Religion and Church.* 9 vols. Edinburgh: T & T Clark, 1849-52.

Paley, William. *Horae Paulinae* (or, *The Truth of Scripture History of St. Paul*). Dublin: Printed for M'Kenzie, 1790.

Rienecker, Fritz. *Linguistic Key to the Greek New Testament.* Grand Rapids: Baker Book House, 1976, 1980.

Vincent, Marvin R. *The Epistles to the Philippians and to Philemon.* Edinburgh: T & T Clark, 1897.

# COLOSSIANS

## Introduction

The genuineness of this epistle is attested by Justin Martyr, *Dialogue with Trypho,* who quotes "the firstborn of every creature" in reference to Christ, from 1:15; Theophilus of Antioch, *To Autolychus,* 2; Irenaeus, 3.14.1, who quotes expressly from this "Epistle to the Colossians" (4:14); Clement of Alexandria, *Stromata,* 1, who quotes 1:9-11, 28; 2:2ff.; 2:8; 3:12, 14; 4:2, 3ff.; Tertullian, *Prescription of Heretics,* 7, who quotes 2:8 and in *The Resurrection of the Body,* 23, quotes 2:12, 20 and 3:1, 2; and Origen, *Against Celsus,* 5.8, who quotes 2:18, 19.

Colosse was a city of Phrygia, on the river Lycus, a branch of the Meander. The church there was mainly composed of Gentiles (cf. 2:13). Alford infers from 2:1 that Paul had not seen its members and therefore could not have been its founder. Colossians 1:7, 8 suggests the probability that Epaphras was the founder of the church there. The date of its foundation must have been subsequent to Paul's visitation, "strengthening in order" all the churches of Galatia and Phrygia (Acts 18:23); for otherwise he must have visited the Colossians, which 2:1 implies he had not. Had Paul been their father in the faith, he would doubtless have alluded to the fact, as in 1 Corinthians 3:6, 10; 4:15; 1 Thessalonians 1:5; 2:1. It is only in Romans, Ephesians, and this epistle that such allusions are lacking; in that to the Romans, because, as in this church of Colosse, he had not been the instrument of their conversion; in that to the Ephesians, owing to the cyclical nature of the epistle. Probably during the "two years" of Paul's stay at Ephesus, when "all which dwelt in Asia heard the word of the Lord Jesus" (Acts 19:10, 26), Epaphras, Philemon, Archippus, Apphia and the other natives of Colosse, became converts at Ephesus and subsequently became the first sowers of the gospel seed in their own city. This will account for their personal acquaintance with, and attachment to, Paul and his fellow ministers, his loving language to them, and their counter salutations to him. So also with respect to "them at Laodicea" (2:1).

This epistle was written at Rome, during Paul's first imprisonment there (Acts 28). In the Introduction to the Epistle to the Ephesians, it was shown that the three epistles, Ephesians, Colossians, and Philemon, were sent at the same time, viz., during the freer portion of his imprisonment. Colossians 4:3, 4 and Ephesians 6:19, 20 imply greater freedom than he had while writing to the Philippians, after the promotion of Tigellinus to be Praetorian Prefect. (See Introduction to Philippians.) This epistle, though carried by the same bearer, Tychicus, who bore that to the Ephesians, was written before that epistle; for many phrases similar in both appear in the more expanded form in the Epistle to the Ephesians (Eph. 6:21).

The reason Paul wrote Colossians was to counteract various theological errors that had crept into the church at Colosse. From the text of Colossians we can infer that the Colossians were infiltrated by a syncretic philosophical system (2:8), a system that combined elements of legalistic Judaism (2:11, 14, 16, 17), asceticism (2:20-23), and Gnosticism (2:3ff.). The gnostic element was the most pronounced and most ardently fought against by Paul.

It is essential to understand Gnosticism if one is to comprehend what lies behind many of Paul's statements in this epistle. Curtis Vaughn has provided an excellent summary of Gnosticism, especially as it relates to the Colossian heresy:

> Gnosticism, in all its forms, was characterized by belief in the evil of matter, in mediating beings, and in salvation through knowledge. Beginning with the assumption that all matter is evil, the Gnostics argued that God didn't create this world and that he has absolutely no contact with it. However, intellectual necessity did not permit them to break completely the bond between divinity and the material world. They therefore taught that God put forth from himself a series of "aeons" or emanations, each a little more distant from him and each having a little less of Deity. At the end of this chain of intermediate beings there is an emanation possessing enough of Deity to make a world but removed far enough from God that his creative activities could not compromise the perfect purity of God . . . . Belief in the inherent evil of matter made it impossible for the Gnostics to accept the real incarnation of God in Christ. Some of them explained it away by denying the actual humanity of Jesus, holding that he only seemed to be human. The body of Jesus, they taught, was an illusion, a phantom, only apparently real. . . . Other Gnostics explained away the incarnation by denying the real deity of Jesus.

Paul combated this denigration of Christ's deity by presenting the preeminent, all-inclusive, and all-sufficient Christ. In this epistle Paul portrays Christ as the Son of God's love (1:13), the Redeemer (1:14), God's invisible image (1:15), the chiefborn of all creation (1:15), the vehicle of creation (1:17), the head of the body (1:18), the beginning (1:18), the firstborn from the dead (1:18), the preeminent One (1:18), the embodiment of all God's fullness (1:19), the mediator of reconciliation (1:20), the wealth of the glorious mystery (1:27), the indweller (1:27), the hope of glory (1:27), the mystery of God (2:2), the storehouse of the treasures of wisdom and knowledge (2:3), the embodiment of all the fullness of the Godhead (2:9), the head of all principality and power (2:10), our copartner in spiritual circumcision, burial in baptism, resurrection, and quickening (2:11-13), the obliterator of offenses (2:14), the conqueror of principalities and powers (2:15), the reality of all shadows (2:16, 17), the exalted One (3:1), the One hidden in God (3:3), our life (3:4), the One who will appear with us in glory (3:4), the constituency of the new man (3:11), the forgiver (3:13), the rewarder of our inheritance (3:24), and the content of Paul's gospel (4:3). What a Christ is presented in the book of Colossians!

The style of this epistle is unique; many Greek phrases occur here that are found nowhere else in the NT—such as: "spoil you" (2:8); "making a shew [show] of them openly" (2:15); "beguile of your reward," and "intruding" (2:18); "will-worship" (or self-imposed worship) (2:23); "filthy communication" (3:8); and "rule" (or arbitrate) (3:15). The loftiness and elaboration of Paul's style correspond to the majestic nature of this theme, the majesty of Christ's person and office, in contrast to the heretical philosophy.

Hence arises his use of unusual phraseology. On the other hand, in the Epistle to the Ephesians, subsequently written, in which he was not so hampered by the exigencies of controversy, he expounds the same glorious truths, so congenial to him, more freely and uncontroversially, in the fuller outpouring of his spirit, with less of the elaborate and antithetical language of system, such as was needed in cautioning the Colossians against the particular errors threatening them. Hence arises the striking similarity of many of the phrases in the two epistles written about the same time and generally in the same vein of spiritual thought; while the unique phrases of the Epistle to the Colossians are such as are natural, considering the controversial purpose of that epistle.

*Chapter* 1

## 1-14 THANKSGIVING AND PRAYER FOR THE COLOSSIANS

➤**1 by** [through] **the will of God**—or, "through God's will." **Timotheus**—Timothy was with Paul in Rome at the time of writing. Paul and Timothy had traveled together through Phrygia, where Colosse was located, and the Colossians associated them in their feelings and prayers. Although neither had visited the church in Colosse, they had, during their earlier travels, met individual Colossians such as Epaphras, Philemon, Archippus, and Apphia who, when converted, returned with the gospel to their native city.

➤**2 Colosse**—written "Colasse" in some of the earliest manuscripts. **saints and faithful brethren**—two descriptions of the same Christians. **and the Lord Jesus Christ**—is present in some ancient manuscripts and absent in others.

➤**3 We**—This means Timothy and Paul. **God and the Father**—or, as in some ancient manuscripts, "God the Father." **always**—According to the Greek, this could also be joined with "We give thanks." They were thankful for the faith, hope, and love of the Colossians. Paul made a similar statement in his letter to the Ephesians (1:15, 16), which was sent at the same time by the same messenger, Tychicus (Eph. 6:21).

➤**4 we heard**—The language implies that Paul had not seen them. Cf. Romans 1:8, where similar language is used of another church that he had not visited; and see Ephesians 1:15.

➤**5 For** [because of] **the hope**—explains why the Colossians loved all the saints (1:4) and per-haps also gives cause for Paul and Timothy's thanksgiving. **the hope which is laid** [stored] **up for you in heaven**—is the hope of being with Christ in glory (3:3). **whereof**—"which," referring to "hope." **the gospel**—Faith, love, and hope are the results of receiving the gospel.

➤**6 Which is come unto you**—lit., "which has come to be present among you." Paul speaks of the Word as a living person, present among the Colossians. **as it is in all the world**—Christ commanded that the gospel should be shared with all nations, and not just with the Jews, as the law had been (Matt. 13:38; 24:14; 28:19). By this time, the gospel had been preached in most of the world known to the apostles. **and bringeth forth fruit** [and groweth]—The earliest manuscripts read, "bearing fruit and growing." The gospel's coming brings continuous fruit-bearing and growth. **knew**—rather, "came to know" experientially and personally. **the grace of God in truth**—i.e., in its truth and with true knowledge (Alford).

➤**7 As ye also learned**—The word "also" is not present in the earliest manuscripts. Those scribes who inserted it thought Paul had preached the gospel to the Colossians as well as Epaphras. But Epaphras alone was the founder of the church there. **Epaphras our dear fellowservant** [slave]—He was one of Paul's coworkers. **who is for you a faithful minister of Christ**—Epaphras had become a Christian at Ephesus during Paul's earlier visit. He returned to his native Colosse and founded the church there. Epaphras may have been arrested because of his own preaching, but it is more likely that he was with Paul voluntarily (Philem. 23; see comments on 4:10).

➤**8 Who also declared unto us your love**—Not only had Epaphras brought the gospel to Colosse, he had brought news of the church there to Paul (Geisler). **in the Spirit**—lit., "in spirit" or "in Spirit." The expression describes either the way in which Epaphras made known their love (probably to Paul or to all the saints) or depicts the sphere of the Colossians' love (probably the latter).

➤**9 pray**—Paul now specifically states what he was praying for (1:3). **knowledge**—Greek, "full and accurate knowledge, thorough knowledge." **of his will**—i.e., his will (or, heart's desire) for his eternal purpose (see comments on Eph. 1:9-11). **in all wisdom and spiritual understanding**—Paul often spoke of the Colossians' hunger for knowledge (1:28; 2:2, 3; 3:10; 4:5, 6). He made it clear that knowledge must be tempered by spiritual understanding if the Christian is to make wise decisions and correct judgments.

➤**10 That ye might walk**—or, conduct your life. The expression (lit., "to walk") connects with "be filled" in 1:9. True understanding of God's will is inseparable from living in harmony with it. **worthy of the Lord unto all pleasing**—Paul reminded the Colossians to behave in a way worthy of their status as God's servants. **being fruitful in every good work**—This is the first evidence that one is living to please and honor the Lord. The second is growing in understanding of God. **increasing in the knowledge of God**—could also be translated "growing by the full-knowledge of God." (The Gk. word for "full-knowledge" or "thorough knowledge" indicates experiential and progressive knowledge.) Knowing God produces growth, and growth produces more experiential knowledge of God. Paul's prayer here is that they might continue to grow (1:6) as more spiritual understanding (1:9) is given them. The full knowledge of God is the real instrument of enlargement in the soul and life of the believer (Alford).

➤**11 Strengthened with all might, according to his glorious power**—lit., "empowered with all power according to the might of his glory" (Eph. 1:9; 3:16; 6:10). This is the power that issues from the mighty, glorious God, who wrought this power in raising Christ from the dead and now transmits the same to the church (see comments on Eph. 1:19-23). **unto** [for] **all patience** [endurance] **and longsuffering**—Both come as a result of the empowering. Even in the midst of persecution and false teaching, Paul reminded the Colossians that they had the

strength to continue steadfastly in their faith. **with joyfulness**—Some translators conjoin this phrase with 1:12, but most prefer to keep it connected with this verse because it shows that God's empowering gives us the ability to endure and suffer with joy.

➤**12 made us meet**—qualified us. **to be partakers of the inheritance**—actually, "for the share of the allotment" or "for the portion of the inheritance." "The allotment" in Greek could be a genitive of apposition, a further expression of the same concept conveyed by "the share" (hence, "the portion which consists in the lot"—Lightfoot); or "the allotment" may denote the total allotment, the complete inheritance, while "the share" signifies the portion of that allotment appointed to each believer—as the Promised Land, Canaan, was apportioned to each of the twelve tribes. In either case, Paul alluded to the Canaan inheritance. The OT saints inherited a portion of the good land; the NT saints inherit Christ as their portion—which image is expanded upon in the next verse. This allotment is **of the saints**—i.e., belonging to the saints; and this allotment is **in light**—in contrast to the realm of darkness (1:13).

➤**13** This verse continues the thought begun in 1:12 in that it is an extension of the same allusion to the OT picture of the Jews possessing their inheritance. The expression **delivered us from the power of darkness** (or, "rescued us from the authority of darkness") alludes to the deliverance of Israel from Pharaoh's Egypt (which typifies Satan's domain), and the expression **translated us into the kingdom of his dear Son** (or, "transferred us into the kingdom of the Son of his love") refers to the transfer of Israel from Egypt into Canaan. As such, "the share of the allotment" is intrinsically related to the kingdom of God's beloved Son. Having been transferred into this kingdom, the NT saints have the Son as their portion. The following verses (14-20) describe this Son, the portion of the saints.

➤**14** This verse indicates that **redemption** is the basis of our having been qualified by the Father (1:12), delivered, and transferred.

15-23 THE PREEMINENT CHRIST

➤**15 Who is**—present tense in Greek, designates the Son's *present* position as the glorified God-man. As such, the focus of this passage is not on the historical Christ as such, nor on the eternal Word, but on "Christ's present glorified state, in which He is exalted in our humanity, but exalted to that glory which He had with the Father before the word was. So that the following description (1:15-20) applies to Christ's whole Person in its essential glory" (Alford). **the image of the invisible God**—or, "the invisible God's image" or, "a visible image of the invisible God" (Conybeare, Montgomery). The expression points to the fact that the Son of God has always been God's expression. He is the One in the Godhead who explains, defines, and shines out God. He is called "the Word" (John 1:1), "the image of God" (2 Cor. 4:4), and "the express image" of God's substance (Heb. 1:3). **the first-born of every creature**—or, "the premier of all creation." Understood as a second, separate description of the Son, this title indicates that the Son in his humanity is now the foremost creature of all creation. The designation in no way indicates that Christ is the first creature created by God (as in the Arian heresy); the very next verse annuls this thought because it asserts that *all* things were created in, through, and for Christ. Thus, Christ could not have been created in Christ. The Greek word for "firstborn" is *prōtotokos*. The first part of the word (*prōto*) can indicate "first in time" (temporal priority) or "first in place" (dignity, preeminence). In this context, the second meaning is in the forefront. Thus, the Son of man is the chiefborn among all God's creatures. (See Exod. 4:22; Deut. 21:16, 17; Ps. 89:23 in the LXX for the use of *prōtotokos* in connection with the idea of preeminence.)

►**16 For by** [in] **him were all** [the] **things created**—a refutation of the Arian notion that Christ was the first item of creation, for he is distinct from all things. Creation came into being **in him** [as the sphere], **by** [through] **him** [as the vehicle], and **for him** [as the end]. **were . . . created . . . were created** [lit., "have been created"]—the first verb (an aorist) indicates the original act of creation; the second (a perfect), the durative state of creation in its relationship to Christ (Lightfoot).

►**17 he** [himself] **is before all things**—This statement shows his eternal preeminence and priority to all creation. **by him all things consist**—Greek, "have held together." Again, the perfect tense is used to show that all things are still in a state of being held together by the Son.

►**18** While verses 15-17 unveil the Son's relationship to the old creation, this verse describes his relationship to the new creation, the church. He is the church's Head and source (beginning). **who is the beginning**—or, who is its beginning (i.e., the church's beginning, the church's source). He is the church's beginning because he is the **firstborn from** [among] **the dead**—The church was created through Christ's resurrection. **in all things**—i.e., in all things in the old and new creation. **have the preeminence**—lit., "be holding the first place."

►**19 For**—introduces the explanation of why he is preeminent. **all** [the] **fulness**—is the plenitude, the completeness, the totality of the Godhead (see 2:9). All of God (including his attributes, characteristics, nature, and being) indwells the Son. Nothing is left out, as is asserted by the statement: all the fullness. To the Gnostics, "fullness," meant the assemblage of emanations, or angelic powers, coming from God. But the true fullness abides in Christ. According to the grammar of this verse, the "fullness" is personified—it functions as a surrogate for "God." As such, this fullness was **pleased** to dwell in the Son. [to] **dwell**—lit., "to permanently settle down."

►**20** This verse is a continuation of 1:19. "The fullness" (God personified) was pleased to dwell in the Son **and to reconcile all things** through the Son to himself. The two infinitives, "to dwell" and "to reconcile" are the activities of "the fullness." God, "the fullness," was in Christ reconciling the world to himself (see 2 Cor. 5:19). **having made peace through the blood of his cross**—cf. Ephesians 2:13-18. **by** [through] **him**—God acting through the instrumental agency of Christ. **to reconcile**—See 2 Corinthians 5:19. **unto himself**—i.e., God. **things in earth, or things in heaven**—Christ is the facilitator for the new creation just as he was for the creation of the universe (1:16). All of creation is maintained by Christ, so it follows that all of creation was affected by his sacrifice. Sin had brought disharmony to the heavens as well as to the earth. Only through Christ and his blood was peace restored in both the heavenly and earthly realms (see 2:15). This strengthens Paul's later argument against angel-worship, for it indicates that angels, like men, are wholly dependent upon Christ for their reconciliation. Thus, only Christ is the true object of worship. Some commentators, however, have gone beyond Paul's primary point and stretched it to say that Paul was speaking of a universal reconciliation in which all men (good and evil) and all angels (good and bad) will be reconciled to God. Countering this notion, F. F. Bruce said,

[I]t is very difficult to press his [Paul's] language to yield anything like universal reconciliation in the sense in which the phrase is commonly used nowadays. It is contrary to the analogy of Scripture to apply the idea of reconciliation in the ordinary sense to fallen angels; and as for Paul, he thinks rather of hostile spiritual powers as emptied of all vitality by the work of Christ and the faith of his people. And even with regard to the human race, to deduce from such words as these that every last man or woman, irrespective of moral record or attitude to God, will at last enjoy eternal bliss would be (to say no more) putting on them a burden of meaning heavier than they can bear.

➤21, 22 And you—While 1:20 deals with the reconciliation of creation, 1:21 and 22 speak of the believers' reconciliation to God. **enemies in your mind by wicked works—** Our alienation from God was due to an unregenerated mind occupied with evil thoughts and producing evil actions. **reconciled in the body of his flesh—**refers to the act of reconciliation that was accomplished by God through Christ's death on the cross. Christ partook of flesh for the sake of suffering death (Heb. 2:14; 1 Pet. 2:24). **through death—**lit., "through the death" (i.e., Christ's death). **holy and unblameable and unreproveable in his sight—**Christ's act of reconciliation puts us in perfect standing with God. One day our actual disposition will match this glorious position, (cf. Eph. 1:4).

➤23 **grounded—**founded (same word used in Eph. 3:17). **settled—**steadfast. **not moved away—**also used in 1 Cor. 15:58. **the hope of** [pertaining to] **the gospel—**See Eph. 1:18. **which ye have heard, and which was preached to every creature** [all creation] **which is under heaven; whereof I Paul am made a minister—**Paul poses three arguments against their being moved away from the gospel: (1) they heard it; (2) it was

preached universally; and (3) Paul's ministry was for this gospel. Concerning the universality of the gospel, Pliny, not many years subsequent to the writing of this epistle, wrote to the Emperor Trajan (B. X. Ep. 97) saying, "Many of every age, rank, and sex are being brought to trial. For the contagion of that superstition [Christianity] has spread over not only cities, but villages and the country."

## 24-29 PAUL'S SUFFERING FOR THE CHURCH

➤24 **fill up—**or, complete. **that which is behind** [lacking] **of the afflictions of Christ . . . for his body's sake—**This expression shows that Paul believed that he must suffer for the church's sake (see 1:28–2:2), and that such suffering was an addition (or, a complement) to the suffering Christ underwent to produce the church.

➤25 **Whereof—**"which," referring to the church. **dispensation—**or, stewardship; it is a rendering of the Greek word *oikonomia* (lit., "household management"). **given to me for you—**This perfectly expresses the nature of stewardship (cf. Eph. 3:2). Paul was entrusted with the task of giving to the believers what he had received from God; thus, his stewardship was very essential to God's NT economy. **to fulfil** [complete] **the word of God—**means "to give its [God's word] complete development" (Lightfoot) or "to present the Word of God in all its fullness" (Vaughn) or "to give full scope to the Word of God" (Robertson)— hence, to fully make known the word of God, and to make the word of God fully complete. Without Paul's ministry concerning God's plan for Christ and the church, the word of God would be incomplete.

➤26 **the mystery—**is in apposition to "the word of God" (1:25); thus, the word of God that Paul made known was the mystery. The Greek word for "mystery" (*mystērion* means "a secret revealed to the initiates"—hence, mysterious to those without, a secret to those within. According to the parallel passage in Ephesians 3:1-6 the mystery hidden from the ages involves the joining together of Jewish and Gentile Christians in one body.

➤27 **the riches of the glory—**or, the glorious wealth (see Eph. 3:8, 16). **which—**refers to the riches. The wealth of the mystery is **Christ in you,** the hope of glory—an appositive to "Christ in you," indicates that the indwelling Christ is our hope of participating in the coming glorification.

➤28 preach—proclaim or announce. warning—is connected with repentance, refers to one's conduct, and is addressed primarily to the heart. teaching—is connected with faith, refers to doctrines, and is addressed primarily to the intellect. in all wisdom—with all the wisdom that we possess. present—at Christ's coming. every man—every believer. perfect—mature, complete, fullgrown: perfectly instructed in doctrine, and full grown and matured in faith and practice. in Christ—in living union with Christ.

➤29 striving—or, contending, struggling—the Greek word *agōnizomai* was used in connection with athletic competition, especially wrestling. mightily—lit., "in power."

Chapter *2*

## 1-23 PAUL'S STRUGGLE IN PRAYER FOR THE COLOSSIANS' CONTINUED FAITH IN CHRIST AND WARNING THAT THEY NOT BE INFLUENCED BY FALSE TEACHING

➤1 what great conflict—how great a struggle (the same word used in 1:29). for you—at Colosse. and for them at Laodicea—This church was also being influenced by the false teachers, so Paul included them in this letter—as well as sent them another one (4:16). and for as many as have not seen my face in the flesh—This included Christians in Hierapolis (4:13). Paul considered himself in debt to all the Gentile believers (Rom. 1:14) and longed to be with them (Rom. 1:13). His presence would have been a comfort to them (2:2; Acts 20:38). To make up for his absence, he prayed earnestly for them (see 2:5).

➤2 That their hearts might [may] be comforted [encouraged]—He wanted them to be comforted and encouraged. Paul felt that those whom he had not been able to visit would be comforted to know that he was interested in them and was praying diligently on their behalf. They would also be relieved of their anxiety concerning the doctrinal teachings of Epaphras since Paul endorsed them as true. When writing to churches where he had personally taught, Paul addressed their particular situation in detail. To those that he had not visited, he wrote more general principles of Christ-

tianity. being knit together in love—or, "having been united together in love," thus describing the means by which the saints would be encouraged. unto [so that they may have] all riches of the full assurance of understanding—This describes the result or goal—the encouragement produced through the uniting together in love yields a rich and full understanding of God's mystery, Christ. The accumulation of phrases implies the importance that Paul gave to this matter. They had some knowledge of the truth, but Paul wanted them to fully understand the truth (see 1:6, 9, 10). to the acknowledgement—lit., "unto full knowledge," or resulting in thorough knowledge. the mystery of God, and of the Father, and of Christ—This is a late, conflated reading. The two earliest manuscripts (the Chester Beatty Papyrus, P46, and Codex Vaticanus) preserve the earliest (and probably original) reading, "the mystery of God, Christ." Christ himself is God's mystery, God's secret revealed to the believers.

➤3 In whom are hid [hidden] all the treasures of wisdom and knowledge—"Two thoughts are contained in this statement: First, all the treasures of wisdom and knowledge are in Christ. The false teachers claimed to have, through their relation with a supposed hierarchy of supernatural beings, a higher knowledge than that possessed by ordinary believers. Against this, Paul argues that all wisdom and knowledge are in Christ and that their treasures are accessible to every believer. Second, the treasures of wisdom are in Christ in a hidden way. 'Hidden' does not, however, mean that they are concealed but rather that they are laid up or stored away as a treasure" (Vaughn).

➤4 Paul is here referring to the false teachers, who attempted to mix Oriental theosophy, angel worship, and Jewish asceticism with pure Christianity.

➤5 For—This argument was to prevent the Colossians from being misled and was based on the respect they would have had for Paul's personal authority had he been there. your order—This refers to 2:2, where they were "knit together in love," into a well-organized, orderly body (cf. 1 Cor. 14:33, 40; Eph. 4:16). the stedfastness of your faith—The Colossians were getting along well because of their strong faith. Their faith was a solid foundation for the building of the church.

➤6 received Christ Jesus—They had not merely received the doctrines of Christ by their faith, but Christ himself. walk—conduct your life.

in him—in union with him. They were to live their lives in union with the indwelling Christ. This is the essential point of Paul's letter to the Colossians.

➤7 Rooted—actually, "having been rooted," a perfect participle, emphasizing present result of past action. In this portion (2:6-8), the language describes Christ as if he were land. built up—actually, "being built up," a present action based upon the effect of the rooting. stablished—lit., "being established." After a Christian is rooted in Christ, he can experience an ongoing process of being built up into Christ's body (see 2:19; Eph. 4:16). the faith—is the totality of the Christian faith, as taught by the apostles. The Colossians needed to know what constituted the true faith and be established therein.

➤8 spoil you—expanded, "carry you off as spoil" or, "lead you away as prey" (see Darby) or, "take you captive" (TEV, NIV)—alluding to the time when the Israelites were led captive from Canaan to Babylon (cf. 2:6, 7 where Paul likens Christ to the land and see comments on 1:13). A Christian must remain rooted in Christ and built up into his body, then he will not be in a position to be carried off as spoil. philosophy—lit., "the philosophy," the gnostic philosophy that was infesting the church at Colosse. rudiments—elementary principles which are "the elemental spirits" (see comments on Gal. 4:3).

➤9 in him dwelleth all the fulness of the Godhead bodily—"Godhead" (theotetos in Gk.), used only here in the NT, designates the totality of God's nature and person. The Greek word could also be translated as "Deity" but not as "divinity" (theiotes in Gk.), used in Romans 1:20, because divinity emphasizes only the divine nature. The Godhead encompasses God's nature and person. All the fullness of the Godhead dwells (or, permanently resides) in the very body of Jesus, the God-man. Through the incarnation, all of the Godhead took up bodily residence in Jesus.

➤10 ye are complete in him—The Colossians lacked nothing outside of Christ; in him they had everything they needed—contrary to the gnostic teaching that pointed to so many other things apart from Christ. head of all principality and power—lit., "head of all rule and authority." Cf. Ephesians 1:21. Since Christ is the head of all the angelic rulers, it is absurd to worship or venerate any angel.

➤11 The circumcision spoken of in this verse is spiritual; it is characterized as a putting off the

body . . . of the flesh. [The words "of the sins" in KJV are not found in the earliest manuscripts.]—If "the body" is the physical body, then "the body of the flesh" is the body in its fallen condition—the body become sinful flesh. But if "the body" is another way of saying "the sum total," then "the body of the flesh" is the "accumulation of corruptions" (see Calvin).

➤12, 13 As our mystical participation in Christ's crucifixion became our spiritual circumcision, so our mystical participation in Christ's burial is linked with our baptism. Furthermore, we partake of Christ's resurrection by believing that we were united with him in that event by God's power (cf. Eph. 1:19, 20). Cf. 2:13 with Ephesians 2:4, 5. In both passages, Paul speaks of our being dead in . . . sins. To cure our death, God made us alive; to deliver us from sins, he quickened us together with Christ. In 2:11-13, we see that we were united with Christ in crucifixion (called circumcision), burial, vivification, and resurrection.

➤14 Blotting out—i.e., cancelling. The Greek word underlying this expression was used in NT times to describe the washing out of writing on a papyrus (Moulton and Milligan) and the cancelling of a decree of law (Darby). handwriting—according to the Greek, was a technical term for a written acknowledgment of debt (Rienecker), called "a certificate of debt" in NASB. of ordinances—describes what was written in the bill of debt—i.e., the legal demands. that was against us—according to the Greek, the handwriting (not the ordinances) was against us—i.e., our debts against the law were charged against us. nailing it to his cross—One ancient method of cancelling bonds was to strike a nail through the writing.

➤15 spoiled—actually, "put off" or "disarmed"—lit., "stripped [them] for himself" (middle voice in Gk.). Some have interpreted the middle voice verb here as suggesting that Christ stripped off from himself the rulers and the authorities who had attached themselves to him in an attempt to defeat him. But this idea is unique (perhaps even alien) to the NT; and furthermore, it is more in keeping with the context for Paul to say that Christ stripped off (i.e., disarmed, spoiled) the rulers and authorities and in so doing exposed them to open shame. he made a show [public spectacle] of them—lit., "he exposed them openly." triumphing over them—is an image Paul used in 2 Corinthians 2:14-16, in which he depicts the triumphal procession of the victors leading their captives to their doom. **in it**—or, by it (the cross).

►**16 Let no man therefore judge you**—because you are complete in Christ, and God has dispensed into him everything that is essential to the Christian life. **meat . . . drink**—See Romans 14:1-17. **holyday**—a yearly feast, of which there were three (see 1 Chron. 23:31). **new moon**—a monthly observance. **sabbath**—a weekly observance.

►**17 a shadow of things to come**—The OT observances foreshadowed Christ and the spiritual realities his coming brought. **the body**—means the substance, the reality—as contrasted to the shadow. The OT ordinances, festivals, holy days, etc., were like a shadow without a body. Christ is the body, the reality, of all the OT shadows.

►**18 beguile you of your reward**—lit., "be an umpire against you"—which means "give judgment against you so as to deprive you of your prize." **in a voluntary humility**—or, "by delighting in humility." This sort of humility must have been self-absorbing and self-gratifying, and a kind of pretentious piety. **worshipping** [or, veneration] **of angels**—Their "humility" made them unable to come directly to God, so they prayed to angels, justifying this by the fact that the law was given by angels. This practice continued for some time in Phrygia, so that in A.D. 360 the Council of Laodicea specifically spoke against angel-worshipers in its 35th *canon*. Even as late as Theodoret's time there were oratories to Michael the archangel, and the modern Greeks have a legend of Michael opening a chasm to save the Colossians from a threatening flood. Scripture clearly opposes the idea of "patrons" or "intercessors" (1 Tim. 2:5, 6). True Christian humility comes from realizing that our only worth is due to Christ's intervention on our behalf. **things which he hath not seen**—All the earliest manuscripts read, "things which he has seen." The gnostic ascetics gloried in their visions. The language admits that the visions must have been real, or else Paul would have qualified his statement. But these people trusted in their visions and senses rather than holding on to Christ, the Head, by faith (2:19).

►**19 not holding the Head**—i.e., not being connected to the Head, Christ. [out] **from which** [whom]—the head is the unique source of **all the body's** growth and function. **having nourish-**

**ment ministered, and knit together**—better, "being fully supplied and united together." All the body of Christ receives the supply and is united together by the function of the **joints and bands;** it is not the joints (or, junctures) and bands (or, ligaments) that are supplied (as in KJV). (The Gk. word for "being fully supplied" agrees grammatically with "body.") The joints and bands, by connecting all the members of the body to one another, allow the nourishment (which comes from the head) to circulate to all the body. **increaseth with the increase of God**—actually, "grows with the growth of God" (i.e., grows with the growth that partakes of God—Lightfoot).

►**20 if ye be dead with Christ**—if you died with Christ (see Rom. 6:2; Gal. 2:20). **rudiments**—elementary principles. The underlying Greek word has a variety of meanings, several of which could fit in this context: (1) elementary principles of teaching, (2) elemental spirits, and (3) heavenly bodies (which were associated with personal, celestial beings).

►**21** Paul here gives instances of the ordinances (2:20) in the words of their impostors.

►**22 Which**—referring to the things handled, touched, and tasted. **perish with the using**—"perish as they are used" (RSV). **after**—according to, connected to "ordinances" in 2:20.

►**23 a show of wisdom**—lit., "an expression of wisdom," or perhaps, "a reputation for wisdom" (Wuest). The gnostic philosophy had but an appearance or reputation for wisdom; true wisdom is in Christ. **will worship**—better, "self-imposed religion," which is man-made religion. **not in any honour to the satisfying of the flesh**—better, "not of any value against the indulgence of the flesh." Asceticism cannot really annul fleshly indulgence.

# Chapter 3

**1-25 CHRISTIANS ARE ALIVE IN CHRIST AND DEAD TO THEIR OLD LIFE. PAUL SUGGESTS SOME HEAVENLY GOALS AND GIVES ADVICE**

►**1** Whereas chapter two was mostly a criticism of false teachers, this chapter affirms the Christian's new position in Christ. **If** [since] **ye then be risen with Christ**—According to the Greek, there is no doubt about this. Christians are joined with Christ in his resurrection (see Rom. 6:2; Eph. 2:6). **where Christ sitteth**—Christ is at God's right hand (Eph. 1:20), representing those who belong to him. The Christian was formerly alive to the world and separated from God; he is now dead to the world and reconciled to God.

➤**2 Set your affection on things above**— The love of Christ is a powerful magnet to draw our affections up to him. This love motivates us to holiness.

➤**3** The Greek aorist tense implies, "For you have died once for all." The Christian died in Christ's death (2:20). **your life is hid**—like a seed buried in the earth (cf. "planted" in Rom. 6:5). Our real life is hidden from the world, just as Christ's glory is hidden. When Christ returns to earth (3:4), our hidden life will be revealed as truly reflecting God's image (Neander). After we died with Christ, we now have a new threefold life, a life that is (1) **hidden,** (2) **with Christ,** (3) **in God**—i.e., our new spiritual life is a hidden, inner life, that is now in union with Christ who has brought us to be with him in God.

➤**4 Christ ... our life**—Christ himself is our new, implanted, divine life. But this life is now hidden. One day, when Christ is manifested in glory, we will also be manifested in glory, for this divine life will have saturated our entire being and thereby glorified us (see Rom. 8:11, 18, 19, 30).

➤**5 Mortify**—put to death. A necessary consequence of having died with Christ is the daily "putting to death" of evil desires (cf. 2:11). **members ... upon the earth**—fleshly instruments of lust. These can be deadened by the power of the Holy Spirit (Rom. 6:19; 8:13; Gal. 5:24, 25). **fornication, uncleanness**—See Ephesians 5:3, 4. **inordinate affection**—passion. **evil concupiscence**—bad desire. **covetousness, which is idolatry**—See comments on Ephesians 5:5.

➤**6 on the children of disobedience**—This phrase is found in several ancient manuscripts, but the two most ancient (the Chester Beatty Papyrus, P46, and Codex Vaticanus) do not contain it.

➤**7 walked**—conducted your life. **some time**—"then" or "once." **lived in them**—lived in these things (itemized in 3:5).

➤**8 put off**—or, put away the things mentioned in 3:5 and the things itemized in this verse.

➤**9 old man**—a literal rendering, is "old self" or "old nature" in various modern versions. Actually, the old man is one's old, unregenerated humanity—including the old self, nature, and life.

➤**10 the new man**—a literal translation, has been rendered as "new self" or "new nature" in various modern versions. The new man is one's new, regenerated humanity—including a new spirit, a new nature, and a new life. The new man here (as in Eph. 4:24) is primarily individual, whereas the new man in Ephesians 2:15 is corporate (the "one new man" composed of Jewish and Gentile believers). The new man here is "the regenerate man formed after Christ" (Lightfoot). But there is also a sense in which this new man is corporate—for as each and every believer is renewed to the image of Christ, the same image is expressed by all in one new humanity, a humanity void of distinctions. **renewed**—lit., "being renewed," which indicates an ongoing process. **knowledge**—Greek, "full knowledge," or, "thorough, experiential knowledge"—The Greek word conveys the idea of personal, ongoing knowledge. The new man is being renewed to a full and personal knowledge of Christ **after** [in accordance with] **the image of him** [i.e., the new man]—In other words, the new man is being renewed into Christlikeness, and such renewing simultaneously brings the new man into a personal, experiential knowledge of its Creator, Christ.

➤**11 Where there is neither**—i.e., where there is no place for the following: **Greek nor Jew** [denoting racial distinction], **circumcision not uncircumcision** [indicating religious distinction], **Barbarian, Scythian** [denoting some cultural/national distinctions], **bond** [slave], **free** [indicating some class distinction]. **Christ is all, and in all**—"Christ has dispossessed and obliterated all distinctions of religious prerogative and intellectual preeminence and so-called caste; Christ has substituted Himself for all these; Christ occupies the whole sphere of human life and permeates all its developments" (Lightfoot).

➤**12 the elect of God**—There is no article in the Greek: "God's elect" (cf. 1 Thess. 1:4).

➤**13 Forbearing**—as to present offenses. **forgiving**—as to past offenses. **quarrel**—Greek, "cause of blame," "cause of complaint." **Christ**— The earliest manuscripts read, "Lord."

➤**14 perfectness**—or, completion. A good thought-for-thought rendering of this verse is, "And over all these virtues put on love, which binds them all together in perfect unity" (NIV). Love is the crowning virtue that must unite all the virtues previously mentioned.

►**15 peace of God**—The earliest manuscripts read, "the peace of Christ." **rule**—actually, "act as umpire" or "arbitrate." (The same root word was used in 2:18.) The peace of Christ should act as our umpire when anger, envy, and such passions arise, and restrain them. **to the which**—refers to "peace." **ye are** [were] **called in one body**—The unity of the body is a strong reason for peace among the members.

►**16 the word of Christ**—the message proclaimed by Christ (i.e., the gospel) or the word about Christ. **dwell in you richly**—indwell your being richly. **in all wisdom**—in most versions is conjoined by punctuation with **teaching. in psalms and hymns and spiritual songs**—is joined by punctuation with **teaching and admonishing** in some versions and with **singing** in others. It should be noted that the Bible indicates that singing accompanied prophecy and was itself, on occasion, prophecy—a speaking forth of God's word (see Exod. 15:20, 21; 1 Sam. 10:5; 1 Chron. 25:1-3; 1 Cor. 14:24-26).

►**17 in the name of the Lord Jesus**—i.e., in the conscious realization of his presence and person or, in the authority of being his representative.

3:18–4:1 ADVICE FOR WIVES,
HUSBANDS, FATHERS, CHILDREN,
MASTERS AND SLAVES (See Eph.
5:22–6:9, which covers the same material
more thoroughly.)

►**18 own**—not present in earliest manuscripts—borrowed from Ephesians 5:22.

►**19** Cf. Ephesians 5:22ff.

►**20 unto the Lord**—According to the earliest manuscripts, "in the Lord." Cf. Ephesians 6:1.

►**21 provoke**—irritate. Cf. Ephesians 6:4.

►**22, 23** Cf. Ephesians 6:5-8.

►**24 the reward of the inheritance**—the recompense of inheriting God's kingdom (see 1:12).

►**25 But**—should read "For," according to the earliest manuscripts.

*Chapter* **4**

1-6 PAUL'S FINAL ADVICE
TO THE COLOSSIANS

►**1** This verse, thematically speaking, belongs with the end of chapter three. **Masters, give . . . that which is just and**

**equal**—The responsibility between slaves and masters is reciprocal (Eph. 6:9; Philem. 16). **knowing that ye also have a Master**—Masters and slaves stand as equals before God, their Master.

►**2 Continue in prayer**—The Greek means "persist in prayer" (cf. Eph. 6:18). **and watch in the same with thanksgiving**—The Christian is to be thankful for God's responses to himself and others, whether they seem to be pleasant or unpleasant at the time (1 Cor. 14:17; Phil. 4:6; 1 Thess. 5:18).

►**3 for us**—This refers to Paul and Timothy (1:1). **that God would open unto us a door of utterance**—In Eph. 6:19, Paul asks for wisdom and ability in preaching. Here, he is asking for the opportunity to preach, preferably by his release from prison. **the mystery of Christ**—See 1:27. **for which**—referring to the mystery. **I am also in bonds**—Paul was not only God's slave but was also in chains at Rome (Eph. 6:20).

►**4** Some interpreters think Paul was asking for his freedom as though it were the only way that he could spread the gospel. Though the Colossians and others prayed to this end, there are indications that Paul had many opportunities to proclaim Christ even in prison (Phil. 1:12, 13; cf. 2 Tim. 2:9).

►**5 Walk in wisdom**—A double meaning is implied here. The Christian must be wise in his dealings with unbelievers, and in the way in which he shares Christ with them. **them that are without**—This refers to those outside the Christian church (1 Cor. 5:12; 1 Thess. 4:12). The Christian fellowship will make allowances for the mistakes of their brothers, but the world will not. The Christian's behavior toward unbelievers should be above reproach. **redeeming the time**—buying up the opportunity.

►**6 Let your speech be alway**[s] **with grace**—cf. 3:16; Eph. 4:29. Even the smallest actions and words of the Christian should reflect the Holy Spirit's leading. (See Luke 4:22; John 7:46, referring to Jesus' speech.) **seasoned with salt**—Don't be insipid or frivolous in your conversation (Matt. 5:13; Mark 9:50; Eph. 4:29). (Cf. the salted offering, Lev. 2:13.) **that ye may know how ye ought to answer every man**—This will be true of conversation that is gracious as well as sensible (1 Pet. 3:15).

## 7-18 THE COMING OF TYCHICUS AND ONESIMUS. PERSONAL SALUTATIONS AND GREETINGS

➤**7 Tychicus**—This messenger brought letters to the Colossians and the Ephesians, so he was well known among them.

➤**8** Paul, knowing that his presence at Colosse would be a great encouragement, but being unable to get there, sent Tychicus. **that he might know your estate**—This reading is supported by some very ancient manuscripts; whereas others read, "that you may know our state." Although both readings are defensible, the second is more suitable to the context. **comfort your hearts**—This concerned their troubles and Paul's imprisonment.

➤**9 Onesimus . . . who is one of you**—i.e., Onesimus was a native of Colosse. He was a slave who ran away from Philemon (an elder in the church at Colosse) and was saved through Paul in prison. The Epistle to the Colossians and the Epistle to Philemon were written in the same period and sent with the same envoy from Paul.

➤**10 Aristarchus**—This Macedonian from Thessalonica (Acts 27:2) was arrested with Gaius during a disturbance in Ephesus (Acts 19:23-41). He accompanied Paul to Asia (Acts 20:4) and later to Rome (Acts 27:2). **fellow-prisoner**—In Philemon 24, he is referred to as Paul's fellow worker and here as his fellow prisoner. Epaphras also is called Paul's fellow worker (1:7) and his fellow prisoner (Philem. 23), leading some to suggest that Paul's friends voluntarily shared his imprisonment by turns, Aristarchus being with him when he wrote this letter, and Epaphras when he wrote to Philemon. The Greek is literally "fellow captive," an image taken from warfare. **Marcus** [Mark]—This was John Mark (Acts 12:12-25), the Gospel writer. **sister's son to Barnabas**—Barnabas, known to the Colossians, had chosen Mark as his and Paul's traveling companion of their first missionary journey. The book of Acts gives us a few facts about Mark. The home of Mark's mother was a meeting place for Christians in Jerusalem (Acts 12:12). The family was from Cyprus (Acts 4:36), accounting for Barnabas's, choice of Cyprus as the first stop on their journey (Acts 13:4) and for Mark's eagerness

to make the journey. Mark went as far as Perga, in Pamphylia, and from there returned to his mother in Jerusalem (Acts 13:13). Because Mark did not go farther, Paul did not take him on his second journey (Acts 15:37-39). **touching whom**—referring to Mark. **ye received commandments**—This advice may have been conveyed verbally by Tychicus. (The past tense was used to denote the time when a letter would be read.) Paul had been upset with Mark for his desertion on their earlier journey (Acts 13:13), but tells the Colossians that his confidence has been restored. The Colossians needed this recommendation as Mark was to visit them as a teacher.

➤**11 Justus**—This was a common Jewish name meaning "righteous." **who are of the circumcision**—i.e., Jewish Christians. Very few of such labored together with the apostle to the uncircumcision. **a comfort**—The Greek indicates comfort in the dangers of discussion or debate; a different word is used to mean comfort with respect to internal problems.

➤**12 Epaphras**—See 1:7 and comments. **labouring fervently**—struggling, wrestling (same word used in 1:29; 2:1). **perfect**—This refers to maturity as a Christian (1:28; 2:2; 3:14). **complete**—Some ancient manuscripts read "fully assured" (cf. Rom. 4:21).

➤**13 he hath a great zeal for you**—Paul wanted to provide a motive for the Colossians' own concern. **Laodicea . . . Hierapolis**—These are probably other local churches founded by Epaphras. These two cities, with Colosse, were destroyed by an earthquake in A.D. 62. Laodicea was named for Laodice, queen of Antiochus II. Located on the river Lycus, it was "the chiefest city to Phrygia Pacatiana." Hierapolis was six Roman miles north of Laodicea.

➤**14 Luke, the beloved physician**—Luke probably treated Paul for his illness during his travels in Phrygia and Galatia. He was with Paul during his last imprisonment (2 Tim. 4:11). **Demas**—This man is here listed with Paul's fellow workers (Philemon 24), but he later deserted (2 Tim. 4:10).

➤**15** The textual problem in this verse is complex. Paul first says, "the brothers in Laodicea greet you." According to Paul's terminology, "the brothers in Laodicea" equals "the church in Laodicea" (cf. Phil. 1:2; 4:21) because all the Christians in a particular locality comprise the church in that locality. Then Paul adds, "and Nymphas." This is a special salutation: "Greet the church—and especially Nymphas." Then Paul adds, "and the church at (his, her, or their) house." Three different pronouns appear in the manuscripts: "his" in Codex Bezae and the majority of later manuscripts, "her" in Codex Vaticanus and other manuscripts, and "their" in Codices Sinaiticus, Alexandrinus, and Ephraemi Rescriptus. If Nymphas was a man, it is quite correct to say "the church in his house"; if Nymphas was a woman, it is of course correct to say "the church in her house." Unfortunately, Nymphas's sex cannot be determined from the Greek. Therefore, the textual critic must select the most likely and/or earliest reading—which in this case is either "her" or "their." Those scholars who defend the originality of "their" say it refers to "the ones with Nymphas" (see Alford, M'Clintock, and Strong). Others say "their" refers to "the brothers in Laodicea" and is equal to the church in Laodicea. How could the church in Laodicea (the brothers in Laodicea) have the church in their house? Because of this problem, several critics have opted for the reading "her."

What seems plain is that Paul was asking the Colossian believers to greet the brothers in Laodicea (which is another way of saying, "Greet the church in Laodicea") and especially greet Nymphas and the meeting (of believers) at Nymphas's house. Within the local church proper, there could be several meetings, several *ecclesiai,* several assemblies of believers—

each of which could genuinely be called an *ecclesia* (an assembly). Paul was sending a greeting to the entire church at Laodicea and to a particular gathering of believers who meet at Nymphas's house (see Rom. 16:5; 1 Cor. 16:19, 20 for a similar kind of greeting to a particular assembly of saints within a local church proper). If the entire church met at Nymphas's house, it would be redundant for Paul to say, "Greet the brothers in Laodicea *and* the church at Nymphas's house."

►**16 the epistle from Laodicea**—is the epistle coming from Laodicea (see NASB) to Colosse. This letter was probably a circular from Paul to various churches in Asia—perhaps the same letter traditionally known as "Ephesians" (see Introduction).

►**17 And say**—This directive was given to both leaders and regular members in the Colossian church. **Archippus**—was singled out for special encouragement (2 Tim. 4:5).

►**18 The salutation by the hand of me Paul**—Paul's own signature shows that the letter, though written by a secretary, was from him. (See comments on Gal. 6:11.) **Remember my bonds**—Paul had already mentioned his imprisonment (4:3, 10) as a reason for the Colossians to love and pray for him. This last reminder would again bring them to consider how he had struggled for them even while in chains and written an epistle to liberate them from erring theology and point them back to Christ as supreme. **Grace be with you**—Greek, "the grace" every Christian enjoys in some degree, that flows from God in Christ by the Holy Spirit (2 Cor. 13:14).

BIBLIOGRAPHY

Alford, Henry. *The Greek New Testament.* 1852. Reprint. Grand Rapids: Guardian Press, 1976.

Bruce, F. F. "The Epistle to the Colossians, to Philemon, and to the Ephesians" in *The New International Commentary on the New Testament.* Grand Rapids: Eerdmans, 1984.

Calvin, John. *The Epistles of Paul the Apostle to the Galatians, Ephesians, Philippians and Colossians.* 1546? Translated by T. H. L. Parker, and edited by David W. and Thomas F. Torrance. Grand Rapids: Eerdmans, 1965.

Darby, John N. *New Translation.* Addison, Ill: Bible Truth Publishers, n.d.

Geisler, Norman. "Colossians" in *The Bible Knowledge Commentary.* Wheaton, Ill.: Victor Books, 1983.

Lightfoot, J. B. *St. Paul's Epistles to the Colossians and to Philemon.* New York: MacMillan & Co., 1879.

M'Clintock and Strong. *Cyclopaedia of Biblical, Theological,* *and Ecclesiastical Literature.* New York: Harper, 1894.

Moulton and Milligan, *The Vocabulary of the Greek New Testament.* Grand Rapids: Eerdmans, 1930.

Robertson, A. T. *Word Pictures in the New Testament.* Nashville: Broadman Press, 1932.

Vaughn, Curtis. "Colossians" in *Expositor's Bible Commentary.* Grand Rapids: Zondervan, 1978.

Wuest, Kenneth. *Ephesians and Colossians in the Greek New Testament.* Grand Rapids: Eerdmans, 1953.

Note: Certain portions of this commentary on Colossians were adapted from a work written by the New Testament editor Philip W. Comfort, entitled *From Text to Translation,* "Translating Ephesians and Colossians Phrase by Phrase"; Vol. 3 in "Studies in the Greek New Testament for English Readers." Wheaton, Ill., 1986.

# 1 THESSALONIANS

## Introduction

The authenticity of this epistle is attested by Irenaeus, *Against Heresies*, 5.6.1, quoting 5:23; Clement of Alexandria, *Paidagogos*, 1.88, quoting 2:7; Tertullian, *The Resurrection of the Body*, sec. 24, quoting 5:1; Gaius, according to Eusebius's *Ecclesiastical History*, 6.20; Origen, *Against Celsus*, 3.

At the time Paul wrote this epistle, Thessalonica was the capital of the Roman second district of Macedonia (Livy, 45. 29). It lay on the bay of Therme and has always been, and still is, under its modern name Thessaloniki, a place of considerable commerce. After his imprisonment and scourging at Philippi, Paul (2:2) went to Thessalonica; and in company with Silas (Acts 17:1-9) and Timothy (Acts 16:3; 17:14; cf. 1:1; 3:1-6; 2 Thess. 1:1) founded the church there. The Jews, as a whole, rejected the gospel when Paul preached it for three successive Sabbaths (Acts 17:2); but a few "believed and consorted with Paul and Silas, and of the devout [i.e., proselytes to Judaism] Greeks a great multitude, and of the chief women not a few." The believers received the word joyfully, notwithstanding trials and persecutions (1:6; 2:13) from their own countrymen and from the Jews (2:14-16). Paul's stay at Thessalonica was probably not limited to the three weeks specified in Acts 17:2—for his laboring there "with his hands" for his living (2:9; 2 Thess. 3:8), his receiving supplies there more than once from Philippi (Phil. 4:16), his making many converts from the Gentiles (1:9), and his appointing ministers all imply a longer residence. As at Pisidian Antioch (Acts 13:46), at Corinth (Acts 18:6, 7), and at Ephesus (Acts 19:8, 9), after having preached the gospel to the Jews who rejected it, Paul then turned to the Gentiles. He most likely held Christian meetings in the house of Jason (Acts 17:5), perhaps "the kinsman" of Paul mentioned in Romans 16:21. His great subject of teaching seems to have been the coming of Christ to establish his kingdom (as we may infer from 1:10; 2:12, 19; 3:13; 4:13-18; 5:1-11, 23, 24), and that they should walk worthy of it (2:12; 4:1). When Paul was in Thessalonica he must have preached about Jesus' kingship, for the charge which the assailants of Jason's house brought against him and the other brethren was, "These do contrary to the decrees of Caesar, saying that there is another *king*, one Jesus" (Acts 17:7). As it had happened during the ministry of the Lord Jesus himself (John 18:33-37; 19:12; cf. Matt. 26:64), the enemies of Christ perverted the doctrine of Christ's kingship into a charge of treason against Caesar. As a result, Paul and Silas were forced to flee under the cover of night to Berea. Timothy had probably preceded them there (Acts 17:10, 14). Despite the persecution, the church in Thessalonica had been planted, and the gospel spread from there throughout Macedonia, Achaia, and elsewhere (1:7, 8). Later, after having planted a Scripture-loving church in Berea, Paul again was forced to flee because the Thessalonian Jews had followed him there. Timothy and Silas then remained in Berea, while Paul proceeded by sea to Athens. While in Athens he more than once "longed to visit" the Thessalonians to see personally their spiritual state and "perfect that which was lacking in their faith" (3:10); but "Satan [probably using the Thessalonian Jews as his instruments] hindered" him (2:18; cf. Acts 17:15).

Timothy's account of the Thessalonian church was highly favorable. They abounded in faith and love and reciprocated his desire to see them (3:6-10). Still, as nothing human on earth is perfect, there were some defects. Some had too exclusively dwelt on the doctrine of Christ's coming kingdom so as to neglect their present human responsibilities (4:11,12). Some who had lost relatives by death needed comfort and instruction concerning their doubts as to whether they who died before Christ's coming would have a share with those still alive at the time of his coming. Some among them needed to be warned against adultery (4:3-7) and against revelry (5:5-8). There were symptoms in some of a lack in respectful love and subordination to their ministers (5:12, 13); others treated slightingly the manifestations of the Spirit in those possessing spiritual gifts (5:19). The object of this epistle was to give spiritual admonition on these subjects, to commend what deserved commendation, and to testify of his love for them.

Paul probably wrote this epistle from Corinth, where Timothy and Silas rejoined him (Acts 18:5) soon after he arrived there (2:17) in A.D. 50/51.

It was written not long after the conversion of the Thessalonians (1:8, 9), while Paul could speak of himself as only "taken from them for a short season" (2:17). Thus this epistle was first in date of all Paul's extant epistles (unless Galatians was written in A.D. 49; see Introduction to Galatians). First Thessalonians is written in the joint names of Paul, Silas, and Timothy, the three founders of the Thessalonian church. The plural first person "we" is used everywhere, except in 2:18; 3:5; 5:27. ("We" is the true reading in 4:13.)

Paul's style in this letter is calm and equable in accordance with the subject matter, which deals only with Christian duties in general, taking for granted the great doctrinal truths were not as yet disputed. There was no deadly error as yet to call forth his more vehement bursts of feeling and impassioned argument. The earlier epistles, as we should expect, are moral and practical. It was not until Judaistic and legalizing errors arose at a later period that he wrote those epistles (e.g., Romans and Galatians), which unfold the doctrines of grace and justification by faith. The Prison Epistles confirm the same truths. Last of all, the Pastoral Epistles are suited to the more developed ecclesiastical constitution of the church. They give directions as to bishops and deacons and correct abuses and errors of later growth.

The prevalence of the Gentile constituency in this church is shown by the fact that 1 and 2 Thessalonians are among the very few of Paul's writings in which no OT quotations occur.

*Chapter* 1

## 1-10 THE ADDRESS AND SALUTATION

Paul expresses his thanksgiving for the Thessalonians' faith, hope, and love; their first reception of the gospel; and their good report among those around them.

➤**1 Paul**—He did not add "an apostle" because with the Thessalonians, as with the Philippians, his apostleship was understood. **Silvanus**—otherwise known as Silas. Acts 15:22 and 32 mention him as a church leader and a gifted speaker. His age and position cause him to be placed before **Timotheus** [Timothy]— then a youth (Acts 16:1; 1 Tim. 4:12). Both Silvanus and Timothy helped start the Thessalonian church and thus are included in the address (cf. 2 Cor. 1:19). (Later in life, Silvanus was with Peter—for 1 Pet. 5:12 tells us that Silvanus was Peter's amanuensis [secretary] for his first epistle.) **unto the church of the Thessalonians**—The church in any given locality belongs to the Christians in that locality. Elsewhere, Paul spoke of the churches as "the churches of the saints" (1 Cor. 14:33). The local church does not belong to a group of elders or any other kind of leaders. **in God the Father and in the Lord Jesus Christ**—This blessed union is the mark of Christianity. **Grace . . . peace**—This is the salutation in all Paul's epistles except the three "pastoral" ones which include "mercy."

➤**2** cf. Romans 1:9; 2 Timothy 1:3. Here and following, each verse builds on and amplifies the preceding one. Paul often employed this technique when he was deeply gratified by the growth of the people—as if he were seeking by words heaped on words to convey some idea of his exuberant feelings toward them.

➤**3 work of faith**—i.e., the working reality of your faith, its eagerness in receiving the truth, and in manifesting itself by its fruit. **labour of love**—The Greek implies toil or troublesome labor, stimulated by love. For instances of self-denying labors of love, see Acts 20:35; Romans 16:12. **patience of hope**—lit., "endurance of hope," the persevering endurance of trials, which is based upon hope. **hope in** [of] **our Lord Jesus Christ**—i.e., the hope of his coming (1:10). The Thes-

salonians' faith, love, and hope were outstanding manifestations of their spiritual regeneration.

➤**4 Knowing, brethren beloved, your election of God**—Greek, "knowing, brethren, beloved of God, your election." Christians have been elected (or, chosen) by God to be his sons and have eternal life (see Eph. 1:3, 4; 2 Thess. 2:13).

➤**5 our gospel**—the gospel preached by Paul, Silvanus, and Timothy. **not . . . in word only, but also in power, and in the Holy Ghost** [Spirit]—The words of the gospel preached to the Thessalonians were empowered by the Holy Spirit; thus, these words generated faith and **much assurance. what manner of men we were among you**—speaks of their entire conduct, both in preaching the gospel and living it (see 2:10-12).

➤**6 ye became followers of us, and of the Lord**—They were following Paul's example of following the Lord. **having received the word in** [the midst of] **much affliction**—See 2:14; 3:2-5; Acts 17:5-10. **joy of** [from] **the Holy Ghost** [Spirit]—The Thessalonians endured their trials because of the joy they had from receiving the Holy Spirit.

➤**7 ensamples**—lit., "types" or, models. The word is plural in some ancient manuscripts and singular in others. Collectively speaking, the church at Thessalonica was a model to the other churches in the region. (The church at Philippi was the only church in the region to be founded before Thessalonica.) **Macedonia and Achaia**—were the two provinces into which Greece had been divided since 142 B.C.

➤**8 from you sounded out the word of the Lord**—They had not actually gone out themselves, but their story and reputation were repeated by Christian merchants of Thessalonica who traveled widely.

➤**9 what manner of entering in we had**— "what a welcome we had among you" (RSV). **turned to God from idols**—Notice the order: they did not turn from idols to God, but to God from idols. Their conversion was a positive turn to the living God, from lifeless idols. **the living and true God**—A contrast is drawn between the God they now worship and the false gods they once served.

➤**10 to wait for his Son from heaven**—At the end of each chapter in 1 Thessalonians, Paul mentions the return of Christ. **whom he raised**

**from the dead**—This is a confirmation of his deity and divine sonship (Rom. 1:4). **delivered [is delivering] us from the wrath to come**—when Christ comes to execute judgment on those who do not believe.

Chapter 2

1-20 PAUL'S MANNER OF PREACHING, AND THEIRS OF RECEIVING, THE GOSPEL. PAUL'S DESIRE TO REVISIT THEM FRUSTRATED BY SATAN.

➤**1** From here to 2:12 Paul discusses how he and his fellow workers spread the word; from 2:13 to 2:16 he reviews how the Thessalonians received the message. **brethren**—Paul, the former Gentile-hating Pharisee, uses this phrase more than twenty times in the Thessalonian letters. **our entrance in unto you**—"our visit to you." **was not in vain**—The Greek for "was" expresses rather "has been and is," implying the permanent and continuing character of their preaching.

➤**2 we had suffered . . . at Philippi**—See Acts 16:19-40. Here Paul and Silas were wrongly accused of breaking the Roman law, cruelly beaten and thrown in prison. **bold**—cf. Acts 4:29; Ephesians 6:20. **with much contention**—"as of competitors in a contest" (cf. Col. 1:29; 2:1). This indicates the struggle was with external forces rather than internal or personal ones. (See Acts 17:1-10.)

➤**3 exhortation**—or, encouragement. **not of deceit [error], nor of uncleanness, nor in guile**—Paul was not an impostor seeking fame and self-gratification, as were so many of the Gentile teachers of his day (see Phil. 1:16; 2 Pet. 2:10, 14; Jude 8; Rev. 2:14, 15). Estius tells us that Simon Magus and Cerinthus taught for such motives.

➤**4 allowed**—The original Greek meaning would be "approved by trial." Paul, however, attests that this approval does not come from any personal merit but only from the grace and mercy of God (Acts 9:15; 1 Cor. 7:25; 2 Cor. 3:5; 1 Tim. 1:11, 12). **not as pleasing men**—which is a frequent tactic of false teachers (Gal. 1:10). A false teacher is not concerned with conveying truth as much as eliciting a desired effect from his audience. **God, which trieth**

**our hearts**—This continues the image of approval by trial. God was constantly testing and re-examining Paul's motives to keep them as pure as possible.

➤**5 cloak of covetousness**—"a mask to cover up greed" (NIV).

➤**6 we might have been burdensome**—with respect to demanding financial support (see 2:9; 2 Cor. 11:9; 12:16; 2 Thess. 3:8). Twice Paul received supplies from Philippi while at Thessalonica (Phil. 4:16).

➤**7 we were**—The Greek is "we were made," affirming again that one is what is only by God's grace. **gentle**—The Greek says "mild in bearing with the faults of others," as a parent would with his children (Tittmann). Some of the earliest manuscripts read "babes" instead of "gentle," but this was probably due to an early transcriptional error. The last letter (*n*) of the Greek word preceding "gentle" (*ēpioi*) was inadvertently duplicated and added to it, thus making the Greek word for "babes" (*nēpioi*). Paul never referred to himself and the other apostles as babes, and the verse itself makes it very evident that the Thessalonians were the babes Paul cared for as a nursing mother (*GAM*). **among you**—The Greek here is "in the midst of you," i.e., the talking and sharing we did together was in a context of mutual daily life and work. **even as a nurse**—a suckling mother. **cherisheth**—caring for. **her children**—Greek, "her own children."

➤**8 being affectionately desirous of you**—The Greek implies "to connect oneself with another; to be closely attached to another." **were willing**—were pleased. **to have imparted unto you . . . our own souls**—As a nursing mother is ready to impart not only her milk to her children, but her life to them, so the apostles not only imparted the spiritual milk of the word to the Thessalonians, but were willing to give them their very souls (see John 15:13). **ye were**—you became.

➤**9 our labour**—at tentmaking (Acts 18:3). **night and day**—The Jews reckoned the day from sunset to sunset, thus "night" comes before "day" (cf. Acts 20:31). Evidently they often worked overtime. **we would not be chargeable unto any of you**—i.e., not become a financial burden to you (cf. 2 Cor. 11:9, 10). **we preached unto you**—See Acts 17:1-4.

➤**10 Ye are witnesses**—They had seen his outward conduct. **and God**—God attests to the inward conduct. **holily**—toward God. **justly**—toward men. **we behaved ourselves**—lit., "we were made to be"—by God.

➤**11 exhorted** [encouraged] . . . **comforted** [consoled] . . . **charged** [solemnly witnessed]—Paul's words were carefully chosen. He exhorted, consoled, and solemnly witnessed to the Thessalonians. **as a father**—A loving parent teaches with gentle sternness.

➤**12 who hath called you**—a reading supported by some ancient manuscripts; whereas, other ancient manuscripts read "who is calling you." **into his kingdom**—The idea of the "kingdom" is found frequently in Paul's writings. The kingdom is both present and future. Men can enter the kingdom here and now, experiencing a part of its joys, but will only apprehend it fully at the end of the age. **glory**—that you may share Christ's glory (John 17:22; Col. 3:4).

➤**13 ye received it . . . as . . . the word of God**—Paul was consistently grateful that they had accepted his message as the word of God, even though he had not adjusted his message to suit their wishes. **which effectually worketh also in you**—This is evidenced in 2:14, where they showed patient endurance in the midst of persecution (cf. Gal. 3:5; 5:6).

➤**14 followers** [imitators] **of the churches of God in Judaea**—with respect to their suffering at the hands of Jews. **in Christ Jesus**—an expression that exclusively characterizes Christians (as opposed to Jews). **your own countrymen**—This includes the Jews settled at Thessalonica, from whom the persecution originated, and the Gentiles there, who were incited by the Jews. About this time, Paul also wrote of suffering persecution from the Jews at Corinth (Acts 18:5, 6, 12).

➤**15 their own**—These words are not present in the earliest manuscripts. **prophets**—See Matthew 21:33-41; 23:31-37; Luke 13:33. **they please not God, and are contrary to all men**—It is hard to tell by this if Paul meant they were willfully turning against God and man out of purely destructive desires, or only seeming to do so by zealously protecting their own faith. They did seem to have a bad reputation, for Josephus, in *Apion* 2.14 calls the Jews

"Atheists and misanthropes, the dullest of barbarians" and Tacitus in *Histories* 5.5 says "They have a hostile hatred of all other men." Perhaps they were only against God and man in that their persecution of the Christians limited the outreach of the gospel (2:16).

➤**16 for the wrath is come upon them**—The Greek has a past tense, as if some form of punishment had already begun. Already in A.D. 48 a riot had occurred at the Passover in Jerusalem where 30,000 Jews were slain.

➤**17 being taken from you**—perhaps referring to the suddenness of their departure (see Acts 17:10).

➤**18 I Paul**—He slightly distinguishes himself here to make plain that this was his own intention, possibly when he went on alone to Athens. He met Timothy there and sent him to Thessalonica. **Satan hindered us**—On a different occasion, "the Spirit of Jesus" (Acts 16:7, RSV) forbade or hindered Paul's group in traveling as they planned. But in this case he states it is Satan who stopped them, either through evil men, some of whom had already driven them out of Thessalonica (Acts 17:13ff.), or else by some more direct messenger from Satan (2 Cor. 12:7).

➤**19-20** The thought and spirit of these two verses are captured in Constable's comments on them:

He [Paul] voiced a rhetorical question to heighten the intensity of his fervor. In effect he asked what would be the greatest blessing he could possibly receive at the judgment seat of Christ. They were! They were everything that was worth anything to Paul. They were his *hope;* their development was what he lived for as a parent lives to see his children grow up to maturity, to produce and reproduce. They were his *joy;* they filled his life with sunshine as he thought of what they used to be, what they had become, and what they would be by the grace of God. They were his *crown;* they themselves were the symbol of God's blessing on his life and ministry. They were his *glory and joy,* and not only his but also the glory and joy of his companions in labor. Paul said in essence, "When life is over and we stand in the presence of our

Lord Jesus at His coming, you Thessalonians will be our source of glory and joy; you mean that much to us."

## Chapter 3

### 1-13 PAUL'S CONCERN FOR THE THESSALONIANS AND JOY OVER TIMOTHY'S REPORT OF THE STEADFASTNESS OF THEIR FAITH

➤**1, 2 forbear**—"endure" the suspense (the Gk. is applied to a watertight vessel): "When we could no longer contain ourselves in our yearning desire for you." **we thought it good to be left at Athens alone; and sent Timotheus**—Apparently, Paul and Silas stayed in Athens, and together decided to send Timothy to Thessalonica. (After Paul went to Athens alone, he must have asked Silas and Timothy to come from Berea to join him.) **minister of God, and our fellow-labourer**—The earliest manuscripts read "fellow worker with God" but were very likely altered with ensuing copying to avoid such a bold expression. (Similar phrases are used in 1 Cor. 3:9; 2 Cor. 6:1.) Paul spoke highly of one who was only recently brought into the ministry. Perhaps he wished to impress the Thessalonians with a high respect for the delegate sent them and to encourage Timothy, who seems to have been timid (1 Tim. 4:12; 5:23).

➤**3 moved**—shaken, beguiled away. In some contexts, the word was used in Greek of a dog wagging the tail, or fawning—so as to allure, fascinate, flatter, beguile, or draw aside from the right path (Rienecker). Therefore Tittmann explains it, "That no man should, amidst his calamities, be *allured* by the flattering hope of a more pleasant life to abandon his duty."

➤**4 we told you before that we should** [are about to] **suffer tribulation** [persecution]—Paul had forewarned them of the inevitable sufferings they would encounter; and forewarned, they should have been forearmed.

➤**5 forbear**—See comments on 3:1. **to know**—Greek, "to come to know"; hence, to learn. **your faith**—the condition of your faith in the midst of persecution. **the tempter have tempted you**—Satan, the tempter, tempted Jesus (Matt. 4:1-11) and he continues to tempt

Jesus' servants (see Luke 22:3; 1 Cor. 7:5) (*NIVSB*). Satan takes advantage of the believers' sufferings to tempt them with the hope that he can get them to deviate from their faith or even deny their faith. **our labour be in vain**—See Isaiah 49:4; 1 Corinthians 3:8.

➤**6 now when Timotheus came from you unto us**—"But Timotheus having just now come from you unto us" (Alford). Paul was writing this from Corinth (see Acts 18:5), where Timothy had just joined him. **faith and charity** [love]—See 1:3; cf. 2 Thessalonians 1:3.

➤**7** This verse is better translated: "Therefore, brothers, in all our distress and persecution we were encouraged about you because of your faith" (NIV). At the time of writing, Paul was suffering persecution from the Jews (Acts 18:1-11).

➤**8 now we live**—We are revived (Ps. 22:26; 2 John 3, 4). **if ye stand fast**—The joy the apostles were experiencing would continue if the Thessalonians remained strong in their faith (3:10; Phil. 4:1).

➤**9 joy**—It was "comfort" in 3:7; now it is "joy". Paul was joyful before God that the Thessalonians' faith had triumphed.

➤**10 Night and day**—Paul seemed often to have spent the night in meditation and prayer (2 Tim. 1:3). **praying**—The Greek word indicates "petitioning." **perfect**—Greek, "adjust," "outfit," "furnish"; the word means to bring to completion or perfection by repairing or furnishing what is faulty and/or lacking. Evidently some of their doctrinal views were not quite correct, and they were still not conducting themselves as they should (4:1-9). Paul usually praised the good first and later tried to correct the wrong.

➤**11** This verse is clearer when translated: "Would that [optative mood in Gk.] God himself, even our Father, and our Lord Jesus Christ, direct our way unto you." In the Greek the verb is singular, implying that the subject, the Father and Son, are one in essential being. Paul's prayer was answered when, five years later, he returned to Macedonia. Paul characteristically inserted brief prayers in his writings, often concerning his journeys (Rom. 1:10; 15:32).

➤**12 the Lord**—the Lord Jesus. **love one toward another**—See John 13:34, 35;

Romans 13:8; 1 Thessalonians 4:9; 1 John 3:11, 23.

➤**13 unblameable in holiness**—We must have holiness to stand before God in that day (Heb. 12:14). God has predestined his sons to attain to this blamelessness and holiness (Eph. 1:4, 5). **coming**—Greek, *parousia;* the word was used in NT times to describe the visitation of royalty. **with all his saints**—i.e., all the redeemed, all the believers. Perhaps this means that Christ's believers, having been taken to his presence, will accompany him when he returns to earth.

*Chapter* 4

**1-12 EXHORTATIONS TO CHASTITY, BROTHERLY LOVE, AND TO MAKE A DECENT LIVING**

➤**1 Furthermore**—The Greek says, "As to what remains." **how ye ought to walk** [to conduct your lives] **and to please God**—This does not mean that everything about the Thessalonians' lives was wrong. They were living in a way pleasing to God, but Paul wanted them to do even better.

➤**2 commandments we gave you**—Paul used the strong term "commandments" in writing to this fairly new church, knowing they would take it in the right spirit and that they would understand he was speaking with divine authority. **by the Lord Jesus**—by his authority and direction.

➤**3 this is the will of God, even your sanctification**—God wills our sanctification (see comments on 3:13). **abstain from fornication**—Paul knew the cultural context surrounding the Thessalonians, wherein sexual immorality was often not considered a sin, but a means of consecrating oneself to a god or goddess. Therefore, Paul made a point of specifically denouncing it (cf. Acts 15:20).

➤**4 possess his vessel**—Does the term "vessel" refer to a man's wife or a man's personal life? Those who insist it refers to the Christian's personal life do so on the basis that the other interpretation would show Paul to have a low view of marriage. Thus, they take "vessel" to mean one's body (see Rom. 9:22, 23; 2 Cor. 4:7), and they take "possess" to mean "control." But the Greek word behind "possess" can

hardly mean "control"; it most naturally means "acquire." Thus, Paul was speaking of acquiring a wife in terms of obtaining a vessel. This terminology roughly corresponds to 1 Peter 3:7 and accords well with common Jewish phraseology. **in sanctification**—See Romans 6:19; 1 Corinthians 6:15, 18. **honour**—See Hebrews 13:4.

➤**5 lust**—passion. **even as the Gentiles**—The Graeco-Roman world did not demand sexual purity of men. **which know not God**—and so know no better. A people's morals correspond to the objects they worship (Deut. 7:26; Ps. 115:8; Rom. 1:23, 24).

➤**6 defraud his brother**—by committing fornication with a woman engaged to a Christian brother or by committing adultery with the wife of a Christian. **in any matter**—lit., "in the matter"—the matter at hand concerning marital relations.

➤**7 God hath ... called us ... unto holiness**—God called us to become sanctified by the sanctifying work of the Holy Spirit, working from inside out, from our spirit to our soul to our body (5:23). Sanctification or holiness is a major theme in this epistle.

➤**8 despiseth not man, but God**—Again Paul emphasized that they were to be held accountable to God, not men. They could not justify themselves by the lesser mores of their culture. **hath also given**—lit., "also giving." The present tense signifies that God continues to give his Spirit.

➤**9 taught of God**—See John 6:45; Hebrews 8:11; 1 John 2:20, 27.

➤**11 study**—actually, "be diligent." **to be quiet**—in direct opposition to the world's ambition, which is to fill life with great activity and much noise (cf. 2 Thess. 3:11, 12). **work with your own hands**—This might indicate that the Thessalonian converts were basically working-class people. Evidently their expectation of the coming of Christ led some enthusiasts to stop work, thereby becoming a financial burden to others (cf. 4:12). As this subsequently got worse, Paul reproved them even more harshly (2 Thess. 3:6-12).

➤**12 honestly**—becomingly, as becomes your Christian profession. **have lack of nothing**—i.e., not have to beg from others for our living. Rather than depending on others we should work in order to help others (cf. Eph. 4:28).

## 13-18 THE RAPTURE OF DECEASED AND LIVING BELIEVERS AT CHRIST'S COMING

➤**13** A leading topic of Paul's preaching at Thessalonica was perhaps the coming kingdom (Acts 17:7). Evidently, some either misunderstood or willfully perverted the message, sowing fear in the people's hearts by saying that friends and relatives who had recently died would not share in the kingdom as would those that remained alive. This is the error that Paul tries to correct here (cf. 5:10). **them which are asleep**—a euphemism for death, or more specifically, the state (or condition) of the dead. Scripture speaks of "the dead in Christ" (i.e., the Christians who have died) as those whose bodies (but not souls and spirits—for one's soul and spirit goes to be with Christ at the time of death) are in a calm and holy sleep, awaiting to be awakened at the resurrection. Believers who have died prior to the resurrection are now with Christ in spirit (see Acts 7:59; 2 Cor. 5:6-8; Phil. 1:21-23). In that day, Christ will resurrect and glorify the believers' bodies and thereby make a full and visible display of his glorious church. **that ye sorrow not**—i.e., have sorrow, as those who have no hope of resurrection. **as others** [the rest] **which have no hope**—Catullus, the Roman poet, said, "When once our brief day has set, we must sleep one everlasting night." The sepulchral inscriptions of heathen Thessalonica express the hopeless view of those who have died—as Aeschylus, the Greek tragedian, wrote, "Of one once dead there is no resurrection." Also, whatever ideas the philosophers of that time had about the existence of the soul (or, spirit) after death, they had none whatever of the body (Acts 17:18, 20, 32).

➤**14** Here the teaching is repeated: the Christians who have died will return with Christ. Disembodied souls are not spoken of; the original Greek reference is to sleeping bodies awaking and returning. The facts of Christ's experience are repeated. He died and then rose: so believers shall die and rise with him.

➤**15 by** [in] **the** [a] **word of the Lord**—i.e., "by virtue of a direct revelation from the Lord to me." Just how he received this word and under what conditions he received it, Paul did not indicate. **we which are alive and remain unto the coming of the Lord**—means whichever of us are alive and still on earth when the Lord comes. **shall not prevent**—i.e., shall not go before. **them which are asleep**—the deceased believers. Evidently the Thessalonians believed that those who were alive at the time of Christ's coming would meet him before those who had already died. Paul corrected this. Christians of all ages will rise at Christ's return. Living Christians in every age should live in expectation of his coming (Matt. 25:13; Rom. 13:11; 1 Cor. 15:51; James 5:9; 1 Pet. 4:5, 6).

➤**16 the Lord himself shall descend**—See Acts 1:11. **with a shout**—The Greek signifies "a signal shout," "war shout," "a shout of command." Jesus is here presented as a victorious king, beginning his last battle for victory over the forces of evil. **with the voice of the archangel**—This is distinct from the "signal shout." Perhaps Michael is meant (Jude 9; Rev. 12:7), who has responsibility for guarding the people of God (Dan. 10:13). **trump** [trumpet-call] **of God**—Cf. Exodus 19:16; Psalm 47:5. A trumpet call accompanied God's appearance when his people were called to convocation (Num. 10:2, 10; 31:6). Here it will be used to call them together at Christ's return (cf. Ps. 50:1-5; Matt. 24:31; 1 Cor. 15:52). **the dead in Christ shall rise first**—The deceased Christians will rise before the Christians who are still alive.

➤**17 we which are alive and remain**—See comments on 4:15. **shall be caught up together with them**—The living Christians will join the deceased Christians—now resurrected—in a corporate rapture. Both groups of Christians will have had their bodies glorified just prior to the rapture (see 1 Cor. 15:51, 52; Phil. 3:20, 21). **in the clouds**—Greek, "in clouds." Christ was taken in a cloud at his ascension (Acts 1:9). He will return the same way (Rev. 1:7). The clouds are spoken of as God's chariots (Ps. 104:3; Dan. 7:13). **in the air**—rather, "into the air"; caught up into the region just above the earth, where the meeting (cf. Matt. 25:1, 6) shall take place between them ascending and their Lord descending toward the earth. **and so shall we ever be with the Lord**—This is a general statement describing the believers' eternal privilege of having unbroken, everlasting fellowship with their Lord Jesus Christ (see Rev. 21:3, 4; 22:3, 4).

Paul did not go over the other events foretold for the end times such as Christ's reign on earth (1 Cor. 6:2, 3) and the final judgment, because they were not really relevant to his discussion here.

➤**18 comfort one another**—in your mourning for the dead (4:13)—or simply, "encourage one another" with the truth of **these words.**

# *Chapter* 5

## 1-28 LIVING IN ANTICIPATION OF CHRIST'S RETURN

➤**1 times**—the general and indefinite term for chronological periods. **seasons**—specific segments of time. **ye have no need**—those who watch do not need to be told when the hour will come for they are always ready (Bengel).

➤**2 as a thief in the night**—Paul used the same image Christ used about the suddenness of his coming (see Matt. 24:43; cf. also 2 Pet. 3:10). Signs will precede the coming to confirm the hope of those who keep their eyes open, but the coming itself will be sudden (Matt. 24:32-36; Luke 21:25-30, 35).

➤**3 they**—the men of the world, unbelievers. **Peace**—See Judges 18:7, 9, 27, 28; Jeremiah 6:14; Ezekiel 13:10. **then**—the coming will transpire at the very moment when they least expect it. (Cf. the case of Belshazzar in Daniel 5:1-5,6, 9, 26-28; Herod in Acts 12:21-23.) **destruction**—not annihilation, but ruin. **as travail**—labor pains, from which there is no escape to the woman about to give birth. The coming destruction cannot be avoided (see Amos 9:2, 3; Rev. 6:15, 16).

➤**4 not in darkness**—not in darkness of understanding (cf. Eph. 4:18). **that day**—the day of the Lord's coming (Heb. 10:25). **overtake you as a thief**—Christians should not be surprised by Christ's coming, as one would be surprised by a thief. The unbelievers will be surprised.

➤**5 children** [sons] **of light . . . children** [sons] **of the day**—This is taken from a Hebrew idiom, suggesting that as sons resemble their fathers, so our enlightened character resembles God's light (Luke 16:8; John 12:36).

➤**6 sleep**—referring to spiritual apathy (Rom. 13:11; Eph. 5:14). **watch**—or, be vigi-lant. **sober**—refraining from carnal indulgences (1 Pet. 5:8).

➤**7 For they that sleep sleep in the night; and they that be drunken are drunken in the night.**—This verse is meant to be taken literally. The implication is that we as Christians should remain watchful for signs of Christ's return and act in a way that would stand unashamed in the full light of day.

➤**8 faith and love; and . . . hope**—These are the three most important virtues (cf. 1:3; 1 Cor. 13:13). The breastplate consists of faith and love, the helmet of hope. These two parts of armor defend the two vital parts—the heart and the head (cf. Isa. 59:17; Eph. 6:14-17). A Christian needs faith in Christ and love for the saints as a protection against the enemy's attacks. And the hope of salvation (Rom. 13:11) guards the believer's thoughts from the enemy's assaults.

➤**9 appointed us**—In God's eternal purpose Christians were not appointed to experience the coming wrath. **to obtain**—or, "to receive" (NIV). The verb in Greek can be taken actively (to gain, to win, to possess, etc.) or passively (to receive). This salvation (or, deliverance from the wrath) is obtained by believers' acceptance of the divine appointment. The context seems to indicate that it involves man's cooperation with the divine appointment.

➤**10 died for us**—on our behalf. **whether we wake or sleep**—whether we be found at Christ's coming alive or in our graves. **together**—In the Greek, this refers to the togetherness of the living and deceased believers. **with him**—with Christ.

➤**11 comfort**—encourage. **edify one another**—build up one another by speaking one to another about the Lord's coming. **even as also ye do**—it was already their practice.

➤**12 know**—regard, respect, realize their responsibilities, treat them accordingly (cf. 1 Cor. 16:18) and liberally take care of their needs (1 Tim. 5:17). Since the Thessalonian church was new and the ministers were novices, Paul must have thought it necessary to put the church's responsibility to its leaders in proper focus. **them which labour**—i.e., have a life of labor. [who] **are over you**—i.e., those who take the lead and oversee, which would be the elders, who are also called overseers. **admonish**—or, warn, not with arbitrary authority, but gently and truly (2 Tim. 2:14, 24, 25; 1 Pet. 5:3). The same group of people is said to labor, take the lead, and admonish.

**►13 esteem them . . . for their work's sake**—The nature of the elders' work is worthy of esteem, love, and respect. **be at peace among yourselves**—speaks of peace among the workers, the workers and church members, and the church members.

**►14 unruly**—disorderly, idle. The word characterizes those who would not work but expected to be supported by everyone else (2 Thess. 3:6, 11). In Greek this word means "rankbreakers." **the feeble-minded**—lit., "the little souled," the faint-hearted. **the weak**—spiritually. Paul himself helped the weak (1 Cor. 9:22). **be patient**—cf. 2 Corinthians 10:1; 2 Peter 3:15.

**►15** cf. Romans 12:17; 1 Peter 3:9.

**►16, 17** The joy and constant prayer seem to go together (Eph. 6:18; Phil. 4:4, 6). **Pray without ceasing**—pray continually. "Continual prayer is not prayer that prevails without any interruption, but prayer that continues whenever possible" (Constable).

**►18** Romans 8:28 and Ephesians 5:20 teach, as this verse does, that what appears to be adverse is not really so.

**►19 Quench not the Spirit**—Do not throw cold water on those who, with extraordinary inspiration from the Spirit, stand up to speak in tongues, or reveal mysteries, or pray. Perhaps Paul was warning the Thessalonian ministers and elders, who, not receiving much respect themselves, might tend to resent the more dramatic gifts of others. Albeit, caution was needed (see 5:21).

**►20 prophesyings**—either inspired teachings or predictions of future events (see 1 Cor. 14:5ff.).

**►21** We should not discourage the full use of the gifts of the Spirit; but we should be aware that some might not be genuine and therefore should be avoided. Some members of the church are given the power to tell whether or not it was the Spirit of God speaking through a person (1 Cor. 12:10; 14:29; 1 John 4:1). Another sure test is to try the alleged revelation against Scripture, as the Bereans did (Acts 17:11). **hold fast that which is good**—Joined with the previous words, this statement means

that the church should keep whatever prophecies (or other speakings) prove to be good.

**►22 Abstain from all appearance of evil**—This speaks of avoiding those who *appear* to be Spirit-inspired prophets. However specious the form or outward appearance of such prophets and their prophesyings, Christians are to avoid it—for the falseness is a kind or form of evil (Thomas).

**►23 sanctify you**—make you holy. **wholly**—"through and through" (NIV). **whole**—entire, encompassing a man's total being. **spirit and soul and body**—All three constitute man "entire." The spirit enables man to contact the divine Spirit and is that part of man quickened by God's Spirit at the time of regeneration (John 3:6; Rom. 8:16). The soul of man is man's personality and inward, animating essence. Man's body, of course, is man's physical being. God works from the inside out to sanctify one's entire being. **blameless**—The goal of God's sanctifying work is to preserve each believer in holiness. **the coming**—the *parousia,* the Second Coming.

**►24 Faithful**—He will be faithful to his covenant promises (John 10:27-29; 1 Cor. 1:9; 10:13; Phil. 1:6). **he that calleth**—i.e., God who calls. **do it**—He will keep our spirit, soul, and body blameless until Christ returns (5:23; Rom. 8:30; 1 Pet. 5:10).

**►25 pray for us**—Paul made the same request in the epistles to the Romans, Ephesians, Philippians, Colossians, Philemon, and in 2 Corinthians. Interestingly, he omitted such a request in 1 Corinthians and Galatians, epistles of rebuke and censure.

**►26 an holy kiss**—This was a custom of salutation in Paul's day, as it remains in some cultures today. It was a token of Christian fellowship (cf. Luke 7:45; Acts 20:37) from which grew a custom in the early church of passing the kiss through the congregation at the holy communion (Justin Martyr, *Apology,* 1.65; *Apostolic Constitutions,* 2.57)—the men kissing men and the women kissing women.

**►27 this epistle be read**—The Greek indicates that this epistle be read aloud to **all the . . . brethren**—meaning the entire church, at a specific time and place. **holy**—This word appears in some of the earliest manuscripts but is absent in others. Since "holiness" is a major theme of this epistle, it would seem natural for Paul to include it in the salutation. On the other hand, scribes, for the very same reason, may have been tempted to add it.

➤28 grace—All of Paul's epistles conclude with a benediction invoking grace. Amen—is absent from some ancient manuscripts.

BIBLIOGRAPHY
Alford, Henry. *The Greek New Testament*. 1852. Reprint. Grand Rapids: Guardian Press, 1976.
Bengel, John A. *New Testament Word Studies*. 1742. Reprint. Grand Rapids: Eerdmans, 1971.
Constable, Thomas L. "First Thessalonians" in *The Bible Knowledge Commentary*. Wheaton, Ill.: Victor Books, 1983.

Rienecker, Fritz. *Linguistic Key to the Greek New Testament*. Grand Rapids: Baker Book House, 1976, 1980.
Thomas, Robert L. "First Thessalonians" in the *Expositor's Bible Commentary*. Grand Rapids: Zondervan, 1978.
Tittmann, J. A. *Remarks on the Synonyms of the New Testament*. Edinburgh: T & T Clark, 1833-37.

# 2 THESSALONIANS

## Introduction

The genuineness of 2 Thessalonians is attested by Polycarp (*Epistle to the Philippians*, sec. 11), who alludes to 3:15; Justin Martyr, *Dialogue with Trypho*, who alludes to 2:3; Irenaeus, who quotes 2:8; Clement of Alexandria, who quotes 3:2, as Paul's words (*Stromata*, 1.5; *Paidagogos*, 1.17); Tertullian (*The Resurrection of the Body*, chap. 24) who quotes 2:1, 2, as part of Paul's epistle.

The accounts from Thessalonica, after the sending of the first epistle, presented the faith and love of the Christians there as on the increase and their constancy amidst persecutions unshaken. One error of doctrine, however, resulting in practical evil, had sprung up among them. The apostle's description of Christ's sudden second coming (1 Thess. 4:13 ff., and 5:2) and the *possibility* of its being at any time led them to believe it was *actually* at hand. Some professed to know by "the Spirit" (2:2) that it was so; others alleged that Paul had said so when with them. A letter, too, purporting to be from the apostle to that effect, seems to have been circulated among them. (That 2:2 refers to such a spurious letter, rather than to Paul's first epistle, appears likely from the statement in 3:17 concerning his autograph salutation's being the mark whereby his genuine letters might be known.) Some neglected their daily business to wait for the coming of the Lord. This error, therefore, needed rectifying and forms a leading topic of the second epistle. Paul tells them that before the Lord comes there must first be a great apostasy, and the man of lawlessness must be revealed; and that the Lord's sudden coming is no ground for neglecting daily business; that to do so would only bring scandal on the church and was contrary to his own practice among them (3:7-9); and that the faithful must withdraw themselves from such disorderly people (3:6, 10-15). Thus, there are three divisions of the epistle: (1) 1:1-12; commendations of the Thessalonians' faith, love, and patience amid persecutions. (2) 2:1-17; the error as to the immediate coming of Christ corrected, and the previous rise and downfall of the man of lawlessness foretold. (3) 3:1-16; exhortations to orderly conduct in their whole walk, with prayers for them to the God of peace, followed by his autograph salutation and benediction.

As the epistle is written jointly with Timothy and Silas, and as they were with Paul while at Corinth and not with him for a long time subsequent to his leaving that city, it follows that the place of writing must have been Corinth. The Second Epistle to the Thessalonians was written shortly after the first, A.D. 51.

The style of the Second Epistle to the Thessalonians is not different from that of most of Paul's other writings, except in the prophetic portion of it (2:1-12), which is distinguished from them in subject matter. As is usual in his more solemn passages, his diction here is more lofty, abrupt, and elliptical. The former epistle dwells mostly on the second coming of Christ with respect to the rapture (1 Thess. 4 and 5); this epistle dwells mostly on the aspect of everlasting destruction to the wicked and him who shall be the final consummation of wickedness, the man of lawlessness. Paul had not given an erroneous impression as to Christ's speedy coming when he wrote his first epistle because he had already told them when he was with them the same truths about the apostasy that he reiterates in the second epistle (2:5). Several points of coincidence occur between the two epistles, confirming the genuineness of the latter: cf. 3:2 with 1 Thessalonians 2:15, 16; 2:9 with 1 Thessalonians 2:18 and 3:5; 3:6, 14 with 1 Thessalonians 5:14.

Paul probably then visited Thessalonica on his way to Asia (Acts 20:4) and took with him from there Aristarchus and Secundus. Aristarchus became his "companion in travel" and shared with him his perils at Ephesus and his shipwreck and was his "fellow prisoner" at Rome (Acts 27:2; Col. 4:10; Philem. 24). According to tradition he became bishop of Apamea.

*Chapter* **1**

## 1-12 INTRODUCTION. THANKSGIVING FOR THE THESSALONIANS' GROWTH. PRAYER FOR THEIR PERFECTION AND FOR THEIR READINESS AT THE LORD'S COMING

➤**1 in God our Father**—even more endearing than the expression in 1 Thessalonians 1:1, "in God the Father."

➤**2 from God our Father**—"our" is present in some early manuscripts, while absent in others.

➤**3 We are bound**—Greek, "We owe it as a debt." Since their prayer in 1 Thessalonians 3:12 that the Thessalonians' love might grow and overflow had been dramatically answered, they must thank God for it. Paul and his fellow workers were practicing what they preached in 1 Thessalonians 5:18. **meet**—right, fitting, proper.

➤**4 glory in you**—boast of you. **in** [among] **the churches**—Paul, now at Corinth, boasted of the faith of the Macedonian churches (2 Cor. 10:15-17). **persecutions and tribulations**—Macedonian Jews were stirring up the courts and the people against the Christians (Acts 17:6, 8).

➤**5 Which is a manifest token** [evidence] **of the righteous judgment of God**—This joins with the previous verse. The Thessalonians' perseverance proves God's righteous judgment (Thomas). David (Ps. 73:1-14) and Jeremiah (12:1-4) were perplexed at the wicked prospering and the godly suffering. But Paul makes this fact a matter of consolation. It is a proof of the future judgment, which will rectify the present anomalies—by rewarding the now suffering saints and by punishing the persecutors. **that ye may be counted worthy of the kingdom of God**—Christians' sufferings prepare them for God's kingdom. "Worthy" implies that, though men are justified by faith, they shall be judged according to their works (Rev. 20:12; cf. 1 Thess. 2:12; 1 Pet. 1:6, 7; Rev. 20:4).

➤**6 Seeing it is a righteous thing**—continuing the idea of God's righteous judgment in 1:5. **to recompense** [pay back] **tribulation**—God would requite tribulation for the tribulation the Macedonian Jews had caused the believers in Thessalonica.

➤**7 rest**—The Greek is "relaxation," a loosening of the tension they had been in. **us**—Paul, Silas, and Timothy, who had also been suffering persecution. **when the Lord Jesus shall be revealed**—lit., "at the unveiling of the Lord

Jesus." **mighty angels**—this means the angels by whom Jesus makes his might known (Matt. 13:41, 49).

➤**8 In flaming fire**—recalling the divine manifestation in the burning bush (Exod. 3:2) and the giving of the Law at Mount Sinai (Exod. 19:18). Also, it shall accompany Christ's presence in the kingdom (Dan. 7:9, 10). Fire is a symbol of glory and vengeance (Heb. 10:27; 12:29; 2 Pet. 3:7, 10). **them that know not God**—Gentiles (see Gal. 4:8; Eph. 2:12; 1 Thess. 4:5). **obey not the gospel**—primarily the unbelieving Jews (Rom. 10:3, 16); secondarily, all who obey not the truth (Rom. 2:8). **Christ**—This word is not present in the earliest manuscripts.

➤**9 Who shall be punished with everlasting destruction**—lit., "who will pay the penalty, eternal destruction." The penalty is severe, namely, eternal ruin. The Greek word for "destruction" (*olethros*) does not mean annihilation—which, of course, could not be eternal—but means loss of everything worthwhile. "Just as endless life belongs to Christians, endless destruction belongs to those opposed to Christ" (Thomas). **from the presence of the Lord**—indicates separation or exclusion from the Lord's presence. To be separated from the Lord's presence is to experience eternal death. **and from the glory of his power**—Those separated from Christ's presence will also be excluded from participating in Christ's glorious and powerful appearance in his kingdom (see next verse).

➤**10 When he shall come to be glorified in his saints**—Christ will be glorified in his believers when he returns to establish his kingdom on earth. Christ in the believers, previously the hope of glory (Col. 3:4), will then be the reality of glory shining out through all the transformed and transfigured saints. **to be admired**—by other people. **in all them that believe**—Christ in the believers will be admired because he will be glorified in them. **because our testimony among you was** believed—A parenthetical statement affirming the Thessalonians' portion in the just-mentioned glory *because* they had believed the gospel. **in that day**—joins with the first part of this verse, as shown by the preceding parentheses in the KJV.

➤**11 worthy of this calling**—This refers to the entire scope of God's calling, according to which Christians are destined to inherit the kingdom (see 2 Tim. 1:9). **fulfil all the good pleasure of his goodness, and the work of faith with power**—could also be rendered, "may fulfill every good resolve and work of faith by his power" (RSV).

➤**12 the name**—a metonymy for "person." The person of the Lord Jesus Christ would be representatively glorified in his believers. **glorified in you, and ye in him**—speaking of mutual, reciprocal glorification (see John 13:31; 17:21-24). **the grace of our God and the Lord Jesus Christ**—According to the Greek this could read, "the grace of our God and Lord, Jesus Christ (cf. NIV mg.). There is a Greek grammatical rule (called the Granville Sharpe rule) that says when one article governs two nouns joined by the Greek conjunction *kai* (and), the total expression forms one unit and thus describes one substantive (see Dana and Mantey). However, some scholars do not consider 2 Thessalonians 1:12 to be in the same category as Titus 2:13 and 2 Peter 1:1 because the word "Lord" in Greek (*kurios*) was often written without an article and could therefore function as a separate substantive. (See comments on Titus 2:13 and 2 Pet. 1:1.)

*Chapter* 2

## 1-18 CORRECTION OF THE THESSALONIANS' ERRORS CONCERNING THE IMMINENCE OF CHRIST'S COMING. AN ANNOUNCEMENT OF THE COMING APOSTASY AND EXHORTATIONS TO STEADFASTNESS

➤**1 Now**—This marks a change from Paul's prayers to some teaching. **our gathering together unto him**—The final gathering together of the saints to Christ, at his coming (see Matt. 24:31; 1 Thess. 4:17). The Greek noun is nowhere else found in the NT except in Hebrews 10:25, said of the assembling together of believers for the universal gathering.

➤**2 shaken**—lit., "tossed," as ships tossed by an agitated sea (cf. Eph. 4:14). **in mind**—rather as the Greek, "from your mind," i.e., agitated emotionally. **by spirit**—by a person professing to have a spirit of prophecy

(1 Cor. 12:8-10; 1 John 4:1-3). The Thessalonians had been warned to test such prophecies (1 Thess. 5:20, 21). **by word**—or, by report, as from Paul. **by letter as from us**—The Thessalonians received a letter, which was allegedly from Paul, that taught them that the Lord had already come (Constable). Therefore, Paul provided a test by which the readers could know if a letter of his was genuine (see 3:17).

➤**3 Let no man deceive you by any means**—Christ, in Matthew 24:4, gives the same warning in connection with the same event. Paul had already indicated three ways (2:2) in which they might be deceived. (Cf. other ways, 2:9, and Matt. 24:5, 24.) **falling away**—The Greek is *"the* falling away," or "apostasy." "The word 'apostasy', as used in the Septuagint and NT, points to a deliberate abandonment of a former professed position" (Thomas). **man of sin**—This reading is supported by some early manuscripts, but the two earliest manuscripts (Codex Vaticanus and Codex Sinaiticus) read, "man of lawlessness" or "man of rebellion" (NIV). Just as Christ embodied righteousness, so the "man of lawlessness" will embody lawlessness and rebellion. This man seems to be the one described in Daniel 11:36: "The king will do exactly as he pleases, claiming to be greater than every god there is, even blaspheming the God of gods, and prospering—until his time is up" (TLB). (See also Dan. 7:8, 25.) **the son of perdition**—lit., "the son of destruction" (i.e., destined to destruction), a title given to only one other person—Judas, the traitor (John 17:12). This is the antichrist who will come up out of the earth "with two little horns like those of a lamb but a fearsome voice like the Dragon's" (Rev. 13:11, TLB). "He will take over the kingdom by flattery and intrigue. . . his method will be deceit" (Dan. 11:21, 23, TLB).

➤**4 Who opposeth and exalteth himself above all that is called God, or that is worshipped**—Daniel 11:36, 37 is referred to here. The words originally applied to Antiochus Epiphanes (who desecrated the Jewish temple) will be even more applicable to the man of lawlessness. Each of the previous world kingdoms had one extraordinary person as its embodiment (Babylon had Nebuchadnezzar, Dan. 2:38 ff.; Medo-Persia had Cyrus; Greece had Alexander and Antiochus Epiphanes, the

forerunner of the antichrist). The final age will find its embodiment in the antichrist. **he as God sitteth in the temple of God, showing himself that he is God**—Pretending to be God, the antichrist will desecrate a rebuilt Jewish temple by setting up an image of himself in the temple and then demanding to be worshiped as God. This is what is otherwise known in Scripture as the abomination that causes desolation (see Dan. 9:26, 27; 11:31; 12:11; Matt. 24:15). This act of desecration will take place halfway through the seventieth prophetic week of Daniel 9:24-27, when the covenant made earlier with the Jewish people is broken (Thomas).

➤**5** Paul spoke of Christ's coming when he was with the Thessalonians; he must have provided them with similar details about the events preceding Christ's coming.

➤**6 now ye know**—by Paul having told them. **what withholdeth**—lit., "that which is holding back," or "what is restraining" (RSV). Paul said that the Thessalonians knew what it was; but since he did not identify it here, we do not know. Some scholars have said that it could be a veiled reference to the Roman Empire, or the Jewish state, or some great force in the struggle between good and evil that keeps back the antichrist until his time comes. Other scholars have said that this great power must be God, or more specifically, the Holy Spirit (see Alford). The Holy Spirit indwelling Christ's body, the church, is now that force that keeps the full force of the lawless one in check. Once the church is removed from this earth, through the rapture, that restraining power no longer will be present to keep the lawless one back—and, consequently, he will be fully revealed. The Spirit's "function of restraining evil through the body of Christ (John 16:7-11; 1 John 4:4) will cease similar to the way he terminated his striving in the days of Noah (Gen. 6:3). At that point the reins will be removed from lawlessness and the satanically inspired rebellion will begin" (Thomas).

➤**7 the mystery of iniquity doth already work**—lit., "the mystery of lawlessness is already at work." In the NT "mystery" does not mean that which is mysterious, but that which is secret. It is hidden from the eyes of men and is that which man in all his searching is unable to discover. **only he who now letteth will let**—"only he who now restrains it will do so" until he be taken out of the way—"When the church leaves the earth in the rapture, the Holy Spirit will be taken out of the way in the sense that His unique lawless-restraining ministry through God's people will be removed . . . " (Constable).

►8 that Wicked—the lawless one (see comments on 2:3, 7). the Lord—a reading supported by several early manuscripts; whereas other early manuscripts read, "the Lord Jesus." consume . . . and . . . destroy—Antichrist's manifestation and destruction are declared in the same breath. At his greatest heights, he is nearest his fall. with the spirit [or, breath] of his mouth—a powerful weapon according to the OT (Exod. 15:8; Ps. 33:6; Isa. 30:27, 28). destroy with the brightness of his coming—The Greek for "destroy" means abolish. The Greek for "brightness" is *epiphaneia* (lit., "epiphany"). The word suggests a divine appearance. Some time during the *parousia* (which is a gradual coming, comprised of various events), Christ will make an epiphany, a personal appearance. (See 1 Tim. 6:14; 2 Tim. 1:10; 4:1, 8; Titus 2:13 where the same Greek word, *epiphaneia*, is used.)

►9 whose coming—referring to the personal appearance (Gk., *parousia*) of the lawless one. after the working of Satan—according to Satan's operation. His power, his life force, comes from Satan. As Christ is to God, so the antichrist is to Satan, his visible embodiment and manifestation. power and signs and lying wonders—In Matthew 24:24 Jesus implied that the miracles would be real, though demoniac, like the mysterious powers of the Egyptian sorcerers. They would not be like the ones Christ performed, in character, power, or purpose. The Antichrist will attempt to imitate Christ's works as a proof of divinity. But no matter how dramatic a copy he might make, it will be a flawed forgery.

►10 And with all deceivableness of unrighteousness in them that perish—This could be translated, "and with all wicked deception for those who are to perish" (RSV). The people who are perishing (cf. 2 Cor. 2:15, 16; 4:3) will be deceived by the antichrist's wicked deceit. because they received not the love of the truth—i.e., "they refused to love the truth" (NIV). that they might be saved—The truth, the embodiement which is Jesus

(John 14:6), saves those who love it (see Eph. 4:21).

►11 strong delusion—or, "the power of error" (TEV). a lie—lit., "the lie," which the antichrist embodies and displays. Once they have completely refused the truth, God justly lets them go their own way and settle into believing Satan's great lie (cf. 1 Kings 22:22, 23; Ezek. 14:9; Job. 12:16; Matt. 24:5, 11; 1 Tim. 4:1).

►12 damned—judged. pleasure in unrighteousness—cf. Rom. 1:32; 2:8.

►13 God hath from the beginning chosen you to salvation—This reading is supported by some early manuscripts; whereas others read, "God has chosen you as firstfruits to salvation." In Greek the expression "from the beginning" (*ap archēs*) could have easily been confused for the Greek word for "firstfruits" (*aparchēn*), or vice versa. (In the early manuscripts no space was left between the words.) The first reading looks legitimate because it was customary for the NT writers (especially Paul) to speak of God's choosing his elect from the beginning, even before the foundation of the world (see Eph. 1:4; 2 Tim. 1:9). The second reading also seems genuine because Paul had the habit of calling the first converts (in certain geographical regions) the "firstfruits" (see Rom. 16:5; 1 Cor. 16:15). Nevertheless, most modern translations contain the first reading and note the second in the margin (*GAM*). through sanctification of the Spirit—God's choice of each believer is made effective and real by the sanctifying work of the Spirit. The Spirit works in the chosen person until he or she believes the truth. This same operation is described in 1 Peter 1:2, in which it is said that the sanctifying Spirit causes the elect to become obedient to Jesus Christ and receive the sprinkling of his cleansing blood.

►14 to the obtaining of the glory of our Lord Jesus Christ—i.e., to share in Jesus Christ's glory (see John 17:22, 24; Rom. 8:17, 29; 2 Tim. 2:10).

►15 stand fast, and hold the traditions—The Thessalonians had strayed away from what Paul had earlier taught them, letting themselves be taken in by some dubious revelations and forged letters allegedly from Paul. The Greek word for "traditions" means "that which is passed on"—rendered, "the teachings we passed on to you" in the NIV. These teachings, divinely inspired, were passed on to the Thessalonians by word and by letter. They were to be kept and guarded.

➤**16, 17** According to the Greek, both Jesus Christ and the Father function as the God who has **loved us,** [given us] **everlasting consolation** [or, eternal encouragement], and [a] **good hope through** [our participation in] **grace**—Paul asks that both the Son and Father comfort their hearts and establish (or strengthen) them in every good work and word (which is the order of the words in the earliest manuscripts).

*Chapter* 3

1-18 REQUEST FOR PRAYER, WARNING AGAINST IDLENESS, AND FINAL GREETINGS

➤**1 Finally**—lit., "as to what remains." **the word of the Lord**—"the Lord's message" (TEV). **may have free course**—lit., "may run," or spread rapidly (TLB, NIV). **and be glorified**—receive glory, be honored, by being accepted by those who hear. **as it is with you**—see 1 Thessalonians 1:6; 4:10; 5:11.

➤**2 unreasonable . . . men**—lit., "men . . . out of place"; i.e., inept, more than ordinarily bad. Paul was now at Corinth being persecuted by the Jews (cf. Acts 18:5-9; 1 Thess. 2:15, 16). **all men have not faith**—lit., "the faith" of the Christian. Paul was reminding the Thessalonians that not all men accept the gospel as readily as they did (1 Thess. 1:5, 6); the Jews in Corinth were far from it.

➤**3 the Lord is faithful**—in contrast to those who do not have faith (3:2). Faith on the part of men answers to faithfulness on the part of God. **stablish you**—or, strengthen you (see 2:17).

➤**4 we have confidence in the Lord**—who is faithful, trustworthy (3:3).

➤**5 the Lord**—probably refers to the Lord God. **direct**—lit., "clear the obstacles." **love of God**—meaning "God's love" or "love to God"—both are defensible. **patient waiting for Christ**—The Greek is the "patience (endurance) of Christ" (2:4; 1 Thess. 1:3). Christ set the example (Alford).

➤**6 we command you**—Paul had expressed faith in their obedience (3:4); here he put it to a particular test. **withdraw**—Paul had addressed the same problem in 1 Thessalonians 5:14, but now that it had gotten more out of hand he had to use stricter discipline. **walketh disorderly**—lives in idleness. Some of the Thessalonians, anticipating the Lord's imminent return, stopped their regular employment. **the tradition**—See comments on 2:15.

➤**7 follow**—lit., "imitate."

➤**8 eat any man's bread**—i.e., live at anyone's expense. **wrought with labour and travail**—In both letters to the Thessalonians Paul noted that he and his coworkers maintained themselves by working. In this second letter Paul pointed out that they did so especially to set a good example. In the first, their motive was represented as insuring that no one would get the idea they were preaching for monetary gain (1 Thess. 2:5, 9). The Philippians, however, did not think it was a burden to contribute to Paul's support (Phil. 4:15, 16) even while he was in Thessalonica (Acts 16:15, 34, 40). Paul also refused support at Corinth, to show himself different from the false teachers. At the writing of this letter, Paul was working with Aquila making tents (Acts 18:3).

➤**9** See 1 Corinthians 9:4-6; Galatians 6:6.

➤**10 if any would not** [is not willing to] **work, neither should he eat**—This is a saying that Paul picked up and applied to their particular situation. The saying was in common use, appearing in Hebrew in *Bereshith Rabba* and in the book *Zeror.*

➤**11 disorderly**—living in idleness. **busybodies**—meddlers in the affairs of others. Idleness is the parent of meddling (1 Tim. 5:13).

➤**12 with quietness they work**—"to work quietly for their living" (NEB).

➤**13 be not weary**—do not get tired.

➤**14 that he may be ashamed**—The Greek reads, "he may be made to turn and look into himself"—in other words, be forced into healthy introspection.

➤**15 Yet count him not an enemy, but admonish him as a brother**—Do not shun him in contemptuous silence, but tell him why he is being avoided (Matt. 18:15; 1 Thess. 5:14).

➤**16 the Lord of peace**—The same title is given to Christ as to the Father, the "God of Peace" (Rom. 15:33; 16:20; 2 Cor. 13:11). **peace**—This is the peace which he alone can give; inward and outward, now and in the future (Rom. 14:17). **always**—at all times. **by all means**—in every way.

➤**17** The letter was written by an amanuensis (secretary), perhaps Silas or Timothy, and only this closing salutation was written in Paul's own hand (cf. Rom. 16:22; 1 Cor. 16:21;

Col. 4:18). **the token**—"the distinguishing mark" (NIV), showing that this letter was not a forgery (see 2:2).

➤**18 grace**—Paul closed every letter with a prayer that his recipients would be blessed with the Lord's grace. **Amen**—is not present in the earliest manuscripts.

BIBLIOGRAPHY

Alford, Henry. *The Greek New Testament.* 1852. Reprint Grand Rapids: Guardian Press, 1976.

Dana and Mantey. *A Manual Grammar of the Greek New*

*Testament.* New York: MacMillan, 1957.

Thomas, Robert L. "Second Thessalonians" in the *Expositor's Bible Commentary.* Grand Rapids: Zondervan, 1978.

# GENERAL INTRODUCTION TO THE PASTORAL EPISTLES

The Pastoral Epistles (1 Timothy, 2 Timothy, and Titus) were the three last epistles written by Paul. Paul's authorship was affirmed in our earliest records of church history. Clement of Rome, at the end of the first century, quotes 1 Timothy 2:8 in his first *Epistle to the Corinthians* (chap. 29). The epistles are in the second century Peshitta version of the Scriptures. The Muratorian *Fragment on the Canon of Scripture,* written at the close of the second century, acknowledges them as such. Irenaeus in *Against Heresies* quotes 1 Timothy 1:4, 9; 6:20; 2 Timothy 4:9-11; Titus 3:10. Clement of Alexandria in *Stromata* quotes 1 Timothy 4:1, 10; 2 Timothy (as to deaconesses); Titus 1:12. Tertullian in *Prescription of Heretics* quotes 1 Timothy 1:18; 6:13, 20; 2 Timothy 1:14; 2:2; Titus 3:10, 11. Eusebius, the church historian includes the three in the "universally acknowledged" Scriptures. Portions of the Pastoral Epistles are alluded to by several second-century church fathers: Ignatius, Polycarp, Hegesippus, Athenagoras, and Justin Martyr.

Paul's authorship of the Pastoral Epistles was never questioned, until the nineteenth century—when various German scholars posited several arguments against Pauline authorship. First, they showed that the historical incidents in the Pastoral Epistles do not coincide with the historical incidents in Acts. This is true, but the argument does not disprove Pauline authorship. Rather, it shows that Paul must have written the Pastoral Epistles after his first imprisonment (which, historically speaking, is as far as Acts goes). Most scholars now recognize that 1 Timothy and Titus were written some time between Paul's first and second imprisonments in Rome.

The second argument against Pauline authorship has to do with style and vocabulary. Quite simply, some scholars do not believe Paul wrote the Pastoral Epistles because there are so many new words and expressions not found in his previous epistles. The careful student of Paul's epistles, however, will have seen that Paul's vocabulary and style of writing passed through various phases of development. His early epistles (1 and 2 Thessalonians, 1 and 2 Corinthians, and Romans) resemble one another in style and vocabulary. His Prison Epistles (Ephesians, Philippians, Colossians, and Philemon) are noticeably similar. And his Pastoral Epistles bear remarkable likeness to one another.

The occasions and conditions for each writing brought forth new expressions to meet the need.

The third argument raised against Pauline authorship focuses on the Pastoral Epistles' treatment of Gnosticism. Previous scholars have argued that the Gnosticism spoken against was a well-defined, second-century Gnosticism. But many present-day scholars now recognize that Gnosticism was already very well formulated in the first century. Paul had already refuted a type of Gnosticism in his Epistle to the Colossians. In the Pastoral Epistles he speaks out against another type (see 1 Tim. 6:20), a type mingled with Jewish legalism and fables (1 Tim. 1:7; 4:3; Titus 1:10, 14; 3:9), false doctrine about the resurrection (2 Tim. 2:17, 18), and certain teachings that produced questionings and strife (1 Tim. 1:4; 2 Tim. 2:23-26; 4:3, 4; Titus 1:14). All in all, the Gnostic teachings generated impiety and godlessness. To counter the errors, Paul exhorted Timothy and Titus to provide healthy, sound teachings that produce godliness and practical piety.

A fourth argument given against Pauline authorship concerns the matter of church organization. The scholars opposed to Pauline authorship have said that the ecclesiastical structure portrayed in the Pastoral Epistles represents a second-century structure, not one of the first century. However, it seems that such scholars have not made an important clarification concerning the NT perspective on the position (or function) of bishops (also called overseers) and elders (also called presbyters). According to the NT, elders functioned as overseers; in other words, the presbyters were the bishops. (See Acts 20:17 and 28 where Paul speaks of the elders at Ephesus as being the overseers of the church there. See also 1 Peter 5:1, 2 where the elders are charged to function as overseers.) After the first century, many churches appointed one elder to take the lead among the others; he was given the title "bishop." But this was not the practice in the first century, and Paul did not present this structure in the Pastoral Epistles. Quite simply, Paul spoke of elders, deacons, and deaconesses. Such church functions were present from the earliest days of the church.

The Epistles to Timothy and Titus have been called "Pastoral" because of the advice given by Paul to Timothy and Titus about pastoring (or, shepherding) the local churches under their care. Of the three Pastoral Epistles, the first to be written was 1 Timothy (written around A.D. 63), followed by Titus (written around A.D. 65/66), and then finally 2 Timothy (written just prior to Paul's death, which was in A.D. 68).

# 1 TIMOTHY

## Introduction

First Timothy was written by Paul to encourage Timothy to take care of the church, the house of the living God (3:15), in his absence. Paul directed Timothy to combat false teachers and their teaching anything different from what the apostles had taught (1:3-20). He also gave Timothy instructions about the worship in church meetings, the selection of qualified elders and deacons, the appointment of widows to church care and church service, and his relationships with sisters and older brothers in the church. (See chapters 2–5). This is followed by a personal appeal to Timothy, as a man of God, to fight the good fight of faith until the time of the Lord's appearing (see chapter 6).

*Chapter* 1

### 1-20 INTRODUCTION. WARNING AGAINST FALSE TEACHERS. PAUL'S APPRECIATION OF GRACE

➤**1 an apostle . . . by the commandment of God**—This expresses God's authority in commissioning Paul to the apostleship. In the earlier epistles the phrase is, "by the *will* of God." The implication here is that it was necessary for him to be an apostle; it was not an optional matter for Paul. (See Rom. 16:26 for a similar expression.) **God our Saviour**—referring to the Father (see Luke 1:47; 1 Tim. 2:3; 4:10; 2 Tim. 1:9; Titus 1:3; 2:10; 3:4; Jude 25). It was a Jewish expression of devotion, drawn from the OT (cf. Ps. 106:20, 21). **our hope**—See Colossians 1:27; Titus 1:2; 2:13.

➤**2 my own son**—lit., "a genuine child" (cf. Acts 16:1; 1 Cor. 4:14-17). **mercy**—added here to Paul's usual salutation: "Grace and peace." In Galatians 6:16 "peace" and "mercy" occur together. There are many similarities of style between the Epistle to the Galatians and the Pastoral Epistles (see Introduction), possibly because Paul had the same purpose in writing these letters, i.e., to correct false teachers, especially regarding the right and wrong use of the law (1:8, 9). "Mercy" is a free gift of love, expressed toward the miserable. "Grace" corresponds to the sins of men; "mercy" to men's misery. God pours out his grace to men as they are guilty, while he gives mercy to those who are miserable. **Jesus Christ**—The earlier manuscripts reverse the order, making it "Christ Jesus." In the Pastoral Epistles "Christ" is often put before "Jesus" in order to emphasize that Jesus fulfilled the messianic promises of the OT (well known to Timothy—2 Tim. 3:15).

➤**3 As I besought thee to abide still at Ephesus**—Timothy acted as a substitute for Paul in overseeing the church at Ephesus, and so his job was temporary. The office of superintending overseer, needed in Ephesus or Crete because the presiding apostle was absent, later became a permanent office when the apostle died. Paul was now urging Timothy for the second time to remain in Ephesus. **teach no other doctrine**—than what

Paul taught (cf. Gal. 1:6-9). Paul's prophetic warnings against the teachers, given years before (Acts 20:29), were now actually happening (cf. 6:3).

➤4 fables—legends about the origin and propagation of angels, such as the false teachers taught at Colosse (Col. 2:18-23). Paul elsewhere speaks of "Jewish fables" (Titus 1:14) and "old wives' fables" (4:7; 2 Tim. 4:4). endless genealogies—It was common for the Jews to trace their descent from the patriarchs (Abraham, Moses, etc.). Paul would not object to this nor would he call them "fables." Gnostic genealogies of spirits ("lists of Gnostic emanations"—as they called them) had slipped into the practice of tracing ancestors. The people doing this, while strictly obeying the Law of Moses, added to it a theosophic, ascetic tendency, pretending to see in it mysteries deeper than others could see. The "seeds," not the "full grown" Gnosticism of the post-apostolic age, existed then. The word "endless" refers to the tedious, unprofitableness of their lengthy genealogies (cf. Titus 3:9). Paul, opposing the Gnostic notion of past ages, countered their belief with his proclamation in 1:17: "He is the King of the ages, the unseen one who never dies; he alone is God and full of wisdom" (TLB). questions—of mere speculation (Acts 25:20), impractical, causing only curious discussions (see 6:4; 2 Tim. 2:14, 23). godly edifying—The earliest manuscripts read "the stewardship [or, economy] of God." Conybeare translates it, "the exercising of the stewardship of God." The believers should be exercised in promoting God's economy by carrying out the divine stewardship (see RSV, NEB mg). in faith—The carrying out of God's stewardship should be done in faith.

➤5 Now—or, "but," in contrast to the doctrine of the false teachers. the end—the goal, the aim. the commandment—Greek, "the charge," referring to 1:3. charity—love. Paul wanted Timothy to urge the church to be filled with love. Love is the totality and goal of both the law and the gospel. And love fulfills the spirit of the law in all things (Rom. 13:10). The foundation is faith (1:4), while the "end" is love (1:14). out of—springing as from a fountain. pure heart—a heart purified by faith (Acts 15:9; 2 Tim. 2:22; Titus 1:15). good conscience—or, a clear conscience. This comes by

the effect of a stable faith in Christ (1:19; 3:9). (Contrast 4:2 and Titus 1:15; with Acts 23:1.) A good conscience springs from unfeigned faith, while a bad conscience comes from an unstable faith. faith unfeigned—not a weak, hypocritical, unproductive faith, but faith working by love (Gal. 5:6). The false teachers drew men away from genuine faith to wicked ideas (1:4) and foolish talk (1:6).

➤6 From which—refers to the items mentioned in 1:5. having swerved—lit., "having missed the mark to be aimed at." It is translated "erred" in 6:21. They had not aimed at attaining the above-mentioned traits, and they had "turned away from the truth" (2 Tim. 2:18). vain jangling—vain talking (see 6:20; Titus 1:10; 3:9).

➤7 Desiring to be teachers of the law—the Jewish law (Titus 1:14; 3:9). These Judaizers appear to be distinct from those who were resisted by Paul in the Epistles to the Galatians and Romans, for they made the works of the law necessary to justification and so opposed the gospel of grace. The Judaizers spoken of here corrupted the law with "fables," which led to the subversion of morals and truth. Their error was not in meeting the obligation of the law but in abusing it by incredible and immoral interpretations of it. understanding neither what they say, nor whereof they affirm—They understood neither their own assertions about the law nor the law itself (Alford).

➤8 the law is good, if a man use it lawfully—God intended that the law be used as a means of revealing the sin in the ungodly (1:9, 10; cf. Rom. 7:7-12; Gal. 3:21), not as a means of a "righteous man" reaching higher perfection than could be reached by the gospel alone (4:8; Titus 1:14). This was the perversion of the false teachers.

➤9 the law is not made for a righteous man—not made for those whose sins are forgiven on the basis of Christ's righteousness, and whose lives are filled with the Holy Spirit. The law gives no inward power to be sanctified. As a man follows the leading of the Holy Spirit, he does not need the law, which is only an outward rule (Rom. 6:14; Gal. 5:18, 23). But the man made right before God does not always make himself completely available to the inward leading of the Spirit, and so for this reason morally needs the outward law to show him his sin and God's requirements. The reason why the Ten Commandments no longer have power to condemn the Christian is not that they have no authority over him, but that Christ has fulfilled them for us (Rom. 10:4). **disobedient**—insubordinate, unruly (Titus 1:6); those who oppose the law for whom it was made. **ungodly**—impious; those who do not respect God and openly sin against him. **unholy and profane**—those inwardly impure, and those deserving exclusion from participation in services of the sanctuary; sinners against the third and fourth commandments. **murderers of fathers . . . mothers**—sinners against the fifth commandment. **manslayers**—sinners against the sixth commandment.

➤**10 whoremongers**—fornicators; sinners against the seventh commandment. **them that defile themselves with mankind**—"sexual perverts" (TEV). **menstealers**—"slave traders" (NIV) or "kidnappers" (TLB); sinners against the eighth commandment. **any other thing**—answers to the tenth commandment in its widest aspect. Paul does not specifically describe this commandment because his purpose is to bring out the grosser forms of sin. The tenth commandment is deeply spiritual— so spiritual that the sense of sin (in its subtlest form of "evil desires") was brought home to Paul's own conscience (Rom. 7:7). By this Paul demonstrates that those would-be teachers of the law, while bragging of a higher perfection through it, bring themselves down from the gospel to the level of the grossly "lawless." It was for the lawless that the law was designed. So in practice, the greatest sticklers for the law as a means of moral perfection are those who fall completely from the morality of the law. The gospel of grace is the only way for man to become free from sin and right before God.

➤**11 According to the glorious gospel of the blessed God**—This is what frees the Christian from the law, The gospel reveals God's glory (Eph. 1:16, 17; 3:16) in making the believer "righteous" through the righteousness of Christ, without law (1:9), even by imparting that righteousness whereby the believer hates those sins the law is directed against (1:9, 10). The term "blessed" indicates immortality and supreme happiness. All blessings come from the blessed God. This term, as applied to God, occurs here and in 6:15 only. It appropriately speaks of the

"glorious gospel of the blessed God" in contrast with the curse of those under the law (1:9; Gal. 3:10). **which was committed to my trust**— Greek, "committed in trust to me."

➤**12** The honor of having the gospel ministry committed to him suggests the following digression in which he confesses that he was no better (1:13) than the lawless ones described above (1:9, 10), until the grace of the Lord visited him (1:13, 14). **I thank**—Greek, "I have (feel) thanks" or "I feel gratitude." **who hath enabled me**—lit., "who is empowering me." In effect Paul was saying, "It is not in my own strength that I bring this doctrine to men, but as strengthened and served by Him who saved me" (Theodoret). **counted me faithful**—God knew in advance that Paul would be faithful to the trust given to him. Paul's thanking God for this shows that the merit of his faithfulness was due solely to God's grace and not to his own natural ability (1 Cor. 7:25). **putting me into**— or, appointing me.

➤**13 before**—formerly. **blasphemer**—See Acts 26:9-11. **persecutor**—See Acts 22:4, 5, 19, 20; 26:10, 11; Galatians 1:13. **injurious**— meaning "insolence and violence" (Earle). **I obtained mercy**—God's mercy and Paul's need of it stand in sharp contrast (Ellicott). This sense of mercy was continually in Paul's mind (see comments on 1:2). Those who have experienced mercy can best give mercy (Heb. 5:2, 3). **because I did it ignorantly**—Ignorance in itself does not deserve to be excused, but it is a more excusable reason for unbelief than pride or purposely hardening oneself against the truth (cf. John 9:41; Acts 26:9). The word "because" does not imply that ignorance was a sufficient reason for the mercy given; rather, it shows how it was possible that such a sinner could receive mercy. God's compassion is the sole reason for the mercy shown to Paul (Titus 3:5). **in unbelief**—The ground of ignorance lies in unbelief, which implies that guilt accompanies ignorance. But there is a great difference between one's honest zeal for the law and one's willing rebellion against the Spirit of God (Matt. 12:22-32; Luke 11:52).

➤**14 the grace . . . was exceeding abundant**—"But the more we see our sinfulness, the more we see God's abounding grace forgiving us" (Rom. 5:20, TLB). **faith**—Even our faith is a gift of Christ's grace. **love**—Whereas Paul once scoffed at Christ and persecuted his people, now he loved Christ and his people because of Christ Jesus.

➤**15 faithful**—trustworthy, worthy of credit, because God is true to his word (1 Cor. 1:9; 1 Thess. 5:24; 2 Thess. 3:3; Rev. 21:5; 22:6). The expression "this is a faithful saying" is mentioned only in the Pastoral Epistles (see 4:9; 2 Tim.; 2:11; Titus 3:8); "the repeated formula is always attached to a maxim (relating either to doctrine or practice) on which full reliance can be placed" (Earle). **all acceptation** [reception]—received by all believers with their heart, soul, and mind. Unlike the false teachers (1:7), Paul knew what he was talking about, and by his simple style and message (the fundamental truth of salvation through Christ), he refuted the illusive and impractical speculations of false teachers (1 Cor. 1:18-29). **Christ Jesus came into the world to save sinners**—even renowned sinners like Saul of Tarsus. His situation was without rival since Christ's ascension, with respect to the greatness of the sin and the greatness of the mercy. The consenter to Stephen's death (the first Christian martyr) would become the preeminent champion of Stephen's message concerning Christ. **of whom I am chief**—This statement could be part of the maxim—and if so, it was something said by many early Christians, not just Paul—or an addendum reflecting Paul's personal feelings. Most commentators consider the words to be exclusively Paul's. Note, Paul did not say, "I was chief" but "I am chief," for he considered himself still to be so (1 Cor. 15:9; Eph. 3:8; cf. Luke 18:13). To each believer his own sins will always appear greater than those of others, which he will never know like his own. **chief**—foremost (the same Gk. word in 1:16). Where there was mercy for him, the greatest of sinners, there is mercy for all who come to Christ (Matt. 18:11; Luke 19:10).

➤**16 that in me**—as an example. **first**—foremost. As Paul was the foremost in sin, so God made him the foremost sample of mercy. **show**—display. **all longsuffering**—God had unlimited patience in enduring Saul, the persecutor. **a pattern**—an example, a model. The Greek word was used to mean a sketch or an outline, which afterwards would need to be filled in with details. Paul's life was such an outline; each Christian's life needs to fill in the details of the sketch Paul provided (Alford). **to**

**life everlasting**—This is the ultimate aim faith always keeps in view (Titus 1:2).

➤**17** This verse is an appropriate conclusion to the beautifully simple presentation of the gospel, of which Paul's own life is a living example. This praise comes from Paul's experiential sense of God's grace. **the King eternal**—lit., "King of the ages" (see Exod. 15:18, LXX; Ps. 145:13). The eternal King gives his believers eternal life (1:16). **immortal**—The earliest manuscripts read, "incorruptible." **invisible**—God, Spirit by nature, is invisible (6:16; Exod. 33:20; John 1:18; Heb. 11:27). Jesus Christ is his visible expression (John 1:1, 14, 18; Col. 1:15; Heb. 1:5). **only wise God**—The earliest manuscripts do not contain the word "wise." It was added later, probably borrowed from Romans 16:27. God is "the only God." **for ever and ever**—The thought of eternity (terrible as it is to unbelievers) is delightful to those assured of grace (Bengel).

➤**18** Paul continues the subject begun in 1:3. **This charge I commit unto thee**—as a sacred deposit, a sacred trust (cf. 6:20) that must be passed on to others (cf. 2 Tim. 2:2). Timothy was to fulfill his calling as a Christian and as a minister; then he could stop those who were teaching wrong doctrine (1:3). **according to the prophecies which went before on** [respecting] **thee**—i.e., the information given by prophets about Timothy at his ordination (4:14) probably by Silas, one of Paul's companions and a prophet (Acts 15:32). Such prophetic information, as well as the good report given about Timothy by the brothers (Acts 16:2), may have convinced Paul to take him as his companion. There are similar prophecies regarding others: Acts 13:1-3 (in connection with the laying on of hands); Acts 11:28; 21:10, 11; cf. 1 Cor. 12:10; 14:1; Eph. 4:11. In Acts 20:28 it is specifically said that the Holy Spirit had made the Ephesian elders overseers. Clement of Rome said that the apostles usually had a "trial by the Spirit," in order to determine who were to be overseers and deacons in several beginning churches. Clement of Alexandria said that overseers in the churches near Ephesus were marked out for ordination by a revelation of the Holy Spirit to John. **war a good warfare**—See 6:12; 2 Timothy 4:7.

➤**19 Holding faith, and a good conscience**—The loss of a clear conscience results in the loss of faith in Christ. **which**—in Greek refers to "conscience." **put away**—thrust away. **made shipwreck**—with respect to the faith. Faith is the vessel in which they had professedly embarked, of which "good conscience" is the anchor. Early Christians used this image, comparing the course of faith to navigation. The Greek does not imply that **faith** can be shipwrecked, but that a person can be shipwrecked with respect to the faith.

➤**20 Hymenaeus**—No doubt he is the Hymenaeus of 2 Timothy 2:17. Although he was given over to Satan (the ruler of all those outside the church, Acts 26:18, and the one who punishes when God allows, 1 Cor. 5:5; 2 Cor. 12:7), Hymenaeus probably was later restored to the church and troubled it again. Paul, as an apostle, pronounced the sentence to be carried out at Ephesus; it very likely involved the excommunication of wrongdoers (cf. Matt. 18:17, 18). The sentence not only had spiritual effects (being given over to Satan's control), but physical effects also. Some kind of sickness usually resulted in order to bring the offender to repentance and salvation. **Alexander**—is probably "the coppersmith" who did Paul "much evil" when Paul visited Ephesus. It is likely that Alexander was given to Satan because he fought against Paul's words (2 Tim. 4:14, 15). Hymenaeus was given to Satan because he preached the lie that the resurrection of the dead had already occurred (2 Tim. 2:18). The Alexander mentioned could be the same mentioned at the riot in Ephesus (Acts 19:33). **learn**—Greek, "be disciplined." **not to blaspheme**—the name of God and Christ. Though the apostles had the power of excommunication, accompanied with physical infliction miraculously sent (2 Cor. 10:8), ministers today have no power except that of excluding from church fellowship those who have habitually lived in sin.

# Chapter 2

## 1-15 INSTRUCTION ON CORPORATE WORSHIP

➤**1 therefore**—taking up the general subject of the epistle in continuation of the charge (1:3, 18). **first of all**—signifies the importance Paul gives to prayer. **supplications**—prayers for personal needs, petitions (Wuest). **prayers**—a general term including all kind of prayers. **intercessions**—specific requests made on behalf of others. **for all men**—Just as Christ died for all men, Christians should pray for all men.

➤**2 For kings**—Christians had been accused of showing no concern or interest to the ruling powers (Acts 17:7; Rom. 13:1-7). Therefore, Paul exhorted them to pray for those in government offices (cf. Titus 3:1). **for all that are in authority**—or, are in places of high responsibility. Christians had more direct contact with lesser rulers than with the king. **quiet**—tranquil (within). **peaceable**—free from outside political agitation or persecution. **godliness**—godly and pious living. **honesty**—The word means, "reverenced, venerable, exhibiting a dignity which arises from moral elevation, and thus invites reverence" (Vincent).

➤**3 this**—praying for all men. **is good and acceptable in the sight of God**—not in the sight of men, as if it were their favor that we aimed for (2 Cor. 8:21). **our Saviour**—He who is our Savior wills that all should be saved (2:4; Rom. 5:18); and so we should carry out God's will by praying for men's salvation. More would be saved if we prayed more. God wills salvation to all, even to those who do not as yet believe, if they will believe (cf. 4:10; Titus 2:11).

➤**4 Who will**—Greek, "who wishes" or "who desires." Since God wishes for everyone's salvation, men should wish the same; and if someone wishes for it, pray for it. Prayer makes things happen (Chrysostom). **to come unto the knowledge**—to come into a thorough, experiential knowledge (see 1 Cor. 13:12; Phil. 1:9). **the truth**—the saving truth that is in Jesus Christ (John 17:3, 17).

➤**5 one God**—"The oneness of God has a bearing on the practical question of man's salvation. It is possible for all men to be saved, because over them there are not many gods that can exercise conflicting will-power towards them, but one only. One Godhead stands over against one humanity; and the Infinite and the finite can enter into relations one with the other, since they are linked by a mediator who is both God and man" (White). **one mediator between God and men**—There is a great gulf between God and all people that can only be bridged by Christ, the mediator. **the man**—Greek, "man," absolutely and generically, not a mere individual man, but the second head of humanity representing and embodying in himself the whole human race and nature. Christ affects the whole race because there is only one mediator made to be the representative man for all men (cf. Rom. 5:15; 1 Cor. 8:6; 2 Cor. 5:19; Col. 2:14). Christ's being man was necessary to his being a mediator, sympathizing with man through experiental knowledge of our nature (Isa. 50:4; Heb. 2:14; 4:15). Even in everyday experience, almost all blessings are not given directly from God but through various other means. Moses was a mediator for Israel (Num. 14; Deut. 9), Abraham for Abimelech (Gen. 20:7), and Job for his friends (Job 42:10). All these instances forecast the great mediation for all by the one mediator, Christ. And yet, he was also God (cf. 3:16).

➤**6 gave himself**—through his death. **a ransom**—The word "ransom" in Greek is *antilutron*— made up of *anti* (signifying substitution) and *lutron* (the word used for the ransom of a slave or prisoner). "The *antilutron* is a payment given instead of the slave or prisoner, that is, in substitution for the slave or prisoner. The person holding the slave or prisoner is satisfied with the payment as a substitute for the slave he owns or the prisoner he holds" (Wuest). According to Galatians 3:13, Christ redeemed us from the curse of the law. The law held us captive to its demands, and no one but Christ could pay the price to release us from this bondage. **for all**—on behalf of all, signifying benefaction (cf. Titus 2:14); for all, not merely for a select few (cf. 2:1 where Paul urges prayer for everyone). **to be testified**—Greek, "the testimony." **in due time**—Greek, "in its own time," i.e., "in its proper time" (NIV).

➤**7 Whereunto**—Greek, "for which," referring to "the testimony" (2:6). **I am ordained**—lit., "I was placed" or "I was appointed" (see 1:12). **a preacher**—actually, "a herald" (see 1 Cor. 1:21; 9:27; 15:11; 2 Tim. 1:11; Titus 1:3). In 1:16 Paul refers to himself as an example to show everyone the gospel; here he refers to himself as a herald of the gospel to the Gentiles (Gal. 2:7, 9; Eph. 3:1-12; Col. 1:23). **I speak the truth . . . and lie not**—This is characteristic of Paul's strong spirit, which encountered frequent challenge (Rom. 11:1; 2 Cor. 11:13).

➤**8 men**—lit., "the males," as distinguished from the females. Paul had something different to say to the women in 2:9-12 (cf. 1 Cor. 11:14, 15; 14:34, 35). But the emphasis is not so much on "men" as it is on "prayer," taken up from 2:1. **lifting up holy hands**—Some of the early Christians turned up their palms toward heaven as they prayed, a typical pose for those in great need of help. Solomon did the same (1 Kings 8:22; Ps. 141:2). The Jews washed their hands before prayer (Ps. 26:6). Paul figuratively (cf. Job 17:9; James 4:8) referred to this tradition (cf. Isa. 1:15, 16). To be clean before God is a quality needed for effective prayer (Ps. 24:3, 4). **without wrath**—See Matthew 5:23, 24; 6:14, 15. **doubting**—or, disputing (see Phil. 2:14). Such things hinder prayer (Luke 9:46; Rom. 14:1; 1 Pet. 3:7).

➤**9, 10** Paul was directing his comments to women in public worship, though the rules would apply in other situations also. **modest apparel**—Women tend to want fancy and expensive clothing; and at Ephesus the wealth of some (6:17) would lead them to dress luxuriously. **shamefacedness**—modesty, respectful timidity, humility (Wuest). **good works**—in contrast with the preceding phrase. Women are to be noticed not for their outward beauty but for their inward beauty, as expressed toward others in good works (cf. 1 Pet. 3:3).

➤**11 Let the woman learn in silence with all subjection**—Women were not to teach (2:12) in public (Acts 18:25, 26), nor could they ask questions in a public meeting (1 Cor. 14:34, 35).

➤**12 usurp authority**—exercise authority.

➤**13 Adam was first formed, then Eve**—Eve was created for Adam (1 Cor. 11:8, 9).

➤**14 Adam was not deceived, but the woman being deceived was in the transgression**—Adam was not fooled by Satan, but he was persuaded by Eve (Gen. 3:17). Eve said, "The serpent tricked me" (Gen. 3:13, TLB). Last in creation, Eve was first in sin. The serpent knew Eve was weaker and so tempted her, not Adam. Eve gave in to the temptations and trickery of Satan, while Adam gave in to his love for her. Satan stands first to be judged before God, the woman next, and the man last (Gen. 3:14-19). In Romans 5:12, Adam is represented as the first sinner, but there is no reference to Eve; thus, Adam is regarded as the head of the sinning race. And so here (2:11) and there (Gen. 3:16), the woman's "subjection" is represented as the result of her being deceived.

➤**15 Notwithstanding she shall be saved in childbearing**—lit., "through childbearing." Among the several interpretations of this statement, Vine offers the one most suitable to the context: "By means of begetting children and so fulfilling the design appointed for her through acceptance of motherhood . . . she would be saved from becoming a prey to the social evils of the time and would take her part in the maintenance of the testimony of the local church." **if they**—The pronoun shifts from the singular to the plural, as Paul shifted from plural "women" in 2:10 to singular "woman" in 2:11. **continue** [remain] **in faith**—the basic way to salvation (1:5). Faith is in relation to God. **charity**—or, love, stands in relation to our fellowman. **holiness**—sanctification. **sobriety**—See 2:9. The role of women in early Christianity was that of quiet receptiveness and faithful activity in family life.

*Chapter* 3

## 1-16 OVERSEERS AND DEACONS IN THE CHURCH

➤**1 This is a true saying**—"a faithful saying" (see comments on 1:15), a fitting introduction for what follows. **desire**—aspire (lit., "to stretch one's self forward to grasp something"). The role of an overseer in Paul's day, accompanied with difficulties and often persecution, would not seem to the world as a good aspiration. **the office of a bishop**—The Greek is "the function of oversight"; hence an overseer. Elders functioned as overseers of the local church (see Acts 20:17, 28 where the words "elders" and "overseers" are used to describe the same people).

➤**2** The existence of church organization and elders at Ephesus is presupposed (5:17, 19). The fact that the church was already taking care of widows (chap. 5) supports this. Paul's directions to Timothy, the apostle in residence, pertains to filling vacancies among elders or adding more to their number. New churches in the area would also need elders. Episcopacy, or

rule by elders, was adopted in apostolic times as the most convenient form of government. The eldership followed the pattern of the Jewish synagogue. Elders ruled the synagogue (Acts 4:8; 24:1) and were also called overseers. **the husband of one wife**—This contradicts the Catholic position of celibacy. Paul was writing (1) to prohibit polygamy, (2) to prohibit remarriage after divorce, or (3) to urge an overseer to be completely dedicated to his wife (as it is in the Greek, "a one-woman man"). All three interpretations are defensible (see Litfin), but the second seems preferred by several commentators, especially the earliest exegetes. A similar restriction occurs in 5:9, but the opposite, that women should have been married only once. The common feeling among the Gentiles, as well as the Jews (cf. Anna in Luke 2:36, 37), was that those in the important position of influence and leadership, as elders were, should be free from any type of judgment or criticism. In this context the stress is laid on the reputation of the candidate in the eyes of those he is to lead (Titus 1:16). Paul's words also indicate that the man who has a wife and a good family is preferred over a bachelor. Such a man with family responsibilities would be able to relate more easily to those with families, and so he would teach both by word and example (3:4, 5). The Jews teach that a priest should be married and have children in order to remain sensitive and merciful. **vigilant**—temperate, sober. **sober**—sensible. **good behaviour**—orderly. The new man in Christ has attitudes and expressions that are set against confusion, disorder, violence, laziness, harshness, and meanness (cf. Phil. 4:8).

➤**3 Not given to wine**—not an excessive drinker. **no striker**—i.e., not violent. **not greedy of filthy lucre**—not found in any of the earliest manuscripts, it is a late interpolation, taken from Titus 1:7 (see comments there). **patient**—forbearing. **not a brawler**—lit. "not a fighter."

➤**4 One that ruleth well**—presides over. **his own house**[hold]—as contrasted with the church (the household of God—3:5, 15), which he might be called to lead. **having his children in subjection with all gravity**—cf. Titus 1:6. The fact that such a person can rule his children well means he is likely to lead the church well.

**➤5 if a man know not how to rule his own house, how shall he take care of the church of God?**—rather, "a church," a local church. How can one who cannot fulfill the less demanding role fulfill the greater and more difficult?

**➤6 Not a novice**—This shows that the church at Ephesus was established for some time. This role was absent in the Epistle to Titus because the church in Crete had just been started. The new Christian has not been disciplined and matured by problems and temptations. **lifted up with pride**—translates one Greek word meaning "wrapt in smoke," so inflated with self-conceit and exaggerated ideas of his own self-importance that, he cannot see himself or others in the true light (cf. 6:4; 2 Tim. 3:4). **fall into the condemnation of the devil**—into the same condemnation (or, judgment) as Satan fell into. Pride was the cause of Satan's downfall (Isa. 14:12-15; John 12:31; 16:11; 2 Pet. 2:4; Jude 6).

**➤7 a good report**—just as Paul was influenced by the good report of Timothy, whereby he chose him as his companion (Acts 16:2). **them which are without**—those outside the church and/or the Gentiles. An elder should have a good reputation even among those not in the church. **lest he fall into reproach and the snare of the devil**—i.e., the reproach of men and the devil's trap. "Satan likes nothing better than to disgrace God's work and God's people by trapping church leaders in sin before a watching world" (Litfin). If an elder is accused of wrongs, even if he did not do them, he will gain a bad reputation and thus lose the respect he needs to lead the flock. When Paul gave these general directions, he assumed that candidates for the eldership would have the gift of the Spirit (4:14), true faith, and that they would show these qualities by their actions.

**➤8 deacons**—The deacons were chosen by the voice of the people. Cyprian (*Epistle,* 2.5) says that a good elder never departed from the old tradition of consulting the people. The deacon's duty was to read the Scriptures in church, to instruct the new converts in Christian truths, to assist the elders at the Lord's Supper, to receive gifts and offerings, and to teach and instruct. Just as an assistant (called a "Chazzan") covered and uncovered the Ark in the synagogue, so the deacon in the early church put the coverings

on the Communion table. **grave**—serious, respectable. **doubletongued**—They must not say one thing to one man and something different to another; they must be consistent. Deacons were constantly in touch with people and so might have a tendency to do this. **not greedy of filthy lucre**—"not pursuing dishonest gain" (NIV). This is especially important, for part of the deacon's job was to collect money and distribute gifts.

**➤9 holding**—having, keeping, retaining; hence, being faithful to. **the mystery of the faith**—the secret of the Christian faith known only to those initiated into it by the revealing work of the Holy Spirit. **in a pure conscience**—with a clear conscience. The deacons needed to maintain a good conscience with regard to their participation in the Christian faith as a testimony to the local church members and to the unbelievers, who would not know the secret but could observe the behavior.

**➤10 be proved**—not by a period of probation, but by a searching inquiry directed by Timothy. If they were approved, then they would be chosen as deacons. **let them use the office of a deacon**—lit. "let them minister [function as a deacon]."

**➤11 their wives**—means the women or, more likely, "deaconesses," for there is no reason why rules would be made for the wives of deacons and not for the wives of elders. Also, a closer translation would render it "wives," omitting "their," which is not in the Greek. Probably there were deaconesses in the church at Ephesus, yet there is no mention of them in this epistle except here. If "deaconesses" were meant in this verse, then Paul would have been writing to all the persons in church service. The qualifications for both sexes seem to be similar. **faithful in all things**—This not only refers to their job as deaconesses but to all areas of life.

**➤12 Let the deacons be the husbands of one wife**—See comments on 3:2. **ruling their children and their own houses well**—Paul continually emphasized the practical side of Christianity in the Pastoral Epistles. As the miraculous gifts began to decline, other criteria had to be used in choosing officers—moral character being one of them (see Acts 6:3). Less emphasis is placed on personal excellence in the case of the deacon than in that of the elder (see comments on 3:2, 3).

►**13 used the office of a deacon**—functioned as a deacon. **purchase** [acquire] **to themselves a good degree**—lit., "a step," indicating "order, rank, position." The good standing thus gained could speak of future reward or of esteem from fellow church members.

►**14 These things write I unto thee, hoping to come unto thee shortly**—Because Paul was not sure when he would visit Timothy (3:15), he provided for Timothy's longer stay (without him) by giving him the following rules to guide him. These rules are general instructions to him as an evangelist, having been given special abilities from God (4:14). This verse supports the theory that this First Epistle to Timothy was not written after Paul's visit and departure from Ephesus (Acts 19, 20); for after visiting Ephesus he decided to spend the summer in Macedonia (1 Cor. 16:58) and the winter in Corinth. The epistle was probably written after his first imprisonment at Rome (Acts 28), at Corinth, where he might have been thinking of going to Epirus before returning to Ephesus.

►**15 But if I tarry long**—before coming to Timothy. **how thou oughtest to behave**—The Greek does not specify the substantive. Most likely, Paul was speaking of how the church members (not Timothy) ought to behave themselves. **the house of God**—"God's household," a local assembly. **the church of the living God**—lit. "an assembly of the living God." God is the ruler of the church (2 Tim. 2:19-21). The fact that Timothy's basic duty concerns God's church is the strongest motive to faithfulness for one overseeing the church. We work and suffer because of our hope in the living God (4:10). The work in one local church adds to the building of the great church of God, in which each person is a living stone (1 Pet. 2:5). **the pillar and ground** [bulwark] **of the truth**—The church is the pillar of the truth, as the continued existence (historically) of the truth rests on it, for it supports and preserves the word of truth. The person who adheres to the truth belongs to the church. Christ alone is the ground of truth in the highest sense (1 Cor. 3:11), while the apostles are foundations in a secondary sense (Eph. 2:20; Rev. 21:14). The church rests on the truth as it is in Christ; not the truth on the church. The importance of Timothy's position is emphasized by reminding him that the church is God's church and that it preserves and holds his truth (cf. Matt. 16:18). Paul set this in opposition to the coming heresies that he dealt with next (4:1ff.).

►**16 without controversy**—lit. "confessedly"; hence, "by common agreement" or "by common profession" (Earle). **great is the mystery of godliness**—or, piety. The revealed secret of godly living is found in Christ who was God lived out in the flesh. To the ungodly there is no answer—Christ is shrouded in mystery to them. But to the godly, Christ is a mystery revealed (see 1 Cor. 2:7-14; Col. 1:27). Paul now proceeds to describe this "mystery" in detail. It is possible that what follows was used as a hymn (Eph. 5:19; Col. 3:16), because it contains some of the characteristics of a Christian hymn: short, unconnected sentences with the words similarly arranged, the ideas related by opposites. The order of opposites is reversed in each new phrase, e.g., flesh and spirit, angels and nations, world and glory. **God**—The hand of the original scribes of Codex Sinaiticus, Codex Alexandrinus, and Codex Ephraem Rescriptus wrote "[he] who," which was then changed by later scribes, in all three manuscripts, to read "God." Few textual problems have occasioned so much stir and controversy as this one—especially in the nineteenth century. Many scholars entered the debate—and not without good reason, inasmuch as this verse is related to the doctrine of incarnation. When the reading in the TR and KJV ("God was manifest in the flesh") was challenged by another reading ("he who was manifest in the flesh"), some may have thought the doctrine of God becoming man was being undermined. Not so. The scholars who defended the reading with "he who" primarily did so because they realized that the second reading was a manifest emendation. In the three manuscripts just mentioned, a later scribe changed *hos* ("he who") to *theos* ("God"). In the original text, the subject of the verse is simply "who"—which most translators render as "he" and which most commentators identify as Christ (GAM). **manifest in the flesh**—Jesus Christ is God incarnate; he himself in the flesh to men (John 1:1, 14). Jesus Christ, the God-man, manifested his deity in and through his humanity. God was once manifested in the flesh of Christ and now continues to be manifested in Christ's body, the church. Thus, the church is not just maintaining an historical testimony to Christ's incarnation but it is also continuing a living manifestation of God's expression on earth (3:15). Alford said, "It is not the objective fact of God being manifested, of which the Apostle is speaking, but the life of God lived in the church—the truth of which the congregation of believers is the pillar and basement, as identical with Him who is its centre and heart and stock, as unfolded once for all in the unfolding of Him." **justified in the Spirit**—Christ, who came to earth as a man, seemed to be just like other men and, in fact, took the load of all their sins. But having died to sin and having risen again (remaining spotless and pure), Christ gained for himself and his people justification or righteousness with God (Isa. 50:8; John 16:10; Acts 22:14; Rom. 4:25; 6:7, 10; Heb. 9:28; 1 Pet. 3:18; 4:1; 1 John 2:1). By his resurrection, Christ's true, divine identity was proven, and thus he was "justified" (i.e., vindicated). And since the resurrection was empowered by the Spirit (Rom. 8:11) and Christ's resurrection state is characterized in Scripture as "Spirit" (1 Cor. 15:45; 1 Pet. 3:18)—in contrast to his life on earth which is characterized as "flesh"—it is fitting to say that he was justified in the Spirit. Romans 1:3, 4 posits the same point, for it speaks of Christ *in the flesh* as the son of David and as the Son of God through resurrection, by the Spirit of holiness. Christ's resurrection, by and in the Spirit, vindicated his divinity. Previous to his resurrection, Christ's identity was justified by the Spirit empowering his words and works, but few realized it. The resurrection was the final and ultimate proof. **seen of** [by] **angels**—This could refer to the times when angels served Christ during his earthly ministry (Matt. 4:11; Luke 22:43), or to Christ's exaltation to heaven in the presence of the angels (cf. Phil. 2:9-11; Col. 2:15), or to the fact that the angels desired to look into the events of Christ's incarnation, suffering, and glorification (1 Pet. 1:12), **preached unto the Gentiles**—After Christ's resurrection and exaltation, Christ was preached by the believers to the nations (see Matt. 28:19; Rom. 16:25, 26). **believed on in the world**—The gospel message was believed and continues to be believed. **received up into**

**glory**—referring to Christ's ascension (Mark 16:19; Luke 24:51; Acts 1:11).

Chapter **4**

1-16 INSTRUCTIONS TO TIMOTHY ABOUT ERRONEOUS TEACHINGS, GODLY LIVING, AND PREACHING THE WORD

➤**1 Now**—or "But," in contrast to the mystery of godliness. **the Spirit speaketh**—the prophets in the church, whose prophecies rested on those of the OT (Dan. 7:25; 8:23ff.; 11:30, 31), on Jesus of the NT (Matt. 24:11-24), and also on Paul himself (2 Thess. 2:3). (See also 2 Pet. 3:3; 1 John 2:18; Jude 18.) **expressly**—"in actual words," "in words actually offered" (Gk., *rhētos*). This shows that Paul referred to actual prophecies of the Spirit with which Timothy was familiar. **in the latter times**—refers to the times following the times in which he is now writing; this is not the distant future, but times immediately after these. The beginnings of the turning away from the faith were already noticeable (Acts 20:29); they were indicators of the coming last days (2 Tim. 3:1). **depart from the faith**—the apostasy or abandonment of one's faith was about to begin in the church. In 2 Thessalonians 2:3 (written earlier), the apostasy of the Jews from God (in joining the heathen against Christ's church) is the basis upon which the prophecy arises. But here, in the Pastoral Epistles, the prophecy is connected with gnostic errors, which had already been sown in the church (2 Tim. 2:18) (Auberleen). Apollonius Tyanaeus, a heretic, came to Ephesus during Timothy's lifetime. **giving heed**—See 1:3, 4; Titus 1:14. **seducing spirits**—working in the heretical teachers. (cf. the use of "the spirit of error" opposed to "the spirit of truth" in 1 John 4:2, 3, 6.) **doctrines of devils**—i.e., teaching suggested by demons (cf. James 3:15).

➤**2** This verse should be translated, "through the pretensions of liars whose consciences are seared" (RSV). This verse, continuing the idea of 4:1, shows how some will be deceived to depart from the faith. The means by which the false teachers deceive is their false sanctity (4:3). **their conscience seared with a hot iron**—The words "hot iron" have been added by the KJV translators. The Greek says, "branded in their conscience." The metaphor is from the practice of branding slaves or criminals, the latter on the brow. These deceivers are not acting under delusion but are acting deliberately against conscience. They wear the form of godliness and contradict their profession by their crooked conduct (2 Tim. 3:5). "The brand is not on their brow but on their conscience" (Vincent). The image also depicts searing something with a cauter.

➤3 Forbidding to marry . . . to abstain from meats—A concern to curb sensual appetites has often led to false spiritualism. While the man with a pure heart sees purity in everything, the man with an evil heart finds evil in everything, for his dirty mind affects all that he sees and hears (Titus 1:15). By a false spiritualism (2 Tim. 2:18), which made moral perfection consist of abstaining from outward things, they pretended to attain a higher perfection. They prohibited marriage (cf. Matt. 19:10-12 with 1 Tim. 5:14) and the eating of meat (using the OT distinction as to clean and unclean—cf. Col. 2:16, 17; 20-23). Their outward denial of marriage and meat made them look holy, but they were not actually spiritual (Col. 2:23). The historian Eusebius (*Ecclesiastical History,* 4.29) quotes a statement from Irenaeus (1.28). He said that Satunninus, Marcion, and the Encratites preached abstinence from marriage and animal meats. Paul warned against such beliefs (cf. 6:20; 2 Tim. 2:17, 18). **which God hath created to be received with thanksgiving of [by] them which believe and know the truth**—Even though food was created by God for all mankind (Ps. 104:14; Matt. 5:45), only those who believe God and know the truth of God's creation enjoy God's provision with genuine thankfulness to the Creator. This is opposed to those who abstain from food, or to those who eat it, but are not thankful for it.

➤4 For every creature [creation] of God is good—See Genesis 1:31; Romans 14:14, 20. Gnostics opposed the creation scheme. Judaism started the error about meat-eating (Acts 10:11-16; 1 Cor. 10:25, 26), and then oriental Gnostics added new elements. **nothing to be refused, if it be received with thanksgiving**—Meats are pure in themselves but become impure by being received without thanksgiving (Rom. 14:6; Titus 1:15).

➤5 For it is sanctified by the word of God and prayer—Prayers of consecration (setting apart as sacred or holy) mainly consisted of portions from God's Word. The *Apostolic Constitutions* give this ancient prayer of grace, basically consisting of Scripture: "Blessed art thou, O Lord, who feedest me from my youth, who givest food to all flesh: Fill our hearts with joy and gladness, that we, having all sufficiency, may abound unto every good work in Christ Jesus our Lord, through whom glory, honor, and might, be to thee for ever. Amen" (7.49).

➤6 put the brethren in remembrance of these things—i.e., suggest these things to the brothers. The things are the truths stated in 4:4, 5, in opposition to the errors forecast in 4:1-3. **minister**—servant. **nourished**—Greek, "being nourished," "continually fed" (cf. 2 Tim. 1:5, "still trusting"; 3:14, "keep on believing"—TLB). **the words of faith**—in opposition to the "devil-inspired" teaching which Timothy was to refute (cf. 1:10, 11; 6:3; Titus 1:9; 2:1). **thou hast attained**—actually, "you have followed" (see 2 Tim. 3:10).

➤7 refuse—have nothing to do with such talk (2 Tim. 2:23; Titus 3:10). **profane and old wives' fables**—See 1:3, 4, 9; Titus 1:14. They are profane, or godless, because they lead away from godliness (cf. 1:4-7; 6:20; 2 Tim. 2:16; Titus 1:1, 2). **exercise thyself rather unto godliness**—This is not the exercise of asceticism, like those with devil-inspired ideas (4:3, 8; cf. 2 Tim. 2:22, 23; Heb. 5:14; 12:11), but the exercise of practical piety (6:11, 12).

➤8 bodily exercise profiteth little—i.e., is profitable to a small extent; viz., to a small part of one's being (the body). Bodily exercise in this context means the exercise of self-control over fleshly desire (see Col. 2:23). **godliness is profitable unto all things**—i.e., profitable not just to one portion of man's being but to every portion of it, bodily and spiritual, temporal and eternal (Alford). **having promise of the life that now is, and of that which is to come**—i.e., "holding promise for the present life and the life to come" (NIV). God's life enriches our lives now and guarantees us eternal life.

➤9 This is a faithful saying—See 1:15; 2 Timothy 2:11. This confirms the statement in 4:8 and leads into the rest of 4:9, 10. **acceptation**—reception.

➤**10 we both labour and suffer reproach, because we trust in the living God**—Godly men seem to suffer in this life, yet Paul had balanced this with what he said in 4:8. They work hard and suffer much because they have placed, and do place, their hope in the living God. Their hard work and suffering are consistent with what they have from the living God, even in this present life (Mark 10:30, "a hundred times over . . . with persecutions!" (TLB), and much more in the life to come. **who is the Saviour of all men, specially of those that believe**—If God died for all, and is in that sense the Savior of all, consider how much more he is the Savior "for those who have accepted his salvation" (TLB).

➤**12 Let no man despise thy youth**—Be respected in spite of your youth! (cf. Titus 2:15). Timothy was very young when he joined Paul (Acts 16:1-3). About eleven years passed until the time after Paul's first imprisonment. Timothy was still young, especially compared with Paul, whose place he was filling. As a young man, he was to treat the older men as if they were his father (5:1). His duties in reprimanding, encouraging, and ordaining were normally the responsibilities of an older man. **be thou an example**—for this is the best way to gain respect as a young man.

➤**13 Till I come**—Then Timothy's job would be taken over by Paul (1:3; 3:14). **reading**—The tradition of reading Scripture aloud in corporate meetings was transferred from the Jewish synagogue to the Christian church (see Luke 4:16-20; Acts 13:15; 15:21; 2 Cor. 3:14). The NT Gospels and Epistles, recognized as being inspired by those who had the gift of discerning spirits, were read in the church along with the OT (1 Thess. 5:21, 27; Col. 4:16). The Scriptures are central to the teachings and ministry of the church.

➤**14 Neglect not the gift that is in thee**—by letting it lie unused. In 2 Timothy 1:6 the gift is expressed as the flame of the Holy Spirit; this needs to be stirred up in order to be used effectively. The gift of the Spirit would qualify Timothy for the work of winning others to Christ, or would enable him to discern the spirits, a gift needed especially by an overseer. **given thee by prophecy**—given by God, accompanied by a prophet's message (see comments on 1:18). **with the laying on of the hands of the presbytery** [body of elders]— The same was done in Joshua's case (Num. 27:18-20; Deut. 34:9). In 2 Timothy 1:6, the apostle mentions only his own laying on of hands. But Paul's purpose there is to remind Timothy of the special part that he played in the transmitting of this gift. In this case he mentions that the neighboring elders took part in this ceremony, but he was in charge.

➤**15 Meditate**—or, practice. TLB says, "put these abilities to work." These abilities are of no use unless they are used. **give thyself wholly to them**—or, be totally absorbed in them. This is the secret of doing one's task well. Other pursuits come and go, but this task never goes out of style; it is never obsolete. A minister must first be his own scholar before he can be another's teacher. **profiting**—actually, "advance." Timothy needed to advance in the Christian life, and especially toward the realization of the ideal of a Christian minister (4:12).

➤**16 Take heed unto thyself, and unto the doctrine**—"Watch your life and doctrine closely" (NIV). The teaching of an elder will "go in one ear and out the other" unless he lives what he teaches. **continue in them**—In faithfully doing his duty to others, the minister receives God's blessing.

*Chapter* **5**

## 1-25 INSTRUCTIONS TO TIMOTHY ABOUT WIDOWS AND ELDERS

➤**1 Rebuke not an elder**—an older man. As Timothy was instructed to conduct himself so that others would not think little of him because he was young (4:12), so here he is instructed to keep in mind his young age and behave with modesty and respect toward those older than he.

➤**2 with all purity**—respectful treatment of the other sex will promote purity.

➤**3 Honour widows that are widows indeed**—i.e., that are really widows, unlike those in 5:4 who have children or relatives to take care of them and those who are always seeking pleasure (5:6). But these widows are those most likely to trust completely in God, to pray constantly, and to carry out the duties assigned to church widows (5:5). Care for widows, at one time a responsibility of the Jewish economy, came to the Christian tradition, as well (Deut. 14:29; 16:11; 24:17, 19).

➤4 **let them learn first to show piety at home**—not at the church, where the widow would be a comparative stranger. The widow has a claim on her own children, prior to her claim on the church; and so the children and grandchildren should fulfill this prior claim by supporting her with material necessities. **requite their parents**—including progenitors, i.e., their grandmother or mother. Some widows claimed church support even though they had children or grandchildren to support them.

➤5 **desolate**—without children or grandchildren to support her. **trusteth in God, and continueth in supplications and prayers**— This verse specifies another qualification for a widow receiving church support. In addition to being "desolate," she must be looking to God for his help (through supplication) and continue in prayer. Her being poor and alone would enable her to devote the rest of her life to God and the church (see 1 Cor. 7:33, 34). Compare Anna, who was an eighty-four-year-old widow, who "never left the Temple but stayed there night and day, worshiping God by praying and often fasting" (Luke 2:36, 37, TLB). Such a person would be most deserving of the church's help, for she would be promoting the cause of Christ's church by praying for it.

➤6 **But she that liveth in pleasure**—This is in contrast to the Christian widows in 5:5, and therefore one who in no way deserves support from the church. **is dead while she liveth**—They are dead in the Spirit while alive in the flesh (Matt. 8:22; Eph. 5:14).

➤7 **that they may be blameless**—i.e., the widows who receive support.

➤8 **But**—refers back to what was said in 5:4. **if any provide not for his own** [relatives], **and specially for those of his own house[hold], he hath denied the faith**—Faith without love and its works is dead. If in any case a duty of love is plain, it is in relation to one's own relatives. To fail in so clear an obligation is a plain lack of love and therefore lack of faith. **worse than an infidel** [unbeliever]— The unbelievers are taught by nature to provide for their own family, and they generally recognize this duty. The Christian who fails to do this is worse (Matt. 5:46, 47). He has less excuse

with his greater light than the unbeliever who may break the laws of nature.

➤9 **Let not a widow be taken into the number under threescore** [sixty] **years old**— i.e., enrolled; added to the list of widows who received support and who prayed for the church (5:5) and did good deeds (5:10). These women, who were not deaconesses, were chosen at a younger age (forty was the age fixed at the Council of Chalcedon in A.D. 451). They were a band of widows set apart to the service of God and the church. Traces of such a class appear in Acts 9:41. Dorcas herself was one. As it was better that an elder should be married only once, so it was in the case of this class of widows. Tertullian, Hermas, and Chrysostom mention this class of widows in their writings. The widows were to be sixty years or older and were to resemble the elders both in the respect paid to them and in their duties. They ministered to other widows and orphans—a ministry to which their own experiential knowledge of the feelings of such people had equipped them. They were supported by the church, but they were not the only widows so supported (5:3, 4). **having been the wife of one man**—in order not to offend and thus turn away the Jews and heathen who regarded second marriages with disfavor (see 3:2; Titus 1:6).

➤10 **Well reported of for good works**— This corresponds to 3:7 with respect to an elder: "he must be well spoken of by people outside the church" (TLB). **she has brought up children**—This qualification would prepare her for taking proper care of orphan children. **lodged strangers**—See 3:2; Titus 1:8. **washed the saints' feet**—The washing of feet was one way these women showed their kindness to other Christians (cf. John 13:3-12). **relieved the afflicted**—either through financial or other help. **followed . . . good**—See 1 Thessalonians 5:15; cf. instances in Matthew 25:35, 36.

➤11 **The younger widows**—are those under sixty years of age (5:9). **refuse**—to put them on the list. **wax wanton against Christ**— i.e., "their sensual desires overcome their dedication to Christ" (NIV), or they "disregard their vow to Christ" (TLB). See 2 Chronicles 26:16. **they will**—they desire.

➤12 **damnation**—actually, "judgment." **they have cast off their first faith**—i.e., their pledge to Christ and his church. There could be no hardship at sixty years and upwards in not marrying again (see 5:9) in order to serve Christ better. No rules existed against remarriage for ordinary widows (1 Cor. 7:39). The special class of widows (see 5:9) did not remarry because the single life was holier than a married life, but because the interests of Christ's cause made it desirable (see 3:2). Their first pledge was to Christ, but now they wanted to transfer that first pledge to a husband (cf. 1 Cor. 7:3, 34).

►13 idle—See 2 Thessalonians 3:11. from house to house—of the members of the church (cf. 2 Tim. 3:6). tattlers—gossips. busybodies—This usually comes from idleness.

►14 I will [give counsel] therefore that the younger women [widows] marry—This statement is not inconsistent with 1 Corinthians 7:40; for the events surrounding the two cases were distinct (cf. 1 Cor. 7:26). Marriage is advised to prevent inordinate passion, laziness, and other evils mentioned in 5:11-13. Naturally, where there was no inclination toward these evils, marriage would not be so important. Paul speaks of what is generally desirable, expecting that problems like this would arise. bear children—See 2:15. In this way they would gain one of the qualifications (5:10) for later becoming one of the widows mentioned in 5:9, 10. guide the house—lit. "be lord of the household"—which means to be the master of the household affairs. give none occasion to the adversary [the opposer] to speak reproachfully—See 3:7; 6:1; Titus 2:5, 10. It is generally agreed that the opposer here is not Satan but some human adversary; but because the next verse speaks of Satan, some commentators think the opposer here and Satan in 5:15 are one and the same.

►15 some are already turned aside after Satan—not by falling away from the faith but by such errors mentioned in 5:11-13. Because of this, others have said things against them (5:14).

►16 If any man or woman that believeth have widows—as relatives. let them relieve them—of their burdens. let not the church be charged—burdened with the care of the widows. widows indeed—really widows (see 5:3).

►17 the elders that rule well be counted worthy of double honour—i.e., "be highly appreciated and paid well" (see 1 Cor. 9:14; Gal. 6:6; 1 Thess. 5:12). especially they who labour in the word and doctrine—The elders who labor in teaching the word should be highly respected.

►18 For the scripture saith—The first statement quoted ("Thou shalt not muzzle the ox that treadeth out the corn") comes from Deuteronomy 25:4; the second statement ("the labourer is worthy of his reward") comes from Luke 10:7, the words of Jesus. If Paul extends the phrase, "For the scripture saith," to this second clause, then he would be recognizing the Gospel of Luke as inspired Scripture. There is good reason to think this to be the case, for Luke's Gospel was probably in circulation for eight or nine years prior to the writing of 1 Timothy. However, if "For the scripture saith," applies only to the passage quoted from Deuteronomy 25:4, then his quotation would be that of a common proverb, quoted also by the Lord (Matt. 10:10).

►19 before two or three witnesses—A judicial conviction was not permitted in Deuteronomy 17:6; 19:15, unless at least two or three witnesses testified (cf. Matt. 18:16; John 8:17; 2 Cor. 13:1; 1 John 5:6, 7). In this case, it was not for Timothy to punish judicially, but to correct with stern language. It was important that there be two or three witnesses, for in an elder's dealings with those who disagreed in the faith (Titus 1:9), he would be constantly subject to false accusations. A strong testimony was required against elders who, in order to be efficient, were to be without blame (3:2; Titus 1:6). Verses 21 and 24 imply that Timothy had the power of judgment in the church. He would not condemn any except on the testimony of two or three witnesses, but in ordinary cases he would correct them (as the law of Moses also allowed) on the testimony of only one witness. But in the case of elders he would require two or three witnesses even before correcting them, for their character of innocence stands higher, and they are exposed to envy and false accusation more than others (Bengel).

►20 rebuke before all—publicly before the church (Matt. 18:15-17; 1 Cor. 5:9-13; Eph. 5:11). Not until this "rebuke" was ignored was the offender to be excommunicated. that others also may fear—See Deuteronomy 13:11; Acts 5:11.

►21 I charge thee—cf. 2 Timothy 4:1. before God, and the Lord Jesus Christ—

They will testify against you if you ignore what I say. **and the elect angels**—in opposition to the angels who sinned (2 Pet. 2:4). Angels take part by action and sympathy in the affairs of the earth (Luke 15:10; 1 Cor. 4:9). **observe these things**—refers to 5:19, 20. **without preferring one before another, doing nothing by partiality**—No one deserves preferential treatment. Prejudices are not to interfere.

➤**22 Lay hands suddenly on no man**—most likely, referring to a prohibition against hasty ordination, although it could refer to restoring an offender by the laying on of hands (see NEB mg). The way to avoid scandals with elders is to be very cautious and discerning as to the character of the candidate before he is ordained. **neither be partaker of other men's sins**—For in so doing you become in some degree responsible for his sins. **keep thyself pure**—Keep yourself clear of participating in other men's sins by rebuking those that do sin (5:20).

➤**23 Drink no longer water, but use a little wine**—This is a modification of the previous warning to stay away from sin. Elders and deacons were warned against drinking (3:3, 8). Timothy seems to have had a tendency to unnecessary ascetical strictness at this point. Paul means to say that Timothy is not to drink water only, but is to use a little wine, as needed for his health, and condemns by inference the rules among various groups that prohibit the use of wine.

➤**24, 25** Two kinds of sins are specified: first, those sins that everyone knows about; and second, those sins which are hidden until the judgment day. So in 5:25 there are two classes of good works: those that everyone sees and those that are hidden. After Paul has told Timothy (1) to rebuke those that sin in front of the church (5:20); (2) to stay away from all sin (5:22); and (3) to use a little wine for medicinal purposes (5:23), he then returns to the subject of Timothy's being forceful as an overseer. He must rebuke sin, whether in elders or others, in order to avoid participation in men's sins by ordaining ungodly candidates. So he says that there are two classes of sins, as there are two classes of good works: the evident and the hidden. The evident should be acted upon immediately when the situation arises, whether to rebuke in general or to ordain ministers in

particular. As to the hidden, only the final judgment can decide.

*Chapter* **6**

**1, 2 INSTRUCTIONS TO SLAVES**
➤**1 servants** [slaves] **. . . count their own masters worthy of all honour**—See Titus 2:9. This command is natural, for there was a danger of Christian slaves feeling that they were above their heathen masters. **that the name of God and his doctrine be not blasphemed**—Heathen masters would say, "What kind of a God is the God of the Christians?" if they observed disrespect from those who worshiped him (Rom. 2:24; Titus 2:5, 10).

➤**2 they that have believing masters, let them** [the slaves] **not despise them** [the masters], **because they** [the masters] **are brethren**—The Christian slave who has a Christian master should not despise him for maintaining him in slavery, but rather love him as a brother in Christ and serve him.

**3-10 WARNINGS AGAINST HETERODOXY AND MONEY-LOVING**
➤**3 teach otherwise**—Greek, "teach heterodoxically." Any teaching not in line with the apostles' teaching was heterodox. **wholesome**—Greek, "healthy." **words of our Lord Jesus Christ**—words spoken by Paul, inspired by the Lord Jesus Christ.

➤**4 proud**—See 3:6. While **knowing nothing** of the truth which is according to godliness, he thinks his knowledge is the highest (1:7). **doting about questions and strifes of words**—The Greek word for "doting" means "being sick"—as opposed to being healthy (6:3). Such people have a morbid craving for controversy.

➤**5 Perverse disputings**—The earliest manuscripts read, "perpetual disputings (or, wranglings)." **men of corrupt minds**—The corrupt mind is the source of strife. **destitute of the truth**—deprived of the truth (cf. Titus 1:14). **supposing that gain is godliness**—i.e., imagining that the practice of piety would be a way of advancing one's worldly interests.

➤**6 godliness with contentment is great gain**—Although material wealth in this world makes a man rich, it will not make him truly rich.

**►7** This verse is drawn from OT verses like Job 1:21 and Ecclesiastes 5:15.

**►9 will be rich**—desire to be rich, i.e., desire to have more than food and clothing. They are resolved to have riches at any cost (Prov. 28:20, 22). This is fatal to being happy and good (6:6). Rich men are not told to throw away their riches, but not to "trust" in them and to "do good" with them (6:17, 18; Ps. 62:10). **fall into temptation and a snare** [trap]—Once one is caught in this trap of wanting wealth, no matter what it takes, one falls deeper and deeper into sin, finally ending up in **destruction and perdition**—lit. "ruin and destruction."

**►10 For the love of money is the root of all evil**—not money itself, but the love of it is the root of all evil. The wealthy may be rich not in a bad sense, while the poorest may covet in a bad sense (Ps. 62:10). Love of money is not the sole root of evil, but it is a leading root of bitterness. **erred from the faith**—See 1:19; 4:1. **pierced themselves through with many sorrows**—cf. Proverbs 1:32.

## 11-21 PAUL'S CHARGE TO TIMOTHY

**►11 man of God**—This phrase applies primarily to Timothy as a minister (cf. 2 Pet. 1:21), just as the term was used for Moses (Deut. 33:1), Samuel (1 Sam. 9:6), Elijah, and Elisha. It applies secondarily to him as a Christian born of God (James 1:18; 1 John 5:1), no longer a man of the world. He is God's property, not his own; he was bought with a price and so has relinquished all rights to himself. Christ's work is to be his greatest work, and he is to be Christ's living representative. **flee these things**—i.e., the love of money with its evil results (6:9, 10). **follow after**—pursue (cf. 2 Tim. 2:22).

**►12 Fight the good fight of faith**—Some scholars think this letter was written from Corinth, where contests or national games were continually held. The word for "fight" refers to such a contest (see also 1 Cor. 9:24-26; 2 Tim. 4:7). **lay hold on eternal life**—just as one would hold tightly the crown or garland (the victor's prize) that he would receive for a good fight (cf. Phil. 3:12-14; 2 Tim. 4:7, 8). **a good profession**—the good confession, the confession of the Christian faith. This is probably the confession for which Timothy was set apart as

a minister, or the confession he made at the time of his baptism.

**►13 quickeneth**—Greek, "preserves life," a different word than the one that means "give life" or "quickeneth." The God who preserves life can preserve Timothy in his spiritual struggle and warfare. **before Pontius Pilate witnessed a good confession**—It was Christ's part to witness, Timothy's part to confess. The confession was Christ's testimony that he was king and his kingdom was truth (John 18:36, 37). Christ, in witnessing to this truth, attested to the truth of the whole of Christianity. So Timothy's confession or profession included the whole of the Christian truth.

**►14 keep this commandment**—See 1:5. **without spot, unrebukeable** [without reproach]—cf. Ephesians 5:27; James 1:27; 2 Peter 3:14. **the appearing**—Greek "epiphany," meaning "a divine appearance" or "an appearance of Deity" (see 2 Thess. 2:8; Titus 2:13). The church's attitude is that of constant expectation of his appearing (1 Cor. 1:8; Phil. 1:6, 10).

**►15 Which**—refers to "the appearing" in 1:14. **in his times**—or, in its own time. God regulates the appropriate time for all his actions (see Matt. 24:36). **he shall show**—The pronoun here has been added; the actual subject of the clause is "the blessed and only Potentate," whom most commentators designate as God the Father. **Potentate**—Greek *dynastēs* (cf. "dynasty"), meaning "ruler," "sovereign," or "possessor of power" (Cremer, Earle). **King of kings**—lit., "King of the ones reigning." **Lord of lords**—lit., "Lord of the ones lording." The two titles are applied to Christ in Revelation 17:14 and 19:16. They are used for God in the OT in Deuteronomy 10:17; Psalm 136:3; Daniel 4:34, LXX (Earle).

**►16 Who only hath immortality**—i.e., who alone is not subject to death. The word "immortality" (lit., "not dying") appears only here and in 1 Corinthians 15:53, 54 in the NT. **dwelling in the light which no man can approach**—After life comes the mention of light, as in John 1:4. That light is unapproachable by creatures, unless God himself admits them to it. It is unapproachable because of its tremendous brightness. If a person cannot stare at the sun, which is a small part of creation, how much less can mortal man look on the inexpressible glory of God (Ps. 104:2; 1 John 1:5). **whom no man hath seen, nor can see**—See Exodus 23:20; John 1:18; Colossians 1:15; Hebrews 11:27; 1 John 4:12. Perhaps even in their perfect state no creature will ever fully see God. Yet the saints, in some sense, will have the joy of seeing him (Matt. 5:8; 1 Cor. 13:12; Rev. 22:4).

➤**17** Paul resumes the subject of 6:5, 10. God's immortality alone is rich in glory. Therefore, his people should not lust for money (cf. 6:14-16). From speaking of the desire to be rich, Paul continues to those who are rich and addresses (1) their attitude toward money, (2) the use of their wealth, and (3) the results of using their money for God's work. **high-minded**—Pride is often the character of the rich (Rom. 12:16). **nor trust in uncertain riches**—Such trust would be trusting in uncertainty (Prov. 23:5). **who giveth us richly**—He gives both the things on earth and in heaven, for the body and the soul. **all things to enjoy**—Enjoyment consists in giving, not in taking and possessing for ourselves only.

➤**18 rich in good works**—Richness in faith produces good works (James 2:5). **ready to distribute**—"share with others" (TLB). **willing to communicate**—ready contributors. See Galatians 6:6; Hebrews 13:16.

➤**19 Laying up in store for themselves a good foundation**—This treasure is wisely laid in heaven whereas our earthly treasures are wisely distributed and shared with others (6:18). **against the time to come**—"for the future." **lay hold on eternal life**—The life now lived cannot be called a safe investment, for its

goods are only temporal: life itself is like a vapor (James 4:14). Only eternal life is secure and lasting.

➤**20 O, Timothy**—is a personal appeal, showing Paul's affection for Timothy. **keep that which is committed to thy trust**—Greek, "guard the deposit," i.e., that which Paul put into Timothy and committed to his care (see 1:18; 2 Tim. 1:12, 14; 2:2). **avoiding**—or, "turn away from," just as others have turned away from the truth (1:6; 5:15; 2 Tim. 4:4). **profane**—Cf. 4:7; 2 Timothy 2:16. **vain babblings**—empty utterances. **oppositions**—Some of these arguments centered around the heresy of dualistic oppositions (Alford), i.e., between the good and evil principle, eventually developed in Gnosticism. **science falsely so called**—Greek, "falsely named knowledge," a reference to Gnosticism (Gk., *gnōsis*). The Gnostics claimed to have special knowledge (Col. 2:8, 18, 23), which they taught in several churches. In order to guard against their errors, certain creeds were formulated. They were called symbols (or "watchwords") and were used as a test whereby the true believers could distinguish orthodoxy from heterodoxy and heresy. Perhaps 6:20 and 2 Timothy 1:13, 14 imply the existence of some short formulas of doctrine then in existence.

➤**21 Which**—refers to "the falsely named knowledge" (6:20). **professing**—belief in Gnosticism. **erred**—lit., "missed the mark" (see 1:6). **concerning the faith**—the Christian faith. **Grace**—All of Paul's epistles conclude with a benediction of grace. **Amen**—is not present in the earliest manuscripts.

BIBLIOGRAPHY

Alford, Henry. *The Greek New Testament.* 1852. Reprint. Grand Rapids: Guardian Press, 1976.

Auberlen, Karl. *The Epistles of Paul.* New York: Charles Scribners, 1870.

Bengel, John A. *New Testament Word Studies.* 1742. Reprint. Grand Rapids: Eerdmans, 1971.

Cremer, Hermann. *Biblico-Theological Lexicon of the New Testament Greek.* Edinburgh: T & T Clark, 1878.

Earle, Ralph. "First Timothy" in the *Expositor's Bible Commentary.* Grand Rapids: Zondervan, 1978.

Ellicott, Charles J. *Commentaries, Critical and Grammatical, on the Epistles of St. Paul.* Boston: Draper, 1866.

Litfin, A. Duane. "First Timothy" in *The Bible Knowledge Commentary.* Wheaton, Ill.: Victor Books, 1983.

Vincent, M. R. *Word Studies in the New Testament.* 1886. Reprint. Grand Rapids: Eerdmans, 1946.

Vine, W. E. *An Expository Dictionary of New Testament Words.* Westwood, New Jersey: Revell, 1940.

White, Newport J. D. "First and Second Epistles to Timothy" in the *Expositor's Greek Testament.* Grand Rapids: Eerdmans, 1979.

Wuest, Kenneth. *Word Studies in the Greek New Testament: The Pastoral Epistles.* Grand Rapids: Eerdmans, 1954.

# 2 TIMOTHY

## Introduction

Paul, in the interval between his first and second imprisonment, after having written 1 Timothy from Macedonia, returned to Ephesus as he had intended, by way of Troas, where he left the books, etc. with Carpus (4:13). From Ephesus he went to Crete for a short visit and returned, and then wrote to Titus. Next he went by Miletus to Corinth (4:20), and then to Nicopolis (Titus 3:12), whence he proceeded to Rome. From prison there he wrote the Second Epistle to Timothy, shortly before his martyrdom. It is not certain where Timothy was at this time. Some of the internal evidence favors the view of his having been then at Ephesus: (1) Paul's salutation to Priscilla and Aquila, who generally resided in Ephesus (4:19); (2) Paul's mention of the household of Onesiphorus, who were said to have ministered to Paul at Ephesus (1:14-16); (3) also, the Hymenaeus of 2:17 seems to be the same as the Hymenaeus at Ephesus (1 Tim. 1:20); and (4) probably "Alexander the coppersmith" (4:14) is the same as the Alexander joined with Hymenaeus in 1 Timothy 1:20. Thus, Timothy was probably in Ephesus when Paul wrote this epistle.

Paul did not write 2 Timothy during his first imprisonment, but during his second. This is substantiated by the following points: (1) Paul's first imprisonment, described in Acts 28, was much milder than that of the imprisonment in which he wrote 2 Timothy. In the former, he had liberty to lodge in his own hired house and to receive all comers, guarded only by a single soldier. In the latter, he was so closely confined that Onesiphorus had difficulty finding him; he was chained, his friends had forsaken him, and he had narrowly escaped sentence of execution from the Roman emperor. He was probably under military custody, as in his former imprisonment, though of a severer kind (1:16-18; 2:9; 4:6-8, 16, 17). (2) The visit to Troas (4:13) can hardly have been that mentioned in Acts 20:5-7, the last before his first imprisonment. For if it were, the interval between that visit and the first imprisonment would be seven or eight years, a long period for him to be without his cloak and parchments. Paul's leaving Trophimus sick at Miletus (4:20) could not have been on the occasion mentioned in Acts 20:15, for subsequent to that, Trophimus was with Paul in Jerusalem (Acts 21:29). (3) The words (4:20), "Erastus abode at Corinth," imply that Paul had shortly before been at Corinth where he left Erastus. But before his first imprisonment, Paul had not been at Corinth for several years;

and in the interval Timothy had been with him so that Timothy did not need to be told about that visit (Acts 20:2, 4). For all these reasons the imprisonment, during which he wrote 2 Timothy, is shown to be his second imprisonment. So Clement of Rome (B.1.5), the disciple of Paul, states, "In the east and west, Paul as a preacher instructed the whole world [i.e., the Roman Empire] in righteousness, and having gone to the extremity of the west, and having borne witness before the rulers (of Rome), he so was removed from the world." This implies that he fulfilled his design (Rom. 15:24-28) of a missionary journey into Spain. The canon of the New Testament, compiled about A.D. 170 (called Muratori's *Canon*), also mentions "the journey of Paul from Rome to Spain."

Paul's martyrdom is said to have occurred in Nero's reign (see Eusebius' *Ecclesiastical History*, 2.22; and Jerome's *Catalog of Scriptures*). About five years elapsed between the first imprisonment, A.D. 63 (Acts 28), and his martyrdom, A.D. 68, the last year of Nero's reign. He was probably arrested by the magistrates in Nicopolis (Titus 3:12) in Epirus in the winter, on a double charge: first, of being one of the Christians who had conspired (as was alleged by Nero's partisans) to set fire to Rome (A.D. 64); second, of introducing a novel and unlawful religion. All his friends except Luke left him—Demas from "love of this present world," the others from various causes (4:10, 11). On the first charge he seems to have been acquitted. His liberation from his first imprisonment took place in A.D. 63, the year before the great fire at Rome, which Nero made the pretext for his persecution of the Christians. Every cruelty was heaped on them: some were crucified; some were covered with the skins of wild beasts and hunted to death by dogs; some were wrapped in pitch-robes and set on fire by night to illuminate the circus of the Vatican and gardens of Nero. But now (A.D. 67 or 68) some years had elapsed since the first excitement that followed the fire. Hence, Paul, being a Roman citizen, was treated in his trial with a greater respect for the forms of the law and was very likely acquitted (4:17) on the first charge. Alexander the coppersmith seems to have been a witness against him (4:14). Had he been condemned on the first charge, he would probably have been burnt alive, as the preceding martyrs were, for arson. His judge was the city Prefect. Clement of Rome specifies that Paul's trial was not before the emperor but "before the rulers." No advocate ventured to plead his cause, no patron appeared for him who under ordinary circumstances might have aided him. He was remanded for the second stage of his trial. He did not expect this to occur until the following "winter" (4:21), whereas it probably took place about mid-summer—if in Nero's reign, not later than June. In the interim, Luke was his only constant companion. One friend from Asia, Onesiphorus, had diligently sought him and visited him in prison, undeterred by the danger. Linus, too, the future leading elder of Rome, Prudens, and Claudia were among his visitors. Tychicus, before he was sent by Paul to Ephesus (4:12), perhaps carried this epistle to Timothy.

Paul wrote this epistle because he was anxious to see his disciple Timothy before his (Paul's) death. And he also wanted Timothy to bring Mark with him (1:4; 4:9, 11, 21). But feeling how uncertain it was whether Timothy should arrive in time, he felt it necessary also to give him by letter a last warning as to the heresies, the seeds of which were then being scattered in the churches. Therefore, he wrote a series of exhortations to faithfulness, zeal for sound doctrine, and patience amidst trials.

*Chapter* 1

## 1-18 INTRODUCTION. THANKSGIVING TO GOD AND ENCOURAGEMENT TO TIMOTHY

➤**1 according to the promise of life . . . in Christ**—Paul's apostleship came into existence because of the promise of life Paul found in Christ Jesus. This "promise of life in Christ" (cf. 1:10; 2:8) was needed to spur Timothy to fortitude in the midst of trials and to boldness in undertaking the journey to Rome, which would be attended with much risk (1:8).

➤**2 my dearly beloved son**—In 1 Timothy 1:2 and Titus 1:4, written at an earlier period than this epistle, the expression used in the Greek is, "my genuine son." Paul felt very close to Timothy and loved him dearly.

➤**3 I thank God**—Greek, "I feel gratitude to God." **whom I serve from my forefathers**—The Greek word for "serve" means "to serve with worship" or "to serve by worship." Paul here asserts his own conscientious service of God as he had received it from his progenitors. Paul appreciated his spiritual heritage (see Acts 22:3; 24:14). As he walked in the faith of his forefathers (Acts 23:1; 24:14; 26:6, 7; 28:20), so Timothy should persevere firmly in the faith shared by his parent and grandparent. **with pure conscience**—with a clean conscience. **that . . . I have remembrance of thee**—"how unceasing I make my mention concerning thee" (cf. Philem. 4). The cause of Paul's feeling thankful is, not that he remembers Timothy unceasingly in his prayers, but for what Timothy is in faith (1:5) and grace. **night and day**—See comments on 1 Timothy 5:5.

➤**4 desiring**—Greek, "with yearning as for one much missed." **mindful of thy tears**—not only at our parting (Acts 20:37), but perhaps also at other occasions. **that I may be filled with joy**—to be reunited with you.

➤**5 When I call to remembrance**—This increased his "desire to see" Timothy. The earliest manuscripts read, "When I called to remembrance," implying that some recent incident had reminded him of the sincerity of Timothy's faith. **which**—refers to "faith." **dwelt**—lit., "indwelt," or "made its dwelling" (cf. John 14:23). **first**—before it dwelt in thee. Lois was the farthest back of the progenitors of Timothy whom Paul knew. **mother Eunice**—Timothy's mother was a Jew

who believed in Jesus Christ. But his father was a Greek, i.e., a heathen (Acts 16:1). The faith of one parent sanctified the child (3:15; 1 Cor. 7:14). Eunice was probably converted at Paul's first visit to Lystra (Acts 14:6). It is an undesigned coincidence, and so a mark of truth, that in Acts 16:1 the belief of the mother alone is mentioned, just as here praise is bestowed on the faith of the mother, while of the father no notice is taken (Paley). The mention of the faith of Timothy's mother and grandmother is intended to be an incentive to stir up his faith. **I am persuaded**—perfect tense in Greek, "I have been persuaded." **in thee also**—indwells you also. Since faith is spoken of as an indweller, faith is thus personified—or perhaps identified as the indwelling Spirit of Christ (see 1:7).

➤**6 Wherefore**—Greek, "for which cause," viz., because you have inherited, did once possess, and I trust ("am persuaded") still possess, such unfeigned faith (Alford). **stir up**—lit., "bring to life the fire again"; hence, "rekindle," "fan into flame," "revive the spark of"—the opposite of "quench" or extinguish (1 Thess. 5:19). Paul does not doubt the existence of real faith in Timothy, but he desires it to be put into active exercise. Timothy seems to have become somewhat remiss from being so long without Paul (2:22). **gift of God**—the spiritual grace received for his ministerial office, either at his original ordination, or at his consecration to the particular office of overseeing the Ephesian church (1 Tim. 4:14). This gift, of and from the Spirit (1:7), had become dormant; the flame had died down to cooling embers. Timothy needed to fan the flame, to give it life again. **by the putting on of my hands**—In 1 Timothy 4:14, it is "with the laying on of the hands of the presbytery [the body of elders]." Thus, the elders must have accompanied Paul in laying hands on Timothy.

➤**7** Paul's statement in this verse implies that Timothy needed the exhortation "to stir up the gift of God in him," due to his timidity. God did not give us **the spirit of fear**—The spirit which he gave us was not the spirit of timidity (lit., "cowardice," which is weakness), but of "power" (exhibited in a fearless "testimony" for Christ—1:8). Power is the invariable accompaniment of the gift of the Holy Spirit (Luke 24:49; Acts 1:8; cf. Acts 6:5, "full of faith and of the Holy Spirit" with 6:8, "full of faith and power"). Fear is the result of "the spirit of bondage" (Rom. 8:15). Fear within exaggerates the causes of fear without. "The spirit of power" is the Spirit of God imparting power to love to the spirit of men. **love**—which moves the believer while "speaking the truth" with power, when giving his testimony for Christ (1:8). **a sound mind**—or, "sober-mindedness," a virtue that young man like Timothy especially needed (2:22; 1 Tim. 4:12; Titus 2:4, 6). These three gifts are preferable to any miraculous powers.

➤**8 therefore**—seeing that God has given us such a spirit. **Be not thou therefore ashamed**—The Greek subjunctive here, with the negative, implies action completed at one time, not continued action that the present imperative would express—thus implying that because of Timothy's constitutional timidity (1:7) Paul felt it necessary to stir him up. **of the testimony of our Lord**—i.e., "to testify of our Lord" (NIV). **our**—connects Timothy and Paul together in the testimony both should give for their common Lord. The testimony Christ gave before Pilate (1 Tim. 6:12, 13) is an incentive to the believer that he should, after his Lord's example, witness a good testimony or confession. **nor of me his prisoner**—Christ's prisoner (see Eph. 3:1). Timothy might have easily been tempted to be ashamed of someone in prison, especially since not only worldly shame, but also great risk, attended any recognition of Paul the prisoner. **be thou partaker**—with me. **of the gospel**—rather, as in the Greek, "for the gospel," i.e., suffer for the gospel (2:3-5; Philem. 13). **according to the power of God**—exhibited in having saved and called us (1:9). God who has done the greater act of power (i.e., saved us) will surely do the less (carry us safe through afflictions borne for the gospel).

➤**9 saved us**—a definite and complete act (see Eph. 2:8). **called us with an holy calling**—or, called us *to* a holy calling, i.e., "called us to a holy life" (NIV). The call comes wholly from God and claims us wholly for God. "Holy" implies the separation of believers from the rest of the world unto God. **not according to**—not having regard to our works in his election and calling of grace (Rom. 9:11; Eph. 2:8, 9). **his own purpose**—The origination of salvation was of his own purpose, flowing from his own goodness, not for our works coming first, but wholly because of his own gratuitous,

electing love (Theodoret and Calvin). **grace . . . given us**—according to God's eternal purpose, we were graced in his beloved Son (see Eph. 1:4-6). **in Christ**—believers being regarded by God as in him (Eph. 1:4; 3:11). **before the world began**—Greek, "before the times [periods] of ages"; the enduring ages of which no end is contemplated (1 Cor. 2:7; Eph. 3:11). We were graced in Christ before the world began because God saw us in his Son, as his sons (see Eph. 1:3-6).

➤**10 But . . . now . . . manifest**—in contrast to its concealment until now in the eternal purpose of God "before the world began" (1:9; Eph. 1:4; 3:9-11; Col. 1:16; Titus 1:2, 3). **appearing**—Greek, "epiphany," a visitation of Deity. **abolished death**—Greek, "taken away the power from death" (Tittmann). The Greek article before "death" implies that Christ abolished death, not only in some particular instance, but in its very essence, being, and idea, as well as in all its aspects and consequences (John 11:26; Rom. 8:2, 38; 1 Cor. 15:26, 55; Heb. 2:14). The carrying out of the abolition of death into full effect is to be at the resurrection (Rev. 20:14). **brought . . . to light**—making visible by the gospel what was before hidden in God's purpose. **life**—of the Spirit, acting first on the soul here, about to act on the body also at the resurrection. **immortality**—Greek, "incorruptibility" of the new life, not merely of the risen body (Alford). **through**—by means of—the gospel, which brings to light the life and incorruption purposed by God from eternity, but manifested now first in Christ, who in his own resurrection has given the pledge of his people's final triumph over death. Before the revelation of the gospel, man had but a glimmering idea of the possibility of a future being of the soul, but not the faintest idea of the resurrection of the body (Acts 17:18, 32). If Christ were not "the life," the dead could never live; if he were not the resurrection, they could never rise; had he not the keys of hell and death (Rev. 1:18), we could never break through the bars of death or the gates of hell (Pearson).

➤**11 Whereunto**—lit., "for which," for the propagation of which gospel. **I am appointed**—Greek, "I was appointed." **preacher**—Greek, "herald." **teacher of the Gentiles**—See 1 Timothy 2:7. He brought forward his own example in this verse and in 1:12, as a pattern for Timothy.

►12 **For the which cause**—for the gospel cause of which Paul was appointed a preacher (1:10, 11). **I am not ashamed**—so Timothy also should not be ashamed (1:8). **I know**— The Greek word (*oida*) speaks of absolute knowledge, knowledge void of doubt (Wuest). **whom**—I know what a faithful, promise-keeping God he is (2:13). It is not, I know how I have believed, but, I know *whom* I have believed. **believed**—rather, "trusted," carrying out the metaphor of a depositor depositing his pledge with one whom he trusts. **am persuaded**—See Romans 8:38. **he is able**—in spite of so many foes around me. **to keep that which I have committed unto him**—Greek, to guard "my deposit." The deposit we commit to God's safekeeping is our entire being— body, soul, and spirit (1 Thess. 5:23; 1 Pet. 4:19)—and our entire life and work as Christians. There is one deposit (his revelation) committed by God to us that we ought to keep (1:13, 14) and transmit to others (2:2); there is another committed by God to us that we should commit to his keeping, viz., ourselves and our eternal portion. **that day**—the day of his appearing (1:18; 4:8).

►13 **Hold fast the form**—rather as Greek, "Have (i.e., keep) a pattern of sound (lit., "healthy") words which thou hast heard from me, in faith and love." "Keep" suits the reference to a deposit in the context. The Greek for "form" is translated "pattern" in 1 Timothy 1:16, the only other passage where it occurs (see comments there). **in faith and love**—Timothy needed to keep the healthy words by remaining in faith and love.

►14 This verse is clearer when translated, "That godly deposit keep through the Holy Spirit indwelling us." The deposit here is the teaching Paul committed to Timothy's trust, even the stewardship of the gospel. **in us**—in all believers. The indwelling Spirit enables us to guard the deposit of his word committed to us by God.

►15 **all they which are in Asia**—Proconsular Asia. All who are there now, when they were in Rome turned from Paul. In contrast to Onesiphorous they did not stand with Paul but forsook him (4:16). It is possible that they forsook him when he was apprehended in

Nicopolis, where they had escorted him on his way to Rome, but from which they turned back to Asia. A hint to Timothy, now in Asia, not to be like them, but rather to imitate Onesiphorous, and to come to Paul (4:21). **Phygellus and Hermogenes**—specified perhaps, as being persons from whom such cowardly conduct could least be expected; or, as being well known to Timothy, and spoken of before in conversations between him and Paul, when the latter was in Asia Minor.

►16 **The Lord give mercy**—even as Onesiphorous had abounded in works of mercy. **the house**[hold] **of Onesiphorous**—He himself was then absent from Ephesus, which accounts for the form of expression (4:19). God blesses not only the righteous man himself but all his household. **my chain**—Paul in the second imprisonment, as in his first, was bound by a chain to the soldier who guarded him.

►17 **found me**—in the crowded metropolis. So in turn may he "find mercy of the Lord in that day."

►18 **The Lord**—who rewards a kindness done to his disciples as if done to himself (Matt. 25:45). **of**—from the Lord; "the Lord" is emphatically put instead of "from himself" for solemnity and emphasis. **in how many things**—"how many acts of ministry he rendered." **unto me**—not present in the oldest manuscripts, so that the "ministered" may include services rendered to others as well as to Paul. **thou knowest very well**—because Onesiphorous was a member of the church at Ephesus.

Chapter **2**

## 1-26 A GOOD SOLDIER, ATHLETE, FARMER, AND WORKMAN APPROVED OF GOD

►1 **Thou therefore**—following Paul's example (1:8, 12) and that of Onesiphorous (1:16-18), and shunning that of those who forsook Paul (1:15). **be strong**—lit., "be continually empowered." **in the grace**—the element in which the believer's empowering exists.

►2 **among**—Greek, "through," i.e., with the attestation of many witnesses, viz., the elders and others present at his ordination or consecration (1 Tim. 4:14; 6:12). **commit**—in trust, as a deposit (1:14). **faithful**—the quality most needed by those having a trust committed to them. **who**—Greek, "[persons] such as shall be competent to teach [them to] others also." Timothy not only has to keep the deposit for himself but to transmit it to others, who in their turn shall fulfill the same function. Our knowledge of the gospel of Christ is not based on oral tradition, for the chain of succession—from then until now—would have too many faults. We have the deposit in God's written word.

➤**3 Thou therefore endure hardness**—The earliest manuscripts simply read, "Endure hardship with" (me). "Take thy share in suffering" (Conybeare and Howson).

➤**4 No man that warreth**—"No one while serving as a soldier." **the affairs of this life**—"the businesses of life" (Alford), commercial, or affairs other than military. **him who hath chosen him**—the general who at the first enlisted him as a soldier. Paul himself worked at tentmaking (Acts 18:3). Therefore what is prohibited here is not all occupations other than full-time Christian work, but the becoming entangled, or over-engrossed in those occupations.

➤**5 And**—"Moreover." **strive for masteries**—"strive in the games" (Alford), alluding to the great national games of Greece. **yet is he not crowned, except**—even though he gain the victory. **strive lawfully**—observing all the conditions of both the contest and the preparation for it, viz., as to self-denying diet, anointing, exercise, self-restraint, chastity, decorum, etc. (1 Cor. 9:24-27).

➤**6 must be first partaker**—The right of "first partaking of fruits" belongs to him "who is laboring."

➤**7 Consider what I say**—Consider the force of the illustrations I have given of the soldier, the contender in the games, and the farmer, as applying to you and your ministry. **and the Lord give thee understanding**—The oldest manuscripts read, "for the Lord will give you understanding." Timothy would understand Paul's words when he applied them to himself and when he sought the Lord for their meaning. Paul was not urging intellectual perception but personal appropriation of the truths metaphorically expressed.

➤**8** Rather as Greek, "Remember Jesus Christ, raised from the dead." Remember Christ risen, so as to follow him. As he was raised after death, so if Timothy would share his risen "life," he must now share his "death" (2:11). The Greek perfect passive participle ("having been raised") implies a permanent character acquired by Jesus as the risen Savior. Christ's resurrection is put prominently forward as the reality that should strengthen Timothy to steadfastness in sharing Paul's sufferings for the gospel's sake. **of the seed of David**—Romans 1:3, 4 parallels this passage in that both speak of Jesus' human lineage from the seed of David and of his divine designation through resurrection. **my gospel**—that which I always taught.

➤**9 Wherein**—"in which," referring to the gospel. **bonds**—imprisonment. **word . . . not bound**—Though Paul was bound, his tongue and pen were not (4:17; Acts 28:31). Even more so, the gospel proclaimed by others could not be stopped by any kind of shackles (see Phil. 1:18).

➤**10 Therefore**—Because of the anxiety Paul felt that the gospel should be expanded (2:9). **endure**—not merely "I passively suffer," but "I actively and perseveringly endure," and "am ready to endure patiently all things." **the elect's sakes**—for the sake of the church, all the members of Christ's spiritual body (Col. 1:24). **they . . . also**—as well as Paul himself. **salvation . . . glory**—not only salvation from wrath, but glory in reigning with him eternally (2:12). Glory is the full expansion and expression of salvation (Acts 2:47; Rom. 8:21-24, 30; Heb. 9:28).

➤**11** Greek, "Faith is the saying." **if we be dead**—lit., "if we died." The Greek aorist tense implies a state once for all entered into in past time—here, referring to the time of Christ's crucifixion. **with him**—in union with Christ (see Rom. 6:3, 8; Col. 2:12). **we shall also live with him**—in eternity, in glory. The symmetrical form of "the saying," (2:11-13) and the rhythmical balance of the parallel clauses make it likely that these words formed part of a church hymn (see comments on 1 Tim. 3:16) or an accepted formula, perhaps first uttered by some of the Christian "prophets" in the public assembly (1 Cor. 14:26). The phrase "faithful is the saying," which seems to have been the usual formula (cf. 1 Tim. 1:15; 3:1; 4:9; Titus 3:8), in such cases favors this.

►**12 suffer**—rather, as the Greek is the same as in 2:10, "If we endure [with him]" (Rom. 8:17). **reign with him**—The special privilege of the elect church, now suffering with Christ, is then to reign with him (see 1 Cor. 6:2). To reign with Christ in his kingdom is the reward for suffering for his sake now (see Rev. 3:21; 5:10; 20:4, 5). **deny**—with the mouth. As "believe" with the heart follows (2:13). Cf. the opposite, "confess with thy mouth" and "believe in thine heart" (Rom. 10:9, 10). **he also will deny us**—This speaks of the possibility of apostasy (cf. 1 Tim. 4:1; Heb. 10:38, 39; 2 John 9) and of the Lord's rejection of those who deny him (see Matt. 10:33) (Litfin).

►**13 If we believe not**—or, if we are unfaithful. **he abideth faithful**—he remains faithful. **he cannot** [it is an impossibility that he should] **deny himself**—He cannot be unfaithful to his word so as to deny those who deny him, even though they be unfaithful to their profession of faith in him (Rom. 3:3). The NIV says, "Christ cannot disown himself"— "therefore He will not deny even unprofitable members of His own body. True children of God cannot become something other than children, even when disobedient and weak. Christ's faithfulness to Christians is not contingent on their faithfulness to him" (Litfin).

►**14 charging**—Greek, "testifying continually." **before the Lord**—See 1 Timothy 5:21. **that they strive not about words**—lit., "not to fight with words," "not to have a war of words" (2:23, 24; 1 Tim. 6:4). **to no profit**—lit., "profitable for nothing." **to the subverting**—sure to subvert (overturn) the hearers: the opposite of "edifying" (building up).

►**15 Study**—Greek, "Be earnest" or "Be diligent." **to show**—Greek, "present," as in Romans 12:1. **thyself**—as distinguished from those whom Timothy was to charge (2:14). **approved**—tested by trial, the opposite of "reprobate" or disapproved (Titus 1:16). **not to be ashamed**—by his work not being "approved" (Phil. 1:20). **rightly dividing**— lit., "cutting straight." The word means to cut along a straight line, to cut a straight road, or to keep a straight course. "The metaphor could be that of plowing a straight furrow [cf. NEB] or of a road maker driving his road straight [see

Bengel] or of a mason squaring and cutting a stone to fit in its proper place [see Moulton and Milligan]" (Reinecker). The word is found in Proverbs 3:6; 11:5 (LXX), where it is used with *hodous* and means "cut a road across country (that is forested or otherwise difficult to pass through) in a straight direction" so that the traveler might go directly to his destination (BAG). Thus, Paul's statement would mean, "guide the word of truth along a straight path (like a road that goes straight to its goal), without being turned aside by words, debates, or impious talks" (ibid.).

►**16 shun**—lit., "stand above," separate from, and be superior to. **vain**—empty. **increase**—Greek, "advance"; lit., "cut forward," an image from pioneers cutting away all obstacles before an advancing army. **more ungodliness**— Greek, "a greater degree of impiety."

►**17 will eat**—lit., "will have pasture." The cancerous progress of mortification is the image. They pretend to give rich spiritual pasture to their disciples: the only pasture is that of a spiritual cancer feeding on their inner being. **canker**—a "cancer" or "gangrene." **Hymenaeus**—See comments on 1 Timothy 1:20. After his excommunication he seems to have been readmitted into the church and again to have troubled it.

►**18 erred**—Greek, misaimed (see comments on 1 Tim. 6:21). **the resurrection is past already**—has already taken place. The beginnings of the subsequent gnostic heresy already existed. They "wrested" (2 Pet. 3:16) Paul's own words (Rom. 6:4; Eph. 2:6; Col. 2:12) "to their own destruction," as though the resurrection was merely the spiritual raising of souls from the death of sin. Cf. 1 Corinthians 15:12, where Paul shows all our hopes of future glory rest on the literal reality of the resurrection. To believe it past (as the Seleucians or Hermians did, according to Augustine, *Ep.* 119.55, *ad Januarium,* sec. 4), is to deny it in its true sense. **overthrow**—trying to subvert "the foundation" on which alone faith can rest secure (2:19; cf. Titus 1:11).

►**19 Nevertheless**—Notwithstanding the subversion of their faith, "the firm foundation of God standeth" fast (so the Gk. ought to be translated). The "foundation" here is "the church"—1 Corinthians 3:10-15; Ephesians 2:19-22; 1 Timothy 3:15 (Alford), "the ground" or basement support "of the truth" (1 Tim. 3:15), Christ himself being the ultimate "foundation" (1 Cor. 3:11). The "house" (2:20) answers to the "foundation"; it is made up of the elect whom "the Lord knoweth" (acknowledges, recognizes—Ps. 1:6; Matt. 7:23; John 10:14; 1 Cor. 8:3) as "his," and who persevere to the end, though others "err concerning the faith" (Matt. 24:24; John 10:28; 1 John 2:19). **seal**—an inscription indicating ownership and destination. Inscriptions were often engraven on a "foundation" stone (Rev. 21:14) (Alford). This will agree with the view that "the foundation" is the church (Eph. 2:20). "The one seal bears two inscriptions, two mutually complimentary parts or aspects: (a) the objective fact of God's superintending knowledge of His chosen; (b) the recognition by the consciousness of each individual of the relation in which he stands to God, with its imperative call to holiness" (White). **depart**—lit., "stand away." **from iniquity**—See Isaiah 52:11. In both clauses there may be an allusion to Numbers 16:5, 26, LXX. God's part and man's part are marked out. God chooses and knows his elect; our part is to believe, and by the Spirit depart from all iniquity, an unequivocal proof of our being the Lord's (cf. Deut. 29:29; Luke 13:23-27).

➤**20 in a great house**—i.e., the visible professing Christian church (1 Tim. 3:15). Paul is speaking, not of those without, but of the (visible) family of God (Calvin). As in the parable of the dragnet (Matt. 13:47-49), which gathers together of every kind under the waves, good and bad cannot be distinguished until brought to shore, so believers and unbelievers continue in the same church until the judgment makes the everlasting distinction. "The ark of Noah is a type of the Church: as in the former there were together the leopard and the kid, the wolfe and the lamb; so in the latter, the righteous and sinners, vessels of gold and silver, with vessels of wood and earth" (Jerome, *Against Lucifer,* 302; cf. Matt. 20:16). **vessels of gold . . . silver**—precious and able to endure fire. **of wood and earth**—worthless, fragile, and flammable (1 Cor. 3:12, 15; 15:47). **some . . . some**—the former . . . the latter. **to dishonour**—"for ignoble use" (NIV). See Proverbs 16:4; Romans 9:17-23.

➤**21 If a man . . . purge himself from these**—The Greek says"If one [e.g., you, Timothy] purify himself [so as to separate] from among these" (vessels unto dishonor). **sanctified**—set apart as wholly consecrated to the Lord. **and meet**—suitable. Some of the earliest manuscripts omit "and." **the master's**—the Lord's. Paul himself was such a vessel: once one among those of earth, but afterwards he became one of gold. **prepared unto every good work**—See 3:17; Titus 3:1; cf. Titus 1:16.

➤**22 Flee**—Avoid occasions of sin. There are many lusts from which our greatest safety is in flight (Gen. 39:12). But judging from the self-restrained character of Timothy (1 Tim. 3:2, 3), it is not likely that Paul was speaking of sexual passion. Probably Paul was alluding to the strife and vainglory that accompany youth (see 1 Tim. 4:12). **righteousness**—the opposite of "iniquity," i.e., unrighteousness (2:19; cf. 1 Tim. 6:11). **peace, with**—rather, put no comma—"peace with them that call on the Lord out of a pure heart" (Eph. 6:5; Col. 3:22). We are to love all men, but it is not possible to be at peace with all men, for this needs unity of purpose and opinion; they alone who call on the Lord sincerely (as contrasted with the false teachers who had only the form of godliness, 3:5, 8; Titus 1:15, 16) have this unity (Theodoret).

➤**23 See Titus 3:9. unlearned**—Greek, "undisciplined," not tending to promote the discipline of faith and morals (Prov. 5:23); "uninstructive," in contrast with "instructing" (2:25).

➤**24 not strive**—"The servant of the Lord" must imitate his master in not striving contentiously, though uncompromising in earnestly contending for the faith (Jude 3; Matt. 12:19). **gentle unto all men**—"patient" (Greek, "patient in bearing wrongs") in respect to adversaries. **apt to teach**—implying not only solid teaching and ease in teaching, but patience and assiduity in it (Bengel).

➤**25 instructing**—Greek, "disciplining," instructing with correction, which those who deal in uninstructive or undisciplined questions need (see 2:23; 1 Tim. 1:20). **those that oppose themselves**—Greek, "those opposing" what Timothy says. **if . . . peradventure**—Greek, "if at any time." **repentance**—which they need as a prerequisite for appropriating the full knowledge (so the Greek for "acknowledgment") of the truth (1 Tim. 2:4).

➤**26 recover themselves**—Greek, "return to soberness," viz., from the spiritual intoxication whereby they have fallen into the snare of the devil. **the snare of the devil**—See Ephesians 6:11 ("the wiles of the devil") and 1 Timothy 3:7; 6:9. **taken captive by him at his will**—lit., "having been caught by him for the will of that one." There is some difficulty explaining this statement because one cannot be sure if "that one" (Gk., *ekeinou*) refers to "the devil" or to "God" in 2:25. Normally, this Greek demonstrative pronoun points to the farthest antecedent (in this case, "God"). This exegesis is supported by many scholars who would say that this statement means that "they who had been taken captive by the devil may recover themselves out of his snare, so as to serve the will of God" (White).

## Chapter 3

### 1-9 WARNING AGAINST GODLESSNESS IN THE LAST DAYS

➤**1 also**—Greek, "but." **last days**—preceding Christ's second coming (2 Pet. 3:3; Jude 18). "The latter times," 1 Timothy 4:1, refer to a period not so remote as "the last days." **perilous times**—lit., "difficult times," in which it is difficult to know what is to be done; hence, "grievous times." **shall come**—Greek, "shall be imminent"; "shall come unexpectedly" (Bengel).

➤**2 men**—The people described in the next verses (3:2-9) are probably in Christianity but not genuine Christians. Cf. Romans 1:29ff., where much the same sins are attributed to heathen men. **lovers of their own selves**—one word in Greek (*philautoi*), found only here in the NT. **covetous**—lit., "money-loving," a distinct Greek word (*philarguroi*). **boasters**—empty boasters (Alford), boasting of having what they have not. **proud**—lit., "showing themselves above" their fellows. **blasphemers**—rather, "evil-speakers," "revilers." **disobedient to parents**—The character of the times will be especially reflected in the manners of the young (Bengel). **unthankful**—The obligation to gratitude is next to that of

obedience to parents. **unholy**—irreligious (Alford).

➤**3 trucebreakers**—rather as the Greek is translated in Romans 1:31, "implacable." **false accusers**—slanderers (1 Tim. 3:11; Titus 2:3). **incontinent, fierce**—at once both soft and hard: indulging themselves without restraint and inhuman to others. **despisers**—lit., "no lovers of good," the opposite of "a lover of good" (Titus 1:8).

➤**4 Traitors**—betrayers. **heady**—hasty in action and in passion. **highminded**—lit., "puffed up" with pride, as with smoke blinding them. **lovers of pleasure**—one word in Greek: *philēdonoi* ("pleasure-lovers"). **lovers of God**—one word in Greek: *philotheoi* ("God-lovers"). Love of pleasure destroys one's love for God.

➤**5 form**—outward semblance. **godliness**—piety. **denying**—rather as Greek, "having denied," i.e., renounced. **the power**—the living regenerating, sanctifying influence of it. **turn away**—implying that some of such characters, forerunners of the last days, were already in the church.

➤**6 of this sort**—Greek, "of these," such as were described (3:5). **creep into**—stealthily. **silly women**—"weak-willed women" (NIV). **laden** [heaped up] **with sins**—According to the Greek, this describes the "silly women," whose consciences are burdened with sins and so are a ready prey to the false teachers who promise ease of conscience if they will follow them. A bad conscience leads easily to shipwreck of faith (1 Tim. 1:19). **divers** [various] **lusts**—not only fleshly lusts, but passion for change in doctrine and manner of teaching—the running after fashionable men and fashionable tenets, drawing them in the most opposite directions (Alford).

➤**7 Ever learning**—some new point, for mere curiosity, to the disparagement of what they seemed to know before. **the knowledge**—Greek, "the full knowledge." Gnosticism appealed especially to the females (Irenaeus, 1.13.3).

➤**8 Now**—Greek, "But"; it is no wonder there should be now such opponents to the truth, for their prototypes existed in ancient times (Alford). **Jannes . . . Jambres**—traditional names of the Egyptian magicians who resisted Moses (Exod. 7:11, 22), derived from "the unwritten teaching of the Jews" (Theodoret). In *Praeparatio Evangelica* Eusebius quotes from Numenius: "Jannes and Jambres were sacred scribes (a lower order of priests in Egypt) skilled in magic." **resist**—"withstand," the same word in Greek used before (". . . withstood Moses"). The magicians withstood Moses by trying to rival Moses' miracles. So the false teachers shall exhibit lying wonders in the last days (Matt. 24:24; 2 Thess. 2:9; Rev. 13:14, 15). **reprobate**—incapable of testing the truth of the Christian faith (Rom. 1:28) (Bengel). Alford takes it passively: "not abiding the test," rejected on being tested, disapproved (Jer. 6:30).

**►9 they shall proceed no further**—Though for a time (2:16) "they shall advance or proceed (KJV, "increase") unto more ungodliness," yet there is a final limit beyond which they shall not be able to "proceed further" (Job 38:11; Rev. 11:7, 11). They themselves shall "wax worse and worse" (3:13), but they shall at last be for ever prevented from seducing others. **folly**—lit., "without understanding" (used only here and in Luke 6:11 in the NT). **shall be manifest**—Greek, "shall be brought forth from concealment into open day" (see Bengel; 1 Cor. 4:5). **as theirs . . . was**—as that of those magicians was, when not only could they no longer try to rival Moses in sending boils, but the boils fell upon themselves: so as to the lice (Exod. 8:18; 9:11).

## 10-17 PAUL'S CHARGE TO TIMOTHY

**►10 fully known**—lit., "closely followed" and traced, with a view to following Paul as his pattern. The same Greek word appears in Luke 1:3, "having followed all things closely" (RSV) or "have traced the case of these happenings carefully" (Phillips). Timothy knew Paul intimately and was well aware of Paul's Christian biography; it formed a pattern for Timothy's life. As Luke had traced out the life of Jesus, Timothy could have also traced the life of Paul from the time he (Paul) came to Christ. **doctrine**—"teaching." **manner of life**—"conduct," "behavior." **purpose**—The Greek is elsewhere normally used of God's "purpose," but here of Paul's determined purpose to follow the Lord (cf. Acts 11:23). **longsuffering**—toward Paul's adversaries and the false teachers, toward brothers in bearing

their infirmities, and toward the unconverted (4:2; 2 Cor. 6:6; Gal. 5:22; Eph. 4:2; Col. 3:12). **charity**—love. **patience**—endurance.

**►11 afflictions**—sufferings. **which**—Greek, "such as." **at Antioch**—of Pisidia (Acts 13:14, 50, 51). **Iconium**—See Acts 14:1-5. **Lystra**—See Acts 14:6, 19. **out of them all the Lord delivered me**—cf. 4:17. An encouragement to Timothy not to fear persecutions.

**►12 Yea, and**—an additional consideration for Timothy: if he wanted to live godly in Christ, he must make up his mind to encounter persecution. **all that will live**—Greek, "all whose will is to live . . . ." Instead of thinking of persecution as a stumbling block, Timothy should consider it the portion of the godly. **live godly in Christ**—See Galatians 2:20; Philippians 1:21. There is no godliness or piety apart from Christ. The world easily puts up with the mask of a religion that depends on itself, but the piety that derives its vigor directly from Christ is as odious to modern Christians as it was to the ancient Jews (Bengel). **shall suffer persecution**—cf. Galatians 5:11.

**►13** This verse provides a reason why persecutions must be expected, these becoming worse and worse as the end approaches. The breach between light and darkness, so far from being healed, shall be widened (Alford). **evil men**—in contrast to the "godly" (3:12). **seducers**—lit., "conjurors," one who practices magic art, a sorcerer (Rienecker), a charlatan (NEB). Magical arts prevailed at Ephesus (Acts 19:19) and had been renounced by many Ephesians after they accepted Christ. The Ephesians knew about sorcery firsthand. Probably sorcery will characterize the final apostasy (Rev. 13:15; 18:23; 22:15). **wax worse**—lit., "advance in the direction of worse." This verse is not contradictory to 3:9: there the *diffusion* of the evil was spoken of; here its *intensity* (Alford). **deceiving, and being deceived**—"Error feeds on itself" (Litfin).

**►14 But . . . thou**—Resuming the thought begun at 3:10. **learned**—from Paul and from Timothy's mother and grandmother (1:5; 2:2). **assured of**—from Scripture (3:15). **of whom**—plural, not singular, in the oldest manuscripts, "from what teachers." Not only from me, but from Lois and Eunice.

➤**15 from a child**—lit., "from an infant." The tender age of the first dawn of reason is when the most lasting impressions of faith may be made. **the holy scriptures**—lit., "the sacred letters" or "the sacred writings," an expression used by Philo and Josephus to describe the OT, which is what Timothy was taught when he was a child (Earle). **wise unto salvation**—i.e., wise unto the attainment of salvation. **through faith**—as the instrument of this wisdom. Each knows divine things only as far as his own experience extends. He who does not have faith has neither wisdom or salvation.

➤**16 All scripture**—Greek, "every Scripture," i.e., Scripture in its every part. The Greek never speaks of writings in general but only of the sacred Scriptures. The position of the two Greek adjectives ("God-breathed" and "profitable") closely united by "and," forbids our taking the one as an epithet and the other as predicated, so as to be translated as "Every Scripture given by inspiration of God is also profitable." The adjectives are so closely connected that as surely as one is a predicate, the other must be so too. Most of the NT books were written when Paul wrote this his last epistle; so he includes in the clause "All Scripture is God-inspired," not only the OT, in which alone Timothy was taught when a child (3:15), but the NT books according as they were recognized in the churches. Paul means, "All Scripture is God-inspired and therefore useful." Because we see no utility in any words or portion of it, it does not follow it is not God-inspired. It is useful because God-inspired, not God-inspired because useful. One reason for the article's not being before the Greek word for "Scripture" may be that, if it had, it might be supposed that it limited the sense to the "Holy Scriptures" (3:15) of the OT, whereas here the assertion is more general: "*all* Scripture" (cf. Gk., 2 Pet. 1:20). The translation "all Scripture that is God-inspired is also useful" would falsely imply that there is some Scripture that is not God-inspired (*NBD*). **given by inspiration of God**—Greek, *theopneustos* ("God-breathed"), from *theos* ("God") and *pneustos* (from *pneuma*—"breath" or "spirit"). The word means "God-breathed," "God-spirated," or "God-spirited." Although it is difficult to fully recreate the thought of this Greek expression in English, we are fairly sure that Paul

meant to say that all (or, every) Scripture was breathed out from God. This is the primary meaning. But the expression could also mean that the word was inbreathed (or, inspired) by God. The first definition affirms the word's divine origin; the second speaks of God's spiritual presence in the word. Although most scholars (especially in this century) adhere to only the first definition, the second cannot be ruled out. Other NT philologists did not hesitate to tell us that the expression "God-breathed" indicates that God is breathing through the Scripture and the Scripture is breathing out God. Cremer posited this and so did Bengel, the grandfather of NT philologists. He said the Bible "was divinely inspired, not merely while it was written, God breathing through the writers, but also while it is being read, God breathing through the Scripture, and the Scripture breathing Him."

The inspiration gives the divine sanction to all the words of Scripture, though those words were the utterances of the individual writer, and only in special cases were revealed directly by God (1 Cor. 2:13). Inspiration is here predicated of the writings, "all Scripture," not of the persons. The issue is not *how* God has done it but *that* he has done it, that all the sacred writings are everywhere inspired, and that even the very words are stamped with divine sanction—as Jesus used them (e.g., in the temptation and John 10:34, 35), for deciding all questions of doctrine and practice. There are degrees of revelation in Scripture, but not of inspiration. The sacred writers did not even always know the full significance of their own God-inspired words (1 Pet. 1:10-12). Verbal inspiration does not mean mechanical dictation, but all "Scripture is (so) inspired by God," that everything in it, its narratives, prophecies, citations, the whole—ideas, phrases, and words—are such as he saw fit to be there. The present condition of the text is no ground for concluding against the original text's being inspired, but it is a reason why we should use all critical diligence to restore the original inspired text. Again, inspiration may be accompanied by revelation or not, but it is as much needed for writing known doctrines or facts authoritatively, as for communicating new truths (Tregelles). **is profitable**—According to the context of 2 Timothy 3, Paul was not so much defending the divine origin of Scripture as he was promoting the fact that the Scripture is the present medium of divine inspiration. This God-breathed Scripture, Paul tells Timothy, is profitable for teaching, reproof, correction, and instruction. In other words, it is God-breathed in its application. It is not enough to have an academic belief in the divine inspiration of Scripture; we must know it to be divine by our experience and in its application (Comfort). **correction**—Greek, "setting one right." **instruction**—Greek, "disciplining," as a father does his child, or "training" by instruction, warning, example, kindnesses, promises, and chastisements.

➤**17 man of God**—See 1 Timothy 6:11. **perfect**—Greek, "fitted," "furnished," "equipped." The man of God is equipped by the practical appropriation of Scripture. **thoroughly furnished**—or, "fully equipped" (TLB, JB). This repetition (in Gk.) emphasizes the main point: the man of God who is equipped with Scriptures is fully equipped to accomplish every good work.

## Chapter 4

### 1-22 PAUL'S FINAL WORDS

➤**1 charge**—Greek, "solemnly witness," "adjure." What follows is a very solemn charge. **therefore**—omitted in the earliest manuscripts. **the Lord Jesus Christ**—The earliest manuscripts read simply, "Christ Jesus." **shall judge**—See Acts 10:42; 1 Peter 4:5. **the quick**—the living, those alive at the time of his appearing. **appearing**—Greek, "epiphany," suggesting the appearance of Deity to earth and a manifestation of divinity (used also in 1 Tim. 6:14; 2 Tim. 4:8; Titus 2:13). **and his kingdom**—to be established at his appearing, when we hope to reign with him. His kingdom is real now but not visible. It shall then be both real and visible (Luke 22:18, 30; Rev. 1:7; 11:15; 19:6). Now he reigns in the midst of his enemies anticipating the time when they shall be overthrown (Ps. 110:2; Heb. 10:13). Then he shall reign with his adversaries prostrate. The phrase "at his appearing and his kingdom" in the Greek is "both [by] his epiphany and [by] his kingdom." This expression modifies either

Christ's judgment (see TEV) or Paul's charge to Timothy (see RSV).

➤**2 Preach**—lit., "proclaim as a herald." **be instant**—lit., "be standing by"; hence, be attentive, be on guard. **in season, out of season**—i.e., at all seasons; whether the listeners regard the minister's speaking as seasonable or unseasonable. "Just as the fountains, though none may draw from them, still flow on; and the rivers, though none drink of them, still run; so must we do all on our part in speaking, though none give heed to us" (Chrysostom's *Homily*, 30, vol. 5). The expression includes the idea of preaching not merely when convenient but also when inconvenient: night as well as day (Acts 20:31), in danger as well as in safety, in prison and out of prison, everywhere and on all occasions, whenever and wherever the Lord's work requires it. **reprove**—expose. **with**—Greek, "in." See 2:24, 25; 3:10. **doctrine**—The Greek for "doctrine" here is *didachē*, but in 3:16 *didascalia*. *Didascalia* is what one receives; **didachē** is what is communicated (Tittmann).

➤**3 they**—professing Christians. **sound doctrine**—Greek, "the sound [see 1 Tim. 1:10] doctrine" (*didascalias*) or "teaching" of the gospel. **after their own lusts**—"to suit their own desires" (NIV). **heap**—one on another, an indiscriminate mass of false teachers. Variety delights itching ears. **to themselves**—such as will suit their depraved tastes: *populus vult decipi, et decipiatur*—"the people wish to be deceived, so let them be deceived." **itching**—have a craving to hear teachers who give them pleasure (Acts 17:19-21) and who do not offend by truths grating to their ears. "They, as it were, tickle with pleasure the levity of the multitude [Cicero], who comes as to a theater to hear what will delight their ears, not to learn what will do them good" (Seneca's *Epistle*, 10.8).

➤**4 turned**—Greek, "turned aside" (1 Tim. 1:6). It is a righteous retribution, that when men turn away from the truth, they should be turned to fables (see Jer. 2:19). **fables**—1 Tim. 1:4.

➤**5** Since Paul would no longer be there to withstand the evils just mentioned, he urged Timothy to do so. **watch thou**—lit., "with the wakefulness of one sober." **in all things**—on all occasions and under all circumstances (Titus 2:7). **endure afflictions**—suffer hardship (Alford). **evangelist**—a missionary preacher and teacher. **make full proof of**—fulfill in all its requirements, leaving nothing undone (Acts 12:25; Rom. 15:19; Col. 4:17).

➤**6 For I am now ready to be offered**— Greek, "For I am already being poured out [as a drink offering, as a libation]," an appropriate image anticipating the shedding of his blood (cf. Phil. 2:17). Paul's imminent martyrdom should have stimulated Timothy to greater faithfulness. **my departure**—Greek, "lifting up," as in "loosing an anchor"; also "dissolution" (cf. Phil. 1:23).

➤**7 I have fought a good fight**—lit., "I have contested the good contest." The image here speaks of a race (see TEV, NEB; cf. 1 Cor. 9:24; 1 Tim. 6:12). **I have finished my** [the] **course**—i.e., I have crossed the finish line. **kept the faith**—the Christian faith committed to me as a believer and an apostle (cf. 1:14; Rev. 2:10; 3:10).

➤**8 a crown**—rather as Greek, "the crown." the "henceforth" marks the decisive moment: he looks to his state in a threefold aspect: (1) in the past "I have fought"; (2) in the immediate present "there is laid up for me"; (3) in the future "the Lord will give in that day" (Bengel). **crown**—a crown, or garland, given to the successful competitor in wrestling, running, etc. (cf. 1 Pet. 5:4; Rev. 2:10). **of righteousness**— The reward is in recognition of righteousness wrought in Paul by God's Spirit; the crown is prepared for the righteous; but it is a crown that consists in righteousness. Righteousness will be its own reward (Rev. 22:11). A man is justified gratuitously by the merits of Christ through faith; and when he is so justified, God accepts his works and honors them with a reward that is not their due, but is given of grace. "So great is God's goodness to men that He wills that their works should be merits, though they are merely His own gifts" (*Epistle* of Pope Celestine I., 12). **give**—Greek, "will award" in righteous requital as "judge" (Acts 17:31; 2 Cor. 5:10; 2 Thess. 1:6, 7). The righteous heavenly Judge stands in contrast to the unrighteous earthly judges who condemned Paul. **at that day**—the day of his appearing (1:12). The partakers of the first resurrection may receive a crown also at the last day. **not to me only**—Greek, "not only to me." **them also that love his appearing**—perfect tense in Greek: "have continued to love," speaking of an habitual love and desire for Christ's appear-

ing. Note the sad contrast in 4:10, "having loved this present world."

➤**9** Timothy is here asked to come to be a comfort to Paul and also to be strengthened by Paul for carrying on the gospel work after Paul's decease (see 1:4, 8; 4:21).

➤**10 Demas**—once a "fellow laborer" of Paul, along with Mark and Luke (Col. 4:14; Philem. 24). **Galatia**—This reading is supported by a diversity of ancient manuscripts, but two early manuscripts (Codex Sinaiticus and Codex Ephraem Rescriptus) read "Gaul." This latter reading is probably a scribal error ("Galatian" written as "Gallian"—i.e., "Gaul") or a scribal alteration, for in the early centuries of the Christian era Gaul was commonly called Galatia (Metzger). **Titus**—He must have therefore left Crete after "setting in order" the affairs of the churches there (Titus 1:5). **Dalmatia**— part of the Roman province of Illyricum on the coast of the Adriatic. Paul had written to him (Titus 3:12) to come to him in the winter to Nicopolis (in Epirus), intending in the spring to preach the gospel in the adjoining province of Dalmatia. Titus seems to have gone there to carry out the apostle's intention. Whether he went of his own accord, as is likely, or was sent by Paul, which the expression "is departed" hardly accords with, cannot be positively decided. Paul here speaks only of his personal attendants having forsaken him; he had still friends among the Roman Christians who visited him (4:21), though they had been afraid to stand by him at his trial (4:16).

➤**11 Only Luke is with me**—Luke remained Paul's faithful companion to the end. **Mark**—John Mark was probably in, or near, Colosse, for in the Epistle to the Colossians (Col. 4:10), written a few years before this, he was mentioned as about to visit them. Timothy was now absent from Ephesus and somewhere in the interior of Asia Minor; hence he would be sure to join Mark on his journey. **he is profitable to me for the ministry**—Mark had been under a cloud for having forsaken Paul at a critical moment in his missionary tour with Barnabas (Acts 15:37, 40; 13:5, 13). Timothy had subsequently occupied the same post in relation to Paul as Mark once held. Hence Paul, appropriately here, wiped out the past censure by high praise of Mark and may have guarded against Timothy's making self-complacent comparisons between himself and Mark, as though he were superior to the latter (cf. Philem. 24).

►**12** Timothy was to come to Paul, while Tychicus was to be sent by Paul to Ephesus to fill Timothy's vacancy (cf. Titus 3:12). It is possible Tychicus was the bearer of this epistle.

►**13 The cloak that I left**—probably obliged to leave it in a hurried departure from Troas. **Carpus**—a faithful friend to have been entrusted with Paul's precious possessions. The mention of his "cloak" is one of those graphic touches that sheds light on the last scene of Paul's life. In prison during the winter, he needed a cloak to cover him from the cold. **books**—lit., "scrolls" or more likely "papyri," probably to be used for writing. **especially the parchments**—made of animal skins. These parchments were probably already written upon—either containing books of the OT or copies of Paul's NT writings and/or other NT writings (such as the Gospels or Acts).

►**14 Alexander the coppersmith**—or "smith" in general. Perhaps the same as the Alexander at Ephesus (see comments on 1 Tim. 1:20). Having been excommunicated by Paul, he may have sought revenge by accusing Paul before the Roman judges, whether of insurrection or of introducing a new religion (see Introduction). **reward**—The earliest manuscripts read, "will reward" or "will requite." Paul left requital (or, vengeance)to the Lord.

►**16 At my first answer**—i.e., "defense" in court, at my first public examination. Timothy knew nothing of this until Paul now informs him. But during his former imprisonment at Rome, Timothy was with him (Phil. 1:1, 7). This must have been, therefore, a second imprisonment. He must have been set free before the persecution in A.D. 64, when the Christians were accused of causing the conflagration in Rome; for had he been a prisoner then, he certainly would not have been spared. The tradition (see Eusebius's *Ecclesiastical History,* 2.25) that he was finally beheaded accords with his not having been put to death in the persecution of A.D. 64, when burning to death was usually the mode by which Christians were executed. His "first" trial in his second imprisonment may have been on the charge of complicity in the conflagration; his

absence from Rome may have been the ground of his acquittal on that charge; his final condemnation was probably on the charge of introducing a new and unlawful religion into Rome. **stood with me**—Greek, "came forward with me" (Alford) as a friend and advocate. **may** [it] **not be laid to their charge**—The position of "their" in the Greek is emphatic. "May it not be laid to *their* charge," for they were intimidated. Their drawing back from Paul was not from bad disposition so much as from fear; it is sure to be laid to the charge of those who intimidated them.

►**17 the Lord**—the more precious because men deserted Paul. **stood with me**—i.e., was present with me, stronger than "came forward with me" (4:16). **strengthened**—Greek, "put strength in me," "empowered me." **by me**—"through me." **the preaching**—"the gospel proclamation." **might be fully known, and that all the Gentiles might hear**—It seems that this language suggests that Paul was expecting to be released from prison so that he could preach the gospel to the nations—unless, of course, he was preaching the gospel at his final trial. Rome was the capital of the Gentile world, so that a proclamation of the truth to the Romans was likely to go forth to the rest of the Gentile world. **I was delivered out of the mouth of the lion**—lit., "out of a lion's mouth." This could mean he was delivered (1) from trouble (cf. Ps. 22:21; Dan. 6:22), (2) from Satan, the roaring, devouring lion (1 Pet. 5:8), or (3) from Caesar Nero, who was called "the lion"—or all three.

►**18 And the Lord shall deliver me**—Hope draws its conclusions from the past to the future (Bengel). **will preserve me**—lit., "will save" (Ps. 22:21), "will bring me safe to." Jesus is the Lord and the Deliverer (Phil. 3:20; 1 Thess. 1:10). He saves from evil. **heavenly kingdom**—lit., "his kingdom which is a heavenly one." **to whom be glory for ever and ever**—lit., "to whom be the glory into the ages of ages."

►**19 Prisca and Aquila**—See Acts 18:2, 26; Romans 16:3, 4; also 1 Corinthians 16:19 (written from Ephesus, where Aquila and Priscilla were then living). **household of Onesiphorus**—See 1:16.

►**20** In order to depict his desertion, Paul informs Timothy that Erastus, one of his usual companions (Acts 19:22, possibly the same

Erastus as in Rom. 16:23, though how he could leave his official duties for missionary journeys is not clear), stayed behind at Corinth, his native place, or usual residence, of which city he was "chamberlain," or city steward and treasurer (Rom. 16:23); and Trophimus he left behind at Miletus sick. (See Acts 20:4; 21:29.) This verse shows that Paul wrote this epistle in his second imprisonment, not his first, for he did not pass by Corinth or Miletus on his way to Rome when he was about to be imprisoned for the first time. As Miletus was near Ephesus, there is a presumption that Timothy was not at Ephesus when Paul wrote or he would not need to inform Timothy of Trophimus lying sick in his immediate neighborhood. However, Trophimus may not have been still at Miletus at the time when Paul wrote, though he had left him there on his way to Rome. Priscilla and Aquila were most likely at Ephesus (4:19),

and he desired Timothy to salute them; so also Onesiphorus's household (1:16).

➤**21 before winter**—when a voyage, according to ancient means of navigation, would be out of the question; also Paul would need his "cloak" for the winter (4:13). **Linus**—According to an early tradition, Linus was the first bishop of Rome after Peter's death (Irenaeus's *Against Heresies,* 3.3).

➤**22 The Lord Jesus Christ**—The earliest manuscripts read "Lord." **be with thy spirit**—Jesus Christ is with the spirit of each believer because his Spirit, the Spirit of Jesus Christ, indwells each believer (Rom. 8:9-11, 16). Paul pronounced this as a fact for Timothy to appreciate and appropriate. **Grace be with you**—The word "you" is plural in the earliest manuscripts. This benediction was therefore directed to Timothy and the members of the Ephesian church and neighboring churches.

BIBLIOGRAPHY

Alford, Henry. *The Greek New Testament.* 1852. Reprint. Grand Rapids: Guardian Press, 1976.

Bengel, John A. *New Testament Word Studies.* 1742. Reprint. Grand Rapids: Eerdmans, 1971.

Calvin, John. *Commentaries on the Epistles to Timothy, Titus, and Philemon.* 1856. Reprint. Grand Rapids: Eerdmans, 1948.

Comfort, Philip. "Reading the Inspired Word" in *Inspired Word,* Spring 1986.

Conybeare and Howson. *The Life and Epistles of St. Paul.* 1851. Reprint. Grand Rapids: Eerdmans, 1978.

Cremer, Hermann. *Biblico-Theological Lexicon of the New Testament Greek.* Edinburgh: T & T Clark, 1878.

Earle, Ralph. "Second Timothy" in the *Expositor's Bible Commentary.* Grand Rapids: Zondervan, 1978.

Metzger, Bruce M. *A Textual Commentary on the Greek New Testament.* New York: United Bible Societies, 1971, 1975.

Moulton and Milligan. *The Vocabulary of the Greek New Testament.* Grand Rapids: Eerdmans, 1930.

Packer, J. I. on "Inspiration" in *New Bible Dictionary 2nd ed.,* ed. J. D. Douglas. Wheaton, Ill.: Tyndale House Publishers, 1982 (with InterVarsity Press).

Paley, William. *Horae Paulinae* (or, *The Truth of Scripture History of St. Paul).* Dublin: Printed for M'Kenzie, 1790.

Rienecker, Fritz. *Linguistic Key to the Greek New Testament.* Grand Rapids: Baker Book House, 1976, 1980.

Tittmann, J. A. *Remarks on the Synonyms of the New Testament.* Edinburgh: T & T Clark, 1833-37.

Tregelles, Samuel P. *New Testament Historic Evidence.* London: Bagster & Sons, 1852.

White, Newport J. D. "First and Second Epistles to Timothy" in the *Expositor's Greek Testament.* Grand Rapids: Eerdmans, 1979.

Wuest, Kenneth. "The Pastoral Epistles" in *Word Studies in the Greek New Testament.* Grand Rapids: Eerdmans, 1954.

# TITUS
## Introduction

Paul's Epistle to Titus was written probably from Corinth after his first imprisonment, when Paul was on his way to Nicopolis (3:12) in Epirus. Therefore, the Epistle to Titus was written between A.D. 63 and 67. This epistle is much like 1 Timothy; both were written from the same place, Corinth, and at dates not widely apart—1 Timothy shortly after coming to Corinth (before he had planned a journey to Epirus) and the Epistle to Titus afterwards. The journey to Crete and Ephesus for the bearers of his letters would be easy from Corinth, and he could himself easily go into Epirus from there. He had shortly before visited Crete, where a church existed (though without proper organization). He may have laid its foundation during his former visit (Acts 27:7, etc.), when on his way to his first imprisonment at Rome. That he returned to the East after his first imprisonment appears most probable from Philippians 2:24; Philemon 22. However, there may have been seeds of the gospel sown in Crete, even before his first visit, by the Cretans who heard Peter's preaching at Pentecost (Acts 2:11).

But some bad seed fell among the good. Corrupt elements soon showed themselves in the Cretan church similar to those noticed in the Epistles to Timothy: Judaism, false pretensions to science (or Gnosticism), and ungodliness. Paul, on his late visit, had left Titus in Crete to establish church government and ordain elders. Titus had been several times employed by Paul on a mission to the Corinthian churches and may have visited Crete, which was within easy reach of Corinth. Hence the suitableness of his selection by the apostle for the superintendence of the Cretan church. Paul then followed up with instructions by letter those he had already given to Titus in person on the qualifications of elders and the graces becoming the old, young, and women. He also warns him against the unprofitable speculations so rife in Crete. The national character of the Cretans was extremely low, as Epimenides, who was quoted in 1:12, paints it. Livy (44.45) stigmatizes their avarice; Polyblus (6.46.9) their ferocity and fraud; and (6.47.5) their deceit—so much so, that "to Cretanize" is another name for to lie.

Titus was a Greek and therefore a Gentile (Gal. 2:1, 3); he was converted through Paul's ministry (1:4). He accompanied the apostle on the deputation sent from the church of Antioch to Jerusalem to consult the apostles about the circumcision of Gentile converts (Acts 15:2). He himself, unlike Timothy, was not circumcised. He was in company with Paul at Ephesus, from where he was sent to Corinth to commence the collection for the Jerusalem saints and to ascertain the effect of the First Epistle to the Corinthians (2 Cor. 7:6-9; 8:6; 12:18). He next proceeded to Macedonia, where he joined Paul, who had been already eagerly expecting him at Troas (2 Cor. 2:12, 13; 7:6). He was then employed by the apostle in preparing the collection for the poor saints in Judea and became the bearer of the Second Epistle to the Corinthians (2 Cor. 8:16, 17, 23). In this epistle Paul calls him "my partner and fellow helper concerning you." His being located in Crete (Titus 1:5) took place after Paul's first imprisonment and shortly before the second, about A.D. 67, ten years later than the last mention of him in 2 Corinthians, A.D. 57. He probably met Paul, as the apostle desired, at Nicopolis, for his subsequent journey into Dalmatia would be more likely than from the distant Crete (2 Tim. 4:10, written after the Epistle to Titus). In the unsettled state of things then, Titus's commission in Crete was to be but temporary—Paul requiring the presence of Titus whenever Artemas or Tychicus should arrive in Crete to relieve him of his duties there.

*Chapter* **1**

### 1-4 INTRODUCTORY REMARKS

**➤1 servant** [slave] **of God**—This phrase is not found anywhere else in Paul's writings. Paul usually referred to himself as a servant of Christ (see Rom. 1:1; Phil. 1:1). While Romans 1:1 follows with "called to be an apostle," the passage here follows with "apostle of Jesus Christ." The former describes a general designation of the office of an apostle, the latter a special designation, "apostle of Jesus Christ." The expression of Paul's apostolic office in both letters points out the form and content of his message. The special designation here would never have been forged. **according to the faith**—rather, "for the faith." This was Paul's purpose as an apostle (cf. 1:4, 9; Rom. 1:5). **God's elect**—chosen ones of God. For them we should be willing to suffer (2 Tim. 2:10). This choosing has its roots purely in God's will and purpose, not in anything the chosen ones possess (2 Tim. 1:9; Rom. 8:30-33; cf. Luke 18:7; Eph. 1:4; Col. 3:12). All faith on the part of the chosen begins with God, who gives it to them. They do not become chosen by their faith, but receive faith—becoming believers because they are chosen. **and the acknowledging** [full knowledge] **of the truth**—the full knowledge of the truth, the Christian truth (Eph. 1:13). **after** [according to] **godliness**—This knowledge is in opposition to error, both on practical and doctrinal levels (see 1:11, 16; 1 Tim. 6:3). It is also in opposition to natural earthly truth replacing heavenly truth. Heavenly truth results in the growth of divine life. "Godliness" or "piety" is a term pecu-

liar to the Pastoral Epistles. Paul used it in combating the doctrinal errors that led to ungodliness. Godliness means the condition of one who lives a sanctified life in the presence of God so as to express God in his or her living.

**➤2 In hope of eternal life**—lit., "based upon the hope of eternal life." The connection between 1:1 and 1:2 is not clear. Some commentators say that this describes the basis for Paul's apostleship (i.e., his apostleship rested on his hope of eternal life), and others say that this describes the basis of the elect's faith and knowledge (i.e., the Christian's life is grounded in the hope of eternal life). Perhaps Paul meant for Titus (and us) to see both connections (see Hiebert). **promised before the world began**—This is a contracted expression for the promise "purposed before the world began and promised actually in time," the promise springing from the eternal purpose (2 Tim. 1:9). **God . . . cannot lie**—See Romans 3:4; 11:29; Hebrews 6:18.

**➤3 in due times**—lit., "in its own seasons," meaning that God has a fixed time for it (see Acts 1:7). **manifested**—This implies that God's promise (1:2) was previously hidden (cf. Col. 1:26; 2 Tim. 1:9, 10). **through preaching**—"in the [gospel] proclamation." The word preached presents full knowledge (1:1), generates faith (1:1), and gives eternal life (1:2). **committed**—entrusted. **God our Saviour**—lit., "of our Savior God." In the Pastoral Epistles, this expression (or ones similar) appears often: 1 Timothy 1:1; 2:3; 4:10; Titus 1:3; 2:10; 3:4. In each of these verses, the appellation seems to describe God the Father. The OT spoke of God as Savior or Deliverer (see Ps. 24:5; Isa. 12:2; 45:15, 21, LXX), and so did a few other NT writers (Luke 1:47; Jude 25). The Son is also called "Savior" in the Pastoral Epistles (2 Tim. 1:10; Titus 1:4; 2:13; 3:6), and in Titus 2:13 the Son is called "God and our Savior."

➤**4 Titus, mine own son**—The Greek reads, "my genuine child" (see 1 Tim. 1:2). Titus heard and received the gospel from Paul (cf. 1 Cor. 4:17; Philem. 10). **after**—in accordance with. **the common faith**—the faith common to all the people of God, not restricted to Jews only, but included Gentiles such as Titus as well (cf. 2 Pet. 1:1; Jude 3). **Grace, mercy, and peace**—Although some ancient manuscripts support this reading, the two earliest manuscripts (Codices Sinaiticus and Ephraem Rescriptus) do not have the word "mercy." Later copyists could have easily added "mercy" in an attempt to emulate the style of the two other Pastoral Epistles (see 1 Tim. 1:2; 2 Tim. 1:2). **our Saviour**—This title is added to Christ's name only in Paul's Pastoral Letters and in 2 Peter 1:1, 11; 2:20; 3:18.

## 5-9 QUALIFICATIONS FOR ELDERS

➤**5 For this cause I left thee in Crete, that thou shouldest set in order the things that are wanting**—Although Paul began the work in Crete, he was unable to correct all the problems there due to his short stay. There is little doubt that Christianity had existed in Crete for some time because a number of Cretans had heard Paul's message at Pentecost (Acts 2:11). There was a large contingent of Jews in Crete (1:10), and it is probably that those who fled after Stephen's persecution (Acts 11:19) brought the gospel to these Jews as well as to the Jews in Cyprus, Antioch, etc. Furthermore, Paul landed in Crete on his way to Rome when the winds blew the sailing vessels off course (Acts 27:7-12). By all these situations, the gospel was sure to reach Crete. Yet until Paul's later visit, after his Roman imprisonment, the Cretan Christians were without organization, which Paul began to remedy. In writing this letter, Paul was encouraging Titus to complete the task. **ordain**—actually, "appoint." **in every city**—Greek, "from city to city." In each city where there was a local church, Titus was to appoint a group of elders (cf. Acts 14:23).

Concerned that the right type of elders be chosen due to the faltering condition of the Cretan Christians, Paul wanted Titus to choose men who would stop gossip and superstition. His concern here is not only to find elders but to find suitable ones. The following verses bear this out.

➤**6, 7** It is important that all the elders be reputable men in the local assembly. Immorality was a problem among the Cretans, so that an elder had to be able to take a firm stand when this issue came up. The Cretans had been poorly instructed, so the elders had to be knowledgeable and to hold a firm belief in God's truth as expressed in Christ (1:9). **the husband of one wife**—See comments on 1 Timothy 3:2. **having faithful children**—i.e., believing children. If an elder could not lead his own children to believe in the Lord, how could he lead others? **not accused of riot**—"not open to the charge of being profligate" (RSV). It is not enough that the children not be wild; they must also be above suspicion of such behavior. **unruly**—insubordinate. First Timothy 3:4 states this in more positive terms: "children who obey quickly and quietly" (TLB). **bishop**—lit., "overseer" (Gk., *episcopos*). In the NT, elders functioned as overseers (cf. Acts 20:17 and 20:28, where the "elders" of the church at Ephesus are called "overseers"). An overseer (or, bishop) in the post-apostolic times was made higher than the elders; in fact, one elder became the presiding elder and was given the title "bishop." The NT church had no such practice. **must be blameless**—The emphasis is on "must." If an elder is to influence his congregation for good, then it is absolutely necessary that he be blameless himself. **the steward of God**—An elder should serve as God's steward in God's household (the Gk. word for "steward" has the same root as the word for "household"). Stewards are not merely church officers, but God's servants, for church government is a divine appointment. **not selfwilled**—not self-pleasing. An elder must be able to accommodate others in a hospitable manner. The example of Nabal is the antithesis of this. He was "uncouth, churlish, stubborn, and ill-mannered" (1 Sam. 25:3, TLB). **not given to wine, no striker**—See comments on 1 Timothy 3:3, 8. **not given to filthy lucre**—"not pursuing dishonest gain" (NIV). Preaching the gospel should not be a task motivated by a desire to get rich (1 Tim. 3:8). There were those at this time who preached and taught only to make money (1:11; 1 Tim. 6:5; 1 Pet. 5:2).

**►8 a lover of hospitality**—lit., "a lover of foreigners [foreign travelers]"—This was needed especially in those days. (See Rom. 12:13; 1 Tim. 3:2; Heb. 13:2; 1 Pet. 4:9; 3 John 5.) It was customary for traveling Christians to be given lodging by brothers and sisters in the faith. **lover of good men**—Greek, "a lover of all that is good," men or things. One is to fix his thoughts on the true, the good, and the right, thinking pure thoughts, and dwelling on the fine things in others (Phil. 4:8). **sober**—discreet or self-restrained (Alford). (See comments on 1 Tim. 2:9.) **just**—toward men. **holy**—devout, devoted to God (the same Greek word is used in 1 Tim. 2:8). **temperate**—self-controlled. These traits encompass emotions, speech, actions, and vision.

**►9 Holding fast the faithful word**—"He must hold firmly to the trustworthy message" (NIV). **as he hath been taught**—lit., "according to the teaching" which he has received (1 Tim. 4:6; 2 Tim. 3:14). **sound doctrine**—Greek, "healthy teaching." **convince the gainsayers**—reprove those who contradict. An elder must not only teach truth in a positive way, but he must refute those who claim to know other truths. Thus, the propagation of truth is approached in two ways: the first is in teaching, while the second is in defending that teaching against error.

## 10-16 BEWARE OF FALSE TEACHERS

**►10 unruly**—insubordinate. **vain talkers**—cf. 1 Timothy 1:6. **deceivers**—lit., "deceivers of the mind" of others. **specially they of the circumcision**—The source of a number of problems in the Cretan churches was the Judaizers (i.e., false and genuine Jewish Christians who insisted on keeping Jewish laws and customs and enforced them on Gentile Christians). According to Josephus, many Jews were then living in Crete.

**►11 Whose mouths must be stopped**—lit., "muzzled" or "bridled" as is done with an ornery horse or mule (Ps. 32:9). **subvert**—overturn. **whole houses**—entire households. The Judaizers were destroying the faith of entire families (cf. 2 Tim. 2:18). **for filthy lucre's sake**—base gain (1 Tim. 3:3, 8; 6:5).

**►12 One**—This refers to Epimenides of Cnossus, in Crete, around 600 B.C. He was considered a prophet, sent to purify Athens from Cylon's polluted teachings. The following quote is probably taken from Cretica. Paul also quotes from two other heathen writers, Aratus (Acts 17:28), and Meander (1 Cor. 15:33), although he does not mention their names. **One of themselves** [their own]—This enhances Epimenides' authority as a witness. "To Cretanize" was proverbial for "to lie," as "to Corinthianize" meant "to be immoral." **alway[s] liars**—cf. the phrase in 1:2, "that [who] cannot lie" (referring to God). The Cretans loved "fables" (1:14); even the heathen poets laughed at their lying assertion that they had the tomb of Jupiter in their country. **evil beasts**—Since Crete was without wild animals, Epimenides satirized the Cretans by saying that the human inhabitants took their place. **slow bellies**—"lazy gluttons" (RSV, NIV). The Cretans were lazy because they lived only to satisfy physical appetites (Phil. 3:19).

**►13 This witness is true**—The testimony of Epimenides was true. **rebuke them sharply**—The Christians involved in this perversion needed to be severely reproved. **that they may be sound** [healthy] **in the faith**—Those corrupted by false teachers needed to be brought back to health in the faith.

**►14 Jewish fables**—See 1 Timothy 1:4; 4:7; 2 Timothy 4:4. These formed the transition to subsequent Gnosticism. At this point the error was not openly opposed to the faith, but it was unprofitable and tended toward ungodliness. **commandments of men**—This refers to ascetic or total abstinence (1:15; Mark 7:7-9; Col. 2:16, 20-23; 1 Tim. 4:3). **turn from the truth**—This refers to persons who characteristically turn away from truth (2 Tim. 4:4).

**►15 Unto the pure all things are pure**—Things that are external are pure in themselves, for the distinction is not between pure and impure in "things," but rather, in the disposition of the one using those things. This is in opposition to the "commands of men" (1:14), which prohibited certain things as intrinsically impure. To those who are pure in heart by faith (Acts 15:9; Rom. 14:20; 1 Tim. 4:3), all outward things are pure; all things are free to be used. Sin alone contaminates the soul (Matt. 23:26; Luke 11:41). **nothing pure**—either within or without (Rom. 14:23). **mind**—Both mental sense and intelligence are meant here. **conscience**—The motives and actions of a man with an impure conscience are distinctly opposed to the law of God. Throughout the Pastoral Epistles a corrupt conscience and mind are represented as the source of error (1 Tim. 1:19; 6:5).

➤**16 They profess that they know God**— They may know God on a theoretical level but practically have no knowledge of him. **but in works they deny him**—Their actions betray their speech (1 Tim. 5:8; 2 Tim. 2:12; 3:5). They are **abominable** (detestable) themselves, even though they emphasize the corrupting effects of external things (cf. Rom. 2:22). **disobedient**—They do not obey God (3:3; Eph. 2:2; 5:6). **reprobate**—rejected as worthless when tested (see comments on Rom. 1:28; 1 Cor. 9:27; 2 Tim. 3:8).

# Chapter 2

## 1-10 INSTRUCTIONS TO TITUS ON HOW TO TEACH VARIOUS GROUPS OF BELIEVERS

➤**1 But speak thou**—This stands in contrast to the false teachers identified in 1:11, 15, 16. Of this verse and section Calvin said, "He [Paul] deals more in exhortations, because those intent on useless questions needed chiefly to be recalled to the study of a holy, moral life; for nothing so effectually allays men's wandering curiosity as the being brought to recognize those duties in which they ought to exercise themselves." **sound doctrine**—lit., "healthy teaching," teaching that ministers spiritual health.

➤**2 sober**—temperate (1 Tim. 3:2). **grave**— serious, dignified. **temperate**—sensible, self-restrained (1:8; 1 Tim. 2:9). **sound in faith**—healthy in the faith. **charity**—love. **patience**—endurance (see 1 Tim. 6:11). Patience depends on and is supported by hope (1 Cor. 13:7; 1 Thess. 1:3). Older men are especially endowed with these traits, as they are derived by overcoming problems (Rom. 5:3).

➤**3 behaviour as becometh holiness**— reverent demeanor, a quality found in women

dedicated to God (1 Tim. 2:10). **not false accusers**—not slanderers, as are some older women. **not given to much wine**—The Cretans were particularly prone to this problem (1:12). Addiction to drink is slavery (Rom. 6:16; 2 Pet. 2:19). **teachers of good things**— This refers to private teaching, not public (see 1 Cor. 14:34; 1 Tim. 2:11, 12). Older women were to teach goodness to younger women by example.

➤**4 teach the young women to be sober**— or, train the young women. **to love their husbands**—lit., "to be husband-lovers." **to love their children**—lit., "to be child-lovers." Paul wisely advised Titus, a young man, to teach the young women indirectly through the older women.

➤**5 discreet**—sensible. **chaste**—pure. **keepers at home**—Greek, "guardians of the house." The young women were to be conscientious in the responsibilities of home life (Prov. 7:11; 1 Tim. 5:14). **good**—beneficient (Matt. 20:15; Rom. 5:7; 1 Pet. 2:18). They were not to be ungracious or incompetent, but good, frugal housewives. **obedient**—submissive (Eph. 5:21, 22, 24). **their own husbands**—Wives owe subjection to their own husbands (Eph. 5:22; Col. 3:18). **that the word of God be not blasphemed** [spoken against]— The good news must not be discredited by an inconsistent profession of faith (2:8, 10; Rom. 2:24; 1 Tim. 5:14; 6:1).

➤**6 sober minded**—sensible. Nothing is so difficult for a young man as governing his pleasures and impulsive behavior.

➤**7 pattern**—or example. Titus was urged to set the example for the young men, for all teaching is useless unless the teacher's example confirms his word. **in doctrine** [teaching] **showing uncorruptness** [integrity]—so that you will be a pattern for everyone to follow (cf. 2 Cor. 11:3). The truth would be loved as long as Titus loved the truth himself. **gravity**— seriousness. He was to take seriously his responsibility for communicating the truth. **sincerity**—not present in the earliest manuscripts.

➤**8 Sound speech**—lit., "healthy speech." This refers to speech in both public and private affairs. **he that is of the contrary part**—"an opponent" (see 1:9; 2 Tim. 2:25). **may be ashamed**—Power, truth, and innocence can be effective silencers (cf. 2:5, 10; 1 Tim. 5:14; 6:1).

**of you**—in a few ancient manuscripts; most of the ancient manuscripts read "of us."

➤**9 servants**—slaves. **to please them well**—"to give satisfaction" (Alford). Titus was to urge slaves to obey their masters and try their best to please them. The slaves should desire to gain the master's favor by anticipating his wishes and doing more than was required. The relation of master and slave comes up frequently in the NT (Eph. 6:5; Col. 3:22; 1 Tim. 6:1; 1 Pet. 2:18), because in no social situation was there more danger of abusing the truth of Christian equality and freedom. It was natural for the slave who had become a Christian to forget his position and put himself on a level of equality with his master. Each slave was urged to remain as he was when converted (1 Cor. 7:20-24). **not answering again**—not contradicting.

➤**10 not purloining**—not pilfering. **showing all good fidelity**—They should honestly and faithfully do their best (Eph. 6:5, 6; Col. 3:22-24). Non-Christians do not judge the Christian by his words as much as from his actions (Chrysostom). **that they may adorn the doctrine of God our Saviour**—God desires to use those of the lowest social status to bring people to himself; even slaves should not think the influence of their example of no consequence in religious matters. God's love in being our Savior (see 1 Tim. 2:4; 4:10) is the strongest ground for magnifying this truth by our lives.

## 11-15 GOD'S GRACE AS AN INCENTIVE TO GODLINESS

➤**11 the grace of God that bringeth salvation**—lit., "the saving grace of God." **hath appeared**—has been brought to light. With the coming of Christ, the embodiment of grace (John 1:17), God's saving grace came to be manifest to men—after having been kept secret in the past centuries (Col. 1:26; 2 Tim. 1:9, 10). Both the gift of salvation and Christ's glory have appeared (2:13; cf. Rom. 13:12). **to all men**—This refers to those different classes enumerated in 2:2-9, including the Gentiles who were once alienated from God. We thus have an obligation to all men.

➤**12 Teaching**—instructing. **denying**—The Greek aorist tense expresses "denying once for all." **worldly lusts**—Greek, "the lusts

of the world," "all worldly lusts" (Alford) (Gal. 5:16; Eph. 2:3; 1 John 2:15-17; 5:19). We turn from worldly lusts when we refuse to consent to them and obliterate them from our heart and mind. **live soberly, righteously, and godly**—This is the positive side of the Christian life.

➤**13 Looking for**—with constant expectation. This is patient and hopeful waiting (Rom. 8:19). As the object of the Christian's hope becomes more real to him, things that once seemed very attractive have less appeal to him. **blessed**—bringing blessing. **hope**—of Christ's return, of Christ's appearing. The Greek reads, "expecting the blessed hope and appearance," i.e., the hope is the appearance. **the glorious appearing**—Greek, "the appearance of the glory" or "the appearing of the glory." **the great God and our Saviour Jesus Christ**—an inaccurate translation. According to the Greek, it should read "our great God and Savior, Jesus Christ" (see NASB, RSV, NIV). In the Greek, there is one article governing the two titles "God" and "Savior Jesus Christ" joined by the conjunction *kai* ("and"). According to a Greek grammatical rule (called the "Granville Sharpe Rule"—see Dana and Mantey), this structure indicates that the two nouns describe one person. In this case, Jesus Christ is both God and Savior. A similar structure in 2 Peter 1:1 also reveals that Jesus Christ is both God and Savior (see comments there and on 2 Thess. 1:12). In addition to this, there are three reasons why the one called "our great God" is "Jesus Christ." (1) Paul never uses the word "appearing" when speaking of God the Father (cf. John 1:18; 1 Tim. 6:16). This only refers to Christ, with reference to his first coming (2 Tim. 1:10) or his second coming (1 Tim. 6:14; 2 Tim. 4:1, 8). (2) There is no reference to the Father in the passage (see 2:14) but to Christ alone; nor is there any reason for reference to the Father in the passage. (3) The expression "great God," as applied to Christ, fits the context, which refers to "his glorious appearing," just as "the true God" is predicated of Christ in 1 John 5:20. The phrase "great God" occurs nowhere else in the NT but often in the OT. Deuteronomy 7:21 and 10:17 refer to Yahweh, who, as their revealed Lord, led the Israelites through the wilderness. Believers now look for Christ's appearing because they will share in it.

➤**14 Who gave himself for us**—via incarnation and by death. **redeem us**—or, ransom us, i.e., deliver us from bondage by paying the ransom with his blood. **iniquity**—lawlessness. The essence of sin was disobedience to the law, which held us in bondage. Christ's purpose was to rescue us, not merely from death, but from sin itself (see 2:11, 12 for the positive effects). **purify**—cleanse. **a peculiar people**—actually, "a people for his own possession," a people special to God.

➤**15 with all authority**—cf. 1:13. **Let no man despise thee**—cf. 1 Timothy 4:12.

# Chapter 3

## 1-12 LIVING THE CHRISTIAN LIFE

➤**1 Put them in mind**—Though they know their obligations, they are in danger of forgetting them. The struggle between Christianity and paganism and the Jews' rebellion against the Roman Empire could easily cause the Christians to forget their responsibility to obey those in power. Diodorus Siculus mentions the tendency of the Cretans to open rebellion. **to be subject to principalities and powers**—rulers and authorities in civil authority. **to obey magistrates**—simply, "to be obedient" in Greek. **to be ready to every good work**—Romans 13:3 shows that obedience to a civil authority would be honest work since the civil authority's intent is to favor the good and punish the bad.

➤**2 To speak evil of no man**—especially not of those holding public office. **no brawlers**—not contentious. **gentle**—toward those who quarrel with us. We should be understanding and considerate of the other person's point of view (Phil. 4:5). **unto all**—As a result of God's grace to all men the Christian has a responsibility to all men.

➤**3 For we ourselves also were sometimes** [at one time]—Our own past sin should make us compassionate toward others still in sin. The contrast of our former sinfulness with our present deliverance by God's free gift (3:4) is a favorite theme in Paul's writings. We should treat our neighbor as God treated us. **foolish**—Without God's grace, the human life is unreasonable and irrational. The free gift of grace is the only remedy for foolishness. **disobedient**—This refers to an attitude toward God.

**deceived**—led astray. **serving**—as slaves, an image depicting bondage. **hateful, and hating**—hated by men and hating one another.

➤**4 Prior to the appearance of God's love and kindness, all men participated in those things described in 3:3. It was the "kindness and love of God" that saved us, not any goodness on our part. **kindness and love**—God's kindness and love are in opposition to the hateful characteristics of corrupted men (3:3). The Greek word for "kindness" means love toward men, generosity, kindness (Rienecker). The expression "love of God . . . toward men" in Greek means "God's fondness for men." **of God our Saviour**—The Father (1:3) saved us (3:5) "through Jesus Christ our Savior" (3:6). **appeared**—In Greek, the verb form of "epiphany." Christ's first epiphany was a manifestation of God's kindness to men and fondness for them.

➤**5 Not by works of righteousness which we have done**—Since we were without any inherent righteousness, we were necessarily without any righteous works. Only by God's mercy were we saved. **according to his mercy he saved us**—God saved each one of us because he acted out of mercy. Faith is presupposed here as instrumental to our salvation because our actual salvation is spoken of as an "accomplished fact." Paul did not mention faith because his purpose was not to describe man's new state; rather, Paul emphasized the saving agency of God (independent of man's work) in bringing about this new state. **by**—"through," "by means of." **washing**—Greek *loutron*, which can signify the receptacle of washing (the laver) or the act of washing itself. In Ephesians 5:26, the only other NT occurrence of this word, the natural meaning is washing. Here also the action of washing is presented (Hiebert). Many commentators have understood this washing to signify baptism, but such exegesis would lead to the belief in baptismal regeneration. Quite simply, the text says that regeneration is characterized by (or, accompanied by) the action of washing. The regenerative activity of the Holy Spirit is characterized elsewhere in Scripture as also cleansing and purifying (see Ezek. 36:25-27 and see comments on John 3:5). **regeneration**—lit., "birth again," indicating a new birth, an actual regeneration. Such a regeneration is effected by the

Holy Spirit (see John 3:6; Rom. 8:16; Gal. 4:6). **and renewing of the Holy Ghost** [Spirit]— According to the Greek, this phrase is also governed by the one preposition *dia* ("through"). God saved us through (or, by means of) one process with two aspects: the washing of regeneration and renewing of the Holy Spirit. Regeneration washes away the old element and also renews us—giving us a new element (God's life) and a new nature (the divine nature—2 Pet. 1:4). Both the regenerating and the renewing are produced by the Holy Spirit.

➤**6 Which**—referring to the Holy Spirit. The Holy Spirit was poured out not only on the church in general at Pentecost but also upon individuals. **through Jesus Christ our Saviour**—Christ is the means by which we are made acceptable to God, and eligible to receive the gift of his Spirit.

➤**7 being justified by his grace**—Greek, "having been justified by his grace." Justification puts us into the position of becoming God's heirs. And our greatest inheritance is **eternal life.** We *hope* for this inheritance and anticipate it.

➤**8 This is a faithful saying**—This kind of statement is peculiar to the Pastoral Epistles (see 1 Tim. 1:4; 6:4; 2 Tim. 2:23; Titus 1:14). The "saying" is a statement concerning the graciousness of God's gift of salvation (3:4-7). **these things . . . affirm constantly**—i.e., the things Paul has previously detailed. **have believed in God . . . maintain good works**—good works follow faith as evidence of the genuineness of the faith. This parallels the thought in James 2:17, 18.

➤**9** This is a repeated theme in the Pastoral Epistles: see 1 Timothy 1:4; 6:4; 2 Timothy 2:23; Titus 1:14 (Litfin).

➤**10 heretick**—actually, "a man causing factions." Factions occurred when an individual did and taught what he chose, independent of the teaching and practice of the church. This was happening in Crete (3:9). **after the first and second admonition reject**—avoid. The believers should not engage in normal conversation with such people or try to correct them; rather, they should avoid them.

➤**11 subverted**—perverted, warped.

## 12-15 CONCLUDING REMARKS

➤**12 Artemas . . . or Tychicus**—Artemas may have eventually become an elder in the church at Lystra. Paul sent Tychicus to Asia Minor during his first imprisonment (Eph. 6:21) and again during his second imprisonment (2 Tim. 4:12). There is evidence that Tychicus later became an elder at Chalcedon in Bithynia. **Nicopolis**—or, "the city of victory," was named from the battle of Actium in Epirus. This letter was probably written from Corinth in the fall. Paul intended to travel through Etolia and Acarnania and stay in Nicopolis for the winter. (See Introduction.)

➤**13 Zenas**—This is a shortened form of Zenodorus. **lawyer**—This was a Jewish scribe, who still retained the title of his former occupation following his conversion. **Apollos**—Apollos and Zenas were to deliver Paul's letter. In 1 Corinthians 16:12 Apollos is mentioned as intending to visit Corinth; his immediate presence at Corinth (assuming the theory that Paul was in Corinth when he wrote), agrees with this intention. Crete would have been on his way either to Palestine or his homeland, Alexandria. Ironically, Paul and Apollos appear in harmony in the very city where their names had once been used in forming schisms. Paul wanted Apollos to visit sometime before this, but Apollos was unwilling due to partisan rivalry. Hippolytus mentions Zenas as one of the seventy (see Luke 10:1, 17) and afterwards as elder of Diospolis. **nothing be wanting**—They lack nothing for the journey.

➤**14 let ours**—"our people" (NIV), the Christians and fellow members of God's household. **for necessary uses**—"for daily necessities" (NIV) or "for real needs" (TEV). They needed to supply the essential needs of missionaries and other believers (cf. 1:8). **unfruitful**—or, unproductive. "Paul had been stressing the need for good works, not to earn salvation, but to serve others, and he pointedly reiterated it here" (Litfin).

➤**15 those that love us in the faith**—i.e., those who share the same Christian faith as Paul and who love Paul (and his coworkers). **Grace be with you all**—The plural indicates that Paul was addressing an audience greater than just Titus (Litfin) (cf. 1 Tim. 6:21; 2 Tim. 4:22; Philem. 25). **Amen**—is not present in the earliest manuscripts.

## BIBLIOGRAPHY

Alford, Henry. *The Greek New Testament.* 1852. Reprint. Grand Rapids: Guardian Press, 1976.

Calvin, John. *Commentaries on the Epistles to Timothy, Titus, and Philemon.* Edinburgh: Calvin Translation Society. 1856. Reprint. Grand Rapids: Eeerdmans, 1948.

Dana and Mantey. *A Manual Grammar of the Greek New Testament.* New York: MacMillan, 1957.

Hiebert, D. Edmond. *First Timothy.* Chicago: Moody Press, 1967.

Litfin, A. Duane. "Titus" in *The Bible Knowledge Commentary.* Wheaton, Ill.: Victor Books, 1983.

Rienecker, Fritz. *Linguistic Key to the Greek New Testament.* Grand Rapids: Baker Book House, 1976, 1980.

# PHILEMON

## Introduction

The testimonies to this epistle's authenticity are Origen, *Homily 19, on Jeremiah,* which speaks of the letter of Paul to Philemon concerning Onesimus; Tertullian, *Against Marcion,* 5.21; and Jerome, *An Introduction to Philemon,* who argues for it against those who objected to its canonicity on the ground of its subject being beneath an apostle to write about.

Paul's Epistle to Philemon is closely linked with Paul's Epistle to the Colossians. Both were carried by the same bearer, Onesimus (with whom, however, Tychicus is joined in the Epistle to the Colossians—Col. 4:7-9). The persons sending salutations are the same, except one, Jesus called Justus (Col. 4:11). In both Archippus is addressed (v. 2; Col. 4:17), Paul and Timothy stand in the headings, and Paul appears as a prisoner (v. 9; Col. 4:18). Hence it follows, it was written at the same time and place as the Epistle to the Colossians (which was about the same time as the Epistle to the Ephesians), viz., at Rome, during Paul's first imprisonment, A.D. 61 or 62.

Onesimus, of Colosse (called "one of you"—Col. 4:9), slave of Philemon, had fled from his master to Rome after having defrauded him (v. 18). He was brought to Christ by Paul, and being encouraged by him to return to his master, he was furnished with this epistle, recommending him to Philemon's favorable reception—as being now no longer a mere servant but a brother in Christ. Paul ends by requesting Philemon to prepare him a lodging, as he trusted soon to be set free from prison and then to visit Colosse. This epistle is addressed also to Apphia, who is believed to be Philemon's wife because of the letter's domestic subject matter, and to Archippus (a minister of the Colossian church—Col. 4:17), who is believed to be a relative of Philemon for the same reason. In the *Apostolical Canons* (73) Onesimus is said to have been emancipated by his master. Ignatius, *Epistola ad Ephesum,* 1, speaks of him as an elder of the Ephesian church.

Luther's description of this epistle provides a fitting conclusion to the introductory remarks:

> This Epistle shows a right, noble, lovely example of Christian love. Here we see how Paul laid himself out for the poor Onesimus, and with all his means pleaded his cause with his

master, and so set himself as if he were Onesimus, and had himself done wrong to Philemon. Yet all this he did, not with force, as if he had right thereto, but he stripped himself of his right, and thus enforced Philemon to forego his right also. Even as Christ did for us with God the Father, thus also did Paul for Onesimus with Philemon: for Christ also stripped Himself of His right, and by love and humility enforced [?] the Father to lay aside His wrath and power, and to take us to His grace for the sake of Christ, who lovingly pleads our cause, and with all His heart lays Himself out for us; for we are all His Onesimi, to my thinking.

## Chapter 1

### 1-3 GREETING FROM PAUL TO PHILEMON, TO THE CHURCH MEETING IN HIS HOME, TO APPHIA, AND TO ARCHIPPUS

➤**1 Paul, a prisoner of Jesus Christ** [Christ Jesus]—Paul was jailed for preaching the gospel of Jesus Christ (see also 9, 13, 23). In other epistles Paul names himself more formally as an apostle; here, however, he speaks informally, suggesting a more intimate relationship to those addressed. **our dearly beloved, and fellowlabourer**—Philemon (who was from Colosse) participated in building up the church in Colosse while Paul was in Ephesus.

➤**2 Apphia**—She was either Philemon's wife or a close relative; otherwise she would not have been greeted with Philemon in a letter concerning a domestic matter. **Archippus**—He was a minister in the Colossian church. **fellowsoldier**—See 2 Timothy 2:3, 4. Paul frequently alluded to military concepts in his description of the Christian life, emphasizing the necessity for discipline and commitment. **the church in thy house**—In the first two centuries of the church, Christians met in homes. It is not until the third century that we have any record of separate church buildings (Rupprecht, Deibler). Since Philemon was one of those who labored to begin the church at Colosse, it was very natural to have a church meeting in his home. However, it is very unlikely that the entire church at Colosse met in his home. If it did, Paul would have had to address this epistle to all the saints at Colosse. But he already had written a separate epistle to the entire church (the Epistle to the Colossians), which was sent to Colosse

with Onesimus and Tychicus (see Col. 4:7-9 and Introductions to Colossians and to Philemon) at the same time this epistle to Philemon was sent. Thus, it was Paul's intention that the entire church at Colosse read his larger epistle and that the church meeting at Philemon's house read this smaller, personal epistle. Since the believers meeting in Philemon's home would know of Philemon's affairs—especially concerning Onesimus—it was wise for Paul to include them in this epistle. It would keep them from gossiping, and the church could apply extra pressure on Philemon to meet Paul's request (Deibler). At any rate, the church that met in Philemon's home was a house church, a home meeting (or ecclesia), assembling within the confines of the local church at Colosse. The same kind of meetings are spoken of in Romans 16:5; 1 Corinthians 16:19, 20; Colossians 4:15, 16 (see comments on these verses).

➤**3 Grace to you, and peace, from God our Father and the Lord Jesus Christ**—This is a typical Pauline benediction.

### 4-7 PAUL'S THANKSGIVING FOR PHILEMON

➤**4 I thank my God . . . in my prayers**—Here is another example of Paul's steadfastness in prayer support for those with whom he had contact, as well as his attitude of praise. **always**—joins with "I thank my God."

➤**5 Hearing**—Since Paul had not visited the church in Colosse, his knowledge of them was by word of mouth. Yet verse 19 implies that Philemon was converted as a result of Paul's witness at Ephesus or some other place where he had met Paul. **love and faith**—The usual order is faith, then love. However, Paul purposely put Philemon's love first since Paul is encouraging him to act lovingly. **toward the Lord Jesus, and**

**toward all saints**—The Greek words for "toward" are of two different kinds here. The first indicates a love "toward" *(pros)* the Lord; the second indicates "for" *(eis)* his people. (cf. Col. 1:4).

➤**6 the communication of thy faith**—"the sharing of your faith" (RSV, NIV). Paul's prayer is that Philemon will share his faith with the spiritually needy (cf. Heb. 13:16). **may become effectual**—The measure of Philemon's faith was the degree to which it could affect the lives of others. **by the acknowledging of**—Here the Greek means "as they come to a thorough knowledge of." **every good thing which is in you**—The earliest manuscripts read "which is in us," i.e., a recognition of every grace that is actually in us as Christians. In other words, "That your faith may by acts be proved to work by love." **in Christ Jesus**—In Greek, this is "unto Christ Jesus," i.e., to the glory of Christ Jesus. Three of the oldest manuscripts omit "Jesus." Paul is here paving the way for his request on behalf of Onesimus.

➤**7 we have great joy and consolation in thy love**—cf. 2 Corinthians 7:4. Amidst the sufferings Paul had undergone, he received much joy and comfort from Philemon's love. **the bowels**—were thought of by the Greeks as being the place of deepest emotions. **the saints are refreshed by thee**—The cause of Paul's joy and comfort was Philemon's kindness in opening up his house to fellow Christians.

## 8-20 INTERCESSION ON ONESIMUS'S BEHALF

➤**8 I might . . . enjoin thee**—i.e., "I could order you." By virtue of Paul's apostolic authority, or in response to Philemon's obligation to Paul, because of having been converted through his witness (v. 19), Paul could have demanded the favor rather than asked it. But Paul was appealing to his friendship with Philemon rather than to his apostolic authority. **in Christ**—Christ was the source of Paul's apostolic authority.

➤**9 Paul the aged**—or, "Paul, an ambassador" (RSV, NEB, TEB). The Greek word can mean an old man or an ambassador.

➤**10 I beseech thee for my son Onesimus**—In the Greek, the name "Onesimus" is skillfully put last; he puts first a favorable description of the slave who had fallen into disrepute with Philemon. Scripture does not sanction slavery, nor does it begin a political crusade against it. Scripture sets forth principles of love to our fellowmen regardless of social position or external circumstances. **whom I have begotten in my bonds**—i.e., "whom I won to the Lord while here in my chains" (TLB).

➤**11 unprofitable**—Onesimus's name in Greek means "profitable, useful." Paul played on this name in saying that he belied it; he was not only of little use, but had actually wronged his master. **profitable [useful] to thee and to me**—Onesimus became useful in spiritual as well as temporal matters.

➤**12 mine own bowels**—in modern parlance, "my very heart" (NIV). (See comments on v. 7.) Paul loved Onesimus with the intense affection of a parent for a child.

➤**13 Whom I would have retained [kept] with me**—The "I" here is emphatic: "*I*, for my part." Paul was saying, in effect, that since he had such implicit trust in Onesimus as to wish to keep him, Philemon could have this kind of trust as well. **that in thy stead [place] he might have ministered unto me**—Paul recognized here that if Philemon were available to be with Paul, he would have helped him in any way he could; therefore, if Paul had kept Onesimus, Philemon would have been helping Paul vicariously. **in the bonds of [for] the gospel**—Paul endured chains for the sake of the gospel.

➤**14** This verse is clearer when translated: "But I preferred to do nothing without your consent in order that your goodness might not be by compulsion but of your own free will" (RSV). Had Paul kept Onesimus, Philemon would have had no opportunity to show his willingness to send Onesimus back to Paul.

➤**15 perhaps**—Paul now postulates that Onesimus's desertion may have been part of God's providence, the past evil being overruled for the greater good. **receive him**—The Greek means "have him for yourself in full possession."**for ever**—Onesimus's absence, however long it may have been, was short as compared with the devotion now binding him to his master.

➤**16 Not now as a servant** [slave] . . . **a brother beloved**—No longer merely a slave, Onesimus is now also a brother in the Lord. **specially to me**—Paul was Onesimus's spiritual father and experienced his faithful attentions. To offset Philemon's distaste for accepting Onesimus as a brother, Paul first recognized him as his own brother and as the spiritual son of the same God. **much more unto thee**—Onesimus stood in a nearer and more lasting relationship to Philemon than to Paul.

➤**17 partner**—Onesimus should be Philemon's partner in the Christian fellowship of faith, hope, and love. **receive him as myself**—This thought refers back to verse 12.

➤**18 If he hath wronged thee**—Onesimus seems to have confessed some such act to Paul. **put that on mine account**—Paul was ready to make good the loss if necessary. The latter parts of verses 19 and 21 imply that he did not expect Philemon to demand it.

➤**19 I Paul have written it with mine own hand**—"A signature to a deed in ancient or medieval times would commonly take this form. . . .This incidental mention of his autograph, occurring where it does, shows that he wrote the whole letter with his own hand. This procedure is quite exceptional, just as the purpose of the letter is exceptional. In all other cases he appears to have employed an amanuensis, only adding a few words in his own handwriting at the close . . ." (Lightfoot). **I do not say**—lit., "not to say," not to mention. **how thou owest unto me even thine own self besides**—Because of Paul's part in Philemon's conversion, Philemon owed Paul his spiritual life. So if the debt Onesimus owed Philemon were transferred to Paul, the debt would be cancelled.

➤**20 let me have joy**—The "me" is emphatic in the Greek. The Greek word for "joy" (*onaimēn*) can also mean "profit" or "benefit"; the word is cognate to the name "Onesimus." **refresh my bowels**—See comments on verse 7.

## 21-25 CONCLUSION AND GREETINGS

➤**21 Having confidence in thy obedience**—This is an allusion to Paul's apostolic authority (v. 8), which he had chosen not to use; instead, he had asked a favor (v. 9). **do more than I say**—Here is perhaps a hint that Philemon could free Onesimus, in addition to treating him kindly.

➤**22** This prospect of Paul's visiting Colosse would tend to secure a kindly reception to Onesimus, as Paul would know in person how he had been treated. **you**—plural in the Greek. This refers to Philemon, Apphia, Archippus, and the church in Philemon's house. Paul expected to be released from prison; this was also in another letter written during the same imprisonment (Phil. 2:23, 24).

➤**23** The same persons send salutations in the accompanying Epistle to the Colossians, except that "Jesus Justus" is not mentioned here (cf. Col. 4:10-14). **Epaphras my fellow prisoner**—He had been sent by the Colossian church to look after Paul and possibly was cast into prison by the Roman authorities on suspicion. However, he is not mentioned as a prisoner in Colossians 4:12, so that "fellow prisoner" may indicate a faithful companion who has aligned himself with Paul in the eyes of society—so also "Aristarchus, my fellow prisoner" (Col. 4:10).

➤**25 grace . . . be with your spirit**—This is typical of Paul's benedictions; similar ones can be seen in Galatians 6:18 and 2 Timothy 4:22. The grace of our Lord Jesus Christ is with Christians' spirits because the Spirit of Jesus Christ indwells the spirits of the believers. The final expression, "your spirit," is plural in Greek; it is a benediction for all those addressed in verses 1 and 2. **Amen**—is not present in some of the earliest manuscripts.

BIBLIOGRAPHY

Deibler, Edwin C. "Philemon" in *The Bible Knowledge Commentary.* Wheaton, Ill.: Victor Books, 1983.

Lightfoot, J. B. *St. Paul's Epistles to the Colossians and*

*Philemon.* 1879. Reprint. Grand Rapids: Zondervan, 1957.

Rupprecht, Arthur A. "Philemon" in the *Expositor's Bible Commentary.* Grand Rapids: Zondervan, 1978.

# HEBREWS
## Introduction

Since the writer of Hebrews did not identify himself (or, herself), readers throughout the ages have made conjectures about its authorship. Among the candidates who have been named are Paul, Barnabas, Apollos, and Luke.

Clement of Alexandria attributed it expressly to Paul, on the authority of Pantaenus (second century). Clement said that since Jesus is referred to as the "apostle" (3:1), Paul, through humility, does not call himself an apostle of the Hebrews. This is especially appropriate since Paul is known as the apostle to the Gentiles. Clement added that Paul prudently omitted his name on it because the Hebrews to whom it was written were prejudiced against him. (Clement also thought that Paul wrote it in Hebrew and Luke translated it into Greek.) The earliest extant collection of Paul's epistles in one volume, namely the Chester Beatty Papyrus (P46), dated early third century, includes Hebrews as the second book in the collection, following Romans. Origen quoted Hebrews as being an epistle of Paul; however, in his *Homilies,* he regarded the style distinct from that of Paul, and as "more Grecian" but the thoughts as the apostle's—adding that the "ancients who have handed down the tradition of its Pauline authorship must have had good reason for doing so, though God alone knows with certainty who was the actual writer." In the African church, in the beginning of the third century, Tertullian ascribed it to Barnabas. Irenaeus, bishop of Lyons, is mentioned in Eusebius's writings as quoting from this epistle, without expressly referring it to Paul. About the same period, Gaius, the presbyter in the church of Rome, mentions only *thirteen* epistles of Paul, whereas, if the Epistle to the Hebrews were included, there would be *fourteen.* And the Muratorian Canon (end of second century, or beginning of the third) omits mentioning it. Thus, the Latin church did not recognize it as Paul's until a considerable time after the beginning of the third century. In the fourth century, Hilary of Poitiers, Lucifer of Cagliari, Ambrose of Milan, and other Latins, quote it as Paul's, and the fifth Council of Carthage (A.D. 419) formally counted it among his fourteen epistles.

As to the similarity of its style to that of Luke's writings, this is due to Luke's having been so long the companion of Paul. Chrysostom, comparing Luke and Mark, says, "Each imitated his teacher: Luke imitated Paul, flowing along with more than river-fulness; but Mark imitated Peter, who studied brevity of style." Besides, there is a greater use of Hebrew idiom in this epistle than in Luke's writings. There is no clear evidence for attributing the authorship to Luke, or to Apollos, whom some scholars uphold as the author. The grounds alleged for the latter view are its supposed Alexandrian phraseology and modes of thought. But it would be unlikely that the Alexandrian church should have so undoubtingly asserted the Pauline authorship, if Apollos, their own countryman, had really been the author. Nevertheless, it could be admitted that the eloquence of its style and rhetoric is more characteristic of what we presume of Apollos's preaching than what we know of Paul's style of preaching. Furthermore, the writer of Hebrews consistently quoted from the Septuagint, the Greek translation of the Old Testament made in Alexandria, and the writer used the allegorical method of biblical interpretation, a method very popular in Alexandria. But if Apollos was the writer, we have no record from the African church to this effect. Barnabas is also a good candidate because he was a Jew, a Levite (hence, all the references to the priesthood in Hebrews), and a companion of Paul. But, again, Barnabas's authorship cannot be proved.

Those who favor Pauline authorship usually point to 13:19, 23 as showing that this epistle must have been written by Paul during his imprisonment, for he speaks of being restored (i.e., set free from prison) and of Timothy already being freed. But Timothy was not in prison before or during either of Paul's two imprisonments (see Introductions to 1 Timothy and to 2 Timothy). Timothy's release probably came *after* Paul's decease, some time between A.D. 67 and A.D. 70—which is the date most scholars say Hebrews was written. (Hebrews had to have been written before A.D. 70—the time of Jerusalem's destruction—because the author spoke of the Levitical priesthood as still existing.)

If the author was not Paul, the writer displayed a remarkable likeness to Pauline thought, for Hebrews has many expressions similar to those in Paul's epistles. So the divine Son appears as the image, or manifestation of Deity in 1:3, as in other epistles of Paul (Phil. 2:6; Col. 1:15-20); his lowering of himself for man's sake similarly (cf. 2:9 with 2 Cor. 8:9; Phil. 2:7, 8); also his final exaltation (cf. 2:8; 10:13; 12:2 with 1 Cor. 15:25, 27). The word "Mediator" is peculiar to Paul alone (cf. 8:6 with Gal. 3:19, 20). Christ's death is represented as the sacrifice for sin prefigured by the Jewish sacrifices (cf. Rom. 3:22-26; 1 Cor. 5:7 with Heb. 7-10). The phrase "God of peace" is peculiar to Paul (cf. 13:20 with Rom. 15:33; 1 Thess. 5:23). Justification, or "righteous by faith," appears in 11:7; 10:38 and in Romans 1:17; 4:22; 5:1; Galatians 3:11; Philippians 3:9. The word of God is the "sword of the Spirit" (cf. 4:12 with Eph. 6:17). Inexperienced Christians are *children* needing *milk,* i.e., instruction in the *elements,* whereas mature Christians, *as full grown men,* require *strong meat* (cf. 5:12, 13; 6:1 with 1 Cor. 3:1, 2; 14:20; Gal. 4:9; Col. 3:14). Salvation is represented as a *boldness of access to God by Christ* (cf. 10:19 with Rom. 5:2; Eph. 2:18; 3:12). The Christian life is a *race* (cf. 12:1 with 1 Cor. 9:24; Phil. 3:12-14). But such similarities are not conclusive proof for Pauline authorship, for similar parallels can be drawn between Peter's writings and Paul's, and even John's writings. Nevertheless, the similarities demonstrate that the author of Hebrews communicated what Paul himself would have probably said—in essence, if not exact expression.

The author's intention in this epistle is to show the superiority of Christ and the new covenant over Judaism and the old covenant. The new covenant was introduced by one far higher than the angels or Moses, through whom the Jews received the law. And the OT priesthood and sacrifices are inferior to Christ's priesthood and sacrifice. Besides, Christ is the substance of which the former are but the shadow, and type necessarily gives place to the antitype. Now we are no longer kept at a comparative distance from

God, as under the law, but have freedom of access through the opened veil, i.e., Christ's flesh. His readers, Jewish Christians, were in danger of returning to Judaism and the OT economy—and thereby committing apostasy. The writer urges them to see the preeminence of Christ over everything in the old covenant, to not return to Judaism, and to go forward in pursuit of Christ.

As was mentioned before, the Epistle to the Hebrews was written before the destruction of Jerusalem, which would have been mentioned in the epistle had that event gone before (cf. 13:10). The epistle was probably directed to churches in which the Jewish members were the more numerous, as those in Judea and perhaps Alexandria. There were more Jews in Alexandria than any other city, besides Jerusalem. It was from Alexandria that the epistle appears to have come first to the knowledge of Christendom. Moreover, "the Epistle to the Alexandrians," mentioned in the Muratorian Canon may possibly be this Epistle to the Hebrews. The title to the Epistle, "Hebrews," is attested by Pantaenus (in Eusebius's *Ecclesiastical History,* 6.14.4) and Tertullian (*De Pudicitia,* 20). This title is found in the earliest manuscripts. "It is often said that the title was not original, and this may be the case, though it should be added that we have no knowledge of any other title or any time when it lacked this one" (Morris). The word "Hebrew" means "one belonging to Eber," as was Abraham (Gen. 10:21; 11:14ff.); thus, "Hebrews" is patronymic for Abraham and his descendants, the Jews.

*Chapter* **1**

## 1-14 THE SON OF GOD, SUPERIOR TO ANGELS

While God used a number of media and methods to tell us something about himself, he could only make himself fully understood through a person. That person, Christ, has finally come and the highest honors belong to him.

➤**1 sundry times**—Greek, "in many portions." All was not revealed to each single prophet; but one received one portion of revelation, and another prophet another portion of revelation. **divers manners**—various ways, different modes. God used different ways to communicate his word to different men. He communicated through angels, dreams, visions, and direct speech. **in time past**—Four hundred years had passed between the end of the OT and the arrival of God's personal revelation. **the fathers**—The term is not restricted to the patriarchs (Abraham, Isaac, and Jacob) but refers to all who went before in the faith (Heb. 11:4-38). **by the prophets**—lit., "in the prophets." God did not merely use the prophets mechanically but was *in* them when he spoke.

Westcott said, "They were His messengers, inspired by His Spirit, not in their words only but as men."

➤**2 in these last days**—These words were used for the messianic age, and they indicate that it has begun. **by his Son**—lit., "in Son." The preposition in Greek is *en,* and there is no article before "Son." The preposition shows us that the writer was thinking of God's presence *in* his Son. And the lack of article shows that the emphasis is not on Christ's person, but on his relationship to God the Father as Son. The writer proceeded to show us that a son is the ideal medium for God's self-expression. Everything is his; everything was made through him (John 1:3; Col. 1:16), and he has the most honored position. He first revealed who the Son is in himself (1:3) and then who he is in relation to the angels (1:4-14). **heir of all things**—because all things were created through him. **world**—lit., "ages" or "aeons." Here, the word refers to the entire space-time universe.

➤**3 the brightness**—lit., "the shining out." The word expresses the beaming effulgence emanating from a glorious source of light—like the beams of the sun. Christ, as the effulgence of God's glory, is the radiance of God. The Son is the light of light, the beaming out of God—bringing God's glory to be expressed among men. **express image**—The Greek word (*character*) originally meant the instrument used in engraving or stamping (as on coins); it then developed to mean the image so engraved or stamped (Morris). In this context it means that Christ is "the exact representation of his [God's] being" (NIV), "the very stamp of his nature" (RSV). Since God's essence, nature, and being are invisible, the Son's function is to be the express image, the exact visible likeness of God to men. **person**—The Greek word is *hupostasis* (lit., "that which stands under"); the word denotes the underlying substance or essential reality of any particular thing. Christ is the exact impress of God's underlying substance, the visible representation of God's essence. **upholding all things**—or, "carrying all things." Christ does not merely hold up the universe; he carries it along to a desired end and sustains it. **the word**—Greek, "the spoken word," the command. **of his power**—his empowered and empowering word. **by himself**—This is the reading in one early manuscript (the Chester Beatty Papyrus, P46) and several late manuscripts. But all the other early manuscripts do not support this reading. **purged our sins**—lit., "having made a cleansing of sins." This is the first mention of Christ's priestly function, which is the main theme of the book. **sat down on the right hand of the Majesty on high**—See Romans 8:34; Ephesians 3:20; Colossians 3:1. This is not a physical location or position, but the place of highest honor that Christ received after his crucifixion, resurrection, and ascension (Phil. 2:8, 9).

►**4** After the Son's own person has been presented, the writer turns to his relationship to others. **Being made so much better**—Christ was made superior when he was exalted in contrast to being made lower than angels when he was incarnated (3:9). Jesus Christ, the God-man, is now exalted above all angels. In him humanity has been raised to a level higher than ever before.

►**5 Thou art my son, this day have I begotten thee**—This passage, which comes from Psalm 2:7, was quoted in Acts 13:33 as applying to Christ's resurrection. **I will be to him a Father, and he shall be to me a Son**—Taken from 2 Samuel 7:14, this statement, originally spoken to Solomon, finds its true

fulfillment in the Messiah, God's Son, the heir of David's throne.

►**6 again**—This word can be joined with "bringeth" (when he brings again the first-begotten into the world), and thus would indicate a reference to Christ's second coming. **firstbegotten**—firstborn (see Col. 1:18). **world**—inhabited earth. **let all the angels of God worship him**—Although this quotation is similar to Psalm 97:7 (which states that it is Yahweh who is to receive worship), it actually comes from Deuteronomy 32:43 in the Septuagint (which, in this verse, is supported by one of the Dead Sea Scrolls).

►**7 of the angels he saith**—This OT quotation comes from Psalm 104:4. The idea is that God makes his messengers (angels) into winds and his servants into flames (Morris). The servants are therefore expendable but not the Son, who is eternal.

►**8 unto the Son he saith, Thy throne, O God**—The quotation comes from Psalm 45:6. God the Father, in speaking to his Son, calls him "O God." Some translations (see RSV mg., NEB mg.) indicate that this could read, "God is thy throne," but such a reading violates the Greek and obscures Christ's deity. God calls his Son "God" and declares that his throne is everlasting because of his righteousness (see 1:9). **sceptre**—rod.

►**9** This verse continues the quotation of Psalm 45; here it is Psalm 45:7. **therefore God, even thy God, hath anointed thee**—According to the Greek, the first word "God" is an articular vocative; i.e., it functions the same way as in the previous verse (see Marshall). The Father, in speaking to the Son, says, "therefore, O God." The second expression "thy God" refers to God and Father. The verse then could read: "therefore, thy God has anointed thee, O God. . . ." The anointing here is the anointing accompanying inauguration into kingship (1 Sam. 10:1; 1 Kings 19:16). **oil**—typifying the Holy Spirit. Christ was anointed with the Holy Spirit at his baptism (Luke 4:18) and at his enthronement. **above thy fellows**—above your companions—i.e., Christ's brothers (2:11).

►**10-12** In still another passage (Ps. 102:25-27), our author takes words that were spoken of Yahweh and applies them to the Son. The

Son is therefore depicted as the Creator who outlives and outlasts his creation.

➤13 **Sit on my right hand, until I make thine enemies thy footstool?**—The argument of Christ's supremacy over angels is brought to a conclusion with a question built around Psalm 110:1. It was the custom of the time that a victorious king would place his foot on the neck of his defeated enemy to show his complete surrender (Josh. 10:24).

➤14 **ministering spirits**—These words resume the thought of 1:7. These spirits are God's servants and sometimes act for the benefit of human beings, especially for those who are the heirs of salvation. **heirs of salvation**—i.e., "those who will inherit salvation" (NIV).

*Chapter* **2**

1-18 DO NOT NEGLECT
SO GREAT A SALVATION

➤1 **Therefore**—The logical conclusion of the argument that the Son is superior to angels (chap. 1) must now be stated. **lest . . . we should let them slip**—or, lest we drift away. This is the danger we face. The figure is that of a boat that is carried downstream because its anchor was not properly secured (cf. 6:19). Neglect of the gospel message will cause us to drift away unknowingly.

➤2 **the word** [message] **spoken by** [through] **angels**—The reference is to the Mosaic law (Deut. 33:2; Ps. 68:17; Acts 7:53; Gal. 3:19). This is not explicitly stated in the account of Exodus 20, but it is clear from other passages that angels were present at Sinai. They may have performed their normal function as messengers, as has already been stressed in chapter 1. **transgression and disobedience**—Two Greek words are used which cover all types of disobedience—sins of commission as well as of omission.

➤3 **great salvation**—This refers to the gospel. **spoken by the Lord**—This is in contrast to announcement made by angels. **confirmed unto us**—The writer places himself among those we would call second-generation Christians. He, along with his readers, had not heard the gospel directly from the Lord but from his apostles. The apostles confirmed, attested, and

guaranteed Jesus' message. **by them that heard him**—This refers to Christ's apostles.

➤4 **God also bearing them witness, both with signs and wonders**—God provided signs and wonders to show his approval of the apostles' preaching (cf. Mark 16:20). **miracles**—displays of divine power. **gifts of the Holy Ghost** [Spirit]—lit., "distributions of the Holy Spirit," translated "gifts of the Holy Spirit" in RSV, NIV (see 1 Cor. 12:4-11).

➤5 Here our writer takes up again the argument that he set aside for a moment at the end of chapter 1. **the world to come**—lit., "the coming inhabited earth," here referring to Christ's coming kingdom to be established on earth. "It has been claimed that the Dead Sea Scrolls show that the sectarians of Qumran believed that the coming age would be marked by the dominion of Michael and his angelic subordinates. The statement here by the writer of Hebrews forcefully refutes this view" (Hodges).

➤6-8a Psalm 8:4-6 (LXX), the source of this quotation, speaks of man's place in the scheme of creation. The psalm does not reflect reality as it is now, but as it was before it was changed by sin (Gen. 1:26), when God placed man in charge of the created world. Though man's position was forfeited due to the fall, Jesus regained the place that man was meant to fill. **man**—The word in the Hebrew text of Psalm 8:4 is *enosh;* it denotes weak, mortal, and feeble man (Darby's *New Translation* on Gen. 4:26). **son of man**—in the Hebrew text of Psalm 8:4 is *Ben-Adam.* Christ, the son of man, the last Adam, became the man that Adam was supposed to be. **angels**—In the Hebrew text of Psalm 8:5, the word is *Elohim* (gods). But the writer of Hebrews followed the Septuagint, which reads "angels." **crownedst him with glory and honour**—These traits are characteristic of a king. **didst set him over the works of thy hands**—This statement, although a part of Psalm 8:6, may not have been quoted by the writer of Hebrews because the statement is not found in the two earliest manuscripts (the Chester Beatty Papyrus, P46, and Codex Vaticanus). **all things in subjection under his feet**—Jesus quoted this in Matthew 22:44 with reference to his own lordship. Here, it is still speaking of man's ideal position of the federal head of creation, a position that only Christ filled.

►**8b-9 now we see not yet all things put under him**—Shifting from the ideal to the actual, the writer admits that what God had intended for man was not yet realized. **But we see Jesus**—In seeing Jesus we see the man who accomplished God's original intention for man—i.e., to be God's representative head over creation. **Jesus . . . [now] crowned with glory and honour.** Psalm 8 is here applied to Jesus in particular. "As forerunner of man's restored dominion over the earth, he was made lower than the angels for a while but is now crowned with glory and honor at God's right hand. By his perfect life, his death on the cross and his exaltation, he has made possible for redeemed man the ultimate fulfillment of Psalm 8 in the future kingdom when man will regain sovereignty over creation" (*NIVSB*).

►**10 bringing many sons unto glory**—or, "leading many sons into glory." The grammar in the Greek indicates that it is the captain (*archēgon*—accusative) who does the leading (*agagonta*—also accusative). This was pointed out by Marshall in his introduction to the *Greek-English Interlinear New Testament*. As such, Hebrews 2:10 could be rendered as follows: "For it was fitting for him, for whom are all things and by whom are all things, to perfect through sufferings the Leader who leads many sons into glory, *even the Leader* of their salvation." But many commentators take exception to the grammar and call for a special use of the accusative case so as to preserve the meaning (as in the KJV) that it is God the Father who is bringing many sons into glory. **perfect**—This does not mean that he was ever imperfect in the moral sense of the term. The word is not used as a moral term here but communicates the idea of reaching a goal. The only way Jesus could accomplish his purpose was through suffering. **captain**—or, leader, originator—similar to our idea of "pioneer."

►**11 both he that sanctifieth**—the sanctifier, Christ. **they who are sanctified**—the believers undergoing the process of sanctification. **are all of one**—i.e., all come from the same source, namely God. **not ashamed to call them brethren**—Although the sonship is not the same in both cases (Jesus is Son in a unique sense), he considers it no compromise of his place to acknowledge the believers as his brothers.

►**12** The quotation is from a psalm (22:22) that is clearly messianic. It begins with the familiar cry from the cross: "My God, my God, why have you forsaken me?" It continues to describe his suffering until it reaches verse 22, and there it turns to his resurrection. **I will declare thy name unto my brethren**—After Christ's resurrection, he declared to his disciples that his God was now their God and his Father now their Father (see John 20:17; cf. Matt. 28:10). **in the midst of the church**—or, in the midst of an assembly. Since the time of Christ's resurrection, Christ has been in the midst of the church (or, church assembly) as the church meets together to worship the Father. **I [will] sing praise unto thee**—A better rendering of the Greek would be "I will sing of you" or "I will praise you." God the Father is the content of the Son's praise, not just the object.

►**13 I will put my trust in him**—The expression of confidence is from Isaiah 8:17 (LXX). This is followed immediately by a quotation from Isaiah 8:18: "Behold I and the children which God hath given me." There is now a shift from Jesus' "brothers" (2:12) to Jesus' "children." In either case, the main point is that Jesus is identified with his believers because he and they share the same Father and same life.

►**14 children**—The argument that God's method of saving human beings was consistent with his character continues on the basis of this word from 2:13. The nature of the persons to be saved had to be taken into consideration. **flesh and blood**—Earlier Greek manuscripts have these two terms (which together make up a synonym for "human being") in the opposite order. Since this was the nature of those the Son came to save, it was necessary that he have the very same nature. **through death**—The only way he could deal with death was by dying, and the only way he could die was by becoming human. **destroy**—"annul," "render inoperative," but not "annihilate." **the power of death**—The devil possesses the might of death in that "he induces people to sin and to come under sin's penalty, which is death" (*NIVSB*). It was not God's original plan that human beings should die. Death became a part of human experience because of sin (Gen. 2:17; Rom. 5:12). Since death was the punishment for sin (Rom. 6:23), it was necessary for Jesus to die if he wanted to take their punishment and set human beings free.

➤**15 fear of death**—The impact of death on the human mind is such that it causes fear long before it is experienced. This fear may not be conscious; it may be an unconscious dread that is unfaced and undealt with. But Christ dealt with the cause of this fear and took away our bondage to the dread of death. We now can *live* in liberty.

➤**16 took**—The Greek word means "to lay hold on," "to take possession of." "By a metaphor drawn from laying hold of another to rescue him from peril, the word came to mean 'to lay hold for the purpose of helping or succoring.' It is used in the latter sense here" (Wuest). Primarily the passage is speaking of Christ's rescue extended to the seed of Abraham as opposed to angels. But some commentators have seen it as referring to Christ's becoming a man (via the Jewish race) as opposed to becoming an angel. The italicized words in the KJV reflect this interpretation and interpolation.

➤**17 in all things . . . made like unto his brethren**—The likeness is complete. Nothing that is truly human is excluded from it except sin. **might be**—This has the sense of "could become." He became High Priest by suffering (2:10). **merciful**—This is Christ's attitude of compassion or sympathy that comes from his understanding of the experience his people face. **faithful**—This represents his attitude toward God (3:2, 6). **high priest**—This is the first use of a term that appears 17 times in this letter and is not found in any other NT writing with reference to Christ. Jesus is spoken of as a priest in Psalm 110 and Zechariah 6:13, but the letter to the Hebrews is the single definitive discussion of his priesthood. **to make reconciliation** [propitiation] **for the sins of the people**—Christ makes propitiation to God to appease God's wrath against sin (Rom. 1:18; 5:10). This propitiation clears the way for fellowship between God and his people.

➤**18** No man understands himself or others as well as Christ does. Christ does not have an abstract understanding from some detached perspective, but he has the kind that causes him to walk with us and suffer. Because of his purity, his suffering was more intense than

ours. **tempted**—or, tried. **succour**—The Greek word means "run to the aid of one who cries out for help."

*Chapter* 3

## 1-6 JESUS, GREATER THAN MOSES

The consequences of refusing to believe in Christ are far worse than those Israel suffered for refusal to follow Moses. Chapters 1 and 2 show that Jesus is greater than the angels, because (1) he is Son, and (2) he is the first man to function as the ruler of creation in this new age. A new argument, parallel to the former one, begins here as the writer shows that Jesus is superior to Moses.

➤**1 Wherefore**—What is said now is based on the point that has already been made. Since it has been demonstrated that Jesus is superior to the angels, that God has spoken through him, and that he died, rose again, and is now our heavenly High Priest, we ought to make him the focus of our attention. **holy brethren**—referring to 2:11. **partakers**—sharers. The verb form of the same word appears in 2:14. **heavenly calling**—coming to us from heaven and leading us to heaven (cf. Phil. 3:14). **Apostle and High Priest**—This is the only place the word "Apostle" (sent one) is used of Jesus. He was sent by the Father to bring salvation. He is said to have sent the twelve disciples in just the same way as the Father had sent him (John 20:21). We have here, too, the second use of the term that marks Jesus as representative of the people before God. In the previous age, Moses represented God to the people, and Aaron represented the people before God. In this new age Jesus fills both roles.

➤**2** Though the author is about to present evidence that Jesus is superior to Moses, the writer begins with the common ground between himself and his Jewish readers. **Who was faithful**—"Who being faithful"; the Greek indicates that he still is faithful. **appointed him**—lit., "made him." **as also Moses**—Moses wrote down the prophecy that the Messiah-Prophet would be similar to him (Deut. 18:15). Prophets that followed Moses simply called the people back to the teachings Moses had given, so it is obvious that Moses was superior to them. Yet Jesus was similar to Moses and was also his superior. **Moses was faithful in all his house**—probably referring to God's house (see RSV, NIV). The word "all" is not present in several early manuscripts; however, other manuscripts, almost as ancient, do contain "all"—and this word is present in Numbers 12:17 (LXX), the source of this quote. See 3:5 where the quote appears again, exactly as it is in the Septuagint, and affirmed by all the manuscripts.

►**3 more glory than Moses**—We are moved immediately from the similarities between Christ and Moses to a clear statement of Christ's superiority. **builded the house**—The Greek is "prepared the house" or "established the house" (Alford). One who prepares a house equips it with everything needed to make it functional. Moses was responsible for building the tabernacle and furnishing it.

►**4** Every house must have a builder. Although Moses was responsible for the building where he served (Num. 12:7), it was actually God's house—for God was the architect of the tabernacle. If 3:3 presents Jesus as the builder of this house, the truth of this verse is as applicable to the Son as to the Father.

►**5** We move now from the contrast between builder and building to that which exists between servant and Son. **Moses verily was faithful**—Again, the writer stressed a point his readers would find it easy to agree with. **in all his** [God's] **house**—See comments on 3:2. **servant**—The Greek language has more than one word for such a person. This word refers to an attendant who serves of his own will. Such a servant was a man of high position in the household. **a testimony of those things which were to be spoken after**—Moses' servanthood in God's house served as a testimony to what would be spoken in the future about Jesus' servanthood. That is, Moses served as a model of the coming Messiah, of which the writer of Hebrews now speaks.

►**6 But Christ**—This marks the beginning of the contrast. **as a son over his own house**—In the Greek it is simply "his house," but verses 2, 4, and 5 make it clear that "his" means "God's," and what belongs to the Father belongs also to the Son. **whose house are we**—The believers comprise God's house. **if we hold fast**—The writer of Hebrews constantly

warned against negligence. **confidence**—or, courage. **rejoicing of the hope**—in Christ's return. **firm unto the end**—not present in the three earliest manuscripts. The expression was probably taken from 3:14.

**7-11 THE PERIL OF UNBELIEF OUTLINED AGAINST THE BACKGROUND OF PSALM 95**

►**7 Wherefore**—What follows this word is the conclusion of the argument. **Holy Ghost** [Spirit] **saith**—The words of the psalmist are ascribed to the Spirit's authorship, for the Spirit was the inspirer. **To day**—Psalm 95 was used often in worship and devotion, and each time it reminded its users that they should heed what God was saying. It was applicable when God spoke through Moses and the prophets, and it is applicable now as God speaks through his Son (1:2).

►**8 Harden not your hearts**—The Bible indicates that God causes hardening (Rom. 9:18), but this shows us that it is man's doing. **the provocation . . . the day of temptation**—The specific reference is to the event at Rephidim (Exod. 17:1-7).

►**9 tempted me, proved me**—"tried Me by testing Me" (NASB). The Israelites were never quite convinced that God would really take care of them. After every mighty act, they came up with a new doubt.

►**10 I was grieved**—I was angry. God tempered this reaction with patience for a while; but when it became increasingly clear that they had formed a habit of rejecting his way, he said, "They always go astray in their heart; and they did not know My ways" (NASB).

►**11 They shall not enter into my rest**—Canaan was intended first, but the writer will soon argue that there is an application to spiritual rest (chap. 4). This verse concludes what some consider a parenthetical thought. See parentheses in KJV; 3:7 and 3:11.

**12-19 A WARNING AGAINST UNBELIEF**

►**12 Take heed**—This continues the thought of 3:6 and 3:7-11. **an evil heart of unbelief**—unbelief from the heart is true unbelief, not just doubt or questioning (which occur in the mind). Such unbelief is sinful and evil. **departing**—Unbelief ends in desertion. **the living God**—This is the true God, as opposed to gods thought up by human minds.

►**13 exhort one another**—The believers are to encourage and strengthen each other to prevent any hardening of heart.

►**14 we are made**—we have become. **partakers of Christ**—participators in the Christ, partakers of his life and nature. **the beginning of our confidence**—"the confidence we had first" (NIV), when we first believed. The Greek word for "confidence" (*hypostasis*) means "that which underlies," and so speaks of that which is secure and firm.

►**15** This verse is a repetition of 3:8, quoting Psalm 95:7, 8. The words that have been quoted from Psalm 95 must not be forgotten.

►**16** This verse is clearer when translated as two interrogatives: "Who were they who heard and rebelled? Were they not all those Moses led out of Egypt?" (NIV).

►**17, 18** In these verses the question of the hearers' identity is raised again. They were the Israelites who began to resist God almost as soon as they were out of Egypt, who had to wander in the wilderness for forty years, and who failed to enter into the Promised Land and experience God's rest.

►**19 unbelief**—the sole cause of missing God's promised rest.

*Chapter* **4**

## 1-13 THE PROMISE OF GOD'S REST REALIZED THROUGH CHRIST

►**1 a promise being left**—a promise still remaining. When God makes a promise, he does not take it back; but the promise has its corresponding warning. **entering into his rest**—To the Jews, entrance into Canaan and possession of their land as their inheritance constituted entrance into their rest. To the Christian, participation in Christ now and in the future as the portion of their inheritance constitutes their rest (see comments on Col. 1:12, 13).

►**2 unto us was the gospel preached, as well as unto them**—There is a parallel between the readers of this letter and the Jews of Moses' day. Both heard the good news concerning God's promise of entrance into his rest. **not being mixed with faith in them that heard it**—Only a few ancient manuscripts support this reading. The most ancient manuscripts read, "they were not united in faith with those

who heard." The Greek word for "united" or "mixed" agrees grammatically with "those who heard." Thus, this verse is not talking about combining, mixing, or mingling faith with the word; it is talking about the fact that the majority of the Israelites were not united in faith with those who heard the good news (i.e., Moses, Joshua, and Caleb). Moses, Joshua, and Caleb truly heard the word concerning the promise of entering the good land, and they believed it; but the Israelites did not share their faith (*GAM*).

►**3 believed**—belief is the unique qualification for entrance into the rest. **into rest**—Greek, "into *the* rest," which is promised in Psalm 95. **if they shall enter into my rest**—according to the Greek means, "they shall never enter my rest" (see RSV, NIV, NASB). God's rest has been available to men since the creation.

►**4 God did rest the seventh day**—God's rest did not begin and end in a single twenty-four-hour period but is still going on. It does not mean that he has gone into a state of inactivity, but that the period of creation is over.

►**5 in this place**—referring to Psalm 95:11 again.

►**6 remaineth**—It is still available. **they to whom it was first preached**—Israel was given first option under Moses.

►**7 Again, he limiteth a certain day**—God again set another day, a day of rest for God's people. **To day**—The emphasis here is on the repeated "today" of Psalm 95:11, "thus presenting this opportunity to all readers of the psalm for whom the 'Today' becomes their own 'Today' " (Hodges).

►**8 Jesus**—actually, "Joshua." The Greek name *Iēsous* is a translation of the Hebrew word for "Joshua." Psalm 95 would not have spoken of a rest yet to be realized if Joshua had given Israel rest. If it was time to enter the rest in David's day (at least 300 years after Moses), the rest had a larger meaning than the land of Canaan.

►**9 There remaineth therefore a rest to the people of God**—The author used a different word for "rest" in this verse than he has used previously. He switched to the word *sabbatismos* ("sabbath rest")—with reference to God's rest when the creation was finished (4:4), and yet the idea of the *sabbatismos* extends beyond the Sabbath. The writer of Hebrews was probably echoing what Jesus said, "Come unto me all ye that labour and are heavy laden, and I will give you rest" (Matt. 11:28). When we become partakers of Christ (3:14), we have a foretaste of this rest: the full taste of the total rest will come when we are fully with Christ in glory. Then our inheritance will be realized completely.

➤**10** See comments on 4:9.

➤**11 Let us labour**—should read, "Let us be eager." Since there is peril involved in failure to enter the rest, we should be willing to put forth some effort. **the same example of unbelief**—The Israelites provide us with a negative example.

➤**12 For**—We must put forth the necessary effort (4:11) because of the nature of God's communication with us. We will be evaluated by what we have heard God say. **the word of God**—Some have taken these words to refer to God's personal Word (John 1:1), but such a meaning does not fit very well into a context where so much is made of listening to what God says. It is far more probable that it is the spoken and written word that the writer had in mind. **quick**—living. **powerful**—operative, active. **piercing even to the dividing asunder of soul and spirit, and of the joints and marrow**—God's word is able to penetrate so effectively as to divide soul (that which constitutes the natural man) from spirit (that which characterizes the spiritual man). The Israelites did not allow the word to penetrate them (4:2), and so they suffered the loss of their promised inheritance. It is better to have the word expose our natural man than to harden our hearts to the word and suffer the consequences. The overall intent of the image in this verse shows that the word is dynamically active and able to penetrate into the depths of our being, for it is the **discerner** [or, critic] **of the thoughts and intents of the heart.**

➤**13** This verse speaks of man's inability to hide anything from God. Before God, we are **naked and opened**—in Greek this term speaks of having the neck exposed—either to an opponent in wrestling or to a person about to make a sacrificial offering. **with whom we have to do**—with whom is our account. One day we will all stand before God to give account for our lives (Rom. 14:10-12; 2 Cor. 5:10).

## 4:14–5:10 JESUS, THE GREAT HIGH PRIEST

➤**14** Here we return to the main thought of the letter as introduced in 2:17 and 3:1, i.e., Christ's superiority. **passed into** [through] **the heavens**—The high priest used to go through the veil into the Holy of Holies, but Jesus, by his ascension, has gone through the heavens to represent us before the very presence of God.

➤**15** Stated in the positive, this verse tells us that we have a High Priest who has sympathy toward us that comes from his own great suffering. He understands our suffering, but we do not and cannot understand his. He knows temptation and suffering far better than we do, for he faced them on levels we know nothing about. We have never experienced the full force of their power because we surrender to them and reduce the tensions long before they peak. Jesus was tempted but never sinned. We are tempted, and we sin (to be tempted is not sin; to give in to temptation is sin)—due to our **infirmities**—i.e., weaknesses. He is able to sympathize with our weaknesses and give us grace to help us overcome sin in times of temptation.

➤**16 come**—This means to "approach" or "draw near." **boldly**—We can come with confidence. **throne of grace**—One day we must face the throne of judgment (see comments on 4:13); now we can come to the throne of grace. **mercy, and . . . grace**—are now available to all who would come to receive it. **to help**—lit., "to run to the aid of one who cries for help." **time of need**—Life does have its seasons of trials and temptations, with times when we feel particularly in need of Christ's help. He supplies grace and mercy to help us through these times.

*Chapter* **5**

➤**1 high priest**—Jesus qualifies for the position of High Priest because of his genuine humanity, his divine appointment, and his self-sacrifice. The writer here begins with a list of qualifications for the high priesthood in the OT. **taken from among men**—No other creature, lower or higher, could represent human beings. **ordained for men**—He is "appointed" to serve "on behalf of men." **offer both gifts and sacrifices**—These terms indicate sacrificial offerings, and in particular, those offered by the high priest on the day of Atonement.

➤**2 have compassion**—He does not react with extreme emotion. He is not indifferent or filled with rage but has a genuine interest in the persons he is called to represent. **ignorant**—This alludes to those who committed sins done in ignorance—for which there was expiation in the OT economy (see Num. 15:22-31). **out of the way**—being led astray (cf. Isa. 53:6). **compassed with infirmity**—"beset with weakness" (RSV). This speaks of the OT priests, not Jesus Christ.

➤**3 so also for himself, to offer for sins**—The OT high priest, being himself prone to sin and in fact a sinner, made expiatory offerings for himself as well as for the people.

➤**4 no man taketh this honour** [of being the high priest] **unto himself**—According to the OT, only Aaron's family could fill this role. Korah attempted to assume the right to sacrifice and was destroyed for it (Num. 16:5-7).

➤**5 So also Christ glorified not himself to be made an high priest**—Jesus did not simply take the role of High Priest, but acted in accord with the Father's will (John 8:54). **he** [God] **that said unto him**—It was God's will that he should have the office as indicated by the quote from Psalm 2:7. **Thou art my Son, to day have I begotten thee**—This quotation is elsewhere used in the NT to speak of Christ's resurrection (see Acts 13:33). After Christ's resurrection, he was inaugurated into his heavenly position as High Priest.

➤**6 Thou art a priest for ever after** [according to] **the order of Melchisedec**—A quotation of Psalm 110:4, a messianic psalm. In this psalm the Messiah is portrayed as the ruling Lord and eternal Priest. The priesthood according to the order of Melchizedek is explained (and commented upon) in chapter 7.

➤**7 in the days of his flesh**—i.e., "during the days of Jesus' life on earth" (NIV). **offered up prayers and supplication with strong crying and tears**—This must refer to Jesus' agony in Gethsemane. **him that was able to save from death**—lit., "the one able to deliver him out from death." Many expositors have grappled with this statement and offered many explanations. The problem centers around the fact that Jesus did die—so then in what sense did God hear his prayer for deliverance from

death? Many commentators point to the preposition *ek* (out from), in the phrase "from death," to show that Jesus was resurrected out from death and thus was delivered from death. Of all the explanations, this accords well with the context of this chapter (see comments on 5:5) and the parallelism between this verse and Psalm 22, in which the prayer of the crucified Savior was heard and answered—in that God raised him from the dead (see Ps. 22:19-22).

➤**8** Christ learned his obedience not through his divine Sonship, but through his human sufferings. His dedication was such that he was never disobedient to the Father. But he learned experientially in practical sufferings the special obedience needed to qualify him as our High Priest.

➤**9 made perfect**—completed, brought to the goal, through death and resurrection. His perfection was the culmination of his life of suffering and of obedience. **author**—The Greek word also means "cause" or "reason." **eternal salvation**—Christ would still have been God's Son if he had not suffered, but he would not have been the Savior providing eternal salvation. **that obey him**—We should be obedient to the will of God as Christ was.

➤**10** In chapter 7 the author will explain the Melchizedek analogy, but he turns aside from his main argument to deal with another peril. He knew it would take a great deal of spiritual insight to understand this analogy, and that his readers did not yet have this important quality.

## 5:11–6:8 THE PERIL OF FALLING AWAY

➤**11** The discussion of Melchizedek breaks off at this point, and our minds are turned to the fact that it is perilous to make no progress. **hard to be uttered**—lit., "difficult interpretation to speak." The writer experienced difficulty in explaining the spiritual truths, not because of his lack of utterance, but because of the recipients' lack of understanding. **dull of hearing**—Their understanding has been dulled. Instead of making the progress they should have, they have slipped back. One danger of failing to grow is the resulting reversal or decline.

➤**12 for the time**—It has been long enough for them to have shown more progress. **the first principles**—They are still in elementary school, spiritually speaking. They should have gone on to graduate school and become teachers, but they have not even mastered their ABC's. **the ora-cles of God**—The Scriptures of the OT, which were not properly understood. **milk . . . strong meat**—There is one kind of nourishment for those who are just starting out in the Christian life, and there is another for those who are more mature.

➤**13 useth**—partakes. **unskilful**—lacking experience. **the word of righteousness**—the teaching about righteousness, which is difficult for most Christians to grasp (cf. Rom. 1:17; 8:2-4; 2 Cor. 3:9).

➤**14 full age**—mature. The same word is usually translated "perfect" in KJV. **by reason of use**—habit. **to discern both good and evil**—i.e., to distinguish good from evil teachings and practices.

*Chapter* **6**

➤**1 leaving**—or, abandoning. Some scholars think that the list of six elementary teachings that follow (6:1, 2) are directed toward practices of Judaism; other scholars consider them to be teachings concerned with the Christian faith. If all the six teachings concerned Judaism, the writer was exhorting them to abandon them; if they were teachings fundamental to the Christian life, the writer was encouraging them to go beyond them but not totally reject them. **the principles of the doctrine of Christ**—"the elementary teachings about Christ" (NIV). **let us**—the writer considers himself one of the learners. He does not say "you must," but "let us. **let us go on**—lit., "let us be carried along" (Wuest). **unto perfection**—to maturity. The writer does not leave us to wonder what lessons should come first and then be left behind but provides a specific list of six. **not laying again the foundation**—the elementary teachings of Christ are foundational to the faith; having been laid, they do not need to be laid again. **of repentance from dead works**—Dead works are not necessarily evil deeds, but deeds done by persons who are not in right relationship to God. To be a Christian, it is necessary to turn away from every thought of saving one's self. Instead, one must have **faith toward God**—Normally, the NT speaks of "faith in Christ"; so this expression might be directed to Jewish believers.

➤**2 doctrine** [teaching] **of baptisms**—The plural indicates that the writer was not speaking only of the unique Christian baptism, but about various ablutions and cleansings, known to the Jews, and concerning which there needed to be instruction and clarification (cf. John 3:25; Acts 19:1-5). **laying on of hands**—frequently mentioned in the NT in connection with the impartation of the Holy Spirit (Acts 8:17-19) or some other spiritual gift (2 Tim. 1:6). **resurrection of the dead**—The young convert did not have to wait to be instructed in Christian hope. The resurrection of Jesus and its implications for Christians were made clear to them. (It should also be noted, however, that many Jews believed in the resurrection of the dead.) **eternal judgment**—This is another element of both the Christians and the Jews' view of the future. There will be a court at the end of history that will settle human destinies.

➤**3 And this will we do**—i.e., we will leave the elementary teachings and go on to maturity. **if God permit**—If God did not will it so, we would not grow—in spite of all the effort we put into it. Our growth, however, is his will, and he favors and supports it.

➤**4-6** These verses are difficult to interpret because it is not fully clear who the writer is speaking of and what it means to renew them again unto repentance. Some say the people are Jewish Christians who, desiring to return to Judaism, would lose their salvation. Still others say that the people are professing Christians who apostatize from the faith and thus show that they were never really believers (see 1 John 2:19 and the case of Simon Magus in Acts 8). Those who apostatize (fall away) from the faith do so willfully; it is impossible for these people to repent (Morris)—which, of course, means that it is impossible for these people to obtain salvation. Lindsell said, "Whatever view is taken about the state of an apostate prior to his apostasy, the outcome is the same. Whoever openly and consciously rejects Jesus Christ is unregenerate even if he seemed to have been saved earlier. The Arminian would say he had lost his salvation; the Calvinist that he never had it. Either way, the result is identical." **once enlightened**—by the truth of the gospel, by the light of Christ. **tasted of the heavenly gift**—This indicates at least an initial experience of God's gift in Christ (see John 4:10). **partakers**

**of the Holy Ghost** [Spirit]—"shared in the Holy Spirit" (NIV). **tasted the good word of God**—as had the Israelites before they were supposed to go into the Promised Land, but then refused to enter (see comments on 4:2). **the powers of the world to come**—the powers of the coming age, the messianic age. A person can experience many of the same blessings as genuine Christians do and then later reject the faith. Such rejection is called apostasy. **If they shall fall away**—In the Greek this is joined with the other participles ("being enlightened," "tasting," etc.): "and falling away." The falling away is an apostasy, a falling by the way (see 2 Thess. 2:3). It involves a denial of the Christian faith and of Christ himself. [it is impossible] **to renew them again unto repentance**—This is the view from the human side. It should not be taken to mean that God would refuse to forgive those who truly came to him, for that would not be consistent with his character. If those who try Christianity become unsettled and decide against Christ, they are no longer undecided, and their personalities might well crystalize around that decision. It can never be said that God would not forgive them, but it can be said that they would not repent. **crucify to themselves the Son of God afresh**—By their final decision, they join the side of those who put him to death.

➤**7** The peril is now illustrated from nature. **receiveth blessing from God**—If the earth accepts God's blessings and becomes productive, it fulfills its purpose and brings glory to God.

➤**8 rejected**—after having been tested. In this case, there is no lack of blessing. The very same showers fall, but the land does not become productive. It fails in the purpose it was made for. **nigh unto cursing**—near to being cursed (see Gen. 3:17), on the verge of being given up. **whose end**—speaking of the land. The same land can bring forth blessing or bring upon itself cursing. An unfruitful land will be burned. This warning is very similar to the one expressed by Jesus in John 15:6.

## 6:9-20 GOD'S PROMISE AND OATH

➤**9 beloved**—This is an expression of the faithful love that prompts such warnings. **we are** [have been] **persuaded better things of you**—i.e., better than the falling away (spoken of in 6:6) and the cursing (spoken of in 6:8). The writer did not believe his readers in general were apostates or about to be cursed (although some of the Jewish Christians may not have been genuine believers). The writer was hopeful and expectant; the Hebrews were worthy of better things. **things that accompany salvation**—i.e., that come as a result of salvation.

➤**10 God is not unrighteous**—It would not be in keeping with God's character. He forgets forever the sins he has forgiven and has an excellent memory for the good that is done. **your work**—There is no suggestion of salvation by works, but there is still a reward for the work of the Christian. **and labour of love**—Since the words "labour of" are not found in the earliest Greek manuscripts, it is best to drop them. This love toward God is an evidence of salvation, and their treatment of other believers was an expression of love for him.

➤**11 desire**—In the Greek this is a very intense desire. **the full assurance of hope unto the end**—This is not the end of the age, but the end of their own days on earth.

➤**12 be not slothful**—In 5:11 it was noted that their minds had grown dull; here it becomes plain that such growth in reverse can spread if it is not checked. **followers of them who through faith**—This calls for imitation of the examples of faith given in chapter 11. **patience**—This attribute enables people to put up with situations they do not care for. This attitude is characteristic of God (Rom. 2:4). **inherit the promises**—Greek, "those inheriting the promises"; for examples of which, see chapter 11.

➤**13-15 For when God made promise to Abraham**—Abraham is a prime example of one who had nothing but God's promise (see Gen. 22:16-18) to go by, and learned that there was nothing to do but be patient and endure until he received what God promised. **sware by himself**—In the making of an oath, a person would swear by someone greater to certify its validity. (A modern example would be a parent cosigning a loan agreement for his or her child.) Since no one is greater than God, he swore by himself.

➤**16 an oath for confirmation is to them an end of all strife**—i.e., "the oath ends all argument" (TLB). It is the function of an oath to place a matter beyond dispute. In the light of the consequences that would follow failure to keep an oath, people expect it to be an indication of truthfulness.

➤17 **Wherein God**—which being the case among men, God, in accommodation to their manner of confirming covenants, added to his sure **word** [his] **oath**—the "two immutable things" in 6:18. **the immutability of his counsel**—"the unchangeableness of his purpose" (NASB).

➤18 **two immutable** [unchangeable] **things**—God's promise and God's oath. **impossible for God to lie**—God has such integrity and such loyalty to his own character that he cannot go against it. **fled for refuge**—This draws upon the OT picture of those who had committed crimes fleeing to the cities of refuge (Num. 35:11). The same expression ("fled for refuge") appears in Deuteronomy 4:42 (LXX). "Here it speaks of the sinner fleeing for refuge from the penalty of sin, to the High Priest who has offered atonement for him and his sin" (Wuest).

➤19 **Which hope we have as an anchor of the soul**—Shifting images, the writer moved from a city of refuge to an anchor in a harbor—both of which speak of security. **sure and stedfast**—"firm and secure" (NIV). **entereth into that within the veil**—Another symbol is combined with that of the anchor. Our anchor is lodged, not in the sea, but inside heaven's Holy of Holies, in the very presence of God. These words remind us of our Lord's priestly function. Christ will be seen as analogous to Melchizedek (5:11) in chapter 7.

➤20 **Whither**—referring to inside the veil. **the forerunner**—Jesus, the one who went before us. **for us**—on our behalf. Jesus' presence in the heavenly Holy of Holies benefits us, for it is there he carries out his heavenly priesthood on our behalf. **Jesus, made an high priest for ever after the order of Melchisedec**—as is fully explained in the next chapter.

# Chapter 7

## 1-28 THE HIGH PRIESTHOOD OF JESUS, DEPICTED BY ANALOGY WITH MELCHIZEDEK AND SHOWN TO BE SUPERIOR TO THAT OF AARON

➤1 **this Melchisedec**—See 6:20; Psalm 110:4. **king . . . priest**—Jesus served both of these functions. **Salem**—Some identify Salem with Jerusalem, but others prefer to think of them as two distinct places. This makes no difference whatever to the meaning of the verse. "Salem" means peace. **most high God**—The Greek here is the equivalent of "El Elyon," an OT title for God that was used by people outside of Israel. It indicates that Yahweh is the true God. **who met Abraham returning from the slaughter of the kings**—Abraham and his associates had just defeated four Canaanite kings (Gen. 14:17); Melchizedek came out to meet Abraham as he was returning from the battle. **blessed him**—As a priest of the true God and as a superior, Melchizedek pronounced a blessing on Abraham.

➤2 **tenth part of all**—Abraham's response, the giving of the tithe, was a recognition of Melchizedek's superiority. **King of righteousness**—The name "Melchizedek" seems to be related to the Hebrew words "king" (*melek*) and "justice" (*sedeq*). **Salem . . . peace**—"Salem" seems to have a connection with *shalom,* meaning "peace."

➤3 **Without father, without mother**—This is an argument from silence, which is unusual because it occurred in a culture where it was very important to keep records of family trees. The fact that the Bible does not tell us who this man's mother and father were seems to require some explanation. In this way, the man is a ready-made figure of speech to use when speaking about Jesus. **without descent**—without a genealogy, without pedigree. **having neither beginning of days, nor end of life**—This statement is parallel to the former ones and is to be explained in the same way. Melchizedek appears in Scripture for the first time in Genesis 14:18, and he disappears at the end of Genesis 14:20. He is never mentioned again except in Psalm 110:4, which this passage of Hebrews is based upon. **made like**—The Greek word means "to make a facsimile," "to produce a model or copy" (see Wuest, Rienecker). In the way the Bible presents Melchizedek, he is a facsimile of the Son of God. **abideth** [remains] **a priest continually**—The last word in Greek means "that which continues throughout"; it speaks of perpetuity and is used again in 10:1, 12, 14. The priesthood of Melchizedek typifies Christ's perpetual, eternal priesthood.

➤**4 consider**—Greek, "view with contemplation." We are to use our minds to think, study, and learn from Melchizedek's priesthood. **even**—This word suggests an element of surprise. **the patriarch Abraham**—Abraham, held in such high respect, was inferior to Melchizedek.

➤**5 sons of Levi**—Levi's sons formed the Levitical priesthood; Aaron's sons served as priests. **have a commandment to take tithes**—The law required that the Levites collect the tithes (see Num. 18:21, 26). **of their brethren, though they came out of the loins of Abraham**—Even though the Levites and the rest of Israel had the same pedigree, the Israelites paid tithes to one tribe, Levi.

➤**6 he whose descent is not counted from them**—Melchizedek had no family ties to the tribe of Levi.

➤**7** The point of this verse is that the one who is blessed is inferior to the one who blesses, and this principle makes Melchizedek superior to Abraham.

➤**8** The second point of Melchizedek's superiority is that his priesthood is enduring, while the Levitical priesthood was transitory. The priesthood according to the order of Melchizedek is perpetuated by Christ.

➤**9 I may so say**—i.e., "it might even be said" (NEB), or "so to speak." "The writer knew that Levi did not literally pay tithes to Melchizedek, but on the principle that an ancestor is greater than his descendants, Abraham's act affirmed Melchizedek's superiority even to the Levitical priests themselves" (Hodges).

➤**10 he was yet in the loins of his father**—Since Levi was a descendant of Abraham, he was united with the patriarch in paying tithes to Melchizedek. This again shows Melchizedek's priesthood as superior to the Levitical priesthood.

➤**11 perfection**—means the completion of salvation that now enables men to have access to God (7:19; 9:9; 10:22) (Hawthorne). **what further need** [of] . . . **another priest**—i.e., why was another priesthood needed? The Levitical priesthood (also called Aaronic) could not provide God's people with perfect access to God, so a different kind of priesthood was needed, a priesthood typified by Melchizedek's.

➤**12** Once a different kind of priesthood comes, there must be a corresponding change in the law, for the two function hand-in-hand.

➤**13 he**—referring to Christ. **of whom these things are spoken**—referring to Psalm 110:4. **pertaineth** [belongs] **to another tribe**—the tribe of Judah (7:14). **of which no man gave attendance at the altar**—No one from any tribe but the tribe of Levi could minister at the altar.

➤**14 our Lord sprang out of Juda**—Jesus was not a member of the tribe of Levi but of Judah (Gen. 49:10), the line of royalty.

➤**15, 16** Not only was Jesus from a different tribe, but he was appointed on a different basis. The hereditary priesthood was a thing of the past. Christ's priesthood was instituted **after the power of an endless life**—lit., "an indissoluble life". Christ's life, being eternal, can never be destroyed, and therefore he has an eternal, indestructible priesthood—as is verified by the citation of Psalm 110:4 in the next verse.

➤**17** All that has been said is an explanation of these words quoted from Psalm 110:4.

➤**18 disannuling**—canceling. **the commandment**—ordaining the Levitical priesthood. **weakness and unprofitableness**—It lacked the power to achieve God's ultimate goal of providing men with access to God.

➤**19 we draw nigh** [near] **unto God**—The law could not reach this ultimate goal, but the new priest has overcome the obstacles between human beings and their God. Christ brought in this better hope and better way.

➤**20, 21 not without an oath he was made priest**—Drawing upon Psalm 110:1, the writer affirmed again the certainty of this new priesthood because it was instituted by a God-given oath.

➤**22 surety**—pledge, guarantee. **better testament**—rather, "better covenant." God's people now have a better covenant than the old one which was imperfect.

➤**23 many priests**—There was not one but many, due to the death of each priest.

➤**24 an unchangeable priesthood**—The word for "unchangeable" means "that which cannot be transgressed"; hence, "inviolable, and so unchangeable" (Abbot-Smith). Christ's priesthood is "an intransmissible priesthood"

(Marshall). Jesus has no successor; he fills the priesthood himself forever.

➤**25 able . . . to save**—His very name, "Jesus," means "Yahweh saves." **to the uttermost**—lit., "to the entirety"; hence, "entirely," "completely," "in all respects." He saves through and through, totally. **come unto God**—This is done by faith. **by him**—Christ is the Mediator (cf. John. 14:6; 1 Tim. 2:6). **ever liveth to make intercession**—Christ lives eternally in God's presence, making intercession for the saints (cf. Rom. 8:34).

➤**26** This verse contains a description of Christ as our High Priest demonstrating that he is perfectly suited to our needs. **holy**—This is not the usual Greek word for "holy" (*hagios*), but the word *hosios*. The former is the word for consecration of dedication, but this word refers to holiness in the sense of piety. **harmless**—or, blameless. He was truly innocent; no man could honestly charge him with any wrong doing. **undefiled**—He lived in close proximity to sinners and faced the same sort of temptations they faced, but the evil did not stain him. **separate from sinners**—actually, "separated from sinners" in his heavenly state as High Priest. **made higher than the heavens**—inasmuch as he passed through the heavens (4:14) and was given the highest place of honor.

➤**27 needeth not daily, as those high priests, to offer up sacrifices**—Some commentators perceive a difficulty here because the high priest did not take part in the daily sacrifice but became involved only on the day of Atonement. But the expression in Greek "day by day" is probably a figurative way of referring to the endless repetition of sacrifices offered throughout the year (Exod. 29:36-42) (*NIVSB*). **this he did once**—and for all. **when he offered up himself**—Christ's one-time offering took care of all sins forever.

➤**28** This verse summarizes the chapter and underscores the superiority of Christ's priesthood over the Levitical priesthood. The latter was under the law and maintained by priests who were themselves sinners. Christ's priesthood, established by God's oath, is sustained by him who has been perfected (not "consecrated," as in KJV) forever (see 2:10).

*Chapter* **8**

## 1-13 CHRIST'S PRIESTHOOD SUPERSEDES THE LEVITICAL PRIESTHOOD, AND THE NEW COVENANT NULLIFIES THE OLD

➤**1 the sum**—the principal point. The main point of the discussion is about to be stated. **We have such an high priest**—He is to be contrasted with all others and shown to be superior. **in the heavens**—The fact that Jesus is in heaven is of utmost importance to the argument.

➤**2 minister**—It is his priestly ministry that the author has in mind. **the sanctuary**—The reference is, in particular, to the Holy of Holies—here, the heavenly sanctuary. **true**—The real place of worship is the one in heaven; the one on earth was only a copy. **tabernacle**—This was the first edifice constructed for the worship of God; Moses and the Israelites, by God's instructions, pitched a tent where God and man could meet. **which the Lord pitched, and not man**—The heavenly tabernacle spoken of here is not necessarily a physical *place*. When the Son of God was incarnated, he "tabernacled" among men (see comments on John 1:14) by dwelling among them in a human body. When the Son of God ascended into heaven, he entered with a glorified body into the immaterial presence of God, where he now intercedes for us. Thus, God himself became his sanctuary (see Ps. 90:1 and comments on John 14:2ff.).

➤**3 ordained to offer gifts and sacrifices**—This was the whole point of being a priest, so it was necessary for Jesus to perform this function.

➤**4 if**—If Jesus were on earth he would not be a priest because he was from the wrong tribe. Only Levites could serve as priests.

➤**5 the example**—Greek, "a copy." "a sketch"; hence, a representation. The earthly tabernacle was a copy, a sketch, a representation of the one in heaven (8:2). **shadow**—an image of the reality. **pattern showed to thee** [Moses] **in the mount**—The plans that were given to Moses (Exod. 25:40; Num. 8:4; Acts 7:44) provided a representation of the sanctuary in heaven.

➤**6 a more excellent** [priestly] **ministry**—
than any earthly ministry. **mediator of a better
covenant**—As the Mediator between God and
man, he will carry into effect God's covenant
with his people. **better promises**—detailed in
8:10, 11.

➤**7** The argument of this verse is similar to
that of 7:11. **if that first covenant had been
faultless**—The first covenant was faulty
because it could not accomplish God's purpose
for humanity. If all human needs could have
been met by the first covenant, no new or
different way of meeting them would be
required.

➤**8 finding fault**—God recognized that his
human creatures had needs that could not be
met by laws and rituals. **he saith**—What follows is a quote from Jeremiah 31:31-34. The
Lord through Jeremiah declared that there
would be a new covenant. **the days come** [are
coming]—This type of language is associated
with the messianic age. **Israel and . . . Judah**—
Both kingdoms, all twelve tribes, would be
involved.

➤**9 Not according to the covenant that I
made with their fathers**—Behavior would
now be governed by God's indwelling presence rather than by regulations imposed from
outside the person. **I took them by the hand**—
He guided them as a mother or father would
guide a child. **I regarded them not**—The
Hebrew text says, "although I was a husband
to them." But here, as usual, the writer followed
the Septuagint. God disregarded his people
because they had disregarded him who was a
husband to them.

➤**10 I will put my laws into their mind**—
This is the first of the promises, which is realized in us by our cooperation with the
indwelling Spirit (see Rom. 8:2-6). **write them
in their hearts**—The will of God will not be
an external code applied by force but will be
expressed in the core of the personality, where
thought and decision take place. **I will be to
them a God, and they shall be to me a people**—
an affirmation of the most solid and sublime
relationship in the universe (see Rev. 21:3).

➤**11 And they shall not teach**—No human
being will need to act as mediator between God
and other human beings, as all will have immediate access to God. **neighbour**—This refers to
a fellow citizen. **brother**—This refers to a rel-

ative. **Know the Lord: for all shall know
me**—Two different Greek words are used here
for "know." The first word (from the Greek
*ginōskō*) means "come to know," "know personally"—it designates an ongoing personal
knowledge; the second word (from the Greek
*oida*) means "perceive," "know absolutely."
Thus, the entire clause could be rendered, "And
they shall not teach . . . , 'come into a personal
knowledge of the Lord, for all shall absolutely
know me . . . ' " **least to the greatest**—In
God's presence there are no distinctions of this
kind.

➤**12** Here follows another promise. **I will
be merciful**—There will be forgiveness of
sins. **their iniquities** [sins] **will I remember
no more**—God will never recall them or use
them against his people.

➤**13 decayeth and waxeth old**—"obsolete
and aging" (NIV). The new covenant makes the
old one obsolete.

## 9
*Chapter*

1-28 A CONTRAST OF THE PRIESTLY
MINISTRIES UNDER TWO COVENANTS

➤**1 ordinances of divine service**—should
read, "regulations for worship" (RSV, NIV),
which were established by God. **worldly sanctuary**—The Greek adjective *kosmikon* in this
context could mean "earthly," "material,"
"mundane"—or perhaps even "orderly," which
is the root meaning of the word *kosmos*. (But
the word "orderly" has been argued against
because it would call for the Greek word
*kosmion*, not *kosmikon*.

➤**2 the first**—the first sanctuary of the tabernacle, called the holy place. **candlestick**—or,
lampstand. On this lampstand made of gold
there were seven lamps (Exod. 25:31-39). The
table was made of acacia wood covered with
gold. Its function was to hold the bread of the
presence (Exod. 25:23-30). **showbread**—This
literally means "the setting out of the bread,"
referring to the "bread of [God's] face" or
"bread of the presence." There were twelve
loaves, one for each of the tribes.

➤**3 second veil**—There were, in fact, two
veils: one at the entrance to the tabernacle and
one in front of the Holy of Holies. **called**—It

was spoken of in this way, but it was only a copy of the real one in heaven.

➤**4 golden censer**—What we have here is a word which had two distinct meanings. It was often used for a censer, or it could refer to the altar of incense. Some see a difficulty in the fact that this altar was not actually located in the Holy of Holies, but outside it (Exod. 30;1-6). On this basis, they prefer the word "censer." It could well be that the altar, since it was the only way of approaching the Holy of Holies, was so intimately connected with it as to be considered a part of it. Thus, to say that the holiest of all **had** the golden incense altar is to say that the altar belonged to it (see 1 Kings 6:22, NIV; cf. Exod. 30:6). **ark of the covenant**—was made of acacia wood and covered with gold. It was in the tabernacle of Moses' day and in Solomon's temple (1 Kings 8:1-6), but it was absent from the second temple. **manna**—There was enough to supply one man for a day (Exod. 16:33). **Aaron's rod that budded**—See Numbers 17:10. **the tables of the covenant**—the two tablets containing the Ten Commandments.

➤**5 cherubim**—The "im" on the end of this word indicates more than one. Two of these golden figures faced each other across the mercy seat with outstretched wings (Exod. 25:18-20). **of glory**—This glory, sometimes called the "Shekinah" (the glory dwelling in the tabernacle), appeared over the mercy seat between the cherubim, to indicate God's presence (Exod. 25:22; Lev. 16:2; Num. 7:89). **mercy seat**—or more literally, "the propitiatory cover," the lid over the ark of the covenant. In the ritual for the day of Atonement, the blood of the sacrifice was sprinkled on the golden lid of the ark (Lev. 16:15). **of which** [things] **we cannot now speak particularly**—in detail, because the author wanted to proceed with his major argument.

➤**6 went always into the first tabernacle, accomplishing the service**—In the morning they went in to trim the lamps and burn sweet spices, and in the evening they lit the lamps and burned incense (Exod. 30:7, 8). On the Sabbath they had to arrange the bread of the presence (Lev. 24:5).

➤**7 once every year**—They actually went in more than once a year, but the point is that it was only on one day of the year that the atonement occurred. That day, the day of Atonement, was the tenth day of Tisri, the seventh month. **not without blood**—The high priest had to offer the blood of a young bull for his own sins (Lev. 16:11-14) and the blood of a goat for the sins of the people (Lev. 16:15). **errors**—lit., "ignorances," which is an appropriate term for sin. "Ignorance of the law is no excuse" because ignorance is a fault. Human beings can and should know the will of God that has been revealed.

➤**8** The Holy Spirit who guided the writer saw to it that these details were included because of the lesson he wanted to teach us. **the holiest of all**—This room represents the immediate presence of God. **first tabernacle was yet standing**—The "first tabernacle" could be "the holy place" (which is called the first tabernacle in 9:2) as contrasted with "the holiest of all" (9:8). The first tabernacle would therefore symbolize the OT economy, while the second tabernacle (9:7) would signify the NT economy. Christ has now opened the way into the holiest of all by his shed blood—this is the signal work of the NT. Other commentators, however, say that the first tabernacle represents the entire OT tabernacle with its accompanying Levitical service because of the expression "was yet standing" (which can also be rendered "is still standing"—RSV). Even while the writer penned these words, the Levitical priesthood was still functioning in this old system. Either way we look at it, the effect of the comparison is the same—for it serves to show the superiority of the NT economy (under Christ's priesthood) over the OT economy.

➤**9 figure**—Greek, "parable"—meaning "it was all symbolic" (NEB). The **gifts and sacrifices** offered in the OT economy could not give the priest (or worshiper) a perfect conscience, a conscience washed of all offense and completely right with God.

➤**10** It is clear that the rituals noted in this verse were external to the person. **meats**—foods (Lev. 11). **drinks**—See Leviticus 10:8, 9. **washings**—See Exodus 29:4. **carnal ordi-**

**nances**—"regulations for the body" (RSV). **time of reformation**—a time of rectification, when the new priestly system would be instituted by Christ.

➤**11** In contrast to the picture he has given of the old system, the writer turns to the priestly work of Jesus. **by** [through] **a greater and more perfect tabernacle**—In the OT the priest passed through the tabernacle to get to the Holy of Holies. By contrast, Christ passed through the more perfect tabernacle into the very presence of God. This more perfect tabernacle could be Christ's glorified body by which and through which he entered into the Father's presence.

➤**12 the blood of goats and calves**—The blood which Jesus offered for sin is contrasted with the blood offered by the priests of the old system. **having obtained**—lit., "having found for himself"; it was a personal experience for him. Through shedding his own blood, Jesus secured our eternal redemption—an act that does not need to be repeated but will last as long as God does.

➤**13 blood of bulls and of goats**—See 10:4. **ashes of an heifer**—These were mixed with water and used to wash away the defilement caused by contact with a dead body. **sanctifieth to the purifying of the flesh**—effected only an outward sanctification and purification.

➤**14 through the eternal Spirit**—a unique expression in the NT, supported by the earliest manuscripts. (Some later manuscripts used "through the Holy Spirit.") The phrase, connected with the verb "offered," indicates the agency by which Christ offered himself on the cross—i.e., he did it through the eternal Spirit. "[As] the Saviour depended upon the power and direction of the Holy Spirit to accomplish the will of the Father in all of His life, so He did in His death" (Hawthorne). The Spirit is called "eternal" to match "the eternal redemption" (9:12) Christ accomplished for us. **offered himself without spot to God**—"He was the one who offered the sacrifice, and he was the sacrifice itself" (*NIVSB*). See 1 Peter 1:19. **purge your conscience**—Christ's sacrifice cleanses the conscience (cf. 9:9). **dead works**—works done in the flesh, which are not animated by the life-giving Spirit. **to**

**serve the living God**—See Romans 12:1; Revelation 22:13.

➤**15** In the following verses the author uses a Greek word (*diathēkē*) that can refer either to a covenant or to a will (testament). In 9:15b-17, the word means "will" (or, "testament"). In 9:15a and 9:18ff., the word means "covenant." **death**—The idea of death, in this context, ties the two meanings of the Greek word *diathēkē* together. Jesus had to go through death to enact this covenant. **for the redemption** [ransom] **of the transgressions** [of those] **that were under** [who existed during the time of] **the first testament** [covenant]—Christ's redemption took care of the sins of the OT believers. Thus, "the death of Christ is retroactive" (Hawthorne). **they which are called**—including both the OT and NT believers. **the promise of eternal inheritance**—See 6:15; 10:36; Acts 20:32.

➤**16, 17** A will is not in force until the person who made it dies, at which time the heirs come into possession of their property.

➤**18** The first covenant could have never operated without death.

➤**19 when Moses had spoken**—See Exodus 24:3-8. **the blood of calves**—Young men were sent to sacrifice these animals. The goats and water are not mentioned in the Exodus 24 account, nor are the hyssop and scarlet wool, which were part of the various rituals. The author is dealing here with a unique ritual that was never repeated again.

➤**20** These are the words Moses spoke on that occasion, adapted from the Septuagint (cf. Luke 22:20).

➤**21** Since there was no tent at that time, the action described here was not part of the Exodus 24 incident, but of a later one described in Exodus 3:25-30 and 40:9, 10.

➤**22 almost all things**—There were some exceptions (Exod. 19:10; Lev. 15:5; 16:26, 28; 22:66; Num. 31:22-24). **without**—lit., "apart from." **shedding of blood**—This is a basic biblical principle; it is a fact rather than a theory. **remission**—forgiveness.

➤**23** The author returns to the thought that was set aside after 9:12. Verses 13-22 provide an explanation of the point about blood. **patterns**—lit., "antitypes," corresponding types. The items of the earthly tabernacle were antitypes of the heavenly things in the heavenly tabernacle. **better sacrifices**—Although the word is plural, the thought points to Christ's once-and-for-all sacrifice.

➤**24 heaven itself**—The important thing is the immediate presence of the Father. **now**—This is the eternal "now," since the ascension. **in the presence of God for us**—Christ is now with the Father serving as High Priest on our behalf.

➤**25** There is a contrast between Jesus and the old system in the number of times the sacrifice had to be made. Jesus made the sacrifice once and for all, and with his own blood—not the blood of others.

➤**26 then must he often have suffered**—That the sacrifice of Jesus should be repeated is unthinkable! **since the foundation of the world**—On such a basis, the history of human sin from Adam onward would have called for continual dying. **once**—There is no need for such repetition. **in the end of the world** [age]—Jesus came at the end of things, in the last age. **put away**—This means to annul or abolish.

➤**27 it is appointed unto men once to die**—God has determined that it shall be so. **judgment**—Men do not come back again to go through various reincarnations and die again and again. Human beings die once, and the next significant event for them will be the judgment.

➤**28 Christ was once offered**—This is the point of parallel. **to bear the sins of many**—See Isaiah 53:12; 1 Peter 2:24. **look for him**—eagerly expect him. **appear the second time**—a clear reference to Christ's second coming. **without sin**—apart from, separate from sin. Having taken care of sin when he came the first time, he will come the second time not to deal with sin—but to execute judgment. **unto salvation**—His second coming will result in the final salvation, the ultimate deliverance.

*Chapter* **10**

## 1-39 A SUMMARY: THE SUPERIORITY OF CHRIST'S SACRIFICE

This chapter concludes the discussion of the transition from the old to the new system. The sacrifice of animals that had no will in the matter is as nothing compared to the voluntary self-sacrifice of Jesus.

➤**1 the law**—referring in this context to the entire OT and its sacrificial system. **a shadow . . . not the very image**—an image drawn from painting: the shadow is the preliminary outline; the image is the finished painting (see Calvin, Morris). The OT was a shadowy outline, a preliminary sketch foreshadowing the reality yet to come and yet to be revealed in the NT. (See Col. 2:17.) **can never with those sacrifices . . . make the comers** [those approaching God] **thereunto perfect**—The sacrifices in the OT economy covered the sins of the worshipers; these sacrifices did not cleanse the worshipers' consciences of guilt so as to make them perfect in the sight of God and therefore able to approach him.

➤**2** If the sacrifices had purified the consciences of the worshipers, then there would be no need for further sacrifices. But the opposite was true.

➤**3 But**—The reality of the situation was quite different. **a remembrance**—Instead of providing relief from guilt feelings, the sacrifices tended to remind people of the wrong they had done.

➤**4 For**—The blood of passive animals did not have any power to change lives. No men on earth were more aware of this fact than Israel's prophets.

➤**5-7** The words of Psalm 40:6-8, quoted here from the Septuagint, are an expression of the Son of God's motive in assuming human form. **a body hast thou prepared me**—In Hebrew text the words are "ears you have dug for me." Some commentators see this as an allusion to the practice of securing ownership of a slave—in which the master would bore a hole in the slave's ear (Exod. 21:6; Deut. 15:17). Applied to Jesus, this image would show Christ's submissive servanthood—his willingness to accomplish redemption to satisfy his Father's desire. Other commentators see the text as saying that the body is the instrument through which the divine command, received by the ear, is carried out (Westcott, Morris). In either view, the central point is that Christ was prepared to become an obedient slave and to show that obedience in sacrificial death. **Then said I, Lo, I come**—In the prophetic voice, Christ himself was speaking of his coming to accomplish redemption. **in the volume of the book**—meaning "the roll of the scroll," referring to the OT law. **to do thy will, O God**—The Son took on a human body in preparation for sacrifice because he wanted to comply with his Father's desire.

➤**8, 9** Since he held this view of sacrifice, Jesus sacrificed himself, thus making the change from the old to the new economy.

➤**10 By** [or, in] **the which will**—The whole work of redemption flows from the will of God, the Father, as the primary cause, who decreed redemption from the foundation of the world. **are sanctified**—"having been sanctified"—indicating the present result of an accomplished act. Sanctification is something that has been done once for all, but its effect still continues. (Cf. 2:11, where sanctification is spoken of as a process, and see comments on 10:14.)

➤**11, 12** In these verses we have a new contrast between Jesus and the former priests. The OT priests had to stand and daily offer many sacrifices—none of which could take away sin (see comments on 10:1). Jesus, by contrast, has **sat down**—because his work is finished; he offered one sacrifice that took away all sins.

➤**13 expecting**—He still awaits the total result of his finished work. **enemies**—We are not told who they are, but death and Satan will certainly be among them (1 Cor. 15:25, 26). **made his footstool**—beneath his feet, which was the usual posture for the defeated. (See comments on 1:13.)

➤**14 by one offering he hath perfected**—Christ's perfect sacrifice gives those who are sanctified a perfect conscience and perfect access to God. **for ever**—Greek, "in perpetuity." Christ's sacrifice is continually effective. **are sanctified**—Greek, "are being sanctified" (an ongoing process). In 10:10 the perfect participle ("having been sanctified") indicates the present result of a past action. Christ sanctified (set us apart to God) by his one sacrifice, and that sanctification has a lasting result—so much so that it continues to work in us, making us holy, setting us apart to God.

➤**15-17** This quotation (also quoted in 8:8-12, in fuller form) from Jeremiah 31:33, 34, is the expression of the Holy Spirit. In chapter 8 the quotation from Jeremiah shows that the new covenant is superior; here it is used to demonstrate that no further sacrifice is needed.

➤**18** This is the conclusion drawn from the OT quotation. **remission of these** [sins]—i.e., forgiveness of sins. **no more offering for sin**—because the once and for all offering has been made.

➤**19** Now that the doctrine has been made clear, the writer turns to the practical appropriation in our daily lives. The argument here is similar to that of 4:14-16. **boldness to enter into**—Every Christian now has the privilege that was once reserved for the high priest. The Christian can do, at any time, what the high priest could do only once a year. The Christian can now come again and again into the very presence of God by the blood of Jesus.

➤**20 new and living way**—The Greek word for "new" is *phosphaton,* meaning "recently killed" or "freshly slain." Because Christ shed his blood to prepare the way for us to enter the Holy of Holies, this way is "a freshly slain way," a way ever fresh because of the eternal efficacy of Jesus' blood. At the same time, this is the living way—for this way leads to our source of spiritual life, namely God himself. Therefore, this way, prepared by Jesus' death, leads to life. **consecrated**—rather, "dedicated" or "inaugurated." "The word is used in the Septuagint of the inauguration (dedication) of the altar, the Temple, the Kingdom (1 Sam. 11:4), a house (Deut. 20:5)" (Rienecker; see also Westcott). **through the veil . . . his flesh**—When Christ's flesh was rent on the cross, the temple veil was rent (see Matt. 27:51; Mark 15:38; Luke 23:45); and from henceforth, the way into God's presence has been open.

➤**21 high priest**—The Greek here, unlike the term used elsewhere in this letter, means "great" or "kingly" High Priest. **the house of God**—or, God's household, the church.

➤**22** This is a reiteration of 4:16; 7:19. **Let us draw near with a true heart**—This is honesty in a person who really is dedicated to God. **full assurance of faith**—implying certainty of acceptance. **sprinkled**—

producing a cleansing. **evil conscience**—a conscience contaminated with sin. **bodies**—referring to the entire being (see 2 Cor. 7:1). **washed**—bathed.

➤**23** This verse reiterates 3:6, 14; 4:14. **profession**—Greek, "confession." **faith**—This is inaccurate; it should read "hope."

➤**24** Christians should be sensitive to and responsible for one another, especially to encourage one another to pursue **love** and **good works.**

➤**25 assembling**—The Greek word used here (*episunagōgē*) is used also in 2 Thessalonians 2:1 but nowhere else in the NT. Christian meetings rise directly out of the need Christians have to receive encouragement from one another (10:24). **manner**—custom, habit. **the day approaching**—The fact that the day of Christ's coming is near should lead Christians to deeper levels of care for one another.

➤**26** The thought expressed here is related to 6:4-6 because both are concerned with apostasy—the denial and rejection of Christ. **sin wilfully**—This is not an isolated failure resulting from weakness or ignorance, but a continual commission of sin by a person who has a full awareness of what he is doing. In the Greek, the word for "sin" is a present participle, indicating ongoing action. For the apostate who continues in deliberate sin there is no more sacrifice for sins. If a person rejects the sacrifice Christ made, there will be no other.

➤**27** Since there are not going to be any more sacrifices, the only event left to look forward to is the judgment (9:27).

➤**28** The basis for this verse is Deuteronomy 17:2-7, which speaks of punishment for idolatry.

➤**29** The contract that exists between the new and the old covenants means that rejecting the new is far more serious. **trodden under foot the Son of God**—"a strong expression for disdain. It implies not only rejecting Christ but also despising him—him who is no less than 'the Son of God' " (Morris). **the blood of the covenant**—i.e., Jesus' blood which enacted the new covenant (Matt. 26:28; Mark 14:24; Luke 22:20; 1 Cor. 11:25). **an unholy thing**—lit., "a common thing." To count Jesus' blood as common is to consider Jesus' death a common death. **done despite**—insulted. **the Spirit of grace**—This title of the Spirit only appears in

one other Bible verse, Zechariah 12:10, a verse that speaks of God's giving the Spirit of grace to the Jews to enable them to recognize and weep for the pierced One—i.e., Jesus the crucified. To reject the crucified One is to insult the Spirit of grace, who reveals him.

➤**30** The words of Deuteronomy 32:35, 36 are not idle words: **vengeance** belongs to the Lord, and he will **judge his people**.

➤**31 It is a fearful thing to fall into the hands of the living God**—Whether it is fearful or not depends upon the individual involved. It would not be a bad experience for those who love God, but it would be the worst thing that could happen to his enemies.

➤**32** With this warning behind him, the author turns to words of encouragement. **call to remembrance**—They should habitually think about the subject suggested. **illuminated**—enlightened with the truth of the gospel. **ye endured a great fight of afflictions**—This experience was intense, and they are constantly to recall it.

➤**33** Those who became Christians suffered a great deal at the hands of the Jews, both personally and in sympathy with others. **gazingstock**—"publicly exposed" (RSV, NIV)—lit., "made into a theatre."

➤**34 ye had compassion of me in my bonds**—The best manuscript evidence indicates that the words "of me" and "my" were added by later copyists—probably in an attempt to make this verse sound like Paul speaking (cf. Phil. 1:7, 13, 14, 27; Col. 4:18). The text should read "you showed sympathy to the prisoners" (NASB). **a better and an enduring substance**—When they lost their earthly possessions, they recognized that the most important things could not be taken from them.

➤**35 cast not away . . . your confidence**—The believer's confidence in Christ is so valuable that nothing must happen to diminish it. **reward**—To have this confidence is part of the reward.

➤**36 ye have need of patience, that, after ye have done the will of God, ye might receive the promise**—They needed perseverance to attain the promise.

➤**37, 38** These verses are adapted from Habakkuk 2:3, 4 (LXX). The first verse (10:37) is taken from Habakkuk 2:3 and given a definite messianic interpretation by adding a definite article before "coming" (as it is in the LXX), making it "the coming one." The second verse (10:38) comes from Habakkuk 2:4 (LXX), except in inverted order. Habbakuk 2:4 became a key verse cited in the NT because it speaks of justification by faith (see Rom. 1:17). This chapter ends with an expression of confidence and a word about justification by faith. The discussion of faith begun here carries over into the next chapter.

➤**39 draw back unto perdition** [destruction]—Hebrews speaks of coming forward, not drawing back—which is the mark of apostasy. **believe to the saving of the soul**—lit., "of faith to the acquisition of the soul," which speaks of saving our souls by faith in Christ—as opposed to losing our souls by being faithless (cf. Matt. 6:26 with Luke 9:25).

*Chapter* **11**

1-40 FAITH DESCRIBED AND ILLUSTRATED WITH EXAMPLES FROM THE OLD TESTAMENT

➤**1** What we have here is not a full definition of faith, but a description of the characteristics of faith. **substance**—The Greek word for this (*hypostasis*—lit., "that which stands under") can mean "substance"—that which gives reality, or it can mean "confidence" (as is rendered in 3:14). Things are made real by faith—which is to say that faith gives us the confidence that the things we have hoped for will be realized. **evidence**—The Greek word here (*elenchos*) means "demonstration" or "proof." **of things not seen**—They are invisible because they are going to happen in the future.

➤**2** The people mentioned in the verses that follow are noteworthy because they had the kind of faith described in 11:1.

➤**3 we understand**—Faith plays a part in our perception; some things can never be known by people who lack faith. **worlds**—The literal meaning of the Greek (*aiōnas*) is "ages." Time is a creation of God, and the author is thinking of everything that exists in the space-time universe. **framed**—prepared, constructed. **by the word of God**—by God's speaking (Gk. *rhēmati*), which concurs with the expression "God said" in Genesis 1. **the things which are seen were not made of things which do appear**—The writer's main point is that "no purely physical explanation of the [creation of the] world is possible" (Westcott). Faith apprehends that which is invisible.

➤**4** This is the only place in the Bible where Genesis 4:4 is explained. Faith made the difference.

➤**5** Enoch passed into heaven without suffering physical death because his faith was pleasing to God (Gen. 5:22-24).

➤**6 without faith it is impossible to please him**—This generalization follows from the rather plain statement that Enoch did, in fact, please God because he walked with God—and a walk with God must be based on faith. **must believe that he is**—No one would approach God if he did not believe he exists. **a rewarder**—God makes himself available to those who **diligently seek him.**

➤**7 warned of God**—The Greek expression always "has reference to a divine communication" (Marshall). **moved with fear**—actually, "being devout." **by the which**—through his faith put into action. **heir of the righteousness which is by faith**—a Pauline thought. Noah was first called righteous in Genesis 6:9, and in 2 Peter 2:5 he is called "a preacher of righteousness."

➤**8** The previous examples have mentioned people who lived before the flood; now our attention is drawn to the founders of the Jewish nation. **a place which he should afterward receive**—Abraham left Ur on the basis of faith in something that was to happen in the future.

➤**9 tabernacles**—He had no permanent residence but was a resident alien in a country that belonged to other people. **same promise**—Each one received the promise from God (Gen. 26:3; 28:23).

➤**10 city which hath foundations**—i.e., a city with permanence (see TEV). This city is the heavenly Jerusalem (11:16; 12:22; 13:14). **builder and maker**—"architect and builder" (NIV).

➤**11 received strength**—receive power (cf. Rom. 4:19-21). God empowered Sarah, overcomingherdoubt(Gen.18:12)and infusing her with faith.

►**12 him as good as dead**—referring to Abraham, for whom, due to his old age, it was humanly impossible to impregnate Sarah (see Rom. 4:19). **stars . . . sand**—The image combines two promises God gave to Abraham concerning the multiplicity of his offspring (Gen. 15:5; 22:17).

►**13, 14** Verses 13-16 provide a summary of the exemplary qualities of the founding fathers. **died**—They died, as they lived, with promises concerning the unseen future. **were persuaded of them**—These words do not appear in the earliest manuscripts. **strangers and pilgrims . . . seek**[ing] **a country**—the heavenly Jerusalem (cf. 10:34; 11:16; Phil. 3:20).

►**15 mindful of that country**—i.e., "if their hearts had been in the country they had left" (NEB). Abraham might well have moved back to Ur.

►**16** God has already prepared the heavenly city for those men of faith (see 12:22).

►**17 offered up**—The perfect tense in Greek indicates "that as far as Abraham was concerned the sacrifice was complete" (Morris). **received**—an unusual word in the NT, meaning "undertake," "assume"—in the legal sense (Moulton and Milligan). Abraham did not passively receive the promises; he assumed responsibility concerning them. **only begotten**—"one of a kind," "unique"—not Abraham's only son, but the only one given to him by God.

►**18** See Genesis 21:12.

►**19** Abraham offered up Isaac, expecting his death because he believed that God was able to raise him from the dead. This, then, became **a figure** of Christ's resurrection from the dead.

►**20 things to come**—This future-oriented faith made Isaac able to do this (see Gen. 27:27-29).

►**21** Jacob's sight was so bad that he could not distinguish the two sons of Joseph. He placed his right hand on the youngest, but this abnormal behavior was a result of faith rather than blindness (Gen. 48:8-20).

►**22 made mention of the departing** [exodus] **of the children of Israel**—This happened while he was dying (Gen. 50:24, 25). In spite of his rise to power, he did not

think of Egypt as a permanent residence but recognized that God would keep his promise and take his people back to Canaan (Exod. 13:19;Josh.24:32).

►**23 by faith . . . parents**—The punctuation in the KJV is misleading; it was Moses' parents who exercised faith. Exodus 2:2 only mentions the mother, but the Septuagint has plural verbs in Exodus 2:2, 3, and therefore indicates both parents. **proper child**—Greek, "beautiful child" or "fine child." This was a clue to them that he would have a great future.

►**24, 25** The great lawgiver was a great example of faith. **refused**—He surrendered the rights that were his as a prince of Egypt. No law imposed this on him; it was a personal decision based on faith. **the pleasures of sin for a season** [time]—He was not the type of man who could be satisfied with short-lived pleasures.

►**26 the reproach of Christ**—It was not unusual for the NT writers to speak of Christ's presence in the times of the OT. Paul mentioned Christ as the Rock that accompanied Israel (1 Cor. 10:4) and as the One whom the Israelites tempted in the wilderness (1 Cor. 10:9, see comments). Jude (v. 4, see comments) speaks of Jesus as being the One who saved the Israelites out of Egypt. Here, the writer speaks of Christ as the One with whom Moses chose to suffer. Given the fact that these writers were writing from a NT perspective, a perspective that viewed Jesus as Yahweh the Savior (the Deliverer), it is not difficult to imagine that they would identify him with Yahweh's deliverance from Egypt.

►**27 not fearing the wrath of the king**—There were times when he did experience fear. He ran away to avoid the consequences of killing an Egyptian (Exod. 2:4), but a man who is in bondage to fear is not able to distinguish when he should run from danger or when he should stand his ground. **seeing him who is invisible**—lit., "seeing the unseen one" (cf. 1 Tim. 1:17; 6:16), which takes us back to the primary description of faith in 11:1.

►**28 he kept** [made] **the passover**—Moses instituted the Passover (see Exod. 12). **the sprinkling of blood**—See Exodus

12:7. The blood sprinkled on the doorpost of each house saved the dwellers from death's angel. To sprinkle the blood was an act of faith.

➤**29 passed through the Red sea**—See Exodus 14.

➤**30** The leader in this event was Joshua; the site was Jericho (Josh. 6).

➤**31 Rahab**—recognized the reality of Israel's God and believed that he would conquer (Josh. 2:9, 11).

➤**32** The examples of faith in the Old Testament could have gone on and on and made this letter much too long. Since we have the OT Scriptures, we can read of these examples on our own, and the writer suggested more names for our consideration.

➤**33 subdued kingdoms**—This was true of Gideon (Judg. 7) and David (2 Sam. 8:1ff.). **wrought righteousness**—as Samuel did (1 Sam. 8:9; 12:3-23; 15:33) and David (2 Sam. 8:15). **obtained promises**—i.e., obtained the fulfillment of promises (see Josh. 21:45; 1 Kings 8:56). **stopped the mouths of lions**—Daniel is remembered for his experience (Dan. 6:22), but so are Samson (Judg. 14:6) and David (1 Sam. 17:34-37).

➤**34 Quenched the violence** [power] **of fire**—See Daniel 3:25-27. **escaped the edge of the sword**—This was the experience of Jephthah (Judg. 12:3), David (1 Sam. 18:11) and Elijah (1 Kings 19:2). **out of weakness were made strong**—Hezekiah is a good example of this (2 Kings 20:5, 6; Isa. 37 and 38). **waxed valiant in fight**—lit., "became strong in war." Barak manifested this (Judg. 4:14, 15). **turned to flight the armies of the aliens**—There is no reason why this may not refer to the heroic deeds of the Maccabees as they are recorded in the books that bear their name.

➤**35 Women received their dead raised to life again**—The widow of Zarephath (1 Kings 17:21, 22) and the woman of Shunem (2 Kings 4:18-25) were blessed in this way. **and**—actually "but," according to the Greek. This indicates a contrast; faith does not necessarily bring deliverance. **obtain a better resurrection**—than that of the women's children raised to life again. **imprisonment**—See 1 Kings 22:26, 27; 2 Chronicles 16:10.

➤**37, 38 stoned**—See 2 Chronicles 24:20-22. **sawn asunder** [in two]—According to tradition, this happened to Isaiah. **sword**—See 1 Kings 19:10. **sheepskins and goatskins**—See 1 Kings 19:13.

➤**39 received not the promise**—Much of what God promised them was still in the future when they died.

➤**40 God having provided** [Gk., "having foreseen"] **some better thing for us**—the partakers of the new covenant. **that they without us should not be made perfect**—"[T]he men of faith in the OT and those in the Christian era alike belong to one people of God who are *together* made perfect" (Hawthorne). The Greek idea behind "perfection" here means "reaching the final end." (The same root word is used in 12:2, translated "finisher.") The OT saints cannot complete the race without the NT saints—it is like a relay race where the last runner must finish before the whole race can be finished (see 12:1).

*Chapter* **12**

**1-29 THE LESSONS LEARNED FROM THE GREAT EXAMPLES OF THE PAST APPLIED TO THE LIFE OF THE PRESENT AND A SUMMARY OF THE TWO COVENANTS**

➤**1 compassed about** [surrounded by] . . . **so great a cloud of witnesses**—The imagery here draws upon an athletic contest, with spectators, in an amphitheater. The great examples of faith in chapter 11 ran the first laps of the race, and they are now watching the present runners with a great deal of interest. **let us lay aside every weight**—In athletics this involves a diet to overcome obesity. **which doth so easily beset us**—It takes all these words to give us the sense of a single Greek word that refers to something so very close to us that it entangles us. It is like getting caught in the hem of our own clothing. **patience**—endurance (10:36).

➤**2 Looking unto** [away to] **Jesus**—The Greek word indicates the act of looking away from things that might distract us. **the author and finisher**—Christ initiated our faith, and he will bring it to its completion (see comments on 11:40). **for the joy that was set before him**—The Greek word behind "for" is *anti,* which usually means "instead of" (thus, Jesus endured the cross instead of participating in a certain joy), but, it can mean "for the sake of" (which is more suitable here). For the joy he would soon experience by returning to the presence of his Father, Jesus endured the cross. **despising the shame**—i.e., disregarding the shame of crucifixion.

►**3 consider**—Christians are to compare their sufferings with those Jesus endured. They will be quick to see that there really is no comparison.

►**4 resisted unto blood**—experienced martyrdom. **striving**—The word in Greek means "wrestling"—thus continuing the imagery of athletic competition. **sin**—(personified) is our opponent (see Rom. 7:8-13).

►**5, 6 forgotten**—It slipped their minds completely. The quotation is from Proverbs 3:11, 12, a passage that unites suffering with sonship. And discipline is the evidence of a father's love.

►**7** The writer of Hebrews could not conceive of fatherly love void of discipline.

►**8 bastards, and not sons**—This is the logical conclusion. The only sons who do not receive discipline are those who are not really sons. Lack of discipline is, then, a sign of illegitimacy.

►**9 gave them reverence**—respected them. **the Father of spirits**—i.e., "our spiritual Father" (TEV, NEB, JB), as contrasted with our earthly fathers (called "fathers of our flesh" in KJV).

►**10** Here we see why God deserves greater respect: **that we might be partakers of his holiness**—The Greek word for "holiness" here is unusual; it points to God's holy character. "The aim of God's chastisement of his people is to produce in them a character like his own" (Morris).

►**11 peaceable fruit of righteousness**—"a harvest of righteousness and peace" (NIV). **exercised**—Again the writer draws upon athletic imagery. A Christian needs to be spiritually exercised in order to make discipline result in spiritual profit.

►**12 lift up**—lit., "straighten." **the hands which hang down**—are wearied. Since the

hands represent strength, tired hands indicate weakness. **feeble knees**—paralyzed knees.

►**13** Proverbs 4:26 (LXX) is quoted here. **paths**—lit., "wheel tracks." These tracks were easy to follow. The exhortation is "exert yourselves to make the course clear for yourselves and your fellow-Christians, so that there be no stumbling and laming" (Vincent). **that which is lame be turned out of the way**—actually, "the lame be turned aside."

►**14 Follow peace with all men**—See Romans 14:19. **and holiness**—See comments on 2:11. **without which no man shall see the Lord**—See Matthew 5:8.

►**15 fail of the grace of God**—"fail to obtain the grace of God" (RSV). Believers should watch out for each other so that none of their number will fail to take Christ's grace and so drop out of the race. **any root of bitterness**—The background for this thought is Deuteronomy 29:18, which focuses on idolatry. But the image here is much broader. Any principle of doctrine or practice so radically corrupt as to spread corruption all around could start as a root of bitterness. **many**—lit., "the many," the whole congregation.

►**16 fornicator**—See 13:4; 1 Corinthians 6:10. **profane person, as Esau**—It is profane to treat God's blessings (the inheritance rights of the firstborn—in the case of Esau) as nothing. **one morsel of meat**—He threw his birthright away for a very limited satisfaction.

►**17** See Genesis 21:30-40. **he found no place of repentance**—i.e., "he could not find a way to change what he had done" (TEV).

►**18** The contrast between the two covenants is brought out again in closing. **mount**—This word is not found in the earliest manuscripts. The text, then, says, "you have not come to what may be touched" (RSV). The scene here described recaptures Exodus 19:12-22.

►**19 the sound of a trumpet**—a signal of God's coming (Exod. 19:16, 19). **intreated that the word should not be spoken to them**—They did not resist the revelations, but they wished God to speak through Moses rather than to them directly (see Exod. 20:19; Deut. 5:23-27).

►**20 that which was commanded**—In Exodus 19:12, 13.

➤**21 terrible**—fearful. **the sight**—This refers to the majesty of God.

➤**22 But**—marks a strong contrast with the experience described in 12:18-21. **ye are come**—perfect tense in Greek, "you have come," indicating the present result of a past action. Since this is not a future event but one already accomplished, the Mount Zion so mentioned cannot be the future, visible New Jerusalem. It must be the invisible city of God now realized in the universal church and in the future made visible on earth. (See 11:10; 12:18.) **city of the living God**—The dwelling place of the living God is now the church (see 1 Tim. 3:15). **the heavenly Jerusalem**—See comments on Galatians 4:24-26 and see Revelation 21:2-27. **an innumerable company of angels**—Cf. Deuteronomy 33:2.

➤**23 general assembly**—Greek, *panēgurei*, meaning "the festal full assembly" (such as were the Olympic games). **church**—or simply "assembly" (*ecclēsia*). **of the firstborn**—plural in Greek, "firstborn ones"—referring to all the genuine believers who, as God's sons, have the full rights of primogeniture. **which are written in heaven**—enrolled as citizens there because their names are written in the Lamb's book of life (Rev. 21:27). **the spirits of just men made perfect**—Before the resurrection—at which time the spirit and glorified body are united—righteous men live with God in spirit and even as spirits. Such people have been perfected (or, matured) before they went to be with the Lord.

➤**24 to Jesus, the mediator of the new covenant**—See 9:15. The Greek word for "new" (*neas*), rather than the usual word, *kaine*. *Neas* refers to something that has come about recently and is contrasted with what happened long ago. **the blood of sprinkling**—The blood of Jesus speaks here with a quite different message than that spoken by Abel's blood (Gen. 4:10).

➤**25 him that speaketh** [is speaking]—God is speaking through his Son (1:1, 2). The danger of rejecting this revelation is far greater than the danger of rejecting that which was given by Moses.

➤**26 Whose voice then shook**—See Exodus 19:18. **saying**—The quotation is from Haggai 2:6 (see also Ps. 68:8). The final shaking that began with the coming of Jesus is going

on now and will be finished when he returns. The entire universe will shake in this final great catastrophe.

➤**27** This is a sifting process that will leave only those things that are eternal.

➤**28 kingdom which cannot be moved**—lit., "an unshakable kingdom." It is this kingdom that will survive the sifting. **grace**—is the source of our Christian life. **reverence** [devoutness] **and godly fear** [awe]—should characterize our service to God.

➤**29 consuming fire**—The source of this quotation is Deuteronomy 4:24. God refines the good and destroys what is worthless.

*Chapter* **13**

## 1-25 CONCLUDING INSTRUCTIONS FOR CHRISTIAN LIVING

➤**1 brotherly love**—The kind of love one has for his or her family should be extended to all members of the church (2 Pet. 1:7).

➤**2 to entertain strangers**—This refers to giving hospitality to those outside the fellowship. **entertained angels**—This illustration comes from the lives of Abraham and Lot (Gen. 18:2; 19:1).

➤**3 as bound with them**—The nature of Christian unity is such that when one suffers all suffer. **as being yourselves also in the body**—There is empathy based on similar personal experiences.

➤**4 Marriage is honourable in** [by] **all**—See 1 Corinthians 7:38; 1 Timothy 4:3. **whoremongers**—fornicators.

➤**5 Let your conversation be without covetousness**—Greek, "let your way [of life] be without love of money." The love of money is just as much an evil desire as the sexual lust that can violate marriage. **I will never leave thee, nor forsake thee**—Such a promise is made in Deuteronomy 31:6 (cf. Gen. 29:15; 1 Chron. 28:20; Matt. 28:20).

➤**6** The quotation comes from Psalm 118:6 and/or Psalm 27:1.

➤**7 Remember them which have the rule over you**—i.e., "remember your leaders" (TLB, NIV, RSV). **whose faith follow** [imitate]—follow in the same way we would emulate the faith of those described in chapter 11.

**the end of their conversation**—i.e., the result of their conduct.

➤**8 Jesus Christ the same yesterday, and to day, and for ever**—Earthly leaders come and go (referring to 13:7), but Jesus Christ remains (Morris). Jesus Christ is the true, paramount leader. He remains the constant giver of life and grace to all who come to him. He is accessible at all times—past, present, and future. We can count on him to be present and available!

➤**9 Be not carried about**—Greek, "carried away." This means to be pulled away as the current of a river would pull a boat that was not tied down. We should rely upon Jesus Christ's permanence and remain attached to him. **divers**—various. **strange**—foreign to the apostolic teaching. **established with grace**—In contrast to the various, strange doctrines that unsettle one's soul, grace strengthens a believer's life. **not with meats**—referring to the teachings of the legalistic Judaizers (*NIVSB*).

➤**10 an altar**—the cross of Christ, whereon his body was offered. The Lord's Table represents this altar, the cross, as the bread and wine represent the sacrifice offered on it. A Jewish priest who does not believe in Christ has no right to partake of the Lord's Table.

➤**11, 12 sanctuary**—The Holy of Holies. The blood was brought into the Holy of Holies on the day of Atonement. **without** [outside] **the camp**—The general rule is given in Leviticus 4:11, 12. **Jesus also . . . suffered without** [outside] **the gate**—Christ died outside of Jerusalem—a picture of how he removed sin.

➤**13 Let us go forth therefore unto him without the camp**—of Judaism, symbolized by Jerusalem. Christians must take their place beside him. The Jews would treat them as outcasts, and they must be willing to have it so, for this is **bearing his reproach.**

➤**14 we seek one to come**—Christians can bear to be outcasts because they are seeking the same ultimate home that Abraham sought (11:10).

➤**15** If, as in 13:10, there is an altar, then there is also a sacrifice. But there is no suggestion in this that Jesus must die again and again. Instead, Christians are to provide a continual sacrifice of praise, which is the fruit offered to God through speaking praises to him (see Isa. 57:19; Hos. 14:2; 1 Pet. 2:5).

➤**16** The sacrifices of verbal praises must be accompanied by self-sacrificial acts of goodness.

➤**17 them that have the rule over you**—The leaders are mentioned three times in this chapter (13:7, 24). **they watch for your souls**—See Acts 20:28; 1 Peter 5:2. **they that must give account**—They will be accountable to him for the way they function in the role he has given.

➤**18 a good conscience**—They were persons of integrity.

➤**19 that I may be restored to you the sooner**—The writer has kept himself well out of the picture to this point, but now we begin to learn about him (see Introduction).

➤**20, 21 the God of peace**—God brings unity out of human discord. **brought again from the dead our Lord Jesus**—See Acts 2:24. **that great shepherd of the sheep**—This title was well known to Jewish readers. See Isaiah 40:11; Ezekiel 34:23; cf. John 10:2, 11, 14; 1 Peter 2:25; 5:4. **blood of the everlasting covenant**—The eternal covenant is the new covenant (cf. Jer. 31:31 with Jer. 32:40).

➤**22 written a letter unto you in few words**—The epistle was brief, considering all that could have been said on the points made.

➤**23 Know ye that our brother Timothy is set at liberty**—"Timothy, who was well known to the recipients of the letter, had recently been released from prison" (*NIVSB*).

➤**24, 25 them that have the rule over you**—lit., "the leading ones." He thinks again of their leaders and sends them greetings. **They of Italy**—It is not easy to tell whether the writer was writing from Italy or just passing on greetings from believers in Italy (see Introduction).

BIBLIOGRAPHY

Abbot-Smith, G. *Manual Greek Lexicon of the New Testament.* Edinburgh: T & T Clark, 1936.

Alford, Henry. *The Greek New Testament.* 1852. Reprint. Grand Rapids: Guardian Press, 1973.

Calvin, John. *The Epistles of Paul the Apostle to the Hebrews and the First and Second Epistles of St. Peter.* Edinburgh: Oliver & Boyd, 1963.

Darby, John N. *New Translation.* 1871. Reprint. Addison, Ill.: Bible Truth Publishers, n.d.

Hawthorne, Gerald F. "The Letter to the Hebrews" in *Bible Commentary for Today.* Glasgow: Pickering & Inglis, 1979.

Hodges, Zane, C. "Hebrews" in *The Bible Knowledge Commentary.* Wheaton, Ill.: Victor Books, 1983.

Lindsell, Harold. General Editor of *KJV Study Bible.* Wheaton, Ill.: Tyndale House Publishers, 1986, 1989.

Marshall, Alfred. *The Interlinear Greek-English New Testament.* Grand Rapids: Zondervan, 1958 (through Samuel Bagster & Sons).

Morris, Leon. "Hebrews" in the *Expositor's Bible Commentary.* Grand Rapids: Zondervan, 1981.

Rienecker, Fritz. *Linguistic Key to the Greek New Testament.* Grand Rapids: Baker Book House, 1976, 1980.

Vincent, M. R. *Word Studies in the New Testament.* 1886. Reprint. Grand Rapids: Eerdmans, 1946.

Westcott, B. F. *The Epistle to the Hebrews.* London: MacMillan, 1892.

Wuest, Kenneth. "Hebrews" in *Word Studies in the Greek New Testament.* Grand Rapids: Eerdmans, 1954.

# JAMES
## Introduction

The first mention of James's epistle by name occurs early in the third century in a writing by Origen (*Commentary on John,* 1.19; 4.306), who was born c. A.D. 185 and died c. A.D. 254. Clement of Rome (*First Epistle to the Corinthians,* chap. 10; cf. James 2:21, 23; chap. 11, cf. James 2:25) quotes it; so also the *Shepherd of Hermas* quotes 4:7. Irenaeus (*Against Heresies,* 4.16.2) is thought to refer to 2:23. Clement of Alexandria commented on it, according to Cassodorus. None of the Latin fathers before the fourth century quotes it; but soon after the Council of Nicea (A.D. 325), it was admitted as canonical both by the Eastern and Western churches, and was specified as such in the Councils of Hippo and Carthage (A.D. 397). The Epistle of James took a long time to be accepted into the NT canon because of "its untheological nature, its brevity, the question of James's identity, the fact that it was not written by one of the twelve apostles, and its general address (sent to no specific person or church)" (Burdick). But eventually this epistle (along with 2 Peter, 2 and 3 John, Jude, and Revelation) was accepted into the NT canon and read as authoritative Scripture.

Luther's objection to this epistle (which he called "an epistle of straw, and destitute of an evangelic character") was due to his mistaken idea that it opposes the doctrine of justification by faith and not by works, taught by Paul. But the two apostles, while looking at justification from distinct standpoints, mutually complement each other's definitions. Paul saw faith as producing justification, which in turn produces good works. James saw good works as the genuine proof that one had faith and could therefore be assured of justification. The error James confronted was the Jewish notion that their possession and knowledge of God's law would justify them, even though they disobeyed it (cf. 1:22 with Rom. 2:17-25).

The James who wrote this epistle was probably not James, the son of Zebedee, for he was martyred too early (A.D. 44) to have written it (see Acts 12:1, 2). Most scholars have identified this James as Jesus' brother (Mark 6:3; Gal. 1:19), the prominent elder of the church in Jerusalem (Acts 15:13, 19; 21:17-25; Gal. 2:12). The whole character of the epistle coincides with what we know of this James's legalism and Jewishness.

As an elder of Jerusalem writing to the twelve tribes of the dispersion (which came as a result of the persecution noted in Acts 11:19), James set forth the gospel in its relation to the law, which the Jews so reverenced. As Paul's epistles are a commentary on the doctrines flowing from the death and resurrection of Christ, so James' epistle has a close connection with Christ's teaching during his life on earth, especially his Sermon on the Mount. In both the Sermon on the Mount and the Epistle of James, the law is represented as fulfilled in love—and the very language is remarkably similar (cf. 1:2 with Matt. 5:12; 1:4 with Matt. 5:48; 1:5; 5:15 with Matt. 7:7-11; 2:13 with Matt. 5:7, and 6:14, 15; 2:10 with Matt. 5:19; 4:4 with Matt. 6:24; 4:11 with Matt. 7:1, 2; 5:2 with Matt. 6:19). The whole spirit of this epistle breathes the same gospel-righteousness that the Sermon on the Mount inculcates as the highest realization of the law. James's own character as "the Just" disposed him to this coincidence (cf. 1:20; 2:10; 3:18 with Matt. 5:20). It also fitted him for presiding over a church still zealous for the law (Acts 21:18-24; Gal. 2:12). If any could win the Jews to the gospel, he was most likely because he presented a pattern of OT righteousness, combined with evangelical faith (cf. also 2:8 with Matt. 5:44, 48). Practice, not profession, is the test of obedience (cf. 2:17; 4:17 with Matt. 7:21-23). Sins of the tongue, however lightly regarded by the world, are an offense against the law of love (cf. 1:26; 3:2-18 with Matt. 5:22; also any swearing, 5:12; cf. Matt. 5:33-37).

Many scholars confirm an early date for James's epistle, even as early as A.D. 45-50, because the whole orientation of the epistle fits the early history of the church, an era in which many Jewish Christians had not made a complete severance from Judaism. Thus, James uses the terms "the twelve tribes" (1:1) and "the synagogue" (2:2, Gk.); he speaks as an OT prophet (5:1ff.) and as one fond of OT proverbs (cf. 1:5 with Prov. 2:6; 1:19 with Prov. 29:20; 3:18 with Prov. 11:30; 4:13-16 with Prov. 27:1; and 5:20 with Prov. 10:12—Burdick). James's message, as was noted earlier, closely follows Jesus' sermons. His message does not deal with the Jewish/Gentile problems that arose in the fifties and sixties; and he, unlike Peter, Jude, and John (in their epistles), did not deal with false teachings. All these reasons point to an early date. Perhaps the Epistle of James was the first NT book to be written. If not, we are sure that it was written before A.D. 62, the time of James's martyrdom, according to Josephus (Burdick).

*Chapter* **1**

## 1-18 TRIALS AND TEMPTATIONS

▶**1 James**—James, along with Peter and John were missionaries to the Jews. James ministered in Jerusalem, Palestine, and Syria; Peter in Babylon and in Rome; and John in Ephesus and Asia Minor. Peter addressed the Jewish Christians scattered throughout Pontus, Galatia, Cappadocia, Asia, and Bithynia, while James wrote to the Jewish Christians in general. **servant of God**—lit., "slave of God," a title Paul often used to speak of himself. **and of the Lord Jesus Christ**—James used the Lord's name only twice in all his recorded ministry—here, and again in 2:1. It does not appear in any of his speeches (Acts 15:14, 15; 21:20, 21). Bengel feels that this reflects a reluctance to display the fact that he was the Lord's brother by mentioning his name too frequently. Because James was dealing with practical matters rather than doctrinal issues, it was not necessary to use the actual name so often. **twelve tribes**—This designation clearly shows that James's, epistle was sent to the Jews, specifically the Jews in the dispersion. Some of these Jews were believers in Jesus Christ (2:1). **scattered abroad**—lit., "in the dispersion." The dispersion of the Jews was a divine strategy that enabled Christianity to move easily along the natural communication lines existing between these scattered Jews and their religious home in Jerusalem. Wordsworth wrote: "The pilgrim troops of the law became the caravans of the gospel." **greeting**—This particular salutation seems to be James's, personal trademark in the NT. Although it is the usual idiom in thousands of papyri letters known to us (Robertson), it appears only twice in the NT, once previously in the letter to the Gentile Christians drafted by the Jerusalem council in which James played such a major role, and again here in his own letter. The Greek for "greeting" (*chairein*) always includes a sense of joy or happiness. James was encouraging these Jewish Christians to find happiness in their new and difficult circumstances.

➤**2 brethren**—This is James's favorite means of expressing the personal sense of national and Christian identity he feels toward these Jewish Christians. **fall into**—The Greek text implies falling unexpectedly into so many difficulties that a person is completely surrounded. **temptations**—These are not simply appeals to sin but tests designed to produce pure Christian character. Genesis 22:1 uses "tempt" in the same way. James probably had in mind the suffering and sickness that his readers were experiencing (5:13, 14). God's plan is to produce something good out of every such circumstance in a person's life.

➤**3 trying of your faith**—lit., "that which is approved [through testing] in your faith." **patience**—The Greek word suggests a quality of endurance and steady persistence (see Luke 8:15).

➤**4 perfect work**—The full effect of matured patience is the ability to find "joy in bearing the cross" (Menochius) and to endure to the end (Matt. 10:22) (Calvin). **perfect and entire**—The scriptural standard for perfection (or, maturation) is to be fully developed in all the attributes of Christian character, to be complete in every area of life (spirit, soul and body—1 Thess. 5:23), to be a whole man. God's plan is to make complete men. Alford said that "if God's teachings have had a perfect work in you, *you* are perfect."

➤**5 wisdom**—The kind of wisdom James is talking about is described in 3:17. **ask**—See 4:2. **liberally**—The same Greek word is translated "generous" in Romans 12:8. God gives without adding anything that might take away from the graciousness of the gift (Alford). **upbraideth not**—does not reproach. God does not hold our past sins or our present ungratefulness against us, just as he does not refuse to give us what we ask for simply because he knows what we will do with it in the future. When Solomon asked for wisdom, God gave him more than he asked for, even though he was aware of how Solomon would abuse it. The Jews pray: "May I never need to rely on the gifts of men whose resentful attitudes are not worth the trouble of their puny gifts, but give me from your bountiful supply." James must have been thinking of the Sermon on the Mount here (see Introduction). God responds to every genuine request, either by giving what we ask, or else giving something that is much better for us in the long run.

➤**6 let him ask in faith**—Real faith is the persuasion that God can and will give what we ask. Bengel notes that James begins and ends with faith and in between explains what it is and what keeps men from experiencing it. **nothing wavering**—doubting nothing. Instability results when a person is unable to make up his mind whether to believe God or not. The Jews had a history of this fence-sitting kind of faith, which limited God's power in their lives. The Scripture always recommends unreserved commitment and God always rewards it (Acts 10:20; Rom. 4:20). **like a wave of the sea**—James's use of the sea imagery accurately depicts the unstable character of a person who is both driven by external pressures and tossed by his own indecision (Bengel). Wiesinger elaborated further on the metaphor: At one time cast on the shore of faith and hope, at another rolled back into the abyss of unbelief; at one time raised to the height of worldly pride, at another tossed in the sands of despair and affliction. **driven**—The same Greek word (*anemizō*) appears in Isaiah 57:20 (LXX) and Ephesians 4:14. In Ephesians it describes people who are always changing their minds about what they believe.

➤**7, 8** The man who asks without faith is a walking contradiction. His answer will only be as firm as his request. James coined a new expression, "double minded," to describe this kind of man. Here and again in 4:8 he speaks of someone who maintains two entirely opposite mind-sets at the same time—first operating from one, then the other. James seems to be less concerned with the man who pretends to be a Christian and is not, than with this "double minded" man who can't make up his mind once and for all whether he will believe God or not.

➤**9, 10** The basic contrast of these two verses introduces one of the recurring themes of the letter: Christ places all men on a common ground (2:1; 5:13). James may again have alluded to the present circumstances of these Jewish Christians (1:2) when he encouraged those in poor circumstances to consider their rich heritage as sons of God. It has been noted that while he called the poor man a "brother," he referred to the man with wealth as simply a "rich man" (Gk.). There is at least the implication that a man without money has less trouble in being a genuine Christian than a wealthy man who has all that money to think about. The rich man's only hope is to recognize that his money means nothing to God.

**►11** This verse echoes Isaiah 40:6, 7. **sun . . . risen with a burning heat**—This probably refers to "the blistering east wind called Sirocco" (Rienecker), rather than the relatively mild heat of the early sun. Isaiah 40:7 seems to agree with the use of "hot wind" rather than the relatively mild heat of the early sun.

**►12 Blessed**—See Sermon on the Mount (Matt. 5:4, 10, 11). The real blessedness comes from being able to last through a trial and come out victorious (see Job 5:17). **crown**—This is not the laurel crown worn by victorious Greek athletes at their ancient games. Paul used the image in that sense because he knew his audience was familiar with it. However, such contests were considered pagan by Jewish Christians, and James's audience would have frowned at his use of the word in that way. Rather, the crown implied kingship to Jewish minds (Ps. 21:3). **of life**—Eternal life is the ultimate reward of the Christian's successful struggle. **Lord**—The actual name does not appear in the earliest manuscripts. Some copyists supplied "God," and others "Lord." Either name is adequate to supply the sense. **to them that love him**—cf. 2 Timothy 4:8. The true test of love is endurance.

**►13 I am tempted of God**—James is not here contradicting what he wrote in 1:2, when he said that temptations were tests of good Christian character. Here he merely reverts to the conventional meaning of the word as an allurement to sin. God is not capable of leading men in that direction. He never sends testing in order to make men worse, but in order to make them better (1:16, 17). God is the agent for escape from that kind of temptation (1 Cor. 10:13).

**►14 when he is drawn away of his own lust**—The source of sin is self. Man is not in danger from Satan's suggestions until he incorporates these suggestions into his own being.

**►15** James illustrated the truth by painting the picture of a pregnant prostitute. The woman represents man's evil thoughts and wishes. Conception is initiated when a person's will embraces that idea. Sin is born. The death that results stands in striking contrast to the crown of life that is promised to the man who endures temptation (1:12). The person who takes Satan's evil suggestions into his own mind is fighting Satan in his own territory and is therefore fighting a losing battle. The time to stop sin is when the will is first confronted by these wrong ideas.

**►17 good gift and every perfect gift**—In the Greek text there are two separate words to describe God's giving. The first word (*dosis*) means "the act of giving" and is accompanied by the adjective "good," while the second (*dōrema*) denotes the actual gifts received and is preceded by the adjective "perfect." The first emphasizes the goodness of receiving something from God, and the second, the perfect quality of whatever God gives. God's giving is always good, and his gifts are always perfect. We can be sure that if it is good to receive and perfect to possess, it came from God, **the Father of lights**—He is the source of both physical and spiritual light. This was typified in the Urim, the supernatural lights that shone on the breastplate of the Jewish high priest. **with whom is no variableness, neither shadow of turning**—This is the reading in some ancient manuscripts. Two early manuscripts (Codices Sinaiticus and Vaticanus) read, "no variation which consists in the turning of the shadow," and one early papyrus manuscript (P23) reads, "no variation or turning of the shadow." Due to the complexity of the metaphor, different scribes attempted to clarify the sense, and it is not easy to determine which scribe emended what. The image seems to portray God as an unchanging orb of light—quite unlike the natural sun which, from our perspective, shifts and thus causes shadows. The reading of P23 could possibly evoke the image of an ancient sundial (which told time by the turning of the shadow). If so, James would be indicating that God is changeless *and* timeless. But the context appears to deal only with God's unchanging, steadfast nature (*GAM*). God is not subject to the variations of light caused by the rotations of the planets, nor can even the slightest shadow of an eclipse ever dim his pure intensity. There is never even a hint of change in God (Mal. 3:6).

## 18-27 PUTTING GOD'S WORD INTO PRACTICE

➤**18 Of his own will**—God chose to regenerate us; to do so was pleasing to him. **begat**—lit., "brought us forth" (RSV), conveying the idea of giving birth. **with** [by] **the word of truth**—the gospel that brings salvation (Eph. 1:13). The gospel truth believed and received is the vehicle through which God can regenerate men (cf. 1 Pet. 1:23-25). **a kind of firstfruits**—Christ is, in respect to resurrection, "the firstfruits" (1 Cor. 15:20, 23); believers in respect to regeneration, are, as it were, the firstfruits among all God's creation. The Jewish Christians were familiar with James's use of the word "firstfruits" to describe their relationship in this new family. It recalled the law that required a man to present the first of his children, his animals, and his crop to God. This made the rest of his family and possessions accepted before God. The believers are the first of God's creatures to experience the reconstitution that is planned for all creation (see Rom. 8:20-23).

➤**19 Wherefore**—James here begins his lesson on listening and speaking by reminding the Jews of something they already knew. The earliest manuscripts read here: "you know" (as in Eph. 5:5; Heb. 12:17). Jewish rabbis had long taught that men have two ears in plain view, but only one tongue, and that hidden by a row of teeth. James proceeds from this familiar maxim to explain how to listen properly and what to listen for (1:22-27). **slow to speak**—See Proverbs 10:19; 17:27, 28; Ecclesiastes 5:22. This is a good way to avoid many temptations that come from inside us. The Jews were frequently guilty of sinning by what they said, and James pointed out several instances of this in his letter. He warned them about being too quick to take teaching positions where they would be susceptible to criticism for what they said (3:1). **slow to wrath**—From the context it

appears that James might have meant anger that results from debate. However, Tittmann thinks that James was alluding to a frustrated anger arising from the difficult circumstances these Christians found themselves in (1:2). Regardless of which kind of anger, it is always difficult for God's word to get through to an angry man. Naaman is a good illustration of a man whose quick temper hampered God's word from working in his life (2 Kings 5:11; see also Luke 4:28).

➤**20** Man's angry outbursts cannot ever accomplish the righteousness God wants to produce in us. His purposes are accomplished by peace, not anger (3:18).

➤**21 lay apart**—"put away" (RSV). The Greek implies a once-for-all action just as one throws out soiled clothing. **all filthiness and superfluity of naughtiness** [evil]—We are to get rid of all sorts of evil thoughts and attitudes that find expression in our lives (cf. Eph. 4:31; Col. 3:8). **receive with meekness**—The proper way to receive God's word is not defensively or negatively, but openly as a child (1 Pet. 2:2), not looking for something to argue about, but hungry for spiritual food. **the engrafted word**—The word is engrafted by the Spirit to be livingly incorporated with the believer—as the fruitful shoot is grafted to the maternal wild stock. Because of the engrafting, the wild stock will eventually inherit the goodness of the good source and bear good fruit. This will also happen in the believer; once the word becomes a part of his life, his natural life will gradually absorb the divine characteristics of the engrafted word, which will then be spontaneously expressed in his actual living. **able to save**—This ought to be a lesson for our lazy listening habits, for as Calvin commented, what we are so casual about hearing can actually save our souls. **souls**—your true selves, your entire personality. God's salvation extends to every part of man's inner being.

➤**22** In another allusion to the Sermon on the Mount (Matt. 7:21-29), James qualified his previous advice to "be swift to hear" (1:19). **be ye doers of the word, and not hearers only, deceiving your own selves**—Do not make the mistake of thinking that simply reading (or hearing) the Bible will profit you if you do not do what it says.

➤**23** The rabbis also taught that true discipleship meant learning in order to do, not just for the sake of knowing something else or passing it on to others. **his natural face**—lit., "the face he was born with." God's word accurately exposes the reality of man's inner nature in the same way that a mirror reminds us of the imperfections of our physical features.

➤**24 straightway forgetteth what manner of man he was**—By implication the matter in question is not whether the person has seen what he is really like in the mirror of the word, but whether he has allowed what he has seen to affect his life. Although he does see himself there, he relaxes, lets his mind wander, or turns his attention somewhere else, thereby forgetting what he looked like. Merely running the words through one's mind does not allow the word to do its complete work in a person's life (Ezek. 33:31).

➤**25 looketh**—According to the Greek, this verb means "to stoop down beside [something] in order to take a better look." The word is used in this way in Luke 24:12; John 20:5, 11. The word is used in general to indicate a close and attentive look (see 1 Pet. 1:12). What a difference between that and the person who looks and then walks away! (1:24). This kind of inspection requires careful scrutiny, almost curious spying into the word. Bengel admitted that this sort of curiosity is good if it leads to productive living. **perfect law of liberty**—Christ established a new law for right living that called for even holier habits than the old laws of Moses. The difference now is that the men respond to this new law because they want to, not because they are told to. Once a man is set free from his old sin-nature by the Spirit of God, he feels free to obey God because he loves him (see 2:8, 10, 12; John 8:31-36; 15:14, 15; 1 Cor. 7:22; Gal. 5:1, 13; 1 Pet. 2:16).

➤**26, 27** The chapter concludes with an example of obeying God's laws. **religious . . . religion**—The Greek word for "religion" appears only once more in the NT (Acts 26:5), where Paul was recalling his careful observance of Pharisaic customs prior to conversion. In both instances the word is used to refer to the outer form of a faith that is empty of any inner reality. A religious person could perform many religious practices yet still be void of Christ in his or her life. True religion—or, devotion to

God—should be expressed in acts of mercy (taking care of orphans and widows) and in self-purification. (See Mic. 6:7, 8.) **bridleth not his tongue**—Knowing how to speak well is not nearly as important as knowing what to say and where and when to say it (3:2, 3; Ps. 39:1). This is a work for God to do. It is not something that could be legislated by the old law. Calvin said that people who are not bothered by the obvious sins may seem very spiritual, but they often draw attention to their own "spirituality" by pointing out the weaknesses of others. All this is done out of an apparent eagerness to serve God, but deep down inside they only do it because they enjoy talking about others. **religion**—In a final parallelism, James points out the positive and negative aspects of genuine religion. On the positive side, one is to be pure or unpolluted and to minister to others in such ways as taking care of orphans and widows. On the negative side, he is to live without fault and to remain unsoiled and undirtied by his contacts with the world. **before God and the Father**—God sets the standard for purity and faultlessness, and that is what counts. No man-made standard will ever do. **fatherless [orphans] and widows**—God the Father takes a special interest in people who do not have any family (Ps. 68:5). **and**—The conjunction does not appear in the original text, suggesting the close relationship between public ministry and personal purity.

*Chapter* 2

## 1-26 FAVORITISM AND THE FUTILITY OF FAITH WITHOUT ACTION

➤**1 brethren**—James spoke out against the kind of discrimination that favored the rich over the poor. He appealed to their common bond as members of a community of Christians. **our Lord Jesus Christ, the Lord of glory**—In the Greek, this reads, "our Lord Jesus Christ, the glory." Because "glory" is an apposition to "Lord Jesus Christ," he himself is the glory (cf. Luke 2:32). Or the text can be understood to mean that Christ is glorious (see NIV). It is the splendor of Christ that gives Christians any dignity they have, not what they might happen to own. That is why showing favoritism is so contrary to one's belief in

Christ. The Christian without a lot of money should be treated just as well as the Christian who has everything. **respect of persons**—"favoritism" (TLB). This is the practice of showing partiality toward certain people by offering them preferential treatment.

➤**2 assembly**—lit., "synagogue." The use of this word shows that James was writing to Jewish Christians who still considered their assembly to be a synagogue. No other NT writer spoke of the assembly of Christian brothers as a synagogue. The reaction of orthodox Jews to Christianity soon forced Christians to abandon use of the word in this sense altogether (Rev. 3:9). While a "synagogue" implied any assembly or meeting of people regardless of common interest, the Greek word for "church" meant any group or community of people who are bound together by mutual ties whether they were actually assembling together or not. The Jewish term emphasized the place where people meet, while the Greek word pointed to the people themselves.

It was natural that Jewish Christians should associate many of the forms and much of the terminology of their former religion with their new faith in Christ. Christian churches were built like synagogues. The Communion Table stood in the east end where the Ark had been. James's use of the word "synagogue" reflects the same tendency, but in these verses he is concerned about the unhealthy practices that had been carried over into the Christian church by too close an association with the synagogue. The Jews had become accustomed to being seated in the synagogue according to the kind of job they had. This naturally drew attention to the wealthier people and those with more prominent and prestigious professions. They were ushered to the front seats to show off their finery. And when some of them became Christians, this practice was perpetuated in their meetings. So James spoke out against such favoritism.

➤**2, 3 A man with a gold ring . . . and ye have respect to him**—The man gets all the attention just because he's well dressed. **Stand thou there**—The poor man gets standing room only or a spot on the floor.

➤**4 Are ye not then partial in yourselves**—"have you not discriminated among yourselves" (NIV). **judges of evil thoughts**—

could be rendered "judges with evil thoughts" (RSV, NIV).

➤**5 poor of this world**—According to the earliest manuscripts, these people who are poor "in respect to the world," as opposed to "the rich in the world" (1 Tim. 6:17). More Christians come from the lower classes than higher up in society (1 Cor. 1:25-28). **rich in faith**—Their riches consist in faith. They are "rich toward God" (Luke 12:21). **the kingdom . . . promised**—See Luke 12:32; 1 Corinthians 2:9; 2 Timothy 4:8.

➤**6 despised**—lit., "dishonored." "To dishonor the poor is to dishonor those whom God honors, and so to invert the order of God" (Calvin). **rich men**—James is speaking of the rich as a class. **oppress you**—lit., "abuse their power against you." Those with money take advantage of their wealth and influence to give the little man a hard time. **draw** [drag] **you before the judgment seats**—Alford suggested that it is usually the same ones the poor give special treatment to, who end up hauling them into court. These people are looking for any excuse to corner Christians in court, if not because of their faith then for some other reason.

➤**7 they blaspheme**—probably speaking of the rich Jews who speak against Jesus Christ. **worthy name**—"noble name" (TLB). Christians need to guard the good name of Jesus'—it is the name with which they are marked (see Acts 11:26; 15:17; 1 Pet. 4:14-16). Real Christians identify closely with his name because they actually belong to him (1 Cor. 3:23).

➤**8 the royal law according to the scripture**—the law of love (Lev. 19:18), the most lofty, majestic, and supreme law (called "royal"). Since Jewish Christians still respected and obeyed the law (Acts 15:1; 21:18-24; Rom. 2:17; Gal. 2:12), James pointed to the fact that the law commands love for one's neighbor. This love cancels the favoritism denounced in 2:2-7.

➤**9 sin**—Showing favoritism to the rich can never be justified, for it is a violation of the law.

➤**10 offend** [stumble] **in one point**—James did not use the Greek word for "fall," as in Romans 11:11. Instead, he chose the word "stumble," which implies that not even falling, just stumbling a little is enough to be totally guilty in God's eyes. It is impossible to pick and choose which laws we will obey. When God says "obey," he means obey all of them. **is guilty of all**—See Matthew 5:18, 19; 23:25.

➤**11 he** [God] **that said**—"He is the One who gave the whole law; therefore, they who violate his will in one point, violate it all" (Bengel). It is as impossible to divide up his law into bits and pieces as it is to divide up God himself. Both are complete units. **Do not commit adultery ... Do not kill**—In keeping with his illustration (2:1-9) James cited the two most glaring examples of failing to love one's neighbor (see Exod. 20:13, 14). Favoritism is actually another (2:9).

➤**12** This is the conclusion of James's discussion on favoritism. **judged by the law of liberty**—i.e., the gospel law of love, which is not a law of external constraint, but of internal, free, instinctive inclination. Once God's mercy sets a person free from the demands of the law, he or she is free to love and obey God willingly, not out of any compulsion or command. However, Christ actually wants us to love our neighbor in more ways than the old law ever required.

➤**13** This reverses the lesson of Matthew 5:7. If those who have been kind and merciful will be rewarded with happiness, then those who have not can expect God's judgment (cf. Matt. 18:32-35). "It [the judgment] shall be such toward everyone as everyone shall have been" (Bengel). **rejoiceth against judgment**—"mercy triumphs over judgment" (RSV, NIV). There is reason for this victory celebration, for God now extends mercy to men rather than judgment. People must take advantage of this mercy while it is available and extend it to their fellowman.

➤**14** In this second part of the chapter, James speaks against those who abused the teaching of justification by faith. James must have been familiar with Paul's preaching on the subject. He and Paul used similar language and an identical illustration in speaking to the problem as they found it in their particular, though very different, circumstances (see Rom. 3–5). Paul was dealing with people who felt they could work their way to salvation; James was speaking to those with Antinomian ("against law") tendencies. The Holy Spirit inspired each man to speak God's word. Paul never contradicted James's message, that a man must evidence what he believes by the way he lives.

In fact, in his later letters, and as the situation demanded, he advocated good living as evidence of a person's faith (Titus 2:14; 3:8). **though a man say he hath faith**—James was careful to distinguish between a man who says he has faith and a man who really does. James was concerned with people who profess a belief they do not really have or that they do not put into practice. **can faith save him?**—i.e., "can the faith [just mentioned] save him?" The Greek indicates that James was speaking of the kind of faith that is professed but not practiced. This is an empty faith, even a false faith; therefore, this faith cannot save a person.

➤**15 a brother or sister**—The implication is that these are Christians for whom other Christians should sense a special responsibility.

➤**16** It is possible to get in the habit of offering superficial sympathy to people in need without ever providing any real help. **one of you**—James pointed his finger to get the message across. **Depart in peace**—The words, as good as they may sound, do not help the problem. When Jesus came across people in need he substantiated his kind words with actions. **be ... warmed**—What the person really needs is clothes (Job 31:20). **be ... filled**—Jesus met people's need for food with plenty to spare (Matt. 15:37). **what doth it profit?**—James started and finished with the same question (2:14): "What good does that do?" (TLB). Words without action certainly do not help the person who needs help. So faith consisting in mere profession is unacceptable to God.

➤**17** This verse is clearer when translated: "So faith by itself, if it has no works, is dead" (RSV). If a person is not demonstrating what he believes by the way he lives, then he does not have faith. It is just like a human body with the life gone out of it (2:26). Yes, there is a body, but what good is it without life?

➤**18** Into the hypothetical argument begun in 2:14 James now introduces someone who shares his position. These are the words of a person who really believes that you cannot have faith without works. His argument is that since no one but God can actually see faith, there must be some way of letting other people know what it means to have it. That way is by good works. God does not need to see the works because he has already justified us by our faith in Christ (Rom. 8:33). Thus, it is not a question of how a person is brought into right standing with God but how other people know that he has. That is why God tested Abraham (Gen. 22:1ff.). God did not justify Abraham because he was willing to sacrifice Isaac. God was satisfied long before by Abraham's faith in the fact that God would give him a son. What God really wanted was for Abraham to show the people around him that he believed God. Good works don't save a person; they just show others that that person is saved. You know a tree is alive when you see the fruit, but you can be sure there was life in it long before you ever saw the fruit or even the leaves.

➤**19 Thou believest that there is one God**—This is the fundamental belief of both Jews and Christians; however, the Jews of James's day were proud of the fact that this is what made them different from the Gentiles. But their faith is not so special—even the demons believe in God, and they shudder at the very thought of God because of the judgment he has prepared for them (Matt. 8:29; Luke 4:34; 2 Pet. 2:4; Jude 6; Rev. 20:10). But this faith is out of fear, not love. There is more to real faith.

➤**20 faith without works is dead**—The earliest manuscripts read, "faith without works is unproductive."

➤**21 Was not Abraham our father justified by works**—God recognized Abraham's willingness to demonstrate his faith in action. Yet James is just as insistent as Paul that God accepted Abraham in the first place because of his faith (2:23), not because of what he did.

➤**22 by works was faith made perfect** [complete]—His actions completed his faith— i.e., they manifested the full development and maturation of his faith. The seed has everything it needs to be a full-grown tree right from the start, but you can hardly say it is complete until you see the towering tree. Good deeds show that our faith is full-grown at last.

➤**23 the scripture**—While Paul used Genesis 15:6 to show that God justified Abraham simply by faith (see Rom. 4), James used the same verse to say that God justified Abraham because of how his faith was put into action. Paul was talking about the seed of faith, while James was talking about full-grown faith. Abraham's willingness to offer Isaac was more than just obedience. It was an expression of faith, and real faith is not full-grown until it is

expressed in action. **called the Friend of God**—Abraham had this kind of reputation because people could see his faith actually being worked out in his life. He showed that he loved God by what he did, and God demonstrated his love for Abraham by justifying him. This kind of friendship with God is still available on the same terms (cf. John 15:14, 15).

➤**24 by works a man is justified, and not by faith only**—This summarizes the preceding verses.

➤**25** James did not use **Rahab** as an example of someone who was saved simply by what she did because obviously she was not. First she had to believe that the Jews would actually defeat her country's well-trained forces. She had to believe it so strongly that she would be ready to risk her life to prove it. When Rahab hid the Hebrew spies, she was putting that faith into action. That is why her action is recorded as an illustration of faith (Heb. 11:31), rather than an example of obedience, because it is clear that she did not obey God in everything she did. And that is exactly why the writer of Hebrews and James chose to use the story of a prostitute alongside that of the patriarch Abraham when they talked about faith. They wanted to show that God accepts anyone as long as he comes by faith. James was especially anxious to show the difference between people who say the right things and people who really believe God and prove it by what they do. Abraham and Rahab are good examples of that kind of faith.

➤**26 For as the body without the spirit is dead, so faith without works is dead also**—It almost seems as if James had things backwards when he compared faith to the human body and good deeds to the human spirit. Actions seem much more physical than faith. But what he was trying to illustrate is the futility of faith that never expresses itself in real life. It is just like a dead body. The body is there, but without the spirit it is lifeless and therefore useless (see 2:20).

*Chapter* **3**

## 1-12 CONTROLLING THE TONGUE

➤**1 be not many masters**—lit., "become not many teachers." Do not be too quick to take teaching positions where you will be more open to criticism for what you say. Do not offer your services but wait to be asked. There are only certain individuals who have the ability to instruct others properly. But many Jews had the idea that talking about what they believed was enough; that made it easy to be a teacher, and many assumed teaching positions in the community. Everybody took his turn. James suggests here that it was bad enough when just those with the gift of teaching were criticized for what they said, but when these self-appointed teachers got into the act it was even worse. **we shall receive the greater condemnation**—James included himself when he reminded those who accept the responsibility of teaching to expect a stricter punishment than the ones they teach if they abuse their position (Luke 12:42-46).

➤**2 we offend all**—lit., "we cause all to stumble." James sees the teaching situation as the most difficult place to be consistently free from blame in what you say. That is why not many should become teachers, especially those who have trouble with their tongue.

➤**3 bits in the horses' mouths**—This is the first of two examples James uses to illustrate the importance of controlling the tongue.

➤**4** The tongue, like the bit in a horse's mouth and the rudder of a ship, is small in comparison to what it controls. Yet the ship is completely at the mercy of the pilot's whims and wishes, just as the horse is compelled to respond to the rider who holds the reins. We usually speak with the same sort of impulsive instinct that motivates the pilot or the rider.

➤**5, 6 how great a matter a little fire kindleth**—"what a great forest is set on fire by a small spark" (NIV). The Greek verb implies a habitual action. It "keeps on being set on fire again and again" (see Prov. 16:27). **a world of iniquity**—"a world of wrong" (TEV). **the course of nature**—or, "the wheel of nature," referring to the entirety of human existence (Burdick). **fire of hell**—James used the same Greek word for "hell" as Matthew did in 5:22. The particular word "Gehenna" appears only these two times in Scripture and shows again how familiar James was with the Sermon on the Mount. (See comments on Matthew 5:22.)

➤**7 every kind**—Man has tamed all sorts of dangerous dispositions and peculiar natures in the animal world. Notice that James classifies wild life in four families: animals, birds, rep-

tiles, and fish. **tamed of mankind**—With gentle but firm patience man has been able to subdue animal nature and even to improve it for his own use. However, the Greek case leaves room for an alternate reading here, which suggests that the animal world has "allowed itself" to be tamed by man.

➤**8 the tongue can no man tame**—Not a single person with those same qualities of patience, gentleness, and firmness can tame the tongue of another member of the human race, or even his own. It is now that the impact of what James has said in verse 2 becomes apparent. **unruly**—The Greek suggests something that is restless and incapable of restraint. Estius observed that despite a double barricade of lips and teeth the tongue is always breaking through the barrier to lash out and destroy people. **deadly**—lit., "death-bearing." The tongue is something that carries death wherever it goes.

➤**9 men . . . are made after the similitude of God**—according to God's likeness. All men are included in this statement since they are all made like God, even though one wouldn't know it by looking at most men. Although man has lost much of his God-likeness, there is still enough there to hint at what he once was like and what he can be again through the work of Christ. (Bengel illustrated this by pointing to Absalom who, though out of favor with his father, was still recognized by the people as the king's son.) We ought to respect the potential in man for restoration to his original God-like state. The Alexandrian Christians understood two distinct ideas from the phrase that describes man's creation in the "image and likeness" of God (Gen. 1:26). The "image" was that God-like part of man he had never lost while the "likeness" was that God-like part of man he has yet to acquire. By "image" they meant man's physical and intellectual nature, and by "likeness" they meant his moral being.

➤**10 Out of the same mouth proceedeth blessing and cursing**—Aesop once wrote that the tongue was, equally, the best and worst of things. That is why in his fables a man is able to blow both hot and cold breaths at the same time. Psalm 62:4 develops a similar contrast. **my brethren**—Again James appeals to them as fellow Christians and Jews (1:2). **these things ought not so to be**—The tone seems mild, but by leaving his audience to consider the probable consequences of this kind of action for themselves, James's short statement actually has a very powerful punch.

➤11 **fountain**—James pictured man's inner being (his heart) as a fountain or spring that shoots out fresh water and bitter from the same opening. Both types of springs were common in Palestine and are sometimes found very close to each other, but fresh water and bitter water never come out of the same hole. Only Christ can change the bitter water of our words into fresh and sweet ones, just as God changed the water at Marah (Exod. 15:23).

➤12 Through the image of the spring James was able to make a subtle transition from talking about the mouth to talking about the heart, which is the real root of the problem. **Can the fig tree . . . bear olive berries? either a vine, figs?**—The obvious answers are, "No, it's impossible." The image was adapted from the Sermon on the Mount where Jesus said that you can't get figs from thistles or grapes from thorns (Matt. 7:16, 17). In the natural world it is impossible for a plant to produce something that is inconsistent with its nature. Similarly, if a man who has been saying bitter, evil things suddenly says something sweet, you can be sure the sweet words just aren't real.

## 13-18 TWO KINDS OF WISDOM

➤13 **Who is a wise man?**—See Psalm 34:12, 13. **let him show out of a good conversation**—actually, "let him show it by his good life" (NIV). Wisdom is expressed in action, not words. As with faith (2:18), good deeds demonstrate wisdom, not merely good words. **meekness of wisdom**—In Greek, a genitive of quality: "a wise meekness" (cf. 3:17).

➤14 **if ye have bitter envying** [jealousy]— The Greek indicative mood suggests that this was the case with them. The phrase might equally read "bitter jealousy," as it once did, in order to differentiate between the proper jealous concern God had for his people and the selfish jealousy of humans. **strife**—rivalry. James is thinking of the kind of selfish ambition that results in rivalry. Like bitterness and jealousy it springs from inside and soon bubbles out in words and actions (see 3:11). **glory not**—do not exult over, do not boast. **and lie not against the truth**—To talk as if you are wise and good when your life denies it is an outright

lie. Paul condemned this sort of bragging in other Jewish Christians (Rom. 2:17, 23).

➤15 **This wisdom descendeth not from above**—In opposition to the true wisdom and illumination that comes from above (1:17), this "wisdom" is rooted and bound in the very nature of the earth itself—it is **earthly. sensual**—natural, pertaining to man's soul. The same Greek word is used to describe men who do not have the Spirit living in them (Jude 19). **devilish**—demon-like. This wisdom originates in hell (cf. 3:6) and cannot be real wisdom since God alone is the source of true wisdom (1:5).

➤16 **envying**—jealousy. The jealous man must be first in everything and cannot stand to see anyone else in the limelight instead of himself. He vents this vicious disposition on anyone who happens to get ahead of him in anything. But he is really attacking God who made each of us different. **strife**—rivalry. **confusion**—"disorder" (TLB, NIV). Luke 21:9 has the translation "insurrection" (TLB, NEB), while 2 Corinthians 6:5 speaks of "angry mobs" (TLB). This can be either the chaotic disorder of a group of people or the turmoil within an individual himself. There is no comparison between such disoriented living and the peace and gentleness that come with true wisdom (3:17).

➤17 **wisdom that is from above**—i.e., wisdom originating from God. **first pure**—God's wisdom stands in opposition to everything that is earthly, natural, and demon-like (3:15). The fact that it is first pure distinguishes it from other kinds of wisdom that make themselves at home in the world but are not at all concerned about purity—a theme James constantly emphasizes (1:27; 4:4, 8; see also 1 Pet. 1:22). In the Christian life, personal purity always comes before public ministry. **peaceable**— Unless a person is pure in God's eyes, he or she cannot be at peace with men. **gentle**—forbearing. A gentle person never makes demands on other people. **easy to be intreated**—compliant, considerate, "open to reason" (RSV). It is not difficult to get along with a person who is reasonable, flexible, and compliant. **full of mercy**—This is the kind of person who is sensitive to other people's needs and finds practical ways of meeting them. **good fruits**—While the wisdom of the world results in "every evil work" (3:16), God's wisdom produces good deeds. **without partiality**—could also be rendered "without uncertainty" (RSV). The Greek James uses here is the opposite expression of the word he uses to describe the man who sometimes believes God and sometimes does not (1:6). God's wisdom in a man gives him confidence in what he is and where he is going. He is always the same. He avoids favoritism at all costs (2:1, 4, 9), and he is exactly what he says he is. **without hypocrisy**—God's wisdom makes genuine men, not fakes.

➤**18** Just as 3:16 summarizes the results of the worldly wisdom that has been described in 3:15, so 3:18 summarizes the consequences of living according to the wisdom of God that is described in 3:17. The regrettable results of the wisdom of the world are reaped immediately, but "a harvest of goodness" takes time to ripen. **them that make peace**—"Peacemakers." In keeping with the husbandry metaphor, Estius describes peacemakers as men who "cultivate peace." Calvin suggests that real peacemaking may sometimes involve exposing other people's sins rather than mildly covering them up. However, this ought to be done gently, as a doctor diagnoses a disease, not coldly as the court would condemn a criminal.

*Chapter* **4**

1-17 PROBLEMS WITH THE TONGUE AND HOW TO HANDLE THEM. WHERE QUARRELS COME FROM, WHAT CRITICISM REALLY MEANS, AND WHY BRAGGING ABOUT THE FUTURE NEVER PAYS

➤**1** We naturally assume that all our troubles come from our circumstances or other people, but James was quick to point out that the trouble is really ourselves. **wars and fightings**—The harsh reality of what life is really like stands in jarring contrast to James's proposal for peace in 3:18. **come they not hence**—James suggested they already knew what caused the quarrels if they would only admit it. **of your lusts** [pleasures] **that war in your members**—There is a full-scale war going on inside us. Because we insist on having our own way, we naturally come into conflict with other people, but in the end we are only fighting ourselves and God's Spirit.

➤**2 Ye lust** [desire], **and have not**—This desire is not a pleasure (4:1) but a craving. It is

setting your mind on something that is always just out of reach. **ye kill**—James probably did not have actual murder in mind; but by Christ's standards, the envy and hate that such desires spawn are just as bad (cf. Matt. 5:21, 22). David and Ahab are examples of men who wanted something so desperately that they actually did kill to get it. Wrong desires lead to wrong attitudes that often end up in wrong actions. **because ye ask not**—God responds to prayer, not fighting. People who grab for everything they can get and then hold grudges when they don't get what they want are hardly the type of people God listens to. If they did start asking God instead of fighting for everything, they would soon stop fighting. This verse then answers the questions posed in 4:1.

➤**3 Ye ask**—God wants us to ask for what he wants (1:5), not what we want or think we need (cf. Matt. 6:31, 32). That way, our needs are taken care of and we stop wanting the things we do not need. And that would bring an end to all the quarreling and fighting.

➤**4 Ye adulterers**—These words are not present in the three earliest manuscripts. **adulteresses**—This refers to all those who love the world rather than God. God's love and concern for humanity is like the love of a husband for his wife. Like a husband, he will not tolerate a wife who is unfaithful (see Jer. 31:32). The **world** system includes evil desires, "quarrels and fights" (4:1), hate and greed (4:2), and all selfish pleasures (4:3). These are God's enemies, and he won't stand for any of them coming between himself and a Christian. **whosoever therefore will be**—The Greek language implies resolution here. If this is what you want out of life, you can count on being God's enemy (1 John 2:15). Although there is no guarantee that you will succeed in what you set out to accomplish, you can be sure that God will be against you all the way. How much better to go through life as "the friend of God" (2:23) rather than his enemy!

➤**5** The second part of this verse is very difficult to translate. But before looking at the translation, it must be pointed out that the earliest manuscript evidence supports the reading, "the spirit he caused to live in us tends towards envy" (NIV). In the margin of the NIV there are two alternative readings: "God jealously longs for the spirit that he made to live in us" and "the Spirit he caused to live in us longs jealously." There has been considerable discussion as to whether the spirit here is actually the Holy Spirit or simply man's natural human spirit. The word for "spirit" in Greek has an article, which usually means "the divine Spirit," but not always. However, the real confusion seems to center around the meaning of "jealousy." If this is an impure jealousy, then James must be speaking of man's natural spirit, since the Holy Spirit is incapable of such a wrong feeling. If, on the other hand, it is the positive kind of jealousy that a husband might have for the faithful love of his wife, then, as 4:4 suggests, God's Holy Spirit is quite capable of such love. Another problem with interpreting this verse is that no one knows what OT Scripture(s) James was alluding to. At best, we can say that the thought of James 4:5 approximates the thought of Exodus 20:5 and 34:14.

➤6 James was quoting Proverbs 3:34. **resisteth**—God only responds in this way to men who have already set themselves against him, just as Pharaoh did. He is always opposed to pride, since that is what led Satan to rebel against him in the first place. **the proud**—The Greek language describes a proud man as one who "sets himself above" his friends and, by doing that, actually opposes God who made men equal. **the humble**—These are people who are satisfied with who they are as God made them, with what he gave them, and with where he placed them.

➤7 **Submit yourselves therefore to God**—See 4:6, 10 (cf. 1 Pet. 5:6). **Resist the devil**—The warfare imagery is striking. James has already listed the weapons of resistance: faith, humility, prayer, and God's wisdom. Now he urges these Jewish Christians to stand up to Satan and fight. **he will flee from you**—This is more than the reassurance of another man—it is God's personal guarantee that Satan will leave.

➤8 **Draw nigh** [near] **to God**—Satan is against anyone who has a desire to get close to God. That is why the Christian must consciously cling to him (Deut. 30:20). **he will draw nigh** [near] **to you**—God always responds to those who sincerely seek him, but he cannot come close to people who deliberately keep their distance from him. **Cleanse your hands**—Hands represent what a person does.

Clean actions are a must in the Christian life. **purify your hearts**—As the hands represent what a person is on the outside, the heart symbolizes what a man is on the inside. It is in the heart that the "whole army of evil desires" (4:1, TLB) is at war, and it is here that the "evil pleasures of this world" (4:4, TLB) are first admitted. God wants men whose attitudes as well as actions are clean and pure.

➤9 **Be afflicted**—lit., "be miserable"; hence, "Be sorrowful" (NEB, TEV). God is looking for real repentance instead of the frivolous attitude we so often have toward sin. The language implies a deep, intense sorrow like the mourning at a funeral. In 5:1, James tells the rich men to "weep and howl." It is not enough simply to say you are sorry when you are dealing with God (Isa. 22:12, 13; Luke 6:25). **heaviness**—lit., "fallen eyes" and comparable to our expression, "his face was fallen." Someone who is genuinely sorry for his sin will have a look of utter dejection and will be ashamed to look anyone in the eye.

➤10 **in the sight of the Lord**—One of the surest ways to stay humble is to realize that we are never out of God's sight for even a minute. Deep roots grow tall trees, and God drives men down before he lifts them up. This principle can also be applied to the development of leaders in the local church (1 Pet. 5:6).

➤11 James now moves on to the matter of criticism, as he continues his instruction on the theme of trouble with control of the tongue. Whether it is criticism or quarreling, all the trouble we get into with our tongues can be traced right back to the selfish desires inside ourselves (4:1). **brethren**—James subtly suggests the inconsistency of criticizing someone one minute and then calling him a brother the next. **if thou judge the law, thou art not a doer of the law, but a judge**—A person who criticizes or judges someone else is actually doing the job God's law was designed to do. God is quite capable of pointing out people's problems through his word. He sees everything and allows what he allows for a reason. He doesn't need any help. This is the last time the law is mentioned in the New Testament, and even here James is really talking, not about the old Jewish law, but about "the perfect law of liberty" (1:25) that Christ came to put into effect.

➤**12 There is one lawgiver, who is able to save and to destroy**—Some men foolishly think they can administer laws that God made. They are trying to play God, but they have none of his power to back up their decisions. **who art thou**—The Greek is very emphatic here: "*and* who are *you?*" It is the height of self-conceit for anyone to be the judge of someone else, for in so doing such a person is really claiming superiority to God and to other people whom God created equal. **another**—The earliest manuscripts read "your neighbor."

➤**13** James introduces another kind of trouble with the tongue: bragging about the future. **Go to now**—an expression meaning, "come now" (RSV). **To day or to morrow**—Some manuscripts read "today and tomorrow." The first implies that the speaker feels he is free to go whenever he wants, while the second, that he is free to go for as long as he wants. Both indicate how much he thinks he is the absolute master of his own destiny. **into such a city**—lit., "into this city." The speaker has a specific place in mind where he is going. He adds to the list of freedoms he claims to have, the freedom to go wherever he wants. **continue there a year**—Now this individual insists he will stay as long as he wants. The implication of the verse is that after the year is up, he has every intention of mapping out the next year of his life in identical detail. **buy and sell, and get gain**—He continues to assert the right to every area of his life by announcing that not only will he go wherever he wants, whenever he wants, and stay as long as he wants—he now maintains that he will do whatever he wants. The materialistic aim of his whole trip indicates how far he has shut God out of his plans.

➤**14** Because we have no way of knowing how long we will live, we can hardly plan any of the other details of our lives. All of these things are just as uncertain as the hour of our death. **a vapour**—or, "a mist" (RSV, NIV), which appears, then vanishes. Such is the transitoriness of our earthly existence.

➤**15 ye ought to say**—There is a substitute for the unwise words of 4:13. **If the Lord will**—With regard to his travel plans, Paul used this expression (Acts 18:21; 1 Cor. 4:19)—but not always (Acts 19:21; Rom. 15:28; 1 Cor. 16:5, 8). "Yet it is obvious, whether Paul explicitly stated it or not, he always condi-

tioned his plans on the will of God" (Burdick). **we shall live, and do this, or that**—The speaker in 4:13 always assumed that he would be alive. James said that we can never make that assumption. A person must realize that just being alive is a gift of God.

➤**16, 17** Assuming the certainty of your future is just another kind of pride that displeases God. James punctuates this very practical lesson with another statement on his favorite theme: **to him that knoweth to do good, and doeth it not, to him it is sin**—A person does not get anywhere with God by merely knowing what he wants, but by doing what he says. There is not a bit of difference between people who know God's word and do not obey it and those who have never even heard it. God calls them all sinners. The danger in hearing what God says so often and not doing it is that one gets calloused and loses his sensitivity to sin.

# Chapter 5

## 1-20 A WARNING TO RICH MEN, AND FINAL ADVICE ON PATIENCE AND PRAYER

➤**1 Go to now**—lit., "come now." This is a strong attention-getter. **ye rich men**—He was addressing men who were known for how much money they had rather than for the good they could have done with it. James was probably speaking out against rich Jews, less for their sake than for the sake of the Christians who were being persecuted by them (Bengel). James warns them to repent because of the coming misery. "Verses 1-6 are similar to OT declarations of judgment against pagan nations, interspersed in books otherwise addressed to God's people" (*NIVSB*). **your miseries** [hardships] **that shall come upon you**—lit., "that are coming upon you."

➤**2 corrupted**—Because the wealth was gotten by cheating poor people, God had destined it to be destroyed.

➤**3 cankered**—rusted, corroded. **shall be a witness against you**—The rusting coins and rotted clothes will prove that their whole lives were spent accumulating something that did not do them any good. **eat your flesh as it were fire**—Just as the process of decay devoured their wealth, the awareness of the futility of all they have done will eat away at their minds. **heaped treasure together for the last days**— See Luke 12:19. The rich man's act of treasuring up wealth is matched by God's act of storing up wrath, which will be poured out when God comes to judge the world.

➤**4 Behold**—James now reinforces the seriousness of what he has been saying. Though they may not want to hear him, they should know that God has heard the cries of the people they have oppressed. **the hire . . . kept back by fraud**— i.e., "wages withheld by fraud." What these rich men were doing was holding back wages that were due. The cheating was not outright stealing since the workers were paid eventually, but James's accusation recalls Deuteronomy 24:14, 15. A man deserves wages for the work he has done, and to delay payment is as serious as not paying at all. If the worker is in need and cries to God, God will look on what the employer has done as stealing. It is a double crime since, as rich men, they should have shared with the poor rather than taken from them what was rightfully theirs. **the Lord of sabaoth**—"the Lord of hosts" (RSV, cf. TLB). It is not strange that the only direct NT use of this familiar OT title should appear in a letter to Jewish Christians. The choice of this particular name of God is especially appropriate in this context since the rich oppress the poor because they think no one will stand up for them, while in fact, the Lord of all the hosts of heaven and earth is their defender, and he is coming back to make things right (5:7).

➤**5 Ye have lived in pleasure**—The Greek indicates a life of leisure, luxury, and sensual pleasure to the extreme. **on the earth**—The scene of their sin will now become the place of their punishment, and instead of pleasure there will be pain. **nourished your hearts**— They gorged themselves with every imaginable pleasure, and their animal appetites were never satisfied until they were completely sated. They lived to eat rather than ate to live. **day of slaughter**—Like well-fed animals that have been fattened for market, these rich men have eaten to their heart's content without realizing that they have just been fattening themselves for their own slaughter, when God comes to judge them. An alternate interpretation suggests that it was from the slaughter of poor and innocent victims that they had made

themselves fat. Such an interpretation is quite consistent with the context of 5:4 and 5:6.

➤**6 Ye have condemned and killed the just [man]**—Naturally, James was thinking of what they had done to Christ, but he is also aware of the continuing persecution of Jewish Christians. James himself, later known as James the Just, became a victim of one of their uprisings. **he doth not resist you**—Either such men did not have the power, or else, in keeping with the character of Christ, who never defended himself when falsely arrested (Isa. 53:7), they did not even try to defend themselves.

➤**7 Be patient**—In view of the coming judgment (5:1, 3), James encouraged them to follow the example of their brothers who died without defending themselves (5:6). **brethren**—James now makes a deliberate point of turning from the rich men to the Christians. In the rest of the chapter he is talking to Christians. **the coming [parousia] of the Lord**—Then their patient suffering will be over, and it will have been worth the wait. **the husbandman** [farmer] **waiteth**— He puts up with all kinds of work and trouble without immediate results because he knows he will harvest a crop worth all the effort (Ps. 126:3 and Gal. 6:9 use the same harvest image). **early and latter rain**—In Palestine these are all fall and spring rains—both of which are needed for a successful crop (Burdick).

➤**8 the coming of the Lord draweth nigh** [has drawn near]—The perfect tense of the Greek verb here expresses the idea of something that is present and imminent. In other words, the Christian should be continually conscious that Christ's coming is near. Nothing can make you forget your present problems faster than to remember that he could come any minute, and yet that knowledge should be a constant awareness and settled fact in the mind of every Christian.

➤**9 Grudge not one against another**—The Greek verb here is "groan." This is not open criticism of someone, but a muffled mutter, a complaint under your breath that says you disapprove of someone or something but don't have the courage to confront him with it. James wants these Christians to exhibit the same kind of patience in putting up with the shortcomings of their brothers as they do in tolerating the injustices of non-Christians (5:6). Some Christians find it harder to put up with other Christians than with people of the world. **lest ye be** condemned—See Matthew 7:1. **the judge standeth before the door**—Other Scriptures use the same expression (Gen. 4:7; Matt. 24:33; Ps. 24:7). When Christ comes the second time, he will come as the Judge.

➤**10 the prophets**—These are men who had rich ministries because they were willing to bear anything for God.

➤**11 count them happy** [blessed]—James's confidence comes from his familiarity with God's promises (Matt. 5:10). **endure**—suffering. In the end, those who have had a hard time here on earth, not those who have had all the pleasure (5:5), will be really happy. **patience**—There are two kinds of patience. The Greek word here is similar to, but not the same as, the word for "patience" in 5:10. This word can be translated "endurance." Many people exhibit a very passive patience in accepting their lot in life, while others actively endure what God has for them. That is the kind of patience these prophets demonstrated. James uses the same Greek word in 1:3 when he talks about patience that actively grows. **Job**—James uses a living example of someone who endured his sufferings. **the end of the Lord**—"what the Lord finally brought about" (NIV). A believer cannot always see the good in what God has for him or her until it is all over. He wants us to learn to endure every tough experience to the end, so he can show us the good that will come of it. **the Lord is very pitiful, and of tender mercy**—compassionate. His tenderness is expressed in his compassion and pity for us. God shows us his tenderness by not giving us more troubles than we can handle, and he proves his mercy by taking us out of all troubles in the end (Bengel).

➤**12 swear not**—Swearing should be the farthest thing from a Christian who is practicing patience. Even in difficult situations (5:10, 11) the Christian should have his tongue under control (Matt. 5:33-37). In 5:13 James implies that when troubles come you should talk to God about them, instead of blaming him for them. **yea be yea . . . nay, nay**—A Christian's word should be so good he doesn't need anything extra to convince people of it. **condemnation**—judgment. Swearing is as serious in God's sight as anything else (2:10) and will be punished just as severely with God's judgment.

➤**13** In tough times Christians can call on God instead of cursing him. They have the example of

Job (5:10) and the prophets (5:11). **sing psalms**—See Ephesians 5:19; Colossians 3:16.

➤**14 call for the elders**—The fact that this is plural rules out the practice of some who think that sending one representative to pray for the sick is sufficient. "The prayers of the elders over the sick would be much the same as though the whole church which they represent should pray" (Bengel). **anointing him with oil**—Some commentators consider this anointing with oil to be a sacramental anointing, but others consider it a medicinal anointing. In defense of the medicinal anointing, Burdick wrote the following:

> There are a number of reasons for understanding this application of oil as medicinal rather than sacramental. The word *aleipsantes* ("anoint") is not the usual word for sacramental or ritualistic anointing. James could have used the verb *chriō* if that had been what he had in mind. The distinction is still observed in modern Greek, with *aleiphō* meaning "to daub," "to smear," and *chriō* meaning "to anoint." Furthermore, it is a well-documented fact that oil was one of the most common medicines of biblical times. See Isaiah 1:6 and Luke 10:34. Josephus (*Antiquities,* 17, 172 [vi. 5]) reports that during his last illness Herod the Great was given a bath in oil in hopes of effecting a cure. The papyri, Philo, Pliny, and the physician Galen all refer to the medicinal use of oil. Galen described it as "the best of all remedies for paralysis" (*De Simplicium Medicamentorum Temperamentis,* 2.10ff.). It is evident, then, that James is prescribing prayer and medicine.

**in the name of the Lord**—According to the Greek, this phrase most likely joins with the verb "pray" and the participle "having anointed." The entire action of praying and anointing is to be done in the Lord's name.

➤**15 the prayer of faith**—It is not the oil (5:14) but the prayer of faith that heals. **save**—can also and, in this case, should be translated "heal." **and if he have committed sins, they shall be forgiven**—Not everybody is sick because of sin in his life, but if someone is, and he has enough faith to believe God will heal his body, God will forgive the sin as well. The word "committed" means literally "in a state of having committed sin," which suggests that in this case he was living with the physical consequences of the sin he had committed. God often deals with sin and sickness together (Isa. 33:24; Matt. 9:2-5; John 5:14).

►16 The earliest manuscripts begin this verse with "therefore." Because God is willing and able to heal us, we should be willing to admit the areas of our lives where we need his healing help. **faults**—actually, "sins." The only sins we should confess to one another are those in which we have sinned against fellow Christians (see Matt. 5:23, 24; Luke 7:14). All other sins should be confessed in private to God (1 John 1:7). **that ye may be healed**—We confess our sins and pray for one another in order that we may be made whole people, in our bodies as well as our souls. **The effectual fervent prayer of a righteous man**— This man is the exact opposite of the doubtful minded man of 1:6. He is intense, sincere, and one who has been "energized" by the Holy Spirit for a special task (Hammond). Although the righteous man's prayer is always heard, the particular context suggests that he prays for the healing of another Christian, and that because of the earnest character of his Christian life, his prayer will be answered. Here is a man who puts faith into action (2:24).

►17 Elias [Elijah] **was a man subject to like passions as we are**—The implication is that since Elijah was a mere man, any one of us can experience the same kind of power in prayer that he did. **prayed earnestly**—lit., "prayed with prayer." It is a Hebrew expression that emphasizes the genuineness and earnestness of his prayer. (Cf. Jesus' words "with desire have I desired" in Luke 22:15—a similar Hebraism.) **that it might not rain**—The OT does not tell us directly that Elijah prayed for no rain, but it is implied in 1 Kings 17:1. His prediction was based

on the conviction that God would answer what he had already prayed for. Because he was so deeply concerned about the dishonor that God's people were bringing on him by worshiping idols (1 Kings 19:10), he asked for a punishment that would affect them all. When they admitted their error, he asked God to take away the drought (1 Kings 18). **three years and six months**—1 Kings 18:1; Luke 4:25. It was three years since he had visited Zarephath; God's prophecy had probably come to him five or six months before that visit. This is the exact period of time that the two witnesses of Revelation 11:6 will have "power to shut heaven, that it rain not."

►18 **he prayed again, and the heaven gave rain**—When Elijah asked God for something, there was action. **the earth brought forth her fruit**—The earth produced again what God had held back because of his people's sin.

►19 Christians have the authority to reclaim for God anyone who has slipped into error if they agree to ask God on his or her behalf (see Matt. 18:18-20). **err**—"wander" (RSV, NIV), "stray" (NEB). **the truth**—the truth concerning the person and work of Jesus Christ and the reality of this truth lived out in a Christian life. **one convert him**—lit., "turn him around," or "bring him back" (NIV). A Christian can help a wayward believer by turning him back to the truth (cf. 1 John 5:16).

►20 **shall save a soul from death, and shall hide a multitude of sins**—A Christian's love and concern for someone else can bring that person to the place where he will see that Christ's death on the cross covers his sins before God. The possibility that a Christian can have a part in such a tremendous task so excited James that he repeated himself (see 5:19).

BIBLIOGRAPHY

Alford, Henry. *The Greek New Testament*. 1952. Reprint. Grand Rapids: Guardian Press, 1976.

Bengel, John A. *New Testament Word Studies*. 1742. Reprint. Grand Rapids: Eerdmans, 1971.

Burdick, Donald W. "James" in the *Expositor's Bible Commentary*. Grand Rapids: Zondervan, 1981.

Calvin, John. *Calvin's Commentaries: A Harmony of the Gospels Matthew, Mark, and Luke and the epistles of James and Jude*. Grand Rapids: Eerdmans, 1972.

Estius, Gulielmus. *In omnes Di Pauli epistdas, item in catholicas comenturri*. Dauci, Ex officiana Typographica Baltzaris Belleri, 1716.

Rienecker, Fritz. *Linguistic Key to the Greek New Testament*. Grand Rapids: Baker Book House, 1976, 1980.

Robertson, A. T. *Word Pictures in the New Testament*. Nashville: Broadman Press, 1932.

Tittmann, J. A. *Remarks on the Synonyms of the New Testament*. Edinburgh: T & T Clark, 1833-37.

Wordsworth, John. *The Ministry of Grace*. New York: Longmans, Greer, 1901.

# 1 PETER

## Introduction

The genuineness of Peter's first epistle is attested by 2 Peter 3:1—also by Polycarp (c. 70–160), who, in writing to the Philippians, quotes many passages: in chapter 2 he quotes 1:1, 21, and 3:9; in chapter 5, 2:11. Eusebius says of Papias (*Ecclesiastical History*, 3.39) that he, too, quotes Peter's first epistle. Irenaeus (*Against Heresies*, 4.9.2) expressly mentions it; and in 4.16.5, quotes 2:16. Clement of Alexandria (in *Stromata*, 1.3) quotes 2:11, 12, 15, 16; and then 1:21, 22; and in 1.4 he quotes 3:14-17; and then 4:12-14. Origen (in Eusebius's *Ecclesiastical History*, 6.25) mentions this epistle; in *Homily* 7, on Joshua, vol. 2, he mentions both epistles; and in his *Commentary* on Psalm 3 and on John, he mentions 3:18-21. Eusebius states it as the opinion of those before him that this was among the universally acknowledged epistles. The internal evidence is equally strong. The author calls himself the apostle Peter (1:1) and "a witness of Christ's sufferings," and an "elder" (5:1). The energy of the style harmonizes with the warmth of Peter's character; and, as Erasmus says, this epistle is full of apostolic dignity and authority and is worthy of the leader among the apostles.

Simon, or Simeon, was a native of Bethsaida on the Sea of Galilee, son of Jonas or John. With his father and his brother Andrew he carried on trade as a fisherman at Capernaum, his subsequent residence. He was brought to Jesus by his brother Andrew, who had been a disciple of John the Baptist, but was pointed to the Savior as "the Lamb of God" by his master. Jesus, on first beholding him, gave him the name by which chiefly he is known, indicative of his subsequent character and work in the church: "Peter" (Greek) or "Cephas" (Aramaic)—both meaning "a stone." The major incidents in his apostolic life are well known: his walking on the troubled waters to meet Jesus, but sinking through doubting; his bold and clear acknowledgment of the divine person and office of Jesus, notwithstanding the difficulties in the way of such belief, whence he was then also designated as *the stone,* or *rock;* his passing from one extreme to the opposite, in reference to Christ's offer to wash his feet; his self-confident assertion that *he* would never forsake his Lord, whatever others might do, followed by his denial of Christ thrice; his deep penitence; Christ's full forgiveness and prophecy of his faithfulness unto death, after he had received from him a profession of love. These incidents illustrate his character as zealous, pious, and ardently attached to the Lord, but at the same time impulsive in feeling, rather than calmly and continuously steadfast. Prompt in action and ready to avow his convictions boldly, he was hasty in judgment, precipitate, and too self-confident in the assertion of his own steadfastness; the result was that, though he abounded in courage, his moral courage was too easily overcome by fear of man's opinion. A wonderful change was wrought in him by the restoration he experienced after his fall, through the grace of his risen Lord. His zeal and ardor became sanctified, being chastened by a spirit of humility.

After the ascension, he took the lead in the church; on the descent of the Holy Spirit at Pentecost, he exercised "the keys" of Christ's kingdom by opening the door of the church through preaching the gospel to thousands of Israelites. Furthermore, he opened an entrance to the Gentiles through his preaching of the gospel to Cornelius. In light of these special functions, Peter could have thought highly of himself. But there is no instance on record of Peter's having ever claimed or exercised supremacy.

Peter was probably in Rome at the time he wrote this epistle. The use of "Babylon" in 5:13 was most likely a code word for "Rome" (see comments on 5:13). According to First Clement 5:4-7, Peter and Paul were victims of persecution. "The common understanding is that the passage refers to the persecution by Nero at Rome . . . which began after the disastrous fire in the city of Rome on 19 July 64" (Blum). Peter must have written this epistle before this persecution, sometime between A.D. 62 and 64.

Peter wrote this first epistle to "the sojourners of the dispersion" (1:1, Gk.). This dispersion consisted primarily of Jewish Christians (see Acts 11:19); but, of course, there were Gentile Christians in the churches Peter addressed. Verses such as 1:14; 2:9, 10; 3:6; and 4:3 show this. Thus he, the apostle of the circumcision, sought to unite Jew and Gentile, promoting thereby the same work and doctrine as Paul the apostle of the uncircumcision. The provinces named by Peter in the opening verse were in the order proceeding from northeast to south and west: Pontus, Galatia, Capadocia, Asia, and Bithynia. Pontus was the country of the Christian Jew Aquila. To Galatia, Paul paid two visits, founding and confirming churches. Crescens, his companion, went there about the time of Paul's last imprisonment, just before his martyrdom. Men of Cappadocia, as well as of "Pontus" and "Asia," were among the hearers of Peter's effective sermon at Pentecost; these people probably brought the gospel home to their native land. Proconsular "Asia" included Mysia, Lydia, Caria, Phrygia, Pisidia, and Lycaonia. In Lycaonia were the churches of Iconium, founded by Paul and Barnabas. In Pisidia was Antioch, where Paul was the instrument of converting many but was driven out by the Jews. In Caria was Miletus. In Phyrgia, where Paul preached while visiting Galatia and its neighborhood, were the churches of Laodicea, Hierapolis, and Colosse. In Lycia, there were churches in Philadelphia, Sardis, Thyatira, and Ephesus. In Mysia was Pergamos. Of "Bithynia," no church is expressly named elsewhere in Scripture. When Paul "assayed to go into Bithynia," the Spirit would not let him (Acts 16:7). But afterwards, as can be inferred from 1:1, the Spirit brought the gospel to that country, possibly by Peter's ministry. Peter may have also brought the gospel to the northern parts of Galatia. The Christians in all the regions Peter mentioned were experiencing persecution and reproach arising from their being so unlike their heathen neighbors.

Peter wrote this epistle to console the persecuted and prepare them for a greater approaching ordeal, and to exhort all—husbands, wives, servants, elders, and people—to live godly lives in the presence of the heathen so that they could not reproach Christianity but rather be won to Christ. Peter himself explained why he wrote this epistle: "I have written briefly, exhorting, and testifying that this is the true grace of God

685

1  PETER  1

wherein ye stand" (5:12). The expression "exhorting and testifying" refers to Peter's *exhortations* throughout the epistle grounded on *testimony* that he bore to the gospel truth, already well known to his readers by the teaching of Paul in those churches (Alford). Therefore, Peter did not set forth a complete statement of this gospel in this epistle. He reaffirmed it with his own style and expression.

*Chapter* 1

### 1-12 A GLORIOUS SALVATION

➤**1 Peter**—The Greek form of the name Cephas meaning "rock." **an apostle of Jesus Christ**—Peter immediately states his position as an apostle of Christ. In this letter he will speak on the basis of the Lord's authority, not on his own. **to the strangers scattered throughout**— lit., "to the sojourners of the dispersion" (cf. James 1:1). It refers specifically to the Jews scattered thoroughout the world since the Babylonian exile (Ps. 147:2). Since Peter was an apostle to the Jews, he was primarily addressing them. But he had more than their physical circumstances in mind. Their spiritual calling as followers of Christ made them strangers and pilgrims on earth, looking for the heavenly Jerusalem, their real home. Since Gentile Christians are the spiritual Israel, they too have the same high calling. In fact, Peter plainly referred to Christian Gentiles in this epistle (1:14; 2:10, 11; 4:3). In the light of the Christian's calling, he must never comfortably settle himself and forget that he is a traveler. When  the Jews were scattered at the Babylonian captivity, they spread the knowledge of the one true God throughout the nations in preparation for Christ's first coming. Today, when Christians are scattered throughout an unbelieving world, they diffuse the knowledge of Christ in preparation for his second coming. **Pontus, Galatia, Cappadocia, Asia, and Bithynia**—These provinces were all in Asia Minor. Peter started in the northeast with Pontus, then moved south to Galatia, southeast to Cappadocia, west to Asia and back north to Bithynia, just west of Pontus. If, as some believe, the letter was written from Babylon, this may have been the order in which those provinces were viewed from the East. Some commentators, however, feel that the letter originated in Rome. See comments on 5:13.

Peter was once again ministering to the people he had preached to at Pentecost (Acts 2:9, 10).

➤**2 Elect**—Although Christians are strangers on earth, they do belong to God for they are his chosen, his elect. It is these whom Peter addressed. **according to the foreknowledge of God the Father**—God's foreknowledge cannot be separated from his love (1:20). Together they form the basis from which God's divine choosing takes place. God's foreknowledge is not his perception of some action being taken outside his control. And it does not negate man's liberty; in fact, it does not impose any absolute constraint. The fact that God knows all things beforehand, even ordains all things beforehand, does not mean that he forces the actions of his creatures, leaving them no choice. For example, Jesus was foreknown (the same Greek word for "foreordained" in 1:20) to be the sacrificial lamb. But this wasn't contrary to his own will. Rather, in a self-conscious act he rested his will in his Father's. The Hebrew and Greek words for "know" include the ideas of approving and acknowledging for oneself. The Hebrew emphasizes the oneness of loving and choosing by having one word for both. Peter will turn from this lofty theme of election to talk about the new birth and the practical outworking of the Christian life. From that point, he will turn again to show his readers how the new birth has opened up the living hope of eternal life. **through sanctification of the Spirit**—The Spirit comes to the elect to sanctify them and bring them to obey the gospel. This sanctifying work of the Spirit begins before salvation (see John 16:7-11) and continues after salvation. God the Father grants salvation by his gracious and sovereign election; the Son earns it by shedding his blood; and the Holy Spirit applies the Son's merit to the believer through the gospel. **unto obedience**—to the gospel (Rom. 1:5). **sprinkling of the blood of Jesus Christ**—This refers to the initial cleansing of the believer by Christ's blood (Heb. 10:22) and to the day-by-day cleansing from sin through Christ's blood (1 John 1:7).

➤**3** Like Paul, Peter opened his epistle by giving thanks to God for his great salvation. In so doing he looked forward to the future (1:3-9) and back into the past (1:10-12). **abundant mercy**—The fullness of God's mercy is evidenced by the fact that it reaches men when they are guilty and his enemies. **hath begotten us again**—Greek, "has regenerated us." Formerly we were dead in our sins, but now we have a new life. **a lively hope**—a living hope. This hope gives life and looks for life as its object. "Living" is a favorite expression of Peter's (cf. 1:23; 2:4, 5). **by the resurrection of Jesus Christ from the dead**—The connection between our sonship and the resurrection also appears in Luke 20:36 and Acts 13:33. Christ's resurrection is the cause of our own. By rising from the dead he made the necessary power available (1 Cor. 15:22); our resurrection, furthermore, will be patterned after his. A believer is born again from his natural state into the life of grace and after that is ushered into the life of glory. The believer's resurrection may be seen as another kind of birth or nativity—a coming out of the womb of the earth into immortality and eternal life. More than any of the other writers, Peter emphasizes the resurrection of Christ.

➤**4 inheritance**—According to 1:9, the inheritance is the "salvation of your souls." **incorruptible, and undefiled, and that fadeth not away**—This inheritance does not have within it the germs of death. It stands in stark contrast to all the imperfection that surrounds us. Contemplating it can help us glimpse those things which we cannot yet fully comprehend. It is unstained, untouched by any kind of sin. Even Israel's inheritance had been defiled, but not so the treasure that awaits the believer. **reserved**—is in the perfect tense in Greek, expressing a fixed and lasting state "which has been and is reserved." Although the heirs are still surrounded by dangers, the inheritance is completely secure, beyond the reach of Satan (1:5; John 17:12). Peter goes on with the picture of our inheritance: **in heaven for you**—Not only is the inheritance secure in heaven from all misfortune, but it is also safe from misappropriation. No one will mistakenly receive it.

➤**5 kept** [guarded] **by the power of God**—Peter here answers a logical objection: What use is that salvation reserved for us in heaven, safe and sound, if we down here are being tossed around like a wrecked vessel on a stormy sea? If the inheritance is going to be kept (1:4), then the heirs must be guarded so they can be sure of reaching it. Remember that the inheritance belongs only to those who endure to the end, those who are kept in God's mighty power because they are trusting in him (cf. Luke 8:13). God himself is our only guarding power (Jude 1; Phil. 1:6; 4:7). The believer lives spiritually in God, and God lives in him. God works organically in and through us so that we, insofar as we let God do his work, are also living in him. The power of God is no external force working on the believer from the outside, as though the believer were a robot. **through faith**—We should not flatter ourselves by thinking that we will be guarded by God if we are not walking by faith. Through faith salvation is both received and kept. **unto salvation**—Salvation will not only be ours by title because of what Christ has done, but it will be expressed and demonstrated, finally and completely, in our lives. **ready to be revealed in the last time**—When Christ is revealed, that salvation will be revealed. The preparations for that time began when Christ came. Salvation has already been accomplished and waits for the time God has chosen to reveal it.

➤**6 Wherein**—lit., "In which," referring to the prospect of obtaining a final salvation. **rejoice**—This prospect is cause enough for great rejoicing now. It can be real to us now even before it is fully experienced. **though now for a season if need be, ye are in heaviness**—When troubles first confront us, we are naturally distressed, but the anticipation of joy ahead can make those troubles seem almost like a thing of the past. **manifold temptations**—"all sorts of trials" (JB).

➤**7** This verse describes the purpose of the trials. **the trial of your faith . . . more precious than of gold that perisheth**—If gold, which will eventually perish, is tried with fire in order to remove the dross and test its genuineness, how much more does your faith, which will never perish, need to pass through a similarly fiery trial to remove whatever is defective and to test its genuineness and true value. **found unto praise and honour and glory at the appearing of Jesus Christ**—When Christ is revealed as Lord on the last day, the sons of God will also be revealed (1:15; Rom. 8:19; 1 John 3:2).

➤**8 Whom having not seen, ye love**—Usually it is firsthand knowledge of people that produces love for them, yet Jesus said that those who have not seen him and yet have believed are all the more blessed (John 20:29). **joy unspeakable**—We have this joy now in our present state, in contrast to our future state when we shall see him face-to-face. **full of glory**—We have part of that glory now because of Christ's presence in our lives; we also have part of that heavenly glory in our anticipation.

➤**9 Receiving the end of your faith, even the salvation of your souls**—We are guaranteed that we will receive the crowning fulfillment of our faith: full and complete salvation. At present we have received only the title to it and its down payment. In 1:10 Peter speaks of salvation being already present, although it was not present for the prophets. This verse, therefore, must refer to our present deliverance from God's wrath. **of your souls**—The immortal soul was lost in the fall, so salvation primarily concerns the soul. At the coming of Christ, the body too will share in redemption, but the soul is saved now.

➤**10 of which salvation the prophets have enquired and searched diligently**—This salvation is so wonderful that the prophets and even the angels (1:12) earnestly inquired into it. The Spirit of Christ has testified to it since the beginning of the world. Much more has been revealed to us than what the prophets could determine by all their inquiry and research. They wanted to know more about what they had been told. Since they were already certain that redemption would come but could not fully see how it would come, they wanted to see the one and same Christ whom we see fully in spirit. In private, the prophets must have pondered the hidden and far-reaching implications of their own prophecies, since these were Spirit-inspired rather than self-initiated. **who prophecied of the grace that should come unto you**—When Christ came, grace came (John 1:16, 17).

➤**11 Searching what or what manner of time**—In what era would Christ the Messiah come? What events and features would characterize the time of his coming? These were the questions in the prophets' minds. **the Spirit of Christ**—This title of the Spirit appears in Romans 8:9. (Acts 16:7 contains the phrase "the Spirit of Jesus" and Phil. 1:19, the "Spirit of Jesus Christ.") Because the Son of God was to become our Christ, he revealed himself in the OT by his Spirit in and through the prophets. **the sufferings of Christ**—The sufferings foretold in regard to Christ were the pains he underwent on the cross to become our Savior. **the glory** [glories] **that should follow**—Christ's resurrection, ascension, coming judgment, and kingdom are the glories that follow his sufferings on the cross (3:18-22; 5:1).

➤**12 Unto whom it was revealed, that not unto themselves, but unto us** ["you" in the earliest manuscripts] **they did minister**—The prophets were also told that these revelations of the future were given not for their time but for ours. Far from disheartening them, this only encouraged them to proclaim through the Spirit the message they had received for the partial good of their own generation and the full benefit of posterity (cf. Rev. 22:10). Their prophecies did contain instruction about the promised Redeemer, but the full understanding was not available until the Messiah came. The "time" was revealed to Daniel (Dan. 9:25, 26). The prophets had the great honor of having Christ's Spirit speak in them, but the privileges of our age are even greater and should move us to an even deeper commitment to Christ (1:13ff.). **things, which are now reported unto you by them that have preached the gospel**—What the prophets predicted concerning Christ, the apostles preached and elucidated. **with** [by] **the Holy Ghost** [Spirit] **sent down from heaven**—The apostles, including Peter, were given the Holy Spirit to preach the gospel (Luke 24:49; Acts 1:5-8; 2:4). **which things the angels desire to look into**—The angels have no intuitive knowledge of redemption. The Greek here indicates that the angels would like to bend over so as to look deeply into and see to the bottom of these things. Just as the cherubim in the Holy of Holies of the temple stood bending over the mercy seat (the emblem of redemption), the angels gaze intently upon and desire to fathom the depths of the "great mystery of godliness, God manifest in the flesh, justified in the Spirit, seen of angels" (1 Tim. 3:16). The angels' ministry to Christians naturally makes them want to penetrate this mystery that reflects the glory of God's love, justice, wisdom, and power. They can only know the part that is revealed in the church, since they don't have the direct share in salvation that we have.

## 13-25 OUR REDEMPTION AND REGENERATION: THE BASIS FOR HOLINESS

➤**13 gird up the loins of your mind, be sober**—Since the prophets had foretold the great privileges of the gospel and even the angels are anxious to understand them better, we should, as believers, show the same kind of earnest and alert concern. The believer should always have his mental powers collected and ready for Christ's return. We are to be "sober," having the spiritual self-restraint to resist those temptations that would draw us away from God. **hope to the end**—lit., "perfectly hope," so that there be nothing deficient in your hope. **for the grace that is to be [being] brought unto you at [in] the revelation of Jesus Christ**—When Christ was first revealed, he came full of grace and truth (John 1:16). His first coming commenced the age of grace. His second coming will complete the age of grace by bringing to the heirs of grace (3:7) their full and complete benefits.

➤**14** Peter now moves on to discuss obedience (1:14), holiness (1:14, 16), and reverential fear (1:17). **obedient children**—Obedience is to be characteristic of our nature. Our nature is to reflect our Father's nature. We are to obey him because we are his children (cf. 1:17). We are to have the obedience of faith (1:22) as well as the obedience of practice (1:16, 18). **not fashioning yourselves according to the former lusts in your ignorance**—This refers to the state of both Jews and Greeks when they were ignorant of God. The process of sanctification, being made more like Christ, is described negatively in this verse—we are told what *not* to do. Then 1:15 describes it positively (cf. Eph. 4:22-24). The believer has put on the "new man," the new nature Christ has given him in which sin does not exist. But the believer still has to contend with the flesh, the "old man" in which sin has power. A lifelong conflict arises from this situation for the believer. The new man prevails, at first only in part and sporadically, but in the end, com-

pletely. The unbeliever knows only the conflicts of the flesh, and he does not have the power to conquer or control them.

➤**15 as he which hath called you is holy, so be ye holy**—Greek, "become holy." God is our model for holiness. Since he has invited us to be his children, we are to assimilate and reflect his character. Peter frequently uses God's call as a motivating factor. We are to assimilate God's holy nature in all that we do, in the whole course of our lives as well as in our inner character. Christians have already been declared holy and set aside for consecration by their faith in Christ. They are now to work at fleshing out that holiness in their day-by-day walk and behavior.

➤**16 Because it is written**—Peter quoted Scripture (Lev. 11:44, 45; 19:2; 20:7) to substantiate his point, which is the authoritative source in questions of doctrine and practice. **Be ye holy; for I am holy**—According to the Greek, the first verb is a future indicative ("You will be holy"), not an imperative. Thus, this is more of a promise than a command. We are holy only to the extent to which we have been made so by God himself. Since God promises that we will be holy, he is himself the source for our holiness. We draw our holiness from his nature.

➤**17 who without respect of persons judgeth**—"who judges impartially" (RSV, NIV) (cf. Luke 20:21; Acts 10:34; Rom. 2:11; James 2:1). God does not accept the Jews above the Gentiles. When it comes to judgment, he is completely unbiased. The Father judges through his Son, who is his representative and who exercises the authority delegated to him (John 5:22). **every man's work**—Each man's work is a complete whole, whether good or bad. The specific works we do demonstrate the general character of our life-work. If we live by faith and love we will please God and escape his condemnation. **fear**—Our fear is not to be slavish or paranoid. We find the proper balance in the fact that God is both our loving Father and our judge, which inspires a fear motivated by reverence. This kind of fear is not opposed to our assurance of God's care and love, but rather to that false kind of security that causes us to take God for granted, to become sloppy in our Christian life and to offend God's holiness. Fear keeps us alert so that we do not fall into that trap. It is true, as 1 John states, that perfect love has no fear in it, but in our present imperfect state we need to have a certain amount of fear to go along with our love. This fear of God will defeat all other fears. When the believer fears God, he has nothing else to fear.

➤**18** Another factor which should make us afraid to displease God is the enormous cost God paid to buy us back from our indebtedness to sin. **ye were not redeemed with corruptible things, as silver and gold**—Gold and silver are themselves liable to corruption. They cannot free anyone from spiritual or physical death. Contrast this with Christ's precious blood in 1:19. In OT days before Christ came, the Israelites were ransomed with half a shekel each, which went toward purchasing the lamb for the daily sacrifice (Exod. 30:12-16; Num. 3:44-51). But the Lamb who redeems believers, the spiritual Israel, does so with the price of his own blood. The church is redeemed from sin and the curse of death by Christ's blood (Matt. 20:28; 1 Tim. 2:6; Titus 2:14; Rev. 5:9). All these passages convey the idea of substitution—one person taking the place of another—to be a stand-in or a ransom. Man is a slave "sold under sin"; he is condemned under the curse of sin and death. The ransom, therefore, was paid as an adequate substitution for our sin. An Israelite who was sold as a bond-servant because of a debt could be redeemed by one of his brethren. Since we were unable to redeem ourselves, Jesus took on our nature so that he could become our nearest kin and brother and also be our Redeemer and God. Holiness is the natural outcome of our redemption from our old evil ways—the one by whom we are redeemed is also the one for whom we are redeemed. **from your vain conversation received by tradition from your fathers**—or "from the empty way of life handed down to you from your forefathers" (NIV). "Some maintain that the recipients must have been pagans because the NT stresses the emptiness of pagan life (Rom. 1:21; Eph. 4:17). Others think they were Jews since Jews were traditionalists who stressed the influence of father as teacher in the home. In light of the context of the whole letter, probably both Jews and Gentiles are addressed" (*NIVSB*).

➤**19 precious**—This means "of inestimable value." **without blemish and without spot**—Although Christ was fully human, he remained pure and sinless in himself, and spotless—uninfected by the sins of others that surrounded him. Living in our sinful world did not corrupt him. Nothing marred him or kept him from being our Redeemer. The paschal lamb was without defect (Exod. 12:5); so Christ, the real Passover Lamb (1 Cor. 5:7) had no blemishes or spots. Israel's redemption from bondage in Egypt required the blood of the paschal lamb; our redemption from sin and its curse required the blood of Christ.

➤**20 foreordained**—lit., "foreknown," but in this context means "foreordained" or "predestined" (Kelly). **before the foundation of the world**—"The redemption was in the plan of God before the world began" (Blum). The great things that God has done for us—planning Christ's redemptive sacrifice and completing it in our time—place an additional incentive and obligation on us to keep on living a holy life. Redemption was no mere afterthought, no last-minute remedy God devised for an evil that he never dreamed would come up. In fact, God not only chose Christ before the foundation of the world, he chose us too (1:2). **was manifest in these last times for you**—Although Christ has existed throughout eternity, he was not revealed until his incarnation. The "last times" began with Christ's first coming and will continue until his second coming.

➤**21 Who by** [through] **him do believe in God**—This verse includes all who have responded in faith to God because of Christ's coming. To believe *in* (Gk., *eis*) God expresses a putting of one's trust in God. To believe *on* (Gk., *epi,* dative case) God expresses the confidence which one places on God, as resting on him. When we know God the Father spiritually, we must also know the Son, for it is by him alone that we can come to the Father. We have life in Christ; if we do not know him, we do not know God. The only living way to God is through Christ and his sacrifice. **that** [who] **raised him up from the dead**—The fact that God raised Jesus from the dead is the special ground for our faith because: (1) in doing so, God openly declared that he accepted Christ as our righteous substitute; and (2) through his resurrection and glorification, Jesus received the power to give believers faith through the Holy Spirit. The same power enabling us to believe is the power which raised Christ from the dead. Our faith must not only be in Christ but by and through Christ. **that your faith and hope might be in God**—This is the object and the effect of God's raising Christ. Peter stated this as an objective fact and actual result and not as an exhortation (except in an indirect sense). Our faith flows from Christ's resurrection; our hope from the fact that God **gave him glory.** Apart from Christ, we could only have feared, not hoped and believed in God.

➤**22 have purified your souls**—The verb here is actually a perfect participle in Greek, which expresses the lasting result of a past action. At the time we obeyed the truth of the gospel our hearts were purified (Acts 15:9). **in obeying the truth**—of the gospel (1:2; Rom. 1:5). **through the Spirit**—This phrase is not present in the earliest manuscripts. **unfeigned**—unhypocritical. **love of the brethren**—Our love for Christian brothers and sisters is different from ordinary love. Love for other Christians is the evidence of our regeneration (1:23; 1 John 3:14). Our cleansing from selfishness and hatred enables us to love. **love one another with a pure heart fervently**—We are to love each other intensely, from the heart and not hypocritically. The adjective "pure" is found in some ancient manuscripts but is absent in others.

➤**23** The brotherhood of Christians flows from the new and lasting life they have each received from and through Christ. This fact is used here to motivate love for our Christian brothers and sisters. Natural relationships give rise to natural affection. In the same way, spiritual relationships give rise to abiding spiritual love. **Being born again**—lit., "having been regenerated." **not of corruptible seed, but of incorruptible**—which speaks of the divine, eternal life, a life that cannot corrupt. This is the life with which we were regenerated. **by the word of God**—God's divine life (seed) is implanted in us through the agency of God's word. **which liveth and abideth for ever**—God's word is "living and enduring" (NIV). "God's word is living because it imparts life (cf. Ps. 33:9; Isa. 55:10-11; Heb. 4:12). His word endures because the God who speaks it is the eternal, faithful, powerful one who keeps his promises" (Blum).

➤**24, 25** These verses are a quotation of Isaiah 40:6-8. Verse 24 depicts our natural

human frailty in contrast to the everlasting "word of the Lord" in 1:25. If we had only our old life, born of the flesh, we would simply fade as grass. **the flower of grass**—refers to all the wisdom, strength, riches, learning, honor, beauty, art, virtue, and righteousness humans can achieve apart from God. But this kind of flowering is transitory. **the word of the Lord . . . this is the word which by the gospel is preached**—In 1:23 the Greek expression for "word" is *logos*—referring primarily to the written message. Here the Greek term is *rhēma*—referring primarily to the spoken word. The spoken word is the gospel preached, the gospel proclaimed (see comments on Rom. 10:14 and note the use of *rhēma*). "The word of the Lord" is the gospel message about the Lord. This word can regenerate men. Peter adapted the OT text (which says "word of God") to its NT context.

*Chapter* 2

1-3 EXHORTATIONS TO GROWTH

➤**1 laying aside**—putting away. The Greek is in the aorist tense, indicating that this is to be done once for all. The command is addressed only to Christians; those who, having a new God-given nature within them, are able to throw off the old, sin-riddled nature that binds them externally. As they experience more of the mighty inner strengthening of his Holy Spirit (Eph. 3:16), they will be able to grow and progressively change into the new people they were meant to be. Verse 1 resumes the exhortation begun in 1:22: Seeing that you have been cleansed, don't get tangled up again in any evil ways. That would be completely contrary to the new life (1:23) received from Christ and to the warm and fervent love Christians should have for each other (1:22). **all malice, and all guile, and hypocrisies, and envies, and all evil speakings**—All these evils are related. They form a network of sins against love. Hatred can lead to dishonesty, pretending to be what one is not, which is the opposite of the open, honest love. Hatred can also easily make us jealous of others or desirous of speaking against them.

➤**2 As newborn babes, desire the sincere [pure] milk of the word**—The last three words are a translation of one Greek word, *logikon,* which has also been translated "spiritual" (RSV, NIV). A born- again person should have a natural desire for the pure (in contrast to 2:1) milk of the word that will nourish him and help him grow toward the fullness of salvation. **grow thereby**—The earliest manuscripts read "grow into salvation." Christians experience ongoing salvation (or, deliverance)—from the time of new birth until the time Christ returns, when salvation will be consummated. The same word that the Spirit uses to bring us to salvation is the word that nourishes us in our continual deliverance.

➤**3 tasted that the Lord is gracious**—cf. Psalm 34:8. When we first taste the Lord's kindness, our appetite is whetted for more. And he doesn't disappoint us; he provides fuller and richer experiences of his grace.

## 4-10 LIVING STONES IN GOD'S BUILDING

➤**4 To whom coming**—The present tense verb ("coming" or better, "approaching") indicates that we are to continue to draw near by faith (the Greek here is the same as in Heb. 10:22). **a living stone**—The quote is taken from Psalm 118:22. See Peter's speech in Acts 4:11. Peter (whose name means "stone") desired that all others should be living stones built on Christ, the true Foundation Stone. Peter here clearly states that Christ, and not he himself (Peter), is the foundation for the church. Christ is *living* in the sense that he has had life in himself from the beginning and also because he has been raised from the dead. He is our source of life; unlike any earthly rock, he lives and gives life (cf. 1 Cor. 10:14). **disallowed** [rejected] **. . . of** [by] **men**—Christ himself also referred to this (Matt. 21:42). **but chosen of God, and precious**—drawn from Isaiah 28:16. Although men have rejected Christ, he is the unique stone of God's building, honored by God and chosen specially for that purpose.

➤**5 Ye also, as lively** [living] **stones**—We are living because we partake of the life of the "living stone" (2:4; 1 Cor. 3:11). Many names assigned to Christ in the singular are assigned to Christians in the plural: Son/sons, High Priest/priests, King/kings, Lamb/lambs. **are built up**—Greek, "are being built up"—conveying the same idea as Ephesians 2:22. Peter

grounded his exhortations in this chapter on his readers' awareness of the high privilege that comes from being a part of the building God is constructing. No doubt these words reflect on Christ's great promises to Peter: "I will build my church" (Matt. 16:18). Peter was seeing this promise being fulfilled in the churches he was writing to. **a spiritual house**—God, who is Spirit (John 4:24), dwells in a spiritual house, the body of Christ (Eph. 2:22), not a physical temple. **an holy priesthood**—referring to a company of priests. **to offer up spiritual sacrifices, acceptable to God**—See Psalms 4:5; 50:13, 14; 51:17, 19; Isaiah 56:7; Hosea 14:2; Philippians 4:18. [through] **Jesus Christ**—Even though our service is imperfect, we should never doubt our acceptance in and through Christ. That would be doubting the acceptability of Christ's sacrifice on our behalf. While extolling the dignity of Christians in this verse, Peter also indicates that Jesus is the one who restored us to our high position.

➤**6 in the scripture**—Isaiah 28:16 (also quoted in Rom. 9:33). **corner stone**—See comments on Ephesians 2:20. **shall not be confounded**—shall not be put to shame (same Greek as Rom. 9:33; 10:11).

➤**7 This verse applies the scripture quoted in 2:6 first to the believer and then to the unbeliever. he is precious**—The preciousness of Christ belongs to Christians. **disobedient**—actually, "unbelieving"; the rest of the verse applies to them. **the stone which the builders disallowed** [rejected], **the same is made** [came to be] **the head of the corner**—This is taken from Psalm 118:22 (also quoted in Matt. 21:42; Acts 4:11). Those who reject Christ are, in spite of themselves and without their knowledge, contributing to his becoming the Cornerstone. A magnet has two poles: one repels and the other attracts. In the same way, the gospel draws those who will believe and drives away those who will not.

➤**8 The quotation in this verse is from Isaiah 8:14. a stone of** [causing] **stumbling**—The stumbling refers not only to the fact that some would be offended with Christ, but also to the fact that they would be judged and punished for their rejection of him (cf. Jer. 13:16). **whereunto also they were appointed**—God does not ordain that certain people would be disobedient, but he does give them up to the consequences of their disobedience. The consequence of disobedience has been predetermined; those who disobey will suffer God's judgment. Through the same Christ whom they reject, sinners themselves will be rejected. The lost will lay all the blame of their ruin on their own sinfulness, not on God's decree. The saved shall give all the credit for their salvation to God's electing love and grace.

►9 This verse contrasts the privilege and destiny of believers with that of unbelievers (2:8). The statements that follow are taken from various OT texts, primarily Exodus 19:5, 6; Isaiah 43:20, 21. **a chosen generation**—Christians are a group distinct from the rest of the world, unified by their common spiritual origin and election (Isa. 43:20). **a royal** [kingly] **priesthood**—a priesthood consisting of kings (see Exod. 19:6; Isa. 61:6; Rev. 1:6). **an holy nation**—a nation distinct from all the others because of its devotion to God (Exod. 19:6). **a peculiar people**—lit., "a people for possession." Christians are God's special treasure, the ones he has specially chosen and purchased (cf. Exod. 19:5; Isa. 43:21). **that ye should show forth the praises** [virtues] **of him who hath called you**—We are to publish abroad the virtues (the moral excellences) of our God. Christians have no right to sing their own praises because, like everyone else, they were in darkness and have only been brought out into the light through God's grace. **out of darkness into his marvellous light**—This expression does not come from any OT verse. Peter added it to accentuate the contrast between our former life in darkness and our new life in the light (Acts 26:18; Col. 1:12, 13).

►10 This verse is an adaption of Hosea 1:9, 10; 2:23. In the Hosea context, the verses describe God's rejection of Israel followed by a future restoration (Blum). Paul applied the verses to the Gentiles (Rom. 9:25, 26); now Peter applies them to the NT church.

## 11-25 OBEDIENCE TO AUTHORITY AND SUFFERING FOR CHRIST

►11 Peter had already asked his fellow Christians to walk worthily of their high calling; in the next four verses he exhorts them to bring glory to God in the example they set for unbelievers. **strangers and pilgrims**—lit., "sojourners and aliens," settlers having a house

in a city where they are not citizens. They are strangers, visitors staying awhile in a foreign land. **fleshly lusts**—These are listed in Galatians 5:19ff. They include not only obvious sins but all the thoughts of a mind not renewed by God. **which war against the soul**—Once a person has been born again, he finds that evil pleasures not only stand in his way, they actively war against his soul or mind. Since they are bent on his destruction, he must keep away from them. The moment he gives way, his strength is gone.

►12 Christians have to know how to handle themselves in their conduct with non-Christians (2:12), in their conduct as citizens (2:13), servants (2:18), wives and husbands (3:1, 7), and under any circumstances (3:8). Furthermore, Christians must be able to communicate their commitment articulately (3:15, 16). **conversation** [conduct] **honest among the Gentiles**—Before their unsaved neighbors, Christians are to act in a becoming and proper way that honors their Lord. **whereas they speak against you as evildoers, they may by your good works, which they shall behold, glorify God**—Act in such a way that at some time in the future they will glorify God for your good works. The Greek says "they shall be eyewitnesses of," "shall behold on close inspection." Unbelievers judge Christianity by mere hearsay. Our actions should unsettle this preconceived attitude. Tertullian described how the "good works" of the early church contrasted with the surrounding society. Many delighted in the bloody gladiatorial spectacles, but Christians were excommunicated if they even went to them. No Christian was found in jail for crime, only for their faith. Slaves were excluded from many religious services, while some of the leaders in the Christian church were slaves. The Christian law of love—doing to others what you wanted them to do to you—gradually undermined the foundations of slavery. When others deserted their relatives in the plague, the Christians ministered to the sick and dying. When the dead were left unburied after a battle and the wounded were cast into the street, the disciples rushed in to relieve the suffering. Christians are to do good, not so that their name will be praised, but so that God's name will be praised. The conduct of Christians is to be so exemplary that it leads unbelievers to form a high estimate of the God Christians serve.

➤**13 Submit yourselves to every ordinance of man**—Peter did not leave any room for his readers to become arrogant about the great privileges and exalted position they have as Christians. He told them to submit to human authorities **for the Lord's sake**—Jesus wants us to follow the example he has set in submission. Although all things are subject to Christ, even he subjected himself to Roman rulers. Since Christians are his earthly representatives, his honor is at stake (cf. Rom. 13:5). **the king, as supreme**—The Roman emperor was the supreme ruler in the Roman provinces to which this epistle was addressed. The Jewish zealots refused to obey him. The distinction Peter drew between the king and the king's officers may imply that if the king commands one thing and his officers another, the king is to be obeyed. Scripture does not recommend one form of government over another. Rather, it simply asks Christians to submit to the government under whose authority they find themselves. It does not discuss the question of what constitutes justified political authority.

➤**14 governors**—subordinates of the emperor, those Caesar sent to preside over the province. **for the punishment of evil doers**—The rest of this verse outlines the true functions of those in authority. While no authority or form of government carries out these functions perfectly, most governments more closely approximate them than a state of anarchy would. Peter is speaking here of what is done by public authority. **the praise of them that do well**—In his letter to the emperor Trajan, Pliny says of Christians, "I have found in them nothing else save a perverse and extravagant superstition." Many recognize the moral value of those who live by Christian principles. This can mitigate persecution in the long run (3:13).

➤**15** In this verse Peter gives the grounds for his directing them to be obedient (2:13). **to silence**—lit., "to muzzle," "to stop the mouth." **the ignorance of foolish men**—Since these people don't know God, they misunderstand God's children. They may misconstrue their actions, being more influenced by appearance than by reality. Many non-Christians undoubtedly are more prone to open their mouths than their eyes or ears concerning Christianity, but

this shouldn't anger Christians. Rather, Christians should make every effort to live so righteously that even one prejudiced will have to admit he can hold nothing against them but their faith. This may even help such persons reconsider Christianity in a more positive light.

➤**16 As free**—The Lord has made us free, but only free to do God's will. Verse 15 says that living good lives is a major part of God's will. It is the natural fruit of being set free from sin. **not using your liberty as a cloak of maliciousness**—We are not to use our liberty as a cloak to hide evil actions, but we are to conduct ourselves in love as **the servants of God.**

➤**17 Honour all men**—This states the general principle; the rest of the verse applies it to three different groups. We are to give everyone the honor he deserves. Christ has dignified humanity by assuming it himself. Therefore, we should be considerate of and honor humanity in each person, no matter how humble. **Love the brotherhood**—The present tense indicates that in addition to our general love for all mankind, we are to love other members of God's family habitually and with special affection. **Fear God. Honour the king**—Although we are to show proper respect for the government, ultimately God alone is to be feared.

➤**18 Servants**—This refers to household servants. The Greek word for slave is not used. It probably includes freedmen remaining in their master's house. Since masters were not usually Christians, Peter limited his comments to the servants who were often persecuted by unbelieving masters. Peter wanted them to submit regardless of their master's character. **be subject**—The exhortation in this verse is linked with those going before. The submission, Peter said, is to extend to all circumstances. **good and gentle**—Some masters can be considerate, overlooking understandable errors and not exercising justice without mercy. Others, however, are **froward**—i.e., harsh and perhaps even perverse. Nevertheless, the disposition and behavior of our superiors should not influence the way we attend to our responsibilities.

➤**19 thankworthy**—Greek, *charis;* in the context it means "that which is admirable" (Rienecker). **if a man for conscience toward God endure grief**—Our reaction should be the opposite of what comes naturally—we are to rejoice in the Lord if, under a tough and cruel master, we suffer for following God's way. We are to strive to please God, not men, and be more concerned about our response to the injustice we have suffered than to the injustice itself.

►**20 what glory** [credit] **is it, if, when ye be buffeted for your faults, ye shall take it patiently?**—There is no particular merit in accepting in a right spirit the suffering we deserve. **if, when ye do well, and suffer for it . . . this is acceptable with God**—We please God if we suffer for doing right. It is not that we earn some kind of merit in his eyes, but we know that our actions receive his approval. This may be cold comfort to some, so Peter goes on to point out Christ's example to encourage us in our suffering.

►**21** As the life of Christ teaches, patient endurance of undeserved sufferings is acceptable to God. Furthermore, we have been **called** to his suffering. **Christ also suffered for us**— A few early manuscripts (Codex Vaticanus and P81) read, "Christ died for us" (see comments on 3:18). Christ's dying for us is the highest example of "doing good" (2:20). We must suffer patiently, even though we are innocent, just as Christ did. While Christ's sufferings are an example, we must not forget that they are primarily sufferings for our benefit, a fact that permanently obliges us to please him. **an example**—Greek, "an underwriting," which was a model of handwriting set up by masters for their pupils to copy. The word was used, as here, as a figure of speech for a model of conduct for imitation (Rienecker). **follow his steps**—Imitate his example of patience and innocence.

►**22** Sinlessness, when it comes to our speech, is a mark of perfection (cf. 2 Cor. 5:21; Heb. 7:26).

►**23 when he was reviled, reviled not again**—Servants are apt to answer back (Titus 2:9), but not Christ. **threatened not**—Since Christ is Lord, he could have threatened his oppressors with divine judgment, but he did not. **committed himself to him**—Peter seems to have Isaiah 53:7, 8 in mind here (cf. Jer. 11:20). Romans 12:19 describes our corresponding duty. We, like Christ, are to leave our case in God's hands, for he always **judgeth righteously.** We do not do this hoping that God

will execute our revenge. Christ has told us that we are to pray for our enemies. Confidence in God's righteous judgment gives tranquility and consolation to the oppressed.

►**24 Who his own self**—No one but Christ could have done this. The fact that he voluntarily undertook the work of redemption is implied. The idea of his substitution for us is underlined: **bare our sins**—The Greek term can mean both carrying and/or offering up (a sacrifice). Isaiah 53:12 says, "He bore the sins of many." This emphasizes the idea of Christ's taking our sins on himself. Here Peter joins with that the idea of Christ's offering up those sins in the sacrifice of himself. By presenting his body as a sacrifice, Christ offered up on the cross the guilt of the sins he was carrying on our behalf, just as an OT priest would make an offering at the altar. This implies two things: (1) Christ has borne the guilt, curse, and punishment of our sins, for they were laid upon him. (2) He has offered up those sins along with himself on the altar. In the OT, sins were first laid upon the sacrificial animal; then the animal was offered up. **his own body on the tree**— which was the proper place for one who carried the curse of sin, for the Scripture says, "Cursed is everyone that hangeth on a tree (Deut. 21:23; Gal. 3:13). Christ took our curse and destroyed it by his death. **that we, being dead to sins**— Because of Christ's death, we are delivered from sin, just as a slave who dies is delivered from service to his master. This is our spiritual standing by faith in Christ's death; our actual deliverance from particular sins depends on the degree to which we have been made like Christ. **should live unto righteousness**—or, "live for righteousness" (NIV), a truth explained in Romans 5:17, 21; 6:3-14. As a result of Christ's death, we are freed from sin to live a life of righteousness (cf. Isa. 53:11). **by whose stripes ye were healed** [cured]—See Isaiah 53:5. Christ's stripes (which is another way of saying "Christ's suffering") have become our cure— from sin, from the curse, and from death.

►**25 ye were as sheep going astray**—The imagery continues to draw upon Isaiah 53, specifically 53:6. **Shepherd and Bishop**—lit., "shepherd and overseer." Christ shepherds us and oversees us, which is the function of church elders (see comments on 5:2). Christ, as the true

Head of the church, watches over our souls—
he keeps his sheep from going astray.

## Chapter 3

### 1-7 WIVES AND HUSBANDS

➤**1** Peter now turns his attention to wives,
calling for submissive behavior from them. **be
in subjection**—or, be submissive. **they also
may without the word be won** [gained] **by the
conversation** [conduct] **of the wives**—The
wife's behavior can bring her unbelieving husband to faith apart from his hearing the word
preached.

➤**2 chaste conversation**—pure conduct.
**fear**—or, reverence. Her conduct is to be pure
and reverential, free from all impurity and recognizing her husband's proper authority.

➤**3 not . . . that outward adorning**—It is
all too easy for women to be overly concerned
about their appearance, to spend too much time
and energy trying to make a good impression
with jewelry or beautiful clothes, or hairstyles.

➤**4 the hidden man** [person]—Peter was
not saying that women should make themselves plain, but that they should not become
overly involved in their physical appearance.
Outward beauty is not scorned but rather seen
in the right perspective: it is much more important to develop a beautiful inner character. Peter
does not forbid the use of jewelry or stylish
clothes, only their abuse. A well-dressed woman
can be humble and a plain, austere woman can be
proud. **of the heart, in that which is not corruptible**—i.e., in that deepest, hidden part of you
which has been born again and been adorned
with the Holy Spirit. **a meek and quiet
spirit**—A woman who has this spirit does not
go around making disturbances; rather she quietly bears the disturbances that others cause (cf.
1 Tim. 2:9-11). A woman with such a spirit is
gentle in her feelings and relationships and
quiet in her words, bearing, and action. **which
is in the sight of God of great price**—We need
to remember that God observes our hearts, not
just our outer appearance. Since Christ's life-
blood is precious to us (1:19), we should try to
live in a way that is precious, or pleasing to
God.

➤**5** the "meek and quiet spirit" of 3:4 was
seen in the saintly women of old (cf. Prov.

31:30). They were saintly because they trusted
in God and knew how to submit to the authority
God had established.

➤**6** Sarah is a good example of what a
woman's attitude should be toward her husband. **calling him lord**—See Genesis 18:12.
**not afraid with any amazement**—The Greek
word for "amazement" is "fluttering alarm,"
"consternation." Proverbs 3:25 (LXX) uses the
same word, which Peter probably referred to.
Peter instructed wives to do good and not be
afraid (he repeats the same advice to all Christians in 3:13-16). Fear may be more of a problem for most women. So Peter assures them that
they do not need to fear anyone if they do
right—not even if their unbelieving husbands
have a sudden outbreak of temper in response
to their goodness.

➤**7 ye husbands, dwell with them according to knowledge**—Husbands are to acknowledge the proper relation of the sexes in God's
design and act with tenderness, wisdom, and
understanding. **giving honour unto the wife,
as unto the weaker vessel**—Both husband and
wife are vessels God has made to fulfill his
purposes (see Rom. 9:23). Both are weak, but
the woman is weaker. The husband's sense of
his own weakness and his realization that his
wife is equally God's vessel should lead him to
act with tender and wise consideration toward
her. **being heirs together of the grace of life**—
The man should give honor to the woman
because God gives honor to them both as
fellow-heirs of the riches in Christ (cf. 1:4).
**that your prayers be not hindered**—Dissensions prevent the united prayers on which many
of God's blessings depend.

### 8-17 SUFFERING FOR DOING GOOD

➤**8** This verse is a general summary of our
duties to one another, after the detailed list of
special duties that began in 2:18. **be ye all of
one mind**—in the faith. **having compassion
one of another**—Enter into the joys and sorrows of others. **love as brethren**—lit., "loving
the brothers." **be pitiful, be courteous**—compassionate and humbleminded. We are to open
our hearts to each other and make a conscious
effort to be truly humble in our relationships.

➤**9 Not rendering evil for evil**—This forbids taking revenge by word or actions. **contrariwise blessing**—When we obey God in

faith, he will bless us so that we may in turn bless others.

➤**10-12** These verses are a quotation of Psalm 34:12-16. **he that will love life, and see good days**—Peter is here addressing those who love life (present and eternal) and want to continue to do so, not involving themselves in troubles that will make this life a burden and cause them to forfeit eternal life. **refrain his tongue from evil**—Our natural tendency is to do just the opposite, to lose control of our tongue. **eschew evil**—turn away from evil. Keeping control of our tongue involves turning away from speaking evil and being deceitful. **seek peace, and ensue** [pursue] **it**—We must pursue peace because in this fallen world it is hard to find and often eludes us. **For the eyes of the Lord are over the righteous**—The fact that God is constantly watching over us is the guarantee of the blessed, good life that is promised the meek in the present and future. **his ears are open unto their prayers**—cf. 1 John 5:14, 15. **but the face of the Lord is against them that do evil**—which is to say that the Lord is opposed to evil doers.

➤**13** According to the Greek this verse should read, "Who will do you evil if you are eager to do good?"

➤**14 But and if ye suffer for righteousness' sake**—Peter goes on to speak about exceptions to the principle he has set down in 3:13. Peter tells how the truly wise would respond to these situations. **be not afraid of their terror**—We are to look to God and not fear the terror that other men can impose upon us (cf. Isa. 8:12, 13). God alone is to be feared; if we fear him, we have nothing else to fear.

➤**15 sanctify the Lord God in your hearts**—The earliest manuscripts read, "Sanctify Christ [as] Lord in your hearts." In the midst of persecution from unbelievers, a Christian should maintain his inward sanctity, looking to the indwelling Christ to prepare him to give a defense for his faith. **ready always to give an answer**—lit., "an apology," which means "a verbal defense." We are called to be ready and able to give a reasonable defense of the faith to which we have committed ourselves. Our faith is not a leap in the dark; it is belief in response to evidence. It involves the mind as well as the will and emotions. This does not mean that every Christian must be a

learned scholar and apologist for the Christian faith. But each Christian is called to understand and be able to clearly explain his own reasons for being a Christian and his own grasp of the faith. **asketh you a reason of** [for] **the hope that is in you**—Unbelievers can see that Christians live according to a hope that gives them strength and joy in hardships. Unbelievers who lack that hope will naturally be attracted to it, inquiring about the secret of that hope. The believer has to be ready to tell them. **with meekness and fear**—This joins with "give an answer." Those who inquire about our Christian hope should be answered with "gentleness and respect" (3:16, NIV). We are not to be arrogant—thinking that we have all the answers. Rather, we are to act with respect toward men and reverence for God.

➤**16 Having a good conscience**—Only if we have a good conscience can we be ready to explain why we believe as we do. Profession without practice carries no weight. But those who have a good conscience can afford to speak in a gentle and respectful way. **speak evil of you, as of evildoers**—The Greek expresses malice shown in deeds as well as in words. **your good conversation in Christ**—It is our walk as Christians, not as citizens, that calls forth malice (cf. 4:4, 5, 14).

➤**17** Some might object to suffering by the innocent, saying that suffering is better borne if deserved. Peter replied that it is better *not* to deserve it, so that by doing good and yet being spoken against, you prove yourself a true Christian (Gerhard). **if the will of God be so**—If we honor God's will as our highest law, we have the comfort of knowing that suffering comes to us only by God's appointment (4:19). Christ proved this in his life, and we can prove it in ours, although our natural inclination is to avoid suffering.

18-22 THE SUFFERINGS OF CHRIST

➤**18** The glorious results of Christ's innocent suffering confirm Peter's point in 3:17. **Christ also hath once suffered**—Only one early manuscript (Codex Vaticanus) reads "suffered"; all the other early manuscripts read, "died" (see comments on 2:21). Christ was the anointed One of God, the just One who died for the unjust. In 2:21 Christ's sufferings were shown to be an example for us; here they are proof of the value of suffering innocently. He died once for all; he will not suffer again. **for sins**—he died for our sins once and for all (Heb. 9:28). **that he might bring us to God**—The result of Christ's death is that he unites us with him in having access to God. At present, because of Christ's death, resurrection, and ascension, we have access spiritually into the very presence of God; in the future, we will actually dwell in his presence. **being put to death in the flesh**—indicating an end to his earthly mode of existence. **quickened by the Spirit**—or, made alive in spirit—suggesting a new mode of existence: in spirit. Christ died to his former mode of life but lived on in another. His spirit did not die and have to be brought to life again; rather, although he had lived and died fully as a man, he began to live a spiritual, "resurrection" life (3:21) in which he has the power to bring us to God. In short, this verse speaks of Christ's two modes or spheres of existence—one, "in flesh" and the other, "in spirit" (see Blum). Life "in flesh" ended by death on the cross; then Christ entered a resurrected state of being, called "in spirit." Actually, at the time of his resurrection, Christ became life-giving spirit (1 Cor. 15:45). In the NT Epistles "the Spirit" is often used as another way of designating the risen Christ (see Rom. 8:9-11; 2 Cor. 3:11, 18) and another way of contrasting his new spiritual mode of existence from his previous sphere of existence in the flesh (see Rom. 1:3, 4; 1 Tim. 3:16).

▶**19 By which**—Greek, "in which," referring to "spirit" in 3:18. If "in spirit" refers to Christ's resurrected state of existence, the action that follows must have come after the time of Christ's resurrection. **he went and preached unto the spirits in prison**—The verb here is not "preached the gospel" but rather "proclaimed" or "heralded." It seems possible, therefore, that Christ was simply making the announcement of his finished work on the cross. His declaration confirmed the testimony of Enoch and Noah. By doing this, it confirmed the condemnation of those who had refused to believe (3:20), while assuring the salvation of Noah and believers. However, the word can in fact mean "preach the gospel," and that is precisely the word (*evangelizo*) Peter uses in 4:6, a verse that must be considered in exegeting 3:18-20. **spirits in prison**—

Who are these spirits? And where were (are) these spirits? They may be the spirits of disobedient men because the next verse could allude to those who disobeyed the gospel preached to them by Noah (Raymer). These spirits, therefore, might be the spirits of the men who disobeyed God and who are awaiting their judgment (cf. Heb. 12:23). This view is greatly strengthened by Peter's words in 4:6: "For this cause was the gospel preached also to them that are dead, that they might be judged according to men in the flesh, but live according to God in the spirit." Another view is that the spirits are fallen angels who instigated gross immorality in the days of Noah—such were those "sons of God" spoken of in Genesis 6:2 (Blum, Kelly). Many commentators favor this view because 2 Peter 2:4, 5 links "the angels that sinned" with the diluvian judgment God enacted in the days of Noah. According to 2 Peter 2:4, 5, these angels of God were cast into Tartarus, a place of confinement prior to their judgment. Tartarus, therefore, is the prison Peter here refers to (Wuest). Some time after Christ was "made alive in the spirit," he made a proclamation to these spirits. The time of this proclamation is not stated, and therefore all comments about such time are conjectures.

Some commentators have conjectured that these verses do not mean that Christ went in person to these spirits after his death, rather that he went "in spirit" at some other time. As he "came and preached peace" by his Spirit in the apostles and ministers after his death and ascension, so, before his incarnation, he preached in the spirit through Noah to the antediluvians. Christ, who in our times came in the flesh, came in the spirit through Noah in his times. In 1:11, Peter spoke of the Spirit of Christ in the OT prophets—Noah was one of those prophets. As attractive as this interpretation appears, it is riddled with many inconsistencies. But, then again, we cannot absolutely affirm any of the above interpretations. Perhaps it is best to join Luther in admitting our inability to adequately exegete this passage.

▶**20 Which sometime were disobedient**—Greek, "to those then disobeying," referring to the "spirits" in 3:19. **longsuffering of God waited in the days of Noah**—God's waiting went on for the 120 years of grace, while Noah was building the ark. The end of his waiting came with the death of the disobedient in the flood. **while the ark was a preparing** [being prepared]—See Hebrews 11:7. Building the ark took a long time since Noah had few to help him—almost everyone disregarded God's warnings. This lengthy opportunity to reconsider God's warnings makes the people's refusal to believe more inexcusable. **eight souls** [persons]—Noah, Noah's wife, and their three sons and their wives. **were saved by** [through] **water**—The same water which drowned the unbelieving buoyed up the ark in which the eight were saved. They were safely preserved from the water although they had to be in the water.

➤**21 The like figure**—Greek, "which antitype," referring grammatically to "the water" (1:20). The water is antitypical of water baptism. Water baptism saves (or, delivers) us from God's judgment on the world—just as the water delivered Noah from the world in which he lived. To the unbelievers in Noah's day, the water brought judgment; to Noah and his family it brought deliverance. The flood was a baptism for Noah, just as the passage through the Red Sea was a baptism for the Israelites (1 Cor. 10:2). Through the baptism of the flood, Noah and his family were transferred from the old world to the new; from immediate destruction to a lengthened probation; from the harassment of the unbelievers to communion with God; from the alienation of creature and Creator to the privileges of the covenant. The same happens to believers now in the spiritual baptism described in Scripture. **not the putting away of the filth of the flesh**—i.e., "not the removal of dirt from the body" (NIV). The water of baptism itself does not save; repentance and faith in God, of which baptism is the sign and seal, do this, as Peter explains here. **the answer**—The Greek word (*eperotēma*) was used at the time of the NT to mean "pledge"—i.e., an agreement to certain conditions or demands (Rienecker), or the word can mean "appeal" (NASB). The person who gets baptized does so with the pledge to live out the reality of baptism and/or an appeal to do so. This pledge or appeal should be done in **good conscience toward God by** [through] **the resurrection of Jesus Christ**—This phrase joins with "saves you" (see the appropriate use of parentheses in KJV). Our baptism unites us

with Christ's death and resurrection. Christ's resurrection is the source of the believer's new spiritual life and power. (See Rom. 6:2-11 for a fuller statement of the believer's being baptized into Christ's death and resurrection.)

➤**22 Who is gone into heaven, and is on the right hand of God**—See Psalm 110:1; Romans 8:34, 38; 1 Corinthians 15:24-28. **angels and authorities and powers being made subject unto him**—See Ephesians 1:20-22; 3:10, 11; Colossians 1:16; 2:10-15. As a result of the sufferings Jesus patiently and voluntarily endured on our behalf, God has raised him to the place of highest honor at his right hand. His lordship is acknowledged by all of creation (cf. Phil. 2:5-11).

*Chapter* 4

1-19 PARTNERS WITH CHRIST IN SUFFERING

➤**1 as Christ hath suffered . . . arm yourselves likewise with the same mind**—Like Christ, we are to suffer patiently and willingly all that God sends our way. **he that hath suffered in the flesh hath ceased from sin**—Since Christ by his death is legally free from sin, the Christian, having died in Christ, is one with him and legally free as well from the penalty of sin. We are no longer bound by its penalty; in practice we must strive to be free from its power. Suffering can be of help here. As Christ's sufferings led to death and resurrection, so our suffering can help us die to sin and self and enter more fully into a new life of service to God.

➤**2** This verse describes both the negative and positive aspects of our new life: **no longer should live . . . in the flesh to** [in] **the lusts of men**—the negative, self-denying part. **but to the will of God**—the positive, affirming part.

➤**3 the time past of our life may suffice us to have wrought the will of the Gentiles**—i.e., "you have spent enough time in the past doing what pagans choose to do" (NIV). An evil past cannot be recalled and relived righteously. It can, however, be repudiated and replaced by an affirmation to live in God's way in the future. Peter lists some of those evil things, which include all types of unbridled conduct and excesses.

➤**4 they think it strange that ye run not with them**—Unbelieving friends will often not understand why an old way of life has been abandoned. **speaking evil of you**—Lack of understanding often leads to contempt and any number of unjust accusations.

➤**5** Those who call us falsely to account now will themselves have to give an account of their evil-speaking and manner of life to God, who will justly condemn them (Jude 15).

➤**6 for this cause was the gospel preached also to them that are dead**—This can mean that the gospel was preached to those who had already died (see comments on 3:19) or that it was preached to those who heard it while living and are now dead. The gospel has been preached to those who have died, is being preached to those who are alive now, and will be preached to those who are alive when Christ comes in judgment. "Dead" must be taken in the same literal sense as "dead" in 4:5; it does not refer to those dead in their sins. Peter, reflecting the attitude of the church in every age, expects Christ to come at any time and judge both the living and the dead. The dead who during their lifetimes have had the gospel preached to them can be judged in the same way as those who are living now and those who will be living when Christ comes. Those who have escaped condemnation by believing God's revealed truth **live according to God in the spirit**—i.e., "live in the spirit like God" (RSV), although they have died (Luke 20:38). In this they are like Christ in life and death. He says "live," not "made alive" or "quickened," for God has already given the dead in Christ life with him when Christ was raised from the dead (Eph. 2:5). Peter had in mind only those who have been within reach of the gospel, or who may have known God through his ministers in OT and NT times. He was probably not dealing with the question of what happens to those who have never heard the gospel. Like Paul, Peter argued that those who are alive at Christ's coming will have no advantage over the dead. The dead will be raised, along with the living.

➤**7 the end of all things is at hand**—The evil ways of the wicked and the sufferings of the righteous will soon be past (Bengel). The Lord will come as unexpectedly as a thief. He could come to judge the world at any moment.

But his patience and his desire that the gospel should be preached as a witness to all nations have caused him to delay the time of his coming. **be ye therefore sober, and watch unto prayer**—Our perspective should make our conduct stand in stark contrast to that of those who don't know God (4:3).

➤**8 have fervent charity** [love] **among yourselves**—This is not saying that love is more important than prayer (4:7). Rather, love is the life-giving, motivating spirit without which all other Christian responsibilities are lifeless. Peter realized that this love already existed among his readers; he urged them to continue and deepen that love. **charity** [love] **shall cover the multitude of sins**—This is quoted from Proverbs 10:12 (cf. Prov. 17:9). Love does not harshly condemn or expose faults. It patiently bears another's burdens, forgiving and forgetting past offenses.

➤**9 Use hospitality**—be hospitable (Rom. 12:13; Heb. 13:2). Peter was not commending superficial socializing but the heartfelt hospitality that is a practical expression of Christian love. We are to specially share our homes with those who are in need, not just with our select group of friends. Our sharing is to be cheerful—we are not to secretly begrudge having to show hospitality, and we are not to remind our guests of what a great favor we are doing them. We are simply and sincerely to share ourselves and our possessions.

➤**10 every man hath received the** [a] **gift**—The gifts or abilities God gives vary according to degree and kind, but no Christian is left out (Rom. 12:3-6). **minister the same** [gift] **one to another**—These gifts are the common property of the Christian community. Each individual has been entrusted with his gift to help build up that community. The gifts are not for selfish use. **as good stewards of the manifold grace of God**—All Christians have been given a measure of grace (Rom. 12:3) concerning which they are to function as stewards who distribute that portion for the benefit of the other members in Christ's body. As we exercise our gift for the good of the body, we show a new side of God's many faceted grace. For a parable related to this theme, see Matthew 25:14-30.

➤**11 let him speak as the oracles of God**—The prophet, teacher, or preacher in the church is called to speak God's words, not his own. God has entrusted this gift to him, and he is bound to exercise it for the good of the body (4:10). Jesus provides us with the pattern: Matthew 7:29; John 12:49; 14:10 (cf. Paul, 2 Cor. 2:17). **minister . . . as of the ability** [strength] **which God giveth** [supplies]—Helping others through concrete action is another sphere of spiritual ministry. If this is our gift, we are to exercise it depending on the store of God's strength. (This refers more to physical power than to moral or intellectual ability: the word is used in the same sense as in Mark 12:30.) **that God in all things may be glorified**—This is the ultimate goal of all a Christian's activity. **through Jesus Christ**—Christ is the Mediator through whom all blessings come to us and also through whom all our praises ascend to God.

►**12 think it not strange concerning the fiery trial**—It is easy to be both bewildered and surprised when God allows his children to be severely tried. These trials are like the fire by which metals are tested and their dross removed (see 1:7). Therefore, these trials don't come our way by accident; they are part of the design God is working out in our lives.

►**13 rejoice, inasmuch as ye are partakers of Christ's sufferings**—When we willingly suffer for Christ's sake, in the way that he suffered, we partake of his sufferings. **exceeding joy**—At present we can, with some effort, rejoice in the midst of suffering (1:6, 8); but when Christ's glory is revealed, our joy will know no limits and we will be forever free from suffering.

►**14 If ye be reproached for the name of Christ, happy are ye**—cf. 3:14; 4:16. The emphasis is on suffering in the name of Christ because we belong to Christ, in contrast with the sufferings mentioned in 4:15. Our suffering should be on Christ's account, not on account of our own sins (2:20). Being "reproached" may be for some a more severe kind of suffering than the loss of possessions or physical pain. **the spirit of glory and of God**—The same Spirit that rested on Christ will rest on us. Believers can cope with curses and insults because God's glorious Spirit rests on them as it did upon Christ. If we are reproached for Christ's sake, we can be happy because the Spirit and the glory that is inseparable from it will be ours before God (Calvin).

►**15 a busybody in other men's matters**—Christians might mistakenly feel that they should step out of their own calling and set themselves up as judges on the conduct of non-believers. Peter forbids this, along with the more obvious types of wrongdoing.

►**16** The name **Christian** was first used as a term of contempt against the believers at Antioch. In the Greek, it is found in only three places in the NT: here; Acts 11:26; 26:28. In the early days of the church, believers had no distinctive name. Among themselves they were called "brothers" (Acts 6:3); "believers" (Acts 6:1); "followers of the way"; "saints." The Jews (who denied that Jesus was the Christ and so would never originate the name "Christian") called them "Nazarenes." In Antioch, when Gentiles were converted and wide missionary work began, the believers could no longer be considered a Jewish sect, so the Gentiles called them by the new name, "Christian." This name marked a new stage of development in the history of the church. This epistle dates from the time when "Christian" had become a usual designation for followers of Christ. Nevertheless, a Christian (lit., "one of Christ") bore reproach for his faith in Christ. **let him not be ashamed**—Although it is generally considered shameful to be insulted or laughed at, it is not a dishonor to suffer for Christ. Suffering for our own faults is no honor (4:15; 2:20) and suffering for Christ is no shame (5:14; 3:14). **let him glorify God on this behalf**—Greek, "let him glorify God by this name." Peter might have gone on to say that we should personally count it a great honor to suffer innocently, but instead he says that we should attribute praise and honor to God, not ourselves, since God has accounted us worthy of identifying with the name of Christ.

►**17** This is another consolation for Christians. All men will be judged by God. God's own family are first, as they suffer in this life. They can praise God for that suffering because it is a proof of their sonship (Heb. 12:8) and a pledge from God that they will escape from his terrible judgment on those who have rejected the gospel. **must begin at the house of God**—Peter was probably alluding to Ezekiel 9:6 (cf. Amos 3:2; Jer. 25:29). "The persecutions that believers were undergoing were divinely sent judgment intended to purify God's people"

(*NIVSB*). **if it first begin at us, what shall the end be of them that obey not the gospel**—If even the godly experience God's chastening judgments now, how much more shall unbelievers be doomed by God's condemnatory judgments in the end.

➤**18** This verse is a quotation of Proverbs 11:31 (LXX). **if the righteous scarcely be saved**—The righteous always face trying chastisements, some to a greater, some to a lesser, degree. In spite of the trials, the righteous man has the certainty of knowing that his salvation and his hope for the future are settled. The phrase here, "scarcely be saved" refers to the severity of the ordeal and the probability (from a strictly human viewpoint) that the Christian could not endure it. From a divine perspective, Christ's righteousness and God's eternal covenant make the outcome sure. **the ungodly and the sinner**—Those who have no regard for God and love sin will have no hope in the face of judgment.

➤**19** God's children know that they face sufferings only according to his will, and that those sufferings chasten them so that they will not perish with the unbelieving world. Therefore, they can trust God cheerfully amid sufferings and keep on doing good. **commit the keeping of their souls**—i.e., "entrust their souls" (RSV). **unto a faithful Creator**—God will never fail to keep his covenant promises with his people. The one who made us will also preserve us. Although sin destroyed the original spiritual relationship between creature and Creator, faith restores it. The believer who lives in the will of God (4:2) can rest securely on his Creator's faithfulness.

# Chapter 5

## 1-9 THE SHEPHERDING OF GOD'S PEOPLE

➤**1 who am also an elder**—Peter was putting himself on the same level with those whom he was exhorting; in this way, his exhortations would carry more weight. In true humility and for the gospel's sake, Peter did not emphasize his position as an apostle, by virtue of which he presided over the elders. **a witness of the sufferings of Christ**—As an eyewitness of Christ's sufferings, Peter was well qualified to exhort his readers to patiently suffer for welldoing as Christ had done (4:19; 2:20). Peter may also be tactfully implying his claim to apostleship, since being an eyewitness to Christ's ministry was a prerequisite for apostleship (Acts 1:21, 22; 2:32; 10:39). **also a partaker of the glory that shall be revealed**—Christ's promise assures us that this hope is true. Peter, James, and John had a brief taste of that glory at the transfiguration.

➤**2 Feed the flock of God**—The Greek says "tend as a shepherd God's flock." This is to be done by providing spiritual food and by instilling discipline through prayer, exhortation, governing and setting an example. Peter never forgot the injunction Christ gave him: "Feed my lambs . . . take care of my sheep" (John 21:16, TLB). Peter invited the elders to share with him in this duty (cf. Acts. 20:28). **taking the oversight**—or, "serving as overseers" (NIV). These words are not found in two early manuscripts (Codex Vaticanus and Codex Sinaiticus—original hand), but other ancient manuscripts include these words, namely the Bodmer Papyrus (P72), Codex Alexandrius, Codex Sinaiticus (by the hand of a corrector), and other reliable witnesses. The testimony supporting the inclusion of the Greek word for "overseeing" is strong—both externally and internally. If the word were not originally in the text, it is difficult to explain why scribes would have added it. On the contrary, it is easy to see why the scribes of the fourth-century manuscripts, Vaticanus and Sinaiticus, omitted it. These scribes may have had the misconception that elders (Gk. "presbytery"—5:1) could not function as overseers. At that time in church history (fourth century), the offices of elder and overseer (i.e., bishop) were differentiated. The overseer or bishop was elevated to a rank above an elder. This contradicts the teaching in the NT. Paul told the elders at Ephesus that the Holy Spirit had made them overseers (bishops) of the flock of God (Acts 20:17, 28). And here Peter charges the elders that they should shepherd the flock of God by overseing it (i.e., by functioning as bishops). Thus, the function of an elder was to oversee the church (Alford, Comfort). **not by constraint, but willingly**—Although the duty and necessity for caring for the church is laid upon the elders, willingness keeps it from being burdensome. The true elder and minister of God's counsel both practices and teaches the things of the Lord. He is not righteous just because he is an elder, but rather he is chosen to be an elder because he is righteous. **not for filthy lucre**—"not for shameful gain" (RSV). See Isaiah 56:11; Titus 1:7. **but of a ready mind**—Be ready to promptly and heartily serve the Lord, without selfish motives, but as the Israelites gave their wholehearted services willingly to the sanctuary.

➤**3 Neither as being lords**—Elders are not to lord it over the flock of God (5:2). Peter left no room for pride or oppression. The flock, after all, belongs to God himself. The elders are his stewards or servants and are bound to exercise their function in humility. **God's heritage**—Greek, "the lots"—i.e., do not lord it over those allotted to you (or, entrusted to your care). Darby thought the word meant "your possessions," to which he added this note: "No doubt the saints were in his [Peter's] thoughts; but the character of the elders' conduct is what is in question. If there were no article, it would mean 'not like persons who lord it over possessions': here it is more applied. Do not be as persons lording it over your possessions, viewing the saints as something belonging to you." **being ensamples** [examples] **to the flock**—A good example is a powerful tool for leaders and teachers (1 Tim. 4:12; Titus 2:7). Jesus is, of course, our perfect example.

➤**4 Here** we see the reward the elders will receive for being good examples to their flock (5:3). **when the chief Shepherd shall appear**—Christ alone is the chief Shepherd, the master Shepherd, under whose headship all other shepherds of the church labor. **a crown of glory that fadeth not away**—The ancient Greeks awarded a garland of victory as the prize in their games. It was woven of ivy, parsley, myrtle, olive, or oak. Our crown or reward will be different from theirs because it never fades. Its "leaves" will not fade away (cf. 1:4) because it is a crown of life. It is not, however, to be confused with the kingly crown that Jesus alone shall wear as Lord of Lords. The fact that we will share eternally in this majestic monarch's glory and honor is astounding (cf. 5:1; 4:13).

➤**5 younger** [men]—could refer to younger men in general or to deacons. Deacons were originally the younger men in the church and

elders were the older. Having exhorted the elders not to lord it over those committed to their care, Peter now turns to the deacons, urging them to submit cheerfully to the authority of the elders. **all of you**—This is directed to the entire church. **be subject**—This verbal expression is not present in all the earliest manuscripts. **be clothed** [lit., "tie on with a fast knot"] **with humility**—gird on humility as the slave dress. This part of the verse, then, could be translated, "Clothe yourselves with humility toward each other." Jesus provides us with a graphic example of this. He girded himself with a towel to perform the lowly task of washing the disciples' feet. Peter played an important part in that scene, so he naturally would have it in mind. **God resisteth the proud, and giveth grace to the humble**—This is taken, as is James 4:6, from Proverbs 3:34.

➤**6 Humble yourselves therefore under the mighty hand of God**—That "mighty hand" may send sufferings into our lives (3:17; 4:1), but we are to accept those chastisements, continuing to walk in humble obedience and dependence on him. **that he may exalt you in due time**—We have this as God's promise and must patiently wait for God to act according to his own timing.

➤**7 Casting all your care** [anxiety] **upon him**—The Greek participle is in the aorist tense, indicating that we are to give our anxieties over to God once for all. We can do so only because we have first humbled ourselves before God (5:6). Only then can we confidently rest in his goodness. Freedom from anxiety goes along with humble submission to God. **for he careth for you**—lit., "because it matters to him concerning you" (Marshall). Since God is concerned about us, we can give him our cares and worries. (Cf. Ps. 22:10; 37:5; 55:22 [to which Peter here alludes]; Luke 12:22, 28; Phil. 4:6.)

➤**8** Christ warned Peter to watch against Satan, but Peter forgot, fell, and denied Christ. Peter may very well have had this admonition in mind. **Be sober, be vigilant**—Anxiety (5:7) may cause us to lose control of ourselves, but we are called to be self-restrained. Freedom from anxiety may lead us into a false sense of security, so Peter warns us to watch out for Satan's attack. This is the proper kind of concern Christians should have. God provides—

we need not be anxious. Satan attacks—we need to be on the alert (Bengel). **your adversary the devil**—An adversary is an opponent in a court of justice. Satan is also called the accuser (Rev. 12:10), the enemy (Matt. 13:39), and a murderer from the beginning (John 8:44). He works against the gospel and its agents. **as a roaring lion**—Satan has an insatiable and violent desire to devour all those who follow Christ. Because of man's sin, Satan had taken the role to accuse men before God (Job. 1:6ff.; 2:1ff.). But Christ, the advocate, by his redemptive act, has fulfilled all the demands justice makes on men. Whoever believes in Christ and the effectiveness of his death does not need to fear Satan's attacks. **walketh about**—See Job 1:7; 2:2. Before his final defeat and eternal punishment (Matt. 25:41; Rev. 20:2, 3), Satan (the prince of the satanic forces in the air) is permitted by God to roam about the world **seeking whom he may devour**. Satan tries to entangle us in anxieties (5:7) and other traps, with a view toward destroying us completely.

➤**9 Whom resist stedfast in the faith**—We stand firm by being established in the truth, putting on God's whole armor, and praying (Eph. 6:10-18). Satan's ultimate power to destroy extends only to the unbelievers; he cannot destroy the faithful. (Remember God holds on to us; it's not a matter of our trying to keep hold on him—1 John 5:18.) Our trust in the Lord gives strength for prayer, a great weapon against the enemy. **knowing that the same afflictions** [sufferings] **are accomplished in your brethren that are in the world**—Other Christian brothers around the world are suffering too; therefore, you share nothing beyond the common lot of Christians. Remember Job's sufferings—it is a sign of God's pleasure, not his displeasure, when he allows Satan to harass us. Fellow Christians have the same battle of faith and prayer against Satan. Since the world is under Satan's influence, it is naturally a scene of tribulation (John 16:33).

10-14 CONCLUSION

➤**10** This verse assures that God will finally complete and perfect the gracious work he has already begun in the believers after they have undergone a necessary period of suffering. **the God of all grace**—God is the source of all kindness and favor (4:10), who, in his grace, completes the work he has begun. **called us unto his eternal glory by Christ Jesus**—From the beginning, God has called us to this glory. He will not let his purposes fall short of completion. Four elements are joined together: the call, the glory to which we are called, the suffering on our way to that glory and, finally, God's grace expressed through Christ, the ground of our calling. **after that ye have suffered a while**—This is a part of God's calling and a required preliminary to the glory Christians will share in Christ. It is, however, a short and insignificant time when compared with that glory (2 Cor. 5:17). **make you perfect** [restore you], **stablish, strengthen, settle you**—Although we are called to be alert and to resist the foe, God himself must do everything in and through us. God initiated his redemptive work in us; ultimately, he alone must complete it. In the process we will be able to stand firm (5:9) in the strength God gives us. Peter may have in mind Christ's charge to him: "When you have repented and turned to me again, strengthen and build up the faith of your brothers" (Luke 22:32, TLB).

➤**11 To him**—This emphatically says that the power is his and his alone. **glory and dominion**—This is the reading in one early manuscript (Codex Sinaiticus) and many later ones. Three other early manuscripts read instead, "power."

➤**12 Silvanus**—Silvanus, or Silas, had been Paul's and Timothy's companion (Acts 15:22-33; 15:40–18:5; 1 Thess. 1:1, 2 Thess. 1:1). Silvanus is never mentioned as Paul's companion after Paul's last journey to Jerusalem. Since Silvanus may have had a close relationship with the Asian churches, it is possible that he assumed oversight of them after Paul's departure, left to go with Peter, and was now being sent back to them with this epistle. **a faithful brother unto you, as I suppose** [regard]—Peter did not know firsthand about Silvanus's relationship with the churches, but he gave him an endorsement based on his personal experience. **exhorting, and testifying that this is the true grace of God**—Peter had dealt more with practical exhortation than formal doctrine. His testimony to these truths confirmed what these churches had previously heard from Paul and Silvanus. Since Paul was no longer in this area, his teachings had been called into question by some (2 Pet. 3:15, 16). God's grace is the keynote of Paul's teaching. Peter confirms it here. As a result of the sufferings Peter's readers had experienced, they needed a confirmation of this truth so that they would be encouraged and not fall back. **wherein ye stand**—According to the earliest manuscripts, this is a command to stand firm (see RSV, NASB, NIV) in their present commitment to the gospel (1:8, 21; 2:7-9).

►**13 The church that is at Babylon, elected together with you**—Greek, "the co-chosen (feminine gender—referring to a woman or a 'church,' which is feminine in Greek) in Babylon." There is a diversity of opinion on who is being referred to here: Peter's wife, the church in Babylon, or the church at Rome (cryptically or symbolically called "Babylon"). "The last view is best because (1) according to early church tradition Peter was in Rome; (2) there is no evidence for Peter's having been in Egypt or Mesopotamia; and (3) the reference may be cryptic because of persecution, or it may be an allusion to the 'exile' of God's people on the pattern of the exile of ancient Israel in Babylon" (Blum).

**Marcus my son**—Mark, my son (in the faith). Mark had been Paul's companion; but because he turned back on a journey, he was replaced by Silvanus (Silas). By the time of this epistle, however, Mark had been restored to a place of esteem both in the eyes of Paul and Peter. He was like a son to Peter and was respected just as Silvanus was. Second Timothy 4:11 and Colossians 4:10 indicate that Mark had a spiritual connection with the Asian churches, so he naturally saluted them. (For more on the relationship between Mark and Peter see the Introduction to the Gospel of Mark.)

►**14 Greet ye one another with a kiss of charity** [love]—See Romans 16:16. This is the token of love for other Christians. **Peace be with you**—Paul's usual closing benediction was "Grace be with you." "Peace" (flowing from salvation) was Christ's own salutation after the resurrection (Luke 24:36; John 20:21). **all that are in Christ**—Those who are "in Christ" are those who believe in him and are living in union with him. . . . **Jesus. Amen**— The last two words of this epistle in the KJV text are present in some ancient manuscripts but not in others.

BIBLIOGRAPHY

Alford, Henry. *The Greek New Testament.* 1852. Reprint. Grand Rapids: Guardian Press, 1976.

Bengel, John A. *New Testament Word Studies.* 1742. Reprint. Grand Rapids: Eerdmans, 1971.

Blum, Edwin A. "First Peter" in the *Expositor's Bible Commentary.* Grand Rapids: Zondervan, 1981.

Calvin, John. *The Epistles of Paul the Apostle to the Hebrews and the First and Second Epistles of St. Peter.* 1554. Reprint. Edinburgh: Oliver & Boyd, 1963.

Darby, John N. *New Translation.* 1871. Reprint. Addison, Ill. Bible Truth Publishers, n.d.

Gerhard, Johann. *Commentary on Peter's Epistles and John's Epistles.* Hamburg: n.p., 1660.

Kelly, J. N. D. *A Commentary on the Epistles of Peter and Jude* (in The Harper New Testament Commentaries). New York: Harper & Row, 1969.

Luther, Martin. *The Epistles of St. Peter and St. Jude.* c. 1530; translated 1904. Reprint. Grand Rapids: Kregel, 1982.

Raymer, Roger M. "First Peter" in *The Bible Knowledge Commentary.* Wheaton, Ill.: Victor Books, 1983.

Rienecker, Fritz. *Linguistic Key to the Greek New Testament.* Grand Rapids: Baker Book House, 1976, 1980.

Wuest, Kenneth. "First Peter" in *Word Studies in the Greek New Testament.* Grand Rapids: Eerdmans, 1954.

# 2 PETER
## Introduction

Peter's authorship of this epistle has been questioned throughout the centuries for several reasons. The most fundamental are as follows: (1) The epistle was not readily accepted in the early church. (2) The writing style of this epistle is different from 1 Peter. (3) Peter's name was connected with many gnostic pseudepigrapha: *The Gospel of Peter, The Acts of Peter, The Teaching of Peter, The Letter of Peter to James, The Preaching of Peter.* (4) Second Peter shares the same material found in Jude. Scholars have used all these points (and more) to disprove Peter's authorship. (For more information on these arguments, plus others, see Bauckham's *Jude, 2 Peter.*) But each point can be countered.

The Second Epistle of Peter, though not universally accepted in the earliest centuries of the church, was nevertheless recognized in the second and third centuries in certain regions. Origen (c. 185–254) was the first to attribute it to Peter. The Gospel of Truth and the Apocryphon of John (both second-century writings) refer to 2 Peter. And the Bodmer Papyrus (P72), an early third-century manuscript, contains 1 and 2 Peter together, with Jude. This arrangement shows that at least some Christians considered 2 Peter as authoritative as 1 Peter, an epistle readily received by the early church (Blum).

Second Peter is written in a different style from 1 Peter; this is quite apparent in the Greek. Two reasons may account for this: (1) Sylvanus, Peter's amanuensis for 1 Peter, exercised his literary skills in helping Peter compose that letter; and Peter himself wrote the second epistle. (2) The nature of 2 Peter called for a different style.

One of the reasons that 2 Peter was not readily accepted in the second and third centuries of the church was that so many pseudepigrapha bearing his name were being produced. The church, therefore, acted with caution; but it did finally act to receive 2 Peter and canonize it—for, with time, it became very clear what was false and what was genuine.

Several scholars have pointed out that since 2 Peter 2–3:3 heavily relies on Jude 4-18, Peter could not have written 2 Peter because an apostle of his stature would not borrow from a lesser servant's work. This argument, however, is not conclusive because it has not been fully shown that Jude was written before 2 Peter. Besides, both Peter and Jude could have been drawing from a common source applicable to both the situations they were addressing.

Weightier than all these arguments, we have the testimony of the writer himself. The writer identifies himself as Simon Peter (1:1); he relates Christ's prophecy concerning his death (1:14); he mentions his presence at the transfiguration of Christ (1:16-18); he speaks of himself as the author of the former epistle (3:1); and he identifies himself as a brother who loved Paul (3:15). Either the writer was Peter or an impostor. If an impostor wrote this epistle, it should be rejected entirely from the NT canon. But it cannot be rejected, for the entire epistle has the ring of apostolic authority and the marks of divine inspiration.

Second Peter was written between A.D. 66 and 68, just prior to Peter's martyrdom. Peter may have been in Rome at the time he wrote this epistle. His reason for writing this letter is set forth in 3:17, 18: "Ye therefore, beloved, seeing ye know these before, beware lest ye also, being led away with the error of the wicked, fall from your own stedfastness. But grow in grace, and in the knowledge of our Lord and Saviour Jesus Christ. To him be glory both now and for ever. Amen." This statement shows Peter's twofold purpose: (1) to warn his readers against false teachings (see chapter 2) and (2) to encourage them to grow in their personal and practical knowledge of their Lord and Savior, Jesus Christ (see 1:2, 8; 2:20).

*Chapter* **1**

## 1-11 ADDRESS AND ENCOURAGEMENT FOR PARTAKING OF THE DIVINE NATURE, KNOWING CHRIST EXPERIENTIALLY AND ENTERING INTO THE KINGDOM

➤**1 Simon Peter**—This mention of his original name accords with the design of the second epistle, which is to combat false teachers by setting forth the true knowledge of Christ via the testimony of original apostolic eyewitnesses like himself. This was not required in Peter's first epistle. **a servant**—This term means "slave." Paul employed it in Romans 1:1. **to them**—He here addresses a wider range of readers (all believers) than in the first epistle—while also including those he addressed in the first epistle, as 3:1 shows. **obtained like precious** [equally precious] **faith with us**—All Christians possess the same, equally precious faith. **through the righteousness of God and our Saviour Jesus Christ**—The Greek grammar here calls for another translation: "through the righteousness of our God and Savior, Jesus Christ" (see NASB, RSV, NIV). This rendering reveals the resplendent truth that Jesus Christ is both our God and Savior. The same truth is unveiled in the Greek text of Titus 2:13 (see comments there, and note details about the Greek construction appearing both here and in

2 Thess. 1:12; Titus 2:13). We have obtained the equally-precious faith by virtue of Christ's righteousness, not our own.

➤**2 knowledge**—Greek, "full knowledge." One of the prominent themes in this epistle is Peter's exhortation to the believers to attain a fuller, more thorough knowledge of Jesus Christ (1:8; 2:20; 3:18). This knowledge leads to grace and peace.

➤**3 According as**—"Seeing that" (Alford). This verse provides a further explanation of 1:2. **his divine power**—Christ's divine power, for he is God (1:1) (Robertson). **given unto us all things that pertain unto life and godliness**—i.e., "everything we need for life and godliness" (NIV). Christ's divine power has provided us with the spiritual dynamo to live a spiritual life, with godliness. **through the knowledge of him**—This goes back to 1:2. Knowing Christ is the major vehicle for appropriating his divine power. **called us to glory and virtue**—Greek, "called us to his own glory and virtue" (a reading supported by several ancient manuscripts), or "called us by [or, through] his own glory and virtue" (a reading supported by the two earliest manuscripts—the Bodmer Papyrus, P72, and Codex Vaticanus). Both readings make good sense because Christ called us *by* his own glory and virtue (excellent character), and he called us *to* participate in his own glory and virtue (see 1:4).

➤**4 Whereby**—Greek, "through which things," probably referring to "glory and virtue" (1:3). Christ's glory and virtue are transmitted to us by his divine power—so that we might participate in them, which is actually a participation in his divine nature. The participation in Christ's excellencies now is accompanied by many **precious promises** yet to be realized. The foremost promise concerns Christ's *parousia,* his second coming (3:13). When this promise is fulfilled, so will be many others—such as our co-glorification with Christ (2 Thess. 1:10) and our full perfection (Col. 1:28). **by these**—i.e., promises. **partakers of the divine nature**—The divine nature is the nature that characterizes God, the nature that is expressed in holiness, virtue, righteousness, love, grace, glory, etc. (see 1:5-7). By being regenerated with the divine nature, believers can partake of these characteristics of the divine nature. **having escaped the corruption that is in the world**—By being made partakers of the divine nature, we escape the corrupting elements in the world. **through lust**—Lust leads to sin and sin to corruption.

➤**5 And beside this**—Greek, "also for this very thing." For the actual participation in the divine nature and escape from the world's corruption, we need to give **all diligence** to **add** [or, supply] **to your faith** several aspects of the divine nature. All Christians begin with a deposit of the equally-precious faith (1:1). But each Christian is responsible to draw upon the divine power and divine nature to add the characteristics of the divine nature to his or her actual living. **virtue**—means "moral excellence," an attribute not innate to any human—it is a divine attribute available for the believer's appropriation. **knowledge**—Greek, "personal and experiential knowledge" of God and his Son, Jesus Christ (1:1; cf. John 17:3).

➤**6 temperance**—self-control. **patience**—or, endurance. **godliness**—or, piety.

➤**7 brotherly kindness**—lit., "brotherliness"; hence, "brotherly affection" (RSV) or "brotherly love" (TEV). **charity**—Greek, *agape,* designating volitional, self-sacrificial love. All the characteristics mentioned in 1:5-7 are not naturally found in the fallen nature of man; they must be developed in Christians by the divine Spirit (see Gal. 5:22, 23) and from God's nature.

➤**8 nor unfruitful in the knowledge of our Lord Jesus Christ**—To experientially know Jesus Christ is to appropriate his divine nature manifest in the characteristics listed in 1:5-7. This knowledge, then, is not mere intellectual understanding but experiential appropriation. (The Greek word used here and in 1:2; 2:20—*epignosis*—speaks of full, experiential knowledge; cf. also 3:18 where *gnosis* is used.)

➤**9** A Christian who lacks the items mentioned in 1:5-7 **is blind** or shortsighted; he has failed to realize that Christ **purged** (cleansed) him from his **old sins**—in order to make him a partaker of the divine nature (1:4).

➤**10 brethren**—It is affection for them that constrained him to urge them so earnestly. **give diligence**—The Greek aorist implies one lifelong effort. **to make your calling and election sure** [secure, confirmed]—We were elected (chosen) and called to participate in Christ's glory and virtue. We must attend to this calling, to confirm its reality in our lives. The proving of our calling is spoken of not in respect to God, whose counsel is steadfast and everlasting, but in respect to our response. There is no uncertainty on his part. We, however, must confirm our election by evidencing the characteristics of the divine nature in our lives (1:4-7, 11). Peter joined election to calling, for the calling is the effect and proof of God's election (Rom. 8:28, 30, 33). We are aware of his calling before we are aware of being chosen; therefore calling is put first.

➤**11 an entrance shall be ministered** [supplied] **unto you abundantly into the everlasting kingdom**—If the characteristics of the divine nature are manifest in our lives, we can be sure that we will "receive a rich welcome into the eternal kingdom" (NIV).

## 12-21 PETER AFFIRMS THE GOSPEL OF CHRIST AND THE SCRIPTURES

➤**12 I will not be negligent to put you always in remembrance**—This reading is supported by some ancient manuscripts, but the earliest read, "I intend always to put you in remembrance" or "I will regard you as always needing to be reminded." This idea of "always" perhaps explains why he wrote the second epistle so soon after the first. He must have thought there needed to be more admonition on account of the increasing infiltration of falsehood into the churches (2:1, 2).

➤**13 this tabernacle**—Peter's body (see comments on 2 Cor. 5:1-4). **to stir you up**—Peter needed to make the most of his short time for the good of Christ's church. He wanted to arouse their desire to know Christ and to partake of his divine nature.

➤**14 I must put off this my tabernacle, even as our Lord Jesus Christ hath showed** [made clear to] **me**—See John 21:18, 19 and comments.

➤**15 my decease**—lit., "my exodus." **have these things always in remembrance**—He was not talking of mere memorization. The truth should be held in earnest remembrance.

➤**16 For**—What follows are reasons why he was so insistent that these things should be remembered after his death. **not followed cunningly devised fables**—The gospel message was not on a par with heathen mythologies and gnostic fables and genealogies, germs of which already existed in the mixture of Judaism with Oriental philosophy in Asia Minor. **when we made known unto you**—Peter himself had not personally taught the churches in Pontus, Galatia, etc., but he was one of the apostles whose testimony was taken to them and to the church in general. **the power and coming** [Gk. *parousia*] **of our Lord Jesus Christ**—A sample of his power was displayed at the transfiguration and the disciples were given a preview of his parousia and its attendant glory. The Greek for "coming" (*parousia*) is usually used of Christ's second advent. [We] **were eyewitnesses of his majesty**—Peter, James, and John witnessed Christ's majesty on the mount of transfiguration (see Matt. 16:28–17:8).

➤**17** See Matthew 17:5.

➤**18** See Matthew 17:1-6.

➤**19 We**—The reference is to all believers. **have also a more sure word of prophecy**—The Greek says, "We have the prophetic word [made] more sure." In context (see 1:16-18), Peter had just told his readers that he (along with two other disciples) was an eyewitness of Jesus Christ's transfiguration—at which time he distinctly heard the Father's voice declaring Jesus Christ to be his beloved Son. This experience affirmed the prophetic word. Jesus' transfiguration and the Father's declaration confirmed the fact that Jesus was the Messiah

predicted by the prophets. Thus, Peter could say, "We have the prophetic word confirmed (or, certified)"—following which he said, "to which you do well to take heed, as to a lamp shining in a dark place, until the day dawns and the day star rises in your hearts." The apostles' experience on the Mount of Transfiguration confirmed to them the accuracy of the OT. We have not had the same experience, but we have the same word, which has now been confirmed. We must take heed to it as to a lamp that shines in the darkness until we, too, are illumined. **take heed, as unto a light that shineth**—The Word was the shining light for OT believers until a gleam of the "dawn" was given at Christ's first coming and especially in his transfiguration. So the prophetic words in the OT are a light unto us still, until "the dawn" bursts forth full at the second coming of "the Son of righteousness." **in a dark place**—The Greek implies squalor and murkiness, having neither water nor light; such, spiritually, is the world, and the heart in its natural state. **until the day dawn**—Until the day of Christ's second coming (Rom. 13:12), we need to heed the shining lamp, the Scriptures. **the day star**—[lit., *phōsphoros*] **arise in your hearts**—Christ is the Day Star, as elsewhere he is called the bright morning Star (Rev. 22:16) and the rising Sun (Luke 1:78). Presently, Christ shines in our hearts; when he comes, he will arise in our hearts and bring us into a perfect day. His outward coming will be matched by an inward rising, "an illuminating transformation" (Blum).

➤**20 prophecy of the scripture**—i.e., Scripture containing prophecy. **is of any private interpretation**—lit., "is of its own unraveling" or "is of its own interpretation." Some commentators have thought that the expression "no prophecy of Scripture is of its own interpretation" refers to the reader's interpretation of the Scripture and indicated that the reader must not interpret the Scripture privately and/or the reader must not interpret any portion of Scripture by itself but by all of Scripture, so that Scripture can interpret Scripture. But the context of 1:21 indicates that Peter was not speaking of the reader of Scripture but of the speaker of Scripture, the prophet. This verse tells us that the Scripture (specifically the OT prophecies) did not originate with any man nor was it interpreted by the prophets themselves as they delivered the message. False prophets produced false prophecies from their own inspiration (see Ezek. 13:2, 17 in NASB), but genuine prophets did not interpret the message as God gave it to them; they simply spoke what was spoken to them and recorded the God-originated, Spirit-motivated words (see 1:21).

➤**21 holy men of God spake as they were moved** [carried] **by the Holy Ghost** [Spirit]— Some ancient manuscripts support this reading, but most of the earliest manuscripts read "men spoke from God as they were carried [along] by the Holy Spirit." The second reading tells us the source from which the men spoke—they spoke *from God,* without interpreting the message according to their own understanding (see comments on 1:20).

*Chapter* 2

## 1-22 THE RISE OF FALSE PROPHETS

➤**1 But**—What follows is set in contrast to the men to whom the Holy Spirit gave messages from God (1:21). **there were false prophets**—See 2 Kings 18:19; Isaiah 9:13-17; Jeremiah 5:31; 23:30-32. **there shall be false teachers**—This is prophesied throughout the NT: Matthew 24:4, 5, 11; Acts 20:29, 30; 2 Thessalonians 2:1-3; 1 Timothy 1:3-7; 4:1-3; 2 Timothy 3:1-8; 1 John 2:18-23; 2 John 7-11; Jude 3, 4. **damnable heresies**—"destructive heresies" (RSV, NIV). The Greek word for "heresies" usually means "parties" or "sects" in the NT, but Peter used the word here in the sense we are most accustomed to—i.e., "teachings contrary to orthodox doctrine." **denying the Lord that bought them**—Even the ungodly were bought by his blood. If they had believed in Christ's redemption, they might have been saved. Their denial will bring about their own **swift destruction.**

➤**2 pernicious ways**—Greek, "licentiousnesses." False doctrine and immoral practice generally go together (2:18, 19). **the way of truth shall be evil spoken of**—They will blaspheme the truth of Christianity by laying on it the blame of their own evil practices (cf. 1 Pet. 2:12).

➤**3 through covetousness shall they with feigned words make merchandise of you**— The false prophets would entice and lure unsuspecting believers with their fabrications and

then exploit them for their own use and satisfaction.

➤**4 God spared not the angels that sinned**— This could refer to God's judgment of the angels (called "sons of men") who had sexual relations with women (Gen. 6:1-4) or to the original sin of the angels who rebelled against God. The context (see 2:5) favors the first view. **cast them down to hell**—Greek, "consigning them to Tartarus." "Tartarus, thought of by the Greeks as a subterranean place lower than Hades where divine punishment was meted out, was so regarded in Jewish apocalyptic as well" (*BAG*). **chains of darkness**—This reading is supported by some early manuscripts; other early manuscripts read, "pits of darkness" or "gloomy pits."

➤**5 spared not the old world**—See 3:6; Genesis 8:23. **Noah the eighth person**—i.e., Noah and seven others. **a preacher of righteousness**— The righteous man preached righteousness. **the flood upon the world of the ungodly**—See Genesis 6:5–8:19. This verse parallels 1 Peter 3:20.

➤**6 Sodom and Gomorrha**—See Genesis 19: 24, 25. **ensample**—example (cf. Jude 7).

➤**7, 8 vexed**—Greek, "tormented." **filthy conversation**—"filthy lives" (NIV), "licentiousness" (RSV). See Genesis 19:4-9. Peter reminded us of Lot's righteousness (see Gen. 18:24-32), not of his sin in the cave.

➤**9 temptations**—"Trials" is more accurate. **to be punished**—The Greek tense indicates ongoing action—"being punished."

➤**10** The first part of this verse could be rendered, "This is especially true of those who follow the corrupt desire of their sinful natures and despise authority" (NIV). The heretics of Peter's day were guilty of inordinate lusts and rebellion against authority (cf. 3:8; Jude 8, 16, 18). **Presumptuous**—Greek, "darers." **not afraid to speak evil of dignities**—lit., "glorious ones" (angels). Jude 8 conveys the same thing.

➤**11 angels . . . bring not railing accusation against them before the Lord**—In the presence of the Lord, the Judge, the angels reverentially abstain from judgment. Judgment belongs to God, not the angels. So the superior angels dare not speak evil even of the bad angels. By contrast, how awful the presumption of those who speak evil of the "glorious ones" (2:10).

➤**12 But**—This is in contrast with the angels (2:11). **as natural brute** [irrational]

**beasts**—They are like animals whose lives are controlled by instinct. **made to be taken** [captured] **and destroyed**—As with animals, their destiny is to be caught and killed. **speak evil of the things that they understood not**—The same idea is found in Jude 10.

➤**13 receive the reward of** [for] **unrighteousness**—They will be recompensed judgment for their unrighteousness. **Spots . . . and blemishes**—They bring blame on the church. **deceivings**—or, deceits (a reading supported by several early manuscripts). Other early manuscripts read, "love feasts." The two Greek words could have easily been confused one for the other: *apatais* ("deceits"), *agapais* ("love feasts"). The expression "love feasts" is used in a parallel passage in Jude 12. The heretics (or, false teachers) Peter has been describing were blemishes on the love feasts of the early churches. Prior to the Lord's Supper, the early churches enjoyed a feast with one another, called a "love feast" (see 1 Cor. 11:21; Jude 12). The false teachers present at such feasts would defile the church because they were full of lust and sin (see 2:14).

➤**14 Having eyes full of adultery**—lit., "having eyes full of an adultress," meaning to desire every woman they see (Blum). The false teachers brought this lust with them into the church meetings (see comments on 2:13). **that cannot cease from sin**—"insatiable for sin" (RSV). **beguiling unstable souls**—alluring (into their traps) unsteady people, people not founded in the truth (cf. 2 Tim. 3:6). **an heart they have exercised with covetous practices**—i.e., "hearts trained in greed" (RSV).

➤**15 the way of Balaam**—is the way of preaching to get money (see Num. 22–24; Deut. 23:4). **loved the wages of unrighteousness**—As a result, Balaam was willing to curse Israel whom God had blessed. And he gave the evil counsel that the only way to bring God's curse on Israel was to entice them to fleshly lust and idolatry (see Num. 31:16; Jude 11; Rev. 2:14).

➤**16 rebuked for his iniquity**—His own beast convicted him of his iniquity (see Num. 22:22ff.). It was not the words of the donkey (for it merely deprecated his beating it), but the miraculous fact of its speaking at all that withstood Balaam's perversity of desiring to go after God had forbidden him. Thus, indirectly

the donkey, and directly the angel rebuked his obstinancy; the donkey turned aside at the sight of the angel, but Balaam, after God had plainly forbade him, persevered in wishing to go for gain. Thus the donkey, in a sense, scolded and rebuked his madness.

➤**17 wells without water**—Their proud boasts are found in trial to be but vanity; promising water, yet yielding none. **clouds**—a reading supported by some early manuscripts and many later ones. The earliest manuscripts read "mists." Mists driven by a tempest is a fit emblem for the children of darkness. **the mist of darkness**—actually, "the gloom of darkness" (cf. 2:4).

➤**18 they speak great swelling words of vanity**—lit., "bombastic words of vanity" (Kelly). **they allure . . . those that were clean** [really] **escaped** [other manuscripts read, "have barely escaped"] **from them who live in error**—Hardly had they escaped from them who live in error when they were lured by the wicked into sin again. The heretics "take for their targets new converts to Christianity from paganism" (Blum).

➤**19 While they promise them liberty, they themselves are the servants of corruption**—The freedom they offer is a bondage, for they are controlled by wanton desires, and "a man is a slave to whatever controls him" (TLB).

➤**20 they**—This could refer to the new converts (2:18) or to the false teachers (also 2:18) or to both (see Kelly, Blum). Whomever Peter had in mind, they had **escaped the pollutions of the world** by coming to know **the Lord and Saviour Jesus Christ,** but then became **entangled** again with the world. Such people are like the soil that received the seed (the gospel message), but then they became entangled with the world and so their growth was choked (see Mark 4:18, 19). **the latter end is worse with them than the beginning**—See Matthew 12:45.

➤**21 the holy commandment**—The commandments themselves do not make one holy, but they should be kept unbroken. **to turn**—The connotation here is of admitting that there is no turning back. **delivered**—passed on—"an important NT term for the transmission of the Christian faith (cf. 1 Cor. 15:3)" (Blum).

➤22 according to the true proverb, The dog is turned to to its own vomit again—The saying concerning the dog comes from Proverbs 26:11; the saying concerning the pig (the sow that was washed to her wallowing in the mire) is extrabiblical. The false teachers "cleaned up on the outside, experiencing an outward moral regeneration, like the sow, went back to their wallowing in the gross forms of sin from which they had been outwardly delivered . . . " (Wuest). Eventually, these people reverted to their real nature (Blum).

Chapter 3

## 1-7 PURPOSE OF THE LETTER

➤1 second epistle—The Second Epistle of Peter, though more general in its address than the first, included especially the same persons to whom the First Epistle of Peter was particularly addressed. stir up your pure minds—See 1:13.

➤2 words . . . spoken before by the holy prophets—See 1:19-21. and of the commandment of us the apostles of the Lord and Saviour—Taken together with the previous statement, Peter was affirming the authority of both the OT (the prophets) and NT (the apostles).

➤3 the last days—This expression characterizes the time period between Christ's first and second comings. scoffers—to which the earliest manuscripts add, "scoffing." walking after their own lusts—Cf. 2:10; Jude 16, 18.

➤4 Where is the promise of his coming?—Cf. Psalm 10:11. all things continue as they were from the beginning of the creation—They set nature and its law above the God of nature and his revelation and argue from the past continuity of nature's phenomena to the conclusion that there can be no further interruption to them. This was the sin of the antediluvians and will also be that of the scoffers in the last days. The scoffers here are not necessarily atheists, nor do they maintain that the world existed from eternity. They are willing to recognize a God, but not a God of revelation. From a seeming delay, they reason against the fulfillment of God's word at all.

➤5 Here begins a refutation of the scoffers' challenge in 3:4. willingly are ignorant of—lit., "this escapes them of their own will" (Alford)—"They deliberately ignore this fact"

(RSV). by the word of God the heavens were of old—God created the heavens by his word (Gen. 1:6). At the same time, he separated the waters by an expanse, so as to make water above and below (see Gen. 1:6, NASB). the earth standing out of the water and in [through] the water—The earth was created by God bringing it out of the water (Gen. 1:2, 6-10). The earth was also sustained by or through the supply of water (Gen. 2:6).

➤6 God would use water also to flood the earth in judgment. the world that then was—referring to the people inhabiting the earth at the time of Noah. being overflowed—being inundated. perished—was destroyed (Gen. 7:23).

➤7 by the same word—that created and that brought the flood; that same word will pronounce judgment by fire. The heavens and earth "are reserved for fire" (NIV).

## 8-14 SURETY OF THE DAY OF THE LORD

➤8 beloved, be not ignorant of this one thing—In addition to the refutation drawn from the history of the deluge (1:5-7), Peter added another point, addressed now to believers. God's delay in fulfilling his promise is not like men's delays because of inability or fickleness. He is, rather, waiting so more sinners will have time to repent (3:9). one day . . . a thousand years—Cf. Psalm 90:4 where Moses says, "A thousand years are but as yesterday to you!" (TLB). Peter viewed God's eternity in relation to the last day; that day seems to us to be long in coming, but with the Lord the interval is neither long nor short. Eternity transcends all measures of time. To his divine knowledge all future things are present. He does not require long delays for the performance of his work. He can do the work of a thousand years in one day. He is not "slow," but always has the power to fulfill his promises.

➤9 slack—or, slow. The term carries connotations of late, tardy, exceeding the due time, as though that time were already come. But God is not dragging, rather he is patiently waiting for people to come to repentance so that they do not have to perish.

➤10 The certainty, suddenness, and concomitant effects of the coming of the day of the Lord are here presented. the day of the Lord—This expression comprehends a whole series of events, beginning with Christ's advent, and ending with the destruction of the wicked, the final judgment. **as a thief in the night**—Peter remembered and repeated his Lord's image (Luke 12:39, 41) used in a conversation in which he took a part (cf. 1 Thess. 5:22; Rev. 3:3, 16:15). **with a great noise**—The language depicts a rushing noise, like that of a whizzing arrow, or the crash of a devouring flame. **the elements shall melt with fervent heat**—See 3:7. **the works that are therein**—i.e., "the works upon the earth" (RSV). **shall be burned up**—This reading is supported by some ancient manuscripts. Two of the earliest manuscripts (Codices Sinaiticus and Vaticanus) read, "will be found out" (i.e., will be exposed). The earliest manuscript (Bodmere Papyrus, P72) reads, "will be found dissolved."

➤11 **dissolved**—See comments on 3:10. **what manner of persons ought ye to be in all holy conversation** [conduct] **and godliness**—Since the earth and everything in it will be dissolved, we must take care of what each one of us will take into eternity—the fruit of a godly and holy life.

➤12 **Looking for and hasting**—The Greek may mean, "hastening the day of God," not that God's eternal appointment of the time is changeable, but that God appoints us as instruments to accomplish those events that must transpire before the day of God can come. By praying for his coming, furthering the preaching of the gospel, and bringing to God those whom he waits to save, we "hurry" the coming of the day of God. **heavens**—Both upper and lower regions of the sky are included. **on fire shall be dissolved**—See 3:7.

➤13 As the flood was the baptism of the earth, eventuating in a renovation, so the baptism with fire shall purify the earth, making it the renovated abode of regenerated man, wholly freed from the curse. **his promise**—See Isaiah 65:17; 66:22. **new heavens**—This suggests a new atmosphere surrounding the renovated earth (Rev. 21:1). **new earth**—See Isaiah 65:17; 66:22; Revelation 21:1. **righteousness**—Righteousness will be the essential feature in that coming world.

➤14 **peace**—God will effect this in its full dimensions. **without spot, and blameless** [blemishless]—See Ephesians 1:4; Jude 24.

## 15-18 THE PURPOSE OF THE LORD'S TARRYING

➤15 **the longsuffering of our Lord is** [for] **salvation**—God has held back Christ's coming so that more people can be saved. **beloved brother Paul**—It is wonderful to see that Peter expressed his love for Paul, even though Paul, on one occasion, severely rebuked Peter (Gal. 2:11ff.). **Paul also ... hath written unto you**—Several of Paul's epistles (Galatians, Ephesians, Colossians) were sent to churches in the same region (see 1 Pet. 1:1).

➤16 **in all his epistles**—The Pauline Epistles had by this time become the common property of all the churches. **hard to be understood**—Though some of Paul's statements are hard to understand, his basic message is clear—at least, to the spiritual man. **unlearned**—These men were not lacking in human learning but in knowledge imparted by the Holy Spirit. The humanly learned have often been deficient in spiritual learning, and they have originated many heresies (cf. 2 Tim. 2:23). **wrest**—twist. The Greek suggests straining and twisting of what is straight in itself (cf. 2 Tim. 2:18). **as ... also the other scriptures**—Paul's epistles were, therefore, by this time recognized in the church as "Scripture." **unto their own destruction**—See 2:1.

➤17 **led away**—This is the term used by Paul of Barnabas's being carried away (Gk., "led away with"), along with Peter and the other Jews, in their hypocrisy (Gal. 2:13). **fall from your own stedfastness** [stability]—The same word is used in 1:12 ("established").

➤18 **grow in grace**—This means grow in the appropriation of grace or grow in your spiritual life by means of grace. **in the knowledge of our Lord and Saviour Jesus Christ**—The knowledge spoken of here is progressive, experiential, and personal; it is knowledge that can grow. We need to grow in our actual, personal knowledge of Jesus Christ; such knowledge is the greatest protection against false teachings. This is the theme of this epistle (see comments on 1:2, 8). **for ever**—Greek, "to an eternal day"—i.e., a day that has no end. **Amen**—This word is not present in the earliest manuscripts.

BIBLIOGRAPHY

Alford, Henry. *The Greek New Testament*. 1852. Reprint. Grand Rapids: Guardian Press, 1976.

Bauckham, Richard J. *Jude, 2 Peter* (in the Word Biblical Commentary series). Waco, Tex.: Word, 1983.

Blum, Edwin A. "Second Peter" in the *Expositor's Bible Commentary*. Grand Rapids: Zondervan, 1981.

Kelly, J. N. D. *A Commentary on the Epistles of Peter and Jude* (in The Harper New Testament Commentaries). New York: Harper & Row, 1969.

Robertson, A. T. *Word Pictures in the New Testament*. Nashville: Broadman Press, 1932.

Wuest, Kenneth. *In These Last Days: Studies in the Greek Text of 11 Peter, 1, 11, 111 John and Jude*. Grand Rapids: Eerdmans, 1954.

# 1 JOHN

## Introduction

Our records of early church history show that the first epistle of John was readily received and recognized as John's writing. Polycarp, the disciple of John (*Epistle to the Philippians,* chap. 7), quotes 4:3. Eusebius (*Ecclesiastical History,* 3.39) says of Papias, a disciple of John and a friend of Polycarp: "He used testimonies from the First Epistle of John." Irenaeus, according to Eusebius (*Ecclesiastical History,* 5.8), often quoted this epistle. So in his work (*Against Heresies,* 3.15.5, 8) Irenaeus quotes from John by name (2:18, etc.); and in 3.16.7, he quotes 4:1-3, 5:1, and 2 John 7, 8. Clement of Alexandria (*Stromata,* 2.66) refers to 5:16. Tertullian in *Against Marcion,* 5.16 refers to 4:1; and in *Against Praxeas,* chapter 15, to 1:1. Cyprian (Epistle 28) quotes 2:3, 4; in *De Oratione Domino 5* he quotes 2:15-17; in *De Opere and Eleemos,* 1:8; and in *De Bene Patientiae 2,* 2:6. The Muratorian Fragment on the Canon shows acceptance of two of John's epistles (probably the first and second). Origen (according to Eusebius's *Ecclesiastical History,* 6.25) spoke of the first epistle as genuine and "probably the second and third, though all do not recognize the latter two." Eusebius (in *Ecclesiastical History,* 3.24) said that John's first epistle and Gospel were acknowledged without question by those of his day, as well as by the ancients. So also Jerome in his *Catalogue of Scriptures.*

The similarities between John's Gospel and John's epistles are so remarkable that no one could doubt that all four of these writings were done by the same person. The syntax, vocabulary, and the thematic developments are so strikingly similar that even the inexperienced reader can tell that John's epistles were penned by the writer of the Gospel of John. One reason for this similarity in style is that John probably wrote the epistles shortly after he compiled his Gospel. The Gospel was written c. A.D. 90, and all three epistles were written most likely c. A.D. 90-95. (See introduction to the Gospel of John.)

Many scholars think that John wrote these epistles to certain local churches in Asia—especially to those around Ephesus, the church in which John functioned as an elder in his latter days. (The same churches probably include those mentioned in Rev. 1:11.) One of the reasons that prompted his first epistle was that a heretical faction had developed within the church, a faction that promoted heretical teachings concerning the person of Christ. Scholars have identified this heresy as Docetism generally and pointed specifically to Cerinthus as the perpetrator of the specific brand of Docetism. The Docetists denied that Jesus had actually partaken of flesh and blood; they denied that God had come in the flesh (see 4:1-3). According to Irenaeus, Cerinthus "represented Jesus as having not been born of a virgin, but as being the son of Joseph and Mary according to the ordinary course of human generation, while he nevertheless was more righteous, prudent, and wise than other men. Moreover, after his baptism, Christ descended upon him in the form of a dove from the Supreme Ruler, and that then he proclaimed the unknown Father, and performed miracles. But at last Christ departed from Jesus, and that then Jesus suffered and rose again, while Christ remained impassible, inasmuch as he was a spiritual being" (*Contra Haereses*, 3.4). John refuted the Cerinthian heresy in 5:5-8 (see comments there).

The heretical faction within the church (or, churches) John was addressing eventually left the fellowship—and, in so doing, exposed the reality that they did not genuinely belong to God's family (2:18, 19). But their false teachings still lingered in the minds of the faithful; so John wrote to clear the air of all the falsehoods and bring the believers back to pure beginning of the gospel and to the basics of the Christian life. John urged his readers (1) to have fellowship with God in the light, (2) to confess their sins, (3) to love God, (4) to love their fellow Christians, (5) to abide in Christ, (6) to purify themselves from worldly lusts, (7) to know God personally and experientially, (8) to appreciate the gift of eternal life, (9) to follow the Spirit of truth (and the anointing) in discerning false teachings, and (10) to esteem Jesus Christ as the true God. Above all these items, John stressed how necessary it was for the early believers to maintain a proper relationship with those who had been with Jesus. In the prologue (1:1-4) to this epistle, he invites all the believers to participate in the one apostolic fellowship. Fellowship is a two-way, simultaneous experience: with fellow believers and with God. This is to safeguard against pseudo-spirituality and extreme individualism. Throughout this epistle, it appears that John addressed his comments to those who were claiming to have a relationship with God and yet had left the fellowship of believers and did not love their brothers in Christ.

John's first epistle has a very unusual thematic structure. Tenney said, "First John is symphonic rather than logical in plan; it is constructed like a piece of music rather than like a brief for a debate. Instead of proceeding step by step in unfolding a subject, as Paul does in Romans, John selects a theme, maintains it throughout the book, and introduces a series of variations, any one of which may be a theme in itself."

*Chapter* **1**

### 1-4 INTRODUCTION: AN INVITATION TO PARTICIPATION IN THE NEW TESTAMENT FELLOWSHIP

➤**1-4** When John opened his gospel, he fondly recollected how he (and the other disciples, for whom he was a spokesman) beheld the Son's glory, the glory as of a unique Son from the Father (1:14). And then he picturesquely described the unique Son, himself

God, dwelling on the Father's bosom (1:18). The opening of John's first epistle also contains a personal testimony, which reads as follows:

That which was from the beginning, [that] which we have heard, [that] which we have seen with our eyes, [that] which we have looked upon, and our hands have handled, of [concerning] the Word of life; (For [indeed] the life was manifested, and we have seen it, and bear witness and show [announce] unto you that eternal life, which was [face to face] with the Father, and was manifested unto us;) that which we have seen and heard declare [announce] we [also] unto you, that ye also may have fellowship with us: and truly our fellowship is with the Father, and with his Son Jesus Christ. And these things write we unto you, that your ["our"—in the earliest manuscripts] joy may be full.

The first words may strike us as odd. Instead of saying, "*He who* was from the beginning," "*he whom* we have seen," etc., he said **That which was from the beginning,** etc. John probably did this because the relative pronoun is more inclusive; it encompasses everything concerning the Word of life, everything pertaining to (Gk., *peri*) the Word of life from the beginning. It includes the Word's person and his work. It must also include that eternal fellowship that existed between the Word and the Father. (Note: as in John 1:1, the Greek text suggests that the Word was "face to face with" the Father.) The Word of life, who was face to face with the Father, was manifested to the disciples. John heard, saw, beheld, and even handled God in the flesh (John 1:14). At the same time, John came to know the One called "eternal life" (see John 1:4; 11:25; 14:6), who was always with the Father, in fellowship with him.

When the Son entered into time, his fellowship with the Father also entered into time. Thus, to have heard Jesus was to have heard the Father speaking in the Son (John 14:10, 24), to have seen Jesus was to have seen the Father (John 14:8-10), and to have known Jesus was to have known him who was one with the Father (John 10:30, 38). During the days of his ministry, Jesus was introducing the Father to the disciples and initiating them into this fellowship. Then once the disciples were regenerated by the eternal life, they actually entered into fellowship with the Father and the Son. Having been brought into this participation, the apostles became the new initiators— introducing this fellowship to others and encouraging them to enter into fellowship with them. Whoever would enter into the fellowship with the apostles would actually be entering into their fellowship with the Father and the Son. Thus, the unique fellowship

between the Father and the Son began in eternity, was manifest in time through the incarnation of the Son, was introduced to the apostles, and then through the apostles was extended to each and every believer. When a person becomes a son of God (through the regeneration of the Holy Spirit), he enters into this one ageless, universal fellowship—a fellowship springing from the Godhead, coursing through the apostles, and flowing through every genuine believer who has ever been or will ever be. This is the fellowship that John was inviting his readers to participate in. Their participation in this fellowship would give John (including the community with him) and his readers fullness of joy. (The earliest manuscripts read "our joy," while later manuscripts read "your joy." "Our joy" means "the joy of us all"—John and the readers.)

## 5-10 WALKING IN THE LIGHT

➤**5 This then is the message which we have heard of him**—Just as Christ passed on the message he heard from the Father, so the apostles in turn are passing on the same message, that they heard from the Son. John did not use the term "gospel," but he did use such words as "witness" or "testimony," "word," "truth," and "message." **God is light**—Just as physical life and growth depend on light, so spiritual life and growth are impossible apart from God, the true light (see 2:8). The expression "God is light," said Vincent,

is a statement of the absolute nature of God. Not *a* light, nor *the* light, with reference to created beings, as *the light of men, the light of the world,* but simply and absolutely, *God is light,* in His very nature. . . . The expression is not a metaphor. . . . Light is immaterial, diffusive, pure and glorious. It is the condition of life. Physically, it represents *glory;* intellectually, *truth;* morally, *holiness.* As immaterial it corresponds to God as *spirit;* as diffusive, to God as *love;* as the condition of life, to God as *life;* as pure and illuminating, to God as *holiness* and *truth.*

**and in him is no darkness at all**—or, "No, not even one speck of darkness." Hebrews 1:3 asserts that God's Son shines out with God's glory or brightness. Every word and deed of

Christ's life on earth reflected this pure light of God.

➤**6 If we say that we have fellowship with him, and walk in darkness, we lie**—We cannot live both in the darkness of sin and in the light of fellowship with God, in whom is "no darkness at all." Our lives of holiness and love must back up our claim of having fellowship with God.

➤**7 But if we walk**—speaking of a constant, daily, habitual living—**in the light, as he is in the light**—Alford notes that this is not merely imitating God but growing more like him in character. **we have fellowship one with another**—Most commentators say that this fellowship is the fellowship among believers that results from each believer having fellowship with God. In other words, the natural result of living in the light, in fellowship with God, is a joyful relationship with other Christians. **the blood of Jesus** ["Christ" is not present in the earliest manuscripts] **his Son cleanseth us from all** [every] **sin**—This is a continual cleansing from daily sins that issue from our fallen natures as we live in the world under constant attack from Satan. It is the blood of Jesus, shed on the cross, which cleansed us completely and brought us into fellowship with God; now the same blood of Jesus keeps us clean from all sin that would mar that fellowship. (See comments on John 13:10.)

➤**8 that we have no sin**—"Have" refers not to the sinful life before conversion but to the present experience of the believer, who must still struggle against his sinful nature. Augustine observed that confession of sin is a sign that truth, which is itself light, has already begun to illuminate our sin-darkened lives. **we deceive ourselves**—We certainly cannot fool God, but by refusing to admit our sin we can cheat ourselves of fellowship with him. **the truth**—that we are sinful and God is holy.

➤**9 If we confess our sins**—Confession of sins is necessary for maintaining continual fellowship with God. **he is faithful**—We can depend on God to be true to his word and to his promises to forgive us. **and just**—He acts on the basis of his justice, not on the basis of how we think he feels about us. Christ has satisfied God's righteous demands on us, so that now

God is bound to forgive all who believe in his Son. We can depend on this. **forgive us our sins**—or, remit (lit., "send away") our sins. **cleanse**—purify us from sin's filthiness, so that we become more and more free from the presence of sin in our lives. **from all unrighteousness**—or, from every unrighteous act.

➤**10 we have not sinned**—This verse parallels 11:8, except that here the focus is on the actual acts of sin growing out of our sinful nature. **we make him a liar**—Cf. 1:6, "we lie" and 1:8, "we deceive ourselves." **his word is not in us**—See 2:14; cf. John 8:55; 10:35; 17:6, 14, 17.

Chapter **2**

## 1, 2 JESUS IS THE PROPITIATION FOR OUR SINS

➤**1 My little children**—This expresses the tender affection of a father for his own children, so that the phrase could read, "My own dear children." **that ye sin not**—or, "not sin at all" (according to the Gk.). In order to "walk in the light" (1:5, 7), the first step is to confess sin (1:9), and the second is to forsake all sin (2:1). John emphasized our sinfulness in chapter 1 in order to make us despise our sin and try to stay free from it. **And if any man sin**—since we are all liable to occasional sins. We should not condone these sins, but while condemning them we should not fear to confess them to God, since **we have an advocate with** [Gk. *pros*]—the same preposition used in 1:2, "face to face with." **the Father**—The term "advocate" is a translation of the Greek word *parakletos* (lit., "paraclete"). The word means "one who is called to our side." This could be a comforter, a consoler, or a defense attorney—an advocate. In John 14:26 and 15:26, the Holy Spirit is called our *parakletos,* our comforter. Here, Christ is called our *parakletos,* our advocate. While the Holy Spirit works within us to comfort and help us, Christ represents us before the Father in heaven. The two Paracletes work together in perfect harmony (cf. Rom. 8:26, 27, 34). **Jesus Christ the righteous**—Christ's righteousness stands in contrast to our sinfulness. Because Christ fulfilled the law and paid sin's penalty for us, he can plead for us on the basis of justice as well as mercy. When God raised Christ from the dead, he accepted once for all Christ's plea for our acquittal (see Rom. 4:23-25). As Luther exclaimed, "The righteousness of Christ stands on our side; for God's righteousness is, in Jesus Christ, ours."

➤**2 he is the propitiation**—The Greek word is *hilasmos,* the noun form of the verb *hilaskomai,* which in classical Greek meant "to appease" but in the NT means "to atone" or "to expiate." Westcott said, "The scriptural conception of the verb is not that of appeasing one who is angry with a personal feeling against the offender, but of altering the character of that which, from without, occasions a necessary alienation, and interposes an inevitable obstacle to fellowship. Such phrases as 'propitiating God,' and 'God being reconciled' are foreign to the language of the New Testament." First John 4:10 says that God demonstrated his love to us by sending his Son to become "the propitiation for our sins." Just as in the OT God met his people when the blood of the sin offering was sprinkled on the altar, so Christ's death brought us into fellowship with God. Our fellowship with God is always based solidly on the *fact* of Christ's atoning death for us. **and not for ours only, but also for the sins of the whole world**—John was reminding all believers that Christ's atoning sacrifice is sufficient for the sins of every person in the world. Luther brings this point home: "Thou, too, art part of the world, so that thine heart cannot deceive itself and think, The Lord died for Peter and Paul, but not for me."

## 3-11 A NEW COMMANDMENT: LOVE ONE ANOTHER

➤**3 hereby we do know that we know him**—Greek, "by this we come to experientially know that we have experientially known him" (see Wuest). Our knowledge of Christ must be personal, experiential, and practical—not just theoretical. Practical knowledge of Christ has practical application in our daily walk (as John is about to assert). "To know about Christ, to understand the doctrine of His person and work is mere theory; we get to know Him and to know that we know Him by practice of His precepts" (Smith). **if we keep his commandments**—In this letter John lists several proofs that we know Christ and belong to him. Here he insists that obedience is one

clear indication. John does not mean that we should follow a list of rules without one slip, but that we should wholeheartedly accept and submit to God's will as he has shown it to us in his word.

➤**4** This verse illustrates the principle set out in 2:3. If we do not obey Christ, it is obvious that we do not belong to him.

➤**5** Here obedience is linked not merely with knowing God but with loving him. As we obey Christ, our love and knowledge will grow together toward completeness and maturity. **hereby know we that we are in him**—By our progress toward this perfect love and obedience we will know that we are living in union with Christ.

➤**6** Again, we are told that our actions must be consistent with our words. **ought . . . to walk**—i.e., should live. **as he walked**—i.e., as he lived. Christ's life on earth, demonstrating his love for others, is held up as our model and example.

➤**7 Brethren**—The earliest manuscripts read "Beloved," which fits in well with the theme of love. **no new commandment . . . but an old commandment**—This commandment is to love one another (3:11), the main principle of living as Christ lived (2:6). This commandment is laid out more explicitly in 2:9, 10. **ye had from the beginning**—from the time the disciples first heard Jesus' command to love one another (John 13:34).

➤**8 a new commandment**—The commandment of love is new and different from the old system of the law. (The Greek word for "new," *kainē*, designates what is new in quality, not in time.) Although the inner spirit of the law was love, and Christ asserted that love fulfilled the law, still the emphasis in the law was on outward conformity to certain regulations. The Christian rule of love is new because love to others is motivated by our love to Christ, who first loved us. We are able to love even our enemies because we realize that Christ loved us when we were his enemies. Jesus called this the *new* commandment in John 13:34, 35; 15:12. **which thing** [fact] **is true in him and in you**—"The expression 'which thing' indicates the love which is enjoined by the commandment. That it is *true* signifies that it receives its fulfillment, is made good. It was (and is) true **in him**—as not only had the commandment been given by Him but it had also been exhibited in His example. It is also true in the children of God because it is to be received and fulfilled by them" (Vine). The new commandment of love finds concrete expression in the daily life of the believer in union with Christ. This love was first shown by Christ in his life on earth, and it is only because he first fulfilled the commandment of love that we can now fulfill it. **because the darkness is past** [is passing], **and the true light now shineth** [already shines]— "Although 'the true light' is already shining, the darkness has not passed completely away; it is in process of 'passing away.' Thanks to the victory of Christ, the outcome of the conflict between light and darkness is a foregone conclusion, but the conflict is still going on. Hence the tension of Christian life in the present world, a tension reflected throughout this epistle, not to say throughout the whole New Testament" (Bruce).

➤**9** In these next few verses, notice the absolute contrast drawn between light and darkness, love and hate, God and the world. Luke 9:50 and 11:23 remind us that we are either *for* or *against* God. As Bengel warned, "Where love is not, there hatred is, for the heart cannot remain a void." To hate one's brother is an indication that such a person never came into the light; **He . . . is in darkness even until now.**

➤**10** Living in love is living in the light, since the gospel both illuminates our minds and warms our hearts to love. **none occasion of stumbling in him**—i.e., "there is nothing in him that will cause someone else to sin" (TEV). He who hates his brother is both a stumbling block to himself and also causes others to stumble (Bengel). John had in mind Jesus' words in John 11:9, 10.

➤**11 walketh** [lives] **in darkness**—This refers to both his *state* of being in a darkness he has never come out of and also to his *outward actions* that reflect that darkness. **knoweth not whither he goeth**—i.e., he does not perceive the final destination and therefore the way to get there. **that darkness hath blinded his eyes**— The darkness has not only surrounded him, it blinded him long ago.

## 12-19 A WORD TO THE FATHERS, YOUNG MEN, AND CHILDREN

➤**12 little children**—a general term, with no reference to age but rather to John's love for those to whom he writes. Christ spoke the same phrase to his disciples in John 13:33. **your sins are** [have been] **forgiven**—All of God's children alike enjoy this forgiveness.

➤**13** In 2:13 and 14 John addresses three different classes among his readers, and his remarks are appropriate for each group (see comments on 2:18). He speaks to the older men as knowing Christ, having a knowledge befitting their maturity. Perhaps many had known Jesus in person as well as by faith. The young men are described with a more active term, as having overcome (or, conquered) the enemy. The young children (here the word does denote age) are seen in relation to God as their Father, whom of course they could know only through the Son (Matt. 11:27).

➤**14** This verse first repeats the message of 2:13 to the fathers and then amplifies the message to the young men. **have known**— have come to know experientially. **him that is from the beginning**—i.e., Christ, the eternal Word of life (1:1, 2). Notice that John now speaks of "him [who was] from the beginning," and not "that which was from the beginning" (as in 1:1). **young men . . . are strong, and the word of God abideth in you, and ye have overcome** [conquered] **the wicked one**—This strength is not the natural physical vigor of young men but the power of God's Word in them through the Holy Spirit (Isa. 40:30, 31). They can enjoy this power and this victory over Satan, John goes on to affirm, only by freeing themselves from the grasp of the evil things of the world. Since Satan is in control of the world (5:19), believers must constantly guard against his assaults by becoming saturated with God's word (see John 17:15-17). John may have been referring particularly to the steadfastness of the young people under Domitian's persecution. He may also have had in mind one young man whom he brought to repentance and watched over until his baptism. However, as several early church historians wrote, the young man joined wicked friends and eventually became captain of a band of robbers. Years later John heard of the youth's fall and visited the captain, who remorsefully ran from him. John pursued him, reminding him that his sins were forgiven through Christ. The young man not only returned to Christianity but also persuaded several of his robber friends to repent and believe.

➤**15 Love not the world**—which is under the power of Satan, whom the young men have overcome. Having already won the fight (4:4), they are to continue their victory by not being trapped into loving the world. **neither the things that are in the world**—This statement would convict any man who denies that he loves the world but cares keenly about some particular thing the world offers, such as riches, honors, or pleasures. **If any man love the world, the love of the Father is not in him**—God and the sinful world are such opposites that it is impossible to love both at once.

➤**16 all that is in the world**—can be put into one of three categories. **the lust of the flesh**—any kind of fleshly desire, but especially "the craze for sex" (TLB), to which young people are particularly liable. **the lust of the eyes**—Satan tempted Christ this way by showing him all the kingdoms of the world. Achan was guilty of this sin (Josh. 7:21). **the pride of life**—or, "the pride in possessions." "Many commentators have noted that the three evils mentioned here were the elements in Satan's temptation both of Eve (Gen. 3) and of our Lord (Luke 4)" (see Vine).

➤**17 the world passeth away**—lit., "is passing away" (see comments on 2:8). **and the lust thereof**—in its threefold manifestation (2:16). **he that doeth the will of God**—as opposed to satisfying the evil desires listed above. **abideth for ever**—just as God lives for ever (Cyprian). In contrast to the three evil desires of the world, which are already fading away, the one who does God's will remains forever united to God.

➤**18 Little children**—This begins the second address to the third group of God's family. The first address is in 2:13. The second address contains a repeated word to the fathers (2:14), an extended word to the young men (2:14b-17), and an exhortation to the children (2:18). **it is the last time**—Greek, "it is a last hour." The *NIVSB* provides a good explanation on this term:

> With other NT writers, John viewed the whole period beginning with Christ's first coming as the last days (see Acts 2:17; 2 Tim. 3:1; Heb. 1:2; 1 Pet. 1:20). They understood this to be the "last" of the days because nei-

ther former prophecy nor new revelation concerning the history of salvation indicated the coming of another era before the return of Christ. The word "last" in "last days," "last times" and "last hour" also expresses a sense of urgency and imminence. The Christian is to be alert, waiting for the return of Christ (Matt. 25:1-13).

➤**as ye have heard**—from the apostles (for example, see 2 Thess. 2:3-10). **that antichrist shall come**—lit., "that Antichrist is coming." The Antichrist is the one who is "instead of Christ" (lit.); he claims to himself what belongs to Christ and poses as a substitute for Christ. The person called "Antichrist" is perhaps the same as "the man of lawlessness" in 2 Thessalonians 2:3 and "the beast" in Revelation 13:1-10. **are there many antichrists**—Greek, "many antichrists have arisen," as precursors to the one Antichrist. These many antichrists are the false teachers who deny (1) that Jesus is the Christ (2:22), (2) that Jesus is God's Son (2:23), and (3) that Jesus was God manifest in the flesh (4:2; 2 John 7). They are deceivers and liars.

➤**19 They went out from us**—As Augustine commented, it is a relief to the church when members who have already left the truth and cut themselves off from spiritual fellowship finally leave publicly. But not until the resurrection will the church be completely free of such people. **they were not of us**—They did not really belong in God's family. **they would . . . have continued with us**—if they had ever actually belonged to the church and to Christ. True believers will choose to remain or persevere (Calvin). Augustine asserts that each person must choose either to be in Christ or to be an antichrist. We cannot completely understand the way God's election harmonizes with man's free will. Man's own evil will chooses the way to hell, and each man will have only himself to blame for his destiny; while God's grace brings people to himself, apart from their own merit. **might be made manifest that they were not all of us**—Their departure from the fellowship showed that "not one of them ever belonged to us" (JB). False teaching, while not desirable, tests those who belong to Christ and those who do not (1 Cor. 11:19).

## 20-27 THE ANOINTING OF THE SPIRIT

➤**20 an unction**—i.e., "an anointing" (same word used in 2:27). The reason Christians can withstand the false teachers' attacks is they have the **anointing.**—The term "anointing" describes the impartation of the Holy Spirit (see Isa. 61:1; Acts 10:38; 2 Cor. 1:21, 22). As Christians, now indwelt by the Holy Spirit, we are joined to Christ, "the Anointed One" and share in his anointing (2 Cor. 1:21, 22). Therefore, we can know all things with respect to truth and falsehood. We know all that we need to know in order to resist the temptations of false teachers and to live godly lives.

➤**21 ye know**—The Greek word indicates absolute knowledge. **no lie is of the truth**—You not only know the truth about the Father and the Son, but you can also detect what is false, what does not measure up to the standard of the truth you know.

➤**22 Who is a liar but he that denieth Jesus is the Christ?**—The great central truth of all truth is that *Jesus is the Christ,* the Son of God. To deny this is blatant heresy. Cerinthus, an avowed enemy of John the apostle, denied that Jesus was the Christ. He spoke of "Jesus" and "the Christ" as two separate beings who were united only from the time of Jesus' baptism to the time he was crucified—at which point, Cerinthus said, "the Christ" left Jesus (see Introduction and comments on 5:5-8). **He is antichrist, that denieth the Father and the Son**—The essence of the antichristian spirit is denial that Jesus is Christ. Those who reject the Son can never know the Father, since the Father is known only by the Son (Matt. 11:27).

➤**23 Whosoever denieth the Son, the same hath not the Father**—since, as Calvin remarked, God gave himself to us completely in Christ. See Colossians 2:9, 10—"For in Christ there is all of God in a human body; so you have everything when you have Christ, and you are filled with God through your union with Christ" (TLB). The second clause in the KJV is italicized because the words were not present in the Greek text underlying the KJV. But this second clause is, in fact, present in all the earliest Greek manuscripts. **acknowledgeth**—Greek, "confesses."

➤**24 Let that therefore abide in you, which ye have heard**—The truth they heard about the Father and the Son should be like a seed not merely dropped in, but actually taking root in their lives (3:9). **from the beginning**—the time you first heard the gospel. **ye also shall continue in the Son, and in the Father**—By clinging to the truth about God the Father and Christ his Son, we can be sure we will never be separated from fellowship with God, and we will gradually become more like Christ.

➤**25 promise that he hath promised us**—See John 3:15, 36; 6:40, 47, 57; 17:2, 3 for examples of promises related to eternal life. **eternal life**—Our new life of belonging to Christ is only the beginning of a joyful, never-ending fellowship with him.

➤**26 These things have I written unto you concerning them**—As in 2:12-14 and 21, John took pains to make clear his purpose in writing and to affirm the practical importance of his teachings. **seduce you**—lit., "lead you astray"—into error, away from what they had been taught from the beginning (2:24).

➤**27 the anointing . . . abideth in you**—This resumes John's thought in 2:20. The active, indwelling presence of the Holy Spirit is the anointing that abides in us. **ye need not that any man teach you**—Christians can tell the lying antichrists, "We do not need another teacher, because the Holy Spirit, the Spirit of truth, is our teacher; so we will remain in Christ and in what he has taught us" (cf. Jer. 13:34; John 6:45; 16:13). This does not mean a Christian will turn away from the counsel of faithful ministers, but he will be able to discern and reject what is false (2:21). The better we know the truth, the more easily will we be able to identify a lie. **teacheth you of all things**—essential for salvation and concerning the basic NT truths. The point here is not that a believer will know and understand everything, since his mind is finite and fallible, but rather that through the Spirit he knows enough to keep him from throwing away his faith in Christ and believing the lies of the false teachers. **even as it hath taught you, ye shall abide in him**—The primary function of the Holy Spirit is to teach us to abide in Christ.

## 2:28–3:10 THE CHILDREN OF GOD AND THE CHILDREN OF THE DEVIL

➤**28 little children, abide in him**—John repeated this command still another time, and the term of endearment reveals how deep was his loving concern for these Christians. He was so anxious for their spiritual lives that he said over and over, "Abide [or, remain] in him; don't let anyone lead you away from him." **he shall appear**—Greek, "he shall be manifested." Although we already have fellowship with Christ through his indwelling Spirit, a time is coming when we will see him face to face, in all his glory (3:2). **we may have confidence and not be ashamed before him at his coming**—This is in contrast with 4:17 (see comments there). John's statement implies that Christ may come at any time, so we must always be ready.

➤**29 he is righteous**—i.e., God is just—in giving men proper standards of behavior, keeping his promises, rewarding men for good deeds, and punishing them for evil. **every one that doeth righteousness is** [has been] **born of him**—John's logic here is: God is righteous, and therefore he is the source of righteousness. If a man's actions demonstrate his righteousness, we know he acquired this righteousness from God by being given a new nature. Instead of believing, as did the Pelagians, that we become children of God by doing right, John said that doing right is a sign that we have already become God's children—since we cannot do right on our own.

## Chapter 3

➤**1 Behold**—John is here calling attention to the wonderful fact, carried over from the last verse (2:29), that God has actually begotten us as his children. **what manner of**—in Greek is *potapēn*, "from what country, race or tribe?" The word speaks of something foreign. The translation could read, "Behold, what foreign kind of love the Father has bestowed upon us." The love of God is foreign to the human race. It is not found naturally in humanity (Wuest). Smith suggests, "from what far realm? What unearthly love . . . how other-worldly." **hath bestowed**—has given. **sons of God**—Greek, "children of God," ones born of God—the word emphasizes birth rather than infancy. After these words, the Greek text has the words, "and we are." God gives us both the title

and the reality; when he *calls us* his children, that is what he *makes us* to be. Great as he is, God has brought us into the loving, intimate relationship of children with their Father. **because it knew him not**—or, it did not recognize him. The world is determined not to know God, and it even refused to recognize Christ as God's Son (John 1:10), so we can hardly expect it to understand our special relationship with God as his children.

➤**2 Beloved**—or, "loved ones." Because God loved us, we love one another. **now**—in contrast to "later on." Even though the world does not recognize us as God's children, it is true right now, so we are looking forward to the time when God will publicly announce that we belong to him. **sons of God**—Greek, "children of God" (see comments on 3:1). **it doth not yet appear what we shall be**—John is here saying that something inconceivably wonderful is waiting for us, even more glorious than what we now have as God's children. **but we know**—We already have a hint of what this future glory will be like, though the world is completely ignorant of it, and this is what we know already: Christ will be revealed to us and in us in all his glory, as the very likeness of God (2 Cor. 4:4), and we will be like him. In the same way believers will be revealed to the world as God's children, sharing in Christ's glory and beauty. Since we have been born into God's family, we enjoy God's kindness and blessings through Christ; but the time is coming when we will also fully share in his glory. What a contrast there is between the fall of the human race through Adam's sin and the restoration of humanity through Jesus Christ! Eve's and Adam's desire to know as much as God (Gen. 3:5-7) showed sinful pride, but through Christ we will finally know him as well as he knows us and see him as he truly is. Since Adam, we have all been slaves to sin and death, but soon they will be conquered completely and will never harm us again. The devil fell by trying to get God's power; man fell by wanting God's knowledge; but if we desire God's goodness, we will grow more and more like him. **we shall be like him**—By constantly gazing at Christ, we will become like him and reflect his glory (see 2 Cor. 3:17, 18). **see him as he is**—The Greek word for "see" involves more than a merely physiological occurrence;

it means "perceiving," "recognizing," even "appreciating" (Tittmann).

➤**3 And every man that hath this hope**— i.e., the hope that he will be like Christ. **purifieth himself**—We can do this only through Christ's Spirit in us, since as Jesus said, "Without me ye can do nothing" (John 15:5). God himself is making us pure so that he can live within us. **even as he is pure**—completely spotless, free from any stain of sin.

➤**4** Sin is incompatible with the new nature derived from the new birth. John here presents negatively the same truth he expressed positively in 3:1-3. Since being born of God demands self-purification, then a life of sin, or a continual lack of purity, is evidence that one is not really God's child. **committeth sin**—lit., "doing sin," in contrast with "doing righteousness" (3:7). **for sin is the transgression of the law**—Here is a basic definition of sin. The Greek word for sin means "missing the mark," and God's law is this mark or standard that we aim at and miss. If God had not told us what we should be like, we would never have realized how sinful we are. We notice how crooked a line is when it is put next to a straight ruler.

➤**5** This verse lists still another proof that sin and sonship are incompatible: children of God do not keep on sinning. **he was manifested to take away our sins**—This was the whole purpose for Christ's becoming a man, and he fulfilled the OT picture of the scapegoat by taking away our sins once for all. **in him is no sin**—present tense, like 3:3, "he *is* pure," and 3:7, "he *is* righteous." Therefore we are to be so.

➤**6** John now reasons that since Christ is completely free from sin, those who belong to him will also stay away from sin. **abideth in him**—or, "remains in him," as a branch lives in the vine, drawing its life from the vine. **sinneth not**—"is not [continually] sinning." As much as we live in Christ is as much as we will be free from sin. This complete union with Christ and complete separation from sin is the ideal of the Christian. Living in sin and living in God are mutually exclusive, like darkness and light. Believers actually do fall into sin (1:8-10; 2:1, 2), but these sins do not come from, or belong to, our life in Christ. We do not sin as long as we are living in Christ. **whosoever sinneth**—Greek, "everyone who keeps on sin-ning." **hath not seen him, neither known him**—John was again presenting the ideal. He was not saying that one who sins even once has never known God; but he insists that as far as we continue in sin, to that degree we do not know God.

➤**7** Verses 7, 8 repeat the same truth, with the addition that as far as we sin, so far we still belong to Satan. **he that doeth righteousness is righteous, even as he is righteous**—It is not doing righteousness that makes us righteous, but rather our righteousness imputed to us by Christ that naturally leads to doing righteous acts. In the same way, a tree that bears good fruit is a good tree; it is not that the fruit makes the tree good, but it shows that it is good.

➤**8 He that committeth sin**—Greek, "He that is doing [practicing] sin." **is of the devil**—"The Devil is the source of sin, and therefore the one who leads a sinful life is spiritually connected with him" (Vine). It is in this sense that the person who continually sins belongs to the devil. The devil cannot create or produce children, but men become children of the devil by imitating him. **the devil sinneth from the beginning**—The devil sinned even before the creation of the world; and ever since, as the prince of this world, he has been both sinning and causing men to sin. **destroy**—to break down (see Eph. 2:14), to undo. **the works of the devil**—sin, and all its awful consequences. John argued that Christians cannot be involved in what Christ came to destroy.

➤**9 Whosoever is born of God doth not commit sin** [does not keep practicing sin]; **for his seed** [i.e., God's life] **remaineth in him: and he cannot sin** [is not able to sin] **because he is born of God**—When we are "born again," a new life is born within us. The new life or nature which is "born of God" does not sin and is entirely incompatible with sin. It gives us a hatred for sin, and though at times we may give in to sin, we are continually fighting against it. Sin is still active, but it no longer has complete control over us. The normal direction of a Christian's life is against sin and toward God; the new nature is not in control, although the old sinful nature is not yet completely dead and still causes us to sin occasionally. The Holy Spirit works, through the word of God, to sanctify us or to make us holy and pure, as Christ is (3:3). (See 5:18.)

➤**10 the children of God . . . the children of the devil**—As was noted earlier, there is no middle ground: we belong either to God or to the devil. **doeth not righteousness is not of God**—See 2:29; 3:7. **neither he that loveth not his brother**—The presence or absence of brotherly love is a sure way to tell a true child of God from a pretender.

11-24 LOVE ONE ANOTHER

➤**11 the message**—This is not a command, as in the old system of the law, but an announcement of something good. The message announced to us from God is that we are to love our brothers in God's family, who are fellow children of God.

➤**12 Not as Cain, who was of that wicked one, and slew his brother . . . Because his own works were evil, and his brother's righteous**—Cain's murder of his brother was caused by envy and hatred of his brother's righteous life. Even then there was a clear division between God's children, those who chose to love and obey him, and Satan's children, those who deliberately defied and rejected God.

➤**13 Marvel not**—The surprise would be if the world did love Christians. **the world**—represented by Cain (3:12). **hate you**—as Cain hated his own brother enough to murder him. The world hates us because it can see the difference between our godly lives and its own evil.

➤**14 we have passed from death unto life**—This radical change is also described in Colossians 1:13. **because we love the brethren**—Our love does not cause us to have eternal life, but it is evidence that we already have it. We must each ask ourselves if we have this love; if we do, then we can be sure that we have eternal life, and that this will be publicly revealed when Christ comes. **abideth in death**—This is the condition we are all in by nature, and one who does not have love shows that he has not passed from death to life.

➤**15 hateth**—This is the same as "loveth not" (3:14); there is no middle ground. Love and hatred, light and darkness, life and death: if we have one, we necessarily lack the other. **is a murderer**—If we hate someone, we wish he were dead, and God sees the inner desire as equal to the outward act that would result from it. **no murderer hath eternal life**—This statement is in the present tense, not the future. He is spiritually dead now, for his hatred is proof that he does not have God's life.

➤**16 he laid down his life for us**—Christ's example shows us that real love involves self-sacrifice which, as 3:17-19 points out, must result in self-sacrificial actions. **we ought to lay down our lives for the brethren**—We do this by becoming truly concerned about the needs of our Christian brothers, and by unselfishly giving time, effort, prayer, and possessions to supply those needs. Such an attitude would result in actually dying for a brother if this were ever necessary. Our lives should not be more precious to us than God's own Son was to him.

➤**17 whoso hath this world's good** [life's possessions]—If we are to give our very lives for our brothers, we certainly should not hold back money or anything we own. **seeth**—not glancing casually, but deliberately beholding. **shutteth up his bowels of compassion**—in modern idiom, "closes his heart" (RSV). **how dwelleth the love of God in him?**—If we respond in love to God's love for us, we will put our neighbor's needs before our own comforts or luxuries.

➤**18** Jerome said that even when John was very old and had to be carried to the church meetings, he continued to remind the believers of Christ's command: "My little children, love one another." The brothers grew tired of always hearing the same instruction, but John insisted that this was the command of the Lord (see John 13:34), and that if we could attain just this one thing, it would be enough.

➤**19 hereby we know that we are of the truth**—We will know that "the truth is the source from whence spring our thoughts, motives, and conduct" (Vine) when we love in deed and in reality. **and shall assure our hearts**—If we are demonstrating love by our actions, we will not constantly be wondering whether God will accept us. **before him**—We are always before the Lord, since he sees and knows our hearts. A confident assurance that God accepts us should be the ordinary, daily experience of the believer.

➤**20** This verse is ambiguous in the original Greek and has been interpreted in two ways. Some see it as consoling the believer whose heart (or, conscience) accuses him of sin in general, since he has the one sign of sonship, love. Peter, for example, remorseful because he had betrayed Christ, could only say, "Lord, you know all things, you know I love you" (John 21:17). Others believe that the phrase "God is greater than our hearts" intensifies John's warning. The condemning voice of our conscience merely echoes the judgment of God, who knows our lives better than we do. Thus we cannot gloss over or excuse our sin as insignificant. Either way—by claiming God's forgiveness through Christ, we can come confidently to God, recognizing that his grace and mercy are greater than our guilt.

➤21 If our hearts do not condemn us, we have confidence (or, boldness) to approach God. John was not speaking to anyone whose conscience does not accuse him, since some deaden their consciences by continual, deliberate sin (1 Tim. 4:2)—he was speaking to Christians who know Christ's commands and test themselves by them.

➤22 whatsoever we ask, we receive of him—as a matter of fact, according to God's promise. Christ taught his disciples to pray, "May your will be done on earth." The prayer of the believer will be in accord with God's will, or if not, the believer will desire to submit to God's will. because we keep his commandments—not that we are earning a hearing for our prayers. Rather, our obedience is the result of the Holy Spirit working in us, teaching us to desire God's will, so that our prayers grow out of this accord between God's will and ours.

➤23 this is his commandment—not two separate commands, but one, since faith and love cannot be separated. We cannot love one another without having faith in Christ, nor truly believe in him without having love for other believers. believe on the name of his Son Jesus Christ—i.e., accept, once for all, all that the gospel tells us about who Christ is and what he has done for us; and on the basis of this, trust him personally.

➤24 dwelleth in him [Christ], and he in them—This mutual indwelling is a mysterious reality for all those who are united to Christ (see 2:28; John 14:20; 15:5; 17:21-23). we know that he [Christ] abideth in us, by the Spirit which he hath given us—We know by experience (see the Gk.) that the indwelling

Spirit provides us with the presence of the indwelling Christ. For the Spirit to abide in us is to have Christ abide in us (see Rom. 8:9-11). When Christ gave us his Spirit to abide in us, he gave us himself to live in us (see John 14:16-20 and comments; see also 1 Cor. 15:45; 2 Cor. 3:17, 18 and comments). This mentioning of Christ's Spirit prepares the way for 4:1-3, which deals with the spirit of truth versus the spirit of error.

*Chapter* 4

## 1-6 DISCERNING FALSE PROPHETS

➤1 Beloved—John used this affectionate phrase several times to call attention to an important subject. every spirit—which presents itself in the person of a prophet. The Spirit of truth and the spirit of error speak through men as their organs. try—i.e., test, prove. The test we are to use is given in 4:2, 3. The responsibility for testing the spirits rests not merely on scholars or church leaders but on every Christian. many false prophets—another name for the many antichrists (2:18, 19).

➤2 Hereby—i.e., by the following test. know ye the Spirit of God—i.e., know whether or not God's Spirit is speaking through various prophets. Every spirit—This refers to the spirit of the person speaking. that confesseth that Jesus Christ is come in the flesh—There are two parts to this truth: that Jesus is God's Christ, and that he became a man. He did not merely appear to be a man; he actually became a man, with a human body. John's "statement is directed against the Gnostic error promulgated by Cerinthus, that the Christ descended into an already existing man" (Vine). The Word *became* flesh (John 1:14), and he has ever remained human. "The verb is in the perfect tense in the Greek ('has come'); it represents an abiding effect. From His incarnation onward, Christ was, and ever is, possessed of true Manhood" (Vine).

➤3 every spirit that confesseth not . . . is not of God—See comments on 4:3. that spirit of antichrist—The word has been supplied to fill in what is lacking in the Greek text. The spirit operating in the false prophets is the spirit of the antichrist (2:18), the spirit of error (4:6). whereof ye have heard—from your Christian teachers. **even now already is it in the world**—in the false teachers.

➤**4 Ye are of God**—In emphatic contrast with the false teachers who are enemies of Christ. **have overcome them**—See 5:4, 5. **greater is he that is in you**—God, who indwells us (4:12, 13). **he that is in the world**—i.e., the antichrist, or Satan himself, the prince of this world.

➤**5 They are of the world**—The false teachers have the spirit and teaching of Satan, and they are possessed and controlled by him. **therefore speak they of the world, and the world heareth them**—Since their life and teaching fit right in with the evil pattern of the world, they are popular. (Cf. John 15:18, 19.)

➤**6 We**—the true teachers of Christ, in contrast to "them," the false teachers. **are of God**—Therefore, we speak of God, in contrast to those who "speak of the world" (4:5). **he that knoweth God**—personally, experientially. **heareth us**—See John 15:20. **the spirit** [Spirit] **of truth**—i.e., the Holy Spirit, who proceeds from God and teaches the truth (John 14:17, 26; 15:26; 16:13-15; 1 John 2:20, 27). **the spirit of error**—i.e., the spirit that comes from Satan and leads people into error.

## 7-21 GOD IS LOVE; WE SHOULD LOVE ONE ANOTHER

➤**7** John now continues with and elaborates on a major theme in this epistle: love among Christians demonstrates love *for* God and love *from* God, for God is love. **love is of God**—God is love (4:8) and the source of all love. Jesus Christ, sent from God the Father, embodied love and demonstrated it in his life on earth, while the Holy Spirit produces love as his fruit in our lives. **every one that loveth**—fellow believers. **is born of God**—See John 1:12, 13. **knoweth God**—lit., "is getting to know God." This is a continual, growing, spiritual knowledge based on actual experience of God in our lives.

➤**8 He that loveth not**—A person who does not love Christians has never known the God Christians love. **knoweth not God**—Greek "did not come to know God"—not only does this person not know God now, but he has *never* known him. **God is love**—We cannot turn this around to say, "Love is God," or even weaken it by saying, "God is loving," as if this were just one of God's attributes. Rather, God is love in his very essence. If a man does not love, he does not know God.

➤**9 In this was manifested the love of God toward us**—i.e., the supreme manifestation of God's love was demonstrated in sending his Son to die for us, that we might live in him. **God sent his only begotten Son into the world**—The great proof of God's love, and the motive for our love, is that he sent his only Son, who is life, so that we could live through him.

➤**10 Herein is love**—love in its highest ideal. The love was all on God's side, not at all on ours. **not that we loved God**—We did not love him, even though he is supremely worthy of our love. **but that he loved us**—even though we were totally unworthy. **sent his Son**—God's love for us was summed up in the act of sending his Son to die for our sins. **the propitiation for our sins**—See comments on 2:2.

➤**11 if God so loved us, we ought also to love one another**—God's supreme love for us is the motive of our love to one another. Since we are born of God, we should resemble our Father, who is love. As we grow in appreciation of God's love for us, our love for him and for other Christians, also his children, will grow too.

➤**12 No man hath seen God at any time**—but we can see his children. Our love to God is to be directed in acts of love toward his children. That is why 4:11 says that God's love for us leads to our love for one another. **If we love one another, God dwelleth in us**—Apart from God's life in us, we could not love one another (see 4:16). **his love**—that is, our love to him (an object genitive in Gk.). We know that our love for God is growing stronger because we can see its results in our loving actions toward each other. **is perfected in us**—i.e., develops toward maturity and completeness.

➤**13** Although we cannot see God, we know he lives in us because he has given us his Spirit. Where God's Spirit is, there God is. This one Spirit lives in each member of the church, and love is his first fruit in our lives (Gal. 5:22).

➤**14 we**—the apostles, eyewitnesses of Christ's life on earth, and appointed by him to tell others about him (1:1-3). The internal evidence of the Holy Spirit in us is borne out of the external evidence of the fact that the Father sent the Son to be the Savior of the world.

**seen**—contemplated, studied attentively (see 3:17). **sent**—or, as in the Greek, "has sent," since it is not merely a past fact, but one which still continues in its effects and consequences.

►**15 Whosoever shall confess**—The Greek verb tense implies that this is done once for all. **that Jesus is the Son of God**—and therefore "the Savior of the world" (4:14). **God dwelleth in him, and he in God**—The person who believes in Christ is indwelt by God and simultaneously dwells in God. This mutual indwelling, experienced by the Father and Son (John 10:38; 14:10; 17:21), is a special privilege for the believers (see John 14:20; 15:5; 17:21-24).

►**16 we**—John and his readers, rather than just the apostles. **have known** [by experience] **and believed**—Note the intimate connection of faith and knowledge. True faith is a faith of knowledge and experience; true knowledge is a knowledge of faith. **the love that God hath**—This involves not only God's love *to* us, but also *through* us, producing a responsive love in us toward him and toward other Christians.

►**17 our love made perfect**—i.e., mature, complete. This perfection happens as our relationship with God, who is love, grows. His perfect love becomes free to work completely in and through us. **boldness**—or, confidence, which is the opposite of "fear" (4:18). The result of living with Christ and growing more perfect in love is confidence in the day of judgment, which is so terrible to other men (Acts 24:25; Rom. 2:16). **because as he is, so are we in this world**—We share in Christ's nature, both in his love and his righteousness, and are his representatives in the world: "little Christs," as Luther put it; in the world but not of it. God imputes Christ's righteousness to us through justification and also imparts his righteousness to us through sanctification. Our confidence in the day of judgment is based not merely on God's love apart from his justice, but on the fact that his love and justice united to make us like him, and thus legitimately beyond reach of judgment.

►**18 fear hath torment**—i.e., "fear has to do with punishment" (RSV, NIV). Based on consciousness of guilt, fear anticipates the deserved punishment and thus suffers a foretaste of that punishment even now. Perfect love involves confidence (4:17) and is incompatible with fear. Christ's death was to deliver us from slavery to fear (Heb. 2:14, 15).

►**19 We love him**—The last word is not present in the earliest manuscripts; it reads simply, "We love." Our love, whether for God or for others, is based on his love for us, which eliminates all dread (4:19). **because he first loved us**—See 4:9, 10.

►**20 he that loveth not his brother whom he hath seen, how can he love God whom he hath not seen?**—If we do not love our Christian brothers, who are God's visible representatives, how can we love the invisible God? In Christ we see God as he is and man as he ought to be. By faith in Christ, we learn to love God's children as being like him.

►**21** Not only is it natural to love God's children if we love God (4:20); it is also God's command. If we love God, we surely will obey him by loving our brothers. (See comments on 2:7ff. and see John 13:34.)

*Chapter* 5

## 1-21 FAITH IN THE SON OF GOD: THE WAY TO VICTORY AND ETERNAL LIFE

►**1** This verse continues the command to love our brothers, God's children, who are defined as those who believe that Jesus is the Christ. **Jesus is the Christ**—As the Christ (the anointed One), Jesus was a Prophet who revealed the way of salvation, a Priest who worked out that salvation, and a King who gave that salvation to us. **every one that loveth him that begat**—i.e., God the Father. **loveth him also that is begotten**—i.e., any and all of God's children. **of him**—of God the Father.

►**2** Just as our love for our brothers is the sign and test of our love for God, so our love for God (tested by obedience, 5:3) is the only basis of our love for our brothers. **we know**—not merely by outward signs, but by consciously knowing that we love God because we obey him. John was not contradicting what he said in 4:20, 21, but insisting that love for God and love for our brothers cannot be separated. We cannot love God without loving our brothers; we can know we love God, as well as our brothers, if we are obeying him. John first urged the effect (love for our brothers); now he urges the cause (love for God).

➤**3 his commandments are not grievous** [heavy, burdensome]—as so many think they are. The stronger our faith (5:4), the easier it is to overcome our natural rebellion against God's commands. The believer who finds God's way hard has never really grasped by faith his privileges as God's child.

➤**4 For**—This word indicates that 5:4 gives the reason to support the statement in 5:3. Although we experience a struggle and conflict in our lives between our sinful nature and the new nature that wants to obey God, we know that our new nature will grow stronger and ultimately win out. Meanwhile, we have a joy in obeying God that also makes it easier. **whatsoever is born of God**—The Greek term for "whatsoever" is *pan to* ("everything"). John used this collective neuter to designate the collective unit of believers, not just a single believer. In the next verse he speaks of the individual. This same pattern—of first speaking of the collective body of believers and then of each individual believer—is found in John 6:37, 39; 17:2, 24 (see comments there).

➤**5** This verse confirms 5:4 with a triumphant question defying all contradiction. It is by believing that we become one with Jesus Christ and so share in his victory over the world. We conquer because the One in our hearts is stronger than any evil in the world (4:4).

➤**6 This is he that came by water and blood, even Jesus Christ**—This phrase "water and blood" in this context can mean one of two things: (1) the phrase takes us back to Christ's death on the cross, at which time he was pierced—and out flowed blood and water (John 19:35). John witnessed this, and asserted the importance of this occurrence. Cerinthus and the Docetists denied Christ's true and lasting humanity. But John saw Jesus shed his blood and die (see comments on 4:2). (2) The phrase "water and blood" could refer to Christ's baptism (water) and crucifixion (blood). F. F. Bruce affirmed this in his commentary:

The sequence "water and blood" is not accidental, but corresponds to the historical sequence of our Lord's baptism and passion.

Cerinthus, we recall, taught that "the Christ" (a spiritual being) came down on the man Jesus when He was baptized but left Him before He died. The Christ, that is to say, came through *water* (baptism) but not through *blood* (death). To this misrepresentation of the truth John replies that the One whom believers acknowledge to be the Son of God (verse 5) came "not with the water only but with the water and with the blood": the One who died on the cross was as truly the Christ, the Son of God, as the One who was baptized in Jordan.

➤**it is the Spirit that beareth witness**— The Spirit bears witness to the truth of Christ's life and work (see John 16:13-15). **the Spirit is truth**—See John 15:26; 16:13.

➤**7, 8** The words "in heaven, the Father, the Word, and the Holy Ghost [Spirit]: and these three are one. And there are three that bear witness in earth" are spurious. This famous passage, called "the heavenly witness," has been the object of much discussion. It came from a gloss on 1 John 5:8 which explained that the three elements (water, blood, and Spirit) symbolized the Trinity. This gloss, evidently, found its way into the text in the form quoted above. The passage has a Latin origin. Its first appearance was in the work of Priscillian, a fourth-century Spanish heretic. It showed up in the writings of other Latin fathers from the fifth century onward, and it found its way into more and more copies of the Latin Vulgate. But "the heavenly witnesses" can not be found in any Greek manuscript prior to the eleventh century, and it was never cited by any Greek father. Erasmus did not include "the heavenly witnesses" in the first two editions of his Greek New Testament. He was criticized for this by defenders of the Latin Vulgate. Erasmus, in reply, said that he would include it if he could see it in any one Greek manuscript. In turn, a manuscript (most likely the Montfort Manuscript, MS 61) was especially produced to contain the passage. Erasmus kept his promise; he included it in the third edition. From there it became part of the Textus Receptus and hence was translated in the KJV (*GAM*). First John 5:7, 8 should read as follows: "For there are three that testify: the Spirit, the water, and the blood; and the three are in agreement" (NIV).

►9 **If we receive the witness of men**—The law required two or three witnesses as adequate testimony to decide what was true. John said that if we believe men, who sometimes make mistakes, we can surely rely on the threefold witness of God (5:8).

►10 **hath the witness in himself**—through the Holy Spirit in them (Rom. 8:16), telling them that Jesus is God's Son. **hath made him a liar**—Those who do not believe should realize that by rejecting what God has so plainly told us, they are calling God a liar. **believeth not**—This has two aspects: refusing to believe what God has said about his Son, and in consequence, refusing to believe in Christ who, because he is God's Son, is the only one who can save men. What better reason can we have for believing than that God says it is true? **record**—testimony.

►11 **hath given to us eternal life**—once for all, when he sent his Son for us. **life is in his Son**—Jesus Christ is life (John 1:4; 14:6; Col. 2:9) and we can have life in him (2 Tim. 1:10). As the "second Adam," Christ has restored all believers to the life of union with God that was lost through sin.

►12 **hath the Son**—Not only do we belong to Christ, but Christ also belongs to us. Our intimate relationship with Christ is pictured by the unity of a husband and wife; indeed, we are the "bride of Christ." **hath life**—Through faith we have Christ and have eternal life now; we possess a new nature and enjoy fellowship with God. But though this life is real now, it is only partial, since our bodies still tie us to sin and death. This life will be completed when our souls are united with perfect bodies and we are fully united with God.

►13 **These things**—referring to the content of the letter. **have I written . . . that ye may know that ye have eternal life**—As he did toward the end of his Gospel (John 20:30, 31), John explicitly states his purpose for writing: that his readers may be sure they have eternal life, and this security is the basis for the other aim of John's letter—that they will be full of joy (1:4).

►14 **this is the confidence**—This confidence that God listens to our prayers is based on the confidence that we are his children, and that we do have eternal life (5:13). **according to his will**—Since we have placed our wills in

line with God's will, this is no restriction on our prayers. The Holy Spirit in us teaches us to understand God's will more completely, and he makes us able to pray in line with God's will.

►15 **if we know that he hear us . . . we know that we have the petitions that we desired of him**—Hannah, for example, had enough confidence in God's answer to be glad before she received what she asked for.

►16 Verses 16, 17 "illustrate the kind of petition we can be sure God will answer" (*NIVSB*). **that sin not unto death . . . a sin unto death**—What is the difference between the sin unto death and the sin not unto death? "The distinction is one which John's readers were expected to recognize. But it is difficult to see how they could recognize the distinction except by the result. Elsewhere in the NT instances occur of sins which caused the death of the persons committing them, when these persons were church members" (Bruce)—see Acts 5:1-11; 1 Cor. 5:5; 11:30. But John may not have been thinking of physical death as much as sin that leads to spiritual death. The *NIVSB* says this:

> In the context of this letter directed against Gnostic teaching, which denied the incarnation and threw off all moral restraints, it is probable that the "sin that leads to death" refers to the Gnostics' adamant and persistent denial of the truth and to their shameless immorality. This kind of unrepentant sin leads to spiritual death.

►17 **All unrighteousness is sin**—including the sin committed by believers (1:7, 9; 3:4), but not every sin is the sin that ends in death. The sin that ends in death includes both the *act* of deliberately denying that Jesus is the Christ, the Son of God, and the *state* of spiritual death that deliberately rejects Christ, destroying faith and love. How can we pray that God will give life to a person who rejects the grace of God in Christ, which is the only way to life? Adamant resistance to the Holy Spirit's plain testimony to Jesus Christ as Lord and Savior cannot be forgiven (Matt. 12:31, 32).

►18 **whosoever is born of God sinneth not**—Greek, "everyone having been begotten of God does not keep on sinning." See comments on 3:9. **he that is begotten of God keepeth himself**—or, the begotten of God (i.e.,

God's Son—see TLB, TEV) keeps him (the one born of God) safe. The difference in translations comes from an underlying textual variation. Early manuscript support can be cited for both readings. The reading behind the KJV indicates that the believer, as a son of God, keeps himself from sin. The alternative reading indicates that the Son of God keeps the believer from sin. Many commentators favor this reading because (1) the first clause of this verse already mentions the believer who is born of God, (2) John consistently uses the perfect tense to describe the believer who has become a son of God (2:29; 3:9; 4:7; 5:1; 5:4; 5:18a) whereas here the aorist is used, and (3) there is little or no security in the fact that the believer must keep himself. Rather, it is the One begotten of God, the Son of God, who keeps each believer (*GAM*).

➤**19 the whole world lieth in wickedness**—i.e., "the whole world is in the power of the evil one" (RSV). Only those who are "in God" and "in Jesus Christ his Son" (5:20) have been freed from Satan's power. Even those the world considers wise, great, and respectable are under Satan's domain.

➤**20 the Son of God is come**—and is therefore present with us here and now, and what he has done for us is a living reality in our experience. **and hath given us an understanding**—concerning God (see John 1:18). **that we may know** [experientially, personally] **him that is true**—i.e., God the Father (see John 17:3). Just as the Holy Spirit teaches us about Christ and points to him, so the Son teaches us about and points to the Father. **we are in him that is true, even in his Son Jesus Christ**—To be in God is to be in God's Son; for when we are united to the Son, we are also united to the Father (see John 17:21-24). The second expression "him that is true" refers to "his Son Jesus Christ" (which, grammatically, is an appositive). **This**—Greek, "This One" (*outos*), referring to the person just named, "Jesus Christ." **is the true God**—Jesus Christ is the true God (cf. John 1:1, 18; 20:28; Rom. 9:5; Titus 2:13; 2 Pet. 1:1). **and eternal life**—While the Father is the source of eternal life, Jesus Christ reveals that life (John 1:4; 14:6) and through his death made that life available to us.

➤**21 Little children, keep yourselves from idols**—John closes his letter with a final affectionate caution. Given the context of this epistle, "idols" are probably false teachings presenting false images of Jesus Christ, who is "the true God and eternal life."

BIBLIOGRAPHY
Listed at the end of 3 John.

# 2 & 3 JOHN

## Introduction

These two epistles were evidently written by the same author because of their similarity of tone, style, and sentiment—all of which are also similar to 1 John. Second and 3 John were recognized as Johannine epistles as early as the second century. Irenaeus (*Against Heresies,* 1.16.3) quoted 2 John 10, 11; and in 3.16.8, he quoted 2 John 7, mistaking it, however, as if occurring in 1 John. Clement of Alexandria in *Stromata,* 2.66, intimated knowledge of other epistles of John besides the first epistle; and in fragments of his *Adumbrations* he says, "John's Second Epistle was written to a certain Babylonian named the Elect lady." Dionysius of Alexandria (according to Eusebius's *Ecclesiastical History,* 7.25) observes that John never names himself in his epistles, "not even in the Second and Third Epistles, although they are short epistles, but simply calls himself the presbyter." Alexander of Alexandria cites 2 John 10, 11 as John's (Socrates' *Historia Ecclesiastica,* 1.6). However, it must be admitted that 2 and 3 John took a while to be recognized as Scripture by many of the early fathers. Eusebius (*Ecclesiastical History*) reckoned both epistles among the *Antilegomena* or *controverted* Scriptures, as distinguished from the *Homologoumena* or *universally acknowledged* from the first. Still his own opinion was that the two minor epistles were genuine, remarking as he does in *Demonstratio Evangelica,* 3.5, that in John's "Epistles" he does not mention his own name, or call himself an apostle or evangelist, but an "elder" (2 John 1; 3 John 1). Origen (according to Eusebius's *Ecclesiastical History,* 6.25) mentions the second and third epistles, but adds, "not all admit [implying that most authorities do] their genuineness." These *Antilegomena* were eventually recognized as canonical, soon after the Council of Nicea (A.D. 325). Thus Cyril of Jerusalem (A.D. 349) enumerates fourteen epistles of Paul, and seven Catholic (or, general) epistles. So also Gregory of Nazianzen in A.D. 389. The Councils of Hippo (393) and Carthage (394) adopted a catalogue of NT books exactly agreeing with our canon. Due to their brevity (which Origen notices) and the personal nature of their contents, the Second and Third Epistles of John were less generally read in the earliest Christian churches and were also less quoted by the Fathers; hence, arose their non-universal recognition at first. Their personal nature makes them less likely to be spurious, for there seems no purpose in their being forgeries.

Second John was written to "an elect lady and her children." Some commentators think this was a specific woman (with her children); and some of the same commentators think the Greek word for "lady" (*kuria*) is a proper name, "Cyria" (see TLB). But other commentators think John was using this address as a surrogate for a particular local church (as perhaps Peter also did in 1 Pet. 5:13—see comments). The nature of the epistle points to a corporate personality—the local assembly—rather than a private individual (see comments on verses 5, 6, 8, 10, 12). Third John was written to Gaius. Although the NT mentions several men with the name Gaius (Acts 19:29; 20:4ff.; Rom. 16:23 and 1 Cor. 1:14), it would be difficult to say that any one of these was the same as the Gaius in 3 John. At any rate, Gaius is commended for his Christian walk and hospitality and so is Demetrius, both of whom stand in sharp contrast to Diotrephes, "the one loving to be first" (3 John 9).

## SECOND JOHN

### 1-13 GREETING. THANKSGIVING FOR THE RECIPIENT'S FAITHFULNESS IN THE TRUTH. COMMANDS LOVE, WARNS AGAINST DECEIVERS. CONCLUSION

**➤1 The elder**—In this informal letter John did not stand on his authority as an apostle, but spoke of himself as an elder, one who watched over the believers with loving concern for their spiritual well-being. **the elect lady**—or, the elect Cyria (Gk., *kuria*). Some scholars think that Cyria was a particular Christian woman, perhaps an influential one, whom John wanted to warn against certain false teachers. Other scholars consider that "the elect lady" was a corporate personality, namely, a local church (see Bruce). Since the epistle does not speak of the woman with any particular details (in contrast to 3 John that speaks specifically of Gaius, Diotrephes, and Demetrius), it seems likely that "the elect lady" was a local church. Verses 6, 12, and 13 also point to a corporate recipient (see comments there). **her children**—If the recipient was a woman, these would have been her children; if the recipient was a local church, these would have been the members of the church. **whom I love in the truth**—The elect lady, probably a local church, was loved by all the believers, who had come to know the truth.

**➤2 For the truth's sake**—Jesus Christ is the full expression and embodiment of truth (John 14:6; Eph. 4:21). **which dwelleth**—Truth dwells in us because Christ and the Spirit of truth (John 16:13) dwell in us.

**➤3 Grace be with you**—The only other time John speaks of "grace" is in John 1:16, 17, which says grace came through Jesus Christ,

and from his fullness we have received grace upon grace. **mercy, and peace**—God's mercy is seen in forgiving us and freeing us from sin, and peace is the result. **from God the Father, and from the Lord Jesus Christ** ["the Lord" is not present in the earliest manuscripts], **the Son of the Father**—Grace, peace, and mercy emanate from the Father and his Son to the believers. **in truth and love**—John speaks more directly about truth in verse 4 and about love in verse 5. Truth and love always go hand in hand.

**➤4 I rejoiced greatly that I found of thy children**—probably on one of his missionary tours to supervise and watch over the churches (see v. 12; 3 John 10, 14). **walking in truth**—i.e., living in accordance with the truth they were taught (cf. Eph. 4:21). **received a commandment from the Father**—through the Son (see John 15:15).

**➤5 now I beseech thee**—This strong term implies some degree of authority, as well as John's deep concern. **lady**—See comments on verse 1. **not . . . a new commandment . . . but that which we had from the beginning**—The Christians had been taught this commandment of love from the time they first heard the gospel preached. (See John 13:35; 1 John 2:7; 3:11.) **that we** [should] **love one another**—The plural pronoun supports the idea that John was writing to an entire church, especially since it would be unlikely that he would write such a phrase to an individual woman.

**➤6 The one command to love sums up all of God's commands, and obedience to God's commands is the sure test of love.**

**➤7 After speaking of truth and love, John warns about those who are against the truth and**

against Christ. **deceivers ... who confess not that Jesus Christ is come in the flesh**—John spoke of the same heresy in his first epistle (4:2, 3). The Docetists denied Jesus Christ's real humanity; they promoted the falsehood that Christ only *seemed* to have a human body. **This is a deceiver and an antichrist**—These false teachers foreshadow the final personal Antichrist, who will embody all the evil of earlier antichristian systems and teachers. (See comments on 1 John 2:18ff.; 4:3.)

➤**8 Look to yourselves**—"Watch yourselves" (TEV), since so many are corrupted and deceived by them. Christ warned his disciples, "Don't let anyone fool you. For many will come claiming to be the Messiah and will lead many astray ... so that if it were possible, even God's chosen ones would be deceived" (Matt. 24:4, 5, 24, TLB). **we have wrought**—This reading is supported by one early manuscript (Codex Vaticanus) and many later ones. Several early manuscripts read, "you have wrought." The reading with "we" speaks of the apostles' labors among these believers; the reading with "you" speaks of these believers' own labors. **we receive**—The earliest manuscripts read, "you [plural] receive." **a full reward**—This is not something God owes us or that we deserve, but rather something he will freely give us because of his grace and love. Bengel remarked, "There is no half reward of the saints. It is either lost altogether, or received *in full; in full* communion with God." Although we are all different, we will all be fully blessed, fully happy, in Christ's presence.

➤**9** This verse explains the loss referred to in verse 8: not having God, which results from not staying in Christ's teachings. **abideth not**—lit., "leading forward," hence, "to go before" or "to run ahead." "Perhaps this is a sarcastic reference to the way in which the false teachers themselves proudly claim to be offering 'advanced' teaching. The elder claims that they have 'advanced' beyond the boundaries of true Christian belief" (Rienecker; Marshall). **the doctrine of Christ**—This is the true apostolic teaching concerning Christ, which was based on the teachings the apostles received from Christ. To remain in this teaching is to remain in the Son and the Father (see comments on 1 John 2:22, 23).

➤**10 If there come any unto you**—The Greek verb tense implies that such persons actually do come and are sure to come. True love involves rejecting and completely staying away from what is false. **bring not this doctrine** [teaching]—the one mentioned in verse 9. **receive him not into your house, neither bid him God speed** [give him greeting]—Don't welcome him as a Christian brother, even though he claims to belong to Christ, since he denies his claim by rejecting Christ's truth.

➤**11 is partaker of his evil deeds**—Greek, "shares in his evil works." By encouraging or helping him, we identify ourselves with, and tacitly approve of, what he does. The word "partaker" literally means "have fellowship with." We cannot have fellowship both with God and his children, and with antichrists, God's enemies. John practiced what he preached to the extent that he once left a bathhouse when he heard that the heretic Cerinthus was inside for fear the house would fall in ruins since the enemy of the truth was there. (This story was told by Polycarp, a disciple of John.)

➤**12 write unto you**—plural in Greek, indicating a plural recipient—namely, the members of a particular local church. **to come unto you, and speak face to face**—lit., "speak mouth to mouth." John's love for the believers was not satisfied merely by writing a letter; he still longed to visit them personally and discuss the truths of the gospel more fully.

➤**13 The children of thy elect sister greet thee**—Since the sister was not named, John was probably referring to the sister church where he was staying. The phrase is very similar to one in verse 1. **Amen**—is not present in the earliest manuscripts.

## THIRD JOHN

1-14 GREETING AND GOOD WISHES TO GAIUS. JOHN EXPRESSES HIS JOY THAT GAIUS IS LIVING BY THE TRUTH AND SHOWING LOVE BY GIVING HOSPITALITY. JOHN EXPOSES PROUD DIOTREPHES. CONCLUSION

➤**1 The elder**—See 2 John 1. **well-beloved Gaius**—John expressed his strong love for Gaius and continually called him "beloved" (in verses 2, 5, and 11). **I love in the truth**—or, "I truly love" (TEV). See 2 John 1.

➤**2** John cared not only about Gaius's soul or spiritual condition but also about his physical health and total well-being. Perhaps John had heard from the brothers (mentioned in v. 3) that Gaius was ill or in a difficult situation owing to Diotrephes' opposition (v. 10).

➤**3 testified of the truth that is in thee**— This truth was his "loyalty to Christ and the gospel by which his life was marked" (Bruce). **thou walkest in the truth**—Gaius conducted his life in the truth—he lived it, in contrast to Diotrephes, whose conduct was contrary to the truth.

➤**4 my children**—members of the church, John's spiritual children. This use of the phrase supports the view that in 2 John the dear woman and her children, and the sister and her children, also refer to local churches. **walk in truth**—i.e., live their lives in accordance with the truth revealed in Christ and the Word.

➤**5 whatsoever thou doest**—i.e., any work you render. **to the brethren, and to strangers**—Gaius lovingly cared for those who served the Lord, even when they were strangers to him.

➤**6 Which** [who] **have borne witness of thy charity** [love] **before the church**—Greek, "before an assembly." Gaius's selfless kindness was held up as an example for others. The traveling Christian workers he had helped mentioned his generous hospitality in an assembly of believers where John was present. **bring forward on their journey after a godly sort**—i.e., "help them on their journey in a way that God would approve" (JB). This help, of course, would include providing needed supplies for the journey.

➤**7 for his name's sake they went forth**— For the sake of Christ they went forth to preach the gospel. The earliest manuscripts read, "For the sake of the Name" (cf. Acts 5:41). **taking nothing**—of their own choice, not because they were not offered anything. **of the Gentiles**—At this time in church history (at least A.D. 80), non-Christians may very well have been considered as being Gentiles—just as previously all non-Jews were categorized as "Gentiles."

➤**8 We**—mature Christians in established churches in contrast to the Gentiles in verse 7.

**that we might be fellowhelpers to the truth**—a beautiful picture of cooperation through hospitality and giving. Believers can help advance the spreading of the truth by helping those who have been sent forth to proclaim the truth of the gospel.

➤**9 wrote**—no doubt urging the church to welcome and help the traveling teachers. This letter is not extant. **unto the church**— the local church of which Gaius was a member. **but Diotrephes . . . loveth to have the preeminence among them**—lit., "loving to be first among them." Diotrephes apparently had an important position in the church, but he was blinded with pride and self-importance (cf. 1 Tim. 3:6). **receiveth us not**—By not receiving John and the brothers John had sent, Diotrephes was not receiving Christ (see Matt. 10:40).

➤**10 if I come**—or, "when I come." See verse 14 for John's anticipation of soon visiting the church Gaius belonged to. **I will remember**—"I will bring up" (RSV) or "I will call attention to" (NIV). John was prepared to publicly denounce Diotrephes before the whole church. **prating against us**—The Greek verb (*phluareō*), used only here in the NT, "has the meaning of making false accusations in a garrulous way" (Vine). **neither doth he himself receive the brethren**—Diotrephes regularly refused to give hospitality to the brothers sent from John. Neander thought the brothers may have been Jews and that Diotrephes was the leader of an anti-Jewish group in the Gentile churches. They recognized Paul as an apostle but opposed John, who was trying through love to unite the various elements in the Gentile churches.

➤**11 follow** [imitate] **. . . that which is good**—illustrated by Demetrius's godly life and contrasted with the bad example of Diotrephes.

➤**12 Demetrius hath good report of all men**—i.e., everyone who knows him. **the truth itself**—The goodness of Demetrius's life is evident when it is compared to the gospel standard of truth, which involves real acts of love and hospitality. **we also bear record**—in addition to the testimony of everyone else, and of the truth itself. **ye know that our record** [testimony] **is true**—See John 19:35; 21:24.

➤**13** See 2 John 12.

►**14 face to face**—lit., "mouth to mouth," an idiom for personal fellowship. **friends**— Although "brothers" is more used in the NT than "friends," it is appropriate in this friendly letter to Gaius. Jesus told his disciples, "Ye are my friends, if ye do whatsoever I command you" (John 15:14). This friendship, grounded in our loving obedience, includes sharing in an intimate knowledge of God as he reveals himself to us through Christ. John was thinking of them as individuals he knew and loved, not merely as a group.

## BIBLIOGRAPHY

Alford, Henry. *The Greek New Testament*. 1852. Reprint. Grand Rapids: Guardian Press, 1976.

Bengel, John A. *New Testament Word Studies*. 1742. Reprint. Grand Rapids: Eerdmans, 1971.

Bruce, F. F. *The Epistles of John: Introduction, Exposition, Notes*. Grand Rapids: Eerdmans, 1970.

Luther, Martin. "Lectures on the First Epistle of St. John" in *Luther's Works*, vol. 30. Translated by W. A. Hansen. St. Louis: Concordia Publishing House, 1967.

Marshall, I. H. "The Epistles of John" in *The New International Commentary*. Grand Rapids: Eerdmans, 1978.

Neander, Johann A. *A General History of the Christian Religion and Church*. 9 vols. Edinburgh: T & T Clark, 1849-52.

Rienecker, Fritz. *Linguistic Key to the Greek New Testament*. Grand Rapids: Baker Book House, 1976, 1980.

Smith, David. "First John" in the *Expositor's Greek Testament*. Grand Rapids: Eerdmans, 1979.

Tenney, Merrill C. *New Testament Survey* (revised by W. M. Dunnett). Grand Rapids: Eerdmans, 1961, 1985.

Tittmann, J. A. *Remarks on the Synonyms of the New Testament*. Edinburgh: T & T Clark, 1833-37.

Trench, R. C. *Synonyms of the New Testament*. Grand Rapids: Eerdmans, 1950.

Vincent, M. R. *Word Studies in the New Testament*. 1886. Reprint. Grand Rapids; Eerdmans, 1946.

Vine, W. E. *The Epistles of John: Light, Love, Life*. Grand Rapids: Zondervan, 1970 (by permission of Oliphants).

Westcott, B. F. *The Epistles of St. John: The Greek Text with Notes and Essays*. London: Macmillan, 1892.

Wuest, Kenneth. *In These Last Days: Studies in the Greek Text of II Peter, I, II, III John and Jude*. Grand Rapids: Eerdmans, 1954.

# JUDE

## Introduction

The writer of this epistle identified himself as Jude, a brother of James. Most commentators agree that this James is not James, the brother of John and son of Zebedee, but James, the brother of Jesus and prominent elder in Jerusalem (Acts 12:17; 15:13; 21:18; Gal. 1:19; 2:9, 12). As such, Jude was also Jesus' brother. In fact, Jude (Greek, "Judas," from the Hebrew word "Judah") is named as one of Jesus' brothers in Matthew 13:55 and Mark 6:3. Jude did not believe that his brother Jesus was the Christ, the Son of God, until after Jesus' resurrection (see John 7:5; Acts 1:14). Instead of introducing himself as the brother of Jesus, he called himself a brother of James (an eminently known figure—especially to Jewish Christians) and "a slave of Jesus Christ" (Gk.). This shows his humility.

If 2 Peter cited Jude (instead of vice versa—see Introduction to 2 Peter), then we have very early evidence of Jude's apostolic authority. Several early church fathers cited Jude and/or alluded to it: Tertullian (*Women's Dress*, 3), Clement of Alexandria (*Stromata*, 3.2.11), and Origen (*Commentary on Matthew* on 13:55; 18:10; 22:23). Origen called Jude an apostle and said, "Jude wrote an epistle of few lines, but one filled full of the strong words of heavenly grace." The Muratorian Canon (c. 200) says that the Epistle of Jude was accepted in the church. The Bodmer Papyrus, P72 (early third century), contains 1 and 2 Peter, together with Jude, thereby showing that Jude was accepted right along with Peter's epistles. However, Eusebius (in *Ecclesiastical History*, 2.23.25) said that Jude was questioned as to its authenticity because few of the ancients quoted it. Thus, Jude was categorized with the *Antilegomena* (the books spoken against)—see *Ecclesiastical History*, 3.25. But Eusebius admitted that Jude was widely used, with the rest of the NT Epistles, in the churches. Eventually, the doubts about Jude were overcome, and the book was recognized by the church. "Didymus of Alexandria (c. 395) defended the book, and since then little objection to its canonicity has been voiced" (Blum).

Jude wrote this epistle primarily to Jewish Christians who were being infected by a form of libertine Gnosticism through heretical teachers. Gnosticism had adherents who practiced asceticism and adherents who lived in carnal self-indulgence. The NT apostles wrote various epistles to counter various gnostic teachings and practices. Jude wrote this short polemic to defend the true faith (v. 3) and to reprove the false teachers (vv. 4-19) who promoted their libertine notions and lived lawless lives.

If Jude wrote this epistle after 2 Peter, it could be dated any time after A.D. 68; if Jude wrote it before 2 Peter, it could be dated as early as A.D. 50-60. (See Introduction to 2 Peter.) The style of Greek is very Hellenistic, and the epistle is filled with rare words. Some scholars have used this as an argument against Jude's authorship—for how could a Galilean have such facility with the Greek language? But recent studies have shown that Jesus, a Galilean and brother of Jude, probably spoke Greek fluently (Hughes). Thus, it follows that there is little reason to doubt that Jude was capable of writing in the style presented in this epistle.

*Chapter* **1**

1-25 ADDRESS. WARNING AGAINST FALSE TEACHERS BY DESCRIBING GOD'S PUNISHMENT OF ISRAEL, THE FALLEN ANGELS, AND SODOM AND GOMORRAH. A COMPARISON OF THE FALSE TEACHERS TO CAIN, BALAAM, AND KORAH. A CALL TO PERSEVERE.

➤**1 the servant of Jesus Christ, and brother of James**—Jude humbly omits reference to himself as Christ's brother, even though he and James (the leader of the Jerusalem church), were half-brothers of Jesus Christ (see Introduction). **sanctified**—The earliest Greek manuscripts read "beloved"; the KJV reading is supported by later manuscripts. The Christians are "beloved by God the Father." **preserved in Jesus Christ**—is better rendered, "kept for Jesus Christ" (RSV, NIV). The thought is "that God the Father preserves the Christian for his Son" (Blum). The phrase "expresses the most positive assurance regarding the future, for He preserves those who trust Him until His coming" (Pentecost). The same idea is presented in verse 24. Before going on to severely warn against dreadful evils, Jude encourages the believers they can rest assured that God will keep them in his love until Jesus Christ returns. **called**—God called us to sonship and to obtaining our eternal inheritance. Therefore, we can be assured that he will bring us into eternal glory (v. 24).

➤**2 Mercy**—Jude mentions mercy first, because it is so necessary to have in the terrible circumstances he is about to describe. This mercy is the mercy of Christ (v. 21). **peace**—This peace comes from the Holy Spirit (v. 20). **love**—i.e., the love of God (v. 21). The Father, the Son, and the Holy Spirit are working together to bring us these blessings.

➤**3** The original thought of this verse is conveyed better in the NIV: "Dear friends, although I was very eager to write to you about the salvation we share, I felt I had to write and urge you to contend for the faith that God has once for all entrusted to the saints." Jude had wanted to write about "the common salvation," but the exigency of the situation forced him to write about the need to contend for the Christian faith that was being attacked by false teachers (vv. 4-18). **the common salvation**—the salvation all Christians have in common through Jesus Christ. It is because we have the same faith in the same Lord that the apostles could write things that are helpful to all Christians, from the first century until now. **earnestly contend**—The word "contend" was used to describe athletic exertion and competitive energy (see 1 Cor. 9:24-27; Phil. 1:27) and it often meant "wrestling." Jude calls upon his readers to fight for the faith. **the faith**—is the Christian faith, the sum total of what Christians believe—especially concerning the work and person of Jesus Christ (cf. v. 4). **which was once [for all] delivered**—The content of what Christians believe—"the faith"—was once for all given by God to the apostles, who taught it and wrote it in the books that now comprise our NT. No other faith or revelation is to supersede it—which is a strong argument for resisting heretical innovators. **saints**—This includes all Christians, since God has called us all to be holy, set apart for him.

➤**4 certain men crept in unawares**—i.e., they secretly slipped into the churches (cf. Gal. 2:4). We must be alert, carefully examining what is taught, that no one can deceive us with clever lies (2 Pet. 2:1). **who were before of old ordained to this condemnation**—or, "whose condemnation was written about long ago." "The reference could be to God's writing down from eternity the destiny (i.e., the reprobation or punishment) of the wicked. But it is more likely that it refers to previously written predictions about the doom of the apostates" (Blum). **ungodly men**—The OT is full of illustrations of such men, some of which Jude goes on to mention. **turning the grace of our God into lasciviousness**—i.e., "change the grace of God into a license for immorality" (NIV). The false teachers used the teaching of God's grace to live free, immoral lives (cf. Gal. 5:13). **denying the only Lord God, and our Lord Jesus Christ**—All the earliest manuscripts read, "denying our only Master and our Lord[,] Jesus Christ." To deny Jesus Christ's lordship is to deny the Christian faith, that faith for which Jude urged the saints to fight. As our Master and Lord, Christ has absolute ownership, with complete right over our lives. Christians must proclaim this truth and live by it.

➤**5 the Lord, having saved** [or, delivered] **the people out of the land of Egypt**—This reading is supported by some ancient manuscripts (including Codex Sinaiticus and Codex Ephraem Rescriptus). Other early manuscripts (including Codex Alexandrinus and Codex Vaticanus) read "Jesus" instead of "Lord." And one early manuscript (the Bodmer Papyrus—P72) reads "God, the Messiah" instead of "Lord." The reading with "Jesus" is probably the one from which all the other variants came because no good reason can be purported to explain why a reading with "God" or "Lord" would be changed to the

unusual name, "Jesus." Given the fact that Jude was writing from a NT perspective, a perspective that viewed Jesus as being Jehovah the Savior, it is not difficult to imagine that Jude would say that Jesus delivered the Israelites out of Egypt. Paul spoke of Christ as present with the Israelites in the wilderness (see 1 Cor. 10:4 and comments on 1 Cor. 10:9), and the writer of Hebrews spoke of Christ as the reward Moses esteemed above the riches of Egypt (Heb. 11:26). Some scholars have said that "Jesus" in this verse indicates "Joshua" (e.g., see NEB mg), as in Hebrews 4:8; but this is generally regarded as unlikely. Joshua led the Israelites into the good land but not out of Egypt; and Joshua certainly did not "destroy them that believed not" (GAM). **saved**—brought them out safely. That the Lord would kill the very ones he had given freedom and safety is a sobering warning to those who despise God's kindness.

➤**6** Here, as in several places, Jude's teaching is very similar to Peter's (2 Pet. 2:4). **And the angels which kept not their first estate, but left their own habitation**—Many commentators say this refers to Genesis 6:1-4, which relates that "the sons of God" (understood by some to mean angels) had sexual relations with women. These angels abandoned their original position (i.e., angelic non-sexuality—angels were not created to reproduce) and habitation (heaven) when they mingled with the women on earth. The Book of Enoch, from which Jude later quotes (v. 14), supports this interpretation. And the context—which speaks of lasciviousness (v. 5), fornication (v. 7), and defiling the flesh (v. 8)—seems to underscore this view. But other commentators prefer to think that Jude was referring to Satan's original fall from heaven, at which time several of the angels that followed him were expelled from heaven. But the rest of Scripture does not indicate that Satan or his angels have been kept in everlasting chains. **he hath reserved in everlasting chains under darkness unto the judgment of the great day**—Commentators who favor the second interpretation given above explain that Jude is not speaking of literal prisons, for the evil angels can travel throughout the world, but they are forever shut out of God's presence and, like prisoners, are awaiting God's inescapable judgment. Even now they exist in an agony of fear, hatred, and complete evil. Commentators who espouse the first interpretation given above indicate that this place of punishment is the same one Peter spoke of in 2 Peter 2:4, called "Tartarus" (see comments on 2 Pet. 2:4).

➤7 **Sodom and Gomorrha**—See comments on 2 Peter 2:6. **going after strange flesh**—i.e., practicing homosexuality. This is the natural result of abusing the gift of sex, rejecting the way God intended it to be enjoyed. Even in the ancient world, the more sophisticated societies came to practice homosexuality without even feeling it was wrong. Such an acceptance clearly shows how far a culture has gone from the truth of God. **are set forth for an example**—See 2 Peter 2:6. **suffering the vengeance of eternal fire**—The complete destruction of these cities, signs of which still remain, is a symbol of the eternal punishment the false teachers will experience.

➤8 **dreamers**—They were asleep spiritually, neither knowing nor caring how seriously they were sinning. **defile the flesh**—through immorality (see v. 4). **despise dominion**—or, despise lordship. **speak evil of dignities**—lit., "blaspheme the glorious ones" (the angels). See comments on 2 Peter 2:10.

➤9 **Michael the archangel**—Michael is the greatest of all the angels (Dan. 10:13, 21) and has a special role in the history and future of Israel. His name means "Who is like God?" Michael and Satan (who is the chief of the fallen angels) have always been in conflict, and Michael will ultimately defeat Satan (Rev. 12:7ff.). **when contending with the devil he disputed about the body of Moses**—This detail can be found in Jewish tradition (based on the apocryphal book, The Assumption of Moses). From the Scriptures, we know that Moses' body was raised because he appeared to the disciples along with Elijah and Jesus on the Mount of Transfiguration (Matt. 17:1-4). Three men in three stages of history were given glorified bodies as examples and promises of the time when all God's people will be raised: Enoch, in the time of the fathers of the human race; Moses, when the law was given and the nation of

Israel was being formed; and Elijah, as one of God's prophets when Israel and Judah had formed two kingdoms. Satan, who has the power of death, argued that Moses' body should not be raised because he had sinned at Meribah. In the same way he continually accuses God's people of sin, but Christ defends us by pointing to his sacrifice that already paid for all our sin. **durst [dare] not bring against him a railing accusation**—because of Satan's former position as a mighty angel. Jude was vividly contrasting the scoffing of the false teachers (v. 8) with the respect that Michael, great as he is, had for Satan even after he had fallen from glory. This was not because he feared Satan, but because he realized that all authority and power come from God.

➤10 **speak evil of those things which they know not**—See 2 Peter 2:12. **as brute beasts**—Like animals, they know nothing except by instinct, and they do whatever comes naturally, whatever leads to physical gratification.

➤11 **Woe unto them!**—Such evil men are under the curse of God. **they have gone in the way of Cain**—The false teachers have the same attitude as Cain, who killed his brother because of his hatred and envy of Abel's godly life. **ran greedily after the error of Balaam for reward**—The Greek describes them as resembling a rushing torrent, hurrying recklessly after money. (See 2 Pet. 2:15.) **perished in the gainsaying of Core**—"perished in the rebellion of Korah" (RSV).

➤12 **spots**—The Greek word, *spilas,* can mean "blemishes" or "rocks." Some translations (KJV, RSV, NEB, NIV, TEV) render it "spots" or "blemishes." This accords with 2 Peter 2:13 and with the verb form of the same Greek word in verse 23 ("spotted"). Other commentators (Alford, Kelly) and translators (see NASB, Weymouth, RSV mg) render it "rocks" or "hidden rocks" (Blum). The first rendering speaks of defilement; the second of hidden danger (like hidden reefs). **in your feasts of charity**—i.e., your love feasts. This was a meal the early churches ate together in connection with the Lord's Supper. See comments on 2 Peter 2:13. **feeding themselves without fear**—They lacked reverence, or any sense of the Lord's presence, when they should have been remembering his death. **clouds**—Cf. 2 Peter 2:17. They claim to be Christians but do not act like it; they claim to have truth but teach lies. Like clouds that bring no rain, or trees without fruit, they are worthless, and only disappoint those who are deceived into expecting anything good from them. **twice dead**—Those who have never heard the gospel, although dead, still have a chance to live, like trees in winter that appear dead but in spring show signs of life. The false teachers have already been offered God's grace and have utterly rejected it, so they have no hope of life at all. Like an uprooted tree, they can never revive but only wait to be burned.

**►13 Raging waves**—See Isaiah 57:20. **wandering stars**—Rather than staying in their place and giving light to the world, the false teachers are like meteors or comets, flashing brightly and then disappearing again in darkness. Despite their show of brilliance, the false teachers are no help; they are unreliable and will not last long.

**►14** Although Jude drew from the apocryphal Book of Enoch, he did say that he was citing Scripture. Paul also quoted non-biblical writers (see comments on Acts 17:28; 1 Cor. 15:33; Titus 1:12). The very earliest prophecies about Jesus Christ tell of his second coming in glory and power, rather than his first coming in lowliness. **Enoch**—See Genesis 5:18-24. **seventh from Adam**—if Adam is counted as the first. **the Lord cometh**—This speaks of Christ's second coming to execute judgment (see 2 Thess. 1:6-10). **saints**—lit., "holy ones," which probably refers to angels (Deut. 33:2; Dan. 4:13-17; 2 Thess. 1:7).

**►15 convince** [reprove] **all that are ungodly**—Enoch's words were true not only of the sinful men of his time but of *all* the ungodly. Enoch's prophecy applied primarily to the flood, but also to God's final judgment. **hard speeches . . . spoken against him**—such as in verses 8, 10, and 16; see also Malachi 3:13, 14 in contrast with Malachi 3:16, 27. Those who mock God's children are regarded by God as speaking against himself.

**►16 murmurers, complainers**—cf. Numbers 11:1; Deuteronomy 28:47. **walking**

**after their own lusts**—The reason they are constantly complaining is that their evil desires are never satisfied, and they can never find contentment. **speaketh great swelling words**—See 2 Peter 2:18. **having men's persons in admiration because of advantage**—i.e., "flattering people to gain advantage."

**►17 remember ye the words which were spoken before of the apostles of our Lord Jesus Christ**—This implies that Jude's readers had known some of the other apostles, probably Peter and Paul. Jude could have been including himself among the apostles because he did not say "told us" but rather "told you" in verse 18. See 2 Peter 3:2.

**►18 How that they told you**—See Acts 20:29; 1 Timothy 4:11; 2 Timothy 3:1; 2 Peter 3:3. **mockers**—In the whole NT this word is found only here and in 2 Peter 3:3, again pointing up the close similarity between the letters of Jude and of 2 Peter. The false teachers Peter and Paul had warned about had already appeared and were causing serious problems in the churches. **in the last time**—This time period lasts from Christ's first coming until his second coming.

**►19 they who separate themselves**—or, they who cause separations. They set themselves up proudly as being wiser and more spiritual than the rest, with a "new doctrine," which is actually heresy. **sensual**—lit., "soulical" or, natural—as opposed to "the spiritual," or "having the Spirit." It is translated, "the natural man," in 1 Corinthians 2:14. In the threefold division of man's being, body, soul, and spirit, the proper state in God's design is that "the spirit," which is the recipient of the Holy Spirit's uniting man to God, should be first and should rule the soul, which stands intermediate between the body and spirit; but in the "natural" man, the spirit is subservient to the natural soul, which is earthly in its motives and aims. **having not the Spirit**—or, not having spirit. In the natural man the spirit, the most excellent part of his being, which ought to be the receiver of the Holy Spirit, is not indwelt by the Holy Spirit; and therefore, his spirit not being in its normal state, he is said not to have the spirit (cf. John 3:5, 6).

►**20 But ye, beloved**—This contrasts with the evil men Jude described in the previous verse. **building up yourselves**—In contrast with those causing separations, the believers need to build up each other. **on your most holy faith**—Those who discard the solid foundation of our faith in Christ only stir up arguments, splitting and weakening the church. But building our lives upon the truth of the gospel makes us strong, both as individuals and as a united body of believers. **praying in the Holy Ghost** [Spirit]—Unlike the false teachers who are devoid of the Spirit, the believers need to pray, being dependent upon the Holy Spirit. The Holy Spirit teaches us how to pray and what to pray for (Rom. 8:26). In verses 20 and 21 Jude brings together faith, hope, and love, and the Father, the Son, and the Holy Spirit.

►**21 Keep yourselves in the love of God**—Jude taught that, although God's love is what keeps us secure, we must exercise ourselves to remain in his love. **looking for**—or, awaiting, because our hope of **eternal life** is certain. **the mercy of our Lord Jesus Christ**—The Scriptures usually speak of mercy in relation to God the Father, but here Jude speaks of Christ's mercy. The Christian inherits **eternal life,** not on the basis of his or her good works, but on the basis of Christ's mercy.

►**22 And of some have compassion, making a difference**—which means "have pity on those who are doubting (or, wavering)." This reading is supported by all the earliest manuscripts. But several other early manuscripts read, "And reprove [or, correct] those who are doubting." The two words look very similar in Greek: *eleate* ("have pity") and *elegchete* ("reprove"); they could have easily been confused one for the other. The idea seems to be that saints are to have pity on or reprove those who have been affected by the false teachings and are now wavering between truth and falsehood. They need to be rescued.

►**23 And others save with fear**—"The faithful are urged to show all possible tenderness for the fallen, but at the same time to have a fear lest they themselves or others whom they influence should be led to think too lightly of the sin whose ravages they are endeavoring to repair" (Mayor). **pulling them out of the fire**—Those who have been wavering and are about to follow the false teachers will share their same judgment—"the vengeance of eternal fire." Such people need to be saved, to be rescued—to be brought to the truth, to be brought into true salvation. **hating even the garment spotted by the flesh**—Christians are to avoid becoming defiled by their contact with those whom they are attempting to rescue. The Christian needs to influence the wavering person, not vice versa. A Christian needs to keep his garment (his Christian behavior) free from any stains (see Rev. 3:4).

►**24, 25** This is Jude's doxology; it is full of hope and encouragement. **keep you from falling**—lit., "guard you without stumbling." **faultless**—unblemished. **before the presence of his glory**—or, "before his glorious presence" (NIV). **To the only wise God**—See Romans 16:27. **our Saviour**—See 1 Timothy 1:1. Many early manuscripts have the phrase "through Jesus Christ our Lord" after "To the only wise God our Saviour." **majesty**—or greatness. **dominion**—or, might. **power**—lit., "authority." Mayor paraphrases this doxology as follows:

> I have bidden you to keep yourselves in the love of God; I have warned you against all impiety and impurity. But do not think that you can attain to the one, or guard yourselves from the other, in your own strength. You must receive power from above, and that it may be so, I offer up my prayer to Him, who alone is able to keep you from stumbling, and to present you before the throne of His glory, pure and spotless in exceeding joy. To Him, the only God and Saviour, belong glory, greatness, might, and authority throughout all ages.

BIBLIOGRAPHY

Alford, Henry. *The Greek New Testament.* 1852. Reprint. Grand Rapids: Guardian Press, 1976.

Blum, Edwin A. "Jude" in the *Expositor's Bible Commentary.* Grand Rapids: Zondervan, 1981.

Hughes, Philip E. "The Languages Spoken by Jesus" in *New Dimensions in New Testament Study*. Grand Rapids: Zondervan, 1974.

Kelly, J. N. D. *A Commentary on the Epistles of Peter and Jude* in The Harper New Testament Commentaries. New York: Harper & Row, 1969.

Mayor, J. B. "The Epistle of Jude" in *The Expositor's Greek Testament*. Grand Rapids: Eerdmans, 1979.

Pentecost, J. Dwight. *Things to Come: A Study in Biblical Eschatology*. Findlay, Ohio: Dunham, 1961.

# REVELATION

## Introduction

The author of Revelation calls himself John (1:1, 4, 9; 22:8). Justin Martyr (c. A.D. 100-165) in his *Dialogue* quotes from Revelation, as the work of John the apostle, with respect to the prophecy of the millennium of the saints, to be followed by the general resurrection and judgment. This testimony of Justin is referred to also by Eusebius (*Ecclesiastical History,* 4.18). Justin, in the early part of the second century, held his controversy with Trypho, a learned Jew, at Ephesus, where John had been living thirty or thirty-five years before. Justin said, "The Revelation had been given to John, one of the twelve apostles of Christ." Melito, a second-century bishop of Sardis (one of the seven churches addressed in Revelation), is said by Eusebius (*Ecclesiastical History,* 4.26) to have written treatises on Revelation. So also Theophilus of Antioch, according to Eusebius's *Ecclesiastical History,* quoted testimonies (c. A.D. 180) from the Revelation of John. Eusebius says the same of Apollonius, who lived in Asia Minor in the end of the second century. Irenaeus (fl. c. A.D. 180), a hearer of Polycarp, the disciple of John, is most decided again and again in quoting Revelation as the work of the apostle John (*Against Heresies,* 4.20.11; 4.21.3; 4.30.4; 5.36.1; 5.30.3; 5.35.2). In 5.30.1, alluding to the mystical number of the beast, 666 (13:18), he says, "We do not hazard a confident theory as to the name of the Antichrist; for if it had been necessary that his name should be proclaimed openly at the present time, it would have been declared by him who saw the apocalyptic vision; for it was seen at no long time back, but almost in our generation, towards the end of Domitian's reign." In his work *Against Heresies,* published ten years after Polycarp's martyrdom, Irenaeus quotes Revelation twenty times, and makes long extracts from it, as inspired Scripture. These testimonies of persons contemporary with John's immediate successors, and more or less connected with the region of the seven churches to which Revelation is addressed, are most convincing. Tertullian of North Africa (c. A.D. 160-220), *Against Marcion* 3.14, quotes the apostle John's descriptions in Revelation of the sword proceeding out of the Lord's mouth (19:14) and of the heavenly city (chap. 21). The Muratorian Fragment of the Canon (c. A.D. 200) refers to John the apostle writing to the seven churches. Hippolytus, bishop of Ostia, near Rome (c. A.D. 240), in *The Antichrist* quotes 17:1-18 as the writing of John the apostle. Among Hippolytus's works, there is specified in the catalogue on his statue a treatise "on the Apocalypse and Gospel according to John." Clement of Alexandria (c. A.D. 155-220), in his *Stromata,* 6.13, alludes to the twenty-four seats on which the elders sit as mentioned by John (4:5); also, in *Quis dives Salvus,* sec. 42, he mentions John's return from Patmos to Ephesus on the death of the Roman tyrant, Domitian (c. A.D. 96). Origen's (c. A.D. 185-254) *Commentary on Matthew* (according to Eusebius's *Ecclesiastical History,* 6.25) mentions John as the author of Revelation, without expressing any doubts as to its authenticity; so also in the same commentary (16.6) he quotes 1:9 and says, "John seems to have beheld the Apocalypse in the island of Patmos." Victorinus, bishop of Pettau in Pannonia, who suffered martyrdom under Diocletian in A.D. 303, wrote the earliest extant commentary on Revelation.

Revelation's canonicity and inspiration (according to Andreas of Cappadocia) are attested to by Papias, a hearer of John and associate of Polycarp. Papias was bishop of Hierapolis, near Laodicea, one of the seven churches mentioned in this book. The epistle of the churches of Lyons and Vienne to the churches of Asia and Phrygia (in Eusebius's *Ecclesiastical History,* 5.1-3) in the persecution under Marcus Aurelius (A.D. 177) quotes 1:5; 3:14; 14:4; and 22:11 as Scripture. (For other instances, see Alford's *Prolegomena,* from which mainly this summary of evidence has been derived.) Athanasius, in his *Festival Epistle,* lists Revelation among the canonical Scriptures, to which none must add and from which none must take away. Jerome (in *Epistola ad Paulinum*) includes Revelation in the canon, adding, "It has as many mysteries as words. All praise falls short of its merits. In each of its words lie hid manifold senses." Thus an unbroken chain of testimony down from the apostolic period confirms its canonicity and authenticity.

The Alogi (*Epiphanius on Heresies,* 51) and Gaius the Roman presbyter (Eusebius's *Ecclesiastical History,* 3.28), toward the end of the second and beginning of the third century, rejected John's Revelation for hypercritical reasons. Gaius, according to Jerome (*De Viris Illustribus,* c. A.D. 210) attributed it to Cerinthus, on the ground of its supporting the millennial reign on earth. Dionysius of Alexandria mentions many before his time who rejected it because of its obscurity and because it seemed to support Cerinthus's dogma of an earthly and carnal kingdom; whence they attributed it to Cerinthus. Dionysius, student of Origen and bishop of Alexandria (c. A.D. 247), admits its inspiration (in Eusebius's *Ecclesiastical History,* 7.10) but attributes it to some John distinct from John the apostle on the ground of its difference of style and character, as compared with John's Gospel and first epistle, and also because the name John is several times mentioned in Revelation, while it is never mentioned in either the Gospel or the first epistle. Moreover, neither does the first epistle make any allusion to Revelation, nor Revelation to the first epistle; and the style is not pure Greek but abounds in grammatical errors. Eusebius wavers in opinion (*Ecclesiastical History,* 24.39) as to whether it is or is not to be ranked among the undoubtedly canonical Scriptures. His antipathy to the millennial doctrine would give an unconscious bias to his judgment on Revelation. Cyril of Jerusalem in *Catecheses,* 4.35, 36 omits Revelation in enumerating the NT Scriptures to be read privately as well as publicly. "Whatever is not read in the churches, that do not even read by yourself; the apostles and ancient bishops of the Church who transmitted them to us were far wiser than you are." Hence, we see that, in his day, Revelation was not read in the churches. Yet in *Catecheses* 1.4 he quotes 2:7, 17; and in *Catecheses* 1.15.13 he draws the prophetical statement from 17:11, that the king who is to humble the three kings (Dan. 7:8, 20) is the eighth king. In chapters 15 and 27 he similarly quotes from 12:3, 4. Alford conjectures that Cyril had at some time changed his opinion, and that these references to Revelation were slips of memory whereby he retained phraseology that belonged to his former, not his subsequent, views. The sixtieth canon (if genuine) of the Laodicean Council in the middle of the fourth century omits Revelation from the canonical books. The Eastern church in part doubted; the Western church, after the fifth century, universally recognized Revelation. Cyril of Alexandria, in *De Adoratione* 146, though implying the fact that some doubted its genuineness, himself accepted it as the work of John. Andreas of Caesarea, in Cappadocia, recognized it as genuine and canonical and wrote the first entire and connected commentary on Revelation. The sources of doubt seem to have been (1) the antagonism of many to the millennial kingdom (20:5, 6) which is set forth in it; and (2) its obscurity and symbolism having caused it not to be read in the churches, or to be taught to the young. But the objective evidence is decidedly for it; the only arguments against it seem to have been subjective.

The personal notices of John in Revelation occur in 1:1, 4, 9; 22:8. Moreover, the writer's addresses to the churches of Proconsular Asia (2:1) agree with the tradition that after John's return from his exile in Patmos, at the death of Domitian, he resided for a long time and then died at last in Ephesus, in the time of Trajan (Eusebius's *Ecclesiastical History,* 3.20, 23). If Revelation were not the inspired work of John, purporting as it does to be an address from their superior to the seven churches of Proconsular Asia, it would have assuredly been rejected in that region, whereas the earliest testimonies in those churches are all in its favor. One person alone was entitled to use the language of authority such as is addressed to the seven angels (messengers) of the churches—namely, John, as the last surviving apostle and overseer of the churches. Also, it accords with John's manner to assert the accuracy of his testimony both at the beginning and end of his book (cf. 1:2, 3 and 22:8, with John 1:14; 21:24; 1 John 1:1, 2). Again, it accords with the view of the writer's being an inspired apostle that he addresses the angels (messengers) of the several churches in the tone of a superior addressing inferiors.

As to the difference of style, as compared with the Gospel and the first epistle, the difference of subject in part accounts for it—the visions of the seer, transported as he was above the region of sense, appropriately taking an abrupt form of expression unlike the grammar and syntax that governed his writings in a calmer and more deliberate character. Moreover, as a Galilean Hebrew, John, in writing a revelation akin to the OT prophecies, naturally reverted to their Hebraistic style. Alford notices, among the features of resemblance between the styles of Revelation and John's Gospel and first epistle: (1) the characteristic appellation of our Lord, peculiar to John exclusively, "the Word of God" (19:13; cf. John 1:1; 1 John 1:1). (2) The phrase, "he that overcometh" (2:7, 11, 17; 3:5, 12, 21; 12:11; 15:2; 17:14; 21:7; cf. John 16:33; 1 John 2:13, 14; 4:4; 5:4, 5). (3) The Greek term (*alēthinos*) for "true," as opposed to that which is shadowy and unreal (3:7, 14; 6:10; 15:3; 16:7; 19:2, 9, 11; 21:5; 22:6). This term, found only once in Luke (Luke 16:11) and four times in Paul (1 Thess. 1:9; Heb. 8:2; 9:24; 10:22), is found nine times in John's Gospel (John 1:9; 4:23, 37; 6:32, 7:28; 8:16; 15:1; 17:3; 19:35), twice in John's first epistle (1 John 2:8; 5:20), and ten times in Revelation (3:7, 14; 6:10; 15:3; 16:7; 19:2, 9, 11; 21:5; 22:6). (4) The Greek diminutive for "Lamb" (*arnion,* lit., "lambkin") occurs twenty-nine times in Revelation, and the only other place where it occurs is John 21:15. In John's writings alone is Christ called directly "the Lamb" (John 1:29, 36). In 1 Peter 1:19, he is called "as a lamb without blemish," in allusion to Isaiah 53:7; so the use of "witness" or "testimony" (1:2, 9; 6:9; 11:7, etc.;

cf. John 1:7, 8, 15, 19, 32; 1 John 1:2; 4:14; 5:6-11), and "keep the word" or "command-ments" (3:8, 10; 12:17; cf. John 8:51, 55; 14:15). Compare also 1 John 2:20, 27 with 3:18 as to the spiritual anointing. The seeming grammatical errors are attributable to that inspired elevation which is above mere grammatical rules and were perhaps designed to arrest the reader's attention by the peculiarity of the phrase, so as to pause and search into some deep truth lying beneath. The vivid earnestness of the inspired writer, handling a subject transcending all others, raises him above servile adherence to ordinary rules of grammar, so that at times he abruptly passes from one grammatical construction to another, as he graphically sets the thing described before the eye of the reader. This is not due to ignorance of grammar, for he "has displayed a knowledge of grammatical rules in other much more difficult constructions" (Winer).

The best authorities among the Fathers state that John was exiled under Domitian (Irenaeus, 5.30; Clement of Alexandria; Eusebius's *Ecclesiastical History,* 3.20). Victorinus says that he had to labor in the mines of Patmos. At Domitian's death, A.D. 96, John returned to Ephesus under the emperor Nerva. He received the Revelation while he was on the island of Patmos. This island is one of the Sporades group of islands. Its circumference is about thirty miles. "It was fitting that when forbidden to go beyond certain bounds of the earth's lands, he was permitted to penetrate the secrets of heaven" (Bede, *Explanations of Apocalypse*).

Tregelles well says, "There is no book of the New Testament for which we have such clear, ample, and numerous testimonies in the second century as we have in favor of the Apocalypse. The more closely the witnesses were connected with the apostle John (as was the case with Irenaeus), the more explicit is their testimony. The doubts that prevailed after ages must have originated either in ignorance of the earlier testimony, or else from some supposed intuition of what an apostle *ought* to have written. The objections on the ground of internal *style* can weigh nothing against the actual evidence. It is in vain to argue, a priori, that John *could* not have written this book when we have the evidence of several competent witnesses that he *did* write it."

Gregory of Nyssa (fourth century) called Revelation "the last book of grace." It completes the volume of inspiration, so that we are to look for no further revelation till Christ himself shall come. Appropriately the last book completing the canon was written by John, the last survivor of the apostles. The NT is composed of the historical books, the Gospels and Acts, the doctrinal epistles, and the one prophetical book, Revelation. The same apostle wrote the last of the Gospels, and probably the last of the Epistles, and the only prophetical book of the NT. All the books of the NT had been written and were read in the church assemblies some years before John's death. His life was providentially prolonged that he might give the final attestation to Scripture. About the year A.D. 100, it is said that the bishops of Asia came to John at Ephesus, bringing him copies of the three Gospels, Matthew, Mark, and Luke, and desiring a statement of his apostolical judgment concerning them; whereupon he pronounced them authentic, genuine, and inspired, and at their request added his own Gospel to complete the fourfold aspect of the Gospel of Christ (cf. the Muratorian Canon).

Eusebius's *Ecclesiastical History,* 3.24; Jerome, *Praemium in Matthaeum;* Victorinus on the *Apocalypse;* and Theodoret, *Mopsuestia*). The canon would be incomplete without Revelation. Scripture is a complete whole, and its component books, written in a period ranging over 1,500 years, are mutually connected. Unity of aim and spirit pervades the whole, so the end is the necessary sequence of the middle, and the middle of the beginning. Genesis presents man and his bride in innocence and blessedness, followed by man's fall through Satan's subtlety, and man's consequent misery, his exclusion from paradise and its tree of life and delightful rivers. Revelation presents, in reverse order, man first liable to sin and death, but afterwards made conqueror through the blood of the Lamb; the first Adam and Eve, represented by the last Adam, Christ, and the church. His spotless bride, in paradise, with free access to the tree of life and the crystal water of life that flows from the throne of God. As Genesis foretold the bruising of the serpent's head by the woman's seed, so Revelation declares the final accomplishment of that prediction (chaps. 19, 20).

Revelation is addressed to the seven churches of Asia, i.e., Proconsular Asia. John's reason for fixing on the number *seven* (for there were more than seven churches in the region meant by "Asia," for instance, Magnesia and Tralles) was doubtless because *seven* is the sacred number implying totality and universality; so it is implied that John, through the medium of the seven churches, addresses the church of all places and ages. The church in its various states of spiritual life or deadness, in all ages and places, is represented by the seven churches, and is addressed with words of consolation or warning accordingly. Smyrna and Philadelphia alone of the seven are honored with unmixed praise, as faithful in tribulation and rich in good works. Well-defined heresies had by this time arisen in the churches of Asia, and the love of many believers had grown cold. Others had advanced to greater zeal, while one believer had sealed his testimony with his blood.

After a brief introduction that sets forth the main subject of the book, viz., to "show unto his servants things which must shortly come to pass," Revelation begins with admonitory addresses to the seven churches from the divine Son of man, whom John saw in his vision (chaps. 1-3). From chapter 4 to the end is mainly prophecy, interspersed with practical exhortations and consolations similar to those addressed to the seven churches, and so connecting the body of the book with its beginning. In fact, chapters 4–22 can be seen as containing expansions of many of the important themes introduced in the first three chapters.

Basically, three schools of interpreters exist: (1) the Preterists, who hold that almost the whole prophecy of Revelation has been fulfilled. (2) The historical interpreters, who hold that it comprises the history of the church from John's time to the end of the world, the seals being chronologically succeeded by the trumpets and the trumpets by the vials. (3) The Futurists, who consider almost the whole prophecy as yet future, and to be fulfilled immediately before Christ's second coming. The first theory was not held by any of the earliest fathers. The Futurist school is open to this great objection: it would leave the church of Christ without prophetical guidance or support under her fiery trials for 1700 or 1800 years. The Jews had a succession of prophets who guided them with the light of prophecy. What their prophets were to them, the apocalyptic Scriptures have been, and are, to the church. Also, there are schools of interpretation with respect to the coming of Christ and the millennial kingdom. (1) The premillennial interpreters believe Christ will return just prior to establishing a millennial kingdom on earth. (2) The amillennial interpreter does not think there will be a literal millennial kingdom (he takes the language in 20:3-6 to be figurative). (3) The postmillennial interpreter thinks the church age will produce the kingdom on earth—after which time Christ will return. Throughout the course of the commentary, on various passages, these various views will be presented. The commentary generally advances the premillennial view.

Alford, following Isaac Williams, draws attention to the parallel connection between Revelation and Christ's discourse on the Mount of Olives, recorded in Matthew 24. The seven seals plainly bring us down to the second coming of Christ, just as the seven trumpets also do (cf. 6:12-17; 8:1, etc.; 11:15), and as the seven vials also do (16:17): all three run parallel and end in the same point. Certain "catchwords" (as Wordsworth calls them) connect the three series of symbols together. They do not succeed one to the other in historical and chronological sequence but move side by side, the subsequent series filling up in detail the same picture the preceding series had drawn in outline. So Victorinus, the earliest commentator on Revelation, says, "The order of the things said is not to be regarded, since often the Holy Spirit, when He has run to the end of the last time, again returns to the same times, and supplies what He has less fully expressed" (7:2).

Moreover, Revelation is connected with the OT, especially Daniel and Ezekiel. Many of the revelations given to Daniel and Ezekiel (and other OT prophets) find their complete fulfillment and actualization in Revelation. Revelation is the end of all prophecy and the consummation of God's eternal plan.

*Chapter* 1

## 1-8 PROLOGUE AND GREETINGS TO THE SEVEN CHURCHES

➤1 **Revelation**—Greek, "apocalypse," meaning "an unveiling." The book of Revelation unveils the triumphant Christ, with his glorious kingdom, the church. Some interpreters define the Revelation as a manifesto of the kingdom of Christ, while others see it as a "traveling manual" of the church for the Gentile Christian times. Others suggest that the Revelation is not a detailed history of the future; it may represent the great epochs and chief worldly powers in developing the kingdom of God. The Revelation should give us understanding about the times; the times should not interpret the Revelation, although it is possible to discern how the times do exert a reflex influence (Auberlen). The book is a series of parallel groupings, not in chronological order. Still there is a live historical development of the kingdom of God. In this book all the other books of the Bible end and meet. According to many interpreters, it is the consummation of all previous prophecy. Daniel foretells the events relating to Christ, the Roman destruction of Jerusalem, and the last Antichrist. But John's Revelation then fills up the intermediate period and describes the millennium and final state beyond the Anti-

christ. Daniel saw the history of God's people in relation to the four world kingdoms. John viewed history from the perspective of the Christian church. The term "apocalypse" applies to no OT book; the book of Daniel is the nearest approach to it, but Daniel was told to seal and shut up the visions until the end of time, while John indicated that the time had come (1:3) to reveal what had been sealed. **of Jesus Christ**—Jesus Christ is the actual source of this revelation, while John is a mere amanuensis (secretary or penman)—he wrote what Jesus revealed to him. God gave the revelation to Jesus Christ, who, in turn, gave the revelation to his servants by sending it through his servant, John. The text, therefore, indicates that it is "the revelation given by God to Jesus Christ so that he could tell his servants about the things which are now to take place very soon" (JB). Strictly speaking, the text does not say that this is "the revelation concerning Jesus Christ"—though many commentators are fond of saying that Revelation is a book that reveals Jesus Christ. This cannot be denied, but it misses the point of Revelation 1:1, which presents Christ as the revealer, not the object of the revelation. Bengel said that Christ revealed many things before he left this earth, but those that were unsuitable for announcement at that time he brought together into the book of Revelation. (See Christ's promise in John

16:13.) **which God gave unto him**—The Father reveals himself and his will in and by his Son. **to show . . . things which must shortly come to pass**—These things are detailed in the rest of Revelation. **unto his servants**—i.e., unto all who serve God (see Rev. 22:3). **shortly**—lit., "with speed." Christ's coming and all the events connected with that coming are often said to be imminent. "The church in every age has always lived with the expectancy of the consummation of all things in its day. Imminency describes an event possible any day, impossible no day" (Johnson). **sent and signified** [i.e., made it known] **it** [the revelation] **by his angel**—This does not happen until 17:1; 19:9, 10. Prior to that, John receives information from others. Jesus Christ begins the Revelation (1:10, 11; see also 4:1). In 6:1 one of the four living creatures acts as his informant; in 7:13 one of the elders reveals information. In 10:8, 9 the Lord and his angel stand by the sea and the earth to reveal information to John. Only at the end (17:1) does the one angel stand by him (cf. Dan. 8:16; 9:21; Zech. 1:19). **unto his servant John**—As one among many of God's servants, John was selected to receive the revelation, record it in writing, and send it to the seven churches in Asia (1:4). Through this medium, God's revelation would reach all God's servants.

➤**2 bare record**—testified. **the word of God**—i.e., the message God gave John to give the churches. **the testimony of Jesus Christ**—This could mean "the testimony concerning Jesus Christ" (as in 1:9; 12:17; 20:4); but more probably it means here "the testimony given by Jesus Christ." Jesus validated the word of God by his own testimony (see 19:10; 22:16-20). The oldest manuscripts omit "and." This would change the meaning to refer to all those things he saw from God and Jesus Christ.

➤**3 Blessed is he that readeth, and they that hear the words of this prophecy**—In ancient days, all reading was done out loud. In this statement, the reader was the public reader in church assemblies; those who "hear" were his hearers. God's blessing has been upon both the reader and the listener. The term "prophecy" relates to the human medium or inspired prophet, the apostle John. God gave the revelation to Jesus. Jesus, by his angel, revealed it to John, who in turn was to make it known to the church. **keep**—i.e., obey, heed (cf. Rom. 2:13).

➤**4 John**—As sole survivor and representative of the apostles and eyewitnesses of the Lord, he needed no other identification except his name in order to be recognized by his readers. (See Introduction.) **seven churches**—seven local churches in Asia Minor, now called Turkey. This does not mean that there were only seven churches in this region. The number "seven" probably refers to the church in its totality and not simply to the seven churches mentioned in 1:11 (Trench). The number "seven" was a sacred number in Jewish numerology, composed of the world number, "four," and the divine number "three." It is the covenant number, the sign of God's covenant relation to mankind and particularly to the church. Thus, the seventh day is the Sabbath Day (Gen. 2:3; Ezek. 20:12). Circumcision, the sign of the covenant, was performed after seven days (Gen. 17:12). Sacrifices, etc. are also related to the seventh day. See Numbers 23:1; 14:29; 2 Chronicles 29:21. Cf. also God's typical acts of his covenant (Josh. 6:4, 15, 16; 2 Kings 5:10). The feasts were arranged by sevens (Deut. 15:1; 16:9, 13, 15). The number seven recurs more times in the Revelation than anywhere else in Scripture. **Asia**—At that time it was a Roman province, governed by a Roman proconsul. The Territory consisted of Phrygia, Mysia, Caria, and Lydia. **Grace . . . and peace**—Paul began most of his epistles in the same way. **from him which is, and which was, and which is to come**—Greek, "from the one being and the one who was and the one coming." The title, describing God the Father, shows him as the eternal, unchangeable, self-existing One, the I AM THAT I AM. **seven Spirits**—"sevenfold Spirit" (TLB, NIV mg). This description of the divine Spirit depicts the sevenfold energy of the Holy Spirit—his perfect, complete, and universal energy. The term "sevenfold" probably corresponds to the earlier reference to "the seven churches." (See comments on 5:6.) Swete, in his classic commentary on the Revelation, suggests that the spirits are seven in number because they operate in the seven churches. The Spirit of God is one in his essence but numerous in his gracious influences. The origin of this expression could have been derived from a currently popular interpretation of Isaiah 11:2, 3, which was taken as a reference to the sevenfold spiritual blessings.

➤**5 from Jesus Christ, who is the faithful witness**—Jesus Christ was a faithful witness throughout his entire ministry. Whatever he heard from the Father he was faithful to speak to men, no matter what the consequences. His faithfulness eventually cost him his life. **the first begotten of the dead**—John immediately established the prominence of Jesus Christ, who not only faithfully revealed all truth but was the first to rise from death (1 Cor. 15:20; Col. 1:18). Lazarus (and others) rose to die again. Christ rose to die no more. This resurrection was a kind of birth (see John 16:20-22 and comments), a new beginning. Other Scriptures affirm this: Psalm 2:7; Acts 13:33; Romans 1:4; Colossians 1:18. According to Romans 1:4, Christ's resurrection revealed his divine sonship as the God-man. So our resurrection and our sonship (or, regeneration) are connected. **prince [ruler] of the kings of the earth**—Jesus is an eternal King, not a temporal sovereign who may rule momentarily, only to be replaced by another king. Jesus attained the kingship of this world by suffering on the cross and then conquering death. See Psalm 2 for a description of God's Son as King. **him that loved us**—The earliest manuscripts have the verb in the present tense, "him who is loving us"—who continues to love us. His love rests eternally on his people. **washed**—This word is found in late manuscripts; the earliest manuscripts read "freed" or "loosed." Even though the two words look very similar (*lusanti* [freed] and *lousanti* [washed]) it is very likely that "freed" (a more difficult reading) was changed to "washed" than vice versa. Christ redeemed us by a ransom (Gk., *lutron*). It seems that this expression is used to refer to the exodus. By his death and resurrection, Christ has delivered his people out of a bondage similar to the Egyptian bondage, only much more terrible—the bondage to sin. It is not mere deliverance, however. It is deliverance from our sins **in [by] his own blood.** The wonder of it all is that Christ, having freed his people from the bondage of sin, made them a kingdom in which every individual is a priest.

➤**6 made us kings and priests unto God**—Greek, "made us a kingdom, priests unto God"; i.e., the kingdom is a kingdom of priests (see Exod. 19:6; 1 Pet. 2:19). The saints together shall constitute the kingdom of God and shall

themselves be kings (cf. 5:10). They will share his king-priest throne in his kingdom. While many interpreters would place the emphasis at the point more on the kingdom than on the priesthood, the emphasis is primarily on a spiritual kingdom, not a materialistic kingdom. Those in the kingdom comprise a kingdom of priests who serve God the Father. And they are kings because they are priests—their priesthood gives them a right to be kings, for they are kings in relation to man, but priests in relation to God. The priest-kings will rule, not because they are holding this office, but simply by virtue of what they are. They will have the power to attract and to convict the heart (Auberlen). **priests unto God**—Priests, above all, have the privilege of near access to the king. The distinction of priests being closer to God than other people will cease. All will have access to the Father. All persons and things will be holy to the Lord. **God and his Father**—There is only one article in the Greek text; therefore, the reference is to one who is both God and Father. **glory and dominion for ever and ever**—The fuller, threefold doxology occurs in 4:11, while the fourfold occurs in 5:13. A sevenfold doxology occurs in 7:12.

➤**7** See Matthew 24:30; Daniel 7:13; Revelation 19:11-21 is the vision corresponding to the prophecy of these Scriptures. **he cometh with clouds**—Jesus was taken up in a cloud at his ascension (Acts 1:9). He will return by the same means (Acts 1:11). **every eye shall see him**—His coming will be personal and visible. **they also which pierced him**—Although a soldier pierced Jesus' side (John 19:34), the party referred to here is plural, not singular. This statement probably speaks of those who were responsible for Jesus' death, namely, the Jews. This accords with Zechariah 12:10, the OT source for this entire verse. **all the kindreds of the earth**—lit., "all the tribes of the land" (referring to the Jews in the land of Israel). **shall wail because of him**—According to Zech. 12:10, they will weep in remorse and repentance for having pierced their Messiah. **Even so [Yes], Amen**—This is God's seal of his own work. This corresponds to the believer's prayer (22:20). The "Amen" comes from Hebrew; the "yes" from Greek. To both Jews and Gentiles his promises and warnings are unchangeable.

➤**8 I am Alpha and Omega**—the first and last letters of the Greek alphabet. This divine title appears again in 21:6 and 22:13. In each context it is difficult to discern if the title applies to God or to Christ or to both. Most likely it can be attributed to the Godhead—God in Christ. God in Christ comprises all that goes between Alpha and Omega, as well as being the first and the last. This expresses God's fullness, comprehensiveness, and all-inclusiveness. **the beginning and the ending**—This is not present in the oldest manuscripts. Later, transcribers inserted the clause, taking it from 21:6. **which is, and which was, and which is to come**—See comments on 1:4. **the Almighty**—Greek, *pantokrator,* meaning "the one who has his hand on everything"—i.e., the one in control of everything. God commands all the hosts of powers in heaven and earth, so he is able to overcome all his foes. The title "almighty," occurs often in Revelation (4:8; 11:17; 15:3; 16:7, 14; 19:6, 15; 21:22), but nowhere else in the NT except in 2 Corinthians 6:18.

9-20 THE SON OF MAN, IN THE MIDST OF THE SEVEN GOLDEN LAMPSTANDS

➤**9 I John**—This is like the expression "I Daniel" in Daniel 7:28; 9:2; 10:2—one of the many features of resemblance between the OT and NT apocalyptic seers. No other Scripture writer uses this phrase. **your brother, and companion in tribulation**—John described himself as their brother and fellow sufferer (lit., "co-sharer in affliction"). **in the kingdom and patience of** [in] **Jesus Christ**—John not only shared their suffering, but he also shared with them in the kingdom and in their patient endurance. The phrase "in Jesus" ("Christ" is not present in the earliest manuscripts) could modify "brother and companion" or "kingdom and patience." **the isle that is called Patmos**—This is a rocky, barren island in the Aegean Sea. Patmos was thirty miles off the West coast of Asia Minor and opposite Ephesus. According to Eusebius, the emperor Domitian had banished John from Ephesus (in A.D. 95) because of his continued witnessing about Jesus. He was released 18 months later by Nerva. He significantly noted that although he was banished from his friends, he was not separated from Jesus. **for the word of God**—John was banished for preaching God's word. **for the**

**testimony of Jesus Christ**—i.e., the testimony John had given to Jesus Christ (see 1 John 1:1-3).

➤**10 I was in the Spirit**—Greek, "I came to be in spirit." In the context of this book, this expression describes a special experience in the Spirit. John was probably in a state of ecstasy: the outer world being shut out and the inner and higher life or spirit being fully controlled by God's Spirit, John was able to enter the invisible, spiritual realm. While the prophet "speaks" in the Spirit, the apocalyptic seer's whole personality was in the Spirit. **the Lord's day**—This is the earliest mention of the "Lord's Day." This was most likely the first day of the week, a day on which Christians gathered to worship and celebrate the Lord's Supper (see Acts 20:17). Ignatius seems to allude to "the Lord's Day," as does Irenaeus. Justin Martyr in his *Apology* (2:98) says, "On Sunday we all hold our joint meeting; for the first day is that on which God, having removed darkness and chaos, made the world, and Jesus Christ our Savior rose from the dead. On the day before Saturday they crucified him, and on the day after Saturday, which is Sunday, having appeared to his apostles and disciples, he taught these things." Tertullian in *De Coron* (3) says, "On the Lord's Day we deem it wrong to fast." Clement of Alexandria, Origen, and Dionysius of Corinth also refer to the Lord's day. **I . . . heard behind me a great** [loud] **voice**—a voice which he had not heard for some sixty years, the voice of Jesus.

➤**11 I am Alpha and Omega, the first and the last**—These words are not present in the earliest manuscripts; they were interpolated into later manuscripts from 22:13. **seven churches which are in Asia**—There were many churches in Proconsular Asia (Miletus, Magnesia, Tralles) in addition to the seven specified. However, the number "seven" is used because it expresses totality and universality. Surely we are to understand that these churches represent the entire group. Ramsay insisted that these cities were centers of seven postal districts of this area in Asia Minor. As a result, they were the best cities for circulating letters intended for other churches in the area. "The seven churches to whom John was directed to write were located on a major Roman road. A letter carrier would leave the island of Patmos (where John was exiled), arriving first at Ephesus. He would travel north to Smyrna and Pergamum, turn southeast to Thyatira, and continue on to Sardis, Philadelphia, and Laodicea—in the exact order in which the letters were dictated" (*Life Application Bible*).

These seven churches are representative churches, embodying the chief spiritual characteristics of the church in all ages, whether faithful or unfaithful. Some interpreters view the churches as representing distinct ages of the church's history. Others view them as individual churches, that had their own distinct problems or virtues. Thus, on one side, there was Smyrna, a church exposed to persecutions unto death. On the other side, Sardis had a name for spiritual life, but it was already dead. Laodicea was lukewarm in Christ's cause. However, Philadelphia had little strength, yet she kept Christ's word and had an open door of usefulness set before her by Christ himself. Ephesus was intolerant of evil and false apostles but had left her first love. Thyatira abounded in works, love, service, and faith, yet a false prophetess seduced many. In another aspect, Ephesus was in conflict with false freedom (the sexual immorality of the Nicolaitans), while Pergamos was in conflict with Balaam-like tempters who promoted free sex and food offered to idols. Philadelphia was in conflict with the Jewish synagogue (legal bondage). Finally, Sardis and Laodicea were without any active opposition to muster their spiritual energies; this was a dangerous position, considering man's natural laziness. In the historic scheme of interpretation, Ephesus represents the closing period of the apostolic age. Smyrna represents intense suffering during the martyr period of the Decian and Diocletian age. Pergamos was the church possessing earthly power but decreasing spirituality from Constantine's time until the seventh century. Thyatira represents the papal church in the first half of the Middle Ages. Sardis represents the church from the close of the twelfth century to the Reformation period. Philadelphia represents the first century of the Reformation, and Laodicea represents the Reformed Church after its first zeal had become stagnant.

➤12 seven golden candlesticks [lampstands]—When John turned to see the one who was speaking, he saw the seven candlesticks. (see Exod. 25:31, 32 for a description of the seven united in one lampstand. See also Zech. 4:2, 11.) The lampstand is not light but rather "holds" the light so that it may give light to all around it. It is not the churches' light but the Lord's. From the Lord the church receives her light. In the OT tabernacle, the lampstands stood in the holy place; since daylight was blocked out, its only light came from the lampstand. By comparison, the Lord God is the churches' only light. Some commentators (e.g., Talbot) insist that the lampstands represent the church as a whole, while others (e.g., Larkin) are more specific—they insist that the lampstands serve as representative churches, referring to various historical church ages.

➤13 in the midst of the seven candlesticks [lampstands]—This implies Christ's continual presence and ceaseless activity among his people on earth. Son of man—Jesus' self-designated, messianic title, a title that emphasizes his humanity and his suffering. His present glory (as Son of man, not merely Son of God) is the result of his humiliation as Son of man. clothed with a garment down to the foot, and girt about the paps [breasts] with a golden girdle—The extension of the robe down to his feet is significant in that it indicates a high rank. The robe and golden girdle seem to be emblems of his priesthood (cf. Exod. 28:2, 4, 31). Aaron's robe and breastplate were "for glory and beauty" and combined the insignia of royalty and priesthood. Christ has exercised his priesthood since the time of his ascension and therefore wears its emblems. As Aaron wore his insignia when he came out from the sanctuary to bless the people (Lev. 16:4, 23, 24), so when Christ shall come again, he shall appear in the similar attire of beauty and glory. The ordinary girding for priests was around the loins; but Josephus (*Antiquities,* 3.7.2) expressly tells us that the Levitical priests were girded higher, around the chest; this was appropriate to calm, majestic movement. The girdle braced the body together and symbolized collected powers. The high priest's girdle was only interwoven with gold, but Christ's is all of gold.

➤14 His head and his hairs were white like wool—In the OT reference (Dan. 7:9), this term applies to the "Ancient of days" (God himself). The white hair signifies purity and glory (Isa. 1:18), not age or decay. **his eyes were as a flame of fire**—This implies consuming indignation against sin. The same description appears in Daniel 10:6, a portion which describes the Son of man; in 2:18, in Christ's message to the church in Thyatira; and in 19:12, in describing the conquering King, Jesus.

➤**15 his feet like unto fine brass**—as if they had been made fiery (red-hot) in a furnace. The same image appears in Daniel 10:6 and Revelation 2:18; it depicts judgment. **his voice as the sound of many waters**—cf. Ezekiel 43:2; see Revelation 14:2. His voice is fearful to his foes.

➤**16 He had in his right hand seven stars**—See 1:20. **out of his mouth went a sharp, twoedged sword**—The sword refers to his keen and accurate judgment on the deeds of man. His word is potent in executing judgment (see 2:12, 16; 19:15, 21). **his countenance was as the sun shineth in his strength**—Christ is presented here in his full, transfigured, resplendent glory (see Matt. 17:2).

➤**17 I fell at his feet as dead**—John was overwhelmed by Christ's glorious presence. (Cf. Dan. 10:9. Also, see Josh. 5:14; Isa. 6:5; Ezek. 1:28.) **laid his right hand upon me**—At the transfiguration the Lord Jesus did the same to the three prostrate disciples, of whom John was one. On that occasion he said, "Be not afraid." The touch of his hand imparted strength and confidence. **I am the first and the last**—He lives from eternity and endures through eternity (see Isa. 41:4; 44:6; 48:12).

➤**18 he that liveth**—Greek, "the living one." **was dead**—Greek, "became dead." **I am alive**—Greek, "I am living." Jesus has life and is the source of life for all his people. In 4:9, 10; 10:6, this same expression describes the Father. Because Jesus passed through death as a man and now lives in resurrection, his people can rest assured that he is the way to resurrection and eternal life. **the keys of hell** [Hades] **and of death**—The order is reversed in the earliest manuscripts. The "keys" are symbolic of authority; the one who has the keys opens and shuts the gates at will (Ps. 9:13, 14; Isa. 38:10; Matt. 16:18). Christ now has authority over death and Hades.

➤**19 the things which thou hast seen**—most likely referring to John's vision of the Son

of man in chapter 1. **the things which are**—probably referring to the *then* present conditions of the seven local churches (chaps. 2–3). **the things which shall be hereafter**—perhaps referring to the rest of the book of Revelation (chaps. 4–22).

➤**20 mystery**—The Greek word signifies a secret revealed to the initiates. Jesus now explains some of the secret symbols of John's first vision. **stars are the angels**—Since the Greek word for "angel" (*angelos*) can also mean "messenger," many commentators are inclined to think that Jesus was referring to human messengers—probably elders in the local churches. But other commentators doubt this interpretation because the word *angelos* is never used in apocalyptic literature with reference to a human messenger (Johnson).

*Chapter* **2**

## 1-7 THE EPISTLE TO THE CHURCH IN EPHESUS

Each of the seven letters included in this and the following chapters begins with "I know" or "I am fully aware." Each also contains a promise from Christ regarding victory through him. Each ends with the admonition "He that hath an ear, let him hear what the Spirit saith unto the churches." The title of our Lord in each case accords with the nature of the address and is taken mainly from the imagery of the vision in 1:4, 5, 12-18. To the church in Ephesus, Jesus presents himself as the one who has the seven stars in his right hand and stands in the midst of the seven lampstands (cf. 1:16 with 2:1); to the church in Smyrna, as the one who became dead and is alive forever more (cf. 1:18 with 2:8); to the church in Pergamos, as the one who has a two-edged sword proceeding out of his mouth (cf. 1:16 with 2:16); to the church in Thyatira, as the one who has eyes as a flame of fire and feet as burnished brass (cf. 1:14, 15 with 2:18); to the church in Sardis, as the one who has the seven Spirits of God and the seven stars (cf. 1:4, 5, 16 with 3:1; see also 4:5; 5:6); to the church in Philadelphia, as the one who has the keys of David (cf. 1:18 with 3:7); and the the church in Laodicea, as the one who is the faithful witness (cf. 1:5 with 3:14).

Each address to each church contains a warning or a promise, and most of the addresses have both. Their order seems to be ecclesiastical, civil, and geographical: Ephesus first, as being the Asiatic metropolis called "the light of Asia" and "the first city of Asia," the nearest to Patmos, where John wrote Jesus' letters to the churches. Next mentioned are the churches on the west coast of Asia; then those in the interior are named. Smyrna and Philadelphia alone received pure praise. Sardis and Laodicea almost solely received condemnation. In Ephesus, Pergamos, and Thyatira, there are some things to praise and others to condemn. Praise is dominant in the letter to Ephesus, while condemnation is dominant in the letters to Pergamos and Thyatira. Therefore, the main characteristics of the various churches, in all times and places, are exposed and appropriately encouraged or warned against. The general outline of each letter follows this pattern: identification of writer, evaluation (whether commendation, criticism, or both), and declaration of promise to those who overcome.

**➤1 Ephesus**—is famous for the temple of Diana, one of the seven wonders of the world. Paul had worked there for three years and had written an epistle to the Ephesian church. He eventually ordained Timothy as overseer there but probably only temporarily. Toward the end of his life, John made Ephesus the center from which he labored and taught. **holdeth**—lit., "holding tightly." **the seven stars**—See comments on 1:20. **who walketh in the midst of the seven golden candlesticks** [lampstands]—See comments on 1:13.

**➤2 I know thy works, and thy labour, and thy patience**—This demonstrates Jesus' omniscience. **canst not bear**—Evil men were a burden; the Ephesian church regarded them as unbearable. We are to share each other's troubles and problems (Gal. 6:2) but are not to tolerate false apostles. **tried**—tested (see 1 Cor. 14:29; 1 Thess. 5:21; 1 John 4:1). **which say they are apostles, and are not**—The churches founded by the apostles had the miraculous gift of discerning spirits (cf. Acts 20:28-30). History is replete with illustrations of this gift being put into action. Tertullian and Jerome refer to a writing alleged to be a canonical history of the Acts of Paul that had been composed by an elder of Ephesus. The apostle John convicted the author and condemned the work.

**➤3** The Ephesians suffered for Jesus without ceasing. According to the earliest manuscripts, this verse should read, "I know you are enduring patiently and bearing up for my name's sake, and you have not grown weary" (RSV).

**➤4** However, this energetic and orthodox church is deficient in love. **thou hast left thy first** [best] **love**—an obvious reference to love for Christ (cf. 1 Tim. 5:12) and probably also to brotherly love. This letter was written during the time of Domitian, and over thirty years had elapsed since Paul had written his letter to the Ephesians. Their warmth of love had turned into a lifeless orthodoxy. (Cf. Paul's view of Christian gifts without love in 1 Cor. 13:1ff.)

**➤5 Remember therefore from whence thou art fallen**—The church is called upon to remember the heights from which it had fallen. **repent**—change your thinking. The Lord here commands them to repent and **do the first works**—i.e., the works motivated by love. This is not a mere "feeling of your first feelings," but doing the works flowing from the same principle as before, "faith which works by love." **I will come unto thee quickly, and will remove thy candlestick** [lampstand] **out of his** [its] **place**—Jesus would take the church away from Ephesus if it did not **repent.** The church would cease to exist as a church (or cease to have any kind of testimony) if it did not remember its "first love."

**➤6** After this necessary censure, Jesus returns to praise the Ephesians for their stand against the works of the Nicolaitans. The Nicolaitans may have been followers of Nicolas, one of the original seven deacons (Acts 6:5). This group was comprised of believing Christians who were antinomians ("against law"). They attempted to introduce false freedom into the church. They had reacted in the opposite direction from legalistic Judaism. Legalism was the first danger the church combated by the council of Jerusalem and by Paul in his letter to the Galatians. These Nicolaitans or followers of "Balaam" (as deduced from 2:14, 15) abused Paul's doctrine of the grace of God by turning it into a plea for sexual freedom (cf. 2 Pet. 2:15, 16, 19; Jude 4:11).

**➤7 He that hath an ear, let him hear what the Spirit saith unto the churches**—This clause precedes the promise in the first three epistles and follows it in the last four. Those with spiritual perception are warned to listen. Note: What Christ says, the Spirit says—for in each epistle the speaking of Jesus Christ is identified as the speaking of the Spirit. Christ is present in the local churches in, through, and as the Spirit (see 1 Cor. 15:45; 2 Cor. 3;17, 18; Rev. 4:5; 5:6—and comments on all the verses). "Churches" is plural and refers to the churches of Asia Minor, as well as to all local churches. **To him that overcometh**—is an expression appearing in similar form both in John's Gospel (16:33) and 1 John (2:13, 14; 5:4, 5). Paul uses a similar image (Rom. 12:21; 1 Cor. 9:24, 25; 2 Tim. 2:5). An overcomer conquers the problems pertaining to his or her local church and remains faithful to the end (1 John 5:5; Rev. 2:26). **give to eat of the tree of life**—The tree of life in paradise (the new Jerusalem), lost by the fall, will be restored by the Redeemer. Allusions to the tree of life occur in Proverbs 3:18; 11:30; 13:12; 15:4; Ezekiel 47:12; and Revelation 22:2, 14. It is interesting to note how closely these introductory addresses are linked to the rest of the book of Revelation. Thus, the "tree of life" appears here and also in 22:1. Deliverance from the "second death" appears in 2:11; 20:14; 21:8. The "new name" (2:17) is mentioned also in 14:1. Revelation 2:26 and 20:4 speak of the believers' authority over the nations. The morning star appears in 2:28 and 22:16. "Clothed in white" (3:5) is also seen in 4:4; 16:15. The book of life (3:5) also occurs in 13:8; 20:15. Revelation 3:12 and 21:10 link the new Jerusalem and its citizenship. **in the midst of the paradise of God**—The words "in the midst" are not present in the earliest manuscripts. In Genesis 2:9 the words "in the midst" are appropriate, for there were other trees in the garden. In this passage the tree of life is simply in the paradise of God, for no other tree is mentioned in it. "Paradise" (a Persian or Semitic word), originally used of any garden of delight, is explained as belonging to God. Therefore, to eat of the tree of life is to partake of eternal life.

## 8-11 THE EPISTLE TO THE CHURCH IN SMYRNA

➤**8 Smyrna**—was located some 35 miles north of Ephesus. The city had great wealth and beauty, possessing a stadium, library, and the largest public theater in Asia Minor. It had the pagan temples of Cybele and Aphrodite. In addition to enslavement to the pagan gods, Caesar worship was also prominent. A large Jewish population lived there and constantly informed the Romans of the Christians' activities. This heightened persecution of the Christians. Polycarp, who was martyred about A.D. 160, more than 80 years after his conversion, was the leading elder of Smyrna. Ignatius, on his way to martydom in Rome, wrote to Polycarp (A.D. 108), who was then bishop of Smyrna. Tertullian and Irenaeus, who talked with Polycarp during his youth, tell us that Polycarp was consecrated bishop of Smyrna by the apostle John. Polycarp's martyrdom was characteristic of the suffering of that period in church history. This has led many commentators to see Smyrna as representing the post-apostolic church age, an age characterized by persecutions. **the first and the last, which** [who] **was dead** [became dead], **and is alive** [lived again]—See 1:17. These are the attributes of Christ most suitable to the church under persecution. As death was the gateway to eternal life for Christ, so it will be for them (2:10, 11). ·

➤**9 thy works**—These words are not present in many early manuscripts. **tribulation**—afflictions through persecution. **poverty**—financial destitution. Perhaps they were poverty-stricken because of the suffering they endured. **but thou art rich**—Contrast the Laodicean church's wealth in the world's eyes as well as her own, with her poverty before God. "There are both poor rich-men and rich poor-men in God's sight" (Trench). **say they are Jews, and are not**—These are Jews by national descent but not spiritually of "the true circumcision." Some Jews blasphemed Christ as "the hanged one." As elsewhere, so at Smyrna Jews bitterly opposed Christianity. At Polycarp's martyrdom they joined the heathen in clamoring for his being thrown to the lions, but when there was an obstacle to this, they began to clamor for his being burned alive; they even carried logs for the pile. **the synagogue of Satan**—This refers to certain Jews in Smyrna who, motivated by Satan, instigated attacks against the church there (Johnson).

➤**10 Fear none of those things which thou shalt suffer**—"The Captain of our salvation never keeps back what those who are faithful witnesses for him may have to bear for his name's sake; never entices recruits by the promise they shall find all things easy and pleasant there" (Trench). **the devil**—meaning "the accuser." He acted through Jewish accusers against Christ and his followers. **ye may be tried**—by the devil's temptations. The same event is often both a temptation by the devil and a trial from God. **ye shall have tribulation ten days**—Some interpreters explain this to be ten years according to a year/day principle. Yet the short time of the persecution is evidently made a ground for consolation. The time of trial will be short; the duration of their joy will be forever. (See the usage of "ten days" for a short time in Gen. 24:55; Dan. 1:12.) **crown of life**—See 2 Timothy 4:8; James 1:12; 1 Peter 5:4. To receive a crown of life is to receive the reward of eternal life.

►**11 shall not be hurt of** [by] **the second death**—refers to the "lake of fire" (21:8). The phrase "second death" is peculiar to Revelation. What does the first death matter if we escape the second death? Augustine commented, "the life of the damned is death." Smyrna (meaning "myrrh") yielded its sweet perfume in being persecuted, even if it meant death. (Myrrh was used in embalming dead bodies [John 19:30] and thereby could typify "death.") Prior to his martyrdom, Polycarp uttered these noble worlds to his heathen judges who wanted him to renounce his faith. He said, "Fourscore and six years have I served the Lord, and he never wronged me; how then can I blaspheme my King and Savior?"

## 12-17 THE EPISTLE TO THE CHURCH IN PERGAMOS

►**12 Pergamos**—was the capital city of Mysia and was located about 55 miles northeast of Ephesus. The Pergamos library (one of the most famous libraries of its day) contained about 200,000 volumes. In fact, parchment, made from the hides of sheep, derived its name from Pergamos. However, this city was also a center of pagan worship; it contained a temple of Asclepius, the snake god of healing. In addition, Greek gods and emperor worship were also prevalent. **hath the sharp sword with two edges**—This is appropriate to his address, which has a penetrating power to con-

vince and convert some (2:13, 17) and to convict and condemn others (2:14-16). The description recalls 1:16 and anticipates 2:16.

►**13 where Satan's seat** [throne] **is**—In an impious mimicry of God's heavenly throne (4:2), Satan set up an earthly throne. Various gods were worshiped in Pergamos, such as Zeus and Asclepius; and emperor-worship was also prevalent. Satan had gained a throne there. **Antipas was my faithful martyr**—According to the context, Antipas (meaning "against all") was martyred through the instigation of Satan. He may have been martyred for his refusal to say "Lord Caesar" instead of "Lord Christ," as the citizens of Roman lands were required to do.

►**14 the doctrine of Balaam, who taught Balac** [Balak] **to cast a stumblingblock before the children of Israel, to eat things sacrificed unto idols, and to commit fornication**—According to Numbers 25:1ff., 31:16, 2 Peter 2:15, and Jude 11, Balaam showed the Midianite women how to lead the Israelites into sin by getting them to eat meat sacrificed to Baal-peor and engage in fornication associated with the worship of Baal-peor. Some of the Christians at Pergamos held to the doctrine of Balaam. They, like the Nicolaitans (see comments on 2:6), adhered to a liberal interpretation of grace. They participated in the practices of the pagans with whom they lived—and subverted by that culture, they succumbed to Satan's scheme.

►**15 the doctrine of the Nicolaitanes** [Nicolaitans]—See comments on 2:6 and 2:14.

►**16 Repent**—Not only the followers of Balaam and the Nicolaitans, but all the church members are called on to change their ways because they did not hate such teaching and practices. **fight against them with the sword of my mouth**—This refers to a war with the followers of Balaam primarily but also includes punishment of the whole church at Pergamos. The sword of his mouth recalls 1:16, but it is also an allusion to the drawn sword with which the angel of the Lord confronted Balaam on his way to curse Israel.

►**17 eat of the hidden manna**—in contrast with the meats offered to idols (2:14). The hidden manna calls to mind the manna hidden in the Ark of the Covenant (Exod. 16:33, 34). In this context, Jesus may have been speaking of himself as the true manna, the bread of life, the bread of God (see John 6:31ff.). Even as the "manna" hidden in the Ark of the Covenant was by divine power preserved from corruption, so Christ and his incorruptible body passes into the heavens and is hidden there until the time of his appearing. Christ himself is the manna "hidden" from the world but revealed to the believer (cf. John 4:32, 34). **white stone . . . a new name . . . which no man knoweth saving** [except] **he that receiveth it**—In ancient times, white stones were given to people (with their names written on them) as invitations to special banquets. (This is similar to the practice in modern times of sending engraved invitations.) If this is what Jesus was alluding to, the white stone with the new name could very well signify an open invitation to his wedding feast (19:9).

## 18-29 THE EPISTLE TO THE CHURCH IN THYATIRA

➤**18 Thyatira**—was the smallest of the cities addressed. It was located forty miles southeast of Pergamos. The city had neither special religious significance nor was it a center of Caesar worship. However, it was an important commercial center. Thyatira was known as a center of world trade and for its dyeing industry (cf. Lydia of Acts 16). The people manufactured a purple dye that came from the madder root and a shellfish called morex. The dye was extremely expensive. **Son of God, who hath his eyes like unto a flame of fire, and his feet are like fine** [burnished] **brass**—Christ's attributes (1:14, 15) again accord with this address. The title "Son of God" is from Psalm 2:7-9, which is referred to in 2:27.

➤**19 I know thy works**—Jesus commended the Christians of Thyatira, giving them full credit for their works, which had increased.

➤**20 sufferest** [permit] **that woman Jezebel, which** [who] **calleth herself a prophetess, to teach and to seduce my servants to commit fornication, and to eat things sacrificed unto idols**—The symbolic "Jezebel" was just as powerfully influential for evil to the church of Thyatira as Jezebel, Ahab's wife, was to him. This self-styled prophetess was as closely attached to the church of Thyatira as a wife is to her husband. As Balaam in Israel's early history, so

Jezebel, daughter of the king of Sidon (1 Kings 16:21), was the great seducer to idolatry in Israel's later history. Like her father, she was swift to violence and murder. She was a dedicated Baal worshiper, as was her father. (His name, Eth-baal, expresses his idolatry.) Jezebel seduced the weak Ahab and Israel beyond calf-worship (worship of the true God, but a violation of the second commandment) to that of Baal (violation of the first and second commandments). She seems to have been a prophetess of Baal (cf. 2 Kings 9:22, 30). The spiritual foe at Thyatira lured God's servants in the same way as the Balaamites and Nicolaitans did (2:6, 14, 15)—to fornication and eating meat offered to idols. By false spiritualism the seducers led their victims to the grossest carnality, as though things done in the flesh were outside of the true man and therefore of no consequence.

➤**21 I gave her space** [time] **to repent of her fornication; and she repented not**—The earliest manuscripts read, "she desired not to repent." Here there is a transfer from literal to spiritual fornication, as appears from 2:22. This idea arose from Yahweh's covenant relationship with Israel as being regarded as a marriage; any transgression against this relationship was harlotry, fornication, or adultery.

➤**22 I will cast her into a bed**—The bed of her sins will be the place of her sickness and anguish. Perhaps a pestilence was about to be sent, or her "bed" would become her eternal grave. **them that commit adultery with her**—i.e., those who participated with her in her adulteries. Her punishment is distinct from theirs; she is to be thrown into a bed and her children are to be **cast . . . into great tribulation.**

➤**23 I will kill her children with death**—This probably contains an allusion to the slaying of Ahab's seventy sons. The judgment is to be as vicious as the sin has been. **and all the churches shall know that I am he which searcheth the reins and hearts**—This depicts Christ's divine omniscience (cf. Ps. 139:1, 2, 23; Jer. 17:10). "Heart" is center of the thought or intellect according to Hebrew thought, while "reins" is literally "kidneys," the center of the emotions.

**I will give . . . according to your works—**
See Matthew 16:27.

➤**24 unto the rest in Thyatira, as many as have not this doctrine—**i.e., those in the church at Thyatira who did not adhere to Jezebel's deception. **the depths of Satan, as they speak** [say]—Gnostic teachers boasted particularily of their knowledge of the mysteries and of the deep things of God, but their knowledge was actually "of Satan"—it was satanically, not divinely, inspired (Beasley-Murray). (Note also 2:9, where Jesus refers to the synagogue of Satan.) Although Gnosticism was not full-grown at this time, some beginnings did exist earlier than the time of John's writing. Many interpreters believe that John's writings were directed against gnostic error. **I will put upon you none other burden—** except to keep from and protest against the above-mentioned Gnostics.

➤**25 hold fast till I come—**the first of several references to Christ's second coming (Johnson).

➤**26 he that overcometh—**or, he that conquers. The overcomers are those who rise above the problems in their particular local church to live a life pleasing to Jesus. **keepeth my works unto the end—**Cf. Matthew 24:13. **him will I give power** [authority] **over the nations—**After Christ's coming the overcomers shall reign over the nations together with Christ (see 3:21; 20:4).

➤**27 he shall rule them with a rod of iron—**Cf. Psalm 2:8, 9. The verb translates literally, "rule as a shepherd," but the expression "rod of iron" indicates that the term "rule" is used here in a destructive sense. Since severity is the primary thought, "rule as a shepherd" seems to be used in the following manner: he who *would* have shepherded them with a pastoral rod shall have to shepherd them with "a rod of iron" because of their unbelief. **as the vessels of a potter shall they be broken—**This vivid image depicts the power of executed judgment. As partners with Christ, the overcomers will join him in executing judgment against the nations.

➤**28 I will give him the morning star—**Christ referred to himself as the morning star in connection with his coming (22:16), and Peter spoke of the day star with reference to

Christ's coming (see 2 Pet. 1:19 and comments). Thus, to receive the morning star must have something to do with participating in the glories of Christ's second coming.

➤**29** See comments on 2:7.

Chapter **3**

## 1-6 THE EPISTLE TO THE CHURCH IN SARDIS

➤**1 Sardis—**This city was located 30 miles southeast of Thyatira. Sardis was a commercial hub for the towns of that area, and wealth poured into the city. Sardis was given to Cybele worship, a Phrygian religion. The followers of Cybele were immoral and crude, not only in their lives but also in their worship. The church in Sardis was like a man who simply appeared to be alive. The church was outwardly existing but inwardly void of life. Jesus' rebuke does not seem to have been in vain, for Melito, bishop of Sardis in the second century, was known for his piety and learning. **the seven Spirits of God—**or, the sevenfold Spirit of God (TLB, NIV mg). The title indicates the Spirit in all its fullness (see 1:4 and comments; 4:5; 5:6; Zech. 3:9; 4:10). A dead church needs the infusion of the sevenfold Spirit of God. **and the seven stars—**See comments on 1:20 and 2:1. **thou hast a name that thou livest, and art dead—** "You have the reputation of being alive, even though you are dead!" (TEV, cf. 1 Tim. 5:6; 2 Tim. 3:5). Sardis was known among the churches for her supposed spiritual vitality, yet the all-knowing Christ pronounced her dead. Laodicea deceived herself as to her true state (3:17), but it is not written that she had a reputation among the other churches as did Sardis.

➤**2 Be watchful, and strengthen the things which remain—**Strengthen those remaining few graces that have not yet become extinct (Alford). **that are ready to die—**The earliest manuscripts read, "which were about ready to die." The church in Sardis, as a whole, was near to spiritual death. Christ's rebuke was intended for deliverance and restoration. **I have not found thy works perfect** [complete] **before God—**In the sight of men, all might appear well, but in God's sight, Sardis was dead. Note that of the seven churches Sardis and Laodicea alone had no conflict with foes without or within the church. This is not to say that either had renounced the appearance of opposition to the world, but both lacked life, freshness, and vitality.

►3 **how thou hast received and heard**—the word of the gospel from the apostles. Sardis is to return to her beginnings so that she will realize how important her original gift was and how much she valued what she first heard and received. **If therefore thou shalt not watch, I will come on thee as a thief**—Christ elsewhere used this language not only to describe his second coming but also his special judgment on churches and peoples. These special judgments anticipate the great last coming. Augustine comments, "The last day is hidden from us, that every day may be observed by us." In his days on earth Christ mentioned this at least twice (Matt. 24:42, 43; Luke 12:39, 40). And the apostles, remembering what Christ said, mention it themselves (1 Thess. 5:2, 4, 6; 2 Pet. 3:10). Revelation 16:15 again mentions Christ's coming as a thief.

►4 **a few names** [persons] **even in Sardis which have not defiled their garments**—This image speaks of those who have not soiled their lives with sin (see 1 Cor. 8:7; 2 Cor. 7:1; 11:2; Jude 23). Cf. also Ephesians 5:27 for Paul's reference to the spotlessness of the church when she shall be presented to Christ. Meanwhile, the church is not to become spotted with any defilement because no defilement shall enter the heavenly city. **they shall walk with me in white**—The promised reward is like the character of those to be rewarded: keeping their garments undefiled and white through the blood of the lamb (7:14) will entitle them to "walk" with him in "white" for eternity. The grace and dignity of long flowing garments is seen to the best advantage when the person "walks." Even so the saint's full character will appear when he serves the Lord perfectly hereafter (22:3). **for they are worthy**—states the reason for the Christians' walking with Jesus. Such worthiness is not their own, but it is given to them from Christ (7:14).

►5 **white raiment**—"White garments are symbolic of righteousness, victory, and the glory of God (3:18; 6:11; 7:9, 13f.; 19:14)" (Johnson). **I will not blot out** [erase] **his name out of the book of life**—Ancient cities kept

registers of their citizens; of course, the names of the dead were erased. So those that have a name indicating that they live but who are actually dead will be blotted out of God's roll of the heavenly citizens and heirs of eternal life. This is not to say that in God's electing decree they were ever in his book of life. But, according to human conceptions, those who had a high name for piety would be supposed to be included in it. Even so, this will do them no good. For references to "the book of life," see 13:8; 17:8; 20:12, 15; 21:27; and Exodus 32:32; Psalm 69:28; Daniel 12:1; and Philippians 4:3. **before my Father, and . . . his angels**—Cf. the similar promise of Christ's confessing before his Father those who confessed him in Matthew 10:32, 33; Luke 12:8, 9.

►6 See comments on 2:7.

## 7-13 THE EPISTLE TO THE CHURCH IN PHILADELPHIA

►7 **Philadelphia**—was located approximately 28 miles southeast of Sardis and was founded by Attalus II c. 140 B.C. Attalus was called the "Philadelphos" ("brother lover"), and the city was named for him. Philadelphia was a city of tremendous potential inasmuch as its mission in earlier days had been to spread Hellenism to the area beyond. It was therefore referred to as the city with the door of opportunity. It was famous for its vineyards and hot springs. The city was destroyed by an earthquake during the reign of Tiberius (A.D. 17). Thereafter, many people lived in the rural area around Philadelphia. Sometimes, the city was called "little Athens" because of the prevalence of idols and paganistic gods within the city. The church in Philadelphia had enjoyed freedom from pagan persecution and from heresies within the church. But, as was true in Smyrna, the Jews had created difficulties for the Christians in Philadelphia. **he that is holy**—as in the OT expression, "The Holy One of Israel." Thus Jesus and the God of the OT are one. None but God is absolutely holy (the Gk. term is *hagios,* "separation from what is common"). **true**—lit., "the true one." The terms "holy" and "true" apply to Christ, but in 6:10 they are used to describe God. His nature answers to his name (John 17:3; 1 Thess. 1:9). **the key of David**—Jesus' faithfulness is described in relationship to possessing the "key of David."

The "key" in David's time had been given to Eliakim; it was a symbol of authority "over the house of David." Eliakim's authority was transferred from Shebna, who was removed as unworthy of the office of chamberlain and treasurer (see Isa. 22:20-22). Christ, the heir of the throne of David, will replace all the less worthy stewards who have abused the trust in God's spiritual house, and he will "reign over Israel forever" (Luke 1:33). The authority to open or close the door to the kingdom rests with Christ, and he decides who is and who is not to be admitted. This power is described in 1:17, 18 by the statement "who has the keys of hell and death." Christ, the true David, has the key of the supreme government upon him. He has the authority to open or close the door to the kingdom, and no one can countermand him.

➤8 an open door—to his kingdom (3:7) and/or to preaching the gospel. thou hast a little strength—Because Philadelphia was weak, she was a fit object for God's power to work through her. and hast kept my word, and hast not denied my name—The verbs are in the aorist tense in Greek, perhaps pointing to a specific time of trial when the church kept Christ's word and did not deny his name.

➤9 I will make—The promise to Philadelphia is greater than to Smyrna. To Smyrna the promise was that the synagogue of Satan would not win over her (see comments on 2:9); to Philadelphia he promised that she should even win over some of the supporters of Satan, who in turn will come and worship before thy feet. The converts will take the very lowest place in the church, doing honor to those they once persecuted.

➤10 Because thou hast kept the word of my patience—i.e., you have kept my word to be patient. Christ himself patiently waits for Satan to be cast out and all enemies to bow before him. I also will keep thee from the hour of temptation [trial]—Jesus offered to reward the faithful according to their faithfulness. which shall come upon all the world, to try them—The trial will bring out the loyalty of those kept by Christ and the hardness of the unbelieving (9:20, 21; 16:11, 21). The particular persecutions that came to Philadelphia shortly thereafter

were the foretaste of the great, last tribulation before Christ's second coming.

➤11 I come quickly—This is a great incentive to remain faithful under the present trials. hold that fast which thou hast—This refers to their patient obedience, which he had just commended them for keeping and which involved the attaining of the kingdom (3:10). They would lose this if they yielded to the temptation of compromise and ease. They were to hold tightly so as not to lose the crown Jesus had given them. Their victory was assured if they held on to it.

➤12 Him that overcometh will I make a pillar in the temple of my God—The reward for the overcomer is to be given a permanent, even eminent, place in God's eternal habitation. he shall go no more out—Under no circumstances will he go out from the temple. The door shall be closed once for all, shutting in the elect forever and shutting out the lost (Matt. 25:10; John 8:35; cf. Isa. 22:23). They will be priests forever unto God (1:6). The historical background of the city and the citizens' custom of writing heroes' names on a pillar in one of the temples serves as the background of this honor and recognition. I will write upon him the name of my God—This suggests that the individual will belong to God in a particular sense (7:3; 9:4; 14:1). The security will be unquestioned. As the name of Yahweh was on the golden plate of the high priest's forehead (Exod. 28:36-38), so the saints and their heavenly royal priesthood shall bear his name openly as people who are set apart for him. Cf. the caricature of this and the brand on the forehead of the beast's followers (13:16, 17) and on the harlot (17:5, cf. 20:4). the name of the city of my God—The saints' citizenship is now hidden, but then it shall be revealed. They will have the right to enter through the gates into the city (22:14). new Jerusalem—"new" in quality, not merely "new" in time. "New" emphasizes that the city is "new and different," superseding the worn-out old Jerusalem and its polity. Bengel states, "John, in the gospel, applies to the old city the Greek name Hierosolyma, but in the Apocalypse, always, to the heavenly city, the Hebrew name Hierousalem. The Hebrew name is the original and holier one; the Greek, on the other hand, is the more secular and political one." **which cometh down out of heaven from my God**—The new Jerusalem, God's eternal habitation with his redeemed people, will not be in heaven, but on the new earth. The new Jerusalem will descend from heaven to the new earth, and every aspect of this city will originate from God. This expression is repeated in 21:2. **I will write upon him my new name**—This is at present incommunicable and known only to God, but it will be revealed and made the believer's own in union with God in Christ. The believer will be entirely Christ's. "New" (in quality) relates to Christ, for he will assume a new character. He will enter with his saints into a kingdom earned by his humiliation as Son of man.

➤**13** See comments on 2:7.

## 14-22 THE EPISTLE TO THE CHURCH IN LAODICEA

➤**14 church of the Laodiceans**—actually, "the church in Laodicea." The situation in the Laodicean church well illustrates the peril of materialism and money. Its geographical location and proximity to Colosse and Hierapolis made it one of the richer commercial cities of the ancient world. The city was destroyed by an earthquake in c. A.D. 17, and its wealthy citizens who refused aid from the state rebuilt it. This suggests that they needed help from neither God nor man. The primary source of monetary gain in this area was from woolen cloth and clothing made from the many black-wool sheep bred there. Laodicea was famous for its worship of Asclepius, the Greek god of healing. Laodiceans had developed a famous medical school and produced an ointment to cure sore ears and a certain powder used in the treatment of diseased eyes. **the Amen, the faithful and true witness**—Jesus' unchanging faithfulness as the Amen ("the One who stands firm") contrasts with Laodicea's wavering of purpose and lukewarmness (3:16). The "faithful and true witness" logically follows the identification of Jesus as "the Amen." "Faithful" means trustworthy (2 Tim. 2:11, 13). "True" is here not truth-speaking but fully realizing all that is comprehended in the word "testimony" (1 Tim.

6:13). Three things are essential for this: (1) to have seen with his own eyes what he attests; (2) to be competent to relate it for others; (3) to be willing to testify truthfully. Jesus met all these conditions. **the beginning of the creation of God**—not he whom God created first, but (as in Col. 1:15-18) the beginner, the originator of all creation. The translation in TEV captures the thought here: "the origin of the creation of God." His being the "origin of creation" is a strong guarantee for his faithfulness.

➤**16 lukewarm, and neither cold nor hot**—The second expression reiterates the first. Lukewarmness characterizes complacency in spiritual matters. Those who are lukewarm are useless to Christ, even tasteless to him—so much so that he will spew them out of his mouth. **I will**—Greek, "I am about to," "I am ready to." The text implies the possibility that Christ might not spit them out—if they repent. **spue thee** [spit you] **out of my mouth**—This statement is the saddest of the condemnations contained within these letters.

➤**17 Because thou sayest, I am rich**—This indicates that self-sufficiency is the fatal danger of a lukewarm state. This statement implies self-praise and self-acquired riches (see Hos. 12:8). **knowest not that thou art wretched, and miserable, and poor**—The "you" is emphatic in the Greek text and shows the Laodiceans' true state to be quite different from what they had pictured it to be—they saw themselves as people of wealth and prosperity. Jesus sees them as wretched, pitiable people who seem to be saying, "We have need of nothing!" And whereas Laodicea boasted of a deeper than common insight into divine things, they were **blind.** They were not absolutely blind, else eye-salve would have been of no use to them (3:18); rather, they were shortsighted.

➤**18** This verse conveys Jesus' gentle and loving irony. Not only were the Laodiceans' convictions untrue, they were in need of the most common necessities of existence. Jesus graciously stooped to their modes of thought and speech. He said in essence, "You are a people ready to listen to any counsel concerning the securing of an advantage; then, listen to my counsel." **buy of me gold tried in the fire**— "Buy" does not imply that we can by any work or merit purchase God's free gift. The very purchase consists in the renunciation of all self-righteousness, such as Laodicea possessed (3:17). They were encouraged to buy "gold purified by fire," gold that had proved its purity and retained its bright gloss. Sterling spiritual wealth, when contrasted with counterfeit spiritual experience, seems to have a brightness the Laodiceans boasted of but failed to possess. Jesus further counseled them to purchase **white raiment** [clothing], a figure likely based upon the fact that Laodicea was famous for its woolen materials and garments. Christ offered infinitely whiter raiment. These garments would clothe the Laodiceans so they would no longer be naked and ashamed. Man can discover his shame, but God alone can cover it so that his naked appearance will be covered. **anoint thine eyes with eye-salve**—Christ had a salve for Laodicea far more valuable than all the expensive eye-salves produced in Laodicea (see comments on 3:14). The "eye" is a reference to the inner man, the mind, the ego. If it is sound and "single," man sees aright spiritually; but if it is unsound, he does not have proper spiritual vision. Our inner man needs the anointing of the Holy Spirit in order to have clear spiritual sight (cf. 1 John 2:20, 27). He first opens our eyes to ourselves and our sinfulness and then to the Savior and his blessedness. Trench comments that Sardis and Laodicea are the only churches in which no specific opponents from without are mentioned, nor is there reference to heresies within the group. Without any foes, either internal or external, the church can become stagnant. ►**19 As many as I love, I rebuke and chasten**—cf. Job 5:17; Proverbs 3:11, 12; Hebrews 12:5, 6. This verse indicates that their wickedness has not quenched the Savior's love for them; Jesus rather indicates that his love prompted him to discipline and punish them. Rather than being antagonistic toward this punishment, the Laodiceans were encouraged to become enthusiastic (zealous) about the things of God.

This is an encouragement to Laodicea not to despair, but to regard the rebuke as a sign for good, if she learns from it. The Greek verb for "love" (*phileō*) here defines the love of gratuitous affection and fondness. However, in referring to Philadelphia (3:9), Jesus used the Greek verb *agapaō*; this defines a volitional, self-sacrificial love.

►**20 Behold, I stand at the door, and knock: if any man hear my voice, and open the door, I will come in to him, and will sup with him, and he with me**—This verse shows Christ outside, seeking to come in and enjoy a meal with the recipient. In context, it does not implicate an invitation to the sinner to receive Christ, but an invitation to the lukewarm Christian to be open to Christ, to allow him to make his home in his or her heart (see Eph. 3:17), and to enjoy intimate fellowship with him. (The idea of enjoying a meal together is first intimated in 3:16, with respect to Jesus' speaking of a "hot" or "cold" drink.)

►**21 to sit with me in my throne**—Cf. 2:26, 27; 20:6; Matthew 19:28; 20:23; John 17:22, 24; 2 Timothy 2:12. Christ is offering a seat with him on the throne to the very same people whom he threatened to spit out of his mouth. Trench suggests that the highest place is within reach of the lowest; the faintest spark of grace may be fanned into the mightiest flame of love. **set down with my Father in his throne**— Jesus mentioned two thrones: "my throne" and the Father's throne. The latter is his Father's, upon which Christ now sits and has sat since his ascension following his victory over death, sin, and the world. No one can sit upon this throne except God and the God-man Jesus Christ, for it is the incommunicable prerogative of God alone. The first throne he mentioned is his as the once humbled and then glorified Son of man. This is the throne that rules over the whole earth at the Lord's return. The victorious saints will share in this throne (1 Cor. 6:2). The church will judge with Christ and reign over the nations. This, the grandest and crowning promise, is placed at the end of all the seven addresses in order to gather each of the addresses into one. It also forms the link to the next part of the book, where the Lamb is introduced while seated on his Father's throne (4:2, 3; 5:5, 6).

Chapter 4

## 1-11 THE VISION OF GOD'S THRONE IN HEAVEN

Chapters 4 and 5 contain one vision in two parts: the vision of God's throne in heaven, and the Lamb with the seven-sealed scroll. This scroll is important to the future of God's people. The first great part of the scroll entails the opening of the seals and the sounding of trumpets (chaps. 4–11). This chapter marks a change in scenes; whereas chapters 1–3 were centered on earth, the following chapters center in heaven.

➤**1 After this I looked**—This marks the transition from the present to the future (see comments on 1:19). The transition is made from the existing state of the seven churches in John's time to what will occur afterwards in relation to John's writing. Chapters 4–10 present the heavenly scene, and chapters 11–21 alternate between heaven and earth. **a door was opened in heaven**—Cf. Ezekiel 1:1; Matthew 3:16; Acts 7:56; 10:11. In those visions the heavens opened and revealed the visions to those on earth. Here, John is transported through an open door into heaven from which he can see things passing on earth and in heaven. **the first voice**—i.e., the voice John had first heard, the voice of Jesus. Just as Jesus has indicated the conditions existing in the seven churches of Asia Minor, he now indicates to John conditions as they exist in heaven. **I will show thee things which must be hereafter**—This refers to what is to occur after the present time, after these things have passed (1:19). In the first chapters the "voice" told him of present conditions within the churches of Asia Minor, but now the "voice" is to show him how things will be hereafter.

➤**2 And immediately I was in the spirit**—See comments on 1:10. John first sees **a throne was set in heaven, and one sat on the throne**—namely, the eternal Father, the Creator (4:11). Cf. also 1:8 with 1:4, where the Father is designated "the one who was, and is, and is to come." When the Son (the Lamb) is

introduced in 5:5-9, a new song is sung that distinguishes the One seated upon the throne from the Lamb. See 5:7 and Daniel 7:13.

➤**3 like a jasper and a sardine** [carnelian] **stone**—The One on the throne cannot be described as he actually is; so we are told what his appearance is like. The stones represent his splendor (see Ezek. 1:4; 8:2; Dan. 7:9.) **a rainbow round about the throne, in sight like unto an emerald**—This rainbow formed a complete circle surrounding the throne vertically. Its various colors, which combined to form one pure solar ray, symbolize the varied aspects of God's providential dealings, uniting in one harmonious hope. The rainbow symbolizes God's consolatory promise in Christ to his people during judgments on his foes. Moreover, the rainbow was the appointed token of God's covenant with all flesh, and his people in particular. The rainbow is always the reminder of God's covenant to restrain his wrath from man on earth (Gen. 9:13). As the rainbow was first reflected on the waters of the world's ruin and continues to be seen only when a cloud is brought over the earth, so another deluge of fire shall precede the new heavens and earth. The Lord is depicted here as being upon his throne, out of which proceed lightnings and thunderings. God will issue the commission to rid the earth of its oppressors, but then in the middle of judgment when men's hearts fail them for fear, the believer will be reassured by the rainbow, the covenant token, around the throne.

➤**4 round about the throne were four and twenty seats** [thrones] **. . . four and twenty elders**—We are to understand that these thrones are lower and smaller than the central throne; therefore, their occupants are subordinate to the One on the central throne. Twenty-four elders are seated on the twenty-four thrones. They are probably not angels, for they wear white robes and have crowns of victory, implying a conflict and endurance. Dispensationalists interpret this as a reference to representatives of redeemed humanity, both OT and NT saints. They insist that Revelation 5:9, 10 is strong evidence for this position. The postmillennialist views the elders as a royal group, the figure itself a symbol of the universal priesthood of Christians. The number "twenty-four" indicates their continual service, as the eternal priesthood of God's people. The amillennialist reminds us that a vision of the triumphant Christ was essential before the other events contained in the Revelation can have meaning. Through this opened door John could see what was occurring in heaven. Therefore, he sees that there is reason for hope in the hour of judgment. Some amillennialists suggest that the twenty-four elders refer to the twelve patriarchs and the twelve apostles. Others simply indicate that this is the number "twelve" (the number of organized religion) doubled. It is readily apparent that the interpretation of the elders is determined by one's basic perspective concerning eschatology, as well as one's method of approaching this book (futurist, historical, preterist, idealist). The interpretations appear close and are similar to each other.

➤5 out of the throne proceeded lightnings and thunderings—demonstrating the omnipotence of God. voices—in the thunderings (cf. Exod. 19:16). The thunderings express God's anger against the ungodly. He not only threatens but predicts special judgments. seven lamps of fire . . . which are the seven Spirits of God—or, the sevenfold Spirit (TLB, NIV mg). The seven Spirits (or, sevenfold) of God, here pictured as seven lamps of burning fire, as it were, emanating from God's throne, must be related to the seven lampstands, the seven local churches (chaps. 2–3). The lampstands have no light of their own; their power and divine energy must come from the sevenfold Spirit of God. The depiction of the Spirit as being sevenfold symbolizes the plenitude and all-extensive availability of the divine Spirit to all the local churches on earth (also depicted by the number seven). See also comments on 5:6.

➤6 [as] a sea of glass like unto crystal— This contrasts with the turbulent "many waters" on which the harlot sits (17:1). John does not say that this was actually a body of water but indicates that it was as (see Gk.) a sea of crystal. For similar figures, see Genesis 1:7, and in the Apocrypha, 2 Enoch 3:3. See comments on 15:2. four beasts—Greek, "four living creatures." See Ezekiel 1 for a similar description. However, in Ezekiel each creature has four faces while each living being here has only one. The living creatures surround the throne.

➤7 like a lion—Perhaps this represents wild animal life. the second . . . like a calf— This may well represent domestic animal life. man . . . eagle—The third represents human life and the fourth may refer to bird life. Therefore, it is revealed to John that the whole creation is pictured as glorified with God and subjected to him. The four living creatures have been variously interpreted: (1) Some have contrasted them with the four world powers represented by the four beasts. (2) The church fathers identified them with the four Gospels: Matthew, the lion; Mark, the ox; Luke, the man; John, the eagle; their symbols express the character of Christ in each Gospel in relation to the world. The lion expresses royalty, and it is Matthew who gives prominence to this feature of Christ. The ox expresses laborious endurance, Jesus' prominent characteristic in Mark's Gospel; man represents the bond of Jesus' sympathy with a whole race of man, which is the dominant feature in Luke's account; and the eagle represents soaring majesty, which is prominent in John's description of Jesus as the Divine Word. (3) Some interpretations use Jewish tradition to explain the four. They see the four referring to the "four standards" under which Israel camped in the wilderness—Judah in the east, Dan to the north, Ephraim to the west, and Reuben to the south; they were respectively a lion, an eagle, an ox, and a man. This depicts the time when the whole earth will be subject to the never-ending rule of God. (4) The redeemed church similarly shall combine in herself human perfections, having a fourfold aspect as follows: kingly righteousness with hatred of evil and judicial equality (lion); laborious diligence in every duty (ox); human sympathy (man); the contemplation of heavenly truth (eagle). As the high soaring intelligence of the eagle forms a complementary contrast to the practical labor of the ox, so the vengeance-seeking lion forms a complementary contrast to the human sympathy of the man.

➤8 John pointed out that the living creatures are involved in ceaseless worship of God; he also noted that their worship recognizes the eternal nature of God in the song they sing— Holy, holy, holy, Lord God Almighty, which [who] was, and is, and is to come. They sing this song day after day and night after night. The refrain, Holy, holy, holy, is the *tris-hagion* of the Greek liturgies. It occurs in Isaiah 6:3 and Psalm 99:3, 5, 9. The three "holies" combine with the threefold description of God's eternal nature: "holy" as he "who was"; "holy," as he "who is"; "holy" as he "who is to come." God showed himself as an object of holy worship in his past creation even more fully in governing all things; and he will, in the highest degree, show himself holy in the consummation of all things. In Isaiah 6:3 there is an added statement: "the whole earth is filled with his glory." However, in Revelation this is put off until the glory of the Lord fills the earth—for then his enemies will be destroyed. **Almighty**—See comments on 1:8.

➤**9, 10** The praise from the four living creatures characterizes the praise that all creation should give to God. The twenty-four elders join the living creatures in worshiping him who lives forever.

➤**11 Thou art worthy, O Lord**—The pronoun "thou" (or, "you") is emphatic in the Greek text. It is *you* who **created all things.** The expression "all things" refers to the universe. The praise here extols the glory of God manifest in his work of creation. Therefore he is worthy of all the worship that they offered to him. **for thy pleasure**—Greek, "on account of your will." For God to *will* is to effect; to determine is to perform; so in Genesis 1:3, "Let there be light. And light appeared." In Hebrew both phrases use the same word, tense, and letters, marking the simultaneous action of will and effect. **they are**—The earliest manuscripts read, "they were."

*Chapter* **5**

## 1-14 THE LAMB OPENS THE SCROLL

The central action of this chapter revolves around a scroll, sealed with seven seals no one on earth or in heaven is worthy to open. John watches breathlessly as a Lamb, which appears to have been slain, steps forward to take the scroll and open it. John learns that this scroll is a writing of destiny. The true action begins with the breaking of the seals.

➤**1 a book**—Greek, "a scroll." His right hand was open and on it lay the scroll. This scroll was written on the inside and on the back, implying fullness and completeness, so that

nothing more needs to be added (22:18). The seven-sealed scroll contains a record of future events concerning the kingdom. God knew its contents, but they were sealed from angel and human sight. **sealed with seven seals**—is an indication of the supreme importance of the book. The number "seven" is often used in Revelation and expresses completeness. Thus, there are seven seals, there are seven trumpets, and there are seven vials.

➤**2 a strong angel**—His strength was displayed when his voice thundered throughout heaven and earth (10:1-3).

➤**3 no man**—Greek, "no one"—not only humans, but any order of beings—angels or evil powers.

➤**4 I wept much, because no man was found worthy to open and to read** [look at] **the book** [scroll]—John had been promised a revelation of those things that were to occur, but now he weeps because there seemed to be no one able to open the book.

➤**5 the Lion of the tribe of Juda**[h]—This designation presents Christ as the fulfillment of the prophecy in Genesis 49:8-10 (see also Ezek. 29:21). He, the Lion descended from Judah, is the royal ruler. **the Root of David**—cf. Isaiah 11:1, 10. This is not a reference to a "sprout" which has come from David's ancient root; this conveys the truth that Christ himself is the root and origin of David. (See comments on Matt. 22:42-45.) As the root of David, he is the Lord of David—and therefore the King of kings. He will rule over Israel and then over the whole earth. **prevailed**—conquered, gained a victory (3:21). His past victory over all the powers of darkness entitles him now to open the book. **to open the book** [scroll], **and to loose the seven seals**—Christ's victory over death qualified him as the unraveler of God's eternal plan.

➤**6 Lamb**—the Greek is *arnion.* It is found only in Revelation and John 21:15. The term expresses affection for Christ. He is the precious Lamb. In other places the Greek word *amnos* is used; it applies to Christ as the sacrificial Lamb (Isa. 53:7, LXX; John 1:29; Acts 8:32; 1 Pet. 1:19). **stood a Lamb as it had been slain**—The living One who had become dead is alive forever more (1:18). He was standing while bearing the marks of one killed. In the middle of heavenly glory the crucified Christ is still the prominent object. The **seven horns** refer to his perfect might, the number "seven" symbolizing perfection. In the OT a horn symbolizes power (Ps. 75:4-7) and royal dignity (Zech. 1:18). **seven eyes . . . the seven Spirits of God**—the sevenfold Spirit of God (TLB, NIV mg). As the seven lamps before the throne represent the Spirit of God in the Godhead, so the seven eyes of the Lamb represent the sevenfold Spirit flowing forth from the glorified God-man. As such, the Spirit and the glorified Christ are united. The sevenfold Spirit emanating from the throne is the Spirit of Christ sent forth to all the churches (see comments on 4:5), and through the churches to all the world. **sent forth into all the earth**—The Greek for "sent forth" (*apostello*) is related to the term "apostle," reminding us of the Spirit-initiated work of Christ's apostles and ministers throughout the world. The Spirit operates through the church to reach the world (see comments on 4:5). The eyes of the Lamb symbolize his all-watchful and wise providence over his church, especially against her enemies.

►**7 he came and took the book** [scroll] **out of the right hand of him that sat upon the throne**—God was on the throne. The scroll was held for anyone who was worthy to take it. The Lamb took it from the Father in token of formal possession of his universal and everlasting dominion as Son of man. This introductory vision gives us, in summary, the completion toward which all the events in the seals, trumpets, and vials converge.

►**8 golden vials full of odours** [incenses], **which** [vials] **are the prayers of saints**—The elders are here seen as carrying with them the prayers of the believers, which are petitions for vengeance and just retribution, according to 8:3, 4.

►**9 they sung a new song**—as praise to Christ's redemptive work, for the theme of redemption is always new, always suggesting fresh thoughts of praise. **redeemed** [purchased] **us to God by thy blood out of every kindred, and tongue, and people, and nation**—Christ's redemption was a purchasing (a paying a price for) the believers whom God had selected out of every race, tongue, and nation.

►**10 kings and priests**—Greek, "a kingdom and priests" (see comments on 1:6). Those who set their crowns in front of the throne do not call themselves kings in the sight of the great King (4:10, 11), even though they have that right. Thus, in 20:6 they are not called kings, but priests. **we** ["they" in the earliest manuscripts] **shall reign on the earth**—This is a new feature, added from 1:6.

►**11** The **angels** form the outer circle, while the redeemed people form the inner circle near the throne.

►**12 to receive power**—The remaining six attributes (the total being seven, representing perfection and completeness) are all, as well as power, listed after one Greek article to mark that they form one complete unit of description, attributed to the Lamb. In the praise recorded in 7:12, each of the seven attributes has an article in the Greek.

►**13** The universal chorus of creation, including the outermost circles as well as the inner, concludes the doxology. Praise is given to God on the throne and to his coequal, the Lamb.

►**14 Amen**—As in 4:11, where the twenty-four elders asserted God's worthiness to receive the glory because he created all things, so here the four living creatures indicate, by their "Amen," that all of creation's glory belongs to him. **And the four and twenty elders fell down and worshipped him**—The picture in heaven is a picture of everyone present worshiping God and the Lamb. All of creation, whether it be animate or inanimate, recognizes the power of God and praises him.

*Chapter* **6**

1-17 THE OPENING OF THE SEALS

This chapter describes the opening of the first six of the seven seals (see 5:1). Many interpreters think that the events connected with the opening of these seals have already taken place, the sixth having been so by the overthrow of paganism and the establishment of Christianity under Constantine's edict of A.D. 312. Other interpreters are equally convinced that the sixth seal concerns future events and is to be broken at the coming of Christ. The millenarian believes that the seals refer to future events; the postmillennialist suggests that the seals represent the gospel as preached from John's time to the final coming of Christ; the amillennialist contends that they depict events that occurred in John's time. In other words, he would insist that the events described by the opening of the various seals are suggestive of conditions and circumstances used by God to defeat the enemies of God's people. Many difficult elements admittedly flow together to form the panorama John describes. Perhaps no one interpreter should be dogmatic at this point; rather, he should see the movement of the message and note that each is representing basically and ultimately a victory for God and his people.

➤1 **the Lamb opened one of the seals**—Remember that "the Lamb" was the only One in heaven worthy to take the book, and now the action begins in that he is worthy also to break one of the seals and reveal the events written in it.

➤2 **a white horse: and he that sat on him**—The rider is seated on a white horse. Some commentators (Walvoord, Swete, Caird, Bruce) argue that this rider is the Antichrist or some other evil force, primarily because the three other horses depict evil powers at work. But other commentators (Alford, Ladd) insist that the rider on the white horse represents Christ (cf. 19:11-16) who brings the saving power of the gospel. The white horse represents conquest, militarism. "White" suggests victory. Perhaps this picture of the horseman is taken from a Parthian cavalryman, the most dreaded enemy of the Roman empire. Roman warriors of that time did not use the bow, which was the favorite weapon of the Parthians. The rider is depicted as having a **crown,** the garland or wreath of a conqueror, on his head. **he went forth conquering, and to conquer**—He is pictured as one gaining a lasting victory. The first four seals are judgments on the earth against the power that opposes the kingdom of God.

➤4 The second **horse** is described as **red,** and the rider has **a great sword.** The color "red" represents blood and the "sword" represents war. This figure heightens the presentation of judgment and punishment which is seen in the opening of the first seal; the scene is intensified in the opening of this seal. The white horse represents victory; the red horse

represents war, the bloody means of carrying out this conquest.

➤5 **a black horse; and he that sat on him had a pair of balances in his hand**—The balance automatically suggests the measuring of food. Warfare makes food scarce; the measure (6:6) indicates that food was especially scarce. Famine generally follows in the wake of warfare.

➤6 Food is doled out bit by bit. Measure—Greek, "choenix." The choenix is the usual ration for a working man. It probably means less than a quart of grain, or as much as would support a man of moderate appetite for one day. **hurt not the oil and the wine**—This could suggest that the rich will still have their commodities, while the poor would suffer—or it could suggest that the famine in general will be limited.

➤8 **a pale horse: and his name that sat on him was Death, and Hell** [Hades] **followed with him**—The paleness suggests sickness (caused by the famine and pestilence—6:5, 6). Sickness leads to death, and death takes its captives to Hades. **Power . . . over the fourth part of the earth**—The "fourth" likely refers to that part of the eastern hemisphere covered by the revived Roman Empire.

➤9 The last three seals relate to the invisible world just as the first four related to the visible world: the fifth concerns the believers who have been martyred, the sixth those who have died as unbelievers or shall be unbelievers at Christ's coming, and the seventh refers to the silence in heaven. **souls**—Greek $psuch\bar{a}s$, which can also mean "persons" or "lives." **the altar**—As the blood of sacrificial victims killed on the altar was poured into the bottom of the altar, so the souls of those sacrificed for Christ's testimony are symbolically represented as underneath it. The sacrificial altar was outside the sanctuary, not inside. So Christ's literal sacrifice and the figurative sacrifice of the martyrs took place, not in the heavenly sanctuary but outside, on earth.

➤10 As the parable of the woman who cried night and day to the unjust judge for justice against her oppressive adversary (Luke 18:1-8), so the elect (not only those on earth, but also those in heaven) cried day and night to God for vengeance against their oppressors. This passage does not need to be restricted to some particular martyrdom; rather, it presents a principle that repeats itself many times prior to Christ's return. **Lord**—in Greek, means "Master"; it implies that he has them, their foes, and all his creatures absolutely at his disposal, as a master has his slaves. Note in 6:11 that the expression "fellow servants" follows. **holy**—Greek, "the holy one." **avenge**—means to exact vengeance for blood. This vengeance is to be brought on those who dwell upon the earth. The reference obviously is to the ungodly, the earthly, as distinguished from the church, whose home and heart are in heavenly places.

➤**11 white robes**—are indicative of light, joy, and triumphant victory over their foes. "White" is also suggestive of the purity and sanctity the Christian enjoys through Christ. **rest yet for a little season**—This suggests that the "rest" is short as compared to eternity. Concerning their **rest,** cf. 14:13; Isaiah 57:2; Daniel 12:13. **their fellow servants also and their brethren, that should be killed as they were, should be fulfilled**—i.e., until their full number shall have been completed. The full blessedness and glory of all the saints shall be simultaneous. The earlier shall not anticipate the later saints.

➤**12** As in 6:4, 6-8, war, famine, and disease are related to that in Matthew 24:6, 7; and 6:9, 10 relate to Matthew 24:9, 10; so this passage, 6:12-17, relates to Matthew 24:29, 30. The imagery describes the significant signs of the immediate coming of the day of the Lord, but the coming itself does not take place until the elect are sealed, and the judgments invoked by the martyrs descend on the earth, the sea, and the trees (chap. 7). The **earthquake** is literally a "shaking" of the heavens, the sea, and the dry land, the shaking of these "shakable" things being the necessary preliminary to the setting up of those things that cannot be shaken (Heb. 12:27, 28). This term is a catchword connecting the sixth seal with the sixth trumpet (11:13), the seventh vial (16:17-21) and also the seventh seal (8:5). (See Joel 2:31.)

➤**13 stars of heaven fell unto the earth, even as a fig tree casteth her untimely figs**—cf. Isaiah 34:4; Nahum 3:12. When this occurs, the church will then be ripe for glorification and the antichristian world for destruc-tion. Concerning the stars falling to the earth, Scripture describes the natural phenomenon as it would appear to the spectator, not in the language of scientific accuracy.

➤**14 the heaven departed as a scroll when it is rolled together**—It was rolled together as a scroll that had been opened but now is rolled up and laid aside. **and every mountain and island were moved out of their places**—See Psalm 121:1; Jeremiah 3:23; 4:24; Nahum 1:5. According to premillennialists, this total disruption will occur before the coming of the new earth. The nonmillennialists would take this as a reference to either temporal or final judgment.

➤**15, 16** All men will attempt to hide so as to conceal themselves from the face of the One sitting on the throne, and from the anger of the Lamb (cf. Hos. 10:8; Luke 23:30).

➤**17 the great day of his wrath**—"their wrath" [God's and the Lamb's] in the earliest manuscripts. After the Lord has exhausted all of his ordinary judgments—war, famine, disease, etc.—and sinners are still impenitent, the "great day" of the Lord itself shall come. Matthew 24 plainly forms a perfect parallelism to the six seals, not only of its events, but also in the order of their occurrence: 24:3, the first seal; 24:6, the second seal; 24:7, the third seal; 24:7, the fourth seal; 24:9, the fifth seal, including evil persecutions, judgments, and gospel preaching to all nations (24:9-28); 24:29, the sixth seal. Needless to say, some interpreters would not think this passage refers to final judgment. Thus, the sixth seal, according to the premillennial interpretation, anticipates the Lord's coming. The ungodly peoples of the earth tremble at the signs of his immediate approach. But before he actually executes his wrath, certain peoples must be protected.

*Chapter* 7

## 1-8 THE SEALING OF THE ELECT

The previous chapter closes with judgment about to come on the enemies of God's people. But the present chapter reveals that this judgment will not come until God's people are protected. Here John describes the sealing of the 144,000 and the great crowd standing before the throne.

➤**1 after these things**—Two divisions in this chapter come in as an episode after the sixth seal and before the seventh seal. These verses indicate that 144,000 are to be sealed, to be protected from the wrath of God. Are the names here to be interpreted literally? If they are not, then to whom do the names refer? All interpreters agree that the interlude in the breaking of the seals is for the purpose of sealing the 144,000, but there are almost as many ideas concerning the identity of the 144,000 as there are interpreters of the passage. **four angels . . . four corners . . . four winds**—the term "four" is a world figure and suggests that whatever is to occur is to occur throughout the world. The judgments to come down on these are in answer to the martyrs' prayer described under the figure of the fifth seal. Note the same judgments under the fifth trumpet, the sealed being excluded (9:4).

➤**2 ascending from the east**—lit., "from the rising of the sun." God's glory is often associated with the east.

➤**3 Hurt not**—by letting loose the destructive winds. **till we have sealed the servants of our God in their foreheads**—This, again, is parallel to Matthew 24:31. Israel, at the eve of the Lord's coming, shall be found reestablished as a nation; for its tribes are distinctly specified, although Joseph is substituted for Dan. From these tribes a believing remnant will be preserved from the judgments which shall destroy all the anti-Christian confederacy (6:12-17) and shall be transfigured with the elect church of all nations. The 144,000 Jews (or whatever number is intended by this symbolic number) shall faithfully resist the seduction of the Antichrist, while the remainder of the nation (restored to Palestine in unbelief) will be his victims. Prior to the Lord's judgments on the Antichrist (and his followers), the Antichrist shall destroy two-thirds of the nation, one-third escaping. By the Spirit's operation through affliction, this group will turn to the Lord. The remnant may form the nucleus on earth of the Israelite nation that is from this time forward to stand at the head of the millennial nations of the world. Israel's spiritual resurrection shall be "as life from the dead" to all the nations. (See Zech. 13, 14;

Matt. 24:34.) **servants**—As has been indicated, some commentators view these servants as being Israelites. Other commentators simply identify these as the righteous of God, and they take the 144,000 as a symbolic number.

➤**4-8 an hundred and forty and four thousand of all the tribes of the children of Israel**—This could refer to 144,000 Jews, 144,000 Jewish Christians (so Seiss, Walvoord), or to the new Israel, composed of Jewish and Gentile believers (so Alford, Caird, Swete). **Juda[h]**—meaning "praise," stands first, since it is Jesus' tribe (5:5; Heb. 7:13, 14). **Benjamin**— the youngest, is last, and with him is associated **Joseph,** next to the last. **Reuben**—as the original firstborn, comes next after Judah, to whom Reuben gave place, having by sin lost his right of primogeniture. Two tribes do not appear in the list: Dan and Ephraim. Both may have been purposely omitted because both fell into idolatry. In fact, they were the first two tribes to fall into gross idolatry (Judg. 17; 18; Hos. 4:17). Ephraim was replaced by Joseph in this list. John may have sought to expose idolatry and beast worship in his day by excluding Dan and Ephraim (Johnson).

## 9-18 PRAISE FROM A GREAT MULTITUDE

➤**9 a great multitude . . . of all nations, and kindreds, and people, and tongues, stood before the throne, and before the Lamb**—This multitude is identified in 7:14 (see comments there). The people are described as **clothed with white robes, and palms in their hands** (cf. 3:5, 18; 4:4; 6:11). The palm-bearing multitude is reminiscent of Christ's entry into Jerusalem. The palm branch is the symbol of joy and triumph. Pieters states that the first group (144,000) represents the church militant and this latter group represents the church triumphant.

➤**10 salvation**—lit., "the salvation." All of the praise for man's salvation is to be given to God. At the time of the Lord's entry into Jerusalem, "salvation" was the cry of a palm-bearing crowd. "Hosanna," the term they shouted, means "save us now." Hosanna is derived from Psalm 118:25. In this psalm the same connection occurs between salvation, the tabernacle of the righteous, and the

Jews' cry—to be repeated by the whole nation at the time of the Messiah's coming: "Blessed is the one who is coming, the one sent by the Lord."

►**11 the angels**—as in 5:11, take up the anthem of praise. This verse suggests the worship the entire group gives God and is also indicative of his worthiness of being worshiped.

►**12** According to the Greek, the definite article appears before each of the nouns, and it therefore should be translated "the blessing and the glory and the wisdom and the thanksgiving and the honor and the power and the might to be to our God forever and forever! Amen."

►**13** One of the elders asked John the identity of these people. The suggestion is that the elder simply addressed himself to John's thoughts. He asked the question that might have arisen in John's mind from what had occurred previously. One of the twenty-four elders (see 4:4) appropriately acts as interpreter of this vision.

►**14** John responded quickly, indicating that the elder was able to answer the question: the apostle did not know the answer (cf. Ezek. 37:3). **These are they which came out of great tribulation**—This is the "tribulation" to which the martyrs were exposed under the fifth seal. It is the same that Christ predicted would precede his coming (Matt. 24:21); it will be followed by the same signs as the sixth seal (Matt. 24:29, 30). In looking back, this also includes all "the tribulation" that the saints of all ages have had to pass through—if one interprets this as being a picture of the day of the Lord. Thus, the seventh chapter is a review of the vision of the sixth seal (chap. 6); it fills out the outline given in that part of it that affects the faithful of that day. In chapter six, their number was waiting to be completed, but here it is completed; they are seen taken out of the earth before judgments on the anti-Christians' apostasy. They and all the Lord's faithful witnesses, including believers of past ages, wait for his coming. Then they will be glorified and will reign together with him. Meanwhile, in contrast with their previous sufferings, they are excluded from the hunger, thirst, and scorching heat of their life on

earth (7:16). The Lamb of God himself feeds and refreshes them (7:17; 14:1-4, 13). (See 1:5; 1 John 1:7; cf. Isa. 1:18; 61:10; Zech. 3:3-5.) **have washed their robes, and made them white in the blood of the Lamb**—The blood of Jesus Christ (i.e., the blood that Jesus shed to secure our redemption) is the only thing that can purify us (see Heb. 7:14; 1 John 1:7; Rev. 12:11; 22:14).

►**15 Therefore are they before the throne of God**—because they are purified (7:14)—for without it they never could have entered God's holy presence. (Cf. 22:14. See also Eph. 5:26, 27.) **serve him**—See 22:3. The "throne" and the temple are connected because we can approach the heavenly King only through priestly mediation: therefore, Christ is at once King and Priest on this throne. **day and night**—means perpetually. Strictly speaking, there will be no night in the new heaven and new earth (22:5). **in his temple**—This is the heavenly analogue to his temple on earth, for strictly there is "no temple therein" (21:22) because "God and the Lamb are the temple" and fill the whole. There is no distinction of sacred and secular places; the city is the temple and the temple the city. **he that sitteth on the throne shall dwell among them**—lit., "will spread his tent over them" (NIV)—i.e., God "will shelter them with his presence" (RSV). The Greek verb is the same one used in John 1:14, "tabernacled" (see comments there).

►**16 they shall hunger no more**—See Isaiah 49:10. **neither thirst any more**—Cf. John 4:13. **neither shall the sun light [fall] on them, nor any heat**—Perhaps this may be a symbolic allusion to the sun of persecution, but it can also be taken quite literally. The entire verse reads like Isaiah 49:10, which comes in a passage that speaks of the blessings in Messiah's kingdom.

►**17 the Lamb which is in the midst of the throne**—See 5:6. **shall feed them**—Greek, "shall shepherd them." **lead them unto living fountains of water**—See 22:1. **and God shall wipe away all tears from their eyes**—See 21:4; cf. Isaiah 25:8; 35:10; 51:11; 65:19. Verses 14-17 are so much like Revelation 21 and 22 that it can hardly be doubted that the scene of the great multitude (7:9-17) is a preview of the blessedness to be experienced by all the redeemed in the new Jerusalem.

*Chapter* 8

## 1-5 THE SEVENTH SEAL AND THE GOLDEN CENSER

➤**1 there was silence in heaven about the space of half an hour**—The half-an-hour silence is the brief pause given to John between the preceding vision and one following: this implies the solemn introduction to the eternal Sabbath, which follows the seventh seal; and on the other hand, the silence ushers in the first of the seven trumpets (8:3-5). In the Jewish temple, musical instruments and singing resounded during the whole time of the offering of the sacrifices, which form the first part of the service; but at the offering of the incense, solemn silence was kept (Ps. 62:1; 65:1), the people praying secretly all the time. The half-hour stillness implies the earnest, adoring expectation with which the blessed spirits and the angels await the unfolding of God's judgments. The "silence in heaven" suggests delayed judgment, but it also emphasizes the dramatic effect. All of heaven is silent to see what will occur. The trumpets summon armies and demand silence, but here they will announce God's activity.

➤**2 seven angels which stood before God**—cf. Luke 1:19. **seven trumpets**—These trumpets sound during the time the martyrs rest, until their fellow servants are martyred. The martyrs pray that those living on earth and persecuting God's people will fall (6:10). All the ungodly, and not merely some portion of them, are meant; all the opponents and obstacles in the way of the kingdom of Christ and his saints (11:15, 18) at the close of the "seven trumpets" are included. Revelation becomes more specific only as it advances farther (13; 16:10; 17; 18). The "seven trumpets" overturned the world kingdoms to make way for Christ's universal kingdom. The first four connect together; the last three alone have the woes attached to them.

➤**3 another angel**—This is not Christ, as many suppose, for he is always designated in Revelation by one of his proper titles. The angel acts merely as a ministering spirit, just as the twenty-four elders have vials full of **incense,** which are **the prayers of all the saints** presented before the Lamb. Christ alone is the Mediator through whom prayer is to be offered to God. The incense accompanies the saints' prayers—both ascend up before God (8:4); thus, the saints praying on earth and the angel's "incensing" in heaven are simultaneous acts. (See comments on 5:8.) **of all saints**—The prayers are both of the saints in heaven and of those militant on earth (6:8). The martyrs' cry is foremost and brings down the ensuing judgments. **upon the golden altar**—i.e., the heavenly incense altar.

➤**4 the prayers of the saints**—ascended up out of the angel's hand into the presence of God. The angel merely burns the incense given him by Christ, the High Priest, so that its smoke blends with the ascending prayers of the saints.

➤**5 and cast it into the earth**—The hot coals on the altar thrown down upon the earth symbolize fiery judgments about to descend on the church's foes. This is in answer to the saints' prayers that have just ascended before God and those of the martyrs (6:8). **voices, and thunderings, and lightnings, and an earthquake**—these phenomena occur as a result of the fiery judgments being thrown down on the earth.

## 6-13 THE FIRST FOUR TRUMPETS AND THE CONSEQUENT PLAGUES

➤**6, 7** The common feature of the first four trumpets is that the judgments resulting from them affect objects within the natural surroundings of the universe—the earth, trees, grass, sea, rivers, fountains, the light of the sun, moon, and stars. The last three, the woe-trumpets (8:13), affect men's lives with pain, death, and hell. Five or six out of the ten correspond exactly to the hail and the fire (Exod. 9:24), the water turned to blood (Exod. 7:19), the darkness (Exod. 10:21), the locusts (Exod. 10:12), and perhaps death (9:18). **hail and fire mingled with blood**—Judgment happens as the result of the second and third vials (16:3, 4). **the third part of trees was burnt up, and all green grass was burnt up**—This is also true in the judgment depicted under the third trumpet, where one-third of the rivers are affected. This is also true in the judgment depicted under the sixth trumpet, where one-third of the men are killed. In Zechariah 13:8, 9 this three-part division appears, but the proportions are reversed: two parts killed, only a third preserved. Here, two-thirds escaped, one-third destroyed. Fire is the predominant element. It is significant to note that one-third of the trees were burnt up, but all green grass was burnt up.

►**8, 9 the second angel sounded, and as it were a great mountain burning with fire was cast into the sea**—This is an allusion to Jeremiah 51:25 and Amos 7:4. **the third part of the sea became blood**—In the parallel second vial, the whole sea (not merely a third) becomes blood. The overthrow of Jericho (a type of the anti-Christian Babylon) and Israel's victory under Joshua (a type of the kingdom of God and of Christ) is perhaps alluded to in the seven trumpets. This judgment ends in the overthrow of all of Christ's foes and the setting up of his kingdom. On the seventh day, at the seventh time, when the seventh priest blew the seven ram's-horn trumpets, the people shouted and the walls fell flat; then followed the destruction of the enemy. In terminology describing a volcanic eruption, these verses depict a blazing "mountain" sent into the sea. Consequently one-third of the ships are destroyed and one-third of the marine life dies.

►**10, 11** Those interpreting this passage symbolically say the **star** that fell **from heaven** represents a chief minister (Arius, according to Bullinger, Bengel; or some future false teacher, if the event is still future) falling from his high place in the church. Instead of shining with heavenly light, the star became a torch lit with earthly fire and smouldering. The star is named **Wormwood** (meaning bitterness). The wormwood, a plant with a bitter taste, symbolizes the bitterness of those in calamity (Jer. 9:15; Lam. 3:19; *NIVSB*). Contrast the converse change of bitter water into sweet at Marah (Exod. 15: 23).

►**12 the third part of the sun**—This is not a total blackout, as in the sixth seal (6:12, 13). This partial obscuration comes between the prayers of the martyrs during the fifth seal and the last overwhelming judgments on the ungodly under the sixth seal (at the eve of

Christ's coming). **the third part of the moon and the third part of the stars**—This darkening of the celestial luminaries is a sign of God's judgment (see Isa. 13:9, 10; Ezek. 32:7, 8; Matt. 24:29).

►**13 an angel**—All the earliest manuscripts read, "an eagle." The flying depicts an ominous warning of impending disaster. **Woe, woe, woe, to the inhabiters of the earth**—The three "woes" correspond to the last three trumpets.

# 9
*Chapter*

## 1-12 THE FIFTH TRUMPET AND THE PLAGUE OF LOCUSTS

►**1** The last three trumpets of the seven are called the "woe-trumpets" (8:13). **a star fall**—Greek, "a star having fallen." When John saw it, it was not in the act of falling but had already fallen. Most likely, the star is an angel, perhaps the same angel who binds Satan in Revelation 20. **the key of the bottomless pit**—Greek, "the shaft of the abyss." The abyss seems to be the subterranean dwelling of demons (Luke 8:31), certain fallen angels (2 Pet. 2:4; Jude 6), and perhaps the dead (Rom. 10:7).

►**2 there arose a smoke out of the pit** [shaft]—Great clouds of smoke come out of the abyss, and the sun seems darkened by their presence. And out of the smoke come great clouds of locusts (9:3).

►**3 locusts . . . unto them was given power, as the scorpions of the earth have power**—These locusts possessed scorpion-like powers (9:5). Locust plagues are among the worst of human calamities (see Exod. 10:1-20; Joel 1:2–2:11).

►**4 they should not hurt the grass of the earth**—The locusts are denied the food on which they ordinarily prey. Therefore, these are not natural and ordinary locusts. Their natural instinct is supernaturally restrained to mark the judgment as being altogether divine. **but only those men which have not the seal of God in their foreheads**—Thus, the first woe does not affect "the servants of God" (7:3; *NIVSB*).

►**5 five months**—"Five months" defines the ordinary lifetime of locusts.

►**6 men seek death, and shall not find it**—See 6:16; cf. Hosea 10:8.

➤**7 the shapes of the locusts were like unto horses prepared unto battle**—Cf. Joel 2:4 for the resemblance of locusts to horses. The plates of a horse armed for battle look like the outer shells of locusts. Ancient writers also mentioned the likeness between the heads of horses and locusts. **crowns like gold**—Alford understood this to mean that the head of a locust actually ends in a crown-shaped fillet having the appearance of gold. **their faces were as the faces of men**—The term "as" implies that these locusts are not actually men. At the same time, they are not natural "locusts." They are probably some kind of supernatural, demonic beings.

➤**8 hair as the hair of women**—An Arabic proverb compares the antennae of locusts to the hair of girls. These locusts have teeth like lions' teeth (Joel 1:6). This figure must refer to their destructiveness.

➤**9 as it were breastlates of iron**—This refers "to thin scales, which appeared as a cuirass of metal plates across the chest and long, flexible bands of steel over the shoulders" (Johnson). **as the sound of chariots**—See Joel 2:5-7.

➤**10** Their power is limited to **five months,** but during this time they are capable of stinging men.

➤**11** The locusts have a **king,** who is **the angel of the bottomless pit** [abyss]. His Hebrew name is *Abaddon,* and his Greek name is *Apollyon.* The term "Abaddon" means "the Destroyer." In the hands of Satan the locusts are supernatural instruments of torment.

➤**12 One woe is past . . . there come two woes more**—Many commentators interpret this as a reference to the judgments about to fall on the ungodly immediately before Christ's second coming (cf. Joel 1:2-7 and 2:1-11; these OT references are, according to the premillennialists, expressly parallel and refer to the great and exceedingly terrible day of the Lord).

## 13-21 THE SIXTH TRUMPET

➤**13 the four horns**—one on each corner of the altar (Exod. 30:1-3). **the golden altar**—See 8:3-5. The martyrs' cry for the avenging of their blood from the altar now reaches its consummation under the sixth seal. This cry ascends to God from "the golden altar" of incense and results in fiery judgments.

➤**14 Euphrates**—The river where Babylon, the ancient foe of God's people, was situated (cf. 16:12). Again, whether from the literal region of the "Euphrates" or from the spiritual Babylon, four angels executing God's judgments will go out, assembling an army of horsemen throughout the four quarters of the earth to slay one-third of all people (9:15).

➤**15** The judgments to be executed by the four angels "had been kept in readiness for that year and month and day and hour, and now they were turned loose to kill a third of all mankind" (TLB). The time element is stated specifically. The third of mankind is distinguished from God's sealed and protected people.

➤**16** This verse numbers the armies as 200 million horsemen. Some commentators think that this army is part of Satan's forces. It is an infernal, demonic army, composed of spirit beings (9:19). Those attacked, therefore, will be without protection. And again, certain commentators think the number of horsemen must be taken literally, although it staggers the imagination to think of 200 million horsemen going into battle. Other commentators think that the number is merely symbolic: 200 million signifies fullness and completion. (The Greek expression is "two myriads of myriads.")

➤**17 them that sat on them, having breastplates of fire, and of jacinth** [hyacinth], **and brimstone: and the heads of the horses were as the heads of lions; and out of their mouths issued fire and smoke and brimstone**—Pagan mythology describes monsters similar to these. McDowell, however, views this as reminiscent of Israel's captivity. Her captors had come from the east (Babylonia and Assyria from the Euphrates). These horsemen provide a dramatic figure of all captivity and suffering brought by man's rebellious spirit toward God. Regardless of the suffering and death caused by man's sin, those individuals who survived the ravages of sin nonetheless refuse to repent (9:21).

➤**18 By these three**—The earliest manuscripts follow with the word "plagues."

➤**19 power is in their mouth . . . tails were like unto serpents**—This depiction underscores the impression that this army is not composed of humans, but of demons or other satanic creatures.

➤ **20 worship devils** [demons], **and idols**— According to 1 Corinthians 10:19, 20 demons are united with idols; therefore, to worship an idol is to worship a demon. The people here are described as continuing in this idolatry.

➤ **21 sorceries**—Greek, *pharmakōn* ("magic arts"). See comments on Acts 19:19. **fornication**—is singular, whereas the other sins are listed in the plural. Other sins are committed at intervals; those who lack purity of heart indulge in perpetual fornication (Bengel). Talbot sees 9:20, 21 as suggesting that man will not repent, even when the devil's power is revealed in such a manifest way. Talbot uses the brand on cattle as an illustration: the burned flesh becomes harder and harder; the same is true of the human heart.

*Chapter* **10**

## 1-11 THE ANGEL AND THE LITTLE SCROLL

Just as an episode was introduced between the breaking of the sixth and seventh seal, so another event takes place after the sounding of the sixth trumpet and before the sounding of the seventh trumpet. Beasley-Murray observes a fourfold purpose in this interlude. The author emphasizes the "certain proximity of the End (10:1-7), the validity of his prophetic ministry (10:8-11), the security of the church (11:1, 2), and the power of its witness in the era of the Antichrist (11:3-13)." The church and her fortunes are the subject of this episode. Even as the judgments on the unbelieving inhabiters of the earth (8:13) were the subject of the fifth and sixth trumpets, this chapter concerns itself with the church and her future. Revelation 6:11 seems to be referred to in 10:6. In 6:11 the martyrs to be avenged were told that they must rest a little longer; in 10:6 they are assured that there should be no more delay. Their prayer shall not have to wait longer, but it will be consummated at the trumpet sounding of the seventh angel (10:7). The little scroll (10:2, 9, 10) is given to John by the angel with the charge that he must prophesy again concerning peoples, nations, tongues, and kings (10:11). Judging from chapter 11, this prophecy seems to affect only those peoples, nations, tongues and kings related to Israel and the church.

➤ **1 another mighty angel**—is distinguished from the mighty angel who asked concerning the former, more complete scroll (5:2). Some commentators identify the "mighty angel" as Christ himself, but others think that "angel" refers to one of authority. **clothed with a cloud**—The cloud is the emblem of God coming in judgment. **a rainbow was upon his head**—The rainbow is the emblem of God's covenant mercy to his people during his judgments upon his enemies. **and his face was as it were the sun**—cf. 1:16; 18:1. **and his feet as pillars of fire**—cf. 1:15; Ezekiel 1:7. Many commentators assert that the angel, as representative of Christ, reflects his glory and bears the insignia attributed to Christ himself in 1:15, 16; 4:3. The "pillars of fire" that led Israel through the wilderness by night symbolize God's presence.

➤ **2 a little book**—Greek, "a little scroll." This "little scroll" is small in comparison with the scroll mentioned in 5:1, which contained the whole vast scheme of God's purposes. This other, described as a "little scroll," contains only a portion, which John was now to make his own (10:9, 11) and then to use in prophesying to others. The posture of the angel is significant; he stands with **his right foot upon the sea, and his left foot on the earth.** Most interpreters concur that the posture of the angel signifies that the message will be for the entire world. In a sense, he stands in authority over all the earth and possesses a message to be given to the entire world. Some commentators point out that the beast with the seven heads will rise out of the sea (13:1), and the beast with the two horns like a lamb will come out of the earth (13:11). The posture of the angel claims both sea and earth as belonging to God and directly under his authority.

➤ **3 cried with a loud voice, as when a lion roareth**—John previously described Christ as the Lion of the tribe of Judah (5:5). **seven thunders uttered their voices**—thunderings mark the opening of the seventh seal (8:1, 5) and also the outpouring of the seventh vial (16:17, 18).

➤ **4 Seal up those things which the seven thunders uttered, and write them not**—The opposite command is given in 22:20. Even though at the time of the end the things sealed in Daniel's time were to be revealed, the voices of these thunders are not to be revealed. Though heard by John, they were not to be imparted by him to others through the Revelation, for they are so terrible that God, in his mercy, withheld them. The godly are thus kept from morbid ponderings over the evil to come, and the ungodly are not driven by despair to utter recklessness of life. John began to write the warnings of the seven thunders, but the voice from heaven told him to seal up those things he heard. There is to be no additional warning. The warning given by the six trumpets had been sufficient; judgment would come without further delay (Summers).

➤5 **lifted up his hand to heaven**—It was customary to lift the hand toward heaven in taking a solemn oath to the God of truth. Perhaps in this part of the vision there is an allusion to Daniel 12 (cf. 10:4 with Dan. 12:4, 9 and 10:5, 6 with Dan. 12:7).

➤6 **and sware by him that liveth for ever and ever**—God lives "into the ages of the ages" (Gk.). **who created heaven, and the things that therein are . . . the earth . . . the sea . . .** This detailed description of God as the Creator is appropriate to the subject of the angel's oath, that is, the consummating mystery of God (10:7). The consummation of all things will surely be brought about with the same almighty power which created all things. **That there should be time no longer**— This is the main point of this declaration. Martyrs will not have to wait any longer for the answer to their prayers. Vengeance will come swiftly.

➤7 **the mystery of God should be** [was] **finished**—The mystery of God is God's secret plan for man (especially the redeemed) revealed in part to the OT prophets and in full to the NT prophets, the last of which is John, who received the final revelation. Some commentators think the mystery of God is the theme of the "small scroll" and also of the remainder of the Revelation. The "mystery" of God's scheme of redemption, once hidden in God's secret counsel and dimly foreshadowed in types and prophecies, is now more clearly revealed according to the gospel-kingdom's development itself. Then finally his servants shall praise him most fully, for the glorious consummation of the secret plan, when God in Christ will take to himself (and for his saints) the kingdom so long ruled by Satan and the ungodly. Thus, this verse is an anticipation of 11:15-18. **as he hath declared** [Gk. "announced the glad tidings"] **to his servants the prophets**—God declared the glad tidings to them. The mystery of God is the "good news." The office of the prophets is to receive the good news from God in order to declare it to others. The final consummation is the great theme of the gospel announced to, and by, the prophets. (Cf. Gal. 3:8.)

➤8 See comments on 10:2. The contents of the little scroll are revealed in 11:1-13.

➤9 **Take it, and eat it up**—i.e., digest it entirely and so let it become part of yourself for the purpose of imparting it more vividly to others. **it shall make thy belly bitter, but it shall be in thy mouth sweet as honey**— Cf. Ezekiel 2:10. Honey, though sweet to the mouth, sometimes turns to bile in the stomach. The thought that God would be glorified (11:3-6, 11-18) gave John the great pleasure. However, afterwards he was overcome with grief at the prophecy of the coming bitter persecutions against God's people (11:7-10).

➤10 **I took the little book** [scroll]—John responded obediently to the command, took the scroll from the angel's hand, and then returned to earth. Some commentators identify the little scroll as the scroll in Daniel 12 containing information relative to the last half of the seventieth week. Other commentators remind us that John sees himself much in the position of Ezekiel. He faces an extremely difficult task in awakening the Christians to the seriousness of their trials and in his own responsibility of encouraging the faithful.

➤11 **And he said unto me, Thou must prophesy again**—The burden was upon John, the servant of God, to prophesy at God's command, as he had already done according to the earlier portion of the Revelation. **many peoples, and nations, and tongues, and kings**—The eating of the scroll (as in Ezekiel's case) marks John's appropriation of the prophetic message, which is about to reveal what will become of the holy city and the church of God. (Events befalling the holy city and the church of God constitute the subject of the remainder of Revelation.)

*Chapter* **11**

## 1-19 THE TWO WITNESSES AND THE SEVENTH TRUMPET

The eleventh chapter is a short summary and/or preview of the more detailed prophecies of the same events to come in chapters 12–20. Thus, we find anticipatory allusions to the later prophecies; cf. 11:7 with the detailed accounts contained in 13:1, 11 and 17:8, for example. The temple is protected, along with its worshipers, but the Court of the Gentiles is left without protection for a period of three and a half years. Some interpreters have taken this to mean that the book was written before the destruction of the temple in A.D. 70, but the overall nature of the book makes this unlikely.

➤**1 there was given me a reed like unto a rod**—i.e., a measuring rule (see Ezek. 40:3; Zech. 2:1, 2). **and the altar, and them that worship therein**—The Greek term translated "temple" is *naos,* the "holy place" of the "sanctuary," in contrast to the general temple enclosure. The term "altar" refers to the altar of incense, for it alone was in the holy place. The measurement of the holy place seems to stand parallel to the sealing of the elect of Israel under the sixth seal. God's elect are symbolized by the sanctuary of Jerusalem (see 1 Cor. 3:16, 17, where the same Gk. word *naos* is used for "temple"). The figure seems to be a symbolic portrayal of God's people. Some commentators, however, think this signals a literal temple in Jerusalem that will stand at the head of the elect church. The measuring implies the exactness of the proportions of the temple to be restored and the definite completeness of the numbers of the Israelite and of the Gentile elections. The literal temple at Jerusalem shall be a typical forerunner of the heavenly Jerusalem. In following chapters John's accurate drawing of the distinction between God's servants and those who bear the mark of the beast is the way in which he fulfills the direction given him to "measure the temple." The fact that the temple is distinguished from those who worship there favors the view that the literal temple is partially meant. There in the restored temple, the Antichrist will put forward his blasphemous claims. The sealed

of the elect church, alone, will refuse his claims. These will comprise the true sanctuary which is here measured, that is, accurately marked and kept by God, whereas the rest will yield to the Antichrist's attraction.

➤**2 the court . . . without [outside] the temple . . . measure it not; for it is given unto the Gentiles: and the holy city shall they tread under foot forty and two months**—The outside of the holy place is left unmeasured (i.e., unprotected), and therefore it will be trampled underfoot by the Gentiles. "Forty-two months" probably refers to the three and a half years of severe tribulation and may be the same period as Daniel's "a time, time and half a time," or three and a half years (see Dan. 7:25; 12:7; Rev. 12:6, 14). Several commentators have pointed out that this period of Gentile domination was foreshadowed by the reign of Antiochus Epiphanes, under whose rule the temple was desolated for three years (168–165 B.C.).

➤**3, 4 And I will give power unto my two witnesses, and they shall prophesy**—The word "power" was supplied to complete the thought in Greek. The possessive pronoun "my" implies that the two were well-known, at least to John. They had the power to prophesy, which means to preach under the inspiration of the Spirit, denouncing judgments against the apostate. The two witnesses are called **the two olive trees, and the two candlesticks standing before the God of the earth**—See Zech. 4:3, 12. Some commentators think that the two olive trees and the two lampstands are symbolic of Joshua and Zerubbabel. Since the **two olive trees** supply the two lampstands with oil, this could mean the two witnesses will supply the church with the Spirit (which is often symbolized by oil—see Isa. 61:1; Zech. 4:6). In the last days God will raise up two inspired witnesses to minister to the remaining persecuted ones. The two candlesticks may indicate the twofold church, Jewish and Gentile, which is supplied by the two witnesses. The actions of the two witnesses are just like those of Moses and Elijah. Moses witnessed for God against Pharaoh, turned the waters into blood, and destroyed Egypt with plagues. Elijah caused fire to devour the enemy and shut up heaven so that it did not rain for three years and six months, the very time (1,260 days) in which the "two witnesses" prophesied. Some interpreters believe that Elijah and Moses will appear again (as Mal. 4:5, 6 seems to imply). Moses and Elijah appeared with Christ at the transfiguration, an experience which foreshadowed his coming kingdom. As to Moses, cf. Deuteronomy 34:5, 6; Jude 9. Many in the early church thought the "two witnesses" to be Enoch (not Moses) and Elijah. This would avoid the difficulty of their dying a second time, for these men had never died—so perhaps they will be the witnesses who are killed. Still, the act of turning rivers and oceans to blood applies best to Moses. An objection to this interpretation is that those blessed and departed servants of God would have to submit to death (11:7-9), and this, in Moses' case, would be a second time, which would contradict Hebrews 9:27. **clothed in sackcloth**—This is a garment of OT prophets, especially when they called people to repent. Their clothes went along with their teachings. So it was in the case of Elijah.

**►5 if any man will hurt them, fire proceedeth out of their mouth, and devoureth their enemies**—This is not to be interpreted literally; rather, it is to be understood as God's making judgment come to pass on their enemies.

**►6** This verse recalls the powerful deeds God did through Elijah and Moses (see 1 Kings 17:1; Exod. 7:17-21).

**►7 the beast that ascendeth out of the bottomless pit** [abyss]—There is a glimpse of the beast in the OT (Dan. 7:3, 11) and subsequent descriptions of him in 13:1 and 17:8. **make war against them**—This alludes to Daniel 7:21, where the same is said of the "little horn" that sprang up among the ten horns of the fourth beast.

**►8 their dead bodies**—Greek, "their corpse." The two fallen in one cause are considered as one. **spiritually**—in a spiritual sense. **Sodom**—is the term applied by Isaiah (1:10) to apostate Jerusalem (cf. Ezek. 16:48). **Egypt**—was the nation upon which the Jews depended; this dependence proved to be their sin. **where also our** ["their" in the earliest manuscripts] **Lord was crucified**—Jerusalem will be the last capital of the world-apostasy and so will receive the last and worst of the judgments ever inflicted on the apostate world.

**►9 and shall not suffer** [allow] **their dead bodies to be put in graves**—"To have his dead body lie in view of all was the worst humiliation a person could suffer from his enemies (Ps. 79:3, 4; Tobit 1:18ff.)" (Johnson). In righteous retribution, the flesh of the anti-Christian host is not buried, but is given to all the fowls to eat (cf. 19:17, 18, 21).

**►10 And they that dwell upon the earth shall rejoice over them, and make merry, and shall send gifts one to another**—The people who had been tormented by the two prophets would celebrate their deaths by exchanging gifts—a common practice in the Near East (Neh. 8:10, 12; Esth. 9:19, 22). **these two prophets tormented them**—The prophets had tormented them with the plagues (11:5, 6).

**►11 And after three days and a half the Spirit of life from God**—This is the same God who breathed life into Israel's dry bones (Ezek. 37:10, 11). **they stood upon their feet**—Cf. Ezekiel 37:10. **And great fear fell upon them which saw them**—This is "fear" such as fell on the soldiers guarding Christ's tomb at his resurrection (Matt. 28:4) when also there was a great earthquake (11:13).

**►12 Come up hither**—The two witnesses, who had been killed and now are raised to life, are invited to come into the very presence of heaven. **And they ascended up to heaven in a cloud**—As the witnesses resembled Christ in their three and a half years of witnessing and their three and a half days of being dead (though not for exactly the same time, nor were they put in a tomb as he was), so also their ascension resembles Christ's. Their ascension characterizes the rapture in which all Christians will participate. **and their enemies beheld them**—The foes must have been openly convicted by God for their unbelief and persecution of his servants. The foes of the witnesses are convicted of their unbelief, even as the foes of the church will be convicted by God for their unbelief when the church is raptured to meet the Lord in the air.

**►13 a great earthquake**—The opening of the sixth seal also resulted in a great earthquake (6:12), but no one repented as a result of that disaster. This earthquake strikes a holy fear in the hearts of those who survive the earthquake (called "the remnant" in KJV—lit., "the rest").

➤**14 the second woe is past**—under the sixth trumpet (9:12-21), including also the prophecy (11:1-13). **behold, the third woe cometh quickly**—It is not mentioned until a sketch of the history of the origin, suffering, and faithfulness of the church in the time of apostasy and persecution is first given. Rather than describing the third woe in detail, the "grand finale" is reviewed in summary fashion; it is the thanksgiving of the twenty-four elders in heaven for the establishing of Christ's kingdom on earth; it is accompanied by the destruction of the destroyers of the earth.

Verses 15-19 describe the sounding of the seventh trumpet and the thanksgiving of the twenty-four elders. The interpreter who follows the recapitulation theory sees the coming of the kingdom with the sounding of this trumpet as concurrent with the breaking of the seventh seal.

➤**15 And the seventh angel sounded**—The world-judgments are complete in six trumpets, but by the fulfillment of the seventh, the world-kingdoms become Christ's. The seventh trumpet, like the seventh seal and seventh vial, brings the consummation and is centered differently from the preceding six; the results are not those that follow on earth but those in heaven. These will include: the great voices and thanksgiving of the twenty-four elders in heaven, the half-hour's silence in heaven, and "It is done" at the seventh vial. The seventh trumpet is followed by the coming of the kingdom of Christ. It is evident from the text that the sounding of the seventh trumpet is to bring the third woe, but no further calamity is described; therefore, it seems that we are to expect additional explanation of the matters to appear later in the writing. (See 14:19, 20 and chap. 18 for a discussion of this.) **great voices in heaven, saying, The kingdoms of this world are become** [became] **the kingdoms of our Lord, and of his Christ; and he shall reign for ever and ever**—The kingdom of the Lord and of Christ will conquer all kingdoms, and all power will be transferred to them. The OT speaks of the Lord's [i.e., Yahweh's] kingdom in Exodus 15:18; Psalm 10:16; Zechariah 14:9. The heavenly voices speak also of Christ's kingdom. The title "Christ" (anointed one) is appropriately used for the first time in Revelation. Though priests and prophets were also anointed, this term is especially applied to him as King (see Ps. 2:2). Some commentators think the glorified Son of man will rule mankind by his remade church in heaven and by his people Israel on earth. It was stated at the close of the sixth trumpet that encouraging visions would be observed before the next great vision. The first was 10:1-11; the second is the vision of the Ark of the Covenant, which leads into the next vision. The seventh trumpet sounds and the voices indicate the dark days have been experienced, but Christ nonetheless is victorious. The outcome of the struggle, beginning with chapter 12, is announced even before the struggle itself begins.

➤**17 We give thee thanks**—especially for conquering the enemy (11:18) and establishing the kingdom. **Lord God Almighty**—See comments on 1:8. **which art** [who is], **and wast, and art to come**—The last clause is not present in the earliest manuscripts. Because the end has actually come, God need not have spoken of one who is still to come in the future. **thou hast taken to thee thy great power, and hast reigned**—God now takes to him the kingdom that is rightfully his.

➤**18** This verse provides a synopsis of the remaining chapters of Revelation. God will unleash his wrath against the nations, judge the dead, reward the righteous, and destroy those (i.e., the beast, the false prophet, the dragon) who had destroyed the earth (Johnson). **The nations were angry**—This alludes to Psalm 99:1, LXX. (See also Ps. 2:2; 48:4.) How impotent is man's anger, standing side by side with that of the all-powerful God! **the time of the dead, that they should be judged**—This proves that the seventh trumpet is at the end of all things; it is when the judgment on Christ's enemies and the reward for which his saints had long prayed will occur.

➤**19** This is a solemn conclusion similar to that of the seventh seal (8:5) and the seventh vial (16:18). It appears that the seven seals, the seven trumpets, and the seven vials are not necessarily consecutive. They parallel and end in the same consummation. They present God's plans for bringing about the grand end under three different aspects, mutually complementing each other. The **temple** is the sanctuary or holy place (Gk. *naos,* a word denoting the innermost portion of the temple), not the whole temple (Gk. *hieron,* a term designating the sacred enclosure of the temple area). **the ark of his testament** [covenant]—As in the first verse the earthly sanctuary was measured, so here the heavenly temple is opened, and the portion corresponding to the Ark of the Covenant in the holiest place below is seen. The covenant of God's faithfulness to save his people and punish his enemies is thus seen. Therefore, this forms a fitting climax to the series of trumpet judgments and serves as an introduction to the episode (chaps. 12, 13) concerning his faithfulness to his church. First, his secret place, the heavenly sanctuary, is opened to encourage his people; then come his judgments on their behalf. This then is parallel to the scene at the heavenly altar at the close of the seals (8:3), the opening of the trumpets at the close of the episode (chaps. 12–15) and opening of the vials (15:7, 8). The outcome of the struggle, which is to begin with chapter 12, is announced prior to its beginning. As a comfort to his people, God reveals the Ark of the Covenant in his heavenly temple. This symbolizes God's faithfulness to his people in Christ (11:15). In Christ, God maintains control of history, a further encouragement to those persecuted by his enemies. Thus, John has reasserted that Christ is King of kings and Lord of lords (Pieters).

*Chapter* **12**

## 1-17 THE WOMAN, HER CHILD, AND THE DRAGON

This parenthetical vision that comes between the sounding of the seven trumpets and the judgments of the seven bowls has been interpreted in various ways. Some interpreters view the woman as Israel during the seven-year tribulation period, others as a figure displaying the composite church—Jews and Gentiles. Still others see the entire course of events from 12:1 through 19:10 as a prophetic forecast of the history of two opposing religious institutions. Each institution is symbolized by a woman that is changed into a city. Many of these same interpreters insist that the parenthetical section is the very core of the book.

Chapters 12–15 describe in detail what had been summarily mentioned in 11:7-10, viz. the persecution of Israel and the church by the beast, and further, the triumph of the faithful and the torment of the unfaithful. Chapters 16–20 describe in detail the judgment of the beast, which was summarized in 11:13, 18.

➤**1 great**—refers to size and significance. **wonder**—or, sign. **in heaven**—is not just in the sky, but in the heaven beyond, referred to in 11:19 (cf. 11:7-9). **woman clothed with the sun ... moon under her feet**—This woman could be a symbol of Israel, the church, or both. Most likely, she represents the composite body of God's people. The church, clothed with the sun, brings the divine light to the world. Thus the seven churches of chapters 1–3 (i.e., the universal church, the woman) are represented as candlesticks. On the other hand, the moon, in ancient cosmology, was part of the sphere of influence of the earth and therefore was connected with earth and sea though it stood above them. Its light was an earthly light. Thus the sea, earth, and moon represent the world in opposition to the kingdom of God—represented by the heaven and sun. Other commentators suggest that the moon stands for Christ's light as it is reflected. The story of 12:1, 2 is similar to the Greek tale of the birth of Apollo and the Egyptian story of the birth of Horus; indeed, the story in modified forms seems to have been told almost universally. The pagans of antiquity would have undoubtedly thought the woman to be a goddess crowned with the twelve stars of the Zodiac. Quite obviously, the Jews would have seen in her their own people, headed by the twelve patriarchs. But the woman represents neither the pagan nor the Jewish meaning but the true people of God in both the Old and New Testaments. **upon her head a crown of twelve stars**—The twelve stars represent the twelve tribes, or the twelve apostles, or both.

➤**2 she being with child cried, travailing in birth, and pained to be delivered**—This image symbolizes the pain and anguish God's people went through to bring forth the Messiah (Isa. 26:17; 66:7, 8; Mic. 4:10). (See comments on John 16:21.)

➤**3 a great red dragon**—Red implies his fiery and murderous rage and the destruction he is determined to bring. This dragon has

**seven heads and ten horns, and seven crowns upon his heads**—The crowns are "diadem" crowns, not the victor's crown. The "diadem" crown was a crown worn by royalty, while the victor's crown (in Gk. the *stephanos*) was given to the victor of an athletic contest. The great red dragon is identified in 12:9, where he is called "the Devil, and Satan." His seven crowns imply the universality of his earthly dominion (cf. the "many crowns" on Christ's head in 19:12) and caricature the seven Spirits of God. The ten horns indicate his many earthly powers.

➤**4 his tail drew the third part of the stars of heaven**—This description shows Satan's great power over the celestial elements. Some commentators think the stars refer to one-third of the angels who will be cast down (or, have already been cast down) to earth with Satan. These commentators use Daniel 8:10, 29 to defend their interpretation, but Daniel is probably referring to saints, not angels. **the dragon stood . . . to devour her child**—So Satan, the dragon, working through his agent, the pharaoh, was ready to devour Israel's males. And Jesus was sought out for destruction by Herod, who killed all the male children in and around Bethlehem.

➤**5 she brought forth a man** [male] **child**—Some interpreters identify the male child as Christ. This would place the church age between 12:5 and 12:6. Others see this as occurring during the tribulation, when the devil will make a supreme effort to destroy the nation that brought Jesus into the world. Still others think that the male child represents a group of martyrs and/or overcomers. The man child may be a corporate entity—perhaps composed of Christ and a group of his followers. The overcomers, according to Revelation 2:27, will be given the responsibility **to rule all nations with a rod of iron.** This ruling will be done by the overcomers with Christ, the ruling One (see Ps. 2:9). And as Christ ascended to the throne, the overcomers will also ascend to the throne. In this chapter, many of the statements can be applied to Christ, to a group of overcomers, or to both.

➤**6 the woman fled into the wilderness**— a place where the people of God are kept safe from the devil's power. This type of flight compares with (but is not necessarily identical

to) Mary's flight with Jesus into Egypt. **a place prepared of** [from] **God**—This statement indicates God's protection of his people. That the place is prepared indicates that the flight is not by human caprice or fear but by the determined counsel and foreknowledge of God. **a thousand two hundred and threescore days**— 1,260 days, or three and a half years (see 12:14).

➤**7 there was war in heaven**—In Job 1 and 2, Satan is presented in heaven among the sons of God, appearing before God as the accuser of the saints (see also Zech. 3:1, 2). But when Christ came to earth as our Redeemer and ascended back to heaven to be our advocate (Rom. 8:33, 34), the accuser, Satan, was thrown out of heaven judicially, never to appear there again in that role. Since then, he and his angels have ranged through the air and the earth; at the second coming of Christ, they will be cast into the bottomless pit and bound for a thousand years and then thrown into the lake of fire forever (20:2, 3, 10). The expression "war in heaven" may appear to be contradictory, but it is true. A contrast is seen in Luke 19:38, where Christ's triumph brings about "peace in heaven." Colossians 1:20 says that Christ has made peace with all things in heaven and earth through the blood of his cross. **Michael and his angels fought against the dragon . . . and his angels**—Satan and his hosts were angels, and it is therefore fitting that they should be encountered and defeated in heaven by faithful angels and their archangel, Michael. On earth the Son of man and his armies of human saints wage the battle against Satan, represented by the beast and the false prophet. They overcome the enemy (19:14-21). Michael is the prince or ruling angel of the Jewish nation. He is the angel of war, while Gabriel is the angel of peace. While the defeat of Satan had been judicially decided at the resurrection and ascension of Christ, the angels of heaven execute that judgment by casting Satan from heaven. Christ's ascension has destroyed Satan's right to stand before God as accuser of the saints. Once before, Michael fought with Satan over the body of the mediator of the old covenant, Moses (Jude 9); now the Mediator of the New Covenant, by the sacrifice of his sinless body, arms Michael with power to renew the conflict and complete the victory.

➤**8 And prevailed not**—Satan and his angels were conquered. **neither was their place found any more in heaven**—i.e., "they lost their place in heaven" (NIV). There are four levels of Satan's ever-deepening downfall: (1) God deprived him of heavenly glory but allowed him access to heaven as man's accuser up until the first coming of Christ. (2) From the time of Christ to the millennium God took his judicial privilege from him and cast him from heaven as the accuser of the elect. Shortly before the millennium, Satan will lose his power against Israel, and Michael will finally banish him. Consequently, he now concentrates his rage and power on earth, particularly toward the end of time (12:12). (3) He will be bound in the abyss during the millennium (20:1-3). (4) After having been loosed for a time, he will be cast forever into the lake of fire (20:10).

➤**9 old** [ancient] **serpent**—alluding to Genesis 3:1, 4. **Devil**—the Greek term for "accuser" or "slanderer." **Satan**—the Hebrew term meaning "adversary," used particularly in a court of justice. These two terms in Greek and Hebrew indicate his twofold objective of accusation and temptation. **deceiveth**—leads astray. **whole world**—in Greek means "habitable world." **he was cast out into the earth**—never again to appear before God in heaven.

➤**10 Now**—as a result of Satan's being cast out from heaven, which came as a result of Jesus' crucifixion, resurrection, and ascension (Matt. 28:18). **salvation**—lit., "the salvation" (cf. Heb. 9:28; Luke 3:6). **the kingdom of our God, and the power** [authority] **of his Christ**—will now be fully manifest and exerted. **accused them before our God day and night**—Prior to Christ's victory and attainment of redemption for God's elect, Satan could accuse God's people.

➤**11 they**—emphatic in the Greek text. They in particular, they alone, **overcame him by the blood of the Lamb, and by the word of their testimony**— The pronoun "him" refers to Satan. The believers overcame Satan (cf. 1 John 2:14, 15) through the blood of Jesus. If Christ had not shed his blood, Satan's accusations would have been unanswerable. But Christ's blood now meets every charge (1 John 1:7; 2:1, 2). The word "testimony" suggests that the Christians become victors on the basis

of their faithful testimony even unto death. Their testimony demonstrates their victory over the beast by virtue of the "blood of the Lamb." By this they declare themselves worshipers of the slain Lamb and overcome the beast, Satan's representative. This anticipates 15:2. **loved not their lives unto the death**—They took so little regard of their own lives that they were willing to submit themselves even to death. John was asserting that the redemptive work of Christ became the primary reason for the saint's victory. It is their testimony that proves his efficacy in their lives.

➤**12 rejoice**—because Satan is cast out of heaven (12:9). **ye that dwell**—lit., "the ones tabernacling" (see 7:15). This refers not only to angels and the souls of the just with God but also to those faithful militants on earth, who in spirit dwell in heaven. They rejoice because Satan is cast out of their home. Not belonging to the world, they exult in the passing of judgment on the prince of this world. John is speaking from the point of view of heaven and looking down on earth when he says that **the devil is come down unto you, having great wrath.** The devil is furious because of his expulsion from heaven. Realizing that **he hath but a short time** until he will be cast down lower, Satan concentrates all his power to destroy as many souls as he can. Though no longer able to accuse the elect in heaven, he can tempt and persecute on earth. The more "the light" becomes victorious, the greater will be the struggles of the powers of darkness; therefore, at the final crisis, the Antichrist will manifest himself with an intensity of wickedness greater than ever before. The expression "a short time" suggests a brief opportunity for his attacks on God's people.

➤**13** This verse continues the narrative of 12:1-6. **he persecuted the woman which brought forth the man child**—The Greek word for "persecuted" can also mean "pursued," which seems to be the meaning here.

➤**14 were given**—by God's providential determination, not by human chances. [the] **two wings of a** [the] **great eagle**—This alludes to Exodus 19:4 and Isaiah 40:30, 31. The image conveys God's provision, protection, and empowering. **where she is nourished for a time, and times, and half a time**—i.e., three and a half years. This woman (God's people, the church) will be nourished in the wilderness for 1,260 days and protected from Satan, the serpent.

➤**15 flood**—Greek, "river."

➤**16 the earth . . . swallowed up the flood**—cf. Numbers 16:30-33, where it is recorded that the earth swallowed up Korah and his men.

➤**17 the dragon . . . went to make war with the remnant** [rest] **of her seed**—the rest of the woman's seed could be all the other believers, as distinguished from Christ, the man child (*NIVSB*) or all the other believers beside the group of overcomers (see comments on 12:5, 11). **which keep the commandments of God, and have the testimony of Jesus** ["Christ" is not present in the earliest manuscripts]—This refers to the believers, who keep God's commands and give testimony to Jesus (or, maintain the testimony Jesus bore—see comments on 1:9).

*Chapter* **13**

## 1-10 THE BEAST OUT OF THE SEA

➤**1 And I stood upon the sand of the sea**—This reading is supported by Codices Sinaiticus and Vaticanus, but two other early codices (Alexandrinus and Ephraem Rescriptus), which are generally considered more reliable in Revelation, read "he stood . . . " Most modern translators follow this reading and consequently place the first part of 13:1 at the end of 12:17 and identify the one standing as the dragon. The beginning of 13:1 would therefore read, "I [John] saw a beast rise up out of the sea. . . ." Standing on the sand of the sea, the dragon gave his power to the **beast** that arose **out of the sea.** In Daniel 7 there are four beasts who come up from the sea. Here the one "beast" could represent all God-opposing world-power throughout history, not restricted to one manifestation alone, e.g., Rome. Or the beast could represent the Antichrist, the head of a specific God-opposing world-power. The first beast expresses the attack of the world-power on the church from outside. The second, which is a revival of the first, is the world-power appearing as the false prophet, working his destructive powers and corrupting the church from within. The "sea" here seemingly represents people—

troubled waves of peoples, multitudes, nations, and tongues. On the other hand, the "earth" (13:11) may symbolize the unified, ordered world of nations with its culture and learning. The creature has **seven heads and ten horns.** The "ten horns" will not be crowned until the final stage of the fourth kingdom (the Roman). This kingdom will continue until the final kingdom (Christ's) destroys and replaces it completely. The ten toes of the two feet of the image in Daniel also represent this last stage. Both dragon and creature wear crowns, but the crowns are on the dragon's heads, while they are on the creature's horns (cf. 12:3; 13:1). Therefore, both heads and horns refer to kingdoms. (Cf. 17:7, 10, 12, where the term "kings" represents the kingdoms, for they are the heads of their kingdoms.) The seven kings are peculiarly powerful and are distinguished from the ten, represented by the horns. In Daniel the "ten" mean the last phase of world-power, for in the image the fourth kingdom is divided into ten parts. They correspond to the seventh head (17:12) and are in the future. **the name** [names] **of blasphemy**—Each head was inscribed with a name of blasphemy—Many Roman emperors deified themselves, taking to themselves the names of "Lord" and "God."

➤**2 leopard . . . bear . . . lion**—This beast unites in itself the God-opposing characteristics of the three preceding kingdoms, resembling respectively the leopard, bear, and lion. Like the fourth beast in Daniel 6, it rises out of the sea and has ten horns, and there are seven heads as Daniel's four beasts had. Thus, the beast would represent in one figure the world-power (which in Daniel is represented by four) of all types and places, not merely of one period and one locality, viewed as opposed to God. This interpretation supports the view that the beast is the vicarious representative of Satan, who is similarly pictured as having seven heads and ten horns. This indicates his universal power in all ages and places of the world. Satan appears as a serpent, the archetype of bestial nature (12:9). Auberlen postulates this interpretation in these words: "If the seven heads meant merely seven Roman emperors, one cannot understand why they alone should be mentioned in the original image of Satan, whereas it is perfectly intelligible if we suppose them to represent Satan's power on earth viewed collectively." Summers finds certain characteristics of the emperor Domitian delineated in these verses. For example, Domitian blasphemed God (13:6), exercised supremacy (13:7), and was worshiped by all except the Christians (13:8). The people who refused to worship him were not able to buy or sell their goods, being refused the right to participate in ordinary commercial activities. Moreover, the names of the emperors (*Augustus, Theos, Soter, Kurios*) were used to influence their subjects at the point of their alleged deity. McDowell, however, disagrees with Summers concerning the identification of the beast and insists that this figure represents Nero who had come back to life. At the time of John there existed a *Nero redivivus* myth indicating that Nero would reappear, although he had long since died.

➤**3 one of**—means "from among." **wounded to death**—To make an impact this is repeated twice again (13:12, 14). The deadly wound may symbolize the temporary paralyzation of the world power. **his deadly wound was healed**—The beast's ascent out of the bottomless pit corresponds to the healing of its wound (17:8). The beast survived, its merely temporary and external wound healed. Now it returns, not only from the sea but from the bottomless pit, where it has gathered more hellish force to turn against Christianity (13:11, 12, 14; 11:7; 17:8). A new and worse heathenism breaks in upon the Christianized world, a heathenism more devilish than the old one of the first heads of the beast. **wondered after**—The world will be amazed at the beast's recovery.

➤**4** John carefully notes that men **worshipped the dragon which gave power** [authority] **unto the beast**—It is very important to notice that the beast received his authority from Satan, the dragon. **Who is like unto the beast? who is able to make war with him?**—These are the very terms used in Exodus 15:11 with reference to God. Some have insisted that this is the Hebrew source of the name of the Maccabees, the opponents of the OT antichrist, Antiochus (parody of the name "Michael," which means "who is like unto God?").

➤**5 power** [authority] **was given unto him to continue forty and two months**—See 11:2, 3; 12:6. The authority he exercises is for a brief time when compared to eternity. This forty-two

months may refer to the last half of the tribulation period.

➤**6 blaspheme his name, and his tabernacle, and them that dwell in heaven**—This reading is supported by some ancient manuscripts, but many of the earliest manuscripts read, "blaspheme his name and his tabernacle, that is, those [dwelling] tabernacling in heaven." According to the syntax in the second reading, the phrase "those dwelling in heaven" is in direct apposition to "his tabernacle." Thus, those who dwell in heaven are God's dwelling place in heaven; the people in heaven and the heavenly place are not two separate entities—as is indicated by the reading in the KJV. In the final chapters of Revelation we learn that the new Jerusalem coming down out of heaven is equated with God's tabernacle—he tabernacles among men (22:1-3). Thus, God's dwelling place and God's people are seen as one entity. He dwells in his people and his people dwell in him (see 21:22) (*GAM*).

➤**7** John notes here that the creature was permitted to make war against the saints and **to overcome them.** He received authority **over all kindreds, and tongues, and nations** (see 17:15).

➤**8 all that dwell upon the earth shall worship him**—those of the beast, earthly, in contrast to those living in heaven (13:6). Only those whose names have been recorded in the slain Lamb's book of life (20:12) will refuse to worship the beast. **the Lamb slain from the foundation of the world**—According to the syntax in the Greek text, the prepositional phrase "from the foundation of the world" modifies "the Lamb slain." This juxtaposition is followed in several other English versions: ASV, NIV, NASB mg, TLB mg. But other translations (RSV, NEB, TEV, JB) conjoined the phrase "from the foundation of the world" with "written in the book of life." The text as stated in the KJV indicates that Christ, the Lamb of God, was foreordained to crucifixion from the foundation of the world. His death on the cross was not an afterthought or merely a remedy; it was the fulfillment of the determined counsel and foreknowledge of God (Acts 2:23; 1 Pet. 1:19, 20).

➤**9** This is a general exhortation consisting of Christ's own words of admonition calling attention to what is being said. It is partly prominent following the parables, and it is also seen at the conclusion of each of the letters to the churches recorded in Revelation 2 and 3.

►**10** Cf. Jeremiah 15:2, which is alluded to in this verse. **he that killeth with the sword must be killed with the sword**—God has appointed the various trials of those who are to be persecuted by the beast. **Here**—This is the time for them to exhibit **patience** [endurance] **and . . . faith** in their bearing of appointed sufferings. This is to be the motto and watchword of the elect during the period of the world kingdom. As the first beast is to be met by endurance and confidence (13:10), the second must be opposed by true wisdom (3:18).

## 11-18 THE SECOND BEAST OUT OF THE EARTH

►**11 Another beast**—a symbol of the false prophet or of religious power in the service of secular authorities (*NIVSB*). He aids the first creature by serving as his prophet. **coming up out of the earth**—out of civilized society, unified and ordered, but for all that, still of earth or earthly. The earth is distinguished from "the sea," the troubled waves of various peoples and nations out of which the world-power and its kingdoms have emerged. The first beast was as a lamb in the sense that it was wounded to death; the second is like the **lamb** in having **two horns like a lamb.** Although this beast seems to caricature Christ, his words are unlike those of the Master. His voice was **as a dragon.** In the first beast, the former paganism of the world-power, which seemed to be wounded to death by Christianity, revives. In its second beast-form it may symbolize Christianized heathenism ministering to the former paganism, supported by earthly culture and learning. The second beast's (or false prophet's) rise comes at the point in time when the beast's deadly wound is healed and he is revived (13:12-14). Just as the former beast corresponds to the first four beasts of Daniel, so the "second beast" (the false prophet) corresponds to the little horn sprouting up among the ten horns of the fourth beast. This anti-Christian horn not only has a blasphemous mouth (13:5) but also a man's eyes (Dan. 7:8). The former characteristic is also in the first beast (13:1, 5), but not the latter. The man's eyes symbolize cunning and intellectual culture, which are very

characteristic of the false prophet (13:13-15; 16:14). The first beast is physical and political; the second beast is a spiritual power, a power of knowledge, ideas, and scientific cultivation. Both are beasts coming from realms below, not from above; they are faithful allies, worldly anti-Christian wisdom of the world serving the anti-Christian power of the world. The dragon is both lion and servant, armed with might and cunning. He gives his external power to the first beast (13:2) and his spirit to the second, so that it speaks with a voice like the dragon's (13:11). The second, coming up out of the earth, is described in 11:7 and 17:8 as ascending out of a bottomless pit. Its infernal nature intensifies its worldly wisdom and culture. Idealism, materialism, deism, pantheism, and atheism spring from these sources. Antichrist is to be the culmination of all these.

►**12** The second beast exalts the first beast and causes those who dwell upon the earth to worship it. The second beast will be a "miracle worker." He will command men to make an image to the first beast, and all who do not worship it will be put to death.

►**13 maketh fire come down from heaven**—This is the same miracle the two witnesses perform and that Elijah performed long ago; the beast (or the false prophet) from the bottomless pit mimics this miracle. Actual miracles, demonic in nature and power and not mere tricks, are to be performed.

►**14 deceiveth them that dwell on the earth**—The people will be deceived into believing the false prophet because of the miracles he will perform. But miracles alone are not enough to warrant belief in a professed revelation unless that revelation is in harmony with God's previously revealed will.

►**15 he had power to give life unto the image of the beast**—In Dura Nebuchadnezzar set up a golden image (probably of himself) to be worshiped. The three Hebrews who refused to worship it were cast into a burning furnace. This, as well as the following examples, is a type of the final apostasy. In his letter to Trajan, Pliny states that he punished those Christians who would not worship the emperor's image with incense and wine. Likewise Julian the apostate set up his own image with the idols of the heathen god in the Forum that the Christians in their reverence to it might seem to worship the idols.

➤**16, 17 a mark . . . no man might buy or sell, save he that had the mark**—The Antichrist will be the head and producer, and the consumer will be powerless in the hands of this ruler. Therefore, it will be necessary to have the mark of the beast on one's right hand or forehead in order to buy or sell. Citizens are to have a brand such as masters stamped on slaves and monarchs on their subjects. Soldiers voluntarily punctured their arms with marks of the general whom they served. Votaries of idols branded themselves with the idols' cipher or symbol. Thus Antiochus Epiphanes branded the Jews with the ivy leaf, the symbol of Bacchus. Contrast God's seal and name in the foreheads of his servants (7:3; 14:1; 22:4; Gal. 6:17).

➤**18 Six hundred threescore and six**—666. This number could symbolize a trinity of imperfection or evil—each digit falling short of seven. Other commentators see the number as representing a particular Roman ruler. Some commentators have continued to follow the interpretation of Irenaeus. Employing the Greek number system, Irenaeus noted that 666 spells out the name of the first Roman ruler, "Lateinos." The mark of the beast, according to this fanciful theory, is the term "Latin." Other commentators believe that 666 refers specifically to Nero. The Greeks and the Hebrews did not use an Arabic system of numbers but used the letter equivalents. Taking the Hebrew consonant equivalents with N=50, R=200, 0=6, N=50, K=100, S=60, and R=200, one arrives at "666" for Nero Caesar.

*Chapter* **14**

1-5 THE LAMB AND THE 144,000

➤**1 a Lamb stood on the mount Sion [Zion]**—This mount Zion is probably the same as the heavenly Jerusalem (Gal. 4:26; Heb. 12:22-24). **hundred forty and four thousand, having his Father's name written in their foreheads**—God's and Christ's name is the seal "upon their foreheads" in 7:3. The 144,000 of Israel are the firstfruits (14:4); "the harvest" (14:15) is the great assembly of Gentile saints. Christ's first act as King is to take them out of

the world before executing judgment on the anti-Christian world. These saints who are to reign with Christ will first suffer with him. The 144,000 could represent spiritual Israel and/or literal Israel. This encouraging vision follows the discouraging reports of the last two chapters. Just as certain ones were marked in chapter 13 by the number "666," even so the individuals of this multitude are marked. However, the mark on their foreheads is not an evil mark but rather the Lamb's name and his Father's name.

➤**2 the voice of many waters**—The voice of his people echoes the great voice of Jesus (1:15). **harpers**—those who stand on the sea and are the 144,000, those who have been translated, or who have died a martyr's death (Larkin).

➤**3 sung . . . a new song**—yet it is as old as God's eternal purpose. The song is a song of victory after conflict with the dragon, beast, and false prophet. It is a song that has never been sung before, for such a conflict had never before been fought; therefore, it is described as "new." Until now the kingdom of Christ on earth had been usurped; now a new song is sung in anticipation of his taking possession of his blood-bought kingdom with his saints (cf. 15:2, 3). **no man could learn that song but the hundred and forty four thousand, which were redeemed from the earth**—The term translated "redeemed" literally means "purchased." It follows that not even the angels can learn that song, for they have not experienced what it is to have been washed in the blood of the Lamb (7:14). Thus, the song certainly concerns redemption (Morris).

➤**4 they which were not defiled with women; for they are virgins**—Some commentators insist that there is a special place for those who have not known marital relations and who kept themselves free from the crowning sin of the day—fornication. Other interpreters think this refers to spiritual fornication—i.e., a forsaking of one's union with Christ by joining oneself to idolatry and/or any kind of heresy. There is no evidence that the NT presents sexual relations in marriage as defiling or unclean. In fact, everything points to the contrary. The idea that sexual relations are defiling came from the ancient world and eventually became prevalent in the church.

(See 1 Cor. 7:46 for Paul's statement concerning sexual relations.) Sharply contrasted with those who have committed spiritual fornication are these 144,000 who **follow the Lamb whithersoever he goeth.** A further characteristic is that they **were redeemed** [purchased] **from among men, being the firstfruits unto God and to the Lamb.** The consecrated offering is the firstfruits offered to God in thanks for his bounty (see Lev. 23:9-14).

►5 A final characteristic of the 144,000 is that **no guile** is found in their mouths, for **they are without fault** [unblemished]. Their purity is with respect to the sincerity of their fidelity to him. They are not absolutely faultless in themselves, but God regarded them as righteous because they faithfully served him by the power of his Spirit within them. This verse alludes to Psalm 15:1, 2.

### 6-19 THE PROCLAMATIONS OF THREE ANGELS. THE GREAT HARVEST.

►6 The first angel proclaims **the everlasting gospel.** This is probably the gospel announcing the glad tidings of the everlasting kingdom of Christ, which is to come to power immediately after the "judgment" of the Antichrist (cf. 14:7). The proclamations of the three angels who proclaim the gospel comprise a summary of events that is amplified in the remaining chapters of Revelation. These include the fall of Babylon (14:8), the judgment on the creature worshipers (14:9-11), the voice from heaven regarding the martyrs (14:13), the vision of the Son of man on a cloud (14:14), the harvest (14:15), and the vintage (14:18). These verses reveal the triumph of the Lamb as being so sure that the angel announces victory even before the battle begins.

►7 **Fear God**—This is a necessary step to embracing the love of God revealed in the gospel. Repentance accompanies faith. **give glory to him**—and not to the beast (cf. 13:4; Jer. 13:16). **for the hour of his judgment is come**—This judgment does not refer to the general judgment but to the judgment upon Babylon, the beast, and his worshipers (14:8-12). **worship him that** [who] **made heaven, and earth**—not the Antichrist, who enters the temple of God and declares himself to be God.

►8 **another angel, saying, Babylon is fallen, is fallen, that great city**—This is the

first reference to Babylon, which is identified with the harlot (the apostate church or Rome). The expression "fallen" anticipates the later judgments described in 18:2. **she made all nations drink of the wine of the wrath of her fornication**—Her fall is the just reward for her impurity, according to the wrath of God. Just as she made the nations drunk with the wine of her impurity, so she herself shall be made drunk with the wine of God's wrath. This is, according to some commentators, the preannouncement of the doom of the Roman Catholic church. For the Roman Catholic church had made the pope to be infallible, made him to be the head of the church, made a woman queen of heaven, caused the world to adore relics, etc. Other interpreters see in these words the doom of imperial Rome symbolized by the name "Babylon," which to the Jews was the epitome of evil. The fall of "Babylon" is so certain that it is looked upon as having already occurred (Summers and McDowell).

►10 **drink of the wine of the wrath of God, which is poured out without mixture**—In ancient times, wine was commonly diluted with water. This wine of God's wrath is undiluted (cf. the figure of Ps. 75:8). Nothing of grace or hope is blended with it. This terrible threat is far worse than the fear of any man's threats. This unmixed cup is already mingled and prepared for Satan and the beast's followers. The Greek term for "wrath" means "boiling indignation," from a root meaning "to boil." **tormented with fire and brimstone** [sulphur] **in the presence of the holy angels**—cf. Isaiah 34:8-10, reminiscent of Genesis 19:24, 25. The person who worships the beast will find that his doom is fixed forever. Those who persist in drinking from the harlot's cup of mixed abominations will be made to drink from the cup of God's unmixed wrath.

►11 **they have no rest day nor night**—cf. 14:13, which depicts a group having rest constantly—rest from sin, weariness, and temptation.

►12 The thought of 13:10 is resumed. The great ordeal of persecution reserved for those who refuse to worship the beast will serve as a test of the faith and patience of the followers of God and Jesus. The term **patience** suggests "persevering endurance." **faith of Jesus**—probably an objective genitive, "faith in Jesus."

➤**13** This verse presents an additional contrast for the sake of emphasis, and it serves as encouragement to cheer those persecuted by the beast. **Blessed are the dead which die in the Lord**—The time for their blessing has come—now that the judgment on the beast and the harvesting of the elect are at hand. The time that the martyrs have longed for is almost come; the full assembly of all their fellow-servants is nearly complete; their time of "waiting for a little while" is almost over, for their eternal rest, the end of their toils (2 Thess. 1:7), is close at hand now. They are blessed in being allowed to sit down to the marriage-supper of the Lamb (19:9), in having a part in the first resurrection (20:6), and in having a right to the tree of life (22:14). Verses 14-16 explain why they in particular are pronounced blessed. **Yea, saith the Spirit**—In Revelation, the Spirit and Christ speak as one (see comments on 2:7). **that they may rest from their labours; and their works do follow them**—Their time of toil is past; they enter on the blessed rest because of their faith evidenced in their works. Their works are specified because of the impending judgment of every man according to his works. His works do not go before the believer, nor even go by his side, but they follow him as a proof that he is Christ's.

➤**14 the Son of man, having on his head a golden crown**—The crown is a *stephanos* crown (Gk.), the garland of victory, not a *diadema* crown (Gk.) such as would be worn by a king. The victory is described in detail (19:11-21). This figure also holds **a sharp sickle.** Many commentators identify this one like a **Son of man** as Christ (see 1:13). This harvest could depict a general inreaping of the believers (see Matt. 9:37, 38; John 4:35-38) or judgment in general (see Matt. 13:30, 40-42), anticipating Armageddon, which does not actually occur until chapter 19.

➤**15** Still **another angel** appeared from **the temple** and called to **him that sat on the cloud.** The Son of man himself is active in the harvest-gathering of the elect; an angel is dispatched to fill the winepress and trample it (14:18-20). **ripe**—lit., "dried." Dried grain is ripe and ready for harvest.

➤**16, 17** See comments on 14:15.

➤**18** A final angel appears, this one coming from the altar (for he has power over fire). The fire is taken from the altar and cast upon the earth, perhaps in answer to the incense-accompanied prayers of the saints (8:5). The grapes and clusters are ready for reaping. The expression translated "ripe" literally means "come to [their] acme."

➤**19** Having gathered the grapes of the earth, the angel cast the grapes **into the great winepress of the wrath of God.** The treading of grapes in the winepress is a familiar OT depiction of God's judgment (see Lam. 1:15; Joel 3:13). Isaiah 63:3 portrays the Messiah as the one who treads the grapes (cf. 19:13).

➤**20 the winepress was trodden without [outside] the city** [of Jerusalem]—The scene of the shedding of Christ's blood may also be the scene of God's vengeance on the enemy of his people. Beasley-Murray, however, views this city as "Babylon the Great" and refers to 11:8 and 18:2 for supporting evidence. **a thousand and six hundred furlongs**—approximately two hundred miles. Sixteen hundred is four hundred times four. The element of "four" in this number may symbolize all four parts of the world—hence, universal judgment. The number also approximates the length of Palestine from Dan to Beersheba (Ladd). Bengel thinks the figure refers to the valley of Kidron, between Jerusalem and the Mount of Olives; the stream in that valley will be discolored with blood for two-hundred miles. This view accords with Joel's prophecy that the valley of Jehoshaphat is to be the scene of the overthrow of the anti-Christian foe (Joel 3:12-14).

*Chapter* **15**

This chapter is a preface to the last seven bowls (vials or flasks) of plagues, and it also contains a record of the song of the victors over the beast. A careful comparison of 16:2 and 15:1 reveals that chapter 15 anticipates the bowls and chapter 16 presents the details. The contents of the bowls consist of events that occur *after* the sounding of the last trumpet (11:15). But it should also be noticed that the contents of the seven bowls are in many ways similar to the effects of the seven trumpets. In most cases, the difference appears to be an amplification of the earlier plagues. The bowls simply constitute a more intense judgment than that which had already been effected by the sounding of the trumpets.

## 1-8 SEVEN ANGELS WITH SEVEN PLAGUES

The chapter is composed of two separate visions: the first (15:2-4) and the second (15:5-8). Verses 2-4 picture the victorious Christians who have emerged from persecution, while verses 5-8 disclose the appearance of the seven angels from the heavenly temple bearing the seven plagues.

➤**1** Verse 1 serves as a headline announcement for the content of chapters 15 and 16. **seven angels having the seven last plagues**—They are last, for with them God's wrath is filled up—lit., "was finished," or "was consummated." The past tense anticipates the future eventuality and emphasizes the absolute surety of the fact that God's wrath will reach its consummation. This verse summarizes the vision that follows. The angels do not actually receive the vials until 15:7, but here in 15:1, by anticipation, they are spoken of as already having them.

➤**2** John saw **a sea of glass mingled with fire.**—This image corresponds to the molten sea or great brazen laver before the mercy-seat of the earthly temple. The presence of fire suggests fiery trial and impending judgment. **them that had gotten the victory over the beast, and over his image**—Greek, "those coming off victorious from [the conflict with] the beast and its image." **mark, and . . . number**—The mark is the number of its name, which the faithful refuse to receive and so are victorious over it. "The sea of glass" is the same as the one described in 4:6. There it was unoccupied, but here it is occupied. Then it was clear but now it is red, symbolizing the fiery trials of its occupants who come out of great tribulation. They have won the victory over the beast. These are the harpers of 14:2. John heard them in the last chapter; now he is able to see them. The victorious are standing on the sea and in the very presence of God. The sea does not keep his people from approaching because they are able to stand "on" the sea (Summers). The saints sing a song to praise God, his power, his deliverance, and his righteous character. The bowls of wrath are soon to be emptied and will present a dreadful experience, but these faithful

Christians need to be fortified first. They need to see how heaven views all of this. These people hold the **harps of God.** These harps surpass the timbrels of Miriam and the Israelite women and suggest a worshipful attitude on the part of God's people.

➤**3** they sing the song of Moses the servant of God, and the song of the Lamb**—The song of the Lamb (i.e., the song which the Lamb shall lead and/or the song concerning the Lamb) is reminiscent of the triumphant OT song of Moses and the Israelites at the Red Sea (Exod. 15:1-22; see also Deut. 32:43). The saints of both the OT and NT are essentially one in their conflicts, difficulties, joys, and triumphs. The two groups are joined in this phrase because Christ's deliverance is similar to the deliverance of Moses, only indescribably greater. Isaiah 12 similarly foretells the song of the redeemed. The elect shall be taken up after their trials and before the vials of wrath are poured on the beast and his kingdom. Noah and his family were taken out of the doomed world before the deluge; Lot was taken out of Sodom before its destruction; some Christians escaped by a special interposition of providence to Pella before the destruction of Jerusalem. The pillar of cloud and fire interposed between Israel and the Egyptian foe with the result that the Israelites arrived safely on the opposite shore before the destruction of the Egyptians. In a similar manner the Lord, coming with the clouds and in flaming fire, shall first catch up his elect people "in the clouds to meet him in the air," and then shall destroy the enemy with fire.

The Lamb leads the song in honor of the Father in the midst of the great congregation. Revelation 14:3 mentions the new song. The singing victors are the 144,000 of Israel, "the first fruits," and the general "harvest" of the Gentiles. This premillennial interpretation magnifies the place of the Jew in a manner that the postmillennialist and nonmillennialist refuse to accept. The postmillennialist notes that in 15:2-4 there is presented the triumph of the saints generally, not just Jews. The nonmillennialist notes that this is a song sung for the purpose of praising God. "Moses" is identified as "the servant of God," but the "Lamb" is more than servant; he is the Son. **Great and marvelous are thy works**—This echoes a part of Moses' last song. The grand conclusion of

God's dealings with his people is the vindication of his justice, all to his own glory. Hence, his servants again and again dwell upon this in their praises (16:7; 19:2; Prov. 16:4; Jer. 10:10; Dan. 4:37). This is especially true at the judgment (Ps. 50:1-6; 145:17). **King of saints**— There is hardly any manuscript support for this reading. Some early manuscripts read "King of ages," and other early manuscripts read "King of nations." "King of ages" is a unique expression; it appears only here and in 1 Timothy 1:17 (Gk.) in the NT. "King of nations," another unique expression, suits the context well, for all the nations shall come and worship him (15:4).

➤**4 Who shall not fear thee, O Lord, and glorify thy name?**—cf. Moses' song in Exodus 15:14-16 concerning the fear which God's judgments strike into the foe. **all nations shall come and worship before thee**—alluding to Psalm 22:27-31 (cf. Isa. 66:23; Jer. 16:19). The conversion of "all nations" will not occur until Christ comes; thus Christ's judgments serve to prepare the hearts of all men to receive Christ's mercy.

➤**5 the temple** [inner sanctuary] **of the tabernacle of the testimony in heaven was opened**—cf. 11:19 and 16:17. The holy of holies has appropriately come into view, and God's faithfulness in avenging his people with judgments on their foes is on the verge of being established. Man needs to catch a glimpse within the holy place to understand the secret source and the end of God's righteous dealings.

➤**6 seven angels . . . having the seven plagues**—This description anticipates the pouring out of the seven vials. **clothed in pure and white linen, and having their breasts girded with golden girdles**—resembling Jesus, the Son of man (1:13).

➤**7 one of the four beasts** [living creatures] **gave unto the seven angels seven golden vials**—The golden flasks are broad shallow cups or bowls. The figure may be drawn from the OT concept of a cup's containing the wrath of God. The breadth of the bowls at their tops would tend to cause their contents to pour out all at once, implying the overwhelming suddenness of the woes. These flasks contain **the wrath of God, who liveth for ever and ever.**

➤**8 the temple** [inner sanctuary] **was filled with smoke from the glory of God**—The smoke filling the sanctuary "refers to the shekinah cloud first associated with the tabernacle and then with the temple. It symbolizes God's special presence and that he is the source of the judgments" (Johnson). (See Exod. 40:34; 1 Kings 8:10; Isa. 6:4; Ezek. 44:4.) **no man was able to enter**—because of God's presence and his manifested glory and power during the execution of these judgments (cf. Exod. 40:35; 1 Kings 8:11). The temple could not be entered until the seven angels had completed pouring out the seven plagues.

*Chapter* **16**

## 1-21 THE SEVEN VIALS (BOWLS)

➤**1 a great** [loud] **voice**—This expression refers to God's "voice," which introduces the seven vials that contain "the last plagues" (15:1). They must therefore belong to the period when the term of the beast's power has expired (close to the coming of the Son of man). The first four are distinguished from the last three, just as with the seven seals and the seven trumpets. The first four are more general and affect the earth, the sea, springs, and the sun—as did the trumpets; the last three are more particular, affecting the throne of the beast, the Euphrates, and the grand consummation. The judgments on the natural bodies affect the whole of them, not merely a part of each as in the case of the previous judgments.

➤**2** John tells us that **the first** [angel] **. . . poured out his vial upon the earth.**—This action recalls the angel's casting fire onto the earth previous to the series of trumpets (8:5). As a result of the outpouring of this bowl of wrath, malignant sores broke out on everyone who had the mark of the beast and was worshiping his image. This is identical to the sixth Egyptian plague (Exod. 9:10, 11), but this flask has no corresponding figure in the trumpet judgments. It has been explained that the sixth Egyptian plague is the first because it was directed against the Egyptian magicians, Jannes and Jambres, so that they could not stand before Moses; so here the plague is sent upon those who had practiced sorcery in worshiping the beast. They submitted to the mark of the beast, so they must bear the mark of the avenging God (cf. 7:3; Ezek. 9:4, 6). The expression "the men which had the mark of the beast" suggests that this first vial comes after the period of the beast's rule.

➤**3** When the contents of the second vial were emptied, the oceans **became as the blood of a dead man: and every living soul died in the sea**—This vial corresponds to the first Egyptian plague (cf. Exod. 7:17ff.). The second trumpet judgment affected only one-third of the ocean (Rev. 8:8), but this judgment spreads through all the oceans.

➤**4** Cf. Exodus 7:17-21 where the same kind of plague is described.

➤**5 the angel of the waters**—i.e., the angel who presides over the waters. **Thou art righteous, O Lord, which art, and wast, and shalt be**—The last clause is not present in the earliest manuscripts. God no longer needs to be addressed as the one who shall come because he has come in vengeance. The third of the three clauses is found in 1:4, 8 and 4:8 but not here and in 11:17 (see comments on each verse).

➤**6** The angel justifies the Lord and the punishment he has brought upon people who have persecuted and killed the saints.

➤**7 I heard another out of the altar say**—lit., "I heard the altar say." The "altar" is here personified. The statement recorded in 16:6 is further substantiated by the altar's cry: **Even so, Lord God Almighty, true and righteous are thy judgments.** From the altar the prayers of saints are presented before God (5:8); beneath it are the souls of martyrs crying for vengeance on the foes of God (6:9).

➤**8** At the fourth trumpet one-third of the sun was darkened (8:12); here with the fourth vial the sun's bright scorching power is intensified.

➤**9 men were scorched with great heat**—These may be the men who had the mark of the beast (16:2). Instead of repenting, these men **blasphemed the name of God;** instead of becoming contrite and repentant, the men became hardened. Pharaoh demonstrated the same tendency.

➤**10** When the content of the fifth vial is poured out on the **seat** [throne] **of the beast,** his **kingdom** lies in **darkness.** It seems that this "throne" mimics God's throne—the dragon had given his throne to the beast (13:2). The term "darkness" parallels the Egyptian plague

of darkness (Exod. 10:21-23). **they gnawed their tongues for pain**—They gnawed their tongues because of pain brought on by the previous plagues, which were even more appalling in the darkness.

➤**11** These suffering men **blasphemed the God of heaven because of their pains and their sores**—This shows there may be an accumulation of plagues, not merely a succession. Yet, the men refused to repent of all their evil deeds.

➤**12** When the sixth angel **poured out his vial,** its contents were directed toward **the great river Euphrates; and the water thereof was dried up, that the way of the kings of the east might be prepared**—The reference to the "Euphrates" similarly occurs in the sixth trumpet (9:14). Some commentators say "the kings of the east" refers to the Parthian army, the ancient foes of Rome. Other commentators think these kings of the east symbolize various forces of evil or even armies of God.

➤**13** John saw **three unclean spirits like frogs come out of the mouth of the dragon . . . the beast, and . . . the false prophet**—The dragon has been identified as Satan, who gives his power and throne to the beast (13:2). The false prophet is ultimately thrown into the lake of fire, with the first beast, as is also the dragon (20:10). The dragon, the beast, and the false prophet form a blasphemous antitrinity, the counterfeit of the Trinity. The dragon acts the part of God the Father, giving his authority to his representative the beast—just as the Father gives his authority to the Son (see John 5:23). And as the ten-horned beast has on its ten horns the crowns (13:1), so Christ has on his head "many crowns." The false prophet speaks not of himself but tells all men to worship the beast and confirms his testimony by miracles—just as the Holy Spirit attests to Christ's divine mission (see John 16:11-13). The unclean spirit **out of the mouth of the dragon** may symbolize the proud opposition to God and Christ. The spirit **from the mouth of the beast** probably characterizes the spirit of the world, the spirit that sets man above God. **out of the mouth of the false prophet**—The spirit out of the false prophet's mouth may depict false spiritualism and religious delusion. Whatever these spirits represent, they are demonic (16:14). They are frog-like because they come from murky marshes of darkness and do their devilish work in the evening shadows. They encourage kings to rise against Jerusalem in order to crush the effort to establish the kingdom of Christ upon earth. Talbot notes that they are similar to seducing demons, only worse.

➤14 John further describes the three evil spirits as **spirits of devils** [demons], **working miracles**—In permitting Satan to do miracles, as in the case of the Egyptian magicians who were his instruments in hardening Pharaoh's heart, God gives the reprobate people over to delusions before their destruction. As Aaron's rod was changed into a serpent, so were those of the Egyptian magicians. Aaron turned the water into blood; so did the magicians. Aaron brought up frogs; so did the magicians. But their powers ended with the frogs. So this will be the last effort of the dragon, beast, and false prophet. These spirits collect together the kings of the earth for **the battle of that great day of God Almighty**—The term "battle" refers to the final conflict for the kingship of the world described in 19:17-21.

➤15 The gathering of the world-kings to the beast, against the Lamb, is the signal for Christ's coming; therefore, he gives the charge to be watching for his coming—to be appropriately dressed in the robes of justification and sanctification (see comments on 22:14). He will come **as a thief,** when men least expect him (see 1 Thess. 5:2 and comments).

➤16 **Armageddon**—This term is derived from *Har,* which means a mountain, and *Megiddo,* in Manasseh in Galilee. In this area God overthrew the Canaanite kings by miraculously aiding Deborah and Barak. Josiah, the ally of Babylon, was also defeated and slain at Megiddo, and the mourning of the Jews at this end time is compared to the mourning for Josiah at Megiddo. "Megiddo" comes from a root meaning to "cut off" and consequently means "slaughter" (cf. Joel 3:2, 12, 14). Just the mention of the famous battleground of Armageddon to a Jew would suggest a battle.

➤17 The contents of the seventh vial are poured **into the air**—the contents are "scattered." **It is done**—This is God's voice concerning the final consummation. (Cf. Jesus' words on the cross when the work of redemp-

tion was completed: "It is finished.") See John 19:30 and Revelation 21:6.

➤18 **voices, and thunders, and lightnings . . . earthquake**—Although similar to the results of the seven seals, these things introduce the consequence of the last vial—the utter destruction of Babylon and then of the anti-Christian armies. **a great earthquake, such as was not since men were upon the earth**—In human history an earthquake is often preceded by a strange quality in the air, such as would result from the vial's being poured upon it.

➤19 **the great city**—was the capital and seat of the apostate church, the spiritual Babylon (of which Rome is the representative, if one literal city is meant). The city in 11:8 is probably different—Jerusalem under Antichrist (the beast). In 11:13 only a tenth of Jerusalem falls, whereas here the city "came to be in three parts" (Gk.) by the "earthquake." **cities of the nations**—other great cities in league with spiritual Babylon. **great Babylon came in remembrance before God**—lit., "Babylon the great was remembered before God" (cf. 18:5). Now the last call to escape from Babylon is given to God's people (cf. 18:4), for she is about to be punished to the last drop of God's anger. **the fierceness of his wrath**—i.e., "the boiling over outburst of his wrath."

➤20 **every island fled away**—is likely parallel to 6:14-17 and by anticipation a description of the last judgment.

➤21 **men blasphemed God because of the plague of the hail**—This refers not to those who died because they cursed God, but to those remaining. The contents of the seventh vial correspond to the seventh Egyptian plague (Exod. 9:23-25).

Chapter **17**

### 1-6 THE HARLOT (PROSTITUTE)

This chapter and the following chapter describe the judgment that is about to be poured out upon the harlot (or prostitute); chapter 19 describes in detail the judgment on the beast and the false prophet, alluded to in 16:13-15 in connection with the Lord's coming.

➤1 **One of the seven angels which had the seven vials** said to John, **Come hither; I will** show unto thee the judgment of the great whore that sitteth upon many waters—See Jeremiah 51:13. Verse 15 identifies the "waters" as "masses of people of every race and nation" (TLB). The harlot is the apostate church, just as the woman (chap. 12) is the faithful church. Satan, having failed by violence, successfully seduces her by the allurements of the world; unlike her Lord, she was overcome by this temptation. Hence, she is seen sitting on the beast, no longer the bride, but the prostitute; no longer is she God's Jerusalem, but she is spiritually Sodom. Many commentators think the harlot is symbolic of ecclesiastical Babylon, not material Babylon. The woman (ecclesiastical Babylon) and the city (material Babylon) do not symbolize the same thing because the woman is destroyed by the ten kings while the same kings lament the destruction of the city. The woman is destroyed three and a half years before the city. Therefore, this is the bride of the Antichrist, Babylon the great. Some commentators specifically identify ecclesiastical Babylon as the Roman Catholic Church; others say it contains both Protestants and Catholics who profess the name of Christ but deny his faith. Other interpreters view the prostitute as symbolizing the Roman hierarchy, the counterfeit, institutional church. Still others say that since Rome was the center of persecuting power, much of the content of the book is given to describing Rome's destruction.

➤2 With whom the kings of the earth have committed fornication, and the inhabitants of the earth have been made drunk with the wine of her fornication—The Greek text suggests that they have become drunk because of the prostitute's fornication (see Jer. 51:7). Therefore, it can be argued that the reference cannot be to pagan Rome, but it must be to papal Rome. But the symbol could also include the whole apostate church—Roman, Greek, and even Protestant, so far as it has been seduced from its first love to Christ (2:4) and has given its affections to worldly idols. The best background for understanding the depiction of God's people becoming a harlot is in Ezekiel 16 and 23 (where Jerusalem is described as a harlot) and Jeremiah 51 (where the Israelites living in Babylon and united to Babylon are described as a harlot). When God's

people forsake him, they are forsaking their marriage union with him and thus committing spiritual fornication.

➤3 So he carried me away in the spirit into the wilderness—Through a spiritual experience John is carried into the wilderness, and there he saw a woman sit[ting] upon a scarlet coloured beast. The "scarlet beast" is probably the same as in 13:1 (see comments there). (See also 17:12-14 and 19:19, 20, as well as 17:13, 14, 16.) Rome, resting on the world-power and ruling it by the claim of supremacy, is the chief representative of this symbol, although not the sole representative. As the dragon is fiery-red, so the animal is also blood-red in color. The "scarlet" serves also as the symbol of kingly authority. full of names of blasphemy—The concept seems to be that "blasphemous names" are written all over the beast, not merely "on his heads," as in 13:1. Under the prostitute's direction, the world-power puts forth blasphemous pretentions worse than those of pagan days. Some commentators think the animal is the Antichrist supporting the apostate church. Eventually, the ten kings of the federated kingdoms will find their power curtailed by the apostate church and will destroy her (Rev. 17:16). This will occur at the time when the worship of the beast is established. Others think the animal represents the Roman Empire. At any rate, this beast is probably the same as the one in 13:1—both are described as having seven heads and ten horns and both are covered with names of blasphemy.

➤4 a golden cup in her hand full of abominations and filthiness of her fornication—The "abominations" refer to idolatrous practices. "Babylon is the archetype of all idolatrous obscenities in the earth" (Johnson).

➤5 A caption was on her forehead. It was characteristic of Roman prostitutes to have their names written on their foreheads (Swete). MYSTERY, BABYLON THE GREAT, THE MOTHER OF HARLOTS AND ABOMINATIONS OF THE EARTH—The expression "mystery" designates a spiritual fact previously hidden and incapable of discovery by mere reason, but now revealed. As the union of Christ and the church is a great "mystery" (a spiritual truth of momentous interest once hidden but now revealed—Eph. 5:31, 32), so the church conforming to the world and thereby becoming a prostitute is also a mystery. The wickedness in the prostitute works, like leaven, as a "mystery," and therefore it is called the "mystery of lawlessness" (2 Thess. 2:7). When the prostitute is destroyed, the wickedness previously working only latently in her shall be revealed in the man of iniquity, the open embodiment of all previous evil. "Babylon" is identified as the "Mother of Harlots [Prostitutes]." This indicates that not only Rome, but other parts of Christendom have become prostitutes. Worldliness, both of extent and content—externally extending over the whole world and internally conforming to the world—is symbolized by the name of the world-city "Babylon"; as the sun shines on all the earth, the woman clothed with the sun is to let her light penetrate to the ends of the earth. But while she is externally Christianizing the world, she permits herself to be seduced by the world; thus, her universality or catholicity is not that of Jerusalem but that of "Babylon," the worldwide prostitute city. Babylon and Jerusalem are the two opposite poles of the spiritual world. The woman's name characterizes the tyrant city as being of the same nature as those cities against which ancient prophets had so vehemently spoken.

➤6 John further notes that **the woman** has become drunk **with the blood of saints, and with the blood of the martyrs of Jesus—** The term "martyrs" refers to the witnesses for Jesus—they were martyred for their witness to Jesus. **when I saw her, I wondered with great admiration** [awe]—the sight of the prostitute evoked the same amazement in John as in Isaiah, Jeremiah, and Ezekiel when they saw Israel become a prostitute.

## 7-18 THE HARLOT ON THE BEAST

This particular section is extremely difficult to interpret because of John's usage of symbolism. The beast incarnates himself in a king who once lived and later reappears (17:10, 11). However, 17:1-6 refer to a city and a nation, not to an individual or even to a series of rulers. Verses 9 and 10 seem to agree with this, noting seven hills on which this city was built. Most interpreters agree that the seven hills figure makes it obligatory to identify Rome with this area. Many expositors interpret 17:8 by refer-

ring to 7:11, thereby arriving at the conclusion that the entire section describes an individual, not a city. Those who follow this approach interpret this section as referring to the *Nero redivivus* myth. If John used sources in compiling the present section under consideration, it is conjectured that the source, or sources, also interpreted the beast as the empire. Therefore, it follows that John probably had the empire in mind. Now if this is true, the first portion of 17:8 must refer primarily not to Nero but to the empire. (See Isa. 27:1 and 30:7, where Isaiah applies similar terminology to the nations antagonistic toward Israel.) Then it follows that God had conquered that power in the beginning, but it now lies dormant. This, however, is to admit that it is on the verge of striking again.

Perhaps John used two symbols to convey his message, one of the beast and another of Nero as described by the *redivivus* myth. If this interpretation is accepted, the beast becomes the power of evil that manifests itself throughout history and in the godless empires; and it was revealed in the Roman Empire in John's day. Till then, it had been somewhat dormant but was soon to arise and reveal itself in a fury of wickedness. It was to be incarnated in the person of Nero, who was to be resurrected. The interpretation of the following verses lend both support and rejection of these basic ideas. Beasley-Murray concludes that John probably fused two symbols, that of the beast and that of the *Nero redivivus* myth. The animal, the power of evil, was then revealing himself in the Roman Empire, particularly in Domitian.

➤7 This verse obviously connects the explanation that follows to the preceding vision.

➤8 **was, and is not**—cf. 17:11. The time when the beast is not alive is the time during which it has the deadly wound. The healing of its wound corresponds to its ascending out of the bottomless pit. The beast, or anti-Christian world-power, returns worse than ever, with satanic powers from hell (cf. 11:7), not merely from the nations (13:1). **go into perdition—** destruction. **whose names were not written in the book of life from the foundation of the world**—Unbelievers, not included in the book of life, will go into perdition. Believers, as the elect of God (1 Pet. 1:2), are foreordained to receive eternal life (Acts 13:48).

➤9 here is the mind which hath wisdom—cf. 13:18; Daniel 12:10, where spiritual discernment is also put forward as needed in order to understand the symbolic prophecy. **The seven heads are seven mountains**—Rome is located on seven hills. The Romans interestingly had a national festival called Septimontium, the Feast of the Seven Hill City. Certain imperial coins also had an inscription of a woman seated on seven hills. Rome's "designation as the city on seven hills is commonplace among Roman writers (e.g., Virgil, Martial, Cicero)" (*NIVSB*). As nature reflects the great realities of the spiritual world, so seven-hilled Rome is a representative of the seven-headed world power of which the dragon has been and is the prince. The seven kings differ from the "ten kings" (17:12). The former are what the latter are not, "mountains," great seats of the world-power.

➤10 **There are seven kings: five are fallen, and one is** [the sixth], **and the other** [the seventh] **is not yet come**—and his reign will be brief. It is important to notice that the first five of the seven are "fallen." Rome was the "one" existing in John's day. The seven kings have been understood to mean seven actual Roman emperors, seven secular empires, or the Roman Empire as a whole (*NIVSB*). "Kings" is the usual scriptural term for kingdoms because these kingdoms are generally represented in character by a prominent head such as Babylon's being represented by Nebuchadnezzar. The other "not yet come" is taken by some to refer to a new empire beginning and continuing in its beast-like anti-Christian power. Its existence is to be brief. When John indicates that five have already fallen, he obviously means that most of the powers have passed.

➤11 **the eighth**—the Antichrist, who now assumes the role as king. The Antichrist will then manifest his fullest and most intense opposition to God. That a personal Antichrist will stand at the head of the anti-Christian kingdom is likely from the analogy of Antiochus Epiphanes, the OT antichrist, referred to as "the little horn" (Dan. 8:9-12). This one is essentially a child of destruction, and hence he has only a little time, once out of the bottomless pit, before he goes to his doom. **is of the seven**—He springs out of the "seven." The eighth is not merely one of the seven restored; it is a new power or person proceeding out of the "seven." At the same time, he will embody all of the God-opposed features of the previous seven, concentrated and consummated. For this reason it is said that there are seven heads, for the eighth is the embodiment of all the seven. He does not fall as the other seven have fallen, but **goeth into perdition** [destruction].

➤12 **ten horns . . . ten kings, which have received no kingdom as yet; but receive power as kings one hour with the beast**—From this verse and 17:14 and 16, it seems that these "ten kings" or kingdoms are contemporaneous with the beast in his final form, i.e., the Antichrist (see Dan. 2:34, 44). The "ten kingdoms" are not, therefore, "ten" that arose in the overthrow of Rome but are to rise out of the last state of the fourth kingdom under the eighth head. These kings received power for only "one hour" (i.e., a short time). Some commentators say this is probably a reference to the three and a half years (11:2, 3; 13:5). Antichrist is in existence long before the fall of Babylon, but it is only at its fall that he obtains the service of the ten kings. At first, he may impose himself on the Jews as the *Messiah,* coming in his own name. Then he may persecute those Jews who refuse his blasphemous pretentions. It is not until the sixth flask, in the latter part of the reign, that he associates the ten kings with himself (having won them over to his side by the aid of miracle-working demons) in war against the Lamb. His connection with Israel appears from his sitting "in the temple of God" (2 Thess. 2:4).

➤13 They **give their power and strength unto the beast**—They become his dependent allies (17:14).

➤14 **These shall make war with the Lamb**—In league with the beast, they will fight the Lamb. This is a summarizing anticipation of 19:19, but this event shall not occur until after they have executed judgment on the prostitute (17:15, 16). **Lord of lords**—anticipates 19:16. Of all kings and all lords, Jesus will be seen to be Lord of lords and King of kings.

➤15 Again, the angel identifies the **waters** as peoples, and multitudes, and nations, and tongues. The "people" show the universality of the spiritual fornication of the apostate church.

Jeremiah (51:13) used the term "waters" to refer to Babylon.

►16 the ten horns . . . shall hate the whore [harlot], and shall make her desolate—They will attack her and leave her naked and ravaged by fire, having first pulled her down from her seat on the animal (17:3) and stripped her of all her gaudy clothing (17:4). As Jerusalem used the world-power to crucify her Savior and then was destroyed by that very power, so the church, having joined the world, will have judgment executed on her by the world-power, the animal and his allies first. And then they will have judgment executed on them by Christ himself in person. burn her with fire—This is the legal punishment for sexual immorality.

►17 For God hath put in their hearts to fulfil his will—To carry out God's plan, they will mutually agree to give their authority to the scarlet beast. The expression "to fulfil" describes the "doing" and "accomplishing" of what God has placed in "their hearts."

►18 The woman is now declared to be that great city, which reigneth over the kings of the earth—The harlot cannot literally be a mere city, but it is called so in a spiritual sense (cf. 11:8). Neither can the beast represent a spiritual power; it must be a world-power. At this point, the harlot is ripe for judgment. The following chapter gives that judgment in detail.

Chapter **18**

1-24 THE FALL OF BABYLON

Chapter eighteen is written in the spirit of OT doom. It has songs similar to those expressed by the OT prophets concerning the hostile nations of that era. The similarities between this chapter and the prophecies against Babylon may be seen by comparing this chapter, Isaiah 13, 21, 47, and Jeremiah 50, 51. For a comparison of this chapter and the prophecy against Tyre, see Ezekiel 26, 27.

►1 after these things I saw another angel came down from heaven, having great power; and the earth was lightened with his glory—See Ezekiel 43:2 for a description of

God's shekinah glory returning to his temple. This verse may allude to this.

►2 Babylon the great is fallen, is fallen—Verse 4 indicates that the actual fall of Babylon is still in the future; nonetheless, these words prophesy her fall. The terms translated "fallen . . . fallen" are aorist in Greek. A. T. Robertson states that these are "prophetic aorists of *pipto* (to fall), repeated like a solemn dirge of the damned." The destruction of Babylon is pictured as being so extensive and complete that she has become the habitation of devils [demons], the hold of every foul [unclean] spirit. This verse echoes Isaiah's pronouncement of doom upon ancient Babylon (Isa. 21:9). Total civilization is so completely obliterated that demons and evil spirits occupy the ruins. The glory of the city has departed, and she lies desolate and deserted.

►3 For all nations have drunk of the wine of the wrath of her fornication—See 14:8. the kings of the earth have committed fornication with her, and the merchants of the earth are waxed rich through the abundance of her delicacies—Some commentators say these are not earthly merchandise, but spiritual commodities, idolatries, and worldly compromises by which the prostitute (the apostate church) has made *merchandise* of men. Other commentators indicate that the Babylon referred to here is commercial Babylon. Still other commentators say that throughout this section the primary emphasis of the writer's message is the fall of Rome. Much of chapter 18 uses OT language in reference to ancient Babylon. In John's day this language had been fulfilled and is here used to picture the destruction of Rome. The first angel announces the fall of Rome because of her spiritual fornication.

►4 Come out of her, my people—This is a quotation from Jeremiah 50:8; 51:6, 45. God calls his people out of Babylon. These people are in great danger; their only safety is in coming out of her at once. In every apostate or world-conforming church there is a remnant of God's invisible and true church, who, if they would be safe, must leave that institution. This is true especially on the eve of God's judgment on apostate Christendom. Just as Lot was warned to come out of Sodom before its destruction, God warns his people to come out of Babylon. The prostitute is not Rome alone but every church that does not remain faithful to Christ.

➤5 **Her sins** are multitudinous, described as being "piled as high as heaven" (TLB). (Cf. Jer. 51:9.)

➤6 She is to be repaid a **double** penalty for her deeds. Contrast with this the *double* joy Jerusalem will receive for her past suffering (Isa. 61:7; Zech. 9:12). Isaiah 40:2 reminds us that Jerusalem had received "double" punishment for her sins.

➤7 She who had lived luxuriously is to know **sorrow,** the sorrow of one who mourns for her dead husband. She would not consider herself a **widow,** for the world-power is her husband and her supporter. **shall see no sorrow**—The words of this verse mark her complete security about the past, present and future. She feels that she will never have to mourn as one bereft of her husband. As Babylon was queen of the East, so Rome has been queen of the West. Augustine's words at this point are famous: "Babylon is a former Rome, and Rome a later Babylon. Rome is a daughter of Babylon, and by her, as by her mother, God has been pleased to subdue the world under one sway."

➤8 The **plagues** will come suddenly, **in one day**—Just that suddenly she will know sorrow instead of feasting, famine instead of her luxurious delicacies (18:3, 7). **She shall be utterly burned with fire**—See comments on 17:16.

➤9 Beginning with this verse, three kinds of people lament over Babylon's fall: kings (18:9), merchants (18:11), seamen (18:17). This lament is very similar to Ezekiel 27, which records Ezekiel's lament for Tyre.

➤10 **Alas, alas, that great city Babylon, that mighty city! for in one hour is thy judgment come**—God's judgment inspires fear even in the worldly, but it is of short duration, for the kings and great men soon follow after the beast (the Antichrist). The term which is translated "mighty" reflects Babylon's glorious past. The mourning of the kings reflects her present. It is significant to note that her complete destruction comes so suddenly, simply in a moment.

➤11 **the merchants of the earth shall weep and mourn over her**— for there is no one left to buy their goods. Now rulers and merchants alike realize that all is gone commercially and that there is no future for them or the power that has made them wealthy.

➤12, 13 See Ezekiel 27:12-22 for a list of goods traded with Tyre. Many of those same items appear in these verses.

➤14 This verse directly addresses Babylon. God declares that all the fancy things they loved so much are now gone. The "autumn-ripe fruits of the lust of the soul" (Gk.) no longer exist for their enjoyment. The term "dainty" refers to that which is "fat" or "sumptuous" in food. These things are described as being gone—**thou shalt find them no more at all.** The expression translated "no more at all" is the double negative (*ou mē*) in the Greek text and is the strongest way of making a negative statement.

➤15 Cf. 18:10.

➤16 This verse describes the former condition of the city in all of her glory.

➤17 John describes how her wealth is destroyed **in one hour** [moment].

➤18 This verse describes the stark reality of all that was seen and also the sorrow occasioned by the destruction of the great city. Great remorse is expressed in the question, **"What city is like unto this great city!"** A similar boast concerning the beast occurs in 13:4. Some interpreters have noted these two facts and suggest that they explain how closely the prostitute and the beast resemble each other.

➤19 The characteristics of sorrow are described by the expression **cast dust on their heads.** Again John repeats the **one hour** in which the city is destroyed.

➤20 In sharp contrast to the attitude of the rulers, merchants, and mariners, there is rejoicing in heaven because **God** has judged the prostitute. The observation of Auberlen is worth repeating:

There is more joy in heaven at the harlot's downfall than that of the two beasts. For the most heinous of all sin is the sin of those who know God's word of grace and keep it not. The worldliness of the church is the most worldly of all worldliness. Hence, Babylon, in Revelation, has not only Israel's sins, but also the sins of the heathen; and John dwells longer on the abominations and judgments of the harlot than on those of the beast. The term "harlot" describes the false church's essential character. She retains her human shape as the *woman,* but does not become a *beast;* she has the form of godliness, but denies its power. Her rightful lord and husband, Jehovah-Christ, and all the joys and goods of his house, are no longer her all in all, but she runs after the visible and vain things of the world, in its manifold forms. The fullest form of her whoredom is where the church wishes to be itself a worldly power, uses politics and diplomacy, makes flesh her arm, uses unholy means for holy ends, spreads her dominion by sword or money, fascinates men by sensual ritualism, becomes "mistress of ceremonies" to the dignitaries of the world, flatters prince or people, and like Israel, seeks the help of one world-power against the danger threatening from another.

➤21 John describes **a mighty angel** who **took up a stone like a great millstone, and cast it into the sea, saying, Thus with violence shall that great city Babylon be thrown down**—This is a symbolic action and perhaps has its roots historically in Jeremiah's similar act with respect to Babylon (51:63, 64).

➤22 There will be no more music or industry in Babylon (see Isa. 24:8; Ezek. 26:13).

➤23 This verse suggests that the happiness once enjoyed by the bridegroom and his bride will not be heard there again (cf. Jer. 25:10). **thy merchants were the great men of the earth**—This was first spoken of Tyre's merchants by Isaiah (23:8). **sorceries**—The "sorceries" should be understood as vice and idolatry, not as literal black magic or witchcraft.

➤24 Jesus applied a similar expression to Jerusalem (Matt. 23:35). Babylon, like Jerusalem, was guilty of killing the prophets and saints (see 6:10; 17:6; 19:2).

Chapter **19**

## 1-6 PRAISE FOR THE DESTRUCTION OF BABYLON

➤1 John uses the expression **after these things** to show a temporal transition (cf. Rev. 7:1 and 18:1). Heaven's praise follows similarly significant events in 4:8; 5:9, etc. The great manifestation of God's power in destroying Babylon calls forth a great shouting of praise in heaven. **Alleluia** [Hallelujah]—This is the first time the word appears in the NT. "Hallelujah" is found first in the Psalms in response to the destruction of the ungodly. "Hallelujah" occurs four times in this passage (cf. Ps. 149:4-9). "Hallelujah" means "praise Jah." Jah is not a contraction of Jehovah, or Yahweh, since it sometimes occurs jointly with the latter term. *Jah* means, "He who is," whereas *Yahweh* is "He who will be, is, and was." It implies God experienced as a present help. **Salvation, and glory, and honour, and power, unto the Lord our God**—God receives all of the honor and credit for the destruction of the prostitute. This expression of praise is thundered out of heaven in praise of the justice of God in destroying this enemy of his people.

➤2 **true and righteous are his judgments**—Cf. 15:3 and 16:7, where the angel of the altar speaks these words. God **hath avenged the blood of his servants**—The term translated "avenged" means literally "exacted in retribution." See Genesis 9:5 for a particular application of this principle. **the blood of his servants**—See 6:10.

➤3 **Alleluia**—Hallelujah (see comments on 19:1). **her smoke rose up for ever and ever** [lit., "into the ages of the ages"]—See Isaiah 34:10; Revelation 14:11.

➤4 **four and twenty elders and the four beasts** [living creatures] **fell down and worshipped**—Compare this time of worship with that described in 4:4-11.

➤5 A response comes from the throne, **Praise our God, all ye his servants, and ye that fear him, both small and great**—Cf. the solemn act of praise performed by the Levites (1 Chron. 16:36; 23:5), especially when the house of God was filled with the divine glory

(2 Chron. 5:13). The cry here possibly comes from one of the four living creatures.

►6 The same group of people mentioned in 19:1 again shout **Alleluia** [Hallelujah]. And the sound of their shout is like **the voice of many waters** (cf. 1:15). The reason for this praise is that the **Lord God omnipotent** [almighty] **reigneth.** His reign is a fact already established. Babylon, the prostitute, had been a great hindrance to his reign. Her overthrow now clears the way for his reign on earth.

## 7-10 THE MARRIAGE OF THE LAMB

►7 **for the marriage of the Lamb is come**—The wedding feast of the Lamb (Jesus Christ) with his bride (the church) is now to begin. In the OT God and his people were described as husband and wife (Isa. 54:5-7; Hos. 2:19), and so also in the NT (Matt. 22:2; 25:6, 10; 2 Cor. 11:2; Eph. 5:25-32). The marriage union between God and his people both in the OT age and NT age will be consummated at the time of this wedding feast (19:9). **his wife hath made herself ready**—lit., "his wife prepared herself." This statement anticipates 21:2, where we see the new Jerusalem "prepared as a bride adorned for her husband." The process of preparation takes a lifetime for each believer and thousands of years for the entire bride. Evidently, the bride is still not ready—or Christ, the bridegroom, would have come for her. Jesus' parables on the entrance into the wedding feast (Matt. 22:2-14); the ten virgins (Matt. 25:1-13), and Paul's portrayal of Christ and the church as husband and wife (Eph. 5:25-32) all speak of the process of preparation.

►8 **to her was granted**—Although in one sense the church must make herself ready for the marriage, in another sense it is not the church, but rather her Lord, who makes her ready by permitting her to wear **fine linen, clean and white.** It is further noted that the **fine linen** represents the **righteousness** [or, righteous deeds] **of saints**—Each saint must have this righteousness. Count Zinzendorf started a hymn with these lines: "God's Christ, who is my righteousness, / My beauty is, my glorious dress." See Isaiah 61:10; Zechariah 3:4, 2 Corinthians 5:21.

►9 **Write, Blessed are they which are called unto the marriage supper of the Lamb**—Those who accept God's calling are the true believers (see Matt. 9:13; Rom. 8:30; 1 Cor. 1:9). In ancient times, "the wedding supper began toward evening of the wedding day and lasted many days, and was a time of great jubilation. Here in Revelation, the wedding is the beginning of the earthly kingdom of God" (Johnson). The celebration and jubilation of this wedding will usher the saints into the millennial kingdom (20:6). **These are the true sayings of God**—"True" means "genuine," veritable sayings which shall be fulfilled. The sayings must relate especially to the visions beginning at 17:1. The statement in 21:6 includes the entire book.

►10 John fell at the angel's feet and intended to worship him (cf. 22:8) because the angel had revealed to him the glory of God's people. But the angel reminds John that he too is simply a fellow servant of God, just as the apostle was and as his brother Christians are who testify of their faith in Jesus. This testifying comes from Jesus, **for the testimony of Jesus is the spirit of prophecy.** It is the result of the same spirit of prophecy in John as in the angel. Angels and apostles alike have the testimony of Jesus by the operation of one and the same Spirit. Therefore, the angel identifies himself as a fellow servant with John (cf. 22:9). This "testimony" includes the historic witness of Jesus as recorded in the Gospels, as well as the continuing witness of his Spirit.

## 11-12 THE WORD OF GOD AND HIS ARMY

►11 **a white horse; and he that sat upon him**—As in 6:2, the rider here also goes forth in righteousness to judge and make war. In ancient times, the horse was used as a war animal. The Lord Jesus will come to wage war against all the evil forces. He will appear visibly from heaven to put an end to the whole present course of the world and to establish his kingdom of glory. He comes to punish the world-power with his justice and to bring redemption, transfiguration, and power over the world to the church. His name **Faithful and True** harmonizes with his purpose and is reminiscent of 3:14. Jesus is depicted as a conqueror in 6:2. There he was depicted as shooting arrows of conviction into man's heart. Here the sword is to make all nations recognize his supremacy. The victorious warrior (19:11–

20:10) has been depicted as Lion, Lamb, and Judge; now he is to be seen as a Warrior. He rides "a white horse," symbolic of victory. Heavenly armies, riding white horses and wearing white linen, follow him.

➤**12** Jesus is described as having **eyes . . . as a flame of fire,** and he wears **many crowns** (diadems) **on his head.** The diadem is a royal crown, not merely a victor's crown or wreath. **he had a name written, that no man knew, but he himself**—cf. Judges 13:18. The same is said of the "new name" of believers (2:17). In this, as in all other respects, the disciple is made like his Lord. The Lord's own "new name" will be theirs and will be "on their foreheads."

➤**13 a vesture dipped on blood**—Perhaps John alluded to Isaiah 63:2 here. The "blood" on his garments reminds us of his own blood, shed for even the ungodly who trample it. Now he sheds the blood, not of the godly, as the prostitute and the beast did, but of the ungodly, including the two just mentioned. **The Word of God**—John had elsewhere called God's Son "the Word" (John 1:1) and "the Word of Life" (1 John 1:1). As "the Word of God," he is the personal expression of God and God manifest in the flesh.

➤**14** This verse describes **the armies . . . in heaven,** composed of angelic beings (cf. 12:7; 14:14-20) and no doubt also of risen saints (cf. 17:14). But the important thing is that the conquest is achieved by the leader, not the followers. They are dressed in white **linen,** symbolic of purity. They also follow **him upon white horses,** still another symbol of victory. They do not appear to be armed.

➤**15** Jesus, the leader of the heavenly armies, has in **his mouth . . . a sharp sword** (see comments on 1:16). This "sword" is used **to smite the nations.** The "sword" is seen as avenging power (cf. 2 Thess. 2:8). **he shall rule them with a rod of iron**—The Greek word translated "rule" means to "tend as a shepherd," but here the word seems to be used in a punitive sense. He would have shepherded them with a pastoral rod and with a golden scepter of his love. But now he will rule them with an iron rod (see comments on 2:27). **he treadeth the winepress of the fierceness and wrath of Almighty God**—See Isaiah 63:3.

➤**16 KING OF KINGS, AND LORD OF LORDS**—See 17:14. Charles is helpful at this point; he writes: "The Seer sees in the vision the divine warrior and his heavenly horsemen—not halting but sweeping downwards from heaven and onwards against the serried armies of the beast, false prophet, and the kings of the earth, and, as they thunder along, their garments stream behind them, and so on the thigh of the leader is disclosed the name: 'King of kings and lord of lords.' "

➤**17** John continues the story by describing **an angel standing in the sun** so as to be conspicuous in the sight of the entire world. The angel called **to all the fowls** [birds] **. . . Come and gather yourselves together unto the supper of the great God**—God invites all the birds of the heavens to partake of the great feast he will prepare for them. The outcome of the battle is never in question because the birds of prey are summoned in this verse and in 19:18. Cf. Ezekiel's vision of the overthrow of Gog and Magog (29:17-20).

➤**18** Contrast the description of this meal and the wedding feast of the Lamb (19:9).

➤**19** This verse describes the gathering of the **beast** and his **armies.** They stand in readiness **to make war against him that sat on the horse, and against his army**—The forces of each side have gathered. The battle is ready to begin, but there is no description of the battle.

➤**20** The beast and his armies are unsuccessful in the "apparent" battle against the King of kings and his forces. The **false prophet** and the **beast** are captured (see comments on 13:1). The false prophet is described as the one who **wrought miracles** that **deceived** all who had accepted **the mark of the beast,** and **worshipped his image** (13:14). Both the beast and the false prophet are cast into the **lake of fire burning with brimstone** [sulphur]—symbolic of utter and complete destruction. Those who **worshipped his image**—lit., "the ones worshiping his image," not an act performed once for all, but those "in the habit of worshiping." These too were thrown alive into the lake of fire that burns with sulphur. Many commentators identify the lake of fire with *Gehenna* (see comments on Matt. 5:22). Satan is subsequently cast into it at the close of the outbreak that follows the millennial kingdom (20:10).

➤21 the remnant—"the rest," i.e., all those besides the beast, false prophet, and the worshipers of the beast's image. This group would then be the kings and their armies (19:19).

Chapter **20**

The twentieth chapter of Revelation brings the various millennial approaches into sharp focus. The premillennialists, both historical (e.g., Ladd) and dispensational (e.g., Larkin, Talbot), view Revelation 20 as an account of the binding of Satan and the establishment of an earthly kingdom. Some interpret the 1,000 years literally; others, although they do think in terms of a literal kingdom, do not necessarily think that it must last exactly one thousand years. Whatever their position on this matter, all premillennialists believe in a literal, earthly reign of Christ. The post-millennialist thinks the millennium precedes the coming of Christ. The world has become better, for the power of Christ has transformed every aspect of life. The non-millennialist, observing that one thousand is the number of completeness, sees the millennium as a symbol of total and complete binding of Satan. It is possibly a period of time between the first and second advents of Christ. Augustine felt that chapter 20 was speaking of the present church age (the period of time between the first and second advents of Christ). Hendrikson associates the binding of Satan (20:1-3) with his ejection from heaven. There are many and various interpretations of the one thousand years. It may refer to the time preceding the Lord's return, an earthly kingdom following his return, or it may be symbolic of Christ's authority; in other words, it may not necessarily refer to a literal thousand years. But it is very likely that the description points to an actual, long-term reign on earth.

1-3 SATAN IS BOUND

➤1 I saw an angel come down from heaven—The destruction of Satan's representatives (the beast and the false prophet to whom he had given his power, throne, and authority) is followed by the binding of Satan himself. The angel holds **the key of the bottomless pit** [abyss] **and a great chain in his hand.** It is obvious that God is in control, not Satan. Satan

himself is not yet made to feel the torment he had inflicted on men; his full torment does not come until he is cast into "the lake of fire and brimstone" (20:10).

➤2 he laid hold on the dragon, that old serpent, which is the Devil, and Satan, and bound him a thousand years—The concept of binding spirits is prominent in Jewish literature: see Tobit 8:3, 1 Enoch 10:4, 11, 12; Jubilee 23:29; Testimony of Levi 18:12. These books describe the imprisoning of a spirit in some underworld prison. Satan's binding at this juncture is not arbitrary, but it is the necessary consequence of the events recorded in 19:20—just as Satan's being cast out of heaven, where he previously had been the accuser of the brethren, was the legitimate judgment passed on him after the death, resurrection, and ascension of Jesus (cf. 12:7-10). The Lord in death overcame him, and by his ascension the righteous Advocate cast out Satan, the accuser, from heaven. Satan had time on earth to make the beast and harlot powerful and then to concentrate all his power on the Antichrist. Christ's appearing will utterly destroy the anti-Christian kingdom. Therefore, his power on earth will end. Satan had attempted to destroy God's people on earth by anti-Christian persecutions (just as he had thought previously to destroy Christ). Now Satan himself is shut up for a thousand years in the abyss, the preparatory prison to the lake of fire, his final doom. As before, Christ's ascension caused Satan to cease to be an accuser in heaven, so during the millennium he ceases to be the seducer and the persecutor on earth. So long as the devil rules in the darkness of the world, we live in an atmosphere impregnated with deadly elements. A mighty purification of the air will be effected by Christ's coming. Though sin will not be absolutely abolished—for men will still be in the flesh—sin will no longer be a universal power, for the flesh will no longer be seduced by Satan. He will not be, as now, the god and prince of the world, nor will the world be under his control; the flesh will be overcome. Christ will reign with his transfigured saints over men in the flesh (Auberlen). **a thousand years**—concurrent with the time of the millennial kingdom (20:6). Talbot, a premillennial dispenationalist, believes that five things must occur before the kingdom is established: (1) The church must be completed. When the last member of this body has been added to the body of Christ, the age of grace will come to a close. (2) The Lord must descend and catch away the waiting church (1 Thess. 4). (3) The Antichrist must arise and rule. (4) The nation of Israel must be regathered in the land of Palestine. (5) Satan must be bound and cast into the bottomless pit.

➤**3 that he should deceive the nations no more**—See 12:9. **after that he must be loosed a little season**—he must be loosed prior to his ultimate destruction.

## 4-6 THE MILLENIAL KINGDOM

➤**4 I saw thrones, and they sat upon them, and judgment was given unto them**—This probably refers to the apostles and to the saints in general. The office of judging had been given to them (see 1 Cor. 6:2). **souls**—Some commentators have used this term as evidence for denying the literalism of the first resurrection as a bodily resurrection. But "souls" expresses their disembodied state (cf. 6:9), as John saw them at first; "and they lived" implies their coming to life in the body again. The phrase in 20:5 ("this is the first resurrection") proves that they must have been visible. For just as surely as "the rest of the dead lived not again" refers to the bodies that had not yet been raised, so must the first resurrection refer to the body. From 6:9 it may be inferred that "souls" is used by the author to refer to disembodied spirits, although it certainly may also speak of persons in general, or even of dead bodies. **beheaded**—lit., "smitten with an ax." This was a Roman punishment. Paul was beheaded and no doubt shall share the "first resurrection" in accordance with his prayer that he "might attain to the resurrection from out of the rest of the dead" (Phil. 3:11, Gk.).

➤**5 the rest of the dead**—i.e., those not participating in the first resurrection. **lived not again**—a reference to their resurrection. **the first resurrection**—refers to the resurrection of the just prior to the establishment of the millennial kingdom. The postmillennialist differs drastically from the premillennial interpretation of these words, noting that the **souls** are those of the righteous dead who live and reign with Christ. Their state is called the "first resurrection." Therefore, the postmillennialist views the first resurrection as the triumphant vindication of God. Summers views "the first

resurrection" as symbolic triumph of the martyrs during the Domitianic persecution. Although they had suffered even to the point of dying for the cause of Christ, they rise by his glorious power. McDowell sees the "first resurrection" as being that of the souls of the saints who arose to be with Christ. This would be similar to the resurrection of the soul of each saint. Augustine viewed the "first resurrection" as a reference to men who were once spiritually dead but are now alive spiritually. The expression "one thousand years" would then refer to the time between the two comings of Christ. McDowell seems to think in terms of the one thousand year reign as a spiritual reign that began with the exaltation of Christ to the right hand of God. This is a long time compared to the "little time" of 12:12 or the three and a half year period (cf. 14:13, 19:9) Satan is given.

➤**6 the second death hath no power**—just as it holds no terror for Christ now that he has been raised by the power of God. The "second death," as explained in 20:14, is the lake of fire, the place of eternal perdition. **priests of God and of Christ**—See 1:6; 22:3, 4. **shall reign with him**—See 22:5. **a thousand years**—hence, the terminology "millennial kingdom." For a discussion of the various views concerning the millennial kingdom, see introductory comments to chapter 20.

## 7-10 SATAN'S FINAL DESTRUCTION

➤**7** See 20:2.

➤**8 Magog**—a general name for the northern nations of Japheth's posterity, whose ideal head is *Gog* (Gen. 10:2). At least one Greek manuscript has only a single Greek article with "Gog and Magog," indicating that the two are marked as having the closest connection. In the prophecy of Ezekiel, "Magog" appears to be the land from which "Gog" came (39:2) and is a nation (39:6). It is therefore possible that "Gog" is to be the leader and "Magog" his people. Some contemporary interpreters note that these nations probably surrounded the southeastern portions of the Black Sea, a rather vague and nebulous area in the knowledge of the Hebrews. Ezekiel 38:6 lists other allies north of the Black Sea.

➤**9 compassed** [encircled] **the camp of the saints . . . and the beloved city** [Jerusalem]— Ezekiel's prophecy of "Gog and Magog" (38 and 39) refers to the attack made by the Anti-christ on Israel before the millennium. But this attack is made after the millennium, so that Gog and Magog must be mystical names represent-ing the final adversaries led personally by Satan. Satan will find many people from all over the earth ready to believe his lie. The revolt will then be worldwide. Armies will encompass the Holy Land and lay siege to Jerusalem. This war will be bloodless, and Satan's enemies will be destroyed by fire. **fire came down from God out of heaven, and devoured them**—Cf. Ezekiel 38:22; 39:6.

➤**10 the devil that deceived them was cast into the lake of fire**—his final doom. The **beast and the false prophet** share the same fate.

11-15 THE JUDGMENT OF THE DEAD

➤**11 a great white throne**—contrasts to the "thrones" of 20:4. "White" suggests purity and justice. Many commentators say that the white throne judgment is the judgment of all people who were not Christians or Jews. They note that the church and Israel have already been judged (Israel's being judged during the tribu-lation). Some commentators also note that this is different from the judgment of the nations, who were judged on earth (Matt. 25:31-46). The judgment of the nations was to determine which nations would have a right to experience the millennium. **him that sat on it**—probably refers to God in Christ (cf. 22:1), that is, the Father represented by the Son, whose judg-ment-seat all must face. The Son has reigned in order to prepare the kingdom for the Father's acceptance; having done this, he shall deliver it to the Father, for it will then be ready for his complete control. Until now, Christ's prophetic mediation had been prominent in his earthly ministry; his heavenly, priestly mediation is prominent between his first and second advents; and his kingly mediation shall be so during the millennium and the general judg-ment. **the earth and the heaven fled away**—in preparation for the new earth and new heaven (21:1). See 2 Peter 3:10-13.

➤**12 the dead**—probably the same as "the rest of the dead" (20:5) who did not share the first resurrection. But those who view this as a general judgment would say that all the dead will be present at this judgment. **small and**

**great**—of the wicked who had died from the time of Adam to Christ's second advent and of all the righteous and wicked who had died during and after the millennium. All these, at this time, will receive their eternal portion. The godly who were transfigured and reigned with Christ during the millennium may also be pres-ent, not to have their portion assigned as if for the first time, but to have it confirmed forever. God's righteousness may then be vindicated in the case of both the saved and the lost, in the presence of an assembled universe. (Cf. Rom. 14:10; 2 Cor. 5:10.) **the books were opened**—Cf. Daniel 7:10, which speaks of the books of God's remembrance of both the evil and the good. The books contain the deeds of individ-uals. This is perhaps a symbolic way of sug-gesting that God keeps an accurate record of all that man does. **the book** [scroll] **of life**—The book of life contains the names of all those people who have received eternal life by faith (see 3:5). **judged . . . according to their works**—See Romans 2:6ff. The general judg-ment is primarily designed for the final vindi-cation of God's righteousness for the whole world, which has been less visible in our dis-pensation. These works are made the eventual test to determine man's eternal fate, thus show-ing God's administration of judgment as alto-gether righteous. Alford writes: "Those books and the book of life bore independent witness to the fact of men being or not being among the saved: the one by inference from the works recorded; the other in inscription or non-inscription of the name in the list. So the books could be as vouchers for the book of life."

➤**13** The underworld is where the souls of the wicked are found until the resurrection. If any righteous died between the first and the second resurrection, they will rise with the wicked. The "sea" may have a symbolic mean-ing. But the literal sense need hardly be deleted; all men are gathered from whatever region their bodies were found.

➤**14 death and hell** [hades]—here person-ified, are described as meeting their final doom. Death, destroyed, will be no more (see 21:4; 1 Cor. 15:54-57), and the place of death, Hades, destroyed. **This is the second death**—The ear-liest manuscripts have an added phrase, "the lake of fire." The "lake of fire" is equivalent to Gehenna. (Cf. 19:10; Matt. 25:41. Cf. also

2 Baruch 86:4 for a parallel.) Being cast into this "lake" is the "second death."

➤15 The person's name who is not recorded in the **book of life** was cast into the lake of fire. The blissful life of the righteous does not receive special mention since their happiness had begun before the final judgment.

Chapter 21

1-27 THE NEW JERUSALEM

The remaining two chapters of Revelation describe the eternal, consummated kingdom of God established with his saints on the new earth. As the world of nations is to be pervaded by divine influence in the millennium, so the world of nature shall be transfigured universally in the eternal state that follows it. The earth was cursed because of man; however, the world is redeemed by the second Adam. The church is now; the kingdom will be in the millennium; and after that there will be the new world where God shall be all in all.

➤1 **a new heaven and a new earth**—After the millennium, the old heaven and old earth will be dissolved and replaced by a new heaven and a new earth (see Mark 13:31; 2 Pet. 3:10-13). John here foresees the fulfillment of this. (See also Isa. 65:17; 66:22.) **the first heaven and the first earth were passed away** [departed]—probably at the same time as the great white throne judgment (20:11). God's originally created heaven and earth will pass away (see Mark 13:31; Heb. 1:10-12; 2 Pet. 3:10-13). **no more sea**—This could be a literal statement or symbolic. The sea represents turmoil and separation—between nations, and between God and men (see chap. 4). In the new earth there will be no more turmoil and separation.

➤2 **I John saw the holy city, new Jerusalem, coming down from God out of heaven**—Following the restoration and renovation of the earth by fire, the "new Jerusalem" descends from heaven. Alford notes that this eternal kingdom is located on a purified earth. It is assumed that the "new Jerusalem" out of heaven is plainly distinct from the earthly Jerusalem, the former capital of Israel. Furthermore, it should be noted that the new Jerusalem descends out of heaven, from God, to the new earth. The new Jerusalem is not in heaven but on earth. This is the city Abraham looked for, the city that has foundations, whose builder and maker is God (Heb. 11:10). This is the city that exists (in some fashion) even now in heaven, for Paul calls it the Jerusalem that is above (Gal. 3:26). And the author of Hebrews said that we have come to the city of the living God, the heavenly Jerusalem (12:22). This heavenly Jerusalem will eventually come down out of heaven from God—perhaps concurrent with the descent of God's people to earth. Thus, the eternal dwelling for God and man will be the new Jerusalem.

God has always desired to have his dwelling place on earth among men, so as to have continual, unbroken fellowship with them. The Lord Jesus asked us to pray for God's kingdom to come on earth as it is in heaven. The new Jerusalem will be the ultimate fulfillment of that prayer. The new Jerusalem will be the place in which God in the Lamb will dwell with his children and from which he will rule the earth. The language of Revelation 21 and 22 indicates that there will still be people on this earth—all of whom will live a life in relationship to the new Jerusalem. The nations outside the new Jerusalem will walk by its light; the kings will bring their glory into the city; the unbelievers will have to stay outside the city; while only those who are written in the Lamb's book of life can participate in it (see comments on 21:24). **prepared as a bride adorned for her husband**—The new Jerusalem is both actual and symbolic. Some commentators have said that the new Jerusalem is only material and physical; it has no inherent symbolism. But it must be admitted that John was given the revelation of the new Jerusalem as that which *depicted* the bride, the wife of the Lamb (21:9). The angel told John that he would see the bride, and then he was shown a city. Thus, the city signifies certain aspects of Christ's bride, which is the church. Revelation 21:9-23 is especially loaded with symbolic language, most of which depicts various characteristics of God's glorified people. But Revelation 21 and 22 are not all symbolic. The language describes real people inhabiting a real city. These people are described in their relationship to God and the Lamb: they see God in the Lamb; they serve him; they have their tears wiped away by his loving hand; they dwell with him; and they worship him.

All things considered, the language of Revelation 21 and 22 indicates that the new Jerusalem is both actual and symbolic. There are actual inhabitants dwelling in a real city; at the same time, the habitation characterizes the inhabitants. In fact, the name "new Jerusalem" designates both the inhabitants and the city itself, just as the name of any city applies to both the people and the premise of that city. For example, Jesus entered Jerusalem (the city) and then exclaimed, "O, Jerusalem, Jerusalem, thou that killest the prophets and stones them which are sent unto thee . . . " (Matt. 23:37). That Jerusalem was both the city and the citizens. So also is the new Jerusalem. But it must be remembered that there is a distinction between city and citizens. In commenting on this matter Alford wrote, "As in our common discourse, the name of the material city stands for the community formed by its inhabitants. But it does not follow in this case, anymore than in ours, that both material city and inhabitants have not a veritable existence."

➤3 Behold, the tabernacle of God is with men, and he will dwell with them, and they shall be his people, and God himself shall be with them—or, as it says in other manuscripts, "God-with-us" (i.e., Emmanuel) will be with people (Rev. 21:3). God will tabernacle with them (lit., "he will pitch his tent among them"). This is what God did when he became the man, Christ Jesus; he tabernacled among men (John 1:14, Gk.). God in the flesh actually walked among men. He could be seen, heard, and touched.

➤4 God then shall wipe away all tears from their eyes; and there shall be no more death—See 20:13; 1 Corinthians 15:26, 54-57. Such things as sorrow and pain have no place in the new Jerusalem, for the former things are passed away.

➤5 I make all things new—The Greek word for "new" here is kaine̅, meaning "new in kind," not neos ("new in time"). Everything in the new (kaine̅) Jerusalem is fresh and new. Morris reminds us that this is one of the few times in Revelation when God himself speaks. More often he speaks through an angel or some unidentified voice. These words from God

himself must have brought much reassurance to the church of John's day.

➤6 Again we hear the words of God: It is done [finished]—The same Greek expression occurs in 16:17. It is better to translate the expression "They are done" (a collective neuter plural in Gk.). All is as sure as if it actually had been fulfilled, for it rests on the word of the unchanging God. Alpha and Omega, the beginning and the end—See comments on 1:18. I will give unto him that is athirst of the fountain of the water of life freely—Cf. 22:17; Isaiah 12:3; 55:1; John 4:13, 14; 7:37, 38. The word "freely" means "gratuitously" (given as a gift). God's love to man is gratuitous. There is every reason in Christ why man should love him, yet man hated him; there was every reason in man why God should hate man, yet God loved man; the very reverse of what might be expected took place in both cases. Even in the new Jerusalem our drinking of the fountain shall be God's gratuitous gift.

➤7 He that overcometh—In Revelation, the believers are called upon to be overcomers—to overcome the deficiencies in their local churches, to conquer Satan, and to maintain the testimony of Jesus until the end. Jesus gave a call to the overcomers in each of his addresses to the seven local churches. The rewards for the overcomers will be fully realized in the new Jerusalem. These rewards are the believers' inheritance. But the best privilege of all is described in this: "I will be his God, and he shall be my son." The expression "I will be his God" suggests that all the blessings implied by the name "God" shall be for believers. The "he" of the second clause is emphatic; "he" in particular and in a peculiar sense above all others is intended. The believer will fully realize the promise that was made in type to Solomon, son of David, and antitypically to the divine Son of David.

➤8 John now describes those who do not inherit the kingdom. The fearful (lit., "cowardly") are those who will not participate in the cause of Christ. unbelieving—unbelievers have no part in God's kingdom. abominable—refers to those participating in idolatry and other abominations (see 17:4). whoremongers—fornicators. sorcerers—i.e., those who practice the magic arts (cf. Acts 19:19). the lake which burneth with fire . . . the second

**death**—See comments on 20:14. This verse is congruous with the general NT teaching about those who are excluded from the kingdom (see Gal. 5:19-21; Eph. 5:5).

➤**9-11** The same angel who had shown Babylon, the prostitute, to John also shows him the new Jerusalem as **the bride, the Lamb's wife.** The city new Jerusalem characterizes and symbolizes the spiritual qualities of its inhabitants. (This is especially evident in Rev. 21:9-23.) This city is called "the bride, the Lamb's wife" because the inhabitants are exactly that. They are the glorified church, the bride of Christ (see Eph. 5:25-32). This city descends **out of heaven from God** and so depicts the heavenly and divine origin of the church (see Eph. 2:6). This city has **the glory of God . . . her light was like unto a stone most precious.** This indicates that the church possesses God's glory (see Eph. 3:21) and exhibits this glory as a light to the world. In the middle of the city God is the light and the Lamb is the lamp (21:23), and the city itself is a receptacle for magnifying the light. **like a jasper stone, clear as crystal**— "Jasper" represents watery crystalline brightness. Its glory is as that of the Creator, whose appearance is described in 4:3 as being like jasper.

➤**12 a wall great and high, and had twelve gates**—See Ezekiel 48:30-35 for a similar description—which, according to some commentators, implies that the millennial Jerusalem (depicted in Ezekiel) shall have its exact antitype in the heavenly Jerusalem that will descend on the regenerated earth. The "wall" denotes the security of the city. It keeps the ungodly from entering, and it also stresses the eternal security of the city's inhabitants. **Twelve angels**—guard the "twelve gates." This is an additional symbol of perfect security, while the "gates" are never closed (21:25), implying perfect liberty and peace. **names of the twelve tribes**—inscribed on the gates. This implies that none but spiritual Israel, God's elect, shall enter the heavenly city.

➤**13** There are three gates on each side. See Ezekiel 48:32 for the notation that Joseph, Benjamin, and Dan (for which Manasseh is substituted in Rev. 7:6) are on the east; Reuben, Judah, and Levi are on the north; Simeon, Issachar, and Zebulun are on the south; Gad, Asher, and Naphtali are on the west.

➤**14 twelve foundations . . . names of the twelve apostles of the Lamb**—Christ himself is the true foundation; the "twelve" are foundations only in regard to their apostolic testimony concerning him (see comments on Eph. 2:20). McDowell stresses that the new Jerusalem is perfect in her glory, observing that there are "twelve gates," "twelve angels," "twelve tribes," "twelve foundations," and "twelve apostles."

➤**15 a golden reed to measure the city, and the gates thereof, and the wall thereof**— In 11:2 lack of measuring the outer courts of the temple implied its being given over to secular and heathen desecration. According to other interpretations, it simply means that these areas are not protected. So here, on the contrary, the city's being measured implies the entire consecration of every part, all things being brought up to the most exact standard of God's holy requirements. And it also refers to God's protection from all evil, even the most minute parts of his holy city.

➤**16 the city lieth foursquare**—i.e., the city is perhaps a cube, as was the holy of holies of the Jewish temple. The measurements given approximate 1,500 miles square, an area occupying one-half of the United States. Other commentators think the structure is pyramidal and not cubal, reasoning that a wall of 216 feet could never support a city 1,500 miles high. If the dimensions are symbolic, they suggest the faultless symmetry of the city, transcending in glory all our most glowing conceptions. The rabbis spoke of the future Jerusalem as extending to Damascus and exalted to the throne of God.

➤**17 the measure of a man, that is, of the angel**—i.e., "by man's measurement, which the angel was using" (NIV).

➤**18 jasper**—See comments on 21:11. **pure gold, like unto clear glass**—This "gold" is transparent, as no earthly gold could possibly be. Excellences will be combined in the heavenly city that now seem imcompatible to earth. The reference to the purity of "gold" may well allude to 3:18.

➤**19** This verse describes the foundations of the wall and their adornment. It is very instructional to observe that the most valuable possessions on earth are used in the high priest's breastplate (Exod. 28:17-20). Both Philo and Josephus conjecture that each of these jewels represented one of the 12 signs of the Zodiac. It is suggested by this correlation of the jewels and the signs that the order of the jewels portrays the progress of the sun as it moves through the 12 signs of the Zodiac, but this movement is in reverse order. See 18:12 for the contrast between this city and the harlot Babylon.

**➤22 I saw no temple therein: for the Lord God Almighty and the Lamb are the temple of it**—The temple is not needed in the city, which is modeled after the holy of holies of the temple. Just as God now dwells in the spiritual church, his **temple** (Gk. *naos,* "sanctuary" (1 Cor. 3:17; 6:19), so the church when perfected shall dwell in him as her "temple" (*naos*). The Greek term *naos* refers to the most sacred portion of the temple. As the church was his sanctuary, so he is to be their sanctuary.

**➤23 no need of the sun, neither of the moon . . . for the glory of God did lighten it, and the Lamb is the light** [lamp] **thereof**— God's glory is the very light of the city, shining through the Lamb, who is the lamp. And the walls of the city magnify the light even more.

**➤24 the nations of them which are saved**—The words "of them which are saved" are not found in any manuscripts. This could mean that John was speaking of nations living around the new Jerusalem (i.e., not included among the redeemed). These nations might be people who live on the new earth and benefit from the new Jerusalem (see 22:2), or these nations might be another description of the believers—for 21:27 says that none can enter into the city whose name is not included in the Lamb's book of life. The **kings** who once had regard only for their own glory will bring their **glory** into the new Jerusalem in order to place it at the feet of their Lord and God.

**➤25** The gates of the city are always open, for it will always be **day;** there is **no night there.** There shall be continual, free passage into the city, so that all who are written in the Lamb's book of life can enter into it.

**➤26** All that is truly glorious and excellent in the earth and its converted nations shall be gathered into this city. While all shall form one bride, there shall be various orders among the redeemed, analogous to the divisions of nations on earth constituting the one great human family. Verses 24-26 basically reproduce Isaiah 60:3-11.

**➤27** The immoral and dishonest will be excluded from this city. All the filth of the old Jerusalem was carried outside the walls and burned; nothing defiled shall enter the heavenly city—it must remain outside (cf. 22:15). The only ones permitted to enter the city will be those whose names **are written in the Lamb's book of life** (see comments on 20:12).

*Chapter* **22**

## 1-5 ETERNAL BLESSINGS FOR GOD'S PEOPLE IN THE NEW JERUSALEM

**➤1 pure river of water of life**—If this is an actual river, it may have its source beneath God's throne somewhere near the summit of the pyramidal mountain in the center of the city. But this river probably symbolizes the flow of Christ's Spirit, out from God, to supply all God's people with life (see John 7:37-39). Whether actual, symbolic, or both, this river is the final reality of the rivers mentioned in Ezekiel 47:1-2 and Zechariah 14:8. **clear as crystal**—Greek, "bright as crystal." **proceeding out of the throne of God and of the Lamb**— The flow of life that supplies all the inhabitants of the new earth has its source from God embodied in the Lamb, for both God and the Lamb, as one, occupy the same central throne. The continuous flow of these waters from the God-man, who is the fountain of life, symbolizes the uninterrupted continuance of "life" derived by the saints from him. This is "life" in fullness of joy, as well as in perpetual vitality. As pure crystal, this "life" is free from every taint.

**➤2 In the midst of the street of it**—Several translations join this phrase with the end of 22:1, as follows: " . . . proceeding out of the throne of God and of the Lamb through the middle of its street . . . " (see ASV, NASB, RSV, NIV, TEV). **and on either side of the river, was there the tree of life**—Greek, "hence and thence of the river a tree of life." Following the picture in Ezekiel 47:7, 12, this language portrays several trees on both sides of the river, all collectively called the tree of life. Some commentators, however, think there is one tree in the midst of the river that extends its branches to both sides. But this interpretation seems more unlikely than the first. In any case, the new Jerusalem, as the restored paradise of God (2:7), contains the tree of life—the tree which was last seen in Genesis 2 and 3. At that time, Adam and Eve could have partaken of the tree of life and gained eternal life, but by their fall they were banished from paradise and severed from the tree of life. Now that tree is reinstated, and the redeemed of God may partake of it freely. **which bare twelve manner of fruits, and yielded her fruit every month**—The fruit varies each month, just as our different seasons now depict their own productions. However, in that day there will be an endless variety. **the leaves of the tree were for the healing of the nations**—Cf. Ezekiel 47:9, 12. This statement can have one of two meanings, depending upon the identification of the nations. If the nations are simply the people living on the new earth benefiting from their association with the new Jerusalem but not participating in it (see comments on 21:24), then the leaves of the tree of life will be for the healing of their ills. If the nations are among the redeemed, the leaves symbolize "the far-reaching effects of the death of Christ in the redeemed community" (Johnson). Walvoord discusses this verse in these words: "The leaves of the tree promote the enjoyment of life in the New Jerusalem, and are not for correcting ills which do not exist."

➤**3 there shall be no more curse**—This statement stands in sharp contrast to the curse pronounced on the original paradise (Gen. 3:14-19). **his servants shall serve him**—in an eternal priesthood.

➤**4 they shall see his face**—His "face" will be revealed in the divine glory of Jesus Christ, the God-man (2 Cor. 4:6). God the Father can only be seen in Christ. They shall see and know him with intuitive knowledge, even as they are known by him (1 Cor. 13:9-12) in "face-to-face fellowship" (cf. 1 Tim. 6:16 with John 14:9). This, of course, involves the transformation of believers into the likeness of Christ. **his name shall be in their foreheads**—Not only shall they personally know their sonship, but they shall be known as sons of God to all the citizens of the new Jerusalem. (See also 3:12 and 19:12.)

➤**5** Cf. 21:24. There shall be **no night** in this city; its inhabitants will have no need for **candles** [lamplight] or **light of the sun; for the**

**Lord God giveth them light** [will shed light on them] **and they shall reign for ever and ever.** See Daniel 7:27; cf. Revelation 20:4.

## 6-21 THE EPILOGUE: JESUS IS COMING

➤**6** This verse begins the epilogue, which contains three prominent themes: (1) the authenticity of the document's visions (22:6, 7, 16-19); (2) the imminence of Christ's return (22:6, 7, 10-12); and (3) the demand for holiness (22:10-15). **These sayings are faithful and true**—This has been repeated three times (see 19:9 and 21:5). We are slow to believe that God is as good as he is. The news seems too good to be true because we are accustomed to the misery of the fallen state of man. The message of this book is no dream of the visionary but constitutes the realities of God's sure work. It seems as if the speaker who addresses John here is Jesus.

➤**7 Behold, I come quickly**—Though some interpreters and translators attempt to translate the term "suddenly," the word translated "quickly" means precisely that. Torrance explains the NT language of imminence in this manner: "The New Testament does not think of the difference between the presence of Christ here and now and His Second Advent so much in terms of a passage of time as the difference between the veiled and the unveiled. That is why the whole New Testament by an inner necessity of personal faith thinks of that day as imminent."

➤**8** Both here and in 19:9, 10, a glorious promise to the church precedes the apostle's falling at the feet of the angel. John verifies that he is the one who **saw these things, and heard them. . . . I fell down to worship before the feet of the angel**—This response of the writer was only natural and to be expected under these circumstances. Bengel thought that John at first intended to worship the angel (19:10) but then began to worship God at the feet of the angel. The angel did not permit even this.

➤**9** The abruptness of the expression "**See thou do it not**" marks the angel's abhorrence of the thought of his being worshiped, however indirectly. Contrast with this the devil's temptation of Jesus, "Fall down and worship me" (Matt. 4:9).

➤**10 Seal not the sayings**—But in Daniel 12:4, 9 (cf. 8:26), the command is, "Seal the book," for the vision shall be "for many days." The fulfillment of Daniel's prophecy was distant, that of John's prophecy is near. The NT marks the time of the end and fulfillment. The church for which John wrote his Revelation needs to be impressed with the nearness of Christ's coming. On the one hand, Revelation points out that Christ's coming is distant, for it shows the succession of the seven seals, seven trumpets, and seven vials. On the other hand, it proclaims, "Behold, I come quickly. . . . " It is noted that the injunction, when compared with that of Daniel, is just the reverse. These words are not to be sealed up for some future generation, but rather they are intended to be read by the people of John's day.

►**11 He that is unjust**—lit., "the one acting unjustly." The expression "filthy" describes the condition of one's unclean soul before God, as opposed to one "holy," consecrated to God. The punishment of sin is sin, and the reward of holiness is holiness. Eternal punishment is not so much an arbitrary law as it is the result of necessarily following in the very nature of things, as the fruit results from the bud. God can lay no worse punishment on ungodly men than to give them up to themselves. The solemn lesson derived from this verse is, "Be converted now in the short time left (22:10ff.) before 'I come'" (22:7, 12), or else remain unconverted forever. The content of 22:11 seems to be dependent upon the last clause of 22:10, "for the time is at hand."

►**12 behold, I come quickly**—Cf. 22:7. God's period of probation for the enemies of his kingdom has now ended. Thus, what a man chooses now will determine his eternal destiny. **my reward is with me**—See Isaiah 40:10; 62:11.

►**13 I am Alpha and Omega, the beginning and the end, the first and the last**—The earliest manuscripts transpose the last two sets of titles. In 1:8 and 21:6, God Almighty is called "the Alpha and Omega"; in 21:6, God is called "the beginning and the end"; in 1:17, the Son of man is called "the first and the last." Here, at the consummation of Revelation, the Son of man distinguishes himself with all three titles, thereby revealing his eternal deity.

►**14 do his commandments**—Even though this reading is supported by many late manuscripts, the earliest manuscripts read, "wash their robes." Therefore, the reference is to the washing of their robes in the blood of the Lamb (7:14). This reading takes away the pretext for the notion of salvation by works. God's first and grand gospel "commandment" is to believe on Jesus. Therefore, our **right to the tree of life** is due, not to our doings, but to what he has done for us. The right or privilege is founded, not on our merits, but on God's grace.

►**15** These words practically repeat 21:8 (see comments there).

►**16 I Jesus have sent mine angel**—for Jesus is Lord of the angels. **to testify unto you**—plural in Greek, referring to the leaders and people in the seven local churches (representing all the churches). **in the churches**—or, "for the churches" (RSV). **I am the root and the offspring of David**—an appropriate title for assuring his church of "the sure mercies of David," promised to Israel first, and through Israel to the Gentiles (see comments on Acts 13:34). As the root of David, he is David's source, David's God; as the offspring of David, he is David's human procreation. Jesus is David's Lord, yet David's son (see comments on Matt. 22:42-45). **the bright . . . morning star**—Jesus' coming as the bright morning star will usher in the dawning of a new age (see 2:28 and comments; and see comments on 2 Pet. 1:19).

►**17 the Spirit and the bride**—In this age, the church age, Christ is united with his church, the bride, by the Spirit (see 1 Cor. 6:17). Thus, the Spirit and the bride in unison sound forth the gospel invitation—while there is yet time, before Christ comes. **Come**—could be a gospel invitation sounded out by the Spirit and the church, or this could be the Spirit and the church asking Jesus to come. **let him that heareth say, Come**—Whoever hears the "Spirit and the bride" say to the Lord Jesus, "Come," joins the bride as a true believer, becomes a part of her, and so stays with her until Jesus comes. Or "hear" means "obey," for until one has obeyed the gospel call he cannot pray to Jesus, "Come." Let him that hears and obeys Jesus' voice join in praying "Come." **him that is athirst come**—As the Spirit and the bride pray to Jesus, "Come," so they urge all who thirst for participation in the full manifestation of redemption glory at his coming to come to him in the meantime and drink of the living waters that flow from the throne of God and of the Lamb (22:1). **whosoever will** [desires], **let him take the water of life freely**—See John 4:10.

➤**18, 19** Although many of John's critics have judged him harshly for concluding his writing with the statement in these verses (amounting almost to an anathema), he was simply following the customary pattern for ancient writers to protect their work against revision and mutilation. The same warning appears in Deuteronomy 4:2; 12:32; Proverbs 30:6. **book** [scroll]—As in the beginning of this writing (1:3), a blessing was promised to the devout and obedient student of it, so now at its close a curse is announced against those who add to the writing or delete from it. **book of life**—All the Greek manuscripts (except two very late ones) read "tree of life." The reading "book of life" is found in the KJV because the KJV basically follows the Greek text compiled by Erasmus (later known as the Textus Receptus). When Erasmus did his work, he did not have any Greek manuscripts containing the last part of Revelation; so he translated from the Latin Vulgate into Greek! And the Latin Vulgate reads "book of life" instead of "tree of life."

➤**20 Surely I come quickly**—These, the final words of Jesus, in Revelation and in the NT, encapsulate the major theme of this book: Jesus' imminent coming. **Amen**—meaning "let it happen"—it is the response of the believers to Jesus' words. **Even so**—These words are not in the earliest manuscripts. **come, Lord Jesus**—This is the corporate cry of all the saints throughout the ages. All those who love Jesus want him to return and begin to reign on earth.

➤**21** This closing benediction, a characteristic Pauline mark in his epistles, was after Paul's death taken up and used by John. The OT ends with a "curse" (Mal. 4:6); the NT ends with a blessing. This verse and its benediction remind us that this writing is an epistle—for all the believers to read and obey. The final word, "Amen," is found in only some of the earliest manuscripts.

It is fitting to finish this book by citing the prayer that Jamieson, Fausset, and Brown wrote to conclude their commentary on the Bible:

> May the Blessed Lord who has caused all holy Scriptures to be written for our learning, bless this humble effort to make Scripture expound itself, and make it an instrument towards the conversion of sinners and the edification of saints, to the glory of His great name and the hastening of His kingdom! Amen.

BIBLIOGRAPHY

Alford, Henry. *The Greek New Testament.* 1852. Reprint. Grand Rapids: Guardian Press, 1976.

Auberlen, Karl. *The Prophecies of Daniel and the Revelations of St. John, Viewed in Their Mutual Relation.* Edinburgh: T & T Clark, 1856.

Beasley-Murray, G. R. "The Revelation" in *The New Bible Commentary Revised.* Grand Rapids: Eerdmans, 1970.

Bengel, John A. *New Testament Word Studies.* 1742. Reprint. Grand Rapids: Eerdmans, 1971.

Bruce, F. F. "The Revelation to John" in *A New Testament Commentary.* Grand Rapids: Zondervan, 1969.

Bullinger, E. W. *Commentary on Revelation.* 1935. Reprint. Grand Rapids: Kregel, 1984.

Caird, G. B. *The Revelation of St. John the Divine* in *The Harper New Testament Commentaries.* New York: Harper & Row, 1966.

Charles, R. H. *A Critical and Exegetical Commentary on the Revelation of St. John.* 2 vols. in The International Critical Commentary series. Edinburgh: T & T Clark, 1920.

Hendriksen, William. *More Than Conquerors; an Interpretation of the Book of Revelation.* Grand Rapids: Baker Book House, 1967.

Johnson, Alan F. "Revelation" in *The Expositor's Bible Commentary.* Grand Rapids: Zondervan, 1981.

Ladd, George E. *A Commentary on the Revelation of John.* Grand Rapids: Eerdmans, 1972.

Larkin, Clarence. *The Book of Revelation.* Glenside, Pa.: Clarence Larkin Estate, n.d.

Life Application Bible. Wheaton, Ill.: Tyndale House Publishers, 1988.

McDowell, Edward A. *The Meaning and Message of the Book of Revelation.* Nashville: Broadman Press, 1951.

Pieters, Albertus. *Studies in the Revelation of St. John.* Grand Rapids: Eerdmans, 1954.

Ramsay, William M. *The Letters to the Seven Churches of Asia.* London: Hodder & Stoughton, 1904.

Robertson, A. T. *Word Pictures in the New Testament.* Nashville: Broadman Press, 1932.

Seiss, Joseph A. *Apocalypse.* Grand Rapids: Zondervan, n.d.

Summers, R. *Worthy Is the Lamb.* Nashville: Broadman, 1951.

Swete, Henry Barclay. *The Apocalypse of St. John.* New York: Macmillan, 1906.

Talbot, Louis. *The Revelation of Jesus Christ.* 1937. Reprint. Grand Rapids: Eerdmans, 1973.

Torrance, Thomas F. *Apocalypse Today.* Greenwood, S.C.: Attic Press, 1960.

Tregelles, Samuel P. *New Testament Historic Evidence.* London: Samuel Bagster & Sons, 1852.

Trench, Richard C. *Commentary on the Epistle to the Seven Churches.* Reprint. Minneapolis: Klock & Klock, 1978.

Walvoord, John F. *The Revelation of Jesus Christ.* Chicago: Moody Press, 1966.

Winer, Johann. *A Grammar of the New Testament Diction.* Edinburgh: T & T Clark, 1860.